If you're wondering why you should buy this new edition of *Politics in America*, here are 10 good reasons!

1. The **2008 presidential campaign and election** are explored throughout the book, including the 2008 primary season, the party conventions, the role of the media, and the historic election of Barack Obama. Figures and tables have also been updated with the latest information on the 2008 election.

2. We have included the **latest examples of key events** related to American politics and government, including recent Supreme Court decisions, and the economic conditions at the end of 2008.

3. The new **Controversy** feature equips you to more effectively debate some of the most provocative issues in American politics, including "The Supremacy Clause: Marijuana for Medical Use?"; "Abortion: The 'Hot Button' Issue"; "Should Violence Against Women Be a Federal Crime?"; "Which Party Does a Better Job?" and "Are We One Nation 'Under God'?"

4. New **Who Gets What? chapter summaries** recap the most important concepts and details of each chapter, presenting them more clearly and in the context of the book's theme—that American politics is a study of "who gets what, when, and how."

5. A new discussion of **federalism and direct democracy** (Ch. 4) looks at the origins of direct democracy in the states, and at the politics of state initiatives.

6. The public opinion and participation chapter now includes information on **public opinion among Hispanics** and the Help America Vote Act (Ch. 5).

7. The use of **paid campaign ads and internet fund raising** connect the media chapter to the 2008 election (Ch. 6).

8. A new discussion of the role of the Supreme Court in **campaign finance** and a look at the **Iowa caucuses** will help you understand some of the more interesting dynamics of the 2008 campaign (Ch. 8).

9. A new section on **outsourcing** explores the bureaucracy's efforts to manage costs and work-load (Ch. 12).

10. **MyPoliSciLab,** a comprehensive, interactive Web site that contains an array of multimedia activities—videos, simulations, exercises, and online newsfeeds—has been completely integrated into this edition to make learning more effective.

PEARSON

ELECTORAL COLLEGE VOTES IN THE 2008 ELECTION

THE UNITED STATES
A political map showing the number of electoral votes per state

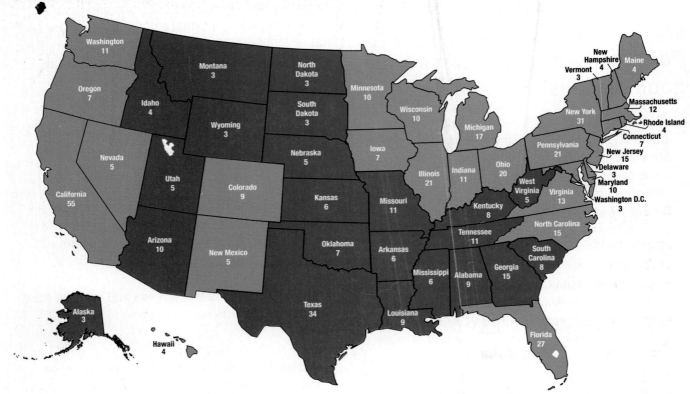

A political map with states drawn in proportion to the number of electoral votes

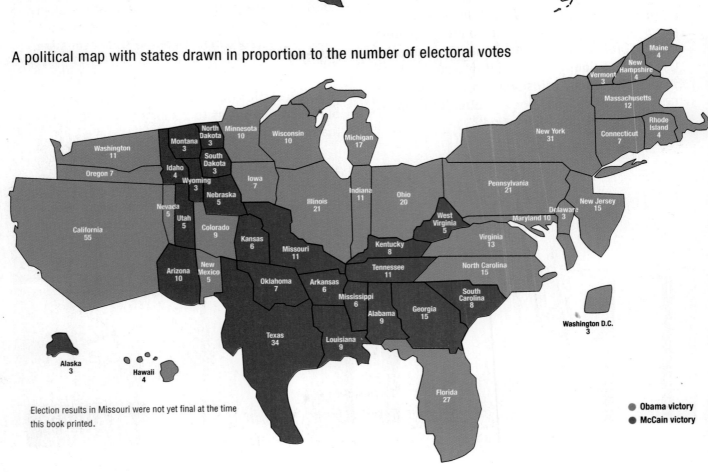

Election results in Missouri were not yet final at the time this book printed.

● Obama victory
● McCain victory

EIGHTH EDITION

POLITICS IN AMERICA

Texas Edition

Thomas R. Dye

Emeritus McKenzie
Professor of Government
Florida State University

Bartholomew H. Sparrow

The University of Texas at Austin

L. Tucker Gibson, Jr.

Trinity University

Clay Robison

Austin Bureau Chief
Houston Chronicle
San Antonio Express-News

Longman

New York   Boston   San Francisco
London   Toronto   Sydney   Tokyo   Singapore   Madrid
Mexico City   Munich   Paris   Cape Town   Hong Kong   Montreal

To our students over the years,
who taught us more than we taught them.

Editor-in-Chief: Eric Stano
Assistant Development Manager: David Kear
Marketing Manager: Lindsey Prudhomme
Associate Development Editor: Donna Garnier
Senior Media Producer: Regina Vertiz
Production Manager: Stacey Kulig
Project Coordination, Text Design, and Electronic Page Makeup: Nesbitt Graphics
Cover Design Manager: John Callahan
Cover Designer: Base Art Co.
Cover Image: Courtesy of iStock
Pearson Image Resource Center/Photo Researcher: Alexander Truitt and Jerry Marshall
Image Permission Coordinator: Debbie Hewitson
Senior Manufacturing Manager: Alfred C. Dorsey
Printer and Binder: Courier Corporation
Cover Printer: Coral Graphics Services

For permission to use copyrighted material, grateful acknowledgment is made to the copyright holders on pp. PC-1–PC-2, which are hereby made part of this copyright page.

Library of Congress Control Number: 2008941538

4 5 6 7 8 9 10—CRK—10

Longman
is an imprint of

www.pearsonhighered.com

ISBN 13: 978-0-13-602724-9
ISBN 10: 0-13-602724-5

Brief Contents

DETAILED CONTENTS

Part Three ★ PARTICIPANTS

People strive for power—to get the most of what there is to get.

Harold Lasswell

5 OPINION AND PARTICIPATION   136

Part Four ★ INSTITUTIONS

Authority is the expected and legitimate possession of power.

Harold Lasswell

10 CONGRESS   320

Part Five ★ OUTCOMES

That political science concentrates upon the influential does not imply the neglect of the total distribution of values throughout the community. . . . The emphasis upon the probability that the few (elite) will get the most does not imply that the many (mass) do not profit from some political changes.

Harold Lasswell

14 POLITICS AND PERSONAL LIBERTY   488

15 POLITICS AND CIVIL RIGHTS   536

16 POLITICS AND THE ECONOMY   576

APPENDIX

PREFACE

olitics is an activity by which people try to get more of whatever there is to get. It is about the struggle over the allocation of values and resources in a society. Simply put, it is about "who gets what, when, and how."

By using Harold Lasswell's classic definition of politics as its unifying framework, *Politics in America, Eighth Edition*, strives to present a clear, concise, and stimulating introduction to the American political system. Politics consists of all of the activities—reasonable discussion, impassioned oratory, campaigning, balloting, fundraising, advertising, lobbying, demonstrating, rioting, street fighting, and waging war—by which conflict is carried on. Managing conflict is the principal function of the political system and power is the ultimate goal.

By examining the struggle for power—the participants, the stakes, the processes, and the institutional arenas—*Politics in America, Eighth Edition*, introduces students to the political struggles that drive democracy.

Why *Politics in America?*

Instructors teaching the introductory American government course often find engaging their students to be the most difficult task facing them. *Politics in America, Eighth Edition*, strikes for a balanced presentation, but "balanced" does not mean boring. It does not mean avoiding controversy. Liberal and conservative arguments alike are set forth clearly and forcefully. Race and gender are given particular attention, not because it is currently fashionable to do so, but because American politics has long been driven by these factors.

Politics in America is designed to invite controversy and spirited discussion into the classroom. It does not hesitate to raise all of the most complicated and sensitive issues: affirmative action and "diversity" in education; civil disobedience; the appropriate use of U.S. military force; the constitutional rights of enemy combatants captured on foreign battlefields or inside the United States; the medical use of marijuana; immigration; the effectiveness of the Electoral College; and other equally challenging controversies, such as the question, Should violence against women be a federal crime?

New to the Eighth Edition

In 2008, the struggle for power in America was as fervent and evident as ever. The longest and most expensive presidential campaign in American history came to an end with the election of Barack Obama, the first African American to occupy the Oval Office. Indeed, the year was marked by intense political conflict, not only in the general election but also in the primary campaigns that lead to the national conventions. And the battle for control of the House and Senate confirmed the Democratic domination of Capitol Hill.

Despite calls for national unity, Americans remain polarized over politics and policy—Democrats versus Republicans, liberals versus conservatives, religious versus secular, supporters of the Iraq war versus its opponents, civil libertarians versus supporters of restrictive measures in the war on terror, supporters of immigration reform versus its opponents, and a host of other conflicts. And race remains an underlying theme in American society.

The Eighth Edition provides coverage of such new topics as:

★ The bitter and prolonged Democratic primary fight between Hillary Clinton and Barack Obama

★ The battle for the White House between Barack Obama and John McCain

★ Washington bails out Wall Street

★ The origins of the war in Iraq, growing opposition to the war, and strategies for exiting the war

A new feature, "Controversy," gets students engaged with some of the most provocative issues in American politics and encourages them to debate the issues. Topics include: "The Supremacy Clause at Work: Marijuana for Medical Use?", "Abortion: The 'Hot-Button' Issue," "Should Violence Against Women Be a Federal Crime?" "Which Party Does a Better Job?", and "Are We One Nation 'Under God'?"

New "Who Gets What" chapter summaries recap the most important concepts and details of each chapter, presenting them in the context of the book's theme—that American politics is truly a study of "who gets what, when, and how."

Additionally, new topics have been added to the "What Do You Think?", "People in Politics," and "Politics Up Close" features.

This balanced and highly readable text uses Harold Lasswell's classic definition of politics—**"who gets what, when and how"**—as a framework for presenting a clear, concise, and stimulating introduction to the American political system. The absorbing narrative examines this struggle for power—the participants, the stakes, the processes, and the institutions—**in a way that provokes thinking and discussion**.

" In countries of Western European civilization wealth and income are inequitably distributed. "

Harold Lasswell

24

▲ Each chapter begins with a quote from Lasswell that **provides a tangible link between the topic of each chapter and the theme of a competition for resources.**

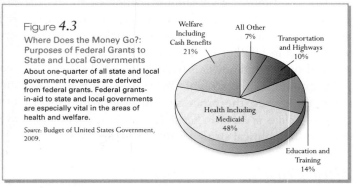

Figure *4.3*

Where Does the Money Go?: Purposes of Federal Grants to State and Local Governments

About one-quarter of all state and local government revenues are derived from federal grants. Federal grants-in-aid to state and local governments are especially vital in the areas of health and welfare.

Source: Budget of United States Government, 2009.

Welfare Including Cash Benefits 21%

All Other 7%

Transportation and Highways 10%

Health Including Medicaid 48%

Education and Training 14%

▲ **The theme of a competition for resources runs throughout *Politics in America***, from the chapter opening pages to the features and figures to the chapter ending summaries.

Controversy

Terrorism's Threat to Democracy

The horrifying images of "9/11" will not be easily forgotten—America's tallest skyscrapers exploding in flames and crumbling to earth—images projected over and over again on the nation's television screens. Commercial airliners, loaded with fuel and passengers, flown at high speeds directly into the symbols of America's financial and military power—the World Trade Center in New York and the Pentagon in Washington. Within minutes, thousands of lives are lost on American soil—more than at any time since the Civil War. After September 11 America found itself in a new war, a war against worldwide networks of terrorists.

The Goal of Terrorism Terrorism is violence directed against innocent civilians to advance political goals. As barbaric as terrorism appears to civilized peoples, it is not without a rationale. Terrorists are not "crazies." Their first goal is to announce in the most dramatic fashion their own grievances, their commitment to violence, and their disregard for human life, often including their own. In its initial phase the success of a terrorist act is directly related to the publicity it receives. Terrorist groups jubilantly claim responsibility for their acts. The more horrendous, the more media coverage, the more damage, the more dead—all add to the success of the terrorists in attracting attention to themselves.

A prolonged campaign of terrorism is designed to inspire pervasive fear among people, to convince them that their government cannot protect them, and to undermine their confidence in their political system. If the government fails to suppress terrorism, people become ever more fearful, more willing to accept restrictions on liberties, and more open to the appeals of demagogues who promise to restore order to protect people at any cost. Or a weakened government

may resort to "negotiations" with the leaders of terrorist groups, implicitly granting them legitimacy and providing them the opportunity to advance their goals.

Security vs. Liberty Threats to national security have historically resulted in challenges to individual liberty. Abraham Lincoln suspended the *writ of habeas corpus* (the requirement that authorities bring defendants before a judge and show cause for their detention) during the Civil War. (Only after the war did the U.S. Supreme Court hold that he had no authority to suspend the writ.[a]

In February 1942, shortly after the Japanese attack on Pearl Harbor, President Franklin D. Roosevelt authorized the removal and internment of Japanese Americans living on the West Coast. The U.S. Supreme Court upheld this flagrant violation of the Constitution;[b] not until 1988 did the U.S. Congress vote reparations and make public apologies to the surviving victims.

New Restrictions on Liberty The "9/11" terrorist attack on America inspired Congress and the president to enact and enforce greater restrictions on individual liberty than the nation had experienced since World War II. Congress passed the Patriot Act with near-unanimous support of Democrats and Republicans. Among other things, the Act allows searches without notice to the suspect; grants "roving" wiretap warrants that allow government eavesdropping on any telephones used by suspects; allows the interception of e-mail; allows investigators to obtain information from credit card companies, banks, libraries, and other businesses; authorizes the seizure of properties used to

[a]Ex parte Milligan (1866).
[b]*Korematsu v. U.S.*, 323 U.S. 214 (1944).

◄ **NEW! Controversy** feature gets students engaged with some of **the most provocative issues in American politics and encourages them to debate the issues.**

A PROVOCATIVE THEME

People in Politics — Bill O'Reilly, "The No Spin Zone"?

Bill O'Reilly assures "fair and balanced" broadcast journalism to Fox News viewers, O'Reilly is frequently loose with the facts; the show is more "entertainment" than "news."

He describes his popular TV show as a "no spin zone" and refers to himself as an "independent." Yet O'Reilly has emerged as the nation's most popular voice of conservatism on television and on radio.

O'Reilly boasts of an Irish Catholic working-class upbringing in Long Island. He graduated from Catholic Marist College, briefly taught in a Miami high school, and earned a master's degree from Boston University in journalism. He bounced around the country as a reporter for various TV stations, and by 1986 he had become a top correspondent for ABC News. He eventually replaced David Frost as anchor of the TV tabloid Inside Edition, but left that job in 1995 to earn a master's

degree from the John F. Kennedy School of Government at Harvard University.

The Fox News network recruited O'Reilly to create a new evening talk show, The O'Reilly Factor. The show quickly grew into the most watched program on cable news, outdistancing even Larry King Live. And O'Reilly's radio talk show competes with Rush Limbaugh for the top spot in talk radio.

O'Reilly mixes humor with bombast. He constantly interrupts guests, both conservatives and liberals, to broadcast his own views. He is convinced that liberal "secularists" are waging war against religion, Christmas, and traditional moral values. Liberal critic Al Franken wrote a satirical mockery of the Fox network and O'Reilly himself, entitled Lies and the Lying Liars Who Tell Them: A Fair and Balanced Look at the Right; O'Reilly prompted Fox News to sue, but the suit was thrown out of federal court. O'Reilly's favorite targets include Hollywood liberals, Jesse Jackson, and the American Civil Liberties Union. The occasional twinkle in his Irish eyes tempers his often venomous commentary.

▲ The **People in Politics** features personalize politics and illustrate that **the participants in the struggle for power are real people**. Students are introduced to some of the key players who have helped shape American politics, as well as their backgrounds and careers.

Politics Up Close — Confidence in American Institutions

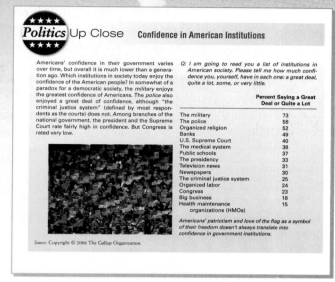

Americans' confidence in their government varies over time, but overall it is much lower than a generation ago. Which institutions in society today enjoy the confidence of the American people? In somewhat of a paradox for a democratic society, the military enjoys the greatest confidence of Americans. The police also enjoyed a great deal of confidence, although "the criminal justice system" (defined by most respondents as the courts) does not. Among branches of the national government, the president and the Supreme Court rate fairly high in confidence. But Congress is rated very low.

Q: I am going to read you a list of institutions in American society. Please tell me how much confidence you, yourself, have in each one: a great deal, quite a lot, some, or very little.

	Percent Saying a Great Deal or Quite a Lot
The military	73
The police	58
Organized religion	52
Banks	49
U.S. Supreme Court	40
The medical system	38
Public schools	37
The presidency	33
Television news	31
Newspapers	30
The criminal justice system	25
Organized labor	24
Congress	23
Big business	18
Health maintenance organizations (HMOs)	15

Americans' patriotism and love of the flag as a symbol of their freedom doesn't always translate into confidence in government institutions.

Source: Copyright © 2006 The Gallup Organization.

▲ **Politics Up Close** illustrates specific **struggles over who gets what** and covers a wide variety of current political conflicts.

Across the USA — Hispanic Population Concentrations

The Hispanic population in the United States is heavily concentrated in a few states—California, Colorado, Arizona, New Mexico, Texas, and Florida. Even within these states Latinos are concentrated in particular counties, especially counties along the southern border as well as Miami-Dade County in Florida (Cubans)

and New York City (Puerto Ricans). This concentration facilitates the continuing use of the Spanish language—in newspapers, television (Univision, TeleMundo), business, and commercial establishments. It often inspires bilingual education in public schools, colleges, and universities.

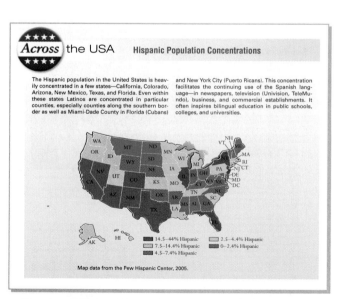

14.5–44% Hispanic
7.5–14.4% Hispanic
4.5–7.4% Hispanic
2.5–4.4% Hispanic
0–2.4% Hispanic

Map data from the Pew Hispanic Center, 2005.

▲ The **Across the USA** collection of **maps summarizes important statistical and demographic information** relevant to American politics in an intuitive, accessible, and visual manner.

Summary
Who Gets What: Ideas in Conflict

Ideas are sources of power. They provide people with guides for determining right and wrong and with rationales for political action. Political institutions are shaped by the values and beliefs of the political culture, and political leaders are restrained in their exercise of power by these ideas.

★ The American political culture is a set of widely shared values and beliefs about who should govern, for what ends, and by what means.

★ Americans share many common ways of thinking about politics. Nevertheless, there are often contradictions between professed values and actual conditions, problems in applying abstract beliefs to concrete situations, and even occasional conflict over fundamental values.

★ Individual liberty is a fundamental value in American life. The classical liberal tradition that inspired the nation's Founders included both political liberties and economic freedoms.

★ Equality is another fundamental American value. The nation's Founders believed in equality before the law; yet political equality, in the form of universal voting rights, required nearly two centuries to bring about.

★ Equality of opportunity is a widely shared value; most Americans are opposed to artificial barriers of race, sex, religion, or ethnicity barring individual advancement. But equality of results is not a widely shared value, most Americans support a "floor" on income and well-being for their fellow citizens but oppose placing a "ceiling" on income or wealth.

★ Income inequality has increased in recent years primarily as a result of economic and demographic changes. Most Americans believe that opportunities for individual advancement are still available, and this belief diminishes the potential for class conflict.

★ A great majority of Americans claim religious affiliation. But there is a growing divide between religious and secular viewpoints on the role of religion in public life. Secularists have challenged many traditional religious practices and symbols, such as the words "under God" in the Pledge of Allegiance.

★ Liberal and conservative ideologies in American politics present somewhat different sets of values and beliefs, even though they share a common commitment to individual dignity and private property. Generally, liberals favor an active, powerful government to provide economic security and protection for civil rights but oppose government restrictions on social conduct. Generally, conservatives favor minimal government intervention in economic affairs and civil rights but support many government restrictions on social conduct.

★ Many Americans who identify themselves as liberals or conservatives are not always consistent in applying their professed views. Populists are liberal on economic issues but conservative in their views on social issues. Libertarians are conservative on economic issues but liberal in their social views.

★ The collapse of communism in Eastern Europe and the former Soviet Union and the worldwide movement toward free markets and democracy have undermined support for socialism throughout the world. Yet Marxism survives in academic circles as a critique of the functioning of capitalism.

▲ **NEW! Who Gets What** chapter summaries recap the most important concepts and details of each chapter, **presenting them in the context of the book's theme**—that American politics is a study of "**who gets what, when, and how**."

"WHO GETS WHAT?"

Marginal learning aids **encourage critical thinking and dispel conventional notions of American politics** by allowing students to compare their initial responses to critical issues in American politics with the responses they have later, as they work through the chapter.

✓ Think About Politics

1. Do you consider yourself politically conservative, moderate, or liberal?
   CONSERVATIVE ○ **MODERATE** ○
   LIBERAL ○

2. Are income differences in America widening?
   YES ○ **NO** ○

3. Is it the government's responsibility to reduce income differences between people?
   YES ○ **NO** ○

4. If incomes were made more equal, would people still be motivated to work hard?
   YES ○ **NO** ○

5. Do Americans today still have the opportunity to significantly improve their condition in life?
   YES ○ **NO** ○

By taking the **Think About Politics** poll at the beginning of each chapter, students understand their own beliefs on these issues before studying the chapter content.

✓ Think Again

Do you consider yourself politically conservative, moderate, or liberal?

The **Think Again** marginal questions in the chapter help students revisit their thinking on issues as they move through the chapter discussion.

What Do You *Think?*

Can You Trust the Government?

Americans are suspicious of big government. Many do not trust the government in Washington to "do what is right." Trust in government has varied over the years, as measured by polls asking, "How much of the time do you think you can trust the government in Washington to do what is right? Just about always? Most of the time? Some of the time? None of the time?" Low levels of trust and confidence in government may represent a profound disaffection with the political system, or a more superficial dissatisfaction with current politicians and political leaders or with policies.[a] Americans' trust in the national government used to be higher. In the 1950s and through the early 1960s, during the Eisenhower, Kennedy, and first years of the Johnson administrations, the public overwhelmingly had confidence in the government. But in the late '60s through the '70s, with the defeat in Vietnam, the Watergate scandal and the forced resignation of President Richard Nixon—the first resignation of a president in U.S. history—public confidence fell, and kept falling.

Throughout this period of decline, television broadcasted many negative images of government and government policy. Television producers want news of scandal, violence, corruption, and incompetence; they want what is simple and sensational, not good news or much in-depth reporting of complicated news (see Chapter 6, "Mass Media: Setting the Agenda"). Meanwhile, more Americans have come to recognize television news anchors and famous reporters than they do presidential candidates or

important members of Congress. And the news anchors and reporters follow their producer's lead: reporting critically, and even cynically, of politicians and the government.

Economic recessions erode public confidence government. People expect the president and Congress to lead them out of "hard times." So while President George H. W. Bush raised public confidence in the early 1990s with the military success of Desert Storm in Iraq, his administration's perceived failure to act decisively to take the United States out of the economic recession of the early 1990s helped to send public confidence in government back down. But then sustained economic growth in the 1990s under President Clinton improved public trust in government.

But public confidence in government can be revived, as it was during the Reagan presidency. President Reagan's popularity may have contributed to the restoration of the public's confidence in government.[b] Americans' trust in government also revived after the terrorist attacks of September 11, 2001. Public trust in government doubled immediately after September 11, as America rallied behind the government for the first time since the Japanese attack on Pearl Harbor on December 7, 1941. American flags and images of Old Glory sprouted from homes and businesses, and on vehicles. Trust in government "to do the right thing" leaped to levels not seen since the early 1970s. But the public trust gradually eroded as the war in Iraq dragged on.

▲ **What Do You Think?** boxes present students with a controversial issue and ask them to take a stance.

A Conflicting *View*

Sometimes It's Right to Disobey the Law

Civil disobedience is the nonviolent violation of laws that people believe to be unjust. Civil disobedience denies the *legitimacy*, or rightfulness, of a law and implies that a higher moral authority takes precedence over unjust laws. It is frequently a political tactic of minorities. (Majorities can more easily change laws through conventional political activity.)

Why resort to civil disobedience in a democracy? Why not work within the democratic system to change unjust laws? In 1963 a group of Alabama clergy posed these questions to Martin Luther King, Jr., and asked him to call off mass demonstrations in Birmingham, Alabama. King, who had been arrested in the demonstrations, replied in his now-famous "Letter from Birmingham City Jail":

> One may well ask, "How can you advocate breaking some laws and obeying others?" The answer is found in the fact that there are unjust laws. I would be the first to advocate obeying just laws. One has not only a legal but a moral responsibility to obey just laws. Conversely, one has a moral responsibility to disobey unjust laws.

King argued that *nonviolent direct action* was a vital aspect of democratic politics. The political purpose of civil disobedience is to call attention or "to bear witness" to the existence of injustices. Only laws regarded as unjust are broken, and they are broken openly, without hatred or violence. Punishment is actively sought rather than avoided, since punishment will further emphasize the injustice of the laws. The objective of nonviolent civil disobedience is to stir the conscience of an apathetic majority and to win support for measures that will eliminate the injustices. By accepting punishment for the violation of an unjust law, persons practicing civil disobedience demonstrate their sincerity. They hope to shame the majority and to make it ask itself how far it is willing to go to protect the status quo. Thus, according to King's teachings, civil disobedience is clearly differentiated from hatred and violence:

Dr. Martin Luther King, Jr., shown here marching in Mississippi with his wife, Coretta Scott King, and others, used civil disobedience to advance the rights of African Americans during the 1950s and 1960s. (Copyright © Flip Schulke)

> One who breaks an unjust law must do it openly, lovingly (not hatefully as the white mothers did in New Orleans when they were seen on television screaming "nigger, nigger, nigger") and with a willingness to accept the penalty. I submit that an individual who breaks a law that conscience tells him is unjust, and willingly accepts the penalty by staying in jail to arouse the conscience of the community over its injustice, is in reality expressing the very highest respect for law.

In 1964 Martin Luther King, Jr., received the Nobel Peace Prize in recognition of his extraordinary contributions to the development of nonviolent methods of social change.

Source: Martin Luther King, Jr., "Letter from Birmingham City Jail," April 16, 1963.

▲ **A Conflicting View** boxes challenge students to rethink conventional wisdom in American politics by presenting them **with views on important topics that clash with popular opinion.**

THINKING CRITICALLY

The *Constitution* of the United States

More than two centuries after its ratification, our Constitution remains the operating charter of our republic. It is neither self-explanatory nor a comprehensive description of our constitutional rules. Still, it remains the starting point. Many Americans who swear by the Constitution have never read it seriously, although copies can be found in most American government and American history textbooks.

Justice Hugo Black, who served on the Supreme Court for 34 years, kept a copy of the Constitution with him at all times. He read it often. Reading the Constitution would be a good way for you to begin (and then reread again to end) your study of the government of the United States. We have therefore included a copy of it at this point in the book. Please read it carefully.

THE PREAMBLE

We the People of the United States, in Order to form a more perfect Union, establish Justice, insure domestic Tranquility, provide for the common defense, promote the general Welfare, and secure the Blessings of Liberty to ourselves and our Posterity, do ordain and establish this Constitution for the United States of America.

"We, the people." Three simple words, yet of profound importance and contentious origin. Every government in the world at the time of the Constitutional Convention was some type of monarchy wherein sovereign power flowed from the top. The Founders of our new country rejected monarchy as a form of government and proposed instead a republic, which would draw its sovereignty from the people.

Under the Articles of Confederation, the legislature was the only functional instrument of government. Therefore, the framers truly believed it was the most important component of the new government.

Section 1 All legislative Powers herein granted shall be vested in a Congress of the United States, which shall consist of a Senate and House of Representatives.

Section 1 established a bicameral (two-chamber) legislature of an upper (Senate) and lower (House of Representatives) organization of the legislative branch.

House of Representatives: Composition, Qualifications, Apportionment, Impeachment Power

Section 2 Clause 1. The House of Representatives shall be com-

▲ An **Annotated Constitution** is included after Chapter 3, providing **extended commentary on key sections and clauses** to give students a deeper insight into the intentions behind this important document.

A *Constitutional* Note

Natural Born Versus Naturalized Citizenship

The 14th Amendment to the Constitution requires the states, and by implication the national government, to treat natural born and naturalized citizens the same: "all persons born or naturalized in United States, and subject to the jurisdiction thereof, are citizens of the United States. . . . No State shall make or enforce any law which shall abridge the privileges or immunities of citizens of the United States. . . . " But there is one key difference between natural born and naturalized citizens written into the original Constitution of 1787: "No Person except a natural born Citizen, or a Citizen of the United States, at the time of the Adoption of this Constitution, shall be eligible to the Office of President. . . ."

Requiring that the President be born in the United States is the only constitutional difference between born and naturalized citizens. Perhaps this difference made more sense in 1787 when many aspiring politicians had only recently moved into the country. But is it relevant today? Does it deny some very qualified people the opportunity to run for the nation's highest office?

▲ **A Constitutional Note** in each chapter expands and integrates topic coverage in the context of the Constitution.

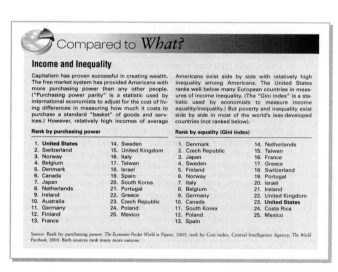

Compared to *What?*

Income and Inequality

Capitalism has proven successful in creating wealth. The free market system has provided Americans with more purchasing power than any other people. ("Purchasing power parity" is a statistic used by international economists to adjust for the cost of living differences in measuring how much it costs to purchase a standard "basket" of goods and services.) However, relatively high incomes of average

Americans exist side by side with relatively high inequality among Americans. The United States ranks well below many European countries in measures of income inequality. (The "Gini index" is a statistic used by economists to measure income equality/inequality.) But poverty and inequality exist side by side in most of the world's less-developed countries (not ranked below).

Rank by purchasing power

1. **United States**	14. Sweden
2. Switzerland	15. United Kingdom
3. Norway	16. Italy
4. Belgium	17. Taiwan
5. Denmark	18. Israel
6. Canada	19. Spain
7. Japan	20. South Korea
8. Netherlands	21. Portugal
9. Ireland	22. Greece
10. Australia	23. Czech Republic
11. Germany	24. Poland
12. Finland	25. Mexico
13. France	

Rank by equality (Gini index)

1. Denmark	14. Netherlands
2. Czech Republic	15. Taiwan
3. Japan	16. France
4. Sweden	17. Greece
5. Finland	18. Switzerland
6. Norway	19. Portugal
7. Italy	20. Israel
8. Belgium	21. Ireland
9. Germany	22. United Kingdom
10. Canada	23. **United States**
11. South Korea	24. Costa Rica
12. Poland	25. Mexico
13. Spain	

Sources: Rank by purchasing power, *The Economist Pocket World in Figures, 2003*; rank by Gini index, Central Intelligence Agency, *The World Factbook, 2003*. Both sources rank many more nations.

◄ Global context is essential to the study of American politics today. **Compared to What?** provides comparisons of the United States with other nations, **challenging students to think differently about such topics as the size of government, tax burdens, voter turnout, and health care.**

RESOURCES IN PRINT AND ONLINE

Name of Supplement	Available in Print	Available Online	Instructor or Student Supplement	Description
American Government Study Site		✗	Both	Online package of practice tests, Web links, and flashcards organized by major topics and matching this book's table of contents. **www.pearsonamericangovernment.com**
Instructor's Manual 0136027261	✗	✗	Instructor	Offers chapter summaries, recent news and pop culture examples, discussion topics, and Web activities.
Test Bank 0136027008	✗	✗	Instructor	Contains over 200 questions per chapter in multiple-choice, true-false, short answer, and essay format. Questions address all levels of Bloom's taxonomy and have been reviewed and edited for accuracy and effectiveness.
MyTest		✗	Instructor	This flexible, online test generating software that includes all questions found in the printed Test Bank.
Study Guide 0136027253	✗		Student	Contains learning objectives, chapter summaries, and practice tests
PowerPoint Presentation		✗	Instructor	Slides include a lecture outline of the text along with graphics from the book. Available on the Instructor Resource Center.*
Digital Transparency Masters		✗	Instructor	These PDF slides contain all maps, figures, and tables found in the text. Available on the Instructor Resource Center.*
Longman Political Science Video Program	✗		Instructor	Qualified college adopters can peruse our list of videos for the American government classroom.
You Decide! Current Debates in American Politics, 2009 Edition 0205684054	✗		Student	This debate-style reader by John Rourke of the University of Connecticut examines provocative issues in American politics today by presenting various sides of key political ideas.
Voices of Dissent: Critical Readings in American Politics, 7th Edition 0205697976	✗		Student	This collection of critical essays by William Grover of Saint Michael's College and Joseph Peschek of Hamline University goes beyond the debate between mainstream liberalism and conservatism to fundamentally challenge the status quo.
Writing in Political Science, 3rd Edition 0321217357	✗		Student	This guide by Diane Schmidt of California State University–Chico takes students through all aspects of writing in political science step by step.
Choices: An American Government Database Reader	✗		Student	This customizable reader allows instructors to choose from a database of over 300 readings to create a reader that exactly matches their course needs. Go to **www.pearsoncustom.com/database/choices.html** for more information.
Ten Things That Every American Government Student Should Read 020528469X	✗		Student	Edited by Karen O'Connor of American University. We asked American government instructors across the country to vote for the ten things beyond the text that they believe every student should read and put them in this brief and useful reader. Available at no additional charge when ordered packaged with the text.
American Government Readings and Cases, Eighteenth Edition 0205697984	✗		Student	Edited by Peter Woll, this long-time best-selling reader provides a strong, balanced blend of classic readings and cases that illustrate and amplify important concepts in American government, alongside extremely current selections drawn from today's issues and literature. Available at a discount when ordered packaged with this text.
Diversity in Contemporary American Politics and Government 0205550363	✗		Student	This reader, edited by David Dulio of Oakland University, Erin E. O'Brien of Kent State University, and John Klemanski of Oakland University, explores the significant role that demographic diversity plays in political outcomes and policy processes.
Penguin-Longman Value Bundles	✗		Student	Longman offers twenty five Penguin Putnam titles at more than a 60 percent discount when packaged with any Longman text. Go to **www.pearsonhighered.com/penguin** for more information.
Longman State Politics Series	✗		Student	These primers on state and local government and political issues are available at no extra cost when shrink-wrapped with the text. Available for Texas, California, and Georgia.

*Instructor Resource Center available at **www.pearsonhighered.com/educator**

IMPROVE RESULTS WITH PEARSON mypoliscilab

Designed to amplify a traditional course in numerous ways or to administer a course online, **MyPoliSciLab** combines pedagogy and assessment with an array of multimedia activities—videos, simulations, exercises, and online newsfeeds—to make learning more effective for all types of students. Now featuring the combined resources, assets, and activities of both Prentice Hall and Longman Publishers, this new release of **MyPoliSciLab** is visually richer and even more interactive than previous iterations—a quantum leap forward in design with more points of assessment and interconnectivity between concepts.

TEACHING AND LEARNING TOOLS

✓ **Assessment**: Comprehensive online diagnostic tools—learning objectives, study guides, flashcards, and pre- and post-tests—help students gauge and improve their understanding.

✓ **E-book:** Identical in content and design to the printed text, an e-book provides students access to their text wherever and whenever they need it.

✓ *UPDATED!* **PoliSci News Review:** A series of weekly articles and video clips—from traditional and non-traditional news sources—recaps the most important political news stories, followed by quizzes that test students' understanding.

✓ *NEW!* **ABC News RSS feed:** MyPoliSciLab provides an online feed from ABC News, updated hourly, to keep students current.

✓ **ABC News Video Clips:** Over 60 high-interest 2- to 4-minute clips provide historical snapshots in each chapter of key political issues and offer opportunities to launch discussions.

✓ *UPDATED!* **Roundtable and Debate Video Clips**: These video clips feature professors discussing key concepts from ideologically diverse perspectives and debating politically charged issues.

✓ **Student Polling:** Updated weekly with timely, provocative questions, the polling feature lets students voice their opinions in nationwide polls and view how their peers across the country see the same issue.

✓ **Political Podcasts:** Featuring some of Pearson's most respected authors, these video podcasts present short, instructive—and even entertaining—lectures on key topics that students can download and play at their convenience.

✓ *NEW!* **Student Podcasts:** The new MyPoliSciLab allows students to record and download their own videos for peer-to-peer learning.

INTERACTIVE ACTIVITIES

✓ **New and Updated Simulations:** Featuring an appealing new graphic interface, these role-playing simulations help students experience political decision-making in a way they never have before—including new "mini activities" that prepare students to make the right decisions.

✓ *NEW!* **Debate Exercises:** These provocative new exercises present classic and contemporary views on core controversies, ask students to take a position, and then show them the potential consequences of taking that stand.

✓ **More Focused Comparative Exercises:** These exercises have been revised in scope to concentrate on a more specific issue when comparing the United States to other political systems, giving students a more concrete foundation on which to analyze key similarities and differences.

✓ **More Interactive Timelines:** With redesigned media and graphics, these timelines let students step through the evolution of some aspect of politics and now include more interactive questions throughout.

✓ **More Dynamic Visual Literacy Exercises:** These revised exercises offer attractive new graphs, charts, and tables and more opportunities to manipulate and interpret political data.

✓ **Expanded Participation Activities:** Reflecting our county's growing political interest, these expanded activities give students ideas and instructions for getting involved in all aspects of politics.

Icons in the margins of this book direct students to activities on MyPoliSciLab related to the topics they are studying.

ONLINE ADMINISTRATION

No matter what course management system you use—or if you do not use one at all, but still wish to easily capture your students' grades and track their performance—Pearson has a **MyPoliSciLab** option to suit your needs. Contact one of Pearson's Technology Specialists for more information or assistance.

A **MyPoliSciLab** access code is no additional cost when packaged with selected Pearson American Government texts. To get started, contact your local Pearson Publisher's Representative at **www.pearsonhighered.com/replocator.**

ACKNOWLEDGMENTS

We would like to thank James Corey of High Point University for preparing the annotated Constitution. We are also indebted to the many reviewers who evaluated the text and contributed invaluable advice.

Danny Adkinson, Oklahoma State University

Weton Agor, University of Texas at El Paso

Lee Almaguer, Midland College

John Bertalan, Hillsborough Community College

Angela Burger, UWC–Marathon Company

Stefanie Chambers, Trinity College

Charles W. Chapman, University of Texas at Brownsville

Frank Colon, Lehigh University

James Corey, High Point University

Irasema Coronado, University of Texas at El Paso

Paul B. Davis, Truckee Meadows Community College

Roy Dawes, University of Southwestern Louisiana

Brian K. Dille, Odessa College

Nelson Dometrius, Texas Tech University

Kevin R. den Dulk, Grand Valley State University

John Ellis, San Antonio College

Larry Elowitz, University of Southwestern Louisiana

Traci Fatimi, Irvine Valley College

Robert Glen Findley, Odessa College

Edward Fox, Eastern Washington University

Marilyn A. W. Garr, Johnson County Community College

Dana K. Glencross, Oklahoma City Community College

Henry Glick, Florida State University

John Green, University of Akron

Dale Herspring, Kansas State University

John C. Hughes, Sr., Oklahoma City Community College

Fred Kramer, University of Massachusetts at Amherst

Dale Krane, University of Nebraska at Omaha

James W. Lamare, Florida Atlantic University

Fred Lokken, Truckee Meadows Community College

Christopher C. Lovett, Emporia State University

Roger Marietta, Darton College

Nancy McGlen, Niagara University

John McGlennon, College of William and Mary

James Meader, Augustana College

Jo Anne Myers, Marist College

Max Neiman, University of California–Riverside

Paul Peretz, California State University, Fullerton

John Pratt, Cedar Valley College

Wayne Pryor, Bazosport College

Bruce Rogers, American River College

Bill Rutherford, Odessa College

Earl T. Sheridan, University of North Carolina

Mark W. Shomaker, Blinn College, Bryan Campus

Robert Small, Massosoit County College

Henry Steck, SUNY–Cortland

Gerald Strom, University of Illinois at Chicago

Albert Waite, Central Texas College

Morris M. Wilhelm, Indiana University Southeast

Thomas R. Dye
Bartholomew H. Sparrow
L. Tucker Gibson, Jr.
Clay Robison

ABOUT THE AUTHORS

Thomas R. Dye, Emeritus McKenzie Professor of Government at Florida State University, regularly taught large introductory classes in American politics. He received his B.A. and M.A. degrees from Pennsylvania State University and his Ph.D. degree from the University of Pennsylvania. He is the author of numerous books and articles on American government and public policy, including *The Irony of Democracy; Politics in States and Communities; Understanding Public Policy; Who's Running America; American Politics in the Media Age; Power in Society; Politics, Economics, and the Public;* and *American Federalism: Competition Among Governments.* His books have been translated into many languages, including Russian and Chinese, and published abroad. Dye has served as president of the Southern Political Science Association, president of the Policy Studies Organization, and secretary of the American Political Science Association. He has taught at the University of Pennsylvania, the University of Wisconsin, and the University of Georgia, and served as a visiting scholar at Bar-Ilan University, Israel; the Brookings Institution in Washington, D.C.; and elsewhere. He is a member of Phi Beta Kappa, Omicron Delta Kappa, and Phi Kappa Phi and is listed in most major biographic directories. Additional information is available at www.thomasrdye.com.

Bartholomew H. Sparrow is a professor of government at the University of Texas at Austin. Sparrow teaches one of the largest American government introductory courses at Texas, as well as upper-division courses on the United States' territorial expansion, the U.S. media as a political institution, and the politics of food in America. He is author of *The Insular Cases and the Emergence of American Empire, Uncertain Guardians: The News Media as a Political Institution,* and *From the Outside In: World War II and the American State.* He is also co-editor of *The Louisiana Purchase and American Expansion, 1803–1898* and *Politics, Discourse, and American Society: New Agendas,* and he has written numerous journal articles, chapters in edited volumes, and book reviews. Sparrow has received the American Political Science Association's Franklin L. Burdette Pi Sigma Alpha and Leonard D. White awards, the Best Paper Award from the Presidency Research Group of the APSA, a Scholar's Award from the Harry S. Truman Library Institute, and fellowships from the Woodrow Wilson International Center for Scholars and the Joan Shorenstein Center on the Press, Politics and Public Policy. He has an A.B. from Dartmouth College, an A.M. from the University of Texas at Austin, and a Ph.D. from the University of Chicago.

L. Tucker Gibson, Jr. is professor of political science at Trinity University, where he teaches introductory courses in American, state, and local politics. His teaching interests also include political parties, interest groups, U.S. legislatures, and public policy. He has served on the Civil Service Commission of the city of San Antonio, assisted local governments across central and south Texas in redistricting their governing bodies, and conducted public opinion research for political candidates, businesses, and corporations. In addition to coauthoring *Politics in America: Texas Edition,* Gibson is the coauthor of *Government and Politics in the Lone Star State: Theory and Practice.*

Clay Robison has covered state government and politics in Texas for more than 35 years as a journalist, first for the *San Antonio Light,* and is now the Austin bureau chief for the *Houston Chronicle* and the *San Antonio Express-News.* He has covered many of the personalities and events that are incorporated in the chapters on Texas government. Robison is the coauthor of *Politics in America: Texas Edition* and *Government and Politics in the Lone Star State: Theory and Practice.*

1 POLITICS
Who Gets What, When, and How

> **"** The study of politics is the study of influence in the influential. . . . The influential are those who get the most of what there is to get. Those who get the most are elite; the rest are mass. **"**

Harold Lasswell

Politics and Political Science

Politics is deciding "who gets what, when, and how."[1] It is an activity by which people try to get more of whatever there is to get—money, prestige, jobs, respect, sex, even power itself. Politics occurs in many different settings. We talk about office politics, student politics, union politics, church politics, and so forth. But political science usually limits its attention to *politics in government.*

Political science is the study of politics, or the study of who gets what, when, and how.[2] The *who* are the participants in politics—voters, special-interest groups, political parties, television and the press, corporations and labor unions, lawyers and lobbyists, foundations and think tanks, and both elected and appointed government officials, including members of Congress, the president and vice president, judges, prosecutors, and bureaucrats. The *what* of politics are public policies—the decisions that governments make concerning social welfare, health care, education, national defense, law enforcement, the environment, taxation, and thousands of other issues that come before governments. The *when* and *how* are the political process—campaigns and elections, political reporting in the news media, television debates, fund raising, lobbying, decision making in the White House and executive agencies, and decision making in the courts.

Political science is generally concerned with three questions. *Who governs? For what ends? By what means?* Throughout this book, we are concerned with who participates in politics, how government decisions are made, who benefits most from those decisions, and who bears their greatest costs (see Figure 1.1).

Politics would be simple if everyone agreed on who should govern, who should get what, who should pay for it, and how and when it should be done. But conflict arises from disagreements over these questions, and sometimes the question of confidence in the government itself underlies the conflict (see *What Do You Think?*: "Can You Trust the Government?").

Politics and Government

What distinguishes governmental politics from politics in other institutions in society? After all, parents, teachers, unions, banks, corporations, and many other organizations make decisions about who gets what in society. The answer is that only **government** decisions can *extend to the whole society*, and only government can *legitimately use force*. Other institutions encompass only a part of society: for example, students and

★ **politics**
Deciding who gets what, when, and how.

★ **political science**
The study of politics: who governs, for what ends, and by what means.

3

Figure *1.1*   Who Gets What, When, and How

Political science is the study of politics. The distinguished political scientist Harold Lasswell entitled his most popular book *Politics: Who Gets What, When and How.* The first topic of politics is "Who?" (that is, who are the participants in politics, both within and outside of government?), "When and how are political decisions made?" (that is, how do the institutions and processes of politics function?), and "What outcomes are produced?" (that is, what public policies are adopted?). Shown here are some of the topics of concern to political science.

Who Governs: Participants

Governmental

President and White House staff
Executive Office of the President, including Office of Management and Budget
Cabinet officers and executive agency heads
Bureaucrats

Congress members
Congressional staff

Supreme Court justices
Federal appellate and district judges

Nongovernmental

Voters
Campaign contributors
Interest-group leaders and members
Party leaders and party identifiers in the electorate
Corporate and union leaders
Media leaders, including press and television anchors and reporters
Lawyers and lobbyists
Think tanks and foundation personnel

When and How: Institutions and Processes

Institutions

Constitution
    Separation of powers
    Checks and balances
    Federalism
    Judicial review
    Amendment procedures
    Electoral system

Presidency
Congress
    Senate
    House of Representatives

Courts
    Supreme Court
    Appellate courts
    District courts

Parties
    National committees
    Conventions
    State and local organizations

Media
    Television
    Press
    Internet

Processes

Socialization and learning
Opinion formation
Party identification
Voting
Contributing
Joining organizations
Talking politics

Running for office
Campaigning
Polling
Fund raising
Parading and demonstrating
Nonviolent direct action
Violence

Lobbying
Logrolling
Deciding
Budgeting
Implementing and evaluating
Adjudicating

Agenda setting
News making
Interpreting
Persuading

What Outcomes: Public Policies

Civil liberties
Civil rights
Equality
Criminal justice
Welfare
Social Security
Health
Education
Energy

Environmental protection
Economic development
Economic stability
Taxation
Government spending and deficits
National defense
Foreign affairs
Homeland Security

faculty in a college, members of a church or union, employees or customers of a corporation. And individuals have a legal right to voluntarily withdraw from *non*governmental organizations. But governments make decisions affecting everyone, and no one can voluntarily withdraw from government's authority (without leaving the country, and thus becoming subject to some other government's authority). Some individuals and organizations—muggers, gangs, crime

★ **government**
Organization extending to the whole society that can legitimately use force to carry out its decisions.

Conflict All Around

Conflict exists in all political activities as participants struggle over who gets what, when, and how. From the streets to the Congress to the campaign trail, participants in the political process compete to further their goals and ambitions.

families—occasionally use physical force to get what they want. But only governments can use force legitimately—that is, people generally believe it is acceptable for the government to use force if necessary to uphold its laws, but they do not extend this right to other institutions or individuals.

Most people would say that they obey the law in order to avoid fines and stay out of prison. But if large numbers of people all decided to disobey the law at the same time, the government would not have enough police or jails to hold them all.

The government can rely on force only against relatively small numbers of offenders. Most of us, most of the time, obey laws out of habit—the habit of compliance. We have been taught to believe that law and order are necessary and that government is right to punish those who disobey its laws.

Government thus enjoys **legitimacy**, or rightfulness, in its use of force.[3] A democratic government has a special claim to legitimacy because it is based on the consent of its people, who participate in the selection of its leaders and the making of its laws. Those who disagree with a law have the option of working for its change by speaking out, petitioning, demonstrating, forming interest groups or parties, voting against unpopular leaders, or running for office themselves. Since people living in a democracy can effect change by "working within the system," they have a greater moral obligation to obey the law than people living under regimes in which they have no voice. However, there may be some occasions when "civil disobedience" even in a democracy may be morally justified (see *A Conflicting View*: "Sometimes It's Right to Disobey the Law").

✓ *Think* Again

Should any group other than the government have the right to use force?

★ **legitimacy**
Widespread acceptance of something as necessary, rightful, and legally binding.

✓ *Think* Again

Is violence ever justified as a means of bringing about political change?

What Do You *Think?*

Can You Trust the Government?

Americans are suspicious of big government. Many do not trust the government in Washington to "do what is right." Trust in government has varied over the years, as measured by polls asking, "How much of the time do you think you can trust the government in Washington to do what is right? Just about always? Most of the time? Some of the time? None of the time?" Low levels of trust and confidence in government may represent a profound disaffection with the political system, or a more superficial dissatisfaction with current politicians and political leaders or with policies.[a] Americans' trust in the national government used to be higher. In the 1950s and through the early 1960s, during the Eisenhower, Kennedy, and first years of the Johnson administrations, the public overwhelmingly had confidence in the government. But in the late '60s through the '70s, with the defeat in Vietnam, the Watergate scandal and the forced resignation of President Richard Nixon—the first resignation of a president in U.S. history—public confidence fell, and kept falling.

Throughout this period of decline, television broadcasted many negative images of government and government policy. Television producers want news of scandal, violence, corruption, and incompetence; they want what is simple and sensational, not good news or much in-depth reporting of complicated news (see Chapter 6, "Mass Media: Setting the Agenda"). Meanwhile, more Americans have come to recognize television news anchors and famous reporters than they do presidential candidates or important members of Congress. And the news anchors and reporters follow their producer's lead: reporting critically, and even cynically, of politicians and the government.

Economic recessions erode public confidence government. People expect the president and Congress to lead them out of "hard times." So while President George H. W. Bush raised public confidence in the early 1990s with the military success of Desert Storm in Iraq, his administration's perceived failure to act decisively to take the United States out of the economic recession of the early 1990s helped to send public confidence in government back down. But then sustained economic growth in the 1990s under President Clinton improved public trust in government.

But public confidence in government can be revived, as it was during the Reagan presidency. President Reagan's popularity may have contributed to the restoration of the public's confidence in government.[b] Americans' trust in government also revived after the terrorist attacks of September 11, 2001. Public trust in government doubled immediately after September 11, as America rallied behind the government for the first time since the Japanese attack on Pearl Harbor on December 7, 1941. American flags and images of Old Glory sprouted from homes and businesses, and on vehicles. Trust in government "to do the right thing" leaped to levels not seen since the early 1970s. But the public trust gradually eroded as the war in Iraq dragged on.

Is it ever right to disobey the law?

The Purposes of Government

All governments tax, penalize, punish, restrict, and regulate their people. Governments in the United States—the federal government in Washington, the 50 state governments, and the more than 87,000 local governments—take nearly 40 cents out of every dollar Americans earn. Each year, the Congress enacts about 500 laws; federal bureaucracies publish about 19,000 rules and regulations, the state legislatures enact about 25,000 laws; and cities, counties, school districts, and other local governments enact countless local ordinances. Each of these laws restricts our freedom in some way.

Why do people put up with governments? An answer to this question can be found in the words of the Preamble to the Constitution of the United States:

> We the people of the United States, in Order to form a more perfect Union, establish Justice, insure domestic Tranquility, provide for the common defense, promote the general Welfare, and secure the Blessings of Liberty to ourselves and our Posterity, do ordain and establish this Constitution for the United States of America.

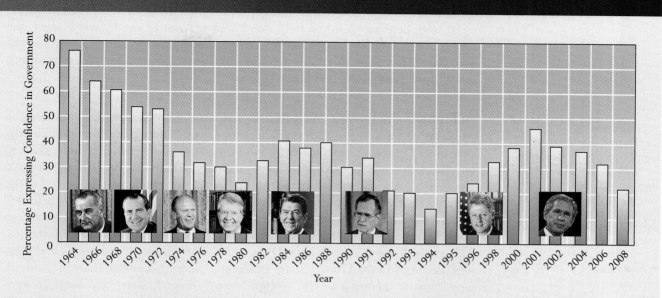

Public Confidence, That the Federal Government Can Be Trusted to "Do What Is Right Most of the Time"

How much of the time do you think you can trust government in Washington to do what is right—just about always, most of the time, or only some of the time?

[a]Timothy E. Cook and Paul Gronke, "The Skeptical American," *Journal of Politics* 67 (Aug. 2005): 784–803

[b]Arthur H. Miller, "Confidence in Government During the 1980s," *American Politics Quarterly* 19 (April 1991): 147–73.

Source: Data from Gallup Opinion Polls (http://www.gallup.com/poll/topics/trust_gov.asd).

General statistics have to be used cautiously, however. ABC News polls after September 11, for example, found that while 68 percent of Americans trusted the government to "do what is right when it comes to handling national security and the war on terrorism," just 38 percent had confidence in the government "when it comes to handling social issues like the economy, health care, Social Security, and education." Public trust in government may depend on what part of the government Americans are being polled about.

To Establish Justice and Insure Domestic Tranquility

Government manages conflict and maintains order. We might think of government as a **social contract** among people who agree to allow themselves to be regulated and taxed in exchange for protection of their lives and property. No society can allow individuals or groups to settle their conflicts by street fighting, murder, kidnapping, rioting, bombing, or terrorism. Whenever government fails to control such violence, we describe it as "a breakdown in law and order." Without the protection of government, human lives and property are endangered, and only those skilled with fists and weapons have much of a chance of survival. The seventeenth-century English political philosopher Thomas Hobbes described life without government as "a war where every man is enemy to every man," where people live in "continual fear and danger of violent death."[4]

To Provide for the Common Defense

Many anthropologists link the origins of government to warfare—to the need of early communities to protect themselves from raids by outsiders and to organize raids against others. Since the Revolutionary War, the U.S. government has been responsible for the country's

★ **social contract**
Idea that government originates as an implied contract among individuals who agree to obey laws in exchange for protection of their rights.

defense. During the long Cold War, when America confronted a nuclear-armed, expansionist-minded, communist-governed Soviet Union, the United States spent nearly half of the federal budget on national defense. With the end of the Cold War, defense spending fell to about 15 percent of the federal budget, but defense spending has begun to creep upward again as the nation confronts the new war on terrorism. National defense will always remain a primary responsibility of United States government.

To Promote the General Welfare   Government promotes the general welfare in a number of ways. It provides **public goods**—goods and services that private markets cannot readily furnish either because they are too expensive for individuals to buy for themselves (for example, a national park, a highway, or a sewage disposal plant) or because if one person bought them, everyone else would "free-ride," or use them without paying (for example, clean air, police protection, or national defense).

Nevertheless, Americans acquire most of their goods and services on the **free market**, through voluntary exchange among individuals, firms, and corporations. The **gross domestic product (GDP)**—the dollar sum of all the goods and services produced in the United States in a year—amounts to more than $15 trillion. Government spending in the United States—federal, state, and local governments combined—amounts to about $4.5 trillion, or an amount equivalent to 30 percent of the gross domestic product.

Governments also regulate society. Free markets cannot function effectively if individuals and firms engage in fraud, deception, or unfair competition, or if contracts cannot be enforced. Moreover, many economic activities impose costs on persons who are not direct participants in these activities. Economists refer to such costs as **externalities**. A factory that produces air pollution or wastewater imposes external costs on community residents who would otherwise enjoy cleaner air or water. A junkyard that creates an eyesore makes life less pleasant for neighbors and passersby. Many government regulations are designed to reduce these external costs.

To promote general welfare, governments also use **income transfers** from taxpayers to people who are regarded as deserving. Government agencies and programs provide support and care for individuals who cannot supply these things for themselves through the private job market, for example, ill, elderly, and disabled people, and dependent children who cannot usually be expected to find productive employment. The largest income transfer programs are Social Security and Medicare, which are paid to the elderly regardless of their personal wealth. Other large transfer payments go to farmers, veterans, and the unemployed, as well as to a wide variety of businesses. As we shall see, the struggle of individuals and groups to obtain direct government payments is a major motivator of political activity.

To Secure the Blessings of Liberty   All governments must maintain order, protect national security, provide public goods, regulate society, and care for those unable to fend for themselves. But *democratic* governments have a special added responsibility—to protect individual liberty by ensuring that all people are treated equally before the law. No one is above the law. The president must obey the Constitution and laws of the United States, and so must members of Congress, governors, judges, and the police. A democratic government must protect people's freedom to speak and write what they please, to practice their religion, to petition, to form groups and parties, to enjoy personal privacy, and to exercise their rights if accused of a crime.

★ **public goods**
Goods and services that cannot readily be provided by markets, either because they are too expensive for a single individual to buy or because if one person bought them, everyone else would use them without paying.

★ **free market**
Free competition for voluntary exchange among individuals, firms, and corporations.

★ **gross domestic product (GDP)**
Measure of economic performance in terms of the nation's total production of goods and services for a single year, valued in terms of market prices.

★ **externalities**
Costs imposed on people who are not direct participants in an activity.

★ **income transfers**
Government transfers of income from taxpayers to persons regarded as deserving.

A Conflicting *View*

Sometimes It's Right to Disobey the Law

Civil disobedience is the nonviolent violation of laws that people believe to be unjust. Civil disobedience denies the *legitimacy*, or rightfulness, of a law and implies that a higher moral authority takes precedence over unjust laws. It is frequently a political tactic of minorities. (Majorities can more easily change laws through conventional political activity.)

Why resort to civil disobedience in a democracy? Why not work within the democratic system to change unjust laws? In 1963 a group of Alabama clergy posed these questions to Martin Luther King, Jr., and asked him to call off mass demonstrations in Birmingham, Alabama. King, who had been arrested in the demonstrations, replied in his now-famous "Letter from Birmingham City Jail":

> One may well ask, "How can you advocate breaking some laws and obeying others?" The answer is found in the fact that there are unjust laws. I would be the first to advocate obeying just laws. One has not only a legal but a moral responsibility to obey just laws. Conversely, one has a moral responsibility to disobey unjust laws.

King argued that *nonviolent direct action* was a vital aspect of democratic politics. The political purpose of civil disobedience is to call attention or "to bear witness" to the existence of injustices. Only laws regarded as unjust are broken, and they are broken openly, without hatred or violence. Punishment is actively sought rather than avoided, since punishment will further emphasize the injustice of the laws.

The objective of nonviolent civil disobedience is to stir the conscience of an apathetic majority and to win support for measures that will eliminate the injustices. By accepting punishment for the violation of an unjust law, persons practicing civil disobedience demonstrate their sincerity. They hope to shame the majority and to make it ask itself how far it is willing to go to protect the status quo. Thus, according to King's teachings, civil disobedience is clearly differentiated from hatred and violence:

Dr. Martin Luther King, Jr., shown here marching in Mississippi with his wife, Coretta Scott King, and others, used civil disobedience to advance the rights of African Americans during the 1950s and 1960s. (Copyright © Flip Schulke)

> One who breaks an unjust law must do it openly, lovingly (not hatefully as the white mothers did in New Orleans when they were seen on television screaming "nigger, nigger, nigger") and with a willingness to accept the penalty. I submit that an individual who breaks a law that conscience tells him is unjust, and willingly accepts the penalty by staying in jail to arouse the conscience of the community over its injustice, is in reality expressing the very highest respect for law.

In 1964 Martin Luther King, Jr., received the Nobel Peace Prize in recognition of his extraordinary contributions to the development of nonviolent methods of social change.

Source: Martin Luther King, Jr., "Letter from Birmingham City Jail," April 16, 1963.

The Meaning of Democracy

Throughout the centuries, thinkers in many different cultures contributed to the development of democratic government. Early Greek philosophers contributed the word **democracy**, which means "rule by the many." But there is no single definition of *democracy*, nor is there a tightly organized system of democratic thought. It is better, perhaps, to speak of democratic traditions than of a single democratic ideology.

★ **democracy**
Governing system in which the people govern themselves, from the Greek term meaning "rule by the many."

Unfortunately, the looseness of the term *democracy* allows it to be perverted by *anti*democratic governments. Hardly a nation in the world exists that does not *claim* to be "democratic." Governments that outlaw political opposition, suppress dissent, discourage religion, and deny fundamental freedoms of speech and press still claim to be "democracies," "democratic republics," or "people's republics" (for example, the Democratic People's Republic of Korea is the official name of communist North Korea). These governments defend their use of the term *democracy* by claiming that their policies reflect the true interests of their people. But they are unwilling to allow political freedoms or to hold free elections in order to find out whether their people really agree with their policies. In effect, they use the term as a political slogan rather than a true description of their government.

The actual existence of **democratic ideals** varies considerably from country to country (see *Compared to What?*: "Freedom and Democracy Around the World"). A meaningful definition of democracy must include the following ideals: (1) recognition of the dignity of every individual; (2) equal protection under the law for every individual; (3) opportunity for everyone to participate in public decisions; and (4) decision making by majority rule, with one person having one vote.

Individual Dignity The underlying value of democracy is the dignity of the individual. Human beings are entitled to life and liberty, personal property, and equal protection under the law. These liberties are *not* granted by governments; they belong to every person born into the world. The English political philosopher John Locke (1632–1704) argued that a higher "natural law" guaranteed liberty to every person and that this natural law was morally superior to all human laws and governments. Each individual possesses "certain inalienable Rights, among these are Life, Liberty, and Property."[5] When Thomas Jefferson wrote his eloquent defense of the American Revolution in the Declaration of Independence for the Continental Congress in Philadelphia in 1776, he borrowed heavily from Locke (perhaps even to the point of plagiarism):

> We hold these truths to be self-evident, that all Men are created equal, that they are endowed by their Creator with certain unalienable Rights, that among these are Life, Liberty and the Pursuit of Happiness.

Individual dignity requires personal freedom. People who are directed by governments in every aspect of their lives, people who are "collectivized" and made into workers for the state, people who are enslaved—all are denied the personal dignity to which all human beings are entitled. Democratic governments try to minimize the role of government in the lives of citizens.

Equality True democracy requires equal protection of the law for every individual. Democratic governments cannot discriminate between blacks and whites, or men and women, or rich and poor, or any groups of people in applying the law. Not only must a democratic government refrain from discrimination itself, but it must also work to prevent discrimination in society generally. Today our notion of equality extends to equality of opportunity—the obligation of government to ensure that all Americans have an equal opportunity to develop their full potential.

Participation in Decision Making Democracy means individual participation in the decisions that affect individuals' lives. People should be free to choose for themselves how they want to live. Individual participation in government is necessary for individual dignity. People in a democracy should not have decisions made *for* them but *by* them. Even if they make mistakes, it is better that they be permitted

---

★ **democratic ideals**
Individual dignity, equality before the law, widespread participation in public decisions, and public decisions by majority rule, with one person having one vote.

Think
Again
Should important decisions in a democracy be submitted to voters rather than decided by Congress?

Compared to *What?*

Freedom and Democracy Around the World

Worldwide progress toward freedom over the past half-century has been impressive. In 1950 there were 22 democracies accounting for 31 percent of the world population that were said to be "free." By 2007, democracy had spread to 90 "free" countries that constituted 47 percent of the world population; an additional 58 countries or 30 percent lived in nations labeled "partly free." But 45 "not-free" authoritarian and totalitarian regimes governed more than 23 percent of the world's population.

The Freedom House is a New York–based think tank that regularly surveys political conditions around the world (see map).

One way to assess the degree of democracy in a governmental system is to consider its record in ensuring political freedoms—enabling citizens to participate meaningfully in government—and individual liberties. A checklist for political freedoms might include whether the chief executive and national legislature are elected; whether elections are generally fair, with open campaigning and honest tabulation of votes; and whether multiple candidates and parties participate. A checklist for individual liberties might include whether

the press and broadcasting are free and independent of the government; whether people are free to assemble, protest, and form opposition parties; whether religious institutions, labor unions, business organizations, and other groups are free and independent of the government; and whether individuals are free to own property, travel, and move their residence.

Worldwide progress toward freedom and democracy made major strides after 1989 as a result of the collapse of communism in Eastern Europe after the demise of the Soviet Union. But in recent years there has been relatively little change in the global state of freedom. And there have been some worrisome trends that present potentially serious threats to the expansion of freedom in the future. Russia's score was downgraded by Freedom House and remains only "partly free." Freedom House denounced then-President Vladimir Putin's increasingly restrictive government. And Freedom House notes a growing pushback against democracy in Venezuela, China, Iran, and Zimbabwe that threatens to erode the gains made in the past 30 years.

Map of Freedom

Map Legend   ■ Free   ☐ Partly Free   ■ Not Free

Source: Reprinted by permission of Freedom House. www.freedomhouse.org

to do so than to take away their rights to make their own decisions. The true democrat would reject even a wise and benevolent dictatorship because it would threaten the individual's character, self-reliance, and dignity. The argument for democracy is not that the people will always choose wise policies for themselves, but that people who cannot choose for themselves are not really free.

Majority Rule: One Person, One Vote   Collective decision making in democracies must be by majority rule, with each person having one vote. That is, each person's vote must be equal to every other person's, regardless of status, money, or fame. Whenever any individual is denied political equality because of race, sex, or wealth, then the government is not truly democratic. Majorities are not always right. But majority *rule* means that all persons have an equal say in decisions affecting them. If people are truly equal, their votes must count equally, and a majority vote must decide the issue, even if the majority decides foolishly.

The Paradox of Democracy

But what if a *majority* of the people decide to attack the rights of some unpopular individuals or minorities? What if hate, prejudice, or racism infects a majority of people and they vote for leaders who promise to "get rid of the Jews" or "put blacks in their place" or "bash a few gays"? What if a majority of people vote to take away the property of wealthy people and distribute it among themselves.[6] Do we abide by the principle of majority rule and allow the majority to do what it wants? Or do we defend the principle of individual liberty and limit the majority's power? If we enshrine the principle of majority rule, we are placing all our confidence in the wisdom and righteousness of the majority of the people. Yet we know that democracy means more than majority rule, that it also means freedom and dignity for the individual. How do we resolve this **paradox of democracy**—the potential for conflict between majority rule and individual freedom?

Limiting the Power of Majorities   The Founders of the American nation were not sure that freedom would be safe in the hands of the majority. In *The Federalist Papers* in 1787, James Madison warned against a direct democracy: "Pure democracy . . . can admit of no cure for the mischiefs of faction. . . . There is nothing to check the inducements to sacrifice the weaker party, or an obnoxious individual."[7] So the Founders wrote a Constitution and adopted a Bill of Rights that limited the power of government over the individual, that placed some

Think Again

In a democracy should "majority rule" be able to limit the rights of members of an unpopular or dangerous minority?

Think Again

Is government trying to do too many things that should be left to individuals?

★ **paradox of democracy**
Potential for conflict between individual freedom and majority rule.

More than Majority Role
The paradox of democracy balances the principles of majority rule against the principle of individual liberty. When the German people voted Adolf Hitler and the Nazi Party into power, did majority rule give the Nazis free rein to restrict the individual liberties of the people? Or did those who abhorred the trespasses of their government have the right to fight against its power?

personal liberties beyond the reach of majorities. They established the principle of **limited government**—a government that is itself restrained by law. Under a limited government, even if a majority of voters wanted to, they could not prohibit communists or atheists or racists from speaking or writing. Nor could they ban certain religions, set aside the rights of criminal defendants to a fair trial, or prohibit people from moving or quitting their jobs. These rights belong to individuals, not to majorities or governments.

★ **limited government**
Principle that government power over the individual is limited, that there are some personal liberties that even a majority cannot regulate, and that government itself is restrained by law.

Totalitarianism: Unlimited Government Power

No government can be truly democratic if it directs every aspect of its citizens' lives. Individuals must be free to shape their own lives, free from the dictates of governments or even majorities of their fellow citizens. Indeed, we call a government with *un*limited power over its citizens totalitarian. Under **totalitarianism**, the individual possesses no personal liberty. Totalitarian governments decide what people can say or write; what unions, churches, or parties they can join, if any; where people must live; what work they must do; what goods they can find in stores and what they will be allowed to buy and sell; whether citizens will be allowed to travel outside of their country; and so on. Under a totalitarian government, the total life of the individual is subject to government control.

★ **totalitarianism**
Rule by an elite that exercises unlimited power over individuals in all aspects of life.

Totalitarian governments undertake to control all agencies of the government, including the military and the police, and virtually all other institutions of society including newspapers, television, schools, churches, businesses, banks, labor unions, and any other organization that might challenge their control. In contrast, democratic societies allow many other institutions to operate independently of the government (see *Politics Up Close*: "Confidence in American Institutions").

Authoritarianism

In many countries throughout the world, a single individual or ruling group monopolizes all *political* power, but allows people to otherwise lead their lives as they wish. **Authoritarianism** is largely concerned with dominating government. People can conduct business and trade, join churches, live where they wish, and otherwise conduct their *private* lives without government interference. They have no role to play in politics, no control over their government, no competitive political parties, no elections, and are otherwise barred from political life. Authoritarianism appears somewhat less oppressive, at least in the everyday lives of the people, than totalitarianism.

★ **authoritarianism**
Monopoly of political power by an individual or small group that otherwise allows people to go about their private lives as they wish.

★ **constitutional government**
A government limited by rule of law in its power over the liberties of individuals.

Constitutional Government   Constitutions, written or unwritten, are the principal means by which governmental powers are limited. Constitutions set forth the liberties of individuals and restrain governments from interfering with these liberties. Consider, for example, the opening words of the First Amendment to the U.S. Constitution: "Congress shall make no law respecting an establishment of religion, or prohibiting the free exercise thereof." This amendment places religious belief beyond the reach of the government. The government itself is restrained by law. It cannot, even by majority vote, interfere with the personal liberty to worship as one chooses. In addition, armed with the power of judicial review, the courts can declare unconstitutional laws passed by majority vote of Congress or state legislatures (see "Judicial Power" in Chapter 13).

Throughout this book we examine how well limited constitutional government succeeds in preserving individual liberty in the United States. We examine free speech and press, the mass media, religious freedom, the freedom to protest and demonstrate, and the freedom to support political candidates and interest groups of all kinds. We examine how well the U.S. Constitution protects individuals from discrimination and inequality. And we examine how far government should go in protecting society without destroying individual liberty (see *Controversy*: "Terrorism's Threat to Democracy" on page 18).

Direct Versus Representative Democracy

In the Gettysburg Address, Abraham Lincoln spoke about "a government of the people, by the people, for the people," and his ringing phrase remains an American ideal. But can we take this phrase literally? More than 300 million Americans are spread over 4 million square miles. If we brought everyone together, standing shoulder to shoulder, they would occupy 70 square miles. One round of five-minute speeches by everyone would take over 3,000 years. "People could be born, grow old, and die while they waited for the assembly to make one decision."[8]

★ **direct democracy**
Governing system in which every person participates actively in every public decision, rather than delegating decision making to representatives.

Direct democracy (also called pure or participatory democracy), where everyone actively participates in every decision, is rare. The closest approximation to direct democracy in American government may be the traditional New England town meeting, where all of the citizens come together face-to-face to decide about town affairs. But today most New England towns vest authority in a board of officials elected by the townspeople to make policy decisions between town meetings, and professional administrators are

By the People
Direct democracy still lives in many New England towns, where citizens come together periodically to pass laws, elect officials, and make decisions about such matters as taxation and land use.

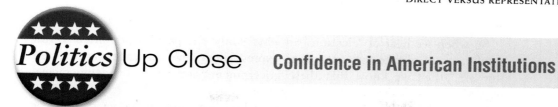

Politics Up Close — Confidence in American Institutions

Americans' confidence in their government varies over time, but overall it is much lower than a generation ago. Which institutions in society today enjoy the confidence of the American people? In somewhat of a paradox for a democratic society, the *military* enjoys the greatest confidence of Americans. The *police* also enjoyed a great deal of confidence, although "the criminal justice system" (defined by most respondents as the courts) does not. Among branches of the national government, the president and the Supreme Court rate fairly high in confidence. But Congress is rated very low.

Q: I am going to read you a list of institutions in American society. Please tell me how much confidence you, yourself, have in each one: a great deal, quite a lot, some, or very little.

	Percent Saying a Great Deal or Quite a Lot
The military	73
The police	58
Organized religion	52
Banks	49
U.S. Supreme Court	40
The medical system	38
Public schools	37
The presidency	33
Television news	31
Newspapers	30
The criminal justice system	25
Organized labor	24
Congress	23
Big business	18
Health maintenance organizations (HMOs)	15

Americans' patriotism and love of the flag as a symbol of their freedom doesn't always translate into confidence in government institutions.

Source: Copyright © 2006 The Gallup Organization.

appointed to supervise the day-to-day town services. The town meeting is vanishing because citizens cannot spend so much of their time and energy in community decision making.

Representative democracy recognizes that it is impossible to expect millions of people to come together and decide every issue. Instead, representatives of the people are elected by the people to decide issues on behalf of the people. Elections must be open to competition so that the people can choose representatives who reflect their own views. And elections must take place in an environment of free speech and press, so that both candidates and voters can freely express their views. Finally, elections must be held periodically so that representatives can be thrown out of office if they no longer reflect the views of the majority of the people.

No government can claim to be a representative democracy, then, unless

1. Representatives are selected by vote of all the people.

2. Elections are open to competition.

3. Candidates and voters can freely express themselves.

4. Representatives are selected periodically.

★ **representative democracy**
Governing system in which public decision making is delegated to representatives of the people chosen by popular vote in free, open, and periodic elections.

So when we hear of "elections" in which only one party is permitted to run candidates, candidates are not free to express their views, or leaders are elected "for life," then we know that these governments are not really democracies, regardless of what they may call themselves.

Throughout this book, as we examine how well representative democracy works in the United States, we consider such issues as participation in elections—why some people vote and others do not—whether parties and candidates offer the voters real alternatives, whether modern political campaigning informs voters or only confuses them, and whether elected representatives are responsive to the wishes of voters. These are the kinds of issues that concern political science.

Who Really Governs?

Democracy is an inspiring ideal. But is democratic government really possible? Is it possible for millions of people to govern themselves, with every voice having equal influence? Or will a small number of people inevitably acquire more power than others? To what extent is democracy attainable in *any* society, and how democratic is the American political system? That is, who really governs?

The Elitist Perspective   "Government is always government by the few, whether in the name of the few, the one, or the many."[9] This quotation from political scientists Harold Lasswell and Daniel Lerner expresses the basic idea of **elitism**. All societies, including democracies, divide themselves into the few who have power and the many who do not. In every society, there is a division of labor. Only a few people are directly involved in governing a nation; most people are content to let others undertake the tasks of government. The *elite* are the few who have power; the *masses* are the many who do not.[10] This theory holds that an elite is inevitable in any social organization. We cannot form a club, a church, a business, or a government without selecting some people to provide leadership. And leaders will always have a perspective on the organization different from that of its members.[11]

In any large, complex society, then, whether or not it is a democracy, decisions are made by tiny minorities. Out of more than 300 million Americans, only a few thousand individuals at most participate directly in decisions about war and peace, wages and prices, employment and production, law and justice, taxes and benefits, health and welfare.

Elitism does *not* mean that leaders always exploit or oppress members. On the contrary, elites may be very concerned for the welfare of the masses. Elite status may be open to ambitious, talented, or educated individuals from the masses or may be closed to all except the wealthy. Elites may be very responsive to public opinion, or they may ignore the usually apathetic and ill-informed masses. But whether elites are self-seeking or public-spirited, open or closed, responsive or unresponsive, it is they and not the masses who actually make the decisions.

Most people do not regularly concern themselves with decision making in Washington. They are more concerned with their jobs, family, sports, and recreation than they are with politics. They are not well informed about tax laws, foreign policy, or even who represents them in Congress. Since the "masses" are largely apathetic and ill informed about policy questions, their views are likely to

Think Again

Is the government run by a few big interests looking out for themselves?

★ **elitism**
Political system in which power is concentrated in the hands of a relatively small group of individuals or institutions.

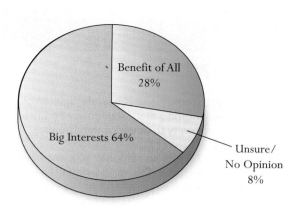

Figure *1.2* Public Opinion About Who Runs the Country

Would you say the government is pretty much run by a few big interests looking out for themselves or that it is run for the benefit of all the people?

Source: CBS/New York Time Poll, July 11, 2004, as reported in The Polling Report, www.pollingreport.com

be influenced more by what they see and hear on television than by their own experience. Most communication flows downward from elites to masses. Elitism argues that the masses have at best only an indirect influence on the decisions of elites.

Opinion polls indicate that many Americans agree with the elitist contention that government is run by "a few big interests" (see Figure 1.2).

The Pluralist Perspective   No one seriously argues that all Americans participate in *all* of the decisions that shape their lives; that majority preferences *always* prevail; that the values of life, liberty, and property are *never* sacrificed; or that every American enjoys equality of opportunity. Nevertheless, most American political scientists argue that the American system of government, which they describe as "pluralist," is the best possible approximation of the democratic ideal in a large, complex society. Pluralism is designed to make the theory of democracy "more realistic."[12]

Pluralism is the belief that democracy can be achieved in a large, complex society by competition, bargaining, and compromise among organized groups and that individuals can participate in decision making through membership in these groups and by choosing among parties and candidates in elections.

Pluralists recognize that the individual acting alone is no match for giant government bureaucracies, big corporations and banks, the television networks, labor unions, or other powerful interest groups. Instead, pluralists rely on *competition* among these organizations to protect the interests of individuals. They hope that countervailing centers of power—big business, big labor, big government—will check one another and prevent any single group from abusing its power and oppressing individual Americans.

Individuals in a pluralist democracy may not participate directly in decision making, but they can join and support *interest groups* whose leaders bargain on their behalf in the political arena. People are more effective in organized groups—for example, the Sierra Club for environmentalists, the American Civil Liberties Union (ACLU) for civil rights advocates, the National Association for the Advancement of Colored People (NAACP) and the Urban League for African Americans, the American Legion and Veterans of Foreign Wars for veterans, and the National Rifle Association (NRA) for opponents of gun control.

According to the pluralist view, the Democratic and Republican parties are really coalitions of groups: the national Democratic Party is a coalition of union members, big-city residents, blacks, Catholics, Jews, and, until recently, southerners; the

★ **pluralism**
Theory that democracy can be achieved through competition among multiple organized groups and that individuals can participate in politics through group memberships and elections.

Controversy

Terrorism's Threat to Democracy

The horrifying images of "9/11" will not be easily forgotten—America's tallest skyscrapers exploding in flames and crumbling to earth—images projected over and over again on the nation's television screens. Commercial airliners, loaded with fuel and passengers, flown at high speeds directly into the symbols of America's financial and military power—the World Trade Center in New York and the Pentagon in Washington. Within minutes, thousands of lives are lost on American soil—more than at any time since the Civil War. After September 11 America found itself in a new war, a war against worldwide networks of terrorists.

The Goal of Terrorism   Terrorism is violence directed against innocent civilians to advance political goals. As barbaric as terrorism appears to civilized peoples, it is not without a rationale. Terrorists are not "crazies." Their first goal is to announce in the most dramatic fashion their own grievances, their commitment to violence, and their disregard for human life, often including their own. In its initial phase the success of a terrorist act is directly related to the publicity it receives. Terrorist groups jubilantly claim responsibility for their acts. The more horrendous, the more media coverage, the more damage, the more dead—all add to the success of the terrorists in attracting attention to themselves.

A prolonged campaign of terrorism is designed to inspire pervasive fear among people, to convince them that their government cannot protect them, and to undermine their confidence in their political system. If the government fails to suppress terrorism, people become ever more fearful, more willing to accept restrictions on liberties, and more open to the appeals of demagogues who promise to restore order to protect people at any cost. Or a weakened government

may resort to "negotiations" with the leaders of terrorist groups, implicitly granting them legitimacy and providing them the opportunity to advance their goals.

Security vs. Liberty   Threats to national security have historically resulted in challenges to individual liberty. Abraham Lincoln suspended the *writ of habeas corpus* (the requirement that authorities bring defendants before a judge and show cause for their detention) during the Civil War. (Only after the war did the U.S. Supreme Court hold that he had no authority to suspend the writ.[a])

In February 1942, shortly after the Japanese attack on Pearl Harbor, President Franklin D. Roosevelt authorized the removal and internment of Japanese Americans living on the West Coast. The U.S. Supreme Court upheld this flagrant violation of the Constitution;[b] not until 1988 did the U.S. Congress vote reparations and make public apologies to the surviving victims.

New Restrictions on Liberty   The "9/11" terrorist attack on America inspired Congress and the president to enact and enforce greater restrictions on individual liberty than the nation had experienced since World War II. Congress passed the Patriot Act with near-unanimous support of Democrats and Republicans. Among other things, the Act allows searches without notice to the suspect; grants "roving" wiretap warrants that allow government eavesdropping on any telephones used by suspects; allows the interception of e-mail; allows investigators to obtain information from credit card companies, banks, libraries, and other businesses; authorizes the seizure of properties used to

[a]Ex parte Milligan (1866).

[b]*Korematsu v. U.S.*, 323 U.S. 214 (1944).

Not Forgotten

The horrifying images of "9/11" will not be easily forgotten—America's tallest skyscrapers exploding and crumbling to earth—images played over and over again on the nation's television screens.

commit or facilitate terrorism; and allows the detention of noncitizens charged with terrorism. President George W. Bush created a new Department of Homeland Security, reorganizing more than forty federal agencies that have a role in combating terrorism.

Terrorism and Democracy   Terrorism has brought mixed blessings to American democracy. It has succeeded in uniting Americans, inspiring patriotism, and increasing their trust in government. But it has also inspired a greater willingness to accept new restrictions on individual liberty. In the past, restrictions on individual liberty have been relaxed when the perceived crisis has subsided. How long will the "war on terrorism" last? Will Americans be asked to sacrifice additional liberties in this war? How far are Americans willing to go in sacrificing individual liberty to achieve national security?

See Robert A. Pape, "The Strategic Logic of Suicide Terrorism," *American Political Science Review* 97 (August 2003): 343–61.

A Conflicting *View*

Complaints About the American Political System

Overall, Americans are very patriotic. Indeed, most polls conducted in United States and other democratic nations show Americans to be the most patriotic citizens in the free world.

Nonetheless, many Americans express serious reservations about their political system. They believe strongly in the ideals of democracy but they are realistic in their appraisal of its weaknesses as well. A majority of Americans describe as "a major problem": elected officials caring more about reelection than what's best for the country; good people being discouraged from running for office because of the high costs of campaigns; citizens who don't stay informed about politics; a decline in moral and ethical standards in government; and the role that money plays in elections and influencing decisions.

Q: As I read each item, tell me how much of a problem you think it is for the political system today: a major problem, somewhat of a problem, or not much of a problem.

	Major Problem	Somewhat of a Problem	Not much of a Problem
Elected officials caring more about getting reelected than doing what is best for the country	76%	19%	4%
The two major political parties not being responsive enough to people's concerns	58%	32%	7%
Good people being discouraged from running for office by the high costs of campaigns	71%	22%	6%
Political contributions having too much influence on elections and government policy	66%	25%	7%
Citizens not making enough effort to vote or stay informed about politics and government	68%	26%	5%
A decline in moral and ethical values in politics	59%	30%	9%
Elected officials spending too much of their time raising money for election campaigns	61%	30%	6%
Elected officials seeking or receiving political contributions while making decisions about issues of concern to those giving money	65%	27%	6%

Source: From *Beyond Red and Blue*, Pew Research Center for the People and the Press, May 20, 2005. Copyright © 2005 by the Pew Research Center. Reprinted by permission.

A *Constitutional* Note

Representative Government, Not Direct Democracy

Nowhere in the Constitution do we find a provision for national referenda voting on any topic, however important for the nation. Indeed, nowhere do we find the word "democracy" in the Constitution. Rather, the founders believed in "republican" government, that is, decision making by representatives of the people, *not* by the people themselves. James Madison wrote, "the public voice, pronounced by representatives of the people, will be more consonant to the public good than if pronounced by the people themselves."

It was not until over a century later that "populism"—a strong political movement mainly in the Midwestern and Western states that appealed especially to farmers—succeeded in getting the initiative and referendum adopted, allowing *state* voters to vote directly on some issues. (The initiative allows citizens to place issues on the ballot by obtaining a certain number of signatures on a petition. The referendum is a popular vote that decides whether the issue

becomes part of the state constitution or state law.) Today about half of the states have the initiative and referendum. (The legislatures of all fifty states can place an issue on the ballot if they choose to do so, usually a change in the state constitution.) But Americans cannot vote directly on *national* issues.

Moreover, some U.S. citizens do not have the right to vote for members of Congress or for the president of the United States. Citizens residing in Puerto Rico, the U.S. Virgin Islands, Guam, and the Northern Marianas can only elect one "delegate" to Congress. (Although "delegates" can propose legislation they cannot cast a tie-breaking vote.) Nor can U.S. citizens of these U.S. territories vote for a U.S. senator or U.S. president. Citizens living in Washington, D.C., were allowed to vote for the U.S. president after the passage of the 23rd Amendment in 1961. They, too, only have a single nonvoting delegate in the House of Representatives and no elected members of the U.S. Senate.

national Republican Party is a coalition of business and professional people, suburbanites, farmers, and white Protestants. When voters choose candidates and parties, they are helping to determine which interest groups will enjoy a better reception in government.

Pluralists contend that there are multiple leadership groups in society (hence the term *pluralism*). They contend that power is widely dispersed among these groups; that no one group, not even the wealthy upper class, dominates decision making; and that groups that are influential in one area of decision making are not necessarily the same groups that are influential in other areas of decision making. Different groups of leaders make decisions in different issue areas.

Pluralism recognizes that public policy does not always coincide with majority preferences. Instead, public policy is the "equilibrium" reached in the conflict among group interests. It is the balance of competing interest groups, and therefore, say the pluralists, it is a reasonable approximation of society's preferences.

VISUAL LITERACY

Using the Census to Understand Who Americans Are

Democracy in America

Is democracy alive and well in America today? Elitism raises serious questions about the possibility of achieving true democracy in any large, complex society. Pluralism is more comforting; it offers a way of reaffirming democratic values and providing some practical solutions to the problem of individual participation in a modern society.

There is no doubt about the strength of democratic *ideals* in American society. These ideals—individual dignity, equality, popular participation in government, and majority rule—are the standards by which we judge the performance of the American political system. But we are still faced with the task of describing the *reality* of American politics.

This book explores who gets what, when, and how in the American political system; who participates in politics; what policies are decided upon; and when and how these decisions are made. In so doing, it raises many controversial questions about the realities of democracy, elitism, and pluralism in American life. But this book does not supply the answers; as a responsible citizen, you have to provide your own answers. At the completion of your studies, you will have to decide for yourself whether the American political system is truly democratic. Your studies will help inform your judgment, but, in the end, you yourself must make that judgment. That is the burden of freedom.

TIMELINE

Major Technological Innovations That Have Changed the Political Landscape

Summary
Who Gets What

Politics is deciding who gets what, when, and how. It occurs in many different settings, but political science focuses on politics in *government*.

★ Political science focuses on three central questions:
Who governs?
For what ends?
By what means?

★ Government is distinguished from other social organizations in that it
Extends to the whole society.
Can legitimately use force.

★ The purposes of government are to
Maintain order in society.
Provide for national defense.
Provide "public goods."
Regulate society.
Transfer income.
Protect individual liberty.

★ The ideals of democracy include
Recognition of individual dignity and personal freedom.
Equality before the law.
Widespread participation in decision making.
Majority rule, with one person equaling one vote.

★ The principles of democracy pose a paradox: How can we resolve conflicts between our belief in majority rule and our belief in individual freedom?

★ Limited government places individual liberty beyond the reach of majorities. Constitutions are the principal means of limiting government power.

★ Direct democracy, in which everyone participates in every public decision, is very rare. Representative democracy means that public decisions are made by representatives elected by the people, in elections held periodically and open to competition, in which candidates and voters freely express themselves.

★ Threats to national security have historically reduced the scope of individual liberty in our nation. The terrorist attack on America of September 11, 2001, inspired greater unity, patriotism, and trust in government among the people. But it also brought greater restrictions on individual liberty.

★ Who really governs? The elitist perspective on American democracy focuses on the small number of leaders who actually decide national issues, compared to the mass of citizens who are apathetic and ill informed about politics. A pluralist perspective focuses on competition among organized groups in society, with individuals participating through group membership and voting for parties and candidates in elections.

★ How democratic is American government today? Democratic ideals are widely shared in our society. But you must make your own informed judgment about the realities of American politics.

Key Terms

politics 3	free market 8	democratic ideals 10	constitutional
political science 3	gross domestic product	paradox of democracy 12	government 14
government 4	(GDP) 8	limited government 13	representative
legitimacy 5	externalities 8	totalitarianism 13	democracy 15
social contract 7	income transfers 8	authoritarianism 13	elitism 16
public goods 8	democracy 9	direct democracy 14	pluralism 17

Suggested Readings

Cronin, Thomas J. *Direct Democracy*. Cambridge, Mass.: Harvard University Press, 1989. A thoughtful discussion of direct versus representative democracy, as well as a review of initiative, referendum, and recall devices.

Dahl, Robert A. *Democracy and Its Critics*. New Haven, Conn.: Yale University Press, 1989. A defense of modern democracy from the pluralist perspective.

Dye, Thomas R., and Harmon Zeigler. *The Irony of Democracy*. 14th ed. New York: Wadsworth, 2008. An interpretation of American politics from the elitist perspective.

Fukuyama, Francis. *Trust*. New York: Free Press, 1995. Argues that the breakdown of trust in America—not only in the government but at a person-to-person level—is burdening the nation with formal rules and regulations, lengthy contracts, bureaucracy, lawyers, and lawsuits.

Katznelson, Ira, Mark Kesselman, and Alan Draper. *The Politics of Power: A Critical Introduction to American Government*. 5th ed. Belmont, Calif.: Wadsworth, 2006. An argument that the United States "is characterized by massive disparities in wealth, income, and political resources."

Lasswell, Harold. *Politics: Who Gets What, When, and How*. New York: McGraw-Hill, 1936. Classic description of the nature of politics and the study of political science by America's foremost political scientist of the twentieth century.

Mills, C. Wright. *The Power Elite*. New York: Oxford University Press, 1956. Classic Marxist critique of elitism in American society, setting forth the argument that "corporate chieftains," "military warlords," and a "political directorate" come together to form the nation's power elite.

Neiman, Max. *Defending Government: Why Big Government Works*. Upper Saddle River, N.J.: Prentice Hall, 2000. A spirited defense of how big government can improve the lives of people.

Putnam, Robert D. *Bowling Alone: The Collapse and Revival of the American Community*. New York: Simon & Schuster, 2001. An argument that Americans are increasingly disconnected from one another, harming the health of democracy.

Roskin, Michael G. *Political Science: An Introduction*. 10th ed. Upper Saddle River, N.J.: Prentice Hall, 2008. A text introduction to the basic theories and concepts of political science.

Suggested Web Sites

American Political Science Association   www.apsanet.org
Association of college and university teachers advises students how to study political science.

Council for Excellence in Government   www.excelgov.org
A Washington-based think tank, relatively unbiased, that regularly publishes polls and studies on key issues facing the nation.

DefenseLink   www.defenselink.gov
Official site of the U.S. Department of Defense, with current news as well as links to Army, Navy, Air Force, Marine, and other defense agencies.

Democracy Net   www.dnet.org
Democracy site of the League of Women Voters linking ZIP codes to your federal, state, and local representatives.

Freedom House www.freedomhouse.org

A think tank monitoring the ongoing evolution of global human rights and liberty; provides an annual world survey covering freedom's progress throughout the state system.

Internet Encyclopedia of Philosophy www.utm.edu/research/iep/

At this site, you can find a concise description of social contract theory along with a discussion of John Locke's writing.

The King Center www.theKingCenter.com

Atlanta-based center commemorates the life and teachings of Martin Luther King, Jr.

National Endowment for Democracy www.ned.org

Private advocacy group for worldwide democracy and human rights.

New Rules Project www.newrules.org

An organization advocating local government solutions and "direct democracy," including the New England town meeting.

The Terrorism Research Center www.terrorism.com

News and information on terrorist attacks around the world and list of terrorist organizations.

U.S. Information Agency www.usinfo.state.gov/products/pubs/whatsdem

Official government site defining democracy, individual rights, and the culture of democracy.

2 POLITICAL CULTURE
Ideas in Conflict

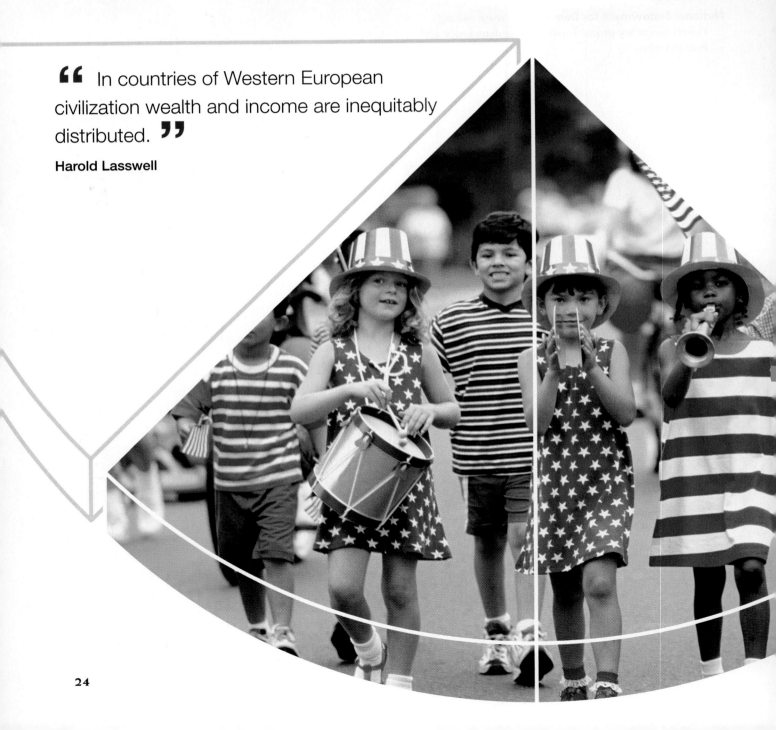

" In countries of Western European civilization wealth and income are inequitably distributed. **"**

Harold Lasswell

Chapter *Outline*

★ Political Culture
★ Individual Liberty
★ Dilemmas of Equality
★ Inequality of Income and Wealth
★ Social Mobility
★ Race, Ethnicity, and Immigration
★ Religion and Secularism in Politics
★ Ideologies: Liberalism and Conservatism
★ Dissent in the United States

Political Culture

Ideas have power. We are all influenced by ideas—beliefs, values, symbols—more than we realize. Political institutions are shaped by ideas, and political leaders are influenced by them.

The term **political culture** refers to widely shared ideas about who should govern, for what ends, and by what means. **Values** are shared ideas about what is good and desirable. Values provide standards for judging what is right or wrong. **Beliefs** are shared ideas about what is true. Values and beliefs are often related. For example, if we believe that human beings are endowed by God with rights to life, liberty, and property, then we will value the protection of these rights. Thus beliefs can justify values.

Cultural descriptions are generalizations about the values and beliefs of many people in society, but these generalizations do not apply to everyone. Important variations in values and beliefs may exist within a society; these variations are frequently referred to as **subcultures** and may arise from such diverse bases as religion, racial or ethnic identity, or political group membership.

Contradictions Between Values and Conditions Agreement over values in a political culture is no guarantee that there will not be contradictions between these values and actual conditions. No doubt the most grievous contradiction between professed national beliefs and actual conditions in America is found in the long history of slavery, segregation, and racial discrimination. The contradiction between the words of the Declaration of Independence that "all men are created equal" and the practices of slavery and segregation became the "American dilemma."[1] But this contradiction does not mean that professed values are worthless; the very existence of the gap between values and behavior becomes *a motivation for change*. The history of the civil rights movement might be viewed as an effort to "bear witness" to the contradiction between the belief in equality and the existence of segregation and discrimination.[2] Whatever the obstacles to racial equality in America, these obstacles would be even greater if the nation's political culture did *not* include a professed belief in equality.

Inconsistent Applications And political culture does not mean that shared principles are always applied in every circumstance. For example,

✔ Think About Politics

1. Do you consider yourself politically conservative, moderate, or liberal?
   CONSERVATIVE ◯ **MODERATE** ◯
   LIBERAL ◯

2. Are income differences in America widening?
   YES ◯ **NO** ◯

3. Is it the government's responsibility to reduce income differences between people?
   YES ◯ **NO** ◯

4. If incomes were made more equal, would people still be motivated to work hard?
   YES ◯ **NO** ◯

5. Do Americans today still have the opportunity to significantly improve their condition in life?
   YES ◯ **NO** ◯

6. Should the U.S. government curtail immigration to America?
   YES ◯ **NO** ◯

7. Should illegal immigrants be denied welfare benefits?
   YES ◯ **NO** ◯

8. Is American culture racist and sexist?
   YES ◯ **NO** ◯

Ask yourself if your answers to these questions are widely shared by most citizens of the United States. Your answers probably reflect not only your own beliefs and values but also those of the political culture to which you belong.

★ **political culture**
Widely shared views about who should govern, for what ends, and by what means.

★ **values**
Shared ideas about what is good and desirable.

25

★ beliefs
Shared ideas about what is true.

★ subcultures
Variations on the prevailing values and beliefs in a society.

people may truly believe in the principle of "free speech for all, no matter what their views might be," and yet when asked whether racists should be allowed to speak on a college campus, many people will say no. Thus general agreement with abstract principles of freedom of speech, freedom of the press, and academic freedom does not always ensure their application to specific individuals or groups.[3]

Conflict The idea of political culture does not mean an absence of conflict over values and beliefs. Indeed, much of politics involves conflict over very fundamental values. The American nation has experienced a bloody civil war, political assassinations, rioting and burning of cities, the forced resignation of a president, and other direct challenges to its political foundations. Indeed, much of this book deals with serious political conflict. Yet Americans do share many common ways of thinking about politics. (However, see *Controversy*: "The Cultural Wars.")

Individual Liberty

★ classical liberalism
Political philosophy asserting the worth and dignity of the individual and emphasizing the rational ability of human beings to determine their own destinies.

No political value has been more widely held in the United States than individual liberty. The very beginnings of our history as a nation were shaped by **classical liberalism**, which asserts the worth and dignity of the individual. This political philosophy emphasizes the rational ability of human beings to determine their own destinies, and it rejects ideas, practices, and institutions that submerge individuals into a larger whole and thus deprive them of their dignity. The only restriction on the individual is not to interfere with the liberties of others.

Political Liberty Classical liberalism grew out of the eighteenth-century Enlightenment, the Age of Reason in which great philosophers such as Voltaire, John Locke, Jean Jacques Rousseau, Adam Smith, and Thomas Jefferson affirmed their faith in reason, virtue, and common sense. Classical liberalism originated as an attack on the hereditary prerogatives and distinctions of a feudal society, the monarchy, the privileged aristocracy, and the state-established church.

Classical liberalism motivated America's Founders to declare their independence from England, to write the U.S. Constitution, and to establish the Republic. It rationalized their actions and provided ideological legitimacy for the new nation. The founders adopted the language of John Locke, who argued that a natural law, or moral principle, guaranteed every person "certain inalienable Rights," among them "Life, Liberty, and Property," and that human beings form a social contract with one another to establish a government to help protect their rights. Implicit in the social contract and the liberal notion of freedom is the belief that governmental activity and restrictions on the individual should be kept to a minimum.

★ capitalism
Economic system asserting the individual's right to own private property and to buy, sell, rent, and trade that property in a free market.

Economic Freedom Classical liberalism as a political idea is closely related to capitalism as an *economic* idea. **Capitalism** asserts the individual's right to own private property and to buy, sell, rent, and trade that property in a free market. The economic version of freedom is the freedom to make contracts, to bargain for one's services, to move from job to job, to join labor unions, to start one's own business. In classical liberal *politics*, individuals are free to speak out, to form political parties, and to vote as they please—to pursue their political interests as they think best. In classical liberal *economics*, individuals are free to find work, to start businesses, and to spend their money as they please—to pursue their economic interests as they think best. The role of government is restricted to protecting private property, enforcing contracts, and performing only those functions and services that cannot be performed by the private market.

Controversy

The Cultural Wars

Is American cultural identity under attack? "Do we have any meaningful identity as a nation that transcends our subnational ethnic, religious, racial identities?"[a]

Historically Americans shared a common set of values and beliefs—"the essential dignity of the individual human being, the fundamental equality of all men, and certain inalienable rights to freedom, justice and fair opportunity."[a] While other nations define themselves by a common ethnicity and ancestry, Americans came from all over the globe and united behind Jefferson's notion of "inalienable rights to life, liberty and the pursuit of happiness." For over two centuries American culture emphasized the rights of the individual, the people as a source of political power, government limited by law, and the free enterprise economy. Political sociologist Seymour Martin Lipset defined the American "civic culture" as including at its core: individual liberty, egalitarianism (of opportunity and respect, not result or condition), individual achievement, popular control of government, and free enterprise economics.[b] Assimilation into American culture meant the personal acceptance of these values and beliefs.

For most of the nation's history, American culture included Christian religion and values. Americans believed in God, right and wrong, good and evil. Americans were the most individualistic people in the world, firmly believing in the notion of the self-made man. Belief in God and country prevailed. Americans were religious and patriotic. Patriotism peaked with President John F. Kennedy's 1961 inaugural address: "Ask not what your country can do for you—ask what you can do for your country." And the American culture included a strong moralism—work hard and play by the rules. Or as a Cuban American advised his fellow immigrants: "Welcome to the capitalist system. Each of you is responsible for the amount of money you have in your pocket. The government is not responsible for whether you eat, or whether you are poor or rich. The government doesn't guarantee you a job or a house. You've come to a rich and powerful country, but it is up to you whether or not you continue living like you did in Cuba."[c]

But in recent years much of American politics is centered on "the cultural wars." American religious and patriotic traditions have come under challenge, particularly in the mass media. The notion of a unifying American culture is now under challenge. The idea of America as a "melting pot" has given way to that of a "mosaic" or "salad" of diverse peoples. America has been "liberated" from the dominant Western European culture. American education has shifted from teaching children the English language and American history and culture, to the teaching of the cultures of different races, ethnic groups, and social classes. The nation's motto, "E Pluribus Unum" ("from many, one") has been redefined to mean "within one, many." "Diversity" and "multiculturalism" are widely praised. Americans have begun to debate whether or not English should be the official language of the country. There is an increased tendency of immigrants to maintain dual identities, loyalties, languages, and even citizenships. America is being transformed into a bilingual, bicultural society. Religion is increasingly excluded from the public forum. Race and ethnicity rather than individual achievement have become recognized criteria for advancement.

Challenges to America's traditional cultural identity have inspired countermovements—support for English-only schooling, opposition to racial preferences, calls for teaching of American history and civics, efforts in universities to restore Western classics to the curriculum, renewed support for Christian values and symbols in public life. The resulting "cultural wars" increasingly define American politics.[d]

[a]Quotations from Samuel P. Huntington, *Who Are We? The Challenges to America's National Identy.* New York: Simon & Schustor, 2004.
[b]Seymour Martin Lipset. *American Exceptionalism.* New York: Norton, 1999.
[c]Huntington, op.cit.
[d]For a contrary view, see Morris P. Fiorina, et al., *Cultural Wars? The Myth of a Polarized America.* New York: Longman, 2006.

The value of liberty in these political and economic spheres has been paramount throughout our history. Only equality competes with liberty as the most honored value in the American political culture.

Dilemmas of Equality

Since the bold assertion of the Declaration of Independence that "all men are created equal," Americans have generally believed that no person has greater

An Early Outsider's Perspective

In the early 1800s, a visiting French historian, Alexis de Tocqueville, identified *equality* as a central American value that distinguished the new nation from European countries.

Comparing Political Landscapes

★ **legal equality**
Belief that the laws should apply equally to all persons.

★ **political equality**
Belief that every person's vote counts equally.

★ **equality of opportunity**
Elimination of artificial barriers to success in life and the opportunity for everyone to strive for success.

worth than any other person. The principle of equal worth and dignity was a radical idea in 1776, when much of the world was dominated by hereditary monarchies, titled nobilities, and rigid caste and class systems.

As early as 1835 the French historian and visitor to America, Alexis de Tocqueville, wrote his classic analysis of American political culture, *Democracy in America*. He identified equality as a fundamental aspect of American society—the absence of a privileged nobility or notions of class that characterize European societies. Yet he also warned of the "tyranny of the majority"—the potential for the majority to trample the rights of minorities and individuals—and he believed that an independent judiciary formed a powerful barrier "against the tyranny of political assemblies."[4]

Belief in equality drove the expansion of voting rights in the early 1800s and ultimately destroyed the institution of slavery. Abraham Lincoln understood that equality was not so much a description of reality as an ideal to be aspired to: "a standard maxim for a free society which should be familiar to all, and revered by all; constantly looked to, constantly labored for, and even though never perfectly attained, constantly approximated and thereby augmenting the happiness and value of life to all people of all colors everywhere."[5] The millions who immigrated to the United States viewed this country as a land not only of opportunity but of *equal* opportunity, where everyone, regardless of birth, could rise in wealth and status based on hard work, natural talents, and perhaps good luck.

Today, most Americans agree that no one is intrinsically "better" than anyone else. This belief in equality, then, is fundamental to Americans, but a closer examination shows that throughout our history it has been tested, as beliefs and values so often are, by political realities.

Political Equality   The nation's Founders shared the belief that the law should apply equally to all—that birth, status, or wealth do not justify differential application of the laws. But **legal equality** did not necessarily mean **political equality**, at least not in 1787, when the U.S. Constitution was written. The Constitution left the issue of voter qualifications to the states to decide for themselves. At that time, all states imposed either property or taxpayer qualifications for voting. Neither women nor slaves could vote anywhere. The expansion of voting rights to universal suffrage required many bitter battles over the course of two centuries. The long history of the struggle over voting rights illustrates the contradictions between values and practices (see the section "Securing the Right to Vote" in Chapter 6). Yet in the absence of the *value* of equality, voting rights might have remained restricted.

Equality of Opportunity   The American ideal of equality extends to **equality of opportunity**—the elimination of artificial barriers to success in life. The term *equality of opportunity* refers to the ability to make of oneself what one can, to develop one's talents and abilities, and to be rewarded for one's work, initiative, and achievement. Equality of opportunity means that everyone comes to the same starting line in life, with the same chance of success, and that whatever differences develop over time do so as a result of abilities, talents, initiative, hard work, and perhaps good luck.

Americans do not generally resent the fact that physicians, engineers, airline pilots, and others who have spent time and energy acquiring particular skills make more money than those whose jobs require fewer skills and less training. Neither do most Americans resent the fact that people who risk their own time and money to build a business, bring new or better products to market, and create jobs for others make more money than their employees. Nor do many

Americans begrudge multimillion-dollar incomes to sports figures, rock stars, and movie stars whose talents entertain the public. And few Americans object when someone wins a million-dollar lottery, as long as everyone who entered the lottery had an equal chance at winning. Americans are generally willing to have government act to ensure equality of opportunity—to ensure that everyone has an equal chance at getting an education, landing a job, and buying a home, and that no barriers of race, sex, religion, or ethnicity bar individual advancement.

Equality of Results   Equality of results refers to the equal sharing of income and material rewards. Equality of results means that everyone starts *and finishes* the race together, regardless of ability, talent, initiative, or work. Those who argue on behalf of this notion of equality say that if individuals are truly equal, then everyone should enjoy generally equal conditions in life. According to this belief, we should appreciate an individual's contributions to society without creating inequalities of wealth and income. Government should act to *transfer* wealth and income from the rich to the poor to increase the total happiness of all members of society.

But equality of results, or absolute equality, is *not* a widely shared value in the United States. This notion of equality was referred to as "leveling" by Thomas Jefferson and generally has been denounced by the nation's political leadership—and by most Americans—then and now:

> To take from one, because it is thought his own industry and that of his fathers has acquired too much, in order to spare to others who have not exercised equal industry and skill, is to violate arbitrarily . . . the guarantee to everyone the free exercise of his industry and the fruits acquired by it.[6]

The taking of private property from those who acquired it legitimately, for no other reason than to equalize wealth or income, is widely viewed as morally wrong. Moreover, many people believe that society generally would suffer if incomes were equalized. Absolute equality, in this view, would remove incentives for people to work, save, or produce. Everyone would slack off, production would decline, goods would be in short supply, and everyone would end up poorer than ever. So some inequality may be essential for the well-being of society.

Thus Americans believe strongly in equality of opportunity but not necessarily equality of results. Americans seek fairness rather than equality of wealth and income.

Fairness   Americans value "fairness" even though they do not always agree on what is fair. Most Americans support a "floor" on income and material well-being—a level that no one, regardless of his or her condition, should be permitted to fall below—even though they differ over how high that floor should be. Indeed, the belief in a floor is consistent with the belief in equality of opportunity; extreme poverty would deny people, especially children, the opportunity to compete in life.[7] But very few Americans want to place a "ceiling" on income or wealth. This unwillingness to limit top income extends to nearly all groups in the United States, the poor as well as the rich. Generally, Americans want people who cannot provide for themselves to be well cared for, especially children, the elderly, the ill, and the disabled. They are often willing to "soak the rich" when searching for new tax sources, believing that the rich can easily afford to bear the burdens of government. But, unlike citizens in other Western democracies, Americans generally do *not* believe that government should equalize incomes.

★ **equality of results**
Equal sharing of income and material goods regardless of one's efforts in life.

Inequality of Income and Wealth

Conflict in society is generated more often by inequalities among people than by hardship or deprivation. Material well-being and standards of living are usually expressed in aggregate measures for a whole society—for example, gross domestic product per capita, income per capita, average life expectancy, infant mortality rate. These measures of societal well-being are vitally important to a nation and its people, but *political* conflict is more likely to occur over the *distribution* of well-being *within* a society. Unequal distributions can generate conflict even in a very affluent society with high levels of income and a high standard of living (see *Compared to What?*: "Income and Inequality").

✓ *Think* Again

Are income differences in America widening?

Inequality of Income   Let us examine inequality of income in the United States systematically. Figure 2.1 divides all American households into two groups—the lowest one-fifth in income and the highest one-fifth—and shows the shares (percentage) of total household income received by each of these groups over the years. (If perfect income equality existed, each fifth of American households would receive 20 percent of all personal income.) The poorest one-fifth received only 4.5 percent of all household income in 1929; today, this group does a little worse, at 3.5 percent of household income. The highest one-fifth received 54.0 percent of all household income in 1929; today, its percentage stands at 50.1.

However, while income differences in the United States have declined over the long run, inequality has actually *increased* in recent years. The income of the poorest households declined from 5.4 to 3.5 percent of total income between 1970 and 2005; the income of the highest quintile rose from 40.9 to 50.1 percent of total income. This reversal of historical trends has generated both political rhetoric and serious scholarly inquiry about both its causes and consequences.[8]

Explaining Recent Increases in Income Inequality   Recent increases in income inequality in the United States are a product of several social and economic trends: (1) the decline of the manufacturing sector of the economy (and the loss of many relatively high-paying blue-collar jobs) and the ascendancy of

Figure *2.1*

Shares of Total Household Income Received by Highest and Lowest Income Groups

Income inequality is growing. Roughly half of total household income in the nation goes to the top 20% of households. Less than 4% of total income goes to the bottom 20% of households.

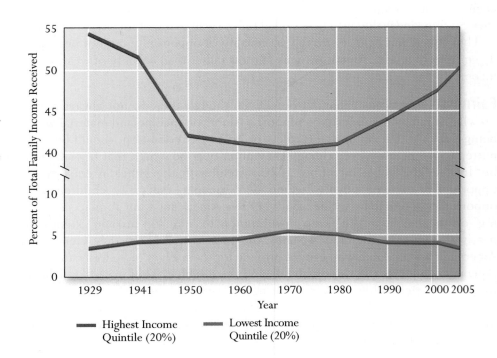

Highest Income Quintile (20%)   Lowest Income Quintile (20%)

Compared to *What?*

Income and Inequality

Capitalism has proven successful in creating wealth. The free market system has provided Americans with more purchasing power than any other people. ("Purchasing power parity" is a statistic used by international economists to adjust for the cost of living differences in measuring how much it costs to purchase a standard "basket" of goods and services.) However, relatively high incomes of average Americans exist side by side with relatively high inequality among Americans. The United States ranks well below many European countries in measures of income inequality. (The "Gini index" is a statistic used by economists to measure income equality/inequality.) But poverty and inequality exist side by side in most of the world's less-developed countries (not ranked below).

Rank by purchasing power

1. **United States**	14. Sweden
2. Switzerland	15. United Kingdom
3. Norway	16. Italy
4. Belgium	17. Taiwan
5. Denmark	18. Israel
6. Canada	19. Spain
7. Japan	20. South Korea
8. Netherlands	21. Portugal
9. Ireland	22. Greece
10. Australia	23. Czech Republic
11. Germany	24. Poland
12. Finland	25. Mexico
13. France	

Rank by equality (Gini index)

1. Denmark	14. Netherlands
2. Czech Republic	15. Taiwan
3. Japan	16. France
4. Sweden	17. Greece
5. Finland	18. Switzerland
6. Norway	19. Portugal
7. Italy	20. Israel
8. Belgium	21. Ireland
9. Germany	22. United Kingdom
10. Canada	23. **United States**
11. South Korea	24. Costa Rica
12. Poland	25. Mexico
13. Spain	

Sources: Rank by purchasing power, *The Economist Pocket World in Figures,* 2003; rank by Gini index, Central Intelligence Agency, *The World Factbook,* 2003. Both sources rank many more nations.

the communications, information, and service sectors of the economy (with a combination of high-paying and low-paying jobs); (2) the rise in the number of two-wage families, making single-wage, female-headed households relatively less affluent; (3) demographic trends, which include larger proportions of aged and larger proportions of female-headed families; and (4) global competition, which restrains wages in unskilled and semiskilled jobs while rewarding people in high-technology, high-productivity occupations.

Social Mobility

Political conflict over inequality might be greater in the United States if it were not for the prospect of **social mobility**. All societies are stratified, or layered, but societies differ greatly in the extent to which people move upward or downward in income and status over a lifetime or over generations. When there is social mobility, people have a good opportunity to get ahead if they study or work long and hard, save and invest wisely, or display initiative and enterprise in business affairs (however, see *A Conflicting View:* "Success Is Determined by the Bell Curve"). Fairly steep inequalities may be tolerated politically if people have a reasonable expectation of moving up over time, or at least of seeing their children do so.

★ **social mobility**
Extent to which people move upward or downward in income and status over a lifetime or over generations.

How Much Mobility?   The United States describes itself as the land of opportunity. The really important political question may be how much real opportunity

Two American?
Income and wealth differences have increased in America in recent years.

exists for individual Americans to improve their conditions in life relative to others. The impression given by Figure 2.1 is one of a static distribution system, with families permanently placed in upper or lower fifths of income earners. But there is considerable evidence of both upward and downward movement by people among income groupings.[9] Almost half of the families in the poorest one-fifth will move upward within a decade, and about half of families in the richest one-fifth will fall out of this top category.

Mobility, Class Conflict, and Class Consciousness   Social mobility and the expectation of mobility, over a lifetime or over generations, may be the key to understanding why **class conflict**—conflict over wealth and power among social classes—is not as widespread or as intense in America as it is in many other nations. The *belief* in social mobility reduces the potential for class conflict because it diminishes **class consciousness**, the awareness of one's class position and the feeling of political solidarity with others in the same class in opposition to other classes. If class lines were impermeable and no one had any reasonable expectation of moving up or seeing his or her children move up, then class consciousness would rise and political conflict among classes would intensify.

Most Americans describe themselves as "middle class" rather than "rich" or "poor" or "lower class" or "upper class." There are no widely accepted income definitions of "middle class." The federal government officially defines a "poverty level" each year based on the annual cash income required to maintain a decent standard of living ($21,200 in 2008 for a family of four). Roughly 12 to 13 percent of the U.S. population lives with annual cash incomes below this poverty line. This is the only income group in which a majority of people describe themselves as poor. Large majorities in every other income group identify themselves as middle class. So it is no surprise that presidents, politicians, and political parties regularly claim to be defenders of America's "middle class"!

Race, Ethnicity, and Immigration

America has always been an ethnically and racially pluralist society. All groups were expected to adopt the American political culture—including individual liberty, economic freedom, political equality, and equality of opportunity—and to learn American history and the English language. The nation's motto

★ **class conflict**
Conflict between upper and lower social classes over wealth and power.

★ **class consciousness**
Awareness of one's class position and a feeling of political solidarity with others within the same class in opposition to other classes.

 Think Again

Is American culture racist and sexist?

A Conflicting *View*

Success Is Determined by the Bell Curve

Most Americans believe in social mobility—the idea that anyone who studies or works hard, saves and invests wisely, and makes good use of his or her talents, initiative, and enterprise can get ahead. But a controversial book, *The Bell Curve* by Richard J. Herrnstein and Charles Murray, sets forth the argument that general intelligence largely determines success in life. General intelligence, the authors contend, is distributed among the population in a bell-shaped curve, with most people clustered around the median, smaller numbers with higher intelligence (a "cognitive elite") at one end, and an unfortunate few trailing behind at the other end (see graph). Over time, say Herrnstein and Murray, intelligence is becoming ever more necessary for the performance of key jobs in the "information society." The result will be the continuing enhancement of the power and wealth of the cognitive elite and the further erosion of the lifestyle of the less intelligent.

Even more controversial than the authors' claim that general intelligence determines success is their contention that general intelligence is mostly (60 percent) genetic. Because intelligence is mostly inherited, programs to assist the underprivileged are useless or even counterproductive.

The cognitive elite, the authors predict, will continue to distance themselves from the masses in

IQ Score

Source: Adapted with the permission of The Free Press, a division of Simon & Schuster Adult Publishing Group, from *The Bell Curve: Intelligence and Class Structure for American Life* by Richard J. Herrnstein and Charles Murray. Copyright © 1994 by Richard J. Herrnstein and Charles Murray. All rights reserved.

knowledge, skills, technical competence, income, and power while social problems will be concentrated among the "dullest." Indeed, they amass statistics showing that educational deficiencies, emotional problems, welfare reliance, early childbirth, and even criminal behavior are disproportionately concentrated in low-intelligence groups (see table).

Cognitive Class		High School Dropout	Women on Welfare Assistance	Mean Age at First Childbearing	Convictions (young white males)
I	Very Bright	0%	0%	27.2 years	3%
II	Bright	0	2	25.6	7
III	Normal	6	8	23.4	15
IV	Dull	35	17	21.0	21
V	Very Dull	55	31	19.8	14

Source: Adapted with the permission of The Free Press, a Division of Simon & Schuster Adult Publishing Group, from *The Bell Curve: Intelligence and Class Structure for American Life* by Richard J. Herrnstein and Charles Murray. Copyright © 1994 by Richard J. Herrnstein and Charles Murray. All rights reserved.

"E Pluribus Unum" (from many, one) is inscribed on its coins. Yet each of America's racial and ethnic groups brings its own traditions and values to the American political culture.

African Americans   Historically African Americans constituted the nation's largest minority. Blacks composed about 20 percent of the population at the time the U.S. Constitution was written in 1787 (although as we shall see in Chapter 3 an enslaved African American was to be counted as only three-fifths of a person in the original Constitution). Heavy European immigration in the late nineteenth century diluted the black population to roughly 12 percent of the nation's total. As late as 1900, most African Americans (90 percent) were still concentrated in the

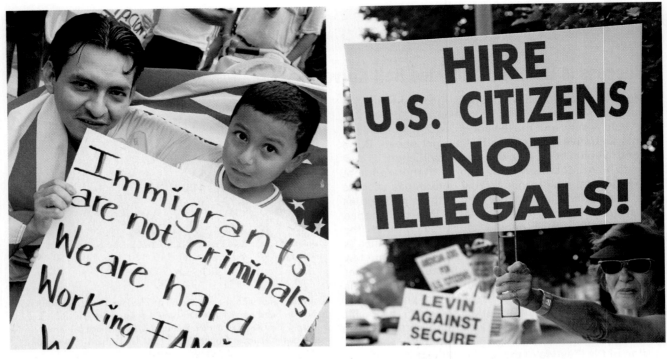

Controversy Over Immigration

Many Hispanic Americans have protested against bills targeting illegal immigrants. Many white Americans, here in Michigan, resent the presence of illegal immigrants.

southern states. But World Wars I and II provided job opportunities in large cities of the Northeast and Midwest. Blacks could not cast ballots in most southern counties, but they could "vote with their feet." The migration of African Americans from the rural South to the urban North was one of the largest internal migrations in our history. Today only about half of the nation's African Americans live in the South—still more than in any other region but less of a concentration than earlier in American history. Today the nation's 37 million African Americans comprise 12.8 percent of the total population of the United States (see Figure 2.2). "African American Politics in Historical Perspective" is discussed in Chapter 15, as

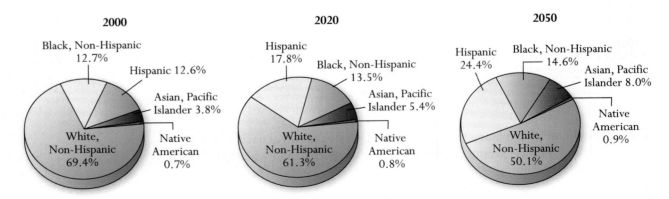

Figure *2.2* Racial and Ethnic Composition of the United States in 2000, 2020, 2050

Current trends in population growth and change suggests that America will become more ethnically and racially diverse over time.

Source: U.S. Bureau of the Census (Middle Series). Two or more races not shown. www.census.gov.

well as the long struggle against slavery, segregation, and discrimination. This struggle has given African Americans a somewhat different perspective on American politics (see "Race and Opinion" in Chapter 5).

Hispanic Americans   Hispanics are now the nation's largest minority. The term *Hispanic* generally refers to persons of Spanish-speaking ancestry and culture; it includes Mexican Americans, Cuban Americans, and Puerto Ricans. Today there are an estimated 45 million Hispanics in the United States, or about 15 percent of the total population. The largest subgroup is Mexican Americans, some of whom are descendants of citizens living in Mexican territory that was annexed to the United States in 1848, but most of whom have come to the United States in accelerating numbers in recent years. The largest Mexican American populations are found in Texas, Arizona, New Mexico, and California. The second-largest subgroup is Puerto Ricans, many of whom move back and forth from the island to the mainland, especially New York City. The third-largest subgroup is Cubans, most of whom have fled from Castro's Cuba. They live mainly in the Miami metropolitan area. The politics of each of these Hispanic groups differs somewhat (see "Hispanic Politics" in Chapter 15).

A Nation of Immigrants   The United States is a nation of immigrants, from the first "boat people" (Pilgrims) to the latest Haitian refugees and Cuban *balseros* ("rafters"). Historically, most of the people who came to settle in this country did so because they believed their lives would be better here, and American political culture today has been greatly affected by the beliefs and values they brought with them. Americans are proud of their immigrant heritage and the freedom and opportunity the nation has extended to generations of "huddled masses yearning to breathe free"—words emblazoned on the Statue of Liberty in New York's harbor. Today about 12 percent of the U.S. population is foreign-born.

DEBATE
Immigration

Immigration policy is a responsibility of the national government. It was not until 1882 that Congress passed the first legislation restricting entry into the United States of persons alleged to be "undesirable" and virtually all Asians. After World War I, Congress passed the comprehensive Immigration Act of 1921, which established maximum numbers of new immigrants each year and set a

★ **immigration policy**
Regulating the entry of non-citizens into the country.

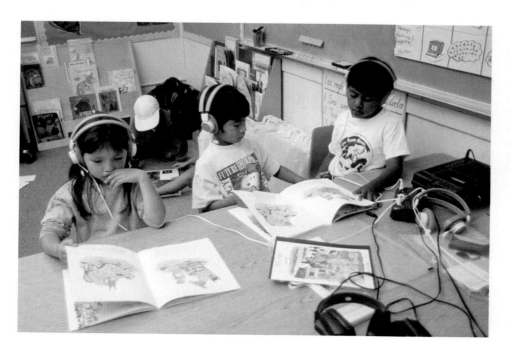

An Education in Diversity
Immigration places responsibility on public schools to provide for the needs of children from different cultures. Here, first grade Latino children use audio equipment to help with reading in a bilingual Spanish-English class in San Rafael, California.

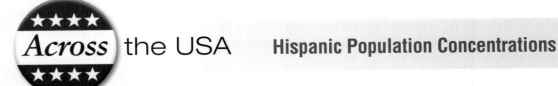

Across the USA   **Hispanic Population Concentrations**

The Hispanic population in the United States is heavily concentrated in a few states—California, Colorado, Arizona, New Mexico, Texas, and Florida. Even within these states Latinos are concentrated in particular counties, especially counties along the southern border as well as Miami-Dade County in Florida (Cubans) and New York City (Puerto Ricans). This concentration facilitates the continuing use of the Spanish language—in newspapers, television (Univision, TeleMundo), business, and commercial establishments. It often inspires bilingual education in public schools, colleges, and universities.

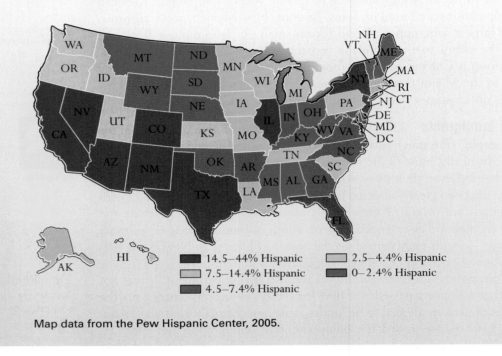

■ 14.5–44% Hispanic	□ 2.5–4.4% Hispanic
□ 7.5–14.4% Hispanic	▨ 0–2.4% Hispanic
▨ 4.5–7.4% Hispanic	

Map data from the Pew Hispanic Center, 2005.

Rights of Passage

The U.S. Coast Guard may intercept boats at sea and return their occupants to their country of origin. But once immigrants reach the U.S. shore, they are entitled to a hearing in any deportation proceedings.

quota for immigrants for each foreign country at 3 percent of the number of that nation's foreign-born who were living in the United States in 1910, later reduced to 2 percent of the number living here in 1890. These restrictions reflected anti-immigration feelings that were generally directed at the large wave of Southern and Eastern European Catholic and Jewish immigrants (from Poland, Russia, Hungary, Italy, and Greece) entering the United States prior to World War I (see Figure 2.3). It was not until the Immigration and Naturalization Act of 1965 that national origin quotas were abolished, replaced by preference categories for close relatives of U.S. citizens, professionals, and skilled workers.

Immigration "reform" was the announced goal of Congress in the Immigration Reform and Control Act of 1986, also known as the Simpson-Mazzoli Act. It sought to control immigration by placing principal responsibility on employers; it set fines for knowingly hiring illegal **aliens**. However, it allowed employers to accept many different forms of easily forged documentation and at the same time subjected them to penalties for discriminating against legal foreign-born residents. To win political support, the act granted **amnesty** to illegal aliens who had lived in the United States since 1982. But the act failed to reduce the flow of either legal or illegal immigrants.

Today, more than a million people per year are admitted *legally* to the United States as "lawful permanent residents" (persons who have needed job skills or who have relatives who are U.S. citizens) or as "political refugees" (persons with "a well-founded fear of persecution" in their country of origin). In addition, each year more than 33 million people are awarded temporary visas to enter the United States for study, business, or tourism (see *What Do You Think?*: "Does Immigration Help or Hurt America?").

Illegal Immigration   The United States is a free and prosperous society with more than 5,000 miles of borders (2,000 with Mexico) and hundreds of

Source: Steve Kelly.

★ **aliens**
Persons residing in a nation who are not citizens.

★ **amnesty**
Government forgiveness of a crime, usually granted to a group of people.

*Over 1 million legal immigrants have been admitted to the United States each year, 2000–2005, leading to an estimate of 11 million for the current decade.

Source: Statistical Abstract of the United States, 2007, p. 8.

Figure *2.3*

Legal Immigration to the United States by Decades

Currently about one million legal immigrants are admitted into the United States each year. Today the nation is experiencing its second great wave of immigration, following the great wave of the early 1900s.

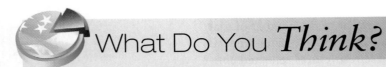

What Do You *Think?*

Does Immigration Help or Hurt America?

There are more immigrants in the United States—that is, foreign-born U.S. residents—than ever before, about 35 million persons. Most of these immigrants, more than 21 million persons, are legal "permanent residents" of the United States. And most Americans think that immigration in general is a good thing:

Q. On the whole, do you think immigration is a good thing or a bad thing for this country today?

Good thing	61%
Bad thing	34%
Mixed or no opinion	5%

Americans are divided as to the *effects* of immigration, however—whether the immigrants make the United States a better place or make it worse off. On the one hand, immigrants do work that others would not do. As the National Restaurant Association's legislative affairs director says, "Restaurants, hotels, nursing homes, agriculture—a very broad group of industries—are looking for a supply of workers to remain productive." He adds that in many parts of the country, workers are not available for such jobs at any price. On the other hand, the strong demand for cheap labor is just that: the demand by employers not to have to pay as much as they would to native-born Americans.

Q. Do you think immigrants mostly help the economy by providing low-cost labor, or mostly hurt the economy by driving wages down for many Americans?

Mostly hurt	48%
Mostly help	42%
Neither	3%
Both	1%
Don't know	5%

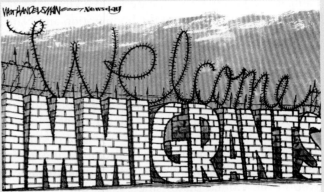

AMERICA'S MIXED MESSAGE...

Americans are more of one mind, though, when it comes to *illegal* immigration in particular—the 10 to 12 million persons in the United States who entered the country illegally. They are not happy with the current immigration policy:

Q. Are you very satisfied, somewhat satisfied, not too satisfied, or not at all satisfied . . . [with] U.S. efforts to deal with illegal immigration?

Very satisfied	2%
Somewhat satisfied	19%
Not too satisfied	29%
Not at all satisfied	48%
Don't know	2%

Furthermore, Americans view illegal immigration as a serious problem.

international air- and seaports. In theory, a sovereign nation should be able to maintain secure borders, but in practice the United States has been unwilling and unable to do so. Estimates of illegal immigration vary widely, from the official U.S. Bureau of Immigration and Citizenship Services estimate of 400,000 per year (about 45 percent of the legal immigration) to unofficial estimates ranging up to 3 million per year. The government estimates that about 4 million illegal immigrants currently reside in the United States; unofficial estimates range up to 15 million or more. Many illegal immigrants slip across U.S. borders or enter ports with false documentation; many more overstay tourist, worker, or student visas.[10] The responsibility for the enforcement of immigration laws rests with **Immigration and Customs Enforcement, ICE** (formerly the Immigration and Naturalization Service [INS]).

Q. *How serious a problem do you think the issue of illegal immigration is for the country right now?*

Very serious	57%
Somewhat serious	32%
Not too serious	8%
Not at all serious	3%
Don't know/no answer	1%

A large majority of Americans also agree that the U.S. government should take a tough stand on illegal immigration.

Q. *When people are caught trying to enter the United States illegally, which do you think should be government policy?*

Immediately sent them back to their home country	61%
Allow them to appeal their case using legal representation and a court hearing	35%
Neither, don't know	4%

Q. *Do you favor or oppose stricter penalties on illegal immigrants?*

Favor	77%
Oppose	18%
Don't know	5%

In addition, over half of Americans (52%) either strongly favor or somewhat favor "deporting all illegal immigrants (45% either somewhat oppose or strongly oppose doing so), and over half of Americans (51%) either strongly favor or somewhat favor building a fence along the U.S.-Mexico border (45% either somewhat oppose or strongly oppose doing so).

Yet Americans are more tolerant of illegal immigrants if they meet various requirements, such as establishing how long they have lived in the United States, paying fees for residing in the U.S. illegally, and speaking the English language, among others.

Q. *Which comes closer to your view about what government policy should be toward illegal immigrants currently living in the U.S. Should the government deport all illegal immigrants back to their home country, allow illegal immigrants to remain in the U.S. in order to work but for only a limited amount of time, or allow illegal immigrants to remain in the U.S. and become U.S. citizens only if they meet certain requirements over a period of time?*

Deport all	24%
Remain in the U.S. in order to work	15%
Remain in the U.S. and become citizens	59%

Q. *Suppose the government does allow illegal immigrants to remain in the U.S. legally and permanently if they meet certain requirements. For each of the following, please say whether it should or should not be a requirement. (Percent saying "should be a requirement.")*

Must have lived in the U.S. for at least five years	74%
Must pay a fine for coming to the U.S. illegally	57%
Must learn to speak English	89%

Source: Various recent national polls reported in Public Agenda, www.publicagenda.com, and in iPoll at the Roper Center.

As a free society, the United States is not prepared to undertake massive roundups and summary deportations of millions of illegal residents. The Fifth and Fourteenth Amendments to the U.S. Constitution require that every *person* (not just citizen) be afforded "due process of law." The government may turn back persons at the border or even hold them in detention camps. The Coast Guard may intercept boats at sea and return persons to their country of origin.[11] Aliens have no constitutional right to come to the United States. However, once in the United States, whether legally or illegally, every person is entitled to due process of law and equal protection of the laws. People are thus entitled to a fair hearing prior to any government attempt to deport them. Aliens are entitled to apply for asylum and present evidence at a hearing of their "well-founded fear of prosecution" if returned to their country. Experience

Politics Up Close   **Could You Pass the Citizenship Test?**

To ensure that new citizens "understand" the history, principles, and form of government of the United States, the CIS administers a citizenship test. Below is a sample of questions from the American government section of the test. Can you answer these questions?

1. What is the supreme law of the land?
2. The idea of self-government is in the first three words of the Constitution. What are these words?
3. What do we call the first 10 amendments to the Constitution?
4. How many amendments does the Constitution have?
5. Who is in charge of the executive branch?
6. Who makes federal laws?
7. What are the two parts of the U.S. Congress?
8. How many U.S. Senators are there?
9. We elect a U.S. Senator for how many years?
10. The House of Representatives has how many voting members?
11. We elect a U.S. Representative for how many years?
12. We elect a President for how many years?
13. In what month do we vote for President?
14. If the President can no longer serve, who becomes President?
15. If both the President and the Vice President can no longer serve, who becomes President?
16. Who is the Commander in Chief of the military?

17. Who signs bills to become laws?
18. Who vetoes bills?
19. What is the highest court in the United States?
20. How many justices are on the Supreme Court?

Answers: 1. The Constitution; 2. We the People; 3. The Bill of Rights; 4. 27; 5. The President; 6. Congress; 7. The Senate and the House of Representatives; 8. 100; 9. Six; 10. 435; 11. Two; 12. Four; 13. November, 14. The Vice President; 15. The Speaker of the House; 16. The President; 17. The President; 18. The President; 19. The Supreme Court; 20. Nine

Source: Bureau of Citizenship and Immigration Services.

★ **illegal immigration**
The unlawful entry of a person into a nation.

has shown that the only way to reduce the flow of **illegal immigration** is to control it at the border, an expensive and difficult, but not impossible, task. Localized experiments in border enforcement have indicated that, with significant increases in personnel and technology, illegal immigration can be reduced by half or more.

Citizenship   Persons born in the United States are U.S. citizens. People who have been lawfully admitted into the United States and granted permanent residence, and who have resided in the United States for at least five years and in their home state for the last six months, are eligible for naturalization as U.S. citizens. Federal district courts as well as offices of the Citizenship and Immigration Services (CIS) may grant applications for citizenship. By law, the applicant must be over age eighteen, be able to read, write, and speak English, possess good moral character, and understand and demonstrate an attachment to the history, principles, and form of government of the United States (see *Politics Up Close:* "Could You Pass the Citizenship Test?").

★ **passport**
Evidence of U.S. citizenship, allowing people to travel abroad and reenter the United States.

Citizens of the United States are entitled to a **passport**, issued by the U.S. State Department upon presentation of a photo plus evidence of citizenship—a birth certificate or naturalization papers. A passport enables U.S. citizens to reenter the country after travel abroad. When traveling abroad, your U.S. passport may be your most valuable possession. A **visa** is a document or stamp on a passport, issued by a foreign country, that allows a citizen of one nation to visit another.

★ **visa**
A document or stamp on a passport allowing a person to visit a foreign country.

Religion and Secularism in Politics

The United States is one of the most religious societies in the world. Over 90 percent of Americans report in polls that they believe in God. Over 80 percent say that prayer is part of their daily lives, and 60 percent say that they attend church at least once a month. Over 80 percent claim some religious affiliation. Evangelical Protestants are the largest single group and the fastest-growing (see Figure 2.4).

At the same time, however, most Americans are concerned about religious leaders exercising influence in political life. Most respondents say it is "not appropriate for religious leaders to talk about their political beliefs as part of their religious activities" (61 percent), "religious leaders should not try to influence how people vote in elections" (64 percent), and "religious groups should not advance their beliefs by being involved in politics and working to affect policy" (54 percent).[12]

American's religious commitments and their belief in the separation of religion from politics sometimes clash.

Challenging Religion in Public Life
There is a growing divide in America between religious faith and **secular** politics on a number of key public issues. The most religious among us, as determined by frequency of church attendance and belief in the literal interpretation of the Bible, generally support limitations on abortion, including parental notification when minors seek abortions, and would prohibit "partial-birth abortions" (intact dilation and extraction). They also support abstinence in sex education; oppose same-sex marriage, support the phrase "under God" in the Pledge of Allegiance; support the display of religious symbols in public places; support the public funding of "faith-based" social service organizations; and generally believe that religion should play an important role in addressing "all or most of today's problems."

★ **secular**
In politics, a reference to opposition to religious practices and symbols in public life.

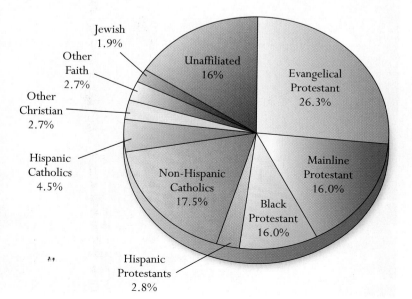

Jewish 1.9%
Other Faith 2.7%
Other Christian 2.7%
Hispanic Catholics 4.5%
Unaffiliated 16%
Evangelical Protestant 26.3%
Non-Hispanic Catholics 17.5%
Mainline Protestant 16.0%
Black Protestant 16.0%
Hispanic Protestants 2.8%

Figure *2.4*
Religious Affiliations of Americans

Americans are a religious people. Over 80 percent claim some religious affiliation. Evangelical Protestants are the largest and fastest-growing religious group in the country.

Source: From Pew Forum on Religion & Public Life Survey of 4,000 U.S. adults in March–May 2004. Copyright © 2004 by The Pew Research Center. Reprinted by Permission.

In contrast, challenges to religion in public life are increasingly being raised in American politics, especially in the courts. Organizations such as the American Civil Liberties Union (see *Politics Up Close*: "The American Civil Liberties Union" in Chapter 14) and Americans United for the Separation of Church and State are challenging many traditional religious practices and symbols in public life. Most of these challenges are based upon the First Amendment's "no establishment of religion" clause (See "Freedom of Religion" in Chapter 14). Among these challenges: removing "under God" from the Pledge of Allegiance and eliminating the national motto "In God We Trust" from our coins; removing religious symbols—Christmas displays, the Ten Commandments, and so on—from public places; supporting the teaching of evolution and opposing the teaching of "creationism" in the schools; opposing the use of public school vouchers to pay for students attending religious schools; supporting gay rights, including same-sex marriages; and threatening to remove tax exemptions from churches whose religious leaders endorse candidates or involve themselves in politics.

Religious/Political Alignments   Interestingly, the religious-versus-secular division on these issues does *not* depend upon *which* religion (for example, Protestants, Catholic, Jewish) that Americans identify themselves. Rather, this division appears to be more closely aligned with the *intensity* of people's religious commitments; in polls, for example, their self-identification as "born-again" or "evangelical"; their frequency of church attendance; and their agreement with statements such as "prayer is an important part of my daily life." An overwhelming majority of Americans (80 percent) say they have "old-fashioned values about family and marriage."

Increasingly, this division between religious and secular viewpoints is coming to correspond with the division between liberals and conservatives in American politics. Religious traditionalists are more likely to describe themselves as conservatives or moderates, while secularists are more likely to describe themselves as liberal in politics.[13]

A large congregation at Calvary Chapel in Fort Lauderdale, Florida, hears a sermon in 2004 regarding faith and morals in politics and government.

Ideologies: Liberalism and Conservatism

An **ideology** is a consistent and integrated system of ideas, values, and beliefs. A political ideology tells us who *should* get what, when, and how; that is, it tells us who *ought* to govern and what goals they *ought* to pursue. When we use ideological terms such as *liberalism* and *conservatism*, we imply reasonably integrated sets of values and beliefs. And when we pin ideological labels on people, we imply that those people are fairly consistent in the application of these values and beliefs in public affairs. In reality, neither political leaders nor citizens always display integrated or consistent opinions; many hold conservative views on some issues and liberal views on others.[14] Many Americans avoid ideological labeling, either by describing themselves as "moderate" or "middle-of-the-road" or by simply declining to place themselves on an ideological scale. But as Figure 2.5 shows, among those who choose an ideological label to describe their politics, conservatives consistently outnumber liberals. (See also *Across the USA*: "Liberalism and Conservatism" on the facing page.)

Despite inconsistencies in opinion and avoidance of labeling, ideology plays an important role in American politics. Political *elites*—elected and appointed officeholders; journalists, editors, and commentators; party officials and interest-group leaders; and others active in politics—are generally more consistent in their political views than nonelites and are more likely to use ideological terms in describing politics.[15]

Modern Conservatism: Individualism plus Traditional Values

Modern **conservatism** combines a belief in free markets, limited government, and individual self-reliance in economic affairs with a belief in the value of tradition, law, and morality in social affairs. Conservatives wish to retain our historical commitments to individual freedom from governmental controls; reliance on individual initiative and effort for self-development; a free-enterprise economy with a minimum of governmental intervention; and rewards for initiative, skill, risk, and hard work. These views are consistent with the early classical liberalism of Locke, Jefferson, and the nation's Founders, discussed at the beginning of this chapter. The result is a confusion of ideological labels: modern conservatives claim to be the true inheritors of the (classical) liberal tradition.

Conservatism is less optimistic about human nature. Traditionally, conservatives have recognized that human nature includes elements of irrationality,

★ **ideology**
Consistent and integrated system of ideas, values, and beliefs.

Are You a Liberal or a Conservative?

What Are American Civic Values?

Think
Again
Do you consider yourself politically conservative, moderate, or liberal?

★ **conservatism**
Belief in the value of free markets, limited government, and individual self-reliance in economic affairs, combined with a belief in the value of tradition, law, and morality in social affairs.

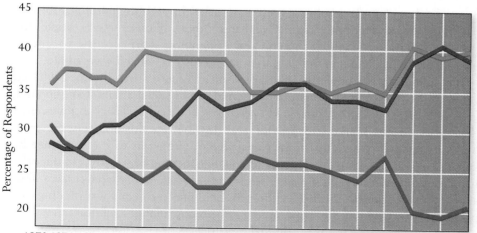

Figure *2.5*

Americans: Liberal, Moderate, Conservative

Americans are more likely to describe themselves as moderates or conservatives than as liberals.

Source: General Social Surveys, National Opinion Research Center, University of Chicago; Updated from *The American Enterprise*, January/February 2000, and Gallup, 2008.

Across the USA   Liberalism and Conservatism

States might be classified in terms of their voters' self-identification in opinion surveys as liberal, moderate, or conservative. The most conservative state is Utah (45 percent conservative, 37 percent moderate, 13 percent liberal). The most liberal states are Massachusetts, New York, and New Jersey.

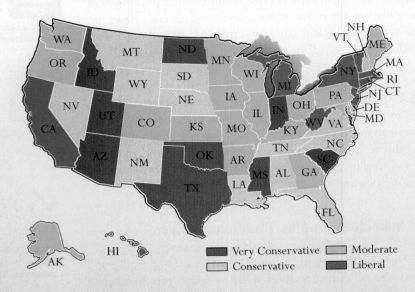

Sources: Data updated from early work of Gerald C. Wright, Robert S. Erikson, and John P. McIver, "Public Opinion and Policy Liberalism in the American States," *American Journal of Political Science* 31 (November 1987): 980–1001. See also Virginia Gray et al. "Public Policy and Organized Interests in the American States," *Political Research Quarterly* 57 (September, 2004), 411–20.

ignorance, hatred, and violence. Thus they have been more likely to place their faith in *law* and *traditional values* than in popular fads, trends, or emotions. To conservatives, the absence of law does not mean freedom but, rather, exposure to the tyranny of terrorism and violence. They believe that without the guidance of traditional values, people would soon come to grief through the unruliness of their passions, destroying both themselves and others. Conservatives argue that strong institutions—family, church, and community—are needed to control individuals' selfish and immoral impulses and to foster civilized ways of life.

It is important to note that conservatism in America incorporates different views of the role of government in economic versus social affairs. Conservatives generally prefer *limited noninterventionist government in economic affairs*—a government that relies on free markets to provide and distribute goods and services; minimizes its regulatory activity; limits social welfare programs to the "truly needy"; keeps taxes low; and rejects schemes to equalize income or wealth. On the other hand, conservatives would *strengthen government's power to regulate social conduct*. They support restrictions on abortion; endorse school prayer; favor a war on drugs and pornography; oppose the legitimizing of homosexuality; support the death penalty; and advocate tougher criminal penalties.

Modern Liberalism: Governmental Power to "Do Good"
Modern **liberalism** combines a belief in a strong government to provide economic security

★ **liberalism**
Belief in the value of strong government to provide economic security and protection for civil rights, combined with a belief in personal freedom from government intervention in social conduct.

People in Politics   Bill O'Reilly, "The No Spin Zone"?

Bill O'Reilly assures "fair and balanced" broadcast journalism to Fox News viewers, O'Reilly is frequently loose with the facts; the show is more "entertainment" than "news."

He describes his popular TV show as a "no spin zone" and refers to himself as an "independent." Yet O'Reilly has emerged as the nation's most popular voice of conservatism on television and on radio.

O'Reilly boasts of an Irish Catholic working-class upbringing in Long Island. He graduated from Catholic Marist College, briefly taught in a Miami high school, and earned a master's degree from Boston University in journalism. He bounced around the country as a reporter for various TV stations, and by 1986 he had become a top correspondent for ABC News. He eventually replaced David Frost as anchor of the TV tabloid *Inside Edition*, but left that job in 1995 to earn a master's degree from the John F. Kennedy School of Government at Harvard University.

The Fox News network recruited O'Reilly to create a new evening talk show, *The O'Reilly Factor*. The show quickly grew into the most watched program on cable news, outdistancing even *Larry King Live*. And O'Reilly's radio talk show competes with Rush Limbaugh for the top spot in talk radio.

O'Reilly mixes humor with bombast. He constantly interrupts guests, both conservatives and liberals, to broadcast his own views. He is convinced that liberal "secularists" are waging war against religion, Christmas, and traditional moral values. Liberal critic Al Franken wrote a satirical mockery of the Fox network and O'Reilly himself, entitled *Lies and the Lying Liars Who Tell Them: A Fair and Balanced Look at the Right*; O'Reilly prompted Fox News to sue, but the suit was thrown out of federal court. O'Reilly's favorite targets include Hollywood liberals, Jesse Jackson, and the American Civil Liberties Union. The occasional twinkle in his Irish eyes tempers his often venomous commentary.

and protection for civil rights with a belief in freedom from government intervention in social conduct. Modern liberalism retains the classical liberalism commitment to individual dignity, but it emphasizes the importance of social and economic security for the whole population. In contrast to classical liberalism, which looked at governmental power as a potential threat to personal freedom, modern liberalism looks on the power of government as a positive force for eliminating social and economic conditions that adversely affect people's lives and impede their self-development. The modern liberal approves of the use of governmental power to correct the perceived ills of society (see *People in Politics*: "Barbara Boxer, Defending Liberalism in Congress"). The prevailing impulse is to "do good," to perform public services, and to assist the least fortunate in society, particularly the poor and minorities. Modern liberalism is impatient with what it sees as the slow progress of individual initiative and private enterprise toward solving socioeconomic problems, so it seeks to use the power of the national government to find solutions to society's troubles.

Modern liberalism contends that individual dignity and equality of opportunity depend in some measure on *reduction of absolute inequality* in society. Modern liberals believe that true equality of opportunity cannot be achieved where significant numbers of people are suffering from hopelessness, hunger, treatable illness, or poverty. Thus modern liberalism supports government efforts to reduce inequalities in society.

Liberals also have different views of the role of government in economic versus social affairs. Liberals generally prefer an *active, powerful government in economic affairs*—a government that provides a broad range of public services; regulates business; protects civil rights; protects consumers and the environment; provides

People In Politics   Barbara Boxer, Defending Liberalism in Congress

Perhaps no one has been more successful in defending liberal causes in Congress than California's outspoken U.S. senator, Barbara Boxer. Her political résumé boasts awards and honors from such organizations as Planned Parenthood (family planning, reproductive health, and abortion rights), the Sierra Club (environmental causes), Mobilization against AIDS, Anti-Defamation League (civil rights), and Public Citizen (consumer affairs).

A graduate of Brooklyn College with a B.A. in economics, Boxer worked briefly as a stockbroker before moving to San Francisco, where she became a journalist and later a campaign aide to a local congressional representative. Her political career is based in Marin County, a trendy, upper-class, liberal community north of San Francisco, where she first won elected office as a member of the County Board of Supervisors. She was elected to the U.S. House of Representatives from her Marin County district in 1982 and quickly won a reputation as one of the most liberal members of the House. Appointed to the House Armed Services Committee, she became a leading critic of defense spending and virtually every weapon requested by the military.

When her state's liberal Democratic senator, Alan Cranston, announced he would not seek reelection to the Senate in the wake of his censure in the Keating Five affair, Boxer sought the open seat. Her opponent, conservative Republican radio and TV commentator Bruce Herschensohn, hammered at Boxer's 143 overdrafts at the House bank, her frequent absenteeism, and her extensive use of congressional perks. But with the help of Clinton's 1992 landslide (47 to 32 percent) victory over George Bush in California, Boxer eked out a 48 to 46 percent victory over Herschensohn. Her victory, together with that of Dianne Feinstein, gave California a historical first—two women U.S. senators.

Boxer quickly emerged as a powerful force in the U.S. Senate on behalf of abortion rights. She led the Senate fight for a federal law protecting abortion clinics from obstruction by demonstrators. On the Environmental and Public Works Committee she helped block efforts to relax federal environmental regulations. She helped lead the fight for the Family Medical Leave Act, passed in the early days of the Clinton administration. She voted against the ban on partial birth abortions passed by Congress. She voted against Senate confirmation of Chief Justice John Roberts and Associate Justice Samuel Alito.

Boxer was a thorn in the side of President George W. Bush. She voted against the 2002 resolution authorizing the president to use force in Iraq. She voted against the confirmation of Condoleezza Rice for Secretary of State. She has been a strong voice in support of gay and lesbian causes; she opposed the Defense of Marriage Act and supports partnerships for same-sex couples.

Following the Democratic victory in the 2006 congressional midterm elections, Boxer assumed the Chair of the Senate Environment and Public Works Committee. She has led the battle to block oil drilling in the Arctic National Wildlife Refuge. She has led in fights to cut further emissions from power plants, to reduce energy consumption, and to curb global warming.

Election results indicate that Boxer is very popular among California voters. She won reelection in 1998 by a solid 10 percentage point margin, and again in 2004 with an unprecedented 20 percentage point margin. Her vote total that year in the nation's most populous state was the highest vote total in the history of direct elections for the U.S. Senate.

generous unemployment, welfare, and Social Security benefits; and reduces economic inequality. But many of these same liberals would *limit the government's power to regulate social conduct.* They oppose restrictions on abortion; oppose school prayer; favor "decriminalizing" marijuana use and "victimless" offenses like public intoxication and vagrancy; support gay rights and tolerance toward alternative lifestyles; oppose government restrictions on speech, press, and protest; oppose the death penalty; and strive to protect the rights of criminal defendants. Liberalism is the prevailing ideology among college professors (see Figure 2.6).

The Ideological Battlefield
If Americans aligned themselves along a single liberal-conservative dimension, politics in the United States would be easier to describe, but far less interesting. We have already defined liberals as supporting a

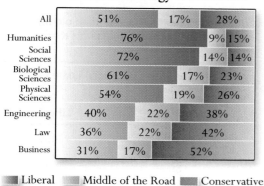

Political Ideology of Professors

Liberal   Middle of the Road   Conservative

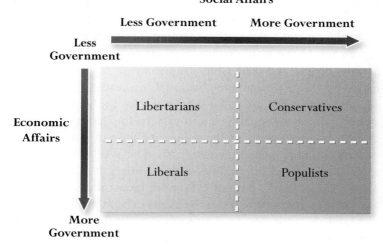

Figure 2.6

Ideology Among Professors

Most professors describe their politics as "liberal," especially professors in the humanities and social sciences.

Source: American Enterprise, vol. 2, July/August 1991, http://www.TAEmag. com. Published by the American Enterprise Institute for Public Policy Research, Washington, D.C.

strong government in economic affairs and civil rights, but opposing government intervention in social affairs. And we have described conservatives as supporting a limited government in economic affairs and civil rights, but favoring government regulation of social conduct. Thus neither liberals nor conservatives are really consistent in their view of the role of government in society, each differentiating between economic and social affairs.

Yet some people consistently support strong government to regulate business and provide economic security, and also to closely regulate social conduct. While few people use the term *populist* to describe themselves, these people may actually make up a fairly large proportion of the electorate. Liberal politicians can appeal for their votes by stressing government intervention to provide economic security, while conservative politicians can appeal to them by stressing the maintenance of traditional social values.

And some people, often referred to as **libertarians**, oppose government intervention in *both* economic affairs and in the private lives of citizens. They are against most environmental regulations, consumer protection laws, antidrug laws, defense spending, foreign aid, and government restrictions on abortion. In other words, they favor minimal government intervention in all sectors of society.

The result may be a two-dimensional ideological battlefield—identifying more or less government intervention and separating economic from social affairs—resulting in four separate groups—liberals, conservatives, populists, and libertarians (see Figure 2.7). (See also *Controversy*: "The Libertarian Party: A Dissenting Voice," in Chapter 7).

★ **libertarian**
Opposing government intervention in both economic and social affairs, and favoring minimal government in all sectors of society.

Figure 2.7

Mapping the Ideological Battlefield

We can classify people's views on whether they prefer more or less government intervention, first, in economic affairs (the vertical axis), and, second, in social affairs (the horizontal axis). The result is a fourfold classification scheme distinguishing types (economic and social) of liberals and conservatives.

Table *2.1* Ideology and Age

Younger people are more likely to describe their views as "liberal" than older people. More people describe their views as "conservative" on economic issues than on social issues.

Thinking about social issues, would you say your views on social issues are conservative, moderate, or liberal?

Age	Conservative	Moderate	Liberal
18–24	27%	36%	36%
25–38	33	34	31
39 plus	40	38	19

Thinking about economic issues, would you say your views on economic issues are conservative, moderate, or liberal?

Age	Conservative	Moderate	Liberal
18–24	33%	40%	26%
25–38	39	39	20
39 plus	47	38	12

Source: Gallup Poll reported May 20, 2003. Copyright © 2003 by The Gallup Organization.

Youth and Ideology   Young people are more likely to hold liberal views than their elders. Especially on social issues, young people age 18–24 are more likely to describe themselves as liberals (see Table 2.1). Older adults are more likely to describe themselves as conservatives on social as well as economic issues.

Dissent in the United States

Dissent from the principal elements of American political culture—individualism, free enterprise, democracy, and equality of opportunity—has arisen over the years from both the *left* and the *right*. The **left** generally refers to socialists and communists, but it is sometimes used to brand liberals. The **right** generally refers to fascists and extreme nationalists, although it is sometimes used to stamp conservatives.

Antidemocratic Ideologies   Antidemocratic ideas have historical roots in movements that originated primarily outside America's borders. These movements have spanned the political spectrum from the far right to the far left.

At the far-right end of this spectrum lies **fascism**, an ideology that asserts the supremacy of the state or race over individuals. The goal of fascism is unity of people, nation, and leadership—in the words of Adolf Hitler: *"Ein Volk, Ein Reich, Ein Führer"* ("One People, One Nation, One Leader"). Every individual, every interest, and every class are to be submerged for the good of the nation. Against the rights of liberty or equality, fascism asserts the duties of service, devotion, and discipline. Its goal is to develop a superior type of human being, with qualities of bravery, courage, genius, and strength. The World War II defeat of the two leading fascist regimes in history—Adolf Hitler's Nazi Germany and Benito Mussolini's fascist Italy—did not extinguish fascist ideas. Elements of fascist thought are found today in extremist movements in both the United States and Europe.

Marxism arose out of the turmoil of the Industrial Revolution as a protest against social evils and economic inequalities. Karl Marx (1818–83), its founder,

★ **left**
A reference to the liberal, progressive, and/or socialist side of the political spectrum.

★ **right**
A reference to the conservative, traditional, anticommunist side of the political spectrum.

★ **fascism**
Political ideology in which the state and/or race is assumed to be supreme over individuals.

★ **Marxism**
The theories of Karl Marx, among them that capitalists oppress workers and that worldwide revolution and the emergence of a classless society are inevitable.

was not an impoverished worker but rather an upper-middle-class intellectual unable to find an academic position. Benefiting from the financial support of his wealthy colleague Friedrich Engels (1820–95), Marx spent years writing *Das Kapital* (1867), a lengthy work describing the evils of capitalism, especially the oppression of factory workers (the proletariat) and the inevitability of revolution. The two men collaborated on a popular pamphlet entitled *The Communist Manifesto* (1848), which called for a workers' revolution: "Workers of the world, unite. You have nothing to lose but your chains."

It fell to Vladimir Lenin (1870–1924) to implement Marx and Engels's revolutionary ideology in the Russian Revolution in 1917. According to **Leninism**, the key to a successful revolution is the organization of small, disciplined, hard-core groups of professional revolutionaries into a centralized totalitarian party. To explain why Marx's predictions about the ever-worsening conditions of the masses under capitalism proved untrue (workers' standards of living in Western democracies rose rapidly in the twentieth century), Lenin devised the theory of imperialism: advanced capitalist countries turned to war and colonialism, exploiting the Third World, in order to make their own workers relatively prosperous.

Communism is the outgrowth of Marxist-Leninist ideas about the necessity of class warfare, the inevitability of a worldwide proletarian revolution, and the concentration of all power in the "vanguard of the proletariat"—the Communist Party. Communism justifies violence as a means to attain power by arguing that the bourgeoisie (the capitalistic middle class) will never voluntarily give up its control over "the means of production" (the economy). Democracy is only "window dressing" to disguise capitalist exploitation. The Communist Party justifies authoritarian single-party rule as the "dictatorship of the proletariat." In theory, after a period of rule by the Communist Party, all property will be owned by the government, and a "classless" society of true communism will emerge.

Socialism

Socialism shares with communism a condemnation of capitalist profit making as exploitative of the working classes. Communists and socialists agree on the "evils" of industrial capitalism: the concentration of wealth, the insensitivity of the profit motive to human needs, the insecurities and suffering brought on by the business cycle, the conflict of class interests, and the tendency

★ **Leninism**
The theories of Vladimir Lenin, among them being that advanced capitalist countries turned toward war and colonialism to make their own workers relatively prosperous.

★ **communism**
System of government in which a single totalitarian party controls all means of production and distribution of goods and services.

★ **socialism**
System of government involving collective or government ownership of economic enterprise, with the goal being equality of results, not merely equality of opportunity.

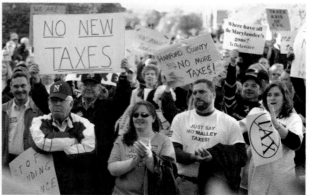

Ideologies in Action
Liberals' concern about efforts to curtail social welfare programs reflects their support of strong government, whereas conservatives' demands for tax cuts reflect their preference for government that encourages self-reliance and individual initiative.

Controversy

Are You a Liberal or a Conservative?

Not everyone consistently takes a liberal or a conservative position on every issue. But if you find that you agree with more positions under one of the following "liberal" or "conservative" lists, you are probably ready to label yourself ideologically.

	You are *Liberal* If You Agree That . . .	You Are *Conservative* If You Agree That . . .
Economic policy	Government should regulate business to protect the public interest.	Free-market competition is better at protecting the public than government regulation.
	The rich should pay higher taxes to support public services for all.	Taxes should be kept as low as possible.
	Government spending for social welfare is a good investment in people.	Government welfare programs destroy incentives to work.
Crime	Government should place primary emphasis on alleviating the social conditions (such as poverty and joblessness) that cause crime.	Government should place primary emphasis on providing more police and prisons and stop courts from coddling criminals.
Social policy	Government should protect the right of women to choose abortion and fund abortions for poor women.	Government should restrict abortion and not use taxpayer money for abortions.
	Government should pursue affirmative action programs on behalf of minorities and women in employment, education, and so on.	Government should not grant preferences to anyone based on race or sex.
	Government should keep religious prayers and ceremonies out of schools and public places.	Government should allow prayers and religious observances in schools and public places.
National security policy	Government should support "human rights" throughout the world.	Government should pursue the "national interest" of the United States.
	Military spending should be reduced now that the Cold War is over.	Military spending must reflect a variety of new dangers in this post–Cold War period.

of capitalist nations to involve themselves in imperialist wars. However, socialists are committed to the democratic process as a means of replacing capitalism with collective ownership of economic enterprise. Socialists generally reject the notion of violent revolution as a way to replace capitalism and instead advocate peaceful, constitutional roads to bring about change. Moreover, many socialists are prepared to govern in a free society under democratic principles, including freedom of speech and press and the right to organize political parties and oppose government policy. Socialism is egalitarian, seeking to reduce or eliminate inequalities in the distribution of wealth. It attempts to achieve equality of results, rather than mere equality of opportunity.

The End of History? Much of the history of the twentieth century was the struggle between democratic capitalism and totalitarian communism. Thus the collapse of communism in Eastern Europe and the Soviet Union, symbolized by the tearing down of the Berlin Wall in 1989 as well as the worldwide movement toward free markets and democracy at the end of the twentieth century,

Extremism, Left and Right

Political extremists on the left and right often have more in common than they would like to admit. Although decidedly different in their political philosophies, both members of radical left wing groups and members of white supremacist groups typically reject democratic politics and assert the supremacy of the "people" over laws, institutions, and individual rights. Gregory Johnson (left) was the catalyst for the flag-burning controversy that still rages from time to time, and the young men on the right are members of a U.S. neo-Nazi group.

has been labeled the **end of history**.[16] Democratic revolutions were largely inspired by the realization that free-market capitalism provided much higher standards of living than communism. The economies of Eastern Europe were falling further and further behind the economies of the capitalist nations of the West. Similar comparative observations of the successful economies of the Asian capitalist "Four Tigers"—South Korea, Taiwan, Singapore, and Hong Kong—even inspired China's communist leadership to undertake market reforms. Communism destroyed the individual's incentive to work, produce, innovate, save, and invest in the future. Under communism, production for government goals (principally a strong military) came first; production for individual needs came last. The result was long lines at stores, shoddy products, and frequent bribery of bureaucrats to obtain necessary consumer items. More important, the concentration of both economic and political power in the hands of a central bureaucracy proved to be incompatible with democracy. Communism relies on central direction, force, and repression. Communist systems curtail individual freedom and prohibit the development of separate parties and interest groups outside of government.

Capitalism does not *ensure* democracy; some capitalist nations are authoritarian. But economic freedom inspires demands for political freedom. Thus market reforms, initiated by communist leaders to increase productivity, led to democ-

★ **end of history**
The collapse of communism and the worldwide movement toward free markets and political democracy.

A *Constitutional* Note

Natural Born Versus Naturalized Citizenship

The 14th Amendment to the Constitution requires the states, and by implication the national government, to treat natural born and naturalized citizens the same: "all persons born or naturalized in United States, and subject to the jurisdiction thereof, are citizens of the United States. . . . No State shall make or enforce any law which shall abridge the privileges or immunities of citizens of the United States. . . . " But there is one key difference between natural born and naturalized citizens written into the original Constitution of 1787: "No Person except a natural born Citizen, or a Citizen of the United States, at the time of the Adoption of this Constitution, shall be eligible to the Office of President. . . ."

Requiring that the President be born in the United States is the only constitutional difference between born and naturalized citizens. Perhaps this difference made more sense in 1787 when many aspiring politicians had only recently moved into the country. But is it relevant today? Does it deny some very qualified people the opportunity to run for the nation's highest office?

racy movements, and those movements eventually dismantled the communist system in Eastern Europe and the old Soviet Union.

Academic Radicalism Marxism survives on campuses today largely as an academic critique of the functioning of capitalism.[17] Contemporary Marxists argue that the institutions of capitalism have conditioned people to be materialistic, competitive, and even violent. The individual has been transformed into a one-dimensional person in whom genuine humanistic values are repressed.[18] Profitability, rather than humanistic values, remains the primary criterion for decision making in the capitalist economy, and thus profitability is the reason for poverty and misery despite material abundance. Without capitalist institutions, life would be giving, cooperative, and compassionate. Only a *radical restructuring* of social and economic institutions will succeed in liberating people from these institutions to lead humanistic, cooperative lives.

To American radicals, the problem of social change is truly monumental, because capitalist values and institutions are deeply rooted in this country. Since most people are not aware that they are oppressed and victimized, the first step toward social change is consciousness raising—that is, making people aware of their misery.

★ **politically correct (PC)**
Repression of attitudes, speech, and writings that are deemed racist, sexist, homophobic (anti-homosexual), or otherwise "insensitive."

The agenda of academic radicalism has been labeled **politically correct** (PC) thinking. Politically correct thinking views American society as racist, sexist, and homophobic. Overt bigotry is not the real issue, but rather Western institutions, language, and culture, which systematically oppress and victimize women, people of color, homosexuals, and others.

Academic radicalism "includes the assumption that Western values are inherently oppressive, that the chief purpose of education is political transformation, and that all standards are arbitrary.[19] In PC thinking, "everything is political." Therefore curriculum, courses, and lectures—even language and demeanor—are judged according to whether they are politically correct or not. Universities have always been centers for the critical examination of institutions, values, and culture, but PC thinking does not really tolerate open discussion or debate. Opposition is denounced as "insensitive," racist, sexist, or worse, and intimidation is not infrequent (see *Controversy*: "Political Correctness Versus Free Speech on Campus" in Chapter 14).

Summary
Who Gets What: Ideas in Conflict

Ideas are sources of power. They provide people with guides for determining right and wrong and with rationales for political action. Political institutions are shaped by the values and beliefs of the political culture, and political leaders are restrained in their exercise of power by these ideas.

★ The American political culture is a set of widely shared values and beliefs about who should govern, for what ends, and by what means.

★ Americans share many common ways of thinking about politics. Nevertheless, there are often contradictions between professed values and actual conditions, problems in applying abstract beliefs to concrete situations, and even occasional conflict over fundamental values.

★ Individual liberty is a fundamental value in American life. The classical liberal tradition that inspired the nation's Founders included both political liberties and economic freedoms.

★ Equality is another fundamental American value. The nation's Founders believed in equality before the law; yet political equality, in the form of universal voting rights, required nearly two centuries to bring about.

★ Equality of opportunity is a widely shared value; most Americans are opposed to artificial barriers of race, sex, religion, or ethnicity barring individual advancement. But equality of results is not a widely shared value; most Americans support a "floor" on income and well-being for their fellow citizens but oppose placing a "ceiling" on income or wealth.

★ Income inequality has increased in recent years primarily as a result of economic and demographic changes. Most Americans believe that opportunities for individual advancement are still available, and this belief diminishes the potential for class conflict.

★ A great majority of Americans claim religious affiliation. But there is a growing divide between religious and secular viewpoints on the role of religion in public life. Secularists have challenged many traditional religious practices and symbols, such as the words "under God" in the Pledge of Allegiance.

★ Liberal and conservative ideologies in American politics present somewhat different sets of values and beliefs, even though they share a common commitment to individual dignity and private property. Generally, liberals favor an active, powerful government to provide economic security and protection for civil rights but oppose government restrictions on social conduct. Generally, conservatives favor minimal government intervention in economic affairs and civil rights but support many government restrictions on social conduct.

★ Many Americans who identify themselves as liberals or conservatives are not always consistent in applying their professed views. Populists are liberal on economic issues but conservative in their views on social issues. Libertarians are conservative on economic issues but liberal in their social views.

★ The collapse of communism in Eastern Europe and the former Soviet Union and the worldwide movement toward free markets and democracy have undermined support for socialism throughout the world. Yet Marxism survives in academic circles as a critique of the functioning of capitalism.

Key Terms

political culture   25
values   25
beliefs   26
subcultures   26
classical liberalism   26
capitalism   26
legal equality   28
political equality   28
equality of opportunity   28

equality of results   29
social mobility   31
class conflict   32
class consciousness   32
immigration policy   35
aliens   37
amnesty   37
illegal immigration   40
passport   40

visa   41
secular   41
ideology   43
conservatism   43
liberalism   44
libertarian   47
left   48
right   48
fascism   48

Marxism   48
Leninism   49
communism   49
socialism   49
end of history   51
politically correct (PC)   52

Suggested Readings

Baradat, Leon P. *Political Ideologies: Their Origin and Impact.* 9th ed. Upper Saddle River, N.J.: Prentice Hall, 2006. Text coverage of evolution of political ideologies over the past three centuries.

de Tocqueville, Alexis. *Democracy in America* (1835). Chicago: University of Chicago Press, 2000. Classic early assessment of American political culture by a French traveler.

Dolbeare, Kenneth M., and Michael S. Cummings. *American Political Thought.* 5th ed. Washington, D.C.: CQ Press, 2004. A compilation of key writings and speeches from Franklin, Madison, Adams, and Paine, to Bill Clinton, Ronald Reagan, Pat Buchanan, and the Green Party.

Ebenstein, Alan, William Ebenstein, and Edwin Fogelman. *Today's Isms: Communism, Fascism, Capitalism, Socialism.* 11th ed. Upper Saddle River, N.J.: Prentice Hall, 2000. A concise description and history of the major isms.

Herrnstein, Richard J., and Charles Murray. *The Bell Curve: Intelligence and Class Structure in American Life.* New York: Free Press, 1994. A controversial argument that success in life is mainly a result of inherited intelligence and that a very bright "cognitive elite" will continue to distance themselves from the duller masses.

Huntington, Samuel P. *The Clash of Civilizations and the Remaking of World Order.* New York: Simon & Schuster, 1996. The nation's leading political scientist assesses the state of world politics after the fall of communism. He explains how conflict between "civilizations," for example, Western versus Islamic, have replaced nations and ideologies as the driving force in global politics today.

Huntington, Samuel P. *Who We Are? The Challenges to America's National Identity.* New York: Simon & Schuster, 2004. A controversial argument that our national identity, including the English language, individualism, and respect for law, is being eroded by the problems of assimilating massive numbers of immigrants. The author argues the need to reassert the core values that make us Americans.

Jacobs, Lawrence R., and Theda Skocpol, eds. *Inequality and American Democracy.* New York: Russell Sage Foundation, 2005. A series of essays on the political consequences of growing income inequality in America.

Love, Nancy S. *Understanding Dogmas and Dreams.* 2nd ed. Washington, D.C.: CQ Press, 2006. An introduction to liberalism, conservatism, socialism, anarchism, fascism, feminism, environmentalism, and globalism.

Ryscavage, Paul. *Income Inequality in America.* Armonk, N.Y.: M.E. Sharpe, 1999. A careful analysis of current trends toward income inequality in the United States.

Takaki, Ronald. *A Different Mirror: A History of Multicultural America.* Boston: Little, Brown and Co., 1993. A thorough and engaging account of how the United States has always been a racially, ethnically, and culturally diverse society.

Wolff, Edward N. *Top Heavy.* 2nd ed. New York: News Press, 2002. A fact-filled report on the increasing inequality of wealth in America, together with a proposal to tax wealth as well as income.

Suggested Web Sites

Americans United for Separation of Church and State
www.au.org
An interest group formed to keep religion out of public places, especially schools.

American Conservative Union www.conservative.org
Conservative news and views and rankings of Congress members on conservative index.

Americans for Democratic Action www.adaction.org
The ADA is the nation's oldest liberal political action organization.

Bill O'Reilly www.billoreilly.com
Popular Web site for conservative views as well as promotion of O'Reilly programs, books, editorials, etc.

Bureau of Citizenship and Immigration Services (CIS)
www.immigration.gov
Official site with information on immigration laws, citizenship requirements, etc.

Center for Equal Opportunity www.ceousa.org
Think tank advocating equality of opportunity over equality of results.

Center for Immigration Studies www.cis.org
Advocacy organization for strengthening enforcement of immigration law.

Family Religious Council www.frc.org
An interest group championing religion, family, and marriage, and government support of these values.

Global Policy Forum   www.globalpolicy.org
Information on many global issues. Click to "social and economic policy" and then to "inequality of wealth and income" for crossnational data.

Heritage Foundation   www.heritage.org
This think tank site includes a ranking of over 150 nations on an "Index of Economic Freedom." The U.S. ranks sixth; Hong Kong ranks first.

Immigration and Customs Enforcement (ICE)
www.ice.gov
Agency responsible for enforcement of immigration and customs laws.

Monticello   www.monticello.org
Biography, letters, and a "Day in the Life" of Thomas Jefferson.

National Association of Scholars   www.nas.org
Association of college and university professors opposed to PC restrictions on campus.

People for the American Way   www.pfaw.org
An influential interest group on the Left which, among other issues, strongly opposes religious symbols in public.

Philosophy Pages   www.philosophypages.com
History of Western philosophy and discussion of major democratic philosophers, including John Locke, Jean Jacques Rousseau, and Thomas Hobbes, among others.

Socialist Party USA   http://sp-usa.org
News and views from America's Socialist party.

U.S. Senator Barbara Boxer   www.senate.gov/~boxer/
The official Web site of U.S. Senator Barbara Boxer of California contains biographical material, information about Boxer's committee assignments, and her stands on various political issues.

Young Americans for Freedom   www.yaf.com
The "YAF" archives site contains background on the conservative organization and conservative views on key issues of the day.

3 THE CONSTITUTION
Limiting Governmental Power

66 The ascendancy of any elite depends upon the success of the practices it adopts. . . . In the Constitution, written and unwritten common embodies the practices which are deemed most fundamental to the governmental and social order. 99

Harold Lasswell

Chapter *Outline*

Think About Politics

1. Was the original constitution of 1787 a truly democratic document?
   YES ◯ NO ◯

2. Should citizens be able to vote directly on national policies such as prayer in public schools or doctor-assisted suicides?
   YES ◯ NO ◯

3. Should a large state like California, with 38 million people, elect more U.S. senators than a small state like Wyoming, with only half a million people?
   YES ◯ NO ◯

4. Should federal laws always supersede state laws?
   YES ◯ NO ◯

5. In which do you have the most trust and confidence?
   PRESIDENT ◯ CONGRESS ◯ SUPREME COURT ◯

6. Should the Constitution be amended to require Congress to pass only balanced budgets?
   YES ◯ NO ◯

7. Should the Constitution be amended to guarantee that equal rights shall not be denied based on sex?
   YES ◯ NO ◯

In a democracy "of the people, by the people, and for the people," who really has the power to govern? Are strong national government and personal liberty compatible? Can majorities limit individual rights? America's Founders struggled with such questions, and in resolving them established the oldest existing constitutional government.

Constitutional Government

Constitutions govern government. **Constitutionalism**—a government of laws, not of people—means that those who exercise governmental power are restricted in their use of it by a higher law. If individual freedoms are to be placed beyond the reach of government and beyond the reach of majorities, then a constitution must truly limit the exercise of authority by government. It does so by setting forth individual liberties that the government—even with majority support—cannot violate.

A **constitution** legally establishes government authority. It sets up governmental bodies (such as the House of Representatives, the Senate, the presidency, and the Supreme Court in the United States). It grants them powers. It determines how their members are to be chosen. And it prescribes the rules by which they make decisions.

Constitutional decision making is deciding how to decide; that is, it is deciding on the rules for policy making. It is not policy making itself. Policies will be decided later, according to the rules set forth in the constitution.

A constitution cannot be changed by the ordinary acts of governmental bodies; change can come only through a process of general popular consent.[1] The U.S. Constitution, then, is superior to ordinary laws of Congress, orders of the president, decisions of the courts, acts of the state legislatures, and regulations of the bureaucracies. Indeed, the Constitution is "the supreme law of the land."

The Constitutional Tradition

Americans are strongly committed to the idea of a written constitution to establish government and limit its powers. In fact, the Constitutional Convention of 1787 had many important antecedents.

The Magna Carta, 1215 English lords, traditionally required to finance the king's wars, forced King John to sign the Magna Carta, a

★ **constitutionalism**
A government of laws, not people, operating on the principle that governmental power must be limited and government officials should be restrained in their exercise of power over individuals.

57

★ **constitution**
The legal structure of a political system, establishing governmental bodies, granting their powers, determining how their members are selected, and prescribing the rules by which they make their decisions. Considered basic or fundamental, a constitution cannot be changed by ordinary acts of governmental bodies.

Comparing Constitutions

document guaranteeing their feudal rights and setting the precedent of a limited government and monarchy.

The Mayflower Compact, 1620 Pilgrim colonists, while still aboard the *Mayflower*, signed a compact, among themselves and other passengers, establishing a "civil body politic . . . to enact just and equal laws . . . for the general good of the colony, unto which we promise all due submission and obedience." After the Pilgrims landed at Plymouth, in what is today Massachusetts, they formed a colony based on the Mayflower Compact, thus setting a precedent of a government established by contract with the governed.

The Colonial Charters, 1624–1732 The charters that authorized settlement of the colonies in America were granted by royal action. For some of the colonies, the British king granted official proprietary rights to an individual, as in Maryland (granted to Lord Baltimore), Pennsylvania (to William Penn), and Delaware (also to Penn). For other colonies, the king granted royal commissions to companies to establish governments, as in Virginia, Massachusetts, New Hampshire, New York, New Jersey, Georgia, and North and South Carolina. Royal charters were granted directly to the colonists themselves only in Connecticut and Rhode Island. These colonists drew up their charters and presented them to the king, setting a precedent in America for written contracts defining governmental power.

The "Charter Oak Affair" of 1685–88 began when King James II became displeased with his Connecticut subjects and issued an order for the repeal of the Connecticut Charter. In 1687 Sir Edmund Andros went to Hartford, dissolved the colonial government, and demanded that the charter be returned. But Captain John Wadsworth hid it in an oak tree. After the so-called Glorious Revolution in England in 1688, the charter was taken out and used again as the fundamental law of the colony. Subsequent British monarchs silently acquiesced in this restoration of rights, and the affair strengthened the notion of loyalty to the constitution rather than to the king.

The Declaration of Independence, 1776 The First Continental Congress, a convention of delegates from twelve of the thirteen original colonies, came together in 1774 to protest British interference in American affairs. But the Revolutionary War did not begin until April 19, 1775. The evening before, British regular troops marched out from Boston to seize arms stored by citizens in Lexington and Concord, Massachusetts. At dawn the next morning, the Minutemen—armed citizens organized for the protection of their towns—engaged the British regulars in brief battles, then harassed them all the way back to Boston. In June of that year, the Second Continental Congress appointed George Washington Commander-in-Chief of American forces and sent him to Boston to take command of the American militia surrounding the city. Still, popular support for the Revolution remained limited, and even many members of the Continental Congress hoped only to force changes—not to split off from Britain.

As this hope died, however, members of the Continental Congress came to view a formal Declaration of Independence as necessary to give legitimacy to their cause and establish the basis for a new nation. Accordingly, on July 2, 1776, the Continental Congress "Resolved, that these United Colonies are, and, of right, ought to be free and independent States." Thomas Jefferson had been commissioned to write a justification for the action, which he presented to the Congress on July 4, 1776. (See *People in Politics:* "Thomas Jefferson and

People in Politics Thomas Jefferson and the Declaration of Independence

Thomas Jefferson's opening words of the Declaration of Independence provide the most succinct summary of the role of government in a free society:

We hold these truths to be self evident, that all men are created equal, that they endowed by their Creator with certain unalienable Rights, that among these are Life, Liberty and the pursuit of Happiness. That to secure these rights Governments are instituted among Men, deriving their just powers from the consent of the governed. That whenever any Form of Government becomes destructive of these ends, it is the Right of the People to alter or abolish it, and to institute new Government. . . .

In this single paragraph, Jefferson asserts natural law and the natural rights derived from it, the social contract as the origin of government, government by the consent of the governed, and the right of revolution.

Jefferson was born into wealth and privilege in Virginia in 1743. He mastered Latin, Greek, and French and at age 14 inherited 5,000 acres of land and dozens of slaves on the plantation that eventually became known as Monticello. He graduated in two years from the College of William and Mary in Williamsburg with highest honors. He practiced law and served in the Virginia House of Burgesses and was sent by Virginia to the Continental Congress. There he was delegated the task of writing the Declaration of Independence, which was formally adopted July 4, 1776. He later served as governor of Virginia and as the American Minister to France, America's most important ally at the time. He did not attend the Constitutional Convention and gave only lukewarm support to the new Constitution, believing that it was flawed for lack of a Bill of Rights. After returning from France, he served as the nation's first Secretary of State under President George Washington.

Jefferson can be credited with founding the American party system. In Washington's cabinet he argued against the policies of Secretary of the Treasury Alexander Hamilton—policies that would strengthen the role of the federal government in business, banking, and commerce. He resigned from the Cabinet and became the principal spokesperson for the emerging Anti-Federalists. He lost the presidency in 1796 to the Federalist candidate John Adams, but won enough electoral votes to become Vice President. Prior to the election of 1800, Jefferson worked closely with Aaron Burr of New York to organize the Democratic-Republican party that would eventually become the Democratic Party. When all his party's electors cast their two votes for Jefferson and Burr, intending that Jefferson should be president and Burr vice president, the two men actually tied for the presidency. The Federalist-controlled House, after thirty-six ballots, and on the advice of Alexander Hamilton, finally elected Jefferson as president and Burr as vice president. Later Burr would kill Hamilton in a duel.

Jefferson's presidency was highlighted by the Louisiana Purchase, which doubled the size of the United States. He hoped that this purchase would provide the American people with farmland "to the hundredth and thousandth generation." When he spoke warmly of the wisdom of "the people," he was actually referring to those who owned and managed their own farms and estates. He believed that only those who owned land could make good citizens. He disliked aristocracy, but he also held the urban masses in contempt. He wanted to see the United States become a nation of free, educated, land-owning farmers. After leaving the presidency, Jefferson plunged into the planning and designing of the University of Virginia. His dream was realized with the opening of the university in 1825.

President John F. Kennedy welcomed forty-nine Nobel Prize winners to the White House in 1962, with his now famous tribute to Jefferson: "I think this is the most extraordinary collection of talent and of human knowledge that has ever been gathered together at the White House—with the possible exception of when Thomas Jefferson dined alone."

the Declaration of Independence.") In writing the Declaration of Independence, Jefferson lifted several phrases directly from the English political philosopher John Locke asserting the rights of individuals, the contract theory of government, and the right of revolution. The declaration was signed first by the president of the Continental Congress, John Hancock. (See Declaration of Independence in the Appendix.)

The Revolutionary War effectively ended when British General Charles Cornwallis surrendered at Yorktown, Virginia, in October 1781. But even as the war was being waged, the new nation was creating the framework of its government.

The Articles of Confederation, 1781–1789   Although Richard Henry Lee, a Virginia delegate to the Continental Congress, first proposed that the newly independent states form a confederation on July 6, 1776, the Continental Congress did not approve the Articles of Confederation until November 15, 1777, and the last state to sign them, Maryland, did not do so until March 1, 1781. Under the Articles, Congress was a single house in which each state had two to seven members but only one vote. Congress itself created and appointed executives, judges, and military officers. It also had the power to make war and peace, conduct foreign affairs, and borrow and print money. But Congress could *not* collect taxes or enforce laws directly; it had to rely on the states to provide money and enforce its laws. The United States under the Articles was really a confederation of nations. Within this "firm league of friendship" (Article III of the Articles of Confederation), the national government was thought of as an alliance of independent states, not as a government "of the people."

Troubles Confronting a New Nation

Two centuries ago the United States was struggling to achieve nationhood. The new U.S. government achieved enormous successes under the Articles of Confederation: It won independence from Great Britain, the world's most powerful colonial nation at the time; it defeated vastly superior forces in a prolonged war for independence; it established a viable peace and won powerful allies (notably, France) in the international community; it created an effective army and navy, established a postal system, and laid the foundations for national unity. But despite these successes in war and diplomacy, the political arrangements under the Articles were unsatisfactory to many influential groups—notably, bankers and investors who held U.S. government bonds, plantation owners, real estate developers, and merchants and shippers.

Financial Difficulties   Under the Articles of Confederation, Congress had no power to tax the people directly. Instead, Congress had to ask the states for money to pay its expenses, particularly the expenses of fighting the long and costly War of Independence with Great Britain. There was no way to force the states to make their payments to the national government. In fact, about 90 percent of the funds requisitioned by Congress from the states were never paid, so Congress had to borrow money from wealthy patriot investors to fight the war. Without the power to tax, however, Congress could not pay off these debts. Indeed, the value of U.S. governmental bonds fell to about 10 cents for every dollar's worth because few people believed the bonds would ever be paid off. Congress even stopped making interest payments on these bonds.

Commercial Obstacles   Under the Articles of Confederation, states were free to tax the goods of other states. Without the power to regulate interstate commerce, the national government was unable to protect merchants from heavy tariffs imposed on shipments from state to state. Southern planters could not ship their agricultural products to northern cities without paying state-imposed tariffs, and northern merchants could not ship manufactured products from state to state without interference. Merchants, manufacturers, shippers, and planters all wanted to develop national markets and prevent the states from imposing tariffs or restrictions on interstate trade.

Currency Problems

Under the Articles, the states themselves had the power to issue their own currency, regulate its value, and require that it be accepted in payment of debts. States had their own "legal tender" laws, which required creditors to accept state money if "tendered" in payment of debt. As a result, many forms of money were circulating: Virginia dollars, Rhode Island dollars, Pennsylvania dollars, and so on. Some states (Rhode Island, for example) printed a great deal of money, creating inflation in their currency and alienating banks and investors whose loans were being paid off in this cheap currency. If creditors refused payment in a particular state's currency, the debt could be abolished in that state. So finances throughout the states were very unstable, and banks and creditors were threatened by cheap paper money.

Western Lands

Men of property in early America actively speculated in western land. But the Confederation's military weakness along its frontiers kept the value of western lands low. A strong central government with enough military power to oust the British from the Northwest and to protect western settlers against Indian attacks could open the way for the development of the American West. The protection and settlement of western land would cause land values to skyrocket and make land speculators rich. Moreover, under the Articles of Confederation each state lay claim to western lands. Indeed, Maryland's ratification of the Articles was withheld until the states with claims to lands west of the Appalachians were ceded to Congress in 1781 for "the good of the whole."

Civil Disorder

In several states, debtors openly revolted against tax collectors and sheriffs attempting to repossess farms on behalf of creditors who held unpaid mortgages. The most serious rebellion broke out in the summer of 1786 in western Massachusetts, where a band of 2,000 insurgent farmers captured the courthouses in several counties and briefly held the city of Springfield. Led by Daniel Shays, a veteran of the Revolutionary War battle at Bunker Hill, the insurgent army posed a direct threat to investors, bankers, creditors, and tax collectors by burning deeds, mortgages, and tax records to wipe out proof of the farmers' debts. Shays's Rebellion, as it was called, was finally put down by a small mercenary army, paid for by well-to-do citizens of Boston.

Reports of **Shays's Rebellion** filled the newspapers of the large Eastern cities. George Washington, Alexander Hamilton, James Madison, and many other prominent Americans wrote their friends about it. The event galvanized property owners to support the creation of a strong central government capable of dealing with "radicalism." Only a strong central government, they wrote one another, could "insure domestic tranquility," guarantee "a republican form of government," and protect property "against domestic violence." It is no accident that all of these phrases appear in the Constitution of 1787.

The Road to the Constitutional Convention

In the spring of 1785, some wealthy merchants from Virginia and Maryland met at Alexandria, Virginia, to try to resolve a conflict between the two states over commerce and navigation on the Potomac River and Chesapeake Bay. George Washington, the new nation's most prominent citizen, took a personal interest in the meeting. As a wealthy plantation owner and a land speculator who owned more than

A Weakness Exposed

In an attempt to prevent the foreclosure of farms by creditors, Revolutionary War veteran Daniel Shays led an armed mass of citizens in a march on a western Massachusetts courthouse. This uprising, which came to be known as Shays's Rebellion, exposed the Confederation's military weakness and increased support for a strong central government.

★ **Shays's Rebellion**
An armed revolt in 1786, led by a Revolutionary War Officer Daniel Shays, protesting the discontent of small farmers over debts and taxes, and raising concerns about the ability of the U.S. government under the Articles of Confederation to maintain internal order.

30,000 acres of land upstream on the Potomac, Washington was keenly interested in commercial problems under the Articles of Confederation. He lent his great prestige to the Alexandria meeting by inviting the participants to his house at Mount Vernon. Out of this conference came the idea for a general economic conference for all of the states, to be held in Annapolis, Maryland, in September 1786.

★ **Annapolis Convention**
A 1786 meeting at Annapolis, Maryland, to discuss interstate commerce, which recommended a larger convention—the Constitutional Convention of 1787.

The **Annapolis Convention** turned out to be a key stepping-stone to the Constitutional Convention of 1787. Instead of concentrating on commerce and navigation between the states, the delegates at Annapolis, including Alexander Hamilton and James Madison, called for a general constitutional convention to suggest remedies to what they saw as defects in the Articles of Confederation.

On February 21, 1787, the Congress called for a convention to meet in Philadelphia for the "sole and express purpose" of *revising* the Articles of Confederation and reporting to the Congress and the state legislatures "such alterations and provisions therein as shall, when agreed to in Congress and confirmed by the states, render the federal Constitution adequate to the exigencies of government and the preservation of the union." Notice that Congress did not authorize the convention to write a new constitution or to call constitutional conventions in the states to ratify a new constitution. State legislatures sent delegates to Philadelphia expecting that their task would be limited to revising the Articles and that revisions would be sent back to Congress and state legislatures for their approval. But that is not what happened.

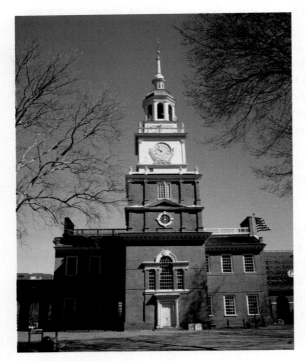

Independence Hall in Philadelphia

The meeting place of the second Continental Congress in 1776 and later the Constitutional Convention in 1787. Now a major tourist attraction in Philadelphia.

The Nation's Founders The fifty-five delegates to the Constitutional Convention, which met in Philadelphia in the summer of 1787, quickly discarded the congressional mandate to merely "revise" the Articles of Confederation. The Virginia delegation, led by James Madison, arrived before a quorum of seven states had assembled and used the time to draw up an entirely new constitutional document. After the first formal session opened on May 25 and George Washington was elected president of the convention, the Virginia Plan became the basis of discussion. Thus, at the very beginning of the convention, the decision was made to scrap the Articles of Confederation altogether, write a new constitution, and form a new national government.[2]

The Founders were very confident of their powers and abilities. They had been selected by their state legislatures (only Rhode Island, dominated by small farmers, refused to send a delegation). When Thomas Jefferson, then serving in the critical post of ambassador to France (the nation's military ally in the Revolutionary War), first saw the list of delegates, he exclaimed, "It is really an assembly of demigods." Indeed, among the nation's notables, only Jefferson and John Adams (then serving as ambassador to England) were absent. The eventual success of the convention, and the ratification of the new Constitution, resulted in part from the enormous prestige, experience, and achievements of the delegates themselves.

Above all, the delegates at Philadelphia were cosmopolitan. They approached political, economic, and military issues from a "continental" point of view. Unlike most Americans in 1787, their loyalties extended beyond their states. They were truly nationalists.[3]

Consensus in Philadelphia

The Founders shared many ideas about government, based on **the Enlightenment**. We often focus our attention on *conflict* in the Convention of 1787 and the compromises reached by the participants, but the really important story of the Constitution is the *consensus* that was shared by these men of influence.

Natural Rights to Liberty and Property

The Founders had read John Locke and absorbed his idea that the purpose of government is to protect individual liberty and property. (See *People in Politics*: "John Locke, Guiding the Founders.") They believed in a **natural law**, superior to any human-made laws, that endowed each person with certain **inalienable rights**—the rights to life, liberty, and property. They believed that all people were equally entitled to these rights. Most of them, including slave owners George Washington and Thomas Jefferson, understood that the belief in personal liberty conflicted with the practice of slavery and found the inconsistency troubling.

Social Contract

The Founders believed that government originated in an implied contract among people. People agreed to establish government, obey laws, and pay taxes in exchange for protection of their natural rights. This **social contract** gave government its legitimacy—a legitimacy that rested on the consent of the governed, not with gods or kings or force. If a government violated individual liberty, it broke the social contract and thus lost its legitimacy.

Representative Government

Although most of the world's governments in 1787 were hereditary monarchies, the Founders believed the people should have a voice in choosing their own representatives in government. They opposed hereditary aristocracy and titled nobility. Instead, they sought to forge a republic. **Republicanism** meant government by representatives of the people. The Founders expected the masses to consent to be governed by their leaders—men of principle and property with ability, education, and a stake in the preservation of liberty. The Founders believed the people should have only a limited role in directly selecting their representatives: they should vote for members of the House of Representatives, but senators, the president, and members of the Supreme Court should be selected by others more qualified to judge their ability.

Limited Government

The Founders believed unlimited power was corrupting and a concentration of power was dangerous. They believed in a written constitution that limited the scope of governmental power. They also believed in dividing power within government by creating separate bodies able to check and balance one another's powers.

Nationalism

Most important, the Founders shared a belief in **nationalism**—a strong and independent national (federal) government with power to govern directly, rather than through state governments. They sought to establish a government that would be recognized around the world as representing "We the people of the United States." Not everyone in America shared this enthusiasm for a strong federal government; indeed, opposition forces, calling themselves Anti-Federalists, almost succeeded in defeating the new Constitution. But the leaders meeting in Philadelphia in the summer of 1787 were convinced of the need for a strong central government that would share power with the states.

★ the Enlightenment
Also known as the Age of Reason, a philosophical movement in eighteenth-century Western thought based on a belief in reason and the capacities of individuals, a faith in a scientific approach to knowledge, and a confidence in human progress.

✔ Think Again

Was the original Constitution of 1787 a truly democratic document?

★ natural law
The law that would govern humans in a state of nature before governments existed.

★ inalienable rights
The rights of all people derived from natural law and not bestowed by governments, including the rights to life, liberty, and property.

★ social contract
The idea the government originates from an implied contract among people who agree to obey laws in exchange for the protection of their natural rights.

★ republicanism
Government by representatives of the people rather than directly by the people themselves.

★ nationalism
Belief that shared cultural, historical, linguistic, and social characteristics of a people justify the creation of a government encompassing all of them and that the resulting nation-state should be independent and legally equal to all other nation-states.

People in Politics   John Locke, Guiding the Founders

The English political philosopher John Locke had a profound influence on America's founders. Indeed, the Declaration of Independence may be thought of as a restatement of Locke's basic ideas. Writing in 1690, Locke rejected the notion of the divine right of kings to rule and asserted the rights of human beings who are "by nature free, equal, and independent" to establish their own government by "social contract" to gain security from an unstable "state of nature." In other words, people consent to be governed to protect themselves and their property. But if the government they create becomes arbitrary, enslaves its people, or takes away their property, then the people have the "right of revolution" against such a government. Locke had been read by most of the Founders, who accepted his ideas of a "social contract" as the origin of government, and even a "right of revolution" as a last resort to a despotic government.

Conflict in Philadelphia

Consensus on basic principles of government was essential to the success of the Philadelphia convention. But conflict over the implementation of these principles not only tied up the convention for an entire summer but also later threatened to prevent the states from ratifying, or voting to approve, the document the convention produced.

Representation   Representation was the most controversial issue in Philadelphia. Following the election of George Washington as president of the convention, Governor Edmund Randolph of Virginia rose to present a draft of a new constitution. This Virginia Plan called for a legislature with two houses: a lower house chosen by the people of the states, with representation according to population and an upper house to be chosen by the lower house (see Table 3.1). Congress was to have the broad power to "legislate in all cases to which the separate States are incompetent, or in which the harmony of the United States may be interrupted." Congress was to have the power to nullify state laws that it believed violated the Constitution, thus ensuring the national government's supremacy over the states. The Virginia Plan also proposed a form of **parliamentary government**, in which the legislature (Congress) chose the principal executive officers of the government as well as federal judges. Finally, the Virginia Plan included a curious "council of revision," with the power to veto acts of Congress.

Delegates from New Jersey and Delaware objected strongly to the great power given to the national government in the Virginia Plan, the larger representation it proposed for the more populous states, and the plan's failure to recognize the role of the states in the composition of the new government. After several weeks of debate, William Paterson of New Jersey submitted a counterproposal.[4] The New Jersey Plan called for a single-chamber Congress in which each state, regardless of its population, had one vote, just as under the Articles of Confederation. But unlike the Articles, the New Jersey Plan proposed separate executive and judicial branches of government and the expansion of the powers of Congress to include levying taxes and regulating

★ **parliamentary government**
A government in which power is concentrated in the legislature, which chooses from among its members a prime minister and cabinet.

People In Politics   George Washington, Founder of a Nation

From the time he took command of the American Revolutionary forces in 1775 until he gave his Farewell Address to the nation in 1796 and returned to his Mount Vernon plantation, George Washington (1732–99) was, indeed, "First in war, first in peace, first in the hearts of his countrymen." His military success, combined with his diplomacy and practical political acumen, gave him overwhelming moral authority, which he used to inspire the Constitutional Convention, to secure the ratification of the Constitution, and then to guide the new nation through its first years.

Washington was raised on a Virginia plantation and inherited substantial landholdings, including his Mount Vernon plantation on the Potomac River. He began his career as a surveyor. His work took him deep into the wilderness of America's frontier. This experience later served him well when, at age 21, he was appointed to be an officer in the Virginia militia. In 1754 he led a small force toward the French Fort Duquesne, but after a brief battle at makeshift "Fort Necessity" he was obliged to retreat. In 1755 British Major General Edward Braddock asked the young militia officer to accompany his heavy regiments on a campaign to dislodge the French from Fort Duquesne. Braddock disregarded Washington's warnings about concealed ways of fighting in the New World; Braddock's parading redcoat forces were ambushed by the French and Indians near Pittsburgh, and the general was killed. Washington rallied what remained of the British forces and led them in a successful retreat back to Virginia.

Washington was viewed by Virginians as a hero, and at age 22 he was appointed by the Virginia Assembly "Colonel of the Virginia Regiment and Commander in Chief of all Virginia Forces." But regular British officers ridiculed the militia forces and asserted their authority over Washington. British General John Forbes occupied Fort Duquesne, renamed it Fort Pitt, and gave Washington's men the task of garrisoning it.

In 1759, having completed his service in the French and Indian Wars, Washington left his military post and returned to plantation life. He married a wealthy widow, Martha Custis, expanded his plantation holdings, and prospered in western land speculation.

The Virginia legislature elected Washington to attend the First Continental Congress in September 1774. Washington was the most celebrated veteran of the French and Indian Wars who was still young enough (42) to lead military forces in a new struggle. John Adams of Massachusetts was anxious to unite the continent in the coming contest, and he persuaded the Second Continental Congress to give the Virginian command of the American Revolutionary forces surrounding the British army in Boston in 1775.

Throughout the Revolutionary War Washington persevered by employing many of the tactics later defined as the principles of guerrilla warfare. By retreating deep into Pennsylvania's Valley Forge, Washington avoided defeat and saved his army. His bold Christmas night attack against Hessian troops at Trenton, New Jersey, encouraged French intervention on America's behalf. Slowly Washington was able to wear down the British resolve to fight. In the end, he succeeded in trapping a British army at Yorktown, Virginia. Assisted by a French naval blockade, he accepted the surrender of Lord Cornwallis and 8,000 of his men on October 19, 1781.

Perhaps Washington's greatest contribution to democratic government occurred in 1783 in Newburgh, New York, near West Point, where the veterans of his Continental Army were encamped. Despite their hardships and ultimate victory in the Revolutionary War, these soldiers remained unpaid by Congress. Indeed, Congress ignored a series of letters, known as the Newburgh Addresses, that threatened military force if Congress continued to deny benefits to the veterans. Washington was invited to Newburgh by officers who hoped he would agree to lead a military coup against the Congress. But when Washington mounted the platform he denounced the use of force and the "infamous propositions" contained in their earlier addresses to Congress. There is little doubt that he could have chosen to march on the Congress with his veteran army and install himself as military dictator. World history is filled with revolutionary army leaders who did so. But Washington chose to preserve representative government.

One of the few noncontroversial decisions of the Constitutional Convention in 1787 was the selection of George Washington to preside over the meetings. He took little part in the debates; however, his enormous prestige helped to hold the convention together and later to win support for the new Constitution.

Table 3.1 Constitutional Compromise

A Senate with equal representation according to each state and a House with representation based on population, and a requirement that both bodies must approve legislation before it is enacted into law, was a political compromise between large and small states reached at the Constitutional Conventional of 1787.

The Virginia Plan	The New Jersey Plan	The Connecticut Compromise The Constitution of 1787
Two-house legislature, with the lower house directly elected based on state population and the upper house elected by the lower.	One-house legislature, with equal state representation, regardless of population.	Two-house legislature, with the House directly elected based on state population and the Senate selected by the state legislatures; two senators per state, regardless of population.
Legislature with broad power, laws including veto power over passed by the state legislatures.	Legislature with the same power as under the Articles of Confederation, plus the power to levy some taxes and to regulate commerce.	Legislature with broad power, including the power to tax and to regulate commerce.
President and cabinet elected by the legislature.	Separate multiperson executive, elected by the legislature, removable by petition from a majority of the state governors.	President chosen by an Electoral College.
National judiciary elected by the legislature.	National judiciary appointed by the executive.	National judiciary appointed by the president and confirmed by the Senate.
"Council of Revision" with the power to veto laws of the legislature.	National Supremacy Clause similar to that found in Article VI of the 1787 Constitution.	National Supremacy Clause: the Constitution is "the supreme Law of the Land."

★ **Connecticut Compromise**
A constitutional plan that merged elements of a Virginia plan and a New Jersey plan into the present arrangement of the U.S. Congress: one house in which each state has an equal number of votes (the Senate) and one house in which states' votes are based on population (the House of Representatives).

commerce. Moreover, the New Jersey Plan included a National Supremacy Clause, declaring that the Constitution and federal laws would supersede state constitutions and laws.

Debate over representation in Congress raged into July 1787. At one point, the convention actually voted for the Virginia Plan, 7 votes to 3, but without New York, New Jersey, and Delaware, the new nation would not have been viable. Eventually, Roger Sherman of Connecticut came forward with a compromise. This **Connecticut Compromise**—sometimes called the Great Compromise—established two houses of Congress: in the upper house, the Senate, each state would have two members regardless of its size; in the lower body, the House of Representatives, each state would be represented according to population. Members of the House would be directly elected by the people; members of the Senate would be selected by their state legislatures. Legislation would have to pass both houses to be enacted. This compromise was approved by the convention on July 16.

Slavery   Another conflict absorbing the attention of the delegates was slavery. In 1787 slavery was legal everywhere except in Massachusetts. Nevertheless, the delegates were too embarrassed to use the word *slave* or *slavery* in their debates or in the Constitution itself. Instead, they referred to "other persons" and "persons held to service or labour."

Delegates from the Southern states, where slaves were a large proportion of the population, believed slaves should be counted in representation afforded the states, but not counted if taxes were to be levied on a population basis. Delegates from the Northern states, with small slave populations, believed that "the people" counted for representation purposes should include only free persons. The Connecticut Plan included the now-infamous **Three-Fifths Compromise**: three-fifths of the slaves of each state would be counted for purposes both of representation in the House of Representatives and for apportionment for direct taxes.

Slave owners also sought protection for their human "property" in the Constitution itself. They were particularly concerned about slaves running away to other states and claiming their freedom. So they succeeded in writing into the Constitution (Article IV, Section 2) a specific guarantee: "No person held to Service or Labour in one State . . . escaping into another, shall . . . be discharged from such Service or Labour, but shall be delivered up on Claim of the Party to whom such Service or Labour may be due."

Yet another compromise dealt with the slave trade. The capture, transportation, and "breaking in" of African slaves was considered a nasty business, even by Southern planters. Many wealthy Maryland and Virginia plantations were already well supplied with slaves and thus could afford the luxury of conscience to call for an end to slave importation. But other planters from the less-developed Southern states, particularly South Carolina and Georgia, wanted additional slave labor. The final compromise prohibited the slave trade—but not before the year 1808, thereby giving the planters twenty years to import all the slaves they needed before the slave trade ended.

Voter Qualifications   Another important conflict centered on qualifications for voting and holding office in the new government. Most of the delegates believed that voters as well as officeholders should be men of property. (Only Benjamin Franklin went so far as to propose universal *male* suffrage.) But delegates argued over the specific wording of property qualifications, their views on the subject reflecting the source of their own wealth. Merchants, bankers, and manufacturers objected to making the ownership of a certain amount of land a qualification for officeholding. James Madison, a plantation owner himself, was forced to admit that "landed possessions were no certain evidence of real wealth. Many enjoyed them who were more in debt than they were worth."

After much debate, the convention approved a constitution without any expressed property qualifications for voting or holding office, except those that the states might impose themselves: "The Electors in each State shall have the Qualifications requisite for Electors of the most numerous Branch of the State Legislature." At the time, every state had property qualifications for voting, and women were not permitted to vote or hold office. (The New Jersey Constitution of 1776 enfranchised women as well as men who owned property, but in 1787 a new state law limited the vote to "free white male citizens.")

Resolving the Economic Issues

The Founders were just as concerned with "who gets what, when, and how" as today's politicians are. Important economic interests were at stake in the Constitution. Historian Charles A. Beard pointed out that the delegates to the Constitutional Convention were men of wealth: planters, slaveholders, merchants, manufacturers, shippers, bankers and investors, and land speculators. Moreover, most of the delegates owned Revolutionary War bonds that were now worthless and would remain so unless the national government could obtain the tax revenues to pay them off[5] (see *A Conflicting View*: "An Economic Interpretation of the Constitution"). But it is certainly not true that the Founders acted only out of personal interest. Wealthy delegates were found on both sides of constitutional debates, arguing principles as well as economic interests.[6]

★ **Three-Fifths Compromise**
A compromise in the Constitutional Convention of 1787 between pre- and slave states in which slaves would be counted as three-fifths of a person for both taxation and representation.

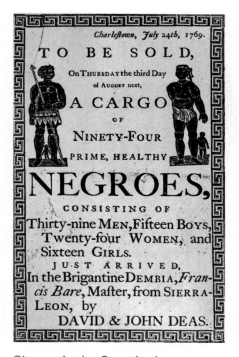

Slavery in the Constitution
Slavery was protected in the Constitution as written in 1787. The buying and selling of slaves was common at the time in the Southern states. The slave trade from Africa to America was given protection for 20 years, until 1808.

★ **taxes**
Compulsory payments to the government.

★ **tariff**
Tax imposed on imported products (also called a customs duty).

Levying Taxes   A central purpose of the Constitution was to enable the national government to levy its own **taxes**, so that it could end its dependence on state contributions and achieve financial credibility. The very first power given to Congress in Article I, Section 8, is the power to tax: "The Congress shall have Power to lay and collect Taxes, Duties, Imposts and Excises, to pay the Debts and provide for the common Defence and general Welfare."

The financial credit of the United States and the interests of Revolutionary War bondholders were guaranteed by Article VI in the Constitution, which specifically declared that the new government would be obligated to pay the debts of the old government. Indeed, the nation's first secretary of the treasury, Alexander Hamilton, made repayment of the national debt the first priority of the Washington administration.

The original Constitution placed most of the tax burden on consumers in the form of **tariffs** on goods imported into the United States. For more than a century, these tariffs provided the national government with its principal source of revenue. Tariffs were generally favored by American manufacturers, who wished to raise the price paid for foreign goods to make their home-produced goods more competitive. No taxes were permitted on *exports*, a protection for southern planters, who exported most of their tobacco and, later, cotton. Direct taxes on individuals were prohibited (Article I, Section 2) except in proportion to *population*. This provision prevented the national government from levying direct taxes in proportion to income until the 16th Amendment (income tax) was ratified in 1913.

The power to tax and spend was given to Congress, not to the president or executive agencies. Instead, the Constitution was very specific: "No Money shall be drawn from the Treasury, but in Consequence of Appropriations made by Law." This is the constitutional basis of Congress's "power of the purse."

Regulating Commerce   The new Constitution gave Congress the power to "regulate Commerce with foreign Nations, and among the several States" (Article I, Section 8), and it prohibited the states from imposing tariffs on goods shipped across state lines (Article I, Section 10). This power created what we call today a **common market**; it protected merchants against state-imposed tariffs and stimulated trade among the states. States were also prohibited from "impairing the Obligation of Contracts"—that is, passing any laws that would allow debtors to avoid their obligations to banks and other lenders.

★ **common market**
Unified trade area in which all goods and services can be sold or exchanged free from customs or tariffs.

Protecting Money   The Constitution also ensured that the new national government would control the money supply. Congress was given the power to coin money and regulate its value. More important, the states were prohibited from issuing their own paper money, thus protecting bankers and creditors from the repayment of debts in cheap state currencies. (No one wanted to be paid for

The Value of a Dollar
Under the Articles of Confederation, each state issued its own currency. Differences in currency regulation from state to state led to financial uncertainty and inflation. By creating a national currency and putting the national government in charge of the money supply, the Founders hoped to restore stability and control inflation.

A Conflicting *View*

An Economic Interpretation of the Constitution

Charles Beard, historian and political scientist, provided the most controversial historical interpretation of the origin of American national government in his landmark book, *An Economic Interpretation of the Constitution of the United States* (1913). Not all historians agree with Beard's economic interpretation, but all concede that it is a milestone in understanding the U.S. Constitution. Beard closely studied unpublished financial records of the U.S. Treasury Department and the personal letters and financial accounts of the fifty-five delegates to the Philadelphia convention. He concluded that they represented the following five economic interest groups, each of which benefited from specific provisions of the Constitution:

★ *Public security interests* (persons holding U.S. bonds from the Revolutionary War; thirty-seven of the fifty-five delegates). The taxing power was of great benefit to the holders of public securities, particularly when it was combined with the provision in Article VI that "all Debts contracted and Engagements entered into, before the Adoption of this Constitution, shall be as valid against the United States under this Constitution, as under the Confederation." That is, the national government would be obliged to pay off all those investors who held U.S. bonds, and the taxing power would give the national government the ability to do so on its own.

★ *Merchants and manufacturers* (persons engaged in shipping and trade; eleven of the fifty-five delegates). The Interstate Commerce Clause, which eliminated state control over commerce, and the provision in Article I, Section 9, which prohibited the states from taxing exports, created a free-trade area, or "common market," among the thirteen states.

★ *Bankers and investors* (twenty-four of fifty-five delegates). Congress was given the power to make bankruptcy laws, to coin money and regulate its value, to fix standards of weights and measures, to punish counterfeiting, to establish post offices and post roads, to pass copyright and patent laws to protect authors and inventors, and to punish piracies and felonies committed on the high seas. Each of these powers is a specific asset to bankers and

investors as well as merchants, authors, inventors, and shippers.

★ *Western land speculators* (persons who purchased large tracts of land west of the Appalachian Mountains: fourteen of the fifty-five delegates). If western settlers were to be protected from the Indians, and if the British were to be persuaded to give up their forts in Ohio and open the way to American westward expansion, the national government could not rely on state militias but must have an army of its own. Western land speculators welcomed the creation of a national army that would be employed primarily as an Indian-fighting force over the next century.

★ *Slave owners* (fifteen of the fifty-five delegates). Protection against domestic insurrection also appealed to the Southern slaveholders' deep-seated fear of a slave revolt. The Constitution permitted Congress to outlaw the *import of slaves* after the year 1808. But most Southern planters were more interested in protecting their existing property and slaves than they were in extending the slave trade, and the Constitution provided an explicit advantage to slaveholders in Article IV, Section 2 (later revoked by the 13th Amendment, which abolished slavery), by specifically requiring the forced return of slaves who might escape to free states.

Beard argued that the members of the Philadelphia convention who drafted the Constitution were, with a few exceptions, immediately, directly, and personally interested in, and derived economic advantages from, the establishment of the new system. But many historians disagree with Beard's emphasis on the economic motives of the Founders. The Constitution, they point out, was adopted in a society that was fundamentally democratic, and it was adopted by people who were primarily middle-class property owners, especially farmers, rather than owners of businesses. The Constitution was not just an economic document, although economic factors were certainly important. Since most of the people were middle class and owned private property, practically all Americans were interested in the protection of property.

goods or labor in Rhode Island's inflated dollars.) If only the national government could issue money, the Founders hoped, inflation could be minimized.

Protecting National Security

At the start of the Revolutionary War, the Continental Congress had given George Washington command of a small regular army—"Continentals"—paid for by Congress, and also had authorized him to take command of state militia units. During the entire war, most of Washington's troops had been state militia. (The "militia" in those days was composed of every free adult male; each was expected to bring his own gun.) Washington himself had frequently decried the militia units as undisciplined, untrained, and unwilling to follow his orders. He wanted the new United States to have a *regular* army and navy, paid for by the Congress with its new taxing power, to back up the state militia units.

War and the Military Forces   Congress was authorized to "declare War," to raise and support a regular army and navy, and to make rules regulating these forces. It was also authorized to call up the militia, as it had done in the Revolution, in order to "execute the Laws of the Union, suppress Insurrections and repel Invasions." When the militia are called into national service, they come under the rule of Congress and the command of the president.

The United States relied primarily on militia—citizen-soldiers organized in state units—until World War I. The regular U.S. Army, stationed in coastal and frontier forts, directed most of its actions against Native Americans. The major

Commander in Chief

The president's role as Commander-in-Chief was designed at the Constitutional Convention with George Washington in mind, as a reflection of his exploits in the Revolutionary War. Here three wartime presidents—Franklin Delano Roosevelt, Lyndon Baines Johnson, and George W. Bush—are shown reviewing troops.

actions in America's nineteenth-century wars—the War of 1812 against the British, the Mexican War of 1846–48, the Civil War in 1861–65, and the Spanish-American War in 1898—were fought largely by citizen-soldiers from these state units.

Commander-in-Chief   Following the precedent set in the Revolutionary War, the new president, whom everyone expected to be George Washington, was made "Commander-in-Chief of the Army and Navy of the United States, and of the Militia of the several States, when called into the actual Service of the United States." Clearly, there is some overlap in responsibility for national defense: Congress has the power to declare war, but the president is Commander-in-Chief. During the next two centuries, the president would order U.S. forces into 200 or more military actions, but Congress would pass an official Declaration of War only five times. Conflict between the president and Congress over war-making powers continues to this day (see the section "Commander-in-Chief" in Chapter 11).

Foreign Affairs   The national government also assumed full power over foreign affairs and prohibited the states from entering into any "Treaty, Alliance, or Confederation." The Constitution gave the president, not Congress, the power to "make Treaties" and "appoint Ambassadors." However, the Constitution stipulated that the president could do these things only "by and with the Advice and Consent of the Senate," indicating an unwillingness to allow the president to act autonomously in these matters. The Senate's power to "advise and consent" to treaties and appointments, together with the congressional power over appropriations, gives the Congress important influence in foreign affairs. Nevertheless, the president remains the dominant figure in this arena.

The Structure of the Government

The Constitution that emerged from the Philadelphia convention on September 17, 1787, founded a new government with a unique structure. That structure was designed to implement the Founders' beliefs in nationalism, limited government, republicanism, the social contract, and the protection of liberty and property. The Founders were realists; they did not have any romantic notions about the wisdom and virtue of "the people." James Madison wrote, "A dependence on the people is, no doubt, the primary control on the government, but experience has taught mankind the necessity of auxiliary precautions." The key structural arrangements in the Constitution—national supremacy, federalism, republicanism, separation of powers, checks and balances, and judicial review—all reflect the Founders' desire to create a strong national government while at the same time ensuring that it would not become a threat to liberty or property.

National Supremacy   The heart of the Constitution is the **National Supremacy Clause** of Article VI:

> This Constitution, and the Laws of the United States which shall be made in Pursuance thereof, and all Treaties made, or which shall be made, under the Authority of the United States, shall be the supreme Law of the Land, and the Judges in every State shall be bound thereby, any Thing in the Constitution or Laws of any State to the Contrary notwithstanding.

This sentence ensures that the Constitution itself is the supreme law of the land and that laws passed by Congress supersede state laws. This National Supremacy Clause establishes the authority of the Constitution and the U.S. government. (See *Controversy*: "The Supremacy Clause at Work: Marijuana for Medical Use?")

Think Again

Should a large state like California, with 36 million people, elect more U.S. senators than a small state like Wyoming, with only half a million people?

★ **National Supremacy Clause**
The clause in Article VI of the U.S. Constitution declaring the Constitution and federal laws "the supreme Law of the Land" superior to state laws and constitutions and requiring state judges to be bound thereby.

Federalism   The Constitution *divides power* between the nation and the states (see Chapter 4). It recognizes that both the national government and the state governments have independent legal authority over their own citizens: both can pass their own laws, levy their own taxes, and maintain their own courts. The states have an important role in the selection of national officeholders—in the apportionment of congressional seats and in the allocation of electoral votes for president. Most important, perhaps, both the Congress and three-quarters of the states must consent to changes in the Constitution itself.

Republicanism   To the Founders, a *republican* government meant the delegation of powers by the people to a small number of gifted individuals "whose wisdom may best discern the true interest of their country, and whose patriotism and love of justice, will be least likely to sacrifice it to temporary or partial considerations."[7] The Founders believed that enlightened leaders of principle and property with ability, education, and a stake in the preservation of liberty could govern the people better than the people could govern themselves. So they gave the voters only a limited voice in the selection of government leaders.

The Constitution of 1787 created *four* decision-making bodies, each with separate numbers of members, terms of office, and selection processes (see Table 3.2). Note that in the *original* Constitution only one of these four bodies—the House of Representatives—was to be directly elected by the people. The other three were removed from direct popular control: state legislatures selected U.S. senators; "electors" (chosen at the discretion of the state legislatures) selected the president; the president appointed Supreme Court and other federal judges.

Democracy?   The Founders believed that government rests ultimately on "the consent of the governed." But their notion of republicanism envisioned decision making by *representatives* of the people, not the people themselves (see *A Conflicting View*: "Let the People Vote on National Issues"). The U.S. Constitution does not provide for *direct* voting by the people on national questions; that is, unlike many

---

Table *3.2* Decision-Making Bodies in the Constitution of 1787

The Constitution of 1787 established four decision-making bodies, only one of which—the House of Representatives—was to be directly elected by the people.

House of Representatives	Senate	President	Supreme Court
Members alloted to each state "according to their respective numbers," but each state guaranteed at least one member.	"Two senators from each state" (regardless of the size of the state).	Single executive.	No size specified in the Constitution, but by tradition nine.
Two-year term. No limits on number of terms that can be served.	Six-year term. No limits on number of terms that can be served.	Four-year term (later limited to two terms by the 22nd Amendment in 1951).	Life term.
Directly elected by "the People of the several States."	Selected by the state legislatures (later changed to direct election by the 17th Amendment in 1913).	Selected by "Electors," appointed in each state "In such Manner as the Legislature thereof may direct" and equal to the total number of U.S. senators and House members to which the state is entitled in Congress.	Appointed by the president, "by and with the Advice and Consent of the Senate."

Controversy

The Supremacy Clause at Work: Marijuana for Medical Use?

Currently, marijuana prohibition applies to everyone across the nation, including the sick and dying. But many doctors, patients, and organizations contend that marijuana, medically known as cannabis, is valuable in the treatment of glaucoma, HIV-AIDS, nausea, and pain relief, especially in cancer patients. As of 2008, twelve states—Alaska, California, Colorado, Hawaii, Maine, Maryland, Montana, Nevada, New Mexico, Oregon, Rhode Island, Vermont, and Washington—have enacted medical marijuana laws re-versing state-level penalties for possession and cultivation when patients possess written documentation from physicians stating that they benefit from its medical use. Wherever the issue has appeared on state referenda, it has passed by large margins. National polls regularly report that 75 percent of the American public support making marijuana legally available to seriously ill patients.

Congress, however, has never exempted the medical use of marijuana from its Controlled Substance Act, which makes it a federal crime "to manufacture, distribute, or dispense, or possess . . . a controlled substance." Various petitions to the federal Drug Enforcement Agency to declassify marijuana as a controlled substance and allow physicians to legally prescribe its use have been rejected.

Clearly, federal law is in direct conflict with the laws of many states on this issue. But the Supremacy Clause of the Constitution clearly requires that federal law prevail over state law in cases of conflict.

The issue reached the U.S. Supreme Court in 2001. The Court recognized that whether or not the activities of individuals or organizations regarding marijuana were legal under California law, they nonetheless violated federal law, notably the Controlled Substance Act. The Court further held that "medical necessity" does not allow anyone to violate the Controlled Substance Act; Congress made no exemption in this act for medical necessity. The

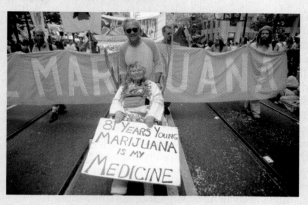

The Supremacy Clause of the Constitution dictates that the laws of Congress prevail over those of the states. Some states have attempted to legalize the use of marijuana for medical purposes. But the laws of Congress have not (yet?) made an exception for such use.

Supreme Court recognized that the states have concurrent powers with the federal government in regulating drugs and medications. However, "Under the Supremacy Clause, any state law, however clearly within a state's acknowledged power, which interferes with or is contrary to federal laws must yield."[a]

Politically, the federal Drug Enforcement Agency realizes that prosecuting seriously ill patients or their doctors for using marijuana medically is very unpopular. Many individuals, especially in those states that have tried to legalize the medical use of marijuana, have continued to use the drug, knowing that they are violating federal law.

[a]*United States v. Oakland Cannabis Buyers Cooperatives* 523 U.S. 483 (2001).

state constitutions today, it does *not* provide for national **referenda**. Moreover, as noted earlier, only the House of Representatives (sometimes referred to even today as "the people's house") was to be elected directly by voters in the states.

These republican arrangements may appear "undemocratic" from our perspective today, but in 1787 the U.S. Constitution was more democratic than any other governing system in the world. Although other nations were governed by monarchs, emperors, chieftains, and hereditary aristocracies, the Founders recognized that government depended on the *consent of the governed*. Later democratic impulses in America greatly altered the original Constitution (see "Constitutional Change" later in this chapter) and reshaped it into a much more democratic document. (See also *What Do You Think?*: "Should We Call a New Constitutional Convention?")

★ **referenda**
Proposed laws or constitutional amendments submitted to the voters for their direct approval or rejection, found in state constitutions, but not in the U.S. Constitution.

What Do You *Think?*

Should We Call a New Constitutional Convention?

Does the United States need a new, more democratic, more perfect Constitution? The U.S. Constitution was drafted more than 220 years ago for a small newly independent federation with about three million persons in 13 member states. Does it work today for the world's most powerful nation with over 300 million persons, 50 states, 5 territories, and global interests? Thomas Jefferson once wrote that "no society can make a perpetual constitution, or even a perpetual law. The earth belongs always to the living generation. . . . Every Constitution then, and every law, naturally expires at the end of 19 years. If it be enforced longer, it is an act of force and not of right." Should we take Jefferson's position to heart? Should we call a new Constitutional Convention?

What are the problems that exist with the present-day U.S. Constitution? Prominent political scientists have pondered this question and voiced the following concerns:

★ The current Constitution gives small population states the same influence in the U.S. Senate as it gives large states. The current constitution severely dilutes the voice of citizens in large population states such as California, Texas, and New York, and greatly amplifies the voice of citizens in small states, such as Wyoming, Alaska, and Vermont.

★ Not only is the Senate a seriously undemocratic body, but the Electoral College (with the number of each state delegation equal to the number of its congressional delegation of members of the House and Senate) also distorts the voice of the American people in presidential elections. George W. Bush was elected president in 2000 despite losing the national popular vote.

★ Members of the U.S. House face very few competitive elections, depriving voters of effective choices for their congressional representatives, largely because members of Congress work with state parties in redistricting to design electoral districts to maximize "safe" seats.

★ Presidents can go to war and send U.S. troops into combat around the world contrary to the wishes of Congress and the American people.

★ U.S. Supreme Court justices sit in office for life, with the power to overturn the decisions of the elected representatives of the nation and the states.

★ The current Constitution does not allow itself to be easily repaired. Amendments cannot even be proposed unless two-thirds of both the House and the Senate agree or unless two-thirds of the state legislatures petition for amendments to a constitutional

convention called by Congress. And should an amendment be proposed, its ratification demands the approval of either three-quarters of the legislatures of the 50 states or agreement and especially called conventions in three-quarters of the states. This means that as few as 13 states—barely a quarter of the American states and potentially a small fraction of the U.S. population—can block the passage of any amendment.

What should be done? Among the recommendations:

★ Grant states up to four senators based on population size.

★ Mandate nonpartisan redistricting for House elections.

★ Expand the size of a house to approximately 1000 members so that representatives can better get to know and represent smaller constituencies.

★ Establish term limits for representatives and senators, thus restoring the founders' principle of frequent rotation in office.

★ Add a Balance Budget Amendment, with appropriate escape clauses, in order to encourage fiscal fairness to future generations.

★ Limit presidential war-making powers and expand Congress's oversight of war-making by incorporating into the Constitution a requirement for congressional assent to ongoing wars at regular intervals.

★ Eliminate lifetime tenure for Supreme Court justices in favor of a single nonrenewable term of 15 years.

★ Grant more populated states additional electors in the Electoral College.

★ Restrict the presidential primary process to the four months preceding the August nominating conventions, thereby sparing voters a year-long campaign

But would a Constitutional Convention create more heat than light, more conflict than consensus, more threats than guarantees to individual liberty? Conflicts over the current hot-button social and cultural issues—immigration, abortion, prayer in schools, gay rights, the death penalty, the rights of criminal defendants, gun control, and the like—may poison debate and make compromise on these topics unlikely. "Any attempt to place constitutional provisions on either side of these cultural grenades would probably explode the process." Efforts to reform the structure of American government and politics would most likely give way to attempts to "strengthen" or "weaken" the Bill of Rights.

Source: Sanford Levinson, *Our Undemocratic Constitution: Where the Constitution Goes Wrong (and How the People Can Correct It).* New York: Oxford University Press, 2006. Larry J. Sabato, *A More Perfect Constitution: 25 Proposals, to Revitalize Our Constitution and Make America a Fairer Country.* New York: Walker & Company, 2007.

Separation of Powers and Checks and Balances

The Founders believed that unlimited power was corrupting and that the concentration of power was dangerous. James Madison wrote, "Ambition must be made to counteract ambition." The **separation of powers** within the national government—the creation of separate legislative, executive, and judicial branches in Articles I, II, and III of the Constitution—was designed to place internal controls on governmental power. Power is not only apportioned among three branches of government, but, perhaps more important, each branch is given important **checks and balances** over the actions of the others (see Figure 3.1). According to Madison, "The constant aim is to divide and

★ **separation of powers**
Constitutional division of powers among the three branches of the national government—legislative, executive, and judicial.

★ **checks and balances**
Constitutional provisions giving each branch of the national government certain checks over the actions of other branches.

The American System of Checks and Balances

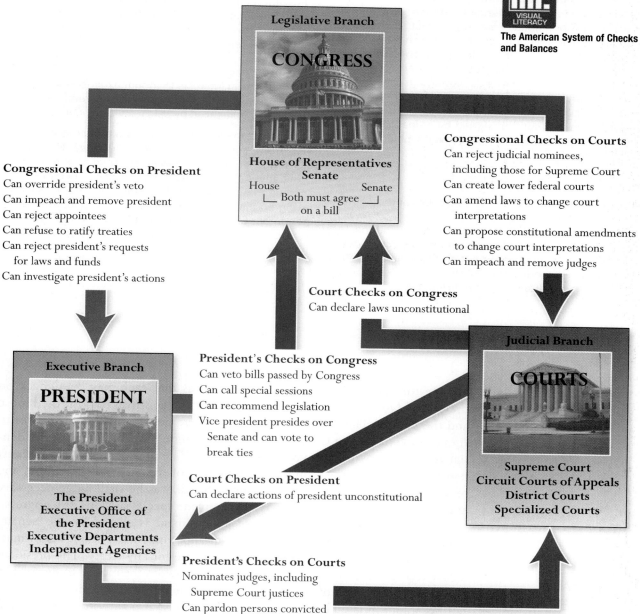

Legislative Branch

CONGRESS

House of Representatives
Senate
House   Senate
⌐ Both must agree ⌐
on a bill

Congressional Checks on President
Can override president's veto
Can impeach and remove president
Can reject appointees
Can refuse to ratify treaties
Can reject president's requests
  for laws and funds
Can investigate president's actions

Congressional Checks on Courts
Can reject judicial nominees,
  including those for Supreme Court
Can create lower federal courts
Can amend laws to change court
  interpretations
Can propose constitutional amendments
  to change court interpretations
Can impeach and remove judges

Court Checks on Congress
Can declare laws unconstitutional

President's Checks on Congress
Can veto bills passed by Congress
Can call special sessions
Can recommend legislation
Vice president presides over
  Senate and can vote to
  break ties

Executive Branch

PRESIDENT

The President
Executive Office of
the President
Executive Departments
Independent Agencies

Court Checks on President
Can declare actions of president unconstitutional

Judicial Branch

COURTS

Supreme Court
Circuit Courts of Appeals
District Courts
Specialized Courts

President's Checks on Courts
Nominates judges, including
  Supreme Court justices
Can pardon persons convicted
  by federal courts

Figure *3.1* Checks and Balances

A Conflicting *View*

Let the People Vote on National Issues

"Direct democracy" means that the people themselves can initiate and decide policy questions by popular vote. The Founders were profoundly skeptical of this form of democracy. They had read about direct democracy in the ancient Greek city-state of Athens, and they believed the "follies" of direct democracy far outweighed any virtues it might possess. It was not until more than 100 years after the U.S. Constitution was written that widespread support developed in the American states for direct voter participation in policy making. Direct democracy developed in states and communities, and it is to be found today *only* in state and local government.

Why not extend our notion of democracy to include nationwide referenda voting on key public issues? Perhaps Congress should be authorized to place particularly controversial issues on a national ballot. Perhaps a petition signed by at least 1 million voters should also result in a question being placed on a national ballot.

Proponents of direct voting on national issues argue that national referenda would

★ Enhance government responsiveness and accountability to the people.
★ Stimulate national debate over policy questions.
★ Increase voter interest and turnout on election day.
★ Increase trust in government and diminish feelings of alienation from Washington.
★ Give voters a direct role in policy making.

Opponents of direct democracy, from our nation's Founders to the present, argue that national referenda voting would

★ Encourage majorities to sacrifice the rights of individuals and minorities.
★ Lead to the adoption of unwise and unsound policies because voters are not sufficiently informed to cast intelligent ballots on many complex issues.
★ Prevent consideration of alternative policies or modifications or amendments to the proposition set forth on the ballot. (In contrast, legislators devote a great deal of attention to writing, rewriting, and amending bills, as well as seeking out compromises among interests.)
★ Enable special interests to mount expensive referendum campaigns; the outcomes of referenda would be heavily influenced by paid television advertising.

How would voters' decisions in national referenda differ from current government policies? National polls suggest that voters would approve of many policy initiatives that Congress has rejected, including a constitutional requirement to balance the budget; making English the official language; a constitutional amendment to limit the terms of Congress members; and a constitutional amendment to allow prayer in public schools.[a]

[a]Gallup. www.gallup.com.

Think Again

In which do you have the most trust and confidence? President, Congress, Supreme Court

arrange the several offices in such a manner as that each may be a check on the other." No bill can become a law without the approval of both the House and the Senate. The president shares legislative power through the power to sign or to veto laws of Congress, although Congress may override a presidential veto with a two-thirds vote in each house. The president may also suggest legislation, "give to the Congress Information of the State of the Union, and recommend to their Consideration such Measures as he shall judge necessary and expedient." The president may also convene special sessions of Congress.

However, the president's power of appointment is shared by the Senate, which confirms cabinet and ambassadorial appointments. The president must also secure the advice and consent of the Senate for any treaty. The president must execute the laws, but it is Congress that provides the money to do so. The president and the rest of the executive branch may not spend money that has not been appropriated by Congress. Congress must also authorize the creation of executive departments and agencies. Finally, Congress may impeach and remove the president from office for "Treason, Bribery, or other High Crimes and Misdemeanors."

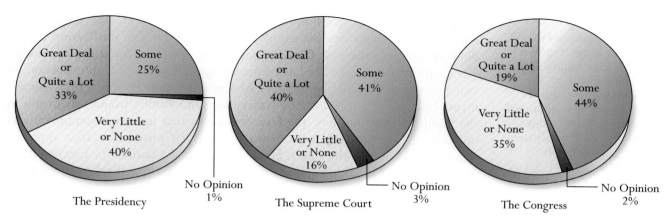

Figure *3.2* Confidence in the Three Branches of Government

"Now I am going to read you a list of institutions in American society. Please tell me how much confidence you, yourself, have in each one—a great deal or quite a lot, some, or very little or none?"

Source: Derived from Gallup, July, 2006.

Members of the Supreme Court are appointed by the president and confirmed by the Senate. Traditionally, this court has nine members, but Congress may determine the number of justices. More important, Congress must create lower federal district courts as well as courts of appeal. Congress must also determine the number of these judgeships and determine the jurisdiction of federal courts. But the most important check of all is the Supreme Court's power of judicial review.

Judicial review, which is not specifically mentioned in the Constitution itself, is the power of the judiciary to overturn laws of Congress and the states and actions of the president that the courts believe violate the Constitution (see "Judicial Power" in Chapter 13). Judicial review, in short, ensures compliance with the Constitution.

Many Federalists, including Alexander Hamilton, believed the Constitution of 1787 clearly implied that the Supreme Court could invalidate any laws of Congress or presidential actions it believed to be unconstitutional. Hamilton wrote in 1787, "[Limited government] . . . can be preserved in no other way than through the medium of courts of justice, whose duty it is to declare all acts contrary to the manifest tenor of the Constitution void."[8] But it was not until *Marbury v. Madison* in 1803 that Chief Justice John Marshall asserted in a Supreme Court ruling that the Supreme Court possessed the power of judicial review over laws of Congress. (See *People in Politics*: "John Marshall and Early Supreme Court Politics" in Chapter 13.) Today the American people express more trust and confidence in the Supreme Court than in either the president or the Congress (see Figure 3.2).

★ **judicial review**
Power of the U.S. Supreme Court and federal judiciary to declare laws of Congress and the states and actions of the president unconstitutional and therefore legally invalid.

Conflict over Ratification

Today the U.S. Constitution is a revered document, but in the winter of 1787–88, the Founders had real doubts about whether they could get it accepted as "the supreme Law of the Land." Indeed, the Constitution was ratified by only the narrowest of margins in the key states of Massachusetts, Virginia, and New York.

★ **ratification**
Power of a legislature to approve or reject decisions made by other bodies. State legislators or state conventions must have the power to ratify constitutional amendments submitted by Congress. The U.S. Senate has the power to ratify treaties made by the president.

★ **Federalists**
Supporters of the ratification of the Constitution, who later coalesced into a political party supporting John Adams for president in 1800.

You Are James Madison

The Founders adopted a **ratification** procedure that was designed to enhance chances for acceptance of the Constitution. The ratification procedure written into the new Constitution was a complete departure from what was then supposed to be the law of the land, the Articles of Confederation, in two major ways. First, the Articles of Confederation required that amendments be approved by *all* of the states. But since Rhode Island was firmly in the hands of small farmers, the Founders knew that unanimous approval was unlikely. So they simply wrote into their new Constitution that approval required only nine of the states. Second, the Founders called for special ratifying conventions in the states rather than risk submitting the Constitution to the state legislatures. Because the Constitution placed many prohibitions on the powers of states, the Founders believed that special constitutional ratifying conventions would be more likely to approve the document than would state legislatures.

Supporters of the new constitution, who become known as **Federalists**, enjoyed some important tactical advantages over the opposition. First, the Constitutional Convention was held in secret; potential opponents did not know what was coming out of it. Second, the Federalists called for ratifying conventions to be held as quickly as possible so that the opposition could not get itself organized. Many state conventions met during the winter months, so it was difficult for some rural opponents of the Constitution to get to their county seats in order to vote (see Figure 3.3 below).

The Federalists also waged a very professional (for 1787–88) media campaign in support of the Constitution. James Madison, Alexander Hamilton, and John Jay issued a series of eighty-five press releases, signed simply "Publius," on behalf of the

Figure *3.3*

The Fight over Ratification

The vote for ratification of the Constitution of 1787 reflects divisions in the country, with support linked to a commercial economy and disapproval to more agricultural sectors.

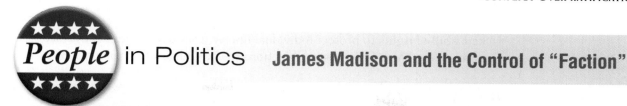

People in Politics   James Madison and the Control of "Faction"

The most important contributions to American democracy by James Madison (1751–1836) were his work in helping to write the Constitution and his insightful and scholarly defense of it during the ratification struggle. Indeed, Madison is more highly regarded by political scientists and historians as a *political theorist* than as the fourth president of the United States.

Madison's family owned a large plantation in Virginia. He graduated from the College of New Jersey (now Princeton University) at 18 and assumed a number of elected and appointed positions in Virginia's colonial government. In 1776 Madison drafted a new Virginia Constitution. While serving in Virginia's Revolutionary assembly, he met Thomas Jefferson; the two became lifetime political allies and friends. In 1787 Madison represented Virginia at the Constitutional Convention and took a leading role in its debates over the form of a new federal government.

Madison's political insights are revealed in *The Federalist Papers*, a series of eighty-five essays published in major newspapers in 1787–88, all signed simply "Publius." Alexander Hamilton and John Jay contributed some of them, but Madison wrote the two most important essays: Number 10, which explains the nature of political conflict (faction) and how it can be "controlled," and Number 51, which explains the system of separation of powers and

checks and balances (both reprinted in the Appendix of this textbook). According to Madison, "controlling faction" was the principal task of government.

What creates faction? Madison believed that conflict is part of human nature. In all societies, we find "a zeal for different opinions concerning religion, concerning government, and many other points," as well as "an attachment to different leaders ambitiously contending for preeminence and power." Even when there are no serious differences among people, these "frivolous and fanciful distinctions" will inspire "unfriendly passions" and "violent conflicts."

Clearly, Madison believed conflict could arise over just about any matter. Yet "the most common and durable source of factions, has been the various and unequal distribution of property." That is, economic conflicts between rich and poor and between people with different kinds of wealth and sources of income are the most serious conflicts confronting society.

Madison argued that factions could best be controlled in a republican government extending over a large society with a "variety of parties and interests." He defended republicanism (representative democracy) over "pure democracy," which he believed "incompatible with personal security, or the rights of property." And he argued that protection against "factious combinations" can be achieved by including a great variety of competing interests in the political system so that no one interest will be able to "outnumber and oppress the rest." Modern pluralist political theory (see Chapter 1) claims Madison as a forerunner.

Constitution. Major newspapers ran these essays, which were later collected and published as *The Federalist Papers*. The essays provide an excellent description and explanation of the Constitution by three of its writers and even today serve as a principal reference for political scientists and judges faced with constitutional ambiguities (see *People in Politics*: "James Madison and the Control of 'Faction'"). Two of the most important *Federalist Papers* are reprinted in the Appendix to this textbook.

Nevertheless, opponents of the Constitution—the **Anti-Federalists**—almost succeeded in defeating the document in New York and Virginia. They charged that the new Constitution would create an "aristocratic tyranny" and pose a threat to the "spirit of republicanism." They argued that the new Senate would be an aristocratic upper house and the new president a ruling monarch. They complained that neither the Senate nor the president was directly elected by the people. They also argued that the new national government would trample state governments and deny the people of the states the opportunity to handle their own political and economic affairs. Virginia patriot Patrick Henry urged the defeat of the Constitution "to preserve the poor Commonwealth of Virginia." Finally, their most effective argument was that the new Constitution

★ **Anti-Federalists**
Opponents of the ratification of the Constitution, who later coalesced into a political party supporting Thomas Jefferson for president in 1800.

lacked a bill of rights to protect individual liberty from government abuse (see *A Conflicting View*: "Anti-Federalist's Objections to the Constitution" on page 84).

A Bill of Rights

It may be hard to imagine today, but the original Constitution had no **Bill of Rights**. This was a particularly glaring deficiency because many of the new state constitutions proudly displayed these written guarantees of individual liberty.

The Founders certainly believed in limited government and individual liberty, and they did write a few liberties into the body of the Constitution, including protection against ex post facto laws, a limited definition of treason, a guarantee of the writ of habeas corpus, and a guarantee of trial by jury (see Chapter 14).

The Federalists argued that there was really no need for a bill of rights because (1) the national government was one of **enumerated powers** only, meaning it could not exercise any power not expressly enumerated, or granted, in the Constitution; (2) the power to limit free speech or press, establish a religion, or otherwise restrain individual liberty was not among the enumerated powers; (3) therefore it was not necessary to specifically deny these powers to the new government. But the Anti-Federalists were unwilling to rest fundamental freedoms on a thin thread of logical inference from the notion of enumerated powers. They wanted specific written guarantees that the new national government would not interfere with the rights of individuals or the powers of the states. So Federalists at the New York, Massachusetts, and Virginia ratifying conventions promised to support the addition of a bill of rights to the Constitution in the very first Congress.

A young member of the new House of Representatives, James Madison, rose in 1789 and presented a bill of rights that he had drawn up after reviewing more than 200 recommendations sent from the states. Interestingly, the new Congress was so busy debating new tax laws that Madison had a difficult time attracting attention to his bill. Eventually, in September 1789, Congress approved a Bill of Rights as ten **amendments**, or formal changes, to the Constitution and sent them to the states. (Congress actually passed twelve amendments. One was never ratified; another, dealing with pay raises for Congress, was not ratified by the necessary three-quarters of the states until 1992.) The states promptly ratified the first ten amendments to the Constitution (see Table 3.3), and these changes took effect in 1791.

The Bill of Rights was originally designed to limit the powers of the new *national* government. The Bill of Rights begins with the command "Congress shall make no law. . . ." It was not until after the Civil War that the Constitution was amended to also prohibit states from violating individual liberties. The Fourteenth Amendment, ratified in 1868, includes the command "No State shall. . . ." It prohibits the states from depriving any person of "life, liberty or property, without due process of law," or abridging "the privileges or immunities of citizens of the United States," or denying any person "equal protection of the laws." Today virtually all of the liberties guaranteed in the Constitution protect individuals not only from the national government but also from state governments.

Constitutional Change

The purpose of a constitution is to govern government—to place limits on governmental power. Thus government itself must not be able to alter or amend a constitution easily. Yet the U.S. Constitution has changed over time, sometimes by formal amendment and other times by judicial interpretation, presidential and congressional action, and general custom and practice.

★ **Bill of Rights**
Written guarantees of basic individual liberties; the first ten amendments to the U.S. Constitution.

★ **enumerated powers**
Powers specifically mentioned in the Constitution as belonging to the national government.

★ **amendments**
Formal changes in a bill, law, or constitution.

✓ *Think* Again

Should the Constitution be amended to guarantee that equal rights shall not be denied based on sex?

Table *3.3*   The Bill of Rights

Thomas Jefferson, in a letter to James Madison in 1787, wrote: "A bill of rights is what the people are entitled to against every government on earth. . . ." This table summarizes and groups rights by their major purpose.

Guaranteeing Freedom of Expression
First Amendment prohibits the government from abridging freedoms of
  speech, press, assembly, and petition.

Guaranteeing Religious Freedom
First Amendment prohibits the government from establishing a religion or
  interfering with the free exercise of religion.

Affirming the Right to Bear Arms and Protecting Citizens from Quartering Troops
Second Amendment guarantees the right to bear arms.
Third Amendment prohibits troops from occupying citizens' homes in
  peacetime.

Protecting the Rights of Accused Persons
Fourth Amendment protects against unreasonable searches and seizures.
Fifth Amendment requires an indictment by a grand jury for serious crimes;
  prohibits the government from trying a person twice for the same crime; prohibits the government from taking life, liberty, or property without due
  process of law; and prohibits the government from taking private property for
  public use without fair compensation to the owner.
Sixth Amendment guarantees a speedy and public jury trial, the right to confront witnesses in court, and the right to legal counsel for defense.
Seventh Amendment guarantees the right to a jury trial in civil cases.
Eighth Amendment prohibits the government from setting excessive bail or
  fines or inflicting cruel and unusual punishment.

Protecting the Rights of People and States
Ninth Amendment protects all other unspecified rights of the people.
Tenth Amendment reserves to the states or to the people those powers neither
  granted to the federal government nor prohibited to the states in the
  Constitution.

Amendments   A constitutional amendment must first be proposed, and then it must be ratified. The Constitution allows two methods of *proposing* a constitutional amendment: (1) by passage in the House and the Senate with a two-thirds vote, or (2) by passage in a national convention called by Congress in response to petitions by two-thirds of the state legislatures. Congress then chooses the method of *ratification*, which can be either (1) by vote in the legislatures of three-fourths of the states, or (2) by vote in conventions called for that purpose in three-fourths of the states (see Figure 3.4).

Of the four possible combinations of proposal and ratification, the method involving proposal by a two-thirds vote of Congress and ratification by three-quarters of the legislatures has been used for all the amendments except one. Only for the 21st Amendment's repeal of Prohibition did Congress call for state ratifying conventions (principally because Congress feared that southern Bible Belt state legislatures would vote against repeal). The method of proposal by national convention has never been used.

In addition to the Bill of Rights, most of the constitutional amendments ratified over the nation's 200 years have expanded our notion of democracy. Today the Constitution includes 27 amendments, which means that only 17 (out of

SIMULATION
You Are Proposing a Constitutional Amendment

TIMELINE
The History of Constitutional Amendments

Figure *3.4*

Constitutional Amendment Process

The Constitution set up two alternative routes for proposing amendments and two for ratifying them. One of the four possible combinations has actually been used for all except one (the 21st) amendment. However, in our time there have been persistent calls for a constitutional convention to propose new amendments permitting school prayer, making abortion illegal, and requiring a balanced national budget.

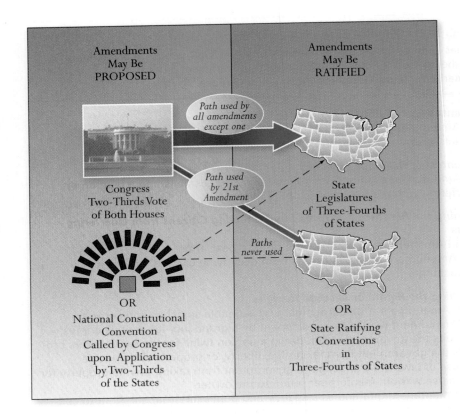

Amendments May Be PROPOSED	Amendments May Be RATIFIED
Congress Two-Thirds Vote of Both Houses	State Legislatures of Three-Fourths of States
Path used by all amendments except one	
Path used by 21st Amendment	
Paths never used	
OR National Constitutional Convention Called by Congress upon Application by Two-Thirds of the States	OR State Ratifying Conventions in Three-Fourths of States

★ **Equal Rights Amendment (ERA)**
Proposed amendment to the Constitution guaranteeing that equal rights under the law shall not be denied or abridged on account of sex. Passed by Congress in 1972, the amendment failed to win ratification by three of the necessary three-fourths of the states.

more than 10,000) proposed amendments have been ratified since the passage of the Bill of Rights. It is possible to classify the amendments that have been ratified into the broad categories of constitutional processes, Prohibition, income tax, individual liberty, and voting rights (see Table 3.4).

Amending the U.S. Constitution requires not only a two-thirds vote in both houses of Congress, reflecting *national* support, but also ratification by three-fourths of the states, reflecting widespread support within the states. The fate of the **Equal Rights Amendment**, popularly known as the ERA, illustrates the need for nationwide consensus in order to amend the Constitution. The Equal Rights Amendment is a simple statement to which the vast majority of Americans agree, according to public opinion polls: "Equality of rights under the law shall not be denied or abridged by the United States or any state on account of sex." Congress passed the ERA in 1972 with far more than the necessary two-thirds vote; both Republicans and Democrats supported the ERA, and it was endorsed by Presidents Nixon, Ford, and Carter as well as most other national political leaders and organizations. By 1978, thirty-five state legislatures had ratified the amendment—three states short of the necessary thirty-eight (three-quarters). (Five states subsequently voted to rescind, or cancel, their earlier ratification. However, because there is no language in the Constitution regarding rescission, there is some disagreement about the constitutionality of this action.) Promising that the "ERA won't go away," proponents of the amendment have continued to press their case. But to date Congress has not acted to resubmit the ERA to the states.

Judicial Interpretations Some of the greatest changes in the Constitution have come about not by formal amendment but by interpretations of the document by federal courts, notably the U.S. Supreme Court.

Table *3.4* Amendments to the Constitution Since the Bill of Rights
The Constitution has been amended a total of 27 times, including the first 10 amendments of the Bill of Rights. This table summarizes and groups subsequent amendments by their major purpose.

Perfecting Constitutional Processes

Eleventh Amendment (1798) forbids federal lawsuits against a state by citizens of another state or nation.

Twelfth Amendment (1804) provides separate ballots for president and vice president in the Electoral College to prevent confusion.

Twentieth Amendment (1933) determines the dates for the beginning of the terms of Congress (January 3) and the president (January 20).

Twenty-second Amendment (1951) limits the president to two terms.

Twenty-fifth Amendment (1967) provides for presidential disability.

Twenty-seventh Amendment (1992) prevents Congress from raising its own pay in a single session.

The Experiment with Prohibition

Eighteenth Amendment (1919) prohibits the manufacture, sale, or transportation of intoxicating liquors.

Twenty-first Amendment (1933) repeals the Eighteenth Amendment.

The Income Tax

Sixteenth Amendment (1913) allows Congress to tax incomes.

Expanding Liberty

Thirteenth Amendment (1865) abolishes slavery.

Fourteenth Amendment (1868) protects life, liberty, and property and the privileges and immunities of citizenship and provides equal protection of the law.

Expanding Voting Rights

Fifteenth Amendment (1870) guarantees that the right to vote shall not be denied because of race.

Seventeenth Amendment (1913) provides for the election of senators by the people of each state.

Nineteenth Amendment (1920) guarantees that the right to vote shall not be denied because of sex.

Twenty-third Amendment (1961) gives the District of Columbia electoral votes for presidential elections.

Twenty-fourth Amendment (1964) guarantees that the right to vote shall not be denied because of failure to pay a poll tax or other tax.

Twenty-sixth Amendment (1971) guarantees that the right to vote shall not be denied to persons 18 years of age or older.

Indeed, through **judicial review**, the U.S. Supreme Court has come to play the central role in giving meaning to the Constitution. Judicial review is the power of federal courts, and ultimately the Supreme Court, to declare laws of Congress and actions of the president unconstitutional and therefore invalid. This power was first asserted by Chief Justice John Marshall in the case of *Marbury v. Madison* in 1803 (see *People in Politics*: "John Marshall and Early Supreme Court Politics" in Chapter 13). It is now an important part of the system of checks and balances (see Figure 3.1). This power is itself an interpretation of the Constitution, because it is not specifically mentioned in the document.

Supreme Court interpretations of the Constitution have given specific meaning to many of our most important constitutional phrases. Among the most important examples of constitutional change through judicial interpretation are the meanings given to the 14th Amendment, particularly its provisions that "No State shall

★ **judicial review**
The power of federal courts to declare laws of Congress and actions of the president unconstitutional.

A Conflicting *View*

Anti-Federalists' Objections to the Constitution

Virginia's **George Mason** was a delegate to the Constitutional Convention of 1787, but he refused to sign the final document and became a leading opponent of the new Constitution. Mason was a wealthy plantation owner and a heavy speculator in western (Ohio) lands. He was a friend of George Washington, but he considered most other political figures of his day to be "babblers" and he generally avoided public office. However, in 1776 he authored Virginia's Declaration of Rights, which was widely copied in other state constitutions and later became the basis for the Bill of Rights. Although an ardent supporter of states' rights, he attended the Constitutional Convention of 1787 and, according to James Madison's notes on the proceedings, was an influential force in shaping the new national government. His refusal to sign the Constitution and his subsequent leadership of the opposition to its ratification made him the recognized early leader of the Anti-Federalists.

Mason's first objection to the Constitution was that it included no Bill of Rights. But he also objected to the powers given to the Senate, which was not directly elected by the people in the original document; to the federal courts; and to the president. He was wary of the Necessary and Proper Clause, which granted Congress the power to "make all laws which shall be necessary and proper" for carrying out the enumerated powers—those specifically mentioned in the Constitution. Mason correctly predicted that this clause would be used to preempt the powers of the states.

In his "Objections to the Constitution" Mason wrote,

There is no declaration of rights; and the laws of the general government being paramount to the laws and constitutions of the several States, the declaration of rights in the separate States are no security.

Senators are not the representatives of the people, or amenable to them.

The judiciary of the United States is so constructed and extended as to absorb and destroy the judiciaries of the several States; thereby rendering law as tedious, intricate and expensive . . .

Under their own construction of the general clause at the end of the enumerated powers, the Congress may . . . extend their power as far as they shall think proper; so that the State Legislatures have no security for the powers now presumed to remain to them; or the people for their rights.

Note that virtually all of Mason's objections to the original Constitution had to be remedied at a later date. The Bill of Rights was added as the first ten amendments. Eventually (1913) the 17th Amendment, for the direct election of U.S. senators, was passed. And Mason correctly predicted that the federal judiciary would eventually render the law "tedious, intricate, and expensive" and that the Necessary and Proper Clause, which he refers to as "the general clause at the end of the enumerated powers," would be used to expand congressional powers at the expense of the states.

Patrick Henry was another prominent Anti-Federalist deserving mention. Henry was a lawyer, superb orator, author of the Virginia Stamp Act resolution, and one of foremost patriots of colonial America. It was on March 23, 1775, during the debate in the House of Burgesses—the Virginia legislature—over whether to commit the Virginia militia against British forces, who were then on the move, that Patrick Henry stated, "Is life so dear, or peace so sweet, as to be purchased at the price of chains and slavery? Forbid it, Almighty God! I know what course others may take; but as for me, give me liberty or give me death." Henry served on the Committees of Correspondence, as a Virginia delegate to the First Continental Congress, and as the first post-colonial governor of Virginia (1776–79), with a total of five terms as Virginia governor. But Henry opposed the Constitution for its lack of a Bill of Rights, like George Mason, and for its grant of too much power to the federal government. Henry thought that Congress, "by the power of taxation—by the raising of an army, and by their control over the militia, have the sword in one hand, and the purse in the other. Shall we be safe without either? . . . Now, Sir, the American spirit, assisted by the ropes and chains of consolidation, is about to convert this country to a powerful and mighty empire."[a]

[a]Speech at the Virginia Ratification Convention, in consideration of the U.S. Constitution, June 5, 7, and 9, 1788.

. . . deprive any person of life, liberty, or property, without due process of law; nor deny to any person within its jurisdiction the equal protection of the laws":

★ Deciding that "equal protection of the laws" requires an end to segregation of the races (*Brown v. Board of Education of Topeka*, 1954, and subsequent decisions).

★ Deciding that "liberty" includes a woman's right to choose an abortion, and that the term *person* does not include the unborn fetus (*Roe v. Wade*, 1973, and subsequent decisions).

★ Deciding that "equal protection of the laws" requires that every person's vote should be weighed equally in apportionment and districting plans for the House of Representatives, state legislatures, city councils, and so on (*Baker v. Carr*, 1964, and subsequent decisions).

Presidential and Congressional Action   Congress and the president have also undertaken to interpret the Constitution. Nearly every president, for example, has argued that the phrase "executive Power" in Article II includes more than the specific powers mentioned afterward. Thomas Jefferson purchased the Louisiana Territory from France in 1803 even though there is no constitutional authorization for the president, or even the national government, to acquire new territory. Presidents from George Washington to Richard Nixon have argued that Congress cannot force the executive branch to turn over documents it does not wish to disclose (see Chapter 11).

Congress by law has tried to restrict the president's power as Commander-in-Chief of the Armed Forces by requiring the president to notify Congress when U.S. troops are sent to "situations where imminent involvement in hostilities is clearly indicated" and limiting their stay to sixty days unless Congress authorizes an extension. This War Powers Resolution (1973), passed by Congress over President Richard Nixon's veto in the immediate aftermath of the Vietnam War, has been ignored by every president to date (see Chapter 11). Yet it indicates that Congress has its own ideas about interpreting the Constitution.

Custom and Practice   Finally, the Constitution changes over time as a result of generally accepted customs and practice. It is interesting to note, for example, that the Constitution never mentions political parties. (Many of the Founders disapproved of parties because they caused "faction" among the people.) But soon after Thomas Jefferson resigned as President Washington's first secretary of state (in part because he resented the influence of Secretary of the Treasury Alexander Hamilton), the Virginian attracted the support of Anti-Federalists, who believed

A *Constitutional* Note

How Democratic Was the Constitution of 1787?

The Constitution established *four* decision-making bodies—the House and the Senate in the legislative branch (Article I); the president in the executive branch (Article II); and the Supreme Court and "such inferior Courts as the Congress may from time to time ordain and establish" in the judicial branch (Article III). But in 1787 only one of these bodies was to be elected by the people—the House of Representatives. The other three bodies were removed from direct popular control: State legislatures selected U.S. Senators; "electors," chosen in a fashion decided by state legislatures, chose the president; and the president appointed the Supreme Court and other federal judges "with the Advice and Consent of the [then

unelected] Senate." Of course, over time state legislatures provided for the direct election of presidential electors and the 17th Amendment provided for the direct election of U.S. Senators.

The Constitution of 1787 also recognized slavery—"persons held to Service or Labor" (Article IV, Section 2)—and even protected it, by requiring states that capture runaway slaves to "deliver up," that is, to return them to their owners. In terms of representation, the Constitution of 1787 distinguishes between "free persons" and three-fifths of "all other Persons" (Article I, Section 2), that is, slaves. And Congress could not prohibit the importation of slaves until after 1808 (Article I, Section 9).

the national government was too strong. When Washington retired from office, most Federalists supported John Adams as his successor. But many Anti-Federalists ran for posts as presidential electors, promising to be "Jefferson's men." Adams won the presidential election of 1796, but the Anti-Federalists organized themselves into a political party, the Democratic-Republicans, to oppose Adams in the election of 1800. The party secured pledges from candidates for presidential elector to cast their electoral vote for Jefferson if they won their post, and then the party helped win support for its slate of electors. In this way the Electoral College was transformed from a deliberative body where leading citizens from each state came together to decide for themselves who should be president into a ceremonial body where pledged electors simply cast their presidential vote for the candidate who had carried their state in the presidential election. (For a full discussion of the current operation of the Electoral College, see *What Do You Think?*: "Should We Scrap the Electoral College?" in Chapter 8.)

Summary
Who Gets What: Limiting Government Power

The true meaning of constitutionalism is the limitation of governmental power. Constitutions govern governments; they are designed to restrict those who exercise governmental power. Constitutions not only establish governmental bodies and prescribe the rules by which they make their decisions, but, more important, they limit the powers of government.

★ The American tradition of written constitutions extends back through the Articles of Confederation, the colonial charters, and the Mayflower Compact to the thirteenth-century English Magna Carta. The Second Continental Congress in 1776 adopted a written Declaration of Independence to justify the colonies' separation from Great Britain. All of these documents strengthened the idea of a written contract defining governmental power.

★ The movement for a Constitutional Convention in 1787 was inspired by the new government's inability to levy taxes under the Articles of Confederation, its inability to fund the Revolutionary War debt, obstacles to interstate commerce, monetary problems, and civil disorders, including Shays' Rebellion.

★ The nation's Founders—fifty-five delegates to the Constitutional Convention in Philadelphia in 1787— shared a broad consensus on liberty and property, the social contract, republicanism, limited government, and the need for a national government.

★ The Founders compromised their differences over representation by creating two co-equal houses in the Congress: the House of Representatives, with members apportioned to the states on the basis of population and directly elected by the people for two-year terms, and the Senate, with two members allotted to each state regardless of its population and originally selected by state legislatures for six-year terms.

★ The infamous slavery provisions in the Constitution— counting each slave as three-fifths of a person for purposes of taxation and representation, guaranteeing the return of escaped slaves, and postponing the end of the slave trade for twenty years—were also compromises. Voter qualifications in national elections were left to the states to determine.

★ The structure of the national government reflects the Founders' beliefs in national supremacy, federalism, republicanism, separation of powers, checks and balances, and judicial review.

★ The original Constitution gave the people very little influence on their government: only members of the House of Representatives were directly elected; senators were elected by state legislatures; the president was elected indirectly by "electors" chosen in each state; and members of the Supreme Court and federal judiciary were appointed for life by the president and confirmed by the Senate. Over time, the national government became more democratic through the expansion of voting rights, the direct election of senators, the emergence of political parties, and the practice of voting for presidential electors pledged to cast their vote for the candidates of one party.

★ The separation of powers and checks and balances written into the Constitution were designed, in Madison's words, "to divide and arrange the several offices in such a manner as that each may be a check on the other." Judicial review was not specifically described in the original Constitution, but the Supreme Court soon asserted its power to overturn laws of Congress and the states, as well as presidential actions, that the Court determined to be in conflict with the Constitution.

★ Opposition to the new Constitution was strong. Anti-Federalists argued that it created a national government that was aristocratic, undemocratic, and a threat to the rights of the states and the people. Their concerns resulted in the Bill of Rights: ten amendments added to the original Constitution, all designed to limit the power of the national government and protect the rights of individuals and states.

★ Over time, constitutional changes have come about as a result of formal amendments, judicial interpretations, presidential and congressional actions, and changes in custom and practice. The most common method of constitutional amendment has been proposal by two-thirds vote of both houses of Congress followed by ratification by three-fourths of the state legislatures.

Key Terms

constitutionalism 57
constitution 58
Shays's Rebellion 61
Annapolis Convention 62
the Enlightenment 63
natural law 63
inalienable rights 63
social contract 63
republicanism 63

nationalism 63
parliamentary government 64
Connecticut Compromise 66
Three-Fifths Compromise 67
taxes 68
tariff 68

common market 68
National Supremacy Clause 71
referenda 73
separation of powers 75
checks and balances 75
judicial review 77
ratification 78
Federalists 78

Anti-Federalists 79
Bill of Rights 80
enumerated powers 80
amendments 80
Equal Rights Amendment (ERA) 82
judicial review 83

Suggested Readings

Beard, Charles. *An Economic Interpretation of the Constitution.* New York: Macmillan, 1913. A classic work setting forth the argument that economic self-interest inspired the Founders in writing the Constitution.

Epstein, Lee, and Thomas G. Walker. *Constitutional Law for a Changing America: Institutional Powers and Constraints.* 6th ed. Washington, D.C.: CQ Press, 2007. Supreme Court cases and explanatory narrative regarding the separation of power, federalism, national and state powers, national security, and so on.

Finkelman, Paul. *Slavery and the Founders.* 2nd ed. Armonk, N.Y.: M.E. Sharpe, 2000. A critical account of the Founders' attitudes toward slavery and the resulting three-fifths' compromise.

Frohren, Bruce, ed. *The American Republic: Primary Sources.* Indianapolis: Liberty Fund Inc., 2002. Excellent collection of earliest American documents, from the Mayflower Compact to the Declaration of Independence.

Madison, James, Alexander Hamilton, and John Jay. *The Federalist Papers.* New York: Modern Library, 1937. These eighty-five collected essays, written in 1787–88 in support of ratification of the Constitution, remain the most important commentary on that document. Numbers 10 and 51 (reprinted in the Appendix) ought to be required reading for all students of American government.

Mason, Alpheus Thomas, and Donald Grier Stephenson, Jr. *American Constitutional Law.* 14th ed. Upper Saddle River, N.J.: Prentice Hall, 2005. The now classic introduction to the Constitution and the Supreme Court through essays and case excerpts.

McDonald, Forrest B. *Novus Ordo Seculorum.* Lawrence: University Press of Kansas, 1986. A description of the intellectual origins of the Constitution and the "new secular order" that it represented.

Peltason, J. W., and Sue Davis. *Understanding the Constitution.* 16th ed. New York: Harcourt Brace, 2004. Of the many books that explain the Constitution, this is one of the best. It contains explanations of the Declaration of Independence, the Articles of Confederation, and the Constitution. The book is written clearly and well suited for undergraduates.

Rossiter, Clinton L. *1787, The Grand Convention*. New York: Macmillan, 1960. A very readable account of the people and events surrounding the Constitutional Convention in 1787, with many insights into the conflicts and compromises that took place there.

Sabato, Larry J. *A More Perfect Constitution*. New York: Walker, 2007. Proposals for a new Constitutional Convention to consider.

Storing, Herbert J. *What the Anti-Federalists Were For*. Chicago: University of Chicago Press, 1981. An examination of the arguments of the Anti-Federalists in opposition to the ratification of the Constitution.

Suggested Web Sites

The Anti-Federalist Papers
www.thisnation.com/library/antifederalist
Essays by Anti-Federalists opposed to the ratification of the Constitution.

Constitution Society   www.constitution.org
Web site includes comprehensive list of founding documents, essays, and commentaries on the Constitution.

Constitutional Law
www.law.cornell.edu/topics/constitutional
Cornell University Law School overview of the Constitution.

The Electoral College Official FEC site
www.fec.gov/pages/ecmenu
Provides brief history of the Electoral College and a description of how it works.

George Washington Papers   http://gwpapers.virginia.edu
The life of George Washington with images, maps, documents, and papers.

The Great Compromise   www.jmu.edu/madison
James Madison University Web site on Madison with information on constitutional compromises, including the slavery compromise.

James Madison   www.jmu.edu/madison
The legacy of Madison organized by topic.

National Constitution Center   www.constitutioncenter.org
Located in Philadelphia's Independence Mall, this museum is devoted to explaining the U.S. Constitution.

Our Documents   www.ourdocuments.gov
National Archives Web site with access to 100 "milestone documents" in American history.

U.S. History   www.ushistory.org
The Independence Hall Association Web site with "Documents of Freedom" including Mayflower Compact, Declaration of Independence, Articles of Confederation, etc.

The *Constitution* of the United States

More than two centuries after its ratification, our Constitution remains the operating charter of our republic. It is neither self-explanatory nor a comprehensive description of our constitutional rules. Still, it remains the starting point. Many Americans who swear by the Constitution have never read it seriously, although copies can be found in most American government and American history textbooks.

Justice Hugo Black, who served on the Supreme Court for 34 years, kept a copy of the Constitution with him at all times. He read it often. Reading the Constitution would be a good way for you to begin (and then reread again to end) your study of the government of the United States. We have therefore included a copy of it at this point in the book. Please read it carefully.

THE PREAMBLE

We the People of the United States, in Order to form a more perfect Union, establish Justice, insure domestic Tranquility, provide for the common defense, promote the general Welfare, and secure the Blessings of Liberty to ourselves and our Posterity, do ordain and establish this Constitution for the United States of America.

"We, the people." Three simple words, yet of profound importance and contentious origin. Every government in the world at the time of the Constitutional Convention was some type of monarchy wherein sovereign power flowed from the top. The Founders of our new country rejected monarchy as a form of government and proposed instead a republic, which would draw its sovereignty from the people.

The Articles of Confederation that governed the United States from 1776 until 1789 started with: "We the under signed Delegates of the States." Early drafts of the new constitution started with: "We, the states . . ." But again, the Founders were not interested in another union of states but rather the creation of a new national government. Therefore, "We, the states" was changed to "We, the people."

The remainder of the preamble describes the generic functions of government.

One of these generic functions of government is to provide for the general welfare. For a good discussion of a right versus entitlement to welfare, see the Constitutional Note at the end of Chapter 17, page 623.

ARTICLE I—THE LEGISLATIVE ARTICLE

Legislative Power

The very first article in the Constitution established the legislative branch of the new national government. Why did the framers start with the legislative power instead of the executive branch?

Under the Articles of Confederation, the legislature was the only functional instrument of government. Therefore, the framers truly believed it was the most important component of the new government.

Section 1 All legislative Powers herein granted shall be vested in a Congress of the United States, which shall consist of a Senate and House of Representatives.

Section 1 established a bicameral (two-chamber) legislature of an upper (Senate) and lower (House of Representatives) organization of the legislative branch.

House of Representatives: Composition; Qualifications; Apportionment; Impeachment Power

Section 2 Clause 1. The House of Representatives shall be composed of Members chosen every second Year by the People of the several States, and the Electors in each State shall have the Qualifications requisite for Electors of the most numerous Branch of the State Legislature.

This section sets the term of office for House members (2 years) and indicates that those voting for Congress will have the same qualifications as those voting for the state legislatures. Originally, states limited voters to white property owners. Some states even had religious disqualifications, such as Catholic or Jewish. Most property and religious qualifications for voting were removed by the 1840s, but race and gender restrictions remained, until the 15th and 19th amendments were passed.

Clause 2. No Person shall be a Representative who shall not have attained to the Age of twenty five Years, and been seven Years a Citizen of the United States, and who shall not, when elected, be an inhabitant of that State in which he shall be chosen.

This section sets forth the basic qualifications of a representative: at least 25 years of age, a U.S. citizen for at least 7 years, and a resident of a state. Note that the Constitution does not require a person to be a resident of the district he or she represents. At the time the Constitution was written, life expectancy was about 43 years of age. So a

person 25 years old was middle aged. Considering today's life expectancy of about 78 years, the equivalent age of 25 would be about 45. The average age of a current representative is 53.

Clause 2 does not specify how many terms a representative can serve in Congress. Calls for Congress members to be term limited have never been enacted. Some states passed legislation to limit the terms of their U.S. representatives. Because of the specificity of the qualifications for office, the USSC ruled in *U.S. Term Limits, Inc. v. Thornton*, 514 U.S. 779 (1995) that term limits for U.S. legislators could not be imposed by any state but would require a constitutional amendment.

Clause 3. Representatives and direct Taxes[1] shall be apportioned among the several States which may be included within this Union, according to their respective Numbers, which shall be determined by adding to the whole Number of free Persons, including those bound to Service for a Term of Years, and excluding Indians not taxed, three fifths of all other Persons.[2] The actual Enumeration shall be made within three Years after the first Meeting of the Congress of the United States, and within every subsequent Term of ten Years in such Manner as they shall by Law direct. The Number of Representatives shall not exceed one for every thirty Thousand, but each State shall have at Least one Representative, and until such enumeration shall be made, the State of New Hampshire shall be entitled to chuse three, Massachusetts eight, Rhode Island and Providence Plantations one, Connecticut five, New York six, New Jersey four, Pennsylvania eight, Delaware one, Maryland six, Virginia ten, North Carolina five, South Carolina five, and Georgia three.

This clause contains the Three-Fifths Compromise wherein American Indians and Blacks were only counted as 3/5 of a person for congressional representation purposes. This clause also addresses the question of congressional reapportionment every 10 years, which requires a census. Since the 1911 Reapportionment Act, the size of the House of Representatives has been set at 435. This is the designated size that is reapportioned every 10 years. Based on changes of population, some states gain and some states lose representatives. This clause also provides that every state, regardless of population, will have at least one (1) representative. Currently, seven states have only one representative.

States are required to draw new congressional district boundaries after each reapportionment if the state gains or loses congressional seat(s). The USSC has ruled that legislative districts must contain an approximate equal number of voters. They have also ruled that minority voters must be protected by the creation of majority-minority districts where minority voters can be concentrated. Redrawing of district lines to promote party interests is not prohibited. Many states redraw district lines to protect incumbents regardless of party.

Clause 4. When vacancies happen in the Representation from any State, the Executive Authority thereof shall issue Writs of Election to fill such Vacancies.

This clause provides a procedure for replacing a U.S. representative in the case of death, resignation, or expulsion from the House. Generally, if less than half a term is left, the governor will appoint a successor. If more than half a term is remaining, most states require a special election to fill the vacancy.

Clause 5. The House of Representatives shall chuse their Speaker and other Officers, and shall have the sole Power of Impeachment.

Only one officer of the House is specified—the Speaker. All other officers are decided by the House. This clause also gives the House authority for impeachments (accusations) against officials of the executive and judicial branches.

Senate Composition: Qualifications, Impeachment Trials

Section 3 Clause 1. The Senate of the United States shall be composed of two Senators from each State, chosen by the Legislature thereof,[3] for six Years and each Senator shall have one Vote.

This clause treats each state equally—all have two senators each. Originally, senators were chosen by state legislators, but since passage and ratification of the 17th Amendment, they are now elected by popular vote. This clause also establishes the term of a senator—6 years—three times that of a House member.

Clause 2. Immediately after they shall be assembled in Consequence of the first Election, they shall be divided as equally as may be into three Classes. The Seats of the Senators of the first Class shall be vacated at the Expiration of the second Year, of the second Class at the Expiration of the fourth Year, and of the third Class at the Expiration of the sixth Year, so that one third may be chosen every second Year and if Vacancies happen by Resignation, or otherwise, during the Recess of the Legislature of any State, the Executive thereof may make temporary Appointments until the next Meeting of the Legislature which shall then fill such Vacancies.[4]

To prevent a wholesale election of senators every six years, this clause provides that one-third of the Senate will be elected every two years. Senate vacancies are filled similar to the House—either appointment by the governor or a special election.

Clause 3. No person shall be a Senator who shall not have attained to the Age of thirty Years, and been nine Years a Citizen of the United States, and who shall not, when elected, be an Inhabitant of that State for which he shall be chosen.

This clause sets forth the qualifications for U.S. senator: at least 30 years old, a U.S. citizen for at least nine years, and a citizen of a state. The equivalent age of 30 today would be 54 years old. The average age of a U.S. senator at present is 58 years.

---

[1]Modified by the 16th Amendment
[2]Replaced by Section 2, 14th Amendment

[3]Repealed by the 17th Amendment
[4]Modified by the 17th Amendment

Clause 4. The Vice President of the United States shall be President of the Senate but shall have no Vote, unless they be equally divided.

The only constitutional duty of the vice president is specified in this clause—president of the Senate. This official only has a vote if there is a tie vote in the Senate; then the vice president's vote breaks the tie.

Clause 5. The Senate shall chuse their other Officers, and also a President pro tempore, in the Absence of the Vice President, or when he shall exercise the Office of President of the United States.

One official office in the U.S. Senate is specified— temporary president, who fills in during the vice president's absence (which is normally the case). All other Senate officers are designated and selected by the Senate.

Clause 6. The Senate shall have the sole Power to try all Impeachments. When sitting for that Purpose, they shall be on Oath or Affirmation. When the President of the United States is tried, the Chief Justice shall preside. And no Person shall be convicted without the Concurrence of two thirds of the Members present.

Judgment in Cases of impeachment shall not extend further than to removal from Office, and disqualification to hold and enjoy any Office of honor, Trust or Profit under the United States, but the Party convicted shall nevertheless be liable and subject to Indictment, Trial, Judgment and Punishment according to Law.

The Senate acts as a trial court for impeached federal officials. If the accused is the president, the Chief Justice of the U.S. Supreme Court presides. Otherwise, the vice president normally presides. Conviction of the charges requires a 2/3 majority vote of those senators present at the time of the vote. Conviction results in the federal official's removal from office and disqualification to hold any other federal appointed office. Removal from office does not bar further prosecution under applicable criminal or civil laws, nor does it apparently bar one from elected office. A current representative, Alcee L. Hastings, was impeached and removed as a federal district judge. He subsequently ran for Congress and represents Florida's 23rd Congressional District.

Congressional Elections: Times, Places, Manner

Section 4 The Times, Places and Manner of holding Elections for Senators and Representatives, shall be prescribed in each State by the Legislature thereof, but the Congress may at any time by Law make or alter such Regulations, except as to the Places of chusting Senators.

The Congress shall assemble at least once in every Year, and such Meeting shall be on the first Monday in December, unless they shall by Law appoint a different Day.[5]

The states determine the place and manner of electing representatives and senators, but Congress has the right to make or change these laws or regulations, except for the election sites. Con-

[5]Changed by the 20th Amendment

gress is required to meet annually, and now, by law, annual meetings begin in January.

Powers and Duties of the Houses

Section 5 Clause 1. Each House shall be the Judge of the Elections, Returns and Qualifications of its own Members, and a Majority of each shall constitute a Quorum to do Business, but a smaller Number may adjourn from day to day, and may be authorized to compel the Attendance of absent Members, in such Manner, and under the Penalties as each House may provide.

This clause enables each legislative branch to essentially make its own rules. Normally, to take a vote, a quorum is necessary. But if no votes are scheduled, fewer than a quorum can convene a session.

Clause 2. Each House may determine the Rules of its Proceedings, punish its Members for disorderly Behaviour, and with the Concurrence of two thirds, expel a Member.

Essentially, each branch promulgates its own rules and punishes its own members. The ultimate punishment is expulsion of the member, which requires a 2/3 vote. Expulsion does not prevent the member from running again.

Clause 3. Each House shall keep a Journal of its Proceedings, and from time to time publish the same, excepting such Parts as may in their Judgment require Secrecy, and the Yeas and Nays of the Members of either House on any question shall, at the Desire of one fifth of those Present, be entered on the Journal.

An official record called the Congressional Record, House Journal, etc., is kept for all sessions. It is a daily account of House and Senate floor debates, votes, and members' remarks. However, a record is not printed if a proceeding is closed to the public for security reasons. Many votes are by voice vote, and if at least 1/5 of the members request, a recorded vote of Yeas and Nays will be conducted and recorded. This procedure permits analysis of congressional roll-call votes.

Clause 4. Neither House, during the Session of Congress shall, without the Consent of the other, adjourn for more than three days, nor to any other Place than that in which the two Houses shall be sitting.

This clause prevents one branch from adjourning for a long period or to some other location without the consent of the other branch.

Rights of Members

Section 6 Clause 1. The Senators and Representatives shall receive a Compensation for their Services, to be ascertained by Law, and paid out of the Treasury of the United States. They shall in all Cases, except Treason, Felony and Breach of the Peace, be privileged from Arrest during their Attendance at the Session of their respective Houses, and in going to and returning from the same, and for any Speech or Debate in either House, they shall not be questioned in any other Place.

This section ensures that senators and congressional representatives will be paid a salary from the U.S. Treasury. This salary is determined by no

other than the legislature. According to the Library of Congress legislative Web site THOMAS "The current salary for members of Congress is $169,300. A small number of leadership positions, like Speaker of the House, receive a somewhat higher salary." In addition, members of Congress receive many other benefits: free health care, fully funded retirement system, free gyms, 26 free round trips to their home state or district, etc. This section also provides immunity from arrest or prosecution for congressional actions on the floor or in travel to and from the Congress. For example, few members of Congress have ever been charged with drunk driving.

Clause 2. No Senator or Representative, shall, during the Time for which he was elected, be appointed to any civil Office under the Authority of the United States, which shall have been created, or the Emoluments whereof shall have been encreased during such time; and no Person holding any Office under the United States, shall be a Member of either House during his Continuance in Office.

This section prevents the United States from adopting a parliamentary democracy, since congressional members cannot hold executive offices and members of the executive branch cannot be members of Congress.

Legislative Powers: Bills and Resolutions

Section 7 Clause 1. All Bills for raising Revenue shall originate in the House of Representatives; but the Senate may propose or concur with Amendments as on other Bills.

This clause specifies one of the few powers specific to the U.S. House—revenue bills.

Clause 2. Every Bill which shall have passed the House of Representatives and the Senate, shall, before it becomes a Law, be presented to the President of the United States; If he approve he shall sign it, but if not he shall return it, with his Objections to that House in which it shall have originated, who shall enter the Objections at large on their Journal, and proceed to reconsider it. If after such Reconsideration two thirds of that House shall agree to pass the Bill, it shall be sent, together with the Objections, to the other House, by which it shall likewise be reconsidered, and if approved by two thirds of that House, it shall become a Law. But in all such Cases the Votes of both Houses shall be determined by yeas and Nays, and the Names of the Persons voting for and against the Bill shall be entered on the Journal of each House respectively. If any Bill shall not be returned by the President within ten Days (Sundays excepted) after it shall have been presented to him, the Same shall be a Law, in like Manner as if he had signed it, unless the Congress by their Adjournment prevent its Return, in which Case it shall not be a Law.

The heart of the checks and balances system is contained in this clause. Both the House and Senate must pass a bill and present it to the president. If the president fails to act on the bill within 10 days (not including Sundays), the bill will automatically become law. If the president signs the bill, it becomes law. If the president vetoes the bill and sends it back to Congress, this body may override the veto by a 2/3 vote in each house. This vote must be a recorded vote.

Clause 3. Every Order, Resolution, or Vote to which the Concurrence of the Senate and House of Representatives may be necessary (except on a question of Adjournment) shall be presented to the President of the United States; and before the Same shall take Effect, shall be approved by him, or being disapproved by him, shall be repassed by two thirds of the Senate and House of Representatives, according to the Rules and Limitations prescribed in the Case of a Bill.

This clause covers every other type of legislative action other than a bill. Essentially, the same procedures apply in most cases. There are a few exceptions. For example, a joint resolution proposing a new congressional amendment is not subject to presidential veto.

Powers of Congress

Section 8 Clause 1. The Congress shall have Power to lay and collect Taxes, Duties, Imposts and Excises, to pay the Debts and provide for the common Defence and general Welfare of the United States, but all Duties, Imposts and Excises shall be uniform throughout the United States.

To borrow Money on the credit of the United States;

To regulate Commerce with foreign Nations, and among the several States, and with the Indian Tribes;

To establish an uniform Rule of Naturalization, and uniform Laws on the subject of Bankruptcies throughout the United States;

To coin Money, regulate the Value thereof, and of foreign Coin, and fix the Standard of Weights and Measures;

To provide for the Punishment of counterfeiting the Securities and current Coin of the United States;

To establish Post Offices and post Roads;

To promote the Progress of Science and useful Arts, by securing for limited Times to Authors and Inventors the exclusive Right to their respective Writings and Discoveries;

To constitute Tribunals inferior to the supreme Court;

To define and punish Piracies and Felonies committed on the high Seas, and Offences against the Law of Nations;

To declare War, grant Letters of Marque and Reprisal, and make Rules concerning Captures on Land and Water;

To raise and support Armies, but no Appropriation of Money to that Use shall be for a longer Term than two Years;

To provide and maintain a Navy;

To make Rules for the Government and Regulation of the land and naval Forces;

To provide for calling for the Militia to execute the Laws of the Union, suppress Insurrections and repel Invasions;

To provide for organizing, arming, and disciplining, the Militia, and for governing such Part of them as may be employed in the Service of the United States, reserving to the States respectively, the Appointment of the Officers, and the Authority of training the Militia according to the discipline prescribed by Congress;

This *extensive* clause establishes what are known as "enumerated," or "expressed" or "specified" powers of Congress. In theory, this serves as a limit or brake on congressional power.

Clause 2. To exercise exclusive Legislation in all Cases whatsoever, over such District (not exceeding ten Miles square) as may, by Cession of particular States, and the Acceptance of Congress, become the Seat of the Government of the United States, and to exercise like Authority over all Places purchased by the Consent of the Legislature of the State in which the Same shall be, for the Erection of Forts, Magazines, Arsenals, dock Yards, and other needful Buildings—And

This clause establishes the seat of the federal government, which was first started in New York but eventually was moved to Washington, D.C., when both Maryland and Virginia ceded land to the new national government, which then established the District of Columbia.

Clause 3. To make all Laws which shall be necessary and proper for carrying into Execution the foregoing Powers, and all other Powers vested by this Constitution in the Government of the United States, or in any Department or Officer thereof.

This clause, known as the "Elastic Clause," provides the basis for the doctrine of "implied" congressional powers, which was first introduced in the U.S. Supreme Court case of *McCulloch v. Maryland*, 1819. This doctrine tremendously expanded the power of Congress to pass legislation and make regulations.

Powers Denied to Congress

Section 9 Clause 1. The Migration or Importation of such Persons as any of the States now existing shall think proper to admit, shall not be prohibited by the Congress prior to the Year one thousand eight hundred and eight, but a Tax or duty may be imposed on such Importation, not exceeding ten dollars for each Person.

This clause was part of the Three-Fifths Compromise. Essentially, the new Congress was prohibited from stopping the importation of slaves until 1808, but it could impose a head tax, not to exceed ten dollars for each slave.

Clause 2. The Privilege of the Writ of Habeas Corpus shall not be suspended, unless when in Cases of Rebellion or Invasion the public Safety may require it.

Congress cannot suspend the writ of habeas corpus except in cases of rebellion or invasion. The writ of habeas corpus permits a judge to inquire about the legality of detention or deprivation of liberty of any citizen.

Clause 3. No Bill of Attainder or ex post facto Law shall be passed.

This provision prohibits Congress from passing either a bill of attainder (forfeiture of property in capital cases) or ex post facto laws (retroactive crimes after passage of legislation). Similar restrictions were enshrined in many state constitutions.

Clause 4. No Capitation, or other direct Tax shall be laid, unless in Proportion to the Census or Enumeration herein before directed to be taken.[6]

This clause prevented Congress from passing an income tax. Only with passage of the 16th Amendment in 1913 did Congress gain this power.

Clause 5. No Tax or Duty shall be laid on Articles exported from any State.

This section establishes free trade within the United States. The federal government cannot tax state exports.

Clause 6. No Preference shall be given by any Regulation of Commerce or Revenue to the Ports of one State over those of another; nor shall Vessels bound to, or from one State, be obliged to enter, clear, or pay Duties in another.

This clause also applies to free trade within the United States. The national government cannot show any preference to any state or maritime movements among the states.

Clause 7. No Money shall be drawn from the Treasury, but in Consequence of Appropriations made by Law, and a regular Statement and Account of the Receipts and Expenditures of all public Money shall be published from time to time.

This provision of the Constitution prevents any expenditure unless it has been specifically provided for in an appropriations bill. At the beginning of most fiscal years, Congress has not completed its work on the budget. Technically, the government cannot spend any money according to this provision and would have to shut down. So Congress normally passes a Continuing Resolution providing temporary authority to continue to spend money until the final budget is approved and signed into law.

Clause 8. No Title of Nobility shall be granted by the United States. And no Person holding any Office of Profit or Trust under them, shall, without the Consent of Congress, accept of any present, Emolument, Office, or Title, of any kind whatever, from any King, Prince, or foreign State.

Feudalism would not be established in the new country. We would have no nobles. No federal official can even accept a title of nobility (even honorary) without permission of Congress.

Powers Denied to the States

This section sets out the prohibitions on state actions.

Section 10 Clause 1. No State shall enter into any Treaty, Alliance, or Confederation, grant Letters of Marque and Reprisal, coin Money, emit Bills of Credit, make any Thing but gold and silver Coin a Tender in Payment of Debts, pass any Bill of Attainder, ex post facto Law, or Law impairing the Obligation of Contracts of grant any Title of Nobility.

This particular clause presents a list of denied powers. Note that these restrictions cannot even be waived by Congress. States are not to engage in foreign relations, nor acts of war. A letter of Marque and Reprisal was used during the Revolutionary War to provide legal cover for privateers. The federal government's currency monopoly is established. The sanctity of contracts is specified. And similar state prohibitions are specified for bills of attainder, ex post facto, etc.

Clause 2. No State shall, without the Consent of the Congress, lay any Imposts or Duties on Imports or Exports, except what may be absolutely necessary for executing its inspection Laws: and the net Produce of all Duties and Imposts, laid by any State on Imports or Exports, shall be for the Use of the Treasury of the United States, and all such Laws shall be subject to the Revision and Controul of the Congress.

[6]Modified by the 16th Amendment

This section establishes the monopoly control of the national government in matters of both national and international trade. The only concession to states is health and safety inspections.

Clause 3. No State shall, without the Consent of Congress, lay any Duty of Tonnage, keep Troops, or Ships of War in time of Peace, enter into any Agreement or Compact with another State, or with a foreign Power, or engage in War, unless actually invaded, or in such imminent Danger as will not admit of delay.

This final section of the Legislative article establishes the war monopoly power of the national government. The only exception to state action is actual invasion or threat of imminent danger.

ARTICLE II—THE EXECUTIVE ARTICLE

This article establishes an entirely new concept in government—an elected executive power.

Nature and Scope of Presidential Power

Section 1 Clause 1. The executive Power shall be vested in a President of the United States of America. He shall hold his Office during the Term of four Years and, together with the Vice President, chosen for the same Term, be elected, as follows.

This clause establishes the executive power in the office of the president of the United States of America. It also establishes a second office—vice president. A four-year term was established, but no limit on the number of terms. A limit was later established by the 22nd Amendment.

Clause 2. Each State shall appoint, in such Manner as the Legislature thereof may direct, a Number of Electors, equal to the whole Number of Senators and Representatives to which the State may be entitled in the Congress: but no Senator or Representative, or Person holding an Office of Trust or Profit under the United States, shall be appointed an Elector.

This paragraph essentially establishes the Electoral College to choose the president and vice president.

Clause 3. The Electors shall meet in their respective States, and vote by Ballot for two Persons, of whom one at least shall not be an Inhabitant of the same State with themselves. And they shall make a List of all the Persons voted for, and of the Number of Votes for each; which List they shall sign and certify, and transmit sealed to the Seat of the Government of the United States, directed to the President of the Senate. The President of the Senate shall, in the Presence of the Senate and House of Representatives, open all the Certificates, and the Votes shall then be counted. The Person having the greatest Number of Votes shall be the President, if such Number be a Majority of the whole Number of Electors appointed; and if there be more than one who have such Majority and have an equal Number of Votes, then the House of Representatives shall immediately chuse by Ballot one of them for President; and if no Person have a Majority, then from the five highest on the List the said House shall in like Manner chuse the President. But in chusing the President, the Votes shall be taken by States, the Representation from each State having one Vote; a quorum for this Purpose shall consist of a Member or Members from two thirds of the States, and a Majority of all the States shall be necessary to a Choice. In every Case, after the Choice of the President, the Person having the greatest Number of Votes of the Electors shall be the Vice President. But if there should remain two or more who have equal Votes, the Senate shall chuse from them by Ballot the Vice President.[7]

This paragraph has been superseded by the 12th Amendment. The original language did not require a separate vote for president and vice president. This resulted in a tied vote in the Electoral College in 1800 when both Thomas Jefferson and Aaron Burr received 73 electoral votes. The 12th Amendment requires a separate vote for each. Only one of the two can be from the state of the elector. This means that it is highly unlikely that the presidential and vice presidential candidates would be from the same state. This question arose in the 2000 election when Dick Cheney, who lived and worked in Texas, had to reestablish his residence in Wyoming, so that he would have a different state residence than Texan George W. Bush.

The original language provided for a House election in the case of no majority vote or a tie vote among the top five candidates. The amendment lowered the number of candidates to the top three. The Senate is to select the vice president if a candidate does not have an electoral majority or in the case of a tie vote. The Senate considers only the top two candidates. The amendment also clarifies that the qualifications of the vice president are the same as those for president.

In the 2008 presidential campaign, some promoted the Hispanic Senator from Florida, Mel Martinez, as a possible running mate for John McCain to help win the Hispanic vote. There was, however, a big problem. Mel Martinez was born in Cuba and thus would not meet the qualification to become president of the United States. Once this was realized, all talk about Martinez disappeared.

Clause 4. The Congress may determine the Time of chusing the Electors, and the Day on which they shall give their Votes; which Day shall be the same throughout the United States.

Congress is given the power to establish a uniform day and time for the state selection of electors.

Clause 5. No Person except a natural born Citizen, or a Citizen of the United States, at the time of the Adoption of this Constitution, shall be eligible to the Office of President, neither shall any Person be eligible to that Office who shall not have attained to the Age of thirty five Years, and been fourteen Years a Resident within the United States.

The qualifications for the offices of president and vice president are specified here—at least 35 years old, 14 years' resident in the United States, and a natural-born citizen or citizen of the United States. The 14th Amendment clarified who is a citizen of the U.S.: a person born or naturalized in the United States and subject to its jurisdiction. But the term "natural-born citizen" is unclear and has never been further defined by the judicial branch. Does it mean

---

[7]Changed by the 12th and 20th Amendments

born in the United States or born of U.S. citizens in the United States or somewhere else in the world? Unfortunately, there is no definitive answer.

See further discussion of this issue in the Constitutional Note at the end of Chapter 2, page 51.

Clause 6. In Case of the Removal of the President from Office, or of his Death, Resignation, or Inability to discharge the Powers and Duties of the said Office, the Same shall devolve on the Vice President, and the Congress may by Law provide for the Case of Removal, Death, Resignation, or Inability, both of the President and Vice President, declaring what Officer shall then act as president, and such Officer shall act accordingly, until the Disability be removed, or a President shall be elected.[8]

This clause has been modified by the 25th Amendment. Upon the death, resignation, or impeachment and conviction of the president, the vice president becomes president. The new president nominates a new vice president, who assumes the office, if approved by a majority vote in both congressional branches. The president is also now able to notify the Congress of his inability to perform his office.

This clause was tested when Richard Nixon resigned as president and Gerald Ford, who was vice president, moved up to become president. President Ford nominated Nelson Rockefeller to become the new vice president, who was approved by a majority vote of the House and Senate. However, Ford assumed the vice presidency because Spiro Agnew, who was elected with Richard Nixon in 1968, also resigned office in 1973. This was an extreme test of the 25th Amendment.

Clause 7. The President shall, at stated Times, receive for his Services, a Compensation which shall neither be encreased nor diminished during the Period of which he shall have been elected, and he shall not receive within that Period any other Emolument from the United States, or any of them.

This section covers the compensation of the president, which cannot be increased or decreased during his office. The current salary is $400,000/year.

Clause 8. Before he enter on the Execution of his Office, he shall take the following Oath or Affirmation—"I do solemnly swear (or affirm) that I will faithfully execute the Office of President of the United States, and will to the best of my Ability, preserve, protect and defend the Constitution of the United States."

This final clause in Section 1 is the oath of office administered to the new president.

Powers and Duties of the President

Section 2 Clause 1. The President shall be the Commander in Chief of the Army and Navy of the United States, and of the Militia of the several States; when called into the actual Service of the United States, he may require the Opinion, in writing, of the principal Officer in each of the executive Departments, upon any Subject relating to the Duties of their respective

Offices, and he shall have the Power to grant Reprieves and Pardons for Offences against the United States, except in Cases of Impeachment.

This clause establishes the president as Commander-in-Chief of the U.S. armed forces. George Washington actually led U.S. armed forces during the Whiskey Rebellion. The second provision provides the basis for cabinet meetings that are used to acquire the opinions of executive department heads. The last provision provides an absolute pardon or reprieve power from the president. The provision was controversial, but legal, when President Gerald Ford pardoned Richard Nixon following the Watergate scandal.

Clause 2. He shall have Power, by and with the Advice and Consent of the Senate to make Treaties, provided two thirds of the Senators present concur, and he shall nominate, and by and with the Advice and Consent of the Senate, shall appoint Ambassadors, other public Ministers and Consuls, Judges of the supreme Court, and all other Officers of the United States, whose Appointments are not herein otherwise provided for, and which shall be established by Law but the Congress may by Law vest the Appointment of such inferior Officers, as they think proper in the President alone, in the Courts of Law, or in the Heads of Departments.

This clause covers two important presidential powers, treaty making and appointments. The president (via the State Department) can negotiate treaties with other nations, but these do not become official until ratified by a 2/3 vote of the U.S. Senate. The president is empowered to appoint judges, ambassadors, and other U.S. officials (cabinet officers, military officers, agency heads, etc.) subject to Senate approval. The Congress can and does delegate this approval to the president in the case of inferior officers. For example, junior military officer promotions are not submitted to the Senate, but senior officer promotions are.

Clause 3. The President shall have Power to fill up all Vacancies that may happen during the Recess of the Senate, by granting Commissions which shall expire at the End of their next Session.

This provision allows recess appointments of the officials listed in Clause 2 above. These commissions automatically expire unless approved by the Senate by the end of the next session. Presidents have used this provision to fill jobs when the nomination process is stalled. Some of these appointments have been very controversial. The regular nomination was stalled because the Senate did not want to confirm the nominee.

Section 3 He shall from time to time give to the Congress Information of the State of the Union, and recommend to their Consideration such Measures as he shall judge necessary and expedient, he may, on extraordinary Occasions convene both Houses, or either of them and in Case of Disagreement between them, with Respect to the Time of Adjournment, he may adjourn them to such Time as he shall think proper, he shall receive Ambassadors and other public Ministers, he shall take Care that the Laws be faithfully executed, and shall Commission all the Officers of the United States.

---

[8]Modified by the 25th Amendment

This section provides for the annual State of the Union address to a joint session of Congress and the American people. The president is also authorized to call special meetings of either the House or Senate. If there is disagreement between the House and Senate regarding adjournment, the president is empowered to adjourn them. This would be extremely rare. The president formally receives other nations' ambassadors. The next to last provision to faithfully execute laws provides the basis for the whole administrative apparatus of the presidency. All officers of the United States receive a formal commission from the president (most of these are signed with a signature machine).

Section 4 The President, Vice President and all civil Officers of the United States, shall be removed from Office on Impeachment for, and Conviction of, Treason, Bribery, or other high Crimes and Misdemeanors.

This section provides the constitutional authority for the impeachment and trial of the president, vice president, and all civil officers of the United States for treason, bribery, or other high crimes and misdemeanors (the exact meaning of this phrase is unclear and is often more political than judicial).

ARTICLE III—THE JUDICIAL ARTICLE

Judicial Power, Courts, Judges

Section 1 The judicial Power of the United States, shall be vested in one supreme Court, and in such inferior Courts as the Congress may from time to time ordain and establish. The Judges, both of the supreme and inferior Courts, shall hold their Offices during good Behaviour, and shall, at stated Times, receive for their Services, a Compensation, which shall not be diminished during their Continuance in Office.

This section establishes the judicial branch in very general terms. It specifically provides only for the Supreme Court. Congress is given the responsibility to flesh out the court system. It initially did so in the Judiciary Act of 1789, when it established 13 district courts (one for each state) and 3 appellate courts. All federal judges hold their offices for life and can only be removed for breaches of good behavior—a very nebulous term. Federal judges have been removed for drunkenness, accepting bribes, and other misdemeanors. To date, no justice of the U.S. Supreme Court has ever been removed.

The salary of federal judges is set by congressional act, but can never be reduced. Although the American Bar Association and the Federal Bar Association consider federal judges' salaries inadequate, most Americans would probably disagree. Federal district judges earn $169,300/year, appellate judges $179,500, and Supreme Court justices $208,100. The Chief Justice is paid $212,100. These are lifetime salaries, even upon retirement.

Jurisdiction

Section 2 The judicial Power shall extend to all Cases, in Law and Equity, arising under this Constitution, the Laws of the United States, and Treaties made, or which shall be made, under their Authority,—to all Cases affecting Ambassadors, other public Ministers and Consuls,—to all Cases of admiralty and maritime Jurisdiction,—to Controversies to which the United States shall be a Party,—to Controversies between two or more States; between a State and Citizens of another State;[9]—between Citizens of different States;—between Citizens of the same State claiming Lands under Grants of different States, and between a State, or the Citizens thereof, and foreign States, Citizens, or Subjects.

In all Cases affecting Ambassadors, other public Ministers and Consuls, and those in which a State shall be Party, the supreme Court shall have original Jurisdiction. In all the other Cases before mentioned, the supreme Court shall have appellate Jurisdiction, both as to Law and Fact, with such Exceptions, and under such Regulations as Congress shall make.

The Trial of all Crimes, except in Cases of Impeachment, shall be by Jury; and such Trial shall be held in the State where the said Crimes shall have been committed; but when not committed within any State, the Trial shall be at such Place or Places as the Congress may by Law have directed.

This section establishes the original and appellate jurisdiction of the U.S. Supreme Court. With the Congress of Vienna's 1815 establishment of "diplomatic immunity," the U.S. Supreme Court no longer hears cases involving ambassadors. Since 1925, the Supreme Court no longer hears every case on appeal but can select which cases it will accept, which is now only about 150 cases per year. This section also establishes the right of trial by jury for federal crimes.

Treason

Section 3 Treason against the United States, shall consist only in levying War against them, or in adhering to their Enemies, giving them Aid and Comfort. No Person shall be convicted of Treason unless on the Testimony of two Witnesses to the same overt Act, or on Confession in open Court.

The Congress shall have Power to declare the Punishment of Treason, but no Attainder of Treason shall work Corruption of Blood, or Forfeiture except during the Life of the Person attainted.

Treason is the only crime defined in the U.S. Constitution. Congress established the penalty of death for treason convictions. Note that two witnesses are required to convict anyone of treason. Even in cases of treasonable conduct, seizure of estates is prohibited.

ARTICLE IV—INTERSTATE RELATIONS

Full Faith and Credit Clause

Section 1 Full Faith and Credit shall be given in each State to the public Acts, Records, and judicial Proceedings of every other State. And the Congress may by general Laws prescribe the Manner in which such Acts, Records and Proceedings shall be proved, and the Effect thereof.

This section provides that the official acts and records of one state will be recognized and given credence by other states, e.g., marriages and divorces.

---

[9]Modified by the 11th Amendment

Privileges and Immunities, Interstate Extradition

Section 2 Clause 1. The Citizens of each State shall be entitled to all Privileges and Immunities of Citizens in the several States.

This clause requires states to treat citizens of other states equally. For example, when driving in another state, one's driver's license is recognized. One area not so clear is that of charging higher tuitions at state educational institutions for out-of-state students.

Clause 2. A person charged in any State with Treason, Felony or other Crime, who shall flee from Justice, and be found in another State, shall on Demand of the executive Authority of the State from which he fled, be delivered up, to be removed to the State having Jurisdiction of the Crime.

Extradition is the name of this clause. A criminal fleeing to another state, if captured, can be returned to the state where the crime was committed. But this is not an absolute. A state's governor can refuse, for good reason, to extradite someone to another state.

Clause 3. No person held to Service or Labour in one State, under the Laws thereof, escaping into another, shall, in Consequence of any Law or Regulation therein, be discharged from such Service or Labour, but shall be delivered up on Claim of the Party to whom such Service or Labour may be due.[10]

This clause was included to cover runaway slaves. It has been made inoperable by the 13th Amendment, which abolished slavery.

Admission of States

Section 3 New States may be admitted by the Congress into this Union but no new State shall be formed or erected within the Jurisdiction of any other State, nor any State to be formed by the Junction of two or more States, or Parts of States, without the Consent of the Legislatures of the States concerned as well as of the Congress.

The Congress shall have Power to dispose of and make all needful Rules and Regulations respecting the Territory or other Property belonging to the United States, and nothing in this Constitution shall be so construed as to Prejudice any Claims of the United States, or of any particular State.

This section concerns the admission of new states to the Union. In theory, no state can be created from part of another state without permission of the state legislature. But West Virginia was formed from Virginia during the Civil War without the permission of Virginia, which was part of the Confederacy. With fifty states now part of the Union, this section has not been used for many decades. The only future use may be in the case of Puerto Rico or perhaps Washington, D.C.

Republican Form of Government

Section 4 The United States shall guarantee to every State in this Union a Republican Form of Government, and shall protect each of them against Invasion, and on Application of the Legislature, or of the Executive (when the Legislature cannot be convened) against domestic Violence.

This section commits the federal government to guarantee a republican form of government to each state and protect the state against foreign invasion or domestic insurrection.

See discussion in the Constitutional Note at the end of Chapter 1, Page 21.

ARTICLE V—THE AMENDING POWER

The Congress, whenever two thirds of both Houses shall deem it necessary, shall propose Amendments to this Constitution, or, on the Application of the Legislatures of two thirds of the several States, shall call a Convention for proposing Amendments, which, in either Case, shall be valid to all Intents and Purposes, as Part of this Constitution, when ratified by the Legislatures of three fourths of the several States, or by Conventions in three fourths thereof, as the one or the other Mode of Ratification may be proposed by the Congress; Provided that no Amendment which may be made prior to the Year One thousand eight hundred and eight shall in any Manner affect the first and fourth Clauses in the Ninth Section of the first Article; and that no State, without its Consent, shall be deprived of its equal Suffrage in the Senate.

Amendment to the U.S. Constitution can be originated by a 2/3 vote in both the U.S. House and Senate or by 2/3 of the state legislatures asking for a convention to propose amendments. Proposed amendments, by either route, must be approved by 3/4 of state legislatures or by 3/4 of conventions convened in the states for purposes of ratification. Only one amendment has been ratified by the convention method—Amendment 21 to repeal the 18th Amendment establishing Prohibition.

Thousands of amendments have been proposed; few have been passed by 2/3 vote in each branch of Congress. The Equal Rights Amendment was one such case, but it was not ratified by 3/4 of state legislatures. There have only been 27 successful amendments to the U.S. Constitution.

ARTICLE VI—THE SUPREMACY CLAUSE

Clause 1. All Debts contracted and Engagements entered into, before the Adoption of this Constitution, shall be as valid against the United States under the Constitution, as under the Confederation.

This clause made the new national government responsible for all debts incurred during the Revolutionary War. This was very important to banking and commercial interests.

Clause 2. This Constitution, and the Laws of the United States which shall be made in Pursuance thereof, and all Treaties made, or which shall be made, under the Authority of the United States, shall be the supreme Law of the Land, and the Judges in every State shall be bound thereby any Thing in the Constitution or Laws of any State to the Contrary notwithstanding.

This is the Supremacy Clause, which provides the basis for the supremacy of the national government.

---

[10]Repealed by the 13th Amendment

Clause 3. The Senators and Representatives before mentioned, and the Members of the several State Legislatures, and all executive and judicial Officers, both of the United States and of the several States, shall be bound by Oath or Affirmation, to support this Constitution, but no religious Test shall ever be required as a Qualification to any Office or public Trust under the United States.

This clause requires essentially all federal and state officials to swear or affirm their allegiance to and support of the U.S. Constitution. Note that a religious test was prohibited for federal office. However, some states used religious tests for voting and office qualification until the 1830s.

ARTICLE VII—RATIFICATION

The Ratification of the Conventions of nine States, shall be sufficient for the Establishment of this Constitution between the States so ratifying the Same.

Done in Convention by the Unanimous Consent of the States present the Seventeenth Day of September in the Year of our Lord one thousand seven hundred and Eighty seven and of the Independence of the United States of America the Twelfth. *In Witness whereof We have hereunto subscribed our Names.*

Realizing the unanimous ratification of the 13 states of the new Constitution might never have occurred, the framers wisely specified that only 9 states would be needed for ratification. Even this proved to be a test of wills between Federalists and Anti-Federalists, leading to publication of the great political work *The Federalist Papers*.

AMENDMENTS THE BILL OF RIGHTS

[The first ten amendments were ratified on December 15, 1791, and form what is known as the "Bill of Rights."]

The Bill of Rights applied initially only to the federal government and not to state or local governments. Beginning in 1925 in the case of *Gitlow v. New York*, the U.S. Supreme Court began to selectively incorporate the Bill of Rights, making its provisions applicable to state and local governments. There are only three exceptions, which will be discussed at the appropriate amendment.

AMENDMENT 1—
RELIGION, SPEECH, ASSEMBLY, AND POLITICS

Congress shall make no law respecting an establishment of religion, or prohibiting the free exercise thereof; or abridging the freedom of speech, or of the press; or the right of the people peaceably to assemble, and to petition the Government for a redress of grievances.

This is the godfather of all amendments in that it protects five fundamental freedoms: religion, speech, press, assembly, and petition. Note that the press is the only business that is specifically protected by the U.S. Constitution. Freedom of religion and speech are two of the most contentious issues and generate a multitude of Supreme Court cases.

AMENDMENT 2—
MILITIA AND THE RIGHT TO BEAR ARMS

A well-regulated Militia, being necessary to the security of a free State, the right of the people to keep and bear Arms, shall not be infringed.

There is also controversy as to the meaning of this amendment. Some believe that it specifically refers to citizen militias, which were common at the time of the Constitution but now have been replaced by National Guard units. Therefore, is the amendment still applicable? Do private citizens need weapons for the security of a free state?

AMENDMENT 3—QUARTERING OF SOLDIERS

No Soldier shall, in time of peace be quartered in any house, without the consent of the Owner, nor in time of war, but in manner to be prescribed by law.

It was the practice of the British government to insist that colonists provide room and board to British troops. This amendment was designed to prohibit this practice. Today, military and naval bases provide the necessary quarters.

AMENDMENT 4—SEARCHES AND SEIZURES

The right of the people to be secure in their persons, houses, papers, and effects, against unreasonable searches and seizures, shall not be violated, and no Warrants shall issue, but upon probable cause, supported by Oath or affirmation, and particularly describing the place to be searched, and the persons or things to be seized.

This is an extremely important amendment to prevent the abuse of state police powers. Essentially, unreasonable searches or seizures of homes, persons, or property cannot be undertaken without probable cause or a warrant that specifically describes the place to be searched, the person involved, and suspicious things to be seized.

AMENDMENT 5—GRAND JURIES,
SELF-INCRIMINATION, DOUBLE JEOPARDY,
DUE PROCESS, AND EMINENT DOMAIN

No person shall be held to answer for a capital, or otherwise infamous crime, unless on a presentment or indictment of a Grand jury, except in cases arising in the land or naval forces, or in the Militia, when in actual service in time of War or public danger; nor shall any person be subject for the same offence to be twice put in jeopardy of life or limb, nor shall be compelled in any criminal case to be a witness against himself, nor be deprived of life, liberty, or property, without due process of law; nor shall private property be taken for public use, without just compensation.

Only a grand jury can indict a person for a federal crime. This provision does not apply to state/local governments. This amendment also covers double jeopardy, or being tried twice for the same crime in the same jurisdiction. Note that since the federal government and state governments are different jurisdic-

tions, one could be tried in each jurisdiction for essentially the same crime. For example, it is a federal crime to kill a congressperson. It is also a state crime to murder anyone. Further, this amendment also covers the prohibition of self-incrimination. Pleading the 5th Amendment is common among defendants. The deprivation of life, liberty, or property by any level of government is prohibited unless due process of law is applied. Finally, private property may not be taken under the doctrine of "eminent domain" unless the government provides just compensation and the taking is for public purposes.

Amendment 6—Criminal Court Procedures

In all criminal prosecutions, the accused shall enjoy the right to a speedy and public trial, by an impartial jury of the State and district wherein the crime shall have been committed, which district shall have been previously ascertained by law, and to be informed of the nature and cause of the accusation, to be confronted with the witnesses against him, to have compulsory process for obtaining witnesses in his favor, and to have the Assistance of Counsel for his defence.

This amendment requires public trials by jury for criminal prosecutions. Anyone accused of a crime is guaranteed the right to be informed of the charges; confront witnesses; to subpoena witnesses for his or her defense; and to have a lawyer for his or her defense. The government must provide a lawyer for a defendant unable to afford one.

Amendment 7—Trial by Jury in Common Law Cases

In Suits at common law, where the value in controversy shall exceed twenty dollars, the right of trial by jury shall be preserved, and no fact tried by a jury shall be otherwise re-examined in any Court of the United States, than according to the rules of the common law.

This amendment is practically without meaning in modern times. Statutory law has largely superseded common law. Federal civil law suits with a guaranteed jury are now restricted to cases that exceed $50,000. The Bill of Rights, which includes the right to trial by jury, applied orginally only to the national government. Beginning in 1925, the Supreme Court began a selective process of incorporating provisions of the Bill of Rights, applicable to state/local governments as well. There are just a few provisions that have not been thus incorporated. Trial by jury is one. Some state/local governments have trials by judges, not by juries.

Amendment 8—Bail, Cruel and Unusual Punishment

Excessive bail shall not be required, nor excessive fines imposed, nor cruel and unusual punishments inflicted.

Capital punishment is covered by this amendment, which also prohibits excessive bail. But this is relative. Million-dollar bails are not uncommon

in some cases. One federal judge offered voluntary castration for sex offenders in lieu of jail time. Higher courts held this to be a cruel or unusual punishment. But it is the death penalty that generates the most heated controversy. Court cases challenging the constitutionality of capital punishment cite this amendment's language prohibiting cruel and unusual punishment. For a period of 4 years, the Supreme Court banned capital punishment. When states modified their statutes to provide a two-part judicial process of guilt determination and punishment, the Supreme Court allowed the reinstitution of capital punishment by the states.

The enumeration in the Constitution of certain rights, shall not be construed to deny or disparage others retained by the people.

This amendment implies that there may be other rights of the people not specified by the previous amendments. Indeed, the Warren Court established the right to privacy even though it is not specifically mentioned in any previous amendment.

Amendment 10—Reserved Powers of the States

The powers not delegated to the United States by the Constitution, nor prohibited by it to the States, are reserved to the States respectively, or to the people.

The 10th Amendment was seen as the reservoir of reserved powers for state governments. If the national government had been limited only to expressed powers in Article 1, Section 8, of the Constitution, this would have been the case. But the doctrine of implied national government powers, which was established by the U.S. Supreme Court in *McCulloch v. Maryland* in 1819, made the intent of this amendment almost meaningless. What reserved powers that were retained by the states were virtually removed by the U.S. Supreme Court's decision in the *Garcia v. San Antonio Metropolitan Transit Authority* case in 1985, which basically told state/local governments not to look to the courts to protect their residual rights but rather to their political representatives. In subsequent cases, the Supreme Court has retreated somewhat from this position when the court found the federal government encroaching in state jurisdictional areas.

Amendment 11—Suits Against the States

[Ratified February 7, 1795]

The Judicial power of the United States shall not be construed to extend to any suit in law or equity, commenced or prosecuted against one of the United States by Citizens of another State, or by Citizens or Subjects of any Foreign State.

Article 3 of the U.S. Constitution originally allowed federal jurisdiction in cases of one state citizen against another state citizen or state. This amendment removes federal jurisdiction in this

area. In essence, states may not be sued in federal court by citizens of another state or country.

AMENDMENT 12—ELECTION OF THE PRESIDENT

[Ratified June 15, 1804]

The Electors shall meet in their respective states, and vote by ballot for President and Vice-President, one of whom, at least, shall not be an inhabitant of the same state with themselves; they shall name in their ballots the person voted for as President, and in distinct ballots the person voted for as Vice-President, and they shall make distinct lists of all persons voted for as President, and of all persons voted for as Vice-President, and of the number of votes for each, which lists they shall sign and certify, and transmit sealed to the seat of the government of the United States, directed to the President of the Senate;—The President of the Senate shall, in presence of the Senate and House of Representatives, open all the certificates and the votes shall then be counted;—The person having the greatest number of votes for President, shall be the President, if such number be a majority of the whole number of Electors appointed; and if no person have such majority, then from the persons having the highest numbers not exceeding three on the list of those voted for as President, the House of Representatives shall choose immediately, by ballot, the President. But in choosing the President, the votes shall be taken by states, the representation from each state having one vote; a quorum for this purpose shall consist of a member or members from two-thirds of the states, and a majority of all states shall be necessary to a choice. And if the House of Representatives shall not choose a President whenever the right of choice shall devolve upon them, before the fourth day of March next following, then the Vice-President shall act as President, as in the case of the death or other constitutional disability of the President.[11] The person having the greatest number of votes as Vice-President, shall be the Vice-President, if such a number be a majority of the whole numbers of Electors appointed, and if no person have a majority, then from the two highest numbers on the list, the Senate shall choose the Vice-President, a quorum for the purpose shall consist of two-thirds of the whole number of Senators, and a majority of the whole number shall be necessary to a choice. But no person constitutionally ineligible to the office of President shall be eligible to that of Vice-President of the United States.

This was a necessary amendment to correct a flaw in the Constitution covering operations of the Electoral College. In the election of 1800, both Thomas Jefferson and Aaron Burr, of the same Democratic-Republican Party, received the same number of electoral votes, 73, for president. Article II of the original Constitution specified that each elector would cast two ballots. It did not specify for whom. This amendment clarifies that the electoral vote must be specific for president and vice president. The original Constitution provided that if no candidate received a majority of electoral votes, the House would decide from the candidates with the top five vote totals. This amendment reduces the candidate field to the top three vote totals. If the House delays in this selection past the fourth day of March, the elected vice president will act as president until the House selects the president. The original Constitution provided that the candidate with the second highest number of electoral votes would become vice president.

This amendment, which requires a separate vote tally for vice president, provides for selection by

the U.S. Senate if no vice presidential candidate receives an electoral vote majority.

AMENDMENT 13—PROHIBITION OF SLAVERY

[Ratified December 6, 1865]

Section 1 Neither slavery nor involuntary servitude, except as a punishment for crime whereof the party shall have been duly convicted, shall exist within the United States, or any place subject to their jurisdiction.

Section 2 Congress shall have power to enforce this article by appropriate legislation.

This is the first of the three Civil War amendments. Slavery is prohibited under all circumstances. Involuntary servitude is also prohibited unless it is a punishment for a convicted crime.

AMENDMENT 14—CITIZENSHIP, DUE PROCESS, AND EQUAL PROTECTION OF THE LAWS

[Ratified July 9, 1868]

Section 1 All persons born or naturalized in the United States, and subject to the jurisdiction thereof, are citizens of the United States and of the State wherein they reside. No State shall make or enforce any law which shall abridge the privileges or immunities of citizens of the United States; nor shall any State deprive any person of life, liberty, or property, without due process of law; nor deny to any person within its jurisdiction the equal protection of the laws.

This section defines the meaning of U.S. citizenship and protection of these citizenship rights. It also establishes the Equal Protection Clause that each state must guarantee to its citizens. It extended the provisions of the 5th Amendment of due process and protection of life, liberty, and property and made these applicable to the states.

Section 2 Representatives shall be apportioned among the several States according to their respective numbers, counting the whole number of persons in each State, excluding Indians not taxed. But when the right to vote at any election for the choice of electors for President and Vice President of the United States, Representatives in Congress, the Executive and Judicial officers of a State, or the members of the Legislature thereof, is denied to any of the male inhabitants of such State, being twenty-one[12] years of age, and citizens of the United States, or in any way abridged, except for participation in rebellion, or other crime, the basis of representation therein shall be reduced in the proportion which the number of such male citizens shall bear to the whole number of male citizens twenty-one years of age in such State.

This section changes the Three-Fifths Clause of the original Constitution. Now all male citizens, 21 or older, will be used to calculate representation in the House of Representatives. If a state denies the right to vote to any male 21 or older, the number of denied citizens will be deducted from the overall state total to determine representation.

Section 3 No person shall be a Senator or Representative in Congress, or elector of President and Vice President, or hold any office, civil or military under the United States, or under any State, who, having previously taken an oath, as a member of

---

[11]Changed by the 20th Amendment

[12]Changed by the 26th Amendment

Congress, or as an officer of the United States, or as a member of any State legislature, or as an executive or judicial officer of any State, to support the Constitution of the United States, shall have engaged in insurrection or rebellion against the same, or given aid or comfort to the enemies thereof. But Congress may by a vote of two-thirds of each House, remove such disability.

This section disqualifies from federal office or elector for president or vice president anyone who rebelled or participated in an insurrection against the Constitution. This was specifically directed against citizens of Southern states. Congress by a 2/3 vote could override this provision.

Section 4 The validity of the public debt of the United States, authorized by law, including debts incurred for payment of pensions and bounties for services in suppressing insurrection or rebellion, shall not be questioned. But neither the United States nor any State shall assume or pay any debt or obligation incurred in aid of insurrection or rebellion against the United States or any claim for the loss or emancipation of any slave, but all such debts, obligations and claims shall be held illegal and void.

Section 5 The Congress shall have power to enforce, by appropriate legislation, the provisions of this article.

These sections guarantee payment of Civil War debts incurred by the U.S. government but declare void any debts incurred by the Confederacy.

AMENDMENT 15—THE RIGHT TO VOTE

[Ratified February 3, 1870]

Section 1 The right of citizens of the United States to vote shall not be denied or abridged by the United States or by any State on account of race, color, or previous condition of servitude.
Section 2 The Congress shall have power to enforce this article by appropriate legislation.

This final Civil War amendment guarantees that voting rights cannot be denied by any states on account of race, color, or previous servitude. Unfortunately, it did not mention sex or gender. Accordingly, all male citizens 21 or over were guaranteed the right to vote by this amendment.

AMENDMENT 16—INCOME TAXES

[Ratified February 3, 1913]

The Congress shall have power to lay and collect taxes on incomes, from whatever source derived, without apportionment among the several States, and without regard to any census or enumeration.

Article 1, Section 9, of the original Constitution prohibited Congress from enacting a direct tax (head tax) unless in proportion to a census. Congress in 1894 passed an income tax law, levying a 2 percent tax on incomes over $4,000. In 1895, the U.S. Supreme Court in a split decision (5–4) found that the income tax was a direct tax not apportioned among the states and was thus unconstitutional. Thus, Congress proposed an amendment allowing it to enact an income tax. Once this amendment was ratified, the flow of tax money to Washington increased tremendously.

AMENDMENT 17—DIRECT ELECTION OF SENATORS

[Ratified April 8, 1913]

The Senate of the United States shall be composed of two Senators from each State, elected by the people thereof, for six years and each Senator shall have one vote. The electors in each State shall have the qualifications requisite for electors of the most numerous branch of the State legislatures.

When vacancies happen in the representation of any State in the Senate, the executive authority of such State shall issue writs of election to fill such vacancies: Provided, That the legislature of any State may empower the executive thereof to make temporary appointment until the people fill the vacancies by election as the legislature may direct.

This amendment shall not be so construed as to affect the election or term of any Senator chosen before it becomes valid as part of the Constitution.

Prior to this amendment, U.S. senators were selected by state legislatures. Now U.S. senators would be selected by popular vote in each state. Further, the governor of each state may fill vacancies, subject to state laws.

AMENDMENT 18—PROHIBITION

[Ratified January 16, 1919, Repealed December 5, 1933 by Amendment 21]

Section 1 After one year from the ratification of this article the manufacture, sale, or transportation of intoxicating liquors within, the importation thereof into, or the exportation thereof from the United States and all territory subject to the jurisdiction thereof for beverage purposes is hereby prohibited.

Section 2 The Congress and the several States shall have concurrent power to enforce this article by appropriate legislation.

Section 3 This article shall be inoperative unless it shall have been ratified as an amendment to the Constitution by the legislatures of the several States, as provided in the Constitution, within seven years from the date of the submission hereof to the States by the Congress.[13]

This amendment was largely the work of the Women's Christian Temperance Union and essentially banned the manufacture, sale, or transportation of alcoholic beverages. Unintended consequences of this attempt to legislate morality were the brewing of "bathtub gin" and moonshine liquor, and the involvement of the mob in importing liquor from Canada. This ill-fated social experiment was corrected by the 21st Amendment. This is also the first amendment for which Congress fixed a period for ratification—7 years.

AMENDMENT 19—WOMEN'S SUFFRAGE

[Ratified August 18, 1920]

The right of the citizens of the United States to vote shall not be denied or abridged by the United States or by any State on account of sex.

Congress shall have power to enforce this article by appropriate legislation .

At long last, women achieved voting parity with men.

---

[13]Repealed by the 21st Amendment

AMENDMENT 20—THE LAME DUCK AMENDMENT

[Ratified January 23, 1933]

Section 1 The terms of the President and Vice President shall end at noon on the 20th day of January, and the terms of the Senators and Representatives at noon on the 3d day of January, of the years in which such terms would have ended if this article had not been ratified, and the terms of their successors shall then begin.

Section 2 The Congress shall assemble at least once in every year, and such meeting shall begin at noon on the 3d day of January, unless they shall by law appoint a different day.

Section 3 If, at the time fixed for the beginning of the term of the President, the President elect shall have died, the Vice President elect shall become President. If a President shall not have been chosen before the time fixed for the beginning of his term, or if the President elect shall have failed to qualify, then the Vice President elect shall act as President until a President shall have qualified, and the Congress may by law provide for the case wherein neither a President elect nor a Vice President elect shall have qualified, declaring who shall then act as President, or the manner in which one who is to act shall be selected, and such person shall act accordingly until a President or Vice President shall have qualified.

Section 4 The Congress may by law provide for the case of the death of any of the persons from whom the House of Representatives may choose a President whenever the right of choice shall have devolved upon them, and for the case of the death of any of the persons from whom the Senate may choose a Vice President whenever the right of choice shall have devolved upon them.

Section 5 Sections 1 and 2 shall take effect on the 15th day of October following the ratification of this article.

Section 6 This article shall be inoperative unless it shall have been ratified as an amendment to the Constitution by the legislatures of three-fourths of the several States within seven years from the date of its submission.

Called the Lame Duck amendment, this amendment fixes the dates for the end of presidential and legislative terms. A new president is elected in November, but the current president remains in office until January 20 of the following year. Thus, the term "lame duck." Legislative terms begin earlier, on January 3.

AMENDMENT 21—REPEAL OF PROHIBITION

[Ratified December 5, 1933]

Section 1 The eighteenth article of amendment to the Constitution of the United States is hereby repealed.

Section 2 The transportation or importation into any State, Territory, or possession of the United States for delivery or use therein of intoxicating liquors, in violation of the laws thereof, is hereby prohibited.

Section 3 This article shall be inoperative unless it shall have been ratified as an amendment to the Constitution by conventions in the several States, as provided in the Constitution, within seven years from the date of the submission hereof to the States by the Congress.

This unusual amendment nullified the 18th Amendment. It ended federal Prohibition; now only state laws regulate liquors.

AMENDMENT 22—NUMBER OF PRESIDENTIAL TERMS

[Ratified February 27, 1951]

Section 1 No person shall be elected to the office of the President more than twice, and no person who has held the office of Presi-

dent, or acted as President, for more than two years of a term to which some other person was elected President shall be elected to the office of the President more than once. But this article shall not apply to any person holding the office of President when this article was proposed by the Congress, and shall not prevent any person who may be holding the office of President, or acting as President, during the term within which this article becomes operative from holding the office of President or acting as President during the remainder of such term.

Section 2 This article shall be inoperative unless it shall have been ratified as an amendment to the Constitution by the legislatures of three-fourths of the several states within seven years from the date of its submission to the states by the Congress.

This amendment could be called the Franklin D. Roosevelt amendment. It was FDR who broke the previous unwritten custom of no more than two-term presidents. Democrat Roosevelt won an unprecedented four terms as president. When the Republicans took control of the Congress in 1948, they pushed through the 22nd Amendment, limiting the U.S. president to a lifetime of two full four-year terms of office.

AMENDMENT 23—PRESIDENTIAL ELECTORS FOR THE DISTRICT OF COLUMBIA

[Ratified March 29, 1961]

Section 1 The District constituting the seat of government of the United States shall appoint in such manner as the Congress may direct:

A number of electors of President and Vice President equal to the whole number of Senators and Representatives in Congress to which the District would be entitled if it were a state, but in no event more than the least populous state, they shall be in addition to those appointed by the states, but they shall be considered for the purposes of the election of President and Vice President, to be electors appointed by a state, and they shall meet in the District and perform such duties as provided by the twelfth article of amendment.

Section 2 The Congress shall have power to enforce this article by appropriate legislation.

This amendment gave electoral votes to the citizens of Washington, D.C., which is not a state and thus not included in the original scheme of state electoral votes. Currently, Washington, D.C., has 3 electoral votes, bringing the total of presidential electoral votes to 538. Puerto Ricans and the residents of Guam, U.S. Virgin Islands, and the Northern Marianas are citizens of the U.S. but have no electoral votes.

AMENDMENT 24—THE ANTI-POLL TAX AMENDMENT

[Ratified January 23, 1964]

Section 1 The right of citizens of the United States to vote in any primary or other election for President or Vice President, for electors for President or Vice President or for Senator or Representative in Congress, shall not be denied or abridged by the United States or any state by reason of failure to pay any poll tax or other tax.

Section 2 The Congress shall have power to enforce this article by appropriate legislation.

The poll tax was a procedure used mostly in Southern states to discourage poor white and

black voters from registering to vote. Essentially, one would have to pay a tax to register to vote. The tax was usually not much. But for a poor white or black voter, this might not be disposable income. As part of the assault against disenfranchisement of voters, the poll tax was abolished. Literacy tests, another device to disqualify voters, were abolished by the Voting Rights Act of 1965.

AMENDMENT 25—PRESIDENTIAL DISABILITY, VICE PRESIDENTIAL VACANCIES

[Ratified February 10, 1967]

Section 1 In case of the removal of the President from office or his death or resignation, the Vice President shall become President.

Section 2 Whenever there is a vacancy in the office of the Vice President, the President shall nominate a Vice President who shall take the office upon confirmation by a majority vote of both Houses of Congress.

Section 3 Whenever the President transmits to the President pro tempore of the Senate and the Speaker of the House of Representatives his written declaration that he is unable to discharge the powers and duties of his office, and until he transmits to them a written declaration to the contrary, such powers and duties shall be discharged by the Vice President as Acting President.

Section 4 Whenever the Vice President and a majority of either the principal officers of the executive departments or of such other body as Congress may by law provide, transmit to the President pro tempore of the Senate and the Speaker of the House of Representatives their written declaration that the President is unable to discharge the powers and duties of his office, the Vice President shall immediately assume the powers and duties of the office as Acting President.

Thereafter, when the President transmits to the President pro tempore of the Senate and the Speaker of the House of Representatives his written declaration that no inability exists, he shall resume the powers and duties of his office unless the Vice President and a majority of either the principal officers of the executive departments, or of such other body as Congress may by law provide, transmit within four days to the President pro tempore of the Senate and the Speaker of the House of Representatives their written declaration that the President is unable to discharge the powers and duties of his office. Thereupon Congress shall decide the issue, assembling within forty-eight hours for that purpose if not in session. If the Congress, within twenty-one days after receipt of the latter written declaration, or, if Congress is not in session, within twenty-one days after Congress is required to assemble, determines by two-thirds vote of both Houses that the President is unable to discharge the powers and duties of his office, the Vice President shall continue to discharge the same as Acting President; otherwise the President shall resume the powers and duties of his office.

During the administration of President Woodrow Wilson, his final year in office, in 1919, was marked by serious illness. It is rumored that his wife acted as president. There was no constitutional provision to cover an incapacitating illness of a president. So this amendment provides a procedure for this eventuality. The president can inform congressional leaders of his incapacitation and the vice president takes over. When he recovers, the president can so inform congressional leaders and he resumes office.

But the amendment also recognizes that the president may not be able or wish to indicate this debilitation; so the vice president and a majority of

cabinet members can inform congressional leaders and the vice president takes over. When the president informs congressional leadership that he is back in form, he resumes the presidency unless the vice president and a majority of the cabinet disagree. Then Congress must decide. The likelihood that this procedure will ever be used is very small.

The most immediate importance of this amendment concerns the office of vice president. The original Constitution did not address the issue of a vacancy in this office. So the 25th Amendment established the procedure, just in time! This amendment was ratified in 1967. In 1973, the sitting vice president, Spiro Agnew, resigned his office. Under the provisions of this amendment, President Nixon nominated Gerald Ford as vice president. A former member of the House, the Congress quickly approved him. But a year later, President Nixon also resigned. Now Vice President Ford became President Ford, and he in turn appointed Nelson Rockefeller as the new vice president. For the first time in our history, we had both a president and vice president, neither of whom was elected by the Electoral College.

AMENDMENT 26—EIGHTEEN-YEAR-OLD VOTE

[Ratified July 1, 1971]

Section 1 The right of citizens of the United States, who are 18 years of age or older, to vote, shall not be denied or abridged by the United States or by any state on account of age.

Section 2 The Congress shall have power to enforce this article by appropriate legislation.

During the Vietnam War, 18-year-olds were being drafted and sent out to possibly die in the service of their country. Yet they did not even have the right to vote. This incongruity led to the 26th Amendment, which lowered the legal voting age from 21 to 18.

AMENDMENT 27—CONGRESSIONAL SALARIES

[Ratified May 7, 1992]

No law varying the compensation for the services of the Senators and Representatives shall take effect until an election of Representatives shall be intervened.

This is a "sleeper" amendment that was part of 12 amendments originally submitted by the first Congress to the states for ratification. The states only ratified 10 of the 12, which collectively became known as the Bill of Rights. But since Congress did not set a time limit for ratification, the other two amendments remained on the table. Much to the shock of the body politic, in 1992, 3/4 of the states ratified original amendment 12 of 12. This reflected the disgust of seeing Congress continuing to increase its salary and benefits. The amendment delays any increase of compensation for at least one election cycle.*

---

*Annotations by James Corey

4 FEDERALISM
Dividing Governmental Power

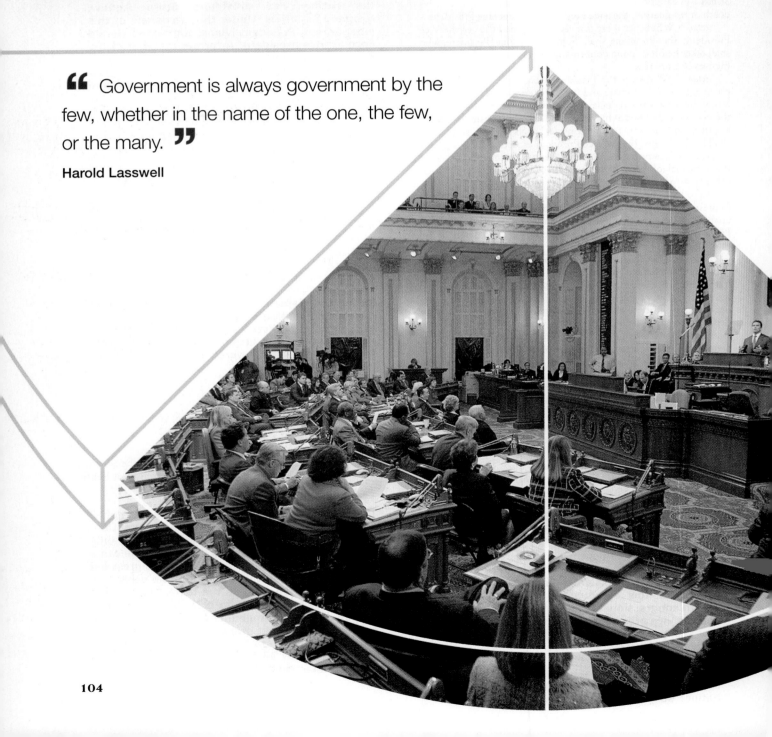

" Government is always government by the few, whether in the name of the one, the few, or the many. **"**

Harold Lasswell

Chapter *Outline*

✓ Think About Politics

1. Which level of government deals best with the problems it faces?
   FEDERAL ◯ STATE ◯ LOCAL ◯

2. In which level of government do you have the most confidence?
   FEDERAL ◯ STATE ◯ LOCAL ◯

3. Should the national government be able to prosecute a high school student for bringing a gun to school?
   YES ◯ NO ◯

4. Should welfare benefits be the same in all states?
   YES ◯ NO ◯

5. Should each state determine its own minimum age for drinking alcohol?
   YES ◯ NO ◯

6. Should each state determine its own maximum highway speed limit?
   YES ◯ NO ◯

7. When the federal government requires states to provide safe drinking water, clean air, or access for the handicapped, should it provide funds to carry out these mandates?
   YES ◯ NO ◯

8. Should violence against women be a federal crime?
   YES ◯ NO ◯

What should be the relationship between the national government and the states? Questions like these lie at the heart of the issue of who gets what, when, and how. They affect employment, transportation, health, education, the very air we breathe. And when there has been disagreement, the nation has been plunged into conflict at best and the bloodiest war in its history at worst.

COMPARATIVE

Comparing Federal and Unitary Systems

Indestructible Union, Indestructible States

In December 1860 South Carolina seceded from the Union and in April 1861 authorized its state militia to expel U.S. troops from Fort Sumter in Charleston harbor. Although there is no provision in the Constitution for states leaving the Union, eleven Southern states—South Carolina, Mississippi, Florida, Alabama, Georgia, Louisiana, Texas, Virginia, Arkansas, Tennessee, and North Carolina, in that order—argued that the Union was a voluntary association and they were entitled to withdraw.[1] President Abraham Lincoln declared these states to be in armed rebellion and sent federal troops to crush the "rebels." The result was the nation's bloodiest war: more than 250,000 battle deaths and another 250,000 deaths from disease and privation, out of a total population of less than 30 million.

Following the Civil War, Chief Justice Salmon P. Chase confirmed what had been decided on the battlefield. "The Constitution in all its provisions looks to an indestructible union, composed of indestructible states."[2]

Federalism divides power between two separate authorities—the nation and the states—each of which enforces its own laws directly on its citizens. Both the nation and the states pass laws, impose taxes, spend money, and maintain their own courts. Neither the nation nor the states can dissolve the Union or amend the Constitution without the consent of the other. The Constitution itself is the only legal source of authority for both the states and the nation, the states do not get their power from the national government, and the national government does not get its power from the states. Both national and state governments derive their power directly from the people.

American federalism differs from a **unitary system** of government, in which formal authority rests with the national government, and whatever powers are exercised by states, provinces, or subdivisions are given to those governments by the national government. Most of the world's governments—including France and Britain—are unitary. Federalism also differs from a **confederation** of states, in which the national government relies on the states for its authority, not the people (see Figure 4.1). Under the Articles of Confederation of 1781, the United States was a confederation. The national government could not even levy taxes; it had to ask the states for revenue. Like the United States, a number of other countries were confederations before establishing federal systems, and today new types of confederations with limited functions are being formed (see *Compared to What?*: "The European Union").

Figure *4.1*

Federal, Confederation, and Unitary Systems of Government

In theory, power in a federal system is divided between a national government and the states; power in a confederation remains with the member states; power in a unitary system is concentrated in the national government. The United States, the European Union, and Great Britain resemble federal, confederation, and unitary systems; but no government completely conforms to these designs.

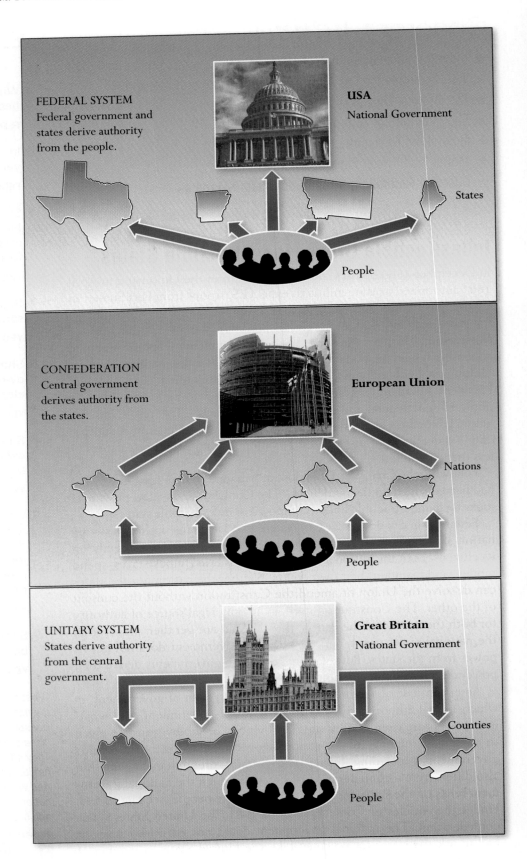

FEDERAL SYSTEM
Federal government and states derive authority from the people.

USA
National Government

States

People

CONFEDERATION
Central government derives authority from the states.

European Union

Nations

People

UNITARY SYSTEM
States derive authority from the central government.

Great Britain
National Government

Counties

People

Table *4.1* How Many American Governments?	
Over 89,000 governments function in the United States. The U.S. Constitution recognizes only the national government and the states. Local governments are created and empowered by state laws and constitutions.	
U.S. government	1
States	50
Counties	3,033
Municipalities	19,492
Townships	16,519
Special districts	37,381
School districts	13,051
All governments	*89,527*

Source: Census of Governments, 2007.

People in the United States often think of the *federal government* when the word *government* comes up. In fact, today there are more than 89,000 American governments. These state and local governments are important in American life, for they provide such essential day-to-day services as schools, water, and police and fire departments (see Table 4.1). However, the U.S. Constitution, the supreme Law of the Land, recognizes the existence of only the national government and the states. Local governments have no guarantees of power—or even existence—under the U.S. Constitution. Whatever powers they have are given to them by their state governments. States can create or abolish local governments, grant or withhold their powers, or change their boundaries without their consent. Some local governments have powers guaranteed in *state* constitutions, and some are even given **home rule**—the power to pass laws affecting local affairs, so long as those laws do not conflict with state or federal laws. About 60,000 of these 89,000 governments have the power to levy taxes to support activities authorized by state law.

In short, the American federal system is large and complex, with three levels of government—national, state, and local—sharing power. Indeed, the numbers and complexity of governments in the United States make **intergovernmental relations**—all of the interactions among these governments and their officials—a major concern of political scientists and policy makers.

Why Federalism? The Argument for a "Compound Republic"

The nation's Founders believed that "republican principles" would help make government responsible to the people, but they also argued that "auxiliary precautions" were necessary to protect the liberties of minorities and individuals. They believed that majority rule in a democratic government made it particularly important to devise ways to protect minorities and individuals from "unjust" and "interested" *majorities*. They believed that federalism would better protect liberty, disperse power, and manage "faction" (conflict).

Protecting Liberty Constitutional guarantees of individual liberty do not enforce themselves. The Founders argued that to guarantee liberty, government should be structured to encourage "opposite and rival" centers of power *within* and *among* governments. So they settled on both *federalism*—dividing powers between the national and state governments—and *separation of powers*—the dispersal of power among branches within the national government.

★ **federalism**
A constitutional arrangement whereby power is divided between national and subnational governments, each of which enforces its own laws directly on its citizens and neither of which can alter the arrangement without the consent of the other.

★ **unitary system**
Constitutional arrangement whereby authority rests with the national government; subnational governments have only those powers given to them by the national government.

★ **confederation**
Constitutional arrangement whereby the national government is created by and relies on subnational governments for its authority.

★ **home rule**
Power of local government to pass laws affecting local affairs, so long as those laws do not conflict with state or federal laws.

★ **intergovernmental relations**
Network of political, financial, and administrative relationships between units of the federal government and those of state and local governments.

Think Again

Which level of government deals best with the problems it faces?

Compared to *What?*

The European Union

The European Union (EU) incorporates features of both federalism and confederation. The EU now includes twenty-seven member nations and embraces more than 455 million people. It grew slowly from a European Economic Community established in 1957 (designed to reduce and eventually abolish all tariffs among member nations), through a European Community established in 1965 (designed to create a single market free of all barriers to the movement of goods, services, capital, and labor), to its much more unified European Union established in 1991.

European Parliament

Deputies of the European Parliament are directly elected every five years by the EU's 455 million citizens. The major political parties operating in each of the member nations nominate candidates. The Parliament oversees the EU budget and passes on proposals to the Council of Ministers and the Commission. The Parliament also passes on new applicants to the EU.

Distribution of Seats in the European Parliament

Austria	18	Latvia	9
Belgium	24	Lithuania	13
Bulgaria	18	Luxembourg	6
Cyprus	6	Malta	5
Czech Republic	24	Netherlands	27
Denmark	14	Poland	54
Estonia	6	Portugal	24
Finland	14	Romania	35
France	78	Slovakia	14
Germany	99	Slovenia	7
Greece	24	Spain	54
Hungary	24	Sweden	19
Ireland	13	United Kingdom	78
Italy	78		

Council of the EU

The Council is the EU's principal decision-making body. It is composed of the foreign ministers of the member nations. Each country takes the presidency for six months; the Council votes by majority, although each country's vote is weighted differently.

The Commission

The Commission of the EU supervises the implementation of EU treaties, implements EU policies, and manages EU funds. It is composed of twenty commissioners appointed by member governments. The five largest countries—France, Germany, Italy, Spain, and the United Kingdom—appoint two commissioners each; the remaining countries appoint one commissioner each.

The Court of Justice

A Court of Justice hears complaints about member governments' treaty violations and interprets EU treaties and legislation. Its fifteen justices are appointed by the member governments and serve six-year terms.

The "Euro"

Perhaps the most far-reaching accomplishment of the EU was the introduction of the "euro"—a single European currency for use in all member states. The euro was first introduced January 1, 1999, and officially replaced old national currencies—such as francs, marks, pesetas, and lira—on January 1, 2002. However, the United Kingdom, Sweden, and Denmark have refused to substitute the euro for their own currency.

The Future of the Union

The future of the EU remains under discussion. A lengthy EU Constitution was to be submitted to the voters in each nation. Ten nations approved it, but in 2005 voters in France and the Netherlands rejected it. Inasmuch as all twenty-five nations must approve it in order for it to go into effect, its future is in serious doubt.

In the compound republic of America, the power surrendered by the people is first divided between two distinct governments, and then the portion allotted to each is subdivided among distinct and separate departments. Hence a double security arises to the rights of the people. The different governments will control each other, at the same time that each will be controlled by itself.[3]

Thus the Founders deliberately tried to create competition within and among governmental units as a means of protecting liberty. Rather than rely on the "better motives" of leaders, the Founders sought to construct a system in which governments and government officials would be constrained by competition with other governments and other government officials: "Ambition must be made to counteract ambition."[4]

At present the EU is more of an economic alliance than a sovereign political state. Voters in member nations may not be as yet willing to enact a common Bill of Rights or depend upon a central government (in Brussels) for the protection of their individual liberties.

How much power will be allocated to the central EU government relative to the powers of member nations? Note that these and similar questions were the same as many of those discussed in the American Constitutional Convention of 1787 (see Chapter 3).

This map, produced by the EU, uses the languages of the nations portrayed. Test yourself by translating these names into English, for example Osterreich = Austria.

Source: Reprinted from www.europa.eu.int/abc/maps/index_en.htm Copyright © European Communities, 1995–2006.

Dispersing Power   Federalism distributes power widely among different sets of leaders, national as well as state and local officeholders. The Founders believed that multiple leadership groups offered more protection against tyranny than a single set of all-powerful leaders. State and local government offices also provide a political base for the opposition party when it has lost a national election. In this way, state and local governments contribute to party competition in the United States by helping to tide over the losing party after electoral defeat at the national level so that it can remain strong enough to challenge incumbents at the next election. And finally, state and local governments often provide a training ground for national political leaders. National leaders can be drawn from a pool of leaders experienced in state and local government.

Politics Up Close   Federalism Is the Enemy of Uniformity

Should taxes and services be uniform throughout the United States? Or should federalism allow variations among the states in tax burdens as well as provided?

Federalism allows citizens in each state to decide levels of public services (schools, transportation, police and fire protection, and so forth, and other state and local functions), as well as how much they pay in state and local taxes. If some voters want more public services and are willing to pay higher taxes for them, and other voters want fewer public services and enjoy lower taxes, then federalism allows for a better match between citizen preferences and public policy. Of course, the result is a lack of uniformity across the states.

Consider, for example, differences in per capita state and local taxes paid by residents of different states.

Ten High-Tax States		Ten Low-Tax States	
New York	$5,258	Utah	$2,734
Connecticut	4,929	Idaho	2,729
New Jersey	4,560	Oklahoma	2,678
Wyoming	4,441	South Carolina	2,664
Massachusetts	4,198	Montana	2,625
Maryland	4,021	South Dakota	2,617
Rhode Island	3,895	Tennessee	2,540
Minnesota	3,813	Arkansas	2,539
Maine	3,792	Mississippi	2,451
California	3,736	Alabama	2,332

States Without Income Taxes

Alaska	New Hampshire[a]	Texas
Florida	South Dakota	Washington
Nevada	Tennessee[a]	Wyoming

States Taxing Individual Income (rate ranges in parentheses)

Alabama (2.0–5.0)	Kentucky (2.0–6.0)	North Carolina (6.0–8.25)
Arizona (2.8–5.0)	Louisiana (2.0–6.0)	North Dakota (2.1–15.6)
Arkansas (1.0–7.0)	Maine (2.0–8.5)	Ohio (0.7–7.5)
California (1.0–9.3)	Maryland (2.0–4.8)	Oklahoma (0.5–6.75)
Colorado (4.6)	Massachusetts (5)	Oregon (5.0–9.0)
Connecticut (3.0–5)	Michigan (4)	Pennsylvania (2.8)
Delaware (2.2–6.0)	Minnesota (5.3–7.8)	Rhode Island (26% federal)[b]
Georgia (1.0–6.0)	Mississippi (3.0–5.0)	South Carolina (2.5–7.0)
Hawaii (1.4–8.25)	Missouri (1.5–6.0)	Utah (2.3–7.0)
Idaho (1.6–7.8)	Montana (2.0–11.0)	Vermont (3.6–9.5)
Illinois (3.0)	Nebraska (2.5–6.8)	Virginia (2.0–5.75)
Indiana (3.4)	New Jersey (1.4–6.4)	West Virginia (3.0–6.5)
Iowa (0.4–9.0)	New Mexico (1.7–6.8)	Wisconsin (4.6–6.8)
Kansas (3.5–6.5)	New York (4.0–7.7)	

[a]State income tax is limited to dividends and interest only, and excludes wage income.
[b]State income taxes determined as a percentage of federal income tax liability.
Source: Data from Council of State Governments, *Book of the States,* 2008 (Lexington, KY: Council of State Governments, 2008).

Increasing Participation   Federalism allows more people to participate in the political system. With more than 87,000 governments in the United States—state, county, municipality, township, special district, and school district—nearly a million people hold some kind of public office.

Improving Efficiency   Federalism also makes government more manageable and efficient. Imagine the bureaucracy, red tape, and confusion if every governmental activity—police, schools, roads, fire fighting, garbage collection, sewage disposal, and so forth—in every local community in the nation were controlled by a centralized administration in Washington. Government can become arbitrary when a bureaucracy far from the scene directs local officials. Thus decentralization often softens the rigidity of law.

Ensuring Policy Responsiveness   Federalism encourages policy responsiveness. The existence of multiple governments offering different packages of benefits and costs allows a better match between citizen preferences and public policy. Americans are very mobile. People and businesses can "vote with their feet" by relocating to those states and communities that most closely conform to their own policy preferences. This mobility not only facilitates a better match between citizen preferences and public policy but also encourages competition between states and communities to offer improved services at lower costs.[5]

Encouraging Policy Innovation   The Founders hoped that federalism would encourage policy experimentation and innovation. Today federalism may seem like a "conservative" idea, but it was once the instrument of liberal reformers. Federal programs as diverse as the income tax, unemployment compensation, Social Security, wage and hour legislation, bank deposit insurance, and food stamps were all state programs before becoming national undertakings. Today much of the current "liberal" policy agenda—mandatory health insurance for workers, child-care programs, notification of plant closings, government support of industrial research and development—has been embraced by various states. The phrase **laboratories of democracy** is generally attributed to the great progressive jurist Supreme Court Justice Louis D. Brandeis, who used it in defense of state experimentation with new solutions to social and economic problems.[6]

★ **laboratories of democracy**
A reference to the ability of states to experiment and innovate in public policy.

Some Important Reservations   Despite the strengths of federalism, it has its problems. First of all, federalism can obstruct action on national issues. Although decentralization may reduce conflict at the national level, it may do so at the price of "sweeping under the rug" very serious national injustices (see *A Conflicting View*: "The Dark Side of Federalism" on page 115). Federalism also permits local leaders and citizens to frustrate national policy, to sacrifice national interest to local interests. Decentralized government provides an opportunity for local NIMBYs (people who subscribe to the motto "Not in My Back Yard") to obstruct airports, highways, waste disposal plants, public housing, drug rehabilitation centers, and many other projects that would be in the national interest.

Think
Again

In which level of government do you have the most confidence?

Minnesota Governor Tim Pawlenty, 2007–2008 national chairman of the National Governors Association, speaks at the annual meeting of the National Governors Association, on Monday, July 23, 2007, in Acme, Michigan.

Controversy

Katrina: Federalism Fails in a Crisis

Hurricane Katrina was the nation's largest natural disaster. Perhaps it was inevitable that government—federal, state, and local—would be unable to respond to such a crisis. But the lack of competence among city, state, and federal officials, the bureaucratic inertia, the disorganized relief that led directly to the deaths of many, all combined to make Katrina "the worst man-made relief disaster ever."[a]

Katrina was a powerful Category Four hurricane when it hit east of New Orleans in 2005, practically leveling the city of Biloxi, Mississippi. The first day New Orleans seemed to be spared, but the next day the levees began to crumble—levees that had protected the below-sea-level "Big Easy" for over a century. Soon water submerged 80 percent of the city and 100,000 people were stranded with little or no food and water and no electricity. For three days emergency efforts floundered badly. Survivors gathered on rooftops and highway flyovers. The country watched on television as babies, old people, the sick, and diabetic died on live television. Reporters got themselves to the scenes of tragedies, but government agents failed to do so. Soon armed looters appeared on the streets.

The first rescuers, including private citizens with small boats, dropped people off on highway overpasses, with 100-degree heat and no water or food. Other makeshift rescue efforts took over 25,000 survivors to the leaking Superdome, where there were no light, no air, and no working toilets. Stories of individual bravery as well as bureaucratic bungling were carried on national television.

No one was in charge. Local, state, and federal leaders failed to lead, bureaucrats battled over turf, and government was paralyzed. The mayor urged residents to evacuate, but tens of thousands, especially the poor, had no cars or other means of transportation. The mayor hesitated to order a mandatory evacuation; when he finally did, hundreds of city buses were underwater. Some nursing homes were overlooked in evacuation efforts and some elderly died unnecessarily.

Meanwhile, the mayor, FEMA officials, the governor, and even the president were giving press conferences boasting of all the aid that was on its way. But the governor refused to request federal troops or to place the Louisiana National Guard under federal authority. President Bush could have done so on his own, but he hesitated, waiting for the governor's request. The governor, a Democrat, feared that Republican federal officials would claim political credit for rescuing the city. She instructed National Guardsmen

Federal, state, and local government agencies performed poorly in response to Hurricane Katrina's devastation of New Orleans and the Mississippi Gulf Coast. Only the U.S. Coast Guard, shown here rescuing survivors, was given high marks for its work during the disaster.

to keep people out of the city; in many instances they interpreted that order to keep out rescue workers from other states. Only the U.S. Coast Guard and military helicopters seemed to perform well—indeed heroically, in many cases rescuing survivors from rooftops.

But FEMA's performance was even worse. FEMA's authority is only to "coordinate" relief efforts in a crisis. FEMA had recently been transformed from an independent agency to a bureau in the Department of Homeland Security. Many newer appointees, including its director, had little or no disaster experience. For three days FEMA sat and waited to be called by the governor. Hundreds of FEMA house trailers sat outside the city unused, as did truckloads of food and water. As flames consumed buildings in New Orleans, FEMA held back 600 firefighters in order to lecture them on equal opportunity, sexual harassment, and customer service.[b] At the airport, frustrated medics waited in empty helicopters to evacuate patients while FEMA delayed over paperwork. When outside doctors and nurses tried to help, FEMA rejected their assistance because they "weren't certified members of a National Disaster Medical Team." "FEMA kept stonewalling us with paperwork. Meanwhile, every 30 or 40 minutes someone was dying."[c] About 150 trucks full of ice purchased for hurricane victims sat uselessly in a parking lot in Maine.[d] The FEMA emergency number was out of service.

[a]*U.S. News and World Report,* September 19, 2005, p. 30.

[b]*Time,* September 19, 2005, p. 18.

[c]*New York Times,* September 18, 2005.

[d]*Ft. Lauderdale Sun Sentinel,* October 7, 2005, p. 1.

The Original Design of Federalism

The U.S. Constitution *originally* defined American federalism in terms of (1) the powers expressly delegated to the national government plus the powers implied by those that are specifically granted, (2) the concurrent powers exercised by both states and the national government, (3) the powers reserved to the states, (4) the powers denied by the Constitution to both the national government and the states, and (5) the constitutional provisions giving the states a role in the composition of the national government (see Figure 4.2).

Delegated Powers   The U.S. Constitution lists seventeen specific grants of power to Congress, in Article I, Section 8. These are usually referred to as the **delegated, or enumerated, powers**. They include authority over war and foreign affairs, authority over the economy ("interstate commerce"), control over the money supply, and the power to tax and spend "to pay the debts and provide for the common defence and general welfare." After these specific grants of power comes the power "to make all laws which shall be necessary and proper for carrying into execution the foregoing powers, and all other powers vested by this Constitution in the government of the United States or in any department or officer thereof." This statement is generally known as the **Necessary and Proper Clause**, and it is the principal source of the national government's **implied powers**—powers not specifically listed in the Constitution but inferred from those that are.

National Supremacy   The delegated and implied powers, when coupled with the assertion of "national supremacy" (in Article VI), ensure a powerful national government. The **National Supremacy Clause** is very specific in asserting the supremacy of federal laws over state and local laws.

> This Constitution, and the laws of the United States which shall be made in pursuance thereof, and all treaties made, or which shall be made, under the authority of the United States, shall be the supreme law of the land, and the Judges in every state shall be bound thereby, any thing in the constitution or laws of any state to the contrary notwithstanding.

Concurrent and Reserved Powers   Despite broad grants of power to the national government, the states retain considerable governing power. **Concurrent powers** are those recognized in the Constitution as belonging to *both* the national and state governments, including the power to tax and spend, make and enforce laws, and establish courts of justice. The Tenth Amendment reassured the states that "the powers not delegated to the United States . . . are reserved to the States respectively, or to the people." Through these **reserved powers**, the states generally retain control over property and contract law, criminal law, marriage and divorce, and the provision of education, highways, and social welfare activities. The states control the organization and powers of their own local governments. Finally, the states, like the federal government, retain the power to tax and spend for the general welfare.

Powers Denied to the States   The Constitution denies the states some powers in order to safeguard national unity. States are specifically denied the power to coin money, enter into treaties with foreign nations, interfere with the "obligation of contracts," levy taxes on imports or exports, or engage in war.

Powers Denied to the Nation and the States   The Constitution denies some powers to both national and state government—namely, the powers to abridge

★ **delegated, or enumerated, powers**
Powers specifically mentioned in the Constitution as belonging to the national government.

★ **Necessary and Proper Clause**
Clause in Article I, Section 8, of the U.S. Constitution granting Congress the power to enact all laws that are "necessary and proper" for carrying out those responsibilities specifically delegated to it. Also referred to as the Implied Powers Clause.

★ **implied powers**
Powers not mentioned specifically in the Constitution as belonging to Congress but inferred as necessary and proper for carrying out the enumerated powers.

★ **National Supremacy Clause**
Clause in Article VI of the U.S. Constitution declaring the constitution and laws of the national government "the supreme law of the land" superior to the constitutions and laws of the states.

★ **concurrent powers**
Powers exercised by both the national government and state governments in the American federal system.

★ **reserved powers**
Powers not granted to the national government or specifically denied to the states in the Constitution that are recognized by the 10th Amendment as belonging to the state governments. This guarantee, known as the Reserved Powers Clause, embodies the principle of American federalism.

POWERS GRANTED BY THE CONSTITUTION

NATIONAL GOVERNMENT
Delegated Powers

Military Affairs and Defense
- Provide for the common defense (I-8).
- Declare war (I-8).
- Raise and support armies (I-8).
- Provide and maintain a navy (I-8).
- Define and punish piracies (I-8).
- Define and punish offenses against the law of nations (I-8).
- Provide for calling forth the militia to execute laws, suppress insurrections, and repel invasions (I-8).
- Provide for organizing, arming, and disciplining the militia (I-8).
- Declare the punishment of treason (III-3).

Economic Affairs
- Regulate commerce with foreign nations, among the several states, and with Indian tribes (I-8).
- Establish uniform laws on bankruptcy (I-8).
- Coin money and regulate its value (I-8).
- Fix standards of weights and measures (I-8).
- Provide for patents and copyrights (I-8).
- Establish post offices and post roads (I-8).

Governmental Organization
- Constitute tribunals inferior to the Supreme Court (I-8, III-1).
- Exercise exclusive legislative power over the seat of government and over certain military installations (I-8).
- Admit new states (IV-3).
- Dispose of and regulate territory or property of the United States (IV-3).

"Implied" Powers
- Make laws necessary and proper for carrying the expressed powers into execution (I-8).

NATIONAL AND STATE GOVERNMENTS
Concurrent Powers

- Levy taxes (I-8).
- Borrow money (I-8).
- Contract and pay debts (I-8).
- Charter banks and corporations (I-8).
- Make and enforce laws (I-8).
- Establish courts (I-8).
- Provide for the general welfare (I-8).

STATE GOVERNMENTS
Reserved to the States

- Regulate intrastate commerce.
- Conduct elections.
- Provide for public health, safety, and morals.
- Establish local government.
- Maintain the militia (National Guard).
- Ratify amendments to the federal Constitution (V).
- Determine voter qualifications (I-2).

"Reserved" Powers

- Powers not delegated to national government nor denied to the States by the Constitution (X).

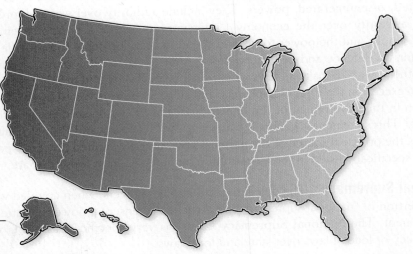

POWERS DENIED BY THE CONSTITUTION

NATIONAL GOVERNMENT

- Give preference to the ports of any state (I-9).
- Impose a tax or duty on articles exported from any state (I-9).
- Directly tax except by apportionment among the states on a population basis (I-9), now superseded as to income tax (Amendment XVI).
- Draw money from the Treasury except by appropriation (I-9).

NATIONAL AND STATE GOVERNMENTS

- Grant titles of nobility (I-9).
- Limit the suspension of habeas corpus (I-9).
- Issue bills of attainder (I-10).
- Make ex post facto laws (I-10).
- Establish a religion or prohibit the free exercise of religion (Amendment I).
- Abridge freedom of speech, press, assembly, or right of petition (Amendment I).
- Deny the right to bear arms (Amendment II).
- Quarter soldiers in private homes (Amendment III).
- Conduct unreasonable searches or seizures. (Amendment IV).
- Deny guarantees of fair trials (Amendment V, Amendment VI, and Amendment VII).
- Impose excessive bail or unusual punishments (Amendment VII).
- Take life, liberty, or property without due process (Amendment V).
- Permit slavery (Amendment XIII).
- Deny life, liberty, or property without due process of law (Amendment XIV).
- Deny voting because of race, color, previous servitude (Amendment XV), sex (Amendment XIX), or age if 18 or over (Amendment XXVI).
- Deny voting because of nonpayment of any tax (Amendment XXIV).

STATE GOVERNMENTS

Economic Affairs
- Use legal tender other than gold or silver coin (I-10).
- Issue separate state coinage (I-10).
- Impair the obligation of contracts (I-10).
- Emit bills of credit (I-10).
- Levy import or export duties, except reasonable inspection fees, without the consent of Congress (I-10).
- Abridge the privileges and immunities of national citizenship (Amendment XIV)
- Make any law that violates federal law (Amendment VI).
- Pay for rebellion against the United States or for emancipated slaves (Amendment XIV).

Foreign Affairs
- Enter into treaties, alliances, or confederations (I-10).
- Make compact with a foreign state, except by congressional consent (I-10).

Military Affairs
- Issue letters of marque and reprisal (I-10).
- Maintain standing military forces in peace without congressional consent (I-10).
- Engage in war, without congressional consent, except in imminent danger or when invaded (I-10).

Figure **4.2** Who Gets What?: The Original Constitutional Distribution of Powers

Under the Constitution of 1787, certain powers were delegated to the national government, other powers were shared by the national and state governments, and still other powers were reserved for state governments alone. Similarly, certain powers were denied by the Constitution to the national government, other powers were denied to both the national and state governments, and still other powers were denied only to state governments. Later amendments especially protected individual liberties.

A Conflicting *View*

The Dark Side of Federalism

Segregationists once regularly used the argument of "states' rights" to deny equal protection of the law to African Americans. Indeed, *states' rights* became a code word for opposition to federal civil rights laws. In 1963 Governor George Wallace invoked the states' rights argument when he stood in a doorway at the University of Alabama to prevent the execution of a federal court order that the university admit two African American students and thus integrate. Federal marshals were on hand to enforce the order, and Wallace only temporarily delayed them. Shortly after his dramatic stand in front of the television cameras, he retreated to his office. Later in his career, Wallace sought African American votes, declaring, "I was wrong. Those days are over."

Federalism in America remains tainted by its historical association with slavery, segregation, and discrimination. In the Virginia and Kentucky Resolutions of 1798, Thomas Jefferson and James Madison asserted the doctrine of "nullification," claiming that states could nullify unconstitutional laws of Congress. Although the original intent of this doctrine was to counter congressional attacks on a free press under the Alien and Sedition Acts of 1798, it was later revived to defend slavery. John C. Calhoun of South Carolina argued forcefully in the years before the Civil War that slavery was an issue for the states to decide and the Constitution gave Congress no power to interfere with slavery in the southern states or in the new western territories.

In the years immediately following the Civil War, the issues of slavery, racial inequality, and African American voting rights were *nationalized*. Nationalizing these issues meant removing them from the jurisdiction of the states and placing them in the hands of the national government. The 13th, 14th, and 15th Amendments to the Constitution were enforced by federal troops in the southern states during the post–Civil War Reconstruction era. But after the Compromise of 1876 led to the withdrawal of federal troops from the southern states, legal and social segregation of African Americans became a "way of life" in the region. Segregation was *denationalized*, which reduced national conflict over race but exacted a high price from the nation's African American population. Segregationists asserted the states' rights argument so often in defense of racial discrimination that it became a code phrase for racism. Not until the 1950s and 1960s were questions of segregation and equality again made into national issues. The civil rights movement asserted the supremacy of national law and in 1954 won a landmark decision in the case of *Brown v. Board of Education of Topeka*, when the U.S. Supreme Court ruled that segregation enforced by state (or local) officials violated the 14th Amendment's guarantee that no state could deny any person the equal protection of the law. Later the *national* Civil Rights Act of 1964 outlawed discrimination in private employment and businesses serving the public.

Only now that national constitutional and legal guarantees of equal protection of the law are in place is it possible to reassess the true worth of federalism. Having established that federalism will not mean racial inequality, Americans are now free to explore the values of decentralized government.

In an attempt to block the admission of two African American students to the University of Alabama in 1963, Governor George Wallace barred the door with his body in the face of U.S. federal marshals. The tactic did not succeed, and the two students were admitted.

individual rights. The Bill of Rights originally applied only to the national government, but the 14th Amendment, passed by Congress in 1866 and ratified by 1868, provided that the states must also adhere to fundamental guarantees of individual liberty.

State Role in National Government

The states are basic units in the organizational scheme of the national government. The House of Representatives apportions members to the states by population, and state legislatures draw up the districts that elect representatives. Every state has at least one member in the

"Look, the American people don't want to be bossed around by federal bureaucrats. They want to be bossed around by state bureaucrats."

Source: © 2002 Robert Mankoff from cartoonbank.com. All Rights Reserved.

Federalism and Regulations

House of Representatives, regardless of its population. Each state elects two U.S. senators, regardless of its population. The president is chosen by the electoral votes of the states, with each state having as many electoral votes as it has senators and representatives combined. Finally, three-fourths of the states must ratify amendments to the U.S. Constitution.

State Obligations to Each Other   To promote national unity, the Constitution requires the states to recognize actions and decisions taken by other states. Article IV requires the states to give "Full Faith and Credit . . . to the public Acts, Records, and judiciary Proceedings of every other State." This provision ensures that contracts, property ownership, insurance, civil judgments, marriages and divorces, among other things, made in one state are recognized in all states (see *Controversy:* "Federalism and Same-Sex Marriage").

The Evolution of American Federalism

American federalism has evolved over 200 years from a state-centered division of power to a national-centered system of government. Although the original constitutional wordings have remained in place, *power has flowed toward the national government since the earliest days of the Republic.* American federalism has been forged in the fires of political conflicts between states and nation, conflicts that have usually been resolved in favor of the national government. (See *Politics Up Close:* "Historical Landmarks in the Development of American Federalism.") Generalizing about the evolution of American federalism is no easy task. But let us try to describe broadly some major periods in the evolution of federalism and then look at five specific historical developments that had far-reaching impact on that evolution.

Whose Call to Make?

Battles over same-sex marriages are currently being fought in state capitals across the country. The Constitution requires every state to give "Full Faith and Credit" to the official acts of other states. But Congress's Defense of Marriage Act relieves states from recognizing same-sex marriages consummated in other states. The Supreme Court may end up deciding the issue. Here, two gay fathers walk with their child in a New York City Gay and Lesbian Pride Day Parade.

Controversy

Federalism and Same-Sex Marriage

Traditionally, states outlawed sodomy (anal penetration, whether practiced by homo- or heterosexuals). The U.S. Supreme Court upheld these laws in 1986: "There is no constitutional right to sodomy."[a] But in 2003 the Supreme Court reversed itself and held that homosexuals' "right to liberty under the Due Process Clause gives them the full right to engage in private conduct without government interference."[b] This decision was an important victory for the gay rights movement in America and generated additional cases involving the legal status of homosexual relations.

Among the issues confronting homosexuals is that of same-sex marriage. The Supreme Court's decision that homosexual activity among consenting adults was a constitutionally protected liberty inspired several state courts to consider whether the denial of marriage to homosexual couples was discriminatory. Anticipating that some state courts might rule that same-sex marriages were constitutionally protected in their states, Congress passed a Defense of Marriage Act in 1996. This act was designed to circumvent the Full Faith and Credit clause of Article IV of the Constitution requiring every state to recognize the public acts and judiciary proceedings of every other state. The act stated that "No state. . . . shall be required to give effect to any public act, record, or judicial proceeding of any other state respecting a relationship between persons of the same-sex that is treated as a marriage. . . ." The Congress relied on the language of the next sentence of Article IV: "The Congress may by general law prescribe the Manner in which such Acts, Records and Proceedings shall be proved, and the Effect thereof." Congress was trying to prevent the recognition of same-sex marriages by all states if one or more states decided to legalize such marriages.

Public opinion is strongly opposed to same-sex *marriage*, but many Americans have no objection to the alternative of *civil unions* for same-sex couples.[c]

Q. Do you think marriages between homosexuals should or should not be recognized by the law as valid, with the same rights as traditional marriages?"

Should be valid	Should not be	Unsure
28%	68%	4%

Q. "Do you think same-sex couples should be allowed to legally marry, should be allowed legally to form civil unions but not to marry, should not be allowed to obtain legal recognition of their relationships?"

Marriage	Civil unions	No legal recognition	Unsure
27%	29%	40%	4%

The Massachusetts Supreme Court in 2003[d] and the California Supreme Court in 2008 both ruled that same-sex couples have a right to marry under their state constitutions.

Yet by 2008, over forty states had laws against same-sex marriages, many adapted by a statewide voter referendum. It is not altogether clear whether the Congress has a power under the language of Article IV to nullify in effect the Full Faith and Credit clause. It is quite possible that the U.S. Supreme Court will hold that it does not, and that states are obliged to recognize same-sex marriages performed lawfully in any state.

Finally, *if* the federal courts, with the approval of the U.S. Supreme Court, were to decide that denying licenses for same-sex marriages violated the Equal Protection Clause of the 14th Amendment to the Constitution, that such denial was discriminatory, *then all* states would be obliged to grant such licenses and recognize such marriages.

Does the Constitution's "full faith and credit clause" oblige all states to recognize same-sex marriages performed in any state? Congress's "Protection of Marriage Act" says no, but the U.S. Supreme Court has yet to speak on the issue. Here television celebrity Rosie O'Donnell leaves the courthouse following her marriage ceremony.

[a] *Bowers v. Hardwick*, 478 U.S. 186 (1986).

[b] *Lawrence v. Texas*, June 26, 2003.

[c] *ABC News Poll*, April 24, 2005, *CNN/USA Today* Poll, March 20, 2005.

[d] *Goodridge v. Department of Health*, 798 N.E 2d 941 (2003).

State-Centered Federalism, 1787–1868   From the adoption of the Constitution of 1787 to the end of the Civil War, the states were the most important units in the American federal system. It is true that during this period the legal foundation for the expansion of national power was being laid, but people looked to the states for resolving most policy questions and providing most public services. Even the issue of slavery was decided by state governments. The supremacy of the national government was frequently questioned, first by the Anti-Federalists (including Thomas Jefferson) and later by John C. Calhoun and other defenders of slavery.

Dual Federalism, 1868–1913   The supremacy of the national government was decided on the battlefields of the Civil War. Yet for nearly a half-century after that conflict, the national government narrowly interpreted its delegated powers, and the states continued to decide most domestic policy issues. The resulting pattern has been described as **dual federalism**. Under this pattern, the states and the nation divided most governmental functions. The national government concentrated its attention on the "delegated" powers—national defense, foreign affairs, tariffs, interstate commerce, the coinage of money, standard weights and measures, post office and post roads, and the admission of new states. State governments decided the important domestic policy issues—education, welfare, health, and criminal justice. The separation of policy responsibilities was once compared to a layer cake, with local governments at the base, state governments in the middle, and the national government at the top.[7]

★ **dual federalism**
Early concept of federalism in which national and state powers were clearly distinguished and functionally separate.

Cooperative Federalism, 1913–64   The distinction between national and state responsibilities gradually eroded in the first half of the twentieth century. American federalism was transformed by the Industrial Revolution and the development of a national economy, by the federal income tax in 1913, which shifted financial resources to the national government, and by the challenges of two world wars and the Great Depression. In response to the Great Depression of the 1930s, state governors welcomed massive federal public works projects under President Franklin D. Roosevelt's New Deal program. In addition, the federal government intervened directly in economic affairs, labor relations, business practices, and agriculture. Through its grants of money, the national government cooperated with the states in public assistance, employment services, child welfare, public housing, urban renewal, highway building, and vocational education.

★ **cooperative federalism**
Model of federalism in which national, state, and local governments work together exercising common policy responsibilities.

This new pattern of federal-state relations was labeled **cooperative federalism**. Both the nation and the states exercised responsibilities for welfare, health, highways, education, and criminal justice. This merging of policy responsibilities was compared to a marble cake: "As the colors are mixed in a marble cake, so functions are mixed in the American federal system."[8] Yet even in this period of shared national-state responsibility, the national government emphasized cooperation in achieving common national and state goals. Congress generally acknowledged that it had no direct constitutional authority to regulate public health, safety, or welfare. Instead, it relied primarily on its powers to tax and spend for the general welfare, providing financial assistance to state and local governments to achieve shared goals. Congress did not usually legislate directly on local matters.

Centralized Federalism, 1964–80   Over the years, it became increasingly difficult to maintain the fiction that the national government was merely assisting the states to perform their domestic responsibilities. By the time President Lyndon B. Johnson launched the Great Society program in 1964, the federal government clearly had its own *national* goals. Virtually all problems confronting

Politics Up Close   Historic Landmarks in the Development of American Federalism

The American federal system is a product of more than its formal constitutional provisions. It has also been shaped by interpretations by the courts of constitutional principles as well as the history of disputes that have occurred over state and national authority.

Marbury v. Madison (1803): Expanding Federal Court Authority

Chief Justice John Marshall, who presided over the Supreme Court from 1801 to 1835, became a major architect of American federalism. Under John Marshall, the Supreme Court assumed the role of arbiter in disputes between state and national authority. It was under John Marshall that the Supreme Court in *Marbury v. Madison* assumed the power to interpret the U.S. Constitution authoritatively.[a] The fact that the referee of disputes between state and national authority has been the *national* Supreme Court has had a profound influence on the development of American federalism. Since the Supreme Court is a *national* institution, one might say that in disputes between nation and states, one of the members of the two contending teams is also serving as umpire. Constitutionally speaking, then, there is really *no* limitation on national as against state authority if all three branches of the national government—the Congress, the president, and the Court—act together to override state authority.

McCulloch v. Maryland (1819): Expanding Implied Powers of the National Government

In the case of *McCulloch v. Maryland*, Chief Justice John Marshall provided a broad interpretation of the Necessary and Proper Clause:

> Let the end be legitimate, let it be within the scope of the Constitution, and all means which are appropriate, which are plainly adopted to the end, which are not prohibited but consistent with the letter and the spirit of the Constitution, are constitutional.[b]

The *McCulloch* case firmly established the principle that the Necessary and Proper Clause gives Congress the right to choose its means for carrying out the enumerated powers of the national government. Today, Congress can devise programs, create agencies, and establish national laws on the basis of long chains of reasoning from the most meager phrases of the constitutional text because of the broad interpretation of the Necessary and Proper Clause.

Dead Soldiers, Civil War, 1865

Secession and the Civil War (1861–65): Maintaining the "Indestructible Union"

The Civil War was, of course, the greatest crisis of the American federal system. Did a state have the right to oppose national law to the point of secession? In the years preceding the Civil War, John C. Calhoun argued that the Constitution was a compact made by the *states* in a sovereign capacity rather than by the *people* in their national capacity. Calhoun contended that the federal government was an agent of the states, that the states retained their sovereignty in this compact, and that the federal government must not violate the compact, under the penalty of state nullification or even secession from the Union.

The issue was decided in the nation's bloodiest war. What was decided on the battlefield between 1861 and 1865 was confirmed by the Supreme Court in 1869: "Ours is an indestructible union, composed of indestructible states."[c] Yet the states' rights doctrines, and political disputes over the character of American federalism, did not disappear with Lee's surrender at Appomattox. The 13th, 14th, and 15th Amendments, passed by the Reconstruction Congress, were clearly aimed at limiting state power in the interests of individual freedom. The 13th Amendment eliminated slavery in the states; the 15th Amendment prevented states from discriminating against blacks in the right to vote; and the 14th Amendment declared that "No State shall make or enforce any law which shall abridge the privileges or immunities of citizens of the United States; nor shall any state deprive any person of life, liberty, or property without due process of law; nor deny to any person

[a]*Marbury v. Madison*, 1 Cranch 137 (1803).
[b]*McCulloch v. Maryland*, 4 Wheaton 316 (1819).
[c]*Texas v. White*, 7 Wallace 700 (1869).

within its jurisdiction the equal protection of the laws." These amendments delegated to Congress the power to secure their enforcement. Yet for several generations these amendments were narrowly construed and added little, if anything, to national power.

The Income Tax and Federal Grants (1913)

With the money provided to Washington by the passage of the 16th (income tax) Amendment in 1913, Congress embarked on cash grants to the states. Among the earliest cash grant programs were the Federal Highway Act of 1916 and the Smith-Hughes Act of 1917 (vocational education). With federal money came federal direction. For example, states that wanted federal money for highways after 1916 had to accept uniform standards of construction and even a uniform road-numbering system (U.S. 1, U.S. 30, and so on). Shortly after these programs began, the U.S. Supreme Court considered the claim that these federal grants were unconstitutional intrusions into areas "reserved" for the states. But the Court upheld grants as a legitimate exercise of Congress's power to tax and spend for the general welfare.[d]

National Labor Relations Board v. Jones and Laughlin Steel Corp. (1937): Expanding Interstate Commerce

The Industrial Revolution in America created a *national* economy with a nationwide network of transportation and communication and the potential for national economic depressions. Yet for a time, the Supreme Court placed obstacles in the way of national authority over the economy, and by so doing the Court created a "crisis" in American federalism. For many years, the Court narrowly construed interstate commerce to mean only the movement of goods and services across state lines, insisting that agriculture, mining, manufacturing, and labor relations were outside the reach of the delegated powers of the national government. However, when confronted with the Great Depression of the 1930s and President Franklin D. Roosevelt's threat to "pack" the Court with additional members to secure approval of his New Deal measures, the Court yielded. In *National*

Labor Relations Board v. Jones and Laughlin Steel Corp. in 1937, the Court recognized the principle that production and distribution of goods and services for a national market could be regulated by Congress under the Interstate Commerce Clause.[e] The effect was to give the national government effective control over the national economy.

Brown v. Board of Education (1954): Guaranteeing Civil Rights

After World War I, the Supreme Court began to build a national system of civil rights that was based on the 14th Amendment. In early cases, the Court held that the 14th Amendment prevented states from interfering with free speech, free press, or religious practices. Not until 1954, in the Supreme Court's landmark desegregation decision in *Brown v. Board of Education* in Topeka, Kansas, did the Court begin to call for the full assertion of national authority on behalf of civil rights.[f] The Supreme Court's use of the 14th Amendment to ensure a national system of civil rights supported by the power of the federal government was an important step in the evolution of the American federal system.

Voting Rights Act (1965) and Bush v. Gore (2000): Federal Oversight of Elections

The Voting Rights Act of 1965 plunged the federal government into direct oversight of state and local as well as federal elections in an effort to end discriminatory practices. The act and subsequent amendments to it require the Justice Department to approve any election law changes in states and communities covered by the act. It provides that intent to discriminate need not be proven if the results demonstrate a discriminatory impact on minorities.

In the contested presidential election of 2000, the U.S. Supreme Court confirmed national oversight of Electoral College voting and vote counting in *Bush v. Gore.*[g] In this landmark case the Court reversed a Florida Supreme Court interpretation of that state's election laws and ruled that voting and vote counting are entitled to Equal Protection and Due Process under the 14th Amendment.

[d]*Massachusetts v. Wellon,* 262 vs. 447 (1923).
[e]*National Labor Relations Board v. Jones and Lauglin Steel Corp.,* 301 vs. 1 (1937).
[f]*Brown v. Board & Education of Topeka, Kansas,* 347 U.S. 483 (1954).
[g]*Bush v. Gore,* 531 U.S. 98 (2000).

Federalism and the Supreme Court

American society—from solid-waste disposal and water and air pollution to consumer safety, home insulation, noise abatement, and even "highway beautification"—were declared to be national problems. Congress legislated directly on any matter it chose, without regard to its *enumerated powers* and without pretending to render only financial assistance. The Supreme Court no longer concerned itself with the reserved powers of the states, and the 10th Amendment lost most of its meaning. The pattern of national-state relations became **centralized federalism**. As for the cake analogies, one commentator observed, "The frosting had moved to the top, something like a pineapple upside-down cake."[9]

New Federalism, 1980–85 New federalism was a phrase frequently applied to efforts to reverse the flow of power to Washington and to return responsibilities to states and communities. (The phrase originated in the administration of Richard M. Nixon, 1969–74, who used it to describe general revenue sharing—making federal grants to state and local governments with few strings attached.) New Federalism was popular early in the administration of President Ronald Reagan, who tried to reduce federal involvement in domestic programs and encourage states and cities to undertake greater policy responsibilities themselves. The result was that state and local governments were forced to rely more on their own sources of revenue and less on federal money. Still, centralizing tendencies in the American federal system continued. While the general public usually gave better marks to state and local governments than to the federal government, paradoxically that same public also favored greater federal involvement in policy areas traditionally thought to be state or local responsibilities. (See: *What Do You Think?:* "Which Level of Government Does the Best Job?")

Representational Federalism, 1985–95 Despite centralizing tendencies, it was still widely assumed prior to 1985 that the Congress could not directly legislate how state and local governments should go about performing their traditional functions. However, in its 1985 *Garcia v. San Antonio Metropolitan Transit Authority* decision, the U.S. Supreme Court appeared to remove all barriers to direct congressional legislation in matters traditionally reserved to the states. The case arose after Congress directly ordered state and local governments to pay minimum wages to their employees. The Court dismissed arguments that the nature of American federalism and the Reserved Powers Clause of the 10th Amendment prevented Congress from directly legislating in state affairs. It said that the only protection for state powers was to be found in the states' role in electing U.S. senators, members of the U.S. House of Representatives, and the president. The Court's ruling asserts a concept known as **representational federalism**: federalism is defined by the role of the states in electing members of Congress and the

★ **centralized federalism**
Model of federalism in which the national government assumes primary responsibility for determining national goals in all major policy areas and directs state and local government activity through conditions attached to money grants.

★ **new federalism**
Attempts to return power and responsibility to the states and reduce the role of the national government in domestic affairs.

★ **representational federalism**
Assertion that no constitutional division of powers exists between the nation and the states but the states retain their constitutional role merely by selecting the president and members of Congress.

Hand in Hand
During the Great Depression of the 1930s, President Franklin D. Roosevelt and the Democratic-controlled U.S. Congress sponsored extended public works within the states. This image of WPA workers bagging a street in anticipation of spring flood is an example of cooperative federalism.

What Do You *Think?*

Which Level of Government Does the Best Job?

Americans appear to be ambivalent about federalism. On the one hand, most surveys show that Americans have greater confidence in their state and local governments than in the federal government. In general, they would prefer that power be concentrated at the state rather than the federal level. They believe that state and local officials get more done than the federal government.

Yet at the same time most Americans want the federal government, rather than state or local governments, to run programs in many specific policy areas, like health care, the environment, and the economy.

Trust and Confidence

Generally speaking, which of the following cares more about the important problems that affect you personally?

The governor, my state legislature	52
The president and Congress	36
Neither	10
Don't know/refused	2

Source: "Immigration, Federalism," Andres McKenna Research. January 15–25, 2004.

And which level of government gets more done?

Local	37
State	31
Federal	27
Don't know/refused	5

For each issue, tell me whether the state government or the federal government should take the lead

Issue	Federal	State	DK/Ref.
Education	24	75	1
Highways and roads	27	73	0
Health care	72	27	1
Crime	27	72	1
Environment	72	28	1
Jobs and the economy	56	43	1

president, not by any constitutional division of powers. The United States is said to retain a federal system because its national officials are selected from subunits of government—the president through the allocation of Electoral College votes to the states and the Congress through the allocation of two Senate seats per state and the apportionment of representatives based on state population. Whatever

These two persons are standing outside the U.S. Supreme Court as the court heard arguments in the *District of Columbia v. Heller* case on March 18, 2008, regarding Washington, D.C.'s ban on handguns. The Court, in a 5–4 decision, ruled that the city's law, as it was written, was in violation of the Constitution and the 2nd Amendment's protection to bear arms.

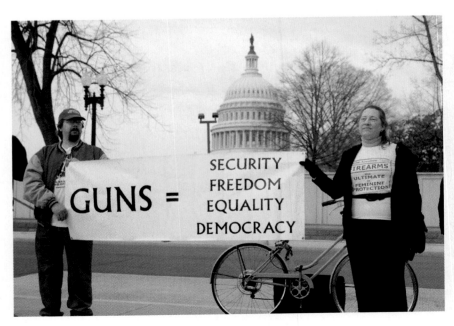

protection exists for state power and independence must be found in the national political process, in the influence of state and district voters on their senators and representatives. In a strongly worded dissenting opinion in *Garcia*, Justice Lewis Powell argued that if federalism is to be retained, the Constitution—not Congress—should divide powers. "The states' role in our system of government is a matter of constitutional law, not legislative grace. . . . [This decision] today rejects almost 200 years of the understanding of the constitutional status of federalism."[10]

Federalism Revived?

In recent years federalism has experienced a modest revival. The U.S. Supreme Court today appears to be somewhat more respectful of the powers of states and somewhat less willing to see these powers trampled upon by the national government.[11]

In 1995 the U.S. Supreme Court issued its first opinion in more than sixty years that recognized a limit on Congress's power over interstate commerce and reaffirmed the Founders' notion of a national government with only the powers enumerated in the Constitution.[12] The Court found that the federal Gun-Free School Zones Act was unconstitutional because it exceeded Congress's powers under the Interstate Commerce Clause. When a student, Alfonso Lopez, was apprehended at his Texas high school carrying a .38 caliber handgun, federal agents charged him with violating the *federal* Gun-Free School Zones Act of 1990.

The U.S. government argued that the act was a constitutional exercise of its interstate commerce power, because "violent crime reduces the willingness of individuals to travel to areas within the country that are perceived to be unsafe." But after reviewing virtually all of the key commerce clause cases in its history, the Court determined that an activity must *substantially affect* interstate commerce in order to be regulated by Congress. Chief Justice William H. Rehnquist, writing for the majority in a 5 to 4 decision in *U.S. v. Lopez*, even cited James Madison with approval: "The powers delegated by the proposed Constitution to the

Think Again

Should the national government be able to prosecute a high school student for bringing a gun to school?

Federalism

You Are a Federal Judge

Brady's Appeal for a Federal Law
Former presidential press secretary James Brady was permanently disabled in the assassination attempt on President Reagan in 1981. Brady and his wife led the effort to pass the Brady Act, which, among other things, ordered state and local officials to conduct background checks on gun purchasers. The Supreme Court held that portion of the act to be an unconstitutional violation of the principle of federalism.

Controversy

Should Violence Against Women Be a Federal Crime?

When a student at VPI (Virginia Polytechnic Institute) was raped, she argued that the attack violated the federal Violence Against Women Act of 1994, a popular bill that passed overwhelmingly in Congress and was signed by President Bill Clinton. The act allowed victims of "gender-motivated violence," including rape, to sue their attackers for monetary damages in *federal* court. The U.S. government defended its constitutional authority to involve itself in crimes against women by citing the Interstate Commerce Clause, arguing that crimes against women interfered with interstate commerce, the power over which is given to the national government in Article I of the Constitution.

But in 2000 the U.S. Supreme Court said, "If accepted, this reasoning would allow Congress to regulate any crime whose nationwide, aggregated impact has substantial effects on employment, production, transit, or consumption. Moreover, such reasoning will not limit Congress to regulating violence, but may be applied equally as well to family law and other areas of state regulation since the aggregate effect of marriage, divorce, and childrearing on the national economy is undoubtedly significant." The Court reasoned that "the Constitution requires a distinction between what is truly national and what is truly local, and there is no better example of the police power, which the Founders undeniably left reposed in the States and denied the central government." In Justice Scalia's opinion, allowing Congress to claim that violence against women interfered with interstate commerce would open the door to federalizing all crime because all crime affects interstate commerce.

Source: U.S. v. Morrison, 259 U.S. 598 (2000).

federal government are few and defined. Those which are to remain in the state governments are numerous and indefinite" (*Federalist*, No. 45).

In another victory for federalism, the U.S. Supreme Court ruled in 1996 in *Seminole Tribe v. Florida* that the 11th Amendment shields states from lawsuits by private parties that seek to force states to comply with federal laws enacted under the commerce power.[13] And in 1999 in *Alden v. Maine*, the Supreme Court held that states were also shielded in their own courts from lawsuits in which private parties seek to enforce federal mandates. In an opinion that surveyed the history of American federalism, Justice Kennedy wrote: "Congress has vast power but not all power. . . . When Congress legislates in matters affecting the states it may not treat these sovereign entities as mere prefectures or corporations."[14]

In defense of federalism, the Supreme Court invalidated a provision of a very popular law of Congress—the Brady Handgun Violence Protection Act. The Court decided in 1997 that the law's command to local law enforcement officers to conduct background checks on gun purchasers violated "the very principle of separate state sovereignty." The Court affirmed that the federal government "may neither issue directives requiring the states to address particular problems, nor command the states' officers, or those of their political subdivisions, to administer or enforce the federal regulatory program" (*Printz v. U.S.*, 521 U.S. 890 (1997).[15] And the Court held that in the Violence Against Women Act, Congress also invaded the reserved police power of the states[16] (see *Controversy*: "Should Violence Against Women Be a Federal Crime?").

Federalism and Direct Democracy

★ **direct democracy**
Decisions are made directly by the people, usually by popular initiative and referenda voting, as opposed to decisions made by elected representatives.

Direct democracy means that the people themselves can initiate and decide policy questions by popular vote. The nation's Founders were profoundly skeptical of this form of democracy; they believed that the "follies" of direct democracy far outweighed any virtues it might possess. The U.S. Constitution has no provision for direct voting by the people on national policy questions. It was not until over 100 years after the Constitution was written that widespread support developed in the American states for direct voter participation in policy making. Direct democracy developed in states and communities and can be found today only in state and local governments.

Origins of Direct Democracy in the States At the beginning of the twentieth century, a strong populist movement in the Midwestern and Western states attacked railroads, banks, corporations, and the politicians that were said to be under their control. The populists were later joined by progressive reformers who attacked "bosses," "machines," and parties as corrupt. The populists believed that their elected representatives were ignoring the needs of farmers, debtors, and laborers. They wanted to bypass governors and legislatures and directly enact popular legislation.

The populists and progressives were responsible for the widespread adoption of three forms of direct democracy: the initiative, referendum, and recall.

Initiative The **initiative** is a device whereby a specific number or percent of voters, through the use of a petition, may have a proposed state constitutional amendment or a state law placed on the ballot for adoption or rejection by the electorate of a state. This process bypasses the legislature and allows citizens to both propose and adopt laws and constitutional amendments. Table 4.2 lists the states that allow popular initiatives for constitutional amendments.

★ **initiative**
Allows a specified number or percentage of voters by use of a petition to place a state constitutional amendment or a state law on the ballot for adoption or rejection by the state electorate.

Table **4.2** Initiative and Recall in the States

Currently eighteen states allow voters by petition to place state constitutional amendments on the ballot. And eighteen states allow voters petition to force a recall vote.

Initiative for Constitutional Amendments (Signatures Required to Get on Ballot)[a]	Recall (Signatures Required to Force a Recall Election)[b]
Arizona (15%)	Alaska (25%)
Arkansas (10%)	Arizona (25%)
California (8%)	California (12%)
Colorado (5%)	Colorado (25%)
Florida (8%)	Georgia (15%)
Illinois (8%)	Idaho (20%)
Massachusetts (3%)	Kansas (40%)
Michigan (10%)	Louisiana (33%)
Mississippi (12%)	Michigan (25%)
Missouri (8%)	Minnesota (25%)
Montana (10%)	Montana (10%)
Nebraska (10%)	Nevada (25%)
Nevada (10%)	New Jersey (25%)
North Dakota (4% of state population)	North Dakota (25%)
Ohio (10%)	Oregon (15%)
Oklahoma (15%)	Rhode Island (15%)
Oregon (8%)	Washington (25%)
South Dakota (10%)	Wisconsin (25%)

[a]Figures expressed as percentage of vote in last governor's election unless otherwise specified; some states also require distribution of votes across counties and districts.
[b]Figures are percentages of voters in last general elections of the official sought to be recalled.

Source: Derived from Council of State Governments, *The Book of the States*, 2007 Edition.

★ referenda
Proposed laws or constitutional amendments submitted to the voters for their direct approval or rejection; found in some state constitutions but not in the U.S. Constitution.

★ recall
An election to allow voters to decide whether or not to remove an elected official before his or her term expires.

Referendum   The referendum is a device by which the electorate must approve decisions of the legislature before these become law or become part of the state constitution. As we noted earlier, most states require a favorable referendum vote for a state constitutional amendment. **Referenda** on state laws may be submitted by the legislature (when legislators want to shift decision-making responsibility to the people), or referenda may be demanded by popular petition (when the people wish to change laws passed by the legislature).

Recall   **Recall** elections allow voters to remove an elected official before his or her term expires. Usually a recall election is initiated by a petition. The number of signatures required is usually expressed as a percentage of votes cast in the last election for the official being recalled (frequently 25 percent). Currently sixteen states provide for recall election for some or all of their elected officials (see Table 4.2). Although officials are often publicly threatened with recall, rarely is anyone ever removed from office through this device. A recall of a state elected official requires an expensive petition drive as well as a campaign against the incumbent. The "granddaddy of all recalls" removed California Governor Gray Davis from office in 2003. The *Terminator* movie star Arnold Schwarzenegger was voted in as his replacement. (See *People in Politics*: "Arnold Schwarzenegger, Governing California.")

Politics of State Initiatives   State initiatives generally reflect popular attitudes rather than the opinions of leaders in business and government. Among the more popular initiatives in recent years: limiting terms for public officials, limiting taxes of various kinds, making English the official language, prohibiting same-sex marriages, allowing gambling, allowing marijuana for medical purposes, and allowing physician-assisted suicide. Of course, citizen initiatives are often backed by "special interests"—specific businesses or industries, religious organizations, the gambling industry, and so on. Often a great deal of money is spent for paid workers to gather the necessary signatures and then later to promote the initiative in the media.

Money and Power Flow to Washington

Over the years, power in the federal system has flowed to Washington because tax money has flowed to Washington. With its financial resources, the federal government has been able to offer assistance to state and local governments and thereby involve itself in just about every governmental function performed by these governments. Today the federal government is no longer one of *enumerated* or *delegated* powers. No activities are really *reserved* to the states. Through its power to tax and spend for the *general welfare*, the national government is now deeply involved in welfare, education, transportation, police protection, housing, hospitals, urban development, and other activities that were once the exclusive domain of state and local government (see *Politics Up Close*: "How Congress Set a National Drinking Age").

Grants-in-Aid   Today grant-in-aid programs are the single most important source of federal influence over state and local activity. A **grant-in-aid** is defined as "payment of funds by one level of government (national or state) to be expended by another level (state or local) for a specified purpose, usually on a matching-funds basis (the federal government puts up only as much as the state or locality) and in

Think Again

When the federal government requires states to provide safe drinking water, clean air, or access for the handicapped, should it provide funds to carry out these mandates?

★ grant-in-aid
Payment of funds from the national government to state or local governments or from a state government to local governments for a specified purpose.

People in Politics Arnold Schwarzenegger, Governing California

The State of California is the second largest government in the United States—second only to the federal government in revenues, spending, and employment. California's population and economy are larger than those of most nations in the world.

Arnold Schwarzenegger had never held political office before his election to the governorship of California in 2003. "Ahnold" (a play on his Austrian accent) came to office in a rare recall election of his predecessor, Gray Davis. (Eighteen states include recall provisions in their constitutions—a petition signed by a specific number of voters that forces incumbent officials to face an election that risks their being ousted before the end of their term.) Davis lost the recall vote and Arnold won over 135 other candidates to become Davis's replacement.

Arnold's father had been a local police chief in Austria and a Nazi Party member before World War II. Arnold donated hundreds of thousands of dollars to the Simon Wiesenthal Center, a Jewish human rights organization, that investigated his father's activities and found no evidence that he had committed any war crimes. Arnold spent his teenage years developing his body in the hope of one day becoming Mr. Universe. At age 20 he fulfilled his dream, becoming the youngest-ever Mr. Universe; he would go on to win that title four more times.

Schwarzenegger moved to the United States in 1968, speaking little English. He continued to win bodybuilding titles, later admitting to the use of performance-enhancing anabolic steroids. Arnold had long planned to move from bodybuilding into movie stardom. He appeared in a few easily forgotten films in the 1970s, and finally made his breakthrough movie *Conan the Barbarian* in 1982. He followed this success with another box office hit *The Terminator* in 1984. In subsequent films, Schwarzenegger tried comedy, but returned to action hero in *Total Recall* in 1990, a widely praised science fiction motion picture.

Arnold married Maria Shriver in 1986. She is the niece of President John F. Kennedy and a successful television newscaster and commentator. They have four children.

Arnold, a registered Republican, revealed an interest in politics by becoming involved with the Special Olympics and serving on President George H. W. Bush's Council on Physical Fitness. As a candidate in the 2003 recall election, Schwarzenegger enjoyed the most name recognition in the crowded field of candidates. He offered few specifics in his campaign for governor: "I'm for the people." He won 48.6 percent of the vote; under the California Constitution, no runoff was required.

Arnold was initially successful in repealing an unpopular vehicle registration fee, but later began to feel a backlash when powerful state unions opposed his various initiatives. He came up against political reality in a special referendum in 2005 in which four ballot measures he sponsored were defeated. His approval ratings sank to dangerous lows. He referred to his Democratic opponents in the legislature as "girlie men." But his political fortunes rose again as he campaigned for reelection in 2006. Despite a poor year nationally for Republicans, Schwarzenegger won reelection with 56 percent of the vote. His victory enhanced his political influence nationwide. He abandoned partisan attacks on the Democratic legislature and transformed himself into a consensus builder. He negotiated agreements on increasing the minimum wage, increasing school spending, and cutting air pollution and saving energy. (He customized his 800 horsepower Hummer into an environmentally clean vehicle.) He restructured his image as an independent-minded governor.

---

accordance with prescribed standards of requirements."[17] No state or local government is *required* to accept grants-in-aid. Participation in grant-in-aid programs is voluntary. So in theory, if conditions attached to the grant money are too oppressive, state and local governments can simply decline to participate and pass up these funds.

About one-quarter of all state and local government revenues currently come from federal grants. Federal grants are available in nearly every major category of state and local government activity. Over 500 separate grant programs are administered by various federal agencies. So numerous and diverse are these grants that state and local officials often lack information about their availability,

Figure *4.3*

Where Does the Money Go?: Purposes of Federal Grants to State and Local Governments

About one-quarter of all state and local government revenues are derived from federal grants. Federal grants-in-aid to state and local governments are especially vital in the areas of health and welfare.

Source: Budget of United States Government, 2009.

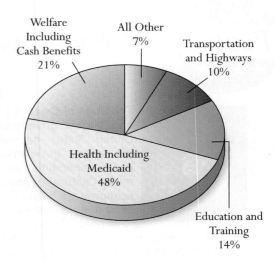

Welfare Including Cash Benefits 21%

All Other 7%

Transportation and Highways 10%

Health Including Medicaid 48%

Education and Training 14%

purpose, and requirements. "Grantsmanship"—knowing where and how to obtain federal grants—is highly valued in state and local governments. Federal grants can be obtained to preserve historic buildings, develop minority-owned businesses, aid foreign refugees, drain abandoned mines, control riots, subsidize school milk programs, and so on. However, welfare (including cash benefits and food stamps) and health (including Medicaid for the poor) account for two-thirds of federal aid money (see Figure 4.3).

Thus many of the special projects and ongoing programs carried out today by state and local governments are funded by grants from the federal government. These funds have generally been dispersed as either categorical grants or block grants.

★ *Categorical Grant*: A grant for a specific purpose or project. The project must be approved by a federal administrative agency. Most federal aid money is distributed in the form of categorical grants. **Categorical grants** can be distributed on a project basis or a formula basis. Grants made on a project basis are distributed by federal administrative agencies to state or local governments that compete for project funds in their applications. Federal agencies have a great deal of discretion in selecting specific projects for support, and they can exercise direct control over the projects. Most categorical grants are distributed to state or local governments according to a fixed formula set by Congress. Medicaid and Food Stamps (see Chapter 17) are the largest categorical grant programs.

★ *Block Grant*: A grant for a general governmental function, such as health, social services, law enforcement, education, or community development. State and local governments have fairly wide discretion in deciding how to spend federal block grant money within a functional area. For example, cities receiving "community development" block grants can decide for themselves about specific neighborhood development projects, housing projects, community facilities, and so on. All **block grants** are distributed on a formula basis set by Congress. Federal administrative agencies may require reports and adherence to rules and guidelines, but they do not choose which specific projects to fund.

★ **categorical grants**
Federal grants to a state or local government for specific purposes or projects; may be allocated by formulas or by projects.

★ **block grants**
Federal grants to state or local governments for general government functions allowing greater flexibility in the use of money.

Politics Up Close How Congress Set a National Drinking Age

Traditionally, the *reserved* powers of the states included protection of the health, safety, and well-being of their citizens. The *enumerated* powers of Congress in the Constitution did not include regulating the sale and consumption of alcoholic beverages. Every state determined its own minimum age for drinking.

But the minimum drinking age became a national issue as a result of emotional appeals by groups such as Mothers Against Drunk Driving (MADD). Tragic stories told at televised committee hearings by grieving relatives of dead teenagers swept away federalism arguments. A few Congress members tried to argue that a national drinking age infringed on state power in a matter traditionally under state control. However, the new law, enacted in 1984, did not directly mandate a national drinking age. Instead, it ordered the withholding of 10 percent of all federal highway funds from any state that failed to raise its minimum drinking age to 21. States retained the rights to ignore the national minimum and give up a portion of their highway funds. (Congress used this same approach in 1974 in establishing a national 55-mile-per-hour speed limit.) Opponents of this device labeled it federal blackmail and a federal intrusion into state responsibilities. For some state officials, then, the issue was not teen drinking but rather the preemption of state authority.

From a purely constitutional perspective, Congress simply exercised its power to spend money for the general welfare; it did not *directly* legislate in an area

reserved to the states. Technically, states remain free to set their own minimum drinking age. Despite heated arguments in many state legislatures, all of the states adopted the 21-year-old minimum national drinking age by 1990.

Appeals by groups such as Mothers Against Drunk Driving (MADD) helped overcome concerns that legislation effectively setting a national drinking age would infringe on state authority.

State–Local Dependency on Federal Grants   Prior to 1980, state and local governments throughout the United States were becoming increasingly dependent upon federal grant money. From 1960 to 1980 federal grants as a percent of state–local spending rose from 14.8 percent to 27.4 percent. President Ronald Reagan made significant cutbacks in the flow of federal funds to state and local governments, and by 1990 federal grants constituted only 18.9 percent of state–local spending (see Figure 4.4). Reagan achieved most of this reduction by transforming categorical grants into block grants and then reducing the size of the block grants below the sum of the categorical grants. But following Reagan's efforts, federal grants again began to creep up under Presidents Bill Clinton and George W. Bush, and today federal grants again account for about one-quarter of all state and local government spending.

"Devolution"   Controversy over federalism—what level of government should do what and who should pay for it—is as old as the nation itself (see *Controversy*: "Liberals, Conservatives, and Federalism"). Beginning in 1995, with a new Republican majority in both houses of Congress and Republicans holding a majority of

Figure *4.4*

State and local Government Dependency on Federal Grants

State and local governments depend on federal grants for about one-quarter of their revenues. This dependency declined somewhat during the Reagan administration in the 1980s but has since returned to previous levels.

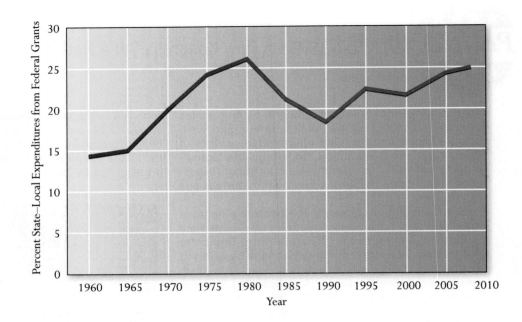

★ **devolution**
Passing down of responsibilities from the national government to the states.

state governorships, debates over federalism were renewed. The new phrase was **devolution**—the passing down of responsibilities from the national government to the states.

Welfare reform turned out to be the key to devolution. Bill Clinton once promised "to end welfare as we know it," but it was a Republican Congress in 1996 that did so. After President Clinton had twice vetoed welfare reform bills, he and Congress finally agreed to merge welfare reform with devolution. A new Temporary Assistance to Needy Families program (see Chapter 17) replaced direct federal cash aid welfare "entitlements." The new program:

★ Establishes block grants with lump-sum allocations to the states for cash welfare payments.

★ Grants the states broad flexibility in determining eligibility and benefit levels for persons receiving such aid.

★ Limits the use of federally aided cash grants for most recipients to two continuing years and five years over their lifetime.

★ Allows states to deny additional cash payments for children born to women already receiving welfare assistance and allowing states to deny cash payments to parents under eighteen who do not live with an adult and attend school.

Since Franklin D. Roosevelt's New Deal, with its federal guarantee of cash Aid to Families with Dependent Children (AFDC), low-income mothers and children had enjoyed a federal "entitlement" to welfare payments. But welfare reform, with its devolution of responsibility to the states, ended this sixty-year-old federal entitlement. Note, however, that Congress continues to place "strings" on the use of federal welfare funds, including a two-year limit on continuing payments to beneficiaries and a five-year lifetime limit.

Political Obstacles to Devolution and Federalism Politicians in Washington are fond of the rhetoric of federalism. They know that Americans generally

Controversy

Liberals, Conservatives, and Federalism

From the earliest days of the Republic, American leaders and scholars have argued over federalism. Political interests that constitute a majority at the national level and control the national government generally praise the virtue of national supremacy. Political interests that do not control the national government but exercise controlling influence in one or more states generally see great merit in preserving the powers of the states.

In recent years, political conflict over federalism—over the division between national versus state and local responsibilities and finances—has tended to follow traditional "liberal" and "conservative" political cleavages. Generally, liberals seek to enhance the power of the *national* government because they believe people's lives can be changed—and bettered—by the exercise of national governmental power. The government in Washington has more power and resources than do state and local governments, which

many liberals regard as too slow, cumbersome, weak, and unresponsive. Thus liberalism and centralization are closely related in American politics.

In contrast, conservatives generally seek to return power to *state and local* governments. Conservatives are skeptical about the "good" that government can do and believe that adding to the power of the national government is not an effective way of resolving society's problems. On the contrary, they argue that "government is the problem, not the solution." Excessive government regulation, burdensome taxation, and inflationary government spending combine to restrict individual freedom, penalize work and savings, and destroy incentives for economic growth. Government should be kept small, controllable, and close to the people.

There is no way to settle the argument over federalism once and for all. Debates about federalism are part of the fabric of American politics.

prefer governments closer to home. Yet at the same time they confront strong political pressures to "DO SOMETHING!" about virtually every problem that confronts individuals, families, or communities, whether or not doing so may overstep the enumerated powers of the national government. Politicians gain very little by telling their constituents that a particular problem—violence in the schools, domestic abuse, physician-assisted suicide, and so on—is not a federal responsibility and should be dealt with at the state or local level of government. So both federal and state politicians compete to address well-publicized problems.[18]

Moreover, neither presidents nor members of Congress are inclined to restrain their own power. Both liberals and conservatives in Washington are motivated to tie their own strings to federal grant-in-aid money, issue their own federal mandates, and otherwise "correct" what they perceive to be errors or inadequacies of state policies.

Coercive Federalism: Preemptions and Mandates

Traditionally, Congress avoided issuing direct orders to state and local governments. Instead, it sought to influence them by offering grants of money with federal rules, regulations, or "guidelines" attached. In theory at least, states and communities were free to forgo the money and ignore the strings attached to it. But increasingly Congress has been guilty of **coercive federalism**, undertaking direct regulation of areas traditionally reserved to the states and restricting state authority to regulate these areas. And it has issued direct orders to state and local governments to perform various services and comply with federal law in the performance of these services.

★ **coercive federalism**
A term referring to direct federal orders (mandates) to state and local governments to perform a service or conform to federal law in the performance of a function.

★ **preemption**
Total or partial federal assumption of power in a particular field, restricting the authority of the states.

★ **total preemption**
Federal government's assumption of all regulatory powers in a particular field.

★ **partial preemption**
Federal government's assumption of some regulatory powers in a particular field, with the stipulation that a state law on the same subject as a federal law is valid if it does not conflict with the federal law in the same area.

★ **standard partial preemption**
Form of partial preemption in which the states are permitted to regulate activities already regulated by the federal government if the state regulatory standards are at least as stringent as the federal government's.

★ **mandates**
Perceptions of popular support for a program or policy based on the margin of electoral victory won by a candidate who proposed it during a campaign; direct federal orders to state and local governments requiring them to perform a service or to obey federal laws in the performance of their functions.

Federal Preemptions   The supremacy of federal laws over those of the states, spelled out in the National Supremacy Clause of the Constitution, permits Congress to decide whether or not there is **preemption** of state laws in a particular field by federal law. In **total preemption**, the federal government assumes all regulatory powers in a particular field—for example, copyrights, bankruptcy, railroads, and airlines. No state regulations in a totally preempted field are permitted. **Partial preemption** stipulates that a state law on the same subject is valid as long as it does not conflict with the federal law in the same area. For example, the Occupational Safety and Health Act of 1970 specifically permits state regulation of any occupational safety or health issue on which the federal Occupational Safety and Health Administration (OSHA) has *not* developed a standard; but once OSHA enacts a standard, all state standards are nullified. A specific form of partial preemption called **standard partial preemption** permits states to regulate activities in a field already regulated by the federal government, as long as state regulatory standards are at least as stringent as those of the federal government. Usually states must submit their regulations to the responsible federal agency for approval; the federal agency may revoke a state's regulating power if that state fails to enforce the approved standards. For example, the federal Environmental Protection Agency (EPA) permits state environmental regulations that meet or exceed EPA standards.

Federal Mandates   Federal **mandates** are direct orders to state and local governments to perform a particular activity or service or to comply with federal laws in the performance of their functions. Federal mandates occur in a wide variety of areas, from civil rights to minimum-wage regulations. Their range is reflected in some recent examples of federal mandates to state and local governments:

★ *Age Discrimination Act, 1986:* Outlaws mandatory retirement ages for public as well as private employees, including police, firefighters, and state college and university faculty.

★ *Asbestos Hazard Emergency Act, 1986:* Orders school districts to inspect for asbestos hazards and remove asbestos from school buildings when necessary.

★ *Safe Drinking Water Act, 1986:* Establishes national requirements for municipal water supplies; regulates municipal waste treatment plants.

★ *Clean Air Act, 1990:* Bans municipal incinerators and requires auto emission inspections in certain urban areas.

★ *Americans with Disabilities Act, 1990:* Requires all state and local government buildings to promote handicapped access.

★ *National Voter Registration Act, 1993:* Requires states to register voters at driver's license, welfare, and unemployment compensation offices.

★ *No Child Left Behind Act, 2001:* Requires states and their school districts to test public school pupils.

★ *Help America Vote Act, 2003:* Requires states to modernize registration and voting procedures and technologies.

★ *Homeland Security Act, 2002:* Requires states and communities as "first responders" to train, equip, and prepare for terrorist attacks.

"Unfunded" Mandates   Federal mandates often impose heavy costs on states and communities. When no federal monies are provided to cover these costs, the

A *Constitutional* Note

How Is National and State Power Divided?

The Constitution gives to Congress—that is, to the national government—seventeen specific grants of power, the so-called "enumerated powers." These are followed by an eighteenth "necessary and proper" power—"to make all laws which shall be necessary and proper for carrying into Execution the foregoing powers, and all other Powers vested by this Constitution in the Government of the United States . . ."(Article I, Section 8). It is this last "implied powers" or "elastic" clause that has been used extensively by the national government to greatly expand its power.

But what of the states? The Founders believed that the Constitution left all other governmental powers to the states. The 10th Amendment solidified that idea: "The powers not delegated to the United States by the Constitution, nor prohibited by it to the States, are reserved to the States respectively, or to the people." The "reserved powers" of the states are limited only by a few paragraphs in the text of the Constitution, notably Article I, Section 10, which, among other things, prohibits the states from entering into treaties with other nations, or coining money, or passing laws impairing the obligation of contracts, or granting any title of nobility, or placing taxes or duties on imports

or exports, or engaging in war with a foreign power "unless actually invaded."

In brief, the original Constitution envisioned the states as having the principal responsibility for the health, safety, education, welfare, law enforcement, and protection of their people. This constitutional "division of power" remains in the Constitution, despite great shifts in power to the national government. Subsequent amendments prohibited slavery in the states (13th Amendment); prohibited states from abridging the privileges or immunities of citizens of the United States, or depriving any person of life, liberty, or property without due process of law, or denying any person within this jurisdiction equal protection of the laws (14th Amendment); or prohibiting citizens the right to vote because of race, color, or previous condition of servitude (15th Amendment); or denying the right to vote for failure to pay any poll tax or other tax (24th Amendment); or denying anyone 18 years of age or older the right to vote on account of age (26th Amendment).

So anyone reading the Constitution, without knowledge of the history of constitutional change in United States, would not really understand the nature of American federalism.

---

mandates are said to be **unfunded mandates**. Governors, mayors, and other state and local officials have often urged Congress to stop imposing unfunded mandates on states and communities. Private industries have long voiced the same complaint. Regulations and mandates allow Congress to address problems while pushing the costs of doing so onto others.

Homeland Security   The Constitution gives the federal government the responsibility for national defense. The terrorist attacks on the World Trade Center in New York and the Pentagon in Washington, on September 11, 2001, began what President George W. Bush described as a long and difficult "war on terrorism." Washington reorganized itself, creating a new Department of Homeland Security (see Chapter 12), and allocated billions of dollars for homeland defenses. But the "first responders" to any terrorist attack are state and local police, fire, medical, and other emergency agencies. States, counties, and cities now face unprecedented and permanent responsibilities in homeland security, even including dealing with the results of nuclear, biological, and chemical attacks. Governors, mayors, city and county officials, and especially police, fire, and emergency officers, have urged the Congress to provide more federal funding and resources to state and local agencies for homeland security. Congress has responded with billions of dollars in additional aid, but states and communities claim that assistance for their "first responders" is inadequate.

★ **unfunded mandates**
Mandates that impose costs on state and local governments (and private industry) without reimbursement from the federal government.

Summary
Who Gets What: Dividing Government Power

The struggle for power between the national government and the states over two centuries has shaped American federalism today. American federalism was designed by the Founders as an additional protection for individual liberty by providing for the division and dispersal of power among multiple units of government.

★ Federalism is the division of power between two separate authorities, the nation and the state, each of which enforces its own laws directly on its citizens and neither of which can change the division of power without the consent of the other.

★ Federalism has also been defended as a means of increasing opportunities to hold public office, improving governmental efficiency, ensuring policy responsiveness, encouraging policy innovation, and managing conflict.

★ However, federalism can also obstruct and frustrate national action. Narrow state interests can sometimes prevail over national interests or the interests of minorities within states. Segregation was long protected by theories of states' rights. Federalism also results in uneven levels of public services through the nation.

★ Power has flowed to the national government over time, as the original state-centered division of power has evolved into a national-centered system of government. Among the most important historical influences on this shift in power toward Washington have been the Supreme Court's broad interpretation of national power, the national government's victory over the secessionist states in the Civil War, the establishment of a national system of civil rights based on the 14th Amendment, the growth of a national economy governed by Congress under its interstate commerce power, and the national government's accumulation of power through its greater financial resources.

★ Federal grants to state and local governments have greatly expanded the national government's powers in areas previously regarded as *reserved* to the states.

★ Federal grants are available for most state and local government activities, but health and welfare account for about two-thirds of these grants. Grant money flows unevenly to the states, causing complaints from states that send more tax dollars then they get back.

★ Although Congress has generally refrained from directly legislating in areas traditionally *reserved* to the states, federal power in local affairs has grown as a result of federal rules, regulations, and guidelines established as conditions for the receipt of federal funds.

★ The Supreme Court in its *Garcia* decision in 1985 removed all constitutional barriers to direct congressional legislation in matters traditionally reserved to the states. Establishing the principle of representational federalism, the Court said that states could defend their own interests through their representation in the national government.

★ Representational federalism focuses on the role of the states in electing national officials—the president through the allocation of Electoral College votes to the states, the Senate through the allocation of two seats for each state, and the House through the apportionment of representatives based on the state's population.

★ Recent efforts at the "devolution" of federal responsibilities for welfare resulted in an end to federal individual "entitlements" to cash welfare payments and their replacement with block grants for cash aid to the states. But Congress continues to place "strings" on the use of federal welfare grants to the states.

Key Terms

federalism 107	laboratories of	implied powers 113	cooperative federalism 118
unitary system 107	democracy 111	National Supremacy	centralized federalism 121
confederation 107	delegated, or enumerated,	Clause 113	new federalism 121
home rule 107	powers 113	concurrent powers 113	representational
intergovernmental	Necessary and Proper	reserved powers 113	federalism 121
relations 107	Clause 113	dual federalism 118	direct democracy 124

Suggested Readings

Dye, Thomas R. *American Federalism: Competition Among Governments*. Lexington, Mass.: Lexington Books, 1990. A theory of "competitive federalism" arguing that rivalries among governments improve public services while lowering taxes, restrain the growth of government, promote innovation and experimentation in public policies, inspire greater responsiveness to the preferences of citizen-taxpayers, and encourage economic growth.

Dye, Thomas R., and Susan A. MacManus. *Politics in States and Communities*. 13th ed. Upper Saddle River, N.J.: Prentice Hall, 2008. A general introduction to state and local government and politics, with an extended discussion of the politics of federalism.

Elazar, Daniel J. *The American Partnership*. Chicago: University of Chicago Press, 1962. Classic study of the historical evolution of federalism, stressing the nation-state sharing of policy concerns and financing, from the early days of the Republic, and the politics behind the gradual growth of national power.

Nagel, Robert F. *The Implosion of Federalism*. New York: Oxford University Press, 2001. America's political institutions are collapsing into the center, reducing the opportunity for competition and participation.

Ostrum, Vincent. *The Meaning of American Federalism*. San Francisco: ICS Press, 1991. A theoretical examination of federalism, setting forth the conditions for a self-governing society and arguing that multiple, overlapping units of government, with various checks on one another's power, provide a viable democratic system of conflict resolution.

O'Toole, Laurence J., ed. *American Intergovernmental Relations*. 4th ed. Washington, D.C.: CQ Press, 2006. A collection of readings, both classic and contemporary, describing the theory, history, and current problems of intergovernmental relations in America.

Peterson, Paul E. *The Price of Federalism*. Washington, D.C.: Brookings Institution, 1995. Historical, theoretical, and empirical perspectives merged into a new, timely model of federalism that would allocate social welfare functions to the national government and education and economic development to states and communities.

Riker, William H. *Federalism: Origin, Operation, Significance*. Boston: Little, Brown and Co. 1964. A classic account of federalism that considers the history of federalism, compares federalism as applied in different countries, and describes and analyses its operational principles.

Van Horn, Carl E. *The State of the States*. 4th ed. Washington, D.C.: CQ Press, 2005. An assessment of the challenges facing state governments as a result of the devolution revolution.

Suggested Web Sites

The Close Up Foundation   www.closeup.org
A nonprofit, nonpartisan citizenship education organization with excellent historical materials about federalism's evolution and information about federalism issues. A related link on the Close Up site contains the complete text of the pro-states' rights 1798 Kentucky and Virginia Resolutions (authored by Jefferson and Madison).

Council of State Governments   www.csg.org
Official Organization of U.S. states, providing information on their governmental structures, officials, and current issues.

European Union Online Official Site   www.europa.eu.int
Describes the structure of the organization, its membership, current issues, and so forth.

National Conference of State Legislatures   www.ncsl.org
This conference site provides information on 50 state legislatures and the issues they confront.

Urban Institute   www.urban.org
Washington think tank offers viewpoints on federalism and issues confronting state/local government.

5 OPINION AND PARTICIPATION

Thinking and Acting in Politics

> **"** People strive for power—to get the most of what there is to get. **"**

Harold Lasswell

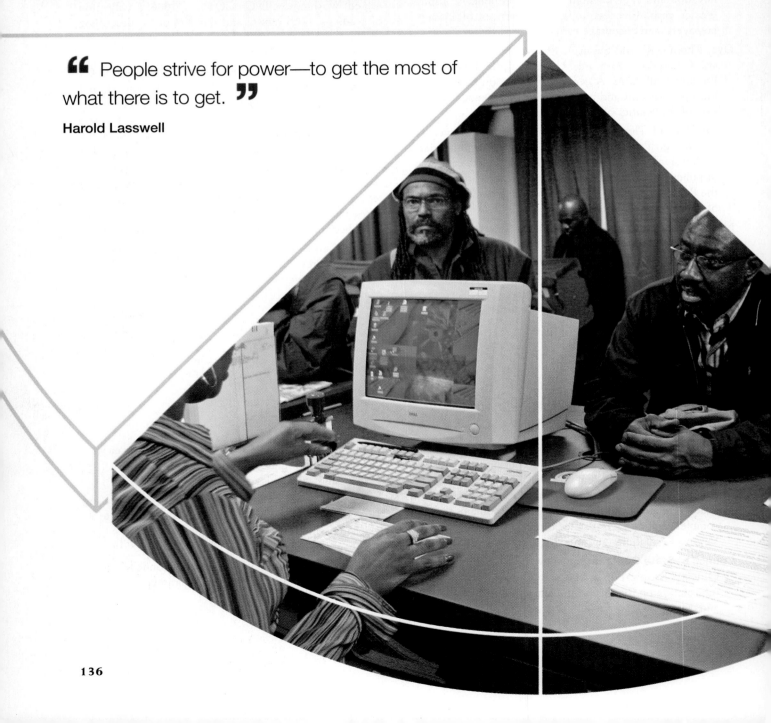

Chapter *Outline*

✔ Think About Politics

1. Should political leaders pay attention to public opinion polls when making decisions for the country?
   YES ◯ NO ◯

2. Do you believe that your representative in Congress cares about your personal opinion on important issues?
   YES ◯ NO ◯

3. Can you name the two U.S. senators from your state?
   YES ◯ NO ◯

4. Is our government really legitimate when only about half the people vote in presidential elections?
   YES ◯ NO ◯

5. Do you identify yourself with the same political party as your family?
   YES ◯ NO ◯

6. Is it appropriate for religious leaders to try to influence how people vote?
   YES ◯ NO ◯

7. Have you ever personally called or written to your representative in Congress?
   YES ◯ NO ◯

8. Do you think you will ever run for public office yourself?
   YES ◯ NO ◯

By thinking about politics and acting on your political opinions—voting, talking to friends, writing letters, joining organizations, attending meetings and rallies, contributing money, marching in demonstrations, or running for office yourself—you are participating in politics.

Politics and Public Opinion

For most Americans, politics is not as interesting as football or basketball, or the sex lives of celebrities, or prime-time television entertainment. Although politicians, pollsters, and commentators frequently assume that Americans have formed opinions on major public issues, in fact, most have not given them very much thought. Nevertheless, **public opinion** commands the attention of politicians, the news media, and political scientists.

Public opinion is given a lot of attention in democracies because democratic government rests on the consent of the governed. The question of whether public opinion *should* direct government policy has confounded political philosophers for centuries. Edmund Burke, writing in 1790, argued that democratic representatives should serve the *interests* of the people, but not necessarily conform to their *will*, in deciding questions of public policy. In contrast, other political philosophers have evaluated the success of democratic institutions by whether or not they produce policies that conform to popular opinion.

Major shifts in public opinion in the United States generally translate into policy change. Both the president and Congress appear to respond over time to *general* public preferences for "more" or "less" government regulation, "more" or "less" government spending, "getting tough on crime," "reforming welfare," and so on.[1] But public opinion is often weak, unstable, ill informed, or nonexistent on *specific* policy issues. Consequently, elected officials have greater flexibility in dealing with these issues—and, at the same time, there is an increase in the influence of lobbyists, interest groups, reporters, commentators, and others who have direct access to policy makers. Moreover, the absence of well-formed public opinion on an issue provides interest groups and the media with the opportunity to influence policy indirectly by shaping popular opinion.

Politicians read the opinion polls. And even though many elected representatives claim that they exercise independent judgment about what

★ **public opinion**
Aggregate of preferences and opinions of individuals on significant issues.

Politics Up Close   Can We Believe the Polls?

Survey research is a flourishing political enterprise. The national news media—notably CBS, NBC, ABC, FOX, and CNN television networks, the *New York Times* and the *Washington Post*, and *Time* and *Newsweek* magazines—regularly sponsor independent national surveys, especially during election campaigns. Major survey organizations—the American Institute of Public Opinion (Gallup), Louis Harris and Associates, National Opinion Research Center (NORC), the Roper Organization, National Election Studies (University of Michigan)—have been in business for a long time and have files of survey results going back many years. Political candidates also contract with private marketing and opinion research firms to conduct surveys in conjunction with their campaigns.

Public opinion surveys depend on the selection of a *random sample* of persons chosen in a way which ensures that every person in the *universe* of people about whom information is desired has an equal chance of being selected for interviewing. National samples, representative of all adults or all voters, usually include only about 1,000 persons. First, geographical areas (for example, counties or telephone area codes) that are representative of all such areas in the nation are chosen. Then residential telephone numbers are randomly selected within these areas. Once the numbers have been selected at random, the poll taker does not make substitutions but calls back several times if necessary to make contact so as not to bias the sample toward people who stay at home. An increasingly troublesome problem in survey research: nearly 15 percent of U.S. households cannot now be reached by the typical telephone survey because they have only a cell phone and no landline telephone. While there is no conclusive evidence yet that cell-only users respond differently to poll questions than landline users, survey researchers must soon address this problem.

Even when random-selection procedures are closely followed, the sample may not be truly representative of the universe. But survey researchers can estimate the *sampling error* through the mathematics of probability. The sampling error is usually expressed as a percentage range—for example, plus or minus 3 percent—above and below the sample response within which there is a 95 percent likelihood that the same response would be found if the entire universe

were questioned. For example, if 65 percent of the survey respondents favor the death penalty and the sampling error is calculated at plus or minus 3 percent, then we can say there is a 95 percent probability that a survey of the whole population (the universe) would produce a response of between 62 and 68 percent in favor of the death penalty.

"Loaded" or "leading" questions are often used by unprofessional pollsters simply to produce results favorable to their side of an argument. An even worse abuse in telephone polling is the "push poll"—questions asked by political campaign workers posing as independent pollsters, deliberately worded to create an opinion—for example, "If you knew that Congressman Smith would soon be indicted for child molestation, would you vote for him?"

Professional pollsters strive for questions that are clear and precise, easily understood by the respondents, and as neutral and unbiased as possible. Nevertheless, because all questions have a potential bias, it is often better to examine *changes over time* in response to identically worded questions. Perhaps the best-known continuing question in public opinion polling is the presidential approval rating: "Do you approve or disapprove of the way____ is handling his job as president?" Changes over time in public response to this question alert scholars, commentators, and presidents themselves to their public standing (see Chapter 11).

A survey can only measure opinions *at the time* it is taken. A few days later public opinion may change, especially if major events that receive heavy television coverage intervene. Some political pollsters conduct continuous "tracking" surveys until election night in order to catch last-minute opinion changes.

An altogether different type of poll is the *exit poll*, during which election day voters are personally interviewed as they leave the voting booth. Exit polls are used by the media to "call" winners early on election night even before all votes are counted. Television networks now jointly contract with an independent company, VNS, to select voting precincts at random, interview voters, and fast-forward the results to the networks. The networks analyze the results and make their own "calls." In response to criticism that early calls reduce voter turnout, the networks have agreed not to call a state result until the polls close in that state.

is best for the nation in their decision making, we can be reasonably sure their "independent judgment" is influenced at least in part by what they think their constituents want. The cynical stereotype of the politician who reads the opinion polls before taking stands on the issues is often embarrassingly accurate.

All this attention to public opinion has created a thriving industry in public opinion polling and **survey research**. Polls have become a fixture of American political life (see *Politics Up Close:* "Can We Believe the Polls?"). But how much do Americans really think about politics? How informed, stable, and consistent is public opinion?

Knowledge Levels   Most Americans do *not* follow politics closely enough to develop well-informed opinions on many public issues (see Figure 5.1). Low levels of knowledge about government and public affairs make it difficult for people to form opinions on specific issues or policy proposals. Many opinion surveys ask questions about topics that people had not considered before being interviewed. Few respondents are willing to admit that they know nothing about the topic or have "no opinion." Respondents believe they should provide some sort of answer, even if their opinion was nonexistent before the question was asked. The result is that the polls themselves "create" opinions.[2]

The "Halo Effect"   Many respondents give "good citizen" or socially respectable answers, whether they are truthful or not, even to an anonymous interviewer. This **halo effect** leads to an *underestimation* of the true extent of prejudice, hatred, and bigotry. Another common example of the halo effect is the fact that people do not like to admit that they do not vote. Surveys regularly report higher percentages of people *saying* they voted in an election than the actual number of ballots cast. Moreover, postelection surveys almost always produce higher percentages of people who say they voted for the winner than the actual vote tally for the winner. Apparently poll respondents do not like to admit that they backed the loser.

Inconsistencies   Because so many people hold no real opinion on political issues, the wording of a question frequently determines their response. People

★ **survey research**
Gathering of information about public opinion by questioning a representative sample of the population.

Comparing Governments and Public Opinion

You Are a Polling Consultant

★ **halo effect**
Tendency of survey respondents to provide socially acceptable answers to questions.

Should political leaders pay attention to public opinion polls when making decisions for the country?

Figure *5.1*

Cause for Concern?: What Americans [Don't] Know about Politics

Politics is not the major interest of most Americans, and as a result knowledge about the political system is limited. Less than one-third of the general public knows the names of their representatives in Congress or their U.S. senators, and knowledge of specific foreign and domestic matters is even more limited.

Source: Data from Robert S. Erikson and Kent L. Tedin, *American Public Opinion*, 7th ed. (New York: Pearson Longman, 2007). p. 62 citing various polls.

Knowledge	Percent
Know the president's term is 4 years	96%
Can name the governor of home state	74%
Can name vice president	78%
Know which party has U.S. House majority	69%
Know there are two U.S. senators per state	52%
Can name their House member	40%
Aware Bill of Rights is first ten amendments to U.S. Constitution	39%
Can name both of their U.S. senators	39%
Can name current U.S. secretary of state	34%
Know term of U.S. House member is 2 years	30%
Can name Chief Justice of United States	8%

Percent

Controversy

Abortion: The "Hot-Button" Issue

Although public opinion may be weak or nonexistent on many policy questions, there are a few "hot-button" issues in politics—issues on which virtually everyone has an opinion and many people feel very intensely about.

Abortion is one such highly sensitive issue. Both *pro-choice* proponents of legalized abortion and *pro-*

life opponents claim to have public opinion on their side. *Interpretation* of the poll results becomes a political activity itself. Consider, for example, responses to the general question posed in the graph pictured here.

Pro-choice forces interpret these results as overwhelming support for legalized abortion; pro-life

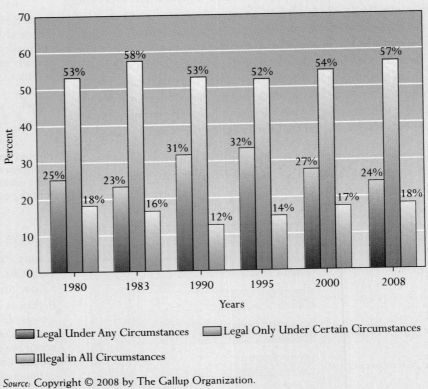

Question: *Do you think abortions should be legal under any circumstances, legal only under certain circumstances, or illegal in all circumstances?*

Legal Under Any Circumstances   Legal Only Under Certain Circumstances
Illegal in All Circumstances

Source: Copyright © 2008 by The Gallup Organization.

respond positively to positive phrases (for example, "helping poor people," "improving education," "cleaning up the environment") and negatively to negative phrases (for example, "raising taxes," "expanding governmental power," "restricting choice").

The wording of questions, combined with weak or nonexistent opinion, often produces inconsistent responses. For example, when asked whether they agreed or disagreed with the statement that "people should have the right to purchase a sexually explicit book, magazine, or movie, if that's what they want to do," an overwhelming 80 percent endorsed the statement. However, when the same respondents were also asked whether they agreed with the opposite statement that "community authorities should be able to prohibit the selling of magazines or movies they consider to be pornographic," 65 percent approved of this view as well.[3]

commentators interpret these results as majority support for restricting abortion. Indeed, public opinion appears to support *specific restrictions* on abortion but oppose a constitutional ban on abortions.

In short, most Americans appear to want to keep some abortions legal, but they believe that government should place certain restrictions on the practice.

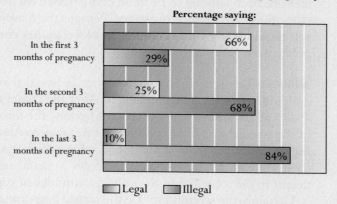

Thinking more generally,
do you think abortion should generally be legal
or generally be illegal during the following stages of pregnancy?

Percentage saying:

In the first 3 months of pregnancy: 66% / 29%
In the second 3 months of pregnancy: 25% / 68%
In the last 3 months of pregnancy: 10% / 84%

☐ Legal   ☐ Illegal

Source: Gallup, CNN, *USA Today*, as reported on Public Opinion Online, *www.publicagenda.org*, October, 2003. Copyright © 2003 by The Gallup Organization.

Salience   People are likely to think more about issues that receive a great deal of attention in the mass media—television, newspapers, magazines. **Salient issues** are those that people think about most—issues on which they hold stronger and more consistent opinions. These are issues that people feel relate directly to their own lives, such as abortion (see *Controversy:* "Abortion: The 'Hot-Button Issue'"). Salient issues are, therefore, more important in politics.

Salient issues change over time. In general, during recessions the most salient issue is "Jobs, Jobs, Jobs!"—that is, unemployment and the economy. During inflationary periods, the issue is "the high cost of living." During wartime, the war itself becomes the public's principal concern. A gasoline shortage can turn public concern toward energy issues. These salient issues drive the political debate of the times.[4]

★ **salient issues**
Issues about which most people have an opinion.

War, Peace, and Public Opinion

Socialization: The Origins of Political Opinions

Where do people acquire their political opinions? Political **socialization** is the learning of political values, beliefs, and opinions. It begins early in life when a child acquires images and attitudes toward public authority. Preschool children see "police officer" and "president" as powerful yet benevolent "helpers." These figures—police officer and president—are usually the first recognized sources of authority above the parents who must be obeyed. They are usually positive images of authority at these early ages:

★ **socialization**
The learning of a culture and its values.

Q: What does the policeman do?
A: He catches bad people.[5]

★ **diffuse support (for the political system)** goodwill toward governmental authority learned early in life.

Even the American flag is recognized by most U.S. preschoolers, who pick it out when asked, "Which flag is your favorite?" These early positive perceptions about political figures and symbols may later provide **diffuse support** for the political system—a reservoir of goodwill toward governmental authority that lends legitimacy to the political order.

Family The family is the first agent of socialization. Children in the early school grades (3 to 5) begin to identify themselves as Republicans or Democrats. These childhood party identifications are almost always the same as those of the parents. Indeed, parent–child correspondence in party identification may last a lifetime.[6] The children who abandon the party of their parents tend to become independents rather than identify with the opposition party. However, party identification appears to be more easily passed on from parent to child than specific opinions on policy questions. Perhaps the reason is that parental party identifications are known to children, but few families conduct specific discussions of policy questions.

School Political revolutionaries once believed that the school was the key to molding political values and beliefs. After the communist revolutions in Russia in 1917 and China in 1949, the schools became the focus of political indoctrination of the population. Today political battles rage in America over textbooks, teaching methods, prayer in schools, and other manifestations of politics in the classroom. But no strong evidence indicates a causal relationship between what is taught in the schools and the political attitudes of students.

Certainly the schools provide the factual basis for understanding government—how the president is chosen, the three branches of government, how a law is passed. But even this elemental knowledge is likely to fade if not reinforced by additional education or exposure to the news media or discussion with family or peers.

The schools *try* to inculcate "good citizenship" values, including support for democratic rules, tolerance toward others, the importance of voting, and the legitimacy (rightfulness) of government authority. Patriotic symbols and rituals abound in the classroom—the flag, the Pledge of Allegiance—and students are taught to respect the institutions of government. Generally the younger the student, the more positive the attitudes expressed toward political authority.[7] Yet despite the efforts of the schools to inspire support for the political system, distrust and cynicism creep in during the high school years. Although American youth retain a generally positive view of the political system, they share with adults increasing skepticism toward specific institutions and practices. During high school, students acquire some ability to think along liberal-conservative dimensions. The college experience appears to produce a "liberalizing" effect: college seniors tend to be more liberal than entering freshmen. But over the years following graduation, liberal views tend to moderate.

Although no direct evidence indicates that the schools can inculcate democratic values, people with more education tend to be more tolerant than those with less education and to be generally more supportive of the political system (see Table 5.1). This pattern suggests that the effects of schooling are gradual and subtle (see also *Controversy:* "College Students' Opinions").

Church Religious beliefs and values may also shape political opinion. *Which* religion an individual identifies with (for example, Protestant, Catholic, Jewish) affects public opinion. So does *how important* religion is in the individual's life. It is difficult to explain exactly how religion affects political values, but we can observe

Table *5.1* Education and Tolerance: A Strong Correlation

Tolerance generally increases with educational level.

	Percentage Responding "Yes" (by highest degree completed)				
	No High School	**High School**	**Junior College**	**College Degree**	**Total**
If such a person wanted to make a speech in your community, should he be allowed to speak? (Yes)					
Atheist (antireligion)	47%	72%	83%	88%	70%
Racist	47	61	68	77	62
Homosexual	52	77	86	90	74
Should such a person be allowed to teach in a college or university? (Yes)					
Atheist (antireligion)	29%	50%	66%	72%	50%
Racist	35	43	52	58	45
Homosexual	41	67	80	84	65

Source: General Social Survey, Cumulative Index, 1971–2004 (Chicago: National Opinion Research Center).

differences in the opinions expressed by Protestants, Catholics, and Jews; by people who say their religious beliefs are strong versus those who say they are not; and between fundamentalists (those who believe in a literal interpretation of the Bible) and nonfundamentalists. Religion shapes political attitudes on a variety of issues, including abortion, drugs, the death penalty, homosexuality, and prayer in public schools[8] (see Table 5.2). Religion also plays a measurable role in political ideology. Fundamentalists are more likely to describe themselves as conservatives than as moderates, and very few accept the liberal label.[9]

At the same time, however, most Americans are concerned about religious leaders exercising influence in political life. Most respondents say it is "not appropriate for religious leaders to talk about their political beliefs as part of their religious activities" (61 percent), "religious leaders should not try to influence how people vote in elections" (64 percent), and "religious groups should *not* advance their beliefs by being involved in politics and working to affect policy" (54 percent).[10]

Think
Again
Is it appropriate for religious leaders to try to influence how people vote?

Table *5.2* Religion and Public Opinion: It's Strength of Conviction, Not Church Affiliation, That Matters

The strength of religious conviction is more important in shaping public opinion than church affiliation.

Opinion	Affiliation			Faith		Belief That the Bible Is . . .		
	Protestant	**Catholic**	**Jew**	**Strong**	**Not Very Strong**	**Literal Word of God**	**Inspired by God**	**Book of Fables**
Abortion for any reason should be legal	36%	35%	79%	26%	47%	23%	44%	67%
Legalize marijuana	19	23	43	14	28	13	23	45
Support death penalty	60	65	69	68	79	69	78	71
Remove book that favored homosexuality from library	42	31	15	46	31	54	24	17
Support prayer in public school	67	60	17	70	57	78	55	33

Source: General Social Survey, Cumulative Index, 2000 (Chicago: National Opinion Research Center). Cross-tabulations by Nikita Desai, Department of Political Science, Purdue University.

Table 5.3 Age and Public Opinion: Opinion and Participation Change with the Years

Younger people express somewhat more liberal opinions than the elderly, but younger people vote less often and show less interest in politics.

	Under 30	55 and Over
Marijuana should be made legal	35%	17%
Allow homosexuals to teach in college	88	61
Allow abortion for any reason	40	28
Describe oneself as:		
Liberal	39	21
Moderate	37	33
Conservative	24	46
Read news about presidential campaign	42	71
Pay attention to national news	33	57
Vote in presidential election	24	65

Source: Questions from *National Election Studies* and *General Social Surveys*, 2004.

Age and Opinion   Age group differences in politics and public opinion are sometimes referred to as the **generation gap**. On most of the issues shown in Table 5.3, older people appear to be more conservative than younger people. Older people are less likely than younger people to favor the legalization of marijuana, to allow abortion for any reason, or to allow homosexuals to teach in college; older people are more likely to identify themselves as "conservative." Younger Americans in general appear to be less interested and involved in politics than older Americans; they are less likely to keep up with political news and, perhaps most importantly, are less likely to vote (see Table 5.3, and the discussion later in this chapter).

★ **generation gap**
Differences in politics and public opinion among age groups.

Democracy and the Internet

Media Influence   Television is the major source of political information for Americans. More than two-thirds report that they receive "all or most" of their news from television, making newspapers, magazines, books, the Internet, and radio secondary to television as a source of political information (see Chapter 6). Moreover, Americans rate television the "most believable" channel of communication.

But the effect of television on opinion is not really in persuading people to take one side of an issue or another. Instead, the principal effect is in *setting the agenda* for thinking and talking about politics. Television does not tell people *what* to think, but it does tell them what to think *about*. Television coverage

Source: PEANUTS reprinted by permission of United Feature Syndicate, Inc.

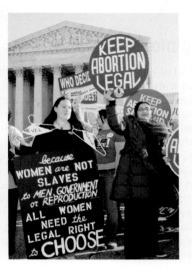

Religion Helps Shape Politics

Top left: Catholics protest a tax-supported museum's showing of feces-smeared painting of the Virgin Mary. Bottom left: Christian social and political activists, led by Rev. Patrick J. Mahoney (right), protest in front of the White House. They wanted President Bush to boycott the opening ceremonies of the Beijing Olympics. They were all later arrested and taken to jail. Right: Pro-choice advocates protest in front of the U.S. Supreme Court during the confirmation of Samuel Alito to the Supreme Court.

determines matters of general public concern. Without coverage, the general public would not know about, think about, or discuss most events, personalities, and issues. Media attention creates issues, and the amount of attention given an issue determines its importance. (We return to the discussion of media power in Chapter 6.)

Ideology and Opinion

Ideology helps to shape opinion. Many people, especially politically interested and active people, approach policy questions with a fairly consistent and integrated set of principles—that is, an *ideology* (see Chapter 2). Liberal and conservative ideas about the proper role of government in the economy, about the regulation of social conduct, about equality and the distribution of income, and about civil rights influence people's views on specific policy questions.

Who Are Liberals and Conservatives? What's the Difference?

To what extent do self-described liberals and conservatives differ over specific issues? Can we predict people's stances on particular issues by knowing whether they call themselves liberal or conservative? Generally speaking, self-described liberals and conservatives do differ in their responses to specific policy questions, although some take policy positions inconsistent with their proclaimed ideology (see Table 5.4). People who describe themselves as liberal generally favor governmental efforts to reduce income inequalities and to improve the positions of African Americans, other minorities, and women. Overall, it appears that ideology and opinion are fairly well linked—that the liberal-conservative dimension is related to opinions on specific policy questions.[11]

Gender and Opinion

A **gender gap** in public opinion—a difference of opinion between men and women—occurs on only a few issues. Interestingly, a gender gap does *not* appear on women's issues: abortion, the role of women in business and politics, whether one would vote for a qualified woman for president, or whether men are better suited for political office. On these issues, men and women do not differ significantly (see Figure 5.2).

★ **gender gap**
Aggregate differences in political opinions between men and women.

Controversy

College Students' Opinions

College students' opinions today appear to be somewhat more conservative then they were a generation ago, in the 1970s. While most students identify themselves politically as "middle-of-the-road," there are somewhat more "conservative" self-identifiers and fewer "liberal" self identifiers than 35 years ago. On policy issues, students today are more likely to support the death penalty, believe the courts are too lenient with criminals, and oppose legalization of marijuana. (However, students are somewhat more liberal on these issues today than in the 1980s and 1990s.) Students in the 1970s confronted an unpopular war in Vietnam, faced a military draft, and were more likely to experiment with drugs and alternative lifestyles. Today's students confront greater economic competition and increased educational requirements for employment. They are more concerned with their financial future than students were a generation ago.

However, college students remain somewhat more liberal than the general population. Moreover, college seniors and graduate students are more liberal than first-year students; students at prestigious Ivy League universities are more liberal than students at state universities and community colleges; and students in humanities and social sciences are more liberal than students in engineering, physical sciences, and business. Over the years following graduation, many of these liberal predispositions tend to moderate.

Political Opinions of College Students

	1972	1995	2000	2007
Political ideology				
Far left	2%	3%	3%	3%
Liberal	33	21	25	28
Middle-of-the road	48	50	51	43
Conservative	16	20	20	24
Far right	1	2	1	2
Policy issues				
Abolish the death penalty	33	21	32	34
Courts are too concerned with rights of criminals	50	73	64	56
Marijuana should be legal	47	34	40	37

Source: Data taken from various issues of the Chronicle of Higher Education, reporting annual polls by the American Council on Education.

However, gender gap differences are apparent on a variety of contemporary issues (see Figure 5.2). Many polls report that women are more likely than men:

★ To favor an activist role for government

★ To oppose U.S. military intervention

★ To support restrictions on firearms

★ To support spending on social programs

★ To support affirmative action

Politically, the most important gender gap is in party identification. Women are more likely to identify themselves as Democrats. This difference emerged in the 1980s, when men were more likely than women to support Republican president Ronald Reagan.[12] (Group differences in party identification are discussed at length in Chapter 7.)

Table **5.4**   Deciding Who Gets What: How Ideology Influences Opinion

Self-described "liberals" and "conservatives" differ over many specific policy questions.

Opinion	Percent Agreeing	
	Liberals	Conservatives
The government should provide "more services even if it means an increase in spending"	89%	39%
The government should guarantee "that every person has a job and good standard of living"	71	16
Favor "government insurance plan which would cover all medical and hospital expenses for everyone"	84	30
The government "should make every effort to improve the social and economic position of blacks"	59	17
Permit abortion "always" or "if needed"	78	44
The government "should make it more difficult to buy a gun"	77	43
Favor diplomacy to solve international problems rather than being ready to use military	84	30
Favor laws to "protect homosexuals from job discrimination"	90	64
Oppose "death penalty for persons convicted of murder"	49	21
The United States "should spend less on defense"	56	12

Source: National Elections Studies, 2004.

Race and Opinion

Opinion over the extent of discrimination in the United States and over the causes of and remedies for racial inequality differs sharply across racial lines. Most whites believe there is very little discrimination toward African Americans in jobs, housing, or education and that differences between whites and blacks in society occur as a result of a lack of motivation among black people. Most African Americans strongly disagree with these views and believe that discrimination continues in employment, housing, and education and that differences between whites and blacks in standards of living are "mainly due to discrimination" (see Figure 5.3).

African Americans generally support a more positive role for government in reducing inequality in society. Approximately two out of every three believe that government should do more to reduce income differences between rich and poor. Blacks favor busing to achieve racial balance in public schools, a view not shared by many whites. Given these preferences for a strong role for government, it is not surprising that more blacks than whites identify themselves as liberals. However, about one-quarter of black people identify themselves as conservative. And indeed, on certain social issues—crime, drugs, school prayers—majorities of black people take conservative positions.

African American perceptions of the criminal justice system are especially negative. Police encounters with black civilians have inspired many of the most destructive riots and demonstrations. Most whites believe the criminal justice system is fundamentally fair; most blacks do not. Whites attribute police brutality to individual malfeasance by officers; blacks see it as racism when the victim is black. Blacks see the disproportionate percentages of blacks in prison as discrimination; whites see it as a product of greater criminality among African Americans.[13]

African Americans are more likely than whites to support governmental actions and programs to improve the position of black people and other minorities. Levels of support for affirmative action depend on the wording of the question, but regardless of wording, blacks are more likely to support racial and minority preferences than whites.

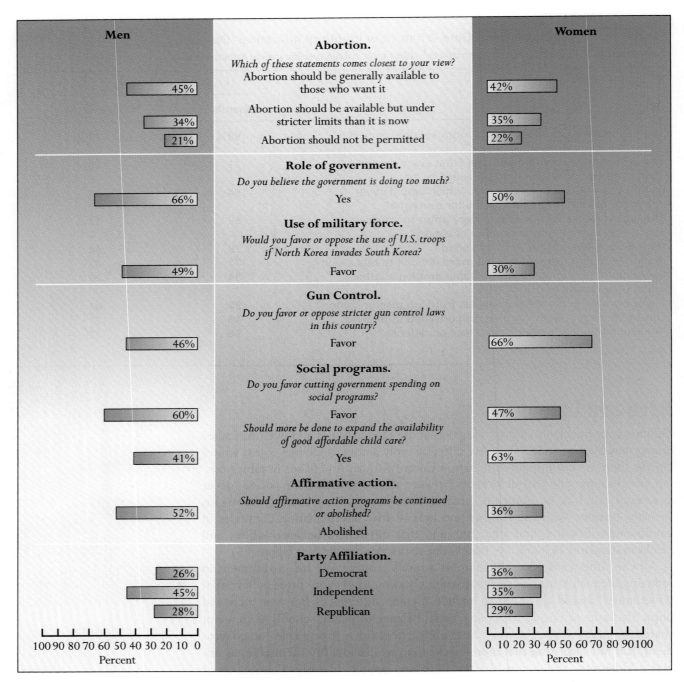

Figure *5.2* The Gender Gap: Differences in Policy Opinions

A gender gap exists in a variety of issues, but not on abortion. Also, women are more likely to identify themselves as Democrats than men do.

Source: Reprinted by permission of Center for American Women and Politics, Eagleton Institute of Politics, Rutgers, The State University of New Jersey. *Note:* The data in this figure was compiled by authors drawing from information collected by the Center for American Women and Politics from a number of surveys conducted by various groups in the mid-1990s. For complete information, go www.cawp.rutgers.edu

Hispanic Opinion

Hispanic voters are a growing force in American politics.[14] (Most Hispanics have no preference regarding the use of Hispanic or Latino to describe their ethnicity.) While Hispanic voter turnout has been low (Hispanics made up only about 6 percent of the voters in the 2004 presidential election, despite

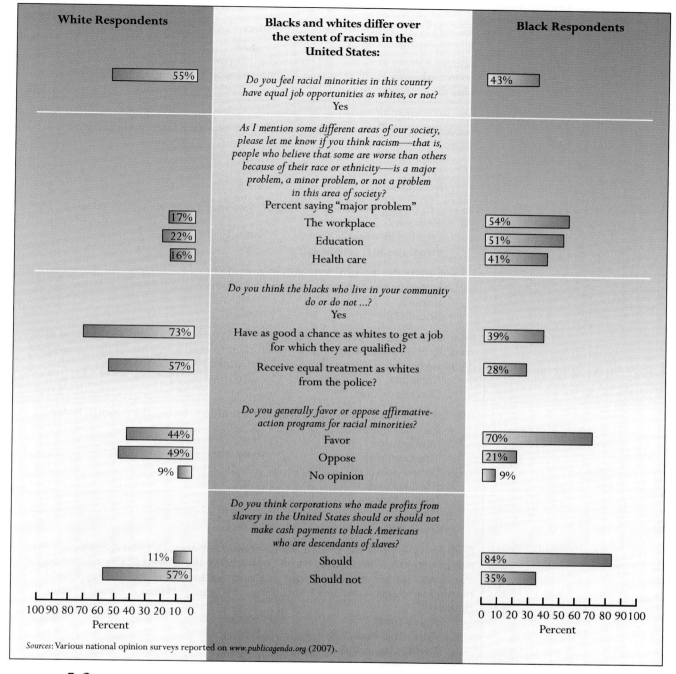

White Respondents	Blacks and whites differ over the extent of racism in the United States:	Black Respondents

Figure 5.3 The Racial Gap: Differences in Policy Opinions

Blacks are more likely than whites to perceive racism in the workplace, education, and health care as a "major problem," and blacks are more likely than whites to support affirmative action programs.

accounting for about 14 percent of the U.S. population), population projections forecast an ever-growing role for Hispanics in national politics (see "Hispanic Politics" in Chapter 15).

Polls suggest that Hispanics are generally conservative on social issues, for example, opposing abortion, opposing racial preferences (see Table 5.5). However, they appear to be liberal on economic issues, for example, favoring government provision of health insurance for all. Hispanics identify Iraq and the war on terror is the most important problem confronting the country followed

Table 5.5 Hispanic Opinion: Policy Preferences of a Growing Demographic

Hispanic opinion tends toward conservatism on social issues and liberalism or economic issues. Hispanic opinion generally favors immigration and believes it helps the economy.

The terms Hispanic *and* Latino *are both used to describe people who are of Hispanic or Latin origin or descent. Do you happen to prefer Hispanic or Latino?*

Hispanic	22%
Latino	11%
No preference	67%

Do you think abortion should be legal in all cases, illegal in most cases, or illegal in all cases?

Legal in all cases	40%
Illegal in most or all cases	58%

Do you think the government should provide health insurance for Americans without insurance, or is this something the government should not do?

Should	83%
Should not	14%

Should colleges sometimes take a student's racial and ethnic background into consideration when deciding which student to admit, or should they select students without considering their racial or ethnic backgrounds?

Consider	40%
Don't consider	18%

What do you think is the most important problem facing the country today?

Iraq/war on terror	32%
Immigration	19%
The economy	16%
Crime/violence	5%
Social issues	8%
Health care	1%
Other	7%
Don't know	12%

Some people think the United States should allow more Latin Americans into this country to work legally; some people think the United States should allow the same number as it does now; and some others think it should reduce the number who come and work in this country legally. Which is closer to your opinion?

Allow more	48%
Allow the same number	32%
Reduce the number	18%
Don't know	8%

Some people say undocumented or illegal immigrants help the economy by providing low-cost labor. Others say they hurt the economy by driving wages down. Which is closer to your view?

Help the economy	72%
Hurt the economy	21%
Don't know	7%

Source: Pew Hispanic Center, Latino Immigration Study, 2007. www.pewhispanic.org

by immigration and the economy. They generally believe that immigration helps the economy, and they oppose reducing the number of Latinos who come to work in this country legally.

Compared to *What*

World Opinion About the USA

Global public opinion has become increasingly unfavorable toward the United States in recent years. World opinion sympathized with the United States immediately following the terrorist attack of September 11, 2001. But since then, U.S. military involvement in Iraq has led to increasingly unfavorable views of America.

The Pew Global Attitudes Project reports that favorable ratings of America are lower in 26 of 33 countries for which trends are available. Yet the United States continues to receive favorable ratings from about half of the nations surveyed in 2007. Nevertheless, unfavorable attitudes are rising among the populations of many of our traditional allies. And negative views of the United States continue to prevail in much of the Muslim world.

Favorable	Views of The United States	Unfavorable
80%	United States	18%
78%	Israel	20%
61%	Poland	31%
61%	Japan	36%
59%	India	28%
58%	South Korea	38%
56%	Mexico	41%
55%	Canada	42%
53%	Italy	38%
51%	Great Britain	42%
46%	Sweden	49%
45%	Czech Republic	50%
44%	Brazil	51%
41%	Russia	48%
39%	France	60%
34%	China	57%
34%	Spain	60%
30%	Germany	66%
29%	Indonesia	66%
21%	Egypt	78%
20%	Jordan	78%
15%	Pakistan	68%
9%	Turkey	83%

Source: Selected nations from Pew Global Attitudes Project, 2007. www.pewglobal.org

Conflicting Views

Students at Augustana College react to the verdict in the nationally televised trial of O. J. Simpson for murder. Simpson was found not guilty by the jury. The verdict focused national attention on the great differences between the beliefs of whites and African Americans about the role of racism in the criminal justice system.

Think Again

Do you believe that your representative in Congress cares about your personal opinion on important issues?

Policy and Opinion

Does public opinion determine government policy? It is widely assumed that in a democracy, government policy will be heavily influenced by public opinion. Yet, as noted earlier, public opinion is weak or nonexistent on many policy questions; it is frequently inconsistent and unstable; and it is poorly informed about many policy issues. Under these circumstances, political leaders—presidents and members of Congress, bureaucrats, judges, and other public officials—are relatively unconstrained by mass opinion in policy decisions (see *What Do You Think?* "Should Government Leaders Pay More Attention to Public Opinion?"). Moreover, in the absence of well-formed public opinion on an issue, other political actors—lobbyists and lawyers, interest-group spokespersons, journalists and commentators, television reporters and executives—can influence public policy by communicating directly with government officials, claiming to represent the public. They can also influence public policy indirectly by molding and shaping public opinion.

The weakness of public opinion on many policy issues increases the influence of elites, that small group of people who are interested and active in public affairs, who call or write their elected representatives; who join organizations and contribute money to causes and candidates; who attend meetings, rallies, and demonstrations; and who hold strong opinions on a wide variety of public issues. According to political scientist V. O. Key, Jr., the linkage between ordinary citizens and democratic government depends heavily on "that thin stratum of persons referred to variously as the political elite, the political activists, the leadership echelons, or the influentials."[15] Thus political *participation* appears to be the essential link between opinion and policy.

Individual Participation in Politics

Democracies provide a variety of ways for individuals to participate in politics. People may run for, and win, public office; take part in marches, demonstrations, and protests; make financial contributions to political candidates or causes;

What Do You *Think?*

Should Government Leaders Pay More Attention to Public Opinion?

In 1774 the British parliamentarian Edmund Burke told his Bristol constituents: "Your representative owes you, not his industry only, but his judgment; and he betrays, instead of serving you, if he sacrifices it to your opinion." Since then, "Burkean representation" has come to refer to political delegates using their own judgment in decision making, without paying much or any attention to public opinion polls. Indeed, many politicians boast of their own courage and independence and of their willingness to ignore public opinion polls on major issues. And political experts in higher education and the media repeatedly point out that the American public is woefully ill informed about political facts—whether about American government or the world at large—that the public is unstable and vacillating in its opinions and priorities, and that Americans are often highly emotional in their responses to difficult and complex issues. Shaping policy to public opinion would be irresponsible and possibly downright dangerous.

But other experts believe that the country would be much better off if politicians paid more attention to public opinion. A number of political scientists point out that public opinion is much more stable and much more reasonable than policy makers and the media would have us believe. There is evidence in polling data over a 30-year period that shows the wisdom and steadfastness of the American public with respect to important issues in U.S. foreign policy—one of the chief areas in which policy makers are wary of the public's judgment.[a] Despite the fact that Americans have limited political knowledge and pay only scant and often fleeting attention to politics, they take reasonable positions: they seek international justice and domestic prosperity and not just security from attack, and they seek to pursue such goals in cooperation with other countries—multilaterally, that is—rather than on their own. The American public (77 percent) agrees that the United Nations "needs to be strengthened." Over four-fifths of Americans believe that the United States should pursue international diplomatic efforts together with other nations to prevent and apprehend terrorists and terrorist suspects (80–89 percent), and the public overwhelmingly supports the use of U.S. troops for humanitarian operations (76–81 percent).

Polls show that the American public certainly believes that the country would be much better off if politicians paid more attention to public opinion.

Q. If the leaders of the nation followed the views of the public more closely, do you think that the nation would be better off or worse off than it is today?

Better	81%
Worse	10%

Indeed, most Americans believe that members of Congress should "read up on the polls" in order to "get a sense of the public's views."

Q. Please tell me which statement you agree with most: (A) When members of Congress are thinking about how to vote on an issue, they should read up on the polls, because this can help them get a sense of the public's views on the issue. (B) When members of Congress are thinking about how to vote on an issue, they should not read the polls, because this will distract them from thinking about what is right.

Should read polls	67%
Should not read polls	26%

But other evidence shows that most members of Congress do not put much stake in public opinion. When members of Congress were asked, "*Do you think the American public knows enough about the issues you face to form wise opinions about what should be done about these issues, or not,*" fewer than one-third (31 percent) said "Yes," whereas almost half (47 percent) said "No" (17 percent answered "Maybe").

In-depth interviews with senior congressional staff personnel reveal much the same thing: only 13 percent of the staffers thought that the purpose of public opinion was to lead public policy; 36 percent reported that public opinion information was used to educate or lead members of Congress; and 31 percent thought that the purpose of collecting information on public opinion was both to lead and to respond.[b] Political scientists Lawrence R. Jacobs and Robert Y. Shapiro found that members of Congress did not so much use information on public opinion to guide their decisions, but rather used it for their own tactical reasons; they ignored public opinion polls when public opinion conflicted with their decisions, and they publicized their agreement with public opinion when poll results meshed with their own judgments.

Still other research suggests that to put responsibility on the American public is misplaced, since Americans themselves don't trust the good judgment of their fellow citizens. Political scientists John Hibbing and Elizabeth Theiss-Morse report that Americans believe that elected officials are both more

[a]Benjamin I. Page with Marshall M. Bouton, *The Foreign Policy Disconnect: What Americans Want from Our Leaders but Don't Get.* Chicago: University of Chicago Press, 2006.

[b]Lawrence R. Jacobs and Robert Y. Shapiro, *Politicians Don't Pander: Political Manipulation and the Loss of Democratic Responsiveness.* Chicago: University of Chicago Press, 2000.

informed and more intelligent than the American public.[c] In fact, they believe that "people don't have enough time or knowledge to make political decisions" (65 percent) and that they "can't be too careful in dealing with people" (60 percent).

But Americans don't care for their political leaders either, leaders who they see as more selfish and more divided than themselves. Rather, the public seems to want "stealth democracy"—democracy but not the conflict and debate that goes along with it.

[c]John R. Hibbing and Elizabeth Theiss-Morse, *Stealth Democracy: Americans' Beliefs about How Government Should Work.* New York: Cambridge University Press, 2002.

Think Again

Do you think you will ever run for public office yourself?

★ **suffrage**
Legal right to vote.

attend political meetings, speeches, and rallies; write letters to public officials or to newspapers; wear a political button or place a bumper sticker on their car; belong to organizations that support or oppose particular candidates or take stands on public issues; attempt to influence friends while discussing candidates or issues; and vote in elections. Individuals may also participate in politics passively, by simply following political issues and campaigns in the media, acquiring knowledge, forming opinions about public affairs, and expressing their views to others. These forms of political participation can be ranked according to their order of frequency (see Figure 5.4). Only a little more than half of the voting-age population vote in presidential elections, and far fewer vote in congressional and state and local elections.

Securing the Right to Vote

Popular participation in government is part of the very definition of democracy. The long history of struggle to secure the right to vote—**suffrage**—reflects the democratizing of the American political system.

The Elimination of Property Qualifications, 1800–40

The Constitution of 1787 left it to the states to determine voter qualifications. The Founders generally

Figure 5.4

Political Participation: How— and How Many—People Get Involved

Only a small percentage of the American people are actively engaged in the political process, yet they receive most of the media attention. Less than 1 percent of the population runs for office at any level of government, and only about half of all voting-age Americans bother to go to the polls even in a presidential election.

Source: National Election Studies Cumulative File. See also M. Margaret Conway, *Political Participation in the United States,* 3rd ed. (Washington, D.C.: CQ Press, 2000).

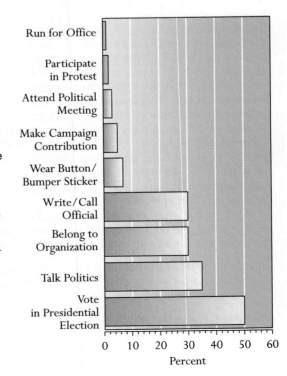

believed that only men of property had a sufficient "stake in society" to exercise their vote in a "responsible" fashion. However, the Founders could not agree on the wording of **property qualifications** for insertion into the Constitution, so they left the issue to the states, feeling safe in the knowledge that at the time every state had property qualifications for voting. Yet over time, Jeffersonian and Jacksonian principles of democracy, including confidence in the judgment of ordinary citizens, spread rapidly in the new Republic. The states themselves eliminated most property qualifications by 1840. Thus before the Civil War (1861–65), the vote had been extended to virtually all *white males* over 21 years of age.

★ **property qualifications**
Early American state requirement of property ownership in order to vote.

The 15th Amendment, 1870   The first important limitation on state powers over voting came with the ratification of the 15th Amendment: "The right of citizens of the United States to vote shall not be denied or abridged by the United States or by any state on account of race, color, or previous condition of servitude." The object of this amendment, passed by the Reconstruction Congress after the Civil War and ratified in 1870, was to extend the vote to former black slaves and prohibit voter discrimination on the basis of race. The 15th Amendment also gave Congress the power to enforce black voting rights "by appropriate legislation." The states retain their right to determine voter qualifications, *as long as they do not practice racial discrimination*, and Congress has the power to pass legislation ensuring black voting rights.

Continued Denial of Voting Rights, 1870–1964   For almost 100 years after the adoption of the 15th Amendment, white politicians in the southern states were able to defeat its purposes. Social and economic pressures and threats of violence were used to intimidate many thousands of would-be black voters.

There were also many "legal" methods of disenfranchisement, including a technique known as the **white primary**. So strong was the Democratic Party throughout the south that the Democratic nomination for public office was tantamount to election. Thus *primary elections* to choose the Democratic nominee were the only elections in which real choices were made. If black people were prevented from voting in Democratic primaries, they could be effectively disenfranchised. Therefore, southern state legislatures resorted to the simple device of declaring the Democratic Party in southern states a private club and ruling that only white people could participate in its elections—that is, in primary elections. Blacks were free to vote in "official" general elections, but all whites tacitly agreed to support the Democratic, or "white man's," Party in general elections, regardless of their differences in the primary. Not until 1944, in *Smith v. Allwright*, did the Supreme Court declare the white primary unconstitutional and bring primary elections under the purview of the 15th Amendment.[16]

★ **white primary**
Democratic Party primary elections in many southern counties in the early part of the twentieth century that excluded black people from voting.

Despite the 15th Amendment, many local registrars in the south succeeded in barring black registration by an endless variety of obstacles, delays, and frustrations. Application forms for registration were lengthy and complicated; even a minor error, such as underlining rather than circling in the "Mr.—Mrs.—Miss" set of choices, as instructed, would lead to rejection. **Literacy tests** were the most common form of disenfranchisement. Many a black college graduate failed to interpret "properly" the complex legal documents that were part of the test. White applicants for voter registration were seldom asked to go through these lengthy procedures.

The Civil Rights Act, the 24th Amendment, and the Voting Rights Act, 1964–65   The Civil Rights Act of 1964 made it unlawful for registrars to apply unequal standards in registration procedures or to reject applications because of

★ **poll taxes**
Taxes imposed as a prerequisite to voting; prohibited by the 24th Amendment.

★ **literacy test**
Examination of a person's ability to read and write as a prerequisite to voter registration, outlawed by Voting Rights Act (1965) as discriminatory.

★ **19th Amendment**
The 1920 constitutional amendment guaranteeing women the right to vote.

immaterial errors. It required that literacy tests be in writing and made a sixth-grade education a presumption of literacy. In 1970 Congress outlawed literacy tests altogether.

The 24th Amendment to the Constitution, ratified in 1964, made **poll taxes**—taxes required of all voters—unconstitutional as a requirement for voting in national elections. In 1966 the Supreme Court declared poll taxes unconstitutional in state and local elections as well.[17]

In early 1965 civil rights organizations led by Martin Luther King, Jr., effectively demonstrated against local registrars in Selma, Alabama, who were still keeping large numbers of black people off the voting rolls. Registrars there closed their offices for all but a few hours every month, placed limits on the number of applications processed, went out to lunch when black applicants appeared, delayed months before processing black applications, and used a variety of other methods to keep blacks disenfranchised. In response to the Selma march, Congress enacted the strong Voting Rights Act in 1965. The U.S. attorney general, upon evidence of voter discrimination, was empowered to replace local registrars with federal registrars, abolish the **literacy test**, and register voters under simplified federal procedures. Southern counties that had previously discriminated in voting registration hurried to sign up black voters just to avoid the imposition of federal registrars. The Voting Rights Act of 1965 proved to be very effective, and Congress has voted to extend it over the years.

The 19th Amendment, 1920   Following the Civil War, many of the women who had been active in the abolitionist movement to end slavery turned their attention to the condition of women in the United States. As abolitionists, they had learned to organize, conduct petition campaigns, and parade and demonstrate. Now they sought to improve the legal and political rights of women. In 1869 the Wyoming territory adopted women's suffrage; later, several other western states followed suit. But it was not until the **19th Amendment** was added to the U.S. Constitution in 1920 that women's right to vote in all elections was constitutionally guaranteed.

The 26th Amendment, 1971   The movement for 18-year-old voting received its original impetus during World War II. It was argued successfully in Georgia in

Opening the Voting Booth

Passage of the Voting Rights Act of 1965 opened the voting booth to millions of black voters formerly kept from the polls by a variety of discriminatory regulations in the south. Here African Americans in rural Alabama in 1966 line up at a local store to cast their votes in a primary that focused on an issue central to their existence—segregation.

PRESIDENT WILSON SAYS:
"This is the time to support Woman Suffrage."

1944 that because 18-year-olds were being called upon to fight and die for their country, they deserved to have a voice in the conduct of government. However, this argument failed to convince adult voters in other states; qualifications for military service were not regarded as the same as qualifications for rational decision making in elections. In state after state, voters rejected state constitutional amendments designed to extend the vote to 18-year-olds.

Congress intervened on behalf of 18-year-old voting with the passage of the **26th Amendment** to the Constitution. The states quickly ratified this amendment in 1971 during a period of national turbulence over the Vietnam War. Many supporters of the amendment believed that protests on the campuses and streets would be reduced if youthful protesters were given the vote.

★ **26th Amendment**
The 1971 constitutional amendment guaranteeing 18-year-olds the right to vote.

The National Voter Registration Act, 1993

The National Voter Registration Act of 1993, popularly known as the "Motor Voter Act," mandates that the states offer people the opportunity to register to vote when they apply for driver's licenses or apply for welfare services. States must also offer registration by mail, and they must accept a simplified registration form prepared by the Federal Election Commission. Finally, it bars states from removing the names of people from registration lists for failure to vote. Did the "**Motor Voter Act**" work? Careful research indicates that it succeeded in increasing voter registration, but its effects on actual turnout at the polls were very limited.[18] Apparently, easy registration does not automatically increase voter turnout.

★ **"Motor Voter Act"**
Federal mandate that states offer voter registration at driver's licensing and welfare offices.

Why Vote?

Deciding whether to cast a vote in an election is just as important as deciding which candidate to vote for. *About 40 percent of the voting-age population in the United States typically fails to vote, even in presidential elections.* Voter **turnout**—the number of actual voters in relation to the number of people eligible to register and vote—is even lower in off-year congressional and state elections, when presidential elections are not held. Turnout in local elections (for example, city, county, school board) is even lower when these elections are held separately from national elections. Voter turnout in presidential elections steadily declined for several decades (see Figure 5.5). The three-way presidential race in 1992 temporarily reversed

★ **turnout**
Number of voters who actually cast ballots in an election, as a percentage of people eligible to register and vote.

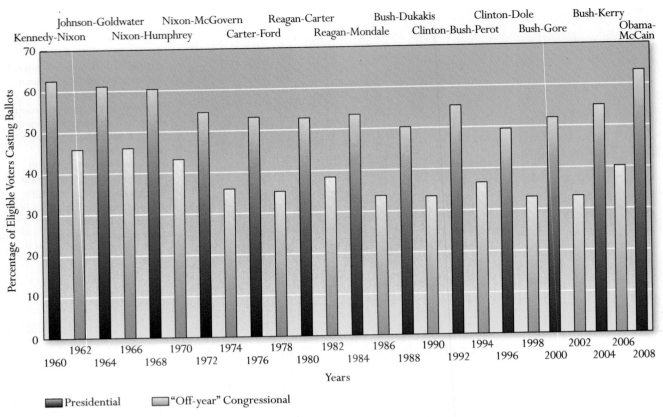

Figure *5.5* Trending Upward: Voter Turnout in Presidential and Congressional Elections

Voter turnout is always higher in years with a presidential election. However, voter turnout has generally declined since 1960, even in presidential election years. The exception came in 1992, when intense interest in the contest between George H. W. Bush and Bill Clinton—spiced by the entry of independent Ross Perot—led to a higher-than-normal turnout. In 1996 fewer than half of voting-age Americans bothered to cast ballots. However, in 2004 and 2008 voter turnout rose to levels not seen since the 1960s.

the downward trend. But in 2004 and 2008 voter turnout surged to levels not seen since the 1960s. Various explanations have been offered: the expected closeness of these elections in key states, the experience of 2000 when only a few votes in Florida decided the outcome, the war in Iraq, the financial crises in 2008, and the historic opportunity in that year to elect an African American president.

Why vote? Usually, this question is asked in the negative: Why do so many people fail to register and vote? But greater insight into the question of voter participation can be obtained if we try to understand what motivates the people who do go to the polls.

The Rational Voter From a purely "rational" perspective, an individual should vote only if the costs of voting (time spent in registering, informing oneself about the candidates, and going to the polls) are *less* than the expected value of having the preferred candidate win (the personal benefits gained from having one's candidate win), multiplied by the probability that one's own vote will be the deciding vote. Why vote when registering, following the political news, and getting to the polls take away time from work, family, or leisure activity? Why vote when the winner will not really change one's life for the better, or even do things much differently from what the loser would have done? Most important, why vote when the chance that one individual vote will determine who wins is very small? Thought of in this fashion, the wonder is that millions of Americans continue to vote.

The "rational" model can explain voter turnout only by adding "the intrinsic rewards of voting" to the equation. These rewards include the ethic of voting, patriotism, a sense of duty, and allegiance to democracy. People exercise their right to vote out of respect for that right rather than for any personal tangible benefit they expect to receive. They can look at the voting returns on television later in the evening, knowing they were part of an important national event. These psychological rewards do not depend on whether a single vote determines the outcome. Millions of people vote out of a sense of duty and commitment to democracy.

The Burden of Registration Voter **registration** remains an obstacle to voting, despite the easing of requirements for registration by many states. Not only must citizens care enough to go to the polls on election day; they must also expend time and energy, weeks before the election, to register. This may involve a trip to the county courthouse and a procedure more complicated than voting itself. Approximately 85 percent of *registered voters* turn out for a presidential election, but this figure represents only about 50 percent of the *voting-age population*. This discrepancy suggests that registration is a significant barrier to participation (see *A Conflicting View*: "Easy Voting Encourages Fraud").

★ **registration**
Requirement that prospective voters establish their identity and place of residence prior to an election in order to be eligible to vote.

Burdensome Voting Deciding upon voting times, places, equipment, and ballots is the responsibility of state governments, most of which pass on this responsibility to their county governments. County elected or appointed "supervisors of elections" function throughout the nation preparing ballots and handling the streams of voters on election day. Nationwide, over 1 million "poll workers," usually volunteers from the local Democratic and Republican party organizations, assist in the voting process and later the counting of votes.

The contested 2000 presidential election spotlighted many of the flaws of ballots and vote counting throughout the nation. That election revealed the variety of voting methods used among the states and even within the same state.[19] Some states and counties use traditional paper or mark-sense ballots, others older lever machines and punch-card ballots, while still others are progressing toward touch screen and other electronic voting equipment. Paper and punch-card ballots regularly produce "overvotes" (where voters mark or punch votes for more than one candidate for the same office) or "undervotes" (where voters fail to make a selection for a particular office), or otherwise spoil their ballot. These ballots are "uncounted"; nationwide, they usually amount to about 2 percent of all ballots cast. Many state laws are fuzzy regarding when and how to conduct "recounts"—requiring election officials to undertake a second or third counting of the ballots. Reformers generally recommend touch screen voting machines, carefully designed ballot layouts, better training of poll workers, uniform rules for recounts, and better voter education programs, including sample ballots distributed well before election day. However, even electronic voting is subject to error. Opponents of "black box" voting argue that every vote on a single machine may be lost to computer error or malfunction. They urged the use of ballots that leave a "paper trail."

Some states now require photo identification at the polling place in order to ensure that voters are who they say they are. But opponents of photo ID argue that it has a disparate impact on poor and minority voters. The U.S. Supreme Court upheld the photo ID requirement in 2008.[20]

Help America Vote Act Congress passed a Help America Vote Act in 2002 in reaction to the controversy surrounding the 2000 presidential election (see *Politics Up Close*: "*Bush v. Gore* in the U.S. Supreme Court" in Chapter 13). The Act

A Conflicting *View*

Easy Voting Encourages Fraud

Since the civil rights battles of the 1960s, the nation has been primarily concerned with expanding voter participation—to bring more people, especially minorities, into the political process. These efforts have led to an easing of the burdens of registration—registration by mail, mass registration drives, registration on the same day as voting, and so forth—as well as an easing of the burdens of voting itself—absentee voting, voting by mail, voting over an extended period, and so forth. Voting via the Internet is also being advocated in many jurisdictions. Yet there is no strong evidence to suggest that these innovations lead to higher voter turnouts.

There are nearly 200,000 voting precincts in the United States. Usually representatives of both the Democratic and Republican parties are present at each precinct to ensure the honesty of the vote. Voters who have previously registered show their voter cards or present other identification and then sign their names on the voter registration lists. This ensures that the voters are who they say they are, and that they do not vote more than once.

But registration by mail and absentee voting are rising over time. Voter registration cards are widely distributed, to be filled out by persons eligible to vote, and then collected and sent to the county election office. As the election nears, registered voters may request an absentee ballot, to be filled out and mailed to the county election office.

Increasingly, party operatives as well as independent "get-out-the-vote" organizations are going to nursing homes, assisted-living facilities, and other institutions housing the elderly, as well as large condominium projects, filling out registration forms for the residents as well as absentee ballot requests, and then "helping out" in marking the ballots, collecting them, and mailing them en masse to voting offices. It has been charged that some groups collecting registration forms and absentee ballots conveniently discard those that do not match the group's preferences.[a]

Few states have the resources, and many politicians lack the will, to investigate and prosecute voter fraud. Finding the right balance between promoting greater participation and maintaining the integrity of the electoral system is creating political conflict in many states and cities today.

[a]See Larry J. Sabato and Glenn R. Simpson, *Dirty Little Secrets: The Persistence of Corruption in American Politics*. New York: Random House, 1996.

authorizes federal aid to the states to help replace punch cards and lever voting machines and establishes minimum election administration standards throughout the country. States devise their own plans for upgrading voting practices, so

Too Confusing?

Voter registration is designed to prevent fraud, but it also tends to discourage people from exercising their right to vote. Spanish language registration forms, where they are used, may ease the burden of registration for some.

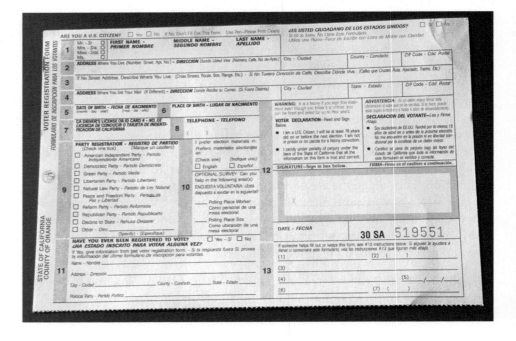

considerable variations remain among the states. The Act also mandates that each polling place have at least one voting system for individuals with disabilities, including the blind and visually impaired. It requires states to develop and maintain statewide voter registration lists. It requires that individuals who are determined at a polling place to be ineligible to vote he allowed to cast a provisional ballot, to be counted later if the voter is subsequently found to be eligible. It also requires that voting systems provide the opportunity for voters to change or correct any errors in their ballot before it is cast and counted.

The Politics of Voter Turnout

Politics drives the debate over easing voter registration requirements. Democrats generally favor minimal requirements—for example, same-day registration, registration by mail, and registration at welfare and motor vehicle licensing offices. They know that nonvoters are heavily drawn from groups that typically support the Democratic Party, including the less-educated, lower-income, and minority groups. Republicans are often less enthusiastic about easing voting requirements, but it is politically embarrassing to appear to oppose increased participation. It is not surprising that the Motor Voter Act of 1993 was a product of a Democratic Congress and a Democratic president, Bill Clinton.[21]

Voting Turnout: Who Votes in The United States?

The Stimulus of Competition   The more lively the competition between parties or between candidates, the greater the interest of citizens and the larger the voter turnout. When parties and candidates compete vigorously, they make news and are given large play by the mass media. Consequently, a setting of competitive politics generates more political stimuli than does a setting with weak competition. People are also more likely to perceive that their votes count in a close contest, and thus they are more likely to cast them. Moreover, when parties or candidates are fighting in a close contest, their supporters tend to spend more time and energy campaigning and getting out the vote.

Political Alienation   People who feel politics is irrelevant to their lives—or who feel they cannot personally affect public affairs—are less likely to vote than people who feel they themselves can affect political outcomes and that these outcomes affect their lives. Given the level of **political alienation** (two-thirds of respondents agree with the statement, "Most public officials are not really interested in the problems of people like me"),[22] it is surprising that so many people vote. Alienation is high among voters, and it is even higher among nonvoters.

★ **political alienation**
Belief that politics is irrelevant to one's life and that one cannot personally affect public affairs.

Intensity   Finally, as we might expect, people who feel strongly about politics and who hold strong opinions about political issues are more likely to vote than people who do not. For example, people who describe themselves as *extreme* liberals or *extreme* conservatives are more likely to vote than people who describe themselves as moderates.

Age and Turnout   Young people do not vote in the same proportions as older people (see Figure 5.6). After the electorate was expanded by the 26th Amendment to include persons 18 years of age and over, voter turnout actually dropped, from 60.9 percent in the 1968 presidential election to 55.2 percent in the 1972 presidential election, the largest turnout decline in successive presidential elections.

Party Organization   Strong party organizations can help increase turnout. But strong party organizations, or machines, that canvassed neighborhoods, took citizens to the courthouse to register them, contacted them personally during

Figure 5.6

Who's Voting? Voter Turnout by Social Groups

Women are slightly more likely to vote than men. Voter turnout increases with education, age, and income. Major efforts to "get out the vote" in the African American community have raised voter turnout to nearly that of whites, but turnout among Hispanics continues to lag.

Source: U.S. Bureau of the Census, *Statistical Abstract of the United States,* 2007. Data for 2004 presidential election.

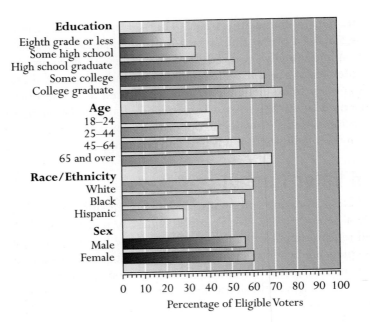

campaigns, and saw to it that they got to the polls on election day have largely disappeared (see Chapter 7).

Regardless of the explanations offered, it is interesting to note that most European democracies report higher voter turnout rates than the United States (see *Compared to What?:* "Voter Turnout in Western Democracies").

Voters and Nonvoters

Who votes and who doesn't? The perceived benefits and costs of voting apparently do not fall evenly across all social groups. Nonvoting would generate less concern if voters were a representative cross section of nonvoters. But voters differ from nonvoters in politically important ways.

Voters are better educated than nonvoters. Education appears to be the most important determinant of voter turnout (see Figure 5.5). It may be that schooling promotes an interest in politics, instills the ethic of citizen participation, or gives people a better awareness of public affairs and an understanding of the role of elections in a democracy. Education is associated with a sense of confidence and political *efficacy*, the feeling that one can indeed have a personal impact on public affairs.

Age is another factor affecting voter participation. Perhaps because young people have more distractions, more demands on their time in school, work, or new family responsibilities, nonvoting is greatest among 18- to 24-year-olds. In contrast, older Americans are politically influential in part because candidates know they turn out at the polls.

High-income people are more likely to vote than are low-income people. Most of this difference stems from the fact that high-income people are more likely to be well educated and older. But poor people may also feel alienated from the political system—they may lack a sense of political efficacy; they may feel they have little control over their own lives, let alone over public affairs. Or poor people may simply be so absorbed in the problems of life that they have little time or energy to spend on registering and voting.[23]

Income and education differences between participants and nonparticipants are even greater when other forms of political participation are considered.

Compared to *What?*

Voter Turnout in Western Democracies

Other Western democracies regularly report higher voter turnout rates than the United States (see figure). Yet in an apparent paradox, Americans seem to be more supportive of their political institutions, less alienated from their political system, and even more patriotic than citizens of Western European nations. Why, then, are voter turnouts in the United States so much lower than in these other democracies?

The answer to this question lies primarily in the legal and institutional differences between the United States and the other democracies. First of all, in Austria, Australia, Belgium, and Italy, voting is *mandatory*. Penalties and the level of enforcement vary within and across these countries. Moreover, registration laws in the United States make voting more difficult than in other countries. In Western Europe, all citizens are required to register with the government and obtain identification cards. These cards are then used for admission to the polls. In contrast, voter registration is entirely voluntary in the United States, and voters must reregister if they change residences. Nearly 50 percent of the U.S. population changes residence at least once in a five-year period, thus necessitating reregistration.

Parties in the United States are more loosely organized, less disciplined, and less able to mobilize voters than are European parties. Moreover, many elections in the United States, notably elections for Congress, are not very competitive. The United States organizes congressional elections by district with winner-take-all rules, whereas many European parliaments are selected by proportional representation, with seats allocated to parties based on national vote totals. Proportional representation means every vote counts toward seats in the legislative body. Thus greater competition and proportional representation may encourage higher voter turnout in European democracies.

But cultural differences may also contribute to differences in turnout. The American political culture, with its tradition of individualism and self-reliance and its reluctance to empower government (see Chapter 2), encourages Americans to resolve their problems through their own efforts rather than looking to government for solutions. Government is not as central to Americans as it is to Europeans, and therefore getting to the polls on election day is not seen as so important.

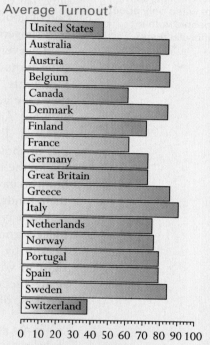

Average Turnout*

United States
Australia
Austria
Belgium
Canada
Denmark
Finland
France
Germany
Great Britain
Greece
Italy
Netherlands
Norway
Portugal
Spain
Sweden
Switzerland

0 10 20 30 40 50 60 70 80 90 100

Percentage Voting in
National Elections

* Percent of voting age population casting ballots, average, in elections, 1991–2000.

Source: Center for Voting and Democracy, 2008. www.fairvote.org Reprinted by permission.

Higher-income, better-educated people are much more likely to be among those who make campaign contributions, who write or call their elected representatives, and who join and work in active political organizations.[24]

Historically, race was a major determinant of nonvoting. Black voter turnout, especially in the South, was markedly lower than white voter turnout. African Americans continue today to have a slightly lower overall voter turnout than whites, but most of the remaining difference is attributable to differences between blacks and whites in educational and income levels. Blacks and whites at the same educational and income levels register and vote with the same frequency. Indeed, in cities where African Americans are well organized politically, black voter turnout may exceed white voter turnout.

The greatest disparity in voter turnout is between Hispanics and others. Low voter participation by Hispanics may be a product of language differences, lack of cultural assimilation, or noncitizenship status.

Nonvoting: What Difference Does It Make?

Think Again

Is our government really legitimate when only about half the people vote in presidential elections?

How concerned should we be about low levels of participation in American politics? Certainly the democratic ideal envisions an active, participating citizenry. Democratic government, asserts the Declaration of Independence, derives its "just powers from the consent of the governed." The legitimacy of democratic government can be more easily questioned when half of the people fail to vote. That is, it is easier to question whether the government truly represents "the people" when only half of the people vote even in a presidential election. Voting is an expression of good citizenship, and it reinforces attachment to the nation and to democratic government. Nonvoting suggests alienation from the political system.

However, the *right* to vote is more important to democratic government than voter turnout. The nineteenth-century English political philosopher John Stuart Mill wrote, "Men, as well as women, do not need political rights in order that they may govern, but in order that they may not be misgoverned."[25] As long as all adult Americans possess the right to vote, politicians must consider their interests. "Rulers and ruling classes are under a necessity of considering the interests of those who have the suffrage."[26] Democratic governments cannot really ignore the interests of anyone who can vote. People who have the right to vote, but who have voluntarily chosen not to exercise it in the past, can always change their minds, go to the polls, and "throw the rascals out."

Voluntary nonvoting is not the same as being denied the suffrage. Politicians can indeed ignore the interests of people denied the vote by restrictive laws or practices or by intimidation or force. But when people choose not to exercise their right to vote, they may be saying that they do not believe their interests are really affected by government. The late Senator Sam Ervin is widely quoted on the topic of nonvoters:

> I'm not going to shed any crocodile tears if people don't care enough to vote. I don't believe in making it easy for apathetic, lazy people. I'd be extremely happy if nobody in the United States voted except for the people who thought about the issues and made up their own minds and wanted to vote.[27]

Protest as Political Participation

Protests, marches, and demonstrations are important forms of political participation. Indeed, the 1st Amendment guarantees the right "peaceably to assemble, and to petition the government for a redress of grievances." A march to the steps of Congress, a mass assembly of people on the Washington Mall with speakers, sign waving, and songs, and the presentation of petitions to government officials are all forms of participation protected by the 1st Amendment.

★ **protests**
Public marches or demonstrations designed to call attention to an issue and motivate others to apply pressure on public officials.

Protests   Protests are generally designed to call attention to an issue and to motivate others to apply pressure on public officials. In fact, protests are usually directed at the news media rather than at public officials themselves. If protesters could persuade public officials directly in the fashion of lobbyists and interest groups, they would not need to protest. Protests are intended to generate attention and support among previously uncommitted people—enough so the ultimate targets of the protest, public officials, will be pressured to act to redress grievances.

A *Constitutional* Note

Who Can Vote?

The Founders generally believed that only property-owning free white males, 21 or older, should be entitled to vote. But they failed to include these qualifications in the original Constitution of 1787. Instead, they left it up to the states to decide who should vote: ". . . the Electors in each State shall have the Qualifications requisite for Electors of the most numerous Branch of the State Legislature" (Article I, Section 2). Why leave it up to the states to decide the voter qualifications for national elections? In committee and in floor discussions the delegates could not agree on what kind of property should qualify a person to vote. Plantation owners argued for qualifications to be expressed in land acreage; bankers wanted them expressed in the size of one's bank account; shippers and businessmen, in the value of their inventories or ships; and so on. In frustration, the delegates dropped the issue into the laps of the states secure in the knowledge that in 1787 all of the states had some form of property qualifications and no state permitted women, slaves, or persons under 21 to vote. But this opening in the Constitution began a long journey toward full voting rights in the United States. Jacksonian democracy swept the nation in the 1840s and property qualifications were dropped by the states themselves. Not until after the Civil War was the Constitution amended to prevent the states from denying the right to vote on account of race (15th Amendment, 1870). The long fight for women's suffrage finally resulted in a constitutional guarantee of women's right to vote (19th Amendment, 1920); poll taxes were constitutionally banned (24th Amendment, 1964); and 18-year-olds secured the constitutional right to vote (26th Amendment, 1971).

Coverage by the news media, especially television, is vital to the success of protest activity. The media not only carry the protesters' message to the mass public but also inform public officials about what is taking place. Protests provide the media with "good visuals"—pictorial dramatizations of political issues. The media welcome opportunities to present political issues in a confrontational fashion because confrontation helps capture larger audiences. Thus protesters and the media use each other to advance their separate goals.

Protests are most commonly employed by groups that have little influence in electoral politics. They were a key device of the civil rights movement at a time when many African Americans were barred from voting. In the absence of protest, the majority white population—and the public officials they elected—were at best unconcerned with the plight of black people in a segregated society. Protests, including a dramatic march on Washington in 1963 at which Martin Luther King, Jr., delivered his inspirational "I Have a Dream" speech, called attention to the injustices of segregation and placed civil rights on the agenda of decision makers.

Protests can be effectively employed by groups that are relatively small in number but whose members feel very intensely about the issue. Often the protest is a means by which these groups can obtain bargaining power with decision makers. Protests may threaten to tarnish the reputations of government officials or private corporations, or may threaten to disrupt their daily activities or reduce their business through boycotts or pressure on customers. If the protest is successful, protest leaders can then offer to end the protest in exchange for concessions from their targets.

Civil Disobedience

Civil disobedience is a form of protest that involves breaking what are perceived as "unjust" laws. The purpose is to call attention to the existence of injustice. In the words of Martin Luther King, Jr., civil disobedience "seeks so to dramatize the issue that it can no longer be

★ **civil disobedience**
Form of public protest involving the breaking of laws believed to be unjust.

Politics Up Close   How to Run for Office

Many rewards come with elected office—the opportunity to help shape public policy, public attention and name recognition, and many business, professional, and social contacts. But there are many drawbacks as well—the absence of privacy; a microscopic review of one's past; constant calls, meetings, interviews, and handshaking; and, perhaps most onerous of all, the continual need to solicit campaign funds.

Before You Run—Getting Involved

Get involved in various organizations in your community:

★ Neighborhood associations.
★ Chambers of commerce, business associations.
★ Churches and synagogues (become an usher, if possible, for visibility).
★ Political groups (Democratic or Republican clubs, League of Women Voters, and so on).
★ Parent-Teacher Associations (PTAs).
★ Service clubs (Rotary, Kiwanis, Civitan, Toastmasters).
★ Recreation organizations (Little League, flag football, soccer leagues, running and walking clubs, for example, as participant, coach, or umpire).

Deciding to Run—Know What You're Doing

In deciding to run, and choosing the office for which you wish to run, you should become thoroughly familiar with the issues, duties, and responsibilities.

★ Attend council or commission meetings, state legislative sessions, and/or committee hearings.
★ Become familiar with current issues and officeholders, and obtain a copy of and read the budget.
★ Learn the demographics of your district (racial, ethnic, and age composition; occupational mix; average income; neighborhood differences). If you do not fit the prevailing racial, ethnic, or age composition, think about moving to another district.
★ Memorize a brief (preferably less than seven seconds) answer to the question, "Why are you running?"

Getting in the Race

Contact your county elections department to obtain the following:

★ Qualifying forms and information.
★ Campaign financing forms and regulations.
★ District and street maps for your district.
★ Recent election results in your district.
★ Election-law book or pamphlet.
★ Voter registration lists (usually sold as lists, or labels, or tapes).

★ Contact your party's county chairperson for advice; convince the party's leaders that you can win. Ask for a list of their regular campaign contributors.

Raising Money

The easiest way to finance a campaign is to be rich enough to provide your own funds. Failing that, you must:

★ Establish a campaign fund, according to the laws of your state.
★ Find a treasurer/campaign-finance chairperson who knows many wealthy, politically involved people.
★ Invite wealthy, politically involved people to small coffees, cocktail parties, dinners; give a brief campaign speech and then have your finance chairperson solicit contributions.
★ Follow up fund-raising events and meetings with personal phone calls.
★ Be prepared to continue fund-raising activities throughout your campaign; file accurate financial disclosure statements as required by state law.

Getting Organized

Professional campaign managers and management firms almost always outperform volunteers. If you cannot afford professional management, you must rely on yourself or trusted friends to perform the following:

★ Draw up a budget based on reasonable expectations of campaign funding.
★ Interview and select a professional campaign-management firm, or appoint a trusted campaign manager.
★ Ask trusted friends from various clubs, activities, neighborhoods, churches, and so on, to meet and serve as a campaign committee. If your district is racially or ethnically diverse, make sure all groups are represented on your committee.
★ Decide on a campaign theme; research issues important to your community; develop brief, well-articulated positions on these issues.
★ Open a campaign headquarters with desks and telephones. Buy a cell phone; use call forwarding; stay in contact. Use your garage if you can't afford an office.
★ Arrange to meet with newspaper editors, editorial boards, TV station executives, and political reporters. Be prepared for tough questions.
★ Hire a media consultant or advertising agency, or appoint a volunteer media director who knows television, radio, and newspaper advertising.
★ Arrange a press conference to announce your candidacy. Notify all media well in advance. Arrange

for overflow crowd of supporters to cheer and applaud.

★ Produce eyecatching, inspirational 15- or 30-second television and radio ads that present a favorable image of you and stress your campaign theme.

★ Prepare and print attractive campaign brochures, signs, and bumper stickers.

★ Hire a local survey-research firm to conduct telephone surveys of voters in your district, asking what they think are the most important issues, how they stand on them, whether they recognize your name and your theme, and how they plan to vote. Be prepared to change your theme and your position on issues if surveys show strong opposition to your views.

On the Campaign Trail

Campaigns themselves may be primarily media centered or primarily *door-to-door* ("retail") or some combination of both.

★ Buy media time as early as possible from television and radio stations; insist on prime-time slots before, during, and after popular shows.

★ Buy newspaper ads; insist on their placement in popular, well-read sections of the paper.

★ Attend every community gathering possible, just to be seen, even if you do not give a speech. Keep all speeches short. Focus on one or two issues that your polls show are important to voters.

★ Recruit paid or unpaid volunteers to hand out literature door-to-door. Record names and addresses of voters who say they support you.

★ Canvass door-to-door with a brief (seven-second) self-introduction and statement of your reasons for running. Use registration lists to identify members of your own party, and try to address them by name. Also canvass offices, factories, coffee shops, shopping malls—anywhere you find a crowd.

★ Organize a phone bank, either professional or volunteer. Prepare *brief* introduction and phone statements. Record names of people who say they support you.

★ Know your opponent: Research his or her past affiliations, indiscretions if any, previous voting record, and public positions on issues.

★ Be prepared to "define" your opponent in negative terms. Negative advertising works. But be fair:

base your comments on your opponent's public record. Emphasize his or her positions that clearly deviate from your district voters' known preferences.

Primary versus General Elections

Remember that you will usually have to campaign in two elections—your party's primary and the general election.

★ Before the primary, identify potential opposition in your own party, try to dissuade them from running.

★ Allocate your budget first to win the primary election. If you lose the primary, you won't need any funds for the general election.

★ In general elections, you must broaden your appeal without distancing your own party supporters. Deemphasize your party affiliation unless your district regularly elects members of your party; in a close district or a district that regularly votes for the opposition party, stress your independence and your commitment to the *district's* interests.

On Election Day

Turning out your voters is the key to success. Election day is the busiest day of the campaign for you and your staff.

★ Use your phone bank to place as many calls as possible to party members in your district (especially those who have indicated in previous calls and visits that they support you). Remind them to vote; make sure your phone workers can tell each voter where to go to cast his or her vote.

★ Solicit volunteers to drive people to the polls.

★ Assign workers to as many polling places as possible. Most state laws require that they stay a specified distance from the voting booths. But they should be in evidence with your signs and literature to buttonhole voters before they go into the booths.

★ Show up at city or county election office on election night with prepared victory statement thanking supporters and pledging your service to the district. (Also draft a courteous concession statement pledging your support to the winner, in case you lose.)

★ Attend victory party with your supporters; meet many "new" friends.

ignored"[28] (see *A Conflicting View:* "Sometimes It's Right to Disobey the Law" in Chapter 1). Those truly engaging in civil disobedience do not attempt to evade punishment for breaking the law but instead willingly accept the penalty. By doing so, they demonstrate not only their sincerity and commitment but also the injustice of the law. Cruelty or violence directed at the protesters by police or others contributes further to the drama of injustice.

Like other protest activity, the success of civil disobedience depends on the willingness of the mass media to carry the message to both the general public and the political leadership.

Violence   Violence can also be a form of political participation. Indeed, political violence—for example, assassinations, rioting, burning, looting—has been uncomfortably frequent in American politics over the years. It is important to distinguish violence from protest. Peaceful protest is constitutionally protected. Often, organized protest activity harnesses frustrations and hostilities, directs them into constitutionally acceptable activities, and thus avoids violence. Likewise, civil disobedience should be distinguished from violence. Civil disobedience breaks only "unjust" laws, without violence, and willingly accepts punishment without trying to escape.

Effectiveness   How effective are protests? Protests can be effective in achieving some goals under some conditions. But protests are useless or even counterproductive in pursuit of other goals under other conditions. Here are some generalizations about the effectiveness of protests:

★ Protests are more likely to be effective when directed at specific problems or laws rather than at general conditions that cannot readily be remedied by governmental action.

★ Protests are more likely to be effective when targeted toward public officials who are capable of granting the desired concession or resolving the specific problem. Protests with no specific targets and protests directed at officials who have no power to change things are generally unproductive.

★ Protests are more likely to succeed when the goal is limited to gaining access or representation in decision making or to placing an issue on the agenda of decision makers.

Civil Disobedience, Uncivil Response

Cruelty or violence directed at peaceful protesters further dramatizes their cause. In Jackson, Mississippi, in 1963, segregationists poured mustard, ketchup, and sugar over lunch counter sit-in protesters. But far more serious violence, including murder, was perpetrated against civil rights protesters in the 1960s.

★ Protests are not always effective in actually getting laws changed and are even less effective in ensuring that the impact of the changes will really improve the conditions that led to the protest.

Public officials can defuse protest activity in a variety of ways. They may greet protesters with smiles and reassurances that they agree with their goals. They may dispense symbolic satisfaction without any tangible results. They may grant token concessions with great publicity, perhaps remedying a specific case of injustice while doing little to affect general conditions. Or public officials may claim to be constrained either legally or financially from doing anything—the "I-would-like-to-help-you-but-I-can't" strategy. Or public officials can directly confront the protesters by charging that they are unrepresentative of the groups they are trying to help.

Perhaps the most challenging and sometimes most effective kind of "protest" is to run for public office (see *Politics Up Close:* "How to Run for Office" on pages 166–67). Whether at the local level, such as the school board, or at the state or national level, the participation of one individual as a candidate—even when not elected—can make a difference in public affairs.

Summary
Who Gets What: Opinion and Participation

Individuals can exercise power in a democratic political system in a variety of ways. They can run for public office, take part in demonstrations and protests, make financial contributions to candidates, attend political events, write letters to newspapers or public officials, belong to political organizations, vote in elections, or simply hold and express opinions on public issues.

Public opinion commands the attention of elected public officials in a democracy, yet many Americans are poorly informed and unconcerned about politics; their opinions on public issues are often changeable and inconsistent. Only a few highly salient issues generate strong and stable opinions.

★ Political socialization—the learning of political values, beliefs, and opinions—starts at an early age. It is influenced by family, school, church, age group, and the media.

★ Ideology also shapes opinion, especially among politically interested and active people who employ fairly consistent liberal or conservative ideas in forming their opinions on specific issues.

★ Race and gender also influence public opinion. Blacks and whites differ over the extent of discrimination in the United States, as well as over its causes and remedies. Men and women tend to differ over issues involving the use of force. In recent years, women have tended to give greater support to the Democratic Party than men have.

★ Securing the right to vote for all Americans required nearly 200 years of political struggle. Key victories included the elimination of property qualifications by 1840, the 15th Amendment in 1870 (eliminating restrictions based on race), the 19th Amendment in 1920 (eliminating restrictions based on gender), the Civil Rights Act of 1964 and Voting Rights Act of 1965 (eliminating racial obstacles), the 24th Amendment in 1964 (eliminating poll taxes), and the 26th Amendment in 1971 (extending the right to vote to 18-year-olds).

★ About half of the voting-age population fails to vote even in presidential elections. Voter turnout has steadily declined in recent decades. Voter registration is a major obstacle to voting. Turnout is affected by competition as well as by feelings of political alienation and distrust of government. Young people have the poorest record of voter turnout of any age group.

★ Voluntary nonvoting is not as serious a threat to democracy as denial of the right to vote. Nevertheless, the class bias in voting may tilt the political system toward the interests of higher-income, better-educated, older whites at the expense of lower-income, less-educated, younger minorities.

★ Protest is an important form of participation in politics. Protests are more commonly employed by groups with little direct influence over public officials. The object is to generate attention and support from previously uncommitted people in order to bring new pressure on public officials to redress grievances. Media coverage is vital to the success of protests.

Key Terms

public opinion 137	generation gap 144	poll taxes 156	registration 159
survey research 139	gender gap 145	literacy tests 156	political alienation 161
halo effect 139	suffrage 154	19th Amendment 156	protests 164
salient issues 141	property	26th Amendment 157	civil disobedience 165
socialization 141	qualifications 155	"Motor Voter Act" 157	
diffuse support 142	white primary 155	turnout 157	

Suggested Readings

Asher, Herbert. *Polling and the Public: What Every Citizen Should Know*. 7th ed. Washington, D.C.: CQ Press, 2007. Explains methods of polling and how results can be influenced by wording, sampling, and interviewing techniques; also covers how polls are used by the media and in campaigns.

Conway, M. Margaret, Gertrude A. Stevernagel, and David Ahern. *Women and Political Participation*. 2nd ed. Washington, D.C.: CQ Press, 2004. An examination of cultural change and women's participation in politics, including treatment of the gender gap in political attitudes and the impact of women's membership in the political elite.

Drexler, Kateri M., and Gwen Garcelon. *Strategies for Active Citizenship*. Upper Saddle River, N.J.: Prentice Hall, 2005. A handbook for becoming active in politics.

Erikson, Robert S., and Kent L. Tedin. *American Public Opinion*, 7th ed. New York: Longman, 2007. A comprehensive review of the forces influencing public opinion and an assessment of the influence of public opinion in American politics.

Greenstein, Fred I. *Children and Politics*. New Haven, Conn.: Yale University Press, 1985. Early research on what children know about politics and how they learned it.

Jacobs, Lawrence R., and Robert Y. Shapiro. *Politicians Don't Pander: Political Manipulation and the Loss of Democratic Responsiveness*. Chicago: University of Chicago Press, 2000. A close study of how politicians use public opinion to suit their own purposes.

Page, Benjamin I., and Robert Y. Shapiro. *The Rational Public*. Chicago: University of Chicago Press, 1992. An examination of fifty years of public opinion polls convinces these authors that American government is generally responsive to the views of the majority.

Stimson, James A. *Tides of Consent: How Public Opinion Shapes American Politics*. New York: Cambridge University Press, 2004. The movement of public opinion over time moves public policy.

Wald, Kenneth D. *Religion and Politics in the United States*. 5th ed. Lantham, MD: Rowman & Littlefield, 2007. An explanation of the impact of religion on American political culture, the policy process, and voting behavior.

Walton, Hanes, and Robert C. Smith. *African American Politics and the African American Quest for Universal Freedom*. New York: Pearson Longman, 2002. A comprehensive American government textbook emphasizing the diversity of African American opinions and behavior.

Zaller, John R. *The Nature and Origins of Mass Opinion*. New York: Cambridge University Press, 1992. An effort to develop and test a conceptual model of how people form political preferences, how political views and arguments diffuse through the population, and how people evaluate this information and convert their reactions into public opinion.

Suggested Web Sites

Americans United for Separation of Church and State
www.au.org

Advocacy organization opposed to religious influence in government.

Center for Voting and Democracy www.fairvote.org

Reform organization devoted to expanding voter participation; Web site includes data on voter turnout nationally and by state.

Center for Women in Politics www.rci.rutgers.edu/~cawp

Extensive information on women officeholders, as well as gender gap data on voting and attitudes on public policy.

Christian Coalition www.cc.org

Organization advocating greater Christian involvement in politics and government.

Gallup www.gallup.com

Oldest public opinion organization, with latest polls and large archive.

National Urban League www.nul.org

Organization devoted to advancing the economic well-being of African Americans, often reflecting opinions of the growing black middle class. Publishes annual *State of Black America*.

The Polling Report www.pollingreport.com

Recent public opinion polls on policy issues, political actors, government institutions, and so on.

The Pollster www.pollster.com

A website summarizing recent polls with links to blogs about polls and polling results.

Protest Net www.protest.net

Radical organization provides calendar of protests against military actions, world trade, animal experiments, and so forth.

Public Agenda Online www.publicagenda.org

Recent opinion polls on a variety of policy issues.

State of the Vote www.stateofthevote.org

Official Web site of the National Association of Secretaries of State (state voting officials) urging young people to register and vote.

6 MASS MEDIA
Setting the Political Agenda

66 To illuminate the mechanisms of propaganda is to reveal the secret springs of social action, and to expose to the most searching criticisms the prevailing dogmas of sovereignty, democracy, honesty, and the sanctity of individual opinion. 99

Harold Lasswell

✓Think About Politics

1. Are media professionals—news reporters, editors, anchors—the true voice of the people in public affairs?

   YES ⃝ NO ⃝

2. Do the media mirror what is really news, rather than deciding themselves what's important and then making it news?

   YES ⃝ NO ⃝

3. Is television your most important source of news?

   YES ⃝ NO ⃝

4. Should the media report on all aspects of the private lives of public officials?

   YES ⃝ NO ⃝

5. Do the media report equally fairly on Democratic and Republican candidates for office?

   YES ⃝ NO ⃝

6. Should the media be legally required to be fair and accurate in reporting political news?

   YES ⃝ NO ⃝

7. Are you more alienated than attracted by the media's coverage of politics?

   YES ⃝ NO ⃝

8. Is your choice of candidates in elections affected by their advertising?

   YES ⃝ NO ⃝

Ask yourself how much of your knowledge about politics in America comes from television and newspapers and the radio. What you know about politics and how you participate are, in fact, largely determined by the power of the media to decide what they want you to know.

★ **mass media**
All means of communication with the general public, including television, newspapers, magazines, radio, books, recordings, motion pictures, and the Internet.

The Power of the Media

Politics—the struggle over who gets what, when, and how—is largely carried out in the **mass media**. The arenas of political conflict are the various media of mass communication—television, newspapers, magazines, radio, books, recordings, motion pictures, and the Internet. What we know about politics comes to us largely through these media. Unless we ourselves are admitted to the White House Oval Office or the committee rooms of Congress or dinner parties at foreign embassies, or unless we ourselves attend political rallies and demonstrations or travel to distant battlefields, we must rely on the mass media to tell us about politics. Furthermore, few of us ever have the opportunity to personally evaluate the character of presidential candidates or cabinet members or members of Congress, or to learn their views on public issues by talking with them face to face. Instead, we must learn about people as well as events from the mass media.

Great power derives from the control of information. *Who knows what* helps to determine *who gets what*. The media not only provide an arena for politics; they are also themselves players in that arena. The media not only report on the struggles for power in society; they are also themselves participants in those struggles. The media have long been referred to as America's "fourth branch" of government—and for good reason.[1]

The Power of Television   Television is the most powerful medium of communication. It is a true *mass* communication medium. Virtually every home in the United States has a television set, and the average home has the set turned on for about 7 hours a day. Television is regularly chosen over other news media by Americans as the most common news source.

Americans turn to *local* TV news broadcasts as their most regular source of news. Daily newspapers are read by less than half of the adult public (see Figure 6.1). The national network evening news shows (*NBC Nightly News, ABC World News Tonight, CBS Evening News*) have lost viewership in recent years. But viewership of CNN, Fox News Cable, CNBC, and MSNBC is rising. Television weekly news magazines, notably CBS's *60 Minutes*, have also become major sources of news for many Americans.

173

Figure *6.1*

Check Your Sources: Where Americans Get Their News

Local TV news has long been America's favorite news source. Nightly network news is losing ground to cable news and the Internet. Newspaper readership is declining but remains a major source of news.

Note: More than one answer accepted in survey, so the sum adds up to well over 100 percent.

Source: Adapted from the Pew Research Center for the People and the Press, "Source of News for Americans," Jan. 2, 2007. www.people-press.org

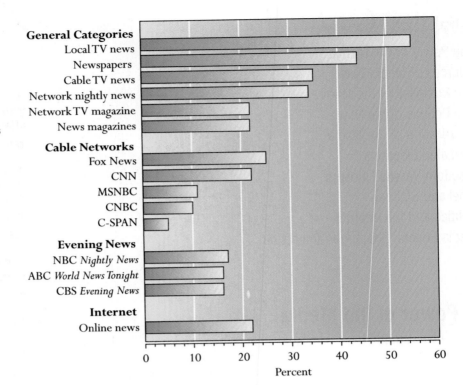

A growing number of Americans, especially young people, are turning to online news sources (see *Politics Up Close*: "The Generation Gap in News").

During a national crisis—for example, the terrorist attack of 9/11—Americans become even more dependent on television for their news. When asked "Where would you go first," for information during a crisis, 66 percent of Americans said they would turn on their TV sets. CNN was mentioned most often.[2]

Believability Television is also rated by Americans as the most *believable* medium of communication. Compared to television news, print sources are generally seen as less believable, with one exception, the *Wall Street Journal*. CNN is rated highest among all news sources (see Figure 6.2). Not many people rate the tabloids as very believable.

You Are the News Editor

Newspapers and Magazines Less than one-half of the adult population reads one of the nation's 1,500 daily newspapers. But the nation's prestige newspapers—the *New York Times*, *Washington Post*, and *Wall Street Journal*—are regularly read by government officials, corporate chiefs, interest-group leaders, and other media people. Stories appearing in these newspapers are generally picked up by daily papers around the country, and these stories almost always appear on national network television.

The leading weekly newsmagazines—*Time*, *Newsweek*, and *U.S. News & World Report*—reach a smaller but more politically attentive audience than do newspapers. Magazines of political commentary—for example, the *Nation* (liberal), *New Republic* (liberal), *National Review* (conservative), *American Spectator* (conservative), *Weekly Standard* (conservative), *Public Interest* (neo-conservative), and *Washington Monthly* (neo-liberal)—reach very small but politically active audiences.

Television's Emotional Communication The power of television derives not only from its large audiences, but also from its ability to communicate emotions as well as information. Television's power is found in its visuals—angry faces in a

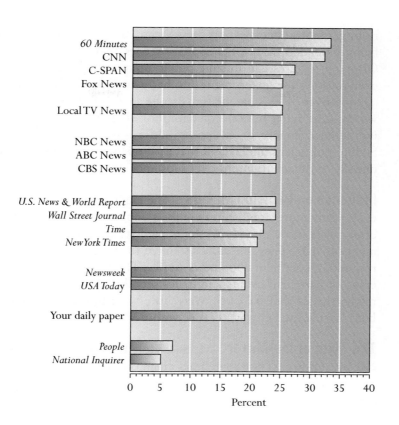

Figure 6.2

Who Do You Believe?: Believability of the Media

Television is rated the "most believable" news source.

Source: Data from Pew Research Center for the People and the Press, June 2, 2005. www.people-press.org

Politics Up Close   The Generation Gap in News

Young people are far less likely to spend time watching the news than older people. Indeed, people 65 and older are nearly twice as likely as those under 30 to watch television news. And older people are more than twice as likely to read a newspaper.

However, young people are more likely than older people to hear radio news, perhaps because radio news periodically interrupts music programming. And young people are the principal consumers of online news. Yet overall, young people are exposed to far less news than seniors.

The News Generation Gap

	18–29	30–49	50–64	65+
Watch TV news	40%	52%	62%	73%
Local TV	28	41	49	52
Network evening news	17	25	38	46
Cable TV news	16	23	30	35
Morning TV news	11	16	21	27
Read newspaper	26	37	52	59
Listen to radio news	34	49	42	29
News magazines	12	13	15	13
Online news	31	30	24	7
No news (yesterday)	33	19	15	12

Source: Pew Research Center for the People and the Press. www.people-press.org Reprinted by permission of Pew Research Center for the People and the Press.

rioting mob, police beating an African American motorist, wounded soldiers being unloaded from a helicopter—scenes that convey an emotional message. Gripping pictures can inflame public opinion, inspire a clamor for action, and even pressure the government into hasty action—the "CNN effect."

Moreover, television focuses on the faces of individuals as well as on their words, portraying honesty or deception, humility or arrogance, compassion or indifference, humor or meanness, and a host of other personal characteristics. Skillful politicians understand that *what* one says may not be as important as *how* one says it. Image triumphs over substance on television.[3]

Influence on Decision Makers   The media's impact on political decision makers is vastly more significant than their impact on ordinary viewers. Media stories often relate more directly to the immediate concerns of politicians and government officials. They are more attentive to these stories; they are often asked to respond or comment upon news stories. They correctly perceive that media coverage of particular events and issues sets the agenda for public discussion. Even media stories that have relatively little widespread public interest can create a buzz "inside the Beltway," that is, within Washington circles.

The Myth of the Mirror   Media people themselves often deny that they exercise great power. They sometimes claim that they only "mirror" reality. They like to think of themselves as unbiased reporters who simply narrate happenings and transmit videotaped portrayals of people and events as they really are. But whether or not the editors, reporters, producers, or anchors acknowledge their own power, it is clear that they do more than passively mirror reality.

Sources of Media Power

Comparing News Media

✓ *Think* Again

Do the media mirror what is really news, rather than deciding themselves what's important and then making it news?

★ **newsmaking**
Deciding what events, topics, presentations, and issues will be given coverage in the news.

Government and the media are natural adversaries. (Thomas Jefferson once wrote that he would prefer newspapers without government to a government without newspapers. But after serving as president, he wrote that people who never read newspapers are better informed than those who do, because ignorance is closer to the truth than the falsehoods spread by newspapers.) Public officials have long been frustrated by the media. But the U.S. Constitution's 1st Amendment guarantee of a free press anticipates this conflict between government and the media. It prohibits government from resolving this conflict by silencing its critics.

Media professionals—television and newspaper reporters, editors, anchors, and producers—are not neutral observers of American politics but rather are active participants. They not only report events but also discover events to report, assign them political meaning, and predict their consequences. They seek to challenge government officials, debate political candidates, and define the problems of society. They see their profession as a "sacred trust" and themselves as the true voice of the people in public affairs.

Newsmaking   Deciding what is "news" and who is "newsworthy"—**news-making**—is the most important source of media power. It is only through the media that the general public comes to know about events, personalities, and issues. Media attention makes topics public, creates issues, and elevates personalities from obscurity to celebrity. Each day, editors, producers, and reporters must select from millions of events, topics, and people those that will be videotaped, written about, and talked about. The media can never be a "picture of the world" because the whole world cannot be squeezed into the picture. The media must decide what is and is not "news."

Democratic presidential candidate U.S. Senator Barack Obama speaks to the travelling media on the tarmac at the airport in Eau Claire, Wisconsin, August 24, 2008.

Politicians have a love-hate relationship with the media. They need media attention to promote themselves, their message, and their programs. They crave the exposure, the name recognition, and the celebrity status that the media can confer. At the same time, they fear attack by the media. They know the media are active players in the political game, not just passive spectators. The media seek sensational stories of sin, sexuality, corruption, and scandal in government to attract viewers and readers, and thus the media pose a constant danger to politicians. Politicians understand the power of the media to make or break their careers.

Agenda Setting

Agenda setting is the power to decide what will be decided. It is the power to define society's "problems," to create political issues, and to set forth alternative solutions. Deciding which issues will be addressed by government may be even more important than deciding how the issues will be resolved. The distinguished political scientist E. E. Schattschneider once wrote, "He who determines what politics is about runs the country."[4]

The real power of the media lies in their ability to set the political agenda for the nation. This power grows out of their ability to decide what is news. Media coverage determines what both citizens and public officials regard as "crises" or "problems" or "issues" to be resolved. Conditions ignored by the media seldom get on the agenda of political leaders. Media attention forces public officials to speak on the topic, take positions, and respond to questions. Media inattention allows problems to be ignored by government. "TV is the Great Legitimator. TV confers reality. Nothing happens in America, practically everyone seems to agree, until it happens on television."[5]

Political issues do not just "happen." The media are crucial to their development. Organized interest groups, professional public relations firms, government bureaucracies, political candidates, and elected officials all try to solicit the assistance of the media in shaping the political agenda. Creating an issue, publicizing it, dramatizing it, turning it into a "crisis," getting people to talk about it, and ultimately forcing government to do something about it are the tactics of agenda setting. The participation of the mass media is vital to their success.[6]

★ **agenda setting**
Deciding what will be decided, defining the problems and issues to be addressed by decision makers.

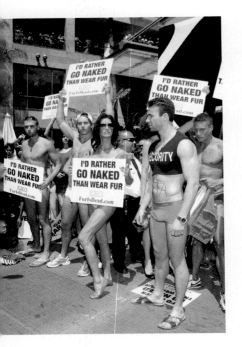

Made for TV

Janice Dickinson and the Dickinson Models march on Hollywood Blvd. for the People for the Ethical Treatment of Animal's (PETA's) "We'd Rather Go Naked Than Wear Fur" campaign on August 20, 2007, in Hollywood, California.

★ **socialization**
The learning of a culture and its values.

VISUAL LITERACY

Use of the Media by the American Public

Interpreting   The media not only decide what will be news; they also interpret the news for us. Editors, reporters, and anchors provide each story with an *angle*, an interpretation that places the story in a context and speculates about its meaning and consequences. The interpretation tells us what to think about the news.

News is presented in "stories." Reporters do not report facts; they tell stories. The story structure gives meaning to various pieces of information. Some common angles or themes of news stories are these:

★ *Good guys versus bad guys*: for example, corrupt officials, foreign dictators, corporate polluters, and other assorted villains versus honest citizens, exploited workers, endangered children, or other innocents.

★ *Little guys versus big guys*: for example, big corporations, the military, or insensitive bureaucracies versus consumers, taxpayers, poor people, or the elderly.

★ *Appearance versus reality*: for example, the public statements of government officials or corporate executives versus whatever contradicting facts hardworking investigative reporters can find.

News is also "pictures." A story without visuals is not likely to be selected as television news in the first place. The use of visuals reinforces the angle. A close-up shot can reveal hostility, insincerity, or anxiety on the face of villains or can show fear, concern, sincerity, or compassion on the face of innocents. To emphasize elements of a story, an editor can stop the action, use slow motion, zoom the lens, add graphics, cut back and forth between antagonists, cut away for audience reaction, and so on. Videotaped interviews can be spliced to make the interviewees appear knowledgeable, informed, and sincere or, alternatively, ignorant, insensitive, and mean-spirited. The media jealously guard the right to edit interviews themselves, rejecting virtually all attempts by interviewees to review and edit their own interviews.

Socializing   The media have power to socialize audiences to the political culture. News, entertainment, and advertising all contribute to **socialization**—to the learning of political values. Socialization through television and motion pictures begins in early childhood and continues throughout life. Most of the political information people learn comes to them through television—specific facts as well as general values. Election coverage, for example, shows "how democracy works," encourages political participation, and legitimizes the winner's control of government. Advertising shows Americans desirable middle-class standards of living even while it encourages people to buy automobiles, detergent, and beer, and entertainment programming socializes them to "acceptable" ways of life. Political values such as racial tolerance, sexual equality, and support for law enforcement are reinforced in movies, situation comedies, and police shows.

Persuading   The media, in both paid advertising and news and entertainment programming, engage in direct efforts to change our attitudes, opinions, and behavior. Newspaper editorials have traditionally been employed for direct persuasion. A great deal of the political commentary on television news and interview programs is aimed at persuading people to adopt the views of the commentators. Even many entertainment programs and movies are intended to promote specific political viewpoints. But most direct persuasion efforts come to us through paid advertising.

Political campaigning is now largely a media battle, with paid political advertisements as the weapons. Candidates rely on professional campaign-management firms, with their pollsters, public relations specialists, advertising-production people, and media consultants, to carry on the fight (see Chapter 8).

Governments and political leaders must rely on persuasion through the mass media to carry out their programs. Presidents can take their message directly to people in televised speeches, news conferences, and the yearly State of the Union message. Presidents by custom are accorded television time whenever they request it. In this way, they can go over the heads of Congress and even the media executives and reporters themselves to communicate directly with the people.

In short, persuasion is central to politics, and the media are the key to persuasion.

The Business of the Media

The business of the media is to gather mass audiences to sell to advertisers. Economic interest drives all media to try to attract and hold the largest numbers of readers and viewers in order to sell time and space to advertisers. Over one-quarter of all prime-time television (8–11 P.M.) is devoted to commercial advertising. Americans get more than one minute of commercials for every three minutes of news and entertainment. Television networks and commercial stations charge advertisers on the basis of audience estimates made by rating services. One rating service, A. C. Nielsen, places electronic boxes in a national sample of television homes and calculates the proportion of these homes that watch a program (the rating), as well as the proportion of homes with their television sets turned on that watch a particular program (the share). Newspapers' and magazines' advertising revenue is based primarily on circulation figures (see Table 6.1).

Table *6.1* Who Reads What? The Largest Circulation U.S. Newspapers and Magazines

USA Today leads all other U.S. newspapers in daily circulation. The *New York Times* and the *Wall Street Journal* follow with over one million readers each day. The most popular magazines—*AARP, Reader's Digest, TV Guide*—have little news content.

Daily Newspapers			Magazines		
Rank	**Newspaper**	**Circulation**	**Rank**	**Magazine**	**Circulation**
1.	*USA Today* (Arlington, VA)	2,222,745	1.	*AARP The Magazine*	22,668,583
2.	*Wall Street Journal* (New York)	2,083,653	2.	*Reader's Digest*	10,155,054
3.	*New York Times* (New York)	1,126,190	3.	*TV Guide*	9,015,866
4.	*Los Angeles Times* (Los Angeles)	843,432	4.	*Better Homes and Gardens*	7,627,256
5.	*New York Daily News* (New York)	688,584	5.	*National Geographic*	6,471,803
6.	*Washington Post* (Washington, D.C.)	678,779	6.	*Good Housekeeping*	4,631,527
7.	*New York Post* (New York)	662,681	7.	*Family Circle*	4,252,730
8.	*Chicago Tribune* (Chicago)	586,122	8.	*Woman's Day*	4,130,507
9.	*Houston Chronicle* (Houston)	521,419	9.	*Ladies' Home Journal*	4,114,353
10.	*Dallas Morning News* (Dallas)	495,469	10.	*TIME*	4,034,272

Source: World Almanac and Book of Facts 2007. New York: World Almanac Books, 2007.

Soft Fluff Versus Hard Programming Lightweight entertainment—"soft fluff"—prevails over serious programming in virtually all media, but particularly on television. Critics of the "boob tube" abound in intellectual circles, but the mass public clearly prefers fluffy entertainment programming. Political scientist Doris Graber writes:

> Although "lightweight" programming draws the wrath of many people, particularly intellectual elites, one can argue that their disdain constitutes intellectual snobbery. Who is to say that the mass public's tastes are inferior to those of elites? . . . Proof is plentiful that the mass public does indeed prefer light entertainment to more serious programs.[7]

And it is the mass public that advertisers want to reach. Channels devoted to highbrow culture, including public television stations, languish with low ratings.

Public Television and Radio The Corporation for Public Broadcasting (CPB) was created by Congress in 1967 to provide "noncommercial high quality programs . . . to inform, enlighten and enrich the public." As a nonprofit government corporation CPB relies on taxpayer funding in annual appropriations from Congress. In turn, it provides the funding for Public Broadcasting Service (PBS) and National Educational Television (NET). PBS had some early successes in programming—*Masterpiece Theatre, Sesame Street*—but in more recent years commercial broadcasting has exceeded PBS in both quality and viewership. Commercial channels—History Channel, Discovery Channel, National Geographic Channel, and others—regularly broadcast high-quality programs to much larger audiences and do not rely on taxpayer funding. Opponents of continued government funding of PBS complain of left-leaning bias in its news and commentary.

News as TV Entertainment Increasingly news is being presented as television entertainment. In recent years there has been a dramatic increase in the number of entertainment-oriented, quasi-news programming, sometimes referred to as the "soft news media."[8] **Soft news** comes mainly in two formats: talk shows, both daytime and nighttime; and tabloid news programs (see Table 6.2). Even late-night entertainment programs—Jay Leno, David Letterman, Conan O'Brien, *Politically Incorrect*—include comedy monologues that occasionally refer to political events or issues.

★ **Soft news**
News featured in talk shows, late-night comedy, and TV news magazines—reaches more people than regular news broadcasts.

Table **6.2** Lighter Fare: TV Soft News Programming

Network news magazines	Network TV soft news
Dateline NBC	*Extra*
20/20	*Entertainment Tonight*
Primetime Live	*Inside Edition*
48 Hours	*Access Hollywood*
60 Minutes	
	Cable TV soft news
Late-night TV talk shows	E! Network
Jay Leno	Black Entertainment Television
David Letterman	MTV News
Conan O'Brien	Evening TV talk shows
Daytime TV talk shows	**Evening TV talk shows**
Oprah Winfrey	*The Colbert Report*
Regis and Kelly	*The Daily Show*
The View	*Politically Incorrect*

Politics Up Close   The *Oprah* Effect

Daytime gab fests and nighttime comedy shows have emerged as critical stomping grounds for presidential candidates. Republican Fred Thompson skipped a New Hampshire debate with his rivals in order to announce his candidacy to Jay Leno on *The Tonight Show*. John McCain announced his own bid on *The Late Show with David Letterman*. Hillary Clinton dined with Ellen Degeneres on daytime TV. And Barack Obama scored the biggest boost when Oprah Winfrey endorsed him on her daytime television show.

Candidates have sought to showcase their lighter sides on late-night programs as far back as 1960 when John F. Kennedy and Richard Nixon visited with Jack Parr on *The Tonight Show*. But talk-show appearances did not become a campaign mainstay until after 1992 when Bill Clinton played the saxophone on the late-night *Arsenio Hall Show*.

What is the political effect of "soft news"—news that is conveyed on entertainment and tabloid news shows, network news magazines, and daytime and nighttime talk shows? Research indicates that the audiences for the shows are less interested in politics than the audiences for hard news shows—nightly network TV news, newspapers, news magazines.[a] But research also shows that exposure to political news, even in an entertaining format, increases political participation, notably voting.[b] There were scores of debates leading up to the election of 2008 but more voters were exposed to the soft news than to formal debates. Candidates enjoy the friendly environs of talk shows where the personal takes precedence over policy. The talk shows provide them with the opportunity to project a friendly image—to get the audiences to like them. As one veteran campaign manager commented, "These are the types of outlets that allow the candidates to connect and communicate who they are as people."[c]

Politicians have a "love-hate" relationship with the media. They need the media to get out their message, just as the media need them to make the news. But both often use each other for their own purposes and neither entirely trusts the other. Here, Republican presidential candidate John McCain (R-AZ) appears on *The Daily Show with Jon Stewart* on Wednesday, May 7, 2008, in New York.

[a]Matthew A. Baum, "Talking the Vote: Why Presidential Candidates Hit the Talk Show Circuit," *American Journal of Political Science* (April 2005): 213–34.

[b]Matthew A. Baum, "The *Oprah* Effect: How Soft News Helps Inattentive Citizens Vote Consistently," *Journal of Politics* 68 (November 2006): 946–59.

[c]*Palm Beach Post*, September 30, 2007.

Soft news is a major source of information for people who are not interested in politics or public affairs. It is true, of course, that most soft news programming favors celebrity gossip, murder trials, sex scandals, disasters, and other human interest stories. But on some high-profile news issues these programs provide an otherwise inattentive public with what little information it absorbs.

60 Minutes attracts more viewers than any other soft news program (see *Politics Up Close: "60 Minutes, News as Entertainment"*). *Dateline* and *20/20* are not far behind. (Arguably these programs are oriented toward a somewhat more sophisticated audience than talk shows or tabloid news programs.) These programs, as well as *Entertainment Tonight* and *Oprah* (see *Politics Up Close: "The Oprah Effect"*), attract more viewers than any of the nightly network newscasts.

Politics Up Close *60 Minutes*, News as Entertainment

Television's longest-running prime-time program is *60 Minutes*. For over 40 years this news/entertainment show has been ranked at or near the top of all prime-time television shows, including dramas, comedies, sports, and other news shows. It was created in 1968 by its now-legendary producer Don Hewitt. He devised reporter-centered, hard-hitting, investigative features centering on scandal and corruption in corporations and governments. The focus is usually on individual wrongdoers who are sometimes the object of confrontational interviews, and at other times ambushed by a reporter and shown mumbling denials or fleeing the camera. The regular cast of *60 Minutes* includes Morley Safer, Steve Croft, Lesley Stahl, Bob Simon, and Scott Pelley. It ends with occasionally humorous comments by its resident curmudgeon, Andy Rooney.

Features stories on nightly news broadcasts seldom exceed two minutes of air time. But features on

60 Minutes run 12 to 15 minutes; each show usually includes three feature stories. The features are designed to entertain, dramatize, and otherwise capture audience attention. The show often includes interviews with celebrities and even with important political figures, for example, Mike Wallace's interviews with the drug dealing Panamanian dictator Manuel Noriega, Russian President Vladimir Putin, and Iran's current leader Mahmoud Ahmadinejad.

60 Minutes demonstrated that news could be presented as entertainment and could capture large audiences. The show has many imitators, including some successful ones—*20/20, Dateline NBC,* and *48 Hours.*

Source: www.cbsnews.com

The media favor bad news over good news. Wars, fires and natural disasters, and crime are all well reported. Here two Amish men read the news of the shooting at a one-room Amish schoolhouse on October 3, 2006, in Nickel Mines, Pennsylvania. But good news about things going well, such as improved health, higher standards of living, or new construction going as planned, get far less attention.

Politicians themselves have come to understand the importance of soft news programming in reaching segments of the public that seldom watch news programs, speeches or debates, or campaign advertising. Presidential candidates welcome invitations to appear with Oprah, or Leno, or Letterman, and try to reformulate their messages in a light, comedic style that fits the program.

The Media Conglomerates Mega-mergers in recent years have created corporate empires that spread across multiple media—television, film, newspapers, music, and the Internet. Conglomerate media corporations combine television broadcasting and cable programming, movie production and distribution, magazine and book publication, music recording, Internet access, and even sports and recreation. The six multinational corporations listed in Table 6.3 currently dominate world media and cultural interests.

The Politics of the News

The politics of the news media are shaped by (1) their *economic interest*, (2) their *professional environment*, and (3) their *ideological leanings*.

Sensationalism The economic interest of the media—the need to capture and hold audience attention—creates a bias toward "hype" in the selection of news, its presentation, and its interpretation. To attract viewers and readers, the media bias the news toward violence, conflict, scandal, corruption, sex, scares of various sorts, and the personal lives of politicians and celebrities. News is selected primarily for its emotional impact on audiences; its social, economic, or political significance is secondary to the need to capture attention.

News must "touch" audiences personally, arouse emotions, and hold the interest of people with short attention spans. Scare stories—street crime, drug use,

Table *6.3*   Who Controls What?: Media Empires in America

Time Warner Inc. (formerly known as AOL Time Warner)

Television: HBO, TNT, TBS, CNN, CNNSI, CNNFN, Cinemax, Time Warner Cable
Motion Pictures: Warner Brothers, New Line Cinema, Castle Rock, Looney Tunes
Magazines: Time, People, Sports Illustrated, Fortune, plus twenty-eight other specialty magazines
Books: Warner Books; Little, Brown Publishing; Book-of-the-Month Club
Music: Warner Brothers Records, Atlantic Records, Elektra
Sports and Entertainment: Atlanta Braves, Atlanta Hawks
Internet: AOL, Netscape, CompuServe

Walt Disney

Television: ABC-TV, plus ten stations; ESPN, ESPN-2, Disney Channel, A&E, E!, Lifetime
Motion Pictures: Walt Disney Pictures, Miramax, Touchstone
Music: Walt Disney Records, Mammoth, Buena Vista Records
Sports and Recreation: Disney theme parks in Florida, California, France, Japan; Disney Cruise Line
Consumer Products: Disney stores, Disney toys

Viacom

Television: CBS, plus forty TV stations: MTV, TNN, Nickelodeon, Showtime, VH1, Nick-At-Nite, Spike TV, BET, Comedy Central
Motion Pictures: Paramount Pictures, Spelling, Viacom
Books: Simon & Schuster, Scribner, Free Press
Radio: Infinity Broadcasting
Music: Famous Music Publishing
Sports and Recreation: SportsLine, plus five Paramount parks

NewsCorp (Fox)

Television: Fox Network plus thirty-five TV stations; Fox News, Fox Entertainment, Fox Sports, Fox Family Channel, National Geographic Channel, DirecTV
Motion Pictures: 20th Century Fox, Searchlight
Books: HarperCollins
Newspapers: New York Post, Wall Street Journal
Magazines: TV Guide
Music: Mushroom Records
Internet: MySpace

Sony

Television: Game Show Network, *Jeopardy, Wheel of Fortune*
Motion Pictures: Columbia Pictures, Sony Pictures, Tri Star
Music: Columbia Records, Epic Records, Sony, Nashville
Sports and Recreation: Sony Theaters

NBC-Universal

Television: NBC Network plus thirteen TV stations; CNBC, MSNBC, Telemundo, Bravo, USA, SciFi
Motion Pictures: Universal Pictures
Sports and Recreation: Universal Studios theme parks in California and Florida
Music: Motown, Geffen, MCA

Source: Thomas R. Dye, *Who's Running America? The Bush Restoration,* 6th ed. (Upper Saddle River, N.J.: Prentice Hall, 2002). Updated by the author.

AIDS, nuclear power plant accidents, global warming, and a host of health alarms—make "good" news, for they cause viewers to fear for their personal safety. The sex lives of politicians, once by custom off-limits to the press, are now public "affairs." Scandal and corruption among politicians, as well as selfishness and greed among business executives, are regular media themes.[9]

Negativism   The media are biased toward bad news. Bad news attracts larger audiences than good news. Television news displays a pervasive bias toward the negative in American life—in government, business, the military, politics, education, and everywhere else. Bad-news stories on television vastly outnumber good-news stories.

Good news gets little attention. For example, television news watchers are not likely to know that illegal drug use is declining in the United States, that both the air and water are measurably cleaner today than in past decades, that the nuclear power industry has the best safety record of any major industry in the United States, and that the aged in America are wealthier and enjoy higher incomes than the nonaged. The violent crime rate is down 50 percent since 1990. Teenage pregnancies and abortion rates are both down significantly. Television has generally failed to report these stories or, even worse, has implied that the opposite is true. Good news—stories about improved health statistics, longer life spans, better safety records, higher educational levels, for example—seldom provides the dramatic element needed to capture audience attention. The result is an overwhelming bad-news bias, especially on television.[10]

Muckraking   The professional environment of reporters and editors predisposes them toward an activist style of journalism once dubbed **muckraking**. Reporters today view themselves as "watchdogs" of the public trust. They see themselves in noble terms—enemies of corruption, crusaders for justice, defenders of the disadvantaged. "The watchdog function, once considered remedial and subsidiary . . . [is now] paramount: the primary duty of the journalists is to focus attention on problems and deficits, failures and threats."[11] Their professional models are the crusading "investigative reporters" who expose wrongdoing in government, business, the military, and every other institution in society—except the media.

The "Feeding Frenzy"   Occasionally, muckraking episodes grow into "**feeding frenzies**"—intense coverage of a scandal or event that blocks out most other news. Political scientist Larry Sabato describes the feeding frenzy: "In such situations a development is almost inevitably magnified and overscrutinized, the crush of cameras, microphones, and people, combined with the pressure of instant deadlines and live broadcasts, hype events and make it difficult to keep them in perspective. When a frenzy begins to gather, the intensity grows exponentially . . . Television news time is virtually turned over to the subject of the frenzy."[12] Increasingly stiff competition among the media for attention and the need for round-the-clock cable news to fill long hours contribute to feeding frenzies.

Media Bias

Liberalism in the Newsroom   The activist role that the media have taken upon themselves means that the personal values of reporters, editors, producers, and anchors are a very important element of American politics. The political values of the media are decidedly liberal and reformist. Political scientist Doris A. Graber writes about the politics of the media: "Economic and social liberalism prevails, especially in the most prominent media organizations. So does a preference for an internationalist foreign policy, caution about military intervention, and some suspicion about the ethics of established large institutions, particularly big business and big government."[13] Most Americans agree that media news coverage is biased and the bias is in a liberal direction (see *What Do You Think?*: "Are the Media Biased?").

Liberalism in Hollywood   With a few exceptions, Hollywood producers, directors, writers, studio executives, and actors are decidedly liberal in their political views, especially when compared with the general public. Of the Hollywood elite, more than 60 percent describe themselves as liberal and only 14 percent as conservative,[14] whereas in the general public, self-described conservatives

★ **muckraking**
Journalistic exposés of corruption, wrongdoing, or mismanagement in government, business, and other institutions of society.

★ **"feeding frenzy"**
Intense media coverage of a scandal or event that blocks out most other news.

What Do You *Think?*

Are the Media Biased?

Are the media biased, and if so, in what direction—liberal or conservative? Arguments over media bias have grown in intensity as the media have come to play a central role in American politics.

The American public is more likely to say that the news media are "too liberal" rather than "too conservative" or "about right." Political partisanship helps to shape Americans' feelings toward bias in the news. Republicans and conservatives are much more likely to say that the media are "too liberal" than Democrats and liberals who are more inclined to say that the media is "just about right."

Q: In general do you think the news media is—too liberal, just about right, or too conservative?[a]

	Too Liberal	Just About Right	Too Conservative
All	44%	33%	19%
Democrats	20	53	23
Independents	40	37	19
Republicans	77	17	5
Liberals	16	45	37
Moderates	39	42	15
Conservatives	68	24	6

Over time Americans have lost much trust and confidence in the mass media. In the early 1970s about 70 percent of Americans reported that they had a great deal or a fair amount of trust and confidence in the media, while only about 30 percent reported they had not very much confidence and trust in the media or none at all. Today the percentage of Americans who report having a great deal or a fair amount of trust and confidence in the media is about 47 percent, the percentage of Americans who have not very much trust in the media or none at all has risen to 53 percent. Trust and confidence in the media is also affected by political partisanship: Democrats are much more likely to have a great deal or a fair amount of trust (about 68 percent) than do Independents (40 percent) or Republicans (32 percent). Interestingly, local news is perceived to be less biased and more trusted than national news.

Most journalists are personally liberal and vote Democratic, and the media's coverage of issues such as gun control, affirmative action, abortion, gay rights, and religion in America reveals a leftward slant.[b] Fox News, and the *Wall Street Journal* (now owned by the same News Corp.) are exceptions to the rest of the mainstream media. The elite newspapers (the *New York Times* and the *Washington Post*) the television networks (ABC, CBS, NBC, CNN), and the newsweeklies (*Time* and *Newsweek*) are liberal in tone and content. However, more than one in five Americans say that they get their news from talk radio—the programming of which is reported to be 90 percent conservative.[c]

Yet at the same time, Americans have high expectations of the role of the media in society: they expect the media to protect them from "abuse of power" by government, to hold public officials accountable, and to identify and help solve the problems of society.

[a]Gallup News Service, October 8, 2007.
[b]Bernard Goldberg, *Arrogance: Rescuing America from the Media Elite*. New York: Warner Books, 2003.
[c]Robert F. Kennedy, Jr., *Crimes Against Nature*. New York: Harper Collins, 2005.

outnumber liberals by a significant margin. Hollywood leaders are five times more likely to be Democrats than Republicans, and Hollywood is a major source of Democratic Party campaign funds. On both economic and social issues, the Hollywood elite is significantly more liberal than the nation's general public or college-educated public.[15] (However, see *A Conflicting View*: "Fox News: 'Fair and Balanced'?").

Conservatism on Talk Radio   Talk radio is the one medium where conservatism prevails. The single most listened-to talk radio show is the *Rush Limbaugh Show*, whose host regularly bashes "limousine liberals," "femi-Nazis," "environmental wackos," and "croissant people."[16] Talk radio might be portrayed as "call-in democracy." Callers respond almost immediately to reported news events. Call-in shows are the first to sense the public mood. Callers are not necessarily representative of the general public. Rather they are usually the most intense and outraged of citizens. But their complaints are early warning signs for wary politicians.

A Conflicting *View*

Fox News: "Fair and Balanced"?

For many years conservatives complained about the liberal tilt of television news. But despite their ample financial resources, conservative investors failed to create their own network or purchase an existing one. It was an Australian billionaire, Rupert Murdoch, who eventually came to the rescue of American conservatives.

Murdoch's global media empire, News Corp, includes Fox Network, Fox News Cable, 20th Century Fox, Fox Movie Channel, MySpace, the *New York Post*, the *Times* and the *Sun* of London, HarperCollins Publishing, the *Weekly Standard*, and thirty-five local TV stations. He began his career by injecting glitz and vulgarity into previously dull Australian newspapers he inherited. The formula worked worldwide: The *New York Post* became a noisy tabloid after Murdoch took over (most memorable headline: "HEADLESS BODY FOUND IN TOPLESS BAR"), and Fox TV entertainment airs even more vulgar shows than the mainstream networks.

Murdoch himself is not particularly conservative in his politics. (He has held fundraising events for Hillary Clinton.) But he recognized an unfilled market for conservative views on American television. In 1996 he founded Fox News and hired Roger Ailes (former TV ad producer for Richard Nixon, Ronald Reagan, and George H. W. Bush) to head up the new network. Ailes quickly signed Bill O'Reilly (see *People in Politics* in Chapter 2) for an hourlong nightly conservative talk show. Brit Hume, one of the few prominent TV reporters considered to be a conservative, was made managing editor.

Fox proclaims "fair and balanced" news—"We report, you decide." The implication is that mainstream media has a liberal bias and that Fox is rectifying it with its own fair and balanced reporting. According to Fox, if its reporting appears conservative, it is only because the country has become so accustomed to left-leaning media that a truly balanced network just seems conservative.

Regular news reporting on Fox is not much different than other networks, except that Fox may cover some stories ignored by the mainstream media, for example, political correctness running amok on college campuses, ridiculous environmental regulations, hypocrisy among Hollywood liberals, and so on. But it is the talk and commentary shows that outrage liberals and warm the hearts of conservatives. Liberals bold enough to appear on Fox are badgered mercilessly, while conservative guests are tossed softball questions. The bottom line, financially as well as politically, is that Fox News is now the most watched cable news network, even surpassing CNN. Whatever its flaws, Fox News had added diversity of views to American television.

In 2007, Murdoch invaded the financial world with his purchase of Dow Jones & Co., publishers of the *Wall Street Journal*. Traditionalists worry that Murdoch will popularize the *Journal* and perhaps detract from its prestige and influence in the financial world. But others believe that changes in the *Journal* will be modest and that Murdoch will use it to further expand his media empire.

Televised Incivility and Political Trust Does watching political shows on television, in which hosts, guests, pundits, and others hurl insults at each other, interrupt and shout over each other, and use especially contentious and uncivil language, reduce levels of trust in politicians and government? Programs such as *The O'Reilly Factor, Meet the Press,* and *Hardball* regularly resort to confrontational talk, replete with hyperbole and venomous invective. One experiment, with some viewers watching friendly, polite, and simple political discussions, and other viewers watching rude, emotional, quarrelsome political confrontations, concluded that incivility has a detrimental effect on trust in government and attitudes toward political leaders.[17] Yet it is not likely that televised politics will ever become more civil. Politics for most people cannot compete with entertainment shows for TV audiences, so increasingly political shows are creating dramatic tension and uncivil conflict to gain viewers.

News Versus Entertainment Cable television and the Internet have produced dramatic increases in available political information. Yet overall political knowledge and turnout have not changed noticeably. The key to understanding this apparent paradox is the vast expansion in choices now available to viewers.[18]

People can now choose from numerous cable channels and Web sites. Increasingly there is a division between people who prefer entertainment programming and those who prefer news shows. There is some evidence that people who prefer news shows acquire greater political knowledge and go to the polls more often than those who mainly watch entertainment shows. Greater media choice, then, appears to widen the "knowledge gap." Because people who like news and take advantage of additional information in the media gain political knowledge, while people who prefer entertainment programming learn less about politics, the mean levels of political knowledge in the population have essentially remained constant.

Polarization of the Media

Increasingly, media audiences are becoming politically polarized, with Republicans and conservatives, and Democrats and liberals, choosing to listen to and view separate media outlets. Listeners and viewers are choosing sides in their sources of news (see Table 6.4).

News audiences in the aggregate are somewhat more conservative than the general public. The Pew Research Center reports that of those who regularly watch, read, or listen to the news, conservatives comprise 36 percent, moderates 38 percent, and liberals 18 percent. The favorites of conservatives are the *Rush Limbaugh Show* on radio and the *O'Reilly Factor* on Fox television, followed by religious radio, Fox News, business magazines, and call-in radio shows. Moderates and liberals turn to *Larry King Live*, the nightly ABC, CBS, and NBC news, National Public Radio, and literary magazines.[19]

Table **6.4**   Ideology and News Sources: What Does Your News Say About You?

Liberals and conservatives differ in their sources of news and commentary.

Of those who regularly watch, read or listen to . . .	Conservative	Moderate	Liberal	Don't Know
Rush Limbaugh Show	77%	16%	7%	0%
O'Reilly Factor	72	23	4	1
Religious radio	53	26	12	9
Fox News	52	30	13	5
Business magazines	49	35	14	2
Call-in radio shows	45	33	18	4
Local news	38	41	15	6
Morning news	38	39	17	6
Newspaper	37	41	17	5
Network News Magazines	37	40	17	6
Political magazines	37	29	29	5
CNN	36	39	20	5
Larry King Live	35	41	16	8
CNBC	35	40	18	7
Letterman/Leno	34	41	21	4
MSNBC	33	41	22	4
Nightly Network news	33	41	18	8
NPR	31	33	30	6
Literary magazines	19	38	36	7

Source: Pew Research Center for the People and the Press, June 8, 2004, www.people-press.org
Reprinted by permission of Pew Research Center for the People and the Press.

Mediated Elections

Political campaigning is largely a media activity, and the media, especially television, shape the nation's electoral politics.

The Media and Candidate-Voter Linkage   The media are the principal link between candidates and the voters. At one time, political party organizations performed this function, with city, ward, and precinct workers knocking on doors, distributing campaign literature, organizing rallies and candidate appearances, and getting out the vote on election day. But television has largely replaced party organizations and personal contact as the means by which candidates communicate with voters. Candidates come directly into the living room via television—on the nightly news, in broadcast debates and interviews, and in paid advertising (see Table 6.5).

Media campaigning requires candidates to possess great skill in communications. Candidates must be able to project a favorable media *image*. The image is a composite of the candidate's words, mannerisms, appearance, personality, warmth, friendliness, humor, and ease in front of a camera. Policy positions have less to do with image than the candidate's ability to project personal qualities—leadership, compassion, strength, and character.

The Media and Candidate Selection   The media strongly influence the early selection of candidates. Media coverage creates **name recognition**, an essential quality for any candidate. Early media "mentions" of senators, governors, and other political figures as possible presidential contenders help to sort out the field even before the election year begins. Conversely, media inattention can condemn aspiring politicians to obscurity.

Serious presidential campaigns now begin at least six months to a year before the New Hampshire primary (or almost two years before the November presi-

★ **name recognition**
Public awareness of a candidate—whether they even know his or her name.

Table **6.5**   When It Counts: Sources of Political Campaign News in Presidential Election Years

Over time, network news (ABC, CBS, NBC) has been declining as a major source of campaign news, while cable news (CNN, MSNBC, Fox) has been gaining. The Internet has also gained ground as a source of campaign news.

News Sources	1992	1996	2000	2004
Television	82%	72%	70%	76%
Cable	29	21	36	40
Network	55	36	22	29
Local	29	23	21	12
Newspapers	57	60	39	46
Radio	12	19	15	22
Internet	—	3	11	21
Magazines	9	11	4	6

Note: Respondents were asked, "How did you get most of your news about the presidential election campaign? From television, from newspapers, from radio, from magazines or from the Internet?" Television users were then asked, "Did you get most of your news about the presidential campaign from network TV news, from local TV news, or from cable news networks such as CNN or MSNBC?" Respondents could name two sources.

Source: Pew Research Center for the People and the Press. www.people-press.org

dential election). This early time period, "the invisible primary," is increasingly critical for campaigns.[20] Candidates must position themselves relative to competitors in their own party—build their name recognition, raise poll numbers, and build a campaign war chest. Inasmuch as campaign contributions are just beginning to come in, candidates have relatively little money to spend on paid advertising. They are forced to focus their efforts on attracting media attention by staging media events and issuing press releases. But from the media's perspective, campaign news is neither timely nor immediately relevant. Candidates must try to win media coverage by catering to the conflict and horse race stories preferred by the media. Press releases and speeches focused on issues are most likely to be ignored.[21]

The media sort out the serious candidates early in a race. They even assign front-runner status, which may be either a blessing or a curse, depending on subsequent media coverage. In presidential primaries, the media play the *expectations game*, setting vote margins that the front-runner must meet in order to maintain *momentum*. If the front-runner does not win by a large enough margin, the media may declare the runner-up the "real" winner. This sorting out of candidates by the media influences not only voters, but—more important—financial contributors. The media-designated favorite is more likely to receive campaign contributions; financial backers do not like to waste money on losers. And as contributions roll in, the favorite can buy more television advertising, adding momentum to the campaign.[22]

Popular Voices

Conservative talk-show host Rush Limbaugh has become a symbol of the talk-radio phenomenon.

The Media as Kingmakers In the early months of a campaign, media coverage of candidates and their standing in public opinion polls tend to move together. Candidates who receive heavy media coverage usually do well in the polls. Good poll ratings create more media coverage. Good poll ratings and increased media coverage inspire campaign contributions, which then allow candidates to buy television advertising to further increase their poll numbers. Media-sponsored public opinion polls play an important role in kingmaking. The CBS/*New York Times* poll, the NBC/Associated Press poll, the ABC/*Washington Post* poll, and the CNN/*USA Today* poll are widely reported; they become the benchmarks for voters, telling them who the winners and losers are.

The name of the game for candidates early in the race is *exposure*. Even appearances on entertainment shows, once considered "unpresidential," are now highly valued by political candidates. They vie to appear on *Larry King Live* and on late-night talk shows hosted by Jay Leno, David Letterman, and Conan O'Brien.

Media Effects on the Campaign Political candidates are aware of the importance of the media to their success. Their campaign managers must be "media-savvy" and they must hire media consultants early in the campaign. Candidates are advised to arrange daily newsworthy events to keep their name and image in the news. Television producers, reporters, and editors do not like to receive position papers on substantive issues or to present "talking heads"—shots only of the faces of speakers. Rather they prefer attention-getting, action-oriented, emotion-laden videotape. Candidates and their managers know this and so they attract media attention and resort to *media events*—staged activities designed to polish the image of the candidate. Candidates arrange to appear at police conventions, at schools, at hazardous waste sites, on aircraft carriers, at flag factories, and so on in order to project an image on television of their concern for crime, education, the environment, national defense, patriotism, and the like. (See also "Campaign Strategies" in Chapter 8.)

Reporters crowd around Republican presidential candidate John McCain, senator from Arizona, after a speech at a campaign stop in Des Moines, Iowa, on December 27, 2007.

Supporters of Democratic presidential candidate Barack Obama celebrated his projected win in the Oregon primary at campaign headquarters in Portland, Oregon, on May 20, 2008.

★ **horse-race coverage**
Media coverage of electoral campaigns that concentrates on who is ahead and who is behind, and neglects the issues at stake.

The Media and the Horse Race The media give election campaigns **horse-race coverage**: reporting on who is ahead or behind, what the candidates' strategies are, how much money they are spending, and, above all, what their current standing in the polls is. Such stories account for more than half of all television news coverage of an election. Additional stories are centered on *campaign* issues—controversies that arise on the campaign trail itself, including verbal blunders by the candidate—and *character* issues, such as the sex life of the candidate. In contrast, *policy* issues typically account for only about one-third of the television news stories in a presidential election campaign.[23]

The Bad News Bias The media's bad-news bias is evident in election campaigns as well as in general news reporting. Negative stories about all presidential candidates usually outnumber positive stories. The media generally see their function in political campaigns as reporting on the weaknesses, blunders, and vulnerabilities of the candidates. It might be argued that exposing the flaws of the candidates is an important function in a democracy. But the media's negative reporting about candidates and generally skeptical attitude toward their campaign speeches, promises, and advertisements may contribute to political alienation and cynicism among voters.

The media focus intense scrutiny on the personal lives of candidates—their marriages, sex lives, drug or alcohol use, personal finances, past friendships, military service, club memberships, and other potential sources of embarrassment. Virtually any past error in judgment or behavior by a candidate is given heavy coverage. But the media defend their attention to personal scandal on the ground that they are reporting on the "character issue." They argue that voters must have information on candidates' character as well as on their policy positions.

The Shrinking Sound Bite Reporters and newsroom anchors dominate television broadcasting. They report roughly three-quarters of all campaign news themselves. The candidates are allocated less than 15 percent of the time devoted to campaign news stories. (Other sources—pundits, commentators, voters, and so forth—account for the remaining airtime.) The candidates themselves have very little direct contact with audiences in network news. The average **sound bite**—time allowed the candidates to speak on their own behalf—has shrunk to less than eight seconds!

★ **sound bite**
Concise and catchy phrase that attracts media coverage.

Politics Up Close — Media Coverage of the Presidential Campaign, 2008

Media coverage of "Election '08" was especially heavy. The Center for Media and Public Affairs recorded more stories about the presidential campaign in 2008 than in any other election with the exception of the disputed election of 2000. The Center counted the number and types of stories dealing with the presidential campaign that appeared on national network evening news broadcasts of CBS, NBC, ABC, and Fox. Relatively few stories dealt with the candidates' records or positions on policy issues. Far more stories dealt with the "horserace"—the candidates' standing in the race and their strategies and tactics for winning.[a]

During the long primary season Barack Obama received more media attention and more positive coverage than any other candidate. Hillary Clinton received more negative than positive coverage on all four television networks. John McCain was the early media favorite among Republican candidates, but his coverage turned sour as soon as he wrapped up the nomination. Among the networks, only Fox news delivered relatively balanced stories among the candidates; ABC, CBS, and especially NBC heavily favored Obama.

The presidential campaign accounted for about 50 percent of all news broadcast time during the fall. The nation's financial crisis was the second-leading topic of news stories, receiving about 25 percent of broadcast time.

Obama continued to be the media favorite during the general election campaign. Obama received 65 percent positive coverage on the broadcast networks, while McCain's coverage was only 31 percent positive. Only Fox News gave Obama mostly negative coverage; Fox also gave McCain mostly negative coverage.[a]

Major policy issues received minimal coverage. Candidate discussion of the economic crisis received the most attention; health care, terrorism, Iraq and Afghanistan were seldom mentioned. Overall news coverage of the election was episodic—campaign stories dominated the news for a week or so, only to be replaced by other stories the following week. Sarah Palin dominated the news in early September following the Republican national convention. During the

financial crisis, campaign coverage shifted to the activities of the candidates: McCain "suspended" his campaign and threatened to boycott the first presidential debate; Obama accepted President Bush's invitation to attend the financial summit meeting. The McCain campaign attempted to shift media attention to William Ayers, the 1960s violent radical who was an early associate of Obama in Chicago. "Joe the plumber" became a popular media figure in October when both candidates referred to him repeatedly in the third presidential debate as a representative of working Americans. The activist group ACORN and stories of voter registration fraud received some media attention.

Democrats and Republicans disagreed over the quality of media coverage in the presidential campaign. Most Republicans believe that media coverage was "poor" and tilted toward Obama. In contrast most Democrats believe that media coverage was "good":[b]

Quality of Media Coverage

	Good	Poor	Don't Know
Republicans	38%	61%	1%
Democrats	70%	28%	2%
Independents	47%	53%	—

Late-night talk shows joked about McCain far more often than about Obama. McCain's age was a frequent target: "McCain was asked how he's going to conserve energy. He said by taking three naps a day."
—Jay Leno

a Center for Media and Public Affairs,
   www.cmpa.com

b Pew Research Center for People and Press.

Favorable Network News Stories

	ABC	CBS	NBC	Fox	Total
Obama	57%	73%	56%	28%	65%
McCain	42%	31%	16%	39%	31%

Source: Center for Media and Public Affairs, August 23–October 24, N = 979.

Paid Campaign Ads Candidates cannot allow the news media to define them or their messages. Rather, they must endeavor to do so themselves, and of course they must try to define their opponents in negative terms. Television ads account for the largest portion of campaign spending. Nearly one million political commercials will be aired during a primary and general election cycle, for president, Congress, governorships, and state legislatures. Heavy costs are incurred in the production of ads as well as the purchase of broadcast time. Networks may charge $1 million or more for 30 seconds of nationwide primetime advertising on a popular show.

Television advertising is most effective in motivating supporters to vote. Advertising can do so by creating a favorable image of the candidate, or more likely by creating a negative image of the opponent. But television ads run the risk of creating boredom and frustration among viewers who grow tired of the constant barrage of political ads. To counter these effects, advertising executives and their political consultants must develop interesting and captivating ads, and they must regularly develop new ads in the course of the campaign. Ads may change themes in response to polls or focus groups that indicate new or developing concerns among the electorate. And ads can also be changed to counter attacks from the opposition. As election day approaches, ads are more likely to "go negative," that is, to attack the opponent. The ad battle is the most salient element of an election campaign. (See "Campaign Strategies" in Chapter 8.)

Freedom Versus Fairness

Think Again

Should the media be legally required to be fair and accurate in reporting political news?

Complaints about the fairness of media are as old as the printing press. Most early newspapers in the United States were allied with political parties; they were not expected to be fair in their coverage. It was only in the early 1900s that many large newspapers broke their ties with parties and proclaimed themselves independent. And it was not until the 1920s and 1930s that the norms of journalistic professionalism and accuracy gained widespread acceptance.

The Constitution protects the *freedom* of the press; it was not intended to guarantee *fairness*. The First Amendment's guarantee of freedom of the press was originally designed to protect the press from government attempts to silence criticism. Over the years, the U.S. Supreme Court has greatly expanded the meaning of the free-press guarantee.

No Prior Restraint The Supreme Court has interpreted freedom of the press to mean that government may place no **prior restraint** on speech or publication (that is, before it is said or published). Originally, this doctrine was designed to prevent the government from closing down or seizing newspapers. Today, the doctrine prevents the government from censoring any news items. In the famous case of the Pentagon Papers, the *New York Times* and *Washington Post* undertook to publish secret information stolen from the files of the State Department and Defense Department regarding U.S. policy in Vietnam while the war was still going on. No one disputed the fact that stealing the secret material was illegal. What was at issue was the ability of the government to prevent the publication of stolen documents in order to protect national security. The Supreme Court rejected the national security argument and reaffirmed that the government may place no prior restraint on publication.[24] If the government wishes to keep military secrets, it must not let them fall into the hands of the American press.

★ prior restraint
Government actions to restrict publication of a magazine, newspaper, or books on grounds of libel, obscenity, or other legal violations prior to actual publication of the work.

Press Versus Electronic Media In the early days of radio, broadcast channels were limited, and anyone with a radio transmitter could broadcast on any

People in Politics   Larry King Live

Who turned presidential politics into talk-show entertainment? A strong argument can be made that Larry King was personally responsible for changing the nature of presidential campaigning. It was Larry King who nudged frequent talk-show guest Ross Perot into the presidential arena. And it was Larry King who demonstrated to the candidates that the talk-show format was a good way to reach out to the American people.

Larry King's supremacy in talk-show politics came late in life, after a half-century of hustling and hard knocks, no college education, bouts of gambling followed by bankruptcy, and multiple marriages. King has written five books about himself, describing his rise from Brooklyn neighborhoods; his friendships with Jackie Gleason, Frank Sinatra, and other celebrities; and his hardscrabble life. As he tells it, he hung around a New York radio station for five years before taking a bus to Miami to try his luck first as a disk jockey and later as a sports announcer. After a decade in Miami, he had his own TV interview show, a talk show on radio, and a newspaper column, and he was color commentator for the Miami Dolphins. He lived the fast life, running up huge debts and dealing in shady financial transactions. He was arrested in 1971 on grand larceny charges; they were dropped only because the statute of limitations had expired. He lost his TV and radio shows and his newspaper column. He ended up in Shreveport, Louisiana, doing play-by-play for the World Football League. In 1975 he was bankrupt but back in Miami doing radio. In 1978 he moved to Washington to launch his Mutual Network radio talk show. As radio talk shows gained popularity, so did King. When CNN started 24-hour broadcasting in 1982, the network turned to King to do an evening interview show, *Larry King Live*. At first, the

show merely filled the space between the evening and the late news. A decade later, the show was making news itself.

King's success is directly attributable to his accommodating style. He actually listens to his guests; he lets them speak for themselves; he unashamedly plugs their books, records, and movies. He does *not* attack his guests; he does not assume the adversarial, abrasive style preferred by reporters like Mike Wallace or interviewers like Bill O'Reilly. An old-fashioned liberal himself, King appears comfortable interviewing politicians of every stripe. He lets guests talk about themselves. He tosses "softball" questions: "If I were to interview the president about an alleged sexual affair I wouldn't ask if he'd had one, I'd ask him, 'How does it feel to read these things about yourself?'"

With his emphasis on feelings, emotions, and motives rather than on facts, it is little wonder that King's style attracts politicians . . . or that *Larry King Live* is the highest-rated show on CNN.

frequency. As a result, interference was a common frustration of early broadcasters. The industry petitioned the federal government to regulate and license the assignment and use of broadcast frequencies.

The Federal Communications Commission (FCC) was established in 1934 to allocate broadcast frequencies and to license stations for "the public interest, convenience and necessity." The act clearly instructed the FCC: "Nothing in this Act shall be understood or construed to give the Commission the power of censorship." However, the FCC views a broadcast license and exclusive right to use a particular frequency as a *public trust*. Thus broadcasters, unlike newspapers and magazines, are licensed by a government agency and supposed to operate in the *public interest*.

Decency   Recently the FCC decided to crack down on "indecency" on radio and television, presumably doing so in the "public interest." CBS was fined for the

Super Bowl halftime "wardrobe malfunction" by singer Janet Jackson. "Shock-jock" Howard Stern incurred millions of dollars in fines for himself and his stations before giving up regular programming and moving to unregulated satellite radio. Government suppression of "indecency" is constitutionally permitted over broadcast waves on the theory that these channels are limited, they belong to the public, and government licenses broadcasters. Otherwise, mere "indecency" that does not constitute "obscenity" is constitutionally protected by the 1st Amendment (see Chapter 14).

The Equal-Time Requirement   The FCC requires radio and television stations that provide airtime to a political candidate to offer competing candidates the same amount of airtime at the same price. Stations are not required to give free time to candidates, but if stations choose to give free time to one candidate, they must do so for the candidate's opponents. But this **equal-time rule** does *not* apply to newscasts, news specials, or even long documentaries, nor does it apply to talk shows like *Larry King Live* (see *People in Politics*: "Larry King Live"). Nor does it apply to presidential press conferences or presidential addresses to the nation, although the networks now generally offer free time for a "Democratic response" to a Republican president, and vice versa. A biased news presentation does not require the network or station to grant equal time to opponents of its views. And it is important to note that newspapers, unlike radio and television, have never been required to provide equal time to opposing views.

Libel and Slander

Communications that wrongly damage an individual are known in law as **libel** (when written) and **slander** (when spoken). The injured party must prove in court that the communication caused actual damage and was either false or defamatory. A damaging falsehood or words or phrases that are defamatory (such as "Joe Jones is a rotten son of a bitch") are libelous and are not protected by the 1st Amendment from lawsuits seeking compensation.

Public Officials   Over the years, the media have sought to narrow the protection afforded public officials against libel and slander. In 1964 the U.S. Supreme Court ruled in the case of *New York Times v. Sullivan* that public officials did not have a right to recover damages for false statements unless they are made with "malicious intent."[25] The **Sullivan rule** requires public officials not only to show that the media published or broadcast false and damaging statements but also to

★ **equal-time rule**
Federal Communications Commission (FCC) requirement that broadcasters who sell time to any political candidate must make equal time available to opposing candidates at the same price.

★ **libel**
Writings that are false and malicious and are intended to damage an individual.

★ **slander**
Oral statements that are false and malicious and are intended to damage an individual.

★ **Sullivan rule**
Court guideline that false and malicious statements regarding public officials are protected by the 1st Amendment unless it can be proven they were known to be false at the time they were made or were made with "reckless disregard" for their truth or falsehood.

"INTERESTING.....IT'S LIKE A PORTABLE 500K FILE and YOU DON'T HAVE TO WAIT FOR IT TO DOWNLOAD.... AND YOU SAY IT'S CALLED A NEWSPAPER?"

prove they did so knowing that their statements were false and damaging or that they did so with "reckless disregard" for the truth or falsehood of their statements. The effect of the Sullivan rule is to free the media to say virtually anything about public officials. Indeed, the media have sought to expand the definition of "public officials" to "public figures"—that is, to include anyone they choose as the subject of a story.

"Absence of Malice"   The 1st Amendment protects the right of the media to be biased, unfair, negative, sensational, and even offensive. Indeed, even *damaging falsehoods* may be printed or broadcast as long as the media can show that the story was not deliberately fabricated by them with malicious intent, that is, if the media can show an "absence of malice."

Shielding Sources   The media argue that the 1st Amendment allows them to refuse to reveal the names of their sources, even when this information is required in criminal investigations and trials. Thus far, the U.S. Supreme Court has not given blanket protection to reporters to withhold information from court proceedings. However, a number of states have passed *shield laws* protecting reporters from being forced to reveal their sources.

Politics and the Internet

The development of any new medium of communications invariably affects political life. Just as, first, radio and, later, television reshaped politics in America, today the Internet is having its own unique impact on public affairs. The Internet provides a channel for *interactive mass participation* in politics. It is unruly and chaotic by design. It offers the promise of abundant and diverse information and the opportunity for increased political participation. It empowers everyone who can design a Web site to spread their views, whether their views are profound and public-spirited or hateful and obscene.

Chaotic by Design   During the Cold War, the RAND Corporation, a technological research think tank, proposed the Internet as a communications network that might survive a nuclear attack. It was deliberately designed to operate without any central authority or organization. Should any part of the system be destroyed, messages would still find their way to their destinations. The later development of the World Wide Web language allowed any connected computer in the world to communicate with any other connected computer. And introduction of the World Wide Web in 1992 also meant that users no longer needed computer expertise to communicate. By 1995 Americans were buying more computers than television sets and sending more e-mail than "snail mail." Since then, Internet usage has continued to mushroom (see Figure 6.3).

Political Web Sites Abound   The Internet is awash in political Web sites. The simple query "politics" on a standard search program can return well over a million matches. Almost all federal agencies, including the White House, Congress, the federal judiciary, and executive departments and agencies, maintain Web sites. Individual elected officeholders, including all members of Congress, maintain sites that include personal biographies, committee assignments, legislative accomplishments, issue statements, and press releases. The home pages of the Democratic and Republican parties offer political news, issue positions, opportunities to become active in party affairs, and invitations to send them money. No serious candidate for major public office lacks a Web site; these campaign sites usually include flattering biographies, press releases, and, of course, invitations to

Think Again

Should the media report on all aspects of the private lives of public officials?

TIMELINE
Three Hundred Years of American Mass Media

TIMELINE
Nominating Process

Figure 6.3

Online America: Growth of Internet Users

Internet use has mushroomed over the last decade.

Source: Statistical Abstract of the United States, 2008, p. 718.

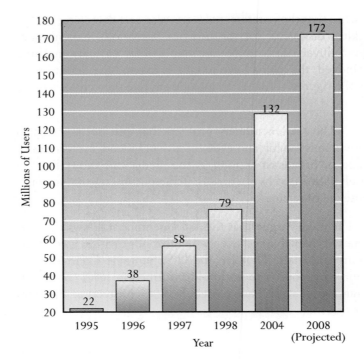

contribute financially to the candidates' campaigns. All major interest groups maintain Web sites—business, trade, and professional groups; labor unions; ideological and issue groups; women's, religious, environmental, and civil rights groups. Indeed, this virtual tidal wave of politics on the Internet may turn out to offer too much information in too fragmented a fashion, thereby simply adding to apathy and indifference.[26]

Internet Fund Raising   All political candidate Web sites solicit credit card campaign contributions. These sites are particularly effective in getting large numbers of small contributions—$10, $25, $50. But candidate Web sites have proven more effective in fund-raising than in vote-getting. In 2004 Democratic presidential candidate Howard Dean was highly successful in soliciting large numbers of small contributions, yet he failed to get votes in the early primaries and was forced to drop out of the race. In 2008 Democratic candidate Barack Obama was very effective in Internet fund raising, surpassing Hillary Clinton and John McCain in dollar amounts and number of contributors.

People who access a candidate's Web site, and especially people who make contributions on it, can be tracked during the campaign to solicit more contributions, and, as election day nears, to urge them to go to the polls. The value of a Web site, then, is primarily in motivating supporters to contribute money and later to cast votes on election day. Web sites, however well designed, seldom turn opponents into supporters.

Internet Uncensored   The Internet allows unrestricted freedom of expression, from scientific discourses on particle physics and information on the latest developments in medical science, to invitations to join in paramilitary "militia" and offers to exchange pornographic photos and messages. Commercial sex sites outnumber any other category on the Web.

Congress unsuccessfully attempted to outlaw "indecent" and "patently offensive" material on the Internet with its Communications Decency Act of 1996. But the U.S. Supreme Court gave the Internet 1st Amendment protection in 1997 in

Barack Obama's campaign web site was the most popular site during the 2008 presidential race. More importantly, it raised record amounts of campaign contributions.

Reno v. American Civil Liberties Union.[27] The Court recognized the Internet as an important form of popular expression protected by the Constitution. Congress had sought to make it a federal crime to send or display "indecent" material to persons under 18 years of age (material describing or displaying sexual activities or organs in "patently offensive" fashion). But the Supreme Court reiterated its view that government may not limit the adult population to "only what is fit for children." The Court decision places the burden of filtering Internet messages on parents. Filtering software can be installed on home computers, but a 1st Amendment issue arises when it is installed on computers in public libraries.

The Bloggers The Internet has spawned a myriad of individual Web sites, commonly known as "blogs," that frequently criticize the professional media. The more reputable blog sites fact-check stories in the mainstream media, or publish stories ignored by them, as well as toss in their own opinions. They have been labeled the media's "back-seat" drivers. (One of the earliest and most quoted bloggers is the "Drudge Report," posted by maverick journalist Matt Drudge.) While many bloggers offer little more than their own often-heated opinions, bloggers have forced the mainstream media to cover stories they may not otherwise have covered, as well as forcing some professional journalists to check the accuracy of their stories before publication.

Media Effects: Shaping Political Life

What effects do the media have on public opinion and political behavior? Let us consider media effects on (1) information and agenda setting, (2) values and opinions, and (3) behavior. These categories of effects are ranked by the degree of influence the media are likely to have over us. The strongest effects of the media are on our information levels and societal concerns. The media also influence values and opinions, but the strength of media effects in these areas is diluted by many other influences. Finally, it is most difficult to establish the independent effect of the media on behavior.

Information and Agenda-Setting Effects The media strongly influence what we know about our world and how we think and talk about it. Years ago, foreign-policy expert Bernard Cohen, in the first book to assess the effects of the media on foreign policy, put it this way: "The mass media may not be successful in telling people what to think, but the media are stunningly successful in telling their audience what to think about"[28] (see *Politics Up Close:* "The Media Age").

✔ *Think* Again

Is your choice of candidates in elections affected by their advertising?

Politics Up Close   The Media Age

The print media—newspapers, magazines, and books—have played a major role in American politics since colonial times. But today the electronic media—radio, television, and cable television—dominate in political communication.

Radio was widely introduced into American homes in the 1920s and 1930s, allowing President Franklin D. Roosevelt to become the first "media president," directly communicating with the American people through radio "fireside chats." After World War II, the popularity of television spread quickly; between 1950 and 1960, the percentage of homes with TV sets grew from 9 to 87.

Some notable political media innovations over the years:

★ **1952:** The first paid commercial TV ad in a presidential campaign appeared, on behalf of Dwight D. Eisenhower. The black-and-white ad began with a voice-over—"Eisenhower answers the nation!"—followed by citizens asking favorable questions and Eisenhower responding, and ending with a musical jingle: "I like Ike." Although crude by current standards, it nevertheless set a precedent in media campaigning.

★ **1952:** The "Checkers speech" by Eisenhower's running mate, Richard M. Nixon, represented the first direct television appeal to the people over the heads of party leaders. Nixon was about to be dumped from the Republican ticket for hiding secret slush-fund money received from campaign contributors. He went on national television with an emotional appeal, claiming that the only personal item he ever took from a campaign contributor was his daughters' little dog, Checkers. Thousands of viewers called and wired in sympathy. Ike kept Nixon on the ticket.

★ **1960:** The first televised debate between presidential candidates featured a youthful, handsome John F. Kennedy against a shifty-eyed Richard M. Nixon with a pronounced "five o'clock shadow." Nixon doggedly scored debater points, but JFK presented a cool and confident image and spoke directly to the viewers. The debate swung the popular tide toward Kennedy, who won in a very tight contest. Nixon attributed his defeat to his failure to shave before the broadcast.

★ **1964:** The first "negative" TV ad was the "Daisy Girl" commercial sponsored by the Lyndon Johnson campaign against Republican conservative Barry Goldwater. It implied that Goldwater would start a nuclear war. It showed a little girl picking petals off a daisy while an ominous voice counted down "10-9-8-7…" to a nuclear explosion,

followed by a statement that Lyndon Johnson could be trusted to keep the peace.

★ **1976:** President Gerald Ford was the first incumbent president to agree to a televised debate. (No televised presidential debates were held in the Nixon-Humphrey race in 1968 or in the Nixon-McGovern race in 1972. Apparently Nixon had learned his lesson.) Ford stumbled badly, and Jimmy Carter went on to victory.

★ **1982:** CNN (Cable News Network), introduced by the maverick media mogul Ted Turner, began 24-hour broadcasting.

★ **1991:** The Persian Gulf War was the first war to be fought live on television. (Although film and videotape reports of the Vietnam War had been important molders of public opinion in America, the technology of that era did not allow live reporting.) In the Gulf War, the Iraqi government permitted CNN to continue live broadcasts from Baghdad, including spectacular coverage of the first night's air raids on the city.

★ **1992:** In the presidential election, television talk shows became a major focus of the campaign. Wealthy independent candidate Ross Perot actually conducted an all-media campaign, rejecting in-person appearances in favor of such media techniques as half-hour "infomercials."

★ **1994–95:** The arrest and trial of celebrity O.J. Simpson on murder charges so dominated the national news that more television time was devoted to the O.J. story than to the actions of the president and Congress.

★ **1996:** The presidential election was given less television time and newspaper space than previous elections. Clinton's large lead throughout the campaign, public boredom with Whitewater and other scandals, and Dole's lackluster performance frustrated reporters in search of drama. Network TV news gave Clinton twice as much positive coverage as Dole.

★ **1997–98:** Sex scandals involving Bill Clinton dominated the news and talk shows, but public opinion polls gave the president the highest approval ratings of his two terms in office.

★ **2000:** On election night, the networks prematurely called the presidential election, first for Gore and then for Bush, causing confusion among the public and embarrassment for the networks. A "Florida feeding frenzy" ensued over the next month as television blanketed every phase of that state's recount, from local election officials staring at punch-card ballots to state and U.S. Supreme Court arguments.

★ **2001:** Dramatic television coverage of commercial aircraft crashing into the World Trade Center and videotape

The first televised presidential election debates were in 1960 between Senator John F. Kennedy and Vice President Richard Nixon. Nixon came armed with statistics, but his dour demeanor, "five o'clock shadow," and stiff presentation fared poorly in contrast to Kennedy's open, relaxed, confident air.

of the collapse of the twin giant buildings shocked Americans and inspired the "War on Terrorism."

★ **2003:** Reporters were "embedded" with American troops in the Iraqi War, providing ground-level narratives and video of combat.

★ **2004:** Photos from Abu Ghraib prison in Iraq showing abuse of detainees were broadcast worldwide, inspiring intense opposition in the Muslim world.

★ **2008:** The Internet achieves political dominance as a means of fund raising and as a source of rumor, innuendo, lies, accurate and inaccurate information. Television network news stories favor Democrat Obama over Republican McCain.

However, **information overload** diminishes the influence of the media in determining what we think about. So many communications are directed at us that we cannot possibly process them all. A person's ability to recall a media report depends on repeated exposure to it and reinforcement through personal experience. For example, an individual who has a brother in a trouble spot in the Middle East is more likely to be aware of reports from that area of the world. But too many voices with too many messages cause most viewers to block out a great deal of information.

Information overload may be especially heavy in political news. Television tells most viewers more about politics than they really want to know. Political scientist Austin Ranney writes, "The fact is that for most Americans politics is still far from being the most interesting and important thing in life. To them, politics is usually confusing, boring, repetitive, and above all irrelevant to the things that really matter in their lives."[29]

Effects on Values and Opinions

The media often tell us how we *should* feel about news events or issues, especially those about which we have no prior feelings or experiences. The media can reinforce values and attitudes we already hold. However, the media seldom *change* our preexisting values or opinions. Media influence over values and opinions is reduced by **selective perception**, mentally screening out information or opinions we disagree with. People tend to see and hear only what they want to see and hear. For example, television news concentration on scandal, abuse, and corruption in government has not always produced the liberal, reformist values among viewers that media people expected. On the contrary, the focus of network executives on governmental scandals—Watergate, the Iran-Contra scandal, the sexual antics of politicians, congressional check kiting, and so on—has produced feelings of general political distrust and cynicism toward government and the political system. These feelings have been labeled **television malaise**, a combination of social distrust, political cynicism, feelings of

★ **information overload**
Situation in which individuals are subjected to so many communications that they cannot make sense of them.

★ **selective perception**
Mentally screening out information or opinions with which one disagrees.

Late-night television is now a popular campaign forum. Many viewers get their news from talk shows such as *The Tonight Show* with Jay Leno, pictured here with Democratic presidential candidate Illinois Senator Barack Obama on October 17, 2007.

★ **television malaise**
Generalized feelings of distrust, cynicism, and powerlessness stemming from television's emphasis on the negative aspects of American life.

✓ *Think* Again

Are media professionals—news reporters, editors, anchors—the true voice of the people in public affairs?

powerlessness, and disaffection from parties and politics that seems to stem from television's emphasis on the negative aspects of American life.

The media do not *intend* to create television malaise; they are performing their self-declared watchdog role. They expect their stories to encourage liberal reform of our political institutions. But the result is often alienation rather than reform.

Direct Effects on Public Opinion   Can the media change public opinion, and if so, how? For many years, political scientists claimed that the media had only minimal effects on public opinions and behavior. This early view was based largely on the fact that newspaper editorial endorsements seldom affected people's votes. But serious research on the effects of television tells a different story.

In an extensive study of eighty policy issues over fifteen years, political scientists examined public opinion polls on various policy issues at a first point in time, then media content over a following interval of time, and finally public opinion on these same issues at the end of the interval. The purpose was to learn if media content—messages scored by their relevance to the issue, their salience in the broadcast, their pro/con direction, the credibility of the news source, and quality of the reporting—changed public opinion. Most people's opinions remained constant over time (opinion at the first point in time is the best predictor of opinion at the second point in time). However, when opinion did change, it changed in the direction supported by the media. "News variables alone account for nearly half the variance in opinion change." Other findings include the following:

★ Anchors, reporters, and commentators have the greatest impact on opinion change. Television newscasters have high credibility and trust with the general public. Their opinions are crucial in shaping mass opinion.

★ Independent experts interviewed by the media have a substantial impact on opinion, but not as great as newscasters themselves.

★ A popular president can also shift public opinion somewhat. Unpopular presidents do not have much success as opinion movers, however.

★ Interest groups on the whole have a slightly negative effect on public opinion. "In many instances they seem actually to have antagonized the public and

A *Constitutional* Note

Can the Federal Communications Commission Ban Profanity from Radio and Television?

When the Bill of Rights was passed by the nation's first Congress, the 1st Amendment's reference to freedom of the press could hardly have envisioned radio, television, or the Internet. When radio broadcasting began in the 1920s, there was a scarcity of broadcast frequencies. Stations fought over frequencies and even jammed each other's programming. The industry welcomed the Federal Communications Act of 1934 which created the Federal Communications Commission (FCC) to license stations for the exclusive use of radio frequencies. The law stated that the use of a frequency was a "public trust" and that the FCC should ensure that it was used in "the public interest." Although technology has vastly multiplied radio and television channels, the FCC has continued to fine broadcasters for indecency or profanity. The Supreme Court has continued to uphold the powers of the FCC. "Shock-jock"

radio personality Howard Stern has been fined almost $2 million. Janet Jackson's "wardrobe malfunction" during the 2004 Super Bowl half-time performance also cost her network a large fine. In short, the FCC has retained its power over radio and television despite the fact that its original rationale, the scarcity of broadcast frequencies, has disappeared. We can contrast the control that the Supreme Court allows the government to exercise over radio and television with the freedom the same Court grants to users of the Internet. The Supreme Court held that the Communications Decency Act of 1996, making it a federal crime to send or display "indecent" material to persons under 18 years of age over the Internet, was unconstitutional. The Supreme Court held that the government may not limit the adult population to "only what is fit for children."[a] Commercial sex sites deluge the Internet.

[a]*Reno v. American Civil Liberties Union*, 521 U.S. 471 (1997).

created a genuine adverse effect"; such cases include war protesters, animal rights advocates, and other demonstrators and protesters, even peaceful ones.[30]

Effects on Behavior   Many studies have focused on the effects of the media on behavior: studies of the effects of TV violence, studies of the effects of television on children, and studies of the effects of obscenity and pornography.[31] Although it is difficult to generalize from these studies, television appears more likely to reinforce behavioral tendencies than to change them. For example, televised violence may trigger violent behavior in children who are already predisposed to such behavior, but televised violence has little behavioral effect on average children.[32] Nevertheless, we know that television advertising sells products. And we know that political candidates spend millions to persuade audiences to go out and vote for them on election day. Both manufacturers and politicians create name recognition, employ product differentiation, try to associate with audiences, and use repetition to communicate their messages. These tactics are designed to affect our behavior both in the marketplace and in the election booth.

Political ads are more successful in motivating a candidate's supporters to go to the polls than they are in changing opponents into supporters. It is unlikely that voters who dislike a candidate will be persuaded by political advertising to change their votes. But many potential voters are undecided, and the support of many others is dubbed "soft." Going to the polls on election day requires effort—people have errands to do, it may be raining, they may be tired. Television advertising is more effective with the marginal voters.

Summary
Who Gets What: The Media

The mass media in America not only report on the struggle for power, they are also participants themselves in that struggle.

★ It is only through the media that the general public comes to know about political events, personalities, and issues. Newsmaking—deciding what is or is not "news"—is a major source of media power. Media coverage not only influences popular discussion but also forces public officials to respond.

★ Media power also derives from the media's ability to set the agenda for public decision making—to determine what citizens and public officials will regard as "crises," "problems," or "issues" to be resolved by government.

★ The media also exercise power in their interpretation of the news. News is presented in story form; pictures, words, sources, and story selection all contribute to interpretation.

★ The media play a major role in socializing people to the political culture. Socialization occurs in news, entertainment, and advertising.

★ The politics of the media are shaped by their economic interest in attracting readers and viewers. This interest largely accounts for the sensational and negative aspects of news reporting.

★ The professional environment of newspeople encourages an activist, watchdog role in politics. The politics of most newspeople are liberal and Democratic.

★ Political campaigning is largely a media activity. The media have replaced the parties as the principal linkage between candidates and voters. But the media tend to report the campaign as a horse race, at the expense of issue coverage, and to focus more on candidates' character than on their voting records or issue positions.

★ The 1st Amendment guarantee of freedom of the press protects the media from government efforts to silence or censor them and allows the media to be "unfair" when they choose to be. The Federal Communications Commission exercises some modest controls over the electronic media, since the right to exclusive use of broadcast frequencies is a *public trust*.

★ Public officials are afforded very little protection by libel and slander laws. The Supreme Court's Sullivan rule allows even damaging falsehoods to be written and broadcast as long as newspeople themselves do not deliberately fabricate lies with "malicious intent" or "reckless disregard."

★ Media effects on political life can be observed in (1) information and agenda setting, (2) values and opinions, and (3) behavior—in that order of influence. The media strongly influence what we know about politics and what we talk about. The media are less effective in changing existing opinions, values, and beliefs than they are in creating new ones. Nevertheless, the media can change many people's opinions, based on the credibility of news anchors and reporters. Direct media effects on behavior are limited. Political ads are more important in motivating supporters to go to the polls, and in swinging undecided or "soft" voters, than in changing the minds of committed voters.

Key Terms

mass media   173
newsmaking   176
agenda setting   177
socialization   178
soft news   180

muckraking   184
"feeding frenzy"   184
name recognition   188
horse-race coverage   190
sound bite   190

prior restraint   192
equal-time rule   194
libel   194
slander   194
Sullivan rule   194

information overload   199
selective perception   199
television malaise   200

Suggested Readings

Alterman, Eric. *What Liberal Media?* New York: Simon & Schuster, 2003. A contrarian argument that the media does *not* have a liberal bias but rather bends over backward to include conservative views.

Ansolabehere, Stephen, Roy Behr, and Shanto L-yengar. *The Media Game: American Politics in the Television Age.* New York: Longman, 1993. A comprehensive text assessing the changes in the political system brought about by the rise of television since the 1950s.

Bennett, Lance W. *News: The Politics of Illusion.* New York: Longman, 2007. How presidents, Congress members, interest groups, and political activists try to get their messages into the news.

Fallows, James. *Breaking the News: How the Media Undermine American Democracy.* New York: Pantheon, 1996. An argument that today's arrogant, cynical, and scandal-minded news reporting is turning readers and viewers away and undermining support for democracy.

Goldberg, Bernard. *Bias: A CBS Insider Exposes How the Media Distort the News.* New York: Perennial, 2003. The title says it all.

Graber, Doris A. *Mass Media and American Politics.* 7th ed. Washington, D.C.: CQ Press, 2005. A wide-ranging description of media effects on campaigns, parties, and elections, as well as on social values and public policies.

Patterson, Thomas E. *Out of Order.* New York: Random House, 1994. The antipolitical bias of the media poisons national election campaigns; policy questions are ignored in favor of the personal characteristics of candidates, their campaign strategies, and their standing in the horse race.

Prindle, David F. *Risky Business.* Boulder, Colo.: Westview Press, 1993. An examination of the politics of Hollywood, its liberalism, activism, self-indulgence, and celebrity egotism.

Sabato, Larry J. *Feeding Frenzy: How Attack Journalism Has Transformed American Politics.* New York: Free Press, 1992. A strong argument that the media prefer "to employ titillation rather than scrutiny" and as a result produce "trivialization rather than enlightenment."

West, Darrell M. *Air Wars: Television Advertising in Election Campaigns.* 4th ed. Washington, D.C.: CQ Press, 2005. The evolution of campaign advertising from 1952 to 2004 and how voters are influenced by television ads.

Suggested Web Sites

Accuracy in Media www.aim.org
A self-described watchdog organization critical of liberal bias in the media.

American Journalism Review www.ajr.org
Features articles on current topics in print and television reporting, together with links to newspapers, television networks and stations, radio stations, media companies, and so forth.

Annenberg Public Policy Center www.appcpenn.org
The Annenberg Center of the University of Pennsylvania conducts research on political use of the media, including the Internet.

Center for Media and Public Affairs www.cmpa.com
Studies of news and entertainment media, including election coverage.

Drudge Report www.drudgereport.com
Controversial site that links to stories not always carried by mainstream media. Links to all major media outlets.

Federal Communication Commission www.fcc.gov
The FCC's official Web site with announcements and consumer information.

National Association of Broadcasters www.nab.org
News and views of the media industry from their trade association.

Network Television www.cbsnews.com www.abcnews.com www.cnn.com www.msnbc.com www.foxnews.com
All major networks now maintain news sites on the Web.

Newspaper Web Sites www.usatoday.com www.nytimes.com www.washingtonpost.com www.wallstreetjournal.com
Virtually all major daily newspapers have Web sites that summarize each day's stories. For national news the most frequently consulted sites are *USA Today, Wall Street Journal, New York Times, Washington Post.*

People for the American Way www.pfaw.org
Web site founded by Hollywood "liberals" to combat "right-wing" influence.

Pew Research Center for People and the Press www.people-press.org
Information, including opinion polls, on the media.

Politico www.politico.com
Favorite blog of political junkies, with links to multiple news articles and political commentaries.

7 POLITICAL PARTIES
Organizing Politics

> **❝** For many purposes it is enough to define a political party as an organization specialized with regard to presenting candidates and issues under its own name in elections. **❞**

Harold Lasswell

Chapter *Outline*

The Power of Organization

In the struggle for power, organization grants advantage. Italian political scientist Gaetano Mosca once put it succinctly: "A hundred men acting uniformly in concert, with a common understanding, will triumph over a thousand men who are not in accord and can therefore be dealt with one by one."[1] Thus politics centers on organization—on organizing people to win office and to influence public policy.

Political organizations—parties and interest groups—function as intermediaries between individuals and government. They organize individuals to give them power in selecting government officials—who govern—and in determining public policy—for what ends. Generally, **political parties** are more concerned with winning public office in elections than with influencing policy, whereas *interest groups* are more directly concerned with public policy and involve themselves with elections only to advance their policy interests (see Figure 7.1). In other words, parties and interest groups have an informal division of functions, with parties focusing on personnel and interest groups focusing on policy. Yet both organize individuals for more effective political action.

American Parties: A Historical Perspective

Parties are *not* mentioned in the Constitution. Indeed, the nation's Founders regarded both parties and interest groups as "factions," citizens united by "some common impulse of passion, or of interest, adverse to the rights of other citizens, or to the permanent and aggregate interests of the community." The Founders viewed factions as "mischievous" and "dangerous."[2] Yet the emergence of parties was inevitable as people sought to organize themselves to exercise power over who governs (see Figure 7.2).

The Emergence of Parties: Federalists and Democratic-Republicans
In his Farewell Address, George Washington warned the nation about political parties: "Let me ... warn you in the most solemn manner against the baneful effects of the spirit of party generally."[3] As

✓ Think About Politics

1. Generally speaking, how would you identify yourself: as a Republican, Democrat, Independent, or something else?

   REPUBLICAN ◯ DEMOCRAT ◯
   INDEPENDENT ◯ OTHER ◯

2. Which major political party better represents the interests of people like yourself?

   REPUBLICAN ◯ DEMOCRAT ◯

3. Does the Republican Party favor the rich more than the middle class or poor?

   YES ◯ NO ◯

4. Does the Democratic Party favor the poor more than the middle class or rich?

   YES ◯ NO ◯

5. Which major party does a better job of protecting the Social Security system?

   REPUBLICAN ◯ DEMOCRAT ◯

6. Which major party does a better job of handling foreign affairs?

   REPUBLICAN ◯ DEMOCRAT ◯

7. Should elected officials be bound by their party's platform?

   YES ◯ NO ◯

8. Do we need a third party to challenge the Republican and Democratic parties?

   YES ◯ NO ◯

How much power do political parties really have to determine who gets what in America? We hear the terms Republican and Democratic linked to people and to policies, but do these parties have real power beyond that of organizing for elections?

★ **political organizations**
Parties and interest groups that function as intermediaries between individuals and government.

205

★ **political parties**
Organizations that seek to achieve power by winning public office.

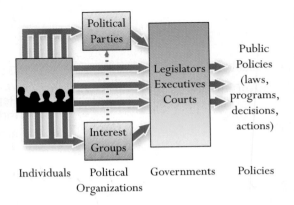

Figure **7.1**

Political Democracy: Organizations as Intermediaries

All political organizations function as intermediaries between individuals and government. Parties are concerned primarily with winning elected office; interest groups are concerned with influencing policy.

TIMELINE

The Evolution of Political Parties in the United States

★ **Federalists**
Those who supported the U.S. Constitution during the ratification process and who later formed a political party in support of John Adams's presidential candidacy.

★ **Anti-Federalists**
Those who opposed the ratification of the U.S. Constitution and the creation of a strong national government.

★ **majority**
Election by more than 50 percent of all votes cast in the contest.

president, Washington stood above the factions that were coalescing around his secretary of the treasury, Alexander Hamilton, and around his former secretary of state, Thomas Jefferson. Jefferson had resigned from Washington's cabinet in 1793 to protest the fiscal policies of Hamilton, notably his creation of a national bank and repayment of the states' Revolutionary War debts with federal funds. Washington had endorsed Hamilton's policies, but so great was the first president's prestige that Jefferson and his followers directed their fire not against Washington but against Hamilton, John Adams, and their supporters, who called themselves **Federalists** after their leaders' outspoken defense of the Constitution during the ratification process. By the 1790s, Jefferson and Madison, as well as many **Anti-Federalists** who had initially opposed the ratification of the Constitution, began calling themselves *Republicans* or *Democratic-Republicans*, terms that had become popular after the French Revolution in 1789.

Adams narrowly defeated Jefferson in the presidential election of 1796. This election was an important milestone in the development of the parties and the presidential election system. For the first time, two candidates campaigned as members of opposing parties, and candidates for presidential elector in each state pledged themselves as "Adams's men" or "Jefferson's men." By committing themselves in advance of the actual presidential vote, these pledged electors enabled voters in each state to determine the outcome of the presidential election.

Jefferson's Democratic-Republicans   Party activity intensified in anticipation of the election of 1800. Jefferson's Democratic-Republican Party first saw the importance of organizing voters, circulating literature, and rallying the masses to their causes. Many Federalists viewed this early party activity with disdain. Indeed, the Federalists even tried to outlaw public criticism of the federal government by means of the Alien and Sedition Acts of 1798, which among other things made it a crime to publish false or malicious writings against the (Federalist) Congress or president or to "stir up hatred" against them. These acts directly challenged the newly adopted 1st Amendment guarantees of freedom of speech and the press. But in the election of 1800, the Federalists went down to defeat. Democratic-Republican electors won a **majority** (more than half the votes cast) in the Electoral College. (See *A Constitutional Note:* "Political Parties and the Constitution" on page 243).

The election of 1800 was a landmark in American democracy—the first time that control of government passed peacefully from one party to another on the basis of an election outcome. As commonplace as that may seem to Americans today, the peaceful transfer of power from one group to another remains a rarity in many political systems around the world.

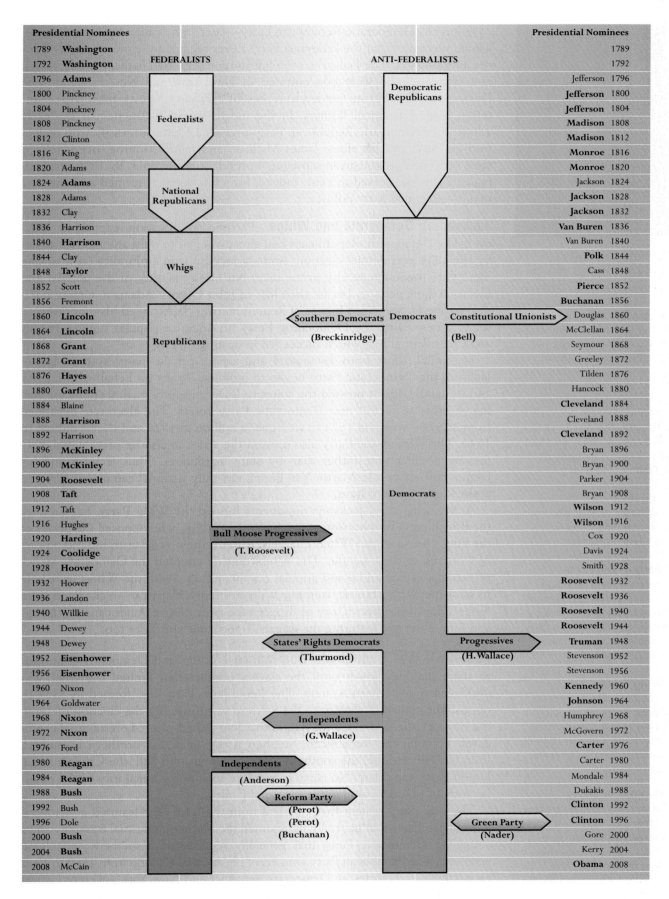

Figure **7.2**   Change and Continuity: The American Party System, 1789–2008

Opening the Party System

A picture of Andrew Jackson late in his life. Andrew Jackson is widely viewed as the founder of the Democratic Party. Jackson was born in Tennessee, the American frontier at the time, and was also a celebrated a military leader who defeated the British in New Orleans in 1815 (after the War of 1812 was officially over), and had led numerous campaigns against the Indians.

★ **plurality**
Election by at least one vote more than any other candidate in the race.

★ **Democratic Party**
One of the main parties in American politics; it traces its origins to Thomas Jefferson's Democratic-Republican Party, acquiring its current name under Andrew Jackson in 1828.

★ **Whig Party**
Formed in 1836 to oppose Andrew Jackson's policies; it elected presidents Harrison in 1840 and Tylor in 1848 but soon disintegrated over the issue of slavery.

★ **Republican Party**
One of the two main parties in American politics, it traces its origins to the antislavery and nationalist forces that united in the 1850s and nominated Abraham Lincoln for president in 1860.

Jefferson's Democratic-Republican Party—later to be called the Democrats—was so successful that the Federalist Party never regained the presidency or control of Congress. The Federalists tended to represent merchants, manufacturers, and shippers, who were concentrated in New York and New England. The Democratic-Republicans tended to represent agrarian interests, from large plantation owners to small farmers. In the mostly agrarian America of the early 1800s, the Democratic-Republican Party prevailed.[4] Jefferson easily won reelection in 1804, and his allies, James Madison and James Monroe, overwhelmed their Federalist opponents in subsequent presidential elections. By 1820, the Federalist Party had ceased to exist. Indeed, for a few years, it seemed as if the new nation had ended party politics.

Jacksonian Democrats and Whigs

Partisan politics soon reappeared, however. The Democratic-Republicans had already begun to fight among themselves by the 1824 presidential election. Andrew Jackson won a **plurality** (at least one more vote than anyone else in the race) but not a majority of the popular and Electoral College vote, but he then lost to John Quincy Adams in a close decision by the factionalized House of Representatives. Jackson led his supporters to found a new party, the **Democratic Party**, to organize popular support for his 1828 presidential bid, which succeeded in ousting Adams.

Jacksonian ideas both *democratized* and *nationalized* the party system. Under Jackson, the Democratic Party began to mobilize voters on behalf of the party and its candidates. It pressed the states to lower property qualifications for voting in order to recruit new Democratic Party voters. The electorate expanded from 365,000 voters in 1824 to well over a million in 1828 and over 2 million in 1840. The Democratic Party also pressed the states to choose presidential electors by popular vote rather than by state legislatures. Thus Jackson and his Democratic successor, Martin Van Buren, ran truly national campaigns directed at the voters in every state.

At the same time, Jackson's opponents formed the **Whig Party**, named after the British party of that name. Like the British Whigs, who opposed the power of the king, the American Whigs charged "King Andrew" with usurping the powers of Congress and the people. The Whigs quickly adopted the Democrats' tactics of national campaigning and popular organizing. By 1840, the Whigs were able to gain the White House, running William Henry Harrison—nicknamed "Old Tippecanoe" from his victory at Tippecanoe over Native Americans in 1811—and John Tyler and featuring the slogan "Tippecanoe and Tyler too."

Post–Civil War Republican Dominance

Whigs and Democrats continued to share national power until the slavery conflict that ignited the Civil War destroyed the old party system. The Republican Party had formed in 1854 to oppose the spread of slavery to the western territories. By the election of 1860, the slavery issue so divided the nation that four parties offered presidential candidates: Lincoln, the Republican; Stephen A. Douglas, the northern Democrat; John C. Breckinridge, the southern Democrat; and John Bell, the Constitutional Union Party candidate. No party came close to winning a majority of the popular vote, but Lincoln won in the Electoral College.

The new party system that emerged from the Civil War featured a victorious **Republican Party** that generally represented the northern industrial economy and a struggling Democratic Party that generally represented a southern agricultural economy. The Republican Party won every presidential election from 1860 to 1912 except for two victories by Democratic reformer and New York governor Grover Cleveland (see *Politics Up Close:* "The Donkey and the Elephant").

Politics Up Close   **The Donkey and the Elephant**

The popular nineteenth-century cartoonist Thomas Nast is generally credited with giving the Democratic and Republican parties their current symbols: the donkey and the elephant. In *Harper's Weekly*'s 1870s cartoons, Nast critically portrayed the Democratic Party as a stubborn mule "without pride of ancestry

nor hope of posterity." During this period of Republican Party dominance, Nast portrayed the Republican Party as an elephant, the biggest beast in the political jungle. Now both party symbols are used with pride.

In the 1870 cartoon on the left, published following the death of Lincoln's Secretary of War E. M. Stanton, Nast shows a donkey (labeled "Copperheads," a disparaging term for the mostly Democratic northerners who were sympathetic to the South during the Civil War) kicking the dead Stanton, who is portrayed as a lion. The 1874 cartoon on the right features the elephant as The Republican Vote and the donkey masquerading as a lion.

Yet the Democratic Party offered a serious challenge in the election of 1896 and realigned the party affiliations of the nation's voters. The Democratic Party nominated William Jennings Bryan, a talented orator and a religious fundamentalist. Bryan sought to rally the nation's white "have-nots" to the Democratic Party banner, particularly the debt-ridden farmers of the South and West. His plan was to stimulate inflation (and thus enable debtors to pay their debts with "cheaper," less valuable dollars) through using plentiful, western-mined "free silver," rather than gold, as the monetary standard. He defeated Cleveland's faction and the "Gold Democrats" in the 1896 Democratic Party convention with his famous Cross of Gold speech: "You shall not crucify mankind upon a cross of gold."

But the Republican Party rallied its forces in perhaps the most bitter presidential battle in history. It sought to convince the nation that high tariffs, protection for manufacturers, and a solid monetary standard would lead to prosperity for industrial workers as well as the new tycoons. The campaign, directed by Marcus Alonzo Hanna, attorney for John D. Rockefeller's Standard Oil Company, spent an unprecedented $16 million (an amount in inflation-adjusted dollars that has never been equaled) to elect Republican William McKinley, advertised as the candidate who would bring a "full dinner pail" to all. The battle also produced one of the largest voter turnouts in history. McKinley won in a landslide. Bryan ran twice again but lost by even larger margins. The Republican Party solidified

On the Attack

Negative advertising has a long history in American politics. In the election of 1896, Republican presidential candidate William McKinley portrayed his Democratic opponent William Jennings Bryan as an unpatriotic destroyer of America's interests, represented by the flag.

★ **GOP**
"Grand Old Party"—popular label for the Republican Party.

★ **New Deal**
Policies of President Franklin D. Roosevelt during the Depression of the 1930s that helped form a Democratic Party coalition of urban working-class, ethnic, Catholic, Jewish, poor, and southern voters.

Think Again

Does the Democratic Party favor the poor more than the middle class or rich?

the loyalty of industrial workers, small-business owners, bankers, and large manufacturers, as well as black voters, who respected "the party of Lincoln" and despised the segregationist practices of the southern Democratic Party.

Republican Split, Democratic Win   So great was the Republican Party's dominance in national elections that only a split among Republicans enabled the Democrat Woodrow Wilson to capture the presidency in 1912. Republican Theodore Roosevelt (who became president following McKinley's assassination and had won reelection in 1904) sought to recapture the presidency from his former protégé, Republican William Howard Taft. At the **GOP** ("Grand Old Party," as the Republicans began labeling themselves) convention, party regulars rejected the unpredictable Roosevelt in favor of Taft, even though Roosevelt had won the few primary elections that had recently been initiated. An irate Teddy Roosevelt launched a third, progressive party, the "Bull Moose," which actually outpolled the Republican Party in the 1912 election—the only time a third party has surpassed one of the two major parties in U.S. history. But the result was a victory for the Democratic candidate, former Princeton political science professor Woodrow Wilson. Following Wilson's two terms, Republicans again reasserted their political dominance with victories by Warren G. Harding, Calvin Coolidge, and Herbert Hoover.

The New Deal Democratic Party   The promise of prosperity that empowered the Republican Party to hold its membership together faded in the light of the Great Depression. The U.S. stock market crashed in 1929, and by the early 1930s, one-quarter of the labor force was unemployed. Having lost confidence in the nation's business and political leadership, in 1932 American voters turned out incumbent Republican President Herbert Hoover in favor of Democrat Franklin D. Roosevelt, who promised the country a **New Deal**.

More than just bringing the Democrats to the White House, the Great Depression marked another party realignment. This time, traditionally Republican voting groups changed their affiliation and enabled the Democratic Party to dominate national politics for a generation. This realignment actually began in 1928, when Democratic presidential candidate Al Smith, a Catholic, won many northern, urban, ethnic voters away from the Republican Party. By 1932, a majority New Deal Democratic coalition had been formed in American politics. It consisted of the following groups:

★ Working classes and union members, especially in large cities.

★ White ethnic groups who had previously aligned themselves with Republican machines.

★ Catholics and Jews.

★ African Americans, who ended their historic affiliation with the party of Lincoln to pursue new economic and social goals.

★ Poor people, who associated the New Deal with expanded welfare and Social Security programs.

★ Southern whites, who had provided the most loyal block of Democratic voters since the Civil War.

To be sure, this majority coalition had many internal factions: southern "Dixiecrats" walked out of the Democratic Party convention in 1948 to protest a party platform that called for an end to racial discrimination in employment. But

Inspiring Confidence
Franklin Roosevelt campaigning among coal miners in West Virginia during the presidential election campaign of 1932. Roosevelt's optimism and "can-do" attitude in the face of the Great Depression helped cement the New Deal Democratic coalition that won him the presidency.

the promise of a New Deal—with its vast array of government supports for workers, elderly and disabled people, widows and children, and farmers—held this coalition together reasonably well. President Harry Truman's **Fair Deal** proved that the coalition could survive its founder, Franklin D. Roosevelt. Republican Dwight D. Eisenhower made inroads into this coalition by virtue of his personal popularity and the Republican Party's acceptance of most New Deal programs. But John F. Kennedy's "New Frontier" demonstrated the continuing appeal of the Democratic Party tradition. Lyndon Johnson's **Great Society** went further than the programs of any of his predecessors in government intervention in the economic and social life of the nation. Indeed, it might be argued that the Great Society laid the foundation for a political reaction that eventually destroyed the old Democratic coalition and led to yet another new party alignment (see Figure 7.3).

★ **Fair Deal**
Policies of President Harry Truman extending Roosevelt's New Deal and maintaining the Democratic Party's voter coalition.

★ **Great Society**
Policies of President Lyndon Johnson that promised to solve the nation's social and economic problems through government intervention.

A New Republican Majority   The American political system underwent massive convulsions in the late 1960s as a result of both the civil rights revolution at home and an unpopular war in Vietnam. Strains were felt in all of the nation's political institutions, from the courts to the Congress to the presidency. And when Lyndon Johnson announced his decision not to run for reelection in 1968, the Democratic Party erupted in a battle that ultimately destroyed its majority support among presidential voters.

At the 1968 Democratic Party convention in Chicago, Vice President Hubert Humphrey controlled a majority of the delegates inside the convention hall, but antiwar protesters dominated media coverage outside the hall. When Chicago police attacked unruly demonstrators with batons, the media broadcast to the world an image of the nation's turmoil. In the presidential campaign that followed, both candidates—Democrat Hubert Humphrey and Republican Richard Nixon—presented nearly identical positions supporting the U.S. military commitment in Vietnam while endorsing a negotiated, "honorable" settlement of the war. But the image of the Democratic Party became associated with the street protesters. Inside the convention hall, pressure from women and minorities led party leaders to adopt changes in the party's delegate-selection process for future conventions to assure better representation of these groups—at the

Think Again

Does the Republican Party favor the rich more than the middle class or poor?

Figure 7.3

Who's Winning?: The Parties in Presidential Voting

Despite the dominance of the Democratic Party in terms of numbers of registered voters, Republicans have managed to win half of the presidential elections since 1960.

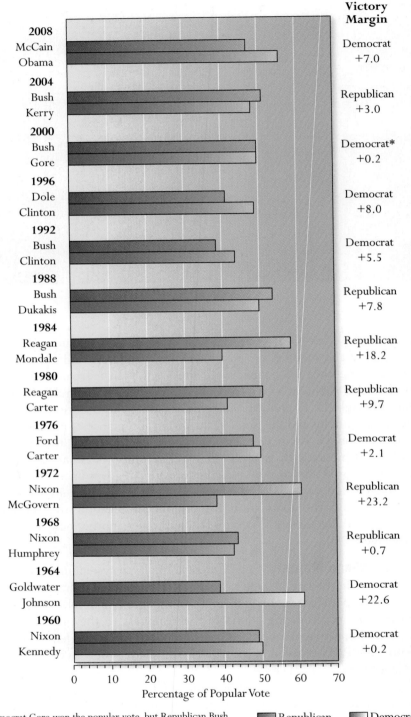

Victory Margin

Year	Candidates	Margin
2008	McCain / Obama	Democrat +7.0
2004	Bush / Kerry	Republican +3.0
2000	Bush / Gore	Democrat* +0.2
1996	Dole / Clinton	Democrat +8.0
1992	Bush / Clinton	Democrat +5.5
1988	Bush / Dukakis	Republican +7.8
1984	Reagan / Mondale	Republican +18.2
1980	Reagan / Carter	Republican +9.7
1976	Ford / Carter	Democrat +2.1
1972	Nixon / McGovern	Republican +23.2
1968	Nixon / Humphrey	Republican +0.7
1964	Goldwater / Johnson	Democrat +22.6
1960	Nixon / Kennedy	Democrat +0.2

Percentage of Popular Vote

* Democrat Gore won the popular vote, but Republican Bush won more Electoral College votes to become president.

Republican   Democrat

expense of Democratic officeholders (see "Making Party Rules" later in this chapter for more details).

In 1972 the Democratic Party convention strongly reflected the views of anti-war protesters, civil rights advocates, feminist organizations, and liberal activists generally. The visibility of these activists, who appeared to be well to the left of both Democratic Party voters and the electorate in general, allowed the Republican Party to portray the Democratic presidential nominee, George McGovern, as an unpatriotic liberal, willing to "crawl to Hanoi" and to sacrifice the nation's honor for peace. It also allowed the Republicans to characterize the new Democratic Party as soft on crime, tolerant of disorder, and committed to racial and sexual quotas in American life. Richard Nixon, never very popular personally, was able to win in a landslide in 1972. The Watergate scandal and Nixon's forced resignation only temporarily stemmed the tide of "the new Republican majority." Democrat Jimmy Carter's narrow victory over Republican Gerald R. Ford in 1976 owed much to the latter's pardon of Nixon.

The Reagan Coalition

Under the leadership of Ronald Reagan, the Republican Party was able to assemble a majority coalition that dominated presidential elections in the 1980s, giving Reagan landslide victories in 1980 and 1984 and George H. W. Bush a convincing win in 1988. The **Reagan Coalition** consisted of the following groups:

★ Economic conservatives concerned about high taxes and excessive government regulation, including business and professional voters who had traditionally supported the Republican Party.

★ Social conservatives concerned about crime, drugs, and racial conflict, including many white ethnic voters and union members who had traditionally voted Democratic.

★ Religious fundamentalists concerned about such issues as abortion and prayer in schools.

★ Southern whites concerned about racial issues, including affirmative action programs.

★ Internationalists and anticommunists who wanted the United States to maintain a strong military force and to confront Soviet-backed Marxist regimes around the world.

Reagan held this coalition together in large part through his personal popularity and his infectious optimism about the United States and its future. Although sometimes at odds with one another, economic conservatives, religious fundamentalists, and internationalists could unite behind the "Great Communicator." Reagan's presidential victory in 1980 helped to elect a Republican majority to the U.S. Senate and encouraged Democratic conservatives in the Democrat-controlled House of Representatives to frequently vote with Republicans. As a result, Reagan got most of what he asked of Congress in his first term: cuts in personal income taxes, increased spending for national defense, and slower growth of federal regulatory activity. With the assistance of the Federal Reserve Board, inflation was brought under control. But Reagan largely failed to cut government spending as he had promised, and the result was a series of huge federal deficits. Reagan appointed conservatives to the Supreme Court and the federal judiciary (see Chapter 13), but no major decisions were reversed (including the *Roe v. Wade* decision, protecting abortion); social conservatives had to be content with the president's symbolic support.

During these years, the national Democratic Party was saddled with an unpopular image as the party of special-interest groups. As more middle-class and working-class voters deserted to the GOP, the key remaining loyal Democratic constituencies were African Americans and other minorities, government

★ **Reagan Coalition**
Combination of economic and social conservatives, religious fundamentalists, and defense-minded anticommunists who rallied behind Republican President Ronald Reagan.

The Power of Unity
President Ronald Reagan created a Republican majority coalition in the 1980s by uniting Republican factions—economic conservatives, social conservatives, religious fundamentalists, and anticommunists—and adding many southern white Democrats.

employees, union leaders, liberal intellectuals in the media and universities, feminist organizations, and environmentalists. Democratic presidential candidates Walter Mondale in 1984 and Michael Dukakis in 1988 were obliged to take liberal positions to win the support of these groups in the primary elections. Later, both candidates sought to move toward the center of the ideological battleground in the general election. But Republican Party strategists were able to "define" Mondale and Dukakis through negative campaign advertising (see Chapter 8) as liberal defenders of special-interest groups. The general conservative tilt of public opinion in the 1980s added to the effectiveness of the GOP strategy of branding Democratic presidential candidates with the "*L word*" (*liberal*).

Clinton and the "New" Democrats

Yet even while Democratic candidates fared poorly in presidential elections, Democrats continued to maintain control of the House of Representatives, to win back control of the U.S. Senate in 1986, and to hold more state governorships and state legislative seats than the Republicans. Thus the Democratic Party retained a strong leadership base on which to rebuild itself.

During the 1980s, Democratic leaders among governors and senators came together in the **Democratic Leadership Council** to create a "new" Democratic Party closer to the center of the political spectrum. The chair of the Democratic Leadership Council was the young, energetic, and successful governor of Arkansas, Bill Clinton. The concern of the council was that the Democratic Party's traditional support for social justice and social welfare programs was overshadowing its commitment to economic prosperity. Many council members argued that a healthy economy was a prerequisite to progress in social welfare. Not all Democrats agreed with the council agenda. African American leaders (including the Reverend Jesse Jackson), as well as liberal and environmental groups, feared that the priorities of the council would result in the sacrifice of traditional Democratic Party commitments to minorities, poor people, and the environment.

In the 1992 presidential election, Bill Clinton was in a strong position to take advantage of the faltering economy under George H. W. Bush, to stress the

Bound by the Job

Left to right: President George W. Bush, former President Bill Clinton, former President Jimmy Carter, and former President George H. W. Bush, at the opening of the Clinton Presidential Center (library) in Little Rock, Arkansas. Shared experiences in the White House can bring Republican and Democratic presidents together.

"new" Democratic Party's commitment to the middle class, and to avoid being labeled as a liberal defender of special interests. At the same time, he managed to rally the party's core activist groups—liberals, intellectuals, African Americans, feminists, and environmentalists. Many liberals in the party deliberately soft-pedaled their views during the 1992 election in order not to offend voters, hoping to win with Clinton and then fight for liberal programs later. Clinton won with 43 percent of the vote, to Bush's 38 percent. Independent Ross Perot captured a surprising 19 percent of the popular vote, including many voters who were alienated from both the Democratic and Republican parties. Once in office, Clinton appeared to revert to liberal policy directions rather than to pursue the more moderate line he had espoused as a "new" Democrat. As Clinton's ratings sagged, the opportunity arose for a Republican resurgence.

Republican Resurgence

A political earthquake shook Washington in the 1994 congressional elections, when the Republicans for the first time in 40 years captured the House of Representatives, regained control of the Senate, and captured a majority of the nation's governorships. For the first time in history Republicans won more seats in the South than the Democrats. This southern swing to the Republicans in congressional elections seemed to confirm the realignment of southern voters that had begun earlier in presidential elections. Just two years after a Democratic president had been elected, the GOP won its biggest nationwide victory since the Great Depression.

Clinton Holds On

Following the Republican victory, the Democratic Party appeared to be in temporary disarray. The new Republican House Speaker, Newt Gingrich, tried to seize national policy leadership; Clinton was widely viewed as a failed president. But the Republicans quickly squandered their political opportunity. They had made many promises in a well-publicized "Contract with America"—a balanced federal budget, congressional term limits, tax cuts, welfare reform, and more—but they delivered little. Majority Leader Bob Dole failed by one vote to pass the Balanced Budget Amendment in the Senate. President Clinton took an unexpectedly hard line toward GOP spending cuts and vetoed several budget bills. When the federal government officially "closed down" for lack of appropriated funds, the public appeared to blame Republicans. Polls showed a dramatic recovery in the president's approval ratings. Clinton skillfully portrayed GOP leaders, especially Newt Gingrich, as "extremists" and himself as a responsible moderate prepared to trim the budget, reduce the deficit, and reform welfare, "while still protecting Medicare, Medicaid, education, and the environment." By early 1996, Clinton had set the stage for his reelection campaign.

Bill Clinton was the first Democratic president to be reelected since Franklin D. Roosevelt. Clinton rode to victory on a robust economy. Voters put aside doubts about Clinton's character, and they ignored Republican Bob Dole's call for tax reductions. Clinton won with 49 percent of the popular vote to Dole's 41 percent and Perot's 8 percent. But Clinton's victory failed to rejuvenate the Democratic Party's fortunes across the country. The GOP retained its majorities in both houses of Congress.

2000—A Nation Divided

The nation was more evenly divided in 2000 between the Democratic and Republican parties than perhaps at any other time in history. Democrat Al Gore won a narrow victory in the popular vote for president. But after a month-long battle for Florida's electoral vote, Republican George W. Bush, former Texas governor and son of the former President Bush, emerged as the winner of the Electoral College vote, 271 to 267 (see Chapter 8).

Newt Gingrich addresses a rally on Capitol Hill on April 7, 1995. Gingrich, from Georgia, led the Republican resurgence of 1994. He served in the U.S. House of Representatives from 1979 to 1999, was co-author of the 1994 Contract with America, and was House Speaker from 1995 to 1999.

Bill Clinton, 42nd President of the United States (1993–2001), delivers his State of the Union address in 1999.

Not only was the presidential vote almost tied, but also both houses of Congress were split almost evenly between Democrats and Republicans. The Republican Party lost seats in the House of Representatives in 1998 and again in 2000. Yet the GOP still retained a razor-thin margin of control of that body. In the Senate, the 2000 election created a historic 50–50 tie between Democrats and Republicans. The vote of the Senate's presiding officer, Republican Vice President Dick Cheney, would have given the GOP the narrowest of control of that body. But in 2001, Vermont's Republican Senator Jim Jeffords decided to switch his support to the Democratic Party, swinging control of the Senate to the Democrats (see Chapter 10).

The Republican Party defied tradition in 2002 by gaining seats in the Senate and expanding its majority in the House. Historically, the party in control of the White House *lost* seats in midterm elections. But in an era in which presidents are not supposed to have coattails, especially in midterm congressional elections, President George W. Bush campaigned energetically across the country for GOP candidates, focusing attention on the war on terrorism. Democratic complaints about the weak economy were muted. Bush's intense efforts appeared to motivate Republican voters; a higher-than-usual midterm voter turnout resulted in Republican victories in hotly contested Senate and House races across the country.

Republicans Take Control   In 2004, the GOP further consolidated its control over the White House, Senate, and House of Representatives. Throughout the 2004 election campaign, polls showed the nation evenly split, with Republican President Bush and Democratic Senator Kerry running neck and neck. There was considerable fear of another contested presidential election and concern that the popular vote winner might again lose in the Electoral College. But Republicans showed unexpected strength, with Bush winning both the popular vote and the Electoral College vote. Turnout was high. (Republican turnout may have been helped by referenda banning same-sex marriage that appeared on the ballot in eleven states; polls consistently show regular churchgoers tending to vote Republican.) Republicans added to their controlling margins in both the House and the Senate. Even the Democratic Senate leader, Tom Daschle of South Dakota, lost his bid for reelection.

Nancy Pelosi (D-CA), Speaker of the U.S. House of Representatives and Henry Reid (D-NV), U.S. Senate Majority Leader, celebrate the midterm election results on November 8, 2006, at a hotel in Washington, D.C.

Democrats Recover—2006   The war in Iraq undermined the Republican Party's hold on congressional voters in 2006. For the first time in 12 years, the GOP lost control of the House of Representatives. They also gave up control of the Senate; Democrats won just enough seats to give them a 51 to 49 margin in that body. Polls suggested that voters had lost confidence in President Bush; his approval ratings remained below 40 percent throughout the election year. Midterm elections are seldom a referendum on national policy, but just enough voters in close House and Senate races decided in favor of "change," bringing back Democratic majorities in both houses of Congress.

Democrats Sweep—2008   Economic instability traditionally has helped Democratic candidates. And not since the Great Depression of the 1930s have Americans experienced so much economic anxiety as they did in 2008. A plunge in housing values, a sharp decline in the stock market, emergency government takeovers of leading banks and investment houses, and Washington's $700 billion bailout of Wall Street all contributed to voter concern over the economy. Republican President George W. Bush suffered the lowest approval ratings of any

People in Politics   Hillary Clinton, Leading the Way for Women

Hillary Rodham Clinton came very close to becoming the first woman President of the United States (see *Politics Up Close*: "Hillary Versus Barack, 2008"). She is the first First Lady ever elected to Congress and the first woman senator from New York.

Hillary Rodham grew up in suburban Chicago, the daughter of wealthy parents who sent her to the private, prestigious Wellesley College. A 1969 honors graduate with a counterculture image—horn-rimmed glasses, long, straggling hair, no makeup—she was chosen by her classmates to give a commencement speech—a rambling statement about "more immediate, ecstatic, and penetrating modes of living."

At Yale Law School Hillary met a long-haired, bearded Rhodes scholar from Arkansas, Bill Clinton, who was just as politically ambitious as she was. Both Hillary and Bill received their law degrees in 1973. Bill returned to Arkansas to build a career in state politics, and Hillary went to Washington as an attorney—first for a liberal lobbying group, the Children's Defense Fund, and later on the staff of the House Judiciary Committee seeking to impeach President Richard Nixon. But Rodham and other Yale grads traveled to Arkansas to help Clinton run, unsuccessfully, for Congress in 1974. Hillary decided to stay with Bill in Little Rock: they married before his next campaign, a successful run for state attorney general in 1976. Hillary remained Hillary Rodham, even as her husband went on to the governorship in 1978.

Her husband's 1980 defeat for reelection as governor was blamed on his liberal leanings; therefore, in his 1982 comeback Bill repackaged himself as a moderate and centrist. Hillary cooperated by becoming Mrs. Bill Clinton, shedding her horn-rims for contacts, blonding her hair, and echoing her husband's more moderate line. These tactics helped propel them back into the governor's mansion. Hillary soon became a full partner in Little Rock's Rose law firm regularly earning more than $200,000 a year (while Bill earned only $35,000 as Arkansas governor). She won national recognition as one of the "100 most influential lawyers in the United States," according to the *American National Law Journal*. She chaired the American Bar Association's Commission on Women and the Profession.

Hillary's steadfast support of Bill during the White House sex scandals and subsequent impeachment by the House of Representatives in all likelihood saved his presidency. Her approval ratings in public opinion polls skyrocketed during the affair. Whatever she thought in private, she never chastised her husband in public and blamed much of the scandal on "a vast right-wing conspiracy."

Her Senate race attracted national media attention as well as campaign contributions from supporters throughout the nation. When New York City's Mayor Rudolph Giuliani announced that he would not run for the Senate, Hillary was relieved to confront a little-known opponent, Congressman Rick Lazio. New York voters were unimpressed with charges that Hillary was not a true New Yorker. She studied New York problems diligently, and overwhelmed Lazio in the campaign. Over $85 million were spent by the candidates, making the campaign the most expensive congressional campaign in history.

Senator Clinton developed a reputation as an advocate for children and families. Her early work with the Children's Defense Fund and Marian Wright Edelman (see *People in Politics*: "Marian Wright Edelman, Lobbying for the Poor" in Chapter 9) was carried forward in her book *It Takes a Village* in 1997. She was prominently mentioned in all of the early 2004 presidential polls, but she declined to run. She crushed her Republican opponent in her 2006 reelection to the Senate, setting the stage for her presidential campaign in 2008. (See *Politics Up Close*: "Hillary Versus Barack, 2008.")

president since Richard Nixon. The stage was set for sweeping Democratic victories in the Senate, House of Representatives, and the White House.

Barack Obama led his party to a decisive sweep, putting Democrats in control of the House, Senate, and White House, creating unified Democratic Party control of the federal government for the first time since 1994. Democrats gained seats in both houses of Congress, but they failed to get the 60-vote margin in the Senate needed to end filibusters—the only check remaining on unified Democratic control of the government in Washington.

Comparing Political Parties

Political Parties and Democratic Government

"Political parties created democracy, and modern democracy is unthinkable save in terms of the parties."[6] Traditionally, political scientists have praised parties as indispensable to democratic government. They have argued that parties are essential for organizing popular majorities to exercise control over government. The development of political parties in all the democracies of the world testifies to the underlying importance of parties to democratic government. But political parties in the United States have lost their preeminent position as instruments of democracy. Other structures and organizations in society—interest groups, the mass media, independent campaign organizations, primary elections, social welfare agencies—now perform many of the functions traditionally regarded as prerogatives of political parties. Nevertheless, the Democratic and Republican parties remain important organizing structures for politics in the United States.

Think Again

Should elected officials be bound by their party's platform?

"Responsible" Parties in Theory In theory, political parties function in a democracy to organize majorities around broad principles of government in order to win public office and enact these principles into law. A "responsible" party should:

★ Adopt a platform setting forth its principles and policy positions.

★ Recruit candidates for public office who agree with the party's platform.

★ Inform and educate the public about the platform.

★ Organize and direct campaigns based on platform principles.

★ Organize the legislature to ensure party control in policy making.

★ Hold its elected officials responsible for enacting the party's platform.

If responsible, disciplined, policy-oriented parties competed for majority support, *if* they offered clear policy alternatives to the voters, and *if* the voters cast their ballots on the basis of these policy options, *then* the winning party would have a "policy mandate" from the people to guide the course of government. In that way, the democratic ideal of government by majority rule would be implemented.

★ responsible party model
System in which competitive parties adopt a platform of principles, recruiting candidates and directing campaigns based on the platform, and holding their elected officials responsible for enacting it.

But Winning Wins over Principle However, the **responsible party model** never accurately described the American party system. The major American parties have been loose coalitions of individuals and groups seeking to attract sufficient votes to gain control of government. *Winning has generally been more important than any principles or policies.* America's major parties must appeal to tens of millions of voters in every section of the nation and from all walks of life. If a major party is to acquire a majority capable of controlling the U.S. government, it cannot limit its appeal by relying on a single unifying principle. Instead, it must form coalitions of voters from as many sectors of the population as it can. Major American parties therefore usually do not emphasize particular principles or ideologies so much as try to find a common ground of agreement among many different people. This emphasis does not mean no policy differences exist between the American parties. On the contrary, each party tends to appeal to a distinctive coalition of interests, and therefore each party expresses somewhat distinctive policy views (see *Controversy*: "Which Party Does a Better Job?").

In their efforts to win, major American political parties strive to attract the support of the large numbers of people near the center of public opinion. Generally more votes are at the center of the ideological spectrum—the middle-of-the-road—

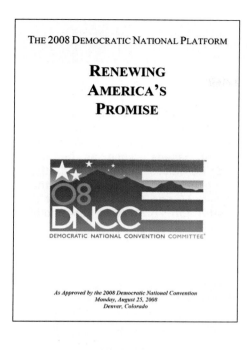

THE 2008 DEMOCRATIC NATIONAL PLATFORM

RENEWING AMERICA'S PROMISE

As Approved by the 2008 Democratic National Convention
Monday, August 25, 2008
Denver, Colorado

The cover of the 2008 Democratic National Platform, containing the political philosophy and issue positions, or "planks," supported by the Democratic Party delegates in Denver, Colorado.

than on the extreme liberal or conservative ends. Thus *no real incentive exists for vote-maximizing parties to take strong policy positions in opposition to each other* (see Figure 7.4).

Party and Ideology   Despite incentives for the parties to move to the center of the political spectrum, the Republican and Democratic parties are perceived by the public as ideologically separate. The electorate tends to perceive the Republican Party as conservative and the Democratic Party as liberal.

Indeed, polls suggest that Republican voters described themselves as conservatives far more often than as liberals. And Democratic voters are more likely to identify themselves as liberals than as conservatives, although many like to think of themselves as moderates (see Table 7.1 on page 221).

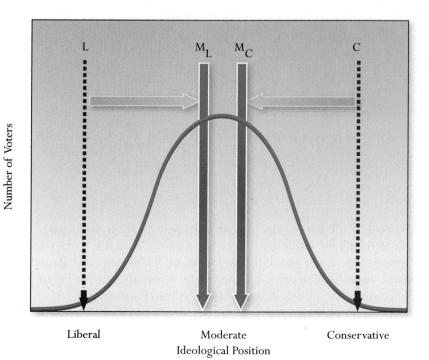

Figure 7.4

Why Parties Drift to the Center

Why don't we have a party system based on principles, with a liberal party and a conservative party, each offering the voters a real ideological choice? Let's assume that voters generally choose the party closest to their own ideological position. If the liberal party (L) took a strong ideological position to the left of most voters, the conservative party (C) would move toward the center, winning more moderate votes, even while retaining its conservative supporters, who would still prefer it to the more liberal opposition party. Likewise, if the conservative party took a strong ideological position to the right of most voters, the liberal party would move to the center and win. So both parties must abandon strong ideological positions and move to the center, becoming moderate in the fight for support of moderate voters.

Controversy

Which Party Does a Better Job?

What do Americans think of the Democratic and Republican parties? Generally speaking, the Democratic Party has been able to maintain an image of "the party of the common people," and the Republican Party has long been saddled with an image of "favoring the rich." And more people have reported a "favorable" image of the Democratic Party.

But the Republican Party is trusted by more people to "do a better job" in handling foreign affairs and

maintaining a strong national defense. It also enjoys a reputation of being better at "holding down taxes."

The Democratic Party enjoys its greatest advantage on "compassion issues" such as helping poor, elderly, and homeless people. And the Democrats have long enjoyed the support of the high-voter-turnout over-65 age group because it is trusted to do a better job "protecting the Social Security system."

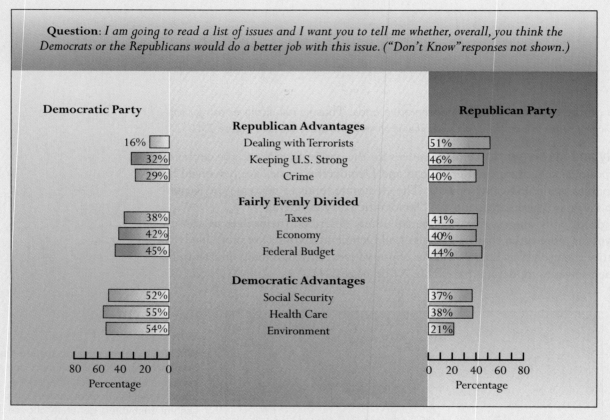

Question: *I am going to read a list of issues and I want you to tell me whether, overall, you think the Democrats or the Republicans would do a better job with this issue.* ("Don't Know" responses not shown.)

	Democratic Party	Republican Party
Republican Advantages		
Dealing with Terrorists	16%	51%
Keeping U.S. Strong	32%	46%
Crime	29%	40%
Fairly Evenly Divided		
Taxes	38%	41%
Economy	42%	40%
Federal Budget	45%	44%
Democratic Advantages		
Social Security	52%	37%
Health Care	55%	38%
Environment	54%	21%

Source: Various polls reported in *The Polling Report,* November 22, 1999. September 10, 2001, January 28, 2002, August 11, 2003, September 18, 2007.

★ **party polarization**
The tendency of the Democratic Party to take more liberal positions and the Republican Party to take more conservative positions on key issues.

This relationship between ideological self-identification and party self-identification is relatively stable over time. It suggests that the parties are not altogether empty jars. Later we will observe that Democratic and Republican party activists (notably, delegates to the party conventions) are even more ideologically separate than Democratic and Republican Party voters.

Democratic and Republican party activists have become more ideologically separate in recent years. And voters have become increasingly aware of this **party polarization**. Indeed many voters are now prepared to say that the

Table **7.1** Who Votes for the Parties? Party and Ideology Among Voters

Self-identified liberals tend to vote Democratic, while conservatives tend to vote Republican.

	All Voters	Democratic Voters	Republican Voters
Liberals	21%	85%	13%
Moderates	45	54	45
Conservatives	34	15	84

Source: As reported at www.CNN.com November 17, 2004.

Democratic Party is more liberal and the Republican Party is more conservative on a variety of high-profile issues, including government services and spending, government provision of health insurance, and government help to African Americans.[7]

The Republican Party tends to include defenders of the free enterprise system and opponents of government regulation, together with strongly religious people who hold traditional views on moral issues. The Republican Party also appeals to people strongly supportive of the military and an assertive foreign policy. The Democratic Party includes liberals with strong views on social issues such as homosexuality, abortion, and environmental protection, as well as reluctance to the use of military force. Yet another part of the Democratic coalition includes the people supportive of the role of government in providing a social safety net—efforts to provide jobs, help to the needy, and economic opportunity for all.

The Erosion of Traditional Party Functions

Parties play only a limited role in campaign organization and finance. *Campaigns are generally directed by professional campaign management firms or by the candidates' personal organizations, not by parties.* Party organizations have largely been displaced in campaign activity by advertising firms, media consultants, pollsters, and others hired by the candidates themselves (see Chapter 8).

Most political candidates today are self-recruited. American political parties also play only a limited role in recruiting candidates for elected office. People initiate their own candidacies, first contacting friends and financial supporters. Often in state and local races, candidates contact party officials only as a courtesy, if at all.

The major American political parties cannot really control who their **nominee**—*the party's entry in a general election race*—*will be.* Rather, party **nominations** for most elected offices are won in **primary elections**. In a primary election, registered voters select who will be their party's nominee in the general election. Party leaders may endorse a candidate in a primary election and may even work to try to ensure the victory of their favorite, but the voters in that party's primary select the nominee.

Candidates usually communicate directly with voters through the mass media. Television has replaced the party organization as the principal medium of communication between candidates and voters. Candidates no longer rely much on party workers to carry their message from door to door. Instead, candidates can come directly into the voters' living rooms via television.

★ **nominee**
Political party's entry in a general election race.

★ **nominations**
Political party's selections of its candidates for public office.

★ **primary elections**
Elections to choose party nominees for public office; may be open or closed.

Politics Up Close   The Appeal of the Republican and Democratic Parties

What explains partisanship among voters? What is it about the Republican and Democratic parties that appeals to voters? A Gallup survey asked Americans—after they identified themselves as Republicans or Democrats (or Independents who said they lean toward either party)—to explain in their own words just what it is about their chosen party that appeals to them most.

Republicans justify their allegiance to the GOP most often with a reference to the party's conservatism or conservative positions on moral issues. Beyond that, Republicans mention the party's conservative economic positions and its preference for smaller government.

In contrast to Republicans who mention conservatism as their rationale for identifying with the GOP, the proportion of Democrats who mention liberalism is comparatively small. Democrats are more likely to say that the Democratic Party appeals to them because it is for the working class, the middle class, or the "common man."

Q. What is it about the Republican Party that appeals to you most? (Asked of Republicans)

Conservative/more conservative (nonspecific)	26%
Conservative family/moral values	15%
Overall platform/philosophy/policies (nonspecific)	12%
Conservative on fiscal/economic issues	10%
Favors smaller government	8%
Favors individual responsibility/self-reliance	5%
Always been a Republican	4%
For the people/working people	3%
Low taxes	3%
Favor strong military	3%
Pro-life on abortion	2%

Q. What is it about the Democratic Party that appeals to you most? (Asked of Democrats)

For the middle class/working class/common man	25%
Social/moral issue positions	18%
Overall platform/philosophy/policies (nonspecific)	14%
Liberal/more liberal (nonspecific)	11%
Help the poor	7%
Always been a Democrat	5%
Antiwar	3%
Health-care reform	2%
Pro-environment/conservation	1%

Note: "Other" and "no opinion" percentages not shown.
Source: Gallup Poll, November 13, 2007. www.gallup.com.

★ **machines**
Tightly disciplined party organizations, headed by a boss, that rely on material rewards—including patronage jobs—to control politics.

★ **patronage**
Appointment to public office based on party loyalty.

★ **divided party government**
One party controls the presidency while the other party controls one or both houses of Congress.

Even if the American parties wanted to take stronger policy positions and to enact them into law, they would not have the means to do so. *American political parties have no way to bind their elected officials to the party platform or even to their campaign promises.* Parties have no strong disciplinary sanctions to use against members of Congress who vote against the party's policy position. The parties cannot deny them renomination. At most, the party's leadership in Congress can threaten the status, privileges, and pet bills of disloyal members (see Chapter 10). Party cohesion, where it exists, is more a product of like-mindedness than of party discipline.

American political parties no longer perform social welfare functions—trading off social services, patronage jobs, or petty favors in exchange for votes. Traditional party organizations, or **machines**, especially in large cities, once helped immigrants get settled in, found **patronage** jobs in government for party workers, and occasionally provided aid to impoverished but loyal party voters. But government bureaucracies have replaced the political parties as providers of social services. Government employment agencies, welfare agencies, civil service systems, and other bureaucracies now provide the social services once undertaken by political machines in search of votes.

Divided Party Government   Finally, to further confound the responsible party model, Americans seem to prefer **divided party government**—where one party controls the executive branch while the other party controls one or both houses

Voters in voting booths in Derry, New Hampshire, during the 2008 primary elections. Over half of eligible voters went to the polls in New Hampshire in 2008, a national record, eight percentage points higher than in the 2000 presidential primary. New Hampshire voters may participate in either Democratic and Republican primaries, no matter which party they are registered with. New Hampshire doesn't have an open primary, though, because people who register as Republican or Democrat on voting day cannot cast ballots in the other party's primary.

of the legislative branch. Over the last forty years, American presidents have been more likely to face a Congress in which the opposition party controls one or both houses than to enjoy their own party's full control of Congress. (Divided party government in the states—where one party controls the governorship and the opposition party controls one or both houses of the state legislature—is also increasing over time.)[8] Divided party control of government makes it difficult for either party to fully enact its platform.

It is noteworthy that American public opinion seems to prefer divided party government over unified party control: *"Do you think it is better when one party controls both the presidency and the Congress, better when control is split between the Democrats and Republicans, or doesn't it matter?"*: Better one party—23.8 percent; Better control split—52.4 percent; Doesn't matter—23.8 percent.[9]

Party Finances

Parties as well as candidates raise hundreds of millions of dollars in every election year. (Later, in Chapter 8, we will examine campaign financing by candidates themselves.) At the national level, contributions to the parties go to the Democratic and Republican National Committees, and to the Democratic and Republican House and Senatorial Committees (see Table 7.2).

The Partisan Tilt of Campaign Contributions
Traditionally the Republican Party was able to raise and spend more money in each election cycle than the Democratic Party. But the dollar differences have narrowed over the years. Perhaps more interesting are the differences in sources of support for each party. Broken down by sector (as in Table 7.3), the Democratic Party relies more heavily on lawyers and law firms, on the TV, movie and music industry (Hollywood),

---

Table 7.2   Where's the Money: Party Finances (in millions)

Parties as well as candidates solicit campaign contributions. At the national level, contributions go to the Democratic and Republican National Committees and to the Democratic and Republican House and Senate Campaign Committees.

	2000	2002	2004	2006	2008
Totals					
Democratic Party	$520	$463	$618	$599	$748
Republican Party	715	691	744	707	$713
National Committees					
Dem. National Com.	260	162	299	131	$206
Rep. National Com.	379	284	330	243	$336
House Party Committees					
Dem. Cong. Camp. Com.	105	103	76	140	$134
Nat'l Rep. Cong. Com.	145	211	156	180	$103
Senate Party Committees					
Dem. Senatorial Camp. Com.	104	143	76	131	$121
Nat'l Rep. Senatorial Camp. Com.	96	125	69	89	$74

Source: Center for Responsive Politics, www.opensecrets.org, 2008 data released October 27, 2008.

Table 7.3   Who Finances to Parties?: Contributors to the Republican and Democratic Parties by Sector

The Democratic Party relies more heavily on contributions from lawyers and law firms, TV, the movie and music industry, teacher and public employee unions, and industrial and building trade unions. The Republican Party relies more heavily on contributions from various business sectors.

Democratic Party	**Republican Party**
1. Lawyers/law firms	1. Real estate
2. Securities/investment	2. Health professionals
3. Real estate	3. Securities/investment
4. TV/movies/music	4. Lawyers/law firms
5. Business services	5. Insurance
6. Health professionals	6. Manufacturing/distributing
7. Education	7. Oil and gas
8. Lobbyists	8. Business services
9. Computers/Internet	9. General contractors
10. Insurance	10. Automotive
11. Public sector unions	11. Computers/Internet
12. Commercial banks	12. Commercial banks
13. Industrial unions	13. Special trade contractors
14. Building trade unions	14. Retail sales
15. Liberal/ideological	15. Food and beverage

Source: Center for Responsive Politics. Candidate committees, miscellaneous, and "retired" excluded from this table. Data from 2004 presidential election.

---

teachers and public sector employee unions, and industrial and building trade unions. Business interests divide their contributions, but they tilt toward the Republican Party, notably the health care industry, insurance, manufacturing, oil and gas, automotive, and general and special contractors.

Parties as Organizers of Elections

Despite the erosion of many of their functions, America's political parties survive as the principal institutions for organizing elections. Party nominations organize electoral choice by narrowing the field of aspiring office seekers to the Democratic and Republican candidates in most cases. Very few independents or third-party candidates are elected to high political office in the United States. **Nonpartisan elections**—elections in which there are no party nominations and all candidates run without an official party label—are common only in local elections, for city council, county commission, school board, judgeships, and so on. Only Nebraska has nonpartisan elections for its unicameral (one-house) state legislature. Party conventions are still held in many states in every presidential year, but these conventions seldom have the power to determine the parties' nominees for public office.

Early Party Conventions   Historically, party nominations were made by caucus or convention. The **caucus** was the earliest nominating process; party leaders (party chairs, elected officials, and "bosses") would simply meet several months before the election and decide on the party's nominee themselves. The early presidents—Thomas Jefferson, James Madison, James Monroe, and John Quincy Adams—were nominated by caucuses of Congress members. Complaints about the exclusion of the people from this process led to nominations by convention—large meetings of delegates sent by local party organizations—starting in 1832. Andrew Jackson was the first president to be nominated by convention. The convention was considered more democratic than the caucus.

For nearly a century, party conventions were held at all levels of government—local, state, and national. City or county conventions included delegates from local **wards** and **precincts**, who nominated candidates for city or county office, for the state legislature, or even for the House of Representatives when a congressional district fell within the city or county. State conventions included delegates from counties, and they nominated governors, U.S. senators, and other statewide officers. State parties chose delegates to the Republican and Democratic national conventions every four years to nominate a president.

Party Primaries   Today, primary elections have largely replaced conventions as the means of selecting the Democratic and Republican nominees for public office.[10] (see *Politics Up Close* "Hillary Versus Barack, 2008") Primary elections, introduced as part of the progressive reform movement of the early twentieth century, allow the party's *voters* to choose the party's nominee directly. The primary election was designed to bypass the power of party organizations and party leaders and to further democratize the nomination process. It generally succeeded in doing so, but it also had the effect of seriously weakening political parties, since candidates seeking a party nomination need only appeal to party *voters*—not *leaders*—for support in the primary election.[11]

Types of Primaries   There are some differences among the American states in how they conduct their primary elections. **Closed primaries** allow only voters who have previously registered as Democrats or Republicans (or in some states voters who choose to register as Democrats or Republicans on primary election day) to cast a ballot in their chosen party's primary. Closed primaries tend to discourage people from officially registering as independents, even if they think of themselves as independent, because persons registered as independents cannot cast a ballot in either party's primary.

★ **nonpartisan elections**
Elections in which candidates do not officially indicate their party affiliation; often used for city, county, school board, and judicial elections.

★ **caucus**
Nominating process in which party members or leaders meet to nominate candidates or select delegates to conventions.

★ **wards**
Divisions of a city for electoral or administrative purposes or as units for organizing political parties.

★ **precincts**
Subdivisions of a city, county, or ward for election purposes.

★ **closed primaries**
Primary elections in which voters must declare (or have previously declared) their party affiliation and can cast a ballot only in their own party's primary election.

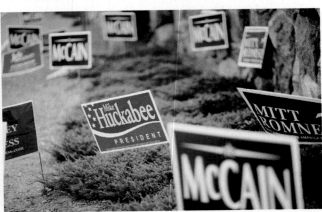

The Driving Force

Parties provide the organizational structure for political campaigns. Top left: The Executive Committee of the Republican National Convention in Chicago in 1880. Conventions emerged as the main way for parties to select candidates in the nineteenth century. Top right: Democratic presidential hopeful Senator John Edwards (D-NC) arriving in Des Moines, Iowa, on August 19, 2007. Bottom left: Republican presidential hopeful and former Massachusetts governor Mitt Romney, campaigning in Milford, New Hampshire, on September 3, 2007. Bottom right: Campaign signs line the street in Bedford, New Hampshire, on October 6, 2007.

★ **open primaries**
Primary elections in which a voter may cast a ballot in either party's primary election.

★ **raiding**
Organized efforts by one party to get its members to cross over in a primary and defeat an attractive candidate in the opposition party's primary.

★ **runoff primary**
Additional primary held between the top two vote-getters in a primary where no candidate has received a majority of the vote.

Open primaries allow voters to choose on election day which party primary they wish to participate in. Anyone, regardless of prior party affiliation, may choose to vote in either party's primary election. Voters simply request the ballot of one party or the other.[12] Open primaries provide opportunities for voters to cross over party lines and vote in the primary of the party they usually do not support. Opponents of open primaries have argued that these types of primary elections allow for **raiding**— organized efforts by one party to get its members to cross over to the opposition party's primary and defeat an attractive candidate and thereby improve the raiding party's chances of winning the general election. But there is little evidence to show that large numbers of voters connive in such a fashion.

Louisiana is unique in its nonpartisan primary elections. All candidates, regardless of their party affiliation, run in the same primary election. If a candidate gets over 50 percent of the vote, he or she wins the office, without appearing on the general election ballot. If no one receives over 50 percent of the primary election votes, then the top two vote-getters, regardless of party, face each other in the general election.[13]

Some states hold a **runoff primary** when no candidate receives a majority or a designated percentage of the vote in the party's first primary election. A runoff

Politics Up Close   Hillary Versus Barack, 2008

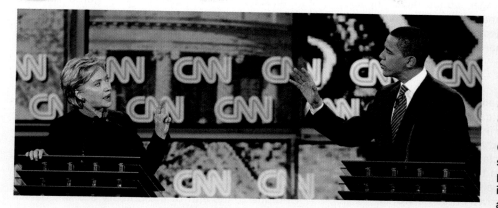

Hillary Clinton was a product of the old Washington establishment. Hillary would challenge the messenger as lacking both programmatic specifics and the necessary experience to bring about "real" change. But Obama stayed on message throughout the campaign. Perhaps more importantly he projected a "rock star" image—a young, fresh, handsome,

The historic clash between Barack Obama and Hillary Clinton brought passion, intensity, and a record voter turnout to the Democratic presidential primaries in 2008. At the beginning of the year, Hillary Clinton was far ahead in the polls and seen as the "inevitable" Democratic nominee. But the excitement began with the very first contest, the Iowa caucuses, where Obama's surprise victory demonstrated his appeal across racial lines. Hillary struck back a week later winning the New Hampshire primary and demonstrating that organization was still an essential component of a presidential primary campaign. She went on to win the Florida and Michigan primaries, but these were hollow victories. The Democratic National Committee had ruled that if Florida and Michigan held their primaries out of order, their delegates would not be seated and their votes not counted at the Democratic convention.

Super Tuesday

Most observers thought that "Super Tuesday," February 5, with its front-loaded 21 state primaries would determine the party's nominee. But instead the outcome reflected the bitter division that was to characterize the race. Clinton won the big states—California, New York, New Jersey, and even Massachusetts (despite Ted Kennedy's endorsement of Obama). But Obama won more states by wider margins and picked up more pledged convention delegates. South Carolina Senator John Edwards, the Democratic vice presidential nominee in 2004, dropped out of the race after finishing a poor third on Super Tuesday.

Barack Moves Ahead

The trend lines began to point in Obama's favor; national polls showed him creeping up in the support of likely Democratic party voters. The Illinois senator's message was simple—"Change"—a message that not only inspired Democrats and Independents unhappy with the Bush administration, but also implied that

new presence on the national scene. He added young people and Independents to his base of African-American voters. The enthusiasm he engendered among his followers inspired them to attend drawn-out party meetings, giving him an advantage in caucus states. Following Super Tuesday, Obama went on to win a string of state primaries and caucuses. Indeed, by "Super Tuesday II," March 4, Hillary appeared on the brink of defeat.

Hillary's Comeback

Hillary clung tenaciously to traditional Democratic voters, appealing especially to white women, lower-income blue-collar workers, and Latinos. Her hopes rested on the Super Tuesday II primaries in Ohio and Texas. She touted her experience, her ability to get things done, and the relative prosperity of the 1990s during her husband's presidency. She won the popular vote in these pivotal states and gave notice that the race for the Democratic nomination was not over.

Obama's Pastor Problem

Even before clips from the sermons of the Reverend Jeremiah Wright were broadcast on cable news channels, Barack Obama knew he had a preacher problem. Wright had been Obama's pastor, friend and spiritual adviser for over 20 years at the Trinity United Church of Christ in Chicago. Wright had officiated at Obama's wedding and baptized both his children. Obama knew of his incendiary racist and anti-American comments and had withdrawn an invitation to Wright to deliver the invocation at his presidential candidacy announcement speech in early 2007. But efforts to keep Wright under wraps were destroyed in March 2008 when video clips emerged of Wright shouting "God damn America."

Obama responded with a carefully crafted address to the nation in which he disavowed the specific comments of his pastor but asked voters to understand the racial contex of Wright's anger. Obama would not "disown" Wright, or the Trinity Church, or black liberation theology. He asked Americans to come to grips with racial divisions and to transcend them, White middle-class Americans may have heard divisive, racist, and unpatriotic pronouncements, but blacks, on the other hand, heard righteous anger about racial injustice. Later, following a National Press Club diatribe by Wright, Obama finally rejected his former pastor. And near the end of the primary contests, Obama left the Trinity Church.

Hillary's Sniper Problem

Just when Hillary appeared to be gaining momentum she sabotaged her own campaign by fibbing about coming under sniper fire in Bosnia in 1996. Videotape of her deplaning revealed that rather than running to avoid sniper fire as she claimed, she calmly attended a ceremony on the open tarmac with a young child presenting her with flowers. Her fib and the conflicting video were widely shown on TV networks.

The Delegate Count

As the primary season wound down in May, Hillary claimed that she was ahead in the popular vote count and that she had won in states that would be crucial for the Democratic nominee in the November general election. But Obama was ahead in pledged

delegates, won in primaries and caucuses, and he had won twice as many states as Clinton. The DNC rules committee voted to reinstate the Michigan and Florida delegations but to limit them to one half of their allotted votes. The decision angered Hillary's supporters. Hillary could only win the nomination by convincing uncommitted superdelegates that she would be a better candidate against Republican nominee John McCain. She argued that her late wins in West Virginia, Kentucky, South Dakota, and Puerto Rico demonstrated Obama's weakness especially among white blue-collar workers and Hispanics. But Obama's late victories in Oregon and Montana again demonstrated his appeal across racial lines. Moreover, the superdelegates were wary of appearing to overturn Obama's legitimate lead in pledged delegates; to do so might split the Democratic party along racial lines.

On June 3, the end of the primary season, Barack Obama proclaimed himself the Democratic nominee. He had won over enough superdelegates that combined with the pledged delegates he had won in primaries and caucuses put him over the top. Four days later, Hillary conceded and urged her supporters to back Barack Obama. The longest and most heated primary contest in modern political history came to a close.

primary is limited to the two highest vote-getters in the first primary. Runoff elections are more common in the southern United States. In most states, only a plurality of votes is needed to win a primary election.

Party Caucuses Some state parties select their candidates, as well as their delegates to the national party conventions, in caucuses rather than primary elections. A caucus is a meeting of party members, usually to select delegates to state or national party conventions. The Iowa presidential caucuses are well publicized as the first presidential contests in the nation. Rather than going to the polls as in primary elections, caucusgoers in each party gather at set times and set locations in schools, churches, libraries, and recreation centers in their neighborhoods. They discuss party platforms, select county committee members, and, most important, in presidential years they indicate their choice for their party's presidential nomination. Because attending a caucus takes more time and effort than voting in a primary election, caucuses tend to be dominated by people with stronger partisan or ideological biases. Caucuses tend to be of advantage to the best-organized candidates—candidates who can persuade and assist supporters in making the extra effort to attend a caucus. Attending a caucus also requires a participant to declare their party affiliation and to openly indicate their support for the candidate of their choice.

★ **general election**
Election to choose among candidates nominated by parties and/or independent candidates who gained access to the ballot by petition.

General Elections Following the parties' selections of their nominees, the **general election** (usually held in November, on the first Tuesday after the first Monday for presidential and most state elections) determines who will occupy elective office. Winners of the Democratic and Republican primary elections must face each other—and any independent or third-party candidates—in the general election. Voters in the general election may choose any candidate, regardless of how they voted earlier in their party's primary or whether they voted in the primary at all.

Independent and minor-party candidates can get on the general election ballot, although the process is usually very difficult. Most states require independent candidates to file a petition with the signatures of several thousand registered voters. The number of signatures varies from state to state and office to office, but it may range up to 5 or 10 percent of *all* registered voters, a very large number that, in a big state especially, presents a difficult obstacle. The same petition requirements usually apply to minor parties, although some states automatically carry a minor party's nominee on the general election ballot if that party's candidate or candidates received a certain percentage (for example, 10 percent) of the vote in the previous general election.

Where's the Party?

The Democratic and Republican parties are found in different political arenas (see Figure 7.5). There is, first of all, the **party-in-the-electorate**—the voters who identify themselves as Democrats or Republicans and who tend to vote for the candidates of their party. The party-in-the-electorate appears to be in decline today. Party loyalties among voters are weakening. More people identify themselves as independents, and more **ticket splitters** divide their votes between candidates of different parties for different offices in the same general election, and more voters cast their ballots without regard to the party affiliation of the candidates than ever before.

The second locus of party activity is the **party-in-the-government**—officials who received their party's nomination and won the general election. The party-in-the-government includes members of Congress, state legislators and local

★ **party-in-the-electorate**
Voters who identify themselves with a party.

★ **ticket splitters**
Persons who vote for candidates of different parties for different offices in a general election.

★ **party-in-the-government**
Public officials who were nominated by their party and who identify themselves in office with their party.

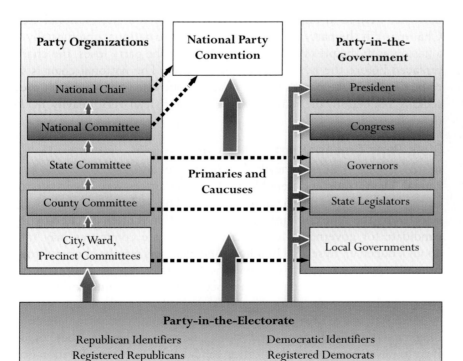

Figure 7.5
Where's the Party?
Even among Americans who strongly identify with a major party, there are differences among those who are strictly members of the party-in-the-electorate (voters), those who are members of the party-in-the-government (elected officials), and those who are members of the party organization (national and state party committee members).

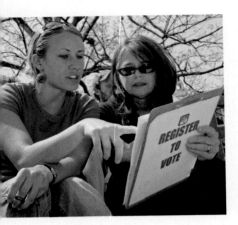

Danielle Wipperfurth, left, of Minneapolis, Minn., gets help from Mary Jo Clark, right, as she registers to vote at Davidson College in Davidson, N.C., Thursday, April 10, 2008.

★ **party organization**
National and state party officials and workers, committee members, convention delegates, and others active in the party.

government officials, and elected members of the executive branch, including the president and governors.

Party identification and loyalty among elected officeholders (the party-in-the-government) are generally stronger than party identification and loyalty among the party-in-the-electorate. Nevertheless, party loyalties among elected officials have also weakened over time. (We examine the role of parties in Congress in Chapter 9 and the president's party role in Chapter 10.)

Finally, there is the **party organization**—national and state party officials and workers, committee members, convention delegates, and others active in the party. The Democratic and Republican party organizations formally resemble the American federal system, with national committees, officers and staffs, and national conventions, 50 state committees, and more than 3,000 county committees with city, ward, and precinct levels under their supervision. State committees are not very responsive to the direction of the national committee; and in most states, city and county party organizations operate quite independently of the state committees. In other words, no real hierarchy of authority exists in American parties.

National Party Structure

The Democratic and Republican national party conventions possess *formal* authority over the parties. They meet every four years not only to nominate candidates for president and vice president but also to adopt a party platform, choose party officers, and adopt rules for the party's operation. Because the convention is a large body that meets for only three or four days, however, its real function is to ratify decisions made by national party leaders, as well as to formally nominate presidential and vice presidential candidates.

The Democratic and Republican national committees, made up of delegates from each state and territory, are supposed to govern party affairs *between* conventions. But the *real* work of the national party organizations is undertaken by the national party chairs and staff. The national chair is officially chosen by the national committee but is actually chosen by the party's presidential candidate (see People in Politics: Howard Dean, Democratic National Committee Chairman). If the party wins the presidency, the national chair usually serves as a liaison with the president for party affairs. If the party loses, the chair may be replaced before the next national convention. The national chair is supposed to be neutral in the party's primary battles, but when an incumbent president is seeking reelection, the national chair and staff lean very heavily in the president's favor.

State Party Organizations

State party organizations consist of a state committee, a state chair who heads the committee, and a staff working at the state capital. Democratic and Republican state committees vary from state to state in composition, organization, and function. The state party chair is generally selected by the state committee, but this selection is often dictated by the party's candidate for governor. Membership on the state committee may range from about a dozen up to several hundred. The members may be chosen through party primaries or by state party conventions. Generally, representation on state committees is allocated by counties, but occasionally other units of government are recognized in state party organizations.

Most state party organizations maintain full-time staffs, including an executive director and public relations, fund raising, and research people. These organizations help to raise campaign funds for their candidates, conduct registration drives, provide advice and services to their nominees, and even recruit candidates to run in

SIMULATION
You Are Redrawing the Districts in Your State

People in Politics — Howard Dean, Democratic National Committee Chairman

Howard Dean won national notoriety in his concession speech in the 2004 Democratic presidential nomination race. He began his speech with a flushed face; clenching his teeth and rolling up his sleeves, he ended his speech with a final cheer that became known in American political folklore as the "Dean Scream." Yet a year later he was elected Chair of the Democratic National Committee.

Dean is the offspring of a wealthy and prominent New York Wall Street investment family. He attended private prep schools and Yale University and received a medical degree from the Albert Einstein College of Medicine in New York in 1978. Together with his physician wife, he opened a medical practice in Burlington, Vermont. But he soon plunged into politics and won election to the Vermont state legislature in 1982. He became that state's lieutenant governor in 1986 but continued to practice medicine. Reportedly he was examining a patient when he received word in 1991 that the then-Governor had died of a heart attack. Dean assumed the governorship and was subsequently elected to five 2-year terms in his own right.

As governor of Vermont Dean focused on health care issues. He developed a "Dr. Dynasaur" program to ensure health coverage for children and pregnant women in the state. His most controversial decision came after the Vermont Supreme Court ruled that same-sex couples were constitutionally entitled to marry or create civil unions. Dean signed the nation's first same-sex civil unions legislation into law.

Dean was the early front-runner, and the early leader in fund raising, in the 2004 Democratic presidential nomination race. Dean was the most vociferous anti–Iraq War candidate. He excelled in his use of the Internet for campaigning and fund raising. Most of his campaign contributions came in small individual donations solicited through his innovative Web site. Yet his skills failed to produce votes in the Iowa caucuses in January 2004. Despite campaigning heavily in that state, Dean finished an embarrassing third behind John Kerry and John Edwards. His concession speech was by his own admission a "crazy, red-faced rant."

Dean was elected Chair of the Democratic National Committee in 2005, despite reservations from some prominent Democrats. His supporters on the Committee were hopeful that he would bring his fund-raising skills to the national Democratic Party. He did not disappoint them. In his first year as Chairman he raised more money than any other DNC Chairperson over a similar period. He also developed what he termed the *50-State Strategy* with the goal of winning elections at every level in every state. He traveled extensively throughout the country in support of Democratic party organizations, including those in heavily Republican districts.

The Democratic Party under Dean captured both houses of Congress in the 2006 midterm elections. Most commentators attributed the Democratic victory to the continuing war in Iraq. But Dean can claim some of the credit.

Dean presided over the DNC decision to penalize Michigan and Florida for jump starting the presidential primary season in 2008. Both states were to be denied the seating of their delegates at the Democratic national convention in September. But the decision angered Democrats in two states that might prove crucial in the November general election. And inasmuch as Hillary Clinton had won these primaries, it appeared as if the DNC was siding with Barack Obama. To halt the threat to Democratic Party unity, Dean and the party's leadership came up with a compromise: the Michigan and Florida delegations would be seated but they could cast only one half of their allotted votes. The squabble did little to enhance Dean's reputation as a party leader.

Dean remains as an angry partisan voice in American politics: "I hate Republicans and everything they stand for."[a]

[a]*New York Daily News*, January 29, 2005.

election districts and for offices where the party would otherwise have no names on the ballot. Services to candidates may include advertising and media consulting, advice on election-law compliance, polling, research (including research on opponents), registration and voter identification, mailing lists, and even seminars on campaign techniques.

Legislative Party Structures The parties organize the U.S. Senate and House of Representatives, and they organize most state legislatures as well. The majority party in the House meets in caucus to select the Speaker of the House as well as the House majority leader and whip (see "Organizing Congress: Party and Leadership" in Chapter 10). The minority party elects its own minority leader and whip. The majority party in the Senate elects the president pro tempore, who presides during the (frequent) absences of the vice president, as well as the Senate majority leader and whip. The minority party in the Senate elects its own minority leader and whip. Committee assignments in both the House and the Senate are allocated on a party basis; committee chairs are always majority-party members.

County Committees The nation's 3,000 Republican and 3,000 Democratic county chairs probably constitute the most important building blocks in party organization in the nation. City and county party officers and committees are chosen in local primary elections; they cannot be removed by state or national party authorities.

National Party Conventions

The Democratic and Republican parties are showcased every four years at the national party **convention**. The official purpose of these four-day fun-filled events is the nomination of the presidential candidates and their vice presidential running mates. Yet the presidential choices have usually already been made in the parties' **presidential primaries** and caucuses earlier in the year. By midsummer, delegates pledged to cast their convention vote for one or another of the presidential candidates have already been selected. Not since 1952, when the Democrats took three convention ballots to select Adlai Stevenson as their presidential candidate, has convention voting gone beyond the first ballot.[14] The possibility exists that in some future presidential race no candidate will win a majority of delegates in the primaries and caucuses, and the result will be a *brokered* convention in which delegates will exercise independent power to select the party nominee. But this event is unlikely.

The Democratic and Republican national conventions are really televised party rallies, designed to showcase the presidential nominee, confirm the nominee's choice for a running mate, and inspire television viewers to support the party and its candidates in the forthcoming general election. Indeed, the national party conventions are largely media events, carefully staged to present an attractive image of the party and its nominees. Party luminaries jockey for key time slots at the podium, and the party prepares slick videotaped commercials touting its nominee for prime-time presentation.

Convention Delegates Convention **delegates** are generally party activists, ideologically motivated and strongly committed to their presidential candidates. Democratic delegates are much more *liberal* than Democratic voters, and Republican delegates are more *conservative* than Republican voters (see Figure 7.6). There is a slight tendency for Democratic and Republican delegates to differ in social backgrounds; usually more African Americans, women, public employees, and union members are found among Democratic delegates than among Republican delegates.

Making Party Rules National party conventions make rules for the party, including rules governing the selection of delegates at the next party convention. Democrats are especially likely to focus on delegate selection rules. In 1972 the

★ **convention**
Nominating process in which delegates from local party organizations select the party's nominees.

★ **presidential primaries**
Primary elections in the states in which voters in each party can choose a presidential candidate for their party's nomination. Outcomes help determine the distribution of pledged delegates to each party's national nominating convention.

★ **delegates**
Accredited voting members of a party's national presidential nominating convention.

Flag-waving delegates from each of the states listen on the floor of the Democratic Convention in the Moscone Center, San Francisco.

Democratic Party responded to charges that African Americans, women, and other minorities were underrepresented among the delegates by appointing a special commission chaired by Senator George McGovern to "reform" the party. The McGovern Commission took "affirmative steps" to ensure that the next convention would include "goals" for the representation of African Americans, women, and other minorities among the delegates in proportion to their presence in the Democratic electorate. The effect of these reforms was to reduce the influence of Democratic officeholders (members of Congress, governors, state legislators, and mayors) at the convention and to increase the influence of ideologically motivated activists. Later rule changes eliminated the *unit vote*, in which all delegates from a state were required to vote with the majority of the state's delegation and which required that all delegates who were pledged to a candidate vote for that candidate unless *released* by the candidate.

Then, in the 1980s, the Democratic Leadership Council pressed the party to reserve some convention delegate seats for **superdelegates**—elected officials and party leaders not bound to one candidate—with the expectation that these delegates would be more moderate than the liberal party activists. The notion was that the superdelegates would inject more balanced, less ideological political judgments into convention deliberations, thus improving the party's chances of victory in the general elections. As a result, many

★ **superdelegates**
Delegates to the Democratic Party national convention selected because of their position in the government or the party and not pledged to any candidate.

Figure 7.6

Ideologies of Party Activists Compared to Voters

Democratic and Republican party activists (convention delegates in 2000) are far more likely to hold divergent liberal and conservative views than voters generally.

Source: As reported in the *New York Times*, August 14, 2000.

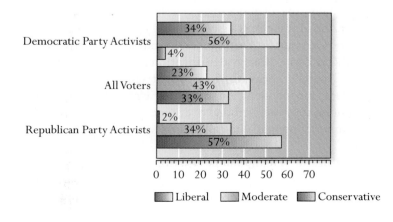

Democratic Party Activists
- 34%
- 56%
- 4%

All Voters
- 23%
- 43%
- 33%

Republican Party Activists
- 2%
- 34%
- 57%

0 10 20 30 40 50 60 70

☐ Liberal   ☐ Moderate   ☐ Conservative

Barack Obama, 2008
Democratic presidential
nominee.

★ **platform**
Statement of principles
adopted by a political party
at its national convention
(specific portions of the
platform are known as
planks); a platform is not
binding on the party's
candidates.

State Control and National Platforms

★ **party identification**
Self-described identification
with a political party, usually
in response to the question,
"Generally speaking, how
would you identify yourself:
as a Republican, Democrat,
independent, or something
else?"

★ **dealignment**
Declining attractiveness of
the parties to the voters, a
reluctance to identify
strongly with a party, and a
decrease in reliance on party
affiliation in voter choice.

Democratic senators, governors, and members of Congress now attend the
convention as superdelegates. If presidential candidates fail to win a majority
of delegates in the primaries and caucus, these superdelegates may control a
nomination.

Party Platforms   National conventions also write party platforms, setting out
the party's goals and policy positions. Because a party's **platform** is not binding on
its nominees, platform *planks* are largely symbolic, although they often provide
heated arguments and provide distinct differences between the parties to present
to voters (see *Politics Up Close*: "Democratic and Republican Platforms: Can You
Tell the Difference?").

Selecting a Running Mate   Perhaps the only suspense remaining in national
party conventions centers on the presidential nominee's choice of a vice presidential running mate. Even a presidential candidate who has decided on a running mate well in advance of the convention may choose to wait until the
convention to announce the choice, otherwise there would be little real "news
value" to the convention, and the television networks would give less coverage to
it. By encouraging speculation about who the running mate will be, the candidate
and the convention manager can sustain media interest. (For a discussion of various strategies in selecting a running mate, see "The Vice Presidential Waiting
Game" in Chapter 11.)

The convention *always* accepts the presidential candidate's recommendation
for a running mate. No formal rules require the convention to do so, but it would
be politically unacceptable for the convention to override the first important
decision of the party's presidential nominee. Convention delegates set aside any
personal reservations they may have and unanimously endorse the presidential
nominee's choice.

Campaign Kickoff   The final evening of the national conventions is really the
kickoff for the general election campaign. The presidential nominee's acceptance
speech tries to set the tone for the fall campaign. Party celebrities, including
defeated presidential candidates, join hands at the podium as a symbol of party
unity. Presidential and vice presidential candidates, spouses, and families assemble under balloons and streamers, amid the happy noise and hoopla, to signal the
start of the general election campaign. TV coverage helps provide the parties
with small postconvention "bumps" in the polls.

Party Voters

Traditionally, the Democratic Party has been able to claim to be the majority
party in the United States (see Figure 7.7). In opinion polls, those who "identify"
with the Democratic Party generally outnumber those who "identify" with the
Republican Party. (**Party identification** is determined by response to the question, "Generally speaking, how would you identify yourself: as a Republican,
Democrat, independent, or something else?") But the Democratic Party advantage among the voters eroded over time, partly as a result of a gradual increase in
the number of people who call themselves independents.

Dealignment   **Dealignment** describes the decline in attractiveness of the political parties to the voters, the growing reluctance of people to identify themselves
with either party, and a decrease in reliance on a candidate's party affiliation in

Politics Up Close — **Democratic and Republican Platforms: Can You Tell the Difference?**

Iraq

A. "To renew American leadership in the world, we would first bring the Iraq war to a responsible end."

B. "The outcome is too critical to our own national security to be jeopardized by artificial or politically inspired timetables that neither reflect conditions on the ground nor respect the essential advice of our military commanders."

Taxes

A. "For families making more than $250,000 we will ask them to give back a portion of the Bush tax cuts to invest in health care and other key priorities."

B. "Along with making the 2001 and 2003 tax cuts permanent so American families will not face a large tax hike, we will advance tax policies to support American families."

Abortion

A. "We strongly and unequivocally support *Roe v. Wade* and a woman's right to choose a safe and legal abortion regardless of ability to pay."

B. "We assert the inherent dignity and sanctity of all human life and affirm that the unborn child has a fundamental right to life which cannot be infringed."

Energy

A. "We know we can't drill our way to energy independence."

B. "We support accelerated exploration, drilling and development of the nation's coasts and onshore fields."

Immigration

A. "Allow immigrants who pay taxes and don't have trouble with the law a path to earn the opportunities and responsibilities of citizenship."

B. "We oppose amnesty. The rule of law suffers if government policies encourage or reward illegal activity."

Other

A. "We support equal rights to democratic self-government and congressional representation for the citizens of our nation's capital."

B. "Judicial activism is a grave threat to the rule of law because unaccountable federal judges are usurping democracy, ignoring the Constitution and its separation of powers, and imposing their personal opinions upon the public."

A. "The key is to make tough choices, in particular, pay-as-you-go budgetary rules."

B. "We favor adoption of the Balanced Budget Amendment [to the Constitution] to require a balanced budget except in time of war."

Source: Excerpts from Democratic [A] and Republican [B] party platforms, 2008.

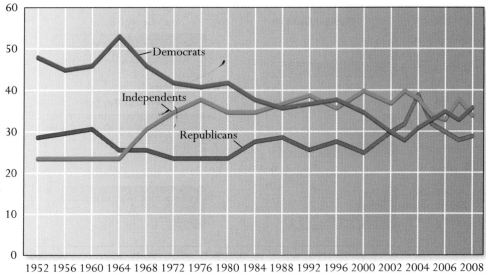

Figure **7.7**

Party Identification in the Electorate

For many years, the Democratic Party enjoyed a substantial lead in party identification among voters. This Democratic lead eroded in the late 1960s as more people began to identify themselves as Independents. Independent identification suggests that many voters have become disillusioned with both parties.

Source: Data from *National Election Studies*, University of Michigan, updated from Gallup Polls.

voter choice. Dealignment is evident not only in the growing numbers of self-described Independents, but also in the declining numbers of those who identify themselves as "strong" Democrats or Republicans. In short, the electorate is less partisan than it once was.

Party Loyalty in Voting Despite the decline in partisan identification in the electorate, it is important to note that *party identification is a strong influence in voter choice in elections.* Most voters cast their ballot for the candidate of their party. This is true in presidential elections (see Figure 7.8) and even more true in congressional and state elections. Those who identify themselves as Democrats are

Figure 7.8

Who Voted How?: Republican, Democratic, and Independent Voters in Presidential Elections

As the percentages here indicate, in recent years registered Democrats have been more likely to "cross over" and vote for a Republican candidate for president than registered Republicans have been to vote for the Democratic presidential candidate.

Source: New York Times.

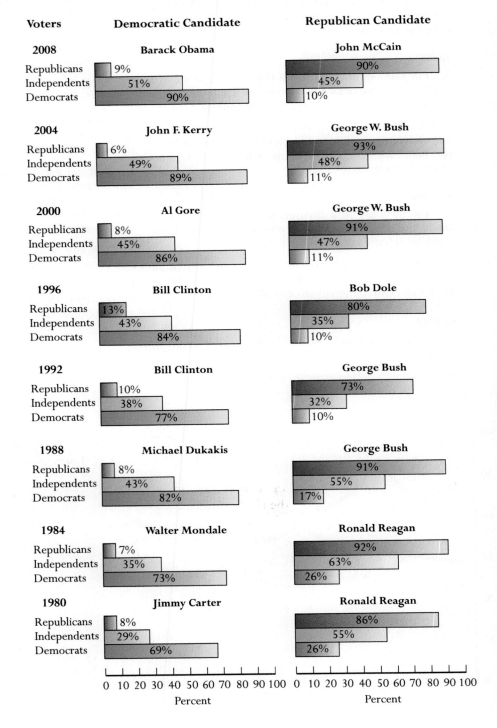

somewhat more likely to vote for a Republican presidential candidate than those who identify themselves as Republicans are to vote for a Democratic presidential candidate. Republican Ronald Reagan was able to win more than one-quarter of self-identified Democrats in 1980 and 1984, earning these crossover voters the label "Reagan Democrats."[15]

Realignment?   Although Democratic Party loyalty has eroded over the last thirty years, it is not clear whether or not this erosion is a classic party **realignment**.[16] Most scholars agree that party realignments occurred in the presidential elections of 1824 (Jackson, Democrats), 1860 (Lincoln, Republicans), 1896 (Bryan, Democrats), and 1932 (Roosevelt, Democrats). This historical sequence gave rise to a theory that realigning elections occur every thirty-six years. According to this theory, the election of 1968 should have been a realigning one. It is true that Richard Nixon's 1968 victory marked the beginning of a 24-year Republican era in presidential election victories that was broken only by Jimmy Carter in 1976. But there was relatively little shifting of the party loyalties of major social groups, and the Democratic Party remained the dominant party in the electorate and in Congress.

The Democratic Party still receives *disproportionate* support from Catholics, Jews, African Americans, less educated and lower income groups, blue-collar workers, union members, and big-city residents. The Republican Party still receives *disproportionate* support from Protestants, whites, more educated and higher income groups, white-collar workers, nonunion workers, and suburban and small-town dwellers (see *Politics Up Close*: "The Donkey and the Elephant" on page 209). Disproportionate support does not mean these groups *always* give a majority of their votes to the indicated party, but only that they give that party a larger percentage of their votes than the party receives from the general electorate. This pattern of social-group voting and party identification has remained relatively stable over the years, even though the GOP has made some gains among many of the traditionally Democratic groups (see Figure 7.9). The only major *shift* in social-group support has occurred among Southern whites. This group has shifted from heavily Democratic in party identification to a substantial Republican preference[17] (see *Across the USA*: "Red States, Blue States").

Third Parties in the U.S. System

Despite the cultural and electoral barriers to victory, **third parties**, more accurately called minor parties, are a common feature of American politics. These parties can be roughly classified by the role they play in the political system.

Ideological Parties   **Ideological parties** exist to promote an ideology rather than to win elections. They use the electoral process to express their views and to rally activists to their cause, and they measure success not by victory at the polls but by their ability to bring their names and their views to the attention of the American public. The socialist parties, which have run candidates in virtually every presidential election in this century, are prime examples of ideological parties in the United States (see also *Controversy*: "The Libertarian Party: A Dissenting Voice").

Protest Parties   **Protest parties** arise around popular issues or concerns that the major parties have failed to address. An important historical example of a protest party is the Populist Party of the late 1800s. It arose as a protest by Midwestern farmers against eastern railroads, "trusts" and monopolies, and the gold standard. The Populists threatened to capture the wave of popular support for railroad regulation, cheap money, and antimonopoly legislation, and thus they

★ **realignment**
Long-term shift in social-group support for various political parties that creates new coalitions in each party.

Do we need a third party to challenge the Republican and Democratic parties?

TIMELINE

Third Parties in American History

★ **third parties**
Political parties that challenge the two major parties in an election.

★ **ideological parties**
Third parties that exist to promote an ideology rather than to win elections.

★ **protest parties**
Third parties that arise in response to issues of popular concern which have not been addressed by the major parties.

Figure 7.9

Who Backs Whom?:
Social-Group Support for
the Democratic and
Republican Parties

The Democratic Party draws
disproportionate support
from low-income, less-
educated, Catholic, Jewish,
and African American voters.
The Republican Party relies
more heavily on support
from high-income, college-
educated, white Protestant
voters.

Note: Independents not shown.

Source: Data from *National Election Studies*, University of Michigan.

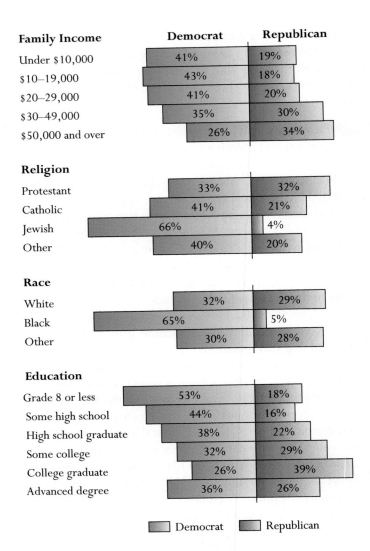

Family Income	Democrat	Republican
Under $10,000	41%	19%
$10–19,000	43%	18%
$20–29,000	41%	20%
$30–49,000	35%	30%
$50,000 and over	26%	34%

Religion	Democrat	Republican
Protestant	33%	32%
Catholic	41%	21%
Jewish	66%	4%
Other	40%	20%

Race	Democrat	Republican
White	32%	29%
Black	65%	5%
Other	30%	28%

Education	Democrat	Republican
Grade 8 or less	53%	18%
Some high school	44%	16%
High school graduate	38%	22%
Some college	32%	29%
College graduate	26%	39%
Advanced degree	36%	26%

Democrat   Republican

endangered the established Democratic and Republican parties. But when the Democratic Party nominated William Jennings Bryan in 1896, the Populist Party officially endorsed Bryan and temporarily disappeared as a significant independent political organization. Populist ideas were set forth again in a new Progressive Party, which nominated Robert M. La Follette for president in 1924; the Democratic and Republican parties both nominated conservative candidates that year, helping La Follette to win almost 17 percent of the popular vote.

Not all major protest movements have been accompanied by the formation of third parties. Indeed, protest leaders have often argued that a third-party effort distracts the movement from a more effective strategy of capturing control of one or both of the major parties. The labor-union-organizing movement of the 1930s and the civil rights and antiwar movements of the 1960s did not spark a separate third party but instead worked largely *within* the dominant Democratic Party to advance their goals.

Single-Issue Parties   **Single-issue parties** have frequently formed around a particular cause. Single-issue parties are much like protest parties, although somewhat narrower in their policy focus. The Greenback Party of the late 1800s shared with the Populists a desire for cheap inflated currency in order to ease the burden of debt and mortgage payments by farmers. But the Greenback Party

★ **single-issue parties**
Third parties formed around
one particular cause.

Across The USA   Red States, Blue States

The Democratic and Republican Parties compete in every state. But sectionalism was and is evident in the strength of the Republican Party in the Mountain, Plains, and Southern states. The Democratic Party is becoming bicoastal—strong in the Northeast and the Pacific Coast. Of the four largest states, California and New York lean Democratic, while Texas and Florida lean Republican. At least this has been the general pattern in presidential elections; congressional and gubernatorial elections are not quite so sectionalized.

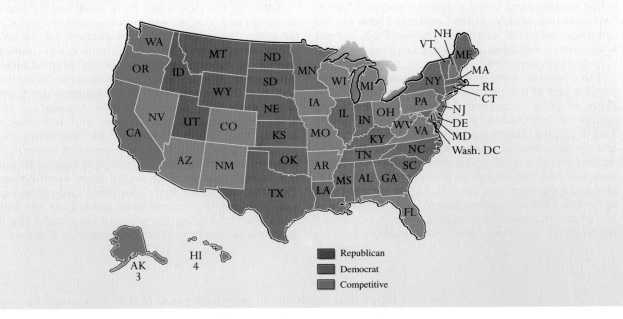

focused on a single remedy: an end to the gold standard and the issuance of cheap currency—"greenbacks."

Perhaps the most persistent of minor parties over the years has been the Prohibition Party. It achieved temporary success with the passage of the Eighteenth Amendment to the U.S. Constitution in 1919, which prohibited the manufacture, sale, or transportation of "intoxicating liquors," only to see its "noble experiment" fail and be repealed by the 21st Amendment.

Today the Green Party provides an example of a single-issue party, with its primary emphasis on environmental protection. However, the Green Party itself contends that it is "part of the worldwide movement that promotes ecological wisdom, social justice, grassroots democracy and non-violence."

Splinter Parties
Finally, many third parties in American politics are really **splinter parties**, parties formed by a dissatisfied faction of a major party. Splinter parties may form around a particular individual, as did the Progressive (Bull Moose) Party of Theodore Roosevelt in 1912. As a popular former president, Teddy Roosevelt won more than 27 percent of the popular vote, outpolling Republican candidate William Howard Taft but allowing Democrat Woodrow Wilson to win the presidency.

Splinter parties also may emerge from an intense intraparty policy dispute. For example, in 1948 the States' Rights (Dixiecrat) Party formed in protest to

★ **splinter parties**
Third parties formed by a dissatisfied faction of a major party.

Controversy

The Libertarian Party: A Dissenting Voice

Would you like to see the federal income tax repealed; the Internal Revenue Service abolished; foreign aid ended; all U.S. troops brought home from overseas; and individual choice "in all matters," from abortion to gun control to drug use? Would you like to eliminate government farm subsidies; end federal support for public broadcasting, science, and the arts; and "privatize" education and "charitize" welfare? These are the campaign promises of the Libertarian Party, whose presidential candidates' names appeared on the ballot in most states since 1992.

The Libertarian Party is unique in its uncompromising commitment to the classical liberal, eighteenth-century ideals of John Locke and Adam Smith. Libertarians oppose all interference by government in the private lives of citizens. They support unregulated free markets and the protection of private property rights. Thus they oppose environmental regulations, consumer protection laws, and laws that infringe on private property or "take" property for government use without just compensation to owners. They also oppose government efforts to regulate private morals—including laws outlawing drug use, prostitution, gambling, and pornography—believing

these activities should be the exclusive choice of consenting individuals. Libertarians are strict noninterventionists in international affairs; they are opposed to the North Atlantic Treaty Organization (NATO) alliance, to foreign aid, to military involvements outside of U.S. territory, and to virtually all spending for national defense.

Although the Libertarian Party candidate for president regularly receives less than 1 percent of the popular vote, Libertarian ideas have entered the nation's policy debates and influenced both major parties. Republican candidates have frequently adopted Libertarian arguments on behalf of deregulation of market activities; Democratic candidates frequently use Libertarian arguments about individual "choice" in the areas of abortion, school prayer, and homosexual activity. And both the Democratic and the Republican parties have vocal "isolationist" wings that borrow Libertarian, noninterventionist arguments against foreign aid, international alliances, and military expenditures. Thus the Libertarian Party, like other ideological parties, functions to promote ideas rather than win elections. The Libertarian Party presidential candidate in 2008 was former Republican Congressman Bob Barr.

the civil rights (fair employment practices) plank in the Democratic Party platform of that year and nominated Strom Thurmond for president. In 1968 George Wallace's American Independent Party won nearly 14 percent of the popular vote. Wallace attacked school desegregation and busing to achieve racial balance in schools, as well as crime in the streets, welfare "cheats," and meddling federal judges and bureaucrats. He abandoned his third-party organization in 1972 to run in the Democratic presidential primary elections. Following some Democratic primary victories, he was shot and disabled for life.

An Anti-Party Party   Many Americans feel disgusted with "politics as usual." They view both the Democratic and Republican parties as ineffective, unprincipled, and even corrupt. They represent a dealignment from the current party system; that is, they have no party loyalty and they usually describe themselves as "Independents." In 1992 Texas billionaire Ross Perot was able to mobilize many of these independents into a third-party challenge to the two-party system. He spent nearly $100 million of his own money to build a nationwide organization, the Reform Party (originally called United We Stand) and to place his name on the ballot of all fifty states. Early in the campaign his poll numbers mushroomed to 35 percent, higher than any other independent candidate's support in the history of modem polling. His political support came mostly from the center of the political spectrum—people who identified themselves as independents. Perot participated in the first three-way presidential television debates and won 19 percent of the popular vote in the general election, the highest percentage won by a third-party candidate since Teddy Roosevelt in 1912. But he failed to win a single electoral vote. Perot ran again in 1996, but

A Dissenting Voice
Ralph Nader, the nation's most visible interest-group entrepreneur, continues his fight against auto companies, speaking here to Toledo residents unhappy with tax breaks given to Daimler-Chrysler to keep its plant in the city. In the 2000 presidential election, Nader was the Green Party's nominee. In 2004 and again in 2008, he ran as an Independent.

when his early poll numbers languished, he was excluded from the presidential debates. On Election Day he won fewer than half of the votes (9 percent) that he had garnered four years earlier, and again failed to win any state's electoral votes. In 2000 the Reform Party imploded in a raucous convention, with rival factions almost coming to blows over control of the microphone. The party officially nominated conservative firebrand Pat Buchanan, but Buchanan's right-wing rhetoric attracted less than 1 percent of the voters. By 2004 many states had dropped the Reform Party from their ballots.

Third-Party Prospects   In recent years, polls have reported that a majority of Americans favor the idea of a third party. But support for the *general* idea of a third party has never been matched by voter support for *specific* third-party or independent presidential candidates (see Table 7.4). Moreover, it is very difficult for a third party or independent candidate to win electoral votes. Only Theodore Roosevelt, Robert M. La Follette, and George C. Wallace managed to win any electoral votes in the past century. The Reform Party, founded by billionaire Ross Perot in 1992, was the latest serious yet unsuccessful attempt to create a nationwide third party.

Table **7.4**   Opposing the Two-Party System: Twentieth-Century Third-Party Presidential Votes

Independent and third-party presidential candidates have failed to win any electoral votes over the last forty years.

Third-Party Presidential Candidates	Popular Vote (percentage)	Electoral Votes (number)
Theodore Roosevelt (1912), Progressive (Bull Moose) Party	27.4%	88
Robert M. La Follette (1924), Progressive Party	16.6	13
George C. Wallace (1968), American Independent Party	13.5	46
John Anderson (1980), Independent	6.6	0
Ross Perot (1992), Independent	18.9	0
Ross Perot (1996), Reform Party	8.5	0
Ralph Nader (2000), Green Party	2.7	0
Ralph Nader (2004), Independent	0.4	0
Ralph Nader (2008), Independent	0.4	0

Why the Two-Party System Persists

The two-party system is deeply ingrained in American politics. Although third parties have often made appearances in presidential elections, no third-party candidate has ever won the Oval Office. (Lincoln's new Republican Party in 1860 might be counted as an exception, but it quickly became a major party.) Very few third-party candidates have won seats in Congress. Many other democracies have multiple-party systems, so the question arises as to why the United States has had a two-party system throughout its history.[18]

Cultural Consensus   One explanation of the nation's continuing two-party system focuses on the broad consensus supporting the American political culture (see Chapter 2). The values of democracy, capitalism, free enterprise, individual liberty, religious freedom, and equality of opportunity are so widely shared that no party challenging these values has ever won much of a following. There is little support in the American political culture for avowedly fascist, communist, authoritarian, or other antidemocratic parties. Moreover, the American political culture includes a strong belief in the separation of church and state. Political parties with religious affiliations, common in European democracies, are absent from American politics. Socialist parties have frequently appeared on the scene under various labels—the Socialist Party, the Socialist Labor Party, and the Socialist Workers Party. But the largest popular vote ever garnered by a socialist candidate in a presidential election was the 6 percent won by Eugene V. Debs in 1912. In contrast, socialist parties have frequently won control of European governments.

On broad policy issues, most Americans cluster near the center. This general consensus tends to discourage multiple parties. There does not appear to be sufficient room for them to stake out a position on the ideological spectrum that would detach voters from the two major parties.

This cultural explanation blends with the influence of historical precedents. The American two-party system has gained acceptance through custom. The nation's first party system developed from two coalitions, Federalists and Anti-Federalists, and this dual pattern has been reinforced over two centuries.

Winner-Takes-All Electoral System   Yet another explanation of the American two-party system focuses on the electoral system itself. Winners in presidential and congressional elections, as well as in state gubernatorial and legislative elections, are usually determined by a plurality, winner-takes-all vote. Even in elections that require a majority of more than 50 percent to win—which may involve a runoff election—only one party's candidate wins in the end. Because of the winner-takes-all nature of U.S. elections, parties and candidates have an overriding incentive to broaden their appeal to a plurality or majority of voters. Losers come away empty-handed. There is not much incentive in such a system for a party to form to represent the views of 5 or 10 percent of the electorate.

Americans are so accustomed to winner-takes-all elections that they seldom consider alternatives. In some countries, legislative bodies are elected by **proportional representation**, whereby all voters cast a single ballot for the party of their choice and legislative seats are then apportioned to the parties in proportion to their total vote in the electorate. Minority parties are assured of legislative seats, perhaps with as little as 10 or 15 percent of the vote. If no party wins 50 percent of the votes and seats, the parties try to form a coalition of parties to establish control of the government. In these nations, party coalition building to form a governing majority occurs *after* the election rather than *before* the election, as it does in winner-takes-all election systems.

★ **proportional representation**
Electoral system that allocates seats in a legislature based on the proportion of votes each party receives in a national election.

A *Constitutional* Note

Political Parties and the Constitution

Political parties had not yet formed in 1787 when the Founders met in Philadelphia to draft the Constitution. Indeed, George Washington and other Founders believed that the new nation might be destroyed by the "baneful effects of the spirit of party." Nowhere in the Constitution do we find any reference to "parties." Indeed, the original Constitution called for presidential electors to cast two votes for president, with the candidate receiving the highest number becoming president and the candidate with the second-highest becoming vice president. But by 1800 parties had formed: the Federalists rallied around John Adams, the second president; and the Democratic-Republicans (often called Republicans, but not to be confused with today's Republican Party) supported Thomas Jefferson.

Candidates for the Electoral College ran under these labels (or sometimes as just Adams's men or Jefferson's men). In the 1800 presidential election the Democratic-Republican party won a majority of electors. But all of them had cast their votes for both Jefferson and his intended vice president Aaron Burr. Thus Jefferson and Burr ended up with the same number of electoral votes, 73, for president. For a while, Burr considered challenging Jefferson for president, but in the end conceded the office. The incident illustrated the failure of the Founders to envision parties as central to the electoral process. Congress and the states were obliged to add the 12th Amendment to the Constitution by 1804 in order to separate "in distinct ballots" the persons voted for as president and vice president.

Legal Access to the Ballot   Another factor in the American two-party system may be electoral system barriers to third parties. The Democratic and Republican nominees are automatically included on all general election ballots, but third-party and independent candidates face difficult obstacles in getting their names listed. In presidential elections, a third-party candidate must meet the varied requirements of fifty separate states to appear on their ballots along with the Democratic and Republican nominees. These requirements often include filing petitions signed by up to 5 or 10 percent of registered voters. In addition, states require third parties to win 5 or 10 percent of the vote in the last election in order to retain their position on the ballot in subsequent elections. In 1980 independent John Anderson gained access to the ballot in all fifty states, as did independent Ross Perot in 1992. But just doing so required a considerable expenditure of effort and money that the major parties were able to avoid.

Summary
Who Gets What: Parties

Organization grants advantage in the struggle for power. Political parties organize individuals and groups to exercise power in democracies by winning elected office.

★ Political parties are not mentioned in the U.S. Constitution, yet they have played a central role in American political history. Major party realignments have occurred at critical points in American history, as major social groups shifted their political loyalties.

★ In theory, political parties are "responsible" organizations that adopt a principled platform, recruit candidates who support the platform, educate the public about it, direct an issue-oriented campaign, and then organize the legislature and ensure that their candidates enact the party's platform.

★ But in the American two-party system, winning office by appealing to the large numbers of people at the center of the political spectrum becomes more important than promoting strong policy positions. American parties cannot bind elected officials to campaign promises anyway.

★ American parties have lost many of their traditional functions over time. Party nominations are won by individual candidates in primary elections rather than through selection by party leaders. Most political candidates are self-selected; they organize their own campaigns. Television has replaced the party as the principal means of educating the public. And government bureaucracies, not party machines, provide social services.

★ Party nominations are won in primary elections as earlier caucus and convention methods of nomination have largely disappeared. Party primary elections in the various states may be open or closed and may or may not require runoff primaries. The nominees selected in each party's primary election then battle each other in the general election.

★ The parties battle in three major arenas. The *party-in-the-electorate* refers to party identification among voters. The *party-in-the-government* refers to party identification and organization among elected officials. The *party organization* refers to party offices at the local, state, and national levels.

★ The Democratic and Republican parties are structured to include national party conventions, national committees with chairs and staff, congressional party organizations, state committees, and county and local committees.

★ Since presidential nominations are now generally decided in primary elections—with pledged delegates selected before the opening of the national conventions and with party platforms largely symbolic and wholly unenforceable on the candidates—the conventions have become largely media events designed to kick off the general election campaign.

★ *Dealignment* refers to a decline in the attractiveness of the parties to the voters, a growing reluctance of people to identify strongly with either party, and greater voter willingness to cross party lines. Despite dealignment, party identification remains a strong influence in voter choice.

★ Opinion polls indicate that most Americans support the general idea of a third party, but throughout the twentieth century no third-party presidential candidate won very many votes.

★ In the United States, many aspects of the political system—including cultural consensus, the winner-take-all electoral system, and legal restrictions to ballot access—place major obstacles in the way of success for third parties and independent candidates. Although never successful at gaining federal office in significant numbers, ideological, protest, single-issue, and splinter third parties have often been effective at getting popular issues on the federal agenda.

Key Terms

Suggested Readings

Hershey, Marjorie. *Party Politics in America*. 12th ed. New York: Longman, 2007. An authoritative text on the American party system—party organizations, the parties-in-government, and the parties-in-the-electorate.

Downs, Anthony. *An Economic Theory of Democracy*. New York: Harper & Row, 1957. The classic work describing rational choice winning strategies for political parties and explaining why there is no incentive for vote-maximizing parties in a two-party system to adopt widely separate policy positions.

Keefe, William J., and Marc J. Hetherington. *Parties, Politics, and Public Policy in America*. 10th ed. Washington, D.C.: CQ Press, 2006. A comprehensive survey of American political parties, from the nominating process to campaign finance and the changing affiliations of voters.

Lowi, Theodore E., and Joseph Romange. *Debating the Two Party System*. Boulder, Colo.: Rowman & Littlefield, 1997. Lowi argues that the two-party system is no longer adequate to represent the people of a diverse nation; Romange counters that two parties help unify the country and instruct Americans about the value of compromise.

Wattenberg, Martin P. *The Decline of American Political Parties, 1952–1992*. Cambridge, Mass.: Harvard University Press, 1994. An authoritative discussion of increasing negative attitudes toward the parties and the growing dealignment in the electorate.

White, John Kenneth, and Daniel M. Shen. *New Party Politics*. 2nd ed. Belmont, Calif.: Wadsworth, 2004. Historical approach to evolution of the American party system.

Suggested Web Sites

Center for Responsive Politics   www.opensecrets.org
Source of information on campaign finances—contributors, recipients, PACs, lobbyists, and so forth.

Democratic Leadership Council/New Democrats Online
www.ndol.org
Moderate Democrats in the House and Senate set forth their views.

Democratic Party Web Site of the Democratic National Committee (DNC)   www.democrats.org
With news, press releases, policy positions, and so forth.

Election World   www.electionsworld.org
Links to party Web sites in many nations of the world, with latest election results.

Franklin D. Roosevelt (FDR) Heritage Center
www.fdrheritage.org
Biography on F.D.R. and information on the New Deal.

Libertarian Party   www.lp.org
This Web site reflects the Libertarian Party's strong ideological commitments to individual liberty, free markets, and nonintervention in world affairs.

MoveOn   www.moveon.org
Web site of the liberal political action committee.

The Polling Report   www.pollingreport.com
Up-to-date polling information from a variety of polls on Democratic and Republican party preferences.

Reagan Information Page   www.presidentreagan.info
Web site celebrating Reagan's presidential achievements.

Reform Party   www.reformparty.org
The Reform Party site provides information about founder Ross Perot and the principles of and news about the party.

Republican Party Web Site of the Republican National Committee (RNC)   www.rnc.org
With GOP news, press releases, policy positions, and so forth.

8 CAMPAIGNS AND ELECTIONS

Deciding Who Governs

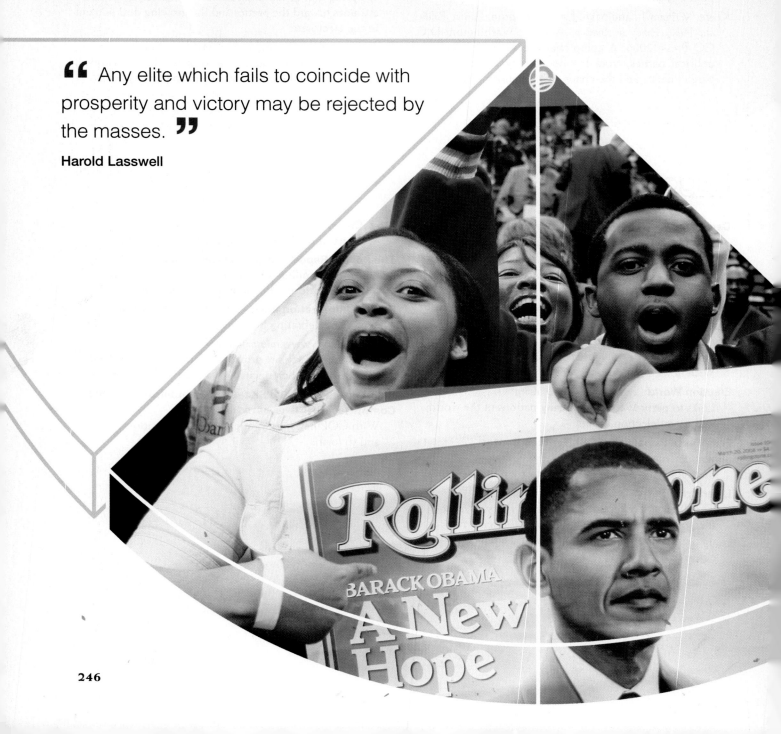

> " Any elite which fails to coincide with prosperity and victory may be rejected by the masses. "
>
> **Harold Lasswell**

Chapter *Outline*

✓ Think About Politics

1. Should elected officials be bound by their campaign promises?
   YES ○ NO ○

2. Do you think that personal ambition, rather than civic duty, motivates most politicians?
   YES ○ NO ○

3. Do career politicians serve their constituents better than those who go into politics for just a short time?
   YES ○ NO ○

4. Should people vote on the basis of a candidate's personal character rather than his or her policy positions?
   YES ○ NO ○

5. Would you vote for a candidate who used negative ads to discredit an opponent?
   YES ○ NO ○

6. Do political campaign contributions have too much influence on elections and government policy?
   YES ○ NO ○

7. Are high campaign costs discouraging good people from becoming candidates?
   YES ○ NO ○

8. Should presidents be elected by direct popular vote?
   YES ○ NO ○

What real power do you have in a democracy? By casting ballots, citizens in a democracy have the power to determine who will represent them, who will make up the government under which they live. You, then, are an integral part of the democratic process every time you vote in an election.

★ **mandate**
Perception of popular support for a program or policy based on the margin of electoral victory won by a candidate who proposed it during a campaign.

Elections in a Democracy

Democratic government is government by "the consent of the governed." Elections give practical meaning to this notion of "consent." Elections allow people to choose among competing candidates and parties and to decide who will occupy public office. Elections give people the opportunity to pass judgment on current officeholders, either by reelecting them (granting continued consent) or by throwing them out of office (withdrawing consent).

In a representative democracy, elections function primarily to choose personnel to occupy public office—to decide "who governs." But elections also have an indirect influence on public policy, allowing voters to influence policy directions by choosing between candidates or parties with different policy priorities. Thus elections indirectly influence "who gets what"—that is, the outcomes of the political process.

Elections as Mandates?   However, it is difficult to argue that elections serve as "policy mandates"—that is, that elections allow voters to direct the course of public policy. Frequently, election winners claim a **mandate**—overwhelming support from the people—for their policies and programs. But for elections to serve as policy mandates, four conditions have to be met:

1. Competing candidates have to offer clear policy alternatives.

2. The voters have to cast their ballots on the basis of these policy alternatives alone.

3. The election results have to clearly indicate the voters' policy preferences.

4. Elected officials have to be bound by their campaign promises.[1]

As we shall see, *none* of these conditions is fully met in American elections. Often candidates do not differ much on policy questions, or they deliberately obscure their policy positions to avoid offending groups of voters. Voters themselves frequently pay little attention to policy issues

Comparing Voting and Elections

in elections but rather vote along traditional party lines or group affiliations, or on the basis of the candidate's character, personality, or media image.

Moreover, even in elections in which issues seem to dominate the campaign, the outcome may not clearly reflect policy preferences. Candidates take stands on a variety of issues. It is never certain on which issues the voters agreed with the winner and on which issues they disagreed yet voted for the candidate anyway.

Finally, candidates often fail to abide by their campaign promises once they are elected. Some simply ignore their promises, assuming voters have forgotten about the campaign. Others point to changes in circumstances or conditions as a justification for abandoning a campaign pledge.

★ retrospective voting
Voting for or against a candidate or party on the basis of past performance in office.

Think Again

Should elected officials be bound by their campaign promises?

Retrospective Voting   Voters can influence future policy directions through **retrospective voting**—votes cast on the basis of the performance of incumbents, by either reelecting them or throwing them out of office.[2] Voters may not know what politicians will do in the future, but they can evaluate how well politicians performed in the past. When incumbent officeholders are defeated, it is reasonable to assume that voters did not like their performance and that newly elected officials should change policy course if they do not want to meet a similar fate in the next election. But it is not always clear what the defeated incumbents did in office that led to their ouster by the voters. Nor, indeed, can incumbents who won reelection assume that all of their policies are approved of by a majority of voters. Nevertheless, retrospective voting provides an overall judgment of how voters evaluate performance in office.

Protection of Rights   Elections also provide protection against official abuse. The long struggle for African American voting rights in the United States was premised on the belief that once black people acquired the right to vote, government would become more responsive to their concerns. In signing the Voting Rights Act of 1965, President Lyndon Johnson expressed this view: "The vote is the most powerful instrument ever devised by man for breaking down injustice and destroying the terrible walls which imprison men because they are different from other men."[3] The subsequent history of racial politics in America (see Chapter 15) suggests that the vote is more effective in eliminating discriminatory laws than it is in resolving social or economic inequities. Nevertheless, *without* the vote, we can be certain that government would have very little incentive to respond to popular needs.

Power and Ambition

Personal ambition is a driving force in politics. Politics attracts people for whom *power*—the drive to shape the world according to one's own beliefs and values—and *celebrity*—the public attention, deference, name recognition, and social status that accompany public office—are more rewarding than money, leisure, or privacy. "Political office today flows to those who want it enough to spend the time and energy mastering its pursuit. It flows in the direction of ambition—and talent."[4]

Think Again

Do you think that personal ambition, rather than civic duty, motivates most politicians?

Communication Skills   Another important personal qualification is the ability to communicate with others. Politicians must know how to talk, and talk, and talk—to large audiences, in press conferences and interviews, on television, to reporters, to small groups of financial contributors, on the phone, at airports and commencements, to their staffs, on the floor of Congress or the state legislature. It matters less what politicians say than how they look and sound saying it. They must communicate sincerity, compassion, confidence, and good humor, as well as ideas.

Professionalism

Politics is increasingly characterized by **professionalism**. "Citizen officeholders"—people with business or professional careers who get into politics part time or for short periods of time—are being driven out of political life by career politicians—people who enter politics early in life as a full-time occupation and expect to make it their career. Politics increasingly demands all of a politician's time and energy. At all levels of government, from city council to state legislatures to the U.S. Congress, political work is becoming full-time and year-round.

★ **professionalism**
In politics, a reference to the increasing number of officeholders for whom politics is a full-time occupation.

Careerism

Professional political careers begin at a relatively early age. **Careerism** in politics begins when ambitious young people seek out internships and staff positions with members of Congress, with congressional committees, in state legislators' or governors' offices, in mayors' offices, or in council chambers. Others volunteer to work in political campaigns. Many find political mentors from whom they learn how to organize campaigns, contact financial contributors, and deal with the media. Soon they are ready to run for local office or the state legislature. Rather than challenge a strong incumbent, they may wait for an open seat to be created by retirement, by reapportionment, or by its holder seeking another office. Over time, running for and holding elective office become their career.

★ **careerism**
In politics, a reference to people who started young working in politics, running for and holding public office, and made politics their career.

Lawyers in Politics

The prevalence of lawyers in politics is an American tradition. Among the fifty-five delegates to the Constitutional Convention in 1787, some twenty-five were lawyers. The political dominance of lawyers continues today, with lawyers filling about half of U.S. Senate seats and nearly half of the seats in the U.S. House of Representatives.

It is sometimes argued that lawyers dominate in politics because of the parallel skills required in law and politics. Lawyers represent clients, so they can apply their professional experience to represent constituents in Congress. Lawyers are trained to deal with statutory law, so they are assumed to be reasonably familiar with the United States Code (the codified laws of the U.S. government) when they arrive in Congress to make or amend these statutes.

But it is more likely that people attracted to politics decide to go to law school fully aware of the tradition of lawyers in American politics. Moreover, political officeholding at the state and local level as well as in the national government can help a struggling lawyer's private practice through free public advertising and opportunities to make contacts with potential clients. Finally, there are many special opportunities for lawyers to acquire public office in "lawyers only" posts as judges and prosecuting attorneys in federal, state, and local governments. Law school graduates who accept modest salaries as U.S. attorneys in the Justice Department or in state or county prosecuting offices can gain valuable experience for later use in either private law practice or politics.

U.S. Senator Barack Obama speaks to reporters in New York, on September 17, 2007.

Most of the lawyers in the Congress, however, have become professional politicians over time. They have left their legal practices behind.

The Advantages of Incumbency

In theory, elections offer voters the opportunity to "throw the rascals out." But in practice, voters seldom do so. **Incumbents**, people already holding public office, have a strong advantage when they seek reelection. The **reelection rates** of incumbents for *all* elective offices—city council, mayor, state legislature, governor, and especially Congress—are very high. Since 1950, more than 90 percent of all members of the House of Representatives who have sought reelection have been successful. The success rate of U.S. Senate incumbents is not as great, but it is still impressive; since 1950, more than 70 percent of senators seeking reelection have been successful.[5]

Why do incumbents win so often? This is a particularly vexing question, inasmuch as so many people are distrustful of government and hold politicians in low esteem. Congress itself is the focal point of public disapproval and even ridicule. Yet people seem to distinguish between Congress as an institution—which they distrust—and their own members of Congress—whom they reelect. The result is something of a contradiction: popular members of Congress serving in an unpopular Congress (see *What Do You Think?*: "Why Do Voters Reelect Members of an Unpopular Congress?"in Chapter 10). Three major advantages tend to enhance incumbents' chances of winning: name recognition, campaign contributions, and the resources of office.

Name Recognition   One reason for incumbents' success is that they begin the campaign with greater **name recognition** than their challengers, simply because they are the incumbent and their name has become familiar to their constituents over the previous years. Much of the daily work of all elected officials, especially members of Congress, is really public relations. Name recognition is a strategic advantage at the ballot box, especially if voters have little knowledge of policy positions or voting records. Voters tend to cast ballots for recognizable names over unknowns. Cynics have concluded that there is no such thing as bad publicity, only publicity. Even in cases of well-publicized scandals, incumbent members of Congress have won reelection; presumably voters preferred "the devil they knew" to the one they did not.

The somewhat lower rate of reelection of Senate versus House members may be a result of the fact that Senate challengers are more likely to have held high-visibility offices—for example, governor or member of Congress—before running for the Senate. Thus Senate challengers often enjoy some name recognition even before the campaign begins. Greater media attention to a statewide Senate race also helps to move the challenger closer to the incumbent in public recognition. In contrast, House challengers are likely to have held less visible local or state legislative offices or to be political novices, and House races attract considerably less media attention than Senate races do.

Campaign Contributions   Incumbents have a strong advantage in raising campaign funds, simply because individuals and groups seeking access to those already in office are inspired to make contributions (see Table 8.1). **Challengers** have no immediate favors to offer; they must convince a potential contributor

★ **incumbents**
Candidates currently in office seeking reelection.

★ **reelection rates**
Percentages of incumbents running for reelection who are successful.

★ **name recognition**
Public awareness of a political candidate—whether they are familiar with his or her name.

★ **challengers**
In politics, a reference to people running against incumbent officeholders.

that they will win office and also that they are devoted to the interests of their financial backers.[6]

Contributing individuals and interest groups show a strong preference for incumbents over challengers. They do not wish to offend incumbent office-holders by contributing to their challengers; doing so risks both immediate retribution and future "freezing out" in the likely event of the challengers' defeat. Thus only when an incumbent has been especially hostile to an organization's interest, or in rare cases where an incumbent seems especially vulnerable, will an interest group support a challenger. Yet challengers need even larger campaign war chests than incumbents to be successful. Challengers must overcome the greater name recognition of incumbents, their many office resources, and their records of constituency service. Thus even if incumbents and challengers had equal campaign treasuries, incumbents would enjoy the advantage.

Resources of Office   Successful politicians use their offices to keep their names and faces before the public in various ways—public appearances, interviews, speeches, and press releases. Congressional incumbents make full use of the **franking privilege** (free use of the U.S. mails) to send self-promotional newsletters to tens of thousands of households in their district at taxpayers' expense. They travel on weekends to their district virtually year-round, using tax-funded travel allowances, to make local appearances, speeches, and contacts.

Members of Congress have large staffs working every day over many years with the principal objective of ensuring the reelection of their members. Indeed, Congress is structured as an "incumbent-protection society" organized and staffed to help guarantee the reelection of its members (see "Home Style" in Chapter 10). Service to constituents occupies the energies of congressional office staffs both in Washington and in local district offices established for this purpose. Casework wins voters one at a time: tracing lost Social Security checks, ferreting out which federal loans voters qualify for and helping them with their applications, and performing countless other personal favors. These individual "retail-level" favors are supplemented by larger-scale projects that experienced members of Congress can bring to their district or state (roads, dams, post offices, buildings, schools, grants, contracts), as well as undesirable projects (landfills, waste disposal sites, halfway houses) that they can keep out of their

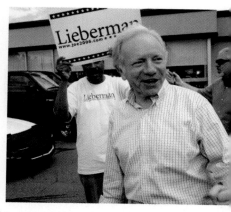

Lose the Primary, Win the General Election
Senator Joe Lieberman (D-CT) lost in his Democratic Party primary for reelection to the U.S. Senate—a rare occurrence for an incumbent. Lieberman was the Democratic vice-presidential candidate on the ticket with Al Gore in 2000. Liberal activists led the way to his defeat, attacking his support of the invasion of Iraq. Lieberman subsequently was reelected as an Independent candidate in the general election.

★ **franking privilege**
Free use of the U.S. mails granted to members of Congress to promote communication with constituents.

Table *8.1*   In the Money: Incumbent Advantage in Fund Raising
Incumbent House and Senate members seeking reelection are able to raise much more than their challengers in campaign contributors.

	2002	2004	2006
Senate			
Average Incumbent Raised	$5,803,639	$7,212,068	$11,317,025
Average Challenger Raised	1,013,314	869,688	1,814,844
House			
Average Incumbent Raised	898,382	982,941	1,270,855
Average Challenger Raised	197,608	171,551	283,075

Source: Center for Responsive Politics; figures for 2002, 2004, and 2006 congressional elections.

district. The longer incumbents have occupied the office, the more favors they have performed and the larger their networks of grateful voters.

Campaign Strategies

Campaigning is largely a media activity, especially in presidential and congressional campaigns. Media campaigns are highly professionalized, relying on public relations and advertising specialists, professional fund raisers, media consultants, and pollsters. Campaign management involves techniques that strongly resemble those employed in marketing commercial products. Professional media campaign management includes developing a **campaign strategy**: compiling computerized mailing lists and invitations for fund-raising events; selecting a campaign theme and coming up with a desirable candidate image; monitoring the progress of the campaign with continual polling of the voters; producing television tapes for commercials, newspaper advertisements, signs, bumper stickers, and radio spots; selecting clothing and hairstyles for the candidate; writing speeches and scheduling appearances; and even planning the victory party.

Selecting a Theme

Finding the right theme or "message" for a campaign is essential; this effort is not greatly different from that of launching an advertising campaign for a new detergent. A successful theme or "message" is one that characterizes the candidate or the electoral choice confronting the voters. A campaign theme need not be controversial; indeed, it need not even focus on a specific issue. It might be as simple as "Change we can believe in"—an attempt to "package" the candidate as fresh, new, and believable.

Most media campaigns focus on candidates' personal qualities rather than on their stands on policy issues. Professional campaigns are based on the assumption that a candidate's "image" is the most important factor affecting voter choice. This image is largely devoid of issues, except in very general terms: for example, "tough on crime," "stands up to the special interests," "fights for the taxpayer," or "cares about you."

Negative Campaigning: "Defining" the Opponent

A media campaign also seeks to "define" the opponent in negative terms. The original negative TV ad is generally identified as the 1964 "Daisy Girl" commercial, aired by the Lyndon B. Johnson presidential campaign (see *Politics Up Close:* "Dirty Politics"). Negative ads can serve a purpose in exposing the record of an opponent. But **negative campaigning** risks an opponent's counterattack charges of "mudslinging," "dirty tricks," and "sleaze."

Research into the opponent's public and personal background ("oppo research") provides the data for negative campaigning. Previous speeches and writings can be mined for embarrassing or mean-spirited statements. The voting record of the opponent can be scrutinized for unpopular policy positions. Any evils that occurred during an opponent's term of office can be attributed to him or her, either directly ("She knew and conspired in it") or indirectly ("He should have known and done something about it"). Personal scandals or embarrassments can be developed as evidence of "character." If campaign managers fear that highly personal attacks on an opponent will backfire, they may choose to leak the information to reporters and try to avoid attribution of the story to themselves or their candidate.

Negative advertising is often blamed on television's dominant role in political campaigns. "The high cost of television means now that you have to go for the

You Are a Media Consultant to a Political Candidate

★ **campaign strategy**
Plan for a political campaign, usually including a theme, an attempt to define the opponent or the issues, and an effort to coordinate images and messages in news broadcasts and paid advertising.

★ **negative campaigning**
Speeches, commercials, or advertising attacking a political opponent during a campaign.

You Are a Campaign Manager: Navigating Negativity: Help Obama Handle Negative Attacks

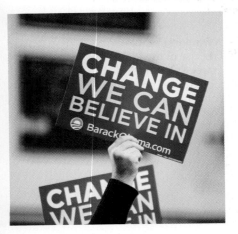

Illinois Senator Barack Obama chose the popular campaign theme of "change" and used the Internet and his campaign Web site, as this sign shows, to his advantage.

Television and Presidential Campaigns

Politics Up Close   Dirty Politics

Political campaigning frequently turns ugly with negative advertising that is vicious and personal. It is widely believed that television's focus on personal character and private lives—rather than on policy positions and governmental experience—encourages negative campaigning. But vicious personal attacks in political campaigns began long before television. They are nearly as old as the nation itself.

"If Jefferson is elected," proclaimed Yale's president in 1800, "the Bible will be burned and we will see our wives and daughters the victims of legal prostitution." In 1864 *Harper's Weekly* decried the "mudslinging" of the day, lamenting that President Abraham Lincoln was regularly referred to by his opponent as a "filthy storyteller, despot, liar, thief, braggart, buffoon, monster, Ignoramus Abe, robber, swindler, tyrant, fiend, butcher, and pirate."

Television's first memorable attack advertisement was the "Daisy Girl" commercial broadcast by Lyndon Johnson's presidential campaign in 1964 against his Republican opponent, Barry Goldwater. Although never mentioning Goldwater by name, the purpose of the ad was to "define" him as a warmonger who would plunge the world into a nuclear holocaust. The ad opens with a small, innocent girl standing in an open field plucking petals from a daisy and counting, "1, 2, 3 . . ." When she reaches 9, an ominous adult male voice begins a countdown: "10, 9, 8 . . ." as the camera closes in on the child's face. At "zero," a mushroom cloud appears, reflected in her eyes, and envelops the screen. Lyndon Johnson's voice is heard: "These are the stakes."

Senator Obama is dressed as a Somali Elder by Sheikh Mahmed Hassan, left, during his visit to Wajir in northeastern Kenya, near the Somali and Ethiopian borders, on August 27, 2006. Obama's deceased father, from whom he was estranged, was Kenyan.

"Attack ads" have multiplied in recent elections at all levels of government. John Kerry had volunteered for Vietnam following his graduation from Yale. In four months as commander of a small "swift boat" he won a Silver Star, a Bronze Star, and three Purple Hearts. But an independent group, Swift Boat Veterans for the Truth, challenged the legitimacy of Kerry's medals in a series of TV ads. Later, the Swift Boat group redirected their attacks toward Kerry's post-Vietnam behavior as a leader in the Vietnam Veterans against the War. These ads showed a young Kerry at a congressional hearing accusing his fellow veterans of terrible atrocities, "murdering civilians, cutting off heads, and burning villages." These ads corresponded to a slight drop in Kerry's poll numbers.

The Internet further facilitates dirty politics. The anonymity of the Net often inspires false and misleading postings. Perhaps the most offensive in 2008 was the recurring assertion that Barack Obama was a Muslim. These postings frequently referred to his middle name, Hussein, and later included a photo of him in African costume (from a 2006 trip to Kenya).

What are the effects of negative advertising? First of all, it works more often than not. Controlled experiments indicate that targets of attack ads are rated less positively by people who have watched these ads. But another effect of negative advertising is to make voters more cynical about politics and government in general. There is conflicting evidence about whether or not negative campaigning by opposing candidates reduces voter turnout.

What, if anything, can be done? Government regulation of political speech directly contravenes the 1st Amendment. American democracy has survived negative campaigning for a long time.

Frames from Lyndon Johnson's 1964 "Daisy Girl" commercial.

VOTE FOR PRESIDENT JOHNSON ON NOVEMBER 3.

Sources: Kathleen Hall Jamieson, *Dirty Politics, Deception, Distraction, and Democracy* (New York: Oxford University Press, 1992); also Stephen Ansolabehere et al., "Does Attack Advertising Demobilize the Electorate?" *American Political Science Review* 88 (December 1994): 829–38; Kim Fridkin Kahn and Patrick J. Kenney, "Do Negative Campaigns Mobilize or Suppress Turnout?" *American Political Science Review* 93 (December, 1999): 877–89.

A woman records a focus group in action at a California advertisement agency. Because of the two-way mirror, the video operator can see the focus group at work, but the persons in the room only see their own reflections.

jugular."[7] A political consultant summarized the current rules of political engagement as follows:

1. Advertise early if you have the money.

2. Go negative early, often, and right through Election Day, if necessary.

3. Appeal to the heart and gut, rather than to the head.

4. Define your opponent to the voters before he or she can define him/herself or you.

5. If attacked, hit back even harder.

6. It's easier to give voters a negative impression of your opponent than it is to improve their image of you.[8]

Using Focus Groups and Polling Focus group techniques can help in selecting campaign themes and identifying negative characteristics in opponents. A **focus group** is a small group of people brought together to view videotapes, listen to specific campaign appeals, and respond to particular topics and issues. Media professionals then develop a campaign strategy around "hot-button" issues—issues that generate strong responses by focus groups—and avoid themes or issues that fail to elicit much interest.

The results of focus group work can then be tested in wider polling. Polling is a central feature of professional campaigning. Serious candidates for national and statewide offices almost always employ their own private polling firms, distinct from the national survey organizations that supply the media with survey data. Initial polling is generally designed to determine candidates' name recognition—the extent to which the voters recognize the candidates—and whatever positive and negative images are already associated with their names.

Campaign polling is highly professionalized, with telephone banks, trained interviewers, and computer-assisted-telephone-interviewing (CATI) software that records and tabulates responses instantly and sends the results to campaign managers. In well-financed campaigns, polling is continual throughout the campaign, so that managers can assess progress on a daily basis. Polls chart the candidate's progress and, perhaps more important, help assess the effectiveness of specific campaign themes. If the candidate appears to be gaining support, the campaign stays on course. But if the candidate appears to be falling in the polls, the campaign manager comes under intense pressure to change themes and strategies. As election day nears, the pressure increases on the trailing candidate to "go negative"—to launch even more scathing attacks on the opponent.

Incumbent Versus Challenger Strategies Campaign strategies vary by the offices being sought, the nature of the times, and the imagination and inventiveness of the candidates' managers. But incumbency is perhaps the most important factor affecting the choice of a strategy. The challenger must attack the record of the incumbent, deplore current conditions in the city, state, or nation; and stress the need for change. Challengers are usually freer to take the offensive; incumbents must defend their record in office and either boast of accomplishments during their term or blame the opposition for blocking them. Challengers frequently opt for the "outsider" strategy, capitalizing on distrust and cynicism toward government.

★ **focus group**
In a political context, a small number of people brought together in a comfortable setting to discuss and respond to themes and issues, allowing campaign managers to develop and analyze strategies.

Think Again

Would you vote for a candidate who used negative ads to discredit an opponent?

News Management News management is the key to the media campaign. News coverage of the candidates is more credible in the eyes of viewers than paid advertisements. The campaign is planned to get the maximum favorable "free" exposure on the evening news. Each day a candidate must do something interesting and "newsworthy," that is, likely to be reported as news. Pictures are as important as words. Candidates must provide good **photo ops** for the media—opportunities where they can be photographed in settings or backgrounds that emphasize their themes. For example, if the theme is patriotism, then the candidate appears with war veterans, at a military base, or at a flag factory. If the theme is education, the candidate appears at a school; if crime control, then with police officers; if environmentalism, then in a wilderness area; if the economy, then at a closed factory or unemployment line or soup kitchen for the homeless.

Themes must be stated in concise and catchy **sound bites** that will register in the viewers' minds. Candidates now understand that the news media will select only a few seconds of an entire day of speech making for broadcast. The average length of a network news sound bite has shrunk from forty-five to seven seconds over the last thirty years. Thus extended or serious discussion of issues during a campaign is sacrificed to the need for one-liners on the nightly news. Indeed, if a campaign theme cannot fit on a bumper sticker, it is too complex.

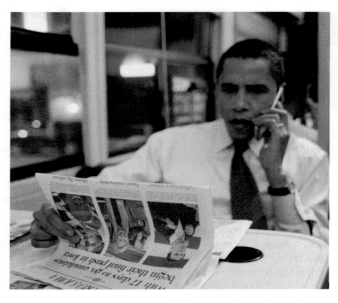

Senator Obama studies news accounts of the Democratic contest in Iowa, on December 18, 2007, in Sioux City. He, Senator Clinton, and Senator Edwards are pictured on the front page of the *Des Moines Register*.

★ **photo ops**
Staged opportunities for the media to photograph the candidate in a favorable setting.

★ **sound bites**
Concise and catchy phrases that attract media coverage.

Paid Advertising Television "spot" ads must be prepared prior to and during the campaign. They involve employing expensive television advertising and production firms well in advance of the campaign and keeping them busy revising and producing new ads throughout the campaign to respond to changing issues or opponents' attacks. Commercial advertising is the most expensive aspect of the campaign. Heavy costs are incurred in the production of the ads and in the purchase of broadcast time. The Federal Communications Commission (FCC) does not permit television networks or stations to charge more than standard commercial rates for political ads, but these rates are already high. Networks and stations are required to offer the same rates and times to all candidates, but if one candidate's campaign treasury is weak or exhausted, an opponent can saturate broadcast airtime.

Paid spot ads on television are usually only 15 or 30 seconds long, owing to the expense of television time. The result is that these ads pay relatively little attention to issues but rather try to appeal to the viewers' emotions. There is some evidence that simply showing enthusiasm for the candidate motivates participation and activates existing supporters to get out and vote, whereas appealing to fear is somewhat more effective in changing behavior, including swinging the votes of undecideds. However, advertis-

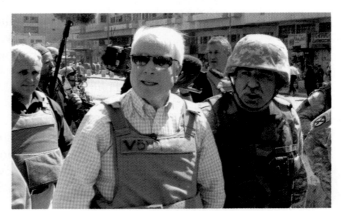

Photo Ops

Staged opportunities for the media to photograph a candidate or politician in a favorable setting, such as this picture of Senator McCain visiting the popular Shorja market in central Baghdad, Iraq, on April 1, 2007.

Paid Media

Advertising that candidates buy in the media, carefully targeted to particular demographics, so as to reach and persuade viewers of their qualities for office. The picture shows a frame from Senator Hillary Rodham Clinton's television ad for her health care plan.

★ **mobilize**

In politics, to activate supporters to work for candidates and turn out on Election Day.

You Are a Campaign Manager: Voter Mobilization and Suppression: Political Dirty Tricks or Fair Games?

Think Again

Are high campaign costs discouraging good people from becoming candidates?

ing campaigns, whether they are directed at inspiring enthusiasm for the candidate or fear of a candidate's opponent, must be kept going over time. Bursts of emotion are likely to fade if the ad campaign does not keep the drumbeat going.[9] An accumulation of short spot ads, all aimed at the same theme, can have a meaningful impact on the course of an election.

Television ads are much maligned by scholars and commentators. And it is easy to identify particular ads that are silly, offensive, uninformative, and even misleading. Nevertheless, there is increasing evidence that paid political advertising does create a somewhat more attentive, more informed, and more-likely-to-vote citizenry. Moreover, paid ads appear to affect people with less political information and less interest in politics more than the better informed and more active citizens. Thus, campaign ads are often petty, sometimes offensive, and seldom uplifting. But they do serve an important political function.[10]

Free Airtime All candidates seek free airtime on news and talk shows, but the need to gain free exposure is much greater for underfunded candidates. They must go to extremes in devising media events, and they must encourage and participate in free televised debates. The debate format is particularly well suited for candidates who cannot match their opponents in paid commercial advertising. Thus well-funded and poorly funded candidates may jockey over the number and times of public debates.

The Effects of Campaigning Campaigns serve primarily to activate a candidate's supporters—to ensure that they go to the polls on Election Day. They serve secondarily to try to persuade undecideds to become supporters. Campaigns are designed to **mobilize** core supporters more than to persuade undecideds or opponents to vote for candidates.[11] Undecideds must be both persuaded *and* mobilized to vote—a more difficult task than simply activating core supporters. Observers may wonder why candidates appear before partisan crowds, visit with supporters, and advertise in areas that appear to support them anyway. "Core party voters are more likely to receive and respond to campaign information, implying that successful campaigns are those that mobilize their supporters enough to translate their natural predispositions into actual votes."

How Much Does It Cost to Get Elected?

Getting elected to public office has never been more expensive (see *Politics Up Close:* "A Brief History of Money in Politics"). The professionalization of campaigning and the heavy costs of television advertising drive up the costs of running for office. Campaign costs are rising with each election cycle (see Figure 8.1).

Congressional Costs The typical winning campaign for a seat in the House of Representatives costs over $1 million. House members seeking to retain their seats must raise this amount *every two years*. The typical winning campaign for a U.S. Senate seat costs over $10 million. But Senate campaign costs vary a great deal from state to state; Senate seats in the larger states may cost $25 million to $50 million or more.

The upward spiral in congressional campaign spending continued through 2006 with over $1.5 *billion* spent by all House and Senate candidates. New York's high-profile Senate race in 2002 between Democrat Hillary Clinton and Republican Rick Lazio attracted a combined $85 million in contributions from across the nation. A new individual spending record was set by multimillionaire Democrat

Politics Up Close   A Brief History of Money in Politics

In 1757, in his race for a seat in the Virginia House of Burgesses, George Washington was reprimanded for purchasing and distributing more than a quart of whiskey per voter in his district. But for the first 50 years or so of American independence, campaign costs were relatively low. The population was small, and only white males who owned property—about one of every five adults—were allowed to vote. But as the population grew, and property requirements were abolished, campaign costs rose. By 1840 the practice of buying votes was well established in the nation's cities.

Rising campaign costs in the early nineteenth century required candidates to begin soliciting funds from businesses, industries, and wealthy individuals. These contributors, in turn, increasingly sought favors from a government that was becoming more and more involved in economic matters. During the Civil War, Abraham Lincoln wrote:

> As a result of the war, corporations have become enthroned, and an era of corruption in high places will follow. The money power of the country will endeavor to prolong its rule by preying on the prejudices of the people until all wealth is concentrated in a few hands.

During the industrial revolution following the Civil War, historian Richard Hofstadter describes what may have been the high-water mark of corruption in American politics: "Capitalists seeking land grants, tariffs, bounties, favorable currency policies, freedom from regulatory legislation and economic reform, supplied campaign funds, fees, and bribes, and plied politicians with investment opportunities." Banks, railroads, and oil and mining companies became the major sources of campaign cash in national politics; in local politics, campaigns were funded by utilities, saloons, gambling halls, houses of prostitution, and racetracks. According to historian George Thayer, "Standard Oil did everything to the Pennsylvania Legislature except refine it." The presidential election of 1896 set a record for campaign spending that would not be surpassed in equivalent dollars until the 1970s. U.S. Senator Marcus Alonzo Hanna, general counsel for John D. Rockefeller's Standard Oil Company, raised between $6 and $7 million for the winner, Republican William McKinley, while his Democratic opponent William Jennings Bryan spent only about a half million dollars.

Political campaign costs rose again following the 17th Amendment (1913), which instituted the direct election of U.S. senators; the 19th Amendment, which won women the right to vote; and the expanding use of primary elections to choose party candidates. Fortunately for politicians who began to need more campaign money to reach more voters, the New Deal vastly increased government involvement in the economy and thereby raised the incentives for business interests to fork over more money to ensure that their interests would be protected in policy making. Labor unions became a major source of campaign funds in 1936 when the newly formed Congress of Industrial Organizations (CIO) contributed a half million dollars to Franklin D. Roosevelt's presidential campaign.

During the 1950s and 1960s, each of the major parties enjoyed the support of wealthy "super-donors"—the Mellons and Rockefellers on the Republican side and the Kennedys and Harrimans on the Democratic side. But a turning point in campaign finance history occurred after the Watergate revelations of secret donations to the 1972 Nixon reelection campaign, especially the $2 million individual contribution by insurance magnate Clement Stone. The result was the passage of the Federal Election Campaign Act, creating the Federal Elections Commission (FEC) and placing limits on direct campaign contributions to candidates by individuals and organizations.

But the reforms envisioned by the act were quickly undermined by an explosion in the number of political action committees, vast increases in unlimited "soft money" contributions to the parties, and the U.S. Supreme Court decision in *Buckley v. Valeo* declaring that individuals (and by implication independent organizations) may spend as much as they wish to express their own views and advance their own candidacies. The result was a skyrocketing of political campaign spending and an even greater dependence on big money.

The Bipartisan Campaign Finance Reform Act of 2002 was designed to close "loopholes" in the earlier reform act. It banned unlimited soft money contributions to the parties, and limited individual contributions to candidates to $2,000 per election ($2,300 in 2008). But contributions to independent organizations ("527s") remained unregulated. These groups were prohibited from coordinating their ads with candidates or parties, but they continue to play a major role in elections (see *Politics Up Close*: "527s: Evading Campaign Finance Reform" on page 267).

Source: Excerpted from *A Brief History of Money in Politics,* Center for Responsive Politics, Washington, D.C., 1999.

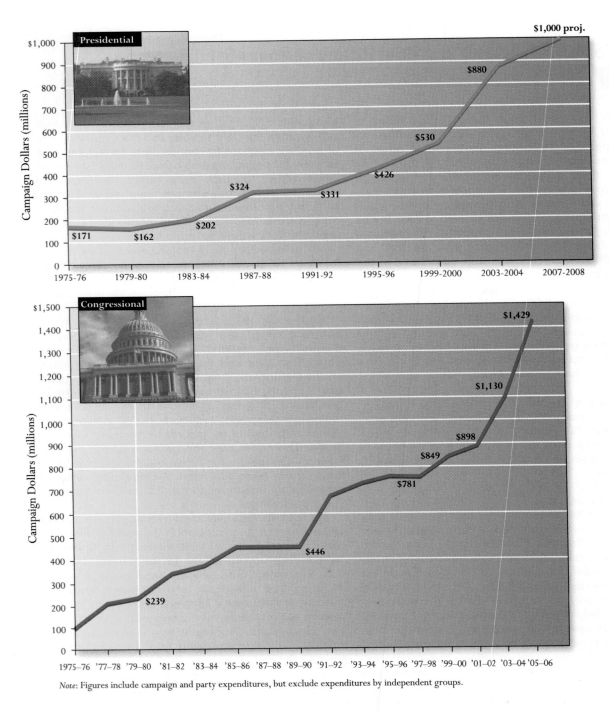

Figure *8.1* Sparing No Expense: The Growing Costs of Campaigns

Source: Data from Center for Responsive Politics, www.opensecrets.org

Jon Corzine in his successful bid for a U.S. Senate seat from New Jersey in 2002; Corzine spent about $60 million of his *own* money.

Spending for House seats also varies a great deal from one race to another. In nearly two-thirds of all House districts, one candidate (almost always the incumbent) outspends his or her opponent by a factor of ten to one or more. Only about 16 percent of House campaigns are financially competitive; that is, neither candidate spends more than twice as much as his or her opponent. In the remaining

84 percent of House campaigns, one candidate spends more than twice as much as his or her opponent.[12]

Raising Campaign Cash

Fund raising to meet the high costs of campaigning is the most important hurdle for any candidate for public office. Campaign funds come from a wide range of sources—small donors, big donors, interest group PACs of every stripe, labor unions, even taxpayers. In some cases, candidates pay their own way (or most of it). More typically, however, candidates for high public office—particularly incumbents—have become adept at running their campaigns using other people's money, not their own.

Public Money Presidential campaigns can be partly funded with taxpayer money through an income tax checkoff system. Each year taxpayers are urged to check the box on their tax forms that authorizes $3 of their tax payment to go to the Federal Elections Commission for distribution to presidential candidates' campaigns as well as to political party conventions. However, taxpayers are becoming less and less willing to allow their tax monies to go into political campaigning (even though the $3 checkoff does not add to the taxpayers' total taxes). Only about 11 percent of taxpayers currently check the box. The Presidential Election Campaign Fund has been in jeopardy of not having enough money to make its promised payments to the candidates and parties.

Presidential candidates may opt out of taxpayer-financed funding if they choose to do so. This allows them to spend as much money as they wish, but they receive no public money. Nonetheless, all presidential candidates, and all candidates for Congress, must abide by federal campaign finance laws (see below).

Small Donations Millions of Americans participate in campaign financing, either by giving directly to candidates or the parties or by giving to political action committees, which then distribute their funds to candidates. For members of Congress, small donors typically make up less than 20 percent of their campaign funds. The proportion is higher for presidential candidates. For donations under $200, contributors' names and addresses are recorded only by the candidates and parties, not passed along to the Federal Election Commission as part of the public record.

Large Individual Donors "Fat cats" are the preferred donors. These are the donors whose names are on the candidates' Rolodexes. They are the ones in attendance when the president, the Speaker of the House, or other top political dignitaries travel around the country doing fund-raisers. They are also the ones who are wined, dined, prodded, and cajoled in a seemingly ceaseless effort by the parties and the candidates to raise funds for the next election.

In its 2002 campaign finance reform legislation, Congress raised the maximum individual contribution to federal candidates to $2,000 (up from $1,000 in the 2000 election). The maximum contribution is indexed to inflation; in 2008 it was $2,300. Fat cats are expected to give the maximum, and indeed even more. They can do so by giving their maximum $2,300 once in the primary election and a second time in the general election. And their spouses can do the same. And, of course, they can also give to the parties and to independent political organizations committed to helping their preferred candidates.

Campaign Finance Regulations

Candidate Self-Financing Candidates for federal office also pump millions into their own campaigns. There are no federal restrictions on the amount of money individuals can spend on their own campaign.[13] Senate and House candidates

Politics Up Close   **How to Spend $10 Million on a Political Campaign**

How do you spend $10 million dollars on a Senate campaign? It may sound like a lot of money, but it can disappear quickly in a heated Senate campaign. Indeed, $11 million is the *average* expenditure of winning senators.

Television advertising is the biggest cost. It may consume 40 to 65 percent of the campaign budget, depending on how many "media markets" (separate cities with groups of TV stations) are in the state and how expensive television time is in each market. Staff salaries may consume a good portion of the budget. Experienced professionals and/or professional campaign manage-

ment firms do not come cheap; volunteers are helpful, but no match for professionals in knowing how to run a campaign. Polling firms are needed throughout the campaign to keep track of progress or decline and to continue to evaluate the effectiveness of campaign themes, policy positions, negative hits on the opponent, and so on. Travel is another large item, whether the candidate and staff fly by private jet or rent a bus. Lawyers and accountants must supervise spending, submit FEC reports, and see that everyone adheres to campaign laws. A typical Senate campaign budget follows.

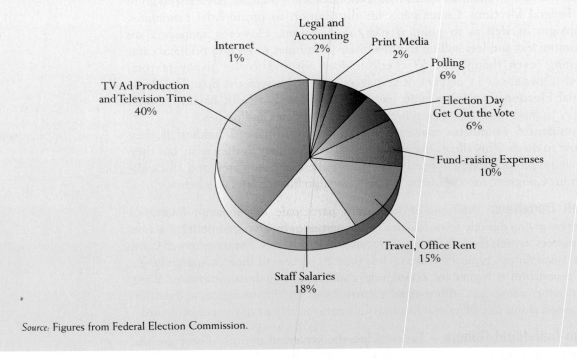

Source: Figures from Federal Election Commission.

★ **issue ads**
Ads that advocate policy positions rather than explicitly supporting or opposing particular candidates.

Think Again

Do political campaign contributions have too much influence on elections and government policy?

frequently put $50,000 to $100,000 or more of their own money into their campaigns, through outright gifts or personal loans. (Candidates who loan themselves the money to run are able to pay themselves back later from outside contributions.)

Issue Ads   Issue ads advocate policy positions rather than explicitly advising voters to cast their ballots for or against particular candidates. But most of these ads leave little doubt about which candidate is being supported or targeted. The Bipartisan Campaign Reform Act of 2002 bans issue ads 60 days before a general election and 30 days before a primary election. However, there are no dollar limits on the size of contributions to sponsoring groups (often referred to as 527s from the section of the Internal Revenue code under which they operate).

What Do Contributors "Buy"?

What does money buy in politics? A cynic might say that money can buy anything—for example, special appropriations for public works directly benefiting the contributor, special tax breaks, special federal regulations. Public opinion views big-money contributions as a major problem in the American political system. Scandals involving the direct (quid pro quo) purchase of special favors, privileges, exemptions, and treatments have been common enough in the past, and they are likely to continue in the future. But campaign contributions are rarely made in the form of a direct trade-off for a favorable vote. Such an arrangement risks exposure as bribery and may be prosecuted under the law. Campaign contributions are more likely to be made without any *explicit* quid pro quo but rather with a general understanding that the contributor has confidence in the candidate's good judgment on issues directly affecting the contributor. The contributor expects the candidate to be smart enough to figure out how to vote in order to keep the contributions coming in the future.

Self-Made Man
New Jersey Governor Jon Corzine at his inauguration in 2006. The multimillionaire Corzine still holds the record for a self-financed U.S. Senate campaign. There are no limits on the amounts of their personal money that candidates can spend on their own campaigns.

The Big-Money Contributors   Big-money contributors—businesses, unions, professional associations—pump millions into presidential and congressional elections. Figure 8.2 lists the top fifty contributors to candidates and parties from 1989 through 2004. Note that union contributions are heavily weighted toward Democrats, as are the contributions of the Association of Trial Lawyers. Businesses and business associations tend to split their contributions between the parties, but Republicans usually get the largest share.

Buying Access to Policy Makers   Large contributors expect to be able to call or visit and present their views directly to "their" officeholders. At the presidential level, major contributors who cannot get a meeting with the president expect to meet at least with high-level White House staff or cabinet officials. At the congressional level, major contributors usually expect to meet or speak directly with their representative or senator. Members of Congress boast of responding to letters, calls, or visits by any constituent, but contributors can expect a more immediate and direct response than noncontributors can. Lobbyists for contributing organizations routinely expect and receive a hearing from members of Congress.

Political Action Committees   Political action committees (PACs) are the most reliable source of money for reelection campaigns in Congress. Corporations and unions are not allowed to contribute directly to campaigns from corporate or union funds, but they may form PACs to seek contributions from managers and stockholders and their families, or union workers and their families. PACs are organized not only by corporations and unions but also by trade and professional associations, environmental groups, and liberal and conservative ideological groups. The wealthiest PACs are based in Washington, D.C. (see "PAC Power" in Chapter 9). PACs are very cautious; their job is to get a maximum return on their contributions, winning influence and goodwill with as many lawmakers as possible in Washington. There's no return on their investment if their recipients lose at the polls; therefore most PACs—particularly business PACs— give most of their dollars to incumbents seeking reelection.

★ **political action committees (PACs)** Organizations that solicit and receive campaign contributions from corporations, unions, trade associations, and ideological and issue-oriented groups, and their members, then distribute these funds to political candidates.

Individual Contributors   Most individual contributors are ideologically motivated. They make their contributions based on their perception of the ideological position of the candidate (or perhaps their perception of the candidate's

Rank	Contributor	Total Contributions (millions)	% Dem.	% Rep.	Rank	Contributor	Total Contributions (millions)	% Dem.	% Rep.
1.	American Federation of State/County/Municipal Employees	$34.9	98%	1%	25.	National Rifle Assn	$14.3	13%	86%
					26.	AFL-CIO	$14.1	88%	11%
					27.	American Bankers Assn	$13.8	39%	60%
2.	National Assn of Realtors	$24.1	50%	49%	28.	Time Warner	$13.4	70%	28%
3.	National Education Assn	$23.4	86%	13%	29.	SBC Communications	$13.0	34%	65%
4.	Assn of Trial Lawyers of America	$23.3	89%	10%	30.	Verizon Communications	$12.6	38%	61%
5.	Communications Workers of America	$22.0	98%	1%	31.	BellSouth Corp	$12.4	43%	56%
					32.	Microsoft Corp	$12.3	58%	41%
6.	Service Employees International Union	$21.9	88%	11%	33.	National Beer Wholesalers Assn	$12.2	30%	69%
7.	Intl Brotherhood of Electrical Workers	$21.5	96%	3%	34.	EMILY's List	$11.8	100%	0%
8.	Carpenters & Joiners Union	$21.0	68%	31%	35.	Sheet Metal Workers Union	$11.7	97%	2%
9.	Teamsters Union	$20.8	85%	13%	36.	Ernst & Young	$11.7	31%	67%
10.	American Medical Assn	$20.6	28%	71%	37.	Lockheed Martin	$11.5	39%	60%
11.	Altria Group (Philip Morris)	$20.6	41%	57%	38.	JP Morgan Chase & Co	$11.5	49%	50%
12.	FedEx Corp	$20.5	33%	66%	39.	RJR Nabisco/ RJ Reynolds Tobacco	$10.9	11%	88%
13.	Laborers Union	$20.5	86%	13%	40.	American Dental Assn	$10.9	43%	56%
14.	United Auto Workers	$19.8	98%	0%	41.	Morgan Stanley	$10.8	34%	65%
15.	AT&T	$19.5	47%	52%	42.	Blue Cross/Blue Shield	$10.8	42%	57%
16.	American Federation of Teachers	$19.3	99%	0%	43.	American Hospital Assn	$10.7	44%	55%
17.	Goldman Sachs	$18.6	50%	49%	44.	National Assn of Insurance & Financial Advisors	$10.6	37%	62%
18.	Machinists & Aerospace Workers Union	$18.4	98%	0%	45.	General Electric	$10.6	46%	53%
19.	United Food & Commercial Workers Union	$18.3	98%	1%	46.	American Institute of CPAs	$10.4	37%	62%
					47.	Union Pacific Corp	$10.1	22%	77%
20.	Citigroup Inc	$17.1	48%	50%	48.	Credit Union National Assn	$10.1	43%	56%
21.	United Parcel Service	$16.9	29%	70%	49.	Deloitte Touche Tohmatsu	$10.1	28%	71%
22.	National Auto Dealers Assn	$16.5	29%	70%	50.	United Steelworkers of America	$10.1	97%	2%
23.	National Assn of Home Builders	$14.9	38%	61%					
24.	National Assn of Letter Carriers	$14.6	71%	27%					

Figure *8.2* Who Gives What?: Fifty Big-Money Contributors, 1989–2004

Source: Data from Center for Responsive Politics, www.opensecrets.org

opponent). They may make contributions to congressional candidates across the country who share their policy views. Liberal and conservative networks of contributors can be contacted through specialized mailing lists—for example, liberals through television producer Norman Lear's People for the American Way. Feminists have been effective in soliciting individual contributions across the country and funneling them very early in a campaign to women candidates through EMILY's List. Ideological contributors may only get the satisfaction of knowing that they are financially backing their cause in the political process. Some contributors simply enjoy the opportunity to be near and to be seen with high-ranking politicians. Politicians pose for photos with contributors, who later frame the photos and hang them in their office to impress their friends, associates, and customers. Contributors are disproportionately high-income, older people with strong partisan views (see Figure 8.3).

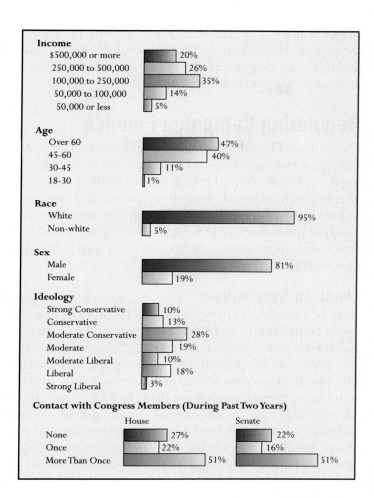

Income
- $500,000 or more — 20%
- 250,000 to 500,000 — 26%
- 100,000 to 250,000 — 35%
- 50,000 to 100,000 — 14%
- 50,000 or less — 5%

Age
- Over 60 — 47%
- 45-60 — 40%
- 30-45 — 11%
- 18-30 — 1%

Race
- White — 95%
- Non-white — 5%

Sex
- Male — 81%
- Female — 19%

Ideology
- Strong Conservative — 10%
- Conservative — 13%
- Moderate Conservative — 28%
- Moderate — 19%
- Moderate Liberal — 10%
- Liberal — 18%
- Strong Liberal — 3%

Contact with Congress Members (During Past Two Years)

	House	Senate
None	27%	22%
Once	22%	16%
More Than Once	51%	51%

Figure *8.3*

Who's Giving?: Characteristics of Individual Political Contributors

Contributors to political campaigns generally are older and have higher incomes than most Americans. Whites and males contribute more than blacks and females, and conservatives contribute more than liberals.

Source: John Green, Paul Herrnson, Lynda Powell, and Clyde Wilcox, "Individual Congressional Campaign Contributors," press release, June 9, 1998, Center for Responsive Politics, www.opensecrets.org Reprinted by permission.

Buying Government Assistance

Many large contributors do business with government agencies. They expect any representative or senator they have supported to intervene on their behalf with these agencies, sometimes acting to cut red tape, ensure fairness, and expedite their cases, and other times pressuring the agencies for a favorable decision. Officials in the White House or the cabinet may also be expected to intervene on behalf of major contributors. There is little question raised when the intervention merely expedites consideration of a contributor's case, but pressure to bend rules or regulations to get favorable decisions raises ethical problems for officeholders (see "Congressional Ethics" in Chapter 10). Corporations that do business with government agencies, and those that are heavily regulated by government agencies, may make contributions simply to "flex their muscles"—to signal bureaucrats that if they wished to do so, they could fight any agency's specific decisions.[14]

Fund-Raising Chores

Fund raising occupies more of a candidate's time than any other campaign activity. Candidates must personally contact as many individual contributors as possible. They work late into the evening on the telephone with potential contributors. Fund-raising dinners, cocktail parties, barbecues, fish frys, and so on, are scheduled nearly every day of a campaign. The candidate is expected to appear personally to "press the flesh" of big contributors. Movie and rock stars and other assorted celebrities may also be asked to appear at fund-raising affairs to generate attendance. Dinners may run to

Senator Hillary Rodham Clinton receives a kiss and a hug from British musician Elton John at a April 9, 2008, fundraising concert for her campaign in New York.

$2,000 a plate in presidential affairs, although often less in Senate or House campaigns. Tickets may be "bundled" to well-heeled individual contributors or sold in blocks to organizations. Fund-raising techniques are limited only by the imagination of the campaign manager.

Regulating Campaign Finance

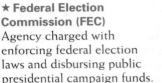

★ **Federal Election Commission (FEC)**
Agency charged with enforcing federal election laws and disbursing public presidential campaign funds.

SIMULATION

You Are a Campaign Manager: McCain Navigates Campaign Financing: Rules and Trends Regarding the "Mother's Milk" of Politics

The **Federal Election Commission (FEC)** is responsible for enforcing limits on individual and organizational contributions to all federal elections, administering the public funding of presidential campaigns, and requiring full disclosure of all campaign financial activity in presidential and congressional elections. Enforcement of these federal election and campaign finance laws lies in the hands of the 6-member FEC. Appointed by the president to serve staggered 6-year terms, commission members are traditionally split 3 to 3 between Republicans and Democrats.

Limits on Contributions The FEC now limits direct individual contributions to a candidate's campaign to $2,300 per election (in 2008) and organizational contributions to $5,000 per election. But there are many ways in which individuals and organizations can legally surmount these limits. Contributors may give a candidate $2,300 for each member of their family in a primary election and then another $2,300 per member in the general election. Organizations may generate much more than the $5,000 limit by bundling (combining) $2,300 additional contributions from individual members. (Soft-money contributions—unregulated amounts given to the national parties officially for "party building" but actually used in support of candidates—were banned in 2002.) Independent organizations can spend whatever they wish in order to promote their political views, so long as these organizations do so "without cooperation or consultation with the candidate of his or her campaign." Finally, as noted, individuals may spend as much of their own money on their own campaigns as they wish.

Candidates often seek the support of celebrities so as to appeal to the public and raise campaign money. Oprah Winfrey embraces Senator Barack Obama at a rally on December 8, 2007, in Des Moines, Iowa. Michelle Obama, the candidate's wife, looks on.

Reporting By law, every candidate for federal office must file periodic reports with the FEC detailing both the income and the expenditures of his or her campaign. Individual contributors who give an aggregate of $200 or more must be identified by name, address, occupation, and employer. All PAC and party contributions, no matter how large or small, must also be itemized. In addition, PACs themselves must file reports with the FEC at least four times a year, detailing both the contributions received by the PAC and the names of candidates and other groups that received the PAC's donations.

Federal Funding of Presidential Elections Federal funding, financed by the $3 checkoff box on individual income tax returns, is available to presidential candidates in primary and general elections, as well as to major-party nominating conventions. Candidates seeking the nomination in presidential primary elections can qualify for federal funds by raising $5,000 from private contributions no greater than $250 each in each of twenty states. In the general election, Democratic and Republican nominees are funded equally at levels determined by the FEC. In order to receive federal funding, presidential candidates must agree to FEC limits on their campaign spending in both primary and general elections.

Federal funding pays about one-third of the primary campaign costs of presidential candidates and all the *official* presidential campaign organization costs in the general election. The parties also receive federal funds for their nominating conventions.

Campaign Finance Reform   Unregulated **soft-money** contributions to the parties grew rapidly during the 1990s. These contributions represented a giant black hole in the original Federal Election Campaign Act of 1974. Contributions made directly to a candidate's campaign—hard money contributions—were limited (originally to $1,000). But individuals, organizations, corporations, and unions could contribute as much as they wanted to the Democratic and Republican national parties. These contributions were supposed to be for party building, voter registration, getting out the vote, and so on, but in fact went into candidate campaigning.

In the 2000 Republican presidential primaries, U.S. Senator John McCain made campaign finance reform his principal issue. He surprised the Republican Party leaders by defeating George W. Bush in the New Hampshire primary that year. Bush and both Democratic and Republican leaders decided to jump on the campaign finance reform bandwagon, although with little real enthusiasm. In 2002 a somewhat reluctant Congress finally passed the Bipartisan Campaign Finance Reform Act (see Table 8.2).

Among other things, this act eliminated soft-money contributions to the parties; increased the individual contribution limit to candidates' campaigns from $1,000 to $2,000 (now $2,300); prohibited independent groups from coordinating their campaign spending with candidates or parties; and did not allow independent groups to mention the name of a candidate in their issue ads.

But contributions to nonprofit independent groups remain unregulated. Big money contributors who can no longer provide large amounts of cash to candidates or to parties *can* establish nonprofit independent groups (known as "527s," referring to their Internal Revenue Service code) to accept big contributions to enable them to produce and broadcast campaign advertisements (see *Politics Up Close* "527s: Evading Campaign Finance Reform").

★ soft money
Previously unregulated contributions to the parties, now prohibited; individual contributions to parties now limited (see Table 8.2).

The Supreme Court and Campaign Finance   The U.S. Supreme Court has recognized that limitations on campaign *contributions* help further a compelling government interest—"preventing corruption and the appearance of corruption" in election campaigns. But the Court has been reluctant to allow governments to limit campaign *expenditures*, because paying to express political views is necessary in the exercise of free speech. In an important early case, *Buckley v. Valeo* (1976), the Court held that limiting a candidate's campaign expenditures that are made from his own personal funds violated the 1st Amendment's guarantee of free speech.

Later, when called upon to consider the constitutionality of the Bipartisan Campaign Reform Act (BCRA), the Court upheld limitations on contributions directly to candidates and to national parties. It also upheld limits on "soft-money" contributions to state and local parties, recognizing that these provisions were designed to prevent circumventions of valid prohibitions on campaign contributions. And the Court also upheld a prohibition on spending for "electioneering communications" by individuals and interest groups that

Table 8.2 Campaign Finance Rules, 2008

General

All federal election contributions and expenditures must be reported to the Federal Election Commission, which may investigate and prosecute violators.

All contributions over $200 must be reported, with name, address, and occupation of contributor.

No foreign contributions can be made.

There are no restrictions on how much individuals may spend on their own campaigns (*Buckley v. Valeo*).

No large contributions (soft money) may be made to the national parties; party contributions by individuals and committees are limited.

Presidential Primaries

Federal matching funds are available for money raised by candidates from individual donors giving $250 or less. To be eligible, the primary candidate must raise $5,000 in each of twenty states in contributions of $250 or less.

Presidential Elections

The federal government will pay the campaign costs of major party candidates (and the costs of party conventions) if the candidates agree to FEC limits. Candidates may opt out of public financing, rely on private contributions, and exceed FEC expenditure limits. (In 2008 Barack Obama rejected public financing.)

Limits on Contributions

Donor	Candidate	PAC	National Party	State/Local Party	Special Limits
Individual	$2,300[a]	$5,000	$28,500	$10,000	$108,300 (Biennial total)
National Party	5,000	5,000	—	—	—
State/Local Party	5,000	5,000	—	—	—
PAC	5,300	5,000	28,500	10,000	—

Millionaire Amendment

If a candidate spends more of his own money beyond specified thresholds (e.g., $350,000 for House candidates), contribution limits for his or her opponent are tripled.

Independent Group Expenditures

Independent individuals or groups airing TV or radio ads must not coordinate with candidates or parties in order to avoid contribution limits.

[a]Contribution limit for 2008. Limits rise with inflation.

Note: This table summarizes the Bipartisan Campaign Finance Reform Act of 2002.

Source: FEC, 2008.

are controlled or coordinated with parties or candidates. The Court struck down an attempt by Congress to prohibit children from making campaign contributions.

But still later, the Supreme Court reconsidered the BCRA's provisions limiting individual and organization electioneering communications. The Court distinguished between "express advocacy" on behalf of a candidate or party and "issue ads" that are *not* the functional equivalent of express advocacy. (In other words, ads that do not urge viewers or listeners to vote for or against a particular candidate or party.) "When it comes to defining what speech qualifies as the functional equivalent of express advocacy, the Court should give the benefit of the doubt to speech, not censorship." The effect of the decision is to permit political contributors to support organizations unaffiliated with a candidate or party, including nonprofit "527" organizations, that air television ads not expressly endorsing a candidate right up to election day.

These decisions not only affect federal campaign finance laws but also the laws of state and local jurisdictions. The Supreme Court has also held that a state law that places too low a limit on how much individuals can contribute to a candidate or party violates the 1st Amendment's guarantee of free speech. When

Politics Up Close   527s: Evading Campaign Finance Reform

The Bipartisan Campaign Finance Reform Act was supposed to eliminate big money contributions from national elections. After years of struggle, reformers thought they had eliminated loopholes that allow individuals, corporations, and labor unions to pump millions of dollars into presidential and congressional campaigns.

But campaign cash is like the Pillsbury doughboy: Push it in one place and it pops out in another. The act banned big soft-money contributions to the parties. But Congress did not block individuals or nonprofit independent groups from spending as much as they want to broadcast their own views. So early in the 2004 election campaign, big-money contributors and politically savvy consultants, especially in the Democratic Party, began to build a network of nonprofit organizations—organizations into which they could funnel millions of dollars and expect to see them broadcast issue ads in favor of their candidates during the campaign. These organizations became popularly known as "527s," in reference to the section in the U.S. Tax Code authorizing them.

George Soros, one of the world's richest men, has given away billions to promote democracy in former Soviet bloc nations, including his birthplace, Hungary. In addition, Soros funds a wide variety of liberal causes through his Open Society Institute. He has given millions to a series of liberal organizations. Among the recipients of his political generosity:

★ MoveOn, an organization originally formed by Silicon Valley entrepreneurs to defend President Bill Clinton against impeachment. It now boasts having over 3 million members and claims to be "one of the largest Political Action Committees in the country."
★ Americans Coming Together (ACT), an organization formed by officers of the AFL-CIO, the Sierra Club, and the Service Employees International Union "to mobilize voters and elect progressive candidates across all America."
★ America Votes, created by former Texas Gov. Ann Richards and her daughter to coordinate get-out-the-vote of anti-George Bush groups. Now a "grassroots voter mobilization effort" for liberal Democratic Candidates.
★ Partnership for America's Families, another group formed by the Service Employees International Union to get "progressive" voters to the polls in big cities.
★ The Media Fund, organized to raise big money to buy TV and radio ads for Democratic Candidates.

By 2008, "527s" were broadcasting TV ads favoring both presidential candidates. Yet these ads did not mention the names of candidates in order to avoid campaign contribution limits.

Vermont placed a $200 limit on campaign contributions for offices in that state, the Court held that limits could not be so low as to prevent challengers from mounting effective campaigns. Vermont's limits were held to be "disproportionately severe."

The Presidential Campaign: The Primary Race

The phrase *presidential fever* refers to the burning political ambition required to seek the presidency. The grueling presidential campaign is a test of strength, character, endurance, and determination. It is physically exhausting and mentally and emotionally draining. Every aspect of the candidates' lives—and the lives of their families—is subject to microscopic inspection by the news media. Most of this coverage is critical, and much of it is unfair. Yet candidates are expected to handle it all with grace and humor, from the earliest testing of the waters through a full-fledged campaign.

Comparing Political Campaigns

Media Mentions   Politicians with presidential ambitions may begin by promoting presidential *mentions* by media columnists and commentators. The media help to identify "presidential timber" years in advance of a presidential race simply by drawing up lists of potential candidates, commenting on their qualifications, and speculating about their intentions. Mentions are likely to come to prominent governors or senators who start making speeches outside their states, who grab the media spotlight on a national issue, or who simply let it be known to the media "off the record" that they are considering a presidential race. Visiting New Hampshire and Iowa and giving speeches there is viewed as "testing the waters" and a signal of presidential ambitions.

Presidential Credentials   Political experience as vice president, governor, U.S. senator, or member of Congress not only inspires presidential ambition but also provides vital experience in political campaigning. However, virtually all presidential candidates testify that the presidential arena is far more challenging than politics at any other level. The experience of running for and holding high public office appears to be a political requirement for the presidency. Some presidential aspirants have tried to make a virtue of their lack of previous political office holding, no doubt hoping to attract support from the many Americans who disdain "politics as usual." But for over a century no major party nominee for president has not previously held office as vice president, governor, U.S. senator, or member of Congress except World War II hero General Dwight D. Eisenhower.

The Decision to Run   The decision to run for president involves complex personal and political calculations. Ambition to occupy the world's most powerful office must be weighed against the staggering costs—emotional as well as financial—of a presidential campaign.

Serious planning, organizing, and fund raising must begin at least 2 years before the general election. A staff must be assembled—campaign managers and strategists, fund raisers, media experts, pollsters, issues advisers and speechwriters, lawyers and accountants—and supporters must be identified in key states throughout the nation. Paid and volunteer workers must be assembled (see Figure 8.4). Leaders among important interest groups must be contacted. A general campaign strategy must be developed, an organization put in place, and several millions of dollars in campaign contributions pledged in advance of the race. Often the decision to run hinges on whether initial pledges of campaign contributions appear adequate. The serious candidate must be able to anticipate contributions of $100 million or more for primary elections. Most of this work must be accomplished in the preprimary season— the months after Labor Day of the year preceding the election, and before the first primary election.

A Strategy for the Primaries   The road to the White House consists of two separate races: the primary elections and caucuses leading to the Democratic and Republican party nominations, and the general election. Each of these races requires a separate strategy. The primary race requires an appeal to party activists and the more ideologically motivated primary voters in key states. The general election requires an appeal to the less partisan, less attentive, more ideologically moderate general election voters. Thus the campaign strategy developed to win the nomination must give way after the national conventions to a strategy to win the November general election.

Primary Campaigns   Primary campaigns come in different varieties. An incumbent president with no serious competition from within his own party can safely glide through his party's primaries, saving campaign money for the general

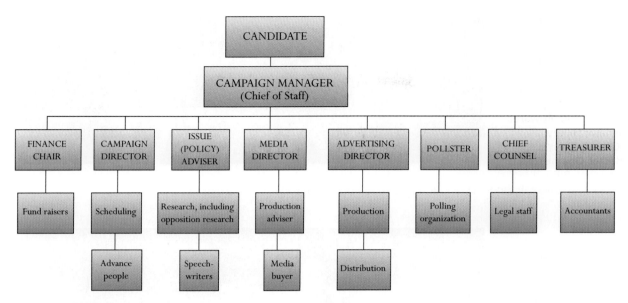

Figure *8.4* Who Does What?: Typical Campaign Organization

Campaign organizations vary, but most assign someone to perform these tasks: funding, scheduling appearances, speechwriting, media production and buying, polling, advertising, legal compliance, and checkwriting, even if, in local campaigns, all these tasks must be performed by the candidate or her or his family members.

election. In contrast, the party out of the White House typically goes through a rough-and-tumble primary (and preprimary) season, with multiple presidential aspirants. And when no incumbent president is running for reelection, both parties experience heavy party infighting among multiple presidential hopefuls. (See *Politics Up Close:* "Hillary Versus Barack, 2008" in Chapter 7.)

Candidates strive during the preprimary season to win media attention, to climb the poll ratings, and raise campaign funds. Early front-runners must beware of stumbles and gaffes; they must be prepared for close scrutiny by the media; and they must expect to be the targets of their competitors. Not infrequently, early front-runners lose their momentum even before the first primary elections.[19]

Primary voters are heavily weighted toward party activists, who are more ideologically motivated than the more moderate voters in general elections. Democratic primary voters are more liberal, and Republican primary voters are more conservative, than the voters in the November general election. Democratic primary voters include large numbers of the party's core constituents—union members, public employees, minorities, environmentalists, and feminists.

Presidential candidates must try to appeal not only to the ideological predispositions of their party's primary voters but also convince them of their "electability"—the likelihood that they can win the party's nomination and more importantly go on to win the presidential election. Often primary voters are torn between voting for their favorite candidate based on his or her ideological and issue positions, or voting for the most electable candidate.

The Iowa Caucuses   Iowa has traditionally held party caucuses even before the New Hampshire primary. Rather than going to the polls and casting ballots as in a primary election, Iowans gather at set times and at set locations in each of

Iowa Caucuses

The Democratic presidential hopefuls appear at the CNN debate on July 23, 2007 in Charleston, South Carolina. From left to right: Senator Mike Gravel (D-AK); Senator Christopher Dodd (D-CT); former Senator John Edwards (D-NC); Senator Hillary Rodham Clinton (D-NY); Senator Barack Obama (D-IL); New Mexico Gov. Bill Richardson; Senator Joseph Biden (D-DE); and Rep. Dennis Kucinich (D-OH).

The ten Republican presidential hopefuls pose before the start of a nationally televised political debate in Columbia, South Carolina. From left to right: Senator John McCain (R-AZ), former New York City Mayor Rudolph W. Giuliani, former Arkansas governor Mike Huckabee, Rep. Duncan Hunter (R-CA), Senator Sam Brownback (R-KS), former Secretary of Health and Human Services and former Wisconsin governor Tommy G. Thompson, former Massachusetts governor Mitt Romney, former Virginia governor Jim Gilmore, Rep. Tom Tancredo (R-CO), and Rep. Ron Paul (R-TX).

1,700 precincts. At the Republican caucuses, a straw vote is taken indicating the voters' choice for presidential nominee. At Democratic caucuses participants divide into groups supporting their preferred presidential nominee. A "viability threshold" eliminates groups with too few members; these members are urged to realign in support of more viable candidates. Finally, a head count is taken which apportions delegates to the county convention and later district conventions. Delegates pledged to a presidential candidate seldom abandon their chosen candidate. The Iowa caucuses, like the New Hampshire primary, inspire retail politics, with presidential candidates shaking hands through small Midwestern towns. The Iowa parties have pledged to keep the Iowa caucuses at least one week ahead of the New Hampshire primary.

The New Hampshire Primary

The primary season begins in the winter snows of New Hampshire, traditionally the first state to hold a presidential primary election. New Hampshire is far more important *strategically* to a presidential campaign than it is in delegate strength. As a small state, New Hampshire supplies fewer than 1 percent of the delegates at the Democratic and Republican conventions. But the New Hampshire primary looms very large in media coverage and hence in overall campaign strategy. Although the popular Democratic Iowa party caucuses are held even earlier, New Hampshire is the nation's first primary, and the media begin speculating about its outcome and reporting early state-poll results months in advance.

The New Hampshire primary inspires **retail politics**—direct candidate contact with the voters. Presidential aspirants begin visiting New Hampshire in the

★ **retail politics**
Direct candidate contact with individual voters.

year preceding the primary elections, speaking at town hall meetings, visiting with small groups, standing outside of supermarkets, walking through restaurants, greeting workers at factories and offices, and so on. These personal contacts bypass the media's filtering and interpreting of the candidate's personality and message. Retail politics is largely confined to New Hampshire, a small state and a year of pre-primary time to reach voters personally. And there is some evidence that voters who actually meet candidates come away with a more favorable view of them.[20]

The "expectations" game is played with a vengeance in the early primaries. Media polls and commentators set the candidates' expected vote percentages, and the candidates and their spokespersons try to deflate these expectations. On election night, the candidates' **spin doctors** sally forth among the crowds of television and newspaper reporters to give a favorable interpretation of the outcome. The candidates themselves appear at campaign headquarters (and, they hope, on national television) to give the same favorable spin to the election results. But the media itself—particularly the television network anchors and reporters and commentators—interpret the results for the American people, determining the early favorites in the presidential horse race.

Iowa and New Hampshire provide the initial *momentum* for the presidential candidates. "Momentum" is more than just a media catchword. The Democratic and Republican winners in these states have demonstrated their voter appeal, their "electability." Favorable results inspire more financial contributions and thus the resources needed to carry the fight into the next group of primary elections. Unfavorable results tend to dry up contributions; weaker candidates may be forced into an early withdrawal.

The Front-End Strategy
A **front-end** strategy places heavy emphasis on the results from Iowa and New Hampshire and other early primary states. This strategy involves spending all or most of the candidate's available resources—time, energy, and money—in these early states, in the hopes that early victories will provide the momentum, in media attention and financial contributions, to continue the race.

Front Loading Primaries, 2008
Traditionally, both the Democratic and Republican parties allowed Iowa and New Hampshire to be the first states in the nation to express their presidential preferences. Yet, over time, resentment grew among other states regarding the influence exercised by these two small states in selecting the early leaders in the presidential race. Governors and state legislatures across the nation began to reschedule their 2008 presidential primaries, pushing their dates earlier into January and February. The Democratic and Republican National Committees sought to prevent a mad scramble among the states to be first in the nation in selecting convention delegates pledged to respective candidates. Both national party committees recognized the traditional first-in-the-nation positions of Iowa and New Hampshire and they also approved of early selections by Nevada and South Carolina. But they sought to restrain all other states from making their selections earlier than the first Tuesday in February. A total of twenty-four states chose to comply and to hold their presidential caucuses and primaries on February 5, "Super Tuesday," including California and New York. But Florida and Michigan chose to jump the gun and hold primary elections in late January. The Democratic National Committee at first voted to deny admission to the national convention to delegates from these states, as a penalty for violating national party rules. Later the DNC rules committee voted to compromise

★ **spin doctors**
Practitioners of the art of spin control, or manipulation of media reporting to favor their own candidate.

★ **front-end strategy**
Presidential political campaign strategy in which a candidate focuses on winning early primaries to build momentum.

★ **front loading**
The scheduling of presidential primary elections early in the year.

New York Senator Hillary Clinton is surrounded by local homeowners and the media as she campaigns in New Hampshire. After finishing third in Iowa, Senator Clinton won New Hampshire.

★ **big-state strategy**
Presidential political campaign strategy in which a candidate focuses on winning primaries in large states because of their high delegate counts.

★ **Electoral College**
The 538 presidential electors apportioned among the states according to their congressional representation (plus three for the District of Columbia) whose votes officially elect the president and vice president of the United States.

DEBATE

Electoral College

VISUAL LITERACY

The Electoral College: Campaign Consequences and Mapping the Results

★ **swing states**
States that are not considered to be firmly in the Democratic or Republican column.

the issue: the Michigan and Florida delegates would be seated at the convention but they could cast only one-half of their elected votes. Finally, after Barack Obama had claimed a majority of delegates, the Democratic convention recognized both state delegations.

Big-State Strategy Presidential aspirants who begin the race with widespread support among party activists, heavy financial backing, and strong endorsements from the major interest groups can focus their attention on the big-state primaries. A **big-state strategy** generally requires more money, more workers, and better organization than a front-end strategy. But the big states—California, New York, Texas, Florida, Pennsylvania, Ohio, and Michigan—have the most delegates.

The Presidential Campaign: The General Election Battle

Buoyed by the conventions—and often by postconvention bounces in the polls—the new nominees must now face the general electorate.

General Election Strategies Strategies in the general election are as varied as the imaginations of campaign advisers, media consultants, pollsters, and the candidates themselves. As noted earlier, campaign strategies are affected by the nature of the times and the state of the economy; by the incumbent or challenger status of the candidate; by the issues, conditions, scandals, or events currently being spotlighted by the media; and by the dynamics of the campaign itself as the candidates attack and defend themselves (see *Politics Up Close:* "Obama Versus McCain, 2008").

Presidential election campaigns must focus on the **Electoral College**. The president is not elected by the national popular vote total but rather by a majority of the *electoral* votes of the states. Electoral votes are won by plurality, winner-take-all popular voting in most of the states. (Exceptions are Nebraska and Maine.) Thus a narrow plurality win in a state delivers *all* of that state's electoral votes. Big-state victories, even by very narrow margins, can deliver big electoral prizes. The biggest prizes are California with 55 electoral votes, New York with 31, and Texas with 34. With a total of 538 electoral votes at stake, *the winner must garner victories in states that total a minimum of 270 electoral votes.* (See *What Do You Think?*: "Should We Scrap the Electoral College?" on page 277.)

Targeting the Swing States In focusing on the most populous states, with their large electoral votes, candidates must decide which of these states are "winnable," then direct their time, energy, and money to these **swing states**. Candidates cannot afford to spend too much effort in states that already seem to be solidly in their column, although they must avoid the perception that they are ignoring these strong bases of support. Neither can candidates waste much effort on states that already appear to be solidly in their opponent's column. So the swing states receive most of the candidates' time, attention, and television advertising money.

Joe Biden, the Democratic vice presidential candidate, makes his acceptance speech before the Democratic National Convention in Denver, Colorado, on August 27, 2008.

Senator John McCain introduces his vice-presidential running mate, Alaska Governor Sarah Palin, at a rally in Dayton, Ohio, just days before the Republican National Convention in St. Paul, Minnesota.

The Presidential Debates   The nationally televised presidential debates are the central feature of the general election campaign. These debates attract more viewers than any other campaign event. Moreover, they enable a candidate to reach undecided voters and the opponent's supporters, as well as the candidate's own partisans. Even people who usually pay little attention to politics may be drawn in by the drama of the confrontation (see *Politics Up Close*: "The Presidential Debates" on page 284).

The debates allow viewers an opportunity to see and hear candidates together and to compare their responses to questions as they stand side by side. The debates give audiences a better view of the candidates than they can get from 30-second commercial ads or 7-second news sound bites. Viewers can at least judge how the candidates react under pressure.

However, the debates emphasize candidate image over substantive policy issues. Candidates must appear presidential. They must appear confident, compassionate, concerned, and good humored. They must not appear uncertain or unsure of themselves, or aloof or out of touch with viewers, or easily upset by hostile questions. They must avoid verbal slips or gaffes or even unpolished or awkward gestures. They must remember that the debates are not really debates so much as joint press conferences in which the candidates respond to questions with rehearsed mini-speeches and practiced sound bites.

Hitting the Talk Shows   Candidates know that more people watch entertainment talk shows then news shows (see Chapter 6). Oprah Winfrey, Larry King, David Letterman, Jay Leno, and Conan O'Brien all have larger audiences than *Meet the Press, Hardball, Hannity and Colmes, The O'Reilly Factor*, and others. Moreover, entertainment hosts rarely ask policy questions but rather toss "softball" queries about family, feelings, and personal qualities. Responding to these questions "humanizes" the candidate. And these entertainment shows reach audiences that have relatively little political knowledge or awareness. This provides an opportunity for a candidate to actually win over

You Are a Campaign Manager: Countdown to 270! Choose Your Candidate and Lead Him to Electoral College Victory

You Are a Campaign Manager: McCain and the Swingers: Help McCain Win Swing States and Swing Voters

Politics Up Close — Campaign '08—Obama Versus McCain

A prolonged war, a troubled economy, and an unpopular Republican president all combined to make 2008 a Democratic year. Barack Obama's theme of "change" resonated well with a disillusioned public. And Obama successfully "defined" his opponent, John McCain, as "four more years of the failed policies of George Bush." McCain sought to distance himself from Bush; he adopted the image of a "reformer" and "maverick" who had challenged the president and his party in the past. He sought to "define" Obama as an inexperienced liberal, beholden to the unpopular Democratic leadership in Congress. But his claims were drowned in a sea of voter anxiety over the economy.

John McCain was running behind in the polls when he stunned political observers with his vice presidential choice, Governor Sarah Palin of Alaska. He hoped to change the dynamics of the race by selecting the first woman to run on a national Republican ticket. (Democrat Geraldine Ferraro was the first woman to run on either party ticket when she ran with Walter Mondale in 1984.) Palin electrified Republican convention goers with her life story as a small town "hockey mom" and a mother of five including a baby with Down syndrome. The youthful, attractive, and socially conservative newcomer described how she first joined the PTA, became a city councilwoman and mayor of Wasilla, Alaska, then fought the Republican establishment of that state to win the GOP gubernatorial nomination, and then went on to become an extremely popular governor. The Palin choice temporarily propelled McCain out of the polling doldrums and into a tie with Obama.

Obama's selection of Delaware Senator Joe Biden provided balance to the Democratic ticket, both in Washington experience and foreign-policy expertise. Biden had served 35 years in Congress and was chairman of the Senate Foreign Relations Committee. Palin captivated Republicans with her folksy charm, but Biden appeared more prepared to assume the presidency.

Obama had already recovered the lead in the polls when the financial crises hit Wall Street and threatened the nation's economic well-being. The economy quickly became the central issue in the campaign. Voters concerned with economic security traditionally turn to Democratic candidates. McCain temporarily "suspended" his campaign to work on the federal bailout of Wall Street. Both candidates supported the bailout, but the polls began to tilt heavily toward Obama.

Economic questions dominated the televised presidential debates. Obama blamed the financial crises on Republican reluctance to regulate the financial industry. He promised to raise taxes on the rich while cutting taxes on the "middle class." He reminded viewers of his early opposition to the war in Iraq and promised to end the war "responsibly." He emphasized diplomacy in dealing with international threats. John McCain blamed the crisis on Democratic support for the failed federal mortgage insurance corporations Fannie Mae and Freddie Mac. He opposed any tax increases, especially during a recession. He called for "victory" in Iraq and took hawkish stands on Iran and Russia. He attacked Obama for his willingness to sit down with dictators "without preconditions."

The Obama campaign shattered all fund-raising records. Obama was the first major party candidate to turn down public financing of his campaign, reversing his earlier stated intention to accept it. By doing so, he was able to accept private contributions that totaled well in excess of the limits that would have prevailed if he accepted federal funds. In contrast, McCain was obliged to accept federal funds and the spending limits that came with them. McCain was outspent by more than two to one.

McCain failed to embrace a single compelling theme comparable to Obama's "Change You Can Believe In." Toward the end of the campaign, McCain adopted "Joe the plumber" as a symbol of working-class Americans who questioned Obama's tax policies. Sarah Palin accused Obama of "palling around with terrorists," a reference to his association with the unrepentant radical William Ayers, a founder of the violent, 60s-era Weather Underground. But most Americans were unmoved. Instead, the looming recession, punctuated by the Wall Street financial scare, occupied their thoughts.

The Obama campaign focused heavily on expanding the electorate, especially adding African American and younger voters. Obama attracted huge and enthusiastic crowds at campaign stops. His Internet site registered millions of e-mail addresses and, perhaps more importantly, generated millions of dollars in small contributions. On election day Obama was able to field hundreds of thousands of workers in a stunningly successful get-out-the-vote effort. The result was a massive voter turnout not seen since the 1960s.

"Campaign '08" ended very close to where it had begun: Obama won by seven percentage points, 53 to 46. The campaign swept away the last racial barrier in American politics, as the country chose Barack Obama as its first African American president.

undecideds and persuadable opposition voters with a likable personality, good humor, and a good rapport with the host.[21] Presidential candidates expend considerable effort to get themselves on as many entertainment talk shows as possible.

The Electoral College Vote   In recent presidential elections, the Democratic candidates (Clinton in 1992 and 1996, Gore in 2000, and Kerry in 2004) have won the Northeastern states, including New York; the upper Midwestern states, including Michigan and Illinois; and, perhaps most important, the West Coast, including California (see *Across the USA*: "How the States Voted"on page 279). Republican presidential candidates (Bush in 1992, Dole in 1996, and Bush in 2000 and 2004) have shown greater strength in the Great Plains and Rocky Mountain states and in the Southeastern states (forming a Republican "L" on the Electoral College map). If these patterns continue in presidential elections, Democrats can depend on two of the four largest Electoral College vote states, California (55) and New York (31). Republicans must win in the other two, Texas (34) and Florida (27). The Electoral College battleground may be states such as Ohio, Pennsylvania, and Missouri—"swing states" that have cast their votes alternatively for Democratic and Republican candidates in recent presidential elections.

Senator Barack Obama, Democratic presidential hopeful, dances with Ellen DeGeneres to the song "Crazy In Love" before taping *The Ellen DeGeneres Show* on October 17, 2007.

Close Calls in Presidential Elections

You Are a Campaign Manager: Lead Obama to Battleground State Victory

You Are a Campaign Manager: Seven Days to Victory: Obama's Last Minute Choices in the Election's Final Week

The Voter Decides

Understanding the reasons behind the voters' choice at the ballot box is a central concern of candidates, campaign strategists, commentators, and political scientists. Perhaps no other area of politics has been investigated as thoroughly as voting behavior. Survey data on voter choice have been collected for presidential elections for the past half century.[22] We know that voters cast ballots for and against candidates for a variety of reasons—party affiliation, group interests, characteristics and images of the candidates themselves, the economy, and policy issues. But forecasting election outcomes remains a risky business.

Party Affiliation   Although many people claim to vote for "the person, not the party," party identification remains a powerful influence in voter choice. Party ties among voters have weakened over time, with increasing proportions of voters labeling themselves as Independents or only weak Democrats or Republicans, and more voters opting to split their tickets or cross party lines than did so a generation ago (see Chapter 7). Nevertheless, party identification remains one of the most important influences on voter choice. Party affiliation is more important in congressional than in presidential elections, but even in presidential elections the tendency to see the candidate of one's own party as "the best person" is very strong.

Consider the three presidential elections (see Figure 8.5). Self-identified Republicans voted overwhelmingly for George W. Bush in 2000 and 2004, and for McCain in 2008. Self-identified Democrats voted overwhelmingly for for Gore in 2000, for Kerry in 2004, and for Obama in 2008.

Because Republican identifiers are outnumbered in the electorate by Democratic identifiers, Republican presidential candidates, and many Republican

Figure 8.5

How We Vote: Party, Ideology, and Nature of the Times in Presidential Voting

Those who identify themselves as members of a major political party are highly likely to vote for the presidential candidates of their party. Likewise, those who identify themselves as liberals are more likely than average to vote for Democrats, and those who identify themselves as conservatives are more likely to vote for Republicans in presidential elections. In addition, voters who see the economic picture as better are more likely to vote for the incumbent, those who are concerned about the nation's economy are more likely to vote against the incumbent.

Source: Election exit polls, Voter News Service, National Election Pool.

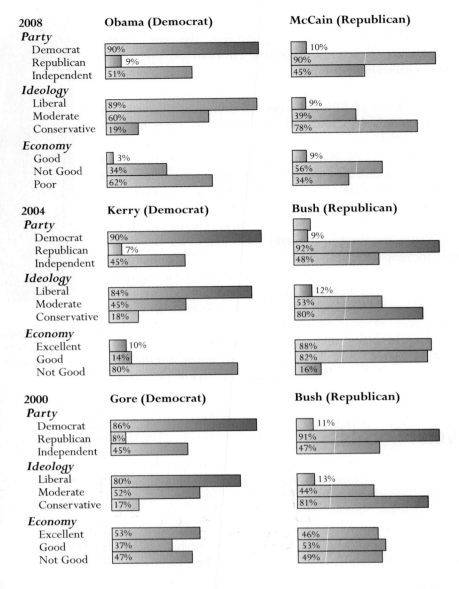

congressional candidates as well, *must* appeal to Independent and Democratic crossover voters.

Group Voting   We already know that various social and economic groups give disproportionate support to the Democratic and Republican parties (see Chapter 7). So it comes as no surprise that recent Democratic presidential candidates have received disproportionate support from African Americans, Catholics, Jews, the less-educated, and union workers; Republican presidential candidates have fared better among whites, Protestants, and better-educated voters (see Figure 8.6 on page 282). That is, these groups have given a larger percentage of their vote to the Democratic or Republican candidates than the candidate received from the total electorate.

Race and Gender Gaps   Among the more interesting group voting patterns is the serious *gender gap* affecting recent Republican candidates. Although Reagan won the women's vote in both 1980 and 1984, his vote percentages among men were considerably higher than among women. George H. W. Bush lost the

What Do You *Think?*

Should We Scrap the Electoral College?

Americans were given a dramatic reminder in 2000 that the president of the United States is *not* elected by nationwide *popular* vote, but rather by a majority of the *electoral votes* of the states.

How the Electoral College Works

The Constitution grants each state a number of electors equal to the number of its congressional representatives and senators combined (see map). Because representatives are apportioned to the states on the basis of population, the electoral vote of the states is subject to change after each 10-year census. No state has fewer than 3 electoral votes, because the Constitution guarantees every state two U.S. senators and at least one representative. The 23rd Amendment granted 3 electoral votes to the District of Columbia even though it has no voting members of Congress. So winning the presidency requires winning in states with at least 270 of the 538 total electoral votes.

Voters in presidential elections are actually choosing a slate of presidential electors pledged to vote for their party's presidential and vice-presidential candidates. The names of electors seldom appear on the ballot, only the names of the candidates and their parties. The slate that wins a *plurality* of the popular vote in a state (more than any other slate, not necessarily a majority) casts *all* of the state's vote in the Electoral College. (This "winner-take-all" system in the states is not mandated by the Constitution; a state legislature could allocate a state's electoral votes in proportion to the split in the popular vote, as happens in Nebraska and Maine. The winner-take-all system in the states helps ensure that the Electoral College produces a majority for one candidate.)

The Electoral College never meets at a single location; rather, electors meet at their respective state capitals to cast their ballots around December 15, following the general election on the first Tuesday after the first Monday of November. The results are sent to the presiding officer of the Senate, the vice president, who in January presides over their count in the presence of both houses of Congress and formally announces the results. These procedures are usually considered a formality, but the U.S. Constitution does not *require* that electors cast their vote for the winning presidential candidate in their state, and occasionally "faithless electors" disrupt the process, although none has ever changed the outcome.

If no candidate wins a majority of electoral votes, the House of Representatives chooses the president from among the three candidates with the largest number of electoral votes, with each state casting *one* vote. The Constitution does not specify how House delegations should determine their vote, but by House rules, the state's vote goes to the candidate receiving a majority vote in the delegation.

The Historical Record

Only two presidential elections have ever been decided formally by the House of Representatives. In 1800 Thomas Jefferson and Aaron Burr tied in the Electoral College because the 12th Amendment had not yet been adopted to separate presidential from vice-presidential voting; all the Democratic-Republican electors voted for both Jefferson and Burr, creating a tie. In 1824 Andrew Jackson won the popular vote and more electoral votes than anyone else but failed to get a majority. The House chose John Quincy Adams over Jackson, causing a popular uproar and ensuring Jackson's election in 1828.

In addition, in 1876, the Congress was called on to decide which electoral results from the Southern states to validate; a Republican Congress chose to validate enough Republican electoral votes to allow Republican Rutherford B. Hayes to win, even though Democrat Samuel Tilden had won more popular votes. Hayes promised the Democratic Southern states that in return for their acknowledgment of his presidential claim, he would end the military occupation of the South.

In 1888, the Electoral College vote failed to reflect the popular vote. Benjamin Harrison received 233 electoral votes to incumbent president Grover Cleveland's 168, even though Cleveland won about 90,000 more popular votes than Harrison. Harrison served a single lackluster term; Cleveland was elected for a second time in 1892, the only president to serve two nonconsecutive terms.

2000—Gore Wins but Loses

Al Gore won the nationwide popular vote, receiving about 500,000 more votes (out of the more than 100 million ballots cast) than George W. Bush. But the vote in several states was extremely close. On election night, Gore was reported to have won 262 electoral votes to Bush's 246—that is, neither candidate had the necessary 270. The key turned out to be Florida's 25 electoral votes. (New Mexico's 5 votes eventually went to Gore.) The Florida secretary of state declared Bush the winner by a few hundred votes out of 6 million cast in that state. The Gore campaign demanded *hand* recounts, especially in heavily Democratic counties in south Florida (including Palm Beach County, where the ballot was said to be confusing to voters). The Bush campaign responded that hand counts are subjective, unreliable, and open to partisan bias. For over a month neither Bush nor Gore would concede the election. Suits were initiated by

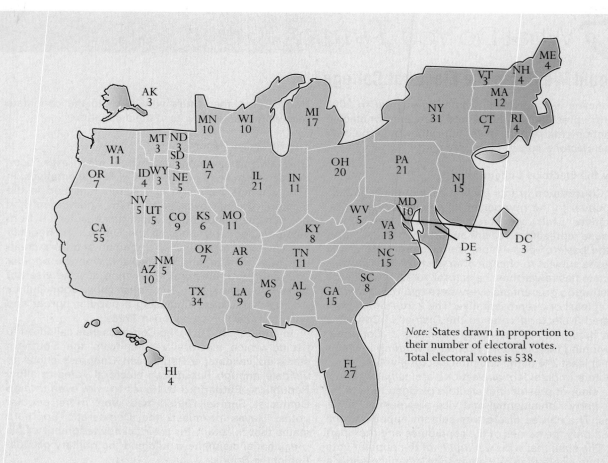

Note: States drawn in proportion to their number of electoral votes. Total electoral votes is 538.

both candidates in both federal and Florida states courts. Finally, the U.S. Supreme Court rejected Gore's appeal; Florida's votes went to Bush and he was declared the winner.

What Would Replace the Electoral College?

Constitutional proposals to reform the Electoral College have circulated for nearly two hundred years, but none has won widespread support. These reform proposals have included (1) election of the president by direct national popular vote; (2) allocation of each state's electoral vote in proportion to the popular vote each candidate received in the state; (3) allocation of electoral votes to winners of each congressional district and two to the statewide winners.

But most reform proposals create as many problems as they resolve. If the president is to be elected by direct nationwide popular vote, should a plurality vote be sufficient to win? Or should a national runoff be held in the event that no one receives a majority in the first election? Would proportional allocation of electoral votes encourage third-party candidates to enter the race in order to deny the leading candidate a majority?

women's vote in both 1988 and 1992. In 1996 the gender gap widened, with 54 percent of women voting for Clinton as opposed to only 38 percent for Dole, and continued in 2000 with women giving Gore 54 percent of the vote as opposed to Bush's 43 percent. Again in 2004 women gave Democrat John F. Kerry 54 percent of their vote, and in 2008 they gave Obama 55 percent of their vote. African Americans have long constituted the most loyal group of Democratic voters, regularly giving the Democratic presidential nominee up to 90 percent or more of their vote. The overall Hispanic vote is Democratic, although a significant portion of Hispanics, notably Cuban Americans in Florida, vote Republican.

Candidate Image In an age of direct communication between candidates and voters via television, the image of candidates and their ability to relate to

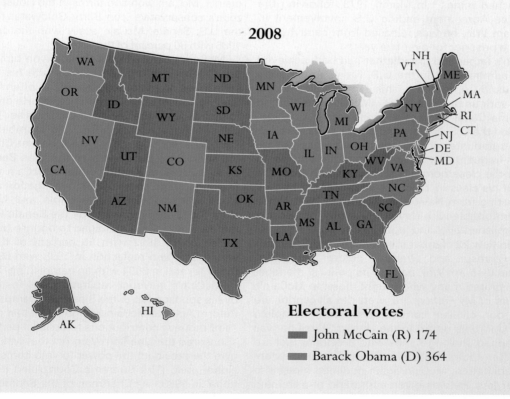

audiences have emerged as important determinants of voter choice. Candidate image is most important in presidential contests, inasmuch as presidential candidates are personally more visible to the voter than candidates for lesser offices.[23]

It is difficult to identify exactly what personal qualities appeal most to voters. Warmth, compassion, strength, confidence, honesty, sincerity, good humor, appearance, and "likability" seem important.

"Character" is often a central feature of media coverage of candidates (see Chapter 6). Reports of extramarital affairs, experimentation with drugs, draft

People in Politics   John McCain, Republican Presidential Nominee

John McCain is a genuine American war hero. Early in the Vietnam War, October 1967, his Navy A-4 Skyhawk fighter-bomber was shot down over Hanoi. He fractured both arms and a leg parachuting into a lake. He was beaten and bayoneted by a mob before being taken to Hanoi's infamous prison, dubbed "the Hanoi Hilton." He was denied medical aid; his beatings and interrogations continued; his captors expected him to die. Only when they learned that his father was a top U.S. Navy Admiral did they give him any medical care. After two years in solitary confinement he was offered an opportunity to return home as a propaganda ploy by his Vietnam captors. McCain refused the offer and his torture began in earnest. Ropes bound him into painful positions and he was beaten every two hours for four days, breaking teeth and bones. He finally signed an anti-American propaganda statement, later acknowledging that "Every man has a breaking point. I had reached mine."[a] In March 1973, following the Paris Peace Agreement ending U.S. involvement in the Vietnam War, he was released from captivity. He had been a prisoner for over five years.

McCain's father and grandfather had both achieved four-star admiral rank in the U.S. Navy. Young John was frequently uprooted as his family followed his father to various naval stations. (McCain was born in the Panama Canal Zone.) Following family tradition, he attended the U.S. Naval Academy at Annapolis, but his undergraduate career was unimpressive. He received frequent disciplinary demerits and fared poorly in the classroom. He graduated fifth from the bottom of his class in 1958. Yet he redeemed himself by graduating from Navy flight school in 1960. While still uncomfortable with Navy regulations, he became an accomplished pilot and flight instructor.

McCain flew 22 combat missions from U.S. aircraft carriers *Forrestal* and *Oriskany* before being shot down. The Vietnam War, notably its political management, frustrated many who fought there. In McCain's book, *Faith of My Fathers*, he wrote "In all candor, we thought our civilian commanders were complete idiots."[b] Upon his return to the United States he was photographed shaking hands with President Richard Nixon. After additional medical treatment and extensive rehabilitation, McCain again qualified himself to fly carrier jets. He was given command of a training squadron at the Naval Air Station in Jacksonville, Florida. He would later serve as a Navy liaison officer to the U.S. Senate, an assignment that introduced him to Washington politics. In 1980 he divorced and remarried; his second wife was the daughter of a wealthy beer distributor in Phoenix, Arizona. In 1981

McCain retired from the Navy as a Captain, having received a Silver Star, Bronze Star, Legion of Merit, Distinguished Flying Cross, and Purple Heart.

When the long-time Arizona Republican Congressman John Rhodes announced his retirement in 1982, McCain decided to run for the open seat. With the support of the Phoenix business community, McCain edged out two experienced state legislators in the Republican primary and then went on to a lopsided victory in the heavily Republican district. McCain won two terms in the House. When Arizona's conservative icon Barry Goldwater retired from the U.S. Senate, McCain easily won the open seat in 1986 with 60 percent of the vote.

McCain's career in the Senate won him the "maverick" label. He regularly broke with his Republican colleagues on major legislation and often fought with leading conservative commentators. He once referred to the leader of the Christian Coalition as "a pompous self-serving son of a bitch." He stumbled badly in 1987 by accepting money from banker Charles Keating and asking the Federal Home Loan Bank Board to delay seizure of Keating's bank. McCain was one of five senators to come under investigation in the affair. None were convicted of a crime, but McCain was cited for "poor judgment" by the Senate Ethics Committee. But McCain managed to bounce back and win reelection in 1992 with 56 percent of the vote. He would later win reelection in 1998 with 69 percent of the vote, and in 2004 with an astonishing 77 percent.

McCain's maverick reputation was fostered in part by his sponsorship of the Bipartisan Campaign Finance Reform Act (the McCain-Feingold bill) that put limits on "soft money" contributions to political parties. He also sponsored the Line Item Veto Act that was intended to give the president the power to veto items of congressional pork. (The Supreme Court ruled it unconstitutional in 1998.) As Chairman of the Senate Commerce Committee McCain took on the tobacco companies, accusing them of targeting teenage smokers.

McCain's "Straight Talk" campaign for the Republican presidential nomination in 2000 clashed with the ambitions of Texas Governor George W. Bush and the Bush family. McCain's surprise win in the early New

[a]*U.S. News and World Report*, May 14, 1973.

[b]John McCain, *Faith of my Fathers*. New York: Random House, 1999, p. 185

Hampshire Republican primary inspired the OOP establishment to turn up the heat on the maverick senator. Bush went on to win the Republican nomination. Relations between McCain and the president remained cool throughout Bush's years in the White House.

McCain voted against Bush's tax cuts in 2001 and 2003, arguing that tax cuts had to be linked to spending cuts. He supported the failed "comprehensive" immigration reform that would have provided legalization of immigrants already in the country, and a guest worker program, combined with increased border enforcement. McCain was a strong supporter of Bush's invasion of Iraq and applauded the president for removing Saddam Hussein from power. But McCain soon began to criticize Defense Secretary Donald Rumsfeld for failing to send enough troops to handle the occupation of Iraq. In 2004 McCain bluntly announced that he had lost confidence in Rumsfeld.

Yet as the war in Iraq became increasingly unpopular, McCain continued to urge victory. He opposed efforts in Congress to cut of funds for the war or to set deadlines for the withdrawal of troops. Instead, he supported the "surge" in troop levels in 2007 and the appointment of General David Petraeus to redirect the war effort (see Chapter 18).

Early in 2007 McCain announced on the *Late Show with David Letterman* that he would seek the Republican presidential nomination in 2008. While he described his health as "excellent," he acknowledged that at 72 he would be the oldest person in history to assume the presidency. (Ronald Reagan was 69 years old at his inauguration following the 1980 election.) Opponents as well as supporters were obliged to recognize his status as a national hero, his patriotism and his personal integrity.

dodging, cheating in college, shady financial dealings, conflicts of interest, or lying or misrepresenting facts receive heavy media coverage because they attract large audiences. But it is difficult to estimate how many voters are swayed by so-called character issues.

Attractive personal qualities can win support from opposition-party identifiers and people who disagree on the issues. John F. Kennedy's handsome and youthful appearance, charm, self-confidence, and disarming good humor defeated the heavy-jowled, shifty-eyed, defensive, and ill-humored Richard Nixon. Ronald Reagan's folksy mannerisms, warm humor, and comfortable rapport with television audiences justly earned him the title "The Great Communicator." Reagan disarmed his critics by laughing at his own personal flubs—falling asleep at meetings, forgetting names—and by telling his own age jokes. His personal appeal won more Democratic voters than any other Republican candidate has won in modern history, and he won the votes of many people who disagreed with him on the issues.

Barack Obama's image as a fresh, young, handsome African American fit comfortably with his theme of "change." His personal charm and eloquence served to overcome whatever lack of experience he brought to the race. Over his years in Congress, John McCain had established his "maverick" image and it fit well with his call for "reform." But his age was visible and it was difficult to shed the image of "too old."

Think Again

Should people vote on the basis of a candidate's personal character rather than his or her policy positions?

The Economy Fairly accurate predictions of voting outcomes in presidential elections can be made from models of the American economy. Economic conditions at election time—recent growth or decline in personal income, the unemployment rate, consumer confidence, and so on—are related to the vote given the incumbent versus the challenger. Ever since the once-popular Republican incumbent Herbert Hoover was trounced by Franklin Roosevelt as the Great Depression of the 1930s deepened, politicians have understood that voters hold the incumbent party responsible for hard economic times.

Perhaps no other lesson has been as well learned by politicians: Hard economic times hurt incumbents and favor challengers. The economy may not be the only important factor in presidential voting, but it is certainly a factor of

Figure *8.6*

How We Vote: Group Voting in Presidential Elections

Democratic presidential candidates regularly do better among African American, Hispanic, lower income, and less educated voters. The gender gap—men tending to vote Republican and women Democratic—first emerged in the Reagan years. Increasingly, white religious voters are casting their ballots for Republican candidates.

Source: Election exit polls, Voter News Service, National Election Pool.

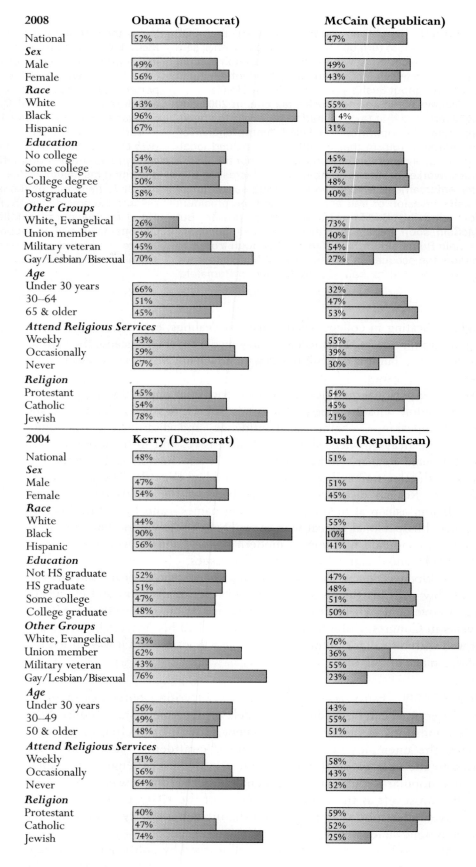

2008	Obama (Democrat)	McCain (Republican)
National	52%	47%
Sex		
Male	49%	49%
Female	56%	43%
Race		
White	43%	55%
Black	96%	4%
Hispanic	67%	31%
Education		
No college	54%	45%
Some college	51%	47%
College degree	50%	48%
Postgraduate	58%	40%
Other Groups		
White, Evangelical	26%	73%
Union member	59%	40%
Military veteran	45%	54%
Gay/Lesbian/Bisexual	70%	27%
Age		
Under 30 years	66%	32%
30–64	51%	47%
65 & older	45%	53%
Attend Religious Services		
Weekly	43%	55%
Occasionally	59%	39%
Never	67%	30%
Religion		
Protestant	45%	54%
Catholic	54%	45%
Jewish	78%	21%

2004	Kerry (Democrat)	Bush (Republican)
National	48%	51%
Sex		
Male	47%	51%
Female	54%	45%
Race		
White	44%	55%
Black	90%	10%
Hispanic	56%	41%
Education		
Not HS graduate	52%	47%
HS graduate	51%	48%
Some college	47%	51%
College graduate	48%	50%
Other Groups		
White, Evangelical	23%	76%
Union member	62%	36%
Military veteran	43%	55%
Gay/Lesbian/Bisexual	76%	23%
Age		
Under 30 years	56%	43%
30–49	49%	55%
50 & older	48%	51%
Attend Religious Services		
Weekly	41%	58%
Occasionally	56%	43%
Never	64%	32%
Religion		
Protestant	40%	59%
Catholic	47%	52%
Jewish	74%	25%

Table *8.3* Public Perception: Obama and McCain images of 2008

Considering the following qualities and characteristics, please state whether you think each one better describes Obama or McCain.

Most Important Quality		Who They Voted For	
Percentage who said:		Obama	McCain
35%	Can bring needed change	89%	9%
20%	Has right experience	6%	93%
12%	Cares about people like me	74%	24%

Table *8.4* What Matters Most?: Issues the Voters Cared about in 2008

Relatively few voters cast their ballots strictly on the issue positions of the candidates. But voters cited these as the "most important" issues in 2008. Presidential Vote of Those Who Listed Issue as "Most Important"

	Most Important Issue		Who They Voted For	
Rank	Percentage who said:		Obama	McCain
1	63%	Economy	53%	45%
2	10%	War in Iraq	59%	39%
3	9%	Terrorism	13%	86%
4	9%	Health care	72%	26%
5	7%	Energy policy	50%	47%

great importance.[24] Some evidence indicates that it is not voters' *own* personal economic well-being that affects their vote but rather voter perception of *general* economic conditions. People who perceive the economy as getting worse are likely to vote against the incumbent party, whereas people who think the economy is getting better support the incumbent.[25]

The economy dominated the 2008 presidential race. Nearly two thirds of voters cited it as the "most important" issue in the election (see Table 8.4), and virtually all of these voters thought the economy was getting worse. These voters broke for Obama over McCain 53 percent to 45 percent. The war in Iraq was cited as most important by only about 10 percent of voters; these voters also tended to support Obama. Voters who thought that terrorism was the most important issue voted heavily for McCain. Voters concerned with health care voted heavily for Obama.

Issue Voting Casting one's vote exclusively on the basis of the policy positions of the candidates is rare. Most voters are unaware of the specific positions taken by candidates on the issues. Indeed, voters often believe that their preferred candidate agrees with them on the issues, even when this is not the case. In other words, voters project their own policy views onto their favorite candidate more often than they decide to vote for a candidate because of his or her position on the issues.

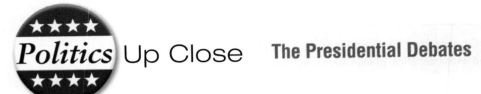

Politics Up Close   The Presidential Debates

Presidential debates attract more viewers than any other campaign activity. Most campaign activities—speeches, rallies, motorcades—reach only supporters. Such activities may inspire supporters to go to the polls, contribute money, and even work to get others to vote their way. But televised debates reach undecided voters as well as supporters, and they allow candidates to be seen by supporters of their opponent. Even if issues are not really discussed in depth, people see how presidential candidates react as human beings under pressure.

Kennedy-Nixon

Televised presidential debates began in 1960 when John F. Kennedy and Richard M. Nixon confronted each other on a bare stage before an America watching on black-and-white TV sets. Nixon was the vice president in the popular presidential administration of Dwight Eisenhower; he was also an accomplished college debate-team member. He prepared for the debates as if they were college debates, memorizing facts and arguments. But he failed to realize that image triumphs over substance on television. By contrast, Kennedy was handsome, cool, confident; whatever doubts the American people may have had regarding his youth and inexperience were dispelled by his polished manner. Radio listeners tended to think that Nixon won, and debate coaches scored him the winner. But television viewers preferred the glamorous young Kennedy. The polls shifted in Kennedy's direction after the debate, and he won in a very close general election.

Carter-Ford

President Lyndon Johnson avoided debating in 1964, and Nixon, having learned his lesson, declined to debate in 1968 and 1972. Thus televised presidential debates did not resume until 1976, when incumbent president Gerald Ford, perceiving he was behind in the polls, agreed to debate challenger Jimmy Carter. Ford made a series of verbal slips. Carter was widely perceived as having won the debate, and he went on to victory in the general election.

Reagan-Carter and Reagan-Mondale

It was Ronald Reagan who demonstrated the true power of television. Reagan had lived his life in front of a camera. It was the principal tool of both of his trades—actor and politician. In 1980 incumbent president Jimmy Carter talked rapidly and seriously about programs, figures, and budgets. But Reagan was master of the stage; he was relaxed, confident, joking. He appeared to treat the president of the United States as an overly aggressive, impulsive younger man, regrettably given to exaggeration. When it was all over, it was clear to most viewers that Carter had been bested by a true professional in media skills.

However, in the first of two televised debates with Walter Mondale in 1984, Reagan's skills of a lifetime seemed to desert him. He stumbled over statistics and groped for words. Reagan's poor performance raised the only issue that might conceivably defeat him—his age. The president had looked and sounded old. But in the second debate, Reagan laid the perfect trap for his questioners. When asked about his age and capacity to lead the nation, he responded with a serious dead-pan expression to a hushed audience and waiting America: "I want you to know that I will not make age an issue in this campaign. I am not going to exploit for political purposes [pause] my opponent's youth and inexperience." The studio audience broke into uncontrolled laughter. Even Mondale had to laugh. With a classic one-liner, Reagan buried the age issue and won not only the debate but also the election.

Bush-Dukakis

In 1988 Michael Dukakis ensured his defeat with a cold, detached performance in the presidential debates, beginning with the very first question. When CNN anchor Bernard Shaw asked, "Governor, if Kitty Dukakis were raped and murdered, would you favor an irrevocable death penalty for the killer?" The question demanded an emotional reply. Instead, Dukakis responded with an impersonal recitation of his stock position on law enforcement. Bush seized the opportunity to establish a more personal relationship with the viewers: Voters responded to Bush, electing him.

Clinton-Bush-Perot

The three-way presidential debates of 1992 drew the largest television audiences in the history of presidential debates. In the first debate, Ross Perot's Texas twang and down-home folksy style stole the show. Chided by his opponents for having no governmental experience, he shot back, "Well, they have a point. I don't have any experience in running up a $4 trillion dollar debt." But it was Bill Clinton's smooth performance in the second debate, with its talk-show format, that seemed to wrap up the election. Ahead in the polls, Clinton appeared at ease walking about the stage and responding to audience questions with sympathy and sincerity. By contrast, George Bush appeared stiff and formal, and somewhat ill-at-ease with the "unpresidential" format.

Clinton-Dole

A desperate Bob Dole, running 20 points behind, faced a newly "presidential" Bill Clinton in their two 1996 debates. (Perot's poor standing in the polls led to his exclusion.) Dole tried to counter his image as a grumpy old man in the first encounter; his humor actually won more laughs from the audience than Clinton's. Dole injected more barbs in the second debate, complaining of "ethical problems in the White House." But Clinton remained cool and comfortable, ignoring the challenger and focusing on the nation's economic health. Viewers, most of whom were already in Clinton's court, judged him the winner of both debates.

Bush-Gore

Separate formats were agreed upon for three debates—the traditional podium, a conference, table, and a town hall setting. Gore was assertive, almost to the point of rudeness, but both candidates focused on policy differences rather than on personal attacks. Viewers gave Gore the edge in these debates but they found Bush more likable. Bush appeared to benefit more in the post-debate polls.

Bush-Kerry

Kerry prepared well for the three debates. He appeared tall, earnest, confident, well-informed, and "presidential." He spoke forcefully, avoiding the qualifying clauses and lengthy sentences that had plagued his speeches in the past. Bush appeared uncomfortable, scowling at Kerry's answers, often repeating himself, and failing to "connect" with his audiences. Polls showed Kerry winning each debate.

Obama-McCain

The debates magnified the contrasts: tall, young, and black versus short, old, and white. Obama, leading in the polls, had only to tie McCain, but he edged the aging Senator in style and presence. McCain accused Obama of compiling "the most liberal voting record in the Senate." Obama shot back: "Mostly that's just me opposing George Bush's wrongheaded policies."

A *Constitutional* Note

Campaign Finance and Free Speech

Both the Congress and the Supreme Court have confronted the issue of whether or not limiting campaign spending has the effect of limiting free speech. In 1976 in *Buckley v. Valeo,* the Supreme Court struck down Congress's limit on what an individual candidate or independent organization could spend to promote its own views in a campaign. "The First Amendment denies government the power to determine that spending to promote one's political views is . . . excessive. In the free society ordained by our Constitution, it is not the government but the people who must retain control over the quantity and range of debate in a political campaign."[a] This decision means that wealthy individuals can spend unlimited amounts on their own campaigns, and independent organizations can spend unlimited amounts as long as their spending is independent of a candidate's campaign. However, the Supreme Court approved limits on *contributions* by individuals and organizations—distinguishing between contributions and expenditures. It approved the Federal Election Commission limits on individual and organizational contributions to political campaigns. Congress sought to remedy the many holes in the original Federal Election Campaign Act of 1974 in its Bipartisan Campaign Reform Act of 2002. It placed limits on "soft money" contributions to political parties, most of which found its way into candidate campaigns. However, Congress did not challenge the Court's *Buckley* decision by trying to prevent individuals or nonprofit organizations from spending money to broadcast their views. Limiting spending for political broadcasting would "place substantial and direct restrictions on the ability of candidates, citizens, and associations to engage in protected political speech."[b] The result was the emergence of independent organizations, known as "527s," in subsequent elections. These organizations spent heavily and played a major role in the presidential campaigns of both parties.

[a]*Buckley v. Valeo,* 424 U.S. 1 (1976).
[b]*McConnell v. Federal Election Commission,* 590 U.S. 93 (2003).

Summary
Who Gets What: Campaigns and Elections

In a democracy, elections decide "who governs." But they also indirectly affect public policy, influencing "who gets what."

★ Although winning candidates often claim a mandate for their policy proposals, in reality few campaigns present clear policy alternatives to the voters, few voters cast their ballots on the basis of policy considerations, and the policy preferences of the electorate can seldom be determined from election outcomes.

★ Nevertheless, voters can influence future policy directions through retrospective judgments about the performance of incumbents, returning them to office or turning them out. Most retrospective voting appears to center on the economy.

★ Personal ambition for power and celebrity drives the decision to seek public office. Political entrepreneurship, professionalism, and careerism have come to dominate political recruitment; lawyers have traditionally dominated American politics.

★ Incumbents begin campaigns with many advantages: name recognition, financial support, goodwill from services they perform for constituents, large-scale public projects they bring to their districts, and the other resources of office.

★ Campaigning for office is largely a media activity, dominated by professional advertising specialists, fund raisers, media consultants, and pollsters.

★ The professionalization of campaigning and the heavy costs of a media campaign drive up the costs of running for office. These huge costs make candidates heavily dependent on financial support from individuals and organizations. Fund raising occupies more of a candidate's time than any other campaign activity.

★ Campaign contributions are made by politically active individuals and organizations, including political action committees. Many contributions are made in order to gain access to policy makers and assistance with government business. Some contributors are ideologically motivated; others merely seek to rub shoulders with powerful people.

★ Presidential primary election strategies emphasize appeals to party activists and core supporters, including the more ideologically motivated primary voters.

★ In the general election campaign, presidential candidates usually seek to broaden their appeal to moderate, centrist voters while holding on to their core supporters. Campaigns must focus on states where the candidate has the best chance of gaining the 270 electoral votes needed to win.

★ Voter choice is influenced by party identification, group membership, perceived image of the candidates, economic conditions, and, to a lesser extent, ideology and issue preferences.

Key Terms

mandate 247	challengers 250	mobilize 256	retail politics 270
retrospective voting 248	franking privilege 251	issue ads 260	spin doctors 271
professionalism 249	campaign strategy 252	political action committees (PACs) 261	front-end strategy 271
careerism 249	negative campaigning 252	Federal Election Commission (FEC) 264	front loading 271
incumbents 250	focus group 254		big-state strategy 272
reelection rates 250	photo ops 255	soft money 265	Electoral College 272
name recognition 250	sound bites 255		swing states 272

Suggested Readings

Abramson, Paul R., John H. Aldrich, and David W. Rohde. *Change and Continuity in the 2004 and 2006 Elections.* Washington, D.C.: CQ Press, 2007. An in-depth analysis of the 2004 presidential and 2006 congressional elections assessing the impact of party loyalties, presidential performance, group memberships, and policy preferences on voter choice.

Ferrar-Myers, Victoria, and Diana Dwyre. *Limits and Loopholes: The Quest for Money, Free Speech and Fair Elections.* Washington, D.C.: CQ Press, 2007. A description of the passage of campaign finance legislation and subsequent court cases.

Fiorina, Morris P. *Retrospective Voting in American National Elections.* Princeton, N.J.: Princeton University Press, 1988. Argues that retrospective judgments guide voter choice in presidential elections.

Flanigan, William H., and Nancy H. Zingale. *Political Behavior of the American Electorate.* 11th ed. Washington, D.C.: CQ Press, 2005. A brief but comprehensive summary of the extensive research literature on the effects of party identification, opinion, ideology, the media, and candidate image on voter choice and election outcomes.

Iyengar, Shanto, and Stephen Ansolabehere. *Going Negative: How Political Advertisements Shrink and Polarize the Electorate.* New York: Free Press, 1996. The real problem with negative political ads is not that they sway voters to support one candidate over another, but that they reinforce the belief that all are dishonest and cynical.

Rosenstone, Steven. *Forecasting Presidential Elections.* New Haven, Conn.: Yale University Press, 1985. A discussion of the models employed to forecast presidential election outcomes based on unemployment, inflation, and personal income statistics.

Sabato, Larry J., and Glenn R. Simpson. *Dirty Little Secrets: The Persistence of Corruption in American Politics.* New York: Random House Times Books, 1996. A political scientist and a journalist combine to produce a lurid report on unethical and corrupt practices in campaigns and elections.

Suggested Web Sites

Campaigns and Elections www.campaignline.com
The Web site for *Campaigns and Elections*, a magazine directed toward candidates, campaign managers, political TV advertisers, political consultants, and lobbyists.

Center for Responsive Politics www.opensecrets.org
The site of an organization devoted to the study of campaign finance laws, the role of money in elections, PACs, "soft money," and special-interest groups.

The Center for Voting and Democracy www.fairvote.org
A site with material on possible changes in the Electoral College.

Federal Election Commission www.fec.gov
The FEC Web site contains ample information on the important regulations and statutes relating to campaign finance.

9 INTEREST GROUPS
Getting Their Share and More

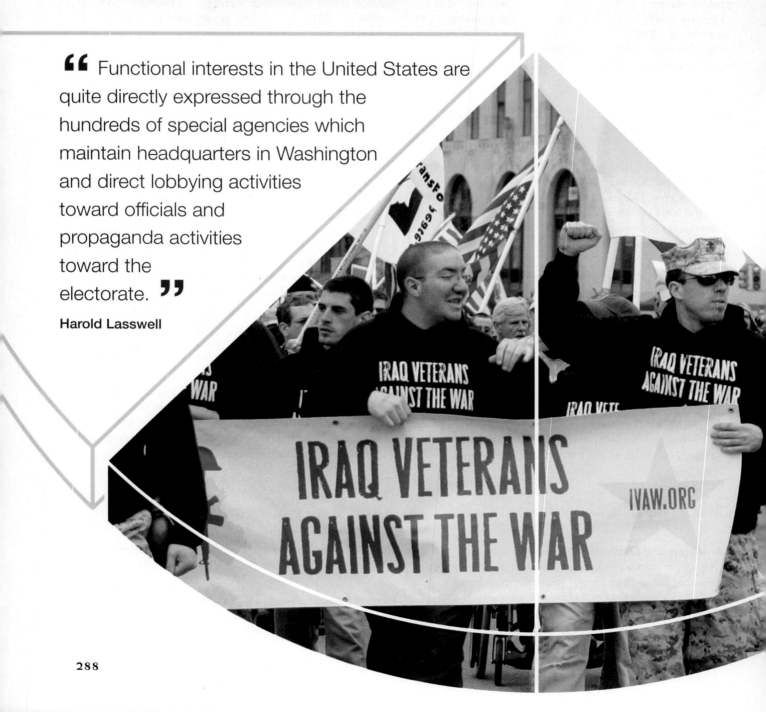

❝ Functional interests in the United States are quite directly expressed through the hundreds of special agencies which maintain headquarters in Washington and direct lobbying activities toward officials and propaganda activities toward the electorate. **❞**

Harold Lasswell

Chapter *Outline*

Interest-Group Power

Organization is a means to power—to determining who gets what in society. Interest groups are organizations that seek to influence government policy. The 1st Amendment to the Constitution recognizes "the right of the people peaceably to assemble and to petition the government for a redress of grievances." Americans enjoy a fundamental right to organize themselves to influence government.

Electoral Versus Interest-Group Systems
The *electoral system* is organized to represent geographically defined constituencies—states and congressional districts in Congress. The *interest-group system* is organized to represent economic, professional, ideological, religious, racial, gender, and issue constituencies. In other words, the interest-group system supplements the electoral system by providing people with another avenue of participation. Individuals may participate in politics by supporting candidates and parties in elections, and also by joining **interest groups**, organizations that pressure government to advance their interests.[1]

Interest group activity provides more *direct* representation of policy preferences than electoral politics. At best, individual voters can influence government policy only indirectly through elections (see Chapter 8). Elected politicians try to represent many different—and even occasionally conflicting—interests. But interest groups provide concentrated and direct representation of policy views in government.

Checking Majoritarianism
The interest-group system gives voice to special interests, whereas parties and the electoral system cater to the majority interest. Indeed, interest groups are often defended as a check on **majoritarianism**, the tendency of democratic governments to allow the faint preferences of a majority to prevail over the intense feelings of minorities. However, the interest-group system is frequently attacked because it obstructs the majority from implementing its preferences in public policy.

Concentrating Benefits While Dispersing Costs
Interest groups seek special benefits, subsidies, privileges, and protections from the government. The costs of these *concentrated* benefits are usually *dispersed* to all

✓ Think About Politics

1. Do special-interest groups in America obstruct the majority of citizens' wishes on public policy?
   YES ⬭ NO ⬭

2. Should people join an interest group such as the American Association of Retired Persons for its discounts, magazines, and travel guides even if they disagree with its policy goals?
   YES ⬭ NO ⬭

3. Should state and local governments use taxpayers' money to lobby Congress to get federal funds?
   YES ⬭ NO ⬭

4. Should former government officials be allowed to lobby their former colleagues?
   YES ⬭ NO ⬭

5. Should interest groups be prohibited from making large campaign contributions in their effort to influence public policy?
   YES ⬭ NO ⬭

6. If a lobbyist makes a campaign contribution to a Congress member, hoping to gain support for a bill, is this a form of bribery?
   YES ⬭ NO ⬭

7. Is organized interest-group activity a cause of government gridlock?
   YES ⬭ NO ⬭

What role do interest groups play in politics? Their organization, their money, and their influence in Washington raise the possibility that interest groups, rather than individuals, may in fact hold the real power in politics. They may be the "who" that determines the "what" that the rest of us get.

★ **interest groups**
Organizations seeking to directly influence government policy.

289

★ **majoritarianism**
Tendency of democratic governments to allow the faint preferences of the majority to prevail over the intense feelings of minorities.

★ **organizational sclerosis**
Society encrusted with so many special benefits to interest groups that everyone's standard of living is lowered.

Comparing Interest Groups

Do special-interest groups in America obstruct the majority of citizens' wishes on public policy?

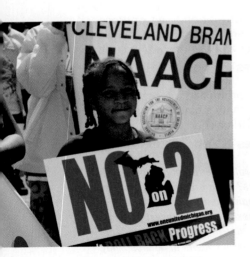

Members of the NAACP march on the Michigan state capitol in Lansing on September 16, 2006, to oppose a ballot initiative that would ban affirmative action by state agencies and public universities.

taxpayers, none of whom individually bears enough added cost to merit spending time, energy, or money to organize a group to oppose the benefit. Thus the interest-group system concentrates benefits to the few and disperses costs to the many. The system favors small, well-organized, homogeneous interests that seek the expansion of government activity at the expense of larger but less well-organized citizen-taxpayers. Over long periods of time, the cumulative activities of many special-interest groups, each seeking concentrated benefits to themselves and dispersed costs to others, result in what has been termed **organizational sclerosis**, a society so encrusted with subsidies, benefits, regulations, protections, and special treatments for organized groups that work, productivity, and investment are discouraged and everyone's standard of living is lowered.

Origins of Interest Groups

James Madison viewed interest groups—which he called "factions"—as a necessary evil in politics. He defined a faction as "a number of citizens, whether amounting to a majority or a minority of the whole, who are united and actuated by some common impulse of passion, or of interest, adverse to the rights of other citizens, or to the permanent and aggregate interests of the community." He believed that interest groups not only conflict with each other but, more important, also conflict with the common good. Nevertheless, Madison believed that the origin of interest groups was to be found in human nature—"a zeal for different opinions concerning religion, concerning government, and many other points"—and therefore impossible to eliminate from politics.[2]

Protecting Economic Interests   Madison believed that "the most common and durable source of factions, has been the various and unequal distribution of property." With genuine insight, he identified *economic interests* as the most prevalent in politics: "a landed interest, a manufacturing interest, a mercantile interest, a moneyed interest, with many lesser interests." From Madison's era to the present, businesspeople and professionals, bankers and insurers, farmers and factory workers, merchants and shippers have organized themselves to press their demands on government (see *Politics Up Close*: "Superlobby: The Business Roundtable").

Advancing Social Movements   Major social movements in American history have spawned many interest groups. Abolitionist groups were formed before the Civil War to fight slavery. The National Association for the Advancement of Colored People (NAACP) emerged in 1909 to fight segregation laws and to rally public support against lynching and other violence against African Americans. Farm organizations emerged from the populist movement of the late nineteenth century to press demands for railroad rate regulation and easier credit terms. The small trade unions that workers formed in the nineteenth century to improve their pay and working conditions gave way to large national unions in the 1930s as workers sought protection for the rights to organize, bargain collectively, and strike. The success of the women's suffrage movement led to the formation of the League of Women Voters in the early twentieth century, and a generation later the feminist movement inspired the National Organization for Women (NOW).

Seeking Government Benefits   As government expands its activities, it creates more interest groups. Wars create veterans' organizations. The first large veterans' group—the Grand Army of the Republic—formed after the Civil War and successfully lobbied for bonus payments to veterans over the years. Today the

Politics Up Close   Superlobby: The Business Roundtable

The Business Roundtable was established in 1972 "in the belief that business executives should take an increased role in the continuing debates about public policy.[a] The organization is composed of the chief executives of the 160 largest corporations in America and is financed through corporate membership fees.

The Roundtable organizes itself into task forces, each headed by the CEO of a major corporation. Among the recent lobbying goals of these task forces: reducing product liability in the courts, opposing limits on executive pay, limiting environmental protection regulations, seeking corporate tax reductions, supporting international trade agreements, and supporting proposals to allow workers to invest part of their Social Security taxes in the stock market.

The power of the Business Roundtable stems in part from its "firm rule" that a corporate chief executive officer (CEO) cannot send a substitute to its meetings. Moreover, corporate CEOs lobby the Congress in person rather than sending paid lobbyists. Members of Congress are impressed when the chair of IBM appears at a congressional hearing on business regulation or when the chair of General Electric speaks to a congressional committee about taxation, or when the chair of Prudential talks to Congress about Social Security, or when the head of B. F. Goodrich testifies before the Senate Judiciary Committee about antitrust policy. One congressional staff member explained, "If a corporation sends its Washington representative to our office, he's probably going to be shunted over to a legislative assistant. But the chairman of the board is going to get in to see the senator." Another aide echoed those sentiments: "Very few members of Congress would not meet with the president of a Business Roundtable corporation."[b]

[a]Quotations about the reasons for the establishment of the Business Roundtable from "The History of the Business Roundtable," 1998.
[b]*Time*, April 13, 1981, pp. 76–77.

American Legion, the Veterans of Foreign Wars, and the Vietnam Veterans of America engage in lobbying the Congress and monitor the activities of the Department of Veterans Affairs. As the welfare state grew, so did organizations seeking to obtain benefits for their members, including the nation's largest interest group, the American Association of Retired Persons (AARP). Over time, organizations seeking to protect and expand welfare benefits for the poor also emerged (see *People in Politics*: "Marian Wright Edelman, Lobbying for the Poor"). Federal grant-in-aid programs to state and local governments inspired the development of governmental interest groups—the Council of State Governments, the National League of Cities, the National Governors Association, the U.S. Conference of Mayors, and so on—so that it is not uncommon today to see state and local governments lobby the national government (cities, towns, and even counties lobby their state governments). Expanded government support for education led to political activity by the National Education Association, the American Federation of Teachers, the American Association of Land Grant Colleges and Universities, and other educational groups.

Responding to Government Regulation   As more businesses and professions came under government regulation in the twentieth century, more organizations formed to protect and further their interests, including such large and powerful groups as the American Medical Association (doctors), the American Bar Association (lawyers), and the National Association of Broadcasters (broadcasters). Indeed, the issue of regulation—whether of public utilities, interstate transportation, mine safety, medicines, or children's pajamas—always causes the formation of interest groups. Some form to demand regulation; others form to protect their members from regulatory burdens.

(a)

(b)

(c)

(d)

(e)

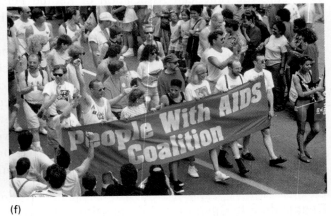

(f)

A History of Protest

From (a) the Whiskey Rebellion of 1794 to (b) violent early union protests such as the Haymarket Riot of 1886 to (c) Carrie Nation's battle to ban liquor and (d) the women's suffrage movement of the late nineteenth and early twentieth centuries to (e) the civil rights marches of the 1960s and (f) the gay rights marches of the 1990s, protest has had a long and strong history for interest groups in the United States. Some protests have been violent and others peaceful, but by addressing key issues of the time, all have prompted public debate, and many have resulted in changes in public policy.

People in Politics Marian Wright Edelman, Lobbying for the Poor

As founder and president of the Children's Defense Fund, Marian Wright Edelman has become legendary in Washington as a persuasive and persistent lobbyist on behalf of civil rights and social welfare legislation. A close friend of the Kennedy family, Edelman regularly testifies at Senate committee hearings, providing rapid-fire statistics on the effects of poverty on African American children. Each year the Children's Defense Fund, with a staff of more than a hundred in its Washington headquarters, produces numerous reports on infant mortality, homelessness, prenatal care, child nutrition, drug use, child abuse, teenage pregnancy, and single-parent households.

Marian Wright grew up in segregated rural South Carolina, the academically gifted daughter of a Baptist minister with a strong commitment to social justice. At an early age, she worked at the Wright House for the Aged, which her father had established. She entered all-black Spelman College in Atlanta and studied abroad at the Sorbonne in Paris and the University of Geneva, intending to take up a career in the foreign service. But Wright changed her career plans when she became involved in the early civil rights struggles in Atlanta. After graduating from Spelman, she entered Yale Law School to prepare herself in civil rights law. Upon her graduation in 1963, she immediately went to work for the NAACP Legal Defense Fund and traveled to Mississippi, where for four years she

undertook the dangerous work of defending civil rights workers. In 1967 she met Peter Edelman, a Harvard Law School graduate and legislative aide to Senator Robert Kennedy; together they persuaded Kennedy to personally tour the most poverty-stricken areas of the Mississippi Delta, where the senator directly confronted hungry children living in miserable conditions.

The following year Wright and Edelman were married and settled in Washington, where she established the Washington Research Project, a public-interest research and lobbying organization on behalf of President Lyndon Johnson's War on Poverty. She maintained her Washington base even while directing the Harvard University Center for Law and Education during the several years that her husband served as vice president of the University of Massachusetts. In 1973 she organized the Children's Defense Fund (CDF) in Washington, "a strong national voice for children and family." The Children's Defense Fund describes its mission: "to leave no child behind." (This CDF slogan become President G. W. Bush's logo for his 2001 education reform act.) It was the principal lobbying group behind the Head Start program as well as federal child care and the Family Leave Act of 1993.

Marian Wright Edelman has been especially effective as an advocate of social welfare programs with her lively style, sense of urgency, and wealth of information about children in poverty. She is a close friend of Hillary Clinton who once worked for the CDF. In 2000 Edelman received the Presidential Medal of Freedom, the nation's highest civilian award.

The Organized Interests in Washington

There are more than 1 million nonprofit organizations in the United States, several thousand of which are officially registered in Washington as lobbyists.[3] Trade and professional associations and corporations are the most common lobbies in Washington, but unions, public-interest groups, farm groups, environmental groups, ideological groups, religious and civil rights organizations, women's groups, veterans and defense-related groups, groups organized around a single issue (for example, Mothers Against Drunk Driving), and even organizations representing state and local governments also recognize that they need to be "where the action is." Among this huge assortment of organizations, many of which are very influential in their highly specialized field, there are a number of well-known organized interests. Even a partial list of organized interest groups (see Table 9.1) demonstrates the breadth and complexities of interest-group life in American politics.

SIMULATION
You Are a Lobbyist

Table *9.1* Major Organized Interest Groups, by Type

Business
Business Roundtable
National Association of
  Manufacturers
National Federation of Independent
  Businesses
National Small Business
  Association
U.S. Chamber of Commerce

Trade
American Bankers Association
American Gas Association
American Hospital Association
American Iron and Steel Institute
American Petroleum Institute
American Truckers Association
Automobile Dealers Association
Edison Electric Institute
Home Builders Association
Motion Picture Association of
  America
National Association of
  Broadcasters
National Association of Realtors
Pharmaceutical Mfrs of America

Professional
American Bar Association
American Medical Association
American Association for Justice
  (trial lawyers)
National Education Association

Union
AFL-CIO
American Federation of State,
  County, and Municipal
  Employees
American Federation of Teachers
International Brotherhood of
  Teamsters
International Ladies' Garment
  Workers Union
National Association of Letter
  Carriers
United Auto Workers
United Postal Workers
United Steel Workers

Agricultural
American Farm Bureau Federation
National Cattlemen's Association
National Farmers Union
National Grange
National Milk Producers Federation
Tobacco Institute

Women
League of Women Voters
National Organization for Women

Public Interest
Common Cause
Consumer Federation of America
Public Citizen
Public Interest Research Groups

Ideological
American Conservative Union
Americans for Constitutional Action
  (conservative)
Americans for Democratic Action
  (liberal)
Federalist Society (conservative)
People for the American Way
  (liberal)
MoveOn (liberal)

Single Issue
Mothers Against Drunk Driving
NARAL Pro-Choice America
National Rifle Association
National Right to Life Committee
PETA
Planned Parenthood Federation of
  America
National Taxpayers Union

Environmental
Environmental Defense Fund
Friends of the Earth
Greenpeace
National Wildlife Federation
National Resources Defense
  Council
Nature Conservancy
Sierra Club
Union of Concerned Scientists

Wilderness Society
Zero Population Growth

Religious
American Israel Public Affairs
  Committee
Anti-Defamation League of B'nai
  B'rith
Christian Coalition
National Council of Churches
U.S. Catholic Conference

Civil Rights
American Civil Liberties Union
American Indian Movement
Gay Lesbian Alliance Against
  Discrimination
Mexican-American Legal Defense
  and Education Fund
National Association for the
  Advancement of Colored People
National Urban League
Southern Christian Leadership
  Conference

Age Related
American Association of Retired
  Persons
National Committee to Preserve
  Social Security
Children's Defense Fund

Veterans
American Legion
Veterans of Foreign Wars
Vietnam Veterans of America

Defense
Air Force Association
American Security Council
Army Association
Navy Association

Government
National Association of Counties
National Conference of State
  Legislators
National Governors Association
National League of Cities
U.S. Conference of Mayors

Business and Trade Organizations Traditionally, economic organizations have dominated interest-group politics in Washington. There is ample evidence that economic interests continue to play a major role in national policy making, despite the rapid growth over the last several decades of consumer and environmental organizations. Certainly in terms of the sheer number of organizations with offices and representatives in Washington, business and professional groups and occupational and trade associations predominate. More than half of the organizations with offices in Washington are business or trade associations, and all together these organizations account for about 75 percent of all of the reported lobbying expenditures.[4]

Business interests are represented, first of all, by large inclusive organizations, such as the U.S. Chamber of Commerce, representing thousands of local chambers of commerce across the nation; the National Association of Manufacturers; the Business Roundtable, representing the nation's largest corporations; and the National Federation of Independent Businesses, representing small business. Specific business interests are also represented by thousands of **trade associations**. These associations can closely monitor the interests of their specialized memberships. Among the most powerful of these associations are the American Bankers Association, the American Gas Association, the American Iron and Steel Institute, the National Association of Real Estate Boards, the American Petroleum Institute, and the National Association of Broadcasters. In addition, many individual corporations and firms achieve representation in Washington by opening their own lobbying offices or by hiring experienced professional lobbying, public relations, or law firms.

★ **trade associations**
Interest groups composed of businesses in specific industries.

Professional Associations

Professional associations rival business and trade organizations in lobbying influence. The American Bar Association (ABA), the American Medical Association (AMA), and the National Education Association (NEA) are three of the most influential groups in Washington. For example, the ABA, which includes virtually all of the nation's practicing attorneys, and its more specialized offspring, the American Association for Justice (trial lawyers), have successfully resisted efforts to reform the nation's tort laws (see *A Conflicting View*: "America Is Drowning in a Sea of Lawsuits," Chapter 13).

Organized Labor

Labor organizations have declined in membership over the last several decades. The percentage of the total workforce belonging to unions has declined from about 37 percent in the 1950s to about 12 percent today. Workers in the private sector have largely avoided unions (see Figure 9.1). The major industrial unions—for example, the United Steelworkers of America, United Automobile Workers, United Mine Workers—have shrunk in membership.

Figure *9.1*
Going Public: Unions and the American Workforce

Source: Statistical Abstract of the United States, 2008.

Controversy

What Groups Deserve Washington's Attention?

Americans distinguish between groups that they believe merit the attention of Washington policymakers and those that do not. The majority of people polled believe that big corporations, Hollywood movie executives, and trial lawyers receive "too much" attention in Washington. In contrast, majorities believe that senior citizens, the poor, small business owners, and veterans receive "too little" attention in the nation's capitol.

Q. Do you think the political leaders in Washington pay too much attention, about the right amount, or too little attention to the needs of each of the following groups?

	Too Much	About Right	Too Little
Big corporations	76%	16%	6%
Hollywood movie executives	74	19	4
Trial lawyers	55	31	10
Defense contractors	53	27	16
Religious conservatives	48	33	17
Gays and lesbians	46	27	24
Labor unions	34	38	26
Hispanics	25	40	32
Doctors	22	49	26
Blacks	16	48	34
Senior citizens	5	28	66
The poor	5	18	77
Small-business owners	3	28	68
Military veterans	2	16	81

Source: Gallup Poll, March, 2007.

Only the unions of government employees—for example, the American Federation of State, Country, and Municipal Employees, the National Education Association—and some transportation and service workers unions—for example, the Teamsters Union, Service Employees International, International Brotherhood of Electrical Workers—have gained members in recent years.

Nevertheless, labor unions remain a major political influence in Congress and the Democratic Party. The AFL-CIO is a federation of sixty-eight separate unions with more than 13 million members. The AFL-CIO has long maintained a large and capable lobbying staff in Washington, and it provides both financial contributions and campaign services (registration, get-out-the-vote, information, endorsements) for members of Congress it favors. Many of the larger individual unions also maintain offices in Washington and offer campaign contributions and services.

Today union influence is greatest among government employees, including teachers. About 38 percent of all public sector employees are unionized. The American Federation of State, County, and Municipal Employees (AFSCME), the National Education Association (NEA), the American Federation of Teachers (AFT), and the Teamsters Union (which recruits public employees in sanitation and transportation) are among the few unions growing in membership.

Labor union political campaign contributions (see "PAC Power" on page 310) remain a major source of union influence in Washington. The AFSCME, NEA, Teamsters, United Auto Workers, United Steel Workers, Electrical Workers, Machinists, and Letter Carriers, as well as the AFL-CIO itself, are regularly ranked among the top contributors in congressional elections. Almost all union campaign contributions go to Democratic candidates.

Farm Organizations Even though the farm population of the United States has declined from about 25 percent of the total population in the 1930s to less than 3 percent today, farmers—especially large agricultural producers and corporate food processors—remain a very potent political force in Washington. Agricultural interests are organized both into large inclusive groups, such as the American Farm Bureau Federation and the National Grange, and into very effective specialized groups, such as the National Milk Producers and the National Cattlemen's Association. Small and low-income farmers are represented by the National Farmers Union.

Women's Organizations Women's organizations date back to the antislavery societies in pre–Civil War America. The first generation of feminists—Lucretia Mott, Elizabeth Cady Stanton, Lucy Stone, and Susan B. Anthony—learned to organize, hold public meetings, and conduct petition campaigns as abolitionists. After the Civil War, women were successful in changing many state laws that abridged the rights of married women and otherwise treated them as "chattel" (property) of their husbands. Women were also prominent in the Anti-Saloon League, which succeeded in outlawing prostitution and gambling in every state except Nevada and provided a major source of support for the 18th Amendment (Prohibition). In the early twentieth century, the feminist movement concentrated on obtaining the vote (suffrage) for women. Today the League of Women Voters—a broad-based organization that provides information to voters—backs registration and get-out-the-vote drives and generally supports measures seeking to ensure honesty and integrity in government.

Interest in feminist politics revived in the wake of the civil rights movement of the 1960s. New organizations sprang up to compete with the conventional activities of the League of Women Voters by taking a more activist stance toward women's issues. The largest of these organizations is the National Organization for Women (NOW), founded in 1966.

Religious Groups Churches and religious groups have a long history of involvement in American politics—from the pre–Civil War antislavery crusades, to the prohibition effort in the early twentieth century, to the civil rights movement of the 1960s. The leadership for the historic Civil Rights Act of 1964 came from the Reverend Martin Luther King, Jr., and his Southern Christian Leadership Conference. Today religious groups span the political spectrum, from liberal organizations such as the National Council of Churches and Anti-Defamation League of B'nai B'rith, to conservative and fundamentalist organizations, such as the Christian Coalition, often referred to as the "religious right" (see *Politics Up Close*: "The Christian Coalition: Organizing the Faithful").

Public-Interest Groups Public-interest groups claim to represent broad classes of people—consumers, voters, reformers, or the public as a whole. Groups with lofty-sounding names, such as Common Cause, Public Citizen, and the Consumer Federation of America, perceive themselves as balancing the narrow,

★ **public-interest groups**
Interest groups that claim to represent broad classes of people or the public as a whole.

"A _very_ special interest to see you, Senator."
©The New Yorker Collection 1993 Joseph Farris from cartoonbank.com. All Rights Reserved.

Politics Up Close   The Christian Coalition: Organizing the Faithful

Christian fundamentalists, whose religious beliefs are based on a literal reading of the Bible, have become a significant political force in the United States through effective organization. Perhaps the most influential Christian fundamentalist organization today is the Christian Coalition, with nearly 2 million active members throughout the country.

Fundamentalist Christians are opposed to abortion, pornography, and homosexuality; they favor the recognition of religion in public life, including prayer in schools; and they despair at the decline of traditional family values in American culture, including motion pictures and television broadcasting. Historically, fundamentalist Protestant churches avoided politics as profane and concentrated evangelical efforts on saving individual souls. Their few ventures into worldly politics—notably the prohibition movement in the early twentieth century—ended in defeat. Their strength tended to be in the southern, rural, and poorer regions of the country. They were widely ridiculed in the national media.

In the 1960s, television evangelism emerged as a religious force in the United States. The Reverend Pat Robertson founded the Christian Broadcasting Network (CBN) and later purchased the Family Channel. But efforts by social conservatives to build a "moral majority" for political action largely failed, as did Robertson's presidential candidacy in 1988. Televangelists, including Jerry Falwell and Tammy Faye Bakker, suffered popular disdain following some well-publicized scandals.

Although officially nonpartisan, the Coalition became an important force in Republican politics; religious fundamentalists may constitute as much as one-third of the party's voter support. The Christian Coalition does not officially endorse candidates, but its voter guides (at right) clearly indicate which candidates reflect the coalition's position on major issues. The political influence of the Christian Coalition in Republican politics, and the "religious right" generally, ensures that most GOP candidates for public office publicly express support for a "profamily" agenda. This agenda includes a constitutional amendment allowing prayer in public schools; vouchers for parents to send their children to private, religious schools; banning late-term abortions as well as banning the use of taxpayer funds to pay for abortions; restrictions on pornography on cable television and the Internet; and opposition to human embryo research and human cloning.

Religious groups can play a key role in elections by informing their members about candidates and getting out the vote. The Christian Coalition is one of the most active religious groups.

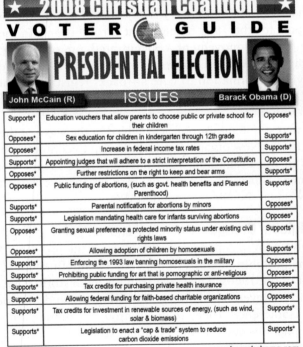

★ **2008 Christian Coalition** ★
VOTER GUIDE
PRESIDENTIAL ELECTION

John McCain (R)   ISSUES   Barack Obama (D)

McCain	Issue	Obama
Supports*	Education vouchers that allow parents to choose public or private school for their children	Opposes*
Opposes*	Sex education for children in kindergarten through 12th grade	Supports*
Opposes*	Increase in federal income tax rates	Supports*
Supports*	Appointing judges that will adhere to a strict interpretation of the Constitution	Opposes*
Opposes*	Further restrictions on the right to keep and bear arms	Supports*
Opposes*	Public funding of abortions, (such as govt. health benefits and Planned Parenthood)	Supports*
Supports*	Parental notification for abortions by minors	Opposes*
Supports*	Legislation mandating health care for infants surviving abortions	Opposes*
Opposes*	Granting sexual preference a protected minority status under existing civil rights laws	Supports*
Opposes*	Allowing adoption of children by homosexuals	Supports*
Supports*	Enforcing the 1993 law banning homosexuals in the military	Opposes*
Supports*	Prohibiting public funding for art that is pornographic or anti-religious	Opposes*
Supports*	Tax credits for purchasing private health insurance	Opposes*
Supports*	Allowing federal funding for faith-based charitable organizations	Opposes*
Supports*	Tax credits for investment in renewable sources of energy, (such as wind, solar & biomass)	Supports*
Supports*	Legislation to enact a "cap & trade" system to reduce carbon dioxide emissions	Supports*

www.johnmccain.com   www.barackobama.com

Each candidate was sent a 2008 Federal Issues Survey by mail and/or facsimile machine. When possible, positions of candidates on issues were verified or determined using voting records and/or public statements, articles or campaign literature. An asterisk (*) indicates such information was used to determine positions and sources are available on request.

Paid for and authorized by the Christian Coalition; PO Box 37030 - Washington, DC 20013

The Christian Coalition is a pro-family, citizen action organization. This voter guide is provided for educational purposes only and is not to be construed as an endorsement of any candidate or party.
Please visit our web site at www.cc.org

★ *Vote on November 4* ★

Photo courtesy: Christian Coalition of America.

People in Politics   Lance Armstrong, Lobbying for Cancer Research

In 1996, Lance Armstrong was 25 and a world-class cyclist when he was diagnosed with testicular cancer—cancer that had spread to his abdomen, lungs, and brain. His prognosis was dim. But Armstrong fought through two surgeries and multiple rounds of chemotherapy, and then began retraining for what was to become an unprecedented career in cycling. He would win an awe-inspiring seven consecutive Tour de France races, from 1999 to 2005, a feat unparalleled in the sports world.

During his treatment and while still recovering, and before he knew his own fate, he created the Lance Armstrong Foundation—initially a charitable organization providing support through education, referrals, and counseling, for people with cancer. Soon the Foundation and Armstrong himself became a voice for the cancer community to be heard nationwide. His goal: to raise awareness of health care policy issues and increase federal funding for cancer research and treatment. Armstrong became a powerful voice in the nation's capital for the National Cancer Institute and the Center for Disease Control. Each year Armstrong holds a meeting with members of Congress and their staffs updating them on the state of cancer research and asking for their support for cancer programs. During the 2008 presidential race, Armstrong invited both Democratic and Republican candidates to a debate on how best to reduce deaths and suffering from cancer and to expand research on cancer survivorship. Armstrong himself now devotes full time to the work of his Foundation.

Mentioned as a possible political candidate in his home state of Texas, Armstrong replied, "I need to run for one office, the presidency of the Cancer Fighters Union of the World." He also said he feared that he would lose lobbying influence if he chose one side or the other in partisan politics.

"selfish" interests of business organizations, trade associations, unions, and other "special" interests. Public-interest groups generally lobby for greater government regulation of consumer products, public safety, campaign finance, and so on. Their reform agenda, as well as their call for a larger regulatory role for government, makes them frequent allies of liberal ideological groups, civil rights organizations, and environmental groups.[5]

Many public-interest groups were initially formed in the 1970s by "entrepreneurs" who saw an untapped "market" for the representation of these interests. Among the most influential public-interest groups are Common Cause, a self-styled "citizens' lobby," and the sprawling network of organizations created by consumer advocate Ralph Nader. Common Cause tends to focus on election-law reform, public financing of elections, and limitations on political contributions. The Nader organization began as a consumer protection group focusing on auto safety but soon spread to encompass a wide variety of causes.

Single-Issue Groups   Like public-interest groups, **single-issue groups** appeal to principle and belief. But as their name implies, single-issue groups concentrate their attention on a single cause. They attract the support of individuals with a strong commitment to that cause (see *People in Politics*: "Lance Armstrong, Lobbying for Cancer Research"). Single-issue groups have little incentive to compromise their position. They exist for a single cause; no other issues really matter to them. They are by nature passionate and often shrill. Their attraction to members is the intensity of their beliefs.

★ **single-issue groups**
Organizations formed to support or oppose government action on a specific issue.

Among the most vocal single-issue groups in recent years have been the organizations on both sides of the abortion issue. NARAL Pro-Choice America describes itself as "pro-choice" and opposes any restrictions on a woman's right to obtain an abortion. The National Right-to-Life Committee describes itself as "pro-life" and opposes abortion for any reason other than to preserve the life of the mother. Other prominent single-issue groups include the National Rifle Association (opposed to gun control) and Mothers Against Drunk Driving (MADD).

★ **ideological organizations**
Interest groups that pursue ideologically based (liberal or conservative) agendas.

Ideological Groups Ideological organizations pursue liberal or conservative agendas, often with great passion and considerable financial resources derived from true-believing contributors. The ideological groups rely heavily on computerized mailings to solicit funds from persons identified as holding liberal or conservative views. The oldest of the established ideological groups is the liberal Americans for Democratic Action (ADA), well known for its annual liberalism ratings of members of the Congress according to their support for or rejection of programs of concern. The American Conservative Union (ACU) also rates members of Congress each year. Overall, Democrats do better on the liberal list and Republicans on the conservative list, although both parties include some Congress members who occasionally vote on the opposite side of the fence from the majority of their fellow party members (see Table 9.2). Other interest groups, such as the AFL-CIO, the National Taxpayers Union, and NARAL Pro-Choice America also rate members of Congress, but these groups have a narrower focus than the ADA and ACU. Yet another prominent ideological group, People for the American Way, was formed by television producer Norman Lear to coordinate the efforts of liberals in the entertainment industry as well as the general public, but it issues no ratings.

Government Lobbies The federal government's grant-in-aid programs to state and local governments (see Chapter 4) have spawned a host of lobbying efforts by these governments in Washington, D.C. Thus state- and local-government taxpayers foot the bill to lobby Washington to transfer federal taxpayers' revenues to states and communities. The National Governors Association occupies a beautiful marble building, the Hall of the States, in Washington, along with representatives of the separate states and many major cities. The National League of Cities and the National Association of Counties also maintain large Washington offices, as does the U.S. Conference of Mayors. The National Conference of State Legislators sends its lobbyists to Washington from its Denver headquarters. These groups pursue a wide policy agenda and often confront internal disputes. But they are united in their support for increased federal transfers of tax revenues to states and cities.

Leaders and Followers

Organizations require leadership. And over time leaders develop a perspective somewhat different from that of their organizations' membership. A key question in interest-group politics is how well organization leaders represent the views of their members.

★ **interest-group entrepreneurs**
Leaders who create organizations and market memberships.

Interest-Group Entrepreneurs People who create organizations and build membership in those organizations—**interest-group entrepreneurs**—have played a major role in strengthening the interest-group system in recent decades. These entrepreneurs help overcome a major obstacle to the formation of strong interest groups—the *free-rider* problem.

Table **9.2**   Under the Influence?: Ideological Interest-Group Ratings for U.S. Senators*

Ideological interest groups rate Congress members according to their votes on issues deemed important to liberals and conservatives.

ADA Americans for Democratic Action (liberal)		ACU American Conservative Union (conservative)	
"Senate Heroes" **95–100% Voting with ADA**		**"The Best and Brightest"** **100% Voting with ACU**	
Stabenow	D-MI	Barrasso	R-WY
Klobuchar	D-MN	Coburn	R-OK
Casey	D-PA	DeMint	R-SC
Akakd	D-HI	Inhofe	R-OK
Durbin	D-IL	Kyl	R-AZ
Bayh	D-IN		
Levin	D-MI	**"The Worst of the Worst"**	
Leahy	D-VT	**0% Voting with ACU**	
Feingold	D-WI	Akad	D-HI
Kohl	D-WI	Biden	D-DE
Harkin	D-IA	Brown	D-OH
Menendez	D-NT	Cardin	D-MD
Sanders	I-VT	Clinton	D-NY
"Senate Losers"		Dodd	D-CT
0–5% Voting with ADA		Durbin	D-IL
Kye	R-AZ	Feinstein	D-CA
Brownback	R-KN	Inouye	D-HI
Coburn	R-OK	Johnson	D-IL
Coburn	R-NV	Kennedy	D-MA
Burr	R-NC	Kohl	D-WI
DeMint	R-SC	Lautenberg	D-NJ
		Leahy	D-VT
		Mikulski	D-MD
		Murray	D-WA
		Reid	D-NV
		Schumer	D-NY
		Whitehouse	D-RI

* Voting in 2007

Sources: Americans for Democratic Action, www.adaction.org; American Conservative Union, www.conservative.org

Free-riders are people who benefit from the efforts of others but do not contribute to the costs of those efforts. Not everyone feels an obligation to support organizations that represent their interests or views. Some people feel that their own small contribution will not make a difference in the success or failure of the organization's goals and, moreover, that they will benefit from any successes even if they are not members. Indeed, most organizations enroll only a tiny fraction of the people they claim to represent. The task of the interest-group entrepreneur is to convince people to join the organization, either by appealing to their sense of obligation or by attracting them through tangible benefits.

★ **free-riders**
People who do not belong to an organization or pay dues, yet nevertheless benefit from its activities.

Marketing Membership   Interest-group entrepreneurs make different appeals for membership depending on the nature of the organization. Some appeal to passion or purpose, as, for example, those who seek to create ideological (liberal

Jack Nicholson on the cover of the March–April 2008 issue of *AARP* magazine, produced by the American Association of Retired Persons.

or conservative) organizations, public-interest organizations committed to environmental or consumer protection or governmental reform, and single-issue organizations devoted to the support or opposition of a single policy issue (gun control, abortion, and so on). Entrepreneurs of these organizations appeal to people's sense of duty and commitment to the cause rather than to material rewards of membership. By using sophisticated computerized mailing lists, they can solicit support from sympathetic people.[6]

Business, trade, and professional organizations usually offer their members many tangible benefits in addition to lobbying on behalf of their economic interests. These benefits may include magazines, journals, and newsletters that provide access to business, trade, and professional information as well as national conventions and meetings that serve as social settings for the development of contacts, friendships, and business and professional relationships. Some organizations also offer discount travel and insurance, credit cards, and the like, that go only to dues-paying members.

It is generally easier to organize smaller, specialized economic interests than larger, general, noneconomic interests. People more easily recognize that their own membership is important to the success of a small organization, and economic interests are more readily calculated in dollar terms.

Large organizations with broad goals—such as advancing the interests of all veterans or all retired people or all automobile drivers—must rely even more heavily on tangible benefits to solicit members. Indeed, some organizations have succeeded in recruiting millions of members (for example, the AARP with 39 million members, the American Automobile Association with 28 million members), most of whom have very little knowledge about the policy positions or lobbying activities of the organization. These members joined to receive specific benefits—magazines, insurance, travel tips, discounts. Leaders of these organizations may claim to speak for millions of members, but it is unlikely that these millions all share the policy views expressed by the leaders.

Organizational Democracy and Leader/Member Agreement   Most organized interest groups are run by a small group of leaders and activists. Few interest groups are governed democratically; members may drop out if they do not like the direction their organization is taking but rarely do they have the opportunity to directly challenge or replace the organization's leadership. Relatively few members attend national meetings, vote in organizational elections, or try to exercise influence within their organization. Thus the leadership may not always reflect the views of the membership, especially in large organizations that rely heavily on tangible benefits to recruit members. Leaders of these organizations enjoy considerable freedom in adopting policy positions and negotiating, bargaining, and compromising in the political arena.

The exception to this rule is the single-issue group. Because the strength of these groups is in the intensity of their members' beliefs, the leaders of such groups are closely tied to their members' views. They cannot bargain or compromise these views or adopt policy positions at variance with those of their members.

Class Bias in Membership   Americans are joiners. A majority of the population belong to at least one organization, most often a church. Yet membership in organized interest groups is clearly linked to socioeconomic status. Membership is greatest among professional and managerial, college-educated, and high-income persons.[7]

Lawyers for Google, Yahoo!, and Cisco Systems, and officials from Human Rights Watch and the Global Internet Freedom Consortium are sworn in before a Senate Judiciary Committee hearing on global internet freedom on Tuesday, May 20, 2000. From left to right: Nicole Wong, Deputy General Counsel for Google, Inc.; Michael Samway, Deputy General Counsel for Yahoo! Inc.; Arvind Ganesan, Program Director for Human Right Watch; Mark Chandler, Senior Vice President, General Counsel, and Secretary for Cisco Systems, Inc.; and Shiyu Zhou, Deputy Director of Global Internet Freedom Consortium.

The Washington Lobbyists

Washington is a labyrinth of interest representatives—lawyers and law firms; independent consultants; public and governmental relations firms; business, professional, and trade associations; and advocates of special causes. It is estimated that more than 15,000 people in Washington fit the definition of **lobbyist**, a person working to influence government policies and actions. This figure suggests at least twenty-eight lobbyists for every member of Congress. Roughly $1.5 *billion* is spent on direct lobbying activities *each year*;[8] this figure does *not* include political campaign contributions. The top spenders for direct lobbying are listed in Table 9.3.

★ **lobbyist**
Person working to influence government policies and actions.

Who Are the Lobbyists?   Lobbyists in Washington share a common goal—to influence the making and enforcing of laws—and common tactics to achieve this goal. Many lobbyists are the employees of interest-group organizations who devote all of their efforts to their sponsors.

Other lobbyists are located in independent law, consulting, or public relations firms that take on clients for fees. Independent lobbyists, especially law firms, are often secretive about whom they represent, especially when they represent foreign governments. Lobbyists frequently prefer to label their activities as "government relations," "public affairs," "regulatory liaison," "legislative counseling," or merely "representation."

In reality, many independent lawyers and lobbyists in Washington are "fixers" who offer to influence government policies for a price. Many are former government officials—former Congress members, cabinet secretaries, White House aides, and the like—who "know their way around." Their personal connections help to "open doors" to allow their paying clients to "just get a chance to talk" with top officials. (Many lobbyists maintain offices on K Street in downtown Washington, D.C.; occasionally, "K Street" is used as a term to describe the Washington lobbying community.)

Some lobbying organizations rely heavily on their campaign contributions to achieve lobbying power; others rely on large memberships, and still others on politically active members who concentrate their attention on a narrow range of issues (see *Politics Up Close*: "Washington's Most Powerful Lobbies").

Table *9.3*   Money Talks: Top Lobbying Spenders, 1998–2007
Direct spending on lobbying (not including campaign contributions) amounts to over $1 billion each year.

Rank	Organization	Total Spending
1	U.S. Chamber of Commerce	$338,324,680
2	American Medical Assn.	$157,247,500
3	General Electric	$149,990,000
4	American Hospital Assn.	$138,084,144
5	Pharmaceutical Researchers & Mfrs. of America	$115,008,600
6	AARP	$112,732,064
7	Edison Electric Institute	$107,132,628
8	National Assn. of Realtors	$103,890,000
9	Business Roundtable	$101,660,000
10	Northrop Grumman	$101,350,474
11	Blue Cross/Blue Shield	$90,163,317
12	Lockheed Martin	$87,797,702
13	Freddie Mac	$86,164,048
14	Verizon Communications	$83,407,022
15	Boeing Co.	$82,038,310
16	General Motors	$77,620,483
17	Philip Morris	$75,500,000
18	Roche Group	$74,888,942
19	Fannie Mae	$73,857,000
20	Ford Motor Co.	$71,312,808

Source: Center for Responsive Politics, www.opensecrets.org

Washington's army of lobbyists includes many former members of Congress. Lobbying is a favorite occupation of former members; they can command much higher salaries as lobbyists than they did as Congress members. Lobbying firms are pleased to have people who know the lawmaking process from the inside and who can easily "schmooze" with their former colleagues.

Regulation of Lobbies   The Constitution's 1st Amendment guarantee of the right "to petition the government for a redress of grievances" protects lobbying. But the government can and does regulate lobbying activities, primarily through disclosure laws. The Regulation of Lobbying Act requires lobbyists to register and to report how much they spend, but definitions of *lobbying* are unclear and enforcement is weak. Many large lobbying groups have never registered as lobbyists. These organizations claim that because lobbying is not their principal activity, they need not register under the law. In addition, financial reports of lobbyists grossly underestimate the extent of lobbying in Congress because the law requires reports of only money spent for *direct* lobbying before Congress, not money spent for public relations or grass-roots mobilization of members to pressure Congress. Another weakness in the law is that it applies only to attempts to influence Congress; it does not regulate lobbying activities in administrative agencies or litigation in the courts.

Tax laws require nonprofit organizations to refrain from direct lobbying in order to retain their tax-free status. Under current tax law, individual contributions to nonprofit charitable and educational organizations are tax deductible, and the income of these organizations is tax free. But these organizations risk losing these tax preferences if a "substantial part" of their activities is "attempting

Fortune magazine sponsored a survey of more than 2,000 Washington "insiders," including members of Congress, their staffs, and White House officials, asking them to rank the most powerful lobbyists in the capital. The results were as follows:

The "Power 25"

1. American Association of Retired Persons
2. American Israel Public Affairs Committee
3. National Federation of Independent Business
4. National Rifle Association of America
5. AFL-CIO
6. Association of Trial Lawyers of America
7. Christian Coalition
8. Credit Union National Association
9. National Right to Life Committee
10. American Medical Association
11. Chamber of Commerce of the U.S.A.
12. Independent Insurance Agencies of America
13. National Association of Manufacturers
14. American Farm Bureau Federation
15. National Restaurant Association
16. National Association of Home Builders of the U.S.
17. National Association of Realtors
18. National Association of Broadcasters
19. Motion Picture Association of America
20. American Bankers Association
21. National Education Association
22. Health Insurance Association of America
23. American Council of Life Insurance
24. National Beer Wholesalers Association
25. Veterans of Foreign Wars of the United States

to influence legislation." Thus, for example, Washington think tanks such as the Brookings Institution, the American Enterprise Institute, and the Heritage Foundation refrain from direct lobbying even though they make policy recommendations. But the line between public affairs "education" and "lobbying" is very fuzzy.

Tightening Lobby Regulations   Recent scandals involving lobbyists (see Ethics" later in this chapter) have led to proposals to curtail gifts by lobbyists to Congress members, including paid vacations, dinners, flights, and so forth. Another reform proposal has been to eliminate "earmarking" of appropriations for specific projects that have been heavily lobbied. Yet, so far, Congress has failed to adopt these reform proposals.

The Fine Art of Lobbying

Any activity directed at a government decision maker with the hope of influencing decisions is a form of **lobbying.** (The term arose from the practice of waiting in the lobbies of legislative chambers to meet and persuade legislators.) For organized interests, lobbying is continuous—in congressional committees, in congressional staff offices, at the White House, at executive agencies, at Washington cocktail parties. If a group loses a round in Congress, it continues the fight in the agency in charge of executing the policy, or it challenges the policy in the courts. The following year it resumes the struggle in Congress: it fights to repeal the offending legislation, to weaken amendments, or to reduce the agency's budget enough to cripple enforcement efforts.

Lobbying techniques are as varied as the imagination of interest-group leaders, but such activities generally fall into seven categories: (1) public relations;

★ **lobbying**
Activities directed at government officials with the hope of influencing their decisions.

(2) access; (3) information; (4) grass-roots mobilization; (5) protests and demonstrations; (6) coalition building; and (7) campaign support. In the real world of Washington power struggles, all these techniques may be applied simultaneously or innovative techniques may be discovered and applied at any time (see Figure 9.2).

Public Relations   Many interest groups actually spend more of their time, energy, and resources on **public relations**—developing and maintaining a favorable climate of opinion in the nation—than on direct lobbying of Congress. The mass media—television, magazines, newspapers—are saturated with expensive ads by oil companies, auto companies, chemical manufacturers, trade associations, teachers' unions, and many other groups, all seeking to create a favorable image for themselves with the general public. These ads are designed to go well beyond promoting the sale of particular products; they portray these organizations as patriotic citizens, protectors of the environment, providers of jobs, defenders of family values, and supporters of the American way of life. Generally, business interests have an advantage in the area of public relations because public relations and sales and marketing activities are synonymous. But paid advertising is less credible than news stories and media commentary. Hence interest groups generate a daily flood of press releases, media events, interviews, reports, and studies for the media. Media news stories appear to favor liberal public interest groups.[9]

Access   "Opening doors" is a major business in Washington. To influence decision makers, organized interests must first acquire **access** to them. Individuals who have personal contacts in Congress, the White House, or the bureaucracy (or who say they do) sell their services at high prices. Washington law firms, public relations agencies, and consultants—often former insiders—all offer their connections, along with their advice, to their clients. The personal prestige of the lobbyist, together with the group's perceived political influence, helps open doors in Washington.

★ **public relations**
Building and maintaining goodwill with the general public.

★ **access**
Meeting and talking with decision makers, a prerequisite to direct persuasion.

Figure **9.2**

How the Game Is Played: A Guide to the Fine Art of Lobbying

Interest groups seek to influence public policy both directly through lobbying and campaign contributions (inside strategy) and indirectly through public relations efforts to mold public opinion (outside strategy).

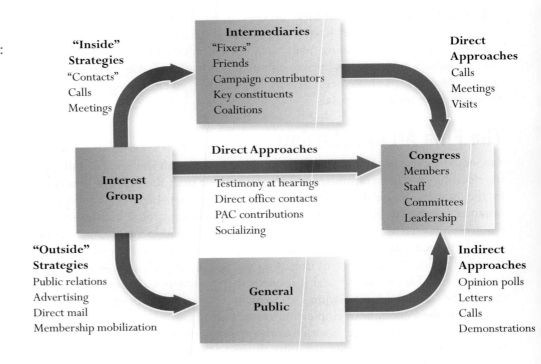

Washington socializing is often an exercise in access—rubbing elbows with powerful people. Well-heeled lobbyists regularly pay hundreds, even thousands, of dollars per plate at fund-raising dinners for members of Congress. Lobbyists regularly provide dinners, drinks, travel, vacations, and other amenities to members of Congress, their families, and congressional staff, as well as to White House and other executive officials. These favors are rarely provided on a direct quid pro quo basis in exchange for votes. Rather, they are designed to gain access—"just a chance to talk."

"Schmoozing," building personal relationships, consumes much of a lobbyist's time and the client's money. It is difficult to know how much this contributes to actual success in passing, defeating, or amending legislation. But, to quote one client: "I figured that half of the money I spend on lobbying is wasted. Trouble is, I don't know which half."[10]

Information Once lobbyists gain access, their knowledge and information become valuable resources to those they lobby. Members of Congress and their staff look to lobbyists for *technical expertise* on the issue under debate as well as *political information* about the group's position on the issue. Members of Congress must vote on hundreds of questions each year, and it is impossible for them to be fully informed about the wide variety of bills and issues they face. Consequently, many of them (and administrators in the executive branch as well) come to depend on trusted lobbyists.

Lobbyists also spend considerable time and effort keeping informed about bills affecting their interests. They must be thoroughly familiar with the "ins and outs" of the legislative process—the relevant committees and subcommittees, their schedules of meetings and hearings, their key staff members, the best moments to act, the precise language for proposed bills and amendments, the witnesses for hearings, and the political strengths and weaknesses of the legislators themselves. In their campaign to win congressional and bureaucratic support for their programs, lobbyists engage in many different types of activities. Nearly all testify at congressional hearings and make direct contact with government officials on issues that affect them. In addition, lobbyists provide the technical reports and analyses used by congressional staffs in their legislative research. Engaging in protest demonstrations is a less common activity, in part because it involves a high risk of alienating some members of Congress.

Experienced lobbyists develop a reputation for accurate information. Most successful lobbyists do not supply faulty information; their success depends on maintaining the trust and confidence of decision makers. A reputation for honesty is as important as a reputation for influence.

Grass-Roots Mobilization Many organized interests lobby Congress from both the *outside* and the *inside*. From the outside, organizations seek to mobilize **grass-roots lobbying** of members of Congress by their constituents. Lobbyists frequently encourage letters and calls from "the folks back home." Larger organized interests often have local chapters throughout the nation and can mobilize these local affiliates to apply pressure when necessary. Lobbyists encourage influential local people to visit the office of a member of Congress personally or to make a personal phone call on behalf of the group's position. And, naturally, members are urged to vote for or against certain candidates, based on their policy stances (see *Politics Up Close*: "AARP: The Nation's Most Powerful Interest Group").

Experienced lawmakers recognize attempts by lobby groups to orchestrate "spontaneous" grass-roots outpourings of cards and letters. Pressure mail is often identical in wording and content. Nevertheless, members of Congress dare not

U.S. Chamber of Commerce President Tom Donohue (left) and China Vice Premier Wang Qishan share a toast after a business partnership signing ceremony at the U.S. Chamber of Commerce in Washington, June 16, 2008.

★ **grass-roots lobbying**
Attempts to influence government decision making by inspiring constituents to contact their representatives.

Politics Up Close   AARP: The Nation's Most Powerful Interest Group

Scott Stantis

The American Association of Retired Persons (AARP) is the nation's largest and most powerful interest group, with more than 39 million members. The AARP's principal interests are the Social Security and Medicare system programs, the nation's largest and most expensive entitlements.

Like many other interest groups, the AARP has grown in membership not only by appealing to the political interests of retired people but also by offering a wide array of material benefits. For a $12.50 annual fee, members are offered a variety of services, including discounted rates on home, auto, life and health insurance; discounted mail-order drugs, tax advisory services; discounted rates on hotels, rental cars, and so on; a newsletter, *The AARP Bulletin*; a semi-monthly magazine, *Modern Maturity*, and for baby boomers now reaching their 50s, a magazine, *My Generation*.

The political power of senior citizens is so great that prospects for limiting current or even future increases in government benefits for the elderly are slim. President G. W. Bush's proposal to allow workers to invest part of their Social Security taxes in private accounts was defeated largely by the work of the AARP. Social Security is said to be the "third rail of American politics—touch it and you're dead."

Critics of the AARP argue that its lobbyists in Washington do not fairly represent the views of the nation's senior citizens, that few of its members know what its lobbying arm does at the nation's capital. Indeed, in the struggle over prescription drug coverage under Medicare in 2003, the AARP leadership was accused of favoring its own interest in selling private insurance over the interests of its members in receiving government-paid insurance. AARP keeps its dues low, and consequently its membership high, through its business ties with insurance companies, its magazine advertising revenue, and commercial royalties revenues for endorsing products and services.

Mike Tidwell of the U.S. Climate Emergency Council and the Chesapeake Climate Action Network speaks about the impact of coal on global warming on Capitol Hill in Washington on June 14, 2007. Protesters brought buckets of coal to protest legislation calling for the liquefaction of coal as a means of reducing American dependency on oil.

ignore a flood of letters and telegrams from home, for the mail shows that constituents are aware of the issue and care enough to sign their names.

Protests and Demonstrations Interest groups occasionally employ protests and demonstrations to attract media attention to their concerns and thereby apply pressure on officials to take action. For these actions to succeed in getting issues on the agenda of decision makers in Congress, in the White House, and in executive agencies, participation by the media, especially television, is essential. The media carry the message of the protest or demonstration both to the general public and directly to government officials (see as "Protest as Political Participation" in Chapter 5).

Organized interest groups most often resort to protests and demonstrations when (1) they are frustrated in more traditional "inside" lobbying efforts; and/or (2) they wish to intensify pressure on officials at a specific point in time. Demonstrations typically attract media attention for a short time only. But media coverage of specific events can carry a clear message—for example, farmers driving tractors through Washington to protest farm conditions; motorcyclists conducting a giant "bike-in" to protest laws requiring helmets; cattle raisers driving steers down the Washington Mall to protest beef prices. The potential drawbacks to such activities are that the attention is short-lived and the group's reputation may be tarnished if the protest turns nasty or violent.

Coalition Building
Interest groups frequently seek to build **coalitions** with other groups in order to increase their power. Coalitions tend to form among groups with parallel interests: for example, the National Organization for Women, the League of Women Voters, and NARAL Pro-Choice America on women's issues. Coalitions usually form temporarily around a single piece of legislation in a major effort to secure or prevent its passage.

★ **coalitions**
A joining together of interest groups (or individuals) to achieve common goals.

Campaign Support
Perhaps the real key to success in lobbying is the campaign contribution. Interest-group contributions not only help lobbyists gain access and a favorable hearing but also help elect people friendly to the group's goals. As the costs of campaigning increase, legislators must depend more heavily on the contributions of organized interests.

Most experienced lobbyists avoid making electoral threats. Amateur lobbyists sometimes threaten legislators by vowing to defeat them at the next election, but this tactic usually produces a hostile reaction among members of Congress. Legislators are likely to respond to crude pressures by demonstrating their independence and voting against the threatening lobbyist. Moreover, experienced members of Congress know that such threats are empty; lobbyists can seldom deliver enough votes to influence the outcome of an election.

Lobbying Ethics
Experienced lobbyists also avoid offering a campaign contribution in exchange for a specific vote.[11] Crude "vote buying" (bribery) is illegal and risks repulsing politicians who refuse bribes. **Bribery**, when it occurs, is probably limited to very narrow and specific actions—payments to intervene in a particular case before an administrative agency; payments to insert a very specific break in a tax bill or a specific exemption in a trade bill; payments to obtain a specific contract with the government. Bribery on major issues is very unlikely; there is too much publicity and too many participants for bribery to be effective.

★ **bribery**
Giving or offering anything of value in an effort to influence government officials in the performance of their duties.

To the skeptical, "lobbying ethics" may seem to be an oxymoron. Lobbyists regularly send Congress members and even their staffs on expensive junkets around the world and entertain them back in Washington with golf outings, free meals at expensive restaurants, luxury skybox seats at sporting events, and a host of other perks. And, of course, they direct their clients' campaign contributions to Congress members who support their cause. Prudent lobbyists report these contributions and avoid any direct communications that would suggest that the contributions were made in exchange for a particular official action. But ethical problems remain. In 2005 lobbyist Jack Abramoff was indicted for defrauding Indian tribes of millions in fees and campaign contributions that had been given by the tribes to gain favorable treatment of their gambling enterprises. Abramoff kept millions for himself, but he also distributed millions to hundreds of Congress members both directly and indirectly through organizations he created. Following his indictment, many Congress members rushed to rid themselves of his contributions by giving them to charity.

PAC Power

★ **political action committees (PACs)**
Organizations that solicit and receive campaign contributions from corporations, unions, trade associations, and ideological and issue-oriented groups, and their members, and then distribute these funds to political candidates.

Organized interest groups channel their campaign contributions through **political action committees (PACs)**. PACs are organized by corporations, labor unions, trade associations, ideological and issue-oriented groups, and cooperatives and nonprofit corporations to solicit campaign contributions and distribute them to political candidates.

Distributing PAC Money Because PAC contributions are in larger lumps than individual contributions, PAC contributions often attract more attention from members of Congress. The PACs listed in Table 9.4 gave millions of dollars to finance the campaigns of their potential allies in 2008.

Most PACs use their campaign contributions to acquire access and influence with decision makers. Corporate, trade, and professional PAC contributions go overwhelmingly to incumbents, regardless of party. Leaders of these PACs know that incumbents are rarely defeated, and they do not wish to antagonize even unsympathetic members of Congress by backing challengers. However, ideological and issue-oriented PACs are more likely to allocate funds according to the candidates' policy positions and voting records. Labor PACs give almost all of their contributions to Democrats. Ideological and issue-oriented PACs give money to challengers

Federal Election Rules, PACs, and the Money Trail

Interest Groups and Campaign Finance

Table *9.4* Deep Pockets: The Big Money PACs in 2007–2008

Interest group PAC contributions account for about 35 percent of House campaign contributions and 20 percent of contributions to Senate campaigns.

Rank	Organization	Total Amount	Dem. Pct.	Repub. Pct.
1	Operating Engineers Union	$2,612,560	86%	14%
2	National Assn. of Realtors	$2,289,750	59%	41%
3	Intl. Brotherhood of Electrical Workers	$2,286,550	98%	2%
4	AT&T Inc.	$2,065,200	36%	64%
5	American Assn. for Justice (trial lawyers)	$1,904,000	95%	5%
6	National Beer Wholesalers Assn.	$1,856,500	52%	48%
7	Machinists/Aerospace Workers Union	$1,840,300	97%	3%
8	American Bankers Assn.	$1,818,520	39%	61%
9	International Assn. of Fire Fighters	$1,787,600	75%	25%
10	National Auto Dealers Assn.	$1,696,000	35%	65%
11	National Air Traffic Controllers Assn.	$1,638,825	77%	23%
12	Air Line Pilots Assn.	$1,634,000	85%	15%
13	Service Employees Inernational Union	$1,631,000	94%	6%
14	Laborers Union	$1,548,500	92%	8%
15	Credit Union National Assn.	$1,530,699	55%	45%
16	American Dental Assn.	$1,530,412	52%	48%
17	Sheet Metal Workers Union	$1,509,010	97%	3%
18	United Parcel Service	$1,502,001	41%	59%
19	Plumbers/Pipefitters Union	$1,467,150	94%	6%
20	American Crystal Sugar	$1,336,500	64%	36%

Source: Based on data released by the FEC on July 28, 2008.

Politics Up Close   EMILY's List

Fundraising is the greatest obstacle to mounting a successful campaign against an incumbent. And the most difficult problem facing challengers is raising money *early* in the campaign, when they have little name recognition and little or no standing in the polls.

EMILY's List is a politically adroit and effective effort to support liberal Democratic women candidates by infusing *early money* into their campaigns. EMILY stands for Early Money Is Like Yeast, because "it makes the dough rise." Early contributions provide the initial credibility that a candidate, especially a challenger, needs in order to solicit additional funds from individuals and organizations. EMILY is a fundraising network of thousands of contributors, each of whom pays $100 to join and pledges to give at least $100 to two women from a list of candidates prepared by EMILY's leaders. Most of the contributors are professional women who appreciate EMILY's screening of pro-choice, liberal women candidates around the country.

EMILY's List was begun in 1985 by a wealthy heir to a founder of IBM, Ellen Malcolm. Women challengers for congressional races traditionally faced frustration in fund raising. Incumbent male officeholders enjoyed a huge fund-raising advantage because contributors expected them to win and therefore opened their wallets to gain access and goodwill. EMILY's List has helped to overcome defeatism among both women candidates and contributors.

Senator Barbara Milkulski, Democrat of Maryland and an early beneficiary of EMILY's List, at a news conference.

EMILY's List supports *only* Democratic women candidates who are strong supporters of abortion rights. When the list was founded, there were no women in the Senate and only a very few in the House. In 2008 there were thirteen women in the Senate (eleven supported by EMILY's List) and forty-nine in the House (forty-three supported by EMILY's list). EMILY's List currently boasts of more than 100,000 member. EMILY's List was an early supporter of Hillary Clinton in the 2008 Democratic presidential primary races.

---

as well as incumbents; in recent years, these groups collectively favored Democrats as women's, environmental, abortion rights, and elderly groups proliferated. (See *Politics Up Close:* "EMILY's List.") Business, trade, and professional PACs usually split their contributions in order to ensure access to both Democrats and Republicans.

PAC money is less important in the Senate than in the House. PAC contributions account for about 35 percent of House campaign contributions; they account for only about 20 percent of Senate campaign contributions. Actually, PACs contribute more *dollars* to the average senator than to the average House member. But because Senate campaigns cost so much more than House campaigns, PAC contributions are *proportionally* less. Senators must rely more on individual contributions than House members do.

Payback   Representatives of organized interest groups say that their PAC contributions are designed to buy access—"a chance to talk"—with members of Congress, their staffs, and executives in the administration (see "What Do Contributors 'Buy'?" in Chapter 8). Both interest groups and government officials usually deny that campaign contributions can "buy" support.

Nevertheless, the pattern of campaign contributions by major industries corresponds closely with the pattern of congressional voting on many key issues. Congress members who receive the largest PAC contributions from an industry group tend to vote in favor of that group's position. Congress members who oppose the industry's position generally receive far less.

Lobbying the Bureaucracy

Lobbying does not cease after a law is passed. Rather, interest groups try to influence the implementation of the law. Interest groups know that bureaucrats exercise considerable discretion in policy implementation (see "Bureaucratic Power" in Chapter 12). Thus many interests spend as much as or more time and energy trying to influence executive agencies as they do Congress.

Lobbying the bureaucracy involves various types of activities, including monitoring regulatory agencies for notices of new rules and regulatory changes; providing reports, testimony, and evidence in administrative hearings; submitting contract and grant applications and lobbying for their acceptance; and monitoring the performance of executive agencies on behalf of group members.

Groups may try to influence the creation of a new agency to carry out the law or influence the assignment of implementation to an existing "friendly" agency. They may try to influence the selection of personnel to head the implementing agency. They may lobby the agency to devote more money and personnel to enforcement of the law (or less, depending on a group's preference). They may argue for strict rules and regulations—or loose interpretations of the law—by the implementing agencies. Lobbyists frequently appear at administrative hearings to offer information. They often undertake to sponsor test cases of administrative regulations on behalf of affected members. In short, lobbying extends throughout the government.[12]

★ **iron triangles**
Mutually supportive relationships among interest groups, government agencies, and legislative committees with jurisdiction over a specific policy area.

Iron Triangles In general, interest groups strive to maintain close working relationships with the departments and agencies that serve their members or regulate their industries. Conversely, bureaucracies seek to nourish relationships with powerful "client" groups that are capable of pressuring Congress to expand their authority and increase their budgets. Both bureaucracies and interest groups seek close working relationships with the congressional committees that exercise jurisdiction over their policy function. Finally, members of Congress seek the political and financial support of powerful interest groups, and members also seek to influence bureaucrats to favor supportive interest groups.

The mutual interests of congressional committee members, organized groups, and bureaucratic agencies come together to form what have been labeled the "iron triangles" of American government. **Iron triangles** refer to stable relationships among interest groups, congressional committees, and administrative agencies functioning in the same policy area. Each of the three sides of these triangles depends on the support of the other two; their cooperation serves their own interests (see Figure 9.3).

In an iron triangle, bureaucracies, interest groups, and congressional committees "scratch each other's backs." Bureaucrats get political support from interest groups in their requests for expanded power and authority and increased budgetary allocations. Interest groups get favorable treatment of their members by the bureaucracy. Congressional committee members get political and financial support from interest groups, as well as favorable treatment for their constituents and contributors who are served or regulated by the bureaucracy.

Iron triangles are more likely to develop in specialized policy areas over which there is relatively little internal conflict. However, conflict, rather than cooperation, is more likely to characterize bureaucratic–congressional–interest-group relationships when powerful, diverse interests are at stake. For example, the Occupational Safety and Health Administration is caught between the demands of labor unions and industry groups. The U.S. Forest Service is caught between the demands of environmental groups and the lumber industry. The Environ-

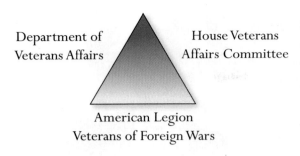

Figure 9.3 It's All Connected: An Example of an Iron Triangle

Department of Veterans Affairs

House Veterans Affairs Committee

American Legion Veterans of Foreign Wars

The iron triangle approach provides a convenient way to look at the interrelationship among interest groups, executive agencies, and congressional committees. As this example shows, veterans' interest groups work closely with both the Department of Veterans Affairs (executive agency) and the House Veterans Affairs Committee.

mental Protection Agency is pressured by environmental groups as well as by industry and agriculture. These kinds of conflicts break open the iron triangles or prevent them from forming in the first place.

Revolving Doors   It is not uncommon in Washington for people in a particular policy field to switch jobs, moving from a post in the government to a job in the private sector, or vice versa, or moving to different posts within the government. In one example, an individual might move from a job in a corporation (Pillsbury or General Mills) to the staff of an interest group (American Farm Bureau Federation), and then to the executive agency charged with implementing policy in the field (U.S. Department of Agriculture) or to the staff of a House or Senate committee with jurisdiction over the field (House Agricultural Committee or Senate Agriculture, Nutrition, and Forestry Committee). The common currency of moves within a network is both policy expertise and contacts within the field.

The term **revolving doors** is often used to criticize people who move from a government post (where they acquired experience, knowledge, and personal contacts) to a job in the private sector as a consultant, lobbyist, or salesperson. Defense contractors may recruit high-ranking military officers or Defense Department officials to help sell weapons to their former employers. Trade associations may recruit congressional staffers, White House staffers, or high-ranking agency heads as lobbyists, or these people may leave government service to start their own lobbying firms. Attorneys from the Justice Department, the Internal Revenue Service, and federal regulatory agencies may be recruited by Washington law firms to represent clients in dealings with their former employers.

Former members of Congress are considered the most viable commodity a lobby firm can offer their clients. The Center for Responsive Politics reports that 125 to 150 former Congress members are lobbyists, many of them among the highest paid in the profession. When asked, lobbyists themselves, especially former members of Congress, acknowledge that their success depends mostly on "schmoozing" with their former colleagues.[13]

Concern about revolving doors centers not only on individuals cashing in on their knowledge, experience, and contacts obtained through government employment, but also on the possibility that some government officials will be tempted to tilt their decisions in favor of corporations, law firms, or interest groups that promise these officials well-paid jobs after they leave government employment.

The Ethics in Government Act limits postgovernment employment in an effort to reduce the potential for corruption. Former members of Congress are not permitted to lobby Congress for one year after leaving that body. Former employees of executive agencies are not permitted to lobby their agency for one year after leaving government service, and they are not permitted to lobby their

★ **revolving doors**
The movement of individuals from government positions to jobs in the private sector, using the experience, knowledge, and contacts they acquired in government employment.

Senator Trent Lott (R-Miss.), right, speaks with Charles Doty before Lott's luncheon address before the Mississippi Manufacturers Association, on December 9, 2004, in Jackson, Mississippi. Lott served in the U.S. Senate from 1989 to 2007, and was twice Senate majority leader, twice Senate minority leader, Senate majority whip, and Senate minority whip. Less than a month after Lott resigned from Senate in December, 2007, he opened a lobbying firm with former Louisiana Senator John Breaux, located just a block from the White House.

★ **litigation**
Legal dispute brought before a court.

★ **amicus curiae**
Person or group other than the defendant or the plaintiff or the prosecution that submits an argument in a case for the court's consideration.

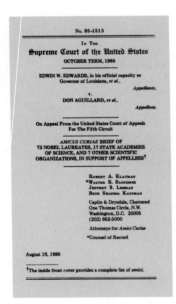

An amicus curiae brief filed by American scientists in opposition to a Louisiana state law mandating the teaching of creation science, "Creationism," in public schools whenever evolution was being taught. The Supreme Court ruled that the Louisiana law was an unconstitutional infringement of the Establishment Clause.

agency for two years on any matter over which they had any responsibility while employed by the government.

Lobbying the Courts

Interest groups play an important role in influencing federal courts. Many of the key cases brought to the federal courts are initiated by interest groups. Indeed, **litigation** is becoming a favored instrument of interest-group politics. Groups that oppose a new law or an agency's action often challenge it in court as unconstitutional or as violating the law. Interest groups bring issues to the courts by (1) supplying the attorneys for individuals who are parties to a case; (2) bringing suits to the courts on behalf of classes of citizens; or (3) filing companion **amicus curiae** (literally "friend of the court") arguments in cases in which they are interested.

The nation's most powerful interest groups all have legal divisions specializing in these techniques. The American Civil Liberties Union is one of the most active federal court litigants on behalf of criminal defendants (see *Politics Up Close:* "The American Civil Liberties Union" in Chapter 14). The early civil rights strategy of the National Association for the Advancement of Colored People (NAACP) was directed by its Legal Defense and Education Fund under the leadership of Thurgood Marshall. The NAACP chose to sponsor a suit by Linda Brown against the Board of Education in her hometown—Topeka, Kansas—in order to win the historic 1954 desegregation decision.[14] NARAL Pro-Choice America is active in sponsoring legal challenges to abortion restrictions. The Environmental Defense Fund and the Natural Resources Defense Council specialize in environmental litigation.

The special rules of judicial decision making preclude direct lobbying of judges by interest groups (see "The Special Rules of Judicial Decision Making" in Chapter 13). Directly contacting federal judges about a case, letter writing, telephoning, and demonstrating outside of federal courtrooms are all considered inappropriate conduct. They inspire more resentment than support among federal judges. However, interest groups have been very active in direct lobbying of Congress over judicial appointments. Key interest groups supporting abortion rights—NARAL Pro-Choice America, People for the American Way, the National Organization for Women, and so on—have played a central role in confirmation battles (see *Controversy:* "The Confirmation of Clarence Thomas" in Chapter 13).

Politics as Interest-Group Conflict

Politics can be viewed as a struggle among interest groups over government policy. Interest groups, rather than individual citizens, can be viewed as the principal participants in American politics.

Pluralism as Democratic Politics   Pluralism (see Chapter 2) is the idea that democracy can be preserved in a large, complex society through individual membership in interest groups that compete, bargain, and compromise over government policy. Individuals are influential in politics only when they act as part of, or on behalf of, groups. (Only leaders of organizations participate directly in policy making.) The group becomes the essential bridge between the individual and the government. Pluralists argue that interest-group politics is a natural extension of the democratic ideals of popular participation in government, freedom of association, and competition over public policy.

Pluralism portrays public policy at any given time as the equilibrium reached in the struggle among interest groups to influence policy (see Figure 9.4). This equilibrium is determined by the relative influence of interest groups. Changes in the relative influence of any interest group can be expected to result in changes in public policy; policy will move in the direction desired by the groups gaining in influence and away from the desires of groups losing influence.

According to this view of political life, government plays a passive role, merely "refereeing" group struggles. Public policy at any given moment represents the "equilibrium" point of the group pressures—the balance of competing interests. The job of politicians is to function as brokers of group interests, arranging compromises and balancing interests.

Balancing Group Power   Pluralism assumes that compromises *can* be arranged and that interests *can* be balanced in relatively stable fashion. It assumes that no single interest will ever become so dominant that it can reject compromise and proceed to impose its will on the nation without regard for the interests of other people. This assumption is based on several beliefs. The first is that interest groups act as a check on each other and that a system of *countervailing power* will protect the interests of all. For example, the power of big business will be checked by the countervailing power of big labor and big government.

A second belief is that *overlapping group membership* will tend to moderate the demands of particular groups and lead to compromise. Because no group can command the undivided loyalty of all its members, its demands will be less drastic and its leaders more amenable to compromise. If the leaders of any group go too far with their demands, those of its members who also belong to other groups endangered by these immoderate demands will balk.

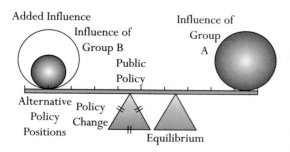

Figure **9.4**

Balancing Act: Understanding The Interest-Group Model

According to pluralist theorists, policy in a democracy is the result of various special-interest groups "reaching equilibrium"—arriving at a compromise position that requires all parties to give up something but gives all parties something they wanted.

A third belief is that radical programs and doctrinaire demands will be checked by the large, unorganized, but potentially significant *latent interest group* that is composed of Americans who oppose extremist politics.

Interest-Group Politics: How Democratic? There are several problems with accepting pluralism as the legitimate heir to classic democratic theory. Democratic theory envisions public policy as the rational choice of *individuals* with equal influence who evaluate their needs and reach a majority decision with due regard for the rights of others. This traditional theory does not view public policy as a product of interest-group pressures. In fact, classic democratic theorists viewed interest groups and even political parties as intruders into an individualistic brand of citizenship and politics. Today critics of pluralism charge that interest groups dominate the political arena, monopolize access to governmental power, and thereby restrict individual participation rather than enhance it.

Another assumption of pluralism is that group membership enhances the individual's influence on policy. But only rarely are interest groups democratically governed. Individuals may provide the numerical strength for organizations, but interest groups are usually run by a small elite of officers and activists. Leaders of corporations, banks, labor unions, medical associations, and bar associations—whose views and agendas often differ from those of their memberships—remain in control year after year. Very few people attend meetings, vote in organizational elections, or make their influence felt within their organizations. Indeed, people believe that "special interest groups" are "what is wrong with government today" (see Table 9.5).

Finally, pluralists hope that the power of diverse institutions and organizations in society will roughly balance out and prevent the emergence of a power monopoly. Yet inequality of power among organizations is commonplace. Examples abound of narrow, organized interests achieving their goals at the expense of the broader, unorganized public. Furthermore, producer interests, bound together by economic ties, usually dominate less well-organized consumer groups and groups based on noneconomic interests. Special interests seeking governmental subsidies, payments, and "entitlements" regularly prevail over the broader yet unorganized interests of taxpayers.

Interest-Group Politics: Gridlock and Paralysis Even if the pluralists are correct that the public interest is only the equilibrium of special-interest claims, some consensus among major interest groups is required if government is to function at all. Democracies require a sense of community and common purpose among the people. If the demands of special interests displace the public interest, government

*Think
Again*

Is organized interest-group activity a cause of government gridlock?

Table **9.5** Too Much Power?: Public Views of Interest Groups

The American public believes that "special interest groups" are the most responsible for "what is wrong with government today."

Among the following, which one or two would you say are most responsible for what is wrong with government today?

Special interest groups	38%
The media	29
Elected officials	24
Political parties	24
The public	14
Government employees	6
Other	8
Not sure	2

Source: As reported in *The Polling Report*, November 11, 2003.

A *Constitutional* Note

Controlling the Effects of Interest Groups

The Constitution's 1st Amendment includes a guarantee of "the right of the people to assemble and petition their government for redress of grievances." The Constitution, then, protects the formation of groups and their right to lobby in Washington on behalf of their own interests. Yet the Founders worried about "the mischiefs of faction," and James Madison, in *Federalist* Number 10, defined a faction as "a number of citizens, whether amounting to a majority or minority of the whole, who are united and actuated by some common impulse of passion, or interests, adverse to the rights of other citizens, or the permanent and aggregate interests of the community." But Madison also understood that "the latent causes of faction are thus sown in the nature of man." A faction could only be destroyed by destroying liberty itself, "by giving to every citizen the same opinions." According to Madison, a wiser and more practical approach would be to control the effects of faction by "first, the delegation of the government [in a republic] to a small number of citizens elected by the rest; secondly, the greater number of citizens and greater sphere of country over which [a republic] may be extended. The influence of factious leaders may kindle a flame within their particular States but will be unable to spread a general conflagration throughout the other States." Today, however, with national means of communication, interest groups are capable of doing exactly what Madison feared. They can mobilize mass opinion, intimidate elected representatives, and dominate the national political arena.

cannot function effectively. Uncompromising claims by conflicting special interests create policy *gridlock*. Yet if politicians try to placate every special interest, the result is confusing, contradictory, and muddled policy—or worse, no policy at all.

Interest-group paralysis and the resulting inability of government to act decisively to resolve national problems weaken popular confidence in government. "The function of government is to govern. A weak government, a government which lacks authority, fails to perform its function, is immoral in the same sense in which a corrupt judge, a cowardly soldier, or an ignorant teacher, is immoral."[15]

Over time, the continued buildup of special protections, privileges, and treatments in society results in "institutional sclerosis." Economist Mancur Olson argues that the accumulation of special interest subsidies, quotas, and protections leads to economic stagnation. Interest groups focus on gaining distributive advantages—a larger share of the pie for themselves—rather than on growth of the whole economy—a larger pie.[16] Major interest groups are more interested in winning income transfers to themselves through government action than in promoting the growth of national income. The more entrenched the interest-group system becomes, the slower the growth of the national economy.

Summary
Who Gets What: Interest Groups

Organizations concentrate power, and concentrated power prevails over diffused power. Interest groups are organizations that seek to influence government policy.

★ The interest-group system supplements the electoral system as a form of representation. The electoral system is designed to respond to broad, majority preferences in geographically defined constituencies. The interest-group system represents narrower, minority interests in economic, professional, ideological, religious, racial, gender, and issue constituencies.

★ Interest groups originated to protect economic interests, to advance social movements, to seek government benefits, and to respond to government activity. As government has expanded into more sectors of American life, more interest groups have formed to influence government policy.

★ Washington lobbying groups represent a wide array of organized interests. But business, trade, and professional associations outnumber labor union, women's, public-interest, single-issue, and ideological groups.

★ Interest-group formation has been aided in recent decades by entrepreneurs who create and build group memberships. They urge people to join organizations either by appealing to their sense of obligation or by providing an array of direct tangible benefits.

★ Most organized groups are dominated by small groups of leaders and activists. Few groups are governed democratically; members who oppose the direction of the organization usually drop out rather than challenge the leadership. Group membership and especially group leadership over-represent educated, upper-middle-class segments of the population.

★ Lobbying activities include advertising and public relations, obtaining access to government officials, providing them with technical and political information, mobilizing constituents, building coalitions, organizing demonstrations, and providing campaign support. Bribery is illegal, and most lobbyists avoid exacting specific vote promises in exchange for campaign contributions.

★ Organized political action committees (PACs) proliferated following the 1974 "reform" of campaign finance laws. Most PAC money goes to incumbents; interest-group leaders know that incumbents are rarely defeated.

★ The mutual interests of organized groups, congressional committees, and bureaucratic agencies sometimes come together to form "iron triangles" of mutual support and cooperation in specific policy areas. In many policy areas, loose "policy networks" emerge among people who share an interest and expertise—although not necessarily opinions—about a policy and are in regular contact with each other.

★ The "revolving door" problem emerges when individuals use the knowledge, experience, and contacts obtained through government employment to secure high-paying jobs with corporations, law firms, lobbying and consulting firms, and interest groups doing business with their old agencies.

★ Interest groups influence the nation's courts not only by providing financial and legal support for issues of concern to them but also by lobbying Congress over judicial appointments.

★ Pluralism views interest-group activities as a form of democratic representation. According to the pluralists, public policy reflects the equilibrium of group influence and a reasonable approximation of society's preferences. Competition among groups, overlapping group memberships, and latent interest groups all combine to ensure that no single group dominates the system.

★ Critics of pluralism warn that interest groups may monopolize power and restrict individual participation in politics rather than enhance it. They note that interest groups are not usually democratically governed, nor are their leaders or members representative of the general population. They warn that accommodation rather than competition may characterize group interaction and that narrow producer interests tend to achieve their goals at the expense of broader consumer (taxpayer) interests.

★ The growing power of special interests, when combined with the declining power of parties and the fragmentation of government, may lead to gridlock and paralysis in policy making. The general public interest may be lost in the conflicting claims of special interests.

Key Terms

Suggested Readings

Berry, Jeffrey M. *The New Liberalism: The Rising Power of Citizen Groups.* Washington, D.C.: Brookings Institution Press, 1999. A description of the increasing number and activities of liberal interest groups in Washington and their success in defeating both business and conservative groups.

Berry, Jeffrey M., and Clyde Wilcox. *The Interest Group Society*. 5th ed. New York: Longman, 2009. Text coverage of organized interests, their relations with parties, PACs, "527s," and more.

Cigler, Allan J., and Burdett A. Loomis, eds. *Interest Group Politics*. 7th ed. Washington, D.C.: CQ Press, 2006. A collection of essays examining interest-group politics.

Goldstein, Kenneth M. *Interest Groups, Lobbying and Participation in America*. New York: Cambridge University Press, 2003. When and why people join interest groups, how they are recruited, and how groups try to influence legislation.

Hernson, Paul S., Ronald G. Shaiko, and Clyde Wilcox. The *Interest Group Connection: Electioneering, Lobbying and Policy-making*. 2nd ed. Washington, D.C.: CQ Press, 2004. Interest group activities in the electoral, legislative, judicial, and policy-making processes.

Lowi, Theodore J. *The End of Liberalism*. New York: Norton, 1969. The classic critique of "interest-group liberalism," describing how special interests contribute to the growth of government and the development of "clientism."

Olson, Mancur. *The Logic of Collective Action*. Cambridge, Mass.: Harvard University Press, 1965. A highly theoretical inquiry into the benefits and costs to individuals of joining groups and the obstacles (including the free-rider problem) to forming organized interest groups.

Olson, Mancur. *The Rise and Decline of Nations*. New Haven, Conn.: Yale University Press, 1982. Argues that, over time, the development of powerful special-interest lobbies has led to institutional sclerosis, inefficiency, and slowed economic growth.

Rozell, Mark J., Clyde Wilcox, and David Madland. *Interest Groups in American Campaigns*. Washington, D.C.: CQ Press, 2005. The role of interest groups in campaigns, including their adjustments to the Bipartisan Campaigns Reform Act of 2002 and the creation of "527s" to circumvent the act.

Suggested Web Sites

AARP www.aarp.org
The AARP site covers issues and provides information relevant to the concerns of citizens who are 50 years of age or older.

AFL-CIO www.alfcio.org
Homepage of labor confederation; includes information on wages, unemployment, strikes, as well as news and press releases on union affairs.

American Farm Bureau www.fb.com
The American Farm Bureau site reveals that the largest farm organization in America represents more than 5 million families in the fifty states and Puerto Rico.

American League of Lobbyists www.alldc.org
Lobbyists have their own Web site, one devoted to "ethical conduct" in the lobbying process and the "advancement of the lobbying profession."

American Medical Association www.ama-assn.org
Professional organization of doctors that both lobbies and publishes medical research in the prestigious Journal of the American Medical Association (JAMA).

Business Roundtable www.businessroundtable.org
Organization representing the largest U.S. corporations.

Children's Defense Fund www.childrendefense.org
Advocacy organization for welfare programs; "the voice of children in America."

Christian Coalition www.cc.org
Organization "defending our godly heritage" by giving "people of faith a voice in government."

EMILY's List www.emilyslist.org
Political network for pro-choice Democratic women that raises early money for women candidates.

NAACP www.naacp.org
Oldest civil rights organization, working on behalf of African Americans.

National Organization for Women www.now.org
An organization of "feminist activists" concerned with abortion rights, lesbian rights, sexual harassment, affirmative action, and electing feminists.

National Rifle Association www.nra.org
The National Rifle Association site is devoted to opposing gun control legislation as well as employing the 2nd Amendment in its antigun control argument.

Public Citizen www.publiccitizen.com
Organization founded by Ralph Nader; devotes its site to "protecting health, safety and democracy" as well as lobbying for "strong citizen and consumer protection laws."

U.S. Chamber of Commerce www.uschamber.com
Representing business, "3 million companies of all sizes."

10 CONGRESS
Politics on Capitol Hill

" Legislatures create vested and sentimental interests which weight national policy in the direction of patchwork rather than mosaic. The local legislator often devotes himself to the advancement of neighborhood projects by striking bargains on national issues. **"**

Harold Lasswell

✓Think About Politics

1. Should members of Congress be limited in the number of terms they can serve?
   YES ⬭ NO ⬭

2. Should congressional districts be drawn to ensure that minorities win seats in Congress in rough proportion to their populations in the states?
   YES ⬭ NO ⬭

3. Do Congress members spend too much time in their home districts seeking reelection?
   YES ⬭ NO ⬭

4. Is the nation better served when the president and the majority in Congress are from the same party?
   YES ⬭ NO ⬭

5. Is it ethical for Congress members to pay special attention to requests for assistance by people who make large campaign contributions?
   YES ⬭ NO ⬭

6. Are there too many lawyers in Congress?
   YES ⬭ NO ⬭

7. Are members of Congress obliged to vote the way their constituents wish, even if they personally disagree?
   YES ⬭ NO ⬭

Who are the members of Congress? How did they get there, and how do they manage to stay there? How did Congress—the official institution for deciding who gets what in America—get its powers, and how does it use them?

The Powers of Congress

The Constitution gives very broad powers to Congress. "All legislative Powers herein granted shall be vested in a Congress of the United States, which shall consist of a Senate and House of Representatives." *The nation's Founders envisioned Congress as the first and most powerful branch of government.* They equated national powers with the powers of Congress and gave Congress the most clearly specified role in national government.

Article I empowers Congress to levy taxes, borrow and spend money, regulate interstate commerce, establish a national money supply, establish a post office, declare war, raise and support an army and navy, establish a court system, and pass all laws "necessary and proper" to implement these powers. Congress may also propose amendments to the Constitution (with a two-thirds vote of both the House and the Senate) and it may admit new states. In the event that no presidential candidate receives a majority of votes in the Electoral College, the House of Representatives selects the president. The Senate has two additional powers: It is called on for advice and consent to treaties, and it confirms presidential nominations to executive and judicial posts. The House has the power to impeach, and the Senate to try any officer of the U.S. government, including the president.

Institutional Conflict Over two centuries, the three separate branches of the national government—the Congress, the presidency and the executive branch, and the Supreme Court and federal judiciary—have struggled for power and preeminence in governing. This struggle for power among the separate institutions is precisely what the Founders envisioned. In writing the Constitution, they sought to create "opposite and rival interests" among the separate branches of the national government. "The constant aim," explained Madison, "is to divide and arrange the several offices in such a manner as that each may be a check on the other"[1] (see Appendix, *The Federalist*, No. 51). From time to time, first the Congress, then the presidency, and occasionally the Supreme Court have appeared to become the most powerful branch of government.

Comparing Legislatures

"The President Initiates, Congress Deliberates" Throughout much of the twentieth century, Congress ceded leadership in national policy making to the president and the executive branch. Congress largely responded to the policy initiatives and spending requests originating from the president, executive agencies, and interest groups. Congress did not merely ratify or "rubber-stamp" these initiatives and requests; it played an independent role in the policy-making process. But this role was essentially a deliberative one, in which Congress accepted, modified, amended, or rejected the policies and budget requests initiated by others.

It is easier for the Congress to obstruct the policy initiatives of the president than it is to assume policy leadership itself. Congress can defeat presidential policy proposals, deny presidential budget requests, delay or reject presidential appointments, investigate executive agencies, hold committee hearings to spotlight improprieties, and generally immobilize the executive branch. It can investigate and question nominees for the Supreme Court and the federal judiciary; it can legislate changes in the jurisdiction of the federal courts; and it can try to reverse court decisions by amending laws or the Constitution itself. The Congress can even threaten to impeach the president or federal judges. But these are largely reactive, obstructionist actions, usually accompanied by a great deal of oratory.

Dividing Congressional Power: House and Senate Congress must not only share national power with the executive and judicial branches of government; it must also share power within itself. The framers of the Constitution took the advice of the nation's eldest diplomat, Benjamin Franklin: "It is not enough that your legislature should be numerous; it should also be divided. . . . One division should watch over and control the other, supply its wants, correct its blunders, and cross its designs, should they be criminal or erroneous."[2] Accordingly, the U.S. Congress is **bicameral**—composed of two houses (see Figure 10.1).

★ **bicameral**
Any legislative body that consists of two separate chambers or houses; in the United States, the Senate represents 50 statewide voter constituencies, and the House of Representatives represents voters in 435 separate districts.

No law can be passed and no money can be spent unless both the House of Representatives and the Senate pass identical laws. Yet the House and the Senate have very different constituencies and terms. The House consists of 435 voting members, elected from districts within each state apportioned on the basis of equal population. (The average congressional district since the 2000 census has a population of about 650,000; the House also includes nonvoting delegates from Puerto Rico, the District of Columbia, Guam, the Virgin Islands, and American Samoa.) All House members face election every 2 years. The Senate consists of 100 members serving 6-year terms, elected by statewide constituencies. Senate terms are staggered so that one-third of senators are elected every 2 years (see Table 10.1).

The House of Representatives, with its 2-year terms, was designed to be more responsive to the American people. Representatives are fond of referring to their chamber as "the people's House," and the Constitution requires that all revenue-raising bills originate in the House. The Senate was designed to be a smaller, more deliberative body, with its members serving 6-year terms. Indeed, the Senate is the more prestigious body. House members frequently give up their seats to run for the Senate; the reverse has seldom occurred. Moreover, the Senate exercises certain powers not given to the House: the power to ratify treaties and the power to confirm federal judges, ambassadors, cabinet members, and other high executive officials.

Domestic Versus Foreign and Defense Policy Congress is more powerful in domestic than in foreign and military affairs. It is freer to reject presidential initiatives in domestic policy areas such as welfare, health, education, the environment, and taxation. But Congress usually follows presidential leadership in

HOUSE OF REPRESENTATIVES   SENATE

Figure *10.1* Corridors of Power: Congress

The architecture and floor plan of the Capitol Building in Washington reflect the bicameral division of Congress, with one wing for the House of Representatives and one for the Senate.

foreign and defense policy even though constitutionally the president and Congress share power in these arenas. The president is "Commander-in-Chief" of the armed forces, but only Congress can "declare war." The president appoints and receives ambassadors and "makes treaties," but the Senate must confirm appointments and provide "advice and consent" to treaties. Historically presidents have led the nation in matters of war and peace.

Table *10.1* Comparing the House and Senate

	House of Representatives	**Senate**
Terms	2 years	6 years
Members	435	100
Elections	All every 2 years	One-third every 2 years
Constituencies	Congressional districts	States
Unique powers	Originate tax bills Bring impeachment charges	Advise and consent to (ratify) treaties by two-thirds vote Confirm appointments Try impeachment charges
Debate on bills	Limited by Rules Committee	Unlimited, except by unanimous consent or vote to close debate (three-fifths)
Member prestige	Modest; smaller personal staffs, fewer committee assignments	High: larger personal staffs, more committee assignments, always addressed as "Senator"
Leadership	Hierarchical, with speaker, majority and minority leaders and whips and committees, especially Rules, concentrating power	Less hierarchical, with each senator exercising more influence on leadership, committees, and floor votes
Committees	Twenty standing and select committees Each member on about five committees Difficult to bypass	Twenty standing and select committees Each member on about seven committees Easier to bypass

The Vietnam experience inspired Congress to try to reassert its powers over war and peace. Military embarrassment, prolonged and indecisive fighting, and accumulating casualties—all vividly displayed on national television—encouraged Congress to challenge presidential war-making power. The War Powers Resolution of 1973, passed over the veto of President Richard Nixon, who was weakened by the Watergate scandal, sought to curtail the president's power to commit U.S. military forces to combat (see "Commander-in-Chief" in Chapter 11). But this legislation has not proven effective, and both Republican and Democratic presidents have continued to exercise war-making powers.

★ **power of the purse**
Congress's exclusive constitutional power to authorize expenditures by all agencies of the federal government.

The Power of the Purse   Congress's real power in both domestic and foreign (defense) policy centers on its **power of the purse**—its power over federal taxing and spending. Only Congress can "lay and collect Taxes, Duties, Imposts and Excises" (Article I, Section 8), and only Congress can authorize spending: "No Money shall be drawn from the Treasury, but in Consequence of Appropriations made by Law" (Article I, Section 9).

Congress jealously guards these powers. Presidents initiate taxing and spending policies by sending their budgets to the Congress each year (see "The Budgetary Process" in Chapter 12 for details). But Congress has the last word on taxing and spending. The most important bills that Congress considers each year are usually the budget resolutions setting ceilings on various categories of expenditures and the later appropriations bills authorizing specific expenditures. It is often in these appropriations bills that Congress exercises its greatest influence over national policy. Thus, for example, the Congress's involvement in foreign affairs centers on its annual consideration of appropriations for foreign aid, its involvement in military affairs centers on its annual deliberations over the defense appropriations bill, and so on.

★ **oversight**
Congressional monitoring of the activities of executive branch agencies to determine if the laws are being faithfully executed.

Oversight of the Bureaucracy   Congressional **oversight** of the federal bureaucracy is a continuing process by which Congress reviews the activities of the executive branch. The *formal* rationale of oversight is to determine whether the purposes of laws passed by Congress are being achieved by executive agencies and whether appropriations established by Congress are being spent as intended. Often the *real* purpose is to influence executive branch decisions, secure favorable treatment for friends and constituents, embarrass presidential appointees, undercut political support for particular programs or agencies, lay the political groundwork for budgetary increases or decreases for an agency, or simply enhance the power of congressional committees and subcommittees and those who chair them.

Oversight is carried out primarily through congressional committees and subcommittees. Individual senators and representatives can engage in a form of oversight simply by writing or calling executive agencies, but committees and their staffs carry on the bulk of oversight activity. Because committees and subcommittees specialize in particular areas of policy making, each tends to focus its oversight activities on particular executive departments and agencies. Oversight is particularly intense during budget hearings. Subcommittees of both the House and the Senate Appropriations Committees are especially interested in how money is being spent by the agencies they oversee.

★ **advice and consent**
The constitutional power of the U.S. Senate to reject or ratify (by a two-thirds vote) treaties made by the president.

Senate Advice and Consent and Confirmation of Presidential Appointments   The Constitution provides that the president must obtain the **advice and consent** of the Senate for treaties "provided that two-thirds of the Senators present concur." In fact, the Senate has seldom provided "advice" to the president regarding treaties prior to their submission to the Senate for "consent." The

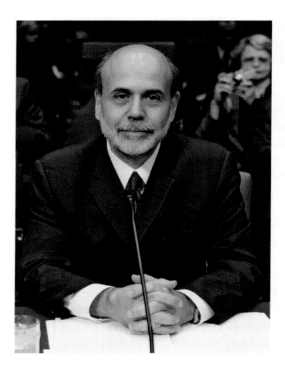

Necessary Confirmation
Senate committee confirmation hearings provide an opportunity for senators to lecture presidential nominees about how they should perform their jobs. The Senate must vote to confirm high executive branch nominees, including the Federal Reserve Board Chairman, Ben Bernanke, shown here testifying in 2005.

president enjoys a high degree of autonomy over U.S. foreign policy (see "Global Leader" in Chapter 11). The process of treaty ratification begins when a president submits an already negotiated treaty to the Senate. Once submitted, treaties are referred to the Senate Foreign Relations Committee. That Committee cannot make changes in the treaty itself; it can either reject the treaty or forward it to the full Senate. The Senate itself cannot make changes in the formal treaty but must accept or reject it. Ratification requires a two-thirds vote. The Senate can, however, express its reservations to a treaty and/or instruct the president in how the treaty is to be interpreted.[3]

The Senate also exercises a special power over the president and the executive branch of government through its constitutional responsibility for approving presidential appointments of key executive officers, including Cabinet members, ambassadors, and other high officials (see "Congressional Constraints on the Bureaucracy" in Chapter 12). And the Senate exercises a special power over the judicial branch through its constitutional responsibility for the **confirmation** of presidential appointments to the federal judiciary including the Supreme Court (see "The Politics of Selecting Judges" in Chapter 13).

Agenda Setting and Media Attention
Congressional hearings and investigations often involve agenda setting—bringing issues to the public's attention and placing them on the national agenda. For agenda-setting purposes, congressional committees or subcommittees need the assistance of the media. Televised hearings and investigations are perhaps the most effective means by which Congress can attract attention to issues as well as to itself and its members.

Hearings and investigations are similar in some ways, but hearings are usually held on a specific bill in order to build a record of both technical information (what is the problem and how legislation might be crafted to resolve it) and political information (who favors and who opposes various legislative options).

★ **confirmation**
The constitutionally required consent of the Senate to appointments of high-level executive officials by the president and appointments of federal judges.

★ **congressional hearings**
Congressional committee sessions in which members listen to witnesses who provide information and opinions on matters of interest to the committee, including pending legislation.

★ **congressional investigation**
Congressional committee hearings on alleged misdeeds or scandals.

★ **subpoena**
A written command to appear before a court or a congressional committee.

★ **contempt**
Willfull disobedience to, or open disrespect of, a court or congressional body.

★ **perjury**
Lying while under oath after swearing to tell the truth.

★ **impeachment**
Formal changes of wrong-doing brought against a government official, resulting in a trial and upon conviction removal from office.

Ticket of admission to the U.S. Senate galleries for the impeachment trial of President Andrew Johnson in 1868.

In contrast, investigations are held on alleged misdeeds or scandals. Although the U.S. Supreme Court has held that there must be some "legislative purpose" behind a **congressional investigation**, that phrase has been interpreted very broadly indeed.[4]

The constitutional rationale for congressional investigations is that Congress is seeking information to assist in its law making function. But from the earliest Congress to the present, the investigating powers of Congress have often been used for political purposes: to rally popular support for policies or programs favored by Congress; to attack the president, other high officials in the adminis-tration, or presidential policies or programs; to focus media attention and public debate on particular issues; or simply to win media coverage and popular recog-nition for members of Congress.

Congressional investigators have the legal power to **subpoena** witnesses (force them to appear), administer oaths, compel testimony, and initiate criminal charges for **contempt** (refusing to cooperate) and **perjury** (lying). These powers can be exercised by Congress's regular committees and subcommittees and by committees appointed especially to conduct a particular investigation.

Congress cannot impose criminal punishments as a result of its investigations. But the information uncovered in a congressional investigation can be turned over to the U.S. Department of Justice, which may proceed with its own criminal inves-tigation and perhaps indictment and trial of alleged wrongdoers in federal courts.

Congressional investigations have long been used as an opportunity for Con-gress to expose wrongdoing on the part of executive branch officials. The first congressional investigation (1792) examined why General Arthur St. Clair had been defeated by the Indians in Ohio; the Crédit Mobilier investigations (1872–73) revealed scandals in the Grant administration; the Select Committee on Campaign Practices, known universally as the "Watergate Committee," exposed the activities of President Richard Nixon's inner circle that led to impeachment charges and Nixon's forced resignation; a House and Senate Joint Select Committee conducted the Iran-Contra investigation in the Reagan admin-istration; the Senate Special Whitewater Committee investigated matters related to Bill and Hillary Clinton's real estate investments in Arkansas.

Impeachment and Removal Potentially Congress's most formidable power is that of impeaching and removing from office the president, other officers of the United States, and federal judges, including Supreme Court justices. Congress can do so only for "Treason, Bribery or other High Crimes and Misdemeanors." The House of Representatives has the sole authority to bring charges of **impeachment**, by a simple majority vote. Impeachment is analogous to a criminal indictment; it does not remove an officer but merely subjects him or her to trial by the Senate. Only the Senate, following a trial, can remove the federal official from office, and then only by a two-thirds vote.

Bill Clinton was the second president in the nation's history to be impeached by the U.S. House of Representatives. (Andrew Johnson was the first in 1867; after a one-month trial in the Senate, the "guilty" vote fell one short of two-thirds needed for removal. President Richard Nixon resigned just prior to an impending impeachment vote in 1974.) The 1998 House impeachment vote split along par-tisan lines, with Republicans voting "yes" and Democrats voting "no." Two Arti-cles of Impeachment were passed, one for perjury before a grand jury and one for obstruction of justice. In the subsequent Senate trial, only 45 senators (less than a majority and far less than the needed two-thirds) voted to convict President Clinton on the first charge, and only 50 voted to convict on the second (see *Politics Up Close*: "Sex, Lies, and Impeachment" in Chapter 11).

Congressional Apportionment and Redistricting

The Constitution states that "Representatives ... shall be apportioned among the several states ... according to their respective Numbers." It orders an "actual enumeration" (census) every 10 years. And it provides that every state shall have at least one representative, in addition to two senators, regardless of population. But the Constitution is silent on the size of the House of Representatives. Congress itself determines its own size; for more than a century, it allowed itself to grow to accommodate new states and population growth. In 1910 it fixed the membership of the House at 435.

The effect of doing so has been to expand the population of House districts over the years. Following the 2000 census, House districts have populations of about 650,000. It is sometimes argued that such large House constituencies prevent meaningful communication between citizens and their representatives. (The Framers originally envisioned House districts of no more than 30,000 people.) But expanding the size of the House would complicate its work, reduce the influence of individual members, require more procedural controls, and probably strengthen the power of party leaders.

Apportionment   Apportionment refers to the allocation of House seats to the states after each 10-year census. The Constitution does not specify a mathematical method of apportionment; Congress adopted a complex "method of equal proportion" in 1929, which so far has withstood court challenges.

Malapportionment   Historically, state legislatures were notorious for their **malapportionment**—congressional (and state legislative) districts with grossly unequal numbers of people. Some congressional districts had twice the average number of people per district, and others had only half as many. In a district twice the size of the average district, the value of an individual's vote was heavily diluted. In a district half the size of the average, the value of an individual's vote was greatly magnified.

Enter the Supreme Court   Prior to 1962, the Supreme Court refused to intervene in apportionment, holding that this question belonged to the state legislatures and that the federal courts should avoid this "political thicket." So the

Think Again

Should congressional districts be drawn to ensure that minorities win seats in Congress in rough proportion to their populations in the states?

★ **apportionment**
The allocation of legislative seats to jurisdictions based on population. Seats in the U.S. House of Representatives are apportioned to the states on the basis of their population after every 10-year census.

★ **malapportionment**
Unequal numbers of people in legislative districts resulting in inequality of voter representation.

On the back wall is the electronic tally board in the U.S. House of Representatives chamber in the Capitol. The board is used to count the votes of the members on the bills up for consideration before the House.

Supreme Court's decision in the landmark case *Baker v. Carr* (1962) came as a surprise. The Court ruled that inequalities in voters' influence resulting from different-size districts violated the Equal Protection Clause of the 14th Amendment. The case dealt with a complaint about Tennessee's state legislative districts, but the Court soon extended its holding to congressional districts as well.[5] "The conception of political equality from the Declaration of Independence to Lincoln's Gettysburg Address, to the 14th, 15th, 17th, and 19th Amendments, can mean only one thing—one person, one vote."[6]

The shift in the Supreme Court's policy raised a new question: How equal must districts be in order to guarantee voters "equal protection of the law"? The courts have ruled that only official U.S. Bureau of the Census figures may be used; estimated changes since the last census may *not* be used. In recent years, the courts have insisted on nearly exact mathematical equality in populations in congressional districts in a state.

"Enumeration"   The U.S. Constitution is very specific in its wording: It calls for an "actual Enumeration" (Article I, Section 2) of the population in each 10-year census. However, the U.S. Bureau of the Census has considered the use of samples and estimates to correct what it perceives to be "undercounts." Undercounting is said to occur when certain populations are difficult to identify and count on an individual basis, populations such as recent non-English-speaking immigrants or residents of neighborhoods likely to mistake government census takers for law enforcement officers or other unwelcome government officials. Political leaders (usually Democrats) of states and cities with large immigrant and minority populations have favored the substitution of samples and estimates for actual head counts. However, the U.S. Supreme Court held in 1999 that the Census Act of 1976 prohibits sampling for purposes of apportioning House members among the states.[7] Congress may use sampling for determining the allocation of grant-in-aid funds if it wishes.

Figure *10.2*

Drawing the Lines: The Original Gerrymander

The term *gerrymander* immortalizes Governor Elbridge Gerry (1744–1814) of Massachusetts, who in 1811 redistricted the state legislature to favor Democrats over Federalists. A district north of Boston was designed to concentrate, and thus "waste," Federalist votes. This political cartoon from the *Boston Gazette*, March 26, 1812, depicted the new district lines as a salamander, dubbing the process the "gerrymander."

Redistricting   Redistricting refers to the drawing of boundary lines of congressional districts following the census. After each census, some states gain and others lose seats, depending on whether their populations have grown faster or slower than the nation's population. In addition, population shifts within a state may force districting changes. Congressional district boundaries are drawn by state legislatures in each state; a state's redistricting act must pass both houses of the state legislature and win the governor's signature (or be passed over a gubernatorial veto). The U.S. Justice Department and the federal judiciary are also deeply involved in redistricting issues, particularly questions of whether or not redistricting disadvantages African Americans or other minorities.

Gerrymandering   Gerrymandering is the drawing of district lines for political advantage (see Figure 10.2). The population of districts may be equal, yet the district boundaries are drawn in such a fashion as to grant advantage or disadvantage to specific groups of voters. Gerrymandering has long been used by parties in control of the state legislatures to maximize their seats in Congress and state legislatures.

Gerrymandering, with the aid of sophisticated computer-mapping programs and data on past voting records of precincts, is a highly technical task. But consider a simple example where a city is entitled to three representatives and the eastern third of the city is Republican but the western two-thirds is Democratic (see Figure 10.3). If the Republicans could draw the district lines, they might draw them along a north–south direction to allow their party to win in one of the three districts. In contrast, if Democrats could draw the district lines, they might draw them along an east–west direction to allow their party to win all three districts by diluting the Republican vote. Such dividing up and diluting of a strong minority to deny it the power to elect a representative is called **splintering**. Often gerrymandering is not as neat as our example; district lines may twist and turn, creating grotesque patterns in order to achieve the desired effects. Another gerrymandering strategy—**packing**—is the heavy concentration of one party's voters in a single district in order to "waste" their votes and allow modest majorities of the party doing the redistricting to win in other districts.

Partisan Gerrymandering   Partisan gerrymandering does not violate federal court standards for "equal protection" under the 14th Amendment. There is no constitutional obligation to allocate seats "to the contending parties in proportion to what their anticipated statewide vote will be."[8] For several years the Supreme Court threatened to intervene to correct partisan gerrymandering,[9] but

★ **redistricting**
Drawing of legislative district boundary lines following each 10-year census.

Congressional Redistricting

★ **gerrymandering**
Drawing district boundary lines for political advantage.

★ **splintering**
Redistricting in which a strong minority is divided up and diluted to prevent it from electing a representative.

★ **packing**
Redistricting in which partisan voters are concentrated in a single district, "wasting" their majority vote and allowing the opposition to win by modest majorities in other districts.

Figure *10.3*
Gerrymandering in Action

Depending on how an area is divided into districts, the result may benefit one party or the other. In this example, dividing the area so one district has virtually all the Republicans gives that party a victory in that district while ceding the other two districts to the Democrats. In contrast, Democrats benefit when Republican voters are divided among the three districts so that their votes are splintered.

Republican Plan
2 Democrats,
1 Republican

	N	
Mostly		Mostly
W Dem.		Rep. E
Voters		Voters
	S	

Democratic Plan
3 Democrats,
0 Republican

	N	
Mostly		Mostly
W Dem.		Rep. E
Voters		Voters
	S	

in 2004 it finally decided that the issue was "nonjusticiable"—there were no "judicially manageable standards for adjudicating [party] claims." The Court decided that "'Fairness' is not a judicially manageable standard."[10] Parties are free to try to advantage themselves in redistricting.

Reredistricting   The redrawing of congressional districts usually occurs after each 10-year census. However, several states have been embroiled in a second round of redistricting, notably Texas. (If one party dominated a state legislature during the first redistricting after the census and drew district lines in a partisan fashion, there is then a strong temptation for the opposition party to undertake a second round of partisan redistricting if it subsequently wins control of the state legislature.) It is theoretically possible that redistricting could be undertaken every time a state legislature changes party control.

In a controversial case, the Supreme Court upheld the practice of reredistricting. After a protracted partisan struggle in 2003, a new Republican majority in the Texas Legislature redrew congressional boundaries that had been drawn by a Democratic-controlled legislature after the 2000 Census. The result was a significant increase in Republican congressional seats and a corresponding decrease in Democratic seats in that state. But the Supreme Court declined to intervene: "Neither the Constitution nor Congress has stated any explicit prohibition on mid-decade redistricting to change districts drawn earlier in conformance with a decennial census.[11] And the Court approved of mid-decade redistricting when racial or ethnic groups appeared to have been disadvantaged by earlier redistricting.

★ **incumbent gerrymandering**
Drawing legislative district boundaries to advantage incumbent legislators.

Incumbent Gerrymandering   Yet another problem confronting state legislatures in redistricting is the preservation of incumbent Congress members, that is, **incumbent gerrymandering**. Incumbents generally have sufficient political clout with their state parties to inspire efforts in the legislature to protect their districts.

Incumbent gerrymandering means drawing district lines in such a way as to ensure that districts of incumbents include enough supporters of their party to provide a high probability of their reelection. But often ensuring incumbents' security and maximizing the party's total number of seats are conflicting goals. It is not always possible to redraw district lines in such a way as to protect incumbents and at the same time ensure the largest number of party seats in a state. Incumbents themselves want the largest number of their party's voters packed in their district. But this tactic may result in losses for their party in other districts that have been robbed of party voters. Redistricting almost always confronts incumbents with new voters—voters who were previously in a different incumbent's district. As a result, incumbents usually have a somewhat more difficult reelection campaign following redistricting than in other elections.[12]

African American members of the 110th Congress on the Capitol steps.

Racial Gerrymandering   Racial gerrymandering to disadvantage African Americans and other minorities violates both the Equal Protection Clause of the 14th Amendment and the Voting Rights Act of 1965. The Voting Rights Act specifies that redistricting in states with a history of voter discrimination or low voter participation must be "cleared" in advance with the U.S. Justice Department. The act extends special protection not only to African

American voters but also to Hispanic, Native American, Alaska Native, and Asian voters.

In 1982 Congress strengthened the Voting Rights Act by outlawing any electoral arrangement that has the effect of weakening minority voting power. This *effects test* replaced the earlier *intent test*, under which redistricting was outlawed only if boundaries were intentionally drawn to dilute minority political influence. In *Thornburg v. Gingles* (1986), the Supreme Court interpreted the effects test to require state legislatures to redistrict their states in a way that maximizes minority representation in Congress and the state legislatures.[13] The effect of this ruling was to require **affirmative racial gerrymandering**—the creation of predominantly African American and minority districts (labeled "majority-minority" districts) whenever possible. Following the 1990 Census, redistricting in legislatures in states with large minority populations was closely scrutinized by the U.S. Justice Department and the federal courts. The result was a dramatic increase in African American and Hispanic representation in Congress (see Figure 10.7 later in this chapter).

★ **affirmative racial gerrymandering**
Drawing district boundary lines to maximize minority representation.

However, the Supreme Court later expressed constitutional doubts about bizarre-shaped districts based *solely* on racial composition. In a controversial 5 to 4 decision in *Shaw v. Reno* (1993), Justice Sandra Day O'Connor wrote, "Racial gerrymandering, even for remedial purposes, may balkanize us into competing racial factions. . . . A reapportionment plan that includes in one district individuals who have little in common with one another but the color of their skin bears an uncomfortable resemblance to political apartheid"[14] (see Figure 10.4). Later the Court held that the use of race as the "predominant factor" in drawing district lines is unconstitutional: "When the state assigns voters on the basis of race, it engages in the offensive and demeaning assumption that voters of a particular race, because of their race, think alike, share the same political interests and will prefer the same candidates at the polls."[15] But the Court has stopped short of saying that *all* race-conscious districting is unconstitutional.

Partisanship Interacts with Race   Racial gerrymandering appears to help Republican congressional candidates. If African American voters are concentrated in heavily black districts, the effect is to "bleach" surrounding districts of Democratic-leaning black voters and thus improve the chances for Republican victories. Republican Party congressional gains in the South during the 1990s may be partly attributed to racial gerrymandering.[16] In what has been described as a "paradox of representation," the creation of majority-minority districts brought more minority members to Congress, but it also led to a more conservative House of Representatives, as Republicans gained seats previously held by white liberal Democrats.[17]

Republican-led efforts to "pack" black (Democratic) voters into relatively few districts suffered a setback in 2003 when the U.S. Supreme Court recognized that doing so might diminish the power of African American voters overall. The Court approved of a plan that "unpacked" some heavily concentrated majority-minority districts in Georgia. The Court reasoned that the result would be to create additional black "influence" districts where African American voters would not be in a majority but would be a large influential voting bloc.[18]

Getting to Capitol Hill

Members of Congress are independent political entrepreneurs—selling themselves, their services, and their personal policy views to the voters in 435 House districts and 50 states across the country. They initiate their own candidacies, raise most of their campaign funds from individual contributors, put together personal campaign organizations, and get themselves elected with relatively

Charles Rangel (D-NY), chairman of the House Ways and Means Committee, talks about the Tax Reduction and Reform Act of 2007, at a news conference in Washington, D.C., on October 25, 2007. Rangel's proposed bill was to increase taxes on executives of hedge funds and private equity firms.

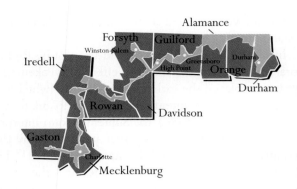

Figure *10.4*

Affirmative Racial Gerrymandering

North Carolina's Twelfth Congressional District was drawn up to be a "majority-minority" district by combining African American communities over a wide region of the state. The U.S. Supreme Court in *Shaw v. Reno* (1993) ordered a court review of this district to determine whether it incorporated any common interest other than race. The North Carolina legislature redrew the district in 1997, lowering its black population from 57 to 46 percent, yet keeping its lengthy connection of black voters from Charlotte to Greensboro.

Think Again

Are there too many lawyers in Congress?

VISUAL LITERACY

Why Is It So Hard to Defeat an Incumbent?

★ open seat
Seat in a legislature for which no incumbent is running for reelection.

little help from their party. Their reelection campaigns depend on their ability to raise funds from individuals and interest groups and on the services and other benefits they provide to their constituents.

Who Runs for Congress?   Members of Congress come from a wide variety of backgrounds, ranging from acting and professional sports to medicine and the ministry. However, exceptionally high percentages of senators and representatives have prior experience in at least one of three fields—law, business, or public service (see Table 10.2). Members of Congress are increasingly career politicians, people who decided early in life to devote themselves to running for and occupying public office.[9] The many lawyers, by and large, are *not* practicing attorneys. Rather, the typical lawyer-legislator is a political activist with a law degree. These are people who graduated from law school and immediately sought public jobs—as federal or state prosecuting attorneys, as attorneys for federal or state agencies, or as staff assistants in congressional, state, or city offices. They used their early job experiences to make political contacts and learn how to organize a political campaign, find financial contributors, and deal with the media. Another group of Congress members are former businesspeople—not employees of large corporations, but people whose personal or family businesses brought them into close contact with government and their local community, in real estate, insurance, franchise dealerships, community banks, and so forth.

Competition for Seats   Careerism in Congress is aided by the electoral advantages enjoyed by incumbents over challengers. Greater name recognition, advantages in raising campaign funds, and the resources of congressional offices all combine to limit competition for seats in Congress and to reelect the vast majority of incumbents (see Advantages of Incumbency" in Chapter 8). The result is an incumbent reelection percentage for House members that usually exceeds 90 percent. The average reelection rate for U.S. senators is more than 80 percent (see Figure 10.5).

Aspirants for congressional careers are well advised to wait for an **open seat.** Open seats in the House of Representatives are created when incumbents retire or vacate the seat to run for higher office. These opportunities occur on average in about 10 percent of House seats in each election. But every 10 years reapportionment creates many new opportunities to win election to Congress. Reapportionment creates new seats in states gaining population, just as it forces out some incumbents in states losing population. Redistricting also threatens incumbents with new constituencies, where they have less name recognition, no history of casework, and perhaps no common racial or ethnic identification. Thus forced retirements and electoral defeats are more common in the first election following each 10-year reapportionment and redistricting of Congress.

Rep. Henry Waxman (D-CA), Chairman of the House Oversight and Government Reform Committee (right) and Ranking Minority Member Tom Davis (R-VA) preside over a hearing on facts of and misperceptions about human growth hormone and performance enhancing substances in Washington, D.C. on February 12, 2008.

Table 10.2   Where Do Our Leaders Come From?: Backgrounds of Congress Members

Occupations

Many Congress members cite more than one occupation, and the largest proportion of members—over 40 percent—have a background in law, with experience in public service and business not far behind. Other occupations represented among Congress members include health care professional (9), homemarker (7), career military (5), actor/entertainer (4), clergy member (3), and former professional sports athlete (2). Although members of Congress cite their occupation, as a practical matter their occupation is being a member of the House of Representatives or U.S. Senate: the average House members has served 10 years, while the average member of the Senate has served an average of 13 years.

	Total
Law	221
Public service	206
Business	193
Education	102
Real estate	39
Agriculture	29
Medicine	16
Labor/blue collar	16
Journalism	15
Law enforcement	10

Religion

Catholics have long been the single largest religious group in Congress. But all Protestants combined—Baptists, Methodists, Presbyterians, Episcopalians, and Lutherans, among others—make up a solid majority; Jews constitute a little under 10 percent of Congress members. Other religions represented include Eastern Orthodox (6), Christian Scientists (5), Unitarians (2), a Quaker (1), and the first Buddhists (2) and Muslim (1) ever elected to the U.S. House of Representatives.

Roman Catholics	153
Baptists	67
Methodists	63
Presbyterians	44
Mormons	15
Episcopalians	38
Lutherans	19
Jews	43
Other religions	93

Figure *10.5*

Familiar Faces: Incumbent Advantage in Congressional Elections

Despite periodic movements to "throw the bums out," voters in most districts and states routinely reelect their members of Congress. In recent years, more than 90 percent of representatives and 80 percent of senators who have sought reelection have been returned to Congress by votes in their districts or states.

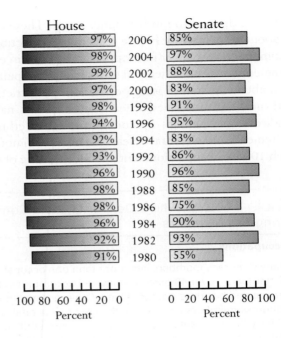

House		Senate
97%	2006	85%
98%	2004	97%
99%	2002	88%
97%	2000	83%
98%	1998	91%
94%	1996	95%
92%	1994	83%
93%	1992	86%
96%	1990	96%
98%	1988	85%
98%	1986	75%
96%	1984	90%
92%	1982	93%
91%	1980	55%

100 80 60 40 20 0   0 20 40 60 80 100
Percent   Percent

Winning Big Not only do incumbent Congress members usually win, they usually also win big. Over 70 percent of House members win by margins of 60 percent or more or run unopposed. (In recent years, 10 to 18 percent of House members have had *no* opposition in the general election.) Senate races are somewhat more competitive. Senate challengers are usually people who have political experience and name recognition as members of the House, governors, or other high state officials. Even so, most Senate incumbents seeking reelection are victorious over their challengers. Most members of Congress, then, sit comfortably in **safe seats**—that is, they regularly win reelection by a large margin of the vote.

★ safe seats
Legislative districts in which the incumbent regularly wins by a large margin of the vote.

Turnover Despite a high rate of reelection of incumbents in Congress, about 15 percent of members arrive new to their jobs each session. **Turnover** occurs more frequently as a result of retirement, resignation (sometimes to run for higher office), or reapportionment (and the loss of an incumbent's seat) than it does as a result of an incumbent's defeat in a bid for reelection. Roughly 10 percent of Congress members voluntarily leave office when their term expires.[20]

★ turnover
Replacement of members of Congress by retirement or resignation, by reapportionment, or (more rarely) by electoral defeat.

Congressional Term Limits? Public distrust of government helped to fuel a movement in the states to limit congressional terms. Several states attempted to limit their state's House members to four 2-year terms and their senators to two 6-year terms. Proponents of congressional **term limits** argued that career politicians become isolated from the lives and concerns of average citizens, that they acquire an "inside the Beltway" (the circle of highways that surround Washington) mentality. They also argued that term limits would increase competition, creating "open-seat" races on a regular basis and encouraging more people to seek public office.

★ term limits
Limitations on the number of terms that an elected official can serve in office. The Constitution (Amendment XXII) limits the president to two terms. There are no limits on the terms of senators or representatives.

Opponents of congressional term limits argued that they infringe on the voters' freedom of choice. If voters are upset with the performance of their Congress members, they can limit their terms by not reelecting them. But if voters wish to keep popular and experienced legislators in office, they should be permitted to do so. Opponents also argued that inexperienced Congress members would be forced to rely more on the policy information supplied them by bureaucrats, lobbyists, and staff people—thus weakening the institution of Congress.

But the U.S. Supreme Court ruled in 1995 that the states themselves cannot limit the terms of their members of Congress. "If the qualifications set forth in the text of the Constitution are to be changed, that text must be amended."[21] In a controversial 5 to 4 decision, the Court held that the Founders intended age, citizenship, and residency to be the *only* qualifications for members of Congress.

It is not likely that the necessary two-thirds of both houses of Congress will ever vote for a constitutional amendment to limit their own stay in office. Thus the Supreme Court's decision effectively killed the movement for congressional term limits.

The Congressional Electorate Congressional elections generally fail to arouse much interest among voters. Indeed, only about 60 percent of the general public can name one U.S. senator from their state, and only about 40 percent can name both of their U.S. senators. Members of the House of Representatives fare no better: less than half of the general public can name their representative. But even constituents who know the names of their congressional delegation seldom know anything about the policy positions of these elected officials or about their votes on specific issues. Turnout in congressional *general elections* averages only about 35 percent in off-year (nonpresidential) elections. Turnout in congressional *primary elections* seldom exceeds 15 to 20 percent of persons eligible to vote. This lack of public attentiveness to congressional elections gives a great advantage to candidates with high name recognition, generally the incumbents (see *What Do You Think?*: "Why Do Voters Reelect Members of an Unpopular Congress?").

Independence of Congressional Voting Congressional voting is largely independent of presidential voting. The same voters who elected Republican presidents in 1968, 1972, 1980, 1984, and 1988 simultaneously elected Democratic majorities to the House of Representatives. And while reelecting Democratic President Bill Clinton in 1996, voters simultaneously reelected Republican majorities in the House and Senate. In 2000, Republicans maintained a razor-thin margin in the House, despite Gore's popular vote victory. Only in 2004 did voters elect a Republican president and *add* to Republican majorities in the House and Senate. It is unlikely that voters deliberately seek to impose *divided party government* on the nation. Rather, they cast their presidential and congressional votes on the basis of differing expectations of presidents versus members of Congress. Divided party government reappeared in Washington in 2006, when Democrats captured control of both houses of Congress, confronting Republican George W.

Bush with a legislature from the opposing party. But divided government ended with the Democratic sweep of the House, Senate, and presidency in 2008.

Congressional Campaign Financing Raising the $1 million it can take to win a House seat or the $5 to $10 million or more for a successful Senate campaign is a major job in and of itself (see Much Does It Cost to Get Elected?" in Chapter 8). Even incumbents who face little or no competition still work hard at fund raising, "banking" contributions against some future challenger. Large campaign chests, assembled well in advance of an election, can also be used to

Should members of Congress be limited in the number of terms they can serve?

Critical Congressional (Mid-Term) Elections

You Are an Informed Voter Helping Your Classmates Decide How to Vote

Senator Robert Byrd (D-WV), born in 1917, and the oldest living member of Congress. As Chairman of the Senate Appropriations Committee, Senator Byrd argues over Iraq spending, on May 15, 2008, at the Capitol. At left is Appropriations Committee staff member Chuck Kieffer.

What Do You *Think*?

Why Do Voters Reelect Members of an Unpopular Congress?

Congress is the least popular branch of government. Public approval of Congress is well below that of the presidency and the Supreme Court. What accounts for this lack of popularity? The belief that members of Congress "spend more time thinking about their own political futures than they do in passing legislation" may contribute to this sentiment.

But public disapproval of Congress may also arise from a misunderstanding of democratic government. "People do not wish to see uncertainty, conflicting options, long debate, competing interests, confusion and compromised imperfect solutions. . . . They often see a patently unrealistic form of democracy."[a]

But in an apparent paradox, most voters *approve of their own* representative (see figure below), even while Congress itself is the object of popular distrust and ridicule. A majority of voters believe that their own representatives "deserve reelection."

This apparent contradiction is explained in part by differing expectations: Americans expect Congress to deal with national issues, but they expect their own representatives to deal with local concerns and even personal problems. Members of Congress understand this concern and consequently devote a great deal of their time to constituent service. Indeed, many members of Congress try to dissociate themselves from Congress, attacking Congress in their own campaigns and contributing to negative images of the institution. Finally, the national news media are highly critical of Congress, but local news media frequently portray local members of Congress in a more favorable light.

Q. *"Do you approve of the way the U.S. Congress is handling its job?"*

Q. *"Do you approve or disapprove of the way the representative from your own congressional district is handling his or her job?"*

My Representative	Year	Congress	Percentage Difference
62%	1978	31%	−31%
60%	1990	38%	−22%
60%	1996	31%	−29%
65%	1998	48%	−17%
62%	2002	40%	−22%
62%	2004	40%	−22%
51%	2006	23%	−34%
69%	2008	18%	−51%

100 80 60 40 20 0
Percent

0 20 40 60 80 100
Percent

[a]John R. Hibbing and Elizabeth Theiss-Morse, *Congress as Public Enemy*. (Cambridge, Eng.: Cambridge University Press, 1995), p. 147. Also cited by Roger H. Davidson and Walter J. Oleszak, *Congress and Its Members*. 9th ed. Washington, D.C.: CQ Press, 2004, p. 487.

frighten off would-be challengers. Campaign funds can be used to build a strong personal organization back home, finance picnics and other festivities for constituents, expand the margin of victory, and develop a reputation for invincibility that may someday protect against an unknown challenger.[23]

Does money buy elections? In about 90 percent of all congressional races, the candidate who spends the most money wins. However, because most winning candidates are incumbents, the money probably reflects the expected political outcome rather than shaping it. But even in open-seat races, the candidate who spends the most money usually wins.

Party Fortunes in Congress

For 40 years (1954–1994) Democrats enjoyed an advantage in congressional races; in fact, the Democratic Party was said to have a "permanent majority" in the House of Representatives (see Figure 10.6). The Republican victory in the congressional election of 1994 was widely described as a political "earthquake." It gave the GOP control of the House for the first time in four decades, as well as control of the Senate. Republicans remained in control of the House and the Senate (except for a brief period in 2001–2002) until the 2006 elections. Democrats strengthened their control in both houses in the 2008 elections.

The Historic Democratic Party Dominance of Congress   The historic Democratic dominance of Congress was attributed to several factors. First, over those four decades more voters identified themselves with the Democratic Party than with the Republican Party (see Chapter 7). Party identification plays a significant role in congressional voting; it is estimated that 75 percent of those who identify themselves with a party cast their vote for the congressional candidate of their party.[24] Second, the Democratic advantage was buttressed by the fact that many voters considered local rather than national conditions when casting congressional

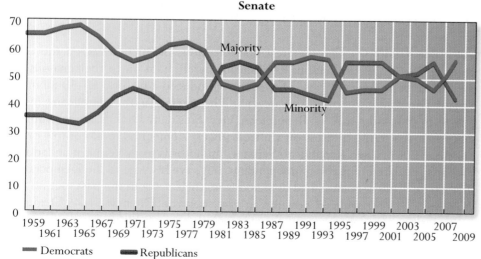

Figure *10.6*

Parties on Capital Hill
Party Control of the
House and Senate

Except for two very brief periods, Democrats continuously controlled both the House of Representatives and the Senate for more than 40 years. The Democratic Party's "permanent" control of Congress was ended in 1994, when Republicans won majorities in both houses. Republicans remained in control of the House for 12 years; Democrats won control in 2006 when frustrations over the war in Iraq hurt Republican candidates. Democrats strengthened their hold on both houses in 2008.

Reversal of Fortune
Newt Gingrich (R-GA) led the Republican Party to victory in the House of Representatives in 1994 after 40 years of Democratic control of that body. He resigned his seat in Congress in 1998 and became a popular author and television commentator.

votes. Voters may have wanted to curtail *overall* federal spending in Washington (a traditional Republican promise), but they wanted a member of Congress who would "bring home the bacon." Although both Republican and Democratic congressional candidates usually promised to bring money and jobs to their districts, Democratic candidates appeared more creditable on such promises because their party generally supported large domestic-spending programs. Finally, Democratic congressional candidates over those years enjoyed the many advantages of incumbency. It was thought that only death or retirement would dislodge many of them from their seats.

The Republican "Revolution"?   The sweeping Republican victory in 1994—especially the party's capturing control of the House of Representatives—surprised many analysts.[25] Just two years after a Democratic president won election and Democrats won substantial majorities in both houses of Congress, the GOP gained its most complete victory in many years. How did it happen?

First of all, the Republican congressional candidates, under the leadership of Newt Gingrich, largely succeeded in *nationalizing* the midterm congressional election. That is, Republican candidates sought to exploit the voters' general skepticism about government and disenchantment with its performance. Voters were often unfamiliar with specific Republican promises, but they correctly sensed that the Republicans favored "less government."

The GOP's capture of control of both houses of Congress in 1994 for the first time in 40 years raised conservatives' hopes of a "revolution" in public policy. The new Republican House Speaker, Newt Gingrich, was the acknowledged leader of the revolution, with Republican Senate Majority Leader Bob Dole in tow. But soon the revolution began to fizzle out. Two key Republican campaign promises failed to pass the Congress: the House failed to muster the necessary two-thirds majority for a constitutional amendment to impose congressional term limits, and the Senate failed to do so on behalf of a balanced budget amendment.

Republicans succeeded in maintaining their control of Congress despite Clinton's reelection in 1996. But Democrats gained House seats in both the 1996 and 1998 congressional elections. Although the GOP retained a slim majority in the House of Representatives, the 1998 midterm election stunned Republicans. They had expected to benefit from Clinton's acknowledged sexual misconduct and the House impeachment investigation. But voters generally sided with Clinton. Democrats were encouraged because historically the party controlling the White House had *lost* seats in midterm elections.

Congress Divided   The congressional elections of 2000 reflected the close partisan division of the nation. Republicans barely held on to their majority in the House of Representatives. The election produced a historic 50–50 tie in the Senate. Formal control of the Senate should have rested with Republicans, owing to the tie-breaking vote of Republican Vice President Dick Cheney. But in a precedent-shattering midsession shift of power, Democrats took control of the Senate in 2001, when Republican Senator Jim Jeffords from Vermont abandoned his party, declared himself an Independent, but gave his vote to the Democrats in the Senate. Other senators had defected from their party in the past, but no previous switch ever produced a change in party control. The new 51–49 Democratic majority took control of all Senate committees as well as the floor of that body.

Bush Leads GOP to Victories in 2002 and 2004   In 2002 President George W. Bush designated himself as "Campaigner-in-Chief," traveling about the country raising campaign money and lending his popularity to Republican House and Senate candidates. His continuing high approval rating throughout the year following the "9/11" terrorist attack on America made him a highly welcomed campaigner in districts and states across the nation. In his campaign stops, Bush talked about the war on terrorism and his need for "allies" in the Congress. President Bush appeared to influence just enough voters in key districts and states to reverse the historic pattern of presidential midterm congressional losses. The GOP won back control of the U.S. Senate and strengthened its majority in the House of Representatives.

Again in 2004 President Bush appeared to help GOP congressional candidates across the country. Republicans increased their control of the Senate from 51 to 55. They picked up several seats of retiring older-generation Southern Democrats. And they even succeeded in defeating the Democratic Senate Minority Leader, Tom Daschle of South Dakota. The 2004 election also made the Senate slightly more "diverse": African American Barack Obama was elected from Illinois, and Hispanic Mel Martinez was elected from Florida. In the House, Republicans also increased their margin of control. President Bush was quick to claim that winning the White House, the Senate, and the House of Representatives meant that the American People supported his "agenda."

Democratic Revival   The war in Iraq seriously eroded President George Bush's popularity and led to the election of a Democratic-controlled House and Senate in the 2006 midterm congressional elections. Republican congressional control had lasted 12 years, and Democrats were anxious to bring their agenda to the Capitol (see *Controversy*: "Divided Versus Unified Party Government").

Congress United for "Change"   In 2008 Democrats not only won the White House but also strengthened their control of both the Senate and the House of Representatives. Republicans had warned voters that this outcome would give unchecked power to Democrats "Obama, Pelosi, and Ried"—referring to the new president, the Speaker of the House, and the Senate Majority Leader. But it is not always certain that united party government ensures complete cooperation between the House, Senate, and White House.

White the theme of "change" prevailed in Washington, specifics of the Democratic agenda remained open to debate. House and Senate Democrats were not prepared to "rubber stamp" every proposal coming from the Democratic

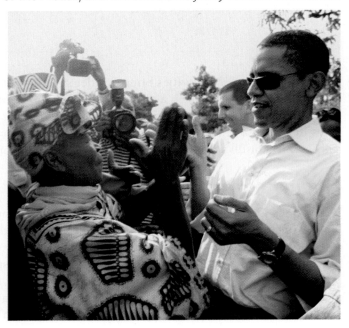

Senator Barack Obama (D-IL) clasps hands with his grandmother, who lives in Kenya. Obama visited Kenya following his election to the U.S. Senate in 2004.

Controversy

Divided Versus United Party Government

Divided government, with a Republican in the White House and Democrats controlling the House and Senate, does not *necessarily* mean policy gridlock, yet that is often the result. Bitter partisanship infected Washington and proved to be a major barrier to cooperation between President George W. Bush and the Democratic-controlled 110th Congress.

The Congress tried but failed to bring an end to the war in Iraq. Because the president is the Commander-in-Chief, there was little that Congress could do by itself to compel changes in strategy in Iraq. In theory, Congress could have cut off funds for the war, but it proved to be too politically risky for Congress to deny funds for American troops in the field. Efforts to place time limits on troop deployments in Iraq also failed.

But President Bush also failed to get Congress to respond to several important initiatives. His "comprehensive" immigration reform proposal—a guest worker program with a promise of citizenship for immigrants who are here now, together with increased border enforcement—failed. Perhaps the most contentious issue between Democrats in Congress and the Republication president was taxation. Bush's first-term tax cuts were set to expire in 2010 and Bush was anxious for Congress to make these cuts permanent. Bush characterized the failure to do so as a "tax increase." Democrats called Bush's cuts "tax cuts for the rich" and opposed making them permanent. Congress and the president did agree to raise the minimum wage and to pass an "economic stimulus" package when faced with a looming recession in 2008. And Congress and the president agreed on a $700 billion bailout of Wall Street.

The Democratic Congress passed some important legislation. It raised the minimum wage; it provided that the U.S. government implement many of the recommendations of the "9/11" Commission; and it passed the Water Resources Development Act of 2007 over President Bush's veto—the bill authorized the wide distributions of federal pork across the United States (something that almost all members of the House and Senate could agree on).

While *bipartisanship* is a popular term used in politics, it rarely describes what actually happens in Washington, especially with divided government.

Beginning in 2009, unified party control of the House, Senate, and White House places the full burden of government on the Democratic Party. Democrats must now bear the full responsibility for governing the nation in very difficult times—an economy in recession, a financial crisis, huge federal deficits, wars in Iraq and Afghanistan, and defending hot-button issues in immigration, taxation, health care, energy, and the environment.

Divided party government is associated with partisanship, bickering, and gridlock. Will unified party government produced major new policy initiatives—the "change" that was promised? Or will other obstacles emerge to block major policy change—institutional competition between the White House and Congress, interest group conflict over the details of policy proposals, personal and "turf" battles among Congress members and committees, and a disciplined minority party in opposition?

president. And larger majorities bring a wider spectrum of views even within the Democratic Party. Moreover, a smaller Republican minority is likely to be more unified and disciplined. Democrats in the Senate do not have the requisite 60 votes to cut off a filibuster. Senate Republicans, united in opposition to specific legislation, can still act as a check on the Democratic majority.

Life in Congress

"All politics is local," declared former House Speaker Thomas P. "Tip" O'Neill, himself once the master of both Boston ward politics and the U.S. House of Representatives. Attention to the local constituency is the key to survival and success in congressional politics. If Congress often fails to deal responsibly with national problems, the explanation lies in part with the design of the institution. House members must devote primary attention to their districts and Senate members to their states. Only *after* their constituencies are served can they turn their attention to national policy making.

The "Representativeness" of Congress The Constitution requires only that members of the House of Representatives be (1) residents of the state they represent (they need not live in their congressional district, although virtually all do so); (2) U.S. citizens for at least 7 years; and (3) at least 25 years old. Senators must also be residents of the state they represent, but they must be at least 30 years old and U.S. citizens for at least 9 years.

★ *African Americans*   African Americans were first elected to Congress following the Civil War—seven black representatives and one black senator served in 1875. But with the end of Reconstruction, black membership in Congress fell to a single seat in the House from 1891 to 1955. Following the Civil Rights Act of 1964 and the Voting Rights Act of 1965, black membership in Congress rose steadily. Redistricting following the 1990 Census resulted in many new "majority-minority" congressional districts. After the 1992 elections, black membership in the House rose dramatically (see Figure 10.7), with most elected from predominantly African American districts.[26] As a result, although African Americans today make up a little more than 12 percent of the U.S. population, they make up about 9 percent of the House membership. African American Carol Moseley Braun of Illinois served in the Senate from 1993 to 1999, and Barack Obama won a Senate seat in the same state in 2004.

★ *Hispanics*   Hispanics now comprise the nation's largest minority, with slightly about 15 percent of the U.S. population. But Hispanic representation in the Congress lags considerably behind their population growth. Currently only about 5 percent of House members are Hispanic, and three Hispanics serve in the U.S. Senate. The Voting Rights Act of 1965 protects "language minorities" as well as racial and ethnic minorities. Prior to the 1990 census and the creation of many court-ordered "majority-minority" congressional districts, very few Hispanics served in the Congress. But with the creation of new Hispanic majority districts, Hispanic representation began to increase in the House of Representatives. Most Hispanic House members come from California, Florida, and Texas.

★ *Women*   Women have made impressive gains in both the House and the Senate in the last decade. The "year of the woman" election in 1992 brought

House Speaker Nancy Pelosi (D-CA) and Senate Majority Leader Senator Harry Reid (D-NV) at an enrollment ceremony at the Capitol. Pelosi signed the Iraq war supplemental funding bill that was to then go to the White House.

Figure *10.7*

Minority Voices: Women, African Americans, and Hispanics in the House of Representatives

Although the House of Representatives is still far short of "looking like America," in recent years the number of African American, Hispanic, and female members has risen noticeably. Particularly impressive advances were made in the 1992 elections, following court-ordered creation of "majority-minority" districts.

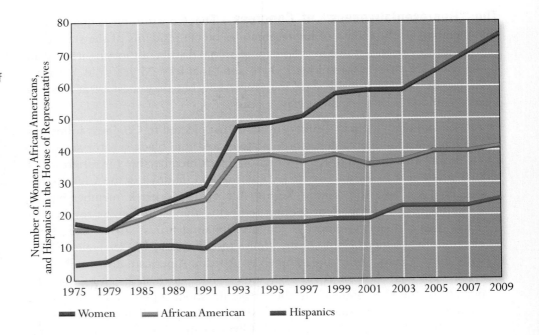

a significant increase in the number of women in the House of Representatives. Since then, women's representation in the House continued upward; seventy-seven women serve in the House in the 111th Congress (2009–2011), divided between sixty Democrats and seventeen Republicans. In the Senate, seventeen women serve. California is represented by two Democratic women, Dianne Feinstein and Barbara Boxer. They are joined by nine other Democratic women senators, and five Republican women senators. Although this is the largest delegation of women ever to serve together in the U.S. Senate, it is still only 17 percent of that body. The number of women in Congress has grown as a result of many factors, including strides that women have made in the workplace and other societal institutions. Yet stereotypes about women as politicians remain. Generally, voters view women as better able to handle "feminine" issues, such as health care, child care and education, but less able to handle "masculine" issues, including the economy and war. In the past, some women candidates tried to counter these stereotypes by emphasizing their toughness, especially on crime. But new evidence suggests that women candidates can use female stereotypes to their advantage by focusing the campaign on gender-owned issues—health, welfare, education, and other compassion issues.[27]

Congressional Staff   Congress is composed of a great deal more than 535 elected senators and representatives. Congressional staff and other support personnel now total some 25,000 people. Each representative has a staff of twenty or more people, usually headed by a chief of staff or administrative assistant and including legislative assistants, communications specialists, constituent-service personnel, office managers, secretaries, and aides of various sorts. Senators frequently have staffs of thirty to fifty or more people. All representatives and senators are provided with offices both in Washington and in their home districts and states. In addition, representatives receive more than $500,000 apiece for office expenses, travel, and staff; and senators receive $2 million or more, depending on the size of their state's population. Overall, Congress spends more than $2 *billion* on itself each year.

Congressional staff people exercise great influence over legislation. Many experienced "Hill rats" have worked for the same member of Congress for many years. They become very familiar with "their" member's political strengths and vulnerabilities and handle much of the member's contacts with interest groups and constituents. Staff people, more than members themselves, move the legislative process—scheduling committee hearings, writing bills and amendments, and tracking the progress of such proposals through committees and floor proceedings. By working with the staff of other members of Congress or the staff of committees and negotiating with interest-group representatives, congressional staff are often able to work out policy compromises, determine the wording of legislation, or even outline "deals" for their member's vote (all subject to later approval by their member). With multiple demands on their time, members of Congress come to depend on their staff not only for information about the content of legislation but also for political recommendations about what position to take regarding it.

Congressional staffers present a container of 2 million mouse cells to Senate Labor, Health and Human Services and Education subcommittee member Senator Arlen Specter (R-PA, center) and Chairman Tom Harkin (D-IO, right).

Support Agencies   In addition to the thousands of personal and committee staff who are supposed to assist members of Congress in research and analysis, four congressional support agencies provide Congress with information:

★ The Library of Congress and its Congressional Research Service (CRS) are the oldest congressional support agencies. Members of Congress can turn to the Library of Congress for references and information. The CRS responds to direct requests of members for factual information on virtually any topic. It tracks major bills in Congress and produces summaries of each bill introduced. This information is available on computer terminals in members' offices.

★ The **Government Accountability Office** (GAO) has broad authority to oversee the operations and finances of executive agencies, to evaluate their programs, and to report its findings to Congress. Established as an arm of Congress in 1921, the GAO largely confined itself to financial auditing and management studies in its early years but expanded to more than five thousand employees in the 1970s and undertook a broad agenda of policy research and evaluation. Most GAO studies and reports are requested by members of Congress and congressional committees, but the GAO also undertakes some studies on its own initiative.

★ The Congressional Budget Office (CBO) was created by the Congressional Budget and Impoundment Act of 1974 to strengthen Congress's role in the budgeting process. It was designed as a congressional counterweight to the president's Office of Management and Budget (see Chapter 14). The CBO supplies the House and Senate budget committees with its own budgetary analyses and economic forecasts, sometimes challenging those found in the president's annual budget.

★ The Government Printing Office (GPO), created in 1860 as the publisher of the *Congressional Record,* now distributes over 20,000 different government publications in U.S. government bookstores throughout the nation.

Power Player
Democratic House Member John Lewis is congratulated for success in passing a Voting Rights Act reauthorization bill. Lewis regularly wins his Atlanta congressional seat by large margins.

Workload Members of Congress claim to work 12- to 15-hour days: 2 to 3 hours in committee and subcommittee meetings; 2 to 3 hours on the floor of the chamber; 3 to 4 hours meeting with constituents, interest groups, other members, and staff in their offices; and 2 to 3 hours attending conferences, events, and meetings in Washington.[28] Members of Congress may introduce anywhere from ten to fifty bills in a single session of Congress. Most bills are introduced merely to exhibit the member's commitment to a particular group or issue. Cosigning a popular bill is a common practice; particularly popular bills may have 100 or 200 cosigners in the House of Representatives. Although thousands of bills are introduced, only 400 to 800 are passed in a session.[29]

Pay and Perks Taxpayers can relate directly to what members of Congress spend on themselves, even while millions—and even billions—of dollars spent on government programs remain relatively incomprehensible. Taxpayers thus were enraged when Congress, in a late-night session in 1991, gave itself a hefty pay raise. Congress claimed the pay raise was a "reform," since it was coupled with a stipulation that members of Congress would no longer be allowed to accept honoraria from interest groups for their speeches and appearances, thus supposedly reducing members' dependence on outside income. Many angry taxpayers saw only a 44 percent pay raise, in the midst of a national recession, for a Congress that was doing little to remedy the nation's problems. By 2008, automatic cost-of-living increases, also enacted by Congress, had raised members' pay to $169,300. House and Senate members receive the same pay. Benefits, including retirement pay, are very generous.

As the pay-raise debate raged in Washington, several states resurrected a constitutional amendment originally proposed by James Madison. Although passed by the Congress in 1789, it had never been ratified by the necessary three-quarters of the states. The 203-year-old amendment, requiring a House election to intervene before a congressional pay raise can take effect, was added as the 27th Amendment when ratified by four states (for a total of thirty-nine) in 1992.

Home Style

Members of Congress spend as much time politically cultivating their districts and states as they do legislating. **Home style** refers to the activities of senators and representatives in promoting their images among constituents and personally attending to constituents' problems and interests.[30] These activities include members' allocations of their personnel and staff resources to constituent services; members' personal appearances in the home district or state to demonstrate personal attention; and members' efforts to explain their Washington activities to the voters back home.

Casework Casework is really a form of "retail" politics. Members of Congress can win votes one at a time by helping constituents on a personal level. Casework can involve everything from tracing lost Social Security checks and Medicare claims to providing information about federal programs, solving problems with the Internal Revenue Service, and assisting with federal job applications. Over time, grateful voters accumulate, giving incumbents an advantage at election

✔ *Think* Again

Do Congress members spend too much time in their home districts seeking reelection?

★ **home style**
Activities of Congress members specifically directed at their home constituencies.

★ **casework**
Services performed by legislators or their staff on behalf of individual constituents.

time. Congressional staff do much of the actual casework, but letters go out over the signature of the member of Congress. Senators and representatives blame the growth of government for increasing casework, but it is also clear that members solicit casework, frequently reminding constituents to bring their problems to their member of Congress.[31]

Pork Barrel and Earmarks

Pork barreling describes the efforts of senators and representatives to "bring home the bacon"—to bring federally funded projects, grants, and contracts that primarily benefit a single district or state to their home constituencies. Opportunities for pork barreling have never been greater: roads, dams, parks, and post offices are now overshadowed by redevelopment grants to city governments, research grants to universities, weapons contracts to local plants, "demonstration" projects of all kinds, and myriad other "goodies" tucked inside each year's annual appropriations bills. **Earmarks** in these appropriations bills specify the particular project for which federal money is to be spent. Members of Congress understand the importance of supporting each other's earmarks, cooperating in the "incumbent-protection society." Even though earmarking and pork barreling add to the public's negative image of Congress as an institution, individual members gain local popularity for the benefits they bring to home districts and states.

Pressing the Flesh

Senators and representatives spend a great deal of time in their home states and districts. Although congressional sessions last virtually all year, members of Congress find ways to spend more than a hundred days per year at home.[32] It is important to be seen at home—giving speeches and attending dinners, fund-raising events, civic occasions, and so on. To accommodate this aspect of home style, Congress usually follows a Tuesday-to-Thursday schedule of legislative business, allowing members to spend longer weekends in their home districts. Congress also enjoys long recesses during the late summer and over holidays.

Puffing Images

To promote their images back home, members make generous use of their **franking privilege** (free mailing) to send their constituents newsletters, questionnaires, biographical material, and information about federal programs. Newsletters "puff" the accomplishments of the members; questionnaires are designed more to flatter voters than to assess opinions; and informational brochures tout federal services members claim credit for providing and defending. Congress's penchant for self-promotion has also kept pace with the media and electronic ages. Congress now provides its members with television studios and support for making videotapes to send to local stations in home districts, and all members maintain Web sites on the Internet designed to puff their images.

Hill Styles and Home Styles

Members of Congress spend their lives "moving between two contexts, Washington and home, and between two activities, governing and campaigning."[33] They must regularly ask themselves how much time they should spend at home with their constituents versus how much time they should spend on lawmaking assignments in Washington. It is no surprise that freshman legislators spend more time in their districts; indeed, very few first-termers move their families to Washington. Long-term incumbents spend more time in Washington, but all Congress members spend more time at home in an election year.

Much of the time spent at home—with small groups of constituents, among contributors, in public speeches, and appearances on radio and television—is devoted to explaining issues and justifying the member's vote on them. "Often members defend their own voting record by belittling Congress—portraying themselves as knights errant battling sinister forces and feckless colleagues."[34]

★ **pork barreling**
Legislation designed to make government benefits, including jobs and projects used as political patronage, flow to a particular district or state.

★ **earmarks**
Provisions in appropriation bills specifying particular projects for which federal money is to be spent.

★ **franking privilege**
Free mail service afforded members of Congress.

Organizing Congress: Party and Leadership

Congress is composed of people who think of themselves as leaders, not followers. They got elected without much help from their party. Yet they realize that their chances of attaining their personal goals—getting reelected and influencing policy—are enhanced if they cooperate with each other.

Party Organizations in Congress   The Democratic and Republican party organizations within the House of Representatives and the Senate are the principal bases for organizing Congress (see Figure 10.8). The leadership of each house of Congress, although nominally elected by the entire chamber, is actually chosen by secret ballot of the members of each party at a "conference" or caucus (see Table 10.3).

The parties and their leaders do not choose congressional candidates, nor can they deny them renomination; all members of Congress are responsible for their own primary and general election success. But party leadership in each chamber can help incumbents achieve their reelection goals. Each party in the House and Senate sponsors a campaign committee that channels some campaign funding to party members seeking reelection, although these Republican and Democratic congressional and senatorial campaign committees contribute less money than either PACs or individuals to the candidates.[35] Rather, good relations between members and their party's leadership are more important in the quest for power and influence in Washington.

Majority status confers great power on the party that controls the House and the Senate. The majority party chooses the leadership in each body, selects the chairs of every committee, and ensures that every committee has a majority of members from the majority party. In other words, if Republicans are in the majority in either the House or the Senate or both, Republicans will occupy all leadership positions, chair every committee, and constitute a majority of the members of every committee, and, of course, the Democrats enjoy the same advantages when they capture a majority of either body. Majority-party members in each house even take in more campaign contributions than minority members.[36]

In the House: "Madam Speaker"   In the House of Representatives, the key leadership figure is the **Speaker of the House,** who serves as both presiding officer of the chamber and leader of the majority party. In the House, the Speaker has many powers. The Speaker decides who shall be recognized to speak on the floor and rules on points of order (with advice from the parliamentarian), including whether a motion or amendment is germane (relevant) to the business at hand. The Speaker decides to which committees new bills will be assigned and can schedule or delay votes on a bill. The Speaker appoints members of select, special, and conference committees and names majority-party members to the Rules Committee. And the Speaker controls both patronage jobs and office space in the Capitol. Although the norm of fairness requires the Speaker to apply the rules of the House consistently, the Speaker is elected by the majority party and is expected to favor that party.

Over the years, different Speakers have displayed different leadership styles. Republican Speaker Newt Gingrich was an ideological leader with a dramatic and aggressive agenda—a "Contract with America"—who contributed to partisan rancor in the House. In contrast, his replacement Republican Speaker Dennis Hastert was a pragmatic leader who dealt with his colleagues in an accommodating fashion.[37] Democratic Speaker Nancy Pelosi led the House in a liberal direction (see *People in Politics:* "Nancy Pelosi, 'Madam Speaker'").

★ **Speaker of the House** Presiding officer of the House of Representatives.

TIMELINE

The Power of the Speaker of the House

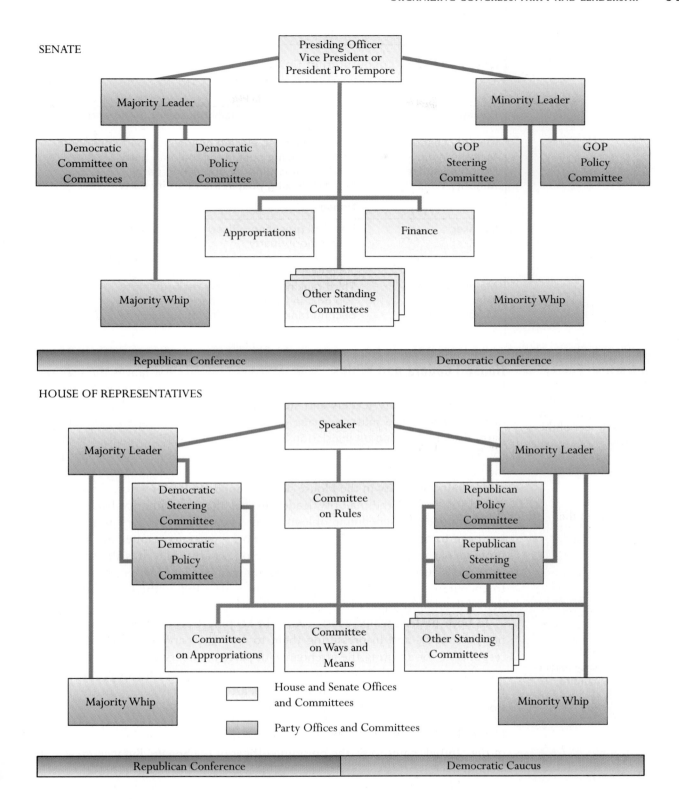

Figure *10.8* How It Works: Organizing the Congress

Aside from naming the Speaker of the House as head of that body's operations and the vice president as overseer of Senate deliberations, the Constitution is silent on the organization of Congress. Political parties have filled this gap: both majority and minority parties have their own leadership, which governs the appointment of members to the various committees, where much of the work of Congress actually takes place.

Table *10.3*   Leadership in Congress

Senate	
President Pro Tempore	An honorary post, usually the senior member of the majority party
Majority Leader	Top Senate post, elected by majority party members
Majority Whip	Second-ranking post in the majority party
Minority Leader	Leader of the minority opposition party
Minority Whip	Second-ranking post in the minority party
House	
Speaker	Powerful presiding officer, elected with the votes of the majority party
Majority Leader	Officially the leader of the majority party but second in power to the Speaker
Majority Whip	Third-ranking leader of the majority party
Minority Leader	Top post in the minority party
Minority Whip	Second-ranking post in the minority party

★ **majority leader**
In the House, the majority-party leader and second in command to the Speaker, in the Senate, the leader of the majority party.

★ **minority leader**
In both the House and Senate, the leader of the opposition party.

★ **whips**
In both the House and Senate, the principal assistants to the party leaders and next in command to those leaders.

House Leaders and Whips   The Speaker's principal assistant is the **majority leader**. The majority leader formulates the party's legislative program in consultation with other party leaders and steers the program through the House. The majority leader also must persuade committee leaders to support the aims of party leaders in acting on legislation before their committees. Finally, the majority leader arranges the legislative schedule with the cooperation of key party members.

The minority party in the House selects a **minority leader** whose duties correspond to those of the majority leader, except that the minority leader has no authority over the scheduling of legislation. The minority leader's principal duty has been to organize the forces of the minority party to counter the legislative program of the majority and to pass the minority party's bills. It is also the minority leader's duty to consult ranking minority members of House committees and to encourage them to adopt party positions and to follow the lead of the president if the minority party controls the White House.

In both parties, **whips** assist leaders in keeping track of the whereabouts of party members and in pressuring them to vote the party line. Whips are also responsible for ensuring the attendance of party members at important roll calls and for canvassing their colleagues on their likely support for or opposition to party-formulated legislation. Finally, whips are involved regularly in the formation of party policy and the scheduling of legislation.

In the Senate: "Mr. President"   The Constitution declares the vice president of the United States to be the presiding officer of the Senate. But vice presidents seldom exercise this senatorial responsibility, largely because the presiding officer of the Senate has very little power. Having only 100 members, the Senate usually does not restrict debate and has fewer scheduling constraints than the House. The only significant power of the vice president is the right to cast a deciding vote in the event of a tie on a Senate roll call. In the usual absence of the vice president, the Senate is presided over by a *president pro tempore*. This honorific position is traditionally granted by the majority party to one of its senior stalwarts. The job of presiding over the Senate is so boring that neither the vice president nor the president pro tempore is found very often in the chamber. Junior

People in Politics   Nancy Pelosi, "Madam Speaker"

Nancy Pelosi is the first woman in the history of the U.S. Congress to serve as Speaker of the House. Following the Democratic victory in the 2006 congressional elections, her Democratic colleagues in the house promoted her from Minority Leader, a post she had held since 2001, to Speaker. Pelosi has represented her San Francisco district since her first election to the Congress in 1986.

Speaker Pelosi comes from a highly political family. Her father, Thomas D'Alesandro, served five terms in Congress and later 12 years as mayor of Baltimore. Pelosi's brother also served as mayor of Baltimore. Young Nancy grew up in Washington and graduated from that city's Trinity College in 1962. She served as a congressional intern to her Maryland senator. She married Paul Pelosi, moved to his hometown of San Francisco, and raised five children. Prior to her election to Congress, she served on the National Democratic Committee.

In her years in Congress, Pelosi built a solid liberal reputation, serving on the powerful Appropriations Committee. But Pelosi's real strength within the Democratic Party has long been her fund-raising ability. Her San Francisco district is the home of some of the party's wealthiest individual donors, and Democrats across the nation rely heavily upon money from California. Pelosi created her own leadership PAC and has handed out millions to her Democratic colleagues. She spends relatively little on her own reelection races in her heavily Democratic district.

In 2002, Pelosi was reelected with an astonishing 80 percent of the vote in her California district. She has continued to win by 80 percent or more of the vote through 2006.

Pelosi is described as hard-driving, yet willing to recognize that her strong liberal views are not necessarily shared by all other Democrats. She has been quoted as saying: "Tell them what you're going to do. Do it. And then tell them what you did." She views her own elevation to the Speaker's position as "a historic moment—for the Congress, and for the women of this country. It is a moment for which we have waited more than 200 years. . . . For our daughters and our granddaughters, the sky is the limit, anything is possible for them."

senators are often asked to assume the chore. Nevertheless, speeches on the Senate floor begin with the salutation "Mr. President," referring to the president of the Senate, *not* the president of the United States.

Senate Majority and Minority Leaders   Senate leadership is actually in the hands of the Senate majority leader, but the Senate majority leader is not as powerful in that body as the Speaker is in the House. With fewer members, all of whom perceive themselves as powerful leaders, the Senate is less hierarchically organized than the House. The Senate majority leader's principal power is scheduling the business of the Senate and recognizing the first speaker in floor debate. To be effective in policy making, the majority leader must be skilled in interpersonal persuasion and communication. Moreover, in the media age, the Senate majority leader must also be a national spokesperson for the party, along with the Speaker of the House. The minority-party leader in the Senate represents the opposition in negotiations with the majority leader over Senate business. With the majority leader, the minority-party leader tends to dominate floor debate in the Senate.

Career Paths within Congress   Movement up the party hierarchy in each house is the most common way of achieving a leadership position. The traditional succession pattern in the House is from whip to majority leader to Speaker. In the Senate, Republicans and Democrats frequently resort to election contests in choosing their party leaders, yet both parties have increasingly adopted a two-step succession route from whip to leader.[38]

Leadership PACs   House and Senate leaders, and members who aspire to become leaders, often ingratiate themselves to their colleagues by distributing campaign funds to them. In recent years, *leadership PACs* have proliferated on Capitol Hill.

In Committee

Much of the real work of Congress is done in committee. The floor of Congress is often deserted; C-SPAN focuses on the podium, not the empty chamber. Members dash to the floor when the bell rings throughout the Capitol signaling a roll-call vote. Otherwise they are found in their offices or in the committee rooms, where the real work of Congress is done.

Standing Committees   The committee system provides for a division of labor in the Congress, assigning responsibility for work and allowing members to develop some expertise (see Table 10.4). The committee system is as old as the Congress itself: the very first Congress regularly assigned the task of wording

---

Table **10.4**   Who Oversees What?: Committees in Congress

Senate

Agriculture, Nutrition, and Forestry	Health, Education, Labor and Pensions
Appropriations	Homeland Security and Environmental Affairs
Armed Services	
Banking, Housing, and Urban Affairs	Judiciary
Budget	Rules and Administration
Commerce, Science, and Transportation	Small Business and Entrepreneurship
Energy and Natural Resources	Select Aging
Environment and Public Works	Select Ethics
Finance	Select Indian Affairs
Foreign Relations	Select Intelligence
	Veterans Affairs

House

Agriculture	Judiciary
Appropriations	Resources
Armed Forces	Rules
Budget	Science
Energy and Commerce	Small Business
Education and the Workforce	Standards of Official Conduct
Financial Services	Transportation and Infrastructure
Government Reform	Veterans Affairs
Homeland Security	Ways and Means
House Administration	Select Intelligence
International Relations	

Joint Committees

Joint Economic Committee
Joint Taxation
Joint Committee on Printing
Joint Committee on the Library

bills to selected members who were believed to have a particular expertise. Soon a system of **standing committees**—permanent committees that specialize in a particular area of legislation—emerged. House committees have forty to sixty or more members and Senate committees fifteen to twenty-five members each. The proportions of Democrats and Republicans on each committee reflect the proportions of Democrats and Republicans in the House and Senate as a whole. Thus the majority party has a majority of members on every committee, and every committee is chaired by a member of the majority party. The minority membership on each committee is led by the **ranking minority member,** the minority-party committee member with the most seniority.

The principal function of standing committees is the screening and drafting of legislation. With 8,000 to 10,000 or more bills introduced each session, the screening function is essential. The standing committees are the gatekeepers of Congress; less than 10 percent of the legislation introduced will pass the Congress. With rare exceptions, bills are not submitted to a vote by the full membership of the House or Senate without prior approval by the majority of a standing committee. Moreover, committees do not merely sort through bills assigned to them to find what they like. Rather, committees—or more often their subcommittees—draft (write) legislation themselves. Committees may amend, rewrite, or write their own bills. Committees are "little legislatures" within their own policy jurisdictions. Each committee guards its own policy jurisdiction jealously; jurisdictional squabbles between committees are common.

The Pecking Order of Committees   The most powerful standing committees, and, therefore, the most sought-after committee assignments, are the Appropriations Committees in the House and the Senate. These committees hold the federal purse strings, arguably Congress's most important power. These committees are closely followed in influence and desirability by the Ways and Means Committee in the House and the Senate Finance Committee; these committees must pass on all tax matters, as well as Social Security and Medicare financing. In the House, the Rules Committee is especially powerful, owing to its control over floor consideration of every bill submitted to the full House. The Senate Judiciary Committee is especially influential because of its influence over all presidential nominees to the federal judiciary, including Supreme Court justices. The Senate Foreign Relations Committee is also a highly valued assignment. Perhaps the *least* desirable committee assignments are those on the Senate Ethics Committee and the House Standards of Official Conduct Committee; members of these ethics panels are obliged to sit in judgment of their own colleagues.

Decentralization and Subcommittees   Congressional **subcommittees** within each standing committee further decentralize the legislative process. At present, the House has about 90 subcommittees and the Senate about 70 subcommittees, each of which functions independently of its full committee (see Table 10.4). Subcommittees have fixed jurisdictions (for example, the House International Relations Committee has subcommittees on Africa, Asia and the Pacific, International Economic Policy, International Operations and Human Rights, and the Western Hemisphere); they meet and schedule their own hearings; and they have their own staffs and budgets. However, bills recommended by a subcommittee still require full standing-committee endorsement before being reported to the floor of the House or Senate. Full committees usually, but not always, ratify the decisions of their subcommittees.

Chairing a committee or subcommittee gives members of Congress the opportunity to exercise power, attract media attention, and thus improve their

★ **standing committee**
Permanent committee of the House or Senate that deals with matters within a specified subject area.

★ **ranking minority member**
The minority-party committee member with the most seniority.

★ **subcommittees**
Specialized committees within standing committees; subcommittee recommendations must be approved by the full standing committee before submission to the floor.

Public Awareness

Congressional committee hearings provide an opportunity for members of Congress to gather information and at the same time promote their own images. Celebrity witnesses increase media coverage. Shown here testifying at a House committee hearing on steroid use in sports are (front to back) baseball stars Curt Schilling, Rafael Palmeiro, Mark McGwire, and Sammy Sosa.

chances of reelection. Often committees have become "fiefdoms" over which their chairs exercise complete control and jealously guard their power. This situation allows a very small number of House and Senate members to block legislation. Many decisions are not really made by the whole Congress. Rather, they are made by subcommittee members with a special interest in the policy under consideration. Although the committee system may satisfy the desire of members to gain power, prestige, and reelection opportunities, it weakens responsible government in the Congress as a whole.

Senator Patrick Leahy (D-VT), Chairman of the Senate Judiciary Committee, speaks on March 29, 2007, at a hearing investigating the firing of eight federal prosecutors by the Justice Department under the Bush administration.

Committee Membership   Given the power of the committee system, it is not surprising that members of Congress have a very keen interest in their committee assignments. Members strive for assignments that will give them influence in Congress, allow them to exercise power in Washington, and ultimately improve their chances for reelection. For example, a member from a big city may seek a seat on Banking, Housing, and Urban Affairs, a member from a farm district may seek a seat on Agriculture, and a member from a district with a large military base may seek a seat on National Security or Veterans Affairs. Everyone seeks a seat on Appropriations, because both the House and the Senate Appropriations committees have subcommittees in each area of federal spending.[39]

Party leadership in both the House and the Senate largely determines committee assignments. These assignments are given to new Democratic House members by the Democratic Steering and Policy Committee; new Democratic senators receive their assignments from the Senate Democratic Steering Committee. New Republican members receive their committee assignments from the Republican Committee on Committees in both houses. The leadership generally tries to honor new members' requests and improve their chances for reelection, but because incumbent members of committees are seldom removed, openings on powerful committees are infrequent.

Seniority

Committee chairs are elected in the majority-party caucus. But the **seniority system** governs most movement into committee leadership positions. The seniority system ranks all committee members in each party according to the length of time they have served on the committee. If the majority-party chair exits the Congress or leaves the committee, that position is filled by the next *ranking majority-party member*. New members of a committee are initially added to the bottom of the ranking of their party; they climb the seniority ranking by remaining on the committee and accruing years of seniority. Members who stay in Congress but "hop" committees are usually placed at the bottom of their new committee's list.

The seniority system has a long tradition in the Congress. The advantage is that it tends to reduce conflict among members, who otherwise would be constantly engaged in running for committee posts. It also increases the stability of policy direction in committees over time. Critics of the system note, though, that the seniority system grants greater power to members from "safe" districts—districts that offer little electoral challenge to the incumbent. (Historically in the Democratic Party, these districts were in the conservative South, and opposition to the seniority system developed among liberal northern Democrats. But in recent years, many liberal Democrats gained seniority and the seniority system again became entrenched [see *People in Politics:* "Ted Kennedy: Liberal Icon in the U.S. Senate"]). The seniority rule for selecting committee chairs has been violated on only a few notable occasions.

Committee Hearings

The decision of a congressional committee to hold public hearings on a bill or topic is an important one. It signals congressional interest in a particular policy matter and sets the agenda for congressional policy making. Ignoring an issue by refusing to hold hearings on it usually condemns it to oblivion. Public hearings allow interest groups and government bureaucrats to present formal arguments to Congress. Testimony comes mostly from government officials, lobbyists, and occasional experts recommended by interest groups or committee staff members. Hearings are usually organized by the staff under the direction of the chair. Staff members contact favored lobbyists and bureaucrats and schedule their appearances. Committee hearings are regularly listed in the *Washington Post* and are open to the public. Indeed, the purpose of many hearings is not really to inform members of Congress but instead to gain publicity and rally public support behind an issue or a bill. The media are the real target audience of many public hearings, with committee members jockeying in front of the cameras for a "sound bite" on the evening news.

Markup

Once hearings are completed the committee's staff is usually assigned the task of writing a report and **drafting a bill**. The staff's bill generally reflects the chair's policy views. But the staff draft is subject to committee **markup**, a line-by-line consideration of the wording of the bill. Markup sessions are frequently closed to the public in order to expedite work. Lobbyists are forced to stand in the hallways, buttonholing members as they go into and out of committee rooms.

It is in markup that the detailed work of lawmaking takes place. Markup sessions require patience and skill in negotiation. Committee or subcommittee chairs may try to develop consensus on various parts of the bill, either within the whole committee or within the committee's majority. In marking up a bill, members of a subcommittee must always remember that the bill must pass both in the full committee and on the floor of the chamber. Although they have considerable freedom in writing their own policy preferences into law,

★ **seniority system**
Custom whereby the member of Congress who has served the longest on the majority side of a committee becomes its chair and the member who has served the longest on the minority side becomes its ranking member.

Government by Committee

Senator Joe Biden (left), shown here when he was Chairman of the Senate Foreign Relations Committee, and Senator Richard Lugar, Ranking Minority Member, speak to reporters after meeting with President Bush about the arms treaty with Russia.

★ **drafting a bill**
Actual writing of a bill in legal language.

★ **markup**
Line-by-line revision of a bill in committee by editing each phrase and word.

People in Politics   Ted Kennedy: Liberal Icon in the U.S. Senate

To the American public, Massachusetts Senator Edward M. "Ted" Kennedy is largely a symbol of his family's legendary triumphs and tragedies. But in the U.S. Senate, Kennedy has established himself over the years as the recognized leader of liberal Democrats and a highly effective legislator.

Ted Kennedy's father, Joseph P. Kennedy, was a wealthy banker and stock market manipulator who provided key financial backing for the 1932 presidential campaign of Franklin D. Roosevelt. FDR later appointed "Old Joe" as ambassador to England. The senior Kennedy fathered nine children, including Joseph P., Jr., who was killed in World War II; President John F. Kennedy, who was assassinated in 1963; Senator Robert F. Kennedy, who was assassinated in 1968; and the youngest, Edward M. "Ted" Kennedy.

Although born to great wealth (he received his first communion from the Pope), Ted Kennedy acquired the sense of competition fostered in the large Kennedy household. In 1951, suspended from Harvard for cheating on an examination, he joined the army and served two years in Germany. He was later readmitted to Harvard from which he graduated in 1956. Rejected by Harvard Law School, he enrolled instead in the University of Virginia Law School and completed his law degree in 1959. When he was just 30 years old, the minimum age for a U.S. senator, he announced his candidacy for the Massachusetts Senate seat formerly held by his brother, who was then president. His 1962 election to the U.S. Senate reflected the esteem that Massachusetts voters have always held for his family.

But Ted's personal life was marred by accident, tragedy, and scandal. He nearly died in a 1964 plane crash in which he suffered a broken back. He was frequently the object of romantic gossip in Washington. In 1969, a young woman died when the car Kennedy was driving plunged off a narrow bridge on Chappaquiddick Island after a late-night party. Missing for 10 hours after the accident, Kennedy later made a dramatic national television appearance claiming that the tragedy had been an accident that he had been too confused to report until the next day. He pled guilty to the minor charge of leaving the scene of the accident. Senate Democrats removed Kennedy from his position as majority party whip.

Kennedy deliberately avoided Democratic presidential battles in both 1972 and 1976, believing that the public's memory of Chappaquiddick was still too fresh. However, in late 1979, with President Jimmy Carter standing at a near all-time low for presidents in opinion polls, Kennedy announced his presidential candidacy. But shortly thereafter, Soviet troops invaded neighboring Afghanistan. Support for the president was equated with support for America, and Carter benefited from this "rally round the flag" effect. Carter defeated Kennedy in the Democratic primaries.

As Chairman of the Senate Health, Education, and Labor Committee, Kennedy has undertaken the lead in a variety of important legislative issues. He helped pass the Family Leave Act of 1993, the Kennedy-Kassebaum Act of 1996 that mandated health insurance "portability" (see Chapter 17), and increases in the minimum wage. He worked with President George W. Bush in passing the No Child Left Behind Act in 2001, and in 2007 cosponsored with Senator John McCain an unsuccessful bill to reform the nation's immigration laws. His support of abortion rights has brought him into conflict with the Roman Catholic church to which he belongs. He is a strong supporter of national healthcare, gun control, and environmental protection. He supported the overthrow of the Taliban regime in Afghanistan in 2001, but he has been a leading critic of the war in Iraq since its beginning.

In 2006 Ted Kennedy was elected to his eighth full term as a US Senator from Massachusetts with fully 70 percent of the vote. In May, 2008, he was diagnosed with a malignant brain tumor.

especially on the details of the legislation, they must give some consideration to the views of these larger bodies. Consultations with party leadership are not infrequent.

Most bills die in committee. Some are voted down, but most are simply ignored. Bills introduced simply to reassure constituents or interest groups that a representative is committed to "doing something" for them generally die quietly. But House members who really want action on a bill can be frustrated by committee inaction. The only way to force a floor vote on a bill opposed by a committee is to get a majority (218) of House members to sign a **discharge petition**.

★ **discharge petition**
Petition signed by at least 218 House members to force a vote on a bill within a committee that opposes it.

Out of hundreds of discharge petition efforts, only a few dozen have succeeded.[40] The Senate also can forcibly "discharge" a bill from committee by simple majority vote; but because senators can attach any amendment to any bill they wish, there is generally no need to go this route.

On the Floor

A favorable "report" by a standing committee of the House or Senate places a bill on the "calendar." The word *calendar* is misleading, because bills on the calendar are not considered in chronological order and many die on the calendar without ever reaching the floor.

Respect Your Elders
Seniority is a valuable resource in the U.S. Senate. Senators Ted Kennedy (D-MA) and Robert Byrd (D-WV) together have served over 80 years in the Senate.

House Rules Committee   Even after a bill has been approved by a standing committee, getting it to the floor of the House of Representatives for a vote by the full membership requires favorable action by the Rules Committee. The Rules Committee acts as a powerful "traffic cop" for the House. In order to reach the floor, a bill must receive a rule from the Rules Committee. The Rules Committee can kill a bill simply by refusing to give it a rule. A **rule** determines when the bill will be considered by the House and how long the debate on the bill will last. More important, a rule determines whether amendments from the floor will be permitted and, if so, how many. A **closed rule** forbids House members from offering any amendments and speeds up consideration of the bill in the form submitted by the standing committee. A **restricted rule** allows certain specified amendments to be considered. An **open rule** permits unlimited amendments. Most key bills are brought to the floor of the House with fairly restrictive rules. In recent sessions, about three-quarters of all bills reaching the floor were restricted, and an additional 10 to 15 percent were fully closed. Only a few bills were open.[41]

Senate Floor Traditions   The Senate has no rules committee but relies instead on a **unanimous consent agreement** negotiated between the majority and minority leader to govern consideration of a bill. The unanimous consent agreement generally specifies when the bill will be debated, what amendments will be considered, and when the final vote will be taken. But as the name implies, a single senator can object to a unanimous consent agreement and thus hold up Senate consideration of a bill. Senators do not usually do so, because they know that a reputation for obstructionism will imperil their own favorite bills at a later date. Once accepted, a unanimous consent agreement is binding on the Senate and cannot be changed without another unanimous consent agreement. To get unanimous consent, Senate leaders must consult with all interested senators. Unanimous consent agreements have become more common in recent years as they have become more specific in their provisions.

The Senate cherishes its tradition of unrestricted floor debate. Senators may speak as long as they wish or even try to **filibuster** a bill to death by talking nonstop and tying up the Senate for so long that the leadership is forced to drop the bill in order to go on to other work. Senate rules also allow senators to place a "hold" on a bill, indicating their unwillingness to grant unanimous consent to its consideration. Debate may be ended only if *sixty* or more senators vote for

★ **rule**
Stipulation attached to a bill in the House of Representatives that governs its consideration on the floor, including when and for how long it can be debated and how many (if any) amendments may be appended to it.

★ **closed rule**
Rule that forbids adding any amendments to a bill under consideration by the House.

★ **restricted rule**
Rule that allows specified amendments to be added to a bill under consideration by the House.

★ **open rule**
Rule that permits unlimited amendments to a bill under consideration by the House.

★ **unanimous consent agreement**
Negotiated by the majority and minority leaders of the Senate, it specifies when a bill will be taken up on the floor, what amendments will be considered, and when a vote will be taken.

★ **filibuster**
Delaying tactic by a senator or group of senators, using the Senate's unlimited debate rule to prevent a vote on a bill.

★ **cloture**
Vote to end debate—that is, to end a filibuster—which requires a three-fifths vote of the entire membership of the Senate.

cloture, a process of petition and voting that limits the debate. A cloture vote requires a petition signed by sixteen senators; 2 days must elapse between the petition's introduction and the cloture vote. If cloture passes, then each senator is limited to 1 hour of debate on the bill. But getting the necessary sixty votes for cloture is difficult. Democrats, although a minority in the Senate, defeated cloture motions in order to derail President Bush's nominees for federal judgeships (see *Controversy*: "Should Presidential Appointments of Judges, Including Supreme Court Justices, Be Thwarted by Senate Filibusters?").

Senate floor procedures also permit unlimited amendments to be offered, even those that are not germane to the bill. A **rider** is an amendment to a bill that is not germane to the bill's purposes.

★ **rider**
Amendment to a bill that is not germane to the bill's purposes.

These Senate traditions of unlimited debate and unrestricted floor amendments give individual senators considerably more power over legislation than individual representatives enjoy.

Floor Voting   The key floor votes are usually on *amendments* to bills rather than on their final passage. Indeed, "killer amendments" are deliberately designed to defeat the original purpose of the bill. Other amendments may water down the bill so much that it will have little policy impact. Thus the true policy preferences of senators or representatives may be reflected more in their votes on amendments than their vote on final passage. Members may later claim to have supported legislation on the basis of their vote on final passage, even though they earlier voted for amendments designed to defeat the bill's purposes.

Members may also obscure their voting records by calling for a voice vote—simply shouting "aye" or "nay"—and avoiding recording of their individual votes. In contrast, a **roll-call vote** involves the casting of individual votes, which are reported in the *Congressional Record* and are available to the media and the general public. Electronic voting machines in the House allow members to insert their cards and record their votes automatically. The Senate, truer to tradition, uses no electronic counters.

★ **roll-call vote**
Vote of the full House or Senate at which all members' individual votes are recorded and made public.

Conference Committees   The Constitution requires that both houses of Congress pass a bill with identical wording. However, many major bills pass each house in different forms, not only with different wording but sometimes with wholly different provisions. Occasionally the House or the Senate will resolve these differences by reconsidering the matter and passing the other chamber's version of the bill. But about 15 percent of the time, serious differences arise and bills are assigned to **conference committees** to reach agreement on a single version for resubmission to both houses. Conference committees are temporary, with members appointed by the leadership in each house, usually from among the senior members of the committees that approved the bills.

★ **conference committees**
Meetings between representatives of the House and Senate to reconcile differences over provisions of a bill passed by both houses.

Conference committees can be very powerful. Their final bill is usually (although not always) passed in both houses and sent to the president for approval. In resolving differences between the House and the Senate versions, the conference committee makes many final policy decisions. Although conference committees have considerable leeway in striking compromises, they focus on points of disagreement and usually do not change provisions already approved by both houses. Figure 10.9 summarizes the lawmaking process.

How a Bill Becomes a Law

Decision Making in Congress

How do senators and representatives decide how they will vote on legislation? From an almost limitless number of considerations that go into congressional decision making, a few factors recur across a range of voting decisions:

Controversy

Should Presidential Appointments of Judges, Including Supreme Court Justices, Be Thwarted by Senate Filibusters?

The Constitution gives the president the power to make judicial appointments, including appointments to the Supreme Court, "by and with the Advice and Consent of the Senate." The Constitution requires only a majority vote of the Senate to consent to the president's appointment.

But from the earliest days of the Senate the idea of "unlimited debate" was enshrined in Senate rules and customs. For over a century, the "filibuster" was honored as "insurance against the will of a majority of states being imposed over the wishes of a minority of states." Over the years, liberals and progressives in the Senate came to loathe the filibuster rule. President Woodrow Wilson (formerly a political science professor at Princeton University and author of a book on Congress) persuaded the Senate to adopt a "cloture rule" (see previous page) which called for cutting off debate with a two-thirds vote of senators present and voting. For decades afterward, liberals sought to completely eliminate the filibuster, as it became an important tool of opponents of civil rights legislation. (The Civil Rights Act of 1964 was passed only after a successful cloture vote ended a Southern filibuster.) In 1975 the Senate lowered the vote requirement for cloture to sixty, that is, three-fifths rather than two-thirds.

By the 1990s filibusters became more common as partisanship in the Senate began to rise. Democrats and Republicans both regularly threatened filibusters to stop legislation they opposed. This meant that controversial bills could not get through the Senate without sixty votes, rather than a simple majority of fifty-one.

Senate Democrats began to use the filibuster to thwart judicial nominees submitted by Republican President George W. Bush. Republican Senate Majority Leader Bill Frist argued that such a use violated the Constitution, which requires only a majority vote for judicial confirmations. Several key appeals for court nominations were held up by Democrats threatening filibusters. Republicans had only fifty-five members in the Senate, not the sixty needed to end debate. So in 2005 Frist threatened "the nuclear option"—having the presiding officer of the Senate, Republican Vice President Richard Cheney, declare the filibuster rule for judicial nominations to be unconstitutional. This ruling would then be upheld by a simple majority vote of the Senate.

But a temporary truce was fashioned in which several Bush judicial appointments were confirmed and

Senate filibusters can be ended only by persuasion or by a three-fifths vote (60 members). Inasmuch as at least one filibustering member must remain continuously on the floor of the Senate, beds are often prepared in Senate offices for periodic alternating-member breaks.

the filibuster rule was undisturbed. Senators promised to use it only under "extraordinary circumstances," a phrase left undefined. Republicans promised not to use the nuclear option unless the Democrats fail to abide by the agreement.

Generally, Americans appear to support the filibuster, even against judicial nominees:

Q. *"As you know there are 100 senators. How many senators' votes should it take to move ahead to confirm a Supreme Court nominee? Should a majority of 51 votes be required, or is this something that should require a larger majority of 60 votes?"*

51 votes	60 votes	Unsure
31%	64%	5%

Q. *"How do you feel about this issue? Do you favor or oppose changing the rules of the Senate to stop the use of filibusters against judicial nominees?"*

Favor	Oppose	Unsure
28%	37%	35%

Source: From *Beyond Red and Blue*, Pew Research Center for the People and the Press, May 20, 2005. Copyright © 2005 by the Pew Research Center. Reprinted by permission.

HOUSE

SENATE

Bill Introduction

Subcommittee Hearings

Committee Action

Floor Action

Conference Action

Presidential Decision

Bill is introduced and assigned to a committee, which refers it to the appropriate subcommittee.

Bill is introduced and assigned to a committee, which refers it to the appropriate subcommittee.

Subcommittee
Subcommittee holds hearings and "marks up" the bill. If the bill is approved in some form, it goes to the full committee.

Committee
Full committee considers the bill. If the bill is approved in some form, it is "reported" to the full House and placed on the House calendar.

Subcommittee
Subcommittee holds hearings, debates provisions and "marks up" the bill. If a bill is approved, it goes to the full committee.

Committee
Full committee considers the bill. If the bill is approved in some form, it is "reported" to the full Senate and placed on the Senate calendar.

Rules Committee
Rules Committee issues a rule to govern debate on the floor. Sends it to the full House.

Full House
Full House debates the bill and may amend it. If the bill passes and it is in a form different from the Senate version, it must go to a conference committee.

Leadership
Majority and minority leaders negotiate "unanimous consent" agreements scheduling full Senate debate and vote on the bill.

Full Senate
Full Senate debates the bill. Senate may amend it. If the bill passes and is in a form different from the House version, it must go to a conference committee.

Conference Committee
Conference committee of senators and representatives meets to reconcile differences between bills. When agreement is reached, a compromise bill is sent back to both the House and the Senate.

President
President signs or vetoes the bill. Congress can override a veto by a two-thirds majority vote in both the House and Senate.

LAW

Figure *10.9*   Running the Gauntlet: How a Bill Becomes a Law

This diagram depicts the major hurdles a successful bill must overcome in order to be enacted into law. Few bills introduced travel this full path; less than 10 percent of bills introduced are passed by Congress and sent to the president for approval or veto. Bills fail at every step along the path, but most die in committees and subcommittees, usually from inaction rather than from being voted down.

party loyalty, presidential support or opposition, constituency concerns, interest-group pressures, and the personal values and ideologies of members themselves.

Party Voting
Party appears to be the most significant influence on congressional voting. **Party votes** are roll-call votes on which a majority of voting Democrats oppose a majority of voting Republicans. Traditionally, party votes occurred on roughly *half* of all roll-call votes in Congress. Partisanship in Congress, as reflected in the percentage of party votes, rose during the 1990s but may be moderating somewhat today (see Figure 10.10).

Party unity is measured by the percentage of Democrats and Republicans who stick by their party on party votes. Both Democratic and Republican Party unity have remained at fairly constant levels (85–95 percent) in both the House and the Senate over the past 10 years. This is higher than in previous decades when party unity was regularly 50–60 percent in both the House and Senate. Greater party unity suggests increased partisan polarization in Congress.

Sources of Partisanship
Why do Democrats and Republicans in Congress vote along party lines? First of all, the Democratic Party has become more liberal and the Republican Party has become more conservative over the years. Conservative Democrats, once very common in southern politics, are rapidly disappearing. At the same time, the ranks of liberal Republicans, mostly from the Northeast, have thinned. Second, the decline in voter turnout, especially in primary elections, has added to the importance of well-organized and ideologically motivated groups. In primary elections Republicans must be more concerned with pleasing conservative activists (e.g., the Christian Coalition, National Right-to-Life Committee, National Rifle Association, and so on), and Democrats must be more concerned with pleasing liberal groups (National Education Association, American Federation of State, County, and Municipal Employees, Sierra Club, and so on). And third, the rising costs of campaigning make members ever more dependent upon the financial support of these interests.

You Are a Member of Congress

★ **party votes**
Majority of Democrats voting in opposition to a majority of Republicans.

★ **party unity**
Percentage of Democrats and Republicans who stick with their party on party votes.

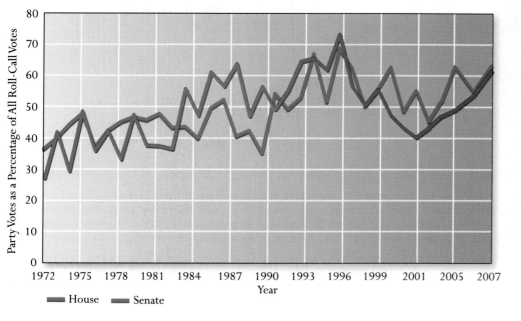

Figure *10.10*

Partisan Politics: Party Voting in Congress
Partisanship varies over time in Congress. For many years, between 30 and 40 percent of votes in the House and Senate were party votes—votes on which a majority of Democrats were in opposition to a majority of Republicans— but during the 1990s the percentage rose, indicating an increasingly partisan environment in Congress.

Note: Data indicate the percentage of all recorded votes on which a majority of voting Democrats opposed a majority of voting Republicans.

Source: Based on data from *Congressional Quarterly Weekly Report*, January 14, 2008, p. 148.

★ **bipartisanship**
Agreement by members of both the Democratic and the Republican parties.

★ **divided party government**
One party controls the presidency while the other party controls one or both houses of Congress.

Conflict between the parties occurs frequently on domestic social and economic issues—welfare, housing and urban affairs, health, business regulation, taxing, and spending. Traditionally, **bipartisanship** was the goal of both presidents and congressional leaders on foreign and defense policy issues. Since the Vietnam War, however, Democrats in the Congress have been more critical of U.S. military involvements (and defense spending in general) than have Republicans.

Presidential Support or Opposition

Presidential influence in congressional voting is closely tied to party. Presidents almost always receive their greatest support from members of their own party (see Figure 10.11). Indeed, policy gridlock is often associated with **divided party government**—either a Republican president

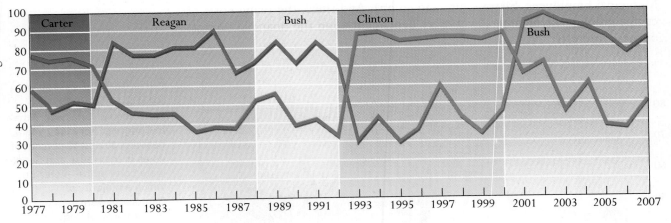

Figure *10.11*   Presidental Influence: Congressional Voting in Support of the President

Presidents always receive more support in Congress from members of their own party. Democratic Presidents Jimmy Carter and Bill Clinton could count on winning large majorities of Democratic members' votes, Republican Presidents Ronald Reagan, George H. W. Bush, and George W. Bush won large majorities of GOP members' votes. Percentages indicate congressional votes supporting the president on votes on which the president took a position.

Source: Norman J. Ornstein, Thomas E. Mann, and Michael J. Malbin, *Vital Statistics on Congress 1999–2000* (Washington, D.C.: CQ Press, 2000), pp. 254–55; and *Congressional Quarterly Weekly Report,* December 11, 1999, p. 2987; January 12, 2002, p. 136; December 14, 2003, p. 3275; January 3, 2004, p. 53; December 11, 2005, p. 2946; January 14, 2008, p. 137.

and a Democratic-controlled Congress, or a Democratic president and a Republican-controlled Congress.

The decentralization of power in the congressional committee system also limits the president's ability to influence voting. The president cannot simply negotiate with the leadership of the House and Senate but instead must deal with scores of committee and subcommittee chairs and ranking members. To win the support of so many members of Congress, presidents often must agree to insert pork into presidential bills, promise patronage jobs, or offer presidential assistance in campaign fund raising.

If negotiations break down, presidents can "go over the heads" of Congress, using the media to appeal directly to the people to support presidential programs and force Congress to act. The president has better access to the media than Congress has. But such threats and appeals can only be effective when (1) the president himself is popular with the public; and (2) the issue is one about which constituents can be made to feel intensely.

Finally, presidents can threaten to veto legislation. This threat, expressed or implied, confronts congressional leaders, committee chairs, and sponsors of a bill with several options. They must decide whether to (1) modify the bill to overcome the president's objections; (2) try to get two-thirds of both houses to commit to overriding the threatened veto; or (3) pass the bill and dare the president to veto it, then make a political issue out of the president's opposition. Historically, less than 5 percent of vetoes have been overridden by the Congress. Unless the president is politically very weak (as Richard Nixon was during the Watergate scandal), Congress cannot count on overriding a veto. If members of Congress truly want to address an important problem and not just define a political issue, they must negotiate with the White House to write a bill the president will sign.

Constituency Influence

Constituency influence in congressional voting is most apparent on issues that attract media attention and discussion and generate intense feelings among the general public. If many voters in the home state or district know about an issue and have intense feelings about it, members of Congress are likely to defer to their constituents' feeling, regardless of the position of their party's leadership or even their own personal feelings. Members of Congress from *safe seats* seem to be just as attuned to the interests of their constituents as members from competitive seats.

Constituencies may also exercise a subtle influence by conditioning the personal views of members. Many members were born, were raised, and continue to live in the towns they represent; over a lifetime they have absorbed and internalized the views of their communities. Moreover, some members of Congress feel an obligation to represent their constituents' opinions even when they personally disagree.

However, members of Congress have considerable latitude in voting against their constituents' opinions if they choose to do so. Constituents, as noted earlier, lack information about most policy issues and the voting records of their senators and representatives. Even when constituents know about an issue and feel strongly about it, members can afford to cast a "wrong" vote from time to time. A long record of home style politics—casework, pork barreling, visits, public appearances, and so on—can isolate members of Congress from the wrath generated by their voting records. Only a long string of "wrong" votes on issues important to constituents is likely to jeopardize an incumbent.

★ **constituency**
The votes in a legislator's home district.

Think Again

Are members of Congress obliged to vote the way their constituents wish, even if they personally disagree?

Think Again

Is it ethical for Congress members to pay special attention to requests for assistance by people who make large campaign contributions?

★ **trustees**
Legislators who feel obligated to use their own best judgment in decision making.

★ **delegates**
Legislators who feel obligated to present the views of their home constituents.

Interest-Group Influence   Inside the Washington Beltway, the influence of interest groups, lobbyists, and fund raisers on members of Congress is well understood. This influence is seldom talked about back home or on the campaign trail, except perhaps by challengers. Lobbyists have their greatest effects on the *details* of public policy. Congressional decisions made in committee rooms, at markup sessions, and around conference tables can mean billions of dollars to industries and tens of millions to individual companies. Pressures from competing interest groups can be intense as lobbyists buttonhole lawmakers and try to win legislative amendments that can make or break business fortunes. One of the most potent tools in the lobbyist's arsenal is money. The prohibitive cost of modern campaigning has dictated that dollars are crucial to electoral victory, and virtually all members of Congress spend more time than they would like courting it, raising it, and stockpiling it for the next election.

Voters may be wrong when they think that all members of Congress are crooks, but they are not far off the mark when they worry that their own representatives may be listening to two competing sets of constituents—the real constituents back home in the district and the "cash constituents" who come calling in Washington.[42]

Personal Values   It was the eighteenth-century English political philosopher Edmund Burke, himself a member of Parliament, who told his constituents; "You choose a member indeed; but when you have chosen him, he is not a member of Bristol, but he is a member of *Parliament*." Burke defended the classic notion of representatives as **trustees** who feel obligated to use their own best judgment about what is good for the nation as a whole. In this theory, representatives are not obligated to vote the views of their constituents. This notion contrasts with the idea of representatives as **delegates** who feel obligated to vote according to the views of "the folks back home" regardless of their own personal viewpoint. Most legislators *claim* to be trustees, perhaps because of the halo effect generated by the independence implied in the term.

Democratic political philosophers have pondered the merits of trustee versus delegate representation over the centuries, but the question only rarely arises in actual congressional deliberations. In many cases, members' own personal views and those of their constituents are virtually identical. Even when legislators perceive conflicts between their own views and those of their constituents, most attempt to find a compromise between these competing demands rather than choose one role or another exclusively. The political independence of members of Congress—their independence from party, combined with the ignorance of their constituents about most policy issues—allows members to give great weight to their own personal ideologies in voting.

Customs and Norms

Over time, institutions develop customs and norms of behavior to assist in their functioning. These are not merely quaint and curious folkways; they promote the purposes of the institution. Congressional customs and norms are designed to help members work together, to reduce interpersonal conflict, to facilitate bargaining and promote compromise.

Civility   Traditionally, members of Congress understood that uncivil behavior—expressions of anger, personal attacks on character, ugly confrontations, flaming rhetoric—undermined the lawmaking function. Indeed, civility was encouraged by the longstanding custom of members of Congress referring to each other in elaborately courteous terms: "my distinguished colleague from Ohio," "the honorable representative from Pennsylvania," and the like. By custom, even bitter partisan

A Conflicting *View*

Congress Can Act Responsibly

Congress is not always mired in partisanship, squabbling, and gridlock. On occasion it acts responsibly in the national interest. Indeed, consider the following congressional landmarks in U.S. history:

Louisiana Purchase (1803)

President Thomas Jefferson offered to purchase from France nearly 830,000 square miles between the Mississippi and the Rockies for $15 million—about three cents an acre. There is no constitutional provision authorizing the federal government to buy foreign territory, but the Senate, accepting Jefferson's broad interpretation of the Constitution, approved the purchase. The House appropriated the money to consummate the deal. On December 29, 1803, the United States took possession of North America's heartland, doubling the nation's size with territory that would eventually comprise thirteen states.

Homestead Act (1862)

This Civil War–era legislation allowed any family head or adult male to claim 160 acres of government land for a $10 registration fee and a promise to live there continuously for five years. It opened up the midwestern United States for immediate settlement. The act drew thousands of English, Irish, Germans, Swedes, Danes, Norwegians, and Czechs to the United States, pushing settlement farther west.

Social Security Act (1935)

The act was designed to secure "the men, women, and children of the nation against certain hazards and vicissitudes of life," explained President Franklin Roosevelt. The act's best-known measure is the social insurance system that provides monthly checks to the elderly.

National Labor Relations Act (1935)

By declaring workers had a right to join unions and bargain collectively with employers for pay raises and improved working conditions, the act spurred the growth of the nation's major industrial unions. Labor's Magna Carta also provided workers with the legal weapons to improve plant conditions and protect themselves from employer harassment.

G.I. Bill of Rights (1944)

The G.I. Bill of Rights, known officially as the Serviceman's Readjustment Act of 1944, offered to pay tuition for college or trade education to ex–World War II servicemen. It also mandated that they receive up to $500 a year for tuition, books, and supplies. Nearly 8 million veterans took advantage of this first G.I. Bill

and American higher education expanded rapidly as a result. Veterans also made use of the bill's guaranteed mortgages and low interest rates to buy new homes in the suburbs, inspiring a housing boom.

Truman Doctrine (1947) and NATO (1949)

The Truman Doctrine initiated U.S. resistance to expansion of the Soviet Union into Western Europe following World War II, and the NATO treaty has provided the framework for European security for half a century. Truman declared to a joint session of Congress, "I believe that it must be the policy of the United States to support free people who are resisting attempted subjugation by armed minorities or by outside pressures."

Federal Highway Act (1956)

President Dwight D. Eisenhower was right when he said, "More than any single action by the government since the end of the war, this one would change the face of America." The most expensive public-works project in U.S. history, the highway act built the 41,000-mile nationwide interstate highway system.

Civil Rights Act of 1964

Only Congress could end racial segregation in privately owned businesses and facilities. It did so by an overwhelming vote of both houses in the Civil Rights Act of 1964. Injustices endure, but the end of segregated restaurants, theaters, and drinking fountains provided new opportunities for African Americans and helped change white attitudes. In addition, Title VII of the act prohibits gender discrimination and serves as the legal bulwark for women's rights.

Voting Rights Act of 1965

President Lyndon B. Johnson signed this act in the same room in the Capitol where Abraham Lincoln had penned the Emancipation Proclamation. This legislation guaranteed all Americans the most fundamental of all rights—the right to vote. Between the 1964 and 1968 presidential elections, black voter registration increased 50 percent across the nation, even in the reluctant Southern states, giving African Americans newfound political clout.

Medicare and Medicaid (1965)

Congress amended the Social Security Act of 1935 to provide for national health insurance for the aged (Medicare) and for the poor (Medicaid). In 2003 (28 years later) Congress added prescription drug coverage to Medicare.

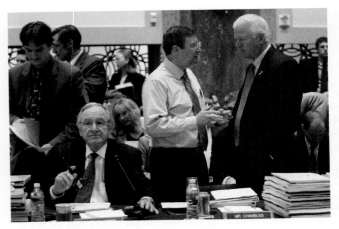

Senate Agriculture Chairman Tom Harkin (D-IA), seated, and Senator Kent Conrad, (D-ND), and Senator Charles E. Grassley (R-IA) and others meet on May 1, 2008, at the start of a House-Senate conference on the farm bill.

enemies in Congress were expected to avoid harsh personal attacks on each other. The purpose of this custom was to try to maintain an atmosphere in which people who hold very different opinions can nevertheless function with some degree of decorum. Unfortunately, many of these customs and norms of behavior are breaking down. Individual ambition and the drive for power and celebrity have led to a decline in courtesy, cooperation, and respect for traditional norms. One result is that it has become increasingly difficult for Congress to reach agreement on policy issues. Another result is that life in Congress is increasingly tedious, conflict-filled, and unpleasant (see *A Conflicting View*: "Congress Can Act Responsibly").

The Demise of the Apprenticeship Norm

Years ago, "the first rule"[43] of congressional behavior was that new members were expected to be seen but not heard on the floor, to be studious in their committee work, and to be cooperative with party leaders. But the institutional norm of apprenticeship has been swept aside as increasingly ambitious and independent senators and representatives arrive on Capitol Hill. Today new members of Congress feel free to grab the spotlight on the floor, in committee, and in front of television cameras. "The evidence is clear, unequivocal, and overwhelming: the [apprenticeship] norm is simply gone."[44] Nevertheless, experienced members are more active and influential in shaping legislation than are new members.[45]

Specialization and Deference

The committee system encourages members of Congress to specialize in particular policy areas. Even the most independent and ambitious members can perceive the advantage of developing power and expertise in an area especially relevant to their constituents. Traditionally, members who developed a special expertise and accumulated years of service on a standing committee were deferred to in floor proceedings. These specialists were "cue givers" for party members when bills or amendments were being voted on. Members are still likely to defer to specialized committee members when the issues are technical or complicated, or when the issue is outside of their own area of policy specialization, but deference is increasingly rare on major public issues.

Bargaining

Bargaining is central to the legislative process. Little could be achieved if individual members were unwilling to bargain with each other for votes both in committees and on the floor. A willingness to bargain is a longstanding functional norm of Congress.

Members of Congress are not expected to violate their consciences in the bargaining process. On the contrary, members respect one another's issues of conscience and receive respect in return. On most issues, however, members can and do bargain their support. "Horse trading" is very common in committee work. Members may bargain in their own personal interest, in the interests of constituents or groups, or even in the interests of their committee with members of other committees. Because most bargaining occurs in a committee setting, it is seldom a matter of public record. The success and reputation of committee chairs largely depend on their ability to work out bargains and compromises.

Bargaining can assume different forms. Explicit trade-offs such as "If you vote for my bill, I'll vote for yours" are the simplest form of bargaining, but implicit understandings may be more common. Members may help other members in anticipation of receiving reciprocal help at some future unspecified time. Moreover, representatives who refuse to cooperate on a regular basis may find little support for their own bills. Mutual "back scratching" allows members to develop a reservoir of IOUs for the future. Building credit is good business for most members; one can never tell when one will need help in the future.

Bargaining requires a certain kind of integrity. Members of Congress must stick to their agreements. They must not consistently ask too high a price for their cooperation. They must recognize and return favors. They must not renege on promises. They must be trustworthy.

Conference-committee bargaining is essential if legislation acceptable to both houses is to be written. Indeed, it is expected that conferees from each house will bargain and compromise their differences. "Every House-Senate conference is expected to proceed via the methods of 'give and take,' 'trading back and forth,' 'pulling and hauling,' 'horse-trading and compromise,' 'splitting the difference,' etc."[46]

Reciprocity   The norm of *reciprocity*—favors rendered should be repaid in kind—supports the bargaining process. Members willing to accept "half a loaf" traditionally accomplished more than those who insisted on a "whole loaf." But the norm of reciprocity may have weakened in recent years.

Logrolling   Perhaps the most celebrated and reviled form of reciprocity, **logrolling** is mutual agreement to support projects that primarily benefit individual members of Congress and their constituencies. Logrolling is closely associated with pork-barrel legislation. Yet it can occur in virtually any kind of legislation. Even interest-group lobbyists may logroll with each other, promising to support each other's legislative agendas.

★ **logrolling**
Bargaining for agreement among legislators to support each other's favorite bills, especially projects that primarily benefit individual members and their constituents.

Leader-Follower Relations   Because leaders have few means of disciplining members, they must rely heavily on their bargaining skills to solicit cooperation and get the work of Congress accomplished. Party leaders can appeal to members' concerns for their party image among the voters. Individual majority members want to keep their party in the majority—if for no other reason than to retain their committee and subcommittee chairs. Individual minority members would like their party to win control of their house in order to assume the power and privileges of committee and subcommittee chairs. Party leaders must appeal to more than partisanship to win cooperation, however.

To secure cooperation, leaders can grant—or withhold—some tangible benefits. A member of the House needs the Speaker's support to get recognition, to have a bill called up, to get a bill scheduled, to see to it that a bill gets assigned to a preferred committee, to get a good committee assignment, and to help a bill get out of the Rules Committee, for example.

Party leaders may also seek to gain support from their followers by doing favors that ease their lives in Washington, advance their legislative careers, and help them with their reelection. Favors from party leaders oblige members to respond to leaders' requests at a later time. Members themselves like to build up a reservoir of good feeling and friendship with the leadership, knowing that eventually they will need some favors from the leadership.

Gridlock   Congress is often criticized for legislative **gridlock**—the failure to enact laws, including appropriations acts, that are widely perceived to have merit. Indeed, much of the popular frustration with Congress relates to gridlock arising from policy and budgetary stalemates. Research has suggested that the following factors contribute to congressional gridlock:[47]

★ **gridlock**
Political stalemate between the executive and legislative branches arising when one branch is controlled by one major political party and the other branch by the other party.

★ Divided party control of the presidency and Congress

★ Divided party control of the House and Senate

The sixteen women senators of the 110th Congress, 2007–2009: (back row) Senators Blanche Lincoln, Kay Bailey Hutchison, Barbara Boxer, Hillary Rodham Clinton, Mary Landrieu, Debbie Stabenow, Susan Collins, Barbara Mikulski, Elizabeth Dole, Amy Klobuchar, and Patty Murray; (front row) Senators Claire McCaskill, Dianne Feinstein, Maria Cantwell, Lisa Murkowski, and Olympia Snowe.

★ Greater ideological polarization (liberal versus conservative) of the parties

★ In the Senate, the willingness of members to filibuster against a bill, requiring 60 votes to overcome the opposition

In contrast, the factors that appear to lessen gridlock and encourage significant legislative accomplishment include

★ Unified party control of the presidency, House, and Senate

★ Larger numbers of moderates among Democrats and Republicans in Congress (as opposed to larger numbers of strong liberals and strong conservatives)

★ Overwhelming public support for new legislation

Note that the constitutional structure of American government—separation of powers and checks and balances, as well as bicameralism—plays a major role in gridlock, as does the American two-party system. Overcoming gridlock requires a willingness of members of both parties in both houses of Congress, as well as the White House, to bargain and compromise over legislation. And it requires strong public opinion in support of congressional action.

Congressional Ethics

Although critics might consider the phrase *congressional ethics* to be an oxymoron, the moral climate of Congress today is probably better than in earlier eras of American history. Nevertheless, Congress as an institution has suffered from well-publicized scandals that continue to prompt calls for reform.

Ethics Rules   Congress has an interest in maintaining the integrity of the institution itself and the trust of the people. Thus Congress has established its own rules of ethics. These rules include the following:

★ *Financial disclosure:* All members must file personal financial statements each year.

★ *Honoraria:* Members cannot accept fees for speeches or personal appearances.

★ *Campaign funds:* Surplus campaign funds cannot be put to personal use. (A loophole allowed members elected before 1980 to keep such funds if they left office before January 1, 1993. A record number of House members resigned in 1992; many of them kept substantial amounts of campaign money.)

★ *Gifts:* Members may not accept gifts worth more than $50 (with annual increases in these amounts for inflation).

★ *Free travel:* Members may not accept free travel from private corporations or individuals for more than four days of domestic travel and seven days of international travel per year. (Taxpayer-paid "junkets" to investigate problems at home or abroad or attend international meetings are not prohibited.)

★ *Lobbying:* Former members may not lobby Congress for at least one year after retirement.

But these limited rules have not gone very far in restoring popular trust in Congress.

Gray Areas: Services and Contributions Congress members are expected to perform services for their political contributors. However, a direct *quid pro quo*—receiving a financial contribution specifically for the performance of official duty—is illegal. Few Congress members would be so foolish as to openly state a price to a potential contributor for a specific service, and most contributors know not to state a dollar amount that would be forthcoming if the member performed a particular service for them. But what if the contribution and the service occur close together? A Senate Ethics Committee once found that a close relationship between a service and a contribution to be an "impermissible pattern of conduct [that] violated established norms of behavior in the Senate . . . [and] was improper and repugnant."[48] But the Ethics Committee offered little in the way of a future guidance in handling services for campaign contributors.

Expulsion The Constitution gives Congress the power to discipline its own members. "Each House may . . . punish its Members for disorderly Behaviour, and, with the Concurrence of two thirds, expel a Member." But the Constitution fails to define *disorderly behavior*.

It seems reasonable to believe that criminal conduct falls within the constitutional definition of disorderly behavior. Bribery is a criminal act: it is illegal to solicit or receive anything of value in return for the performance of a government duty. During its notorious Abscam investigation in 1980, the Federal Bureau of Investigation set up a sting operation in which agents posing as wealthy Arabs offered bribe money to members of Congress while secretly videotaping the transactions. Six representatives and one senator were convicted. But criminal conviction does not automatically result in expulsion from Congress. In the Abscam case, only one defendant, Representative Michael "Ozzie" Myers (D-Pa.), was expelled, becoming the first member to be expelled since the Civil War. (Two other House members and the senator resigned rather than face expulsion, and the other three representatives were defeated for reelection.) Perhaps the most interesting result of the Abscam investigation: Only one member of Congress approached by the FBI, Democratic Senator Larry Presler of South Dakota, turned down the bribe. The powerful chair of the House Ways and Means Committee, Democrat Dan Rostenkowski (Ill.), was indicted by a federal grand jury in 1994 for misuse of congressional office funds; he refused to resign from Congress, but his Chicago constituents voted him out of office. Democratic Representative Mel Reynolds (Ill.) resigned in 1995, following his criminal conviction on charges of sexual misconduct. (A special

Idaho Senator Larry Craig, with his wife Suzanne beside him, announces his resignation from the Senate during a morning news conference on September 1, 2007, in Boise, Idaho. Behind Craig to the left is Idaho Gov. C. L. "Buth" Otter and his wife, Lori. Craig resigned after his arrest on June 11, 2007, for lewd conduct at the Minneapolis-St. Paul Airport. Craig pleaded guilty to the lesser charge of disorderly conduct.

★ **censure**
Public reprimand for wrongdoing, given to a member standing in the chamber before Congress.

election to fill his vacated seat was won by Jesse Jackson, Jr., son of the popular preacher, commentator, and former Democratic presidential contender.) Republican Senator Robert Packwood (Oreg.) resigned in 1995 in order to avoid official expulsion following a Senate Ethics Committee report charging him with numerous counts of sexual harassment of female staff. Representative James A. Traficant (D-Ohio) was expelled in 2002 following his conviction on ten federal corruption charges. And Representative Randy Cunningham (D-Calif.) resigned in 2005 after pleading guilty to charges of accepting $2.4 million in bribes from lobbyists.

Censure   A lesser punishment in the Congress than expulsion is official **censure.** Censured members are obliged to "stand in the well" and listen to the charges read against them. It is supposed to be a humiliating experience and fatal to one's political career. In 1983 two members of Congress, Barney Frank (D-Mass.) and Gerry Studds (D-Mass.), were censured for sexual misconduct with teenage congressional pages. Both were obliged to "stand in the well." In 2002 New Jersey Democratic Senator Robert Torricelli was "severely admonished" by the Senate Ethics Committee for "at least the appearance of impropriety" for improperly accepting gifts and campaign contributions. Torricelli abruptly dropped out of his reelection race.

Lesser forms of censure include a public reprimand or admonition by the Ethics Committee expressing disapproval of the Congress member's behavior. And the Ethics Committee may also order a member to repay funds improperly received.

Scandal and the Loss of Office   One reason for the "thumping" that the Republicans received in 2006 was scandal. Six incumbent Republican representatives were variously linked to scandals, and they all went down to defeat. Six-term congress member J. D. Hayworth lost in his solidly Republican district in Arizona because he received money from the indicted lobbyist Jack Abramoff. Mark Foley, a moderate Republican, had to resign from his Florida seat just before the November election after sexually explicit messages to teenage congressional pages came to light (and Foley had been expected to win reelection by a wide margin). Ten-term veteran Pennsylvania Republican Curt Weldon also went down to defeat under the cloud that his daughter was being investigated by the FBI for Russian business deals. Also in Pennsylvania, four-term Republican Don Sherwood went down to defeat thanks to an assault charge by a woman with whom he had had a five-year affair.

A *Constitutional* Note

Congress as the First Branch

The Founders believed that the Congress would be the first and most powerful branch of government. Thus, Article I establishes the Congress, describes its structure, and sets forth its powers. Note that its powers *are* the enumerated powers of the national government. Following the English precedent of two houses of the legislature, a House of Commons and a House of Lords, the Founders created two separate houses, a House of Representatives and a Senate. They did so in part as a result of the Connecticut Compromise, which balanced large population states in the House with the small population states' demands for equality in the Senate. But the Founders also wanted a Senate elected by state legislatures, not the people, "as a defense to the people against their own temporary errors and delusions." The Founders believed that the Senate would balance the interests and numerical superiority of common citizens with the property interests of the less numerous landowners, bankers, and merchants, who they expected to be sent to the Senate by the state legislatures. This defense against "temporary errors and delusions" of the people was strengthened by different lengths of tenure for the House and Senate. All House members were elected every 2 years, but Senate members were elected for 6-year terms, one-third of the Senate elected every 2 years. The longer terms of the Senate were designed to protect senators from temporary popular movements. Not until the 17th Amendment was ratified in 1913, over a century later, were senators directly elected by the people. In short, the original Constitution of 1787 was careful to limit the role of the people in lawmaking.

Summary
Who Gets What: Congress

The Constitution places all of the delegated powers of the national government in the Congress. The Founders expected Congress to be the principal institution for resolving national conflicts, balancing interests, and deciding who gets what. Today, Congress is a central battleground in the struggle over national policy. Congress generally does not initiate but responds to policy initiatives and budget requests originating from the president, the bureaucracy, and interest groups. Over time, the president and the executive branch, together with the Supreme Court and federal judiciary, have come to dominate national policy making.

★ The Congress represents local and state interests in policy making. The Senate's constituencies are the 50 states, and the House's constituencies are 435 separate districts. Both houses of Congress, but especially the House of Representatives, wield power in domestic and foreign affairs primarily through the "power of the purse."

★ Congressional powers include oversight and investigation. These powers are exercised primarily through committees. Although Congress claims these powers are a necessary part of lawmaking, their real purpose is usually to influence agency decision making, to build political support for increases or decreases in agency funding, to lay the political foundation for new programs and policies, and to capture media attention and enhance the power of members of Congress.

★ Congress is gradually becoming more "representative" of the general population in terms of race and gender. Redistricting, under federal court interpretations of the Voting Rights Act, has increased African American and Hispanic representation in Congress. And women have significantly increased their presence in Congress in recent years. Nevertheless, women and minorities do not occupy seats in Congress proportional to their share of the general population.

★ Members of Congress are independent political entrepreneurs. They initiate their own candidacies, raise their own campaign funds, and get themselves elected with very little help from their party. Members of Congress are largely career politicians who skillfully use the advantages of incumbency to stay in office. Incumbents outspend challengers by large margins. Interest-group political action committees and individual contributors strongly favor incumbents. Congressional elections are seldom focused on great national issues but rather on local issues and personalities and the ability of candidates to "bring home the bacon" from Washington and serve their constituents.

★ Congress as an institution is not very popular with the American people. Scandals, pay raises, perks, and privileges reported in the media have hurt the image of the institution. Nevertheless, individual members of Congress remain popular with their districts' voters.

★ Members of Congress spend as much time on "home style" activities—promoting their images back home and attending to constituents' problems—as they do legislating. Casework wins votes one at a time, gradually accumulating political support back home, and members often support each other's "pork-barrel" projects.

★ Despite the independence of members, the Democratic and Republican party structures in the House and Senate remain the principal bases for organizing Congress. Party leaders in the House and Senate generally control the flow of business in each house, assigning bills to committees, scheduling or delaying votes, and appointing members to committees. But leaders must bargain for votes; they have few formal disciplinary powers. They cannot deny renomination to recalcitrant members.

★ The real legislative work of Congress is done in committees. Standing committees screen and draft legislation; with rare exceptions, bills do not reach the floor without approval by a majority of a standing committee. The committee and subcommittee system decentralizes power in Congress. The system satisfies the desires of members to gain power, prestige, and electoral advantage, but it weakens responsible government in the

Congress as a whole. All congressional committees are chaired by members of the majority party. Seniority is still the major determinant of power in Congress.

★ In order to become law, a bill must win committee approval and withstand debate in both houses of Congress. The rules attached to a bill's passage in the House can significantly help or hurt its chances. Bills passed with differences in the two houses must be reworked in a conference committee composed of members of both houses and then passed in identical form in both.

★ In deciding how to vote on legislation, Congress members are influenced by party loyalty, presidential support or opposition, constituency concerns, interest-group pressures, and their own personal values and ideology. Party majorities oppose each other on roughly half of all roll-call votes in Congress. Presidents receive the greatest support in Congress from members of their own party.

★ The customs and norms of Congress help reduce interpersonal conflict, facilitate bargaining and compromise, and make life more pleasant on Capitol Hill. They include the recognition of special competencies of members, a willingness to bargain and compromise, mutual "back scratching" and logrolling, reciprocity, and deference toward the leadership. But traditional customs and norms have weakened over time as more members have pursued independent political agendas. And partisanship and incivility in Congress have risen in recent years.

★ Congress establishes its own rules of ethics. The Constitution empowers each house to expel its own members for "disorderly conduct" by a two-thirds vote, but expulsion has seldom occurred. Some members have resigned to avoid expulsion; others have been officially censured yet remained in Congress.

Key Terms

Suggested Readings

Davidson, Robert H., Walter J. Oleszek, and Frances E. Lee. *Congress and Its Members*. 11th ed. Washington, D.C.: CQ Press, 2007. Authoritative text on Congress covering the recruitment of members, elections, Home styles and Hill styles, leadership, decision making, and relations with interest groups, presidency, and courts. Emphasizes tension between lawmaking responsibilities and desire to be reelected.

Fenno, Richard F. *Home Style*. Boston: Little, Brown, 1978. The classic description of how attention to constituency by members of Congress enhances their reelection prospects. Home style activities, including casework, pork barreling, travel and appearances back home, newsletters, and surveys, are described in detail.

Herrnson, Paul S. *Congressional Elections: Campaigning at Home and in Washington*. 5th ed. Washington, D.C.: CQ Press, 2007. Interviews with candidates, campaign aides, and political consultants to paint a comprehensive portrait of congressional campaigns.

Jacobson, Gary C. *The Politics of Congressional Elections*. 7th ed. New York: Longman, 2009. Coverage of congressional campaigns and elections with reference to questions of responsibility and representation.

Jones, Charles O. *Separate but Equal Branches: Congress and the Presidency*. 2nd ed. Washington, D.C.: CQ Press, 1999. Presidential–congressional relations under Johnson, Nixon, Ford, Carter, Reagan, Bush, Sr. and Clinton.

Oleszek, Walter J. *Congressional Procedures and Policy Processes*. 7th ed. Washington, D.C.: CQ Press, 2007. The definitive work on congressional rules, procedures and traditions and their effect on the course and content of legislation.

Ornstein, Norman J., Thomas E. Mann, and Michael J. Malbin. *Vital Statistics on Congress*. Washington, D.C.: CQ Press, 2008. Published biennially. Excellent source of data on members of Congress, congressional elections, campaign finance, committees and staff, workload, and voting alignments.

Sinclair, Barbara. *Unorthodox Lawmaking*. 3rd ed. Washington, D.C.: CQ Press, 2007. A description of the various detours and shortcuts a major bill is likely to take in Congress, including case studies.

Stathis, Stephen W. *Landmark Legislation 1774–2002*. Washington, D.C.: CQ Press, 2003. A summary of major congressional legislation over 225 years, in a single volume.

Suggested Web Sites

Congressional Budget Office   www.cbo.gov
The Web site of the CBO is an excellent source of data on federal finances, economic projections, and the budgetary process.

Congressional Quarterly (CQ)   www.cq.com
The *Congressional Quarterly Weekly Report* provides the most comprehensive coverage of events in Congress, including key issues, House and Senate roll call votes, backgrounds of members, and political and election information. The CQ Press is a major publisher of books on politics and government.

Government Accountability Office   www.gao.gov
The GAO Web site provides the latest reports evaluating government programs and spending.

Library of Congress   http://thomas.loc.gov
The Thomas system allows the tracing of bills from their introduction, through the committee system, floor schedule vote, and so on.

Roll Call   www.rollcall.com
This online magazine covers a variety of current topics about Congress but is especially strong on stories dealing with running for Congress and/or campaign financing.

U.S. House of Representatives   www.house.gov
Official Web site of the House, with schedule of floor and committee actions, legislative information, and links to every Representative's Web site and every committee Web site.

U.S. Senate   www.senate.gov
Official Senate Web site, with floor and committee schedules, Senate news, and links to each senator's Web site.

11 THE PRESIDENT
White House Politics

66 Research on power elites. . . . Who are they? What are their perspectives? In what arenas do they function? What base values are at their use? How successful are they in influencing outcomes and effects? **99**

Harold Lasswell

Chapter *Outline*

Presidential Power

Americans look to their president for "Greatness." The presidency embodies the popular "great man" view of history and public affairs—attributing progress in the world to the actions of particular individuals. Great presidents are those associated with great events: George Washington with the founding of the nation, Abraham Lincoln with the preservation of the Union, Franklin D. Roosevelt with the nation's emergence from economic depression and victory in World War II (see *What Do You Think?*: "How Would You Rate the Presidents?"). People tend to believe that the president is responsible for "peace and prosperity" as well as for "change." They expect their president to present a "vision" of America's future and to symbolize the nation.

The Symbolic President   The president personifies American government for most people. People expect the president to act decisively and effectively to deal with national problems. They expect the president to be "compassionate"—to show concern for problems confronting individual citizens.[1] The president, while playing these roles, is the focus of public attention and the nation's leading celebrity. Presidents receive more media coverage than any other person in the nation, for everything from their policy statements to their favorite foods to their dogs and cats.

Managing Crises   In times of crisis, the American people look to their president to take action, to provide reassurance, and to protect the nation and its people. It is the president, not the Congress or the courts, who is expected to speak on behalf of the American people in times of national triumph and tragedy.[2] The president gives expression to the nation's pride in victory. The nation's heroes are welcomed, its scientists, writers, and poets are recognized, and its championship sports teams are feted in the White House Rose Garden.

The president also gives expression to the nation's sadness in tragedy and strives to help the nation go forward. How presidents respond to crises often defines their place in history. Franklin D. Roosevelt raised public morale during the Great Depression of the 1930s by reassuring Americans that "the only thing we have to fear is fear itself." Later he led the nation into war following the Japanese attack on Pearl Harbor, December 7, 1941, "a day which will live in infamy." When the *Challenger*

What Do You *Think*?

How Would You Rate the Presidents?

From time to time, historians have been polled to rate U.S. presidents (see table). The survey ratings given the presidents have been remarkably consistent. Abraham Lincoln, George Washington, and Franklin Roosevelt are universally recognized as the greatest American presidents. It is more difficult for historians to rate recent presidents; the views of historians are influenced by their own (generally liberal and reformist) political views. Richard Nixon once commented, "History will treat me fairly. Historians probably won't."

Historians may tend to rank activist presidents who led the nation through war or economic crisis higher than passive presidents who guided the nation in peace and prosperity. Initially Dwight Eisenhower, who presided in the relatively calm 1950s, was ranked low by historians. But later, after comparing his performance with those who came after him, his steadiness and avoidance of war raised his ranking dramatically.

Federalist Society (2000)	Arthur M. Schlesinger, Jr. (1962)	Robert Murray (1982)	Arthur M. Schlesinger, Jr. (1996)	W. J. Ridings, S. B. McIver (1997)
Great	**Great**	**Presidential Rank**	**Great**	**Overall Ranking**
1. Washington	1. Lincoln	1. Lincoln	1. Lincoln	1. Lincoln
2. Lincoln	2. Washington	2. F. Roosevelt	2. Washington	2. F. Roosevelt
3. F. Roosevelt	3. F. Roosevelt	3. Washington	3. F. Roosevelt	3. Washington
	4. Wilson	4. Jefferson		4. Jefferson
Near Great	5. Jefferson	5. T. Roosevelt	**Near Great**	5. T. Roosevelt
4. Jefferson		6. Wilson	4. Jefferson	6. Wilson
5. T. Roosevelt	**Near Great**	7. Jackson	5. Jackson	7. Truman
6. Jackson	6. Jackson	8. Truman	6. T. Roosevelt	8. Jackson
7. Truman	7. T. Roosevelt	9. J. Adams	7. Wilson	9. Eisenhower
8. Reagan	8. Polk	10. L. Johnson	8. Truman	10. Madison
9. Eisenhower	9. Truman (tie)	11. Eisenhower	9. Polk	11. Polk
10. Polk	10. J. Adams	12. Polk		12. L. Johnson
11. Wilson	11. Cleveland	13. Kennedy	**High Average**	13. Monroe
		14. Madison	10. Eisenhower	14. J. Adams
Above Average	**Average**	15. Monroe	11. J. Adams	15. Kennedy
12. Cleveland	12. Madison	16. J. Q. Adams	12. Kennedy	16. Cleveland
13. Adams	13. J. Q. Adams	17. Cleveland	13. Cleveland	17. McKinley
14. McKinley	14. Hayes	18. McKinley	14. L. Johnson	18. J. Q. Adams
15. Madison	15. McKinley	19. Taft	15. Monroe	19. Carter
16. Monroe	16. Taft	20. Van Buren	16. McKinley	20. Taft
17. L. Johnson	17. Van Buren	21. Hoover		21. Van Buren
18. Kennedy	18. Monroe	22. Hayes	**Average**	22. G.H.W. Bush
	19. Hoover	23. Arthur	17. Madison	23. Clinton
Average	20. B. Harrison	24. Ford	18. J. Q. Adams	24. Hoover
19. Taft	21. Arthur	25. Carter	19. B. Harrison	25. Hayes
20. J. Q. Adams	21. Eisenhower (tie)	26. B. Harrison	20. Clinton	26. Reagan
21. G.H.W. Bush	23. A. Johnson	27. Taylor	21. Van Buren	27. Ford
22. Hayes		28. Tyler	22. Taft	28. Arthur
23. Van Buren	**Below Average**	29. Fillmore	23. Hayes	29. Taylor
24. Clinton	24. Taylor	30. Coolidge	24. G.H.W. Bush	30. Garfield
25. Coolidge	25. Tyler	31. Pierce	25. Reagan	31. B. Harrison
26. Arthur	26. Fillmore	32. A. Johnson	26. Arthur	32. Nixon
	27. Coolidge	33. Buchanan	27. Carter	33. Coolidge
Below Average	28. Pierce	34. Nixon	28. Ford	34. Tyler
27. B. Harrison	29. Buchanan	35. Grant		35. W. Harrison
28. Ford		36. Harding	**Below Average**	36. Fillmore
29. Hoover	**Failure**		29. Taylor	37. Pierce
30. Carter	30. Grant		30. Coolidge	38. Grant
31. Taylor	31. Harding		31. Fillmore	39. A. Johnson
32. Grant			32. Tyler	40. Buchanan
33. Nixon				41. Harding
34. Tyler			**Failure**	
35. Fillmore			33. Pierce	
			34. Grant	
Failure			35. Hoover	
36. A. Johnson			36. Nixon	
37. Pierce			37. A. Johnson	
38. Harding			38. Buchanan	
39. Buchanan			39. Harding	

Note: These ratings result from surveys of scholars ranging in number from 55 to 950.

Sources: Arthur Murphy, "Evaluating the Presidents of the United States," *Presidential Studies Quarterly* 14 (1984): 117–26; Arthur M. Schlesinger, Jr., "Rating the Presidents: Washington to Clinton," *Political Science Quarterly* 112 (1997): 179–90; William J. Ridings and Stuart B. McIver, *Rating the Presidents.* Secaucus, N.J.: Citadel Press, 1997; "Federalist Society—*The Wall Street Journal* Survey on Presidents (2000)," www.opinionjournal.com/hail/rankings.html

spaceship disintegrated before the eyes of millions of television viewers in 1986, Ronald Reagan gave voice to the nation's feelings about the disaster: "I want to say something to the schoolchildren of America who were watching the live coverage of the shuttle's takeoff. I know it is hard to understand, but sometimes painful things like this happen. The future doesn't belong to the faint-hearted. It belongs to the brave." And the terrorist attack on America, September 11, 2001, inspired President George W. Bush to issue a call to the nation:

> Tonight we are a country awakened to danger and called to defend freedom. Our grief has turned to anger, and anger to resolution. Whether we bring our enemies to justice, or bring justice to our enemies, justice will be done.[3]

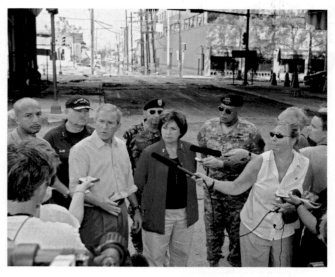

Showing Concern in a Crisis

Crisis management is a key presidential responsibility. People look to the president for reassurance in times of national tragedy. President Bush is shown here during one of his many visits to the New Orleans area following Hurricane Katrina in 2005.

Providing Policy Leadership The president is expected to set policy priorities for the nation. Most policy initiatives originate in the White House and various departments and agencies of the executive branch and then are forwarded to Congress with the president's approval. Presidential programs are submitted to Congress in the form of messages, including the president's annual State of the Union Address, and in the Budget of the United States Government, which the president presents each year to Congress.

As a political leader, the president is expected to mobilize political support for policy proposals. It is not enough for the president to send policy proposals to Congress. The president must rally public opinion, lobby members of Congress, and win legislative battles. To avoid being perceived as weak or ineffective, presidents must get as much of their legislative programs through Congress as possible. The president is responsible for "getting things done" in the policy arena.

Managing the Economy The American people hold the president responsible for maintaining a healthy economy. Presidents are blamed for economic downturns, whether or not governmental policies had anything to do with market conditions. The president is expected to "Do Something!" in the face of high see also 579 unemployment, declining personal income, high mortgage rates, rising inflation, high gasoline prices, or a stock market crash. Herbert Hoover in 1932, Gerald Ford in 1976, Jimmy Carter in 1980, and George Bush in 1992—all incumbent presidents defeated for reelection during recessions—learned the hard way that the general public holds the president responsible for hard economic times. Presidents must have an economic "game plan" to stimulate the economy—tax incentives to spur investments, spending proposals to create jobs, plans to lower interest rates.

Managing the Government As the chief executive of a mammoth federal bureaucracy with 2.8 million civilian employees, the president is responsible for implementing policy, that is, for achieving policy goals. Policy making does not end when a law is passed. Policy implementation involves issuing orders, creating organizations, recruiting and assigning personnel, disbursing funds, overseeing work, and evaluating results. It is true that the president cannot perform all of these tasks personally. But the ultimate responsibility for implementation—in the words of the Constitution, "to take Care that the Laws be faithfully executed"—rests with the president.

The Global President Nations strive to speak with a single voice in international affairs; for the United States, the global voice is that of the president. As Commander-in-Chief of the armed forces of the United States, the president is a

People in Politics   George W. Bush: A Turbulent Presidency

George W. Bush suffered an especially turbulent presidency. From the disputed election of 2000, to the terrorist attack on America of September 11, 2001, to the war against Al Qaeda and the Taliban in Afghanistan, to the prolonged, unpopular war in Iraq, Bush experienced the highs and lows of his office. In domestic affairs Bush achieved success in bringing about tax reductions and educational reform, but he failed in trying to reform Social Security and immigration. His approval ratings skyrocketed after "9/11" but plunged to record lows as casualties mounted in the Iraq War.

Prepping for President

George W. Bush was born into his family's tradition of wealth, privilege, and public service. Bush's grandfather, investment banker Prescott Bush, was a U.S. senator from Connecticut and chairman of the Yale Corporation. Bush's father, the forty-first president, had established himself in the oil business before going into politics—first as a Houston congressman, then as Republican National Chairman, director of the CIA, Ambassador to China, and vice president under President Ronald Reagan. George "Dubya" followed in his father's footsteps to Yale University, but he was not the scholar-athlete that his father had been. Rather, he was a friendly, likable, heavy-drinking fraternity president. Upon graduation in 1968, he joined the Texas Air National Guard, completed flight school, but never faced combat in Vietnam. He earned an MBA degree from Harvard Business School and returned to Texas to enter the oil business himself. Later, he would purchase a major interest in the Texas Rangers baseball team.

Bush had never held public office before running for governor of Texas in 1994. But he had gained valuable political experience serving as an unofficial advisor to his father during his presidential campaigns. And he learned how to tap into Republican big-money campaign contributors. He heavily outspent the incumbent governor, Democrat Ann Richards, winning the governorship with 54 percent of the vote. Dubya's governing style fit comfortably with the Texas "good old boys" in both parties. Although the Texas legislature was controlled by Democrats, Bush won most of his legislative battles. His style was to meet frequently and privately with his Democratic opponents and to remain on friendly terms with them. He easily won reelection as governor in 1998.

First-Term Successes

Bush came to the Oval Office with the legitimacy of his election under challenge. He sought to reassure Americans by appointing experienced people to his White House staff and his cabinet. He chose Richard Cheney as his vice president to add experience to his administration; Cheney had served Bush's father as Secretary of Defense during the Gulf War. Bush also brought the former Chairman of the Joint Chiefs of Staff, Colin Powell, into his administration as Secretary of State. Donald Rumsfeld, Gerald Ford's Secretary of Defense, was reappointed to his old job. National Security Advisor Condoleezza Rice brought a reputation for brillance and independence to her position. It was clear that Dubya was not afraid of being overshadowed by "heavyweights" in his administration.

"9/11"

The terrorist attack on America, September 11, 2001, became the defining moment in the presidency of George W. Bush. He grew in presidential stature; his public appearances and statements reassured the American people. He promptly declared a "War on Terrorism" against both the terrorist organizations and the nations that harbor and support them. Military action in Afghanistan followed quickly. Bush showed no hesitation, no indecision, no willingness to negotiate with terrorists. His approval ratings skyrocketed: 90 percent of Americans approved of the way he was handling his job. The rapid collapse of the Taliban regime in Afghanistan seemed to confirm the wisdom of Bush's actions.

Bush Policy Initiatives

During his first term, Bush enjoyed the support of a Republican-controlled Congress. He was able to set forth an ambitious policy agenda.

Tax reductions. The centerpiece of Bush's domestic policy were tax cuts in 2001 and 2003 that reduced the top marginal rate from 39.6 percent to 35 percent and gave preferential treatment to capital gains and corporate dividends. Despite budget deficits and increased spending for defense and homeland security, Bush steadfastly refused to make the same mistake his father had made in raising taxes. Bush argued that his tax cuts strengthened the economy.

Education reform. The No Child Left Behind Act redefined the federal government's role in education by setting standards of performance, requiring measures of achievement based on testing, and by threatening sanctions, including the transfer of pupils out of failing schools.

Health care. The addition of prescription drug coverage to Medicare for seniors in 2003 was the largest expansion of federal entitlements since the creation of Medicare in 1965.

Social Security. Bush tried unsuccessfully to focus Congress and the nation on Social Security reform. He traveled the country urging a partial diversion of payroll taxes into private accounts that would invest in stocks and bonds, in the expectation of significantly higher returns for retirement. His efforts failed and concern over Social Security was soon overshadowed by the Iraq War.

Homeland security.   The Patriot Act was rushed through Congress just six weeks after the "9/11" terrorist attack. It gave the federal government broad new powers for wiretapping, surveillance, investigation, and the arrest of terrorist suspects. It gave the federal government the power to examine terrorist suspects' records in libraries, bookstores, and universities and on the Internet. In 2002 Bush asked Congress to create a new Department of Homeland Security and undertake a major reorganization of the federal bureaucracy.

National security policy.   Bush believed that the "War on Terrorism" required dramatic changes in national security policy. Bush's national security strategy refocuses U.S. efforts from deterrence and containment of aggression to the preemption of potential threats. As his National Security Advisor put it, "We can't wait for the smoking gun to become a mushroom cloud." In addition, the Bush doctrine emphasized unilateral action in national security policy, "going it alone," rather than the traditional American emphasis on international alliances and UN support.

A Divider—Not a Uniter

George W. Bush came to the Oval Office promising to be "a uniter, not a divider." But his presidency produced just the opposite—an unprecedented level of polarization in Washington and in the American public. In 2004 the difference between his approval among Republicans (89 percent) and Democrats (12 percent) was an unprecedented 77 percentage points. A partisan gap of 70 points or higher continued throughout his tenure. And polls indicated that in Bush's 2004 reelection, 95 percent of Republicans voted for him but only 7 percent of Democrats did so. This was the highest level of partyline voting in recent history. Bush won reelection with a slim 51 percent of the popular vote.

The War in Iraq

But the Bush legacy is defined by the Iraq War. "Operation Iraqi Freedom" enjoyed widespread public support at its beginning in March 2003. Saddam Hussein's regime in Baghdad had violated at least a dozen UN resolutions regarding inspections for weapons of mass destruction. Bush stated that the purpose of military action in Iraq was elimination of weapons of mass destruction and a "regime change" to ensure that Saddam would not aid and assist terrorists around the world. Congress voted overwhelmingly to support military action.

The U.S. military captured Baghdad in just 21 days. British forces captured the port city of Basra. Bush landed on an aircraft carrier to declare "Mission accomplished!" But the real war was just beginning.

Over time, as U.S. fatalities mounted into the thousands, Americans became disenchanted with the president's handling of affairs (see Figure 11.2 on p. 391). Critics at home, including many in Congress, complained bitterly that Bush had misled them regarding the existence of weapons of mass destruction in Iraq. Intensive searches of the country produced no evidence that Saddam had such weapons at the time of the invasion. Years after capturing Baghdad, Iraq remained in chaos. Civil war engulfed the country: both Sunnis and Shiites fought Americans even as they began to fight among themselves. Violence continued unabated. No real "exit strategy" emerged from the White House or the Pentagon. Yet Bush argued forcefully that an abrupt withdrawal ("cut and run") would encourage radical Islamic terrorists around the world: "Iraq would become a safe haven from which terrorists could plan attacks against American interests abroad and our allies. Middle East reformers would never again fully trust American assurances of support for democracy and human rights in the region."

The election of a Democratic-controlled Congress in 2006 appeared as a popular rejection of Bush's war policies. Yet the president successfully fought off efforts by the Democrats to cut off funds for the war, or to set a fixed date for the withdrawal of American troops from Iraq. And Bush ignored the recommendations of the prestigious Iraq Study Group to negotiate with Syria and Iran and to begin a phased withdrawal from Iraq (see "The War in Iraq" in Chapter 18). Instead he ordered a "surge" in U.S. troop levels and appointed a new commander of U.S. forces in Iraq, General David Petraeus. Critics charged that Bush was stubbornly oblivious to the "facts on the ground"; supporters praised his steadfast commitment to victory.

Fiscal Crisis

But a troubled economy eventually replaced the war in Iraq as a chief concern of Americans. The nation worried as banks faltered, investment firms teetered on bankruptcy, the stock market plunged, and unemployment rose. Bush responded with a proposal for a $700 billion bailout of the failed Wall Street banks and investment firms—an attempt to stabilize the financial sector of the economy and by so doing avoid a deep recession. Congress bickered over the details of the Bush administration plan but eventually approved the major parts of it. But the bailout itself was not popular with the general public and Bush was widely blamed for the crisis.

Last Days in Office

Bush never regained his early popularity. In his final year in office his approval rating plunged below 30 percent. The 2008 presidential election campaign overshadowed the lame-duck president. Democratic candidate Barack Obama sought to tie Republican candidate John McCain to the "failed policies of George Bush," while McCain sought to "distance" himself from Bush. Obama's victory and the Democratic sweep in Congress was in large measure a rejection of George Bush and his administration.

powerful voice in foreign affairs. Efforts by Congress to speak on behalf of the nation in foreign affairs and to limit the war-making power of the president have been generally unsuccessful. It is the president who orders American troops into combat (see *People in Politics*: "George W. Bush: A Turbulent Presidency").

Constitutional Powers of the President

Presidential Leadership: Which Hat Do You Wear?

Popular expectations of presidential leadership far exceed the formal constitutional powers granted to the president. Compared with the Congress, the president has only modest constitutional powers (see Table 11.1). Nevertheless, presidents have pointed to a variety of clauses in Article II to support their rights to do everything from doubling the land area of the nation (Thomas Jefferson) to routing out terrorists from Afghanistan and invading Iraq (George W. Bush).

Who May Be President?   To become president, the Constitution specifies that a person must be a natural-born citizen at least 35 years of age and a resident of the United States for 14 years.

Initially, the Constitution put no limit on how many terms a president could serve. George Washington set a precedent for a two-term maximum that endured

---

Table **11.1**   Modest Formal Powers: The Constitutional Powers of the President

The formal constitutional powers of the president are very modest, especially compared to popular expectations of presidential leadership.

Chief Executive
Implement policy: "take Care that the Laws be faithfully executed" (Article II, Section 3)
Supervise executive branch of government
Appoint and remove executive officials (Article II, Section 2)
Prepare executive budget for submission to Congress (by law of Congress)

Chief Legislator
Initiate policy: "give to the Congress Information of the State of the Union, and recommend to their Consideration such Measures as he shall judge necessary and expedient" (Article II, Section 3)
Veto legislation passed by Congress, subject to override by a two-thirds vote in both houses
Convene special session of Congress "on extraordinary Occasions" (Article II, Section 3)

Chief Diplomat
Make treaties "with the Advice and Consent of the Senate" (Article II, Section 2)
Exercise the power of diplomatic recognition: "receive Ambassadors" (Article II, Section 3)
Make executive agreements (by custom and international law)

Commander-in-Chief
Command U.S. armed forces: "The president shall be Commander-in-Chief of the Army and Navy" (Article II, Section 2)
Appoint military officers

Chief of State
"The executive Power shall be vested in a President" (Article II, Section 1)
Grant reprieves and pardons (Article II, Section 2)
Represent the nation as chief of state
Appoint federal court and Supreme Court judges (Article II, Section 2)

until Franklin Roosevelt's decision to run for a third term in 1940 (and a fourth term in 1944). In reaction to Roosevelt's lengthy tenure, Congress proposed the 22nd Amendment, ratified in 1951, which officially restricts the president to two terms (or one full term if a vice president must complete more than 2 years of the previous president's term).

Presidential Succession

Until the adoption of the 25th Amendment in 1967, the Constitution had said little about presidential succession, other than designating the vice president as successor to the president "in Case of the Removal,. . . Death, Resignation, or Inability" and giving Congress the power to decide "what Officer shall then act as President" if both the president and vice president are removed. The Constitution was silent on how to cope with serious presidential illnesses. It contained no provision for replacing a vice president. The incapacitation issue was more than theoretical: James A. Garfield lingered months after being shot in 1881; Woodrow Wilson was an invalid during his last years in office (1919–20); Dwight Eisenhower suffered major heart attacks in office; and Ronald Reagan was in serious condition following an assassination attempt in 1981.

The 25th Amendment stipulates that when the vice president and a majority of the cabinet notify the Speaker of the House and the president pro tempore of the Senate in writing that the president "is unable to discharge the powers and duties of his office," then the vice president becomes *acting* president. To resume the powers of office, the president must then notify Congress in writing that "no inability exists." If the vice president and a majority of cabinet officers do not agree that the president is capable of resuming office, then the Congress "shall decide the issue" within 21 days. A two-thirds vote of both houses is required to replace the president with the vice president.

The disability provisions of the amendment have never been used, but the succession provisions have been. The 25th Amendment provides for the selection of a new vice president by presidential nomination and confirmation by a majority vote of both houses of Congress. When Vice President Spiro Agnew resigned in the face of bribery charges in 1973, President Richard Nixon nominated the Republican leader of the House, Gerald Ford, as vice president; and when Nixon resigned in 1974, Ford assumed the presidency and made Nelson Rockefeller, governor of New York, his vice president. Thus Gerald Ford's 2-year tenure in the White House marked the only time in history when the man serving as president had not been elected to either the presidency or the vice presidency. (If the offices of president and vice president are both vacated, then Congress by law has specified the next in line for the presidency as the Speaker of the House of Representatives, followed by the president pro tempore of the Senate, then the cabinet officers, beginning with the secretary of state.)

Impeachment

The Constitution grants Congress the power of **impeachment** over the president, vice president, and "all civil Officers of the United States" (Article II, Section 4). Technically, impeachment is a charge similar to a criminal indictment brought against an official. The power to bring charges of impeachment is given to the House of Representatives. The power to try all impeachments is given to the Senate, and "no Person shall be convicted without the Concurrence of two thirds of the Members present" (Article I, Section 3). Impeachment by the House and conviction by the Senate only remove an official from office; a subsequent criminal trial is required to inflict any other punishment.

The Constitution specifies that impeachment and conviction can only be for "Treason, Bribery, or other High Crimes and Misdemeanors." These words indicate that Congress is not to impeach presidents, federal judges, or any other offi-

★ **impeachment**
Equivalent of a criminal charge against an elected official; removal of the impeached official from office depends on the outcome of a trial.

cials simply because Congress disagrees with their decisions or policies. Indeed, the phrase implies that only serious criminal offenses, not political conflicts, can result in impeachment. Nevertheless, politics was at the root of the impeachment of President Andrew Johnson in 1867. Johnson was a Southern Democrat who had remained loyal to the Union. Lincoln had chosen him as vice president in 1864 as a gesture of national unity. A Republican House impeached him on a party-line vote, but after a month-long trial in the Senate, the "guilty" vote fell one short of the two-thirds needed for removal.[4] And partisan politics played a key role in the House impeachment and later Senate trial of Bill Clinton (see *Politics Up Close*: "Sex, Lies, and Impeachment").

Presidential Pardons   The Constitution grants the president the power to "grant Reprieves and Pardons." This power derives from the ancient right to appeal to the king to reverse errors of law or justice committed by the court system. It is absolute: the president may grant pardons to anyone convicted of a *federal* crime for any reason. The most celebrated use of the presidential pardon was President Ford's blanket pardon of former President Nixon "for all offenses against the United States which he, Richard Nixon, has committed or may have committed or taken part in." Ford defended the pardon as necessary to end "the bitter controversy and divisive national debate," but his actions may have helped cause his defeat in the 1976 election.

Executive Power   The Constitution declares that the "executive Power" shall be vested in the president, but it is unclear whether this statement grants the president any powers that are not specified later in the Constitution or given to the president by acts of Congress. In other words, does the grant of "executive Power" give presidents constitutional authority to act as they deem necessary *beyond* the actions specified elsewhere in the Constitution or specified in laws passed by Congress?

Contrasting views on this question have been offered over two centuries. President William Howard Taft provided the classic narrow interpretation of executive power: "The president can exercise no power which cannot be fairly and reasonably traced to some specific grant of power or justly implied and included within such express grant as proper and necessary to its exercise."[5] Theodore Roosevelt, Taft's bitter opponent in a three-way race for the presidency in 1912, expressed the opposite view: "My belief was that it was not only his right but his duty to do anything that the needs of the nation demanded, unless such action was forbidden by the Constitution or by the laws."[6] Although the constitutional question has never been fully resolved, history has generally sided with those presidents who have taken an expansive view of their powers.

Some Historical Examples   U.S. history is filled with examples of presidents acting independently, beyond specific constitutional powers or laws of Congress. Among the most notable:

★ George Washington issued a Proclamation of Neutrality during the war between France and Britain following the French Revolution, thereby establishing the president's power to make foreign policy.

★ Thomas Jefferson, who prior to becoming president argued for a narrow interpretation of presidential powers, purchased the Louisiana Territory despite the fact that the Constitution contains no provision for the acquisition of territory, let alone authorizing presidential action to do so.

Think Again

Should presidents have the power to take actions not specifically authorized by law or the Constitution that they believe necessary for the nation's well-being?

Comparing Executive Branches

Politics Up Close   Sex, Lies, and Impeachment

Bill Clinton is the second president in the nation's history (following Andrew Johnson in 1867) to be impeached by the U.S. House of Representatives. (President Richard Nixon resigned just prior to an impeachment vote in 1974.)

Clinton's impeachment followed a report to the House by Independent Counsel Kenneth Starr in 1998 that accused the president of perjury, obstruction of justice, witness tampering, and "abuse of power." The Starr Report describes in graphic and lurid detail Clinton's sexual relationship with young White House intern Monica Lewinsky.

Does engaging in extramartial sex and lying about it meet the Constitution's standard for impeachment—"Treason, Bribery, or other High Crimes and Misdemeanors"? Perjury—knowingly giving false testimony in a sworn legal proceeding—is a criminal offense. But does the Constitution envision more serious misconduct? According to Alexander Hamilton in the *Federalist*, No. 65, impeachment should deal with "the abuse or violation of some public trust." Is Clinton's acknowledged "inappropriate behavior" a private affair or a violation of the public trust?

How are such questions decided? Despite pious rhetoric in Congress about the "search for truth," "impartial investigation," and "unbiased constitutional judgment," the impeachment process, whatever the merits of the charges against a president, is *political*, not judicial.

The House vote to impeach Clinton on December 19, 1998 (228 to 205), was largely along partisan lines, with all but five Republicans voting "yes" and all but five Democrats voting "no." And the vote in Clinton's Senate "trial" on February 12, 1999, was equally partisan. Even on the strongest charge—that Clinton had tried to obstruct justice—the Senate failed to find the president guilty. Removing Clinton failed to win even a majority of Senate votes, far less than the required two-thirds. All forty-five Democrats were joined by five Republicans to create a 50–50 tie vote that left Clinton tarnished but still in office.

Most Americans believed the president had a sexual affair in the White House and subsequently lied about it; however, they also *approved* of the way Clinton was performing his job as president. Indeed, the public appeared to rally around the president following the allegations of sexual misconduct.

Various explanations have been offered for this apparent paradox—a public that believed the president had an affair in the White House and lied about it, yet gave the president the highest approval ratings of his career. Many Americans believe that private sexual conduct is irrelevant to the performance of public

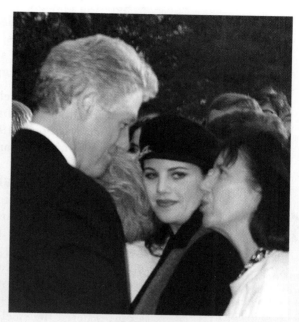

President Clinton greets well-wishers, including Monica Lewinsky, at a Democratic Party event in January 1996. Clinton's acknowledged "inappropriate behavior," and his efforts to conceal his relationship with Lewinsky were the subjects of the impeachment investigation opened against him by the House in 1998.

duties. Private morality is viewed as a personal affair about which Americans should be nonjudgmental. Some people said, "If it's okay with Hillary, why should we worry?" Haven't we had adulterous presidents before, from Thomas Jefferson to John F. Kennedy, presidents who were ranked highly in history? And many Americans believe that "they all do it."

Others argue, nonetheless, that private character counts in presidential performance, indeed, that it is a prerequisite for public trust. The president, in this view, performs a symbolic role that requires dignity, honesty, and respect. A president publicly embarrassed by sexual scandal, diminished by jokes, and laughed at by late-night television audiences cannot perform this role. The acceptance of a president's adulterous behavior, according to one commentator, lowers society's standards of behavior. "The president's legacy . . . will be a further vulgarization and demoralization of society."[a]

[a]Gertrude Himmelfarb, "Private Lives, Public Morality," New York Times, February 9, 1998.

★ Andrew Jackson ordered the removal of federal funds from the national bank and removed his secretary of the treasury from office, establishing the president's power to *remove* executive officials, a power not specifically mentioned in the Constitution.

★ Abraham Lincoln, asking, "Was it possible to lose the nation yet preserve the Constitution?" established the precedent of vigorous presidential action in national emergencies: he blockaded southern ports, declared martial law in parts of the country, and issued the Emancipation Proclamation—all without constitutional or congressional authority.

★ Franklin D. Roosevelt, battling the Great Depression during the 1930s, ordered the nation's banks to close temporarily. Following the Japanese attack on Pearl Harbor in 1941, he ordered the incarceration without trial of many thousands of Americans of Japanese ancestry living on the West Coast.

Think Again

Should Congress have the authority to call home U.S. troops sent by the president to engage in military actions overseas?

Checking Presidential Power   President Harry Truman believed that "the president has the right to keep the country from going to hell," and he was willing to use means beyond those specified in the Constitution or authorized by Congress. In 1952, while U.S. troops were fighting in Korea, steelworkers at home were threatening to strike. Rather than cross organized labor by forbidding the strike under the terms of the Taft-Hartley Act of 1947 (which he had opposed), Truman chose to seize the steel mills by executive order and continue their operations under U.S. government control. The U.S. Supreme Court ordered the steel mills returned to their owners, however, acknowledging that the president may have inherent powers to act in a national emergency but arguing that Congress had provided a legal remedy, however distasteful to the president. Thus the president can indeed act to keep the country from "going to hell," but if Congress has already acted to do so, the president must abide by the law.[7]

The most dramatic illustration of the checking of presidential power was the forced resignation of Richard M. Nixon in 1974 (for details, see *Politics Up Close*: "Watergate and the Limits of Presidential Power"). Nixon's conduct inspired the intense hostility of the nation's media, particularly the prestigious *Washington Post*. His high public approval ratings following the Vietnam peace agreement plummeted. A Democratic-controlled Senate created a special committee to investigate **Watergate** that produced damaging revelations almost daily. Congressional Republicans began to desert the embattled president. The Supreme Court ordered him to turn over White House audiotapes to a special investigator, tapes that implicated Nixon in cash payments to the men who had burglarized the Democratic National Committee offices during his 1972 reelection campaign. Facing the enmity of the media, the loss of public approval, opposition from his own party in the Congress, and the failure of his constitutional claim of "executive privilege" in the Supreme Court, Nixon became the only president of the United States ever to resign that office.

★ **Watergate**
The scandal that led to the forced resignation of President Richard M. Nixon. Adding "-gate" as a suffix to any alleged corruption in government suggests an analogy to the Watergate scandal.

★ **executive privilege**
Right of a president to withhold from other branches of government confidential communications within the executive branch; although posited by presidents, it has been upheld by the Supreme Court only in limited situations.

Executive Privilege   Over the years, presidents and scholars have argued that the Constitution's establishment of a separate executive branch of government entitles the president to **executive privilege**—the right to keep confidential communications from other branches of government. Public exposure of internal executive communications would inhibit the president's ability to obtain candid advice from subordinates and would obstruct the president's ability to conduct negotiations with foreign governments or to command military operations.

But Congress has never recognized executive privilege. It has frequently tried to compel the testimony of executive officials at congressional hearings. Presidents have regularly refused to appear themselves at congressional hearings and have frequently refused to allow other executive officials to appear or divulge specific information, citing executive privilege. The federal courts have generally refrained from intervening in this dispute between the executive and legislative branches. However, the Supreme Court has ruled that the president is not immune from court orders when illegal acts are under investigation. In *United States v. Nixon* (1974), the U.S. Supreme Court acknowledged that although the president might legitimately claim executive privilege where military or diplomatic matters are involved, such a privilege cannot be invoked in a criminal investigation. The Court ordered President Nixon to surrender tape recordings of White House conversations between the president and his advisors during the Watergate scandal.[8] (See *Politics Up Close*: "Watergate and the Limits of Presidential Power.")

Presidential Impoundment   The Constitution states that "no Money shall be drawn from the Treasury, but in Consequence of appropriations made by Law" (Article I, Section 9). Clearly the president cannot spend money *not* appropriated by Congress. But the Constitution is silent on whether the president *must* spend all of the money appropriated by Congress for various purposes. Presidents from Thomas Jefferson onward frequently refused to spend money appropriated by Congress, an action referred to as **impoundment**. But taking advantage of a presidency weakened by the Watergate scandal, the Congress in 1974 passed the Budget and Impoundment Control Act, which requires the president to spend all appropriated funds. The act does provide, however, that presidents may send Congress a list of specific **deferrals**—items on which they wish to postpone spending—and **rescissions**—items they wish to cancel altogether. Congress by *resolution* (which cannot be vetoed by the president) may restore the deferrals and force the president to spend the money. Both houses of Congress must approve a rescission; otherwise the government must spend the money.

Responsibility to the Courts   The president is not "above the law"; that is, his conduct is not immune from judicial scrutiny. The president's official conduct must be lawful; federal courts may reverse presidential actions found to be unconstitutional or violative of laws of Congress. And presidents are not immune from criminal prosecution; they cannot ignore demands to provide information in criminal cases. However, the Supreme Court has held that the president has "absolute immunity" from civil suits "arising out of the execution of official duties."[9] In other words, the president cannot be sued for damages caused by actions or decisions that are within his constitutional or legal authority.

But can the president be sued for *private* conduct beyond the scope of his official duties? In 1997 the U.S. Supreme Court rejected the notion of presidential immunity from civil claims arising from actions outside of the president's official duties.[10] (See *Controversy*: "*Clinton v. Jones*" in Chapter 13.)

Political Resources of the President

The real sources of presidential power are not found in the Constitution. The president's power is the *power to persuade*. As Harry Truman put it, "I sit here all day trying to persuade people to do things they ought to have sense enough to do without my persuading them. … That's all the powers of the president amount to."[11]

The president's political resources are potentially very great. The nation looks to the president for leadership, for direction, for reassurance. The president is the focus

★ **impoundment**
Refusal by a president to spend monies appropriated by Congress; outlawed except with congressional consent by the Budget and Impoundment Control Act of 1974.

★ **deferrals**
Items on which a president wishes to postpone spending.

★ **rescissions**
Items on which a president wishes to cancel spending.

Politics Up Close   Watergate and the Limits of Presidential Power

Richard Nixon was the only president ever to resign the office. He did so to escape certain impeachment by the House of Representatives and a certain guilty verdict in trial by the Senate. Yet Nixon's first term as president included a number of historic successes. He negotiated the first ever strategic nuclear arms limitation treaty, SALT I, with the Soviet Union. He changed the global balance of power in favor of the Western democracies by opening relations with the People's Republic of China and dividing the communist world. In his second term, he withdrew U.S. troops from Vietnam, negotiated a peace agreement, and ended one of America's longest and bloodiest wars. But his remarkable record is forever tarnished by his failure to understand the limits of presidential power.

Richard Nixon was the only president ever to resign the office. He did so in 1974 to avoid impeachment following the Watergate scandal. He is shown here leaving the White House for the last time.

On the night of June 17, 1972, five men with burglary tools and wiretapping devices were arrested in the offices of the Democratic National Committee in the Watergate Building in Washington. Also arrested were E. Howard Hunt, Jr., G. Gordon Liddy, and James W. McCord, Jr., all employed by the Committee to Reelect the President (CREEP). All pleaded guilty and were convicted, but U.S. District Court Judge John J. Sirica believed that the defendants were shielding whoever had ordered and paid for the operation.

Although there is no evidence that Nixon himself ordered or had prior knowledge of the break-in, he discussed with his chief of staff, H. R. Haldeman, and White House advisers John Ehrlichman and John Dean the advisability of payoffs to buy the defendants' silence. Nixon hoped his landslide electoral victory in November 1972 would put the matter to rest.

But a series of sensational revelations in the *Washington Post* kept the story alive. Using an inside source known only as Deep Throat, Bob Woodward and Carl Bernstein, investigative reporters for the *Post*, alleged that key members of Nixon's reelection committee, including its chairman, former Attorney General John Mitchell, and White House staff were actively involved in the break-in and, more important, in the subsequent attempts at a cover-up.

In February 1973 the U.S. Senate formed a Special Select Committee on Campaign Activities—the "Watergate Committee"—to delve into Watergate and related activities. The committee's nationally televised hearings enthralled millions of viewers with lurid stories of "the White House horrors." John Dean broke with the White House and testified before the committee that he had earlier warned Nixon the cover-up was "a cancer growing on the presidency." Then, in a dramatic revelation, the committee—and the nation—learned that President Nixon maintained a secret tape-recording system in the Oval Office. Hoping that the tapes would prove or disprove charges of Nixon's involvement in the cover-up, the committee issued a subpoena to the White House. Nixon refused to comply, arguing that the constitutional separation of powers gave the president an "executive privilege" to withhold his private conversations from Congress. However, the U.S. Supreme Court, voting 8 to 0 in *United States v. Richard M. Nixon*, ordered Nixon to turn over the tapes.

Despite the rambling nature of the tapes, committee members interpreted them as confirming Nixon's involvement in the payoffs and cover-up. Informed by congressional leaders of his own party that impeachment by a majority of the House and removal from office by two-thirds of the Senate were assured, on August 9, 1974, Richard Nixon resigned his office.

On September 8, 1974, new President Gerald R. Ford pardoned former President Nixon "for all offenses against the United States which he, Richard Nixon, has committed or may have committed or taken part in" during his presidency. Upon his death in 1994, Nixon was eulogized for his foreign policy successes.

of public and media attention. The president has the capacity to mobilize public opinion, to communicate directly with the American people, and to employ the symbols of office to advance policy initiatives in both foreign and domestic affairs.

The Reputation for Power A reputation for power is itself a source of power. Presidents must strive to maintain the image of power in order to be effective. A president perceived as powerful, especially by the national media, can exercise great influence abroad with foreign governments and at home with the Congress, interest groups, and the executive bureaucracy. A president perceived as weak, unsteady, bumbling, or error prone will soon become unpopular and ineffective.

Presidential Popularity Presidential popularity with the American people is a political resource. Popular presidents cannot always transfer their popularity into foreign policy successes or legislative victories, but popular presidents usually have more success than unpopular presidents.

Presidential popularity is regularly tracked in national opinion polls. For more than 40 years, national surveys have asked the American public: "Do you approve or disapprove of the way _____ is handling his job as president?" (see Figures 11.1 and 11.2). Analyses of variations over time in these poll results suggest some generalizations about presidential popularity (see Figure 11.1).

Presidential popularity is usually high at the beginning of a president's term of office, but this "honeymoon" period can be very brief. The American public's high expectations for a new president can turn sour within a few months. A president's popularity will vary a great deal during a term in office, with sharp peaks and steep valleys in the ratings. But the general trend is downward.[12] Presidents usually recover some popularity at the end of their first term as they campaign for reelection.

Presidential popularity rises during crises. People "rally 'round the president" when the nation is confronted with an international threat or the president initiates a military action.[13] President George H. W. Bush, for example, registered nearly 90 percent approval during the Persian Gulf War. Likewise, the invasion of Grenada in 1983 and Panama in 1989 rallied support to the president. And the "9/11" terrorist attack on America rallied the American people behind George W. Bush (see Figure 11.2). But prolonged warfare and stalemate erode popular support. In both the Korean and the Vietnam wars, initial public approval of the president and support for the war eroded over time as military operations stalemated and casualties mounted.[14] And President George W. Bush suffered a prolonged erosion of approval as the Iraq War continued.

Major scandals *may* also hurt presidential popularity and effectiveness. The Watergate scandal produced a low of 22 percent approval for Nixon just prior to his resignation. Reagan's generally high approval ratings were blemished by the Iran-Contra scandal hearings in 1987, although he ultimately left office with a high approval rate. But highly publicized allegations of sexual improprieties against President Clinton in early 1998 appeared to have the opposite effect; Clinton's approval ratings went *up*. Perhaps the public differentiates between private sexual conduct and performance in office.

Finally, economic recessions erode presidential popularity. Every president in office during a recession has suffered loss of popular approval, including President Reagan during the 1982 recession. But no president suffered a more precipitous decline in approval ratings than George H. W. Bush, whose popularity plummeted from its Gulf War high of 89 percent in 1991 to a low of 37 percent in only a year, largely as a result of recession.

Think Again

Is presidential performance more related to character and personality than to policy positions?

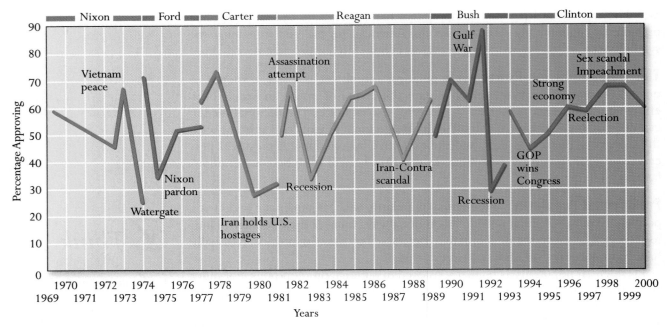

Figure *11.1* • The Battle for Public Approval: Presidential Popularity over Time

Americans expect a great deal from their presidents and are quick to give these leaders the credit—and the blame—for major events in the nation's life. In general, public approval (as measured by response to the question "Do you approve or disapprove of the way is handling the job of president?") is highest at the beginning of a new president's term in office and declines from that point. Major military conflicts generally raise presidential ratings initially but can (as in the case of Lyndon Johnson) cause dramatic decline if the conflict drags on. In addition, public approval of the president is closely linked to the nation's economic health. When the economy is in recession, Americans tend to take a negative view of the president.

★ **White House press corps**
Reporters from both print and broadcast media assigned to regularly cover the president.

Access to the Media   The president dominates the news more than any other single person. All major television networks, newspapers, and newsmagazines have reporters (usually their most experienced and skilled people) covering the "White House beat." The presidential press secretary briefs these reporters daily, but the president also may appear in person in the White House press room at any time. Presidents regularly use this media access to advance their programs and priorities.[15]

The **White House press corps** is an elite group of reporters assigned to cover the president. It includes the prestige press—the *New York Times, Washington Post, Wall Street Journal, Time, Newsweek, U.S. News & World Report,* as well as the television networks—ABC, CBS, NBC, CNN, FOX, and even the foreign press. Indeed, more than 1,800 journalists have White House press credentials. Fortunately, however, not all show up at once (there are only 48 seats in the White House briefing room, and attendance at press conferences is usually about 300). The great majority of daily newspapers have no Washington correspondents, but instead rely on national news services such as the Associated Press.

Formal press conferences are a double-edged sword for the president. They *can* help mobilize popular support for presidential programs. Presidents often try to focus attention on particular issues, and they generally open press conferences with a policy statement on these issues. But reporters' questions and subsequent reporting often refocus the press conference in other directions. Often the lead media story emerging from a press conference has nothing to do with the president's

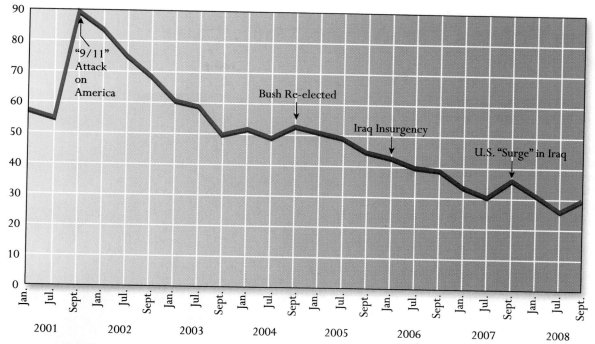

Figure *11.2*   Turbulent Times: George W. Bush's Approval Ratings

Source: Various polls reported in *The Polling Report*.

purpose in holding the conference. The president cannot control questions or limit the subject matter of press conferences.

Presidents may also use direct television addresses from the White House. (President Reagan made heavy use of national prime time television appeals to mobilize support for his programs; he was exceptionally successful in generating telephone calls, wires, and letters to Congress in support of his programs.) President George W. Bush has also used direct addresses to try to mobilize support for the war on terrorism, including military actions in Afghanistan and Iraq.

However, there is some evidence that with the multiplication of channels available to the public, presidential addresses may have less impact today on public opinion than in previous years. Television ratings for presidential addresses have been declining, and in reaction some broadcast networks have declined to cover presidential addresses.[16] Even the State of the Union Address attracts fewer viewers than in the past. Nonetheless, presidents continue to receive more television and press coverage than any other political figure. And a combination of national speeches, press conferences, speeches to various groups around the country, and media interviews, together with public appearances by members of their administrations, can move public opinion in the president's direction.[17]

Personality Versus Policy

A president with an engaging personality—warmth, charm, and good humor—can add to his political power. And, of course, a president who seems distant, uncaring, or humorless can erode his political resources. (Richard Nixon's seeming

People in Politics   Barack Obama, A Call for Change

Barack Obama, handsome, youthful, and charismatic, swept to the White House on the simple promise of "change." And his African American heritage itself symbolized change. The *New York Times* heralded his victory as a historic moment in race relations in America with the headline: "OBAMA: RACIAL BARRIER FALLS IN HEAVY TURNOUT."

Obama's father was born in Nyanza, Kenya, and came to the University of Hawaii as a foreign student. He met and married a fellow student, Ann Durham of Wichita, Kansas. Barack was two years old before they separated and divorced. Barack's inheritance from his father includes his middle name, Hussein. His mother remarried an Indonesian foreign student and the family moved to Jakarta where Barack attended elementary school. At age 10 he returned to Honolulu to live with his maternal grandparents. In his memoir, *Dreams from My Father*, Obama describes his experiences growing up in a white, upper-middle-class, American family. He reflects on his struggles to reconcile the social perceptions of others of his multiracial background. He writes that he used alcohol, marijuana, and cocaine as a teenager "to push questions of who I was out of my mind."

Obama attended Occidental College in Los Angeles for two years before transferring to Columbia University where he majored in political science and international relations. Upon graduation in 1983 he went to Chicago to work as a community organizer in a low-income public housing development. In 1988 he was admitted to Harvard Law school where he complied an enviable record. He was elected president of the *Harvard Law Review,* the first African American to ever receive such an honor. Upon graduation in 1991, he returned to Chicago where he provided legal representation to community organizations and civil rights groups.

Obama married Harvard Law School graduate Michelle Robinson in 1992; they have two daughters. He writes that he was detached from religion until his community work awakened him to "the power of the African American religious traditions to spawn social change." Obama and his wife joined the Trinity United Church of Christ on Chicago's South-side. At Trinity he was mentored by the charismatic and flamboyant pastor, Reverend Jeremiah Wright. Obama's early speaking style was said to be "more Harvard than Chicago"; there was a perception that Obama "wasn't black enough." But he quickly mastered the cadence and phrasing of Wright's sermons, even using the title of a sermon, *The Audacity of Hope,* as the title of his autobiography. (Later Wright's incendiary sermons would become a political burden and

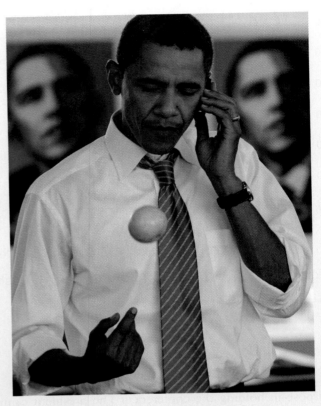

Obama would be obliged to "disown" his pastor and leave the church.) Through his community organizing and church affiliation, Obama gradually assembled a political base in Chicago politics.

Obama was elected to the Illinois State Senate in 1996, representing Chicago's South-side neighborhood of Hyde Park. He served two terms, but often voted "present" on controversial legislation, including anti-abortion bills. His major accomplishment was a law to monitor racial profiling by requiring police to record the race of drivers they stopped. Obama's only political failure came in 2000 when he challenged a Chicago veteran politician, Bobby Rush, for his seat representing Illinois' predominantly black First Congressional District. The Chicago machine and Mayor Richard Daley supported Rush; Obama was soundly defeated. But the defeat taught Obama to work with the machine rather than against it. He made peace with Mayor Richard Daley and won the confidence of Illinois State Senate President, Emil Jones. He sought the financial backing of white liberals including the Pritzker's, owners of Hyatt hotels. He lined up to support of powerful Illinois unions with mostly black membership—teachers, government employees, and service workers. By 2004 Obama was ready to reach for higher office.

In March 2004, Obama won the Democratic primary for an open U.S. Senate seat, winning 53 percent of the vote in a three-way race. He attracted national attention when he delivered the keynote address at the 2004 Democratic National Convention in Boston. His compelling call for unity gained him instant national celebrity: "We are one people, all of us pledging allegiance to the stars and stripes, all of us defending the United States of America." He went on to score a lopsided victory in the November general election of U.S. Senate winning 70 percent of the Illinois vote.

In the Senate Obama was appointed to a much-coveted seat on the prestigious Foreign Relations Committee. He traveled extensively to Eastern Europe, the Middle East, and Africa. His first successful sponsorship of a law came in the Republic of the Congo Relief Act. But he missed over 38 percent of Senate floor votes. He supported comprehensive immigration reform along with Senators Edward M. Kennedy and John McCain; the bill passed in the Senate but failed in the House. He cosponsored a budget transparency act that requires the Office of Management and Budget to create Web site (www.USAspending.gov) that traces federal appropriations. As a member of the Senate Veterans Affairs committee, Obama regularly critized the Bush administration for failing to do enough for veterans returning from Iraq and Afghanistan.

Obama was an early opponent of the war in Iraq, even before he was elected to the U.S. Senate. Indeed, in his primary battles against Senator Hillary Clinton, he critized the New York senator for having initially supported military action in Iraq. Obama was a strong supporter of unsuccessful bills to cap troop levels in Iraq and to set deadlines for the withdrawal of U.S. forces.

In early 2007 Obama stood at the Old State Capitol Building in Springfield, Illinois, where Abraham Lincoln delivered his 1858 House Divided speech, and announced: "In the shadow of the Old State Capitol, where Lincoln once called on a house divided to stand together, where common hopes and common dreams still live, I stand before you today to announce my candidacy for President of the United States of America."

Obama demonstrated his appeal to white voters early in the primary campaign against New York senator Hillary Clinton. He skillfully steered his campaign around the rocks of racial division, distancing himself from the incendiary sermons of his Chicago pastor. And race never really emerged as a central issue in his election.

Obama chose "Change you can believe in" as his campaign theme. He stayed "on message" throughout the long primary battle with New York Senator Hillary Clinton (see *Politics Up Close: "Hillary Versus Barack"* in Chapter 7). Democratic primary voters and caucus goers had a historic choice of either the first woman presidential nominee of a major party or the first African American. Clinton claimed that she won more primary votes than Obama, but the Obama campaign wisely focused on gathering convention delegates. In the end, the unelected superdelegates chose to support the candidate with the most elected delegates, Barack Obama.

Obama carried his message of "change" into the general election campaign. As a young (47-year-old), handsome athletic, African American, he personified change. His image contrasted starkly with the aging (72-year-old) John McCain. Obama led McCain in the polls from the very beginning of the race. Only once, after the Republican convention and McCain's selection of Sarah Palin as his running mate, was McCain temporarily tied with Obama in the polls (see *Politics Up Close: "Campaign '08— Obama Versus McCain"*). McCain's slim chances for victory evaporated with the financial meltdown in September. Obama won 53 percent of the popular vote. "If there is anyone out there who still doubts that America is a place where all things are possible, who still wonders if the dream of our founders is alive in our time, who still questions the power of our democracy, tonight is your answer," declared the new President-elect.

Obama made many promises in his presidential campaign: to end the war in Iraq "responsibly"; to revive the economy; to provide health insurance for all Americans; to aid the development of alternative energy sources; to strengthen civil rights enforcement; to strengthen oversight of the financial community; to provide "middle-class" tax cuts while raising taxes on the wealthy. Perhaps the biggest challenge Obama may face as president is to live up to the expectations that his victory engendered among both black and white Americans.

mean-spiritedness contributed to the collapse of his approval ratings during the Watergate scandal; Jimmy Carter's often cold and distant appearance failed to inspire much popular support for his programs; and George H. W. Bush appeared to be uncaring about the economic circumstances of ordinary Americans.) The public evaluates presidents as much on style as on policy substance.[18] (Perhaps no other president in recent times enjoyed such personal popularity while pursuing relatively unpopular policies as Ronald Reagan.) If the public thinks the president understands and cares about their problems, they may be willing to continue to

A Public Forum

President George W. Bush answers questions during a press conference. These meetings with the press can be a double-edged sword. They give the president an opportunity to present his point of view to the public, but they also allow the press to raise issues a president might rather avoid.

approve of the job he is doing despite policy setbacks. In other words, the public evaluates the president by how much they like him as a person. (President Bill Clinton's likability kept his public approval ratings high during the sex scandal and impeachment effort.) Yet, as we have seen, public approval ratings of presidents can rise or fall based on wars and crises, scandals, and economic prosperity or recession, even while their personal style remains unaltered.

Party Leadership   Presidents are leaders of their party, but this role is hardly a source of great strength. It is true that presidents select the national party chair, control the national committee and its Washington staff, and largely direct the national party convention. Incumbent presidents can use this power to help defeat challengers *within* their own parties. President Ford used this power to help defeat challenger Ronald Reagan in 1976; President Carter used it to help defeat challenger Ted Kennedy in 1980; and President George H. W. Bush used it against challenger Pat Buchanan in 1992. But the role of party leader is of limited value to a president in relations with Congress because the parties have few direct controls over their members (see Chapter 7).

Nevertheless, presidents enjoy much stronger support in Congress from members of their own party than from members of the opposition party (see Figure 10.11 on page 360). Some of the president's party support in Congress is a product of shared ideological values and policy positions. But Republican Congress members do have some stake in the success of a Republican president, as do Democratic members in the success of a Democratic president. Popular presidents may produce those few extra votes that make the difference for party candidates in close congressional districts.

Policy Leadership Presidents feel an obligation to exercise policy leadership—develop a policy agenda, present it to the Congress, sell it to the American people, and lobby it through to success. Presidents are less likely than most politicians to pander to public opinion. Rather, they expect to be able to shape public opinion themselves.[19]

Nevertheless, there are times when presidents prudently decide to follow public opinion, rather than try to change it. First of all, presidents who are approaching a reelection contest become more responsive to public opinion. They are less likely to go off into new policy directions or to support unpopular policies. Generally, presidents present their policy initiatives at the beginning of their terms. This period usually corresponds to a president's high public approval rating. Indeed, throughout a presidential term, the higher their approval rating, the more likely they are to present new policy directions and even to take unpopular policy positions. In contrast, presidents experiencing low approval ratings are much less likely to present new policy initiatives or to pursue unpopular policies.[20]

Chief Executive

The president is the chief executive of the nation's largest bureaucracy: 2.8 million civilian employees, 60 independent agencies, 15 departments, and the large Executive Office of the President. The formal organizational chart of the federal government places the president at the head of this giant structure (see Figure 12.1, "The Federal Bureaucracy," in Chapter 12). But the president cannot command this bureaucracy in the fashion of a military officer or a corporation president. When Harry Truman was preparing to turn over the White House to Dwight Eisenhower, he predicted that the general of the army would not understand the presidency: "He'll sit here and say 'Do this! Do that!' and nothing will happen. Poor Ike—it won't be a bit like the army. He'll find it very frustrating." Truman vastly underestimated the political skills of the former general, but the crusty Missourian clearly understood the frustrations confronting the nation's chief executive. The president does not command the executive branch of government but rather stands at its center—persuading, bargaining, negotiating, and compromising to achieve goals (see *Politics Up Close*: "Contrasting Presidential Styles").

The Constitutional Executive The Constitution is vague about the president's authority over the executive branch. It vests executive power in the presidency and grants the president authority to appoint principal officers of the government "by and with the Advice and Consent of the Senate." Under the Constitution, the president may also "require the Opinion, in writing, of the principal Officer in each of the executive Departments, upon any Subject relating to the Duties of their respective Offices." This awkward phrase presumably gives the president the power to oversee operations of the executive departments. Finally, and perhaps most important, the president is instructed to "take Care that the Laws be faithfully executed."

At the same time, Congress has substantial authority over the executive branch. Through its lawmaking abilities, Congress can establish or abolish executive departments and regulate their operations. Congress's "power of the purse" allows it to determine the budget of each department each year and thus to limit or broaden or even "micromanage" the activities of these departments. Moreover, Congress can pressure executive agencies by conducting investigations, calling administrators to task in public hearings, and directly contacting agencies with members' own complaints or those of their constituents.

Politics Up Close   **Contrasting Presidential Styles**

Every president brings to the White House his own personal administrative style. Some presidents work almost constantly, putting in twelve to fourteen hour days (Carter, Clinton). Others pursue a more leisurely schedule, leaving the Oval Office at 5 or 6 P.M. and spending weekends at the presidential retreat at Camp David or their home (Eisenhower, Reagan, Bush). Some presidents delegate a great deal of responsibility to Cabinet members and White House aides (Eisenhower, Reagan, Bush). Others closely monitor what is happening in executive departments and agencies (Johnson, Carter, Clinton). Some pursue a great many policy initiatives (Clinton), while others focus on a few key priorities (Reagan, Bush). Some are well informed about the specifics of public policy (Carter, Clinton), while others care more about overall goals and directions of their administration (Reagan, Bush). Some operate informally, communicating frequently with staff, Cabinet members, and others (Clinton). Other presidents function in a more business-like fashion, communicating mostly through their chief of staff (Eisenhower, Reagan). Below are the differences between the Bush and Clinton administrative styles as seen by two prominent political scientists.

Differences Between the Bush and Clinton Presidencies

George W. Bush	Bill Clinton
Disciplined White House	Less disciplined White House
Scripted presidency	Unscripted presidency
Strict focus on few key priorities	Wide-ranging policy focus
More reliance on vice president	Less reliance on vice president
Punctuality required for meetings with clear starting and ending times	Meetings start late and seldom end on time
Little use of the bully pulpit	More use of the bully pulpit
Direct public communicator	Skillful public communicator
Frequent reliance on experts to provide policy overviews	Well informed on policy issues
Large responsibilities delegated to aides	Close supervisory role maintained over all top aides
Preference for executive summaries	Enamored of thick briefing books
Regular working days observed insofar as practicable	A "24/7" president

Source: Roger H. Davidson and Walter J. Oleszak, Congress and Its Members. 9th ed. Washington, D.C.: CQ Press, 2004, p. 302.

★ **executive orders**
Formal regulations governing executive branch operations issued by the president.

TIMELINE
The Executive Order Over Time

Executive Orders   Presidents frequently use **executive orders** to implement their policies. Executive orders may direct specific federal agencies to carry out the president's wishes, or they may direct all federal agencies to pursue the president's preferred course of action. In any case, they must be based on either a president's constitutional powers or on powers delegated to the president by laws of Congress. Presidents regularly issue 50 to 100 executive orders each year, but some stand out. In 1942 President Franklin D. Roosevelt issued Executive Order 9066 for the internment of Japanese Americans during World War II. In 1948 President Harry Truman issued Executive Order 9981 to desegregate the U.S. armed forces. In 1965 President Lyndon Johnson issued Executive Order 11246 to require that private firms with federal contracts institute affirmative action programs. A president can even declare a national emergency by executive order, a step that authorizes a broad range of unilateral actions.

President George Bush hosts a meeting in the Oval Office of the White House on Thursday, December 21, 2001.

Executive orders have legal force when they are based on the president's constitutional or statutory authority. And presidents typically take an expansive view of their own authority. (President George Washington issued an executive order declaring American neutrality in the war between France and England in 1793. While the Constitution gave the power to "declare war" to Congress, Washington assumed the authority to declare neutrality.) Federal courts have generally upheld presidential executive orders. However, the Supreme Court overturned an order by President Harry Truman in 1951 during the Korean War seizing the nation's steel mills.[21] Research on the frequency of executive orders suggests that: Democratic presidents issue more orders than Republican presidents; presidents may issue executive orders to circumvent Congress but only when they believe that Congress will not overturn their orders; and presidents issue more executive orders when they are running for reelection.[22]

Appointments   Presidential power over the executive branch derives in part from the president's authority to appoint and remove top officials. Presidents can shape policy by careful attention to top appointments—cabinet secretaries, assistant secretaries, agency heads, and White House staff. The key is to select people who share the president's policy views and who have the personal qualifications to do an effective job. However, in cabinet appointments political considerations weigh heavily: unifying various elements of the party; appealing for interest-group support; rewarding political loyalty; providing a temporary haven for unsuccessful party candidates; achieving a balance of racial, ethnic, and gender representation.[23] The appointment power gives the president only limited control over the executive branch of government. Of the executive branch's 2.8 million civilian employees, the president actually appoints only about 3,000. The vast majority of federal executive branch employees are civil servants—recruited, paid, and protected under civil service laws—and are not easily removed or punished by the president. Cabinet secretaries and heads of independent regulatory agencies require congressional confirmation, but presidents can choose their own White House staff without the approval of Congress.

Presidents have only limited power to remove the heads of independent regulatory agencies. By law, Congress sets the terms of these officials. Federal Communications Commission members are appointed for 5 years; Securities and Exchange Commission members for 5 years; and Federal Reserve Board members, responsible for the nation's money supply, enjoy the longest term of any executive officials—14 years. Congress's responsibility for term length for regulatory agencies is supposed to insulate those agencies, in particular their quasi-judicial responsibilities, from "political" influence.

Budget Presidential authority also derives from the president's role in the budgetary process. The Constitution makes no mention of the president with regard to expenditures; rather, it grants the power of the purse to Congress. Indeed, for nearly 150 years, executive departments submitted their budget requests directly to the Congress without first submitting them to the president. But with the passage of the Budget and Accounting Act in 1921, Congress established the Office of Management and Budget (OMB) (originally named the Bureau of the Budget) to assist the president in preparing an annual Budget of the United States Government for presentation to the Congress. The president's budget is simply a set of recommendations to the Congress. Congress must pass appropriations acts before the president or any executive department or agency may spend money. Congress can and frequently does alter the president's budget recommendations (see Politics of Budgeting" in Chapter 12).

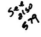

★ cabinet
The heads (secretaries) of the executive departments together with other top officials accorded cabinet rank by the president; only occasionally does it meet as a body to advise and support the president.

The Cabinet The **cabinet** is not mentioned in the U.S. Constitution; it has no formal powers. It consists of the secretaries of the fifteen executive departments and others the president may designate, including the vice president, the Administrator of the Environmental Protection Agency, the Director of the Office of Management and Budget, the Director of National Drug Control Policy, and the Special Trade Representative. According to custom, cabinet officials are ranked by the date their departments were created (see Table 11.2). Thus the secretary of state is the senior cabinet officer, followed by the secretary of the treasury. They sit next to the president at cabinet meetings; heads of the newest departments sit at the far ends of the table.

The cabinet rarely functions as a decision-making body. Cabinet officers in the United States are powerful because they head giant administrative organizations. The secretary of state, the secretary of defense, the secretary of the treasury, the attorney general, and, to a lesser extent, the other departmental secretaries are all people of power and prestige. But seldom does a strong president hold a cabinet meeting to decide important policy questions. More frequently, presidents know what they want and hold cabinet meetings only to help promote their views.

The Constitution requires that "Officers of the United States" be confirmed by the Senate. In the past, the Senate rarely rejected a presidential cabinet nomination; the traditional view was that presidents were entitled to pick their own people and even make their own mistakes. In recent years, however, the confirmation process has become more partisan and divisive, with the Senate conducting lengthy investigations and holding public hearings on presidential cabinet nominees. The intense public scrutiny and potential for partisan attacks, together with financial disclosure and conflict-of-interest laws, may be discouraging some well-qualified people from accepting cabinet posts.

The National Security Council The National Security Council (NSC) is really an "inner cabinet" created by law in 1947 to advise the president and

Table *11.2* The Cabinet Departments

By custom, the fifteen executive departments are ranked by their dates of creation.

Department	Created
State	1789
Treasury	1789
Defense*	1947
Justice	1789
Interior	1849
Agriculture†	1889
Commerce	1913
Labor	1913
Health and Human Services‡	1953
Housing and Urban Development	1965
Transportation	1966
Energy	1977
Education	1979
Veterans' Affairs	1989
Homeland Security	2002

*Formerly the War and Navy Departments, created in 1789 and 1798, respectively.

†Agriculture Department created in 1862, made part of cabinet in 1889.

‡Originally Health, Education, and Welfare; reorganized in 1979, with the creation of a separate Department of Education.

coordinate foreign, defense, and intelligence activities. The president is chair, and the vice president, secretary of state, secretary of defense and secretary of the treasury are participating members. The chair of the Joint Chiefs of Staff and the director of central intelligence serve as advisers to the NSC. The President's national security advisor also sits on the NSC and heads its staff. The purposes of the council are to advise and coordinate policy; but in the Iran-Contra scandal in 1987, a staff member of the NSC, Lt. Col. Oliver North, undertook to *implement* security policy by directly channeling funds and arms to Nicaraguan "contras"

★ **National Security Council (NSC)**
"Inner cabinet" that advises the president and coordinates foreign, defense, and intelligence activities.

Pushing an Agenda

The Constitution designates the president as the nation's chief executive officer. The president names his cabinet secretaries (with the confirmation of the Senate). But the cabinet rarely meets as a body, and when it does, it is usually to allow the president to promote his views. President George W. Bush is shown here with his cabinet in 2005.

fighting a communist-dominated government. Various investigative committees strongly recommended that the NSC staff confine itself to an advisory role.

White House Staff   Today, presidents exercise their powers chiefly through the White House staff. This staff includes the president's closest aides and advisers. Over the years, the White House staff has grown from Roosevelt's small "brain trust" of a dozen advisers to several hundred people.

Senior White House staff members are trusted political advisers, often personal friends or long-time associates of the president. Some enjoy office space in the White House itself and daily contact with the president (see Figure 11.3). Appointed without Senate confirmation, they are loyal to the president alone, not to departments, agencies, or interest groups. Their many tasks include the following:

★ Providing the president with sound advice on everything from national security to congressional affairs, policy development, and electoral politics.

★ Monitoring the operations of executive departments and agencies and evaluating the performance of key executive officials.

★ Setting the president's schedule, determining whom the president will see and call, where and when the president will travel, and where and to whom the president will make personal appearances and speeches.

★ Above all, protecting their boss and steering the president away from scandal, political blunders, and errors of judgment.

The senior White House staff normally includes a chief of staff, the national security adviser, a press secretary, the counsel to the president (an attorney), a director of personnel (patronage appointments), and assistants for political affairs, legislative liaison, and domestic policy. Staff organization depends on each president's personal taste. Some presidents have organized their staffs hierarchically, concentrating power in the chief of staff. Others have maintained direct contact with several staff members.

Chief Legislator and Lobbyist

The president has the principal responsibility for the initiation of national policy. Indeed, about 80 percent of the bills considered by Congress originate in the executive branch. Presidents have a strong incentive to fulfill this responsibility: the American people hold them responsible for anything that happens in the nation during their term of office, whether or not they have the authority or capacity to do anything about it.

Policy Initiation   The Founders understood that the president would be involved in policy initiation. The Constitution requires the president to "give to the Congress Information of the State of the Union," to "recommend to their Consideration such Measures as he shall judge necessary and expedient" (Article II, Section 3). "On extraordinary Occasions" the president may call a recessed Congress into special session. Each year the principal policy statement of the president comes in the State of the Union message to Congress. It is followed by the president's Budget of the United States Government, which sets forth the president's programs with price tags attached. Many other policy proposals are developed by executive departments and agencies, transmitted to the White House for the president's approval or "clearance," and then sent to Congress.

The following labels appear in the diagram:

Director, Intergovernmental Affairs

Deputy Counsel

White House Counsel

Deputy, Legislative Affairs

Director, Legislative Affairs

Director, Political Affairs

Director, Public Liaison

Chair, National Economic Council

First Lady's reception area

First Lady's Office

First Lady's Chief of Staff

Assistant to the President, Domestic Policy

National Security Adviser

Vice President's Office

Vice President's Executive Assistant

Chief of Staff

To residence

Press Secretary

Deputy Communications Director

Communications Director

Cabinet Room

To residence

Roosevelt Room

President's secretaries

President's personal aide

President's study and dining room

President's Oval Office

Figure *11.3*   Corridors of Power: The White House West Wing

Presidents allocate office space in the White House according to their own desires. An office located close to the president's is considered an indication of the power of the occupant. This diagram shows the office assignments during the Clinton administration.

Meeting Congressional Leaders

Presidents are expected to provide policy leadership and to work for congressional passage of their policy proposals. President George W. Bush is shown here with the leadership of both the Democratic and Republican parties in the House and Senate.

Congress may not accept all or even most of the president's proposals. Indeed, from time to time it may even try to develop its own legislative agenda in competition with the president's. But the president's legislative initiatives usually set the agenda of congressional decision making. As one experienced Washington lobbyist put it, "Obviously when the president sends up a bill, it takes first place in the queue. All other bills take second place."[24]

White House Lobbying   Presidents do not simply send their bills to Congress and then await the outcome. The president is also expected to be the chief lobbyist on behalf of the administration's bills as they make their way through the legislative labyrinth. The White House staff includes "legislative liaison" people—lobbyists for the president's programs. They organize the president's legislative proposals, track them through committee and floor proceedings, arrange committee appearances by executive department and agency representatives, count votes, and advise the president on when and how to "cut deals" and "twist arms."

Presidents are not without resources in lobbying Congress. They may exchange many favors, large and small, for the support of individual members. They can help direct "pork" to a member's district, promise White House support for a member's pet project, and assist in resolving a member's problems with the bureaucracy. Presidents also may issue or withhold invitations to the White House for prestigious ceremonies, dinners with visiting heads of state, and other glittering social occasions—an effective resource because most members of Congress value the prestige associated with close White House "connections."[25]

The president may choose to "twist arms" individually—by telephoning and meeting with wavering members of Congress. Arm twisting is generally reserved for the president's most important legislative battles. There is seldom time for a president to contact individual members of Congress personally about many bills in various stages of the legislative process—in subcommittee, full committee, floor consideration, conference committee, and final passage—in both the House and the Senate. Instead, the president must rely on White House staff for most legislative contacts and use personal appeals sparingly.

The Honeymoon   The **honeymoon period** at the very start of a president's term offers the best opportunity to get the new administration's legislative proposals enacted into law. Presidential influence in Congress is generally highest at this time both because the president's personal popularity is typically at its height and because the president can claim the recent election results as a popular mandate for key programs. Sophisticated members of Congress know that votes cast for a presidential candidate are not necessarily votes cast for that candidate's policy positions (see "The Voter Decides" in Chapter 8). But election results signal members of Congress, in a language they understand well, that the president is politically popular and that they must give the administration's programs careful consideration. President Lyndon Johnson succeeded in getting the bulk of his Great Society program enacted in the year following his landslide victory in 1964. Ronald Reagan pushed through the largest tax cut in American history in the year following his convincing electoral victory over incumbent president Jimmy Carter in 1980. Bill Clinton was most successful with the Congress during his first year in office, in 1993, even winning approval for a major tax increase as part of a deficit-reduction package. And George W. Bush succeeded in getting a tax cut through Congress in his first six months in office. Both Democrat Clinton and Republican Bush benefited from having their party control the Congress during their first months in office.

★ **honeymoon period**
Early months of a president's term in which his popularity with the public and influence with the Congress are generally high.

Presidential "Box Scores"   How successful are presidents in getting their legislation through Congress? *Congressional Quarterly* regularly compiles "box scores" of presidential success in Congress—percentages of presidential victories on congressional votes on which the president took a clear-cut position. The measure does not distinguish between bills that were important to the president and bills that may have been less significant. But viewed over time (see Figure 11.4), the presidential box scores provide interesting insights into the factors affecting the president's legislative success.

Presidential Success in Polls and Congress

The most important determinant of presidential success in Congress is party control. Presidents are far more successful when they face a Congress controlled by their own party. Democratic presidents John F. Kennedy and Lyndon Johnson enjoyed the support of Democratic-controlled Congresses and posted average success scores over 80 percent. Jimmy Carter was hardly a popular president, but he enjoyed the support of a Democratic Congress and an average of 76.8 percent presidential support. Republican presidents Richard Nixon and Gerald Ford fared poorly with Democratic-controlled Congresses. Republican president Ronald Reagan was very successful in his first term when he faced a Democratic House and a Republican Senate, but after Democrats took over both houses of Congress, Reagan's success rate plummeted. During the Reagan and Bush presidencies, divided party control of government (Republicans in the White House and Democrats controlling one or both houses of Congress) was said to produce **gridlock**, the political inability of the government to act decisively on the nation's problems. President Bill Clinton's achievements when Democrats controlled the Congress (1993–94), contrasted with his dismal record in dealing with Republican-controlled Congresses (1995–99). Likewise President George W. Bush was very successful when Republicans controlled Congress, but his success evaporated after Democrats gained control.

★ **gridlock**
Political stalemate between the executive and legislative branches arising when one branch is controlled by one major political party and the other branch by the other party.

The Veto Power   The **veto** is the president's most powerful weapon in dealing with Congress. The veto is especially important to a president facing a Congress controlled by the opposition party. Even the *threat* of a veto enhances the president's bargaining power with Congress.[26] Confronted with such a threat, congressional leaders must calculate whether they can muster a two-thirds vote of both houses to override the veto.

★ **veto**
Rejection of a legislative act by the executive branch; in the U.S. federal government, overriding of a veto requires a two-thirds majority in both houses of Congress.

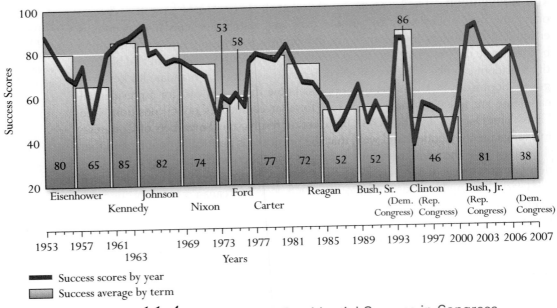

Figure *11.4*   Box Scores: Presidential Success in Congress

Presidential "box scores"—the percentage of times that a bill endorsed by the president is enacted by Congress—are closely linked to the strength of the president's party in Congress. For example, both Dwight D. Eisenhower and Ronald Reagan benefited from having a Republican majority in the Senate in their first terms and suffered when Democrats gained control of the Senate in their second terms. Democratic control of both houses of Congress resulted in significantly higher box scores for Democratic presidents John Kennedy, Lyndon Johnson, and Jimmy Carter than for Republicans Richard Nixon, Gerald Ford, and George H. W. Bush. Clinton was very successful in his first two years, when the Democrats controlled Congress, but when the Republicans won control following the 1994 midterm election, Clinton's box score plummeted. When George W. Bush enjoyed a Republican Congress, he succeeded in passing over 80 percent of his bills. But his success fell dramatically with the election of a Democratic Congress.

★ **pocket veto**
Effective veto of a bill when Congress adjourns within 10 days of passing it and the president fails to sign it.

★ **override**
Voting in Congress to enact legislation vetoed by the president; requires a two-thirds vote in both the House and Senate.

To veto a bill passed by the Congress, the president sends to Congress a veto message specifying reasons for not signing it. If the president takes no action for 10 days (excluding Sundays) after a bill has been passed by Congress, the bill becomes law without the president's signature. However, if Congress has adjourned within 10 days of passing a bill and the president has not signed it, then the bill does not become law; this outcome is called a **pocket veto**.

A bill returned to Congress with a presidential veto message can be passed into law over the president's opposition by a two-thirds vote of both houses. (A bill that has received a pocket veto cannot be overridden because the Congress is no longer in session.) In other words, the president needs only to hold the loyalty of more than one-third of *either* the House or the Senate to sustain a veto. If congressional leaders cannot count on the votes to **override**, they are forced to bargain with the president. "What will the president accept?" becomes a key legislative question.

The president's bargaining power with Congress has been enhanced over the years by a history of success in sustaining presidential vetoes. From George Washington to George W. Bush, more than 96 percent of all presidential vetoes have been sustained (see Table 11.3).

Table *11.3*   Saying No: Presidential Vetoes

Presidential vetoes of bills passed by Congress are seldom overridden. The threat of a veto adds to the president's power in bargaining with the Congress.

President	Total Vetoes*	Vetoes Overridden	Percentage of Vetoes Sustained
F. Roosevelt	633	9	99%
Truman	250	12	95
Eisenhower	181	2	99
Kennedy	21	0	100
L. Johnson	30	0	100
Nixon	43	5	90
Ford	66	12	85
Carter	31	2	94
Reagan	78	8	91
Bush	46	1	98
Clinton	37	2	95
Bush (2001–2006)	1	0	100
Bush (2007)	7	1	86

*Regular vetoes plus pocket vetoes.

Source: Harold W. Stanley and Richard G. Niemi, *Vital Statistics on American Politics, 1999–2000.* Washington, D.C.: CQ Press, 2000, p. 256. Updated by authors.

Line-Item Veto Power Denied   For many years, presidents, both Democratic and Republican, petitioned Congress to give them the **line-item veto**, the ability to veto some provisions of a bill while accepting other provisions. The lack of presidential line-item veto power was especially frustrating when dealing with appropriations bills because the president could not veto specific pork-barrel provisions from major spending bills for defense, education, housing, welfare, and so on. Finally, in 1996 Congress granted the president authority to "cancel" spending items in any appropriation act and any limited tax benefit. Such cancellation would take effect immediately unless blocked by a special "disapproval bill" passed by Congress.

However, opponents of the line-item veto successfully challenged its constitutionality, arguing that it transfers legislative power—granted by the Constitution only to Congress—to the president. The U.S. Supreme Court agreed: "There is no provision in the Constitution that authorizes the president to enact or amend or repeal statutes." The line-item veto, the Court said, "authorizes the president himself to elect to repeal laws, for his own policy reasons" and therefore violates the law-making procedures set forth in Article I of the Constitution.[27]

★ **line-item veto**
Power of the chief executive to reject some portions of a bill without rejecting all of it.

Global Leader

The president of the United States is the leader of the world's largest and most powerful democracy. During the Cold War, the president of the United States was seen as the leader of the "free world." The threat of Soviet expansionism, the huge military forces of the Warsaw Pact, and Soviet-backed guerrilla wars around the world all added to the global role of the American president as the defender of democratic values. In today's post–Cold War world, Western Europe and Japan are formidable economic competitors and no longer routinely defer to

Setting the Tone

The president is recognized throughout the world as the American "head of state"; this power aids him in dominating American foreign and defense policy making. British Prime Minister Tony Blair was one of the very few foreign leaders to support Bush's policies in Iraq, support that eventually led to Blair's replacement.

★ **diplomatic recognition**
Power of the president to grant "legitimacy" to or withhold it from a government of another nation (to declare or refuse to declare it "rightful").

American political leadership. But if a new stable world order based on democracy and self-determination is to emerge, the president of the United States must provide the necessary leadership.

Global leadership is based on a president's powers of persuasion.[28] Presidents are more persuasive when the American economy is strong, when American military forces are perceived as ready and capable, and when the president is seen as having the support of the American people and Congress. America's allies as well as its enemies perceive the president as the controlling force over U.S. foreign and military policy. Only occasionally do they seek to bypass the president and appeal to the Congress or to American public opinion.

Presidents sometimes prefer their global role to the much more contentious infighting of domestic politics. Abroad, presidents are treated with great dignity as head of the world's most powerful state. In contrast, at home presidents must confront hostile and insulting reporters, backbiting bureaucrats, demanding interest groups, and contentious members of Congress.

Foreign Policy   As the nation's chief diplomat, the president has the principal responsibility for formulating U.S. foreign policy. The president's constitutional powers in foreign affairs are relatively modest. Presidents have the power to make treaties with foreign nations "with the Advice and Consent of the Senate." Presidents may negotiate with nations separately or through international organizations such as the North Atlantic Treaty Organization (NATO) or the United Nations, where the president determines the U.S. position in that body's deliberations. The Constitution also empowers the president to "appoint Ambassadors, other public Ministers, and Consuls" and to "receive Ambassadors." This power of **diplomatic recognition** permits a president to grant legitimacy to or withhold it from ruling groups around the world (to declare or refuse to declare them "rightful"). Despite controversy, President Franklin Roosevelt officially recognized the communist regime in Russia in 1933, Richard Nixon recognized the communist government of the People's Republic of China in 1972, and Carter recognized the communist Sandinistas' regime in Nicaragua in 1979. To date, all presidents have withheld diplomatic recognition of the Castro government in Cuba.

Presidents have expanded on these modest constitutional powers to dominate American foreign policy making. In part, they have done so as a product of their role as Commander-in-Chief. Military force is the ultimate diplomatic language. During wartime, or when war is threatened, military and foreign policy become inseparable. The president must decide on the use of force and, equally important, when and under what conditions to order a cease-fire or an end to hostilities.

Presidents have also come to dominate foreign policy as a product of the customary international recognition of the head of state as the legitimate voice of a government. Although nations may also watch the words and actions of the American Congress, the president's statements are generally taken to represent the official position of the U.S. government.

Treaties   Treaties the president makes "by and with the Advice and Consent of the Senate" are legally binding upon the United States. The Constitution specifies that "all Treaties made. . . under the Authority of the United States, shall be the supreme Law of the Land, and the Judges in every State shall be bound thereby" (Article VI). Thus treaty provisions are directly enforceable in federal courts.

Although presidents may or may not listen to "advice" from the Senate on foreign policy, no formal treaty is valid unless "two-thirds of the Senators present concur" to its ratification. Although the Senate has ratified the vast majority of treaties, presidents must be sensitive to Senate concerns. The Senate defeat of the Versailles Treaty in 1920, which formally ended World War I and established the League of Nations, prompted Presidents Roosevelt and Truman to include prominent Democratic and Republican members of the Senate Foreign Relations Committee in the delegations that drafted the United Nations Charter in 1945 and the NATO Treaty in 1949.

Executive Agreements

Over the years, presidents have come to rely heavily on **executive agreements** with other governments rather than formal treaties. An executive agreement signed by the president of the United States has much the same effect in international relations as a treaty. However, an executive agreement does not require Senate ratification. Presidents have asserted that their constitutional power to execute the laws, command the armed services, and determine foreign policy gives them the authority to make agreements with other nations and heads of state without obtaining approval of the U.S. Senate. However, unlike treaties, executive agreements do not supersede laws of the United States or of the states with which they conflict, but they are otherwise binding on the United States.

The use of executive agreements in important foreign policy matters was developed by President Franklin Roosevelt. Prior to his administration, executive agreements had been limited to minor matters. But in 1940, Roosevelt agreed to trade fifty American destroyers to England in exchange for the use of naval bases in Newfoundland and the Caribbean. Roosevelt was intent on helping the British in their struggle against Nazi Germany, but before the Japanese attack on Pearl Harbor in 1941, isolationist sentiment in the Senate was too strong to win a two-thirds ratifying vote for such an agreement. Toward the end of World War II, Roosevelt at the Yalta Conference and Truman at the Potsdam Conference negotiated secret executive agreements dividing the occupation of Germany between the Western Allies and the Soviet Union.

Congress has sometimes objected to executive agreements as usurping its own powers. In the Case Act of 1972, Congress required the president to inform Congress of all executive agreements within 60 days, but the act does not limit the president's power to make agreements. It is easier for Congress to renege on executive agreements than on treaties that the Senate has ratified. In 1973 President Nixon signed an executive agreement with South Vietnamese President Nguyen Van Thieu pledging that the United States would "respond with full force" if North Vietnam violated the Paris Peace Agreement that ended American participation in the Vietnam War. But when North Vietnam reinvaded the south in 1975, Congress rejected President Gerald Ford's pleas for renewed military aid to the South Vietnamese government, and Ford knew that it had become politically impossible for the United States to respond with force.

Intelligence

The president is responsible for the intelligence activities of the United States. Presidents have undertaken intelligence activities since the founding of the nation. During the Revolutionary War, General George Washington nurtured small groups of patriots living behind British lines who supplied him with information on Redcoat troop movements.[29] Today, the Director of National Intelligence (DNI) is appointed by the president (subject to Senate confirmation) and reports directly to the president.

★ **executive agreements**
Agreements with other nations signed by the president of the United States but less formal (and hence potentially less binding) than a treaty because it does not require Senate confirmation.

The Central Intelligence Agency buildings in Langley, Virginia, northwest of Washington, D.C., on the other side of the Potomac River.

★ **covert actions**
Secret intelligence activities outside U.S. borders undertaken with specific authorization by the president; acknowledgment of U.S. sponsorship would defeat or compromise their purpose.

The DNI coordinates the activities of the "intelligence community" (see *Politics Up Close*: "Reorganizing Intelligence After '9/11'" in Chapter 12). Some elements of the intelligence community—the Central Intelligence Agency, the Defense Intelligence Agency, the National Security Agency, the National Reconnaissance Office, and the National Geo-Spacial Agency—deal exclusively with intelligence collection, analysis and distribution. Other elements of the intelligence community are located in the Department of Defense, Department of Homeland Security, Federal Bureau of Investigation, Department of State, Department of Energy, and Department of the Treasury. Indeed, the fragmentation of the intelligence community may be its principal weakness.[30]

The Central Intelligence Agency   The CIA provides intelligence on national security to the president, the DNI, the National Security Council, and other top Washington decision makers. The CIA is responsible for (1) assembly, analysis, and dissemination of intelligence information from all agencies in the intelligence community; (2) collection of human intelligence from abroad; (3) with specific "presidential findings," the conduct of **covert actions**, including paramilitary special operations.

Covert actions refer to activities in support of the national interest of the United States that would be ineffective if their sponsorship were made public. For example, one of the largest covert actions ever undertaken by the United States was the support, for nearly 10 years, of the Afghan rebels fighting Soviet occupation of their country during the Afghanistan War (1978–88). Public acknowledgment of such aid would have assisted the Soviet-backed regime in Afghanistan to claim that the rebels were not true patriots but rather "puppets" of the United States. The rebels themselves did not wish to acknowledge U.S. aid publicly, even

Secret Agreements
The "Big Three," comprised of Prime Minister Winston Churchill of Great Britain (right), Marshal Josef Stalin of the Soviet Union (left), and a gravely ill President Franklin Roosevelt (middle), traveled to Yalta, a port on Russia's Crimean peninsula, and negotiated secret executive agreements dividing Germany among the Allies in 1945. Germany remained divided until 1989, when protesters tore down the Berlin Wall and the Soviet Union under Mikhail Gorbachev acquiesced in the unification of Germany under a democratic government.

though they knew it was essential to the success of their cause. Hence Presidents Carter and Reagan aided the Afghan rebels through covert action.

Covert action is, by definition, secret. And secrecy spawns elaborate conspiracy theories and flamboyant tales of intrigue and deception. In fact, most covert actions consist of routine transfers of economic aid and military equipment to pro-U.S. forces that do not wish to acknowledge such aid publicly. Although most covert actions would have widespread support among the American public if they were done openly, secrecy opens the possibility that a president will undertake to do by covert action what would be opposed by Congress and the American people if they knew about it.

In the atmosphere of suspicion and distrust engendered by the Watergate scandal, Congress passed intelligence oversight legislation in 1974 requiring a written "presidential finding" for any covert action and requiring that members of the House and Senate Intelligence Committees be informed of all covert actions. The president does not have to obtain congressional approval for covert actions; but Congress can halt such actions if it chooses to do so.

Commander-in-Chief

Global power derives primarily from the president's role as Commander-in-Chief of the armed forces of the United States. Presidential command over the armed forces is not merely symbolic; presidents may issue direct military orders to troops in the field. As president, Washington personally led troops to end the Whiskey Rebellion in 1794; Abraham Lincoln issued direct orders to his generals in the Civil War; Lyndon Johnson personally chose bombing targets in Vietnam; and George H.W. Bush personally ordered the 1991 Gulf War cease-fire after 100 hours of ground fighting. All presidents, whether they are experienced in world affairs or not, soon learn after taking office that their influence throughout the world is heavily dependent upon the command of capable military forces.

War-Making Power   Constitutionally, war-making power is divided between the Congress and the president. Congress has the power "to declare war," but the president is the "Commander-in-Chief of the Army and Navy of the United States."

In reality, however, presidents have exercised their powers as Commander-in-Chief to order U.S. forces into military action overseas on many occasions—from John Adams's ordering of U.S. naval forces to attack French ships (1798–99), to Harry Truman's decision to intervene in the Korean War (1951–53), to Lyndon Johnson's and Richard Nixon's conduct of the Vietnam War (1965–73), to George H.W. Bush's Operation Desert Storm (1991), to Bill Clinton's interventions in Bosnia and Kosovo (1998–99), to George W. Bush's military actions in Afghanistan (2001) and Iraq (2003). The Supreme Court has consistently refused to hear cases involving the war powers of the president and Congress.[31]

Thus, although Congress retains the formal power to "declare war," in modern times wars are seldom "declared." Instead, they begin with direct military actions, and the president, as Commander-in-Chief of the armed forces, determines what those actions will be. Historically, Congress accepted the fact that only the president has the information-gathering facilities and the ability to act with the speed and secrecy required for military decisions during periods of crisis. Not until the Vietnam War was there serious congressional debate over whether the president has the power to commit the nation to war.

War Powers Resolution   In the early days of the Vietnam War, the liberal leadership of the nation strongly supported Democratic President Lyndon Johnson's

Soldiers from Bravo Company, Special Troops Battalion, 82nd Airborne Division, Task Force Gladius wait for a CH-47 Chinook helicopter at the landing zone at Forward Operating Base Morales-Frasier in Afghanistan on January 20, 2008.

power to commit the nation to war. By 1969, however, many congressional leaders had withdrawn their support of the war. With a new Republican president, Richard Nixon, and a Democratic Congress, congressional attacks on presidential policy became much more partisan.

Antiwar members of Congress made several attempts to end the war by cutting off money for U.S. military activity in Southeast Asia. Such legislation only passed after President Nixon announced a peace agreement in 1973, however. It is important to note that Congress has *never* voted to cut off funds to support American armies while they were in the field.

Congress also passed the **War Powers Resolution**, designed to restrict presidential war-making powers, in 1973. (President Nixon vetoed the bill, but the Watergate affair undermined his support in Congress, which overrode his veto.) The act has four major provisions:

★ **War Powers Resolution**
Bill passed in 1973 to limit presidential war-making powers; it restricts when, why, and for how long a president can commit U.S. forces and requires notification of and, in many cases, approval by Congress.

Think Again

Should Congress have the authority to call home U.S. troops sent by the president to engage in military actions overseas?

1. In the absence of a congressional declaration of war, the president can commit armed forces to hostilities or to "situations where imminent involvement in hostilities is clearly indicated by the circumstances" only:
   ★ To repel an armed attack on the United States or to forestall the "direct and imminent threat of such an attack."
   ★ To repel an armed attack against U.S. armed forces outside the United States or to forestall the threat of such attack.
   ★ To protect and evacuate U.S. citizens and nationals in another country if their lives are threatened.

2. The president must report promptly to Congress the commitment of forces for such purposes.

3. Involvement of U.S. forces must be no longer than 60 days unless Congress authorizes their continued use by specific legislation.

4. Congress can end a presidential commitment by resolution, an action that does not require the president's signature.

Presidential Noncompliance   The War Powers Resolution raises constitutional questions. A Commander-in-Chief clearly can order U.S. forces to go anywhere. Presumably, Congress cannot constitutionally command troops, yet that is what the act attempts to do by specifying that troops must come home if Congress orders them to do so or if Congress simply fails to endorse the president's decision to commit them. No president—Democrat or Republican—can allow Congress to usurp this presidential authority. Thus, since the passage of the War Powers Resolution, presidents have continued to undertake military actions on their own initiative (see Table 18.1 in Chapter 18).

Politically, it is often important for the president to show the world, and especially enemies of the United States, that he has congressional support for going to war. For this reason, presidents have asked Congress for resolutions in support of using military means to achieve specific goals. President George H.W. Bush asked for and received (by a close vote) a resolution of support to use military force to oust Iraqi forces from Kuwait in 1991. President George W. Bush won strong support for a congressional resolution in 2002 to allow him to use military force to make Saddam Hussein comply with U.N. resolutions. Both presidents claimed that they had the constitutional authority as Commander-in-Chief to use military force even *without* such resolutions. But politically such resolutions strengthen the president when he chooses to use military force. (See "Political Support for War in Iraq" in Chapter 18.)

Presidential Use of Military Force in Domestic Affairs   Democracies are generally reluctant to use military force in domestic affairs. Yet the president has the constitutional authority to "take Care that the Laws be faithfully executed" and, as Commander-in-Chief of the armed forces, can send them across the nation as well as across the globe. The Constitution appears to limit presidential use of military forces in domestic affairs to protecting states "against domestic Violence" and only "on Application of the [state] Legislature or the [state] Executive (when the Legislature cannot be convened)" (Article IV, Section 4). Although this provision would seem to require states themselves to request federal troops before they can be sent to quell domestic violence, historically presidents have not waited for state requests to send troops when federal laws, federal court orders, or federal constitutional guarantees are being violated.

Enforcing the Law

Despite a Supreme Court ruling that segregation in education was illegal, many southern states continued to try to keep their schoolhouse doors closed to black students. Here Elizabeth Eckford, a 15-year-old resident of Little Rock, Arkansas, is denied entry to Central High School by a member of the National Guard under the orders of Governor Orval Faubus. Not until President Dwight Eisenhower sent the 101st Airborne Division to Little Rock were the high court's desegregation orders enforced.

U.S. National Guard soldiers watch as black children go to school on October 3, 1957, in Little Rock, Arkansas.

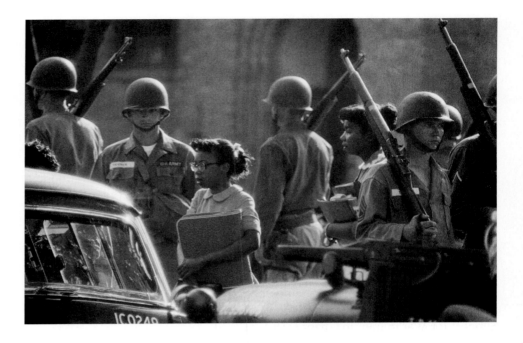

Relying on their constitutional duty to "faithfully execute" federal laws and their command over the nation's armed forces, presidents have used military force in domestic disputes since the earliest days of the Republic. Perhaps the most significant example of a president's use of military force in domestic affairs was Dwight Eisenhower's 1957 dispatch of U.S. troops to Little Rock, Arkansas, to enforce a federal court's desegregation order. In this case, the president acted directly *against* the expressed wishes of the state's governor, Orval Faubus, who had posted state units of the National Guard at the entrance of Central High School to prevent the admission of black students, which had been ordered by the federal court. Eisenhower officially called Arkansas's National Guard units into federal service, took personal command of them, and then ordered them to leave the high school. He then replaced the Guard units with U.S. federal troops under orders to enforce desegregation. Eisenhower's action marked a turning point in the struggle over school desegregation. The Supreme Court's historic desegregation decision in *Brown v. Board of Education of Topeka* might have been rendered meaningless had not the president chosen to use military force to secure compliance.

The Vice-Presidential Waiting Game

Historically, the principal responsibility of the vice president is to be prepared to assume the responsibilities of the president. Eight vice presidents have become president following the death of their predecessor. But vice presidents have not always been well prepared: Harry Truman, who succeeded Franklin Roosevelt while World War II still raged, had never even been informed about the secret atomic bomb project.

Political Selection Process The political process surrounding the initial choice of vice-presidential candidates does not necessarily produce the persons best qualified to occupy the White House. It is, indeed, a "crap shoot"[32]; if it produces a person well qualified to be president, it is only by luck. Candidates may *claim* that they select running mates who are highly qualified to take over as president, but this claim is seldom true.

Traditionally, vice-presidential candidates have been chosen to give political "balance" to the ticket, to attract voters who might otherwise desert the party or stay home. Democratic presidential candidates sought to give ideological and geographical balance to the ticket. Northern liberal presidential candidates (Adlai Stevenson, John Kennedy) selected southern conservatives (John Sparkman, Estes Kefauver, Lyndon Johnson) as their running mates. Walter Mondale selected New York Congresswoman Geraldine Ferraro in a bold move to exploit the gender gap. Liberal Massachusetts Governor Michael Dukakis returned to the earlier Democratic tradition, choosing to run with conservative Texas Senator Lloyd Bentsen. Bill Clinton sought a different kind of balance: Al Gore's military service in Vietnam and his unimpeachable family life helped offset reservations about Clinton's avoidance of the draft and his past marital troubles. Massachusetts Senator John Kerry was viewed as serious, sober, and reserved, so the choice of the cheerful, enthusiastic, and outgoing North Carolinian John Edwards seemed to balance the ticket in both image and geography.

Republican presidential candidates sought to accommodate either the conservative or moderate wing of their party in their vice-presidential selections. Moderate Eisenhower chose conservative Nixon in 1952. Conservative Ronald Reagan turned to his moderate primary opponent George H. W. Bush in 1980, who in 1988 tapped conservative Dan Quayle. But in 2000 George W. Bush chose to add *experience* to the ticket by choosing Dick Cheney, Secretary of Defense in his father's administration.

In 2008 Barack Obama chose Joe Biden, chairman of the Senate Foreign Relations Committee, in an effort to overcome an image of inexperience in foreign affairs. And in a surprise move McCain added excitement to the Republican ticket by selecting Alaska Governor Sarah Palin, social conservative and mother of five children (see *Politics Up Close:* "Choosing Veeps in 2008").

Vice-Presidential Roles   Presidents determine what role their vice presidents will play in their administration. Constitutionally, the only role given the vice president is to preside over the Senate and to vote in case of a tie in that body. Presiding over the Senate is so tiresome that vice presidents perform it only on rare ceremonial occasions, but they have occasionally cast important tie-breaking votes. If the president chooses not to give the vice president much responsibility, the vice presidency becomes what its first occupant, John Adams, described as "the most insignificant office that ever the invention of man contrived or his imagination conceived." One of Franklin Roosevelt's three vice presidents, the salty Texan John Nance Garner, put it more pithily, saying that the job "ain't worth a bucket of warm spit" (reporters of that era may have substituted "spit" for Garner's actual wording).

The political functions of vice presidents are more significant than their governmental functions. Vice presidents are obliged to support their president and the administration's policies. But sometimes a president will use the vice president to launch strongly partisan political attacks on opponents while the president remains "above" the political squabbles and hence more "presidential." Richard Nixon served as a partisan "attack dog" for Eisenhower, and then gave Spiro Agnew this task in his own administration. The attack role allows the vice president also to help cement political support for the president among highly partisan ideologues. Vice presidents are also useful in campaign fund raising. Large contributors expect a personal touch; the president cannot be everywhere at once, so the vice president is frequently a guest at political fund-raising events. Presidents also have traditionally sent their vice presidents to attend funerals of world leaders and placed them at the head of governmental commissions.

Politics Up Close   Joe Biden and Sarah Palin

John McCain was behind in the polls when he surprised political observers with his choice of little-known Alaska Governor Sarah Palin as his vice presidential running mate. Palin was youthful, attractive, folksy, and socially conservative. She captivated Republicans with her life story as a small-town "hockey mom," a mother of five—including a baby with Down syndrome—who first joined the PTA, became Mayor of Wasilla, Alaska, fought the Republican establishment of that state to win the GOP gubernatorial nomination, and then went on to become an extremely popular governor (with over 80 percent approval ratings). McCain hoped that Palin would solidify his base among conservative Republicans and perhaps distract voters from his age. But Palin's inexperience raised questions regarding her qualifications to serve as president.

Barack Obama's selection of Delaware Senator Joe Biden as his running mate balanced the ticket with experience in Washington and foreign-policy expertise. Biden had first won his Senate seat in 1972 as an anti–Vietnam War candidate. He was just 30 years old, the minimum age the Constitution specifies for a member of the Senate. He went on to serve over three decades in the Senate, including prestigious posts as Chairman of the Judiciary Committee and Chairman of the Foreign Relations Committee. He had sought unsuccessfully to be the Democratic presidential nominee himself, even declaring that Obama was not "ready" for the presidency and would need "on-the-job training." Moreover, Biden had voted for the war in Iraq. But his liberal voting record paralleled that of Obama, and his long service in the Senate and his knowledge of foreign affairs provided balance to Obama's relative newness to national politics. Whatever differences Obama and Biden may have had in the past were set aside in order to present a balanced Democratic ticket in 2008.

Vice presidents themselves strive to play a more significant policy-making role, often as senior presidential adviser and confidant. Recent presidents have encouraged the development of the vice presidency along these lines. Walter Mondale, the first modern vice president to perform this function, had an office in the White House next to the president's, had access to all important meetings and policy decisions, and was invited to lunch privately each week with President Carter. Vice President Al Gore was routinely stationed behind President Clinton during major policy pronouncements. Clinton reportedly gave great weight to Gore's views on the environment, on cost savings in government, and on information technology. Gore also spoke out aggressively in defense of Clinton's policies. Thus the senior advisory role is becoming institutionalized over time (see *People in Politics:* "Joe Biden and Sarah Palin").

The Waiting Game   Politically ambitious vice presidents are obliged to play a torturous waiting game. They can use their time in office to build a network of contacts that can later be tapped for campaign contributions, workers, and support in their own race for the presidency, should they decide to run. But winning the presidency following retirement of their former boss requires a delicate balance. They must show loyalty to the president in order to win the president's endorsement and also to help ensure that the administration in which they participated is judged a success by voters. At the same time, vice presidents must demonstrate that they have independent leadership qualities and a policy agenda of their own to offer voters. This dilemma becomes more acute as their boss's term nears its end.

A *Constitutional* Note

How Broad Is the "Executive Power"?

The Constitution states that "The executive Power shall be vested in a President of the United States of America" (Article II). The Constitution also gives the president specific powers; for example "to take care that the laws be faithfully executed"; to appoint and remove executive officials; "to give to the Congress information on the State of the Union and recommend to their Consideration such Measures as he shall judge necessary and expedient"; to veto legislation passed by Congress, subject to override by a two-thirds vote of both houses; to convene special sessions of Congress; to make treaties "with the Advice and Consent of the Senate"; to receive ambassadors; to grant pardons; to appoint federal court and Supreme Court judges, subject to Senate confirmation; and to serve as Commander-in-Chief of the Armed Forces. And the Congress may by law add to the president's powers. But does the Constitution's general grant of "executive power" give the president any powers that are not specified later in the Constitution or given to the president by acts of Congress? Most presidents have asserted a general "executive power," or, as Theodore Roosevelt said, "My belief was that it was not only his right but his duty to do anything that the needs of the nation demanded, unless such action was forbidden by the Constitution or by the laws." But when the Congress has addressed a problem by law, the president is obliged to follow the law, whether he likes it or not.[a] Closely related to the question of executive power is the question of "executive privilege." Can a president withhold information from the Congress or the courts to preserve confidentiality within the executive branch? The Supreme Court has acknowledged a constitutional protection for the "president's need for complete candor and objectivity from advisers" and for "military, diplomatic, or sensitive national security secrets,"[b] But the president cannot withhold information from the courts in a criminal investigation not related to defense or diplomacy, as Richard Nixon found to his dismay in the Watergate affair.

[a]Youngstown Sheet & Tube Co. v. Sawyer, 343 U.S. 579 (1952).
[b]United States v. Nixon, 418 U.S. 683 (1974).

Historically, only a few sitting vice presidents have won election to the White House: John Adams (1797), Thomas Jefferson (1801), Martin Van Buren (1837), and George H.W. Bush (1988). In addition, four vice presidents won election in their own right after entering the Oval Office as a result of their predecessors' death: Theodore Roosevelt (1901), Calvin Coolidge (1923), Harry Truman (1945), and Lyndon Johnson (1963). Only one nonsitting former vice president has been elected president: Richard Nixon (1968, after losing to Kennedy in 1960). Thus out of the forty-eight men who served the nation as vice president through 2008, only nine were ever elected to higher office.

Summary
Who Gets What: The Presidency

The American presidency is potentially the most powerful office in the world. As head of state, the president symbolizes national unity and speaks on behalf of the American people to the world. And as Commander-in-Chief of the armed forces, the president has a powerful voice in national and international affairs. The president also symbolizes government for the American people, reassuring them in times of hardship and crises.

★ As head of the government, the president is expected to set forth policy priorities for the nation, to manage the economy, to mobilize political support for the administration's programs in Congress, to manage the giant federal bureaucracy, and to recruit people for policy-making positions in both the executive and judicial branches of government.

★ Popular expectations of presidential leadership far exceed the formal constitutional powers of the president: chief administrator, chief legislator, chief diplomat, Commander-in-Chief, and chief of state. The vague reference in the Constitution to "executive Power" has been used by presidents to justify actions beyond those specified elsewhere in the Constitution or in laws of Congress.

★ It is the president's vast political resources that provide the true power base of the presidency. These include the president's reputation for power, personal popularity with the public, access to the media, and party leadership position.

★ Presidential popularity and power are usually highest at the beginning of the term of office. Presidents are more likely to be successful in Congress during this honeymoon period. Presidents' popularity also rises during crises, especially during international threats and military actions. But prolonged indecision and stalemate erode popular support, as do scandals and economic recessions.

★ As chief executive, the president oversees the huge federal bureaucracy. Presidential control of the executive branch is exercised through executive orders, appointments and removals, and budgetary recommendations to Congress. But the president's control of the executive branch is heavily circumscribed by Congress, which establishes executive departments and agencies, regulates their activities by law, and determines their budgets each year.

★ Presidents are expected not only to initiate programs and policies but also to shepherd them through Congress. Presidential success scores in Congress indicate that presidents are more successful early in their term of office. Presidents who face a Congress controlled by the opposition party are far less successful in winning approval for their programs than presidents whose party holds a majority.

★ The veto is the president's most powerful weapon in dealing with Congress. The president needs to hold the loyalty of only one more than one-third of either the House or the Senate to sustain a veto. Few vetoes are overridden. The threat of a veto enables the president to bargain in Congress for more acceptable legislation.

★ During the long years of the Cold War, the president of the United States was the leader of the "free world." In the post–Cold War world, the president is still the leader of the world's most powerful democracy and is expected to exercise global leadership on behalf of a stable world order.

★ Presidents have come to dominate foreign policy through treaty making, executive agreements, control of intelligence activities, and international recognition of their role as head of state. Above all, presidents have used their power as Commander-in-Chief of the armed forces to decide when to make war and when to seek peace.

★ The global power of presidents derives primarily from this presidential role as Commander-in-Chief. Constitutionally, war-making power is divided between Congress and the president, but historically it has been the president who has ordered U.S. military forces into action. In the War Powers Resolution, Congress tried to reassert its war-making power after the Vietnam War, but the act has failed to restrain presidents. Presidents have also used the armed forces in domestic affairs to "take Care that the Laws be faithfully executed."

★ The principal responsibility of the vice president is to be prepared to assume the responsibilities of the president. However, the selection of the vice president is dominated more by political concerns than by consideration of presidential qualifications. Aside from officially presiding over the U.S. Senate, vice presidents perform whatever roles are assigned them by the president.

Key Terms

impeachment 379	White House press	honeymoon period 399	diplomatic
Watergate 382	corps 386	gridlock 399	recognition 402
executive privilege 382	executive orders 392	veto 399	executive agreements 403
impoundment 383	cabinet 394	pocket veto 400	covert actions 404
deferrals 383	National Security	override 400	War Powers
rescissions 383	Council (NSC) 395	line-item veto 401	Resolution 406

Suggested Readings

Barber, James David. *The Presidential Character: Predicting Performance in the White House.* 4th ed. Upper Saddle River, N.J.: Prentice Hall, 1992. Barber's original thesis that a president's performance in office is largely a function of active/passive and positive/negative character; includes classifications of twentieth-century presidents through Reagan.

Edwards, George C., and Stephen J. Wayne. *Presidential Leadership*. 7th ed. Belmont, Calif.: Wadsworth, 2006. Comprehensive text covering nomination and election of the president, relations with the public, the media, the bureaucracy, Congress and the courts.

Jacobson, Gary C. *A Divider, Not a Uniter*. New York: Langunton, 2008. Poll data showing that George W. Bush accelerated the polarization of the American people along party lines.

Lowi, Theodore. *The Personal President*. Ithaca, N.Y.: Cornell University Press, 1987. An examination of the presidency from the perspective of the public and its reliance on the president for reassurance in crises.

Pfiffner, James P. *The Modern Presidency*. 5th ed. Belmont, CA: Wordsworth, 2008. Text coverage of institutional relationships between president and the public, White House staff, executive branch, Congress, intelligence community, and so on.

Milkus, Stanley, and Michael Nelson. *The American Presidency: Origins and Development, 1776–2007*. 5th ed. Washington, D.C.: CQ Press, 2003. A comprehensive history of the presidency that argues that the institution is best understood by examining its development over time, describes the significant presidential actions in the early days of the Republic that shaped the office, as well as the modern era in which the president has replaced Congress and the political parties as the leading instrument of popular rule.

Neustadt, Richard E. *Presidential Power*. New York: Wiley, 1960. The classic argument that the president's power is the power to persuade, that the formal constitutional powers of the presidency provide only a framework for the president's use of persuasion, public prestige, reputation for power, and other personal attributes to exercise real power.

Pika, Joseph A., and John Maltese. *The Politics of the Presidency*. 7th ed. Washington, D.C.: CQ Press, 2008. An overview of the institution of the presidency, including George W. Bush as a wartime president.

Schultz, Jeffrey D. *Presidential Scandals*. Washington, D.C.: CQ Press, 1999. An historical survey of scandals in presidential administrations, from George Washington to Bill Clinton.

Suggested Web Sites

American Presidents www.americanpresidents.org
Biographical facts and key events in the lives of all U.S. presidents.

Cabinet www.whitehouse.gov/government/cabinet.html
The White House site provides the names of the current president's cabinet as well as those individuals with "cabinet-rank" status.

Center for the Study of the Presidency
www.thepresidency.org
Studies of the presidency and publication of the scholarly journal *Presidential Studies Quarterly*.

Central Intelligence Agency www.cia.gov
The CIA site provides information about the agency's mission, organization, values, press releases, and congressional testimony along with employment possibilities.

Defense Link www.defenselink.gov
Official site of U.S. Department of Defense, with news and links to Army, Navy, Air Force, and Marine Corps Web sites and other defense agencies and commands.

National Security Council www.whitehouse.gov/nsc
Site provides brief history of NSC plus new releases dealing with national security.

State Department www.state.gov
Official site includes news, travel warnings, international issues, and background notes on countries of the world.

Treaties in Force www.state.gov/www/global/legalaffairs
Complete list of all treaties of the United States in force as of January 1, 2000.

The White House www.whitehouse.gov
This official White House site provides up-to-date information or news about the current president's policies, speeches, appointments, proclamations, and cabinet members.

12 THE BUREAUCRACY

Bureaucratic Politics

" The politician displaces his private motives upon public objects and rationalizes the displacement in terms of public advantage. When this emotional and symbolic adjustment occurs in combination with facility in the acquisition of manipulative skill, the effective politician emerges. "

Harold Lasswell

Chapter *Outline*

✓ Think About Politics

1. Do bureaucrats in Washington have too much power?
   YES ◯   NO ◯

2. Should the federal bureaucracy be managed by nonpartisan professionals rather than people politically loyal to the president?
   YES ◯   NO ◯

3. Should the federal bureaucracy at all levels reflect the gender and minority ratios of the total civilian workforce?
   YES ◯   NO ◯

4. Do you believe the bureaucrats in Washington waste a lot of the money we pay in taxes?
   YES ◯   NO ◯

5. Do you believe the federal government is spending more money but delivering less service?
   YES ◯   NO ◯

6. Do you believe that the overall costs of federal regulatory activity are justified by the benefits?
   YES ◯   NO ◯

7. Do you believe bureaucratic regulations of all kinds are hurting America's competitiveness in the global economy?
   YES ◯   NO ◯

Power in Washington is not only exercised by the president, Congress, and courts, but also by 2.8 million federal bureaucrats—neither elected nor accountable to ordinary citizens—who determine in large measure who gets what in America.

Comparing Bureaucracies

Bureaucratic Power

Political conflict does not end after a law has been passed by Congress and signed by the president. The arena for conflict merely shifts from Capitol Hill and the White House to the **bureaucracy**—to the myriad departments, agencies, and bureaus of the federal executive branch that implement the law. Despite the popular impression that policy is decided by the president and Congress and merely implemented by the federal bureaucracy, in fact policy is also made by the bureaucracy. Indeed, it is often remarked that "implementation is the continuation of policy making by other means." The Washington bureaucracy is a major base of power in the American system of government—independent of Congress, the president, the courts, and the people. Indeed, controlling the bureaucracy has become a major challenge of democratic government.

The Nature of Bureaucracy "Bureaucracy" has become a negative term equated with red tape,[1] paper shuffling, duplication of effort, waste and inefficiency, impersonality, senseless regulations, and unresponsiveness to the needs of "real" people. But bureaucracy is really a form of social organization found not only in governments but also in corporations, armies, schools, and many other societal institutions. The German sociologist Max Weber described bureaucracy as a "rational" way for society to organize itself that has the following characteristics: a **chain of command** (hierarchical structure of authority in which command flows downward); a **division of labor** (work divided among many specialized workers in an effort to improve productivity); and **impersonality** (all persons within the bureaucracy treated on "merit" principles, and all "clients" served by the bureaucracy treated equally according to rules; all activities undertaken according to rules; records maintained to assure rules are followed).[2] Thus, according to Weber's definition, General Motors and IBM, the U.S. Marine Corps, the U.S. Department of Education, and all other institutions organized according to these principles are "bureaucracies."

The Growth of Bureaucratic Power Bureaucratic power has grown with advances in technology and increases in the size and complexity of society. There are a variety of explanations for this growth of power.

★ **bureaucracy**
Departments, agencies, bureaus, and offices that perform the functions of government.

★ **chain of command**
Hierarchical structure of authority in which command flows downward; typical of a bureaucracy.

★ **division of labor**
Division of work among many specialized workers in a bureaucracy.

★ **impersonality**
Treatment of all persons within a bureaucracy on the basis of "merit" and of all "clients" served by the bureaucracy equally according to rules.

You Are a Federal Administrator

Do bureaucrats in Washington have too much power?

You Are a Government Affairs Consultant in Texas

★ **implementation**
Development by the federal bureaucracy of procedures and activities to carry out policies legislated by Congress, it includes regulation as well as adjudication.

1. *Needed Expertise and Technological Advances* Congress and the president do not have the time, energy, or expertise to handle the details of policy making. A related explanation is that the increasing complexity and sophistication of technology require technical experts ("technocrats") to actually carry out the intent of Congress and the president. Neither the president nor the 535 members of Congress can look after the myriad details involved in environmental protection, occupational safety, air traffic control, or thousands of other responsibilities of government. So the president and Congress create bureaucracies, appropriate money for them, and authorize them to draw up detailed rules, regulations, and "guidelines" that actually govern the nation. Bureaucratic agencies receive only vague and general directions from the president and Congress. Actual governance is in the hands of the Environmental Protection Agency, the Occupational Safety and Health Administration, the Federal Aviation Administration, and hundreds of similar agencies (see Figure 12.1).

2. *Symbolic Politics* But there are also political explanations for the growth of bureaucratic power. Congress and the president often deliberately pass vague and ambiguous laws. These laws allow elected officials to show symbolically their concerns for environmental protection, occupational safety, and so on, yet avoid the controversies surrounding actual application of those lofty principles. Bureaucracies must then give practical meaning to these symbolic measures by developing specific rules and regulations. If the rules and regulations prove unpopular, Congress and the president can blame the bureaucrats and pretend that these unpopular decisions are a product of an "ungovernable" Washington bureaucracy (see *Controversy:* What Is your Impression of These Federal Agencies?")

3. *Bureaucratic Explanation* There is also a bureaucratic explanation of the growth in the size and influence of government agencies. Bureaucracy has become its own source of power. Bureaucrats have a personal stake in expanding the size of their own agencies and budgets and adding to their own regulatory authority. They can mobilize their "client" groups (interest groups that directly benefit from the agency's programs, such as environmental groups on behalf of the Environmental Protection Agency, farm groups for the Department of Agriculture, the National Education Association for the Department of Education) in support of larger budgets and expanded authority.

4. *Popular Demands* Finally, it has been argued that "big government" is really an expression of democratic sentiments. People want to use the power of government to improve their lives—to regulate and develop the economy, to guarantee civil rights, to develop their communities, and so on. Conservative opponents of government growth are overlooking popular demands.[3]

Bureaucratic Power: Implementation Bureaucracies are not *constitutionally* empowered to decide policy questions. But they do so, nevertheless, as they perform their tasks of implementation, regulation, and adjudication.

Implementation is the development of procedures and activities to carry out policies legislated by Congress. It may involve creating new agencies or bureaus or assigning new responsibilities to old agencies. It often requires bureaucracies to translate laws into operational rules and regulations and usually to allocate resources—money, personnel, offices, supplies—to the new function. All of these tasks involve decisions by bureaucrats, decisions that drive how the law

Figure *12.1* The Federal Bureaucracy

Although the president has constitutional authority over the operation of the executive branch, Congress creates departments and agencies and appropriates their funds, and Senate approval is needed for presidential appointees to head departments.

Controversy

What Is Your Impression of These Federal Agencies?

Many U.S. government organizations have come under close scrutiny after the terrorist attacks of September 11, 2001, and in the years following. A poll of Americans at the end of 2007 asked the public what their impression was of some key government agencies—ones which politicians and the media regularly bring to the public's attention. Although the poll did not ask about all agencies, it does offer a sense of how Americans view some of the more prominent departments and agencies of the U.S. government.

The Federal Emergency Management Agency, FEMA, was charged with bureaucratic mismanagement during Hurricane Katrina and its aftermath. Survivors endured long lines and inadequate service.

Q. *"Please tell me if you have a favorable or unfavorable impression of _____ Is that very favorable/unfavorable or somewhat favorable/unfavorable?"*

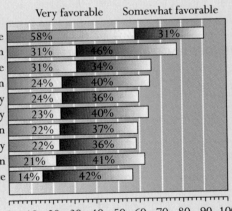

	Very favorable	Somewhat favorable
U.S. Postal Service	58%	31%
Federal Bureau of Investigation	31%	46%
Department of Defense	31%	34%
Social Security Administration	24%	40%
Department of Homeland Security	24%	36%
Environmental Protection Agency	23%	40%
Department of Education	22%	37%
Central Intelligence Agency	22%	36%
Food and Drug Administration	21%	41%
Internal Revenue Service	14%	42%

0 10 20 30 40 50 60 70 80 90 100
Percent

Source: Associated Press/Ipsos-Public Affairs Poll. December 17–December 19, 2007. The Roper Center for Public Opinion Research, University of Connecticut.

will actually affect society. In some cases, bureaucrats delay the development of regulations based on a new law, assign enforcement responsibility to existing offices with other higher priority tasks, and allocate few people with limited resources to the task. In other cases, bureaucrats act forcefully in making new regulations, insist on strict enforcement, assign responsibilities to newly created aggressive offices with no other assignments, and allocate a great deal of staff time and agency resources to the task. Interested groups have a strong stake in these decisions, and they actively seek to influence the bureaucracy.

Bureaucratic Power: Regulation

Regulation involves the development of formal rules for implementing legislation. The federal bureaucracy publishes about 80,000 pages of rules in the *Federal Register* each year. The Environmental Protection Agency (EPA) is especially active in developing regulations governing the handling of virtually every substance in the air, water, or ground. The rule-making process for federal agencies is prescribed by an Administrative Procedures Act, first passed in 1946 and amended many times. Generally, agencies must:

1. Announce in the *Federal Register* that a new regulation is being considered.

2. Hold hearings to allow interested groups to present evidence and arguments regarding the proposed regulation.

3. Conduct research on the proposed regulation's economic and environmental impacts.

4. Solicit "public comments" (usually the arguments of interest groups).

5. Consult with higher officials, including the Office of Management and Budget.

6. Publish the new regulation in the *Federal Register.*

Regulatory battles are important because formal regulations that appear in the *Federal Register* have the effect of law. Congress can amend or repeal a regulation only by passing new legislation and obtaining the president's signature. Controversial bureaucratic regulations often remain in place because Congress is slow to act, because key committee members block corrective legislation, or because the president refuses to sign bills overturning the regulation.

Bureaucratic Power: Adjudication

Adjudication involves bureaucratic decisions about individual cases. Rule making resembles the legislative process, and adjudication resembles the judicial process. In adjudication, bureaucrats decide whether a person or firm is failing to comply with laws or regulations and, if so, what penalties or corrective actions are to be applied. Regulatory agencies and commissions—for example, the National Labor Relations Board, the Federal Communications Commission, the Equal Employment Opportunity Commission, the Federal Trade Commission, the Securities and Exchange Commission—are heavily engaged in adjudication. Their elaborate procedures and body of previous decisions closely resemble the court system. Losers may appeal to the federal courts, but the record of agency success in the federal courts discourages many appeals.

Bureaucratic Power: Administrative Discretion

Much of the work of bureaucrats is administrative routine—issuing Social Security checks, printing forms, delivering the mail. Routines are repetitive tasks performed according to established rules and procedures. Yet bureaucrats almost always have some discretion in performing even the most routine tasks. Discretion is greatest when

★ **regulation**
Development by the federal bureaucracy of formal rules for implementing legislation.

You Are the President of MEDICORP

★ **adjudication**
Decision making by the federal bureaucracy as to whether or not an individual or organization has complied with or violated government laws and/or regulations.

Paper Jam

Jennifer Garbach, left, of Philadelphia, Pennsylvania, and other customers wait in line to mail their parcel packages at the Bustleton branch of the U.S. Post Office in Philadelphia on December 17, 2003.

★ **budget maximization**
Bureaucrats' tendencies to expand their agencies' budgets, staff, and authority.

★ **discretionary funds**
Budgeted funds not earmarked for specific purposes but available to be spent in accordance with the best judgment of a bureaucrat.

You Are the Head of FEMA

cases do not exactly fit established rules, or when more than one rule might be applied to the same case, resulting in different outcomes. The Internal Revenue Service administers the hundreds of thousands of rules developed to implement the U.S. Tax Code, but each IRS auditing agent has wide discretion in deciding which rules to apply to a taxpayer's income, deductions, business expenses, and so on. Indeed, identical tax information submitted to different IRS offices almost always results in different estimates of tax liability. But even in more routine tasks, from processing Medicare applications to forwarding mail, individual bureaucrats can be friendly and helpful or hostile and obstructive.[4]

Bureaucratic Power and Budget Maximization Bureaucrats generally believe strongly in the value of their programs and the importance of their tasks. Senior military officers and civilian officials of the Department of Defense believe in the importance of a strong national defense, and top officials in the Social Security Administration are committed to maintaining the integrity of the retirement system and serving the nation's senior citizens. Beyond these public-spirited motives, bureaucrats, like everyone else, seek higher pay, greater job security, and added power and prestige for themselves.

These public and private motives converge to inspire bureaucrats to seek to expand the powers, functions, and budgets of their departments and agencies. Rarely do bureaucrats request a reduction in authority, the elimination of a program, or a decrease in their agency's budget. Rather, over time, **budget maximization**—expanding the agency's budget, staff, and authority as much as possible—becomes a driving force in government bureaucracies. This is especially true of discretionary funds. **Discretionary funds** are those that bureaucrats have flexibility in deciding how to spend, rather than money committed by law to specific purposes.[5] Thus, bureaucracies continually strive to add new functions, acquire more authority and responsibility, and increase their budgets and personnel. Bureaucratic expansion is just one of the reasons that government grows over time.

The Federal Bureaucracy

The federal bureaucracy—officially part of the executive branch of the U.S. government—consists of about 2.8 million civilian employees (plus 1.4 million persons in the armed forces) organized into 15 cabinet departments, more than 60 independent agencies, and a large Executive Office of the President (see Figure 12.2). The expenditures of *all* governments in the United States—the federal government, the 50 state governments, and some 89,000 local governments—now amount to about $4.5 trillion (roughly 30 percent of the U.S. gross domestic product, or GDP, of $15.0 trillion). About two-thirds of this—about $3.0 trillion a year (about 20 percent of GDP)—is spent by the *federal* government. Government spending in the United States remains relatively modest compared to that of many nations (see *Compared to What?:* "The Size of Government in Other Nations").

Cabinet Departments Cabinet departments employ about 60 percent of all federal workers (see Table 12.1). Each department is headed by a secretary (with the exception of the Justice Department, which is headed by the attorney general)

Figure *12.2*   The Capitol, White House, and Bureaucracy Corridors of Power

This map shows the Capitol, the White House, and the major departments of the federal bureaucracy in Washington, D.C.

who is appointed by the president and must be confirmed by the Senate. Each department is hierarchically organized; each has its own organization chart.

Cabinet status confers great legitimacy on a governmental function and prestige on the secretary, thus strengthening that individual's voice in the government. Therefore the elevation of an executive agency to cabinet level often reflects political considerations as much as or more than national needs. Strong pressures from "client" interest groups (groups principally served by the department), as well as presidential and congressional desires to pose as defenders and

The Size of Government in Other Nations

How does the size of the public sector in the United States compare with the size of the public sector in other economically advanced, democratic countries? There is a great deal of variation in the size of government across countries. Government spending accounts for nearly two-thirds of the total output in Sweden. Government spending exceeds one-half of the total output of Denmark, Netherlands, Finland, Germany, Italy, Austria, Belgium, and France. The high level of government spending in these countries primarily reflects greater public-sector involvement in the provision of housing, health care, retirement insurance, and aid to the unemployed. The sizes of the public sectors in Australia, Japan, and Switzerland are only slightly higher than that of the United States.

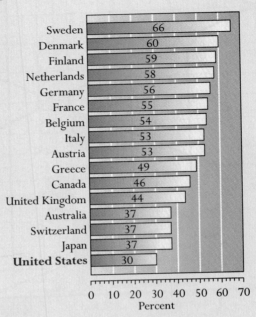

Country	Percent
Sweden	66
Denmark	60
Finland	59
Netherlands	58
Germany	56
France	55
Belgium	54
Italy	53
Austria	53
Greece	49
Canada	46
United Kingdom	44
Australia	37
Switzerland	37
Japan	37
United States	30

Governmental Percentage of Gross Domestic Product

Source: Joint Economic Committee of Congress, "The Size and Function of Government." Washington, D.C.: 1998. United States updated to 2002.

promoters of particular interests, account for the establishment of all of the newer departments. President Woodrow Wilson appealed to the labor movement in 1913 when he separated out a Department of Labor from the earlier business-dominated Department of Commerce and Labor. In 1965 President Lyndon Johnson created the Department of Housing and Urban Development to demonstrate his concern for urban problems. Seeking support from teachers and educational administrators, President Jimmy Carter created a separate Department of Education in 1979 and changed the name of the former Department of Health, Education, and Welfare to the Department of Health and Human Services (perhaps finding the phrase "human services" more politically acceptable than "welfare"). President Ronald Reagan tried, and failed, to "streamline" government by abolishing the Department of Education. But Reagan himself added a cabinet post, elevating the Veterans Administration to the Department of Veterans Affairs in an attempt to ingratiate himself with veterans. President George W. Bush created a new Department of Homeland Security in 2002 in response to the "9/11" terrorist attack on America and the threat of future attacks directly on the soil of the United States.

Cabinet Department Functions
The relative power and prestige of each cabinet-level department is a product not only of its size and budget but also of the importance of its function. By custom, the "pecking order" of departments—and

Table *12.1* Who Does What?: Cabinet Departments and Functions

Department and Date Created	Function
State (1789)	Advises the president on the formation and execution of foreign policy; negotiates treaties and agreements with foreign nations; represents the United States in the United Nations and in more than fifty major international organizations and maintains U.S. embassies abroad; issues U.S. passports and, in foreign countries, visas to the United States.
Treasury (1789)	Serves as financial agent for the U.S. government; issues all payments of the U.S. government according to law; manages the debt of the U.S. government by issuing and recovering bonds and paying their interest; collects taxes owed to the U.S. government; collects taxes and enforces laws on alcohol, tobacco, and firearms and on customs duties; manufactures coins and currency.
Defense (1947: formerly the War Department, created in 1789, and the Navy Department, created in 1798)	Provides the military forces needed to deter war and protect the national security interest; includes the Departments of the Army, Navy, and Air Force.
Justice (1789)	Enforces all federal laws, including consumer protection, antitrust, civil rights, drug, and immigration and naturalization; maintains federal prisons.
Interior (1849)	Has responsibility for public lands and natural resources, for American Indian reservations, and for people who live in island territories under U.S. administration; preserves national parks and historical sites.
Agriculture (1889)	Works to improve and maintain farm income and to develop and expand markets abroad for agricultural products; safeguards standards of quality in the food supply through inspection and grading services; administers rural development, credit, and conservation programs; administers food stamp program.
Commerce (1913)	Encourages the nation's international trade, economic growth, and technological advancement; conducts the census; provides social and economic statistics and analyses for business and government; maintains the merchant marine; grants patents and registers trademarks.
Labor (1913)	Oversees working conditions; administers federal labor laws; protects workers' pension rights; sponsors job training programs; keeps track of changes in employment, price, and other national economic indicators.
Health and Human Services (1953 as Health, Education, and Welfare; reorganized with Education as a separate department in 1979)	Administers social welfare programs for the elderly, children, and youths; protects the health of the nation against impure and unsafe foods, drugs, and cosmetics; operates the Centers for Disease Control; funds the Medicare and Medicaid programs.
Housing and Urban Development (1965)	Is responsible for programs concerned with housing needs, fair housing opportunities, and the improvement and development of the nation's communities; administers mortgage insurance programs, rental subsidy programs, and neighborhood rehabilitation and preservation programs.
Transportation (1966)	Is responsible for the nation's highway planning, development, and construction; also urban mass transit, railroads, aviation, and the safety of waterways, ports, highways, and oil and gas pipelines.
Energy (1977)	Is responsible for the research, development, and demonstration of energy technology; marketing of federal electric power; energy conservation; the nuclear weapons program; regulation of energy production and use; and collection and analysis of energy data.
Education (1979)	Administers and coordinates most federal assistance to education.
Veterans Affairs (1989)	Operates programs to benefit veterans and members of their families.
Homeland Security (2002)	Prevents terrorist attacks within the United States, reduces the vulnerability of the nation to terrorism, and minimizes the damage and assists in recovery from terrorist attacks.

Source: *The United States Government Manual*, Washington, D.C.: Government Printing Office, annual.

A woman filing tax forms while referring to the IRS Web site online. The IRS administers the nation's complex tax code and collects revenues from individuals and businesses in order to pay for government programs and services.

therefore the prestige ranking of their secretaries—is determined by their year of origin. Thus the Departments of State, Treasury, Defense (War), and Justice, created by the First Congress in 1789, head the protocol list of departments. Overall, the duties of the fifteen cabinet-level departments of the executive branch cover an enormous range—everything from providing mortgage insurance, to overseeing the armed forces of the United States (see Table 12.1).

Cabinet Appointments The Constitution requires that "Officers of the United States" be confirmed by the Senate. In the past, the Senate rarely rejected a presidential cabinet nomination; the traditional view was that presidents were entitled to pick their own people and even make their own mistakes. In recent years, however, the confirmation process has become more partisan and divisive, with the Senate conducting lengthy investigations and holding public hearings on presidential cabinet nominees. In 1989 the Senate rejected President Bush's nomination of John Tower as secretary of defense in a partisan battle featuring charges that the former Texas senator was a heavy drinker. The intense public scrutiny and potential for partisan attacks, together with financial disclosure and conflict-of-interest laws, may be discouraging some well-qualified people from accepting cabinet posts.

Independent Regulatory Commissions Independent regulatory commissions differ from cabinet departments in their function, organization, and accountability to the president. Their function is to *regulate* a sector of society— transportation, communications, banking, labor relations, and so on (see Table 12.2). These commissions are empowered by Congress both to make and to enforce rules, and they thus function in a legislative and judicial fashion. To symbolize their impartiality, many of these organizations are headed by *commissions*, usually with five to ten members, rather than by a single secretary. Major policy decisions are made by majority vote of the commission. Finally, these agencies are more independent of the president than are cabinet departments. Their governing commissions are appointed by the president and confirmed by the Senate in the same fashion as cabinet secretaries, but their terms are fixed; they cannot be removed by the president.[6] These provisions are designed to insulate regulators from direct partisan or presidential pressures in their decision making.

A few powerful regulatory agencies remain inside cabinet departments. The most notable are the Food and Drug Administration (FDA), which remains in the Department of Health and Human Services and has broad authority to prevent the sale of drugs not deemed by the agency to be both "safe" and "effective"; the Occupational Health and Safety Administration (OSHA) in the Department of Labor, with authority to make rules governing any workplace in America; and the most powerful government agency of all, the Internal Revenue Service in the Treasury Department, with its broad authority to interpret the tax code, maintain records on every American, and investigate and punish alleged violations of the tax code.

Independent Agencies Congress has created a number of independent agencies outside of any cabinet department. Like cabinet departments, these agencies are hierarchically organized with a single head—usually called an "administrator"—who is appointed by the president and confirmed by the Senate. Administrators have no fixed terms of office and can be dismissed by the president; thus they are independent only insofar as they report directly to the president rather than through a cabinet secretary. Politically, this independence ensures that their interests and budgets will not be compromised by other concerns, as may occur in agencies located within departments. (For more on their operations, see "Regulatory Battles" later in this chapter.)

Table *12.2* Who Does What?: Major Regulatory Bureaucracies

Commission	Date Created	Primary Functions
Federal Communications Commission (FCC)	1934	Regulates interstate and foreign communications by radio, television, wire, and cable.
Food and Drug Administration (FDA)	1930	Sets standards of safety and efficacy for foods, drugs, and medical devices.
Federal Home Loan Bank	1932	Regulates savings and loan associations that specialize in making home mortgage loans.
Federal Maritime Commission	1961	Regulates the waterborne foreign and domestic offshore commerce of the United States.
Federal Reserve Board (FRB)	1913	Regulates the nation's money supply by making monetary policy, which influences the lending and investing activities of commercial banks and the cost and availability of money and credit.
Federal Trade Commission (FTC)	1914	Regulates business to prohibit unfair methods of competition and unfair or deceptive acts or practices.
National Labor Relations Board (NLRB)	1935	Protects employees' rights to organize; prevents unfair labor practices.
Securities and Exchange Commission (SEC)	1934	Regulates the securities and financial markets (such as the stock market).
Occupational Safety and Health Administration (OSHA)	1970	Issues workplace regulations; investigates, cites, and penalizes for noncompliance.
Consumer Product Safety Commission (CPSC)	1972	Protects the public against product-related deaths, illnesses, and injuries.
Commodity Futures Trading Commission	1974	Regulates trading on the futures exchanges as well as the activities of commodity exchange members, public brokerage houses, commodity salespersons, trading advisers, and pool operators.
Nuclear Regulatory Commission (NRC)	1974	Regulates and licenses the users of nuclear energy.
Federal Energy Regulatory Commission (formerly Federal Power Commission)	1977	Regulates the transportation and sale of natural gas, the transmission and sale of electricity, the licensing of hydroelectric power projects, and the transportation of oil by pipeline.
Equal Employment Opportunity Commission (EEOC)	1964	Investigates and rules on charges of racial, gender, and age discrimination by employers and unions, in all aspects of employment.
Environmental Protection Agency (EPA)	1970	Issues and enforces pollution control standards regarding air, water, solid waste, pesticides, radiation, and toxic substances.
Federal Elections Commission (FEC)	1975	Administers and enforces federal campaign finance laws.

Source: FirstGov, www.firstgov.gov/agencies

Environmental Protection Agency and Sunoco workers motor by a boom on the Kentucky River after an oil spill on January 27, 2005 in Carrollton, Kentucky, after a pipeline dumped about 53,000 gallons of crude oil into the river. The Environmental Protection Agency, or EPA, is one of the most powerful independent agencies of the U.S. government.

One of the most powerful independent agencies is the Environmental Protection Agency (EPA), which is responsible for implementing federal legislation dealing with clean air, safe drinking water, solid waste disposal, pesticides, radiation, and toxic substances. EPA establishes and enforces comprehensive and complex standards for thousands of substances in the environment. It enjoys the political support of influential environmental interest groups, including the Environmental Defense Fund, Friends of the Earth, National Audubon Society, National Wildlife Federation, Natural Resources Defense Council, Sierra Club, and the Wilderness Society.

The "Fed" The Federal Reserve System is the most independent of all federal government agencies. The function of the "Fed" is to regulate the supply of money and thereby avoid both inflation and recession (see Chapter 16). The Federal Reserve System is independent of either the president or Congress. Its seven-member Board of Governors is appointed for *14-year terms*. Members are appointed by the president, with the consent of the Senate, but they may not be removed from the board except for "cause." No member has ever been removed since the creation of the board in 1913. The chairman of the board serves only a 4-year term, but the chairman's term overlaps that of the president, so that new presidents cannot immediately name their own chair (see *People in Politics:* "Ben Bernanke Managing the Nation's Money").

Government Corporations Government corporations are created by Congress to undertake independent commercial enterprises. They resemble private corporations in that they typically charge for their services. Like private corporations, too, they are usually governed by a chief executive officer and a board of directors, and they can buy and sell property and incur debts.

Presumably, government corporations perform a service that the private enterprise system has been unable to carry out adequately. The first government corporation was the Tennessee Valley Authority, created by President Franklin Roosevelt during the Depression to build dams and sell electricity at inexpensive rates to impoverished citizens in the mid-South. In 1970 Congress created Amtrak to restore railroad passenger service to the United States. The U.S. Post Office had originally been created as a cabinet-level department, but in 1971 it became the U.S. Postal Service, a government corporation with a mandate from Congress to break even.

People in Politics   Ben Bernanke, Managing the Nation's Money

Ben Bernanke, formerly a professor of economics at Princeton University, was nominated to serve as Chairman of the Board of Governors of the Federal Reserve System by President George W. Bush and confirmed by the U.S. Senate in 2006. It is Bernanke's job to guide "the Fed" in managing the nation's money supply to avoid both inflation and recession.

Bernanke excelled in public schools in Dillon, South Carolina; he achieved the highest SAT score in the state. He graduated summa cum laude from Harvard University in 1975 and earned his Ph.D. degree in economics from MIT in 1979. He taught at Stanford University and then Princeton University and served as editor of the *American Economic Review*. He wrote textbooks on both micro and macro economics. He served as Chairman of the Council of Economic Advisors before being appointed to head the Fed.

Bernanke replaced Alan Greenspan who had served under four presidents—Reagan, Bush, Sr., Clinton, and Bush, Jr. During Greenspan's years inflation averaged only a modest 3% per year and unemployment averaged only 5.5% (This compares with an inflation rate of 6.5% and an unemployment rate of 6.8% in the 18 years prior to Greenspan assuming the post.) But Greenspan was later criticized for having allowed the mortgage industry to make too many substandard housing loans, resulting in an excess of foreclosures and losses for lending banks. Nonetheless upon taking office, Bernanke promptly announced his intention to "maintain continuity" with Greenspan's policies.

Fed Chairman Ben Bernanke attracts media attention as he prepares for testimony before a congressional Committee.

Bernanke promised more open and transparent Fed policy making, but was obliged to back away from his promise when his statements about the future directions of Fed policy drastically affected stock market prices. Yet he began to give economic forecasts four times a year with projections of the expected pace of economic growth, the anticipated unemployment rate, and how the Fed reads the "tea leaves" of inflationary risks.

Bernanke, together with Treasury Secretary Henry Paulson, developed the $700 billion Wall Street bailout plan hurriedly passed by Congress in 2008. Bernanke testified that the bailout was essential in avoiding a deep recession.

Contractors and Consultants   How has the federal government grown enormously in power and size, yet kept its number of employees at roughly the same level in recent years? The answer is found in the spectacular growth of private firms that live off federal contracting and consulting fees. Nearly one-fifth of all federal government spending flows through private contractors: for supplies, equipment, services, leases, and research and development. An army of scientists, economists, education specialists, management consultants, transportation experts, social scientists, and others are scattered across the country in universities, think tanks, consulting firms, and laboratories. Many are concentrated in the "beltway bandit" firms surrounding Washington, D.C.

The federal grant and contracting system is enormously complex; an estimated 150,000 federal contracting offices in nearly 500 agencies oversee thousands of outside contractors and consultants.[7] Although advertised bidding is sometimes required by law, most contracts and grants are awarded without competition through negotiation with favored firms or "sole source contracts" with organizations believed by bureaucrats to be uniquely qualified. Even when federal agencies issue public requests for proposals (RFPs), often a favored contractor has been alerted and advised by bureaucrats within the agency about how to win the award.

Bureaucracy and Democracy

Traditionally, conflict over government employment centered on the question of partisanship versus competence. Should the federal bureaucracy be staffed by people politically loyal to the president, the president's party, or key members of Congress? Or should it be staffed by nonpartisan people selected on the basis of merit and protected from "political" influence?

The Spoils System Historically, government employment was allocated by the **spoils system**—selecting employees on the basis of party loyalty, electoral support, and political influence. Or, as Senator William Marcy said in 1832, "They see nothing wrong in the rule that to the victors belong the spoils of the enemy."[8] The spoils system is most closely associated with President Andrew Jackson, who viewed it as a popular reform of the earlier tendency to appoint officials on the basis of kinship and class standing. Jackson sought to bring into government many of the common people who had supported him. Later in the nineteenth century, the bartering and sale of government jobs became so scandalous and time-consuming that presidents complained bitterly about the task. When President James Garfield was shot and killed in 1881 by a disgruntled job seeker, the stage was set for reform.

The Merit System The **merit system**—government employment based on competence, neutrality, and protection from partisanship—was introduced in the Pendleton Act of 1883. The act created the Civil Service Commission to establish a system for selecting government personnel based on merit, as determined by competitive examinations. In the beginning, "civil service" coverage included only about 10 percent of total federal employees. Over the years, however, more and more positions were placed under civil service, primarily at the behest of presidents who sought to "freeze in" their political appointees. By 1978 more than 90 percent of federal employees were covered by civil service or other merit systems.

The civil service system established a uniform General Schedule (GS) of job grades from GS 1 (lowest) to GS 15 (highest), with an Executive Schedule added later for top managers and pay ranges based on an individual's time in the grade. Each grade has specific educational requirements and examinations. College graduates generally begin at GS 5 or above; GS 9 through GS 12 are technical and supervisory positions; and GS 13, 14, and 15 are midlevel management and highly specialized positions. The Executive Schedule (the "supergrades") are reserved for positions of greatest responsibility. (In 2008 annual pay ranged from roughly $32,000 to $50,000 for Grades 5–8, up to $75,000 to $138,000 for Grades 13–15, and $186,600 for some Executive Schedule positions.)

About two-thirds of all federal civilian jobs come under the General Schedule system, with its written examinations and/or training, experience, and educational requirements. Most of the other one-third of federal civilian employees are part of the "excepted services"; they are employed by various agencies that have their own separate merit systems, such as the Federal Bureau of Investigation, the Central Intelligence Agency, the U.S. Postal Service, and the State Department Foreign Service. The military also has its own system of recruitment, promotion, and pay.

Spoiled Rotten?

During the administration of Andrew Jackson, the spoils system was perhaps more overt than at any other time in the history of the U.S. federal government. Jackson claimed he was trying to involve more of the "common folk" in the government, but his selection of advisers on the basis of personal friendship rather than qualifications sometimes caused him difficulties.

★ **spoils system**
Selection of employees for government agencies on the basis of party loyalty, electoral support, and political influence.

Think
Again

Should the federal bureaucracy be managed by nonpartisan professionals rather than people politically loyal to the president?

Political Involvement

Congress passed the Hatch Act in 1939, a law that prohibited federal employees from engaging in partisan political activity, including running for public office, soliciting campaign funds, or campaigning for or against a party or candidate. It also protected federal merit system employees from dismissal for partisan reasons. But over the years many federal employees came to believe that the Hatch Act infringed on their rights as citizens. In 1993, a Democratic-controlled Congress repealed major portions of the Hatch Act, allowing civil servants to hold party positions and involve themselves in political fund raising and campaigning. They still may not be candidates for public office in partisan elections, or solicit contributions from subordinate employees or people who do business with—or have cases before—their agencies.

The assassination of President James A. Garfield on June 2, 1881. He lived another two and a half months, dying on September 19, 1881.

★ **merit system**
Selection of employees for government agencies on the basis of competence, with no consideration of an individual's political stance and/or power.

TIMELINE

The Evolution of the Federal Bureaucracy

The Problem of Responsiveness

The civil service system, like most other "reforms," eventually created problems at least as troubling as those in the system it replaced. First of all, there is the problem of a *lack of responsiveness* to presidential direction. Civil servants, secure in their protected jobs, can be less than cooperative toward their presidentially appointed department or agency heads. They can slow or obstruct policy changes with which they personally disagree. Each bureau and agency develops its own "culture," usually in strong support of the governmental function or client group served by the organization. Changing the culture of an agency is extremely difficult, especially when a presidential administration is committed to reducing its resources, functions, or services. Bureaucrats' powers of policy obstruction are formidable: They can help mobilize interest-group support against the president's policy; they can "leak" damaging information to sympathizers in Congress or the media to undermine the president's policy; they can delay and/or "sabotage" policies with which they disagree.

The Problem of Productivity

Perhaps the most troublesome problem in the federal bureaucracy has involved *productivity*—notably the inability to improve job performance because of the difficulties in rewarding or punishing civil servants. "Merit" salary rewards have generally proven ineffective in rewarding the performance of federal employees. More than 99 percent of federal workers regularly receive annual "merit" pay increases. Moreover, over time, federal employees have secured higher grade classifications and hence higher pay for most of the job positions in the General Schedule. This "inflation" in GS grades, combined with regular increases in salary and benefits, has resulted in many federal employees enjoying higher pay and benefits than employees in the private sector performing similar jobs.

At the same time, very poor performance often goes largely unpunished. Once hired and retained through a brief probationary period, a federal civil servant cannot be dismissed except for "cause." Severe obstacles to firing a civil servant result in a rate of dismissal of about one-tenth of 1 percent of all federal employees (see Table 12.3). It is doubtful that only such a tiny fraction are performing unsatisfactorily. A federal executive confronting a poorly performing or nonperforming employee must be prepared to spend more than a year in extended proceedings to secure a dismissal. Often costly substitute strategies are devised to work around or inspire the resignation of unsatisfactory federal employees—assigning them meaningless or boring tasks, denying

President Jimmy Carter at his desk in the Oval Office.

Table **12.3**   Firing a Bureaucrat: What Is Required to Dismiss a Federal Employee

Very few federal civil servants are ever dismissed from their jobs.

* Written notice at least 30 days in advance of a hearing to determine incompetence or misconduct.
* A statement of cause, indicating specific dates, places, and actions cited as incompetent or improper.
* The right to a hearing and decision by an impartial official, with the burden of proof falling on the agency that wishes to fire the employee.
* The right to have an attorney and to present witnesses in the employee's favor at the hearing.
* The right to appeal any adverse action to the Merit Systems Protection Board.
* The right to appeal any adverse action by the board to the U.S. Court of Appeals.
* The right to remain on the job and be paid until all appeals are exhausted.

them promotions, transferring them to distant or undesirable locations, removing secretaries or other supporting resources, and the like.

Civil Service Reform   Presidents routinely try to remedy some of the problems in the system. The Civil Service Reform Act of 1978, initiated by President Jimmy Carter, replaced the Civil Service Commission with the Office of Personnel Management (OPM) and made OPM responsible for recruiting, examining, training, and promoting federal employees. Unlike the Civil Service Commission, OPM is headed by a single director responsible to the president. The act also sought to (1) streamline procedures through which individuals could be disciplined for poor performance; (2) establish merit pay for middle-level managers; and (3) create a Senior Executive Service (SES) composed of about 8,000 top people designated for higher Executive Schedule grades and salaries who also might be given salary bonuses, transferred among agencies, or demoted, based on performance.

But like many other reforms, this act failed to resolve the major problems—the responsiveness and productivity of the bureaucracy. No senior executives were fired, demoted, or involuntarily transferred. The bonus program proved difficult to implement: There are few recognized standards for judging meritorious work in public service, and bonuses often reflect favoritism as much as merit. Because the act created a separate Merit Systems Protection Board to hear appeals by federal employees from dismissals, suspensions, and demotions, rates of dismissal for all grades have not changed substantially from earlier days.

Bureaucracy and Representation   In addition to the questions of responsiveness and productivity, there is also the question of the representativeness of the federal bureaucracy. About 45 percent of the total civilian workforce is female, 16.9 percent is black, and 7.3 percent is Hispanic. However, a close look at *top* bureaucratic positions reveals far less diversity. As Table 12.4 shows, only 9.1 percent of federal "executive" positions (levels GS 16–18) are filled by women, only 6.5 percent by African Americans, and only 3.5 percent by Hispanics. Thus the federal bureaucracy, like other institutions in American society, is *unrepresentative* of the general population in its top executive positions.

✔ *Think* Again

Should the federal bureaucracy at all levels reflect the gender and minority ratios of the total civilian workforce?

Table **12.4** Diversity in the Bureaucracy: Women and Minorities in Federal Employment

Women and minorities are not well-represented at the higher levels of the federal bureaucracy.

	Percentage Female	Percentage White, Non-Hispanic	Percentage African American	Percentage Hispanic
Overall	44.4%	68.6%	16.9%	7.3%
By pay grade				
GS 1–4	64.8	56.7	24.2	9.3
GS 5–8	65.9	59.5	24.6	8.8
GS 9–11	46.2	68.7	16.1	8.7
GS 12–13	—	74.9	13.3	5.5
GS 14–15	32.3	80.7	8.9	3.9
Executive	9.1	86.0	6.5	3.5
U.S. population (2000)	50.9	75.2	12.3	12.5

Note: Table excludes Native Americans, Alaska Natives, and Asian and Pacific Islanders.
Source: Office of Personnel Management. Demographic Profile of the Federal Workforce, 2004. www.opm.gov

Bureaucratic Politics

To whom is the federal bureaucracy really accountable? The president, Congress, or itself? Article II, Section 2, of the Constitution places the president at the head of the executive branch of government, with the power to "appoint Ambassadors, other public Ministers and Consuls, Judges of the Supreme Court, and all other Officers of the United States . . . which shall be established by Law." Appointment of these officials requires "the Advice and Consent of the Senate"—that is, a majority vote in the Senate. The Constitution also states that "the Congress may by Law vest the Appointment of such inferior Officers, as they think proper, in the President alone." If the bureaucracy is to be made accountable to the president, we would expect the president to directly appoint *policy-making* executive officers. But it is difficult to determine exactly how many positions are truly "policy making."

Presidential "Plums"   The president retains direct control over about 3,000 federal jobs. Some 700 of these jobs are considered policy-making positions. They include presidential appointments authorized by law—cabinet and subcabinet officers, judges, U.S. marshals, U.S. attorneys, ambassadors, and members of various boards and commissions. The president also appoints a large number of "Schedule C" jobs throughout the bureaucracy, described as "confidential or policy-determining" in character. Each new administration goes through many months of high-powered lobbying and scrambling to fill these posts. Applicants with congressional sponsors, friends in the White House, or a record of loyal campaign work for the president compete for these "plums." Political loyalty must be weighed against administrative competence.[9]

Rooms at the Top   The federal bureaucracy has "thickened" at the top, even as total federal employment has declined. Over time, departments and agencies have added layers of administrators, variously titled "deputy secretary," "undersecretary,"

SIMULATION
You Are Deputy Director of the Census Bureau

VISUAL LITERACY
The Changing Face of the Federal Bureaucracy

"assistant secretary," "deputy assistant secretary," and so on. Cabinet departments have become top-heavy with administrators, and the same multiplication of layers of executive management has occurred in independent agencies as well.[10]

Whistle-Blowers   The question of bureaucratic responsiveness is complicated by the struggle between the president and Congress to control the bureaucracy. Congress expects federal agencies and employees to respond fully and promptly to its inquiries and to report candidly on policies, procedures, and expenditures. **Whistle-blowers** are federal employees (or employees of a firm supplying the government) who report government waste, mismanagement, or fraud to the media or to congressional committees or who "go public" with their policy disputes with their superiors. Congress generally encourages whistle-blowing as a means of getting information and controlling the bureaucracy, but the president and agency heads whose policies are under attack are often less kindly disposed toward whistle-blowers. In 1989 Congress passed the Whistleblower Protection Act, which established an independent agency to guarantee whistle-blowers protection against unjust dismissal, transfer, or demotion.

Agency Cultures   Over time, every bureaucracy tends to develop its own "culture"—beliefs about the values of the organization's programs and goals and close associations with the agency's client groups and political supporters. Many government agencies are dominated by people who have been in government service most of their lives, and most of these people have worked in the same functional field most of their lives. They believe their work is important, and they resist efforts by either the president or Congress to reduce the activities, size, or budget of their agency. Career bureaucrats tend to support enlargement of the public sector—to enhance education, welfare, housing, environmental and consumer protection, and so on. Bureaucrats not only share a belief in the need for government expansion but also stand to benefit directly from increased authority, staffing, and funding as government takes on new and enlarged responsibilities.

Friends and Neighbors   Bureaucracies maintain their own cultures in part by staffing themselves. Informal practices in recruitment often circumvent civil service procedures. Very few people ever get hired by taking a federal civil service examination administered by OPM and then sitting and waiting to be called for an interview by an agency. Most bureaucratic hiring actually comes about through "networks" of personal friends and professional associates. People inside an agency contact their friends and associates when a position first becomes vacant; they then send their friends to OPM to formally qualify for the job. Thus inside candidates learn about an opening well before it appears on any list of vacant positions and can tailor their applications to the job description. Agencies may even send a "name request" to OPM, ensuring that the preselected person will appear on the list of qualified people. In this way, individuals sometimes move through many jobs within a specific policy network—for example, within environmental protection, within transportation, or within social welfare—shifting between the federal bureaucracy, state or local government, and private firms or interest groups in the same field. Network recruiting generally ensures that the people entering a bureaucracy will share the same values and attitudes of the people already there.

"Reinventing" Government   Reformers lament "the bankruptcy of bureaucracy"—the waste, inefficiency, impersonality, and unresponsiveness of large government organizations. They decry "the routine tendency to protect turf, to resist change, to build empires, to enlarge one's sphere of control, to protect projects and programs regardless of whether or not they are any longer needed."[11] Many bureaucratic reform efforts have foundered, from Hoover Commission studies in the Truman and Eisenhower years to the Grace Commission work in the Reagan Administration. Clinton assigned a "reinventing government" task to Vice President Al Gore. Gore produced a report designed to put the "customer" (U.S. citizen) first, to "empower" government employees to get results, to cut red tape, to introduce competition and a market orientation wherever possible, and to decentralize government decision making.[12]

Outsourcing   Presidential administrations from Bill Clinton to George W. Bush have "outsourced" more and more federal jobs. They have contracted to private companies for work formerly done by the U.S. government. As various departments across the government—from the Department of Defense to the National Park Service—have turned projects over to private businesses, the number of federal jobs has also declined, from 3.1 million in 1992 to 2.7 million in 2007. Among the advantages of outsourcing: private firms bid competitively for contracts, likely resulting in lower costs for the U.S. government—and therefore the American taxpayer. In addition, the private sector has fewer rules and regulations in comparison with operations within the departments and agencies of the federal government. Businesses may be able to undertake and complete projects faster and more efficiently than can governmental organizations. But outsourcing has its disadvantages—in many ways simply the reverse of its advantages. The low-cost bidder may be a foreign-owned company. Should the U.S. government be concerned about which companies get its contracts, and where the employees of those companies live? Also, the private sector may be less accountable than the public sector. Work being done by for-profit companies may cut corners and be less reliable than that being done by the government itself.

> ★ **outsourcing**
> Government contracting with private firms to perform public services.

Presidential Initiative   Presidents can create some new agencies by executive order. Often Congress gives presidents the authority to reorganize agencies by legislation (see *Politics Up Close:* "Reorganizing Intelligence After '9/11'"). But presidents have also acted on their own to create new agencies. Indeed, one study concludes that presidents have created about 40 percent of all new agencies[13]—perhaps the most famous was President Kennedy's Peace Corps. Of course, Congress has the last word, inasmuch as the continuation of a presidentially created agency requires funding and Congress controls the purse strings. It can end an agency's existence by cutting off its funds.

The Budgetary Process

The federal government's annual budget battles are the heart of the political process. Budget battles decide who gets what and who pays the cost of government. The budget is the single most important policy statement of any government.

The president is responsible for submitting the annual *Budget of the United States Government*—with estimates of revenues and recommendations for expenditures—for consideration, amendment, and approval by the Congress. But the president's budget reflects the outcome of earlier bureaucratic battles over who gets what. Despite highly publicized wrangling between the president and Congress each year—and occasional declarations that the president's budget is "DOA" (dead on arrival)—final congressional appropriations rarely deviate by more than 2 or 3 percent from the original presidential budget. Thus the president and the Office of Management and Budget in the Executive Office of the President have real budgetary power.

Do you believe the bureaucrats in Washington waste a lot of the money we pay in taxes?

Politics Up Close   Reorganizing Intelligence After "9/11"

"Imagination is not a gift usually associated with bureaucracies." There were reports at lower levels of the intelligence community prior to "9/11" that Al Qaeda was planning a major attack on the United States, that the World Trade Center might be a target because it had been a target of a car bomb in 1992, that Muslim fanatics were in the country and some had been taking flying lessons, and that various intelligence agencies had considered the possibilities of terrorists using aircraft as weapons. But no specifics were reported—time, location, or individuals involved—and the *9/11 Commission: The National Commission on Terrorist Attacks upon the United States* concluded that no agency or individual was to blame for the failure to anticipate the tragedy. Simply, "No one connected the dots."

9/11 Commission

President Bush authorized the 9/11 Commission in 2002, after pressure mounted in Washington for a thorough investigation of the "9/11" attack. The Commission's Final Report makes for exciting reading; it carefully reconstructs what happened in the days and months prior to the tragedy, as well as the events on that day itself; and it describes what each relevant federal agency knew and did not know about the possibility of such an attack. Finally, the commission issued a series of recommendations regarding reorganization of the intelligence community: to unify the intelligence community and operational planning against terrorists; to unify the many agencies participating in counterterrorism; and to strengthen homeland defense.

The Intelligence Community

The intelligence community consists of a series of agencies, each with a specialized responsibility, together with elements of the Department of Defense, the Department of Homeland Security, the Federal Bureau of Investigation, the Department of State, the Department of Energy, and the Department of the Treasury. The Central Intelligence Agency (CIA) was the lead agency in assembly, analysis, and dissemination of intelligence from all other agencies in the intelligence community. It prepared the President's Daily Briefing (PDB), which summarizes all intelligence reports from all agencies for the president each day. The CIA also prepared National Intelligence Estimates (NIE's)—more thorough studies of specific topics, for example, North Korea's nuclear capabilities. In addition the CIA is charged with responsibility for human intelligence collection (recruiting agents around the world and supervising their work), and it also has

responsibility for covert operations under the direction of the president (see the "Central Intelligence Agency" in Chapter 11). The National Security Agency (NSA) collects and processes foreign signals intelligence—all electronic emissions from radio to satellite communication. The National Reconnaissance Office (NRO) collects information from satellite reconnaissance. The National Imagery and Mapping Agency (NIMA) is responsible for geographic and geospatial intelligence. The Defense Intelligence Agency (DIA) is responsible for delivering tactical military intelligence directly to war fighters as well as to policy makers.

Director of National Intelligence

The key recommendation of the 9/11 Commission was the creation of a new office—the Director of National Intelligence (DNI)—to oversee the entire intelligence community. The new DNI would replace the CIA director's role as the principal intelligence advisor to the president. The CIA director would concentrate on the responsibilities of the CIA itself. The DNI would unify the budget for national intelligence as well as approve and submit nominations for individuals to head various agencies of the intelligence community. The DNI would also manage the nation's counterterrorism effort, with the assistance of a new National Counterterrorism Center, which would assemble and analyze information on terrorists gathered both at home and abroad.

Military Intelligence

The Defense Department objected to giving the DNI budget and personnel responsibility for intelligence agencies located within the department. Army, Navy, Air Force, and Marine intelligence are closely integrated with their respective military commands. The issue was compromised in Congress, with the military retaining direct control over intelligence activities within the Defense Department and the DNI only consulting on these issues. The same compromise was reached regarding intelligence activities in the Department of Homeland Security, Department of State, Department of Energy, and Department of the Treasury.

Integrating Foreign and Domestic Intelligence

Perhaps the most troublesome problem in intelligence and counterterrorism in the past had been the lack of coordination between the CIA and the FBI. Fighting global terrorism requires close surveillance of individuals and terrorist organizations both within and outside of the United States. But in the original National Security Act of 1947, establishing the CIA, this agency was specifically prohibited from engaging in any activities, including surveillance of individual organizations, *inside the borders of the United States*. Only the FBI has the authority to act against terrorists inside the United States. Intelligence reorganization encouraged greater cooperation between these agencies. And the USA PATRIOT Act now permits both agencies to undertake surveillance of communications relevant to terrorism both within the United States and abroad. In a separate reorganization within the FBI, a new National Security Center was established with responsibility for counterterrorism. The DNI was given budgetary and personnel authority over the new center. However, the FBI and the intelligence community each continue to operate largely separately from the other, and it is not clear whether the problems of communication and coordination between these agencies have been resolved.

THE INTELLIGENCE COMMUNITY

How It Works: the Structure of the Intelligence Community

Note: The CIA, DIA, NSA, NRO, and NGA are concerned exclusively with intelligence. The Departments of Defense, Homeland Security, Justice, State, Energy, and Treasury are concerned primarily with other missions but do have some intelligence responsibilities.

The Office of Management and Budget

The Office of Management and Budget (OMB) has the key responsibility for budget preparation. In addition to this major task, OMB has related responsibilities for improving the organization and management of the executive agencies, for coordinating the extensive statistical services of the federal government, and for analyzing and reviewing proposed legislation.[14]

Preparation of the budget begins when OMB, after preliminary consultations with the executive agencies and in accord with presidential policy, develops targets or ceilings within which the agencies are encouraged to build their requests (see Figure 12.3). Budget materials and instructions then go to the agencies, with the request that the forms be completed and returned to OMB. This request is followed by about 3 months of arduous work by agency budget officers, department heads, and the "grass-roots" bureaucracy in Washington, D.C., and out in the field. Budget officials at the bureau and departmental levels check requests from the smaller units, compare them with previous years' estimates, hold conferences, and make adjustments. The heads of agencies are expected to submit their completed requests to OMB by July or August. Although these requests usually remain within target levels, occasionally they include some "overceiling" items (requests above the suggested ceilings). With the requests of the spending agencies at hand, OMB begins its own budget review, including hearings at which top agency officials support their requests as convincingly as possible. Frequently OMB must say "no," that is, reduce agency requests. On rare occasions, dissatisfied agencies may ask the budget director to take their cases to the president.

The President's Budget

In December, the president and the OMB director devote much time to the key document, *The Budget of the United States Government*, which by now is approaching its final stages of assembly. Each budget is named for the **fiscal year** in which it *ends*. The federal fiscal year begins on October 1 and ends the following September 30. (Thus *The Budget of the United States Government Fiscal Year* 2009 begins October 1, 2008, and ends September 30, 2009.) Although the completed document includes a revenue plan with general estimates for taxes and other income, it is primarily an expenditure budget. (Revenue and tax policy staff work centers in the Treasury Department, not in the Office of Management and Budget.) In late January, the president presents Congress with *The Budget of the United States Government* for the fiscal year beginning October 1. After the budget is in legislative hands, the president may recommend further alterations as needs dictate.

House and Senate Budget Committees

The Constitution gives Congress the authority to decide how the government should spend its money: "No money shall be drawn from the Treasury, but in Consequence of Appropriations made by Law" (Article I, Section 9). The president's budget is sent initially to the House and Senate Budget Committees, which rely on their own bureaucracy, the Congressional Budget Office (CBO), to review the president's budget. Based on the CBO's assessment, these committees draft a first **budget resolution** (due May 15) setting forth target goals to guide congressional committees regarding specific appropriations and revenue measures. If proposed spending exceeds the targets in the budget resolution, the resolution comes back to the floor in a reconciliation measure. A second budget resolution (due September 15) sets binding budget figures for committees and subcommittees considering appropriations. In practice, however, these two budget resolutions are often folded into a single measure because Congress does not want to argue the same issues twice.

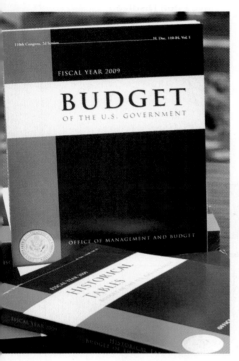

Seeing Red

Copies of the Fiscal 2009 Budget of the U.S. Government, submitted by the Office of Management and Budget in 2008. The budget called for $3.1 trillion in outlays. But because of Democrats controlling Congress, the President's budget has little chance of being enacted without major revisions.

★ **fiscal year**
Yearly government accounting period, not necessarily the same as the calendar year. The federal government's fiscal year begins October 1 and ends September 30.

★ **budget resolution**
Congressional bill setting forth target budget figures for appropriations to various government departments and agencies.

	WHO	WHAT	WHEN
Presidential budget making	President and OMB	OMB presents long-range forecasts for revenues and expenditures to the president. President and OMB develop general guidelines for all federal agencies. Agencies are sent guidelines and forms for their budget requests.	January February March
	Executive agencies	Agencies prepare and submit budget requests to OMB.	April May June July
	OMB and agencies	OMB reviews agency requests and holds hearings with agency officials.	August September October
	OMB and president	OMB presents revised budget to president. President and OMB write budget message for Congress.	November December January
	President	President presents budget for the next fiscal year to Congress.	February
Congressional budget process	CBO and congressional committees	CBO reviews taxing and spending proposals and reports to House and Senate budget committees.	February–April
	Congress; House and Senate budget committees	Committees present first concurrent resolution, which sets overall total for budget outlays in major categories. Full House and Senate vote on resolution. Committees are instructed to stay within Budget Committee's resolution.	May June
	Congress; House and Senate appropriations committees and budget committees	Appropriations committees and subcommittees draw up detailed appropriations bills and submit them to budget committees for second concurrent resolution. The full House and Senate vote on "reconciliations" and second (firm) concurrent resolution.	July August September
	Congress and president	House and Senate pass various appropriations bills (nine to sixteen bills, by major functional category, such as "defense"). Each is sent to president for signature. (If successfully vetoed, a bill is revised and resubmitted to the president.)	September October
Executive budget implementation	Congress and president	Fiscal year for all federal agencies begins October 1. If no appropriations bill for an agency has been passed by Congress and signed by the president, Congress must pass and the president sign a continuing resolution to allow the agency to spend at last year's level until a new appropriations bill is passed. If no continuing resolution is passed, the agency must officially cease spending government funds and must officially shut down.	After October 1

Figure *12.3*   How It Works: The Budget Process

Development, presentation, and approval of the federal budget for any fiscal year takes almost 2 full years. The executive branch spends more than a year on the process before Congress even begins its review and revision of the president's proposals. The problems of implementing the budgeted programs then fall to the federal bureaucracy.

Congressional Appropriations Committees Congressional approval of each year's spending is usually divided into thirteen separate appropriations bills (acts), each covering separate broad categories of spending (for example, defense, labor, human services and education, commerce, justice). These appropriations bills are drawn up by the House and Senate Appropriations Committees and their specialized subcommittees, which function as overseers of agencies included in their appropriations bills. Committee work in the House of Representatives is usually more thorough than it is in the Senate; the committee in the Senate tends to be a "court of appeal" for agencies opposed to House action. Each committee, moreover, has about ten largely independent subcommittees, each reviewing the requests of a particular agency or a group of related functions. Specific appropriations bills are taken up by the subcommittees in hearings. Departmental officers answer questions on the conduct of their programs and defend their requests for the next fiscal year; lobbyists and other witnesses testify. Although committees and subcommittees have broad discretion in allocating funds to the agencies they monitor, they must stay within overall totals set forth in the second budget resolution adopted by Congress.

Appropriations Acts In examining the interactions between Congress and the federal bureaucracy over spending, it is important to distinguish between appropriations and authorization. An **authorization** is an act of Congress that establishes a government program and defines the amount of money it may spend. Authorizations may be for one or several years. However, an authorization does not actually provide the money that has been authorized; only an **appropriations act** can do that. In fact, appropriations acts, which are usually for a single fiscal year, are almost always *less* than authorizations; deciding how much less is the real function of the Appropriations Committees and subcommittees. (By its own rules, Congress cannot appropriate money for programs it has not already authorized.) Appropriations acts include both obligational authority and outlays.

Obligational authority permits a government agency to enter into contracts that will require the government to make payments beyond the fiscal years in question. **Outlays** must be spent in the fiscal year for which they are appropriated.

Continuing Resolutions and "Shutdowns" All appropriations acts *should* be passed by both houses and signed by the president into law before October 1, the date of the start of the fiscal year. However, it is rare for Congress to meet this deadline, so the government usually finds itself beginning a new fiscal year without a budget. Constitutionally, any U.S. government agency for which Congress does not pass an appropriations act may not draw money from the Treasury and thus is obliged to shut down. To get around this problem, Congress usually adopts a **continuing resolution** that authorizes government agencies to keep spending money for a specified period at the same level as in the previous fiscal year.

A continuing resolution is supposed to grant additional time for Congress to pass, and the president to sign, appropriations acts. But occasionally this process has broken down in the heat of political combat over the budget: the time period specified in a continuing resolution has expired without agreement on appropriations acts or even on a new continuing resolution. Shutdowns occurred during the bitter battle between President Bill Clinton and the Republican-controlled Congress over the Fiscal Year 1996 budget. In theory, the absence of either appropriations acts or a continuing resolution should cause the entire federal government to "shut down," that is, to cease all operations and expenditures for lack of funds. But in practice, such shutdowns have been only partial, affecting only "nonessential" government employees and causing relatively little disruption.

★ **authorization**
Act of Congress that establishes a government program and defines the amount of money it may spend.

★ **appropriations act**
Congressional bill that provides money for programs authorized by Congress.

★ **obligational authority**
Feature of some appropriations acts by which an agency is empowered to enter into contracts that will require the government to make payments beyond the fiscal year in question.

★ **outlays**
Actual dollar amounts to be spent by the federal government in a fiscal year.

★ **continuing resolution**
Congressional bill that authorizes government agencies to keep spending money for a specified period at the same level as in the previous fiscal year; passed when Congress is unable to enact final appropriations measures by October 1.

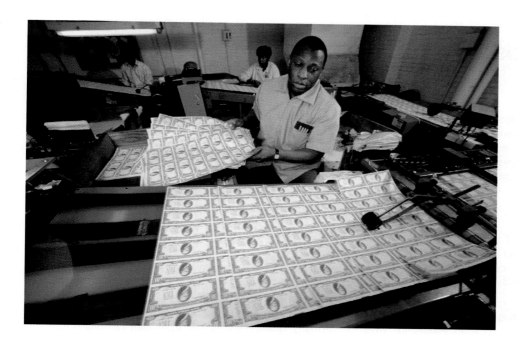

He Doesn't Get to Keep It
Much of the work of the federal bureaucracy is routine, including the printing of money.

The Politics of Budgeting

Budgeting is very political. Being a good "bureaucratic politician" involves (1) cultivating a good base of support for requests among the public at large and among interests served by the agency; (2) developing attention, enthusiasm, and support for one's program among top political figures and congressional leaders; (3) winning favorable coverage of agency activities in the media; and (4) following strategies that exploit opportunities (see *Politics Up Close:* "Bureaucratic Budget Strategies").

Budgeting Is "Incremental"   The most important factor determining the size and content of the budget each year is last year's budget. Decision makers generally use last year's expenditures as a *base;* active consideration of budget proposals generally focuses on new items and requested increases over last year's base. The budget of an agency is almost never reviewed as a whole. Agencies are seldom required to defend or explain budget requests that do *not* exceed current appropriations; but requested increases *do* require explanation and are most subject to reduction by OMB or Congress.

The result of **incremental budgeting** is that many programs, services, and expenditures continue long after there is any real justification for them. When new needs, services, and functions arise, they do not displace older ones but rather are *added* to the budget. Budget decisions are made incrementally because policy makers do not have the time, energy, or information to review every dollar of every budget request every year. Nor do policy makers wish to refight every political battle over existing programs every year. So they generally accept last year's base spending level as legitimate and focus attention on proposed increases for each program.

Reformers have proposed "sunset" laws requiring bureaucrats to justify their programs every 5 to 7 years or else the programs go out of existence, as well as **zero-based budgeting** that would force agencies to justify every penny requested—not just requested increases. In theory, sunset laws and zero-based budgeting would regularly prune unnecessary government programs, agencies,

★ **incremental budgeting**
Method of budgeting that focuses on requested increases in funding for existing programs, accepting as legitimate their previous year's expenditures.

★ **zero-based budgeting**
Method of budgeting that demands justification for the entire budget request of an agency, not just its requested increase in funding.

Politics Up Close — **Bureaucratic Budget Strategies**

How do bureaucrats go about "maximizing" their resources? Some of the most common budgetary strategies of bureaucrats are listed here. Remember that most bureaucrats believe strongly in the importance of their tasks; they pursue these strategies not only to increase their own power and prestige but also to better serve their client groups and the entire nation.

★ *Spend it all:* Spend all of your current appropriation. Failure to use up an appropriation indicates the full amount was unnecessary in the first place, which in turn implies that your budget should be cut next year.

★ *Ask for more:* Never request a sum less than your current appropriation. It is easier to find ways to spend up to current appropriation levels than it is to explain why you want a reduction. Besides, a reduction indicates your program is not growing, an embarrassing admission to most government administrators. Requesting an increase, at least enough to cover "inflation," demonstrates the continued importance of your program.

★ *Put vital programs in the "base":* Put top priority programs into the basic budget—that is, that part of the budget within current appropriation levels. The Office of Management and Budget (OMB) and

legislative committees seldom challenge programs that appear to be part of existing operations.

★ *Make new programs appear "incremental":* Requested increases should appear to be small and should appear to grow out of existing operations. Any appearance of a fundamental change in a budget should be avoided.

★ *Give them something to cut:* Give the OMB and legislative committees something to cut. Normally it is desirable to submit requests for substantial increases in existing programs and many requests for new programs, in order to give higher political authorities something to cut. This approach enables authorities to "save" the public untold millions of dollars and justify their claim of promoting "economy" in government. Giving them something to cut also diverts attention from the basic budget with its vital programs.

★ *Make cuts hurt:* If your agency is faced with a real budget cut—that is, a reduction from last year's appropriation—announce pending cuts in vital and popular programs in order to stir up opposition to the cut. For example, the National Park Service might announce the impending closing of the Washington Monument. Never acknowledge that cuts might be accommodated by your agency without harming basic services.

and expenditures and thus limit the growth of government and waste in government (see *What Do You Think?*: "How Much Money Does the Government Waste?"). But in reality, sunset laws and zero-based budgeting require so much effort in justifying already accepted programs that executive agencies and legislative committees grow tired of the effort and return to incrementalism.

The "incremental" nature of budgetary politics helps reduce political conflicts and maintain stability in governmental programs. As bruising as budgetary battles are today, they would be much worse if the president or Congress undertook to review the value of *all* existing expenditures and programs each year. Comprehensive budgetary review would "overload the system" with political conflict by refighting every policy battle every year.

Budgeting Is Nonprogrammatic Budgeting is *nonprogrammatic* in that an agency budget typically lists expenditures under ambiguous phrases: "personnel services," "contractual services," "travel," "supplies," "equipment." It is difficult to tell from such a listing exactly what programs the agency is spending its money on. Such a budget obscures policy decisions by hiding programs behind meaningless phrases. Even if these categories are broken down into line items (for example, under "personnel services," the line-item budget might say, "John Doaks, Assistant Administrator, $85,000"), it is still next to impossible to identify the costs of various programs.

How Much Money Does the Government Waste?

Politicians, the media, and the public often associate federal bureaucracy and government spending with waste and inefficiency. But it is very difficult to actually determine how much money the government actually wastes. What is "waste" to one person may be a necessary and vital government function for another. Some people may accept some government waste if they think that a government program is necessary; "waste" may be a part of the reality of government. And private companies are themselves often poorly managed or even corrupt. What kind of standard should be applied to the U.S. government, then?

Nearly two-thirds of Americans have over the last two decades described the government as wasting "a great deal" of money—not just "some" or "not very much" (see graph). And they believe that the government wastes more of its domestic spending than its defense spending. But is the public right, that "a lot" of government money is wasted?

The General Accountability Office (GAO) of the U.S. Congress has the authority to audit the operations and finances of federal agencies. The GAO has often found fraud and mismanagement of government operations that come to 10 percent or more of the spending of the agencies that it has reviewed. This suggests that possibly $300 billion of the federal government's $3.1 trillion budget is being wasted. Furthermore government commissions that have studied government operations, such as the Grace Commission during the Reagan administration in the 1980s, put an even higher figure on government waste: more than 20 percent of government spending.

Recent audits by the GAO reveal continued financial mismanagement and abuse throughout the U.S. government. Employees at the Department of Agriculture (USDA) spent millions of dollars on personal purchases with their government credit cards. Investigators estimated that 15 percent of employees abused their government credit cards at a cost of almost $6 million. Taxpayer-funded purchases included Ozzy Osbourne concert tickets, tattoos, bartender school tuition, car payments, lingerie, and cash advances. Meanwhile, some 55,000 USDA credit cards are in circulation, including 1,549 being held by people who no longer work at the USDA.[a]

Other audits found that over a 6-year period the Department of Defense purchased and then left unused some 270,000 commercial airline tickets, at a total cost of $100 million. The Pentagon never even bothered to get refunds for these *fully refundable* tickets. The GAO blamed the Pentagon's system that relied on Defense Department personnel to notify the travel office when purchased tickets were not used. Audits also found that the Pentagon paid twice for the same ticket on about 27,000 transactions between 2001 and 2002: the Defense Department would buy the ticket directly and then also reimburse the employee for the cost of the ticket.[b]

The Army Corps of Engineers, too, has been caught cooking its books. The Corps spends $5 billion annually building dams and other water projects. But it has a serious conflict of interest: the Corps' "strategic vision" inspires managers to increase their budgets as rapidly as they can, but at the same time, the Corps is charged with evaluating the science and economics of each project. The result is that there is every incentive for Corps managers to approve as many proposed projects as possible. GAO and other investigations also found that the Corps' economic studies regularly contained dozens of basic mistakes in arithmetic, simple computer errors, and unrealistic assumptions that artificially inflated the benefits of water projects.[c]

Yet Congress has opposed installing tougher measures of oversight and financial accountability. One reason for Congress's reluctance is that some programs found to have a lot of waste and fraud also happen to be politically popular. Medicare, for instance, which has been found to pay for drugs at as much as eight times the prices of other federal agencies, is a popular program—and, for most senior Americans, an indispensable one. As for the Army Corps of Engineers, they may do wasteful projects, but those same projects meet Congress members' demands for pork-barrel projects that bring in contracts and jobs to their districts around the country.

Q. *How much waste would you say there is in various spending by the United States government: a great deal, some, not not very much, or none at all?*

In domestic spending

Great deal	61%
Some	32%
Not very much	5%
None at all	1%

In military spending

Great deal	43%
Some	41%
Not very much	10%
None at all	3%

[a]www.heritage.org/Research/Budget/bg1840.cfm; U.S. Department of Agriculture, Office of Inspector General, Headquarters Audit Report, "Adequacy of Internal Controls over the Individually Billed Travel Card Program," Report No. 50601-05-HQ, June 19, 2003, at www.usda.gov/oig/webdocs/50601-05-HQ.pdf (March 28, 2005).

[b]U.S. General Accounting Office, *DOD Travel Cards: Control Weaknesses Led to Millions of Dollars in Unused Airline Tickets*, GAO-03-398, March 2004, at www.gao.gov/new.items/d04398.pdf

[c]Michael Grunwald, "An Agency of Unchecked Clout," *The Washington Post*, September 11, 2000; Michael Grunwald, "GAO Details Errors in Army Corps Project," *The Washington Post*, June 11, 2002.

★ **program budgeting**
Identifying items in a budget according to the functions and programs they are to be spent on.

For many years, reformers have called for budgeting by programs. **Program budgeting** would require agencies to present budgetary requests in terms of the end products they will produce or at least to allocate each expense to a specific program. However, bureaucrats are often unenthusiastic about program budgeting; it certainly adds to the time and energy devoted to budgeting, and many agencies are reluctant to describe precisely what it is they do and how much it really costs to do it. Moreover, some political functions are best served by *non*program budgeting. Agreement comes more easily when the items in dispute can be treated in dollars instead of programmatic differences. Congressional Appropriations Committees can focus on increases or decreases in overall dollar amounts for agencies rather than battle over even more contentious questions of which individual programs are worthy of support.

Regulatory Battles

Bureaucracies regulate virtually every aspect of American life. Interest rates on loans are heavily influenced by the Federal Reserve Board. The National Labor Relations Board protects unions and prohibits "unfair labor practices." Safety in automobiles and buses is the responsibility of the National Transportation Safety Board. The Federal Deposit Insurance Corporation insures bank accounts. The Federal Trade Commission orders cigarette manufacturers to place a health warning on each pack. The Equal Employment Opportunity Commission investigates complaints about racial and sexual discrimination in jobs. The Consumer Product Safety Commission requires that toys be large enough that they cannot be swallowed by children. The Federal Communications Commission bans tobacco advertisements on television. The Environmental Protection Agency requires automobile companies to limit exhaust emissions. The Occupational Safety and Health Administration requires construction firms to place portable toilets at work sites. The Food and Drug Administration decides what drugs your doctor can prescribe. The list goes on and on. Indeed, it is difficult to find an activity in public or private life that is not regulated by the federal government (see *A Conflicting View:* "Bureaucratic Regulations Are Suffocating America").

Federal regulatory bureaucracies are legislators, investigators, prosecutors, judges, and juries—all wrapped into one. They issue thousands of pages of rules and regulations each year; they investigate thousands of complaints and conduct thousands of inspections; they require businesses to submit hundreds of thousands of forms each year; they hold hearings, determine "compliance" and "noncompliance," issue corrective orders, and levy fines and penalties. Most economists agree that regulation adds to the cost of living, is an obstacle to innovation and productivity, and hinders economic competition. Most regulatory commissions are independent; they are not under an executive department, and their members are appointed for long terms by a president who has little control over their activities.

Traditional Agencies: Capture Theory
The **capture theory of regulation** describes how some regulated industries come to benefit from government regulation and how some regulatory commissions come to represent the industries they are supposed to regulate rather than representing "the people." Historically, regulatory commissions have acted against only the most wayward members of an industry. By attacking those businesses that gave the industry bad publicity, the commissions actually helped improve the public's opinion of the industry as a whole. Regulatory commissions provided symbolic reassurance to the public that the behavior of the industry was proper. Among the traditional regulatory agencies that have been accused of becoming too close to their regulated industry are the

Think Again

Do you believe bureaucratic regulations of all kinds are hurting America's competitiveness in the global economy?

Think Again

Do you believe that the overall costs of federal regulatory activity are justified by the benefits?

★ **capture theory of regulation**
Theory describing how some regulated industries come to benefit from government regulation and how some regulatory commissions come to represent the industries they are supposed to regulate rather than representing "the people."

A Conflicting *View*

Bureaucratic Regulations Are Suffocating America

Today, bureaucratic regulations of all kinds— environmental controls, workplace safety rules, municipal building codes, government contracting guidelines— have become so numerous, detailed, and complex that they are stifling initiative, curtailing economic growth, wasting billions of dollars, and breeding popular contempt for law and government.

Consider, for example, the Environmental Protection Agency's rules and regulations, now *seventeen volumes* of fine print. Under one set of rules, before any land on which "toxic" waste was once used can be reused by anyone for any purpose, it must be cleaned to near perfect purity. The dirt must be made cleaner than soil that has never been used for anything. The result is that most new businesses choose to locate on virgin land rather than incur the enormous expense of cleaning dirt, and a great deal of land previously used by industry sits vacant while new land is developed.

These and similar examples of "the death of common sense" in bureaucratic regulations are set forth by critic Philip K. Howard, who argues, "We have constructed a system of regulatory law that basically outlaws common sense."[a]

The explosive growth in federal regulations in the last two decades has added heavy costs to the American economy. The costs of regulations do not appear in the federal budget: rather, they are paid for by businesses, employees, and consumers. Indeed, politicians prefer a regulatory approach to the environment, health, and safety precisely because it forces costs on the private sector—costs that are largely invisible to

voters and taxpayers. Yet as the costs of regulation multiply for American businesses, the prices of their products rise in world markets.

How large is the regulatory bill? Proponents of a regulatory activity usually object to estimating its cost. Politicians who wish to develop an image as protectors of the environment, of consumers, of the disabled, and so on, do not want to call attention to the costs of their legislation. Only recently has the Office of Management and Budget (OMB) even attempted to estimate the costs of federal regulatory activity. Overall, regulatory activity costs Americans between $300 billion (OMB estimate) and $700 billion a year (estimate by Center for the Study of American Business), an amount equal to over one-third of the total federal budget.

Regulation also places a heavy burden on innovations and productivity. The costs and delays in winning permission for a new product tend to discourage invention and to drive up prices. For example, new drugs are difficult to introduce in the United States because the Food and Drug Administration (FDA) typically requires up to 10 years of testing. Western European nations are many years ahead in their number of life-saving drugs available; they speak of the "drug lag" in the United States. Critics charge that if aspirin were proposed for marketing today, it would not be approved by the FDA. Recently activists have succeeded in speeding up FDA approval of drugs to treat AIDS, but the agency has continued to delay the introduction of drugs to treat other diseases.

[a]Philip K. Howard, *The Death of Common Sense: How Law Is Suffocating America.* New York: Random House, 1995, pp. 10–11.

Federal Communications Commission (FCC, regulator of the communications industry, including the television networks), the Securities and Exchange Commission (SEC, the securities industry and stock exchanges), the Federal Reserve Board (FRB, the banking industry), and National Labor Relations Board (NLRB, unions).

Agencies need not be actually "captured" by the industries they regulate but rather simply provide "protection" to these industries, especially to the largest corporations within them. Larger corporations are better able to meet agency requirements and to respond to changes in these requirements than smaller corporations or individual firms. In product approval, licensing, permitting, and grant making, for example, larger corporations are better able to jump through bureaucratic hoops.[15]

Commission members often come from the industry they are supposed to regulate, and after a few years in government, the "regulators" return to high-paying jobs in the industry, creating the *revolving door problem* described in Chapter 9. Over the years, then, some industries have come to support their regulatory

Occupational Safety and Health Administration (OSHA) officials, along with others, investigate the collapse of a large building in Hobe Sound, Florida, on July 23, 2004.

bureaucracies. Industries have often strongly opposed proposals to reduce government controls. Proposals to deregulate railroads, interstate trucking, and airlines have met with substantial opposition from both the regulatory bureaucracies and the regulated industries, working together.

The Newer Regulators: The Activists

In recent decades, Congress created several new "activist" regulatory agencies in response to the civil rights movement, the environmental movement, and the consumer protection movement. Unlike traditional regulatory agencies, the activist agencies do not regulate only a single industry; rather, they extend their jurisdiction to all industries. The Equal Employment Opportunity Commission (EEOC), the Environmental Protection Agency (EPA), and the Occupational Safety and Health Administration (OSHA) pose serious challenges to the business community. Many businesspeople argue that EEOC rules designed to prevent racial and sexual discrimination in employment and promotion (affirmative action guidelines) ignore the problems of their industry or their labor market and overlook the costs of training or the availability of qualified minorities. Likewise, many of OSHA's thousands of safety regulations appear costly and ridiculous to people in industry. The complaint about EPA is that it seldom considers the cost of its rulings to business or the consumer. Industry representatives contend that EPA should weigh the costs of its regulations against the benefits to the environment.

Deregulation

★ deregulation
Lifting of government rules and bureaucratic supervision from business and professional activity.

The demand to deregulate American life was politically very popular during President Ronald Reagan's administration in the 1980s. But **deregulation** made only limited progress in curtailing the power of the regulatory bureaucracies. Arguments for deregulation centered on the heavy costs of compliance with regulations, the burdens these costs imposed on innovation and productivity, and the adverse impact of regulatory activity on the global competitiveness of American industry. In 1978 Jimmy Carter succeeded in getting Congress to deregulate the airline industry. Against objections by the industry itself, which *wanted* continued regulation, the Civil Aeronautics Board was stripped of its powers to allocate airline routes to various carriers and to set rates. At the end of 1984, the board went out of existence, the first major regulatory agency ever to be abolished. With the airlines free to choose where to fly and what to charge, competition on heavily traveled routes (such as from New York to Los Angeles) reduced fares dramatically while prices rose on less traveled routes served by a single airline. Overall the cost of airline travel declined by 25 to 30 percent.[16] Competition caused airline profits to decline and financially weak airlines to declare bankruptcy. Also, during the 1980s the Interstate Commerce Commission (ICC), the first regulatory commission ever established by the federal government, dating from 1887, was stripped of most of its power to set railroad and trucking rates. The ICC itself was finally abolished in 1995. Prices to consumers of railroad and trucking services declined dramatically.

Reregulation   Deregulation threatens to diminish politicians' power and to eliminate bureaucrats' jobs. It forces industries to become competitive and diminishes the role of interest group lobbyists. So in the absence of strong popular support for deregulation, pressures to continue and expand regulatory activity will always be strong in Washington.

Airline deregulation brought about a huge increase in airline travel. The airlines doubled their seating capacity and made more efficient use of their aircraft through the development of "hub-and-spoke" networks. Air safety continued to improve; fatalities per millions of miles flown declined; and by taking travelers away from far more dangerous highway travel, overall transportation safety was enhanced. But these favorable outcomes were overshadowed by complaints about congestion at major airports and increased flight delays, especially at peak hours. The major airports are publicly owned, and governments have been very slow in responding to increased air traffic. Congestion and delays are widely publicized, and politicians respond to complaints by calling for reregulation of airline travel.

The political incentives to create new regulatory agencies, grant additional powers to existing agencies, and add to the accumulation of federal regulations are great. Politicians want to be seen "doing something" about any well-publicized problem in America. The media reports accidents, health scares, and environmental dangers. Soon after, politicians are interviewed for their response, and most feel obliged to call for new laws and regulations, with little regard to their likely costs or effectiveness.

Regulating America

Federal regulatory agencies continually add more rules to American life. Roughly 4,000 new rules, all with the force of law, are issued by regulatory agencies each year. The Environmental Protection Agency (EPA) leads in making new rules, closely followed by the Internal Revenue Service (IRS) and the Federal Communications Commission (FCC).

Over 50 federal agencies have rule-making power. These agencies must publish proposed rules in the *Federal Register* and allow time for interested groups to "comment" on them. "Major rules," those estimated to cost Americans at least $100 or more per year in compliance, are sent to the Office of Management and Budget before being finalized.

Multiplying Regulations   Inasmuch as proposed new regulations must be published in the *Federal Register,* the size of this publication is often used as an indicator of overall federal regulatory activity. In 1970, the *Federal Register* included roughly 20,000 pages; by 1980, it had expanded to over 73,000 pages. Only during the presidency of Ronald Reagan, who promised to reduce federal regulatory activity, did the size of the *Federal Register* decline somewhat. But by 2000 it was again over 80,000 pages.

The accumulated regulations of federal government are published in the Code of Federal Regulations. The Code includes all regulations currently in effect. The Code has now expanded to over 150,000 pages, 50 titles, and 205 volumes.

The Costs of Regulation   Regulatory activity incurs costs for American businesses, employers, and consumers—costs which do not appear in the federal budget. (The official budgets of all federal regulatory agencies combined add up to "only" about $20 billion.) Indeed, it is precisely because these costs do *not* appear in the federal budget that politicians prefer a regulatory approach to many of the nation's problems. Regulation shifts costs from the government itself onto the private sector, costs that are largely invisible to voters and taxpayers. Even when agencies themselves are supposed to calculate the costs of their regulations, their calculations vary in quality and almost always underestimate the true costs.[17] One independent estimate of the total costs of federal regulation sets the figure at $700 *billion,* or about 7 percent of the nation's Gross Domestic Product.[18]

Regulations impose costs on Americans in a variety of ways. First of all, there are the direct costs of compliance. Direct costs include everything from adding pollution control devices and making businesses accessible to the disabled, to the overhead costs of paperwork, attorney and accounting fees, and staff time needed to negotiate the federal regulatory maze. Second, there are indirect economic costs—costs incurred by devoting resources to compliance that otherwise would be used to increase productivity. This lost economic output may amount to *$1 trillion* per year.[19] All of these costs, which typically are imposed on businesses, are ultimately passed on to American consumers in the form of higher prices.

Congressional Constraints on the Bureaucracy

Bureaucracies are unelected hierarchical organizations, yet they must function within democratic government. To wed bureaucracy to democracy, ways must be found to ensure that bureaucracy is responsible to the people. Controlling the bureaucracy is a central concern of democratic government. The federal bureaucracy is responsible to all three branches of government—the president, the Congress, and the courts. Although the president is the nominal head of the executive agencies, Congress—through its power to create or eliminate and fund or fail to fund these agencies—exerts its full share of control. Most of the structure of the executive branch of government (see Figure 12.1) is determined by laws of Congress. Congress has the constitutional power to create or abolish executive departments and independent agencies, or to transfer their functions, as it wishes. Congress can by law expand or contract the discretionary authority of bureaucrats. It can grant broad authority to agencies in vaguely written language, thereby adding to the power of bureaucracies, which can then determine themselves how to define and implement their own authority. In contrast, narrow and detailed laws place constraints on the bureaucracy.

In addition to specific constraints on particular agencies, Congress has placed a number of general constraints on the entire federal bureaucracy. Among the more important laws governing bureaucratic behavior are the following:

★ *Administrative Procedures Act (1946):* Requires that agencies considering a new rule or policy give public notice in the *Federal Register,* solicit comments, and hold public hearings before adopting the new measures.

★ *Freedom of Information Act (1966):* Requires agencies to allow citizens (and the media) to inspect all public records, with some exceptions for intelligence, current criminal investigations, and personnel actions (see *Politics Up Close:* "How to Use the Freedom of Information Act").

★ *Privacy Act (1974):* Requires agencies to keep confidential the personal records of individuals, notably their Social Security files and income tax records.

Budget Director Jim Nussle briefs reporters on the fiscal 2009 federal budget on February 4, 2008, in the White House briefing room. The Director of the Office of Management and Budget is one of the most influential government officials, but he seldom appears on national television.

Senate Confirmation of Appointments The U.S. Senate's power to confirm presidential appointments gives it some added influence over the bureaucracy.[20] It is true that once nominated and confirmed, cabinet secretaries and regulatory commission members can defy the Congress; only the president can remove them from office. Senators usually try to impress their own views on presidential appointees seeking confirmation, however. Senate committees holding confirmation

Politics Up Close — How to Use the Freedom of Information Act

The Freedom of Information Act (FOIA) of 1966 requires agencies of the federal government to provide any member of the public records of the agencies. As amended by the Privacy Act of 1974, individuals can obtain their personal records held by government agencies and are given the right to correct information that is inaccurate. The FOIA does not apply to Congress, the federal courts, state and local government agencies (unless a state has a similar law), military plans and weapons, law enforcement investigations, records of financial institutions, or records which would invade the privacy of others. An agency must respond within 10 days to an FOIA request, but it may charge fees for the costs of searching for the documents and duplicating them.

A good request must "reasonably describe" the records that are being sought; it must be specific enough that an agency employee will be able to locate the records within a reasonable amount of time. A good FOIA request letter includes:

Attention: Freedom of Information/Privacy Request
Name and Address of Agency

This is a request under the Freedom of Information Act, 5 U.S.C. Sec.552

I request a copy of the following documents be provided for me.

_____

_____

I am aware that if my request is denied I am entitled to know the grounds for this denial and make an administrative appeal.

I am willing to pay fees for this request up to a maximum of $___. If you estimate that fees will exceed this limit, please inform me first.

Thank you for your prompt attention.

Signature

Address

hearings often subject appointees to lengthy lectures on how the members believe their departments or agencies should be run. In extreme cases, when presidential appointees do not sufficiently reflect the views of Senate leaders, their confirmation can be held up indefinitely or, in very rare cases, defeated in a floor vote on confirmation.

Congressional Oversight   Congressional oversight of the federal bureaucracy is a continuing activity. Congress justifies its oversight activities on the grounds that its lawmaking powers require it to determine whether the purposes of the laws it passed are being carried out. Congress has a legitimate interest in communicating legislative *intent* to bureaucrats charged with the responsibility for implementing laws of Congress. But often oversight activities are undertaken to influence bureaucratic decision making. Members of Congress may seek to secure favorable treatment for friends and constituents, try to lay the political groundwork for increases or decreases in agency appropriations, or simply strive to enhance their own power or the power of their committees or subcommittees over the bureaucracy.

Oversight is lodged primarily in congressional committees and subcommittees (see "In Committee" in Chapter 10) whose jurisdictions generally parallel those of executive departments and agencies. However, all too frequently, agencies are required to respond to multiple committee inquiries in both the House and the Senate.

Congressional Appropriations   The congressional power to grant or to withhold the budget requests of bureaucracies and the president is perhaps Congress's most potent weapon in controlling the bureaucracy. Spending authorizations for executive agencies are determined by standing committees with jurisdiction in various policy areas, such as armed services, judiciary, education, and labor (see Table 10.4 in Chapter 10), and appropriations are determined by the House and Senate Appropriations Committees and, more specifically, their subcommittees with particular jurisdictions. These committees and subcommittees exercise great power over executive agencies. The Defense Department, for example, must seek *authorizations* for new weapons systems from the House and Senate Armed Services Committees and *appropriations* to actually purchase these weapons from the House and Senate Appropriations Committees, especially their Defense Appropriations subcommittees.

Constant Controversy

Protests are frequent in Washington, especially near the White House in Lafayette Park. Topics of protests vary widely. The war in Iraq has spawned more protests in recent years than any other issue.

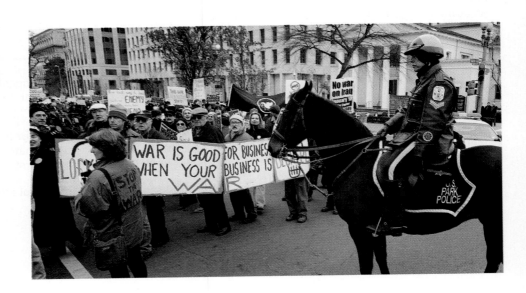

Congressional Investigation   Congressional investigations offer yet another tool for congressional oversight of the bureaucracy. Historically, congressional investigations have focused on scandal and wrongdoing in the executive branch (see "Oversight of the Bureaucracy" in Chapter 10). Occasionally, investigations even produce corrective legislation, although they more frequently produce changes in agency personnel, procedures, or policies. Investigations are more likely to follow media reports of waste, fraud, or scandal than to uncover previously unknown problems. In other words, investigations perform a political function for Congress—assuring voters that the Congress is taking action against bureaucratic abuses. Studies of routine bureaucratic performance are likely to be undertaken by the Government Accountability Office (GAO), an arm of Congress and frequent critic of executive agencies. GAO may undertake studies of the operations of executive agencies on its own initiative but more often responds to requests for studies by specific members of Congress.

Casework   Perhaps the most frequent congressional oversight activities are calls, letters, and visits to the agencies by individual members of Congress seeking to influence particular actions on behalf of themselves or their constituents. A great deal of congressional **casework** involves intervening with executive agencies on behalf of constituents[21] (see Chapter 10). Executive departments and agencies generally try to deal with congressional requests and inquiries as favorably and rapidly as the law allows. Pressure from a congressional office will lead bureaucrats to speed up an application, correct an error, send information, review a case, or reinterpret a regulation to favor a client with congressional contacts. But bureaucrats become very uncomfortable when asked to violate established regulations on behalf of a favored person or firm. The line between serving constituents and unethical or illegal attempts to influence government agencies is sometimes very difficult to discern.

★ **casework**
Services performed by legislators and their staffs on behalf of individual constituents.

Interest Groups and Bureaucratic Decision Making

Interest groups understand that great power is lodged in the bureaucracy. Indeed, interest groups exercise an even closer oversight of bureaucracy than do the president, Congress, and courts, largely because their interests are directly affected by day-to-day bureaucratic decisions. Interest groups focus their attention on the particular departments and agencies that serve or regulate their own members or that function in their chosen policy field. For example, the American Farm Bureau Federation monitors the actions of the Department of Agriculture; environmental lobbies—such as the National Wildlife Federation, the Sierra Club, and the Environmental Defense Fund— watch over the Environmental Protection Agency as well as the National Park Service and U.S. Forest Service. The American Legion, Veterans of Foreign Wars, and Vietnam Veterans "oversee" the Department of Veterans Affairs. Thus specific groups come to have a proprietary interest in "their" specific departments and agencies. Departments and agencies understand that their "client" groups have a continuing interest in their activities.

Many bureaucracies owe their very existence to strong interest groups that successfully lobbied Congress to create them. The Environmental Protection Agency owes its existence to the environmental groups, just as the Equal Employment Opportunity Commission owes its existence to civil rights groups. Thus many

Spinach farmer Dale Huss of Sea Mist Farms, right, inspects spinach plants with Doug Mosebar, president of the California Farm Bureau Federation, September 29, 2006, in a field near Castroville, California. The U.S. Food and Drug Administration's mission is to protect the health of the food—such as spinach—and the drugs consumed by the American public. But the FDA and Congress tend to be most responsive to their biggest clients, such as large agricultural producers and food distributors, fast-food chains, supermarkets, and the major pharmaceutical firms.

bureaucracies nourish interest groups' support to aid in expanding their authority and increasing their budgets (see "Iron Triangles" in Chapter 9).

Interest groups can lobby bureaucracies directly by responding to notices of proposed regulations, testifying at public hearings, and providing information and commentary. Or interest groups can lobby Congress either in support of bureaucratic activity or to reverse a bureaucratic decision. Interest groups may also seek to "build fires" under bureaucrats by holding press conferences, undertaking advertising campaigns, and soliciting media support for agency actions. Or interest groups may even seek to influence bureaucracies through appeals to the federal courts.

Judicial Constraints on the Bureaucracy

Judicial oversight is another source of restraint on the bureaucracy. Bureaucratic decisions are subject to review by the federal courts. Federal courts can even issue *injunctions* (orders) to an executive agency *before* it issues or enforces a regulation or undertakes a particular action. Thus, the judiciary poses a check on bureaucratic power.

Judicial Standards for Bureaucratic Behavior   Historically, the courts have stepped in when agency actions have violated laws passed by Congress, when agencies have exceeded the authority granted them under the laws, when the agency actions have been adjudged "arbitrary and unreasonable," and when agencies have failed in their legal duties under the law. The courts have also restrained the bureaucracy on procedural grounds—ensuring proper notice, fair hearings, rights of appeal, and so on. In short, appeals to the courts must cite failures of agencies to abide by substantive or procedural laws.

Judicial oversight tends to focus on (1) whether or not agencies are acting beyond the authority granted them by Congress; and (2) whether or not they are abiding by

A *Constitutional* Note

Congress and the Budget

The Constitution places "the power of the purse" firmly in the hands of Congress: "No money shall be drawn from the Treasury, but in Consequence of Appropriations made by Law" (Article I, Section 9). The Congress has multiple means of controlling the bureaucracy. It can create, eliminate, or reorganize agencies, and it can alter their functions and rules of operation as it sees fit. And the Senate can confirm or withhold confirmation of presidential appointments. In the exercise of these powers Congress can hold hearings, conduct investigations, and interrogate executive officials. But the power over appropriations for departments and agencies remains the most important instrument of congressional control over the bureaucracy. The president, of course, is head of the executive branch and the Constitution charges him to "take care that the laws be faithfully executed" (Article II, Section 3). Prior to 1921, executive departments and agencies submitted their budgets directly to the Congress with very little presidential input or control. But the Budget and Accounting Act of that year established a Bureau of the Budget which later was placed in the White House directly under the president. The act required all executive agencies to submit their budgets to the Bureau of the Budget, now called the Office of Management and Budget (OMB), and to the president. The president and OMB draw up the *Budget of the United States Government* each year for submission to Congress. The Budget Committees of the House and Senate by resolution set overall totals for budget outlays in major categories. These committees are under no obligation to follow the president's budget recommendations. Later, the Appropriations Committees and subcommittees of each house write up specific appropriations bills. If it wishes, Congress can ignore items in the president's budget and appropriate whatever funds to whatever agencies it chooses. The Appropriations Committees of the House and Senate jealously guard Congress's "power of the purse."

rules of procedural fairness. It is important to realize that the courts do not usually involve themselves in the *policy* decisions of bureaucracies. If policy decisions are made in accordance with the legal authority granted agencies by Congress, and if they are made with procedural fairness, the courts generally do not intervene.

Bureaucrats' Success in Court Bureaucracies have been very successful in defending their actions in federal courts.[22] Individual citizens and interest groups seeking to restrain or reverse the actions or decisions of executive agencies have been largely *unsuccessful*. What accounts for this success? Bureaucracies have established elaborate administrative processes to protect their decisions from challenge on procedural grounds. Regulatory agencies have armies of attorneys, paid for out of tax monies, who specialize in these narrow fields of law. It is very expensive for individual citizens to challenge agency actions. Corporations and interest groups must weigh the costs of litigation against the costs of compliance before undertaking a legal challenge of the bureaucracy. Excessive delays in court proceedings, sometimes extending to several years, add to the time and expense of challenging bureaucratic decisions.

Summary
Who Gets What: The Bureaucracy

The Washington bureaucracy—the departments, agencies, and bureaus of the executive branch of the federal government—is a major base of power in American government. Political conflict does not end when a law is passed by Congress and signed by the president. The arena merely shifts to the bureaucracy.

★ Bureaucratic power has grown with increases in the size of government, advances in technology, and the greater complexity of modern society. Congress and the president do not have the time, resources, or expertise to decide the details of policy across the wide range of social and economic activity in the nation. Bureaucracies must draw up the detailed rules and regulations that actually govern the nation. Often laws are passed for their symbolic value; bureaucrats must give practical meaning to these laws. And the bureaucracy itself is now sufficiently powerful to get laws passed adding to its authority, size, and budget.

★ Policy implementation is the development of procedures and activities and the allocation of money, personnel, and other resources to carry out the tasks mandated by law. Implementation includes regulation—the making of detailed rules based on the law—as well as adjudication—the application of laws and regulations to specific cases. Bureaucratic power increases with increases in administrative discretion.

★ Bureaucracies usually seek to expand their own powers, functions, and budgets. Most bureaucrats believe strongly in the value of their own programs and the importance of their tasks. And bureaucrats, like everyone else, seek added power, pay, and prestige. Bureaucratic expansion contributes to the growth of government.

★ The federal bureaucracy consists of 2.8 million civilian employees in fourteen cabinet departments and more than sixty independent agencies, as well as a large Executive Office of the President. Federal employment is not growing, but federal spending, especially for Social Security, Medicare, and Medicaid, is growing rapidly.

★ Today federal spending amounts to about 20 percent of GDP, and federal, state, and local government spending combined amounts to about 30 percent of GDP.

★ Historically, political conflict over government employment centered on the question of partisanship versus competence. Over time, the "merit system" replaced the "spoils system" in federal employment, but the civil service system raised problems of responsiveness and productivity in the bureaucracy. Civil service reform efforts have not really resolved these problems.

★ The president's control of the bureaucracy rests principally on the powers to appoint and remove policy-making officials, to recommend increases and decreases in agency budgets, and to recommend changes in agency structure and function.

★ But the bureaucracy has developed various means to insulate itself from presidential influence. Bureaucrats have many ways to delay and obstruct policy decisions with which they disagree. Whistle-blowers may inform Congress or the media of waste, mismanagement, or fraud. A network of friends and professional associates among bureaucrats, congressional staffs, and client groups helps create a "culture" within each agency and department. The bureaucratic culture is highly resistant to change.

★ Women and minorities are represented in overall federal employment in proportion to their percentages of the U.S. population. However, women and minorities are not proportionately represented in the higher levels of the bureaucracy.

★ Budget battles over who gets what begin in the bureaucracy as departments and agencies send their budget requests forward to the president's Office of Management and Budget. OMB usually reduces agency requests in line with the president's priorities. The president submits spending recommendations to Congress early each year in *The Budget of the United States Government*. Congress is supposed to pass its appropriations acts prior to the beginning of the fiscal year, October 1, but frequently falls behind schedule.

★ Budgeting is incremental, in that last year's agency expenditures are usually accepted as a base and attention is focused on proposed increases. Incrementalism saves time and effort and reduces political conflict by not requiring agencies to justify every dollar spent, only proposed increases each year. Nonprogrammatic budgeting also helps reduce conflict over the value of particular programs. The result, however, is that many established programs continue long after the need for them has disappeared.

★ Bureaucracies regulate virtually every aspect of our lives. The costs of regulation are borne primarily by business and consumers; they do not appear in the federal budget. In part for this reason, a regulatory approach to national problems appeals to elected officials who seek to obscure the costs of government activity. It is difficult to calculate the true costs and benefits of much regulatory activity. After a brief period of deregulation in the 1980s, regulation has regained popular favor.

★ Congress can exercise control over the bureaucracy in a variety of ways: by creating, abolishing, or reorganizing departments and agencies; by altering their authority and functions; by requiring bureaucrats to testify before congressional committees; by undertaking investigations and studies through the Government Accountability Office; by intervening directly on behalf of constituents; by instructing presidential nominees in Senate confirmation hearings and occasionally delaying or defeating nominations; and especially by withholding or threatening to withhold agency appropriations or by writing very specific provisions into appropriations acts.

★ Interest groups also influence bureaucratic decision making directly by testifying at public hearings and providing information and commentary, and indirectly by contacting the media, lobbying Congress, and initiating lawsuits.

★ Judicial control of the bureaucracy is usually limited to determining whether agencies have exceeded the authority granted them by law or have abided by the rules of procedural fairness. Federal bureaucracies have a strong record of success in defending themselves in court.

Key Terms

bureaucracy 416	budget maximization 420	budget resolution 436	incremental budgeting 439
chain of command 416	discretionary funds 420	authorization 438	zero-based budgeting 439
division of labor 416	spoils system 428	appropriations act 438	program budgeting 442
impersonality 416	merit system 429	obligational	capture theory of
implementation 416	whistle-blowers 432	authority 438	regulation 442
regulation 419	outsourcing 433	outlays 438	deregulation 444
adjudication 419	fiscal year 436	continuing resolution 438	casework 449

Suggested Readings

Gormley, William T., and Steven J. Balla. *Bureaucracy and Democracy: Accountability and Performance.* 2nd ed. Washington, D.C.: CQ Press, 2007. Administrative theory and approaches to bureaucratic relationship in a democracy.

Henry, Nicholas. *Public Administration and Public Affairs.* 10th ed. Upper Saddle River, N.J.: Prentice Hall, 2007. Authoritative introductory textbook on public organizations (bureaucracies), public management, and policy implementation.

Howard, Philip K. *The Death of Common Sense: How Law Is Suffocating America*. New York: Random House, 1995. Outrageous stories of bureaucratic senselessness coupled with a plea to allow bureaucrats flexibility in achieving the purposes of laws and holding them accountable for outcomes.

Kettl, Donald F., and James W. Fesler. *The Politics of the Administrative Process*. 3rd ed. Washington, D.C.: CQ Press, 2005. Introduction to bureaucracy and public administration, including a case appendix with illustrations complementing each chapter.

Kerwin, Cornelius M. *Rulemaking: How Government Agencies Write Law and Make Policy*. 3rd ed. Washington, D.C.: CQ Press, 2003. Argues that rulemaking actually defines the laws of Congress and describes the political activity surrounding rulemaking.

Neiman, Max. *Defending Government: Why Big Government Works*. Upper Saddle River, N. J.: Prentice Hall, 2000. A spirited defense of big government as a product of people's desire to improve their lives.

Osborne, David, and Ted Gaebler. *Reinventing Government*. New York: Addison-Wesley, 1992. The respected manual of the "reinventing government" movement, with recommendations to overcome the routine tendencies of bureaucracies and inject "the entrepreneurial spirit" into them.

Schick, Allen. *The Federal Budget: Politics, Policy, Process*. 3rd ed. Washington, D.C.: Brookings Institution, 2007. A comprehensive explanation of the federal budgetary process.

Smith, Robert W., and Thomas D. Lynch. *Public Budgeting in America*. 5th ed. Upper Saddle River, N.J.: Prentice Hall, 2004. Standard text describing public budget processes, behaviors, and administration.

Wilson, James Q. *Bureaucracy: What Government Agencies Do and Why They Do It*. New York: Basic Books, 1989. In the author's words, "an effort to depict the essential features of bureaucratic life in the government agencies of the United States." Examining what really motivates middle-level public servants, Wilson argues that congressional attempts to "micromanage" government activities hamper the ability of bureaucrats to do their jobs.

Suggested Web Sites

American Society for Public Administration
www.apsanet.org

Organization of scholars and practitioners in public administration. Site includes information on careers, job listings, and so on.

Amtrak www.amtrak.com

The Amtrak Web site provides valuable information about trip planning, reservations, train schedules, and train fares.

Center for Public Integrity www.publicintegrity.org

Reform organization committed to "exposing" corruption, mismanagement, and waste in government.

Code of Federal Regulations www.cfr.law.cornell.edu

All fifty titles of federal regulations can be found at the Cornell Law School site.

Fed World www.fedworld.gov

Run by the U.S. Commerce Department, this site contains information about federal/state–local agency links, government jobs, IRS forms, Supreme Court decisions, and the vast array of governmental services.

Federal Reserve System www.federalreserve.gov

This Federal Reserve System site covers general information about "Fed" operations, including monetary policy, reserve bank services, international banking, and supervisory and regulatory functions.

First Gov www.firstgov.gov

Official Web portal to all federal departments and agencies, information on government benefits, agency links, and so forth.

Food and Drug Administration www.fda.gov

The Food and Drug Administration site is a reflection of the agency's mission "to promote and protect the public health by helping safe and effective products reach the market in a timely way."

Internal Revenue Service www.irs.gov

The tax-collecting IRS is potentially the most powerful of all government agencies, with financial records on every tax-paying American.

Occupational Safety and Health Administration www.osha.gov

This site covers new and information directly related to OSHA's mission "to ensure safe and healthful workplaces in America."

Office of Management and Budget (OMB) www.omb.gov

The OMB site includes all budget documents and information on regulatory oversight.

USA Jobs www.usajobs.gov

This site is the official source for federal employment information.

13 COURTS
Judicial Politics

Chapter *Outline*

- ★ Judicial Power
- ★ Activism Versus Self-Restraint
- ★ Structure and Jurisdiction of Federal Courts
- ★ The Special Rules of Judicial Decision Making
- ★ The Politics of Selecting Judges
- ★ Who Is Selected?
- ★ Supreme Court Decision Making
- ★ Politics and the Supreme Court
- ★ Checking Court Power

Judicial Power

"There is hardly a political question in the United States which does not sooner or later turn into a judicial one."[1] This observation made in 1835 by French diplomat and traveler Alexis de Tocqueville is even more accurate today. It is the Supreme Court and the federal judiciary, rather than the president or Congress, that has taken the lead in deciding many of the most heated issues of American politics. It has undertaken to:

- ★ Eliminate racial segregation and decide about affirmative action.

- ★ Ensure separation of church and state and decide about prayer in public schools.

- ★ Determine the personal liberties of women and decide about abortion.

- ★ Define the limits of free speech and free press and decide about obscenity, censorship, and pornography.

- ★ Ensure equality of representation and require legislative districts to be equal in population.

- ★ Define the rights of criminal defendants, prevent unlawful searches, limit the questioning of suspects, and prevent physical or mental intimidation of suspects.

- ★ Protect private homosexual acts between consenting adults from criminal prosecution.

- ★ Decide the life-or-death issue of capital punishment.

Courts are "political" institutions. Like Congress, the president, and the bureaucracy, courts decide who gets what in American society. Judges do not merely "apply" the law to specific cases. Years ago, former Supreme Court Justice Felix Frankfurter explained why this mechanistic theory of judicial objectivity fails to describe court decision making.

> The meaning of "due process" and the content of terms like "liberty" are not revealed by the Constitution. It is the Justices who make the meaning. They read into the neutral language of the Constitution their own economic and social views. . . . Let us face the fact that five Justices of the Supreme Court are the molders of policy rather than the impersonal vehicles of revealed truth.[2]

✓ Think About Politics

1. Have the federal courts grown too powerful?
   YES ⬭ NO ⬭

2. Is it really democratic to allow federal court judges, who are appointed, not elected, and who serve for life, to overturn laws of an elected Congress and president?
   YES ⬭ NO ⬭

3. Should the Constitution be interpreted in terms of the original intentions of the Founders rather than the morality of society today?
   YES ⬭ NO ⬭

4. Are the costs of lawsuits in America becoming too burdensome on the economy?
   YES ⬭ NO ⬭

5. Should presidents appoint only judges who agree with their judicial philosophy?
   YES ⬭ NO ⬭

6. Should the Senate confirm Supreme Court appointees who oppose abortion?
   YES ⬭ NO ⬭

7. Should the Supreme Court overturn the law of Congress that prohibits federal funding of abortions for poor women?
   YES ⬭ NO ⬭

8. Is there a need to appoint special prosecutors to investigate presidents and other high officials?
   YES ⬭ NO ⬭

Do the Supreme Court and the federal judiciary in fact have the real power to shape public policies in the United States?

Think Again

Have the federal courts grown too powerful?

Comparing Judicial Systems

Comparing Judiciaries

★ **judicial review**
Power of the courts, especially the Supreme Court, to declare laws of Congress, laws of the states, and actions of the president unconstitutional and invalid.

Constitutional Power of the Courts The Constitution grants "the judicial Power of the United States" to the Supreme Court and other "inferior Courts" that Congress may establish. The Constitution guarantees that the Supreme Court and federal judiciary will be politically independent: judges are appointed, not elected, and hold their appointments for life (barring commission of any impeachable offenses). It also guarantees that their salaries will not be reduced during their time in office. The Constitution goes on to list the kinds of cases and controversies that the federal courts may decide. Federal judicial power extends to any case arising under the Constitution and federal laws and treaties, to cases in which officials of the federal government or of foreign governments are a party, and to cases between states or between citizens of different states.

Interpreting the Constitution: Judicial Review The Constitution is the "supreme Law of the Land" (Article VI). Judicial power is the power to decide cases and controversies and, in doing so, to decide what the Constitution and laws of Congress really mean. This authority—together with the guaranteed independence of judges—places great power in the Supreme Court and the federal judiciary. Indeed, because the Constitution takes precedence over laws of Congress as well as state constitutions and laws, it is the Supreme Court that ultimately decides whether Congress, the president, the states, and their local governments have acted constitutionally.

The power of **judicial review** is the power to invalidate laws of Congress or of the states that conflict with the U.S. Constitution. Judicial review is not specifically mentioned in the Constitution but has long been inferred from it. Even before the states had approved the Constitution, Alexander Hamilton wrote in 1787 that "limited government . . . can be preserved in practice no other way than through the medium of courts of justice, whose duty it is to declare all acts contrary to the manifest tenor of the Constitution void."[3] But it was the historic decision of *Marbury v. Madison* (1803)[4] that officially established judicial review as the most important judicial check on congressional power (see *People in Politics*: "John Marshall and Early Supreme Court Politics"). Writing for the majority, Chief Justice Marshall constructed a classic statement in judicial reasoning as he proceeded step by step to infer judicial review from the Constitution's Supremacy (Article VI) and Judicial Power (Article III, Section 1) clauses:

★ The Constitution is the supreme law of the land, binding on all branches of government: legislative, executive, and judicial.

★ The Constitution deliberately establishes a government with limited powers.

★ Consequently, "an act of the legislature repugnant to the Constitution is void." If this were not true, the government would be unchecked and the Constitution would be an absurdity.

★ Under the judicial power, "It is emphatically the province and duty of each of the judicial departments to say what the law is."

★ "So if a law be in opposition to the Constitution . . . the court must determine which of these conflicting rules governs the case. This is the very essence of judicial duty."

People in Politics   John Marshall and Early Supreme Court Politics

John Marshall was a dedicated Federalist. A prominent Virginia lawyer, he was elected a delegate to Virginia's Constitution-ratifying convention, where he was instrumental in winning his state's approval of the document in 1788. Later Marshall served as secretary of state in the administration of John Adams (1797–1801), where he came into conflict with Adams's vice president, Thomas Jefferson.

In the election of 1800, Jefferson's Democratic-Republicans crushed Adams's Federalist Party. But Adams, taking advantage of the fact that his term of office would not expire until the following March,[a] sought to pack the federal judiciary with Federalists. The lame duck Federalist majority in the Senate confirmed the appointments, and John Marshall was sworn in as Chief Justice of the Supreme Court on February 4, 1801. Many of these "midnight appointments" came at the very last hours of Adams's term of office.

At that time, a specified task of the secretary of state was to deliver judicial commissions to new judges. When Marshall left his position as secretary of state to become Chief Justice, several of these commissions were still undelivered. Jefferson and the Democratic-Republicans were enraged over this last-minute Federalist chicanery, so when Jefferson assumed office in March, he ordered his new secretary of state, James Madison, not to deliver the remaining commissions. William Marbury, one of the disappointed Federalist appointees, brought a lawsuit to the Supreme Court, asking it to issue a writ of mandamus ("we command") to James Madison, ordering him to do his duty and deliver the valid commission.

The Judiciary Act of 1789, which established the federal court system, had included a provision granting original jurisdiction to the Supreme Court to issue writs of mandamus. The case, therefore, came directly to new Chief Justice John Marshall, who had failed to deliver the commission in the first place. (Today, we expect justices who are personally involved in a case to "recuse" themselves—that is, not to participate in that case, allowing the other justices to make the decision—but Marshall's actions were typical of his time.)

John Marshall realized that if he issued a direct order to Madison to deliver the commission, Madison would probably ignore it. The Court had no way to enforce such an order, and Madison had the support of President Jefferson. Issuing the writ would create a constitutional crisis in which the Supreme Court would most likely lose power. But if the Court failed to pronounce Madison's actions unlawful, it would lose legitimacy.

Marshall resolved his political dilemma with a brilliant judicial ploy. Writing for the majority in *Marbury v. Madison*, he announced that Madison was wrong to withhold the commission but that the Supreme Court could not issue a writ of mandamus because Section 13 of the Judiciary Act of 1789, which gave the Court *original* jurisdiction in the case, was unconstitutional. Giving the Supreme Court *original* jurisdiction conflicted with Article III, Section 2, of the Constitution, which gives the Supreme Court original jurisdiction only in cases affecting "Ambassadors, other public Ministers and Consuls, and those in which a State shall be a Party." "In all other Cases," the Constitution states that the Court shall have appellate jurisdiction. Thus Section 13 of the Judiciary Act was unconstitutional.

By declaring part of an act of Congress unconstitutional, Marshall accomplished multiple political objectives. He avoided a showdown with the executive branch that would undoubtedly have weakened the Court. He left Jefferson and Madison with no Court order to disobey. At the same time, Marshall forced Jefferson and the Democratic-Republicans to acknowledge the Supreme Court's power of judicial review—the power to declare an act of Congress unconstitutional. (To do otherwise would have meant acknowledging Marbury's claim.) Thus Marshall sacrificed Marbury's commission to a greater political goal, enhancing the Supreme Court's power.

[a]Not until the adoption of the 20th Amendment in 1933 was the president's inauguration moved up to January.

★ "If, then, the courts are to regard the Constitution, and the Constitution is superior to any ordinary act of the legislature, the Constitution, and not such ordinary act, must govern the case to which they both apply."

★ Hence, if a law is repugnant to the Constitution, the judges are duty bound to declare that law void in order to uphold the supremacy of the Constitution.

Linda Brown (foreground) in her classroom in Topeka, taken at about the time of the *Brown v. Board of Education* decision. Brown was refused admittance to a white elementary school, and her family was one of the plaintiffs in the case.

Judicial Review of State Laws   The power of the federal courts to invalidate *state* laws and constitutions that conflict with federal laws or the federal Constitution is easily defended. Article VI states that the Constitution and federal laws and treaties are the supreme law of the land, "any Thing in the Constitution or Laws of any State to the Contrary notwithstanding." Indeed, the Constitution specifically obligates state judges to be "bound" by the Constitution and federal laws and to give these documents precedence over state constitutions and laws in rendering decisions. Federal court power over state decisions is probably essential to maintaining national unity: fifty different state interpretations of the meaning of the Constitution or of the laws and treaties of Congress would create unimaginable confusion. Thus the power of federal judicial review over state constitutions, laws, and court decisions is seldom questioned.

The Supreme Court has used its power of judicial review more frequently to invalidate state laws than laws of Congress. Some of these decisions had impact far beyond the individual states on trial. For example, the historic 1954 decision in *Brown v. Board of Education of Topeka*, declaring segregation of the races in public schools to be unconstitutional, struck down the laws of twenty-one states[5] (see Chapter 12). The 1973 *Roe v. Wade* decision, establishing the constitutional right to abortion, struck down antiabortion laws in more than forty states.[6] In 2003 the Court again struck down the laws of more than forty states by holding that private homosexual acts by consenting adults were protected by the Constitution.[7]

Judicial Review of Laws of Congress   Judicial review is potentially the most powerful weapon in the hands of the Supreme Court. It enables the Court to assert its power over the Congress, the president, and the states and to substitute its own judgment for that of other branches of the federal government and the states. However, the Supreme Court has been fairly restrained in its use of judicial review to void acts of Congress. Prior to the Civil War, the Supreme Court invalidated very few laws of any kind. Since that time, however, the general trend has been for the U.S. Supreme Court to strike down more *state* laws as unconstitutional. In contrast, the Court has been relatively restrained in its rejection of *federal* laws; over two centuries the Court has struck down fewer than 150 of the more than 60,000 laws passed by Congress.

Nevertheless, some of the laws overturned by the Supreme Court have been very important. In *Buckley v. Valeo* (1976)[8] the Court struck down provisions of the Federal Election Campaign Act that had limited the amount individuals could spend to finance their own campaigns or express their own independent political views. In *United States v. Morrison* (2000), the Supreme Court struck down Congress's Violence Against Women Act[9] as an unconstitutional expansion of the interstate commerce power and an invasion of powers reserved to the states (see *Controversy:* "Should Violence Against Women Be a Federal Crime?" in Chapter 4). Overall, however, the Supreme Court's use of judicial review against the Congress has been restrained.

Judicial Review of Presidential Actions   The Supreme Court has only rarely challenged presidential power. The Court has overturned presidential

Politics Up Close   *Clinton v. Jones*

The president is not "above the law"; that is, his conduct is not immune from judicial scrutiny. The president's official conduct must be lawful; federal courts may reverse presidential actions found to be unconstitutional or violative of laws of Congress. And presidents are not immune from criminal prosecution; they cannot ignore demands to provide information in criminal cases.[a] However, the Supreme Court has held that the president has "absolute immunity" from civil suits "arising out of the execution of official duties."[b] In other words, the president cannot be sued for damages caused by actions or decisions that are within his constitutional or legal authority.

But can the president be sued for *private* conduct beyond the scope of his official duties? In 1994 Paula Corbin Jones sued William Jefferson Clinton in federal district court in Arkansas, alleging that he made "abhorrent" sexual advances toward her in Little Rock in 1991 while he was governor and she was a state employee.

The president's lead attorney, Robert Bennett (brother of conservative commentator and former Reagan cabinet official William Bennett), stated that Clinton "has no recollection of ever meeting this woman" and "did not engage in any inappropriate or sexual conduct with this woman." But the president's defense team also argued that the president should be immune from civil actions, especially those arising

from events alleged to occur *before* he assumed office. They argued that the president's constitutional responsibilities are so important and demanding that he must devote his undivided time and attention to them. He cannot be distracted by civil suits; otherwise a large volume of politically motivated frivolous litigation might undermine his ability to function effectively in office. At the very least, the president's attorney argued, the president should be given "temporary immunity" by postponing the case until after he leaves office.

However, in 1997 the U.S. Supreme Court rejected the notion of presidential immunity (as well as temporary immunity) from civil claims arising from actions outside of the president's official duties. Although advising lower courts to give "utmost deference to Presidential responsibilities" in handling the case, the Court held that "the doctrine of separation of powers does not require federal courts to stay all private actions against the president until he leaves office."[c]

Subsequently, after reviewing the case, federal district judge Susan Wright dismissed Jones's charges as insufficient to prove sexual assault or harassment.[d] Clinton later settled the case with a financial payment to Jones, but with no admission or apology. The settlement ended Jones's appeals and avoided possible reopening of the case.

[a]*United States v. Nixon* (1974).
[b]*Nixon v. Fitzgerald* (1982).
[c]*Clinton v. Jones*, May 27, 1997.
[d]*Jones v. Clinton*, April 1, 1998.

policies both on the grounds that they conflicted with laws of Congress and on the grounds that they conflicted with the Constitution. In *Ex parte Milligan* (1866),[10] for example, the Court held (somewhat belatedly) that President Abraham Lincoln could not suspend the writ of habeas corpus in rebellious states during the Civil War. In *Youngstown Sheet & Tube Co. v. Sawyer*, in 1952,[11] it declared President Harry Truman's seizure of the nation's steel mills during the Korean War to be illegal. In 1974 it ordered President Richard Nixon to turn over taped White House conversations to the special Watergate prosecutor, leading to Nixon's forced resignation.[12] And in 1997 the Court held that President Bill Clinton was obliged to respond to a civil suit even while serving in the White House.[13] (See *Politics Up Close: "Clinton v. Jones."*)

Interpreting Federal Laws
The power of the Supreme Court and the federal judiciary does not rest on judicial review alone. The courts also make policy in their interpretation of **statutory laws**—the laws of Congress. Frequently, Congress decides that an issue is too contentious to resolve. Members of Congress cannot

★ **statutory laws**
Laws made by act of Congress or the state legislatures, as opposed to constitutional law.

themselves agree on specific language, so they write, sometimes deliberately, vague, symbolic language into the law—words and phrases like "fairness," "equitableness," "good faith," "good cause," and "reasonableness"—effectively shifting policy making to the courts by giving courts the power to read meaning into these terms.

Activism Versus Self-Restraint

Supreme Court Justice Felix Frankfurter once wrote: "The only check upon our own exercise of power is our own sense of self-restraint. For the removal of unwise laws from the statute books, appeal lies not to the courts but to the ballot and to the processes of democratic government."[14]

Judicial Self-Restraint   The idea behind **judicial self-restraint** is that judges should not read their own philosophies into the Constitution and should avoid direct confrontations with Congress, the president, and the states whenever possible. The argument for judicial self-restraint is that federal judges are not elected by the people and therefore should not substitute their own views for the views of elected representatives. The courts should defer to the judgments of the other branches of government unless there is a clear violation of constitutional principle. The benefit of the doubt should be given to actions taken by elected officials. Courts should only impose remedies that are narrowly tailored to correct specific legal wrongs. As Justice Sandra Day O'Connor argued in her Senate confirmation hearings, "The courts should interpret the laws, not make them . . . I do not believe it is a function of the Court to step in because times have changed or social mores have changed."[15]

Wisdom Versus Constitutionality   A law may be unwise, unjust, or even stupid and yet still be constitutional. One should not equate the wisdom of a law with its constitutionality, and the Court should decide only the constitutionality and not the wisdom of a law. Justice Oliver Wendell Holmes once lectured a younger colleague, 61-year-old Justice Harlan Stone, on this point:

> Young man, about 75 years ago I learned that I was not God. And so, when the people . . . want to do something I can't find anything in the Constitution expressly forbidding them to do, I say, whether I like it or not, "Goddamn it, let 'em do it."[16]

However, the actual role of the Supreme Court in the nation's power struggles suggests that the Court indeed often equates wisdom with constitutionality. People frequently cite broad phrases in the 5th and 14th Amendments establishing constitutional standards of "due process of law" and "equal protection of the laws" when attacking laws they believe are unfair or unjust. Most Americans have come to believe that unwise laws must be unconstitutional. If so, then the courts must be the final arbiters of fairness and justice.

Original Intent   Should the Constitution be interpreted in terms of the intentions of the Founders or according to the morality of society today? Most jurists agree the Constitution is a living document, that it must be interpreted by each generation in the light of current conditions, and to do otherwise would soon render the document obsolete. But in interpreting the document, whose values should prevail—the values of the judges or the values of the Founders? The doctrine of **original intent** takes the values of the Founders as expressed in the text of the Constitution and attempts to apply these values to current conditions. Defenders of original intent argue that the words in the document must be given their historical meaning and that meaning must restrain the courts as well as the

---

✔ *Think* Again

Is it really democratic to allow federal court judges, who are appointed, not elected, and who serve for life, to overturn laws of an elected Congress and president? All of these officials, upon taking office, swear to uphold the Constitution.

★ **judicial self-restraint**
Self-imposed limitation on judicial power by judges deferring to the policy judgments of elected branches of government.

★ **original intent**
Judicial philosophy under which judges attempt to apply the values of the Founders to current issues.

legislative and executive branches of government. That is, the Supreme Court should not set aside laws made by elected representatives unless they conflict with the original intent of the Founders. Judges who set aside laws that do not accord with their personal views of today's moral standards are simply substituting their own morality for that of elected bodies. Such decisions lack democratic legitimacy because there is no reason why judges' moral views should prevail over those of elected representatives.

Judicial Activism   However, the doctrine of original intent carries little weight with proponents of judicial activism. The idea behind **judicial activism** is that the Constitution is a living document whose strength lies in its flexibility, and judges should shape constitutional meaning to fit the needs of contemporary society. The argument for judicial activism is that viewing the Constitution as a broad and flexible document saves the nation from having to pass dozens of new constitutional amendments to accommodate changes in society. Instead, the courts need to give contemporary interpretations to constitutional phrases, particularly general phrases such as "due process of law" (5th Amendment), "equal protection of the laws" (14th Amendment), "establishment of religion" (1st Amendment), and "cruel and unusual punishment" (8th Amendment). Courts have the responsibility to review the actions of other branches of government vigorously, to strike down unconstitutional acts, and to impose far-reaching remedies for legal wrongs whenever necessary.[17]

Stare Decisis   Conflicts between judicial activism and judicial self-restraint are underscored by questions of whether to let past decisions stand or to find constitutional support for overturning them. The principle of **stare decisis**, which means the issue has already been decided in earlier cases, is a fundamental notion in law. Reliance on **precedent** gives stability to the law; if every decision were new law, then no one would know what the law is from day to day. Yet the Supreme Court has discarded precedent in many of its most important decisions: *Brown v. Board of Education* (1954), which struck down laws segregating the races; *Baker v. Carr* (1962), which guaranteed equal representation in legislatures; *Roe v. Wade* (1973), which made abortion a constitutional right; and many other classic cases. Former Justice William O. Douglas, a defender of judicial activism, justified disregard of precedent as follows:

> The decisions of yesterday or of the last century are only the starting points. . . . A judge looking at a constitutional decision may have compulsions to revere the past history and accept what was once written. But he remembers above all else that it is the Constitution which he swore to support and defend, not the gloss which his predecessors may have put on it. So he comes to formulate his own laws, rejecting some earlier ones as false and embracing others. He cannot do otherwise unless he lets men long dead and unaware of the problems of the age in which he lives do his thinking for him.[18]

Rules of Restraint   Even an activist Supreme Court adheres to some general rules of judicial self-restraint, however, including the following:

★ The Court will pass on the constitutionality of legislation only in an actual case; it will not advise the president or Congress on constitutional questions.

★ The Court will not anticipate a question on constitutional law; it does not decide hypothetical cases.

★ The Court will not formulate a rule of constitutional law broader than that required by the precise facts to which it must be applied.

★ **judicial activism**
Making of new law through judicial interpretations of the Constitution.

Supreme Court Chief Justice nominee John Roberts answers questions on September 13, 2005, during his second day of hearings before the Senate Judiciary Committee.

★ **stare decisis**
Judicial precept that the issue has already been decided in earlier cases and the earlier decision need only be applied in the specific case before the bench; the rule in most cases, it comes from the Latin for "the decision stands."

★ **precedent**
Legal principle that previous decisions should determine the outcome of current cases; the basis for stability in law.

★ The Court will not decide on a constitutional question if some other ground exists on which it may dispose of the case.

★ The Court will not decide on the validity of a law if the complainants fail to show that they have been injured by the law.

★ When doubt exists about the constitutionality of a law, the Court will try to interpret the law so as to give it a constitutional meaning and avoid the necessity of declaring it unconstitutional.

★ Complainants must have exhausted all remedies available in lower federal courts or state courts before the Supreme Court will accept review.

★ The Court will invalidate a law only when a constitutional issue is crucial to the case and is substantial, not trivial.

★ Occasionally, the Court defers to Congress and the president, classifies an issue as a political question, and refuses to decide it. The Court has generally stayed out of foreign and military policy areas.

★ If the Court holds a law unconstitutional, it will confine its decision to the particular section of the law that is unconstitutional; the rest of the statute stays intact.

Structure and Jurisdiction of Federal Courts

The federal court system consists of three levels of courts—the Supreme Court, the Courts of Appeals, and the district courts—together with various special courts (see Figure 13.1). Only the Supreme Court is established by the Constitution, although the number of justices is determined by Congress. Article III authorizes Congress to establish such "inferior Courts" as it deems appropriate. Congress has designed a hierarchical system with a U.S. Court of Appeals divided into twelve regional circuit courts, a federal circuit, and ninety-four district courts in the fifty states and one each in Puerto Rico, the U.S. Virgin Islands, Guam, the Northern Marianas, and the District of Columbia. Table 13.1 describes their **jurisdiction** and distinguishes between **original jurisdiction**—where cases are begun, argued, and initially decided—and **appellate jurisdiction**—where cases begun in lower courts are argued and decided on **appeal**.

The Supreme Court is the "court of last resort" in the United States, but it hears only a very small number of cases each year. In a handful of cases, the Supreme Court has original jurisdiction; these concern primarily disputes between states (or states and residents of other states), disputes between a state and the federal government, and disputes involving foreign dignitaries. However, most Supreme Court cases are appellate decisions involving cases from state supreme courts or cases tried first in a U.S. district court.

District Courts   **District courts** are the original jurisdiction trial courts of the federal system. Each state has at least one district court, and larger states have more (New York, for example, has four). There are about eight hundred federal district judges, each appointed for life by the president and confirmed by the Senate. The president also appoints a U.S. marshal for each district to carry out orders of the court and maintain order in the courtroom. District courts hear criminal cases prosecuted by the Department of Justice as well as civil cases. As trial courts, the district courts make use of both **grand juries** (called to hear evidence and, if warranted, to indict a defendant by bringing formal criminal

★ **jurisdiction**
Power of a court to hear a case in question.

★ **original jurisdiction**
Refers to a particular court's power to serve as the place where a given case is initially argued and decided.

★ **appellate jurisdiction**
Particular court's power to review a decision or action of a lower court.

★ **appeal**
In general, requests that a higher court review cases decided at a lower level. In the Supreme Court, certain cases are designated as appeals under federal law; formally, these must be heard by the Court.

★ **district courts**
Original jurisdiction trial courts of the federal system.

★ **grand juries**
Juries called to hear evidence and decide whether defendants should be indicted and tried.

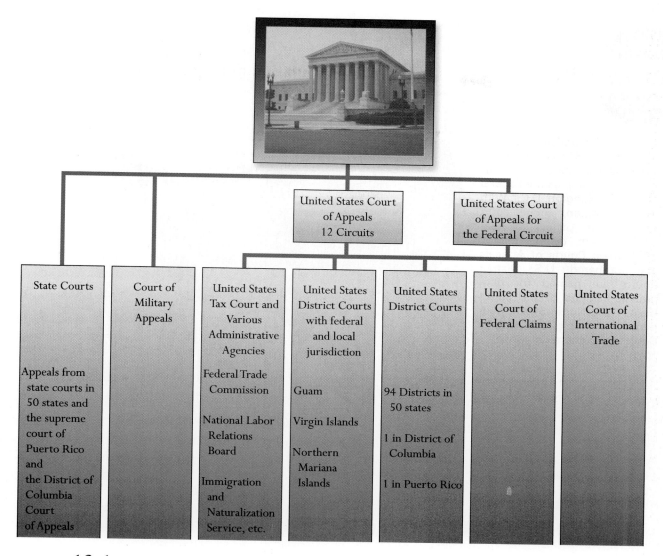

Figure *13.1*   Structure of Federal Courts

The federal court system of the United States is divided into three levels: the courts of original jurisdiction (state courts, military courts, tax courts, district courts, claims courts, and international trade courts), U.S. Courts of Appeals (which hear appeals from all lower courts except state and military panels), and the U.S. Supreme Court, which can hear appeals from all sources.

charges) and **petit** (regular) **juries** (which determine guilt or innocence). District courts may hear 270,000 civil cases in a year and 70,000 criminal cases.

Courts of Appeals   Federal **circuit courts** (see *Across the USA*: "Geographic Boundaries of Federal Courts") are appellate courts. They do not hold trials or accept new evidence but consider only the records of the trial courts and oral or written arguments (**briefs**) submitted by attorneys. Federal law guarantees everyone the right to appeal, so the Courts of Appeal have little discretion in this regard. Appellate judges themselves estimate that more than 80 percent of all appeals are frivolous—that is, without any real basis. There are more than a hundred circuit judges, each appointed for life by the president subject to confirmation by the

★ **petit** (regular) **juries**
Juries called to determine guilt or innocence.

★ **circuit courts**
The twelve appellate courts that make up the middle level of the federal court system.

Across the USA

Geographic Boundaries of Federal Courts

For administrative convenience, the U.S. District Courts are organized into twelve circuits (regions), plus the Federal Circuit (Washington, D.C.). Within each region, circuit court judges form panels to hear appeals from district courts. U.S. Circuit Courts of Appeals are numbered. U.S. District Courts are named for geographic regions of the states (East, West, North, South, Middle), for example, U.S. District Court for Northern California.

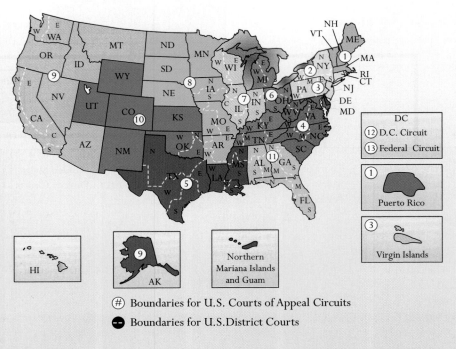

(#) Boundaries for U.S. Courts of Appeal Circuits

(•-) Boundaries for U.S. District Courts

Table *13.1*   Who Decides What?: Jurisdiction of Federal Courts

Supreme Court of the United States	United States Courts of Appeals (Circuit Courts)	United States District Courts
Appellate jurisdiction (cases begin in a lower court); hears appeals, at its own discretion, from:	No original jurisdiction; hear only appeals from:	Original jurisdiction over cases involving:
1. Lower federal courts 2. Highest state courts	1. Federal district courts 2. U.S. regulatory commissions 3. Certain other federal courts	1. Constitution of the United States 2. Federal laws, including federal crimes 3. Civil suits under the federal law 4. Civil suits between citizens of states where the amount exceeds $75,000
Original jurisdiction (cases begin in the Supreme Court) over cases involving:		5. Admiralty and maritime cases 6. Bankruptcy cases 7. Review of actions of certain federal administrative agencies
1. Two or more states 2. The United States and a state 3. Foreign ambassadors and other diplomats 4. A state and a citizen of a different state (if begun by the state)		8. Other matters assigned to them by Congress

Senate. Normally, these judges serve together on a panel to hear appeals. More than 90 percent of the cases decided by the Court of Appeals end at this level. Further appeal to the Supreme Court is not automatic; it must be approved by the Supreme Court itself. Because the Supreme Court hears very few cases, in most cases the decision of the circuit court becomes law.

Supreme Court   The Supreme Court of the United States is the final interpreter of all matters involving the Constitution and federal laws and treaties, whether the case began in a federal district court or in a state court. Appeals to the U.S. Supreme Court may come from a state court of last resort (usually a state's supreme court) or from lower federal courts. The Supreme Court determines whether to accept an appeal and consider a case. It may do so when there is a "substantial federal question" presented in a case or when there are "special and important reasons," or it may reject a case—with or without explaining why.

In the early days of the Republic, the size of the Supreme Court fluctuated, but since 1869 the membership has remained at nine: the Chief Justice and eight associate justices. The Supreme Court is in session each year from October through June, hearing oral arguments, accepting written briefs, conferring, and rendering opinions.

Appeals from State Courts   Each of the fifty states maintains its own courts. The federal courts are not necessarily superior to those courts; state and federal courts operate independently. State courts have original jurisdiction in most criminal and civil cases. Because the U.S. Supreme Court has appellate jurisdiction over state supreme courts as well as over lower federal courts, the Supreme Court oversees the nation's entire judicial system, but the great bulk of cases begin and end in the state court systems. The federal courts do not interfere once a case has been started in a state court except in very rare circumstances. And Congress has stipulated that legal disputes between citizens of different states must involve $75,000 or more to be heard in federal courts. Moreover, parties to cases in state courts must "exhaust their remedies"—that is, appeal their case all the way through the state court system—before the federal courts will hear an appeal. Appeals from state supreme courts go directly to the U.S. Supreme Court and not to a federal district or circuit court. Such appeals are usually made on the grounds that a federal question is involved in the case—that is, a question has arisen regarding the application of the Constitution or a federal law.

Federal Cases   Some 10 million civil and criminal cases are begun in the nation's courts each year (see *A Conflicting View:* "America Is Drowning Itself in a Sea of Lawsuits"). About 270,000 (3 percent) of the cases are begun in the federal courts. About 8,000 are appealed to the Supreme Court each year, but only about 125 of them are openly argued and decided by signed opinions. The Constitution "reserves" general police powers to the states. That is, civil disputes and most crimes—murder, robbery, assault, and rape—are normally state offenses rather than federal crimes and thus are tried in state and local courts.

Federal court caseloads have risen in recent years (see Figure 13.2), in part because more civil disputes are being brought to federal courts. In addition, the U.S. Justice Department is prosecuting more criminal cases as federal law enforcement agencies—such as the Federal Bureau of Investigation (FBI), Drug Enforcement Administration (DEA), Internal Revenue Service (IRS), and Bureau of Alcohol, Tobacco, Firearms, and Explosives (ATF)—have stepped up their investigations. Most of this recent increase is attributable to enforcement of federal drug laws.

★ **briefs**
Documents submitted by an attorney to a court, setting out the facts of the case and the legal arguments in support of the party represented by the attorney.

You Are a Clerk to Supreme Court Justice Judith Gray

Chief Justices of the Supreme Court

Case Overload

A Conflicting *View*

America Is Drowning Itself in a Sea of Lawsuits

America is threatening to drown itself in a sea of lawsuits. Civil suits in the nation's courts exceed *10 million* per year. There are more than 805,000 lawyers in the United States (compared to about 650,000 physicians). These lawyers are in business, and their business is litigation. Generating business means generating lawsuits. And just as businesses search for new products, lawyers search for new legal principles on which to bring lawsuits. They seek to expand legal liability for civil actions—that is, to expand the definition of civil wrongdoings, or torts.

Unquestionably, the threat of lawsuits is an important safeguard for society, compelling individuals, corporations, and government agencies to behave responsibly toward others. Because victims require compensation for *actual* damages incurred by the wrongdoing of others, liability laws protect all of us.

But we need to consider the social costs of frivolous lawsuits, especially those brought without any merit but initiated in the hope that individuals or firms will offer a settlement just to avoid the expenses of defending themselves. Legal expenses and excessive jury awards leveled against corporations increase insurance premiums for businesses and service providers. The Insurance Information Institute estimates that the overall cost of civil litigation in America is many times more than that of other industrial nations, perhaps amounting to over 2 percent of our nation's GDP. For example, the risk of lawsuits forces physicians to practice "defensive medicine," ordering expensive tests, multiple consultations with specialists, and expensive procedures, not because they are adjudged medically necessary, but rather to protect themselves from the possibility of a lawsuit.

Insurance premiums have risen sharply for physicians seeking malpractice insurance, as have premiums for recreation facilities, nurseries and day-care centers, motels, and restaurants.

Reforming the nation's liability laws presents major challenges to the political system. The reform movement can count on support from some normally powerful interest groups—insurance companies, manufacturers, drug companies, hospitals, and physicians. But legal reform is an anathema to the legal profession itself, notably the powerful American Association for Justice (formerly the Association of Trial Lawyers). And lawyers compose the single largest occupational background of Congress members—indeed, of politicians generally.

Figure *13.2*

Overworked?: Caseloads in Federal Courts

Caseloads in the federal courts place a heavy burden on prosecutors and judges. Increases in civil suits in the federal courts are the result of more plaintiffs insisting on taking their cases to the federal level both originally and on appeal. Increases in criminal cases are the result of Congress's decision to make more crimes—especially drug-related crimes—federal offenses and to pursue such criminals more vigorously.

— Civil Cases   — Criminal Cases

Traditionally, federal crimes were offenses directed against the U.S. government, its property, or its employees or were offenses involving the crossing of state lines. Over the years, however, Congress has greatly expanded the list of federal crimes so that federal and state criminal court jurisdictions often overlap, as they do, for example, in most drug violations.

The Special Rules of Judicial Decision Making

Courts are political institutions that resolve conflict and decide about public policy. But unlike Congress, the presidency, and the bureaucracy, the courts employ highly specialized rules in going about their work.

Cases and Controversies   Courts do not initiate policy but rather wait until a case or controversy is brought to them for resolution. A case must involve two disputing parties, one of which must have incurred some real damage as a result of the action or inaction of the other. They do *not* issue policy declarations or decide hypothetical cases. Rather, the courts wait until disputing parties bring a case to them that requires them to interpret the meaning of a law or determine its constitutionality in order to resolve the case. Only then do courts render opinions.

The vast majority of cases do *not* involve important policy issues. Courts determine the guilt or innocence of criminal defendants. Courts enforce contracts and award damages to victims of negligence in **civil cases**. And courts render these decisions on the basis of established law. Only occasionally do courts make significant policy decisions.

Adversarial Proceedings   Underlying judicial decision making is the assumption that the best way to decide an issue is to allow two disputing parties to present arguments on each side. Judges in the United States do not investigate cases, question witnesses, or develop arguments themselves (as they do in some European countries). This **adversarial system** depends on quality of argument on each side, which means it often depends on the capabilities of attorneys. There is no guarantee that the adversarial process will produce the best policy outcomes.

Standing   To bring an issue into court as a case, individuals or firms or interest groups must have **standing**; that is, they must be directly harmed by a law or action. People cannot "go to court" simply because they do not like what the government is doing. Merely being taxpayers does not entitle people to claim that they are damaged by government actions.[19] Individuals or firms automatically have standing when they are prosecuted by the government for violation of laws or regulations. Thus one way to gain standing in order to challenge the legality of a regulation or the constitutionality of a law is to violate the regulation or law and invite the government to prosecute.

To sue the government, plaintiffs must show they have suffered financial damages, loss of property, or physical or emotional harm as a direct result of the government's action. (The party initiating a suit and claiming damages is the **plaintiff**; the party against whom a suit is brought is the **defendant**.) The ancient legal doctrine of **sovereign immunity** means that one cannot sue the government without the government's consent. But by law, the U.S. government allows itself to be sued in a wide variety of contract and negligence cases. A citizen can also personally sue to force government officials to carry out acts that they are required by law to perform or for acting contrary to law. The government does not allow suits for damages as a result of military actions.

★ **civil cases**
Noncriminal court proceedings in which a plaintiff sues a defendant for damages in payment for harm inflicted.

★ **adversarial system**
Method of decision making in which an impartial judge or jury or decision maker hears arguments and reviews evidence presented by opposite sides.

★ **standing**
Requirement that the party who files a lawsuit have a legal stake in the outcome.

★ **plaintiff**
Individual or party who initiates a lawsuit or complaint.

★ **defendant**
Party against whom a criminal or civil suit is brought.

★ **sovereign immunity**
Legal doctrine that individuals can sue the government only with the government's consent.

★ **class action suits**
Cases initiated by parties acting on behalf of themselves and all others similarly situated.

Think Again

Are the costs of lawsuits in America becoming too burdensome on the economy?

★ **contingency fee**
Fee paid to attorneys to represent the plaintiff in a civil suit and receive in compensation an agreed-upon percentage of damages awarded (if any).

Class Action Suits   Class action suits are cases brought into court by individuals on behalf not only of themselves but also of all other persons "similarly situated." That is, the party bringing the case is acting on behalf of a "class" of people who have suffered the same damages from the same actions of the defendant. One of the most famous and far-reaching class action suits was *Brown v. Board of Education of Topeka* (1954). The plaintiff, Linda Brown of Topeka, Kansas, sued her local board of education on behalf of herself and all other black pupils who were forced to attend segregated schools, charging that such schools violated the Equal Protection Clause of the 14th Amendment. When she won the case, the Court's ruling affected not only Linda Brown and the segregated public schools in Topeka but also all other black pupils similarly situated across the nation (see Chapter 12).

Class action suits have grown in popularity. These suits have enabled attorneys and interest groups to bring multimillion-dollar suits against corporations and governments for damages to large numbers of people, even when none of them has individually suffered sufficient harm to merit bringing a case to court. For example, an individual overcharged by an electric utility would not want to incur the expense of suing for the return of a few dollars. But if attorneys sue the utility on behalf of a large number of customers similarly overcharged, the result may be a multimillion-dollar settlement from which the attorneys can deduct their hefty fees.

Legal Fees   Going to court requires financial resources. Criminal defendants are guaranteed an attorney, without charge if they are poor, by the 6th Amendment's guarantee of "Assistance of Counsel" (see Chapter 12).[20] However, persons who wish to bring a *civil* suit against governments or corporations must still arrange for the payment of legal fees. The most common arrangement is the **contingency fee**, in which plaintiffs agree to pay expenses and share one-third or more of the money damages with their lawyers if the case is won. If the case is lost, neither plaintiffs nor their lawyers receive anything for their labors. Lawyers do not usually participate in such arrangements unless the prospects for winning

Justice in Black Robes
The Supreme Court of the United States is the final interpreter of the Constitution and federal laws and treaties. Two members were added to the Court in 2005 and 2006: Chief Justice John Roberts (center, bottom) and Associate Justice Samuel Alito, Jr. (top, right).

the case are good and the promised monetary reward is substantial. Civil suits against the government have increased since Congress enacted a law requiring governments to pay the attorneys' fees of citizens who successfully bring suit against public officials for violation of their constitutional rights.

Remedies and Relief   Judicial power has vastly expanded through court determination of **remedies and relief**. These are the orders of a court following a decision that are designed to correct a wrong. In most cases, judges simply fine or sentence criminal defendants to jail or order losing defendants in civil suits to pay monetary damages to the winning plaintiffs. In recent years, however, federal district court judges have issued sweeping orders to governments to correct constitutional violations. For example, a federal district judge took over operation of the Boston public schools for more than 10 years to remedy *de facto* (an existing, although not necessarily deliberate, pattern of) racial segregation. A federal district judge ordered the city of Yonkers, New York, to build public housing in white neighborhoods. A federal district judge took over the operation of the Alabama prison system to ensure proper prisoner treatment. A federal district judge ordered the Kansas City, Missouri, school board to increase taxes to pay for his desegregation plan.[21]

★ **remedies and relief**
Orders of a court to correct a wrong, including a violation of the Constitution.

Independent Counsels?   The Ethics in Government Act of 1978 (passed in the wake of the Watergate scandal) granted federal courts the power, upon request of the attorney general, to appoint an **independent counsel**, or "**special prosecutor**," to investigate and prosecute violations of federal law by the president and other high officials. This act was challenged in the U.S. Supreme Court as a transferral of executive power ("to take care that the laws be faithfully executed"—Article II) to the judicial branch of government in violation of the separation of powers in the U.S. Constitution. But the Court upheld the law, noting that the attorney general, an executive branch official appointed by the president, had to request the judiciary to appoint the independent counsel.[22]

★ **independent counsel ("special prosecutor")**
A prosecutor appointed by a federal court to pursue charges against a president or other high official. This position was allowed to lapse by Congress in 1999 after many controversial investigations by these prosecutors.

Whatever the original intent of the act, special prosecutors were often accused of *bringing politics into the criminal justice system*. Indeed, special prosecutor Kenneth Starr's dogged pursuit of Bill and Hillary Clinton (in "Whitewater" real estate deals and later the Monica Lewinsky sex scandal) was deemed a "witch hunt" by friends of the president. The First Lady linked Starr to "a vast right-wing conspiracy" trying to reverse the outcome of two presidential elections.

Congress allowed the independent counsel law to lapse in 1999. Democrats, infuriated by Starr's investigations, joined Republicans, who had earlier complained when Reagan and Bush administration officials were the targets of prosecution, in killing the act. Getting rid of the law, said its opponents, will help to "decriminalize" politics in Washington.

The Politics of Selecting Judges

The Constitution specifies that all federal judges, including justices of the Supreme Court, shall be appointed by the president and confirmed by a majority vote of the Senate. Judicial recruitment is a political process: presidents almost always appoint members of their own party to the federal courts. More than 80 percent of federal judges have held some political office prior to their appointment to the court. More important, political philosophy now plays a major role in the selection of judges. Thus the appointment of federal judges has increasingly become an arena for conflict between presidents and their political opponents in the Senate (see *People in Politics*: "John Roberts, Chief Justice").

People in Politics   John Roberts, Chief Justice

As one of the youngest Chief Justices in the history of the Supreme Court, John Roberts has the opportunity to mold the Constitution over the years to come to fit his personal views.

Roberts graduated from a Catholic high school in Indiana first in his class and captain of the football team. After one year at Sacred Heart University, he transferred to Harvard where he majored in history and graduated summa cum laude and Phi Beta Kappa in 1976. He went on to Harvard Law school and served as editor of the *Harvard Law Review*. He then clerked for Supreme Court Justice William Rehnquist.

Robert served in the Reagan administration as a special assistant to the Attorney General and later associate counsel in the White House. He served in the first Bush administration as Deputy Solicitor General and argued some thirty-nine cases for the government before the Supreme Court. President George H. W. Bush nominated him for the U.S. Court of Appeals in 1992, but Congress adjourned without confirming the nomination. During the Clinton years Roberts served as a partner in the Washington law firm of Hogan & Hartson. Then in 2003 he was renominated to the Court of Appeals by President George W. Bush. Although opposed by New York Senator Charles Schumer and Massachusetts Senator Ted Kennedy, he was confirmed by the U.S. Senate.

President Bush originally nominated Roberts to the U.S. Supreme Court in 2005 to fill the vacancy left by the retirement of Justice Sandra Day O'Connor. But following the death of Chief Justice William H. Rehnquist that year, Bush nominated Roberts for the position of Chief Justice. Joseph Alito was nominated to fill the O'Connor vacancy.

Roberts appeared calm and collected during the highly partisan questioning by the Senate Judiciary Committee. Following the custom of nominees to decline to say how they might vote on specific issues before the high court, he nonetheless stated that *Roe v. Wade* "is settled law of the land." That was not enough to win over many Democrats, including Senators Schumer and Kennedy. Yet Roberts was confirmed by a Senate vote of 78 senators to 22.

In his initial decisions on the High Court, Roberts reflected the moderate to conservative views that he expressed in Senate committee hearings. He voted to uphold the ban on partial-birth abortions enacted by the Congress, but gave no indication that he might vote to reverse *Roe v. Wade*.

In Search of Justice?

Class action suits are legal actions undertaken by attorneys on behalf of particular categories of people, such as persons who all bought the same defective product. A sign advertising a class action lawsuit hangs in the Lakeview area of New Orleans a month after Hurricane Katrina, on October 6, 2005, as residents were being allowed back in their homes. Lakeview residents were filing suit because some homeowners insurance companies were classifying the high water from Hurricane Katrina a flood; the residents and their lawyers argued that the broken levees resulting from Katrina were not a flood, and so residents who didn't have flood insurance should still be covered for damages.

The Politics of Presidential Selection   Presidents have a strong motivation to select judges who share their political philosophy. Judicial appointments are made for life. The Constitution stipulates that federal judges "shall hold their Offices during good Behaviour." A president cannot remove a judge for any reason, and Congress cannot impeach judges just because it dislikes their decisions.

This independence of the judiciary has often frustrated presidents and Congresses. Presidents who have appointed people they thought were liberals or conservatives to the Supreme Court have sometimes been surprised by the decisions of their appointees. An estimated one-quarter of the justices of the Supreme Court have deviated from the political expectations of the presidents who appointed them.[23]

It is important to recognize that presidents' use of political criteria in selecting judges has a democratic influence on the courts. Presidents can campaign on the pledge to make the courts more liberal or conservative through their appointive powers, and voters are free to cast their ballots on the basis of this pledge.

Political Litmus Test Traditionally, presidents and senators have tried to discern where a Supreme Court candidate fits on the continuum of liberal activism versus conservative self-restraint. Democratic presidents and senators usually prefer liberal judges who express an activist philosophy. Republican presidents usually prefer conservative judges who express a philosophy of judicial self-restraint. Until very recently, both the president and the Senate denied using any political "litmus test" in judicial recruitment. A **litmus test** generally refers to recruitment based on a nominee's stand on a single issue. Since the Supreme Court ruling on *Roe v. Wade* (1973), however, the single issue of abortion has come to dominate the politics of judicial recruitment. President Clinton was forthright in his pledge to nominate only justices who specifically support the *Roe v. Wade* decision. Republican presidents have denied using a litmus test, but they have insisted that nominees generally support a philosophy of judicial self-restraint.

The Politics of Senate Confirmation All presidential nominations for the federal judiciary, including the Supreme Court, are sent to the Senate for confirmation. The Senate refers them to its powerful Judiciary Committee, which holds hearings, votes on the nomination, and then reports to the full Senate, where floor debate may precede the final confirmation vote.

The Senate's involvement in federal district judgeships traditionally centered on the practice of **senatorial courtesy**. If senators from the president's party from the same state for which an appointment was being considered disapproved of a nominee, their Senate colleagues would defeat the nomination. But if the president and senators from that party agreed on the nomination, the full Senate, even if controlled by the opposition, customarily confirmed the nomination. During the Reagan-Bush years, however, partisan divisions between these Republican presidents and Senate Democrats eroded the tradition of senatorial courtesy.

Supreme Court nominations have always received close political scrutiny in the Senate. Over the last two centuries, the Senate has rejected or refused to confirm about 20 percent of presidential nominees to the high court (see Table 13.2). In the past, most senators believed that presidents deserved to appoint their own judges; the opposition party would get its own opportunity to appoint judges when it won the presidency. Only if the Senate found some personal

✓ *Think* Again

Should presidents appoint only judges who agree with their judicial philosophy?

★ **litmus test**
In political terms, a person's stand on a key issue that determines whether he or she will be appointed to public office or supported in electoral campaigns.

★ **senatorial courtesy**
Custom of the U.S. Senate with regard to presidential nominations to the judiciary to defer to the judgment of senators from the president's party from the same state as the nominee.

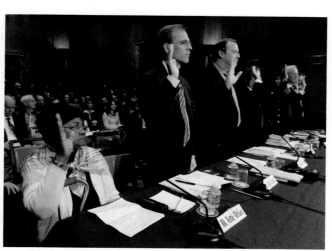

Nettie McGee, 73, a great-grandmother from Chicago with mortgage interest problems, sits as she and others are sworn in on Capitol Hill in Washington, D.C. before testifying before the Senate Judiciary Committee hearing on home foreclosures on December 5, 2007.

Table *13.2*   Senate Confirmation Votes on Supreme Court Nominations since 1950

Nominee	President	Year	Vote
Earl Warren	Eisenhower	1954	NRV[a]
John Marshall Harlan	Eisenhower	1955	71–11
William J. Brennan	Eisenhower	1957	NRV
Charles Whittaker	Eisenhower	1957	NRV
Potter Stewart	Eisenhower	1959	70–17
Byron White	Kennedy	1962	NRV
Arthur Goldberg	Kennedy	1962	NRV
Abe Fortas	Johnson	1965	NRV
Thurgood Marshall	Johnson	1967	69–11
Abe Fortas[b]	Johnson	1968	Withdrawn[c]
Homer Thornberry	Johnson	1968	No action
Warren Burger	Nixon	1969	74–3
Clement Haynsworth	Nixon	1969	Defeated 45–55
G. Harrold Carswell	Nixon	1970	Defeated 45–51
Harry Blackmun	Nixon	1970	94–0
Lewis Powell	Nixon	1971	89–1
William Rehnquist	Nixon	1971	68–26
John Paul Stevens	Ford	1975	98–0
Sandra Day O'Connor	Reagan	1981	99–0
William Rehnquist[b]	Reagan	1986	65–33
Antonin Scalia	Reagan	1986	98–0
Robert Bork	Reagan	1987	Defeated 42–58
Douglas Ginsburg	Reagan	1987	Withdrawn
Anthony Kennedy	Reagan	1988	97–0
David Souter	Bush, Sr.	1990	90–9
Clarence Thomas	Bush, Sr.	1991	52–48
Ruth Bader Ginsburg	Clinton	1993	96–3
Stephen G. Breyer	Clinton	1994	87–9
John G. Roberts, Jr.	Bush, Jr.	2005	78–22
Harriet Miers	Bush, Jr.	2005	Withdrawn
Samuel Alito, Jr.	Bush, Jr.	2005	58–42

[a]No recorded vote.
[b]Elevation to Chief Justice.
[c]Nomination withdrawn after Senate vote failed to end filibuster against nomination; vote was 45 to 43 to end filibuster, and two-thirds majority was required.
Source: Congressional Quarterly's Guide to the US. Supreme Court, 4th ed. (Washington, DC: CQ Press, 2004); updated by the authors.

disqualification in a nominee's background (for example, financial scandal, evidence of racial or religious bias, judicial incompetence) would a nominee likely be rejected. But publicity and partisanship over confirmation of Supreme Court nominees have increased markedly in recent years.[24]

The Bork Battle   The U.S. Senate's rejection of President Ronald Reagan's nomination of Judge Robert H. Bork in 1987 set a new precedent in Senate confirmation of Supreme Court nominees. The Senate rejected Bork because of his views, not because he lacked judicial qualifications. Bork had a reputation for "conservative activism"—a desire better to reflect the "original intent" of the Constitution's Framers by rolling back some of the Supreme Court's broad interpretations of privacy rights, including *Roe v. Wade*, free speech, and equal protection of

What Do You *Think?*

Should Supreme Court Nominees Reveal Their Views on Key Cases Before the Senate Votes to Confirm Them?

U.S. Senators on the Judiciary Committee, questioning presidents' Supreme Court nominees, have traditionally been frustrated by the refusal of nominees to comment on issues that are likely to come before the court in future cases. The nominees have argued that giving specific opinions may impinge upon their judicial impartiality when faced with specific cases. A true judicial approach requires that they examine specific facts in a case, listen to the arguments on both sides, and confer with their colleagues on the Court before rendering an opinion. They should not approach cases with preconceived opinions. Thus, when asked if he supported *Roe v. Wade*, John Roberts simply stated that the case was now precedent in constitutional law and entitled to "due respect." "I should stay away from issues that may come before the court again."

But Democratic Sen. Joseph R. Biden, Jr., insisted that Roberts could at least discuss his views about abortion and the right of privacy, as well as other general legal views. "Without any knowledge of your understanding of the law, because you will not share it with us, we are rolling the dice with you, judge."

Polls reveal that the general public wants to know the Supreme Court nominee's views on important issues.

Q. *"When the Senate votes on a nominee for the U.S. Supreme Court should it consider only that person's legal qualifications and background, or, along with legal background, should the Senate also consider how that nominee might vote on major issues the Supreme Court decides?"*

Legal background only	Issues too	Unsure
36%	51%	10%

Q. *"Before senators vote on whether John Roberts should be confirmed as the Chief Justice of the Supreme Court, how important do you think it is for the Senate to know his position on issues such as abortion and affirmative action?"*

Very Important	Somewhat Important	Not Very Important	Not At All Important	Unsure
46%	31%	9%	13%	1%

Sources: Congressional Quarterly Weekly Report, September 19, 2005, p. 2497; *New York Times*, September 14, 2005.

the law. Unlike previous nominees, Bork was subjected by the Senate Judiciary Committee to extensive case-by-case questioning in nationally televised confirmation hearings. The Democrat-controlled U.S. Senate rejected his nomination. Victory in the Bork battle encouraged liberal interest groups to closely scrutinize the personal lives and political views of subsequent nominees. Indeed, the Bork battle set the stage for an even more controversial political struggle—the confirmation of Justice Clarence Thomas (see *Controversy*: "The Confirmation of Clarence Thomas").

Filibustering Court Nominees   The Constitution requires only a majority vote of the Senate to "advise and consent" to a presidential nominee for a federal court judgeship, including a seat on the Supreme Court. However, recent partisan battles over nominees have centered on the Senate's filibuster rule and the sixty votes required for cloture to end a filibuster.[25] President George W. Bush suffered several key defeats of judicial nominees for seats on the U.S. Court of Appeals by failing to get sixty votes to end filibusters over these nominations. All of his nominations were qualified from a judicial point of view, but all were

Controversy

The Confirmation of Clarence Thomas

Television coverage of Senate confirmation hearings on Clarence Thomas's appointment to the Supreme Court in 1991 captivated a national audience. The conflict raised just about every "hot-button" issue in American politics, from abortion rights and affirmative action to sexual harassment.

Born to a teenage mother who earned $10 a week as a maid, Clarence Thomas and his brother lived in a dirt-floor shack in Pin Point, Georgia, where they were raised by strict, hardworking grandparents who taught young Clarence the value of education and sacrificed to send him to a Catholic school. He excelled academically and went on to mostly white Immaculate Conception Seminary College in Missouri to study for the Catholic priesthood. But when he overheard a fellow seminarian express satisfaction at the assassination of Dr. Martin Luther King, Jr., Thomas left the seminary in anger and enrolled at College of the Holy Cross, where he helped found the college's Black Student Union, and went on to graduate with honors and to win admission to Yale Law School.

Upon graduating from Yale, Thomas took a job as assistant attorney general in Missouri and later became a congressional aide to Republican Missouri Senator John Danforth. In 1981 he accepted the post as head of the Office of Civil Rights in the Department of Education. In 1982 he was named chair of the Equal Employment Opportunity Commission (EEOC), where he successfully eliminated much of that agency's financial mismanagement and aggressively pursued individual cases of discrimination. But at the same time, he spoke out against racial "quotas." In 1989 President Bush nominated him to the U.S. Court of Appeals, and he was easily confirmed by the Senate.

In tapping Thomas for the Supreme Court, the White House reasoned that the liberal groups who had blocked the earlier nomination of conservative Robert Bork would be reluctant to launch personal attacks on an African American. With the opposition fractured, the White House saw an opportunity to push a strong conservative nominee through the Democrat-dominated Senate Judiciary Committee and win confirmation by the full Senate.

Anita Hill

Clarence Thomas

But behind the scenes, liberal interest groups, including the National Abortion Rights Action League, People for the American Way, and the National Organization for Women, were searching for evidence to discredit Thomas. A University of Oklahoma law professor, Anita Hill, a former legal assistant to Thomas both at the Department of Education and later at the Equal Employment Opportunity Commission, charged, in a nationally televised press conference, that Thomas had sexually harassed her in both jobs. Thomas himself flatly denied the charges.

Democrats on the committee treated Hill with great deference, asking her to talk about her feelings and provide even more explicit details of Thomas's alleged misconduct. Given an opportunity to rebut Hill's charges, Thomas did so very emphatically: "This is a circus. It's a national disgrace. And from my standpoint as a black American, as far as I'm concerned, it is a high-tech lynching for uppity blacks who in any way deign to think for themselves."

In the end, there was no way to determine who was telling the truth, and "truth" in Washington is, at any rate, often determined by opinion polls. A majority of blacks as well as whites, and a majority of women as well as men, sided with the nominee.[a] In a fitting finale to the bitter and sleazy conflict, the final Senate confirmation vote was 52 to 48, the closest vote in the history of such confirmations. The best that can be said about the affair was that it placed the issue of sexual harassment on the national agenda.

[a]*Gallup Opinion Reports*, October 15, 1991, p. 209.

considered too conservative by leading Democrats in the Senate. Republicans threatened to try to end the filibuster rule for judicial nominations. They argued that the Constitution itself specifies a "majority vote of the Senate," not a three-fifths vote for confirmation. But ending the filibuster rule, even for only judicial nominations, would challenge a sacred tradition of the Senate. (Some senators referred to it as the "nuclear option.") A shaky compromise was reached in 2005 when some previously rejected Republican appellate court nominees were confirmed, and Democrats in the Senate promised to use the filibuster only in extraordinary cases. The Democrats chose *not* to filibuster the Supreme Court nominations of John Roberts or Samuel Alito.

Who Is Selected?

What background and experiences are brought to the Supreme Court? Despite often holding very different views on the laws, the Constitution, and their interpretation, the justices of the U.S. Supreme Court tend to share a common background of education at the nation's most prestigious law schools and prior judicial experience.

You Are the President and Need to Appoint a Supreme Court Justice

Law Degrees   There is no constitutional requirement that Supreme Court justices be attorneys, but every person who has ever served on the High Court has been trained in law. Moreover, a majority of the justices have attended one or another of the nation's most prestigious law schools (see Table 13.3).

Judicial Experience   Historically, about half of all Supreme Court justices have been federal or state court judges. Many justices have served some time as U.S. attorneys in the Department of Justice early in their legal careers. Relatively

Table *13.3*   The Supreme Court: Background of the Justices

Justice	Age at Appointment	President Who Appointed	Law School	Position at Time of Appointment	Years as a Judge Before Appointment
John Paul Stevens	50	Ford (1976)	Northwestern	U.S. Court of Appeals	5
Antonin Scalia	50	Reagan (1986)	Harvard	U.S. Court of Appeals	4
Anthony M. Kennedy	51	Reagan (1988)	Harvard	U.S. Court of Appeals	12
David H. Souter	50	Bush, Sr. (1990)	Harvard	State Supreme Court	13
Clarence Thomas	43	Bush, Sr. (1991)	Yale	U.S. Court of Appeals	2
Ruth Bader Ginsburg	60	Clinton (1993)	Columbia	U.S. Court of Appeals	13
Stephen G. Breyer	56	Clinton (1994)	Harvard	U.S. Court of Appeals	14
John G. Roberts, Jr., Chief Justice	50	Bush, Jr. (2005)	Harvard	U.S. Court of Appeals	2
Samuel A. Alito, Jr.	55	Bush, Jr. (2005)	Yale	U.S. Court of Appeals	15

few have held elected political office, but one chief justice—William Howard Taft—previously held the nation's highest elected post, the presidency.

Age Most justices have been in their 50s when appointed to the Court. Presumably this is the age at which people acquire the necessary prominence and experience to bring themselves to the attention of the White House and Justice Department as potential candidates. At the same time, presidents seek to make a lasting imprint on the Court, and candidates in their fifties can be expected to serve on the Court for many more years than older candidates with the same credentials.

Race and Gender No African American had ever served on the Supreme Court until President Lyndon Johnson's appointment of Thurgood Marshall in 1967. A Howard University Law School graduate, Marshall had served as counsel for the National Association for the Advancement of Colored People Legal Defense Fund and had personally argued the historic *Brown v. Board of Education* case before the Supreme Court in 1954. He served as solicitor general of the United States under President Lyndon Johnson before his elevation to the high court. Upon Marshall's retirement in 1991, President George H. W. Bush sought to retain minority representation on the Supreme Court, yet at the same time to reinforce conservative judicial views, with his selection of Clarence Thomas.

No woman had served on the Supreme Court prior to the appointment of Sandra Day O'Connor by President Ronald Reagan in 1981. O'Connor was Reagan's first Supreme Court appointment. Although a relatively unknown Arizona state court judge, she had the powerful support of Arizona Republican Senator Barry Goldwater and Stanford classmate Justice William Rehnquist. The second woman to serve on the High Court, Ruth Bader Ginsburg, had served as an attorney for the American Civil Liberties Union while teaching at Columbia Law School and had argued and won several important gender discrimination cases. President Jimmy Carter appointed her in 1980 to the U.S. Court of Appeals; President Bill Clinton elevated her to the Supreme Court in 1993.

Supreme Court Decision Making

The Supreme Court sets its own agenda: it decides what it wants to decide. Of the more than 8,000 requests for hearing that come to its docket each year, the Court issues opinions on only about 150 cases. Another 150 or so cases are decided *summarily* (without opinion) by a Court order either affirming or reversing the lower court decision. The Supreme Court refuses to rule at all on the vast majority of cases that are submitted to it. Thus the rhetorical threat to "take this all the way to the Supreme Court" is usually an empty one. It is important, however, to realize that a refusal to rule also creates law by allowing the decision of the lower court to stand. That is why the U.S. Circuit Courts of Appeals are powerful bodies.

Setting the Agenda: Granting Certiorari Most cases reach the Supreme Court when a party in a case appeals to the Court to issue a **writ of certiorari** (literally to "make more certain"), a decision by the Court to require a lower federal or state court to turn over its records on a case.[26] To "grant certiorari"—that is, to decide to hear arguments in a case and render a decision—the Supreme Court relies on its **rule of four**: four justices must agree to do so. Deciding which cases to hear takes up a great deal of the Court's time.

What criteria does the Supreme Court use in choosing its policy agenda—that is, in choosing the cases it wishes to decide? The Court rarely explains why it accepts or rejects cases, but there are some general patterns. First, the Court

★ **writ of certiorari**
Writ issued by the Supreme Court, at its discretion, to order a lower court to prepare the record of a case and send it to the Supreme Court for review. Most cases come to the Court as petitions for writs of certiorari.

★ **rule of four**
At least four justices must agree to hear an appeal (writ of certiorari) from a lower court in order to get a case before the Supreme Court.

accepts cases involving issues that the justices are interested in. The justices are clearly interested in the area of 1st Amendment freedoms—speech, press, and religion. Members of the Court are also interested in civil rights issues under the Equal Protection Clause of the 14th Amendment and the civil rights laws and in overseeing the criminal justice system and defining the Due Process Clauses of the 5th and 14th Amendments.

In addition, the Court seems to feel an obligation to accept cases involving questions that have been decided differently by different Circuit Courts of Appeals. The Supreme Court generally tries to see to it that "the law" does not differ from one circuit to another. Likewise, the Supreme Court usually acts when lower courts have made decisions clearly at odds with Supreme Court interpretations in order to maintain control of the federal judiciary. Finally, the Supreme Court is more likely to accept a case in which the U.S. government is a party and requests a review, especially when an issue appears to be one of overriding importance to the government. In fact, the U.S. government is a party in almost half of the cases decided by the Supreme Court.

Hearing Arguments   Once the Supreme Court places a case on its decision calendar, attorneys for both sides submit written briefs on the issues. The Supreme Court may also allow interest groups to submit **amicus curiae** (literally, "friend of the court") briefs. This process allows interest groups direct access to the Supreme Court. In the affirmative action case of *University of California Regents v. Bakke* (1978)[27] the Court accepted 59 *amicus curiae* briefs representing more than 100 interest groups. The U.S. government frequently submits *amicus curiae* arguments in cases in which it is not a party. The **solicitor general** of the United States is responsible for presenting the government's arguments both in cases in which the government is a party and in cases in which the government is merely an *amicus curiae*.

Oral arguments before the Supreme Court are a time-honored ritual of American government. They take place in the marble "temple"—the Supreme Court building across the street from the U.S. Capitol in Washington, D.C. (see Figure 13.3). The justices, clad in their black robes, sit behind a high "bench" and peer down at the attorneys presenting their arguments. Arguing a case before the Supreme Court is said to be an intimidating experience. Each side is usually limited to either a half-hour or an hour of argument, but justices frequently interrupt with their own pointed questioning. Court watchers sometimes try to predict the Court's decision from the tenor of the questioning. Oral argument is the most public phase of Supreme Court decision making, but no one really knows whether these arguments ever change the justices' minds.

In Conference   The actual decisions are made in private conferences among the justices. These conferences usually take place on Wednesdays and Fridays and cover the cases argued orally during the same week. The Chief Justice presides, and only justices (no law clerks) are present. It is customary for the Chief Justice to speak first on the issues, followed by each associate justice in order of seniority. A majority must decide which party wins or loses and whether a lower court's decision is to be affirmed or reversed.

Writing Opinions   The *written* opinion determines the actual outcome of the case (votes in conference are not binding). When the decision is unanimous, the Chief Justice traditionally writes the opinion. In the case of a split decision, the Chief Justice may take on the task of writing the **majority opinion** or assign it to another justice in the majority. If the Chief Justice is in the minority, the senior justice in the majority makes the assignment. Writing the opinion of the Court is the central task

★ **amicus curiae**
Literally, "friend of the court"; a person, private group or institution, or government agency that is not a party to a case but participates in the case (usually through submission of a brief) at the invitation of the court or on its own initiative.

★ **solicitor general**
Attorney in the Department of Justice who represents the U.S. government before the Supreme Court and any other courts.

You Are a Young Lawyer

You Are a Supreme Court Justice Deciding a Free Speech Case

★ **majority opinion**
Opinion in a case that is subscribed to by a majority of the judges who participated in the decision.

THE SUPREME COURT

1. Courtyards
2. Solicitor General's Office
3. Lawyers' Lounge
4. Marshal's Office
5. Main Hall
6. Courtroom
7. Conference and Reception Rooms

Figure *13.3* Corridors of Power: The Supreme Court

This cutaway shows the location of the principal offices and chambers of the Supreme Court building.

in Supreme Court policy making. Broadly written opinions may effect sweeping policy changes; narrowly written opinions may decide a particular case but have very little policy impact. The reasons cited for the decision become binding law, to be applied by lower courts in future cases. Yet despite the crucial role of opinion writing in Court policy making, most opinions are actually written by law clerks who are only recent graduates of the nation's prestigious law schools. The justices themselves read, edit, correct, and sometimes rewrite drafts prepared by clerks, but clerks may have a strong influence over the position taken by justices on the issues.

A draft of the opinion is then circulated among members of the majority. Any majority member who disagrees with the reasoning in the opinion, and thus disagrees with the policy that is proposed, may either negotiate changes in the opinion with others in the majority or write a concurring opinion. A **concurring opinion** agrees with the decision about which party wins the case but sets forth a different reason for the decision, proposing, in effect, a different policy position.

Justices in the minority often agree to present a **dissenting opinion**. The dissenting opinion sets forth the views of justices who disagree with both the decision and the majority reasoning. Dissenting opinions do not have the force of law. They are written both to express opposition to the majority view and to appeal to a future Court to someday modify or reverse the position of the majority. Occasionally, the Court is unable to agree on a clear policy position on particularly vexing questions. If the majority is strongly divided over the reasoning behind their decision and as many as four justices dissent altogether from the decision, lower courts will lack clear guidance and future cases will be decided on a case-by-case basis, depending on multiple factors occurring in each case (see, for example, "Affirmative Action in the Courts" in Chapter 15). The absence of a clear opinion of the Court, supported by a unified majority of the justices, invites additional cases, keeping the issue on the Court's agenda until such time (if any) as the Court establishes a clear policy on the issue.

★ **concurring opinion**
Opinion by a member of a court that agrees with the result reached by the court in the case but disagrees with or departs from the court's rationale for the decision.

★ **dissenting opinion**
Opinion by a member of a court that disagrees with the result reached by the court in the case.

Politics and the Supreme Court

The political views of Supreme Court justices have an important influence on Court decisions. Justices are swayed primarily by their own ideological views, but public opinion, the president's position, and the arguments of interest groups all contribute to the outcome of cases.

Liberal and Conservative Voting Blocs Although liberal and conservative voting blocs on the Court are visible over time, on any given case particular justices may deviate from their perceived ideological position. Many cases do not present a liberal-conservative dimension. Each case presents a separate set of facts, and even justices who share a general philosophy may perceive the central facts of a case differently. Moreover, the liberal-versus-conservative dimension sometimes clashes with the activist-versus-self-restraint dimension. Although we generally think of liberals as favoring activism and conservatives self-restraint, occasionally those who favor self-restraint are obliged to approve of legislation that violates their personal conservative beliefs because opposing it would substitute their judgment for that of elected officials. So ideological blocs are not always good predictors of voting outcomes on the Court.

Over time, the composition of the Supreme Court has changed, as has the power of its various liberal and conservative voting blocs (see Table 13.4). The liberal bloc, headed by Chief Justice Earl Warren, dominated Court decision making from the mid-1950s through the end of the 1960s. The liberal bloc gradually weakened following President Richard Nixon's appointment of Warren Burger as Chief Justice in 1969, but not all of Nixon's appointees joined the conservative bloc; Justice Harry Blackmun and Justice Lewis Powell frequently joined in voting with the liberal bloc. Among Nixon's appointees, only William Rehnquist consistently adopted conservative positions. President Gerald Ford's only appointee to the Court, John Paul Stevens, began as a moderate and drifted to the liberal bloc. As a result, the Burger Court, although generally not as activist as the Warren Court, still did not reverse any earlier liberal holdings.

Table *13.4*	How They Vote: Liberal and Conservative Blocs on the Supreme Court			
	The Warren Court	**The Burger Court**	**The Rehnquist Court**	**The Roberts Court***
Liberal	1968 Earl Warren Hugo Black William O. Douglas Thurgood Marshall William J. Brennan Abe Fortas	1975 William O. Douglas Thurgood Marshall William J. Brennan	2004 John Paul Stevens Ruth Bader Ginsburg Stephen G. Breyer	2008 John Paul Stevens Ruth Bader Ginsburg Stephen G. Breyer David Souter
Moderate	Potter Stewart Byron White	Potter Stewart Byron White Lewis Powell Harry Blackmun	Anthony Kennedy Sandra Day O'Connor David Souter	Anthony Kennedy
Conservative	John Marshall Harlan	Warren Burger William Rehnquist	William Rehnquist Antonin Scalia Clarence Thomas	John Roberts Samuel Alito Antonin Scalia Clarence Thomas

*All blocs have been designated by the authors.

The Swing Vote

Supreme Court Justice Anthony Kennedy appears before a House Appropriations financial services and general government subcommittee on March 13, 2008.

★ **U.S. Solicitor General**
The U.S. government's chief legal counsel, presenting the government's arguments in cases in which it is a party or in which it has an interest.

President Ronald Reagan, who had campaigned on a pledge to restrain the liberal activism of the Court, tried to appoint conservatives. His first appointee, Sandra Day O'Connor, turned out to be less conservative than expected, especially on women's issues and abortion rights. When Chief Justice Burger retired in 1986, Reagan seized on the opportunity to strengthen the conservative bloc by elevating Rehnquist to Chief Justice. Reagan also appointed Antonin Scalia, another strong conservative, to the Court. Reagan added Anthony Kennedy to the Court in 1988, hoping to give Rehnquist and the conservative bloc the opportunity to form a majority. Had President Reagan succeeded in getting the powerful conservative voice of Robert Bork on the Court, it is possible that many earlier liberal decisions, including *Roe v. Wade*, would have been reversed. But the Senate rejected Bork; David Souter, the man ultimately confirmed, eventually drifted toward the liberal bloc.

Liberals worried that the appointment of conservative Clarence Thomas as a replacement for the liberal Thurgood Marshall would give the conservative bloc a commanding voice in Supreme Court policy making. But no solid conservative majority emerged. Justices Rehnquist, Scalia, and Thomas were considered the core of the conservative bloc, but they had to win over at least two of the more moderate justices in order to form a majority in a case. President Bill Clinton's appointees, Ruth Bader Ginsburg and Stephen G. Breyer, have consistently supported liberal views on the Supreme Court. On key questions, the moderate bloc has the deciding vote.

While the moderate bloc has held the balance of power on the Court, the Court as a whole has moved in a conservative direction since the high-water-mark of judicial liberalism during the era of Chief Justice Earl Warren (1953–68). Liberalism on the Court—as measured by pro-individual rights decisions against the government in civil liberties cases, pro-defendant decisions in criminal cases, and pro-women and minorities decisions in civil rights cases—has declined significantly since the 1960s.[28] Future appointees to the Court will determine whether the Court continues in a conservative direction.

Public Opinion   "By all arguable evidence of the modern Supreme Court, the Court appears to reflect public opinion about as accurately as other policy makers."[29] And indeed, on the liberal-conservative dimension, it can be argued that Supreme Court decisions have generally followed shifts in American public opinion. However, the Court appears to lag behind public opinion. It is doubtful that the justices read opinion polls; their jobs do not depend on public approval ratings. Rather, it is more likely that the justices, whose nomination and confirmation depended on an elected president and Senate, generally share the views of those who put them on the bench. Thus public opinion affects the Court only indirectly, through the nomination and confirmation process.

Presidential Influence   Even after a president's initial appointment of a Justice to the High Court, a president may exercise some influence over judicial decision making. The Office of the **U.S. Solicitor General** is charged with the responsibility of presenting the government's (the president's) views in cases not only to which the U.S. government is a party, but also in cases in which the president and the Attorney General have a strong interest and present their arguments in amicus curiae briefs. The Solicitor General's Office, in both Democratic and Republican presidential administrations, has compiled an enviable record in Supreme Court cases. When representing federal agencies that are parties to cases, the Solicitors General have won two-thirds of their cases before the Supreme Court over the years. And in cases where the Solicitor General has offered an amicus curiae brief, he has won about three-quarters of the cases. In contrast, the states have won fewer than half of the cases before the Supreme Court in which a state has been a party.

Interest-Group Influence   Interest groups have become a major presence in Supreme Court cases. First of all, interest groups (for example, Planned Parenthood, National Association for the Advancement of Colored People, American Civil Liberties Union) sponsor many cases themselves. They find persons they believe to be directly damaged by a public policy, initiate litigation on their behalf, and provide the attorneys and money to pursue these cases all the way to the Supreme Court. Second of all, it is now a rare case that comes to the Court without multiple amicus curiae briefs filed by interest groups.

How influential are interest groups in Supreme Court decisions? Certainly interest groups have a significant influence in bringing issues before the Supreme Court through their sponsorship of cases. It is unlikely that the Court would have acted when it did on many key issues from racial segregation in 1954 (*Brown v. Board of Education* sponsored by the NAACP) to abortion in 1992 (*Planned Parenthood v. Casey* sponsored by Planned Parenthood) in the absence of interest-group activity. And interest-group *amicus curiae* briefs are now mentioned (cited) in about two-thirds of the written decisions of the Court. However, these briefs may not have much *independent* effect on decisions, that is, they may not have convinced the justices to decide a case one way or another. Several studies have found that interest-group briefs have had very little effect on Supreme Court decisions.[30]

Checking Court Power

Many people are concerned about the extent to which we now rely on a non-elected judiciary to decide key policy issues rather than depending on a democratically elected president or Congress.

Legitimacy as a Restraint on the Judiciary   Court authority derives from legitimacy rather than force. By that we mean that the courts depend on their authority being seen as rightful, on people perceiving an obligation to abide by court decisions whether they agree with them or not. The courts have no significant force at their direct command. Federal marshals, who carry out the orders of federal courts, number only a few thousand. Courts must rely primarily on the executive branch for enforcement of their decisions.

Today most Americans believe that Supreme Court decisions are authoritative statements about the Constitution and that people have an obligation to obey these decisions whether they agree with them or not.[31] Thus public opinion constrains other public officials—from the president, to governors, to school superintendents, to law enforcement officials—to obey Supreme Court decisions. Their constituents do not hold them personally responsible for unpopular actions ordered by the Supreme Court or federal judges. On the contrary, their constituents generally expect them to comply with court decisions.

Compliance with Court Policy   Federal and state court judges must apply Supreme Court policies when ruling on cases in their own courts. Occasionally, lower courts express their disagreement with the Supreme Court in an opinion, even when they feel obliged to carry out the High Court's policy. At times, lower federal and state courts try to give a narrow interpretation to a Supreme Court decision with which they disagree. But judges who seek to defy the Supreme Court face the ultimate sanction of reversal on appeal by the losing party. Professional pride usually inspires judges to avoid reversals of their judgments by higher courts even though a long record of reversals is not grounds for impeachment or removal of a federal judge.

Public officials who defy Supreme Court rulings risk lawsuits and court orders mandating compliance. Persons injured by noncompliance are likely to file suit against noncomplying officials, as are interest groups that monitor official compliance with the policies they support. These suits are expensive, time consuming, and potentially embarrassing to government officials and agencies. Once a court order is issued, continued defiance can result in fines and penalties for contempt of court.

The president of the United States is subject to federal court orders. Historically, this notion has been challenged: early presidents believed they were separate and at least co-equal to the courts and that their own determination about the legality or constitutionality of their own acts could not be overturned by the courts. President Andrew Jackson could—and did—say: "John Marshall has made his decision. Now let him enforce it," expressing the view that the president was not obliged to enforce court decisions he disagreed with.[32] But in the course of 200 years, the courts—not the president—have gained in legitimacy as the final authority on the law and the Constitution. Today a president who openly defied the Supreme Court would lose any claims to legitimacy and would risk impeachment by Congress.

The case of Richard Nixon illustrates the weakness of a modern president who would even consider defying the Supreme Court. When Nixon sought to invoke executive privilege to withhold damaging tapes of White House conversations in the Watergate investigation (see *Politics Up Close*: "Watergate and the Limits of Presidential Power" in Chapter 11), federal district judge John Sirica rejected his claim and ordered that the tapes be turned over to the special prosecutor in the case. In arguments before the Supreme Court, Nixon's lawyers contended that the president would not have to comply with a Supreme Court decision to turn over the tapes. Yet when the Court ruled unanimously against him, Nixon felt bound to comply and released tapes that were very damaging to his cause. But Nixon understood that refusal to abide by a Supreme Court decision would most assuredly have resulted in impeachment. Under the circumstances, compliance was the better of two unattractive choices.

Presidential Influence on Court Policy   The president and Congress can exercise some restraint over court power through the checks and balances built into the Constitution. Using the office's powers of appointment, presidents have effectively modified the direction of Supreme Court policy and influenced lower federal courts as well. Certainly presidents must await the death or retirement of Supreme Court justices and federal judges, and presidents are constrained by the need to secure Senate confirmation of their appointees. However, over time presidential influence on the courts can be significant. During their combined 12 years in the White House, Ronald Reagan and his successor George H. W. Bush were able to fill 70 percent of federal district and appellate court judgeships and six of nine Supreme Court positions with their own appointees. As noted earlier, however, their appointees did not always reflect these presidents' philosophies in rendering decisions. Nevertheless, the federal courts tilted in a somewhat more conservative direction. President Bill Clinton's appointments generally strengthened liberal, activist impulses throughout the federal judiciary, and George W. Bush's appointees generally supported a conservative, restrained judiciary.

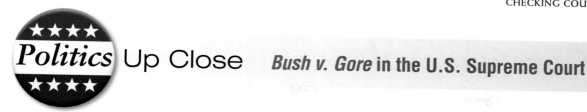

Politics Up Close   *Bush v. Gore* in the U.S. Supreme Court

The presidential election of 2000 was unique in American history in that the outcome was decided by the Supreme Court of the United States. The Supreme Court's decision on December 12, 2000, in *Bush v. Gore*, rested on constitutional issues, but the 5–4 decision of the justices raised the question of the High Court's political partisanship.[a]

"Too Close to Call"

On the morning after Election Day, it became clear that the outcome of the presidential election depended on Florida's twenty-five electoral votes. Florida's Secretary of State (separately elected Republican Katherine Harris) initially reported a margin of 1,784 for George W. Bush out of over 6 million votes cast in the state. But because Florida law provides for a recount when the margin of victory is less than one-half of 1 percent, the recount of machine votes was conducted as well as a count of absentee ballots. Bush's lead was reduced to a slim 930 votes. The Florida Secretary of State declined to accept any recount returns from the counties after November 14, the date set by Florida law as the final date for submission of returns to the Secretary.

Judicial Maneuvering

But immediately after Election Day armies of lawyers descended on Florida's capital city, Tallahassee. The stakes were high—the presidency of the United States. Al Gore's legal team was headed by former Secretary of State Warren Christopher, and the Bush team by former Secretary of State James Baker (although neither argued directly before the courts). The Gore team demanded *manual* recounts of the ballots in the state's three largest (and most Democratic) counties—Miami-Dade, Broward (Fort Lauderdale), and Palm Beach. The case was first argued before a Leon County (Tallahassee) trial judge, who dismissed Gore's petition. But the case was quickly appealed to the Florida Supreme Court (with its seven justices, all appointed by Democratic governors). That Court set aside the state's legal deadline for recounts, and county canvassing boards began a tedious hand count of punch card ballots.

The Bush legal team appealed directly to the U.S. Supreme Court, arguing first of all that the U.S. Constitution gives the power to appoint presidential electors "in such Manner as the *Legislature* thereof may direct" (Article II, Section 1), and that the Florida Supreme Court overreached its authority when it set

aside legislative-enacted provisions of the election laws of the state, including the deadline for recounts. They also argued that hand counts in counties were late, unreliable, subjective, and open to partisan bias. The U.S. Supreme Court responded initially by ordering a halt to the recounts and remanding (sending back) the case to the Florida Supreme Court for clarification as to the grounds on which it had been decided.

The Florida Supreme Court was apparently not intimidated by the U.S. Supreme Court's implied judgment that it had erred in its decision. It ordered a manual recount of all legal votes in the state, especially undercounts (where ballots failed to register a vote for president). It specified that "the intent of the voter" should be the criterion for deciding how to count a ballot. The Florida Supreme Court decision, *Gore v. Harris*,[b] was immediately appealed to the U.S. Supreme Court.

By now more than a month had passed with the nation not knowing who would be its next president. It became clear that Gore had won the nationwide popular vote. But most Americans acknowledged that the popular vote was of secondary importance to the Constitution of the United States in its provisions for choosing the president by state electoral votes. Only the U.S. Supreme Court seemed to possess sufficient legitimacy to resolve the first contested presidential election in over a century.

A Divided Supreme Court

The Supreme Court held that "the use of standardless manual recounts violates the Equal Protection and Due Process Clauses [of the U.S. Constitution]. . . . Moreover, the [Florida] court's interpretation of "legal vote," and hence its decision to order a contest-period recount, plainly departed from the legislative scheme. Florida statutory law cannot reasonably be thought to require the counting of improperly marked ballots. The judgment of the Supreme Court of Florida is reversed."

The narrow 5–4 decision appeared to follow partisan lines, with Justices O'Connor, Kennedy, Rehnquist, Scalia, and Thomas voting in the majority to allow Florida's Secretary of State to certify that state's electoral votes for Bush. Justices Souter, Stevens, Ginsburg, and Breyer dissented, arguing that the U.S. Supreme Court should not interfere with the Florida Supreme Court's order for a manual recount. Indeed, Justice Stevens implied that the Supreme Court's decision would undermine "the nation's confidence in the judge as an impartial guardian of the rule of law."

[a] *Bush v. Gore*, 531 U.S. 98 (2000).
[b] *Gore v. Harris*, Florida Supreme Court December 8, 2000.

A *Constitutional* Note

The Power of Judicial Review

Nowhere in the Constitution do we find any mention of the power of "judicial review." It is true that the Constitution's Supremacy Clause (Article VI, Section 2) makes the Constitution and national laws and treaties "the supreme law of the land, anything in the Constitution or laws of any *state* to the contrary notwithstanding." The Founders clearly believed that federal court power over state decisions was essential to maintaining national unity. But at the *national* level, why should an appointed court's interpretation of the Constitution prevail over the views of an elected Congress and an elected president? All are pledged to uphold the Constitution. The answer is that the Founders distrusted popular majorities and elected officials subject to their influence. So the Founders deliberately insulated the courts from popular majorities; by appointing judges for life terms, they sought to ensure their independence. Alexander Hamilton viewed the federal courts as a final bulwark against threats to principle and property. Writing in *The Federalist* in late 1787 he said:

"Limited government . . . can be preserved in practice no other way than through the medium of courts of justice, whose duty it is to declare all acts contrary to the manifest tenor of the Constitution void." But it was not until the case of *Marbury v. Madison* in 1803 that John Marshall first assumed the power of judicial review. He argued persuasively that (1) the Constitution is declared "the supreme law of the land," and national as well as state laws must be congruent with it; (2) Article III gives the Supreme Court the "judicial power," which includes the power to interpret the meaning of laws and, in case of conflict between laws, to decide which law shall prevail; and (3) the courts are sworn to uphold the Constitution, so they must declare void any law that conflicts with the Constitution. Despite the logic of the argument, judicial review—the ability of an *un*elected judiciary, serving for life, to invalidate laws of Congress and actions of the president—would appear to be an undemocratic feature of the Constitution.

Congressional Checks on the Judiciary The Constitution gives Congress control over the structure and jurisdiction of federal district and appellate courts, but congressional use of this control has been restrained. Only the Supreme Court is established by the Constitution; Article III gives Congress the power to "ordain and establish . . . inferior" courts. In theory, Congress could try to limit court jurisdiction to hear cases that Congress did not wish it to decide. Congress has used this power to lighten the federal courts' workload; for example, Congress has limited the jurisdiction of federal courts in cases between citizens of different states by requiring that the dispute involve more than $75,000. But Congress has never used this power to change court policy—for example, by removing federal court jurisdiction over school prayer cases or desegregation cases. Indeed federal courts would probably declare unconstitutional any congressional attempt to limit their power to interpret the Constitution by limiting jurisdiction.

Likewise, although Congress could, in theory, expand membership on the Supreme Court, the custom of a nine-member Supreme Court is now so deeply ingrained in American government that "court packing" is politically unthinkable. Franklin Roosevelt's unsuccessful 1937 attempt to expand the Supreme Court was the last serious assault on the size of its membership.

A more common congressional constraint on the Supreme Court is amending statutory laws to reverse federal court interpretations of these laws that Congress believes are in error. Thus when the Supreme Court decided that civil rights laws did not mandate a cutoff of *all* federal funds to a college upon evidence of discrimination in a single program but only the funds for that program,[33] Congress amended its own laws to require the more sweeping remedy. Although members of Congress frequently berate the Court for what they see as misreading of the laws, all Congress needs to do to reverse a Court interpretation of those laws is to pass amendments to them.

Constitutional amendment is the only means by which the Congress and the states can reverse a Supreme Court interpretation of the Constitution itself. After the Civil War, the 13th Amendment abolishing slavery reversed the Supreme Court's *Dred Scott* decision (1857) that slavery was constitutionally protected. The 16th Amendment (1913) gave Congress the power to impose an income tax, thus reversing the Supreme Court's earlier decision in *Pollock v. Farmer's Loan*[34] holding income taxes unconstitutional (1895). But recent attempts to reverse Supreme Court interpretations of the Constitution by passing constitutional amendments on the issues of prayer in public schools, busing, and abortion have all failed to win congressional approval. The barriers to a constitutional amendment are formidable: a two-thirds vote of both houses of Congress and ratification by three-quarters of the states. Thus, for all practical purposes, the Constitution is what the Supreme Court says it is.

Congress can impeach federal court judges, but only for "cause" (committing crimes), not for their decisions. Although impeachment is frequently cited as a constitutional check on the judiciary, it has no real influence over judicial policy making. Only five federal court judges have ever been impeached by the House, convicted by the Senate, and removed from office, although two others were impeached and another nine resigned to avoid impeachment. In 1989 Federal District Court Judge Alcee Hastings became the first sitting judge in more than 50 years to be impeached, tried, and found guilty by the Congress. He was convicted by the Senate of perjury and conspiracy to obtain a $150,000 bribe; but a federal district court judge later ruled that he should have been tried by the full Senate, not a special committee of the Senate. Hastings declared the ruling a vindication; in 1992 he won a congressional seat in Florida, becoming the first person ever to become a member of the House after being impeached by that same body. Even criminal convictions do not ensure removal from office, although judges have resigned under fire.

Summary
Who Gets What: The Courts

Great power is lodged in the Supreme Court of the United States and the federal judiciary. These courts have undertaken to resolve many of the most divisive conflicts in American society. The judicial power is the power to decide cases and controversies, and in so doing to decide the meaning of the Constitution and laws of Congress.

★ The power of judicial review is the power to invalidate laws of Congress or of the states that the federal courts believe conflict with the U.S. Constitution. This power is not specifically mentioned in the Constitution but was derived by Chief Justice John Marshall from the Supremacy Clause and the meaning of judicial power in Article III.

★ The Supreme Court has been fairly restrained in its use of judicial review with regard to laws of Congress and actions of presidents; it has more frequently overturned state laws. The federal courts also exercise great power in the interpretation of the laws of Congress, especially when statutory language is vague.

★ Arguments over judicial power are reflected in the conflicting philosophies of judicial activism and judicial self-restraint. Advocates of judicial restraint argue that judges must not substitute their own views for those of elected representatives and the remedy for unwise laws lies in the legislature, not the courts. Advocates of judicial activism argue that the courts must view the Constitution as a living document and its meaning must fit the needs of a changing society.

★ The federal judiciary consists of three levels of courts—the Supreme Court, the U.S. Courts of Appeals, and the U.S. District Courts. The district courts are trial courts that hear both civil and criminal cases. The courts of appeals are appellate courts and do not hold trials but consider only the record of trial courts and the arguments (briefs) of attorneys. More than 90 percent of federal cases end in appeals courts. The Supreme Court can hear appeals from state high courts as well as lower federal courts. The Supreme Court hears only about 200 cases a year.

★ Courts function under general rules of restraint that do not bind the president or Congress. The Supreme Court does not decide hypothetical cases or render advisory opinions. The principle of stare decisis, or reliance on precedent, is not set aside lightly.

★ The selection of Supreme Court justices and federal judges is based more on political considerations than legal qualifications. Presidents almost always appoint judges from their own party, and presidents increasingly have sought judges who share their ideological views. However, because of the independence of judges once they are appointed, presidents have sometimes been disappointed in the decisions of their appointees. In addition, Senate approval of nominees has become increasingly politicized, with problems most evident when different parties control the White House and the Senate.

★ The Supreme Court sets its own agenda for policy making, usually by granting or withholding certiorari. Generally, four justices must agree to grant certiorari for a case to be decided by the Supreme Court. The Supreme Court has been especially active in policy making in interpreting the meaning of the 14th Amendment's guarantee of "equal protection of the laws," as well as of the civil rights and voting rights acts of Congress. It has also been active in defining the meaning of freedom of press, speech, and religion in the 1st Amendment and "due process of law" in the 5th Amendment. The federal courts are active in overseeing government regulatory activity. But federal courts have generally left the areas of national security and international relations to the president and Congress. In addition, the Court tends to accept cases involving questions decided differently by different courts of appeal, cases in which lower courts have challenged Supreme Court interpretations, and cases in which the U.S. government is a party and it requests review.

★ Liberal and conservative blocs on the Supreme Court can be discerned over time. Generally, liberals have been judicial activists and conservatives have been restraintists. Today a moderate bloc appears to hold the balance of power.

★ The Supreme Court risked its reputation for political impartiality when it intervened in the 2000 presidential election and issued a decision that in effect gave Florida's twenty-five electoral votes to George W. Bush and by so doing won him a majority in the Electoral College.

★ Court power derives primarily from legitimacy rather than force. Most Americans believe that Supreme Court decisions are authoritative statements about the Constitution and people have an obligation to obey these decisions whether they agree with them or not. Although early presidents thought of themselves as constitutional co-equals with the Supreme Court and not necessarily bound by Court decisions, today it would be politically unthinkable for a president to ignore a court order.

★ There are very few checks on Supreme Court power. Presidents may try to influence Court policy through judicial nominations, but once judges are confirmed by the Senate they can pursue their own impulses. Congress has never used its power to limit the jurisdiction of federal courts in order to influence judicial decisions.

★ Only by amending the Constitution can Congress and the states reverse a Supreme Court interpretation of its meaning. Congress can impeach federal judges only for committing crimes, not for their decisions.

Key Terms

judicial review 456
statutory laws 459
judicial self-restraint 460
original intent 460
judicial activism 461
stare decisis 461
precedent 461
jurisdiction 462
original jurisdiction 462
appellate jurisdiction 462

appeal 462
district courts 462
grand juries 462
petit (regular) juries 463
circuit courts 463
briefs 465
civil cases 467
adversarial system 467
standing 467
plaintiff 467

defendant 467
sovereign immunity 467
class action suits 468
contingency fee 468
remedies and relief 469
independent counsel, or
  "special prosecutor" 469
litmus test 471
senatorial courtesy 471
writ of certiorari 476

rule of four 476
amicus curiae 477
solicitor general 477
majority opinion 477
concurring opinion 478
dissenting
  opinion 478
U.S. Solicitor
  General 480

Suggested Readings

Baum, Lawrence. *The Supreme Court*. 9th ed. Washington, D.C.: CQ Press, 2006. Readable introduction to the Supreme Court as a political institution, covering the selection and confirmation of judges, the nature of the issues decided by courts, the process of judicial decision making, and the impact of Supreme Court decisions.

Bork, Robert H. *Coercing Virtue*. Washington, D.C.: AEI Press, 2003. An argument that judges, rather than legislators, are making and repealing law and deciding cases with partisan and ideological subjectivity.

Carp, Robert A., Ronald Stidham, and Kenneth L. Manning. *Judicial Process in America*. 7th ed. Washington, D.C.: CQ Press, 2007. Comprehensive coverage of the America judicial system at all levels.

Epstein, Lee, and Thomas G. Walker. *Constitutional Law for a Changing America: Institutional Power and Constraints*. 6th ed. Washington, D.C.: CQ Press, 2007. Commentary and selected excerpts from cases dealing with the structure and powers of government.

Johnson, Charles, and Danette Buickman. *Independent Counsel: The Law and the Investigations*. Washington, D.C.: CQ Press, 2001. A comprehensive history of the independent counsel law and the investigations conducted under it since 1978, from Watergate to Whitewater.

McClosky, Robert G. *The American Supreme Court*. 4th ed. Rev. by Sanford Levinson. Chicago: University of Chicago Press. 2005. Classic work on the Supreme Court's role in constructing the Constitution, with updates to latest cases.

Neubauer, David W., and Stephen S. Weinhold. *Judicial Politics: Law, Courts, and Politics in the United States*. Belmont, Calif.: Wadsworth, 2004. Introduction to the judicial process with controversial cases in each chapter.

U.S. Supreme Court decisions are available at most public and university libraries as well as at law libraries in volumes of *United States Reports*. Court opinions are cited by the names of the parties, for example, *Brown v. Board of Education of Topeka*, followed by a reference number such as 347 U.S. 483 (1954). The first number in the citation (347) is the volume number; "U.S." refers to *United States Reports*; the subsequent number is the page on which the decision begins; the year the case was decided is in parentheses.

Suggested Web Sites

American Bar Association (ABA)   www.abanet.org
ABA news and views; information for law students.

Find Law for Students   http://stu.findlaw.com
Law school information for schools A–Z, state bar information, job listings, law school rankings, and so forth.

Law Info   www.lawinfo.com
Web site offering legal documents, legal help guides, attorney references, and so forth.

Southern Poverty Law Center   www.splcenter.org
Civil rights law firm opposing death penalty, hate groups, display of religion in public places, and so forth.

Southeastern Legal Foundation
www.southeasternlegal.org
Public interest law firm advocating limited government, individual freedom, and the free enterprise system.

Supreme Court Cases   www.law.cornell.edu
This Cornell Law School's Legal Information Institute site contains up-to-date information about important legal decisions rendered by federal and state courts along with an exhaustive online law library available to researchers.

U.S. Courts   www.uscourts.gov
The goal of this site is "to function as a clearinghouse for information from and about the Judicial Branch of the U.S. government." The site covers the U.S. Supreme Court, U.S. Courts of Appeals, U.S. District Courts, and U.S. Bankruptcy Courts.

The U.S. Supreme Court   www.supremecourtus.gov
Official site provides recent decisions, case dockets, oral arguments, and public information.

14 POLITICS AND PERSONAL LIBERTY

> " Liberty is defined not in terms of the absence of responsibility but, on the contrary, presupposing it. "
>
> **Harold Lasswell**

Chapter *Outline*

★ Power and Individual Liberty
★ Freedom of Religion
★ Freedom of Speech
★ Privacy, Abortion, and the Constitution
★ Obscenity and the Law
★ Freedom of the Press
★ Freedom of Assembly and Petition
★ Protecting Property Rights
★ The Right to Bear Arms
★ Rights of Criminal Defendants
★ The Death Penalty

Power and Individual Liberty

To the authors of the Declaration of Independence, individual liberty was inherent in the human condition. It was not derived from governments or even from constitutions. Rather, governments and constitutions existed to make individual liberty more secure.

> We hold these truths to be self-evident, that all men are created equal, that they are endowed by their Creator with certain unalienable Rights, that among these are Life, Liberty and the pursuit of Happiness. That to secure these rights, Governments are instituted among Men, deriving their just powers from the consent of the governed.

The authors of the Bill of Rights (the first ten amendments to the Constitution) did *not* believe that they were creating individual rights, but rather that they were recognizing and guaranteeing rights that belonged to individuals by virtue of their humanity.

Authority and Liberty To avoid the brutal life of a lawless society, where the weak are at the mercy of the strong, people form governments and endow them with powers to secure peace and self-preservation. People voluntarily relinquish some of their individual freedom to establish a government that is capable of protecting them from their neighbors as well as from foreign aggressors. This government must be strong enough to maintain its own existence or it cannot defend the rights of its citizens.

But what happens when a government becomes too strong and infringes on the liberties of its citizens? How much liberty must individuals surrender to secure an orderly society? This is the classic dilemma of free government: People must create laws and governments to protect their freedom, but the laws and governments themselves restrict freedom.

Democracy and Personal Liberty When democracy is defined only as a *decision-making process*—widespread popular participation and rule by majority—it offers little protection for individual liberty. Democracy must also be defined to include *substantive values*—a recognition of the dignity of all individuals and their equality under law. Otherwise, some

✓ Think About Politics

1. Do you think the government has become so large and powerful that it poses a threat to the rights and freedoms of ordinary citizens?
   YES ⬭ NO ⬭

2. Do you believe that using tax funds to pay tuition at church-affiliated schools violates the separation of church and state?
   YES ⬭ NO ⬭

3. Do we have a constitutional right to physician-assisted suicide?
   YES ⬭ NO ⬭

4. Do law-abiding citizens have a constitutional right to carry a handgun for self-protection?
   YES ⬭ NO ⬭

5. Should persons captured on a foreign battlefield in the war on terrorism be entitled to constitutional protections?
   YES ⬭ NO ⬭

6. Do you believe that the seizure of property believed by police to be used in drug trafficking, without a judicial hearing or trial, violates civil liberty?
   YES ⬭ NO ⬭

7. Is the death penalty a "cruel and unusual" punishment?
   YES ⬭ NO ⬭

Government power defends your most basic rights to life, liberty, and the pursuit of happiness while at the same time ensuring that all other Americans have the same rights. The Founders guaranteed individual liberty in the earliest days of our nation through the first ten amendments to the Constitution—our Bill of Rights.

people, particularly "the weaker party, or an obnoxious individual," would be vulnerable to deprivations of life, liberty, or property simply by decisions of majorities (see "The Paradox of Democracy" in Chapter 1). Indeed, the "great object" of the Constitution, according to James Madison, was to preserve popular government yet at the same time to protect individuals from "unjust" majorities.[1]

The purpose of the Constitution—and especially its Bill of Rights, passed by the First Congress in September 1789—is to limit governmental power over the individual, that is, to place personal liberty beyond the reach of government (see Table 14.1). Each individual's rights to life, liberty, and property, due process of law, and equal protection of the law are not subject to majority vote. Or, as Supreme Court Justice Robert Jackson once declared, "One's right to life, liberty, and property, to free speech, a free press, freedom of worship and assembly, and other fundamental rights may not be submitted to vote: they depend on the outcome of no elections."[2]

Comparing Civil Liberties

★ incorporation
In constitutional law, the application of almost all of the Bill of Rights to the states and all of their subdivisions through the 14th Amendment.

Nationalizing the Bill of Rights   The Bill of Rights begins with the words "*Congress* shall make no law . . ." indicating that it was originally intended to limit only the powers of the federal government. The Bill of Rights was added to the Constitution because of fear that the *federal* government might become too powerful and encroach on individual liberty. But what about encroachments by state and local governments and their officials?

The 14th Amendment includes the words "No *State* shall . . ."; its provisions are directed specifically at states. Initially, the U.S. Supreme Court rejected the argument that the 14th Amendment's Privileges or Immunities Clause[3] and the Due Process Clause[4] incorporated the Bill of Rights. But beginning in the 1920s, the Court handed down a long series of decisions that gradually brought about the **incorporation** of almost all of the protections of the Bill of Rights into the "liberty" guaranteed against state actions by the due process clause of the 14th Amendment. In *Gitlow v. New York* (1925), the Court ruled that "freedom of speech and of the press—which are protected by the First Amendment from abridgment by Congress—are among the fundamental personal rights and liberties protected by the due process clause of the 14th Amendment from impairment by the states."[5] Over time, the Court applied the same reasoning in incorporating almost all provisions of the Bill of Rights into the 14th Amendment's Due Process Clause. States and all of their subdivisions—cities, counties, townships, school districts, and so forth—are bound by the Bill of Rights.

Freedom of Religion

Americans are a very religious people. Belief in God and church attendance are more widespread in the United States than in any other advanced industrialized nation. Although many early American colonists came to the new land to escape religious persecution, they frequently established their own government-supported churches and imposed their own religious beliefs on others. Puritanism was the official faith of colonial Massachusetts, and Virginia officially established the Church of England. Only two colonies (Maryland and Rhode Island) provided for full religious freedom. In part to lessen the potential for conflict among the states, the Framers of the Bill of Rights sought to prevent the new national government from establishing an official religion or interfering with religious exercises.[6] The very first words of the 1st Amendment set forth *two* separate prohibitions on government: "Congress shall make no law respecting an *establishment of religion*, or prohibiting the *free exercise* thereof." These two restrictions on government power—the Free Exercise Clause and the Establishment Clause—guarantee separate religious freedoms.

Table *14.1*   How Are We Protected?: Rights Under the Constitution

The Bill of Rights

The first ten amendments to the Constitution of the United States, passed by the First Congress of the United States in September 1789 and ratified by the states in December 1791.

Amendments	Protections
1st Amendment: Religion, Speech, Press, Assembly, Petition	
Congress shall make no law respecting an establishment of religion, or prohibiting the free exercise thereof, or abridging the freedom of speech, or of the press; or the right of the people peaceably to assemble, and to petition the Government for a redress of grievances.	Prohibits government establishment of religion. Protects the free exercise of religion. Protects freedom of speech. Protects freedom of the press. Protects freedom of assembly. Protects the right to petition government "for a redress of grievances."
2nd Amendment: Right to Bear Arms	
A well regulated Militia, being necessary to the security of a free State, the right of the people to keep and bear Arms, shall not be infringed.	Protects the right of people to bear arms and states to maintain militia (National Guard) units.
3rd Amendment: Quartering of Soldiers	
No Soldier shall, in time of peace, be quartered in any house, without the consent of the Owner, nor in time of war, but in a manner to be prescribed by law.	Prohibits forcible quartering of soldiers in private homes in peacetime, or in war without congressional authorization.
4th Amendment: Searches and Seizures	
The right of the people to be secure in their persons, houses, papers, and effects, against unreasonable searches and seizures, shall not be violated, and no Warrants shall issue, but upon probable cause, supported by Oath or affirmation, and particularly describing the place to be searched, and the persons or things to be seized.	Protects against "unreasonable searches and seizures." Requires warrants for searches of homes and other places where there is a reasonable expectation of privacy. Judges may issue search warrants only with "probable cause," and such warrants must be specific regarding the place to be searched and the things to be seized.
5th Amendment: Grand Juries, Double Jeopardy, Self-Incrimination, Due Process, Protection against Government Takings of Property	
No person shall be held to answer for a capital, or otherwise infamous crime, unless on a presentment or indictment of a grand jury, except in cases arising in the land or naval forces, or in the Militia, when in actual service in time of war or public danger; nor shall any person be subject for the same offence to be twice put in jeopardy of life or limb, nor shall he be compelled in any criminal case to be a witness against himself, nor be deprived of life, liberty, or property, without due process of law; nor shall private property be taken for public use, without just compensation.	Requires that, before trial for a serious crime, a person (except military personnel) must be indicted by a grand jury. Prohibits double jeopardy (trial for the same offense a second time after being found innocent). Prohibits the government from forcing any person in a criminal case to be a witness against himself or herself. Prohibits the government from taking life, liberty, or property "without due process of law." Prohibits government from taking private property without paying "just compensation."

(Continued)

Table **14.1**   How Are We Protected?: Rights Under the Constitution *(continued)*

Amendments	Protections
6th Amendment: Fair Trial In all criminal prosecutions, the accused shall enjoy the right to a speedy and public trial, by an impartial jury of the State and district wherein the crime shall have been committed, which district shall have been previously ascertained by law, and to be informed of the nature and cause of the accusation; to be confronted with the witnesses against him; to have compulsory process for obtaining witnesses in his favor, and to have the Assistance of Counsel for his defense.	Requires that the accused in a criminal case be given a speedy and public trial, and thus prohibits prolonged incarceration without trial or secret trials. Requires that trials be by jury and take place in the district where the crime was committed. Requires that the accused be informed of the charges, have the right to confront witnesses, have the right to force supporting witnesses to testify, and have the assistance of counsel.
7th Amendment: Trial by Jury in Civil Cases In Suits at common law, where the value in controversy shall exceed twenty dollars, the right of trial by jury shall be preserved, and no fact tried by a jury, shall be otherwise reexamined in any Court of the United States, than according to the rules of the common law.	Reserves the right to a jury trial in civil cases. Limits the degree to which factual questions decided by a jury may be reviewed by another court.
8th Amendment: Bail, Fines, and Punishment Excessive bail shall not be required, nor excessive fines imposed, nor cruel and unusual punishments inflicted.	Prohibits excessive bail. Prohibits excessive fines. Prohibits cruel and unusual punishment.
9th Amendment: Unspecified Rights Retained by People The enumeration in the Constitution, of certain rights, shall not be construed to deny or disparage others retained by the people.	Protection of unspecified rights (including privacy) that are not listed in the Constitution. The Constitution shall not be interpreted to be a complete list of rights retained by the people.
10th Amendment: Rights Reserved to the States The powers not delegated to the United States by the Constitution, nor prohibited by it to the States, are reserved to the States respectively, or to the people.	States retain powers that are not granted by the Constitution to the national government or prohibited by it to the states.

Rights in the Text of the Constitution

Several rights were written into the text of the Constitution in 1787 and thus precede in time the adoption of the Bill of Rights.

Article I, Section 9: Habeas Corpus, Bills of Attainder, and Ex Post Facto Laws The privilege of the Writ of Habeas Corpus shall not be suspended, unless when in Cases of Rebellion or Invasion the public Safety may require it. No Bill of Attainder or ex post facto Law shall be passed.	Habeas corpus prevents imprisonment without a judge's determination that a person is being lawfully detained. Prohibition of bills of attainder prevents Congress (and states) from deciding people guilty of a crime and imposing punishment without trial. Prohibition of ex post facto laws prevents Congress (and states) from declaring acts to be criminal that were committed before the passage of a law making them so.

(Continued)

Table *14.1*   How Are We Protected?: Rights Under the Constitution *(continued)*

13th and 14th Amendments

The Bill of Rights begins with the words "Congress shall make no law . . ." indicating that it initially applied only to the *federal* government. Although states had their own constitutions that guarantee many of the same rights, for more than a century the Bill of Rights did not apply to state and local governments. Following the Civil War, the 13th, 14th, and 15th (voting rights) Amendments were passed, restricting *state* governments and their local subdivisions. But not until many years later did the U.S. Supreme Court, in a long series of decisions, apply the Bill of Rights against the states.

13th Amendment

Neither slavery nor involuntary servitude, except as a punishment for crime whereof the party shall have been duly convicted, shall exist within the United States, or any place subject to their jurisdiction.	Prohibits slavery or involuntary servitude except for punishment by law; applies to both governments and private citizens.

14th Amendment

All persons born or naturalized in the United States, and subject to the jurisdiction thereof, are citizens of the United States and of the State wherein they reside. No State shall make or enforce any law which shall abridge the privileges or immunities of citizens of the United States; nor shall any State deprive any person of life, liberty, or property, without due process of law; nor deny to any person within its jurisdiction the equal protection of the laws.	Protects "privileges and immunities of citizenship." Prevents deprivation of life, liberty, or property "without due process of law"; this phrase incorporates virtually all of the rights specified in the Bill of Rights. Prevents denial of "equal protection of the laws" for all persons.

Free Exercise of Religion   The **Free Exercise Clause** prohibits government from restricting religious beliefs or practices. Although the wording of the First Amendment appears absolute ("Congress shall make *no* law . . ."), the U.S. Supreme Court has never interpreted the phrase to protect any conduct carried on in the name of religion. In the first major decision involving this clause, the Court ruled in 1879 that polygamy could be outlawed by Congress in Utah Territory even though some Mormons argued that it was part of their religious faith. The Court distinguished between belief and behavior, saying that "Congress was deprived of all legislative power over mere opinion [by the First Amendment], but was left free to reach actions which were in violation of social duties."[7] The Court also employed the Free Exercise Clause to strike down as unconstitutional an attempt by a state to prohibit private religious schools and force all children to attend public schools.[8] This decision protects the entire structure of private religious schools in the nation.

Later, the Supreme Court elaborated on its distinction between religious belief and religious practice. *Beliefs* are protected absolutely, but with regard to religious *practices*, the Court has generally upheld governmental restrictions when enacted for valid secular purposes.[9] Thus the government can outlaw religious practices that threaten health, safety, or welfare. The Free Exercise Clause does *not* confer the *right* to practice human sacrifice or even the ceremonial use of illegal drugs.[10] Individuals must comply with valid and neutral laws even if these laws restrict religious practices.

★ **Free Exercise Clause**
Clause in the 1st Amendment to the Constitution that prohibits government from restricting religious beliefs and practices that do not harm society.

Amish girls play volleyball at their school in Shipshewana, Indiana.

But the Supreme Court has continued to face many difficulties in applying its "valid secular test" to specific infringements of religious freedom. When some Amish parents refused to allow their children to attend any school beyond the eighth grade, the state of Wisconsin argued that its universal compulsory school attendance law had a valid purpose: the education of children. The Amish parents argued that high school exposed their children to worldly influences and values contrary to their religious beliefs. The Supreme Court sided with the Amish, deciding that their religious claims outweighed the legitimate interests of the state in education.[11] When a Florida city attempted to outlaw the Santeria (a mix of Catholicism and voodoo) practice of slaughtering animals in religious ceremonies, the Supreme Court held that the city's ordinance was "not neutral" and "targeted" a particular religious ceremony and was therefore unconstitutional.[12]

Congress attempted to expand upon the Free Exercise Clause with its Religious Freedom Restoration Act in 1993. Congress was dissatisfied with the Supreme Court's willingness to approve of restrictions on religious practices, restrictions that were part of a valid and neutral law. So Congress mandated that:

> Government shall not substantially burden a person's exercise of religion even if that burden results from a rule of general applicability . . . [unless the government can show that the burden] is in furtherance of a compelling government interest; and is the least restrictive means of furthering that compelling government interest.

Most religious groups praised the act. It had near unanimous support in the Congress. But the Supreme Court decided that the act was an unconstitutional effort by Congress to usurp the power of the courts to interpret the meaning of the Constitution:

> When the court has interpreted the Constitution, it has acted within the province of the judicial branch which embraces the duty to say what the law is . . . the Act contradicts vital principles necessary to maintain separation of powers and the federal balance.[13]

So it is the Supreme Court and not the Congress that has the final say regarding the meaning of the Free Exercise Clause—indeed, of the Constitution.

The Supreme Court has upheld government actions that were challenged as infringements of religious freedom in several key cases. The Court approved an Internal Revenue Service action revoking the tax-exempt status of Bob Jones University because of its rules against interracial dating or marriage among its students. The school argued that its rule was based on religious belief, but the Court held that the government had "an overriding interest in eradicating racial discrimination in education."[14] And the Court upheld an Oregon law that prohibited the possession of peyote (a hallucinogenic drug made from cactus plants) against the claims of a Native American church that its use was a religious sacrament.[15] The Court also upheld an Air Force dress code regulation that prevented orthodox Jews from wearing a yarmulke while in uniform. The Court rejected the argument that the regulation violated the Free Exercise Clause, holding instead that "the mission of the military . . . [including fostering] obedience, unity, commitment and esprit de corps" overrides the individual freedom that would protect civilians from such a government regulation.[16]

Think Again

Do you believe that using tax funds to pay tuition at church-affiliated schools violates the separation of church and state?

No Establishment of Religion

Various meanings have been ascribed to the 1st Amendment's **Establishment Clause**.

1. The first meaning—what the writers of the Bill of Rights had in mind—is that it merely prohibits the government from officially recognizing and supporting a national church, like the Church of England in that nation.

2. A second meaning is somewhat broader: the government may not prefer one religion over another or demonstrate favoritism toward or discrimination against any particular religion, but it might recognize and encourage religious activities in general.

3. The most expansive meaning is that the clause creates "a wall of separation between church and state" that prevents government from endorsing, aiding, sponsoring, or encouraging any or all religious activities.

The phrase "separation of church and state" does *not* appear in the Constitution. It was first used by Thomas Jefferson in a letter to a Baptist Church in 1802 assuring them that the federal government would not establish a national church. The current meaning derives from a 1947 decision by Justice Hugo Black, who, writing for the Supreme Court majority, gave the following definition of the **wall-of-separation doctrine**:

> Neither a state nor the Federal Government can set up a church. Neither can pass laws which aid one religion, aid all religions, or prefer one religion over another. Neither can force nor influence a person to go to or to remain away from church . . . or force him to profess a belief or disbelief in any religion. . . . No tax in any amount, large or small, can be levied to support any religious activities or institutions, whatever they may be called, or whatever form they may adopt to teach or practice religion.[17]

Although the Supreme Court has generally voiced its support for the wall-of-separation doctrine, on several occasions it has permitted cracks to develop in the wall. In allowing public schools to give pupils regular releases from school to attend religious instructions given outside of the school, Justice William O. Douglas wrote that the state and religion need not be "hostile, suspicious or even unfriendly."[18]

What Constitutes "Establishment"?

It has proven difficult for the Supreme Court to reconcile this wall-of-separation interpretation of the 1st Amendment with the fact that religion plays an important role in the life of most Americans. Public meetings, including sessions of the Congress, often begin with prayers;[19] coins are inscribed with the words "In God We Trust"; and the armed forces provide chaplains for U.S. soldiers.

The Supreme Court has set forth a three-part **Lemon test** for determining whether a particular law constitutes "establishment" of religion and thus violates the 1st Amendment. To be constitutional, a law affecting religious activity:

1. Must have a secular purpose.

2. As its primary effect, must neither advance nor inhibit religion.

3. Must not foster "an excessive government entanglement with religion."[20]

Using this three-part test, the Supreme Court held that it was unconstitutional for a state to pay the costs of teachers' salaries or instructional materials in parochial schools. The justices argued that this practice would require excessive government controls and surveillance to ensure that funds were used only for secular instruction and thus involved "excessive entanglement between government and religion."

★ **Establishment Clause**
Clause in the 1st Amendment to the Constitution that is interpreted to require the separation of church and state.

★ **wall-of-separation doctrine**
The Supreme Court's interpretation of the No Establishment Clause that laws may not have as their purpose aid to one religion or aid to all religions.

★ **Lemon test**
To be constitutional, a law must have a secular purpose; its primary effect must neither advance nor inhibit religion; and it must not foster excessive government entanglement with religion.

Separation Anxiety
A Menorah lighting ceremony celebrating Chanukah on public property near the White House. The Supreme Court is divided over whether such public displays violate the Establishment Clause of the First Amendment, which is interpreted as requiring the separation of church and state.

However, the Court has upheld the use of tax funds to provide students attending church-related schools with nonreligious textbooks, lunches, transportation, sign-language interpreting, and special education teachers. And the Court has upheld a state's granting of tax credits to parents whose children attend private schools, including religious schools.[21] The Court has also upheld government grants of money to church-related colleges and universities for secular purposes.[22] The Court has ruled that if public buildings are open to use for secular organizations, they must also be opened to use by religious organizations.[23] And the Court has held that a state institution (the University of Virginia) not only can but must grant student activity fees to religious organizations on the same basis as it grants these fees to secular organizations.[24]

The Supreme Court has upheld tax exemptions for churches on the grounds that "the role of religious organizations as charitable associations, in furthering the secular objectives of the state, has become a fundamental concept in our society."[25] It held that schools must allow after-school meetings on school property by religious groups if such a privilege is extended to nonreligious groups.[26] Deductions on federal income tax returns for church contributions are also constitutional. The Supreme Court allows states to close stores on Sundays and otherwise set aside that day, as long as there is a secular purpose—such as "rest, repose, recreation and tranquility"—in doing so.[27]

But the Court has not always acted to "accommodate" religion. In a controversial case, the Court held that a Christmas nativity scene sitting alone on public property was an official "endorsement" of Christian belief and therefore violated the Establishment Clause. However, if the Christian display was accompanied by a Menorah, a traditional Christmas tree, Santa Claus and reindeer, it would simply be "taking note of the season" and not an unconstitutional endorsement of religion.[28] And in another case, the Supreme Court held that a Louisiana law requiring the teaching of "creationism" along with evolution in the public schools was an unconstitutional establishment of a religious belief.[29]

Critics of the Supreme Court have complained of inconsistencies and contradictions in its consideration of cases involving the Establishment Clause. The Court has made some extremely fine distinctions in considering whether the public display of the Ten Commandments is or is not an establishment of religion. The Court held that a law requiring the posting of the Ten Commandments in every classroom in Kentucky was unconstitutional, but a monument to the Ten Commandments on the grounds of the Texas state capital was merely "an acknowledgment of our nation's heritage."[30]

Prayer in the School   The Supreme Court's most controversial interpretation of the Establishment Clause involved the question of prayer and Bible-reading ceremonies conducted by public schools. The practice of opening the school day with prayer and Bible-reading ceremonies was once widespread in American public schools. To avoid the denominational aspects of these ceremonies, New York State's Board of Regents substituted the following nondenominational prayer, which it required to be said aloud in each class in the presence of a teacher at the beginning of each school day: "Almighty God, we acknowledge our dependence upon Thee, and we beg Thy blessings upon us, our parents, our teachers, and our country." New York argued that this brief prayer did not violate the Establishment Clause, because the prayer was denominationally neutral and because student participation in the prayer was voluntary. However, in *Engel v. Vitale* (1962), the Supreme Court stated that "the constitutional prohibition against laws respecting an establishment of a religion must at least mean in this country it is no part of the business of government to compose official prayers for any group of the American people to recite as part of a religious program carried on by government." The Court pointed out that making prayer voluntary did not free it from the prohibitions of the Establishment Clause, and that clause prevented the *establishment* of a religious ceremony by a government agency regardless of whether the ceremony was voluntary.[31]

One year later, in the case of *Abington Township v. Schempp*, the Court considered the constitutionality of Bible-reading ceremonies in the public schools. Here again, even though the children were not required to participate, the Court found that Bible reading as an opening exercise in the schools was a religious ceremony. The justices went to some trouble in the majority opinion to point out that they were not "throwing the Bible out of the schools." They specifically stated that the *study* of the Bible or of religion, when presented objectively and as part of a secular program of education, did not violate the 1st Amendment; but religious *ceremonies* involving Bible reading or prayer established by a state or school did.[32]

"Voluntary" Prayer   State efforts to encourage "voluntary prayer" in public schools have also been struck down by the Supreme Court as unconstitutional. When the state of Alabama authorized a period of silence for "meditation or voluntary prayer" in public schools, the Court ruled that this action was an "establishment of religion." The Court said the law had no secular purpose, that it conveyed "a message of state endorsement and promotion of prayer," and that its real intent was to encourage prayer in public schools.[33] In a stinging dissenting opinion, Justice William Rehnquist noted that the Supreme Court itself opened its session with a prayer and that both houses of Congress opened every session with prayers led by official chaplains paid by the government. In 1992 the Court held that invocations and benedictions at public high school graduation ceremonies were an unconstitutional establishment of religion.[34] And in 2000 the Court ruled that student-led "invocations" at football games were unconstitutional. A Texas school district that allowed students to use its public address system at football games "to solemnize the event" was violating the Establishment Clause. "The Constitution demands that schools not force on students the difficult choice between whether to attend these games or to risk facing a personally offensive religious ritual."[35] (See *Controversy*: "Are We One Nation Under God"?)

The Prayer Problem
Although the Supreme Court ruled in 1962 (*Engel v. Vitale*) that even voluntary prayer in public schools was an unconstitutional violation of the separation of church and state under the 1st Amendment, the question of prayer in schools remains a heated one. Indeed, recent court rulings regarding nondenominational prayers at graduation ceremonies and sporting events have, if anything, further confused the issue.

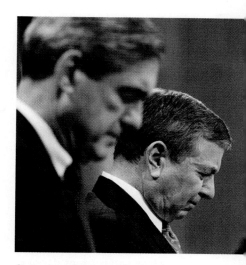

Outgoing Attorney General John Ashcroft bows his head in prayer with FBI Director Robert Mueller, left, during the invocation of his farewell ceremony at the Department of Justice headquarters in Washington, D.C. on January 24, 2005.

School Vouchers

You Are a State Legislator

Do you believe that using tax funds to pay tuition at church-affiliated schools violates the separation of church and state?

What Speech is Protected by the Constitution?

★ **clear and present danger doctrine**
Standard used by the courts to determine whether speech may be restricted; only speech that creates a serious and immediate danger to society may be restricted.

State Vouchers to Attend Religious Schools   Another important issue arising under the Establishment Clause is the granting of educational vouchers to parents to spend at any school they choose, including religious schools. State governments redeem the vouchers submitted by schools by paying specific amounts for each student enrolled. When Ohio initiated a "Scholarship Program" that provided tuition aid to certain students in the Cleveland City School District who could choose to use this aid to attend either public or private or religious schools of their parents' choosing, opponents challenged the program in federal court, arguing that it "advanced a religious mission" in violation of the Establishment Clause. Although parents could use the vouchers to send their children to other public schools or nonreligious private schools, over 90 percent of the students participating in the scholarship program were enrolled in religiously affiliated schools. In 2002 the U.S. Supreme Court held (in a narrow 5–4 decision) that the program did *not* violate the Constitution.[36] The Court reasoned that the program was neutral with respect to religion and provided assistance directly to citizens who, in turn, directed this aid to religious schools wholly as a result of their own independent private choices. The incidental advancement of a religious mission is reasonably attributed to the individual recipients, not the government, "whose role ends with the distribution of benefits."

Freedom of Speech

Although the First Amendment is absolute in its wording ("Congress shall pass no law . . . abridging the freedom of speech"), the Supreme Court has never been willing to interpret this statement as a protection of *all* speech. What kinds of speech does the 1st Amendment protect from government control, and what kinds of speech may be constitutionally prohibited?

Clear and Present Danger Doctrine   The classic example of speech that can be prohibited was given by Justice Oliver Wendell Holmes in 1919: "The most stringent protection of free speech would not protect a man in falsely shouting 'fire' in a theater and causing a panic."[37] Although Holmes recognized that the government may prevent speech that creates a serious and immediate danger to society, he objected to government attempts to stifle critics of its policies, such as the Espionage Act of 1917 and the Sedition Act of 1918. The Sedition Act prohibited, among other things, speech that was meant to discourage the sale of war bonds and "disloyal" speech about the government, the Constitution, the military forces, or the flag of the United States. In the case of *Gitlow v. New York*, the majority supported the right of the government to curtail any speech that "tended to subvert or imperil the government," but Holmes dissented, arguing that "every idea is an incitement. It offers itself for belief and if believed it is acted on unless some other belief outweighs it."[38] Unless the expression of an idea created a *serious and immediate danger*, Holmes argued that it should be tolerated and combated or defeated only by the expression of better ideas.

Holmes's standard for determining the limits of free expression became known as the **clear and present danger doctrine**. Government should not curtail speech merely because it *might tend* to cause a future danger: "The question in every case is whether the words used are used in such circumstances and are of such a nature as to create a clear and present danger that they will bring about the substantive evils that Congress has a right to prevent."[39] Holmes's argument inspired a long struggle in the courts to strengthen constitutional protections for speech and press (see *Politics Up Close*: "The American Civil Liberties Union").

Controversy

Are We One Nation "Under God"?

For over 100 years the Pledge of Allegiance has been recited in public school rooms at the beginning of each day. In 1954, at the height of the Cold War, Congress added the words "under God" after "one nation," to emphasize that the United States acknowledged spiritual values in contrast to "godless communism." President Dwight D. Eisenhower, upon signing the bill, said it would strengthen "those spiritual weapons which forever will be our country's most powerful resource in peace and war."

As early as 1943, the Supreme Court declared that public school pupils could not be *required* to recite the pledge. The opinion was widely praised as an expression of our constitutional freedoms: "If there is any fixed star in our constitutional constellation, it is that no official, high or petty, can prescribe what shall be orthodox in politics, nationalism, religion, or other matters of opinion, or force citizens to confess by word or act their faith therein."[a] Pupils who did not wish to take the pledge were free to stand silent in the classroom while the pledge was being recited.

The Supreme Court was called upon to review the phrase "under God" in 2002 when the father of a public school pupil argued that these words constituted an establishment of religion by an instrument of the government, namely the schools, whether or not his daughter was required to participate in the ceremony. He argued that the pledge with "under God" constituted "a ritual proclaiming that there is a God" and therefore violated the Establishment Clause of the 1st Amendment. The Words "under God" asserted monotheism and possibly offended atheists, the nonreligious, and others who did not wish to swear an oath of allegiance to a monotheistic deity.

The U.S. Court of Appeals for the Ninth Circuit (with jurisdiction for California and other West Coast states and arguably the most liberal Circuit Court in the nation) agreed that the words "under God" were not neutral and represented a swearing of allegiance

to monotheism. The effect of this appeals court's opinion was to remove the words "under God" from the Pledge. However, subsequently it was revealed that the father (who was divorced) did not have custody over his daughter, and that the custodial mother did not wish her daughter to bring suit over this issue. The Supreme Court, therefore, dismissed the case on this technicality and avoided the substantive issue of whether or not the words "under God" in the Pledge of Allegiance violated the Establishment Clause.[b] The effect of the Supreme Court's decision was to retain the words.

It can be argued that these words do not refer to any specific religion or deity but simply acknowledge the nation's religious heritage. References to God have long been part of our national identity. Our coins invoke the blessing "In God We Trust," chaplains are provided for the Armed Forces, prayers open the sessions of both chambers of Congress as well as the Supreme Court itself. A strong majority (84 percent) of Americans support the inclusion of the words "under God" in the Pledge of Allegiance.

[a]*West Virginia Board of Education v. Barnette*, 319 U.S. 624 (1943).
[b]*Elk Grove United School District v. Newdow*, 542 U.S. 277 (2004).

Although Holmes was the first to use the phrase "clear and present danger," it was Justice Louis D. Brandeis who later developed the doctrine into a valuable constitutional principle that the Supreme Court gradually came to adopt. Brandeis explained that the doctrine involved two elements: (1) the clearness or seriousness of the expression; and (2) the immediacy of the danger flowing from the speech. With regard to immediacy he wrote,

Supreme Court Justice Oliver Wendell Holmes.

★ **preferred position**
Refers to the tendency of the courts to give preference to the 1st Amendment rights to speech, press, and assembly when faced with conflicts.

A Threat of Violence
The Supreme Court ruled in 2003 that cross burning was meant to intimidate and was therefore *not* protected as symbolic speech by the 1st Amendment.

No danger flowing from speech can be deemed clear and present, unless the incidence of the evil apprehended is so imminent that it may befall before there is opportunity for full discussion. If there be time to expose through discussion the falsehood and fallacies, to avert the evil by the processes of education, the remedy to be applied is more speech, not enforced silence.

And with regard to seriousness he wrote,

Moreover, even imminent danger cannot justify resort to prohibition [of speech] . . . unless the evil apprehended is relatively serious. Prohibition of free speech and assembly is a measure so stringent that it would be inappropriate as the means for averting a relatively trivial harm to society. . . . There must be the probability of serious injury to the State.[40]

Preferred Position Doctrine   Over the years, the Supreme Court has given the 1st Amendment freedoms of speech, press, and assembly a special **preferred position** in constitutional law. These freedoms are especially important to the preservation of democracy. If speech, press, or assembly are prohibited by government, the people have no way to correct the government through democratic processes. Thus the burden of proof rests on the *government* to justify any restrictions on speech, writing, or assembly.[41] In other words, any speech or writing is presumed constitutional unless the government proves that a serious and immediate danger would ensue if the speech were allowed.

The Cold War Challenge   Despite the Supreme Court's endorsement of the clear and present danger and preferred position doctrines, in times of perceived national crisis the courts have been willing to permit some government restrictions of speech, press, and assembly. At the outbreak of World War II, just prior to U.S. entry into that world conflict, Congress passed the Smith Act, which stated,

It shall be unlawful for any person to knowingly or willfully advocate, abet, advise, or teach the duty, necessity, desirability, or propriety of overthrowing or destroying any government in the United States by force or violence, or by the assassination of any officer of any such government.

Congress justified its action in terms of national security, initially as a protection against fascism during World War II, then later as a protection against communism in the early days of the Cold War.

In 1949 the Department of Justice prosecuted Eugene V. Dennis and ten other top leaders of the Communist Party of the United States for violation of the Smith Act. A jury found them guilty of violating the act, and the party leaders were sentenced to jail terms ranging from one to five years. In 1951 the case of *Dennis v. United States* came to the Supreme Court on appeal. In upholding the conviction of the Communist Party leaders, the Court seemed to abandon Brandeis's idea that "present" meant "before there is opportunity for full discussion."[42] It seemed to substitute clear and *probable* for clear and *present*.

Since that time, however, the Supreme Court has returned to a policy closer to the original clear and present danger doctrine. As the Cold War progressed, Americans grew to view communism as a serious threat to democracy, but not a *present* danger. The overthrow of the American government advocated by communists was not an incitement to *immediate* action. A democracy must not itself become authoritarian to protect itself from authoritarianism. In later cases, the Supreme Court held that the mere advocacy of revolution, apart from unlawful action, is protected by the First Amendment.[43] It struck down federal laws requiring

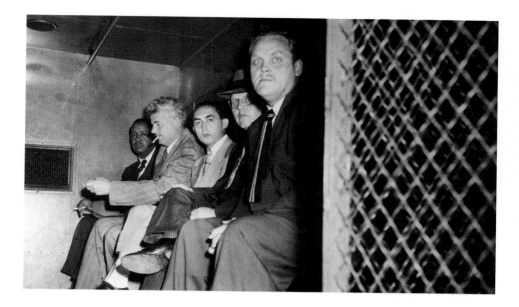

Eugene Dennis and four others of the twelve Communists being returned to their jail cells after being convicted of advocating the overthrow of the government. From left to right: Benjamin Davis, Jr., Eugene Dennis, Gilbert Green, John Williamson, and Gus Hall.

communist organizations to register with the government,[44] laws requiring individuals to sign "loyalty oaths,"[45] laws prohibiting communists from working in defense plants,[46] and laws stripping passports from Communist Party leaders.[47] In short, once the perceived Cold War crisis began to fade, the Supreme Court reasserted the First Amendment rights of individuals and groups.

Symbolic Speech

The First Amendment's guarantees of speech, press, and assembly are broadly interpreted to mean **freedom of expression**. Political expression encompasses more than just words. For example, when Mary Beth Tinker and her brothers were suspended for wearing black armbands to high school to protest the Vietnam War, they argued that the wearing of armbands constituted **symbolic speech** protected by the First Amendment. The Supreme Court agreed, noting that the school did not prohibit all wearing of symbols but instead singled out this particular expression for disciplinary action.[48]

The Supreme Court continues to wrestle with the question of what kinds of conduct are symbolic speech protected by the First Amendment and what kinds of conduct are outside of this protection. Symbolic speech, like speech itself, cannot be banned just because it offends people. "If there is only one bedrock principle underlying the First Amendment, it is that the Government may not prohibit the expression of an idea simply because society finds the idea itself offensive or disagreeable."[49] The Court held that flag burning was "symbolic speech"[50] and therefore protected by the 1st Amendment. In contrast, cross burning was "a form of intimidation and a threat of impending violence"[51] and therefore not protected by the 1st Amendment.

Speech and Public Order

The Supreme Court has wrestled with the question of whether speech can be prohibited when it stirs audiences to public disorder, not because the speaker urges lawless action but because the audience reacts to the speech with hostility. In short, can a speaker be arrested because of the *audience's* disorderly behavior? In an early case, the Supreme Court fashioned a *fighting words doctrine*, to the effect that words that "ordinary men know are likely to cause a fight" may be prohibited.[52] But later the Court seemed to realize that this doctrine, if broadly applied, could create a huge constitutional hole in the First Amendment guarantee of free speech. Authorities could curtail speech simply

★ **freedom of expression**
Collectively, the 1st Amendment rights to free speech, press, and assembly.

★ **symbolic speech**
Actions other than speech itself but protected by the 1st Amendment because they constitute political expression.

because it met with audience hostility. The Court recognized that "speech is often provocative and challenging. It may . . . have profound unsettling effects. . . . That is why freedom of speech, while not absolute, is nevertheless protected against censorship."[53] The Court has also held that the First Amendment protects the use of four-letter words when used to express an idea: "One man's vulgarity may be another's lyric."[54] And the Court has consistently refused to allow government authorities to ban speech *before* it has occurred simply because they believe it *may* create a disturbance.

The Supreme Court has held that reasonable restrictions can be placed on the manner and places of protests. Students may conduct protests on designated places on campus or places which do not interrupt the educational process. Cities can require permits for parades as long as they do not discriminate in the issuance of permits. Authorities cannot selectively ban some protests and parades but not others; authorities cannot regulate the content of signs or speech. The Court upheld a state law that prohibited protests within a 100-foot zone around the entrances to health facilities including abortion clinics.[55]

Campus Speech   Many colleges and universities have undertaken to ban speech that is considered racist, sexist, homophobic, or otherwise "insensitive" to the feelings of women and minorities. Varieties of "speech codes," "hate codes," and sexual harassment regulations that prohibit verbal expressions raise serious constitutional questions, especially at state-supported colleges and universities. The 1st Amendment includes insulting or offensive racist or sexist words or comments in its protection (see *Controversy*: "Political Correctness Versus Free Speech on Campus"). Many of these college and university regulations would not withstand a judicial challenge if students or faculty undertook to oppose them in federal court.

Hate Speech and Hate Crimes   "Hate" speech is usually defined as hostile or prejudicial attitudes expressed toward another person's or group's characteristics, notably sex, race, ethnicity, religion, or sexual orientation. Banning hate speech is now common at colleges and universities, in business employment and sports enterprises, on radio and television, and in the press. But do *government* prohibitions on hate speech violate the 1st Amendment?

Historically the Supreme Court viewed prohibitions on offensive speech as unconstitutional infringements of 1st Amendment freedoms. "The remedy to be applied is more speech, not enforced silence."[56]

The Supreme Court was called upon to review prohibitions on hate speech in 1992 when the city of St. Paul, Minnesota, enacted an ordinance prohibiting any communication that "arouses anger, alarm, or resentment among others on the basis of race, color, creed, religion, or gender." The ordinance defined such expressions as "disorderly conduct" and made them misdemeanors punishable by law. But the Supreme Court, in a unanimous decision, struck down the city's effort to prohibit expressions only because they cause "hurt feelings, offense, or resentment." Speech expressing racial, gender, or religious intolerance is still speech, and it is protected by the 1st Amendment.[57]

However, the Supreme Court is willing to recognize that bias-motivated crimes—crimes intentionally directed at a victim because of his or her race, religion, disability, national origin, or sexual orientation—may be more heavily punished than the same crimes inspired by other motives. The Court held that a criminal defendant's "abstract beliefs, however obnoxious to most people, may not be taken into consideration by a sentencing judge."[58] But a defendant's *motive* for committing a particular criminal act has traditionally been a factor in sentencing, and a defendant's verbal statements can be used to determine motive.

Controversy

Political Correctness Versus Free Speech on Campus

Universities have a very special responsibility to protect freedom of expression. The free and unfettered exchange of views is essential to the advancement of knowledge—the very purpose of universities. For centuries universities have fought to protect academic freedom from pressures arising from the world *outside* of the campus—governments, interest groups, financial contributors—arguing that the university must be a protected enclave for free expression of ideas. But today's threat to academic freedom arises from *within* universities—from efforts by administrations, faculty, and campus groups to suppress ideas, opinions, and language that are not "politically correct" (PC). PC activists seek to suppress opinions and expressions they consider to be racist, sexist, "homophobic," or otherwise "insensitive" to specified groups.[a]

Speech Codes

The experience at the University of Michigan with its "Policy on Discrimination and Discriminatory Harassment" illustrates the battles occurring on many campuses over First Amendment rights. In 1988 a series of racial incidents on campus prompted the university to officially ban "any behavior verbal or physical" that "stigmatized" an individual "on the basis of race, ethnicity, religion, sex, sexual orientation, creed, national origin, ancestry, age, marital status, handicap, or Vietnam-era veteran status" or that created "an intimidating, hostile, or demeaning environment for educational pursuits." A published guide provided examples of banned activity, which included the following:

★ A male student makes remarks in class like "women just aren't as good in this field as men."
★ Jokes about gay men and lesbians.
★ Commenting in a derogatory way about a particular person or group's physical appearance or sexual orientation, or their cultural origins, or religious beliefs.

Free Speech

In 1989 "John Doe," a psychology graduate student studying gender differences in personality traits and mental functions, filed suit in federal court requesting that the University of Michigan policy be declared a violation of the 1st Amendment. (He was permitted by the court to remain anonymous because of fear of retribution.) He was joined in his complaint against the university by the American Civil Liberties Union.

In its decision, the court acknowledged that the university had a legal responsibility to prevent racial or sexual discrimination or harassment. However, it did not have a right to

> establish an anti-discrimination policy which had the effect of prohibiting certain speech because it disagreed with ideas or messages sought to be conveyed....Nor could the University proscribe speech simply because it was found to be offensive, even gravely so, by large numbers of people. . . . These principles acquire a special significance in the University setting, where the free and unfettered interplay of competing views is essential to the institution's educational mission. . . . While the Court is sympathetic to the University's obligation to ensure educational opportunities for all of its students, such efforts must not be at the expense of free speech.[b]

It seems ironic that students and faculty now must seek the protection of the federal courts from attempts by universities to limit speech. Traditionally, universities themselves fought to protect academic freedom. Academic freedom included the freedom of faculty and students to express themselves in the classroom, on the campus, and in writing, on controversial and sensitive topics, including race and gender. It was recognized that students often express ideas that are biased or ill informed, immature, or crudely expressed. But students were taught that the remedy for offensive language or off-color remarks or ill-chosen examples was more enlightened speech, not the suppression of speech.

[a]Dinesh D'Souza, *Illiberal Education: The Politics of Race and Sex on Campus.* (New York: Vintage Books, 1992).
[b]*John Doe v. University of Michigan,* 721 F. Supp. 852 (1989).

Commercial Speech Do 1st Amendment freedoms of expression apply to commercial advertising? The Supreme Court has frequently asserted that **commercial speech** is protected by the 1st Amendment. The Court held that states cannot outlaw price advertising by pharmacists[59] or advertising for services by attorneys[60] and that cities cannot outlaw posting "For Sale" signs on property, even in the interests of halting white flight and promoting racially integrated

★ **commercial speech**
Advertising communications given only partial protection under the 1st Amendment to the Constitution.

neighborhoods. Advertising is the "dissemination of information" and is constitutionally protected.[61]

However, the Court has also been willing to weigh the 1st Amendment rights of commercial advertisers against the public interest served by regulation. In other words, the Court seems to suspend its preferred position doctrine with regard to commercial advertising and to call for a "balancing of interests." Thus the Supreme Court has allowed the Federal Communications Commission to regulate the contents of advertising on radio and television and even to ban advertising for cigarettes. The Federal Trade Commission enforces "truth" in advertising by requiring commercial packages and advertisers to prove all claims for their products.

Libel and Slander Libel and slander have never been protected by the 1st Amendment against subsequent punishment (see "Libel and Slander" in Chapter 6). Once a communication is determined to be libelous or slanderous, it is outside of the protection of the 1st Amendment. The courts have traditionally defined "libel" as a "damaging falsehood." However, if plaintiffs are public officials they must prove that the statements made about them are not only false and damaging but also "made with actual malice"—that is, with knowledge that they are false or with "reckless disregard" of the truth—in order to prove libel.[62]

Privacy, Abortion, and the Constitution

A right of "privacy" is not expressly provided for anywhere in the Constitution. But does the word *liberty* in the 1st and 14th Amendments include a constitutional right to privacy?

Finding a Right to Privacy The U.S. Supreme Court found a right of privacy in the Constitution when it struck down a Connecticut law prohibiting the use of contraceptives in 1965. Estelle Griswold had opened a birth control clinic on behalf of the Planned Parenthood League of that state and was distributing contraceptives in violation of the state statute prohibiting their use. She challenged the constitutionality of the statute, even though there is no direct reference to birth control in the Bill of Rights. The Supreme Court upheld Griswold's challenge, finding a right of privacy, according to Justice William O. Douglas, in the "penumbras formed by the emanations from" the 1st, 3rd, 4th, 5th, 9th, and 14th Amendments. "Various guarantees create a zone of privacy. . . . Would we allow the police to search the sacred precincts of marital bedrooms for telltale signs of the use of contraceptives? The very idea is repulsive to the notion of privacy surrounding the marriage relationship." In concurrent opinions, other justices found the right of privacy in the 9th Amendment: "The enumeration in the Constitution of certain rights, shall not be construed to deny or disparage others retained by the people."[63]

Roe v. Wade The fact that the *Griswold Case* dealt with reproduction gave encouragement to groups advocating abortion rights. In 1969 Norma McCorvey sought an abortion in Texas but was refused by doctors who cited a state law prohibiting abortion except to save a woman's life. McCorvey challenged the Texas law in federal courts on a variety of constitutional grounds, including the right to privacy. McCorvey became "Jane Roe," and the case became one of the most controversial in the Supreme Court's history.[64]

The Supreme Court ruled that the constitutional right of privacy as well as the 14th Amendment's guarantee of "liberty" included a woman's decision to bear or not to bear a child. The Court held that the word "person" in the Constitution did *not* include the unborn child; therefore, the 5th and 14th Amendments' guarantee of "life, liberty, or property" did not protect the "life" of the fetus. The Court also ruled that a state's power to protect the health and safety of the mother could not justify any restriction on abortion in the first 3 months of pregnancy. Between the third and sixth months of pregnancy, a state could set standards for abortion procedures in order to protect the health of women, but a state could not prohibit abortions. Only in the final 3 months could a state prohibit or regulate abortion to protect the unborn.

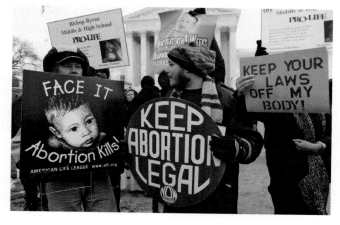

Pro-life and pro-choice demonstrators hold signs side-by-side during the March for Life on January 25, 2005 in Washington, D.C. to protest the 32nd anniversary of the *Roe v. Wade* decision that granted women the constitutional right to abortion.

Rather than end the political controversy over abortion, *Roe v. Wade* set off a conflagration. Congress defeated efforts to pass a constitutional amendment restricting abortion or declaring that life begins at conception. However, when Congress banned the use of federal funds under Medicaid (medical care for the poor) for abortions except to protect the life of a woman, the Supreme Court upheld the ban, holding that there was no constitutional obligation for governments to *pay* for abortions.[65]

Reaffirming *Roe v. Wade*

Abortion has become such a polarizing issue that "pro-choice" and "pro-life" groups are generally unwilling to search out a middle ground. Yet the current Supreme Court appears to have chosen a policy of affirming a woman's right to abortion while upholding modest restrictions, as evidenced by the Court's ruling in *Planned Parenthood of Pennsylvania v. Casey* (1992).[66]

In this case, the Supreme Court considered a series of restrictions on abortion enacted by Pennsylvania: Physicians must inform women of risks and alternatives; women must wait 24 hours after requesting an abortion before having one; and the parents of minors must be notified. It struck down a requirement that spouses be notified. Later, the court struck drawn a parental notification law that did not provide an exception for a judge to withhold notification when it would not be in the best interest of the minor.

Justice Sandra Day O'Connor took the lead in forming a moderate, swing bloc on the Court. Her majority opinion strongly reaffirmed the fundamental right of abortion, both on the basis of the 14th Amendment and on the principle of stare decisis. But the majority also upheld states' rights to protect any fetus that reached the point of "viability." The Court went on to establish a new standard for constitutionally evaluating restrictions: they must not impose an "undue burden" on women seeking abortion or place "substantial obstacles" in her path. All of Pennsylvania's restrictions met this standard and were upheld except spousal notification.

"Partial Birth Abortion"

An abortion procedure known as "intact dilation and evacuation" or "partial birth abortion" has been the object of prohibitions by a number of states and by Congress itself. This procedure, which is used in very few abortions, involves partial delivery of the fetus feet first, then vacuuming out the brain and crushing the skull to ease complete removal. A Nebraska law banning the procedure was declared an unconstitutional "undue burden" on a woman's right to abortion by the Supreme Court in 2002;

the Nebraska law failed to make an exception to save the life of the mother. In response, Congress passed a ban on partial birth abortions in 2003 and President George W. Bush signed it into law. (Earlier bans passed by Congress had been vetoed by President Bill Clinton.) Congress provided an exception—allowing the method if it is necessary to save a mother's life. The Supreme Court upheld this congressional prohibition on partial birth abortions recognizing that government "has the power to restrict abortions after viability if the law contains exceptions for pregnancies endangering the woman's life or health" (*Gonzalez v. Carhart*, April 2007).

Sexual Conduct "Liberty gives substantial protection to adult persons in deciding how to conduct their lives in matters pertaining to sex." This Supreme Court ruling in *Lawrence v. Texas* (2003) struck down a state law against homosexual sodomy. The ruling overturned an earlier case in which the Court held that the Constitution granted no "fundamental right to homosexuals to engage in acts of consensual sodomy."[68] Rather, the Supreme Court decided that "The liberty protected by the Constitution allows homosexual persons the right to choose to enter upon relationships in the confines of their homes and their own private lives and still retain their dignity as free persons."[69]

Other Private Activities How far does the right of privacy extend? The Supreme Court appears to have left this question open to argument. In 1969 the Court held that privacy may be constitutionally protected where there is a "reasonable expectation of privacy," notably in one's own home. The Court overturned a criminal conviction for the "mere private possession of obscene material," that is, the possession and viewing of pornography at home.[70]

Civil Rights and Gay Adoption

Gay Marriage The Supreme Court has not yet spoken out on gay marriages—marriages between persons of the same sex. Several state courts, including the Supreme Court of Massachusetts, have held that the Equal Protection Clause of the 14th Amendment entitles gay couples to marry, that to deny them marriage rights while recognizing heterosexual marriages amounts to discrimination. The issue is complicated by the constitutional provision that requires all states to give "Full Faith and Credit" to judicial proceedings of other states (see *Controversy*: "Federalism and Same-Sex Marriages" in Chapter 4). This provision implies that gay marriages in any state must be recognized in all states. Congress passed a Defense of Marriage Act in 1996 declaring that no state need recognize a gay marriage. But Congress failed to pass a constitutional amendment banning same-sex marriage (see *Controversy*: "Should We Amend the Constitution to Ban Gay Marriages?").

A Right to Die? In most states, for most of the nation's history, it has been a crime to help another person to commit suicide. Michigan's prosecution of Dr. Jack Kevorkian for publicly participating in physician-assisted suicides launched a nationwide debate on the topic. More important, a group of physicians in Washington, along with their gravely ill patients, filed suit in federal court seeking a declaration that their state's law banning physician-assisted suicide violated the "liberty" guaranteed by the 14th Amendment. They argued that mentally competent, terminally ill patients had the "right to die"; that is, they had a privacy right to request and receive aid in ending their life. They relied on the Supreme Court's previous rulings on abortion, contending that Washington's law placed an undue burden on the exercise of a privacy

Controversy

Should We Amend the Constitution to Ban Gay Marriages?

Congress has before it an amendment which says: "Marriage in the United States shall consist only of the union of a man and a woman. Neither this Constitution or the Constitution of any state, nor state or federal law, shall be construed to require that marital status or the legal incidents thereof be conferred upon unmarried couples or groups."

In general, Americans oppose same-sex marriages. Various polls over time indicate that almost two-thirds of the public oppose gay marriages.

Q. *"Should same-sex marriages be recognized by law as valid with the same rights as traditional marriages?"*

Yes 32% No 64%

However, many Americans are reluctant to amend the Constitution to define marriage as strictly between a man and a woman.

Q. *"Do you favor a constitutional amendment that would define marriage as being between a man and a woman, thus barring same-sex marriages?"*

Yes 53% No 44%

Despite protests in support of gay marriage, most states and the Congress in its Protection of Marriage Act declare that a legal marriage can be only "between a man and a woman."

And Americans are divided over whether federal or state laws should govern same-sex marriage.

Q. *"Do you think laws regarding same-sex marriage should be determined by the federal government or individual state governments?"*

Federal 48% State 46%

Source: As reported in *USA Today*, February 25, 2004.

right. But the U.S. Supreme Court held that there is no *constitutional right* to physician-assisted suicide.[71] The Court implied that if the laws governing the practice are to be changed, they must be changed by legislatures, not by reinterpreting the Constitution.

Patients have a right to refuse treatment, even if by so doing they ensure their own deaths. Life-sustaining procedures can be ended at the request of a family member only if there is "clear and convincing evidence" that the patient would not want these procedures.[72] Most states now recognize "living wills" in which people express their wishes while still of sound mind. The absence of a living will, and disputes within the family over what a comatose patient would wish, can cause prolonged and bitter court fights.

Obscenity and the Law

Obscene materials of all kinds—words, publications, photos, videotapes, films— are *not* protected by the 1st Amendment. Most states ban the publication, sale, or possession of obscene material, and Congress bans its shipment in the mails.

Because obscene material is not protected by the 1st Amendment, it can be banned without even an attempt to prove that it results in antisocial conduct. In other words, it is not necessary to show that obscene material would result in a clear and present danger to society, the test used to decide the legitimacy of *speech*. In order to ban obscene materials, the government need only prove that they are *obscene*.

Defining "obscenity" has confounded legislatures and the courts for years, however. State and federal laws often define pornography and obscenity in such terms as "lewd," "lascivious," "filthy," "indecent," "disgusting"—all equally as vague as "obscene." "Pornography" is simply a synonym for "obscenity." *Soft-core pornography* usually denotes nakedness and sexually suggestive poses; it is less likely to confront legal barriers. *Hard-core pornography* usually denotes explicit sexual activity. After many fruitless efforts by the Supreme Court to come up with a workable definition of "pornography" or "obscenity," a frustrated Justice Potter Stewart wrote the now-famous quote in 1974, "I shall not today attempt further to define [hard-core pornography]....But *I know it when I see it.*"[73]

Slackening Standards: *Roth v. United States*

The Court's first comprehensive effort to define "obscenity" came in *Roth v. United States* (1957). Although the Court upheld Roth's conviction for distributing pornographic magazines through the mails, it defined "obscenity" somewhat narrowly: "Whether to the average person applying contemporary community standards, the dominant theme of the material, taken as a whole, appeals to prurient interests."[74]

Note that the material must be obscene to the *average* person, not to children or particular groups of adults who might be especially offended by pornography. The standard is "contemporary," suggesting that what was once regarded as obscene might be acceptable today. Later, the *community standard* was clarified to mean the "society at large," not a particular state or local community.[75] The material must be "considered as a whole," meaning that even if a work includes some obscene material, it is still acceptable if its "dominant theme" is something other than "prurient." The Court added that a work must be "utterly without redeeming social or literary merit" in order to be judged obscene.[76] The Court never really said what a "prurient" interest was but reassured everyone that "sex and obscenity are not synonymous."

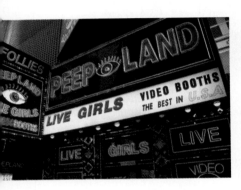

Peepland in New York City. The Supreme Court recognizes "local community standards" in determining what is, or is not, obscene.

Tightening Standards: *Miller v. California*

The effect of the Roth decision, and the many and varied attempts by lower courts to apply its slippery standards, tended to limit law enforcement efforts to combat pornography during the 1960s and 1970s. The Supreme Court itself came under ridicule when it was learned that the justices had set up a movie room in the basement of the Supreme Court building to view films that had been brought before them in obscenity cases.[77]

So the Supreme Court tried again, in *Miller v. California* (1973), to give law-enforcement officials some clearer standards in determining obscenity. Although the Court retained the "average person" and "contemporary" standards, it redefined "community" to mean the *local* community rather than the society at large. It also defined "prurient" as "patently offensive" representations or descriptions of "ultimate sex acts, normal or perverted, actual or simulated," as well as "masturbation, excretory functions, and lewd exhibition of the genitals." It rejected the earlier requirement that the work had to be "utterly without redeeming social value" in order to be judged obscene, and it substituted instead "lacks serious literary, artistic, political, or scientific value."[78]

The effect of the Supreme Court's *Miller* standards has been to increase the likelihood of conviction in obscenity-pornography cases. It is easier to prove that a work lacks serious value than to prove that it is utterly without redeeming merit. Moreover, the *local community standard* allows prosecution of adult bookstores and X-rated video stores in some communities, while allowing the same stores to operate in other communities. The Supreme Court has also upheld local ordinances that ban nudity in public places, including bars and lounges. The Court rejected the argument that nude dancing was "expressive" conduct.[79]

Porn on the Internet

Porn on the Internet New technologies continue to challenge courts in the application of 1st Amendment principles. Currently the Internet, the global computer communication network, allows users to gain access to information worldwide. Thousands of electronic bulletin boards give computer users access to everything from bomb-making instructions and sex conversations to obscene photos and even child pornography. Many commercial access services ban obscene messages and exclude bulletin boards with sexually offensive commentary. Software programs that screen out pornography Web sites are readily available to consumers. But can *government* try to ban such material from the Internet without violating 1st Amendment freedoms?

Congress tried unsuccessfully to ban "indecent" and "patently-offensive" communications from the Internet in its Communications Decency Act of 1996. Proponents of the law cited the need to protect children from pornography. But in 1997 the Supreme Court held the act unconstitutional: "Notwithstanding the legitimacy and importance of the Congressional goal of protecting children from harmful materials, we agree that the statute abridges freedom of speech protected by the First Amendment." Government cannot limit Internet messages "to only what is fit for children." The Supreme Court agreed with the assertion that "as the most participatory form of mass speech yet developed [the Internet] deserves the highest protection from government intrusion."[80] (See also *Politics Up Close*: "Child Pornography").

Freedom of the Press

Democracy depends on the free expression of ideas. Authoritarian regimes either monopolize the media or subject them to strict licensing and censorship of their content. The idea of a free and independent press is deeply rooted in the evolution of democratic government.

No-Prior-Restraint Doctrine

No-Prior-Restraint Doctrine Long before the Bill of Rights was written, English law protected newspapers from government restrictions or licensing prior to publication—a practice called **prior restraint**. This protection, however, does not mean that publishers are exempt from *subsequent punishment* for libelous, obscene, or other illegal publications. Prior restraint is more dangerous to free expression because it allows the government to censor the work prior to publication and forces the defendants to *prove* that their material should *not* be censored. In contrast, subsequent punishment requires a trial in which the government must prove that the defendant's published materials are unlawful.

In *Near v. Minnesota* (1931), a muckraking publication that accused local officials of trafficking with gangsters was barred from publishing under a Minnesota law that prohibited the publication of a "malicious, scandalous or defamatory newspaper." The Supreme Court struck down the law as unconstitutional, affirming the *no-prior-restraint doctrine*. However, a close reading of the majority opinion reveals that the doctrine is not absolute. Chief Justice Charles Evans Hughes noted that prior government censorship might be constitutional "if publication . . . threatened the country's safety in times of war."[81]

★ **prior restraint**
Government actions to restrict publication of a magazine, newspaper, or books on grounds of libel, obscenity, or other legal violations prior to actual publication of the work.

Politics Up Close   Child Pornography

In 1982, the U.S. Supreme Court struck a hard blow against child pornography—the "dissemination of material depicting children engaged in sexual conduct regardless of whether the material is obscene."[a] Such material includes any visual depiction of children performing sexual acts or lewdly exhibiting their genitals. The Court reasoned that films or photographs of sexual exploitation and abuse of children were "intrinsically related" to criminal activity; such material was evidence that a crime has been committed. Thus the test for *child* pornography was much stricter than the standards set for obscene material. It is not necessary to show that the sexual depiction of children is "obscene" (under the *Miller* standards) in order to ban such material; it is only necessary to show that children were used in the production of the material.

But what if the images of children involved in sexual activity are produced by means other than using real children, such as the use of youthful-looking adults or computer-imaging technology? In the Child Pornogra-

phy Prevention Act of 1996, Congress tried to prohibit "any visual depiction, including any photograph, film, video, picture, or computer or computer-generated image . . . [that] is, or appears to be, of a minor engaging in sexually explicit conduct." Congress did not construct this act to meet the *Miller* standards; it prohibited *any* depictions of sexually explicit activity by children, whether or not they contravened community standards or had serious redeeming value.

But the Supreme Court, in a highly controversial (6–3) decision, held that there was an important distinction between actual and virtual child pornography. Virtual child pornography and adults posing as minors do not directly involve the exploitation or abuse of children. The Court held that the congressional definition of child pornography was overly broad; the mere assertion that such material might encourage pedophiles to seduce children was not sufficient to prohibit it. "The First Amendment requires a more precise restriction."[b]

[a]*New York v. Ferber*, 458 U.S. 747 (1982).
[b]*Ashcroft v. Free Speech Coalition*, 535 U.S. 234 (2002).

Angela Jolie as "Fox" and James McAvoy as "Wesley" (driver's mirror) in *Wanted*, released March 28, 2008, by Universal Pictures.

Yet the question of whether or not the government can restrain publication of stories that present a serious threat to national security remains unanswered. For example, can the government restrain the press from reporting in advance on the time and place of an impending U.S. military action, thereby warning an enemy and perhaps adding to American casualties? In the most important case on this question, *New York Times v. United States* (1971), the Supreme Court upheld the right of the newspaper to publish secret documents that had been stolen from State Department and Defense Department files. The material covered U.S. policy decisions in Vietnam, and it was published while the war was still being waged. But five separate (concurring) opinions were written by justices in the majority as well as two dissenting opinions. Only two justices argued that government can *never* restrain any publication regardless of the seriousness or immediacy of the harm. Others in the majority cited the government's failure to show proof in this case that publication "would surely result in direct, immediate, and irreparable damage to our nation or its people."[82] Presumably, if the government had produced such proof, the case might have been decided differently. The media interpret the decision as a blanket protection to publish anything they wish regardless of harm to government or society.

Film Censorship

The no-prior-restraint doctrine was developed to protect the print media—books, magazines, newspapers. When the motion picture industry was in its infancy, the Supreme Court held that films were "business, pure and simple" and were not entitled to the protection of the 1st Amendment.[83] But as films grew in importance, the Court gradually extended 1st Amendment freedoms to cover motion pictures.[84] However, the Supreme Court has not given the film industry the same strong no-prior-restraint protection it has given the press. The Court has approved government requirements for prior submission of films to official censors, so long as (1) the burden of proof that the film is obscene rests with the censor; (2) a procedure exists for judicial determination of the issue; and (3) censors are required to act speedily.[85] To avoid government-imposed censorship the motion picture industry adopted its own system of rating films:

G: suitable for all audiences
PG: parental guidance suggested
PG-13: parental guidance strongly suggested for children under 13
R: restricted to those 17 or older unless accompanied by a parent or guardian
NC-17: no one under 17 admitted

Some city governments have sought to restrict showing of NC-17 films, and their restrictions have been upheld by the Courts.[84]

Radio and Television Censorship

The Federal Communications Commission was created in 1934 to allocate broadcast frequencies and to license stations. The exclusive right to use a particular frequency is a "public trust." Thus broadcasters, unlike newspapers and magazines, are licensed by the government and subject to government rules. Although the 1st Amendment protects broadcasters, the Supreme Court has recognized the special obligations that may be imposed on them in exchange for the exclusive right to use a broadcast frequency. "No one has a First Amendment right to a license or to monopolize a radio frequency; to deny a station license because 'the public interest' requires it, is not a denial of free speech."[87] Thus the Court has upheld FCC-imposed "equal time" and "fairness" rules against broadcasters, even while striking down government attempts to impose the same rules on newspapers.[88]

Media Claims for Special Rights

The news media make various claims to special rights arising out of the 1st Amendment's guarantee of a free press. Reporters argue, for example, that they should be able to protect their news sources and are not obliged to give testimony in criminal cases when they have obtained evidence in confidence. However, the only witnesses the Constitution exempts from compulsory testimony are defendants themselves, who enjoy the 5th Amendment's protection against "self-incrimination." The Supreme Court has flatly rejected reporters' claims to a privilege against compulsory testimony. "We cannot seriously entertain the notion that the First Amendment protects a newsman's agreement to conceal the criminal conduct of his source, or evidence thereof, on the theory that it is better to write about a crime than to do something about it."[89]

Despite these rulings, reporters regularly boast of their willingness to go to jail to protect sources, and many have done so. But the media have also pressured the nation's legislatures for protection. Congress has passed the Privacy Protection Act, which sharply limits the ability of law-enforcement officials to search press offices, and many states have passed **shield laws** specifically protecting reporters from giving testimony in criminal cases.

Disclaimers
Television networks hope to avoid government-imposed censorship by offering warnings such as "viewer discretion advised."

★ **shield laws**
Laws in some states that give reporters the right to refuse to name their sources or to release their notes in court cases; may be overturned by the courts when such refusals jeopardize a fair trial for a defendant.

Freedom of Assembly and Petition

The 1st Amendment guarantees "the right of the people peaceably to assemble, and to petition the government for redress of grievances." The right to organize political parties and interest groups derives from the right of assembly. And freedom of petition protects most lobbying activities.

The Right of Association Freedom of assembly includes the right to form and join organizations and associations. In an important case during the early civil rights movement, the state of Alabama attempted to harass the National Association for the Advancement of Colored People by requiring it to turn over its membership lists to authorities. The Supreme Court held the state's action to be an unconstitutional infringement of the freedom of association.[90] In the 1960s, the Supreme Court struck down attempts by governments to regulate the Communist Party by requiring membership registration, or penalizing individuals for party membership, or by removing party members from privileges other citizens enjoy.[91]

Freedom of association, like freedom of speech and press, is not absolute. Large national organizations, with no firm ideological views, can be forced to abide by antidiscrimination laws. The Court expressly held that the United States Jaycees and later the Rotary Club could not discriminate on the basis of sex. These large, nonideological, nonreligious, nonpolitical groups are granted less protection than "expressive" groups.[92]

"Expressive" groups, including religious organizations, are free to limit participation to persons who subscribe to their views. Antidiscrimination laws, including those protecting homosexuals, cannot force an organization to accept participation by individuals who do not share its expressed views. In a well-publicized case the Supreme Court held that the right of association protected the organizers of Boston's St. Patrick's Day parade from being forced by law to include the "Irish-American Gay, Lesbian and Bisexual Group of Boston."[93] And in another well-publicized case the Supreme Court held that the Boy Scouts are not obliged to accept gays as scouts: "The forced inclusion of an unwanted person in a group infringes the group's freedom of expressive association if the presence of that person affects in a significant way the group's ability to advocate public or private viewpoints."[94]

In another important freedom of association case, the Supreme Court held that California's blanket primary law, a statute that extended participation in party primary elections to all registered voters regardless of their political party affiliation, was unconstitutional.[95] The Court struck down the law holding that it forced political parties to associate with those who do not share their beliefs.

The Supreme Court has also protected the right of students to form organizations. "First Amendment rights...are available to teachers and students. It can hardly be argued that either teachers or students shed their constitutional rights at the school house gate."[96] Attempts by a college or university to deny official recognition to a student organization based on its views violates the right of association.

Protests, Parades, and Demonstrations Freedom of assembly includes the right to peacefully protest, parade, and demonstrate. Authorities may, within reasonable limits, enact restrictions regarding the "time, place, and manner" of an assembly so as to preserve public order, smooth traffic flow, freedom of movement, and even peace and quiet. But these regulations cannot be unevenly applied to groups with different views. Thus authorities may require a permit to parade, but they cannot deny a permit to a group because of the nature of their views or content of their message. For example, the Supreme Court held that city authorities in Skokie, Illinois, acted unconstitutionally in prohibiting the American Nazi Party from holding a march in that city even though it was populated with large numbers of Jewish survivors of the Holocaust.[97]

Picketing Assemblies of people have a high potential for creating a public disturbance. Parades block traffic and litter the streets; loudspeakers assault the ears of local residents and bystanders; picket lines may block the free passage of others. Although the right of assembly is protected by the 1st Amendment, its exercise involves conduct as well as expression, and therefore it is usually subject to greater government regulation than expression alone. The Court has generally upheld reasonable use of public property for assembly, but it has not forced *private* property owners to accommodate speeches or assemblies. Airport terminals, shopping malls, and other open forums, which may or may not be publicly owned, have posed problems for the courts.

Freedom of assembly is currently being tested by opponents of abortion who picket abortion clinics, hoping to embarrass and dissuade women from entering them. Generally the courts have allowed limits on these demonstrations to ensure that people can move freely in and out of the clinics. Freedom of assembly does not include the right to block access to public or private buildings. And when abortion opponents demonstrated at the residence of a physician who performed abortions, the Supreme Court upheld a local ordinance barring assemblies in residential neighborhoods.[98] Physically obstructing access to buildings almost always violates state or local laws, as does the threat or use of force by picketers. The Supreme Court made a distinction between a "fixed buffer zone," prohibiting assembly around a building entrance, and a "floating buffer zone" (of 15 feet), prohibiting demonstrators from approaching individuals in public places. The "fixed" zone was held to be a constitutional limit on assembly but the "floating" zone was held to be an unconstitutional limit on free speech.[99] In 1994 Congress passed a federal law guaranteeing access to abortion clinics, arguing that the federal government should act to guarantee a recognized constitutional right.

Escorts from Planned Parenthood, in orange vests, walk past a group of anti-abortion protestors during a prayer vigil outside the clinic in Washington, D.C. on Saturday, January 21, 2006.

Protesters block Constitution Avenue and access to federal buildings on September 29, 2007, in Washington, D.C. to protest the war in Iraq.

Protecting Property Rights

The 5th Amendment provides specific protection for private property against government confiscation: "nor shall private property be taken for public use without just compensation." This **takings clause** recognizes that occasionally governments—federal, state, or local—may be obliged to take property from private owners for public uses, for example, streets, roads, public buildings, parks and the

★ **takings clause**
The 5th Amendment's prohibition against government taking of private property without just compensation.

★ **eminent domain**
The action of a government to take property for public use with just compensation even if the owner does not wish to sell.

like. But the Founders wanted to be certain that even these "takings" from private owners would have some constitutional protection. Taking land from private owners who do not wish to sell it to the government is known as eminent domain. The 5th Amendment's takings clause guarantees that the taking of private property by the government for public use can only be done with just compensation being paid to the owner. Usually, a city or state tries to purchase land from the owners in a mutually agreed transaction. But if the owners do not wish to sell or do not agree with the government's offered price, the issue is determined by a court in what is known as **eminent domain** proceedings. In these proceedings a city or state must go to court and show that the land is needed for a legitimate public purpose; the court will then establish a fair price (just compensation) based on testimony from the owner, the city or state, and impartial appraisers.

Public Use Takings under eminent domain are valid only when the property is to be put to "public use." But what constitutes a "public use"? Traditionally, public use referred to goods that served the general public, including schools, highways, public buildings, public memorials, and other facilities open to the public generally. Over time, however, the public use clause was given expanded meaning. Eminent domain was used in urban renewal projects to eliminate slums and blighted areas of a city.

But what if the property taken under eminent domain is not a slum or blighted area but rather a residential area not unlike residential areas elsewhere in the city, and the government proposes to give the taken property to private developers to build new residences and offices and facilities for new businesses—"city revitalization"? The city of New London, Connecticut, exercised its eminent domain power by taking a number of residential properties from owners who did not wish to sell for the purposes of economic development. The city proposed to give these properties to private developers for projects that would create new jobs and garner new revenues for the city. The Supreme Court, in reviewing the city's action, acknowledged that "the sovereign may not take the property of A for the sole purpose of transferring it to another private party B, even if A is paid just compensation." The Court seemed to say that if the only beneficiary of the government taking of private property was another private party, it would violate the 5th Amendment's takings clause. But the Court reasoned that economic development was a public purpose, arguing that the definition of "public use" can be "broad and inclusive" and that the legislative body rather than the courts

Susette Kelo's house is all that remains of a block in Fort Trumbull neighborhood in New London, Connecticut, on February 9, 2005. Kelo is fighting against the city's claim of eminent domain over her home.

should make the determination of whether a project would generally serve the public interest.[100] The fact that a taking benefited some private parties more than others did not make it unconstitutional.

This Supreme Court decision allowing an eminent domain taking for sale to private developers seemed to undermine the 5th Amendment's takings clause. It caused a stir among politicians, the media, and the general public. Some states have considered more restrictive definitions of "public use" than the Supreme Court's, a legislative action that the Court said it would allow.

Takings What if the government does not "take" ownership of a property but instead restricts the owner's use of it through regulation? Zoning ordinances, environmental regulations, or building and housing codes may reduce the value of a property to the owner. Should the owner be compensated for the loss of full use?

Courts have recognized that governments can make laws to protect the health, safety, and general welfare of its citizens. Owners of property have never been entitled to any compensation for obeying laws or ordinances with a clear public purpose. Yet it was still argued that some city regulations, especially those designed for beauty and aesthetics, had no relation to public health or safety, but rather they simply enacted somebody's preferences over those of their neighbor. But in 1954 the Supreme Court upheld a very broad interpretation of the police power: "It is within the power of the Legislature to determine that the community should be beautiful as well as healthy, spacious as well as clean, well-balanced as well as carefully patrolled."[101] The Court made it difficult to challenge the constitutionality of local planning and zoning ordinances as a "taking" of private property without compensation even though it reduced the value of property to the owner.

Yet in 1992 the Supreme Court stepped in to hold that a regulation that denies a property owner of *all* economically beneficial use of his land (for example, a state coastal zone management regulation preventing any construction on a beach lot) was a "taking" that requires just compensation to the owner in order to be constitutional.[102] But the court did not address the question of how far governments can go in regulating land use without compensating property owners. Depriving land owners of *all* beneficial uses of their land without compensation is clearly unconstitutional. But what if their use of land is devalued by 50 percent or 25 percent? In recent years both Congress and the federal courts, as well as some states, have undertaken to reconsider "how far" governments can go in depriving property owners of value uses of their land.

The Right to Bear Arms

The 2nd Amendment to the U.S. Constitution states: "A well regulated Militia, being necessary to the security of a free State, the right of the people to keep and bear Arms, shall not be infringed."

Bearing Arms What is meant by the right of the people "to keep and bear arms"? One view is that the 2nd Amendment confers on Americans an *individual* constitutional right, like the 1st Amendment freedom of speech or press. The history surrounding the adoption of the 2nd Amendment reveals the concern of colonists with attempts by despotic governments to confiscate the arms of citizens and render them helpless to resist tyranny. James Madison wrote in *The Federalist*, No. 46, that "the advantage of being armed which the Americans possess over the people of almost every other nation, forms a barrier against the enterprise of [tyrannical] ambition.[103] The 2nd Amendment was adopted with little controversy; most state constitutions at the time, like Pennsylvania's, declared

Think Again

Do law-abiding citizens have a constitutional right to carry a handgun for self-protection?

Gun Rights and Gun Control

Controversy

Gun Control?

New controls on guns are a common policy demand following highly publicized murders or assassination attempts. The Federal Gun Control Act of 1968 was a response to the assassinations of Sen. Robert F. Kennedy and Martin Luther King, Jr., in that year, and efforts to legislate additional restrictions occurred after attempts to assassinate presidents Gerald Ford and Ronald Reagan. Today various federal gun control laws include the following:

★ A ban on interstate and mail-order sales of handguns
★ Prohibition of the sale of firearms to convicted felons
★ A requirement that all firearms *dealers* be licensed by the federal Bureau of Alcohol, Tobacco, Firearms, and Explosives
★ Requirements that manufacturers record the serial number of all firearms and that dealers record all sales
★ Restrictions of private ownership of automatic weapons and military weapons.

Finally there is the *Brady Law* requirement for a five-day waiting period for the purchase of a handgun. (The law was named for James S. Brady, former press secretary to President Ronald Reagan, who was severely wounded in the 1981 attempted assassination of the president.) Handgun dealers must send police agencies a form completed by the buyer; police agencies have five days to make certain the purchaser is not a convicted felon.

Gun Laws and Crime

There is no systematic evidence that gun control laws reduce violent crime. If we compare violent crime rates in jurisdictions with very restrictive gun laws (for example, New York, Massachusetts, New Jersey, Illinois, and the District of Columbia, all of which prohibit the possession of unlicensed handguns by citizens) to crime rates in jurisdictions with very loose controls, we find no difference in rates of violent crime that cannot be attributed to social conditions.[a]

The 2nd Amendment

The Supreme Court ruled in 2008 that the 2nd Amendment right to bear arms was an individual right, not merely the collective right of the states to maintain militia (National Guard) units.[b] The Court specifically ruled that a total prohibition on the possession of handguns was unconstitutional and that individuals had a constitutional right to possess arms "for traditionally lawful purposes, such as self defense within the home." (The Court also held that a trigger lock requirement "makes it impossible for citizens to use arms for the core lawful purpose of self defense and is hence unconstitutional.") But the Court went on to indicate that certain reasonable prohibitions on guns were constitutional: prohibitions on carrying concealed weapons, prohibitions on the possession of firearms by felons and the mentally ill, and prohibitions on the carrying of firearms in sensitive places such as schools and government buildings, or laws imposing conditions and qualifications on the commercial sale of arms.

Public Opinion

Public opinion clearly opposes a nationwide prohibition on the sale of handguns to citizens. Various polls report that 65 to 75 percent of the public does *not* wish to deprive citizens of the right to own guns. However, there is considerable support for various laws respecting gun owners.[c]

[a]Douglas R. Murray, "Handguns, Gun Control Laws and Firearms Violence," *Social Problems* 23 (June 1975, 26–35); James D. Wright and Peter H. Rossi, *Weapons, Crime and Violence in America*. Washington, D.C.: National Institute of Justice, 1981; Gary Kleck, *Targeting Guns*. New York: Aldine de Gruyter, 1997.

[b]*District of Columbia v. Heller*, June 26, 2008.

[c]Various polls from Public Agenda, www.publicagenda.org

	Favor	Oppose
Background checks on people buying guns	92%	6%
Trigger locks on stored guns	81	15
A ban on the sale of assault weapons	71	27
Requiring gun owners to attend a course on gun safety	84	12
A ban on people carrying concealed weapons	49	48

Perhaps most controversial is the proposal to require all gun owners to register with the government. The National Rifle Association (NRA) believes that this is the first step in the government effort to seize all citizen-owned guns. However, the general public seems to favor gun registration.

Requiring gun owners to register with the government	75	24

that "the people have a right to bear arms for the defense of themselves and the state." Early American political rhetoric was filled with praise for an armed citizenry able to protect its freedoms by force if necessary.

State Militias   But many constitutional scholars argued that the 2nd Amendment protects only the collective right of the states to form militias—that is, their right to maintain National Guard units. They focused on the qualifying phrase "a well-regulated Militia, being necessary to the security of a free State." But after years of controversy, the Supreme Court finally decided the issue in 2008: "The Second Amendment protects an individual right to possess a firearm unconnected with service in a militia, and to use that arm for traditionally lawful purposes, such as self defense within the home." (*District of Columbia v. Heller*, June 26, 2008.) A District of Columbia law prohibiting the possession of handguns violated "the ancient right of individuals to keep and bear arms for self-defense." But the Court went on to warn that "Like most rights the Second Amendment right is not unlimited" and that reasonable restrictions on guns may be constitutional (see *Controversy:* "Gun Control?").

Rights of Criminal Defendants

While society needs the protection of the police, it is equally important to protect society from the police. Arbitrary searches and arrests, imprisonment without trial, forced confessions, beatings and torture, secret trials, tainted witnesses, excessive punishments, and other human rights violations are all too common throughout the world. The U.S. Constitution limits the powers of the police and protects the rights of the accused (see Table 14.2). (See also *Controversy:* "Should Victims' Rights Be Added to the Constitution?")

The Guarantee of the Writ of Habeas Corpus   One of the oldest and most revered rights in English common law is the right to obtain a **writ of habeas corpus**, which is a court order directing public officials who are holding a person in custody to bring the prisoner into court and explain the reasons for confinement. If a judge finds that the prisoner is being unlawfully detained, or finds insufficient evidence that a crime has been committed or that the prisoner could have committed it, the judge must order the prisoner's release. Thus the writ of habeas corpus is a means to test the legality of any imprisonment (see *What Do You Think?:* "Are Persons Captured on the Battlefields of Afghanistan and Iraq Entitled to Protections of the U.S. Constitution?").

The writ of habeas corpus was considered so fundamental to the Framers of the Constitution that they included it in the original text of Article I: "The privilege of the Writ of Habeas Corpus shall not be suspended, unless when in Cases of Rebellion or Invasion the public Safety may require it." Despite the qualifying phrase, the Supreme Court has never sanctioned suspension of the writ of habeas corpus even during wartime. President Abraham Lincoln suspended the writ of habeas corpus in several areas during the Civil War, but in the case of *Ex parte Milligan* (1866), the Supreme Court ruled that the president had acted unconstitutionally.[104] (With the war over, however, the Court's decision had no practical effect.) Again, in 1946, the Supreme Court declared that the military had had no right to substitute military courts for ordinary courts in Hawaii during World War II, even though Hawaii was in an active theater of war.[105] State courts cannot issue writs of habeas corpus to federal officials, but federal judges may issue such writs to state officials whenever there is reason to believe that a person is being held in violation of the Constitution or laws of the United States.

The Prohibition of Bills of Attainder and Ex Post Facto Laws   Like the guarantee of habeas corpus, protection against bills of attainder and ex post facto

Bear Arms: A State or an Individual Right?

The 2nd Amendment's "right to bear arms" was interpreted by the Supreme Court to guarantee an individual's right to own guns (as asserted by these protestors), and not merely as a grant of power to the states to maintain National Guard units.

 Think Again

Do you believe that the seizure of property believed by police to be used in drug trafficking, without a judicial hearing or trial, violates civil liberty?

★ **writ of habeas corpus**
Court order directing public officials who are holding a person in custody to bring the prisoner into court and explain the reasons for confinement; the right to habeas corpus is protected by Article I of the Constitution.

You Are a Police Officer

Table *14.2*   Individual Rights in the Criminal Justice Process

Rights	Process
Fourth Amendment: Protection against unreasonable searches and seizures Warranted searches for sworn "probable cause." Exceptions: consent searches, safety searches, car searches, and searches incident to a valid arrest.	**Investigation by law-enforcement officers** Expectation that police act lawfully.
Fifth Amendment: Protection against self-incrimination Miranda rules (see Figure 14.1, p. 526). **Habeas corpus** Police holding a person in custody must bring that person before a judge with cause to believe that a crime was committed and the prisoner committed it.	**Arrest** Arrests based on warrants issued by judges and magistrates. Arrests based on crimes committed in the presence of law enforcement officials. Arrests for "probable cause."
Eighth Amendment: No excessive bail Defendant considered innocent until proven guilty; release on bail and amount of bail depends on seriousness of crime, trustworthiness of defendant, and safety of community.	**Hearing and bail** Preliminary hearing in which prosecutor presents testimony that a crime was committed and probable cause for charging the accused.
Fifth Amendment: Grand jury (federal) Federal prosecutors (but not necessarily state prosecutors) must convince a grand jury that a reasonable basis exists to believe the defendant committed a crime and he or she should be brought to trial.	**Indictment** Prosecutor, or a grand jury in federal cases, issues formal document naming the accused and specifying the charges.
Sixth Amendment: Right to counsel Begins in investigation stage, when officials become "accusatory"; extends throughout criminal justice process. Free counsel for indigent defendants.	**Arraignment** Judge reads indictment to the accused and ensures that the accused understands charges and rights and has counsel. Judge asks defendant to choose a plea: Guilty, *nolo contendere* (no contest), or not guilty. If defendant pleads guilty or no contest, a trial is not necessary and defendant proceeds to sentencing.
Sixth Amendment: Right to a speedy and public trial Impartial jury. Right to confront witnesses. Right to compel favorable witnesses to testify. **Fourth Amendment: Exclusionary rule** Illegally obtained evidence cannot be used against defendant.	**Trial** Impartial judge presides as prosecuting and defense attorneys present witnesses and evidence relevant to guilt or innocence of defendant and make arguments to the jury. Jury deliberates in secret and issues a verdict.
Eighth Amendment: Protection against cruel and unusual punishments	**Sentencing** If the defendant is found not guilty, the process ends. Defendants who plead guilty or no contest and defendants found guilty by jury are sentenced by fine, imprisonment, or both by the judge. Sentences imposed must be commensurate to the crimes committed.
Fifth Amendment: Protection against double jeopardy Government cannot try a defendant again for the same offense.	**Appeal** Defendants found guilty may appeal to higher courts for reversal of verdict or a new trial based on errors made anywhere in the process.

Controversy

Should Victims' Rights Be Added to the Constitution?

The U.S. Constitution includes fifteen specific guarantees of the rights of the accused. It makes no mention of victims' rights.

Liberal California Democratic U.S. Senator Dianne Feinstein and conservative Arizona Republican U.S. Senator Jon Kyl have co-sponsored an amendment to the Constitution that would guarantee to victims of violent crime:

★ To be informed of and not be excluded from critical proceedings including:
arraignment
preliminary hearing
trial
sentencing
appeals hearing
parole hearings
★ To be heard at proceedings involving a release from custody, sentencing, or acceptance of a negotiated plea
★ To notice of any release or escape of the offender
★ To a disposition free from unreasonable delay
★ To an order of restitution from the convicted offender
★ To have the safety of the victims considered in determining a release from custody
★ To notice of the victim's rights.

Supporters of a constitutional amendment, a "Crime Victims' Bill of Rights," argue that each year there are millions of victims of violent crime, many of whom are victimized a second time by the criminal justice system itself. They are not notified of the arrest, arraignment, or trial of the person accused of harming them, nor are they guaranteed a hearing at crucial stages of the judicial process—plea-bargaining, sentencing, or parole. Polls show that victims' rights are overwhelmingly supported by the American people. The Senate Judiciary Committee has approved of the victims' rights amendment to the Constitution, and it has the support of President George W. Bush.

But to date the sponsors of the amendment have failed to gather the necessary two-thirds vote of both houses of Congress to send the amendment to the states for ratification. Opponents argue that more than half the states already have added victims' rights amendments to their state constitutions. They argue that it is unnecessary to further clutter the U.S. Constitution with a lengthy amendment that is likely to cause additional litigation and delay in criminal cases.

CONSTITUTIONAL RIGHTS TODAY

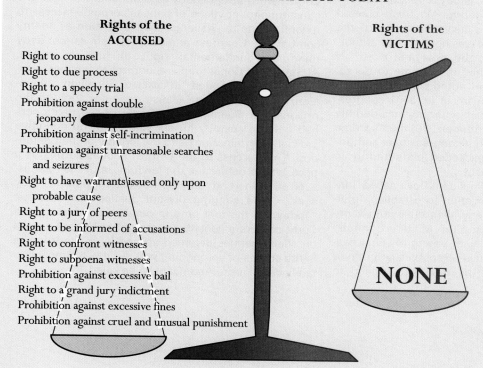

Rights of the ACCUSED

Right to counsel
Right to due process
Right to a speedy trial
Prohibition against double jeopardy
Prohibition against self-incrimination
Prohibition against unreasonable searches and seizures
Right to have warrants issued only upon probable cause
Right to a jury of peers
Right to be informed of accusations
Right to confront witnesses
Right to subpoena witnesses
Prohibition against excessive bail
Right to a grand jury indictment
Prohibition against excessive fines
Prohibition against cruel and unusual punishment

Rights of the VICTIMS

NONE

The Need for a Victims' Rights Amendment
Source: From the Office of U.S. Senator Dianne Feinstein.

What Do You *Think?*

Are Persons Captured on the Battlefields of Afghanistan and Iraq Entitled to the Protections of the U.S. Constitution?

The United States has held 6,000 or more "enemy combatants" captured on the battlefields of Afghanistan and Iraq for several years. Some are held at the U.S. base in Guantánamo Bay, Cuba.

Prisoners of war have never been entitled to constitutional protection. Prisoners of war are uniformed members of the military forces of a nation. (The U.S. held tens of thousands of German and Japanese prisoners of war during World War II.) They are entitled only to "humane treatment" under the Geneva Accords. They are not released until the war is ended.

"Detainees" from the war on terrorism are not officially prisoners of war, inasmuch as they are not uniformed soldiers of any nation. The United States has pledged humane treatment even though the government argues that these detainees are not protected by the Geneva Accords. They are not held on U.S. soil. As military detainees, they were not given lawyers or access to courts or, in most cases, even identified by name.

But in 2004 the Supreme Court held that enemy combatants captured on the battlefield and "imprisoned in territory over which the United States exercises an exclusive jurisdiction and control" are entitled to constitutional rights including habeas corpus—the right to bring their case to U.S. courts. "The fact that petitioners are being held in military custody is immaterial."[a]

In response, President George W. Bush created special military tribunals to hear the cases of the detainees. Initially, Congress was not asked to authorize these tribunals. Rather, the president cited his power as Commander-in-Chief in wartime to do so. He noted that Congress had authorized him to use military force to fight terrorism in its 2001 congressional resolution and that such authority included the creation of special military tribunals. But the Supreme Court held in 2006 that without congressional authorization, the president had exceeded his authority in creating the military tribunals.[b]

Following this decision, President Bush asked Congress for legislative authorization to establish "military commissions" to try "any alien unlawful enemy combatant." Congress passed the Military Commissions Act in October 2006, with voting on final passage largely along party lines—Republicans in favor and Democrats opposed. The new Act applied to aliens, not citizens, and only to "unlawful" enemy combatants (in contrast to lawful prisoners of war who are "regular forces of a state"). It specifically prohibited habeas corpus appeals to U.S. courts. Military commissions were to function under their own procedural rules—rules that did not necessarily afford full constitutional protections for defendants. But defendants could appeal the decisions of military commissions to the U.S. Court of Appeals for the District of Columbia.

But in a controversial 5–4 decision the Supreme Court held that detainees at Guantánamo "have the constitutional privilege of habeas corpus"—access to federal courts to challenge their detention as enemy combatants. Congress and the president cannot deny them the fundamental right of habeas corpus. Although the Constitution recognizes that habeas corpus can be suspended "in cases of Rebellion or Invasion," this Suspension Clause does not apply to the prisoners at Guantánamo. "Some of the petitioners had been in custody for six years with no definitive judicial determination as to the legality of their detention. Their access to the writ [of habeas corpus] is a necessity to determine the lawfulness of their status, even if, in the end, they do not obtain the relief they seek."[c] In a stinging dissent Justice Scalia wrote: "Today, for the first time in our Nation's history, the Court confers a constitutional right to habeas corpus on alien enemies detained abroad by military forces in the course of an ongoing war. . . . It will almost certainly cause more Americans to be killed."

[a]*Rasul v. Bush*, 542 U.S. 466 (2004).
[b]*Hamdan v. Rumsfeld*, 548 U.S. 557 (2006).
[c]*Boumediene v. Bush*, June 12, 2008.

laws was considered so fundamental to individual liberty that it was included in the original text of the Constitution. A **bill of attainder** is a legislative act inflicting punishment without judicial trial. An **ex post facto law** is a retroactive criminal law that works against the accused—for example, a law that makes an act criminal after the act is committed or a law that increases the punishment for a crime and applies it retroactively. Both the federal government and the states are prevented from passing such laws.

The fact that relatively few cases of bills of attainder or ex post facto laws have come to the federal courts does not diminish the importance of these protections. Rather, it testifies to the widespread appreciation of their importance in a free society.

Unreasonable Searches and Seizures

Individuals are protected by the 4th Amendment from "unreasonable searches and seizures" of their private "persons, houses, papers, and effects." The 4th Amendment lays out specific rules for searches and seizures of evidence: "No warrants shall issue, but upon probable cause, supported by Oath or affirmation, and particularly describing the place to be searched, and the persons or things to be seized." Judges cannot issue a **search warrant** just to let police see *if* an individual has committed a crime; there must be "probable cause" for such issuance. The indiscriminate searching of whole neighborhoods or groups of people is unconstitutional and is prevented by the 4th Amendment's requirement that the place to be searched must be specifically described in the warrant. The requirement that the things to be seized must be described in the warrant is meant to prevent "fishing expeditions" into an individual's home and personal effects on the possibility that some evidence of unknown illegal activity might crop up. The only exception is if police, in the course of a valid search for a specified item, find other items whose very possession is a crime—for example, illicit drugs.

But the courts also permit police to undertake various other "reasonable" searches *without* a warrant: searches in connection with a valid arrest; searches to protect the safety of police officers; searches to obtain evidence in the immediate vicinity and in the suspect's control; searches to preserve evidence in danger of being immediately destroyed; and searches with the consent of a suspect. Indeed, most police searches today take place without warrant under one or another of these conditions. The Supreme Court has also allowed automobile searches and searches of open fields without warrants in many cases. The requirement of "probable cause" has been very loosely defined; even a "partially corroborated anonymous informant's tip" qualifies as "probable cause" to make a search, seizure, or arrest.[106] And if the police, while making a warranted search, or otherwise lawfully on the premises, see evidence of a crime "in plain view," they may seize such evidence without further authorization.[107] And the Court recently approved "no-knock searches," reversing a long tradition of requiring police to knock and identify themselves before breaking into a home. However, the Court has held that merely stopping a car for a traffic violation does not give police excuse for a search of the car for drugs.[108]

Wiretapping and Electronic Surveillance

The Supreme Court views wiretapping and electronic surveillance as a search and seizure within the meaning of the 4th Amendment; such law enforcement techniques require "probable cause" and a warrant. The government may not undertake to eavesdrop where a person has "a reasonable expectation of privacy" without first showing probable cause and obtaining a warrant. Congress has also enacted a law prohibiting federal

★ **bill of attainder**
Legislative act inflicting punishment without judicial trial; forbidden under Article I of the Constitution.

★ **ex post facto law**
Retroactive criminal law that works against the accused; forbidden under Article I of the Constitution.

★ **search warrant**
Court order permitting law-enforcement officials to search a location in order to seize evidence of a crime; issued only for a specified location, in connection with a specific investigation, and on submission of proof that "probable cause" exists to warrant such a search.

DEBATE

Privacy and Government Surveillance Powers

A father runs toward his daughter in front of his house in Kansas City, Missouri, as a police tactical team wearing full protective gear goes in.

Civil Liberties and National Security

agents from intercepting a wire, oral, or electronic communication without first obtaining a warrant.

FISA and Domestic Surveillance In the Foreign Intelligence Surveillance Act of 1978 (FISA), Congress created a special FISA court to oversee the collection of electronic intelligence within the United States. It requires all intelligence agencies, including the National Security Agency, which is responsible for the collection of electronic intelligence, to obtain warrants upon a showing that the surveillance is required for investigation of possible attacks upon the nation. The FISA court is secret, and the persons under surveillance are not notified.

Following the 9/11 attack, President Bush authorized the National Security Agency to intercept *international* calls to and from Americans—calls involving known or suspected terrorists—without a FISA warrant. The president claimed that he had inherent constitutional powers as Commander-in-Chief to gather intelligence during war or armed conflict and that the United States is currently at war with international terrorists. Opponents of warrantless surveillance argue that the president is bound by the FISA Act, which specifically requires court warrants for surveillance within the United States, including international calls.

Congress and the president reached a compromise with the FISA Amendments Act of 2008. This act allows the government to undertake warrantless surveillance of suspected terrorists for seven days before obtaining a FISA warrant. It allows wiretapping of international calls and intercepts of international e-mails. It removes requirements for detailed descriptions of the information sought in a request for a FISA warrant. It protects telecommunications companies from lawsuits for "past or future cooperation" with the government in electronic surveillance. It denies the president's claim that his war powers supersedes FISA laws.[110]

Drug Testing "Unreasonable" drug testing violates the 4th Amendment. But the Supreme Court has held that it is reasonable to impose mandatory drug testing on railroad workers, federal law-enforcement agents, and even students participating in athletics.[111] However, when the state of Georgia enacted a law requiring drug testing for candidates for public office, the Court found it to be an "unreasonable" search in violation of the 4th Amendment.[112] Apparently mandatory drug testing in occupations affecting public safety and drug testing in schools to protect children are reasonable, while suspicionless drug testing of the general public is not.

New technologies continuously challenge the right of privacy implied by the 4th Amendment. Here, a video camera monitors a Connecticut preschool.

Arrests

Arrests The Supreme Court permits *arrests without warrants* (1) when a crime is committed in the presence of an officer; and (2) when an arrest is supported by "probable cause" to believe that a crime has been committed by the person apprehended.[113] However, the Court has held that police may not enter a home to arrest its occupant without either a warrant for the arrest or the consent of the owner.[114]

Indictment

Indictment The 5th Amendment requires that an **indictment** be issued by a **grand jury** before a person may be brought to trial on a felony offense. This provision was designed as a protection against unreasonable and harassing prosecutions by the government. In principle, the grand jury is supposed to determine whether the evidence submitted to it by government prosecutors is sufficient to place a person on trial. In practice, however, grand juries spend very little time deliberating on the vast majority of cases. Neither defendants nor their attorneys are permitted to testify before grand juries without the prosecution's permission, which is rarely given. Thus the prosecutor controls the information submitted to grand juries and instructs them in their duties. In almost all cases, grand juries accept the prosecution's recommendations with little or no discussion. Thus grand juries, whose hearings are secret, do not provide much of a check on federal prosecutors, and their refusal to indict is very rare.

★ **indictment**
Determination by a grand jury that sufficient evidence exists to warrant trial of an individual on a felony charge; necessary before an individual can be brought to trial.

★ **grand jury**
Jury charged only with determining whether sufficient evidence exists to support indictment of an individual on a felony charge; the grand jury's decision to indict does not represent a conviction.

Self-Incrimination and the Right to Counsel

Self-Incrimination and the Right to Counsel Freedom from self-incrimination had its origin in English common law; it was originally designed to prevent persons from being tortured into confessions of guilt. It is also a logical extension of the notion that individuals should not be forced to contribute to their own prosecution, that the burden of proof rests on the state. The 5th Amendment protects people from both physical and psychological coercion.[115] It protects not only accused persons at their own trial but also witnesses testifying in trials of other persons, civil suits, congressional hearings, and so on. Thus "taking the Fifth" has become a standard phrase in our culture: "I refuse to answer that question on the grounds that it might tend to incriminate me." The protection also means that judges, prosecutors, and juries cannot use the refusal of people to take the stand at their own trial as evidence of guilt. Indeed, a judge or attorney is not even permitted to imply this to a jury,

SIMULATION
Balancing Liberty and Security in a Time of War

A Conflicting *View*

Terrorism Requires Restrictions on Civil Liberties

The terrorist attack on America of September 11, 2001, was the most horrific violence committed against innocent American citizens in recent times. It created a new examination of Americans' commitment to personal freedoms and their willingness to trade these freedoms for the safety and security of society. All of the polls taken shortly after the attack indicated that Americans were prepared to accept many new restrictions on their freedom—more surveillance of their papers and communications, more searches of their belongings, roundups of suspected immigrants, and even prolonged detention without recourse to the courts. As time passed, however, fewer Americans expressed a willingness to sacrifice basic civil liberties to prevent additional acts of terrorism.[a]

Following the attack, Congress moved swiftly to enact the "PATRIOT" Act, officially the Uniting and Strengthening America Act by Providing Appropriate Tools Required to Intercept and Obstruct Terrorism of 2001. President George W. Bush and Attorney General John Ashcroft successfully lobbied Congress to increase the federal government's powers of search, seizure, surveillance, and detention of suspects. The concerns of civil libertarians were largely swept aside. The act was passed nearly unanimously in the Senate (98–1) and overwhelmingly in the House (357–66), with the support of both Democrats and Republicans. The Act was extended in 2005, with only minor changes.

Among the key provisions of the USA PATRIOT Act:

★ *Roving wiretaps*: Allows wiretaps of any telephones that suspects might use instead of requiring separate warrants for each line.

★ *Internet tracking*: Allows law enforcement authorities to track Internet communications, that is, to monitor individuals on the Internet without obtaining warrants.

★ *Business records*: Allows investigators to obtain information from credit cards, bank records,

consumer purchases, hospitals, libraries, schools and colleges, and so forth, with secret warrants.

★ *Foreign Intelligence Surveillance Court*: A special Foreign Intelligence Surveillance Court, originally established in 1978 to separate intelligence investigations from criminal investigation, may issue search warrants on an investigator's assertion that the information sought is relevant to a terrorist investigation. No showing of "probable cause" is required. The warrant is not made public, in order to avoid "tipping off" the subject.

★ *Property seizure*: Authorizes the seizure of the property of suspected terrorists. Persons whose property is seized bear the burden of proof that the property was not used for terrorist purposes in order to secure the return of their property.

★ *Detention*: Allows the detention of suspected terrorists for lengthy periods without judicial recourse.

★ *Aliens reporting and detention*: Authorizes the Immigration and Customs Enforcement, or ICE (formerly the Immigration and Naturalization Service, or INS) to indefinitely detain illegal aliens suspected of terrorist connections.

★ *Prohibits harboring of terrorists*: Creates a new federal crime—knowingly harboring persons who have committed, or are about to commit, a terrorist act.

What factors affect Americans' willingness to trade off restrictions on civil liberties in order to provide for safety and security from terrorism? Political science research suggests that the greater people's sense of threat, the greater their support for restrictions on civil liberties. The lower people's trust in government, the less willing they are to trade off civil liberties for security. Liberals are less willing to trade off civil liberties than moderates or conservatives. Overall it seems clear that Americans' commitment to civil liberties is highly contingent on their concerns about threats to national or personal security.

[a]Darren W. Davis and Brian D. Silver, "Civil Liberties vs. Security: Public Opinion in the Context of the Terrorist Attacks on America," *American Journal of Political Science* 48 (January 2004): 28–46.

and a judge is obligated to instruct a jury not to infer guilt from a defendant's refusal to testify.

It is important to note that individuals may be forced to testify when they are not themselves the object of a criminal prosecution. Government officials may also extend a **grant of immunity from prosecution** to a witness in order to compel testimony. Under a grant of immunity, the government agrees not to use any of the testimony against the witness; in return, the witness provides information that the government uses to prosecute others who are considered more dangerous or more important than the immune witness. Because such grants ensure that nothing the witnesses say can be used against them, immunized witnesses cannot refuse to answer under the 5th Amendment.

The Supreme Court under Chief Justice Earl Warren greatly strengthened the 5th Amendment protection against self-incrimination and the right to counsel in a series of rulings in the 1960s:

★ *Gideon v. Wainwright (1963)*: Equal protection under the 14th Amendment requires that free legal counsel be appointed for all indigent defendants in all criminal cases.[116]

★ *Escobedo v. Illinois (1964)*: Suspects are entitled to confer with counsel as soon as police investigation focuses on them or once "the process shifts from investigatory to accusatory."[117]

★ *Miranda v. Arizona (1966)*: Before questioning suspects, a police officer must inform them of all their constitutional rights, including the right to counsel (appointed at no cost to the suspect if necessary) and the right to remain silent. Although suspects may knowingly waive these rights, the police cannot question anyone who at any point asks for a lawyer or declines "in any manner" to be questioned. If the police commit an error in these procedures, the accused goes free, regardless of the evidence of guilt.[118] Figure 14.1 shows a typical **Miranda warning** card carried by police to ensure that they issue the proper warnings to those under arrest.

The Exclusionary Rule

Illegally obtained evidence and confessions may not be used in criminal trials. If police find evidence of a crime in an illegal search or if they elicit statements from suspects without informing them of their rights to remain silent or to have counsel, the evidence or statements produced are not admissible in a trial. This **exclusionary rule** is one of the more controversial procedural rights that the Supreme Court has extended to criminal defendants. The rule is also unique to the United States: in Great Britain evidence obtained illegally may be used against the accused, although the accused may bring charges against the police for damages.

The rule provides *enforcement* for the 4th Amendment guarantee against unreasonable searches and seizures, as well as the 5th Amendment guarantee against compulsory self-incrimination and the guarantee of counsel. Initially applied only in federal cases, in *Mapp v. Ohio* (1961) the Supreme Court extended the exclusionary rule to all criminal cases in the United States.[119] A *good faith exception* is made "when law enforcement officers have acted in objective good faith or their transgressions have been minor."[120] And police are *not* prohibited from tricking a suspect into giving them incriminating evidence.[121] But the exclusionary rule is frequently attacked for the high price it extracts from society—the release of guilty criminals. Why punish society because of the misconduct of police? Why not punish police directly, perhaps with disciplinary measures imposed by courts that discover errors, instead of letting guilty persons go free?

Bail Requirements

The 8th Amendment says only that *"excessive* bail shall not be required." This clause does not say that pretrial release on **bail** will be available to all. The Supreme Court has held that "in our society liberty is the norm, and detention prior to trial or without trial is the carefully limited exception." Pretrial

★ **grant of immunity from prosecution**
Grant by the government to an individual of freedom from prosecution on a particular charge in return for testimony by that individual that might otherwise be self-incriminating.

★ **Miranda warning**
Requirement that persons arrested be informed of their rights immediately after arrest.

★ **exclusionary rule**
Rule of law that evidence found in an illegal search or resulting from an illegally obtained confession may not be admitted at trial.

★ **bail**
Release of an accused person from custody in exchange for promise to appear at trial, guaranteed by money or property that is forfeited to court if defendant does not appear.

METROPOLITAN POLICE DEPARTMENT
Warning As To Your Rights

You are under arrest. Before we ask you any questions you must understand what your rights are.

You have the right to remain silent. You are not required to say anything to us at any time or to answer any questions. Anything you say can be used against you in court.

You have the right to talk to a lawyer for advice before we question you and to have him with you during questioning.

If you cannot afford a lawyer and want one, a lawyer will be provided for you.

If you want to answer questions now without a lawyer present, you will still have the right to stop answering at any time. You also have the right to stop answering at any time until you talk to a lawyer.

WAIVER

1. Have you read or had read to you the warning as to your rights?_____

2. Do you understand these rights? _____

3. Do you wish to answer any questions? _____

4. Are you willing to answer questions without having an attorney present? _____

5. Signature of defendant on line below.

_____

6. Time _____   Date _____

7. Signature of officer _____

8. Signature of witness _____

Figure **14.1** "You Have the Right to Remain Silent": The Miranda Warning

Since the U.S. Supreme Court's ruling in the case of *Miranda v. Arizona* in 1966, law-enforcement officials at all levels have routinely carried "Miranda rights" cards, which they read to accused individuals immediately after their arrest. This procedure has largely eliminated defendants' abilities to obtain dismissals and/or acquittals on the basis of ignorance of their rights or lack of proper counsel. The Supreme Court reaffirmed the *Miranda* rule in 2000.

release on bail can be denied on the basis of the seriousness of the crime (bail is often denied in murder cases), the trustworthiness of the defendant (bail is often denied when the prosecution shows that the defendant is likely to flee before trial), or, in a more controversial exception, when release would threaten "the safety of any other person or the community."[122] If the court does not find any of these exceptions, it must set bail no higher than an amount reasonably calculated to ensure the defendant's later presence at trial.

Most criminal defendants cannot afford the bail money required for pretrial release. They must seek the services of a bail bondsman, who charges a heavy fee for filing the bail money with the court. The bail bondsman receives all of the bail money back when the defendant shows up for trial. But even if the defendant is found innocent, the bail bondsman retains the charge fee. (Thus the system is said to discriminate against poor defendants who cannot afford the bondsman's fee.) The failure of a criminal defendant to appear at his or her trial is itself a crime and subjects the defendant to immediate arrest as well as forfeiture of bail. Most states authorize bail bondsmen to find and arrest persons who have "jumped bail," return them to court, and thereby recover the bail money.

Fair Trial   The original text of the Constitution guaranteed jury trials in criminal cases, and the 6th Amendment went on to correct weaknesses the Framers saw in the English justice system at that time—closed proceedings, trials in absentia (where the defendant is not present), secret witnesses, long delays between arrest and trial, biased juries, and the absence of defense counsel. Specifically, the 6th Amendment guarantees the following:

★ The right to a speedy and public trial. ("Speedy" refers to the time between arrest and trial, not the time between the crime itself and trial,[123] but the Supreme Court has declined to set a specific time limit that defines "speedy."[124])

★ An impartial jury chosen from the state or district where the crime was committed.

★ The right to confront (cross-examine) witnesses against the accused.

★ The right of the accused to compel (subpoena) favorable witnesses to appear.

★ The right of the accused to be represented by counsel.

Over the years the courts have elaborated on these elements of a fair trial so that today trial proceedings follow a rigidly structured format. First, attorneys make opening statements. The prosecution describes the crime and how it will prove beyond a reasonable doubt that the defendant committed it. The defense attorney argues either that the crime did not occur or that the defendant did not do it. Next, each side, again beginning with the prosecution, calls witnesses who first testify on "direct examination" for their side, then are cross-examined by the opposing attorney. Witnesses may be asked to verify evidence that is introduced as "exhibits." Defendants have a right to be present during their own trials (although an abusive and disruptive defendant may be considered to have waived his or her right to be present and be removed from the courtroom).[125] Prosecution witnesses must appear in the courtroom and submit to cross-examination (although special protection procedures, including videotaped testimony, may be used for children).[126] Prosecutors are obliged to disclose any information that might create a reasonable doubt about the defendant's guilt,[127] but the defendant may not be compelled to disclose incriminating information.

After all of the witnesses offered by both sides have been heard and cross-examined, prosecution and defense give their closing arguments. The burden of proof "beyond a reasonable doubt" rests with the prosecution; the defense does not need to prove that the accused is innocent, only that reasonable doubt exists regarding guilt. (However, see *A Conflicting View:* "The War on Drugs Threatens Individual Liberty.")

Juries must be "impartial": they must not have prejudged the case or exhibit bias or prejudice or have a personal interest in the outcome. Judges can dismiss jurors for "cause." During jury selection, attorneys for the prosecution and defense are allowed a fixed number of "peremptory" challenges of jurors (although they cannot do so on the basis of race or gender).[128] Jury selection is often regarded by attorneys as the key to the outcome of a case; both sides try to get presumed sympathetic people on the jury. In well-publicized cases, judges may "sequester" a jury (keep them in a hotel away from access to the mass media) in order to maintain impartiality. Judges may exclude press or television to prevent trials from becoming spectacles if they wish.[129] By tradition, English juries have had twelve members; however, the Supreme Court has allowed six-member juries in non-death-penalty cases.[130] Also by tradition, juries should arrive at a unanimous decision. If a jury cannot do so, judges declare a "hung" jury and the prosecutor may schedule a retrial. Only a "not guilty" prevents retrial of a defendant. Traditionally, it was believed that a lack of unanimity raised "reasonable doubt" about the defendant's guilt. But the Supreme Court has permitted nonunanimous verdicts in some cases.[131]

Plea Bargaining

Few criminal cases actually go to trial. More than 90 percent of criminal cases are plea bargained.[132] In **plea bargaining**, the defendant agrees to plead guilty and waives the right to a jury trial in exchange for concessions made by the prosecutor, perhaps the dropping of more serious charges against the defendant or a pledge to seek a reduced sentence or fine. Some critics of plea bargaining view it as another form of leniency in the criminal justice

Benefiting from the Exclusionary Rule

Dollree Mapp was arrested in 1957, but police seized vital evidence against her during an unwarranted, unconstitutional search. In *Mapp v. Ohio* (1961), the U.S. Supreme Court held that evidence obtained illegally could not be used in a criminal trial.

★ **plea bargaining**
Practice of allowing defendants to plead guilty to lesser crimes than those with which they were originally charged in return for reduced sentences.

An Austin, Texas, police officer testifies at a criminal trial as the judge looks on.

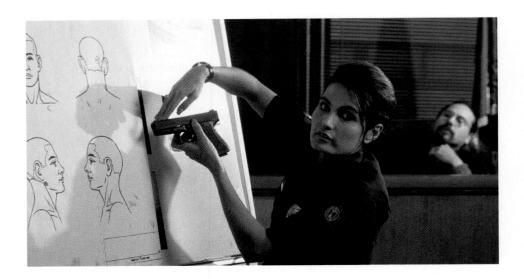

system that reduces its deterrent effects. Other critics view plea bargaining as a violation of the Constitution's protection against self-incrimination and guarantee of a fair jury trial. Prosecutors, they say, threaten defendants with serious charges and stiff penalties in order to force a guilty plea. Still other critics see plea bargaining as an "under-the-table" process that undermines respect for the criminal justice system.

Yet it is vital to the nation's court system that most defendants plead guilty. The court system would quickly break down from overload if any substantial proportion of defendants insisted on jury trials.

Double Jeopardy   The Constitution appears to bar multiple prosecutions for the same offense: "Nor shall any person be subject for the same offense to be twice put in jeopardy of life or limb" (5th Amendment). But very early the Supreme Court held that this clause does not protect an individual from being tried a second time if jurors are deadlocked and cannot reach a verdict in the first trial (a "hung" jury).[133] Moreover, the Supreme Court has held that federal and state governments may separately try a person for the same offense if it violates both federal and state laws.[134] Thus in the well-publicized Rodney King case in 1992, in which police officers were videotaped beating King, a California court found the officers not guilty of assault, but later the U.S. Justice Department won convictions against the officers in a federal court for violating King's civil rights. Finally, a verdict of guilt or innocence in a criminal trial does not preclude a civil trial in which plaintiffs (private citizens) sue for damages inflicted by the accused. Thus O. J. Simpson was found not guilty of murder in a criminal trial but was later found to be responsible for the deaths of two people in a civil trial. Civil courts, of course, can only impose monetary awards; they cannot impose criminal penalties.

The Death Penalty

Think Again

Is the death penalty a "cruel and unusual" punishment?

Perhaps the most heated debate in criminal justice policy today concerns capital punishment. Opponents of the death penalty argue that it violates the prohibition against "cruel and unusual punishments" in the 8th Amendment to the Constitution. They also argue that the death penalty is applied unequally. A large proportion of those executed have been poor, uneducated, and nonwhite. In contrast, many Americans feel that justice demands strong retribution for heinous crimes—a

A Conflicting *View*

The War on Drugs Threatens Individual Liberty

Drug offenses currently account for over half of all prison sentences meted out by federal courts. The average federal sentence for drug crimes—possession, trafficking, or manufacturing of illegal substances—is 7 years; the federal minimum sentence for possession of illegal drugs is 5 years. More than 1.2 million persons are arrested each year for drug violations.[a] The United States imprisons a larger proportion of its population than any other advanced nation.

The greatest threat arising from the "war on drugs," however, is the loss of personal liberty that has accompanied efforts to "take the profit out of crime." Congress passed a Racketeer Influenced and Corrupt Organizations Act (RICO) in 1970, following a 1968 presidential campaign in which President Richard Nixon made "getting tough on crime" a key issue. RICO authorizes federal agents to seize cash, bank accounts, homes, cars, boats, businesses, and other assets on "probable cause" to believe that they were used in criminal activity or were obtained with profits from criminal activity. People may be stopped in an airport terminal, a bus station, or on the street on suspicion of drug trafficking, and have their cash and cars seized by law enforcement agencies. Boats and airplanes are also favored targets of seizure, but RICO also allows the seizure of bank accounts, homes, and businesses. Assets seized by federal law-enforcement agencies—FBI, DEA, Customs Service, Treasury and Justice Departments—are usually retained by these agencies (or the profits of selling these assets at auction), and proceeds are often shared with state and local law-enforcement agencies that cooperated in the investigation. Thus, there is a strong bureaucratic incentive for agencies to concentrate on cases likely to result in forfeiture of these assets—primarily drug cases—and to overlook other law-enforcement activities.

RICO permits the government to seize property *before* any adjudication of guilt. Indeed a subsequent guilty verdict in a criminal trial is not necessary for the government to retain possession of the property seized. The only requirement is that government agents have "probable cause" to believe that the property was used in a crime or was purchased with the profits of crime. People whose property is seized under RICO must initiate a suit against the government. They have the burden of proving that they are innocent of any crime and, more importantly, that officers had no probable cause to seize their property. The proceedings are considered a civil suit by an individual against the government, not a criminal case by the government against the individual. The government, therefore, need not prove "beyond a reasonable doubt" that the person was involved in criminal activity or the property was used in commission of a crime. Rather, the person must prove his or her own innocence and the government's lack of probable cause to seize the property.

In a decision that seriously endangers personal liberty in America, the Supreme Court upheld RICO.[b] The Court ruled that the government's seizure of property is a civil and not a criminal punishment. This means that individuals whose property is seized are not afforded the constitutional rights of criminal defendants. They have no right to "due process of law" (5th Amendment), protection against double jeopardy (5th Amendment), or protection against "excessive fines" (8th Amendment).

Efforts in Congress to reform RICO have consistently failed. Members of Congress wish to avoid being labeled "soft on crime." And law-enforcement agencies—federal, state, and local—lobby heavily against reform.

[a]*Statistical Abstract of the United States,* 2007, p. 202.
[b]*U.S. v. Ursery,* 518 U.S. 267 (1996).

---

life for a life. A mere jail sentence for a multiple murderer or rapist-murderer seems unjust compared with the damage inflicted on society and the victims. In many cases, a life sentence means less than 10 years in prison under the current early-release and parole policies in many states. Convicted murderers have been set free, and some have killed again.

Prohibition Against Unfair Application   Prior to 1971, the death penalty was officially sanctioned by about half of the states. Federal law also retained the death penalty. However, no one had actually suffered the death penalty since

1967 because of numerous legal tangles and direct challenges to the constitutionality of capital punishment.

In *Furman v. Georgia* (1972), the Supreme Court ruled that capital punishment, as then imposed, violated the 8th and 14th Amendment prohibitions against cruel and unusual punishment and due process of law. The justices' reasoning in the case was very complex. Only Justices William J. Brennan and Thurgood Marshall declared that capital punishment itself is cruel and unusual. The other justices in the majority felt that death sentences had been applied unfairly; some individuals received the death penalty for crimes for which many others received much lighter sentences. These justices left open the possibility that capital punishment would be constitutional if it was specified for certain kinds of crime and applied uniformly.[135]

After this decision, a majority of states rewrote their death penalty laws to try to ensure fairness and uniformity of application. Generally, these laws mandate the death penalty for murders committed during rape, robbery, hijacking, or kidnapping; murder of prison guards; murder with torture; and multiple murders. They call for two trials to be held—one to determine guilt or innocence and another to determine the penalty. At the second trial, evidence of "aggravating" and "mitigating" factors must be presented; if there are aggravating factors but no mitigating factors, the death penalty is mandatory.

Death Penalty Reinstated   The revised death penalty laws were upheld in a series of cases that came before the Supreme Court in 1976. The Court concluded that "the punishment of death does *not* invariably violate the Constitution." The majority decision noted that the Framers of the Bill of Rights had accepted death as a common penalty for crime. Although acknowledging that the Constitution and its amendments must be interpreted in a dynamic fashion, reflecting changing moral values, the Court's majority noted that most state legislatures have been willing to reenact the death penalty and hundreds of juries have been willing to impose that penalty. Thus "a large proportion of American society continues to regard it as an appropriate and necessary criminal sanction." Moreover, the Court held that the social purposes of retribution and deterrence justify the use of the death penalty; this ultimate sanction is "an expression of society's moral outrage at particularly offensive conduct."[135]

The Court reaffirmed that *Furman v. Georgia* struck down the death penalty only where it was invoked in "an arbitrary and capricious manner." A majority of the justices upheld the death penalty in states where the trial is a two-part proceeding, provided that during the second part the jury is given relevant information and standards for deciding whether to impose the death penalty. The Court approved the consideration of "aggravating and mitigating circumstances."

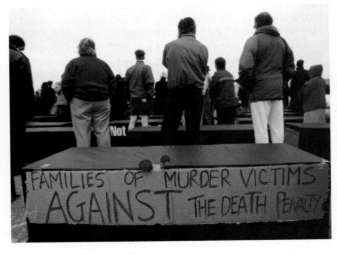

The Death Penalty Debate

Do retribution and deterrence justify the use of the death penalty? Perhaps the most heated debate in criminal justice policy today concerns capital punishment.

Later the Court held that the jury, not a judge acting alone, must find aggravating circumstances in order to impose the death sentence.[137] The Court also called for automatic review of all death sentences by state supreme courts to ensure that none is imposed under the influence of passion or prejudice, that aggravating factors are supported by the evidence, and that the sentence is not disproportionate to the crime. The court disapproved of state laws making

Across the USA   **The Death Penalty**

Today the death penalty is rarely imposed. Twelve states have no death penalty in their laws. An additional seven states have the death penalty in their laws but have not carried out any executions since 1977 (following the Supreme Court's 1976 decision in *Gregs v. Georgia*). The federal government itself has a death penalty, but the execution of Oklahoma City bomber Timothy McVeigh in 2001 marked the first death sentence carried out by the federal government in several decades. There are more than 3,300 prisoners across the country convicted and sentenced to death. Over half of these "death row" inmates have been held for more than 5 years. Executions have slowed as judges and governors have reviewed cases with new DNA evidence.

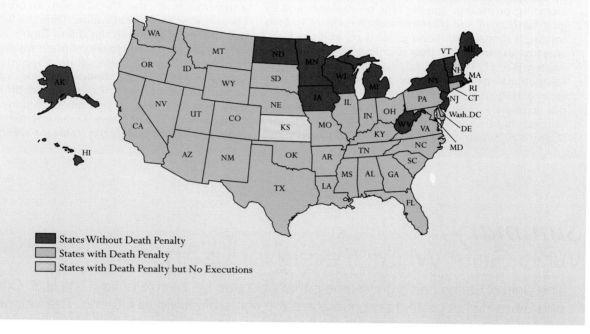

■ States Without Death Penalty
▨ States with Death Penalty
☐ States with Death Penalty but No Executions

the death penalty mandatory in all first-degree murder cases, holding that such laws were "unduly harsh and unworkably rigid." The Court has held that executions of the mentally retarded are "cruel and unusual punishments" prohibited by the 8th Amendment, and that the 8th Amendment prohibits executions of offenders who were under age 18 when their crimes were committed.[138]

Racial Bias   The death penalty has been challenged as a violation of the Equal Protection Clause of the 14th Amendment because of racial bias in the application of the punishment. White murderers are just as likely to receive the death penalty as black murderers. However, some statistics show that if the *victim* is white there is a greater chance that the killer will be sentenced to death than if the victim is black. Nevertheless, the U.S. Supreme Court has ruled that statistical disparity in the race of victims by itself does not bar the use of the death penalty in all cases. There must be evidence of racial bias against a particular defendant in order for the Court to reverse a death sentence.[139]

Race and the Death Penalty

A *Constitutional* Note

The Origins of the Bill of Rights

The Constitution that emerged from the Philadelphia Convention of 1787 did not include a Bill of Rights. This was a particularly glaring omission because the idea of a bill of rights was popular at the time, and most constitutions contain one. The Founders certainly believed in limited government, and they did write a few liberties into the body of the Constitution, including protection against bills of attainder and ex post facto laws, the guarantee of the writ of habeas corpus, a limited definition of treason, and the guarantee of jury trials. But they dismissed the notion of a written Bill of Rights as unnecessary, claiming that the national government, as a government of only enumerated powers, could not exercise any powers not expressly delegated to it. And the power to infringe on free speech or press or otherwise restrain liberty was not among the enumerated powers. It was

therefore not necessary to specifically deny the new government the power to interfere with individual liberty. But this logic was unconvincing to Anti-Federalist opponents of the new Constitution; they wanted much firmer written guarantees of liberty in the Constitution. So Federalist supporters of the Constitution made a solemn promise to add a Bill of Rights as amendments to the Constitution in order to help secure votes for its ratification. Thus the fundamental guarantees of liberty in the Bill of Rights were political concessions made to win support for the Constitution itself. True to their word, supporters of the Constitution, including James Madison, secured the congressional passage of twelve amendments in the very first Congress to be convened under the new Constitution. Ten of these amendments—the Bill of Rights—were ratified by the states by 1791.

Summary
Who Gets What: Personal Liberty

The United States has a government that operates by the rule of law. The U.S. Constitution and Bill of Rights protect and guarantee the rights of individual citizens. The federal government, state governments, and other governing bodies are therefore limited in the degree and under the circumstances in which they can infringe upon these rights. But as a practical matter, the U.S. government and the courts have to balance these individual liberties with the rule of the people—that is, the will of the people as expressed by their elected representatives in Congress and their president, as well as by state legislators and their state governor. Few of the liberties guaranteed in the Constitution and Bill of Rights are absolute. Rather, they are tempered by concerns about Americans' security, personal safety, the preservation of traditional values, and others.

★ Laws and government are required to protect individual liberty. Yet laws and governments themselves restrict liberty. To resolve this dilemma, constitutions seek to limit governmental power over the individual. In the U.S. Constitution, the Bill of Rights is designed to place certain liberties beyond the reach of government.

★ Initially the Bill of Rights applied against only the federal government, not state or local governments. But over time, the Bill of Rights was nationalized, as the Supreme

Court applied the Due Process Clause of the 14th Amendment to all governments in the United States.

★ Freedom of religion encompasses two separate restrictions on government: government must not establish religion or prohibit its free exercise. Although the wording of the First Amendment is absolute ("Congress shall make no law . . ."), the Supreme Court has allowed some restrictions on religious practices that threaten health, safety, or welfare.

★ The Supreme Court's efforts to maintain "a wall of separation" between church and state have proven difficult and controversial. The Court's banning of prayer and religious ceremony in public schools more than 30 years ago remains politically unpopular today.

★ The Supreme Court has never adopted the absolutist position that all speech is protected by the 1st Amendment. The Court's clear and present danger doctrine and its preferred position doctrine recognize the importance of free expression in a democracy, yet the Court has permitted some restrictions on expression, especially in times of perceived national crisis.

★ The Supreme Court has placed obscenity outside the protection of the 1st Amendment, but it has encountered considerable difficulty in defining "obscenity."

★ Freedom of the press prevents government from imposing prior restraint (censorship) on the news media except periodically in wartime, when it has been argued that publication would result in serious harm or loss of life. The Supreme Court has allowed greater government authority over radio and television than over newspapers, on the grounds that radio and television are given exclusive rights to use specific broadcast frequencies.

★ The 1st Amendment guarantee of the right of assembly and petition protects the organization of political parties and interest groups. It also protects the right of people to peacefully protest, parade, and demonstrate. Governments may, within reasonable limits, restrict these activities for valid reasons but may not apply different restrictions to different groups based on the nature of their views.

★ The 2nd Amendment guarantees "the right of the people to keep and bear arms." However, it is frequently argued that this is not an individual right to possess a gun, but rather a collective right of the states to maintain National Guard units.

★ Crime rates in the United States are currently declining. Yet a free society must balance any remedies to the crime problem against potential infringements of the rights of its citizens.

★ The Constitution includes a number of important procedural guarantees in the criminal justice system: the writ of habeas corpus; prohibitions against bills of attainder and ex post facto laws; protection against unreasonable searches and seizures; protection against self-incrimination; guarantee of legal counsel; protection against excessive bail; guarantee of a fair public and speedy trial by an impartial jury; the right to confront witnesses and to compel favorable witnesses to testify; and protection against cruel or unusual punishment.

★ Supreme Court's exclusionary rule helps to enforce some of these procedural rights by excluding illegally obtained evidence and self-incriminating statements from criminal trials. In the 1960s, Court interpretations of the 4th and 5th Amendments strengthened the rights of criminal defendants. Police procedures adjusted quickly, and today there is little evidence that procedural rights greatly hamper law enforcement.

★ Few criminal cases go to trial. Most are plea bargained, with the defendant pleading guilty in exchange for reduced charges and/or a lighter sentence. Although this practice is frequently criticized, without plea bargaining the nation's criminal court system would break down from case overload.

★ The Supreme Court has ruled that the death penalty is not a "cruel and unusual punishment," but the Court has insisted on fairness and uniformity of application.

Key Terms

Suggested Readings

Bruce, Tammy. *The New Thought Police*. New York: Prima Lyfestyles, 2003. A liberal feminist confronts the Left's assault on free speech.

Epstein, Lee, and Thomas G. Walker. *Constitutional Law for a Changing America: Rights, Liberties and Justice*. 6th ed. Washington, D.C.: CQ Press, 2006. An authoritative text on civil liberties and the rights of the criminally accused. It describes the political context of Supreme Court decisions and provides key excerpts from the most important decisions.

Garrow, David. *Liberty and Sexuality: The Right to Privacy and the Making of Roe v. Wade*. New York: Macmillan, 1994. Historical account of the background and development of the right to sexual privacy.

Kobylka, Joseph F. *The Politics of Obscenity*. Westport, Conn.: Greenwood Press, 1991. Comprehensive review of Supreme Court obscenity decisions, arguing that the *Miller* case in 1973 was a turning point away from a more permissive to a more restrictive approach toward sexually oriented material. It examines the litigation strategies of the American Civil Liberties Union and other groups in obscenity cases.

Lewis, Anthony. *Gideon's Trumpet*. New York: Random House, 1964. The classic story of Clarence Gideon and how his handwritten habeas corpus plea made its way to the U.S. Supreme Court, resulting in the guarantee of free legal counsel for poor defendants in felony cases.

Savage, David. *The Supreme Court and Individual Rights*. 4th ed. Washington, D.C.: CQ Press, 2004. An overview of individual rights—freedom of ideas, political participation, due process and criminal rights, equal rights, and personal liberties.

Shiell, Timothy C. *Campus Hate Speech on Trial*. Lawrence, Kans.: University of Kansas Press, 1998. Traditional academic values emphasizing the free exchange of ideas are being sacrificed on campus by anti-hate speech codes.

Sullivan, Harold J. *Civil Rights and Liberties: Provocative Questions and Evolving Answers*. 2nd ed. Upper Saddle River, N.J.: Prentice Hall, 2005. Contemporary issues in civil liberties discussed in a question-and-answer format.

Suggested Web Sites

American Civil Liberties Union (ACLU) www.aclu.org
This American Civil Liberties Union Web site provides ample information about the ACLU as an organization and the issues it deals with.

Americans United for Separation of Church and State
www.au.org
Organization advocating elimination of religious activity from public life.

Anti-Defamation League of B'nai B'rith www.adl.org
Organization opposing anti-Semitism and securing justice for the Jewish people.

Brady Campaign www.bradycampaign.org
The nation's leading gun control organization, with facts, legislation, and a "report card" on each state.

Bureau of Alcohol, Tobacco, Firearms, and Explosives
www.atf.gov
Federal agency responsible for regulation of alcohol, tobacco, firearms, and explosives; site includes publications on gun crimes.

Bureau of Justice Statistics www.ojp.usdoj.gov/bjs
Federal statistics on jails, prisons, probation, and capital punishment. Click to capital punishment for numbers of executions and persons under sentence of death.

Christian Coalition www.cc.org
Organization dedicated to "take America back" from the "judicial tyranny" that would remove religion from public life.

First Amendment Center www.firstamendmentcenter.org
Vanderbilt University center provides sources of information on 1st Amendment issues.

Internet Freedom www.netfreedom.org
Organization opposed to all forms of censorship and content regulation on the Internet.

National Association of Scholars www.nas.org
Advocacy organization opposing speech codes and other PC violations of individual freedom on campuses.

The National Coalition to Abolish the Death Penalty
www.ncadp.org
This site provides information about public policies, institutions, and individuals that collectively work toward the "unconditional rejection of capital punishment."

National Right to Life Committee www.nric.org
Leading anti-abortion organization with information on current legislation and court cases.

Pro-Choice America www.prochoiceamerica.org
Formerly the National Abortion Rights Action League (NARAL), with information on current legislation and court cases.

Right to Keep and Bear Arms www.fkba.org
Organizations advocating self-defense rights with information on legislation, court cases, and related matters.

15 POLITICS AND CIVIL RIGHTS

" There is liberty in a state only when each individual has sufficient self respect to respect others. **"**

Harold Lasswell

Assasination of Dr. Martin Luthe

Think About Politics

1. Does the U.S. Constitution require the government to be color blind with respect to different races in all its laws and actions?
   YES ⬭ NO ⬭

2. If a city's schools are mostly black and the surrounding suburban schools are mostly white, should busing be used to achieve a better racial balance?
   YES ⬭ NO ⬭

3. Are differences between blacks and whites in average income mainly a product of discrimination?
   YES ⬭ NO ⬭

4. Do you generally favor affirmative action programs for women and minorities?
   YES ⬭ NO ⬭

5. Do you believe racial and sexual preferences in employment and education discriminate against white males?
   YES ⬭ NO ⬭

6. Should gender equality receive the same level of legal protection as racial equality?
   YES ⬭ NO ⬭

7. Do dirty jokes and foul language at work constitute sexual harassment?
   YES ⬭ NO ⬭

Equality has long been the central issue of American politics. What do we mean by equality? And what, if anything, should government do to achieve it?

The Politics of Equality

Equality has been the central issue of American politics throughout the history of the nation. It is the issue that sparked the nation's only civil war, and it continues today to be the nation's most vexing political concern.

Conflict begins over the very definition of "equality" (see "Dilemmas of Equality" in Chapter 2). Although Americans agree in the abstract that everyone is equal, they disagree over what they mean by "equality." Traditionally, equality meant "equality of *opportunity*": an equal opportunity to develop individual talents and abilities and to be rewarded for work, initiative, merit, and achievement. Over time, the issue of equality has shifted to "equality of *results*": an equal sharing of income and material rewards. With this shift in definition has come political conflict over the question of what, if anything, government should do to narrow the gaps between rich and poor, men and women, blacks and whites, and all other groups in society.

The nation's long struggle over equality has produced a number of constitutional and legal milestones in civil rights. These are summarized in Table 15.1. Much of the politics of civil rights centers on the development and interpretation of these guarantees of equality.

Slavery, Segregation, and the Constitution

In penning the Declaration of Independence in 1776, Thomas Jefferson affirmed that "All men are created equal." Yet from 1619, when the first slaves were brought to Jamestown, Virginia, until 1865, when the 13th Amendment to the Constitution outlawed the practice, slavery was a way of life in the United States. Africans were captured, enslaved, transported to America, bought and sold, and used as personal property.

Slavery and the Constitution   The Constitution of 1787 recognized and protected slavery in the United States. Article I stipulated that slaves were

---

Table *15.1*   Toward Equality: Guarantees of Civil Rights

13th Amendment (1865)

Neither slavery nor involuntary servitude, except as a punishment for crime whereof the party shall have been duly convicted, shall exist within the United States, or any place subject to their jurisdiction.

14th Amendment (1868)

No State shall make or enforce any law which shall abridge the privileges or immunities of citizens of the United States; nor shall any State deprive any person of life, liberty, or property, without due process of law; nor deny to any person within its jurisdiction the equal protection of the laws.

15th Amendment (1870)

The rights of the citizens of the United States to vote shall not be denied or abridged by the United States or by any State on account of race, color, or previous condition of servitude.

19th Amendment (1920)

The right of the citizens of the United States to vote shall not be denied or abridged by the United States or by any State on account of sex.

Civil Rights Acts of 1866, 1871, and 1875

Acts passed by the Reconstruction Congress following the Civil War. The Civil Rights Act of 1866 guaranteed newly freed persons the right to purchase, lease, and use real property. The Civil Rights Act of 1875 outlawed segregation in privately owned businesses and facilities, but in the Civil Rights Cases (1883), the Supreme Court declared the act an unconstitutional expansion of federal power, ruling that the 14th Amendment limits only "State" actions. Other provisions of these acts were generally ignored for many decades. But the Civil Rights Act of 1871 has been revived in recent decades; the act makes it a federal crime for any person acting under the authority of state law to deprive another of rights protected by the Constitution.

Civil Rights Act of 1957

The first civil rights law passed by Congress since Reconstruction. It empowers the U.S. Justice Department to enforce voting rights, established the Civil Rights Division in the Justice Department, and created the Civil Rights Commission to study and report on civil rights in the United States.

Civil Rights Act of 1964

A comprehensive enactment designed to erase racial discrimination in both public and private sectors of American life. Major titles of the act: I. outlaws arbitrary discrimination in voter registration and expedites voting rights suits; II. bars discrimination in public accommodations, such as hotels and restaurants, that have a substantial relation to interstate commerce; III. and IV. authorizes the national government to bring suits to desegregate public facilities and schools; V. extends the life and expands the power of the Civil Rights Commission; VI. provides for withholding federal funds from programs administered in a discriminatory manner; VII. establishes the right to equality in employment opportunities.

Civil Rights Act of 1968

Prohibits discrimination in the advertising, financing, sale, or rental of housing, based on race, religion, or national origin and, as of 1974, sex. A major amendment to the act in 1988 extended coverage to the handicapped and to families with children.

Voting Rights Act

Enacted by Congress in 1965 and renewed and expanded in 1970, 1975, and 1982, this law has sought to eliminate restrictions on voting that have been used to discriminate against blacks and other minority groups. Amendments in 1975 (1) required bilingual ballots in all states; (2) required approval by the Justice Department or a federal court of any election law changes in states covered by the act; (3) extended legal protection of voting rights to Hispanic Americans, Asian Americans, and Native Americans. The 1982 act provides that *intent* to discriminate need not be proven if the *results* demonstrate otherwise. Although the 1982 extension does not require racial quotas for city councils, school boards, or state legislatures, a judge may under the law redraw voting districts to give minorities maximum representation.

Think Again

Does the U.S. Constitution require the government to be color blind with respect to different races in all its laws and actions?

to be counted as three-fifths of a person for purposes of representation and taxation; it also prohibited any federal restriction on the importation of slaves until 1808. Article IV even guaranteed the return of escaped slaves to their owners. The Founders were aware that the practice of slavery contradicted their professed belief in "equality," and this contradiction caused them some embarrassment. Thus they avoided the word "slave" in favor of the euphemism "person held to Service or Labour" in writing the Constitution.

Anything but Equal
The Supreme Court's 1896 decision in *Plessy v. Ferguson* allowed "separate but equal" public facilities. But segregated facilities were seldom equal, and segregation itself was often a humiliating experience.

Supreme Court Chief Justice Roger Taney, ruling in the notorious case of *Dred Scott v. Sandford* in 1857, reflected the racism that prevailed in early America:

> They had for more than a century before been regarded as beings of an inferior order, and altogether unfit to associate with the white race, either in social or political relations; and so far inferior, that they had no rights which the white man was bound to respect; and that the negro might justly and lawfully be reduced to slavery for his benefit.[1]

Taney's decision in this case interpreted the Constitution in terms of the *original intent* of the Founders. The ruling upheld slavery and the constitutional guarantee given slave owners for the return of slaves escaping to nonslave states.

Emancipation and Reconstruction A growing number of Americans, especially members of the **abolition movement**, disagreed with Taney. In 1860 internal party divisions over the slavery issue led to a four-way race for the presidency and the election of Abraham Lincoln. Although personally opposed to slavery, Lincoln had promised during the campaign not to push for abolition of slavery where it existed. Many Southerners were unconvinced, however, and on December 20, 1860 (three months before Lincoln's inauguration), South Carolina became the first state to secede from the Union, touching off the Civil War.

The Civil War was the nation's bloodiest war. (Combined deaths of Union and Confederate forces matched the nation's losses in World War II, even though the nation's population in 1860 was only 31 million compared to 140 million during World War II.) Very few families during the Civil War did not experience a direct loss from that conflict. As casualties mounted, northern Republicans joined abolitionists in calling for emancipating, or freeing, the slaves simply to punish the Rebels. They knew that much of the South's power depended on slave labor. Lincoln also knew that if he proclaimed the war was being fought to free the slaves, military intervention by the British on behalf of the South was less likely. Accordingly, on September 22, 1862, Lincoln issued his **Emancipation Proclamation**. Claiming his right as Commander-in-Chief of the army and navy, he declared that, as of January 1, 1863, "all persons held as slaves within any State, or designated part of a State, the people whereof shall then be in rebellion

★ **abolition movement**
Social movement before the Civil War whose goal was to abolish slavery throughout the United States.

★ **Emancipation Proclamation**
Lincoln's 1862 Civil War declaration that all slaves residing in rebel states were free. It did not abolish all slavery; that would be done by the 13th Amendment in 1865.

against the United States, shall be then, thenceforward, and forever free." The Emancipation Proclamation did not come about as a result of demands by the people. It was a political and military action by the president intended to help preserve the Union.

The Emancipation Proclamation freed slaves in the seceding states, and the 13th Amendment in 1865 abolished slavery everywhere in the nation. But freedom did not mean civil rights. The post–Civil War Republican Congress attempted to "reconstruct" Southern society. The 14th Amendment, ratified in 1868, made "equal protection of the laws" a command for every state to obey. The 15th Amendment, passed in 1869 and ratified in 1870, prohibited federal and state governments from abridging the right to vote "on account of race, color, or previous condition of servitude." In addition, Congress passed a series of civil rights laws in the 1860s and 1870s guaranteeing the newly freed slaves protection in the exercise of their constitutional rights. Between 1865 and the early 1880s, the success of **Reconstruction** was evident in widespread black voting throughout the South, the presence of many blacks in federal and state offices, and the admission of blacks to theaters, restaurants, hotels, and public transportation.[2]

★ **Reconstruction**
The post–Civil War period when the Southern states were occupied by federal troops and newly freed African Americans occupied many political offices and exercised civil rights.

The Imposition of Segregation
But political support for Reconstruction policies soon began to erode. In the Compromise of 1877, the national government agreed to end military occupation of the South, give up its efforts to rearrange Southern society, and lend tacit approval to white supremacy in that region. In return, the Southern states pledged their support to the Union, accepted national supremacy, and agreed to permit the Republican presidential candidate, Rutherford B. Hayes, to assume the presidency, although the Democratic candidate, Samuel Tilden, had received more popular votes in the disputed election of 1876.

As white Southerners regained political power and blacks lost the protection of federal forces, the Supreme Court moved to strike down Reconstruction laws. In the Civil Rights Cases of 1883, the Supreme Court declared federal civil rights laws preventing discrimination by private individuals to be unconstitutional.[3] By denying Congress the power to protect blacks from discrimination by businesses and individuals, the Court paved the way for the imposition of segregation as the prevailing social system of the South. In the 1880s and 1890s, white Southerners imposed segregation in public accommodations, housing, education, employment

The 13th, 14th, and 15th Amendments to the Constitution, as well as other legislation passed during Reconstruction, opened the ballot box and access to political office to the freedmen of the South. However, these gains were soon largely reversed by Jim Crow laws and segregation.

and almost every other sector of private and public life. By 1895 most Southern states had passed laws *requiring* racial segregation in education and in public accommodations. At the time, more than 90 percent of the African American population of the United States lived in these states.

Segregation became the social instrument by which African Americans were "kept in their place"—that is, denied social, economic, educational, and political equality. In many states, **Jim Crow** followed them throughout life: birth in segregated hospital wards, education in segregated schools, residence in segregated housing, employment in segregated jobs, eating in segregated restaurants, and burial in segregated graveyards. Segregation was enforced by a variety of public and private sanctions, from lynch mobs to country club admission committees. But government was the principal instrument of segregation in both the Southern and the border states of the nation. (For a look at the political reactions of African Americans to segregation, see *Politics Up Close:* "African American Politics in Historical Perspective"on page 548.)

Early Court Approval of Segregation   Segregation was imposed despite the 14th Amendment's guarantee of "equal protection of the laws." In the 1896 case of *Plessy v. Ferguson*, the Supreme Court upheld state laws requiring segregation. Although segregation laws involved state action, the Court held that segregation of the races did not violate the Equal Protection Clause of the 14th Amendment as long as people in each race received equal treatment. Schools and other public facilities that were **separate but equal** were constitutional, the Court ruled.

> The object of the amendment was undoubtedly to enforce the absolute equality of the two races before the law, but in the nature of things it could not have been intended to abolish distinctions based upon color, or to enforce social, as distinguished from political, equality, or a commingling of the two races upon terms unsatisfactory to either. Laws permitting, and even requiring, their separation in places where they are liable to be brought into contact do not necessarily imply the inferiority of either race to the other, and have been generally, if not universally, recognized as within the competency of the state legislatures in the exercise of their police power.[4]

The effect of this decision was to give constitutional approval to segregation; the decision was not reversed until 1954.

Equal Protection of the Laws

The initial goal of the civil rights movement was to eliminate segregation laws, especially segregation in public education. Only after this battle was well under way could the civil rights movement turn to the fight against segregation and discrimination in all sectors of American life, *private* as well as *governmental*.

The NAACP and the Legal Battle   The National Association for the Advancement of Colored People (NAACP) and its Legal Defense and Education Fund led the fight to abolish lawful segregation. As chief legal counsel to the fund, Thurgood Marshall, later to become the first African American to sit on the U.S. Supreme Court, began a long legal campaign to ensure equal protection of the law for African Americans. Initially, the NAACP's strategy focused on achieving the "equal" portion of the separate-but-equal doctrine. Segregated facilities, including public schools, were seldom "equal," even with respect to physical conditions, teachers' salaries and qualifications, curricula, and other tangible factors. In other words, southern states failed to live up even to the segregationist doctrine of separate but equal. In a series of cases, Marshall and other NAACP

Comparing Civil Rights

★ **Jim Crow**
Second-class-citizen status conferred on blacks by southern segregation laws; derived from a nineteenth-century song-and-dance act (usually performed by a white man in blackface) that stereotyped blacks.

★ **separate but equal**
Ruling of the Supreme Court in the case of *Plessy v. Ferguson* (1896) to the effect that segregated facilities were legal as long as the facilities were equal.

The Struggle for Equal Protection

NAACP chief attorney Thurgood Marshall at an NAACP regional meeting in Atlanta in 1955.

Politics Up Close

African American Politics in Historical Perspective

Many early histories of Reconstruction paid little attention to the political responses of African Americans to the imposition of segregation. But there were at least three distinct types of response: accommodation to segregation; the formation of a black protest movement and resort to legal action; and migration out of the South (to avoid some of the worst consequences of white supremacy) coupled with political mobilization of black voters in large Northern cities.

Accommodation

The foremost African American advocate of accommodation to segregation was well-known educator Booker T. Washington (1856–1915). Washington enjoyed wide popularity among both white and black Americans. An adviser to two presidents (Theodore Roosevelt and William Howard Taft), he was highly respected by white philanthropists and government officials. In his famous Cotton States' Exposition speech in Atlanta in 1895, Washington assured whites that blacks were prepared to accept a separate position in society: "In all things that are purely social we can be as separate as the fingers, yet one as the hand in all things essential to mutual progress."[a]

Washington's hopes for black America lay in a program of self-help through education. He himself had attended Hampton Institute in Virginia, where the curriculum centered around practical trades for African Americans. Washington obtained some white philanthropic support in establishing his own Tuskegee Institute in Tuskegee, Alabama, in 1881. His first students helped build the school. Early curricula at Tuskegee emphasized immediately useful vocations, such as farming, teaching, and blacksmithing. One of Tuskegee's outstanding faculty members, George Washington Carver, researched and developed uses for Southern crops. Washington urged his students to stay in the South, to acquire land, and to build homes, thereby helping to eliminate ignorance and poverty.

Protest

While Booker T. Washington was urging African Americans to make the best of segregation, a small group was organizing in support of a declaration of black resistance and protest that would later rewrite American public policy. The leader of this group was W. E. B. Du Bois (1868–1963), a historian and sociologist at Atlanta University. In 1905 Du Bois and a few other black intellectuals met in Niagara Falls, Canada, to draw up a platform intended to "assail the ears" and sear the consciences of white Americans. The

Booker T. Washington

[a]Quoted in Henry Steele Commager, ed., *The Struggle for Racial Equality* (New York: Harper & Row, 1967), p. 19.

lawyers convinced the Supreme Court to act when segregated facilities were clearly unequal. For example, the Court ordered the admission of individual blacks to white public universities where evidence indicated that separate black institutions were inferior or nonexistent.[5]

But Marshall's goal was to prove that segregation *itself* was inherently unequal whether or not facilities were equal in all tangible respects. In other words, Marshall sought a reversal of *Plessy v. Ferguson* and a ruling that separation of the races was unconstitutional. In 1952 Marshall led a team of NAACP lawyers in a suit to admit Linda Brown to the white public schools of Topeka, Kansas, one of the few

W. E. B. Du Bois

Niagara Statement listed the major injustices perpetrated against African Americans since Reconstruction: the loss of voting rights, the imposition of Jim Crow laws and segregated public schools, the denial of equal job opportunities, the existence of inhumane conditions in southern prisons, the exclusion of blacks from West Point and Annapolis, and the federal government's failure to enforce the 14th and 15th Amendments. Out of the Niagara meeting came the idea of a nationwide organization dedicated to fighting for African Americans, and on February 12, 1909, the one hundredth anniversary of Abraham Lincoln's birth, the National Association for the Advancement of Colored People (NAACP) was founded.

Du Bois himself was on the original board of directors of the NAACP, although a majority of the early board members and financial contributors were white. Du Bois was also the NAACP's first director of research

and the editor of its magazine, *Crisis*. The NAACP began a long and eventually successful campaign to establish black rights through legal action. Over the years, this organization brought hundreds of court cases at the local, state, and federal court levels on behalf of African Americans denied their constitutional rights.

Migration and Political Mobilization

World War I provided an opportunity for restive blacks in the South to escape the worst abuses of white supremacy by migrating en masse to Northern cities. Between 1916 and 1918, an estimated half-million African Americans moved north to fill the labor shortage caused by the war effort. Most arrived in big Northern cities only to find more poverty and segregation, but at least they could vote, and they did not encounter laws requiring segregation in public places.

The progressive "ghettoization" of African Americans—their migration from the rural South to the urban North and their increasing concentration in central cities—had profound political, as well as social, implications. The ghetto provided an environment conducive to political mobilization. As early as 1928, African Americans in Chicago were able to elect one of their own to the U.S. House of Representatives. The election of Oscar de Priest, the first black member of Congress from the North, signaled a new turn in American urban politics by announcing to white politicians that they would have to reckon with the black vote in Northern cities. The black neighborhoods would soon provide an important element in a new political coalition that was about to take form: the Democratic Party of Franklin Delano Roosevelt.

The increasing concentration of African Americans in large, politically competitive, "swing" states provided black voters with new political power—not only to support the Democratic Party coalition in national politics but also to elect African Americans to local public office. Today African American mayors serve, or have served, in cities as diverse as New York, Chicago, Los Angeles, Detroit, Philadelphia, Atlanta, Baltimore, and New Orleans.

segregated school systems where white and black schools were equal with respect to buildings, curricula, teachers' salaries, and other tangible factors. In choosing the *Brown* suit, the NAACP sought to prevent the Court from simply ordering the admission of black pupils because tangible facilities were not equal and to force the Court to review the doctrine of segregation itself.

Brown v. Board of Education of Topeka   On May 17, 1954, the Court rendered its historic decision in the case of *Brown v. Board of Education of Topeka*:

Segregation of white and colored children in public schools has a detrimental effect upon the colored children. The impact is greater when it has the sanction of law, for the policy of separating the races is usually interpreted as denoting the inferiority of the Negro

Think Again

If a city's schools are mostly black and the surrounding suburban schools are mostly white, should busing be used to achieve a better racial balance?

In May 1954, the United States Supreme Court ruled that segregation in public schools was unconstitutional. Mrs. Nettie Hunt explains the significance of the ruling to her three-and-a-half-year-old daughter, Nickie, on the steps of the Supreme Court building.

group. A sense of inferiority affects the motivation of a child to learn. Segregation with the sanction of law, therefore, has a tendency to retard the educational and mental development of Negro children and to deprive them of some of the benefits they would receive in a racially integrated school system. Whatever may have been the extent of psychological knowledge of the time of *Plessy v. Ferguson*, this finding is amply supported by modern authority. Any language in *Plessy v. Ferguson* contrary to this source is rejected. . . . We conclude that in the field of public education the doctrine of "separate but equal" has no place. Separate educational facilities are inherently unequal.[6]

The Supreme Court decision in *Brown* was symbolically very important. Although it would be many years before any significant number of black children would attend previously all-white schools in the South, the decision by the nation's highest court stimulated black hopes and expectations. Indeed, *Brown* started the modern civil rights movement. As the African American psychologist Kenneth Clark wrote, "This [civil rights] movement would probably not have existed at all were it not for the 1954 Supreme Court school desegregation decision, which provided a tremendous boost to the morale of blacks by its clear affirmation that color is irrelevant to the rights of American citizens."[7]

Enforcing Desegregation   The *Brown* ruling struck down the laws of twenty-one states as well as congressional laws segregating the schools of the District of Columbia (see Figure 15.1).[8] Such a far-reaching exercise of judicial power was bound to meet with difficulties in enforcement, and the Supreme Court was careful not to risk its own authority. It did not order immediate national desegregation but rather required state and local authorities, under the supervision of federal district courts, to proceed with "all deliberate speed" in desegregation.[9] For more than 15 years, state and school districts in the South waged a campaign of resistance to desegregation. Delays in implementing school desegregation continued until 1969, when the Supreme Court rejected a request by Mississippi officials for further delay, declaring that all school districts were obligated to end their dual school systems "at once" and "now and hereafter" to operate only integrated schools.[10]

Figure *15.1*

Segregation Laws in the United States in 1954

Segregation of the races in public schools was widespread in 1954 before the historic *Brown* decision deciding it was unconstitutional.

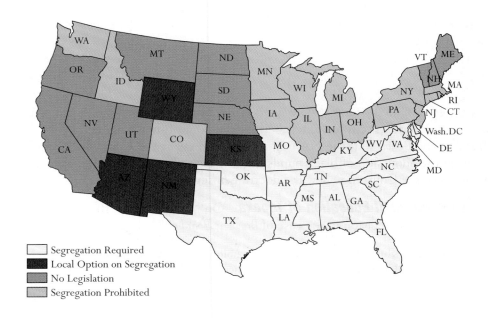

☐ Segregation Required
■ Local Option on Segregation
▨ No Legislation
▨ Segregation Prohibited

Busing and Racial Balancing   Federal district judges enjoy wide freedom in fashioning remedies for past or present discriminatory practices by governments. If a federal district court anywhere in the United States finds that any actions by governments or school officials have contributed to racial imbalances (for example, drawing school district attendance lines that separate black and white pupils), the judge may order the adoption of a desegregation plan to overcome racial imbalances produced by official action. A large number of cities have come under federal district court orders to improve racial balances in their schools through busing.

In the important case of *Swann v. Charlotte-Mecklenburg County Board of Education* (1971), the Supreme Court approved of the following:

★ The use of racial balance requirements in schools and the assignment of pupils to schools based on race.

★ "Close scrutiny" by judges of schools that are predominantly of one race.

★ Gerrymandering of school attendance zones as well as "clustering" or "grouping" of schools to achieve racial balance.

★ Court-ordered busing of pupils to achieve racial balance.[11]

The Court was careful to note, however, that racial imbalance in schools is not itself grounds for ordering these remedies unless it is also shown that some present or past governmental action contributed to the imbalance.

De Facto Segregation   However, in the absence of any past or present governmental actions contributing to racial imbalance, states and school districts are not required by the 14th Amendment to integrate their schools. For example, where central-city schools are predominantly black and suburban schools are predominantly white owing to residential patterns, cross-district busing is not required unless some official action brought about these racial imbalances. Thus in 1974 the Supreme Court threw out a lower federal court order for massive busing of students between Detroit and fifty-two suburban school districts.[12] Although Detroit city schools were 70 percent black and the suburban schools almost all white, none of the area school districts segregated students within their own boundaries.

North and South
Although the first conflicts over integration in the public schools erupted in the segregated Southern states, Northern cities later became the focus of unrest over school integration. When federal judges ordered the busing of schoolchildren outside their neighborhoods in order to achieve racial balances citywide, parents and politicians in some Northern cities responded with a ferocity equal to earlier Southern protests. In Boston, many parents initially boycotted a busing order in 1974, refusing to send their children to school at all or establishing private schools and even attacking busloads of minority children arriving at formerly white schools.

This important decision means that largely black central cities surrounded by largely white suburbs will remain segregated in practice because there are not enough white students living within the city boundaries to achieve integration.

De facto segregation is more common in the Northern metropolitan areas than in the South. The states with the largest percentages of African American students attending schools that have 90 to 100 percent minority enrollments are Illinois, Michigan, New York, and New Jersey. The persistence of de facto segregation, together with a renewed interest in the quality of education, has caused many civil rights organizations to focus their attention on improving the quality of schools in urban areas rather than trying to desegregate these schools.

Many school districts in the South and elsewhere have operated under federal court supervision for many years. How long should court supervision continue, and what standards are to be used in determining when desegregation has been achieved once and for all? The Supreme Court in recent years has undertaken to free some school districts from direct federal court supervision. Where the last vestiges of state-sanctioned discrimination have been removed "as far as practicable," the Supreme Court has allowed lower federal courts to dissolve racial balancing plans even though imbalances due to residential patterns may continue to exist.[13]

★ **de facto segregation**
Racial imbalances not directly caused by official actions but rather by residential patterns.

TIMELINE

The Civil Rights Movement

The Civil Rights Acts

The early goal of the civil rights movement was to eliminate discrimination and segregation practiced by *governments*, particularly states and school districts. When the civil rights movement turned to *private* discrimination—discrimination practiced by private owners of restaurants, hotels, motels, and stores; private employers, landlords, and real estate agents; and others who were not government officials—it had to take its fight to the Congress. The Constitution does not govern the activities of private individuals. Only Congress at the national level could outlaw discrimination in the private sector. Yet prior to 1964, Congress had been content to let the courts struggle with the question of civil rights. New political tactics and organizations were required to put the issue of equality on the agenda of Congress.

Martin Luther King, Jr., and Nonviolent Direct Action   Leadership in the struggle to eliminate discrimination and segregation from private life was provided

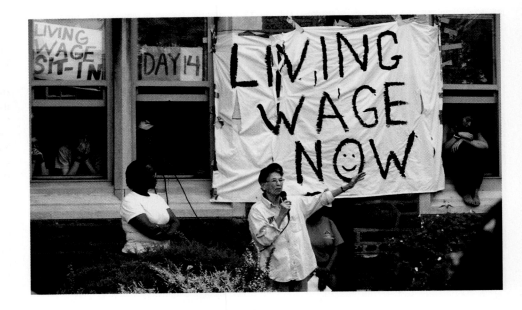

Former Missouri Lt. Gov. Harriett Woods addresses a noon rally in support of the living wage sit-in at Washington University in St. Louis on April 18, 2005. On April 4, 2005, students at the university occupied university buildings for the purpose of raising wages for campus workers such as groundskeepers and food service employees.

by a young African American minister, Martin Luther King, Jr. (see *People in Politics*: "Martin Luther King, Jr., 'I Have a Dream'"). Under King, the civil rights movement developed and refined political techniques for use by American minorities, including **nonviolent direct action**. Nonviolent direct action is a form of protest that involves breaking "unjust" laws in an open, "loving," nonviolent fashion. The purpose of nonviolent direct action is to call attention—to "bear witness"—to the existence of injustice. In the words of Martin Luther King, Jr., such civil disobedience "seeks to dramatize the issue so that it can no longer be ignored"[14] (see also *A Conflicting View*: "Sometimes It's Right to Disobey the Law" in Chapter 1).

King formed the Southern Christian Leadership Conference (SCLC) in 1957 to develop and direct the growing nonviolent direct action movement. During the next few years, the SCLC overshadowed the older NAACP in leading the fight against segregation. Where the NAACP had developed its strategy of court litigation to combat discrimination by *governments*, now the SCLC developed nonviolent direct action tactics to build widespread popular support and to pressure Congress to outlaw discrimination by *private businesses*.

The year 1963 was perhaps the most important for nonviolent direct action. The SCLC focused its efforts in Birmingham, Alabama, where King led thousands of marchers in a series of orderly and peaceful demonstrations. When police attacked the marchers with fire hoses, dogs, and cattle prods—in full view of national television cameras—millions of viewers around the country came to understand the injustices of segregation. The Birmingham action set off demonstrations in many parts of the country. The theme remained one of nonviolence, and it was usually whites rather than blacks who resorted to violence in these demonstrations.

The culmination of King's nonviolent philosophy was a huge yet orderly march on Washington, D.C., held on August 28, 1963. More than 200,000 blacks and whites participated in the march, which was endorsed by many civic leaders, religious groups, and political figures. The march ended at the Lincoln Memorial, where Martin Luther King, Jr., delivered his most eloquent appeal, titled "I Have a Dream." Congress passed the Civil Rights Act of 1964 by better than a two-thirds favorable vote in both houses; it won the overwhelming support of both Republican and Democratic members of Congress.

★ **nonviolent direct action**
Strategy used by civil rights leaders such as Martin Luther King, Jr., in which protesters break "unjust" laws openly but in a "loving" fashion in order to bring the injustices of such laws to public attention.

The Civil Rights Act of 1964

Signed into law on July 4, 1964, the Civil Rights Act of 1964 ranks with the Emancipation Proclamation, the 14th Amendment, and the *Brown* case as one of the most important steps toward full equality for all minorities, including African Americans. Among its most important provisions are the following:

Title II: It is unlawful to discriminate against or segregate persons on the grounds of race, color, religion, or national origin in any public accommodation, including hotels, motels, restaurants, movies, theaters, sports arenas, entertainment houses, and other places that offer to serve the public. This prohibition extends to all business establishments whose operations affect interstate commerce or whose discriminatory practices are supported by state action.

Title VI: Each federal department and agency is to take action to end discrimination in all programs or activities receiving federal financial assistance in any form. This action may include termination of financial assistance to persistently discriminatory agencies.

Title VII: It is unlawful for any employer or labor union to discriminate against any individual in any fashion in employment because of the individual's race, color, religion, sex, or national origin. The Equal Employment Opportunity Commission is established to enforce this provision by investigation, conference, conciliation, persuasion, and, if need be, civil action in federal court.

People In Politics Martin Luther King, Jr., "I Have a Dream"

If a man hasn't discovered something he will die for, he isn't fit to live.[a]

For Martin Luther King, Jr. (1929–68), civil rights was something to die for, and before he died for the cause, he would shatter a century of Southern segregation and set a new domestic agenda for the nation's leaders. King's contributions to the development of nonviolent direct action won him international acclaim and the Nobel Peace Prize.

King's father was the pastor of one of the South's largest and most influential African American congregations, the Ebenezer Baptist Church in Atlanta, Georgia. Young Martin was educated at Morehouse College in Atlanta and received a Ph.D. in religious studies at Boston University. Shortly after beginning his career as a Baptist minister in Montgomery, Alabama, in 1955, a black woman, Rosa Parks, refused to give up her seat to whites on a Montgomery bus, setting in motion a year-long bus boycott in that city. Only 26 years old, King was thrust into national prominence as the leader of that boycott, which ended in the elimination of segregation on the city's buses. In 1957 King founded the Southern Christian Leadership Conference (SCLC) to provide encouragement and leadership to the growing nonviolent protest movement against segregation.

Perhaps the most dramatic application of nonviolent direct action occurred in Birmingham, Alabama, in the spring of 1963. Thousands of African Americans, ranging from schoolchildren to senior citizens, marched in protest. Although the demonstrators conducted themselves in a nonviolent fashion, police and firefighters attacked the demonstrators with fire hoses, cattle prods, and police dogs, all in clear view of national television cameras. Thousands of demonstrators were dragged off to jail, including King. (It was at this time that King wrote his "Letter from Birmingham Jail," explaining and defending nonviolent direct action.) Pictures of police brutality flashed throughout the nation and the world, touching the consciences of many white Americans.

King was also the driving force behind the most massive application of nonviolent direct action in U.S. history: the great "March on Washington" in August 1963, during which more than 200,000 black and white marchers converged on the nation's capital. The march ended at the Lincoln Memorial, where King delivered his most eloquent appeal, titled "I Have a Dream."

I still have a dream. It is a dream deeply rooted in the American dream. I have a dream that one day this nation will rise up and live out the true meaning of its creed: "We hold these truths to be self-evident, that all men are created equal."[b]

It was in the wake of the March on Washington that President John F. Kennedy sent to the Congress a strong civil rights bill that would be passed after his death—the Civil Rights Act of 1964. That same year, King received the Nobel Peace Prize.

White racial violence in the early 1960s, including murders and bombings of black and white civil rights workers, shocked and disgusted many whites in both the North and the South. In 1963 Medgar Evers, the NAACP's state chair for Mississippi, was shot to death by a sniper as he entered his Jackson home. That same year, a bomb killed four young black girls attending Sunday school in Birmingham. On the evening of April 3, 1968, King spoke to a crowd in Memphis, Tennessee, in eerily prophetic terms. "I just want to do God's will. And He's allowed me to go to the mountain. And I've looked over, and I've seen the promised land. I may not get there with you. But I want you to know tonight, that we, as a people will get to the promised land. So I'm happy tonight. I'm not worried about anything. I'm not fearing any man."[c] On the night of April 4, 1968, the world's leading exponent of nonviolence was killed by an assassin's bullet.

[a]Martin Luther King, Jr., speech, June 23, 1963, Detroit, Michigan.
[b]Martin Luther King, Jr., "I Have a Dream" speech, August 28, 1963, at the Lincoln Memorial, Washington, D.C., printed in David J. Garrow, *Bearing the Cross: Martin Luther King, Jr., and the Southern Christian Leadership Conference.* New York: Vintage Books, 1988, pp. 283–84.
[c]Martin Luther King, Jr., speech, April 3, 1968, Memphis, Tennessee, ibid., p. 621.

Speaking Up for Equality
In the civil rights march of 1963, more than 200,000 people marched peacefully on Washington, D.C., to end segregation. It was here that Martin Luther King, Jr., delivered his famous "I Have a Dream" speech.

The Civil Rights Act of 1968   For many years "fair housing" had been considered the most sensitive area of civil rights legislation. Prospects for a fair housing law were poor at the beginning of 1968. However, when Martin Luther King, Jr., was assassinated on April 4, the mood of Congress and the nation changed dramatically. Congress passed a fair housing law as tribute to the slain civil rights leader. The Civil Rights Act of 1968 prohibited discrimination in the sale or rental of a dwelling to any person on the basis of race, color, religion, or national origin.

Equality: Opportunity Versus Results

Although the gains of the civil rights movement were immensely important, these gains were primarily in *opportunity* rather than in *results*. The civil rights movement of the 1960s did not bring about major changes in the conditions under which most African Americans lived in the United States. Racial politics today center around the *actual* inequalities between blacks and whites in incomes, jobs, housing, health, education, and other conditions of life.

Continuing Inequalities   The issue of inequality today is often posed as differences in the "life chances" of blacks and whites. Figures can reveal only the bare outline of an African American's "life chances" in this society (see Table 15.2). The average income of a black family is 62 percent of the average white family's income. Over 24 percent of all black families live below the recognized poverty line, whereas 11 percent of white families do so. The black unemployment rate is more than twice as high as the white unemployment rate. Blacks are less likely to hold prestigious executive jobs in professional, managerial, clerical, or sales work. They do not hold many skilled craft jobs in industry but are concentrated in operative, service, and laboring positions. The civil rights movement opened up new opportunities for African Americans. But equality of *opportunity* is not the same as equality of *results*.

Explaining Inequalities   African American and Hispanic minorities have improved their economic condition in recent years. However, the income

Table *15.2*   Assessing Equality: Minority "Life Chances" in America

Equality of opportunity is not the same as equality of results. Differences remain between white and minority "life chances," for example, in income, poverty, unemployment, and education.

	Median Income of Families			
	1980	1990	2000	2005
White	$47,560	$51,734	$58,167	$56,700
Black	27,519	30,033	36,939	35,158
Hispanic	31,952	32,837	37,779	35,401

	Percentage of Persons below Poverty Level			
	1980	1990	2000	2005
White	10.2%	10.7%	9.5%	10.8%
Black	32.5	31.9	22.5	24.7
Hispanic	25.7	28.1	21.5	21.9

	Unemployment Rate		
	1980	1990	2005
White	6.3%	4.8%	4.4%
Black	14.3	11.4	10.8
Hispanic	10.1	8.2	6.0

	Education: Percentage of Persons over Twenty-Five Who Have Completed High School			
	1970	1980	1990	2005
White	55%	69%	79%	86%
Black	31	51	66	81
Hispanic	32	44	51	59

	Education: Percentage of Persons over Twenty-Five Who Have Completed College			
	1970	1980	1990	2005
White	11%	17%	22%	28%
Black	4	8	11	18
Hispanic	4	8	9	12

Source: Statistical Abstract of the United States, 2008, pp. 449, 448, 374, 143.

 Think Again

Are differences between blacks and whites in average income mainly a product of discrimination?

disparity between whites and minorities has remained about the same. This income gap remains despite a significant narrowing of differences in educational levels between whites and minorities.

Much, but certainly not all, of the disparity in income between whites and minorities disappears when educational levels are taken into account. Comparing the income of whites and minorities *at same educational levels* suggests that some discrimination may remain. Black college graduates on average earn about 81 percent of the income of white college graduates; black high school graduates earn about 81 percent of the income of white high school graduates. Neither African Americans nor Hispanics earn the same income as whites with the same educational background (see Table 15.3).

Table *15.3*   Who Earns What?: White and Minority Income by Educational Attainment

Even at the same educational level, minorities do not earn the same average income as whites.

	Annual Mean Income				
	White	Black	Hispanic	Black/White Ratio	Hispanic/White Ratio
Professional Degree	$115,523	$96,368	$81,186	83%	75%
Bachelor's Degree	52,479	42,285	40,949	81	78
High School Degree	28,145	22,823	24,163	81	86
No High School Degree	19,264	16,516	18,981	86	98

Source: U.S. Bureau of the Census, 2005. Data for 2002.

Policy Choices   What public policies should be pursued to achieve equality in America? Is it sufficient that government eliminate discrimination, guarantee equality of opportunity, and apply color-blind standards to both blacks and whites? Or should government take **affirmative action** to overcome the results of past unequal treatment of blacks—preferential or compensatory treatment to assist black applications for university admissions and scholarships, job hiring and promotion, and other opportunities for advancement in life?

Shifting Goals in Civil Rights Policy   For decades, the emphasis of government policy was on equal *opportunity*. This early nondiscrimination approach began with President Harry Truman's decision to desegregate the armed forces in 1948 and carried through to Title VI and Title VII of the Civil Rights Act of 1964, which eliminated discrimination in federally aided projects and private employment. Gradually, however, the goal of the civil rights movement shifted from the traditional aim of equality of opportunity through nondiscrimination alone to affirmative action involving the establishment of "goals and timetables" to achieve greater equality of results between blacks and whites. While avoiding the term **quota**, the notion of affirmative action tests the success of equal opportunity by observing whether blacks achieve admissions, jobs, and promotions in proportion to their numbers in the population.

Affirmative Action   Affirmative action programs were initially developed in the federal bureaucracy. Federal executive agencies were authorized by the Civil Rights Act of 1964 to develop "rules and regulations" for desegregating any organization or business receiving federal funds. In 1965 President Lyndon B. Johnson signed Executive Order 11246, requiring all federal agencies and businesses contracting with the federal government to practice affirmative action. In 1972 the U.S. Office of Education issued guidelines that mandated "goals" for university admissions and faculty hiring of minorities and women. The Equal Employment Opportunity Commission (EEOC), established by the Civil Rights Act of 1964, is responsible for monitoring affirmative action programs in private employment.

Federal officials generally measure "progress" in affirmative action in terms of the number of disadvantaged group members admitted, employed, or promoted. The pressure to show "progress" can result in relaxation of traditional measures of qualifications, such as test scores and educational achievement. Advocates of affirmative action argue that these measures are not good predictors of performance on the job or in school and are biased in favor of white culture. State and local

★ **affirmative action**
Any program, whether enacted by a government or by a private organization, whose goal is to overcome the results of past unequal treatment of minorities and/or women by giving members of these groups preferential treatment in admissions, hiring, promotions, or other aspects of life.

★ **quota**
Provision of some affirmative action programs in which specific numbers or percentages of positions are open only to minorities and/or women.

governments, schools, colleges and universities, and private employers are under pressure to revise these standards.

Affirmative Action in the Courts

Think Again

Do you generally favor affirmative action programs for women and minorities?

The constitutional question posed by affirmative action programs is whether or not they discriminate against whites in violation of the Equal Protection Clause of the 14th Amendment. A related question is whether or not affirmative action programs discriminate against whites in violation of the Civil Rights Act of 1964, which prohibits discrimination "on account of race," not just discrimination against blacks. Clearly, these are questions for the Supreme Court to resolve.

The *Bakke* Case   In the absence of a history of racial discrimination, the Supreme Court has been willing to scrutinize affirmative action programs to ensure that they do not directly discriminate against whites. In *University of California Regents v. Bakke* (1978), the Supreme Court struck down a special admissions program for

minorities at a state medical school on the grounds that it excluded a white applicant because of his race and violated his rights under the Equal Protection Clause.[15] Allan Bakke applied to the University of California Davis Medical School 2 consecutive years and was rejected; in both years, black applicants with significantly lower grade point averages and medical aptitude test scores were accepted through a special admissions program that reserved sixteen minority places in a class of one hundred.[16] The University of California did not deny that its admissions decisions were based on race. Instead, it argued that its racial classification was "benign," that is, designed to assist minorities. The special admissions program was designed to (1) "reduce the historical deficit of traditionally disfavored minorities in medical schools and the medical profession"; (2) "counter the effects of societal discrimination"; (3) "increase the number of physicians who will practice in communities currently underserved"; and (4) "obtain the educational benefits that flow from an ethnically diverse student body."

Allan Bakke, the plaintiff in the Supreme Court decision to strike down minority admissions quotas, talking to his fellow graduates after receiving his medical school diploma.

The Supreme Court held that these objectives were legitimate and that race and ethnic origin *may* be considered in reviewing applications to a state school without violating the 14th Amendment's Equal Protection Clause. However, the Court also held that a separate admissions program for minorities with a specific quota of openings that were unavailable to white applicants *did* violate the Equal Protection Clause. The Court ordered the university to admit Bakke to its medical school and to eliminate the special admissions program. It recommended that California consider an admissions program developed at Harvard, which considered disadvantaged racial or ethnic background as a "plus" in an overall evaluation of an application but did not set numerical quotas or exclude any person from competing for all positions.

Reaction to the decision was predictable: supporters of affirmative action emphasized the Supreme Court's willingness to allow minority status to be considered a positive factor; opponents emphasized the Supreme Court's unwillingness to allow quotas that exclude whites from competing for some positions. Because **Bakke** had "won" the **case**, many observers felt that the Supreme Court was not going to permit racial quota systems.

★ *Bakke* **case**
U.S. Supreme Court case challenging affirmative action.

What Do You *Think?*

Do You Favor Affirmative Action?

Americans are divided on the issue of affirmative action. Polls reveal that whites are almost equally divided when the question is posed as general support for "affirmative action." In contrast, blacks and Hispanics are strongly supportive of affirmative action programs for racial minorities.

Q. "Do you generally favor or oppose affirmative action programs for racial minorities?"

	Favor	Oppose	Unsure
All	49	43	8
Whites	44	49	7
Blacks	70	21	9
Hispanics	63	28	9

But when the question is phrased in a way that implies minority preference over merit for admission to colleges and universities, then a strong majority of whites favor admission "solely on the basis of merit." Hispanics also favor merit over racial preference, but blacks appeared to be split on the issue.

Q. "Which comes closer to your view about evaluating students for admission into a college or university? Applicants should be admitted solely on the basis of merit, even if that results in few minority students being admitted. Or, an applicant's race and ethnic background should be considered to help promote diversity on college campuses, even if that means admitting some minority students who otherwise would not be admitted."

	Solely Merit	Race/Ethnicity	Unsure
All	69	27	4
Whites	75	22	3
Blacks	44	49	7
Hispanics	59	36	5

Whites believe that black applicants to colleges and universities have the same as or a better chance of admission than white applicants, but blacks believe that white applicants have the advantage.

Q. "If two equally qualified students, one white and one black, applied to a major U.S. college or university, who do you think would have the better chance of being accepted to the college: the white student, the black student, or would they have the same chance?"

	White Student	Black Student	Same Chance	Unsure
All	31	29	36	4
Whites	24	34	38	4
Blacks	67	5	24	4
Hispanics	44	14	38	4

Source: As reported in The Polling Report, www.pollingreport.com

Challenging Affirmative Action

Barbara Grutter and Jennifer Gratz contested the affirmative action policies of the University of Michigan. The Supreme Court rejected Grutter's challenge, holding that the law school's admission policy was "narrowly tailored" to achieve a "compelling interest"—diversity. But the high court upheld Gratz's claim that making race the "decisive factor" in undergraduate admissions was unconstitutional.

Students in Lansing, Michigan, sit on the steps of the Michigan state capitol during an NAACP rally on September 16, 2006, opposing the "Michigan Civil Rights Initiative," which would ban affirmative action by state agencies and public universities.

★ **set-aside program**
Program in which a specified number or percentage of contracts must go to designated minorities.

★ **strict scrutiny**
Supreme Court holding that race-based actions by governments can be done only to remedy past discrimination or to further a "compelling" interest and must be "narrowly tailored" to minimize effects on the rights of others.

Affirmative Action as a Remedy for Past Discrimination The Supreme Court has continued to approve of affirmative action programs where there is evidence of past discriminatory practices. In *United Steelworkers of America v. Weber* (1979), the Supreme Court approved a plan developed by a private employer and a union to reserve 50 percent of higher paying, skilled jobs for minorities. The Court held that "employers and unions in the private sector [are] free to take such race-conscious steps to eliminate manifest racial imbalances in traditionally segregated job categories. We hold that Title VII does not prohibit such . . . affirmative action plans." According to the Court, it would be "ironic indeed" if the Civil Rights Act were used to prohibit voluntary private race-conscious efforts to overcome the past effects of discrimination.[17] In *United States v. Paradise* (1987), the Court upheld a rigid 50 percent black quota system for promotions in the Alabama Department of Safety, which had excluded blacks from the ranks of state troopers prior to 1972 and had not promoted any blacks higher than corporal prior to 1984. In a 5–4 decision, the majority stressed the long history of discrimination in the agency as a reason for upholding the quota system. Whatever burdens imposed on innocent parties were outweighed by the need to correct the effects of past discrimination.[18]

Cases Questioning Affirmative Action However, the Supreme Court has continued to express concern about whites who are directly and adversely affected by government action solely because of their race. In *Firefighters Local Union 1784 v. Stotts* (1984), the Court ruled that a city could not lay off white firefighters in favor of black firefighters with less seniority.[19] In *City of Richmond v. Crosen Co.* (1989), the Supreme Court held that a minority **set-aside program** in Richmond, Virginia, which mandated that 30 percent of all city construction contracts must go to "blacks, Spanish-speaking, Orientals, Indians, Eskimos, or Aleuts," violated the Equal Protection Clause of the 14th Amendment.[20]

Moreover, the Court has held that racial classifications in law must be subject to "**strict scrutiny**." This means that race-based actions by government—any disparate treatment of the races by federal, state, or local public agencies—must be found necessary to remedy past proven discrimination, or to further clearly identified, legitimate, and "compelling" government interests. Moreover, race-based actions must be "narrowly tailored" and "least restrictive" so as to minimize adverse effects on rights of other individuals. In striking down a federal construction contract set-aside program for small businesses owned by racial minorities, the Court expressed skepticism about governmental racial classifications: "There is simply no way of determining what classifications are 'benign' and 'remedial' and what classifications are in fact motivated by illegitimate notions of racial inferiority or simple racial politics."[21]

In addition, the Supreme Court has held that "classifying and assigning school children according to a binary conception of race is an extreme approach in light of this Court's precedents and the nation's history of using race in public schools." The Court held that Seattle's voluntary student assignment plan that relied on race to determine which schools students could attend violated the Equal Protection Clause of the 14th Amendment. Seattle had never segregated by law. The Court held that narrow tailoring requires "serious good faith consideration of workable race-neutral alternatives." Racial diversity may be a "compelling interest" in higher education, but in public schools assignment of pupils must be made on a nonracial basis. "Dividing people by race is inherently suspect because such classifications promote notions of racial inferiority and lead to a politics of racial hostility."

Affirmative Action and "Diversity" in Higher Education

Most colleges and universities in United States—public as well as private— identify "**diversity**," a term that refers to racial, gender, and ethnic representation in the student body and faculty, as an institutional goal.

University administrators argue that students benefit when they interact with others from different cultural heritages. "Students must be engaged with diverse peers if we expect learning and development to occur," and the existence of a racially and ethnically diverse student body is "a necessary condition" for such engagement. There is some evidence that students admitted under policies designed to increase diversity do well in their post-college careers. And there are claims that racial and ethnic diversity on the campus improve students' "self-evaluation," "social-historical thinking," and "intellectual engagement."

But despite numerous efforts to develop scientific evidence that racial or ethnic diversity on the campus improves learning, no definitive conclusions have emerged. Educational research on this topic is clouded by political and ideological conflict. There is no evidence that racial diversity does in fact promote the expression of ideas on the campus or change perspectives or viewpoints of students.

Diversity and Affirmative Action
Even if diversity provides educational benefits, the question arises as to how to achieve it. Diversity is closely linked to affirmative action programs on campuses throughout the nation. When affirmative action programs are designed as special efforts to recruit and encourage qualified minority students to attend college, they enjoy widespread public support. But when affirmative action programs include preferences for minority applicants over equally or better qualified nonminorities, public support falters and constitutional questions arise.

Diversity as a Constitutional Question
The U.S. Supreme Court has held that the Equal Protection Clause of the 14th Amendment requires that racial classifications be subject to "strict scrutiny." This means that race-based actions by governments—any disparate treatment of the racial or ethnic group by federal, state, or local public agencies, including colleges and universities—must be found necessary to advance a "compelling government interest" and must be "narrowly tailored" to further that interest.[23]

The U.S. Supreme Court held in 2003 that diversity may be a compelling government interest because it "promotes cross-racial understanding, helps to break down racial stereotypes, and enables [students] to better understand persons of different races." This opinion was written by Justice Sandra Day O'Connor in a case involving the University of Michigan Law School's affirmative action program. In a 5–4 decision, O'Connor, writing for the majority, said the Constitution "does not prohibit the law school's narrowly tailored use of race in admissions decisions to further a compelling interests in obtaining the educational benefits that flow from a diverse student body."[24]

However, in a case involving the University of Michigan's affirmative action program for *undergraduate admissions*, the Supreme Court held that the admissions policy was "not narrowly tailored to achieve respondents' asserted interest in diversity" and therefore violated the Equal Protection Clause of the 14th Amendment. The Court again recognized that diversity may be a compelling interest, but *rejected an affirmative action plan that made race the decisive factor* for even minimally qualified minority applicants. Yet the Supreme Court restated its support for limited affirmative action programs that use race as a "plus" factor, the position the court has held since the *Bakke* case in 1978.[25]

★ **diversity**
Term in higher education that refers to racial, gender, and ethnic representation among students and faculty.

Support for Affirmative Action

Demonstrators at the Florida state capitol in Tallahassee chant "Shame on Bush" over Governor Jeb Bush's effort to ban racial preferences in university admissions and state contracting.

You Are the Mayor and Need to Make Civil Rights Decisions

Race-Neutral Approaches to Diversity   There is a variety of ways in which diversity can be achieved without using racial preferences in the admission of students. The U.S. Department of Education recommends (1) preferences based on socioeconomic status; (2) recruitment outreach efforts targeted at students from traditionally low-performing schools; and (3) admission plans for students who finish at the top of their high school classes without regard to SAT or ACT scores.[26] California, Texas, and Florida currently give preference to students who stand at or near the top of their class in each of the states' high schools. All three states officially abandoned racial preferences. Yet currently all three states enroll roughly the same numbers of minorities in their colleges and universities that they did before abandoning racial preferences.

The Absence of a Clear Constitutional Principle   The Supreme Court's decisions on affirmative action have not yet established a clear and coherent interpretation of the Constitution. No clear rule of law or constitutional principle tells us exactly what is permissible and what is prohibited in the way of racially conscious laws and practices. Nevertheless, over time some general tendencies in Supreme Court policy can be identified. Affirmative action programs are *more likely to be found constitutional* when

★ They are adopted in response to a past proven history of discrimination.

★ They do not absolutely bar whites or ban them from competing or participating.

★ They serve a clearly identified, legitimate, and "compelling governmental interest."

★ They are "narrowly tailored" to achieve the government's compelling interest and represent the "least restrictive" means of doing so.

It is important to note that the Supreme Court has never adopted the color-blind doctrine, first espoused by Justice Harlan in his *dissent* from *Plessy v. Ferguson,* that "Our Constitution is color-blind, and neither knows nor tolerates classes among the citizens." If the Equal Protection Clause required the laws of the United States and the states to be truly color-blind, then no racial guidelines, goals, or quotas would be tolerated. Occasionally, this view has been expressed in recent minority dissents.

Civil Rights Initiatives in the States   National rethinking of affirmative action was inspired by a citizens' initiative placed on the ballot in California by popular petition and approved by 54 percent of the state's voters in 1996. The California Civil Rights Initiative added the following phrase to that state's constitution:

> Neither the state of California nor any of its political subdivisions or agents shall use race, sex, color, ethnicity or national origin as a criterion for either discriminating against, or granting preferential treatment to, any individual or group in the operation of the State's system of public employment, public education or public contracting.[27]

The key words are "or granting preferential treatment to. . . ." Opponents argued that a constitutional ban on preferential treatment of minorities and women eliminates affirmative action programs in government, prevents governments from acting to correct historic racial or gender imbalances, and denies minorities and women the opportunity to seek legal protections in education and employment. Opponents challenged the California Civil Rights Initiative in federal courts, arguing that by preventing minorities and women from seeking preferential treatment under law, the initiative violated the Equal Protection Clause of the

A Conflicting *View*

The Constitution Should Be Color-Blind

In 1896 a single voice spoke out against *all* racial classifications—Supreme Court Justice John Harlan opposing segregation: "Our Constitution is color-blind and neither knows nor tolerates classes among the citizens." He was *dissenting* from the Supreme Court's majority opinion in the infamous case of *Plessy v. Ferguson*, which approved the segregationist doctrine of "separate but equal." Unfortunately, the ideal of a color-blind society remains almost as elusive today as it was more than a hundred years ago.

Martin Luther King Jr. had a dream that "our children will one day live in a nation where they will not be judged by the color of their skin but by the content of their character." Can that dream be made a reality?

Over time, the civil rights movement shifted its focus from *individual rights* to *group benefits*. Affirmative action programs classify people by group membership, thereby challenging a belief widely held in the United States—that people be judged on individual attributes such as character and achievement, rather than on race or gender. Racial and gender preferences are currently encountered in hiring and promotion practices in private and public employment and in college and university admissions, scholarships, and faculty recruitment.

Affirmative action programs divide Americans into two classes—those who enjoy legally mandated preferential treatment and those who do not. Majority support for civil rights laws is weakening under growing resentment among those who are denied preferential treatment.

Some early supporters of affirmative action have come to view race-conscious programs as no longer necessary. They argue that disadvantages in society today are based more on class than on race. If preferences are to be granted at all, in their view, they should be based on economic disadvantage, not race.

Misgivings also have been expressed by a few African American scholars about the unfair stigmatizing of the supposed beneficiaries of affirmative action—a resulting negative stereotyping of blacks as unable to advance on merit alone. Race-conscious government policies, they argue, have done more harm than good. African American economist Glenn Loury claims that proponents of affirmative action have an inferiority complex: "When blacks say we have to have affirmative action, please don't take it away from us, it's almost like saying, you're right, we can't compete on merit. But I know that we can compete." Conservative columnist William Bennett says that "toxic" race relations, aggravated by affirmative action, have led to damaging forms of new segregation: "Affirmative action has not brought us what we want—a color-blind society. It has brought us an extremely color-conscious society. In our universities we have separate dorms, separate social centers. What's next—water fountains? That's not good and everybody knows it."

Many argue that affirmative action has caused the civil rights movement to lose widespread public support and instead become contentious and divisive. In fact, civil rights has become such a hot topic that most elected officials now prefer to avoid it. As one anonymous member of Congress put it, "The problem is political correctness—you can't talk openly."

Source: Quotations reported in *Newsweek*, February 13, 1996.

14th Amendment. But a Circuit Court of Appeals held, and the U.S. Supreme Court affirmed, that "[A] ban on race or gender preferences, as a matter of law or logic does not violate the Equal Protection Clause in any conventional sense . . . Impediments to preferential treatment do not deny equal protection."[28] The Court reasoned that the Constitution allows some race-based preferences to correct past discrimination, but it does not prevent states from banning racial preferences altogether.

Following success in California, the organizer of that initiative, former California Board of Regents member Ward Connerly, created a nationwide organization to advance similar efforts in other states. The American Civil Rights Institute was instrumental in winning a constitutional amendment banning racial preferences in the state of Washington in 1998. Later, the threat of a ballot initiative in Florida caused Governor Jeb Bush to ban race-based preferences in state universities and state contracting by executive order in 2000. And in 2006, voters in Michigan approved an initiative banning racial preferences by a margin of

58 to 42 percent. This Michigan Civil Rights Initiative was opposed by the state's political leadership, including both the Democratic and Republican candidates for governor. The initiative was spearheaded by Jennifer Gratz, who had earlier prevailed in her Supreme Court case against the University of Michigan's affirmative action program in undergraduate admissions.

Hispanics in America

Hispanics—a term the U.S. Census Bureau uses to refer to Mexican Americans, Puerto Ricans, Cubans, and others of Spanish-speaking ancestry and culture—are now the nation's largest minority (see Table 15.4). The largest Hispanic subgroup is Mexican Americans. Some are descendants of citizens who lived in the Mexican territory annexed to the United States in 1848, but most have come to the United States in accelerating numbers in recent years. The largest Mexican American populations are found in Texas, Arizona, New Mexico, and California. Puerto Ricans constitute the second largest Hispanic subgroup. Many still retain ties to the island and move back and forth from Puerto Rico to New York. Cubans make up the third largest subgroup; most have fled from Fidel Castro's Cuba and live mainly in the Miami metropolitan area. Each of these Hispanic groups has encountered a different experience in American life. Indeed, some evidence indicates that these groups identify themselves separately, rather than as Hispanics as a single group.[29]

If all Hispanics are grouped together for statistical comparisons, their median family income level is well below that of whites (see Table 15.2). Hispanic poverty and unemployment rates are also higher than those of whites. The percentage of Hispanics completing high school and college education is well below that of both whites and blacks, suggesting language or other cultural obstacles in education. Yet within these overall racial comparisons, there are wide disparities among subgroups as well as among individuals.

The Mexican American Civil Rights Movement

Mexican Americans   The Mexican American population in the southwestern United States is growing very rapidly; it doubled in size between 1980 and 2000. For many years, agricultural business encouraged immigration of Mexican farm

---

Table **15.4**   The Changing Face of America: The Projected Population in 2010

Hispanics constitute the largest minority group in the United States, followed by African Americans.

	Number (000)	Percent of Population (%)
White[a]	201,112	65.1
Hispanics	47,756	15.5
African Americans	40,454	13.1
Asians	14,241	4.6
All other races[b]	9,246	3.0
Total Population	308,936	100

[a]White alone not of Hispanic origin.
[b]Includes American Indian and Alaska Native, Pacific Islanders, and persons identified as being of two or more races.

Source: U.S. Bureau of the Census, estimates as of March 18, 2004.

laborers willing to endure harsh conditions for low pay. Many came to the United States as *indocumentados*—undocumented, or illegal, aliens. In the Immigration Reform Act of 1986 Congress offered amnesty to all undocumented workers who had entered the United States prior to 1982.

Economic conditions in Mexico and elsewhere in Central America continue to fuel immigration, legal and illegal, to the United States. But with lower educational levels, average incomes of Mexican American families in the United States are lower and the poverty rate is higher than the general population. Although Mexican Americans have served as governors of Arizona and New Mexico and have won election to the U.S. Congress, their political power does not yet match their population percentages. Mexican American voter turnout is lower than other ethnic groups, perhaps because many are resident aliens or illegal immigrants not eligible to vote, or perhaps because of cultural factors that discourage political participation.[30]

Puerto Ricans

Residents of Puerto Rico are American citizens because Puerto Rico is a commonwealth of the United States. Puerto Rico's commonwealth government resembles that of a state, with a constitution and elected governor and legislature, but the island has no voting members of the U.S. Congress and no electoral votes for president. As citizens, Puerto Ricans can move anywhere in the United States; many have immigrated to New York City.

Median family income in Puerto Rico is higher than anywhere else in the Caribbean, but only half that of the poorest state in the United States. Puerto Ricans have not fared as well economically as other Hispanic groups within the United States: Puerto Ricans have lower median family incomes and higher poverty percentages, in part perhaps because of lower workforce participation. One explanation centers on the history of access to federal welfare programs on the island and the resulting social dependency it fostered among some Puerto Rican families.[31]

Puerto Ricans have long debated whether to remain a commonwealth of the United States, apply for statehood, or seek complete independence from the United States. As citizens of a commonwealth, Puerto Ricans pay no U.S. income tax (although their local taxes are substantial) while receiving all the benefits that U.S. citizens are entitled to—Social Security, welfare assistance, food stamps, Medicaid, Medicare, and so forth. If Puerto Rico chose to become a state, its voters could participate in presidential and congressional elections, but its taxpayers would not enjoy the same favorable cost-benefit ratio they enjoy under commonwealth status. Some Puerto Ricans also fear that statehood would dilute the island's cultural identity and force English on them as the national language.

As a state, Puerto Rico would have two U.S. senators and perhaps six U.S. representatives. The island's majority party, the Popular Democratic Party, is closely identified with the Democratic Party, so most of these new members would likely be Democrats. But the island's New Progressive Party, identified with the Republican Party, supports statehood, and many GOP leaders believe their party should appeal to Hispanic voters. If Puerto Ricans were to choose independence, a new constitution for the Republic of Puerto Rico would be drawn up by the islanders themselves.

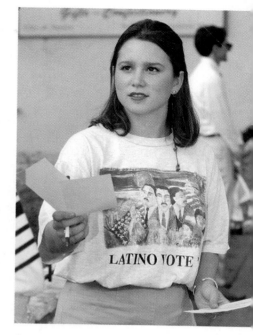

Getting Out the Vote

Despite efforts to improve Hispanic voter turnout, it still remains significantly lower than that of Anglos or of African Americans.

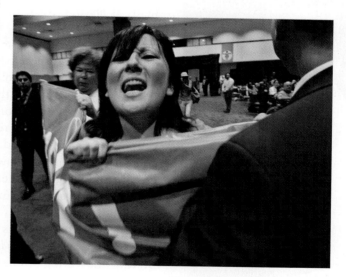

The Immigration Battle

Feelings run high over immigration reform at a 2006 meeting of the National Council of La Raza. The NCLA is the nation's largest Hispanic civil rights organization.

Only Congress can admit a new state, but Congress is unlikely to act without the full support of Puerto Ricans themselves. Several nonbinding referenda votes have been held in Puerto Rico over the years. Opinion today appears to be closely divided, with commonwealth status edging out statehood by a small margin; independence has never received more than one percent of the vote.

Cuban Americans   Many Cuban Americans, especially those in the early waves of refugees from Castro's revolution in 1959, were skilled professionals and businesspeople, and they rapidly set about building Miami into a thriving economy. Although Cuban Americans are the smallest of the Hispanic subgroups, today they are better educated and enjoy higher incomes than the others. They are well organized politically, and they have succeeded in electing Cuban Americans to local office in Florida and to the U.S. Congress.

Hispanic Politics

Mexican Americans constitute the largest portion, nearly three-quarters, of the nation's Hispanic population. Most reside in the Southwestern United States—California, Texas, Arizona, New Mexico, and Colorado. Puerto Ricans in New York, and Cubans and other Central and South Americans in Florida, constitute only about one-quarter of the Hispanic population. Thus generalizations about Hispanic politics are heavily influenced by Mexican Americans.

Organizing for Political Activity   For many decades American agriculture encouraged Mexican American immigration, both legal and illegal, to labor in fields as *braceros*. Most of these migrant farm workers lived and worked under very difficult conditions; they were paid less than minimum wages for backbreaking labor. Farm workers were not covered by the federal National Labor Relations Act and therefore not protected in the right to organize labor unions. But civil rights activity among Hispanics, especially among farm workers, grew during the 1960s under the leadership of Cesar Chavez and his United Farm Workers union. Chavez organized a national boycott of grapes from California vineyards that refused to recognize the union or improve conditions. *La Raza*, as the movement was called, finally ended in a union contract with the growers and later a California law protecting the right of farm workers to organize unions and bargain collectively with their employers. More important, the movement galvanized Mexican Americans throughout the Southwest to engage in political activity.[32]

However, inasmuch as many Mexican American immigrants were noncitizens, and many were *indocumentados* (undocumented residents of the United States), the voting strength of Mexican Americans never matched their numbers in the population. The Immigration Reform and Control Act of 1986 granted amnesty to illegal aliens living in the United States in 1982. But the same act also imposed penalties on employers who hired illegal aliens. The effect of these threatened penalties on many employers was to make them wary of hiring Hispanics, especially as permanent employees. At the same time, industries in need of cheap labor—agriculture, health and hospitals, restaurants, clothing manufacturers, and so on—continued to encourage legal and illegal immigration to fill minimum and even subminimum wage level jobs with few if any benefits.

Los Angeles mayor Antonio Villaraigosa attends the launch party of the highly anticipated "The Simpsons Ride" on May 17, 2008, at Universal Studios Hollywood.

Hispanic Political Power Most Hispanics today believe that they confront less prejudice and discrimination than their parents. Nonetheless, in 1994 California voters approved a referendum, Proposition 187, that would have barred welfare and other benefits to persons living in the state illegally. Most Hispanics opposed the measure, believing that it was motivated by prejudice. A federal court later declared major portions of Proposition 187 unconstitutional. And the U.S. Supreme Court has held that a state may not bar the children of illegal immigrants from attending public schools.[33]

Mexican American voter turnout remains weak. Various explanations have been advanced for the lower voter participation of Mexican Americans. Language barriers may still discourage some voters, even though ballots in many states are now available in Spanish. Illegal immigrants, of course, cannot vote. Lower education and income levels are also associated with lower voter turnout. Nonetheless, Hispanic voting is on the increase throughout the nation, and both Democratic and Republican candidates are increasingly aware of the importance of the Hispanic vote.

Overall, most Hispanics identify with the Democratic Party (see Fig 15.2). Mexican Americans in the Southwestern states and Puerto Ricans in New York have traditionally supported Democratic candidates, while the strong anticommunist heritage among Cuban Americans has fostered a Republican voting tradition in Florida. Hispanics are generally conservative on social issues (opposing abortion, opposing racial preferences, favoring government vouchers to pay parochial school tuitions) but liberal on economic issues (favoring government provision of health insurance for all, favoring a larger federal government with many services).[34]

The Voting Rights Act of 1965, as later amended and as interpreted by the U.S. Supreme Court, extends voting rights protections to "language minorities," including Hispanics (see "Congressional Apportionment and Redistricting" in Chapter 10). Following redistricting after the 1990 census, Hispanic representation in Congress rose substantially; today there are twenty-three Hispanic members of the House of Representatives—about 5 percent, still well below the

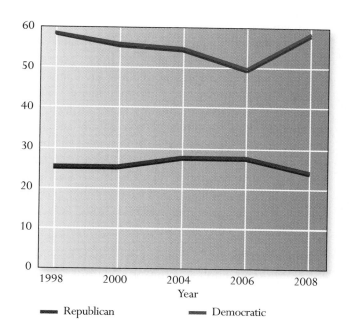

Figure *15.2*

A Return to Form: Hispanic Party Preferences, 1998–2008

After some loosening of their historic ties to the Democratic Party earlier in the decade, Hispanic voters returned to that party in 2008.

Source: Data from pew Hispanic center, www.pewhispanic.org

14 percent of the U.S. population which is Hispanic. Hispanics have been elected governors of Arizona, New Mexico, and Florida.

Native Americans: Trail of Tears

Christopher Columbus, having erred in his estimate of the circumference of the globe, believed he had arrived in the Indian Ocean when he first came to the Caribbean. He mistook the Arawaks there for people of the East Indies, calling them *Indios*, and this Spanish word passed into English as "Indians"—a word that came to refer to all Native American peoples. But at the time of the first European contacts, these peoples had no common ethnic identity; hundreds of separate cultures and languages were thriving in the Americas. Although estimates vary, most historians believe 7 million to 12 million people lived in the land that is now the United States and Canada; 25 million more lived in Mexico; and as many as 60 million to 70 million in all lived in the Western Hemisphere, a number comparable to Europe's population at the time.

In the centuries that followed, the Native American population of the Western Hemisphere was devastated by warfare, by famine, and, most of all, by epidemic diseases brought from Europe. Overall, the Native population fell by 90 percent, the greatest known human disaster in world history. By 1910 only 210,000 Native Americans lived in the United States. Their population has slowly recovered to the current 2.8 million (less than 1 percent of the U.S. population). Many live on reservations and trust lands, the largest of which is the Navajo and Hopi enclave in the Southwestern United States (see *Across the USA*: "Native American Peoples").

The Trail of Broken Treaties   In the Northwest Ordinance of 1787, Congress, in organizing the western territories of the new nation, declared, "The utmost good faith shall always be observed toward the Indians. Their lands and property shall never be taken from them without their consent." And later, in the Intercourse Act of 1790, Congress declared that public treaties between the United States government and the independent Native nations would be the only legal means of obtaining Indian land.

As president, George Washington forged a treaty with the Creeks: in exchange for land concessions, the United States pledged to protect the boundaries of the Creek nation and to allow the Creeks themselves to punish all violators of their laws within these boundaries. This semblance of legality was reflected in hundreds of treaties that followed. (Indeed, in recent years some Native American nations have successfully sued in federal court for reparations and return of lands obtained in violation of the Intercourse Act of 1790 and subsequent treaties.) Yet Native lands were constantly invaded by whites. The resulting Native resistance typically led to wars that ultimately resulted in great loss of life among warriors and their families and the further loss of Native land. The cycle of invasion, resistance, military defeat, and further land concessions continued for a hundred years.

"Indian Territories"   Following the purchase of the vast Louisiana Territory in 1803, President Thomas Jefferson sought to "civilize" the Natives by promoting farming in "reservations" that were located west of the Mississippi River. But soon, peoples who had been forced to move from Ohio to Missouri were forced to move again to survive the relentless white expansion. President James Monroe designated as "Indian territory" most of the Great Plains west of the Missouri

Native Americans Voices
The American Indian Movement, AIM, has emerged as the leading activist organization supporting Native Americans.

Across the USA   Native American Peoples

This map shows the locations of the principal Native American reservations in the United States. Tribal governments officially govern these reservations. (Alaska Natives, including Aleuts and Eskimos, live mostly in 200 villages widely scattered across rural Alaska; twelve regional Native American corporations administer property and mineral rights on behalf of Native peoples in that state.)

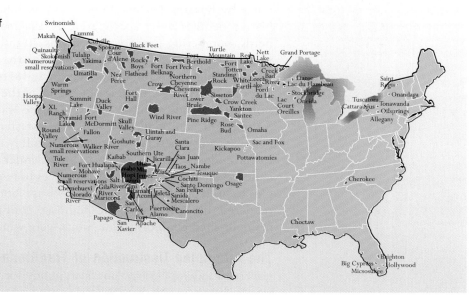

River. Native peoples increasingly faced three unattractive choices: assimilation, removal, or extinction.

In 1814 the Creeks, encouraged by the British during the War of 1812 to attack American settlements, faced an army of Tennessee volunteer militia led by Andrew Jackson. At the Battle of Horseshoe Bend, Jackson's cannon fire decimated the Creek warriors. In the uneven Treaty of Fort Jackson, the Creeks, Choctaws, and Cherokees were forced to concede millions of acres of land.

By 1830 the "Five Civilized Tribes" of the Southeastern United States (Cherokees, Chickasaws, Choctaws, Creeks, and Seminoles) had ceded most but not all of their lands. When gold was discovered on Cherokee land in northern Georgia in 1829, whites invaded their territory. Congress, at the heeding of the old "Indian fighter" President Andrew Jackson, passed the Removal Act, ordering the forcible relocation of the Natives to Oklahoma Indian Territory. The Cherokees tried to use the whites' law to defend their land, bringing their case to the U.S. Supreme Court. When Chief Justice John Marshall held the Cherokees were a "domestic dependent nation" that could not be forced to give up its land, President Jackson replied scornfully, "John Marshall has made his decision. Now let him enforce it." He sent a 7,000-strong army to pursue Seminoles into the huge Florida Everglades swamp and forced 16,000 Cherokees and other peoples on the infamous "Trail of Tears" march to Oklahoma in 1838.

A Native American drawing by Amos Bad Heart Bull shows Chief Crazy Horse being assassinated by soldiers at an American post in 1877. Handwritten text on the drawing provides details of the killing.

"Indian Wars"   The "Indian Wars" were fought between the Plains nations and the U.S. Army between 1864 and 1890. Following the Civil War, the federal government began to assign boundaries to each nation and authorized the Bureau of Indian Affairs (BIA) to "assist and protect" Native peoples on their "reservations." But the reservations were repeatedly reduced in size until subsistence by hunting became impossible. Malnutrition and demoralization of the Native peoples were accelerated by the mass slaughter of the buffalo; vast herds, numbering perhaps as many as 70 million, were exterminated over the years. The most storied engagement of the long war occurred at the Little Bighorn River in Montana on June 25, 1876, where Civil War hero General George Armstrong Custer led elements of the U.S. Seventh Cavalry to destruction at the hands of Sioux and Cheyenne warriors led by chiefs Crazy Horse, Sitting Bull, and Gall. But "Custer's last stand" inspired renewed army campaigns against the Plains peoples; the following year, Crazy Horse was forced to surrender. In 1881, destitute Sioux under Chief Sitting Bull returned from exile in Canada to surrender themselves to reservation life. Among the last peoples to hold out were the Apaches, whose famous warrior Geronimo finally surrendered in 1886. Sporadic fighting continued until 1890, when a small malnourished band of Lakota Sioux were wiped out at Wounded Knee Creek.

The Attempted Destruction of Traditional Life

The Dawes Act of 1887 governed federal Native American policy for decades. The thrust of the policy was to break up Native lands, allotting acreage for individual homesteads in order to assimilate Natives into the white agricultural society. Farming was to replace hunting, and traditional Native customs were to be shed for English language and schooling. But this effort to destroy culture never really succeeded. Although Native peoples lost more than half of their 1877 reservation land, few lost their communal ties or accumulated much private property. Life on the reservations was often desperate. Natives suffered the worst poverty of any group in the United States, with high rates of infant mortality, alcoholism, and other diseases. The Federal Bureau of Indian Affairs (BIA), notoriously corrupt and mismanaged, encouraged dependency and regularly interfered with religious affairs and customs.

The New Deal

The New Deal under President Franklin D. Roosevelt came to Native Americans in the form of the Indian Reorganization Act of 1934. This act sought to restore Native tribal structures by recognizing these nations as instruments of the federal government. Landownership was restored, and elected Native tribal councils were recognized as legal governments. Efforts to force assimilation were largely abandoned. The BIA became more sensitive to Native culture and began employing Native Americans in larger numbers. Yet the BIA remained "paternalistic," frequently interfering in tribal "sovereignty."

The American Indian Movement

The civil rights movement of the 1960s inspired a new activism among Native American groups. The American Indian Movement (AIM) was founded in 1968 and attracted national headlines by occupying Alcatraz Island in San Francisco Bay. Violence flared in 1972 when AIM activists took over the site of the Wounded Knee battle and fought with FBI agents. Several Native nations succeeded in federal courts and Congress at winning back lands and/or compensation for lands taken from them in treaty violations.

Native Americans Today The U.S. Constitution (Article I, Section 8) grants Congress the full power "to regulate Commerce . . . with the Indian Tribes." States are prevented from regulating or taxing Native peoples or extending their courts' jurisdiction over them unless authorized by Congress. The Supreme Court recognizes Native Americans "as members of quasi-sovereign tribal entities"[35] with powers to regulate their own internal affairs, establish their own courts, and enforce their own laws, all subject to congressional supervision. Thus, for example, many Native peoples chose to legalize gambling, including casino gambling, on reservations in states that otherwise prohibited the activity. As citizens, Native Americans have the right to vote in state as well as national elections. Those living off reservations have the same rights and responsibilities as other citizens. Ben Nighthorse Campbell, former U.S. senator from Colorado, was the only tribal member (Northern Cheyenne) to serve in Congress.

The Bureau of Indian Affairs in the Department of the Interior continues to supervise reservation life, and Native Americans enrolled as members of nations and living on reservations are entitled to certain benefits established by law and treaty. Nevertheless, these peoples remain the poorest and least healthy in the United States, with high incidences of infant mortality, suicide, and alcoholism. Approximately half of all Native Americans live below the poverty line.

The Rights of Disabled Americans

Disabled Americans were *not* among the classes of people protected by the landmark Civil Rights Act of 1964. Throughout most of the nation's history, little thought was given to making public or private buildings or facilities accessible to blind, deaf, or mobility-impaired people.[36] Not until the Education of Handicapped Children Act of 1975 did the federal government mandate that the nation's public schools provide free education to handicapped children.

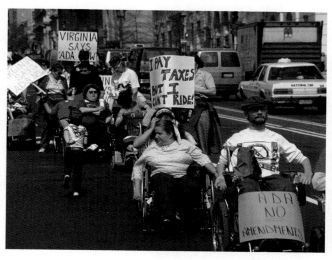

Americans with Disabilities Act The Americans with Disabilities Act (ADA) of 1990 is a sweeping law that prohibits discrimination against disabled people in private employment, government programs, public accommodations, and telecommunications. The act is vaguely worded in many of its provisions, requiring "reasonable accommodations" for disabled people that do not involve "undue hardship." This means disabled Americans do not have exactly the same standard of protection as minorities or women, who are protected from discrimination *regardless* of hardship or costs. (It also means that attorneys, consultants, and bureaucrats will make handsome incomes over the years interpreting the meaning of these phrases.) Specifically the ADA includes the following protections:

★ *Employment*: Disabled people cannot be denied employment or promotion if, with "reasonable accommodation," they can perform the duties of the job. Reasonable accommodation need not be made if doing so would cause "undue hardship" on the employer.

Enabling the Disabled
The most recent Americans to pressure Congress and the courts for protection of rights long denied them are the nation's disabled citizens. In 1990 disability rights activists succeeded in getting Congress to pass the Americans with Disabilities Act, which mandates the removal of many barriers that have kept handicapped people from working, traveling, and enjoying leisure activities. Nevertheless, many obstacles remain. Here, activists demonstrate in favor of the act.

★ *Government programs*: Disabled people cannot be denied access to government programs or benefits. New buses, taxis, and trains must be accessible to disabled persons, including those in wheelchairs.

★ *Public accommodations*: Disabled people must enjoy "full and equal" access to hotels, restaurants, stores, schools, parks, museums, auditoriums, and the like. To achieve equal access, owners of existing facilities must alter them "to the maximum extent feasible"; builders of new facilities must ensure that they are readily accessible to disabled persons unless doing so is structurally impossible.

★ *Communications*: The Federal Communications Commission is directed to issue regulations that will ensure telecommunications devices for hearing- and speech-impaired people are available "to the extent possible and in the most efficient manner."

Mental and Learning Disabilities   The ADA protects the rights of people with learning and psychiatric disabilities, as well as physical disabilities. The U.S. Equal Employment Opportunity Commission has received almost as many complaints about workplace discrimination against the mentally disabled as it has received from people claiming back injuries.[37] But it is far more difficult for employers to determine how to handle a depressed or anxiety-ridden employee than an employee with a visible physical disability. How can employers distinguish uncooperative employees from those with psychiatric disorders?

The American Council on Education reports that the percentage of students in colleges and universities claiming a "learning disability" has jumped from 3 to 10 percent.[38] A recent decision by the U.S. Department of Education that "attention deficit disorder" is covered by the ADA is expected to result in another significant rise in students claiming disabilities. Colleges and universities are required to provide special accommodations for students with disabilities, including tutors, extra time on examinations, oral rather than written exams, and the like.

Gender Equality and the 14th Amendment

The historical context of the 14th Amendment implies its intent to guarantee equality for newly freed slaves, but the wording of its Equal Protection Clause applies to "any person." Thus the text of the 14th Amendment could be interpreted to bar any gender differences in the law, in the fashion of the once proposed yet never ratified Equal Rights Amendment. But the Supreme Court has not interpreted the Equal Protection Clause to give the same level of protection to gender equality as to racial equality. Indeed, in 1873 the Supreme Court specifically rejected arguments that this clause applied to women. The Court once upheld a state law banning women from practicing law, arguing that "the natural and proper timidity and delicacy which belongs to the female sex evidently unfits it for many of the occupations of civil life. . . . The paramount destiny and mission of women are to fulfill the noble and benign offices of wife and mother. This is the law of the Creator."[39]

Early Feminist Politics   The earliest active feminist organizations grew out of the pre–Civil War antislavery movement. There the first generation of feminists—including Lucretia Mott, Elizabeth Cady Stanton, Lucy Stone, and Susan B. Anthony—learned to organize, hold public meetings, and conduct petition campaigns. After the Civil War, women were successful in changing many state

The First Feminists
Elizabeth Cady Stanton addresses a meeting. Stanton, with Lucretia Mott and others, organized one of the defining moments in feminist politics in the United States—the Seneca Falls convention of 1848. Participants at the convention approved a Declaration of Sentiments, modeled on the Declaration of Independence, that demanded legal and political rights for women, including the right to vote.

laws that abridged the property rights of married women and otherwise treated them as "chattel" (property) of their husbands. By the early 1900s activists were also successful in winning some protections for women in the workplace, including state laws limiting women's hours of work, working conditions, and physical demands. At the time, these laws were regarded as "progressive."

The most successful feminist efforts of the 1800s centered on protection of women in families. The perceived threats to women's well-being were their husbands' drinking, gambling, and consorting with prostitutes. Women led the Anti-Saloon League, succeeded in outlawing gambling and prostitution in every state except Nevada, and provided the major source of moral support for the 18th Amendment (Prohibition).

In the early twentieth century, the feminist movement concentrated on women's suffrage—the drive to guarantee women the right to vote. The early suffragists employed mass demonstrations, parades, picketing, and occasional disruption and civil disobedience—tactics similar to those of the civil rights movement of the 1960s. The culmination of their efforts was the 1920 passage of the 19th Amendment to the Constitution: "The right of citizens of the United States to vote shall not be denied or abridged by the United States or by any State on account of sex." The suffrage movement gave rise to the League of Women Voters; in addition to women's right to vote, the League has sought protection of women in industry, child welfare laws, and honest election practices.

Judicial Scrutiny of Gender Classifications

In the 1970s, the Supreme Court became responsive to arguments that sex discrimination might violate the Equal Protection Clause of the 14th Amendment. In *Reed v. Reed* (1971), it ruled that sexual classifications in the law "must be reasonable and not arbitrary, and must rest on some ground of difference having fair and substantial relation to . . . important governmental objectives."[40] This is a much more relaxed level of scrutiny than the Supreme Court gives to racial classification in the law.

The Supreme Court continues to wrestle with the question of whether some gender differences can be recognized in law. The question is most evident in laws dealing with sexual activity and reproduction. The Court has upheld statutory rape laws that make it a crime for an adult male to have sexual intercourse with an underage female, regardless of her consent. "We need not to be medical doctors to discern that young men and young women are not similarly situated with respect to the problems and the risks of sexual intercourse. Only women may become pregnant, and they suffer disproportionately the profound physical, emotional and psychological consequences of sexual activity."[41]

Women's participation in military service, particularly combat, raises even more controversial questions regarding permissible gender classifications. The Supreme Court appears to have bowed out of this particular controversy. In upholding Congress's draft registration law for men only, the Court ruled that "the constitutional power of Congress to raise and support armies and to make all laws necessary and proper to that end is broad and sweeping."[43] Congress and the Defense Department are responsible for determining assignments for women in the military.

Title IX and Women's Athletics

Perhaps no other gender-related law has had more impact on the nation's colleges and universities than **Title IX**, part of the Education Act Amendments of 1972. Title IX prohibits discrimination against women in college and university athletic programs. But what exactly does this mean? It was not until 1978 that the federal government attempted to set forth regulations concerning intercollegiate athletics. Among the stated

Think Again

Should gender equality receive the same level of legal protection as racial equality?

TIMELINE

Women's Struggle for Equality

Levelling the Playing Field

Southern California's Megan Ohai, right, battles UCLA's Erin Hardy during the NCAA Women's College Cup national semifinal soccer game on Friday, December 7, 2007 in College Station, Texas.

★ **Title IX**

A provision in the Federal Education Act forbidding discrimination against women in college athletic programs.

goals of these regulations were (1) financial support substantially proportionate to the number of male and female athletes; (2) the provision of opportunities to participate in athletics for men and women substantially proportionate to their enrollments; (3) or, where these conditions were not met, a continuing practice of program expansion for female athletes. Football was recognized as unique, because it produces the revenues needed to maintain the entire athletic program of most colleges and universities, so football programs could continue to out-spend women's athletics.

The results of Title IX have been impressive. In 2005, there were more than 150,000 female student athletes, a dramatic increase over the 30,000 when the law was passed in 1972. Women's teams in the National Collegiate Athletic Association nearly doubled from about 4,800 to 8,400.

But to maintain the proportionality required by the law, the number of men's sports at many universities have failed to expand and indeed many have been cut, especially nonrevenue producing sports such as wrestling. Critics of the law have urged that it be amended to account for perceived differences in interest in athletics between male and female college students.

★ **Equal Rights Amendment (ERA)**
A proposed constitutional amendment, passed by Congress but never ratified by three-quarters of the states, that would have explicitly guaranteed equal rights for women.

The Equal Rights Amendment   The proposed **Equal Rights Amendment** to the U.S. Constitution, passed by Congress in 1972 but never ratified by the states, was worded very broadly: "Equality of rights under the law shall not be denied or abridged by the United States or any State on account of sex." Had it been ratified by the necessary thirty-eight states, it would have eliminated most, if not all, gender differences in the law. Without the ERA, many important guarantees of equality for women rest on laws of Congress rather than on the Constitution.

Gender Equality in the Economy

As cultural views of women's roles in society have changed and economic pressures on family budgets have increased, women's participation in the labor force has risen. The gap between women's and men's participation in the nation's workforce is closing over time.[42] With the movement of women into the workforce, feminist political activity has shifted toward economic concerns—gender equality in education, employment, pay, promotion, and credit.

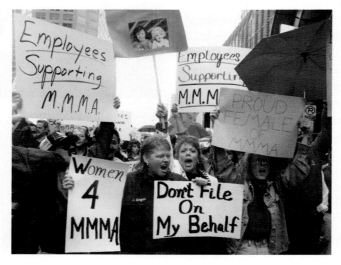

Mitsubishi Motors assembly plant workers Julie Morgan (left), Gretchen Feiste (center) and Sarah Armstrong (right), carry signs during a protest in front of the U.S. Equal Employment Opportunity Commission's Chicago offices. The company provided transportation for hundreds of workers to show up to demonstrate against the federal agency, and paid them for a day's work. Twenty-nine women filed suit with the EEOC against Mitsubishi Motors Manufacturing of America Inc. (MMMA), claiming sexual harassment at the Normal, Illinois, plant.

Gender Equality in Civil Rights Laws   Title VII of the Civil Rights Act of 1964 prevents sexual (as well as racial) discrimination in hiring, pay, and promotions. The Equal Employment Opportunity Commission, the federal agency charged with eliminating discrimination in employment, has established guidelines barring stereotyped classifications of "men's jobs" and "women's jobs." The courts have repeatedly struck down state laws and employer practices that differentiate between men and women in hours, pay, retirement age, and so forth.

The Federal Equal Credit Opportunity Act of 1974 prohibits sex discrimination in credit transactions. Federal law prevents banks, credit unions, savings and loan associations, retail stores, and credit card companies from denying credit because of sex or marital status. However, these businesses may still deny credit for a poor or nonexistent credit rating, and some women who have always maintained accounts in their husband's name may still face credit problems if they apply in their own name.

The Earnings Gap   Despite protections under federal laws, women continue to earn substantially less than men do. Today women, on average, earn about 76 percent of what men do (see Figure 15.3). This earnings gap has been closing very slowly: In 1985 women earned an average 68 percent of men's earnings. The earnings gap is not primarily a product of **direct discrimination**; women in the same job with the same skills, qualifications, experience, and work record are not generally paid less than men. Such direct discrimination has been illegal since the Civil Rights Act of 1964. Rather, the earnings gap is primarily a product of a division in the labor market between traditionally male and female jobs, with lower salaries paid in traditionally female occupations.

★ **direct discrimination**
Now illegal practice of differential pay for men versus women even when those individuals have equal qualifications and perform the same job.

The Dual Labor Market and "Comparable Worth"   The existence of a "dual" labor market, with male-dominated "blue-collar" jobs distinguishable from female-dominated "pink-collar" jobs, continues to be a major obstacle to economic equality between men and women. These occupational differences result from cultural stereotyping, social conditioning, and training and education—all of which narrow the choices available to women. Although significant progress has been made in reducing occupational sex segregation (see Figure 15.4), many observers nevertheless doubt that sexually differentiated occupations will be eliminated in the foreseeable future.

As a result of a growing recognition that the wage gap is more a result of occupational differentiation than direct discrimination, some feminist organizations

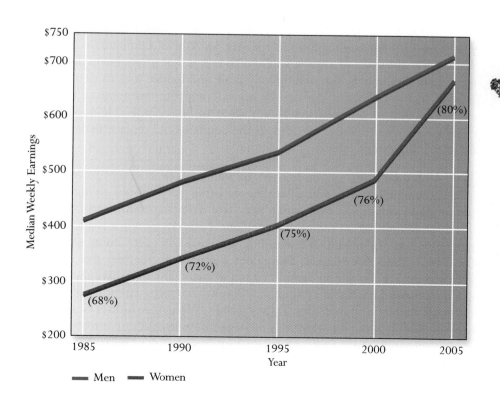

Figure *15.3*

The Earnings Gap: ... n Weekly Earnings ... n and Women

The continuing "earnings gap" between men and women reflects a division in the labor market between traditionally male higher paying occupations and traditionally female lower paying positions.

Note: Figures in parentheses indicate the ratio of women's to men's median weekly earnings.

Source: Bureau of Labor Statistics, www.bls.gov

Figure *15.4*

Where Women Work: Gender Differentiation in the Labor Market

Most of the earnings gap between men and women in the U.S. labor force today is the result of the different job positions held by the two sexes. Although women are increasingly entering "white-collar" occupations long dominated by men, they continue to be disproportionately concentrated in "pink-collar" service positions. "Blue-collar" jobs have been the most resistant to change, remaining a male bastion, although women bartenders now outnumber men.

Sources: Statistical Abstract of the United States, 2008.

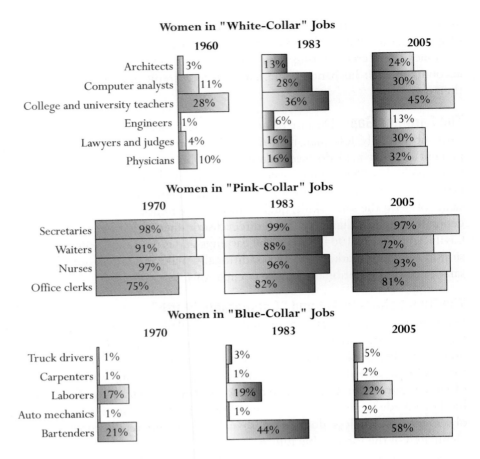

★ **comparable worth**
Argument that pay levels for traditionally male and traditionally female jobs should be equalized by paying equally all jobs that are "worth about the same" to an employer.

★ **glass ceiling**
"Invisible" barriers to women rising to the highest positions in corporations and the professions.

have turned to a new approach—the demand that pay levels in various occupations be determined by **comparable worth** rather than by the labor market. Comparable worth goes beyond paying men and women equally for the same work and calls for paying the same wages for jobs of comparable value to the employer. Advocates of comparable worth argue that governmental agencies or the courts should evaluate traditionally male and female jobs to determine their "worth" to the employer, perhaps by considering responsibilities, effort, knowledge, and skill requirements. Jobs adjudged to be "comparable" would be paid equal wages. Government agencies or the courts would replace the labor market in determining wage rates.

The "Glass Ceiling" The barriers to women's advancement to top positions in the corporate and financial worlds are often very subtle, giving rise to the phrase **glass ceiling**. In explaining "why women aren't getting to the top," one observer argues that "at senior management levels competence is assumed. What you're looking for is someone who fits, someone who gets along, someone you trust. Now that's subtle stuff. How does a group of men feel that a woman is going to fit? I think it's very hard." Or, as a woman bank executive says, "The men just don't feel comfortable."[44] And at all levels, increasing attention has been paid to sexual harassment (see *What Do You Think?* "What Constitutes Sexual Harassment?"). Finally, it is important to note that affirmative action efforts by governments—notably the EEOC—are directed primarily at entry-level positions rather than senior management posts.

What Do You *Think?*

What Constitutes Sexual Harassment?

Various surveys report that up to one-third of female workers say they have experienced sexual harassment on the job.[a] But it is not always clear exactly what kind of behavior constitutes "sexual harassment."

The U.S. Supreme Court has provided some guidance in the development of sexual harassment definitions and prohibitions. Title VII of the Civil Rights Act of 1964 makes it "an unlawful employment practice to discriminate against any individual with respect to his [sic] compensation, terms, conditions or privileges of employment because of such individual's race, color, religion, sex, or national origin." In the employment context, the U.S. Supreme Court has approved the following definition of sexual harassment:

> Unwelcome sexual advances, requests for sexual favors, and other verbal or physical conduct of a sexual nature constitute sexual harassment when (1) submission to such conduct is made either explicitly or implicitly a term or condition of an individual's employment; (2) submission to or rejection of such conduct by an individual is used as the basis for employment decisions affecting such individual; or (3) such conduct has the purpose or effect of unreasonably interfering with an individual's work performance or creating an intimidating, hostile, or offensive working environment.[b]

There are no great difficulties in defining sexual harassment when jobs or promotions are conditional on the granting of sexual favors. But several problems arise in defining a "hostile working environment." This phrase may include offensive utterances, sexual innuendoes, dirty jokes, the display of pornographic material, and unwanted proposals for dates. First, it would appear to include speech and hence raise 1st Amendment questions regarding how far speech may be curtailed by law in the workplace. Second, the definition depends more on the subjective feelings of the individual employee about what is "offensive" and "unwanted" than on an objective standard of behavior easily understood by all. Justice Sandra Day O'Connor wrestled with the definition of a "hostile work environment" in *Harris v. Forklift* in 1993. She held that a plaintiff need not show that the utterances caused psychological injury but that a "reasonable person," not just the plaintiff, must perceive the work environment to be hostile or abusive. Presumably a single incident would not constitute harassment; rather, courts should consider "the frequency of the discriminatory

conduct," "its severity," and whether it "unreasonably interferes with an employee's work performance."[c]

What behaviors does a "reasonable person" believe to be sexual harassment? Some polls indicate that women are somewhat more likely to perceive sexual harassment in various behaviors than men (see figure). But neither women nor men are likely to perceive it to include repeated requests for a date, the telling of dirty jokes, or comments on attractiveness—even though these behaviors often inspire formal complaints.

Many university policies go well beyond both Supreme Court rulings and opinion polls in defining what constitutes sexual harassment, including the following: "remarks about a person's clothing" "suggestive or insulting sounds," and "leering at or ogling of a person's body."

Q: *"Here is a list of some different situations. We're interested in knowing whether you think they are forms of sexual harassment—not just inappropriate or in bad taste, but sexual harassment."*

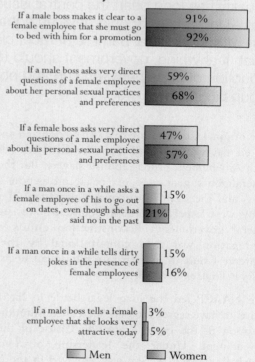

Definitely is sexual harassment:

If a male boss makes it clear to a female employee that she must go to bed with him for a promotion — Men 91%, Women 92%

If a male boss asks very direct questions of a female employee about her personal sexual practices and preferences — Men 59%, Women 68%

If a female boss asks very direct questions of a male employee about his personal sexual practices and preferences — Men 47%, Women 57%

If a man once in a while asks a female employee of his to go out on dates, even though she has said no in the past — Men 15%, Women 21%

If a man once in a while tells dirty jokes in the presence of female employees — Men 15%, Women 16%

If a male boss tells a female employee that she looks very attractive today — Men 3%, Women 5%

☐ Men   ☐ Women

[a]*Washington Post National Weekly Edition,* March 7, 1993.
[b]*Mentor Savings Bank v. Vinson,* 477 U.S. 57 (1986).
[c]*Harris v. Forklift Systems,* 510 U.S. 17 (1993).

Source: Roper Organization as reported in *American Enterprise,* September/October 1993, p. 93.

A *Constitutional* Note

The 14th Amendment

The Constitution of 1787 not only recognized slavery by counting slaves as three-fifths of a person for apportionment of representatives and direct taxes (Article I, Section 2) but also protected slavery by requiring states to return escaped slaves to their owners (Article IV, Section 2). (The Founders appear to have been embarrassed by the word *slave* and employed the euphemism "person held to service or labor.") Following the Civil War the 13th Amendment prohibited slavery and the 15th Amendment prohibited states from denying the right to vote on account of race, color, or previous condition of servitude. But it was the 14th Amendment that eventually became the basis of the civil rights movement in America and the source of the most important guarantees of equality:

> No State shall make or enforce any law which shall abridge the privileges or immunities of citizens of the United States; nor shall any state deprive any person of life, liberty, or property, without due process of law; nor deny to any person within its jurisdiction the equal protection of the laws.

What are the meanings of words such as "liberty," "due process of law," and "equal protection of the laws"? Constitutionally, the history of the civil rights movement centers around definitions of these terms, as does the history of the women's movement.

Summary
Who Gets What: Civil Rights

Equality has long been the central issue of American politics. Today, most Americans agree that all individuals should have an equal opportunity to make of their lives whatever they can without artificial barriers of race, class, gender, or ethnicity. Political conflict arises over what, if anything, government should do to achieve greater equality of results—the reduction of gaps between rich and poor, men and women, blacks and whites, and other groups in society.

★ The original Constitution of 1787 recognized and protected slavery. Not until after the Civil War did the 13th Amendment (1865) abolish slavery. But the 14th Amendment's guarantee of "equal protection of the laws" and the 15th Amendment's guarantee of voting rights were largely ignored in Southern states after the federal government's Reconstruction efforts ended. Segregation was held constitutional by the U.S. Supreme Court in its "separate but equal" decision in *Plessy v. Ferguson* in 1896.

★ The NAACP led the long legal battle in the federal courts to have segregation declared unconstitutional as a violation of the Equal Protection Clause of the 14th Amendment. Under the leadership of Thurgood Marshall, a major victory was achieved in the case of *Brown v. Board of Education of Topeka* in 1954.

★ The struggle over school desegregation continues even today. Federal courts are more likely to issue desegregation orders (including orders to bus pupils to achieve racial balance in schools) in school districts where present or past actions by government officials contributed to racial imbalances. Courts are less likely to order desegregation where racial imbalances are a product of residential patterns.

★ The courts could eliminate *governmental* discrimination by enforcing the 14th Amendment of the Constitution; but only Congress could end private discrimination through legislation. Martin Luther King, Jr.'s, campaign of nonviolent direct action helped bring remaining racial injustices to the attention of Congress. Key legislation includes the Civil Rights Act of 1964, which bans discrimination in public accommodations, government-funded programs, and private employment; the Voting Rights Act of 1965, which authorizes strong federal action to protect voting rights; and the Civil Rights Act of 1968, which outlaws discrimination in housing.

★ Today, racial politics center around continuing inequalities between blacks and whites in the areas of income, jobs, housing, health, education, and other conditions of life. Should the government concentrate on "equality of opportunity" and apply "color-blind" standards to both blacks and whites? Or should government take "affirmative action" to assist blacks and other minorities to overcome the results of past unequal treatment?

★ Generally the Supreme Court is likely to approve of affirmative action programs when these programs have been adopted in response to a past proven history of discrimination, when they are narrowly tailored so as not to adversely affect the rights of individuals, when they do not absolutely bar whites from participating, and when they serve clearly identified, compelling, and legitimate government objectives.

★ Economic conditions in Mexico and other Spanish-speaking nations of the Western Hemisphere continue to fuel large-scale immigration, both legal and illegal, into the United States. But the political power of Mexican Americans, the nation's largest Hispanic group, does not yet match their population percentage. Their voter turnout remains lower than that of other ethnic groups in the United States.

★ Since the arrival of the first Europeans on this continent, Native American peoples have experienced cycles of invasion, resistance, military defeat, and land concessions. Today Native American peoples collectively remain the poorest and least healthy of the nation's ethnic groups.

★ The most recent major civil rights legislation is the Americans with Disabilities Act of 1990, which prohibits discrimination against disabled persons in private employment, government programs, public accommodations, and communications.

★ The Equal Protection Clause of the Fourteenth Amendment applies to "any person," but traditionally the Supreme Court has recognized gender differences in laws. Nevertheless, in recent years the Court has struck down gender differences where they are unreasonable or arbitrary and unrelated to legitimate government objectives.

★ Gender discrimination in employment has been illegal since the passage of the Civil Rights Act of 1964. Nevertheless, differences in average earnings of men and women persist, although these differences have narrowed somewhat over time. The earnings gap appears to be mainly a product of lower pay in occupations traditionally dominated by women and higher pay in traditionally male occupations. Although neither Congress nor the courts have mandated wages based on comparable worth of traditional men's and women's jobs in private employment, many governmental agencies and some private employers have undertaken to review wage rates to eliminate gender differences.

★ The Equal Protection Clause does not bar government from treating persons in various income classes differently. However, governments must treat every individual in a class equally, and the classifications must not be "arbitrary" or "unreasonable." The poor cannot demand benefits or services as a matter of constitutional rights; but once government establishes a social welfare program by law, it must provide equal access to all persons "similarly situated."

Key Terms

abolition movement   539
Emancipation
   Proclamation   539
Reconstruction   540
Jim Crow   541
separate but equal   541

de facto
   segregation   546
nonviolent direct
   action   547
affirmative action   551
quota   551

Bakke case   552
set-aside
   program   554
strict scrutiny   554
diversity   555
Title IX   567

Equal Rights
   Amendment (ERA)   568
direct discrimination   569
comparable worth   570
glass ceiling   570

Suggested Readings

Barker, Lucius J., and Mack H. Jones. *African Americans and the American Political System.* 4th ed. Upper Saddle River, N.J.: Prentice Hall, 1999. Comprehensive analysis of African American politics, examining access to the judicial arena, the interest-group process, political parties, Congress, and the White House.

Bowen, William G., and Derek Curtis Bok. *The Shape of the River.* Princeton, N.J.: Princeton University Press, 1999. An argument by two university presidents that preferential treatment of minorities in admissions to prestigious universities has led to the subsequent success in life by the beneficiaries of the preferences.

Conway, M. Margaret, Gertrude A. Steurnagel, and David W. Ahern. *Women and Political Participation.* 2nd ed. Washington, D.C.: CQ Press, 2004. A wide-ranging review of changes in American political culture brought about by women's increasing political clout. Continuing gender differences in representation are explored.

Fox-Genovese, Elizabeth. *Feminism Is Not the Story of My Life.* New York: Doubleday, 1995. Critique of radical feminism for failing to understand the central importance of marriage and motherhood in women's lives, and a discussion of how public policy could ease the clashing demands of work and family on women.

Harrison, Brigid C. *Women in American Politics.* Belmont, Calif.: Wadsworth, 2003. Comprehensive text on role of women in interest groups, parties, elections, Congress, the executive branch, and the judiciary.

Hero, Rodney E. *Latinos and the U.S. Political System.* Philadelphia: Temple University Press, 1992. General history of political participation of major Latino groups, arguing that different cultural behaviors limit their ability to participate in the interest-group system and policy-making process as currently structured.

LeMay, Michael, *Perennial Struggle: Race, Ethnicity and Minority Group Relations in the United States,* 2nd ed. Upper Saddle River, N.J.: Prentice Hall, 2005. A description and assessment of minority group strategies—accommodation, separatism, radicalism—in coping with their political and economic status.

Sigelman, Lee, and Susan Welch. *Black Americans' Views of Racial Inequality.* Cambridge, Mass.: Cambridge University Press, 1991. Analysis of survey research showing that black perceptions of racial inequality in America are considerably different from white perceptions. Although remaining optimistic about the future, blacks see discrimination as commonplace and are much more likely than whites to attribute black-white differences in education, occupation, and income to racism.

Thernstrom, Stephen, and Abigail Thernstrom. *America in Black and White.* New York: Simon & Schuster, 1997. Information-rich analysis tracing social and economic progress of African Americans and arguing that gains in education and employment were greater *before* the introduction of affirmative action programs.

Walton, Hanes, and Robert C. Smith. *American Politics and the African-American Quest for Freedom.* 3rd ed. New York: Longman, 2005. Comprehensive text arguing the profound influence that African-Americans have on American politics.

Suggested Web Sites

ADA Home Page www.usdoj.gov/crt/ada
Federal agency site with guide to disability rights laws.

American Council on Education www.acenet.edu
Information on a wide range of educational issues, including diversity, testing, admissions, and so forth.

American Indian Movement www.aimovement.org
Advocacy organization for Native Americans, with news and views on treaties and treaty violations.

Brown Matters www.brownmatters.org
Chronology of *Brown v. Board of Education,* 1957.

Bureau of Indian Affairs www.doi.gov/bureau-Indian-affairs
Government agency with responsibility for administration of 562 federally recognized tribal governments in the United States.

Center for Individual Rights www.cir-usa.org
Advocacy organization opposing racial preferences.

Equal Employment Opportunity Commission (EEOC)
www.eeoc.gov
Federal EEOC site with information on what constitutes discrimination by age, disability, race, ethnicity, religion, gender; how to file a charge; and guidance for employers.

Feminist.Com www.feminist.com
Web site promoting women's business development, with information and advice.

FIRE: Foundation for Equal Rights in Education
www.thefire.org
Advocacy organization defending individual rights on campus and opposing racial preferences.

The King Center http://thekingcenter.com
Biography of M. L. K., Jr., together with news and information from Atlanta King Center.

La Raza www.nclr.org
National Council of La Raza. Issue positions, programs, news, dedicated to improving life experiences of Hispanic Americans.

Mexican American Legal Defense League
www.maldef.org
Advocacy and litigation on behalf of Latinos, with information on cases dealing with immigration rights.

NAACP Legal Defense Fund www.naacpldf.org
Founded in 1940 by Thurgood Marshall to provide legal assistance to poor African Americans. Originally affiliated with the NAACP; now a separate organization.

National Organization for Women (NOW) www.now.org
Advocacy organization for feminist activists working to protect abortion rights, end discrimination against women, and "eradicate racism, sexism, and homophobia."

Pew Hispanic Center www.pewhispanic.org
Research and surveys on the U.S. Hispanic population.

U.S. Commission on Civil Rights www.usccr.gov
National clearinghouse on information regarding discrimination because of race, color, religion, sex, age, disability, or national origin. Publishes reports, findings, and recommendations.

U.S. Department of Justice, Civil Rights Division
www.usdoj.gov/crt
Responsible for enforcement of U.S. civil rights laws. Site includes information on cases.

16 POLITICS AND THE ECONOMY

> **"** Some men of substantial property will see that the preservation of American business depends upon a healthy middle class of business and professional Americans. **"**
>
> **Harold Lasswell**

Chapter *Outline*

★ Politics and Economics
★ Economic Decision Making
★ The Performance of the American Economy
★ Economic Globalization
★ Government Spending, Budget Priorities, and Debt
★ The Tax Burden
★ Tax Politics

Politics and Economics

Earlier, we observed that one of America's foremost political scientists, Harold Lasswell, defined "politics" as "who gets what, when, and how." One of America's foremost economists, Paul Samuelson, defined "economics" as "deciding what shall be produced, how, and for whom."[1] The similarity between these definitions is based on the fact that both the political system and the economic system provide society with means for deciding about the production and distribution of goods and services. The political system involves *collective* decisions—choices made by communities, states, or nations—and relies on government coercion through laws, regulations, taxes, and so on to implement them. A free-market economic system involves *individual* decisions—choices made by millions of consumers and thousands of firms—and relies on *voluntary exchange* through buying, selling, borrowing, contracting, and trading to implement them. Both politics and markets function to transform popular demands into goods and services, to allocate costs, and to distribute goods and services.

One of the key questions in any society is how much to rely on government versus the marketplace to provide goods and services. This question of the proper relationship between governments and markets—that is, between politics and economics—is the subject of political economy. The United States is primarily a free-market economy, but the federal government strongly influences economic activity.

Economic Decision Making

Economic decision making involves both fiscal and monetary policy. **Fiscal policy** refers to the taxing, spending, and borrowing activities of the national government. Fiscal policy making takes place within the same system of separated powers and checks and balances that governs other areas of federal policy making (see "Separation of Powers and Checks and Balances" in Chapter 3), with both the Congress and the president sharing responsibility.

Monetary policy refers to decisions regarding the supply of money in the economy, including private borrowing, interest rates, and banking activity. Monetary policy is a principal responsibility of the powerful and independent Federal Reserve Board. Congress established the Federal Reserve Board in 1913 and its power rests on congressional legislation. Congress could, if it wished, reduce its power or even abolish the Fed. But no serious effort has ever been undertaken to do so.

✓ Think About Politics

1. Do you believe government efforts to manage the economy usually make things better or worse?

   BETTER ◯ WORSE ◯

2. Do you believe the government should spend more during recessions to ease economic hardship even if it means larger government deficits?

   YES ◯ NO ◯

3. Do you think the trend toward a global economy is a good thing or a bad thing for the United States?

   GOOD THING ◯ BAD THING ◯

4. Which is more important: holding down the size of government or providing needed services?

   HOLDING DOWN THE SIZE OF GOVERNMENT ◯
   PROVIDING NEEDED SERVICES ◯

5. Do you think the federal government should increase spending on Social Security and Medicare for the elderly?

   YES ◯ NO ◯

6. Do you believe all wage earners should pay the same percentage of income in taxes (a flat tax)?

   YES ◯ NO ◯

7. Would you favor ending all deductions if income taxes could be lowered to no more than 19 percent?

   YES ◯ NO ◯

What is the proper relationship between government and the economy? How much influence should the government exercise over the production and distribution of goods and services in this country?

★ **fiscal policy**
Economic policies involving taxing, spending, and deficit levels of the national government.

★ **monetary policy**
Economic policies involving the money supply, interest rates, and banking activity.

Comparing Economic Policy

Making Economic Policy

Congress, the President, and Fiscal Policy The Constitution of the United States places all taxing, borrowing, and spending powers in the hands of Congress. Article I grants Congress the "Power to lay and collect Taxes, Duties, Imposts and Excises, to pay the Debts and provide for the common Defence and general Welfare of the United States," and "to borrow Money on the Credit of the United States." It also declares that "No Money shall be drawn from the Treasury, but in Consequence of Appropriations made by Law." For nearly 150 years the power to spend was interpreted in a limited fashion: Congress could only spend money to perform powers specifically enumerated in Article I, Section 8, of the Constitution. But the Supreme Court has since ruled that the phrase "to pay the Debts and provide for the common Defence and general Welfare" may be broadly interpreted to authorize congressional spending for any purpose that serves the general welfare. Thus today there are no constitutional limits on Congress's spending power. Congress's borrowing power has always been unlimited constitutionally; *there is no constitutional requirement for a balanced budget.*

The Constitution gives the president no formal powers over taxing and spending or borrowing, stating only that the president shall ". . . recommend to [Congress's] Consideration such Measures as he shall judge necessary and expedient" (Article II, Section 3). From this meager constitutional grant of power, however, presidents have gradually acquired leadership over national economic policy. The principal instrument of executive economic policy making is the Budget of the United States Government, which the president submits annually to Congress. The budget sets forth the president's recommendations for spending for the forthcoming fiscal year; revenue estimates, based on existing taxes or recommendations for new or increased tax levels; and estimates of projected deficits and the need for borrowing when, as has usually been the case of late, spending recommendations exceed revenue estimates (see Figure 12.4, "The Budgetary Process," for more detail).

The President's Economic Team The *president's* recommendations to Congress regarding taxing, spending, and borrowing are influenced by advice received from three sources:

1. The Office of Management and Budget (OMB), responsible for preparing the Budget of the United States Government, exerts a powerful influence on the expenditure side of the budget. OMB supervises the year-long process of checking, reviewing, and modifying the budget requests of every federal department and agency.

2. The Department of the Treasury and the secretary of the Treasury have the principal responsibility for estimating revenues and, if requested by the president, for drawing up new tax proposals and forecasting how much revenue they might produce. The Treasury Department also manages the nation's huge national debt—the result of past annual deficits. The Treasury must continually sell **government bonds** to banks and other investors, both foreign and domestic, in order to cover payments on previous deficits as well as to fund current deficits. In doing so, the Treasury Department determines interest rates on federal bonds, and it pays out interest charges on the national debt—charges that now amount to 9 percent of all federal spending.

★ **government bonds**
Certificates of indebtedness that pay interest and promise repayment on a future date.

3. The Council of Economic Advisers (CEA), which forecasts economic conditions and recommends economic policies, is composed of three professional economists and a small staff. In theory, the CEA gives the president unbiased forecasts of economic trends and impartial analyses of

economic issues. It does so principally in the annual Economic Report of the President, which the CEA prepares. But because the president chooses the members of the CEA, it often produces economic reports that reflect the president's thinking.

The Fed and Monetary Policy

Most economically advanced democracies have central banks whose principal responsibility is to regulate the supply of money, both currency in circulation and bank deposits. And most of these democracies have found it best to remove this responsibility from the direct control of elected politicians. Politicians everywhere are sorely tempted to inflate the supply of money in order to fund projects and programs with newly created money instead of new taxes. Nations pay for this approach with a general rise in prices and a reduction in goods and services available to private firms and individuals—inflation. Indeed, nations whose control of the money supply has fallen victim to irresponsible governments have experienced inflation rates of 500 to 1,000 percent per year, which is to say that their money became worthless.

Pain at the Pump
Senator Chuck Schumer (D-NY) holding a news conference at a gas station to bash Republicans over high gas prices.

The Federal Reserve System of the United States is largely independent of either the president or Congress. Its independent status is a result not only of law but also of its structure. It is run by a seven-member board of governors who are appointed by the president, with the consent of the Senate, for 14-year terms. Members may not be removed from the board except for "cause"; no member has ever been removed since the creation of the board in 1913. The board's chair serves only a 4-year term, but the chair's term overlaps that of the president, so that new presidents cannot immediately name their own chair.

The task of the **Federal Reserve Board (the Fed)** is to regulate the money supply and by so doing to help avoid both inflation and recession. The Fed oversees the operation of the nation's twelve Federal Reserve Banks, which actually issue the nation's currency, called "Federal Reserve Notes." The Federal Reserve Banks are bankers' banks; they do not directly serve private citizens or firms. They hold the deposits, or "reserves," of banks; lend money to banks at "discount rates" that the Fed determines; buy and sell U.S. Government Treasury bonds; and assure regulatory compliance by private banks and protection of depositors against fraud. The Fed determines the reserve requirements of banks and otherwise monitors the health of the banking industry. The Fed also plays an important role in clearing checks throughout the banking system.

★ **Federal Reserve Board (the Fed)**
Independent agency of the executive branch of the federal government charged with overseeing the nation's monetary policy.

The Fed's influence over the economy is mainly through monetary policy—increasing or decreasing the supply of money and hence largely determining interest rates. When **inflation** threatens, the Fed typically acts to limit ("tighten") the supply of money and raise interest rates by (1) raising the reserve requirement of banks and thereby reducing the amount of money they have to loan out; or (2) raising the discount rate and thereby the cost of borrowing by banks; or (3) selling off government bonds to banks and others in "open market operations," thereby reducing the funds banks can lend to individuals and businesses. When **recession** threatens, the Fed typically acts to expand ("ease") the money supply and lower interest rates by taking the opposite of each action just described.

★ **inflation**
Rise in the general level of prices; not just the prices of some products.

★ **recession**
Decline in the general level of economic activity.

Although it is the Fed that makes monetary policy, voters typically hold the president responsible for recessions. Hence presidents frequently try to persuade ("jawbone") the independent Fed into lowering interest rates, especially in an election year, believing a temporary stimulus to help win the election is worth whatever inflationary effects it might create after the election.

The Performance of the American Economy

Underlying the power of nations and the well-being of their citizens is the strength of their economy—their total productive capacity. The United States produces about $14 *trillion* worth of goods and services in a single year for its 300 million people—more than $46,000 worth of output for every person.

★ gross domestic product (GDP)
Measure of economic performance in terms of the nation's total production of goods and services for a single year, valued in terms of market prices.

Economic Growth   Gross domestic product (GDP) is a widely used measure of the performance of the economy.[2] GDP is a nation's total production of goods and services for a single year valued in terms of market prices. It is the sum of all the goods and services that people have been willing to pay for, from wheat production to bake sales, from machine tools to maid service, from aircraft manufacturing to bus rides, from automobiles to chewing gum. GDP counts only final purchases of goods and services (that is, it ignores the purchase of steel by car makers until it is sold as a car) to avoid double counting in the production process. GDP also excludes financial transactions (such as the sale of bonds and stocks) and income transfers (such as Social Security, welfare, and pension payments) that do not add to the production of goods and services. Although GDP is expressed in current dollar prices, it is often recalculated in constant dollar terms to reflect real values over time, adjusting for the effect of inflation. GDP estimates are prepared each quarter by the U.S. Department of Commerce; these figures are widely reported and closely watched by the business and financial community.

★ economic cycles
Fluctuations in real GDP growth followed by contraction.

Growth in real (constant dollar) GDP measures the performance of the overall economy. Economic recessions and recoveries are measured as fluctuations or swings in the growth of GDP. For example, a recession is usually defined as negative GDP growth in two or more consecutive quarters. Historical data reveal that periods of economic growth have traditionally been followed by periods of contraction, giving rise to the notion of **economic cycles**. Prior to 1950, economic cycles in the United States produced extreme ups and downs, with double-digit swings in real GDP. In recent decades, however, economic fluctuations have been more moderate. The United States still experiences economic cycles, but many economists believe that countercyclical government fiscal and monetary policy has succeeded in achieving greater stability (see Figure 16.1).

★ unemployment rate
Percentage of the civilian labor force who are not working but who are looking for work or waiting to return to or to begin a job.

Unemployment   From a political standpoint, the **unemployment rate** may be the most important measure of the economy's performance. The unemployment rate is the percentage of the civilian labor force who are looking for work or waiting to return to or begin a job. Unemployment is different from not working; people who have retired or who attend school and people who do not work because of sickness, disability, or unwillingness are not considered part of the labor force and so are not counted as unemployed. People who are so discouraged about finding a job that they have quit looking for work are also not counted in the official unemployment rate. The unemployed do include people who have been terminated from their last job or temporarily laid off from work, as well as people who voluntarily quit and those who have recently entered or reentered the labor force and are now seeking employment.

The unemployment rate is measured each month by the U.S. Department of Labor. It does so by contacting a random sample of more than 50,000 households in many locations throughout the country. Trained interviewers ask a variety of questions to determine how many (if any) members of the household are either

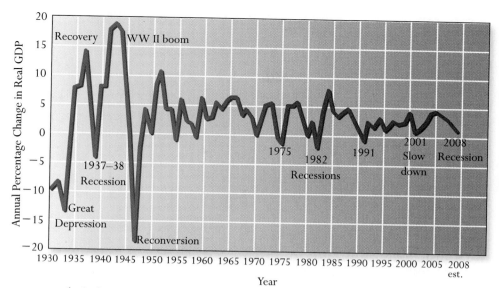

Figure *16.1*

Growth Cycles: Economic Growth in America

The tendency for periods of economic growth to alternate with periods of contraction has led to the concept of the business cycle—the idea that at least some fluctuation is normal, even healthy, helping to keep the economy growing in the long run by keeping prices from getting too high. In recent decades, government intervention in the economy appears to have succeeded in reducing, although not in altogether eliminating, the depths of recessions to which the nation was formerly prone.

Source: Data from Bureau of Economic Analysis, 2008.

working or have a job but did not work at it because of sickness, vacation, strike, or personal reasons (employed); or whether they have no job but are available for work and actively seeking a job (unemployed). The unemployment rate fluctuates with the business cycle, reflecting recessions and recoveries (see Figure 16.2).

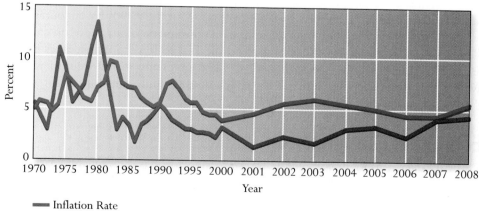

Figure *16.2*

A Double Negative: Unemployment and Inflation in America

Economic growth during the 1980s lowered both the inflation and unemployment rates, freeing the nation from the stagflation (combined inflation and high unemployment) that had characterized much of the 1970s. Unemployment rose during the recession of 1990–91 and again in 2002–2003. Inflation has remained relatively low in recent years.

Source: Data from Bureau of Labor Statistics, 2008.

How Bad Can It Get

Just how bad can inflation get? Between the two world wars, inflation in Germany reached such levels that the nation's currency was often weighed, rather than counted, in order to speed transactions.

Generally, unemployment lags behind GDP growth, going down only after the recovery has begun. Following years of economic growth in the 1990s, the nation's unemployment rate fell to near record lows, below 5 percent. The economic slowdown of 2001–2002 temporarily pushed unemployment above 5 percent again (see Figure 16.2).

Inflation   Inflation erodes the value of the dollar because higher prices mean that the same dollars can now purchase fewer goods and services. Thus inflation erodes the value of savings, reduces the incentive to save, and hurts people who are living on fixed incomes. When banks and investors anticipate inflation, they raise interest rates on loans in order to cover the anticipated lower value of repayment dollars. Higher interest rates, in turn, make it more difficult for new or expanding businesses to borrow money, for home buyers to acquire mortgages, and for consumers to make purchases on credit. Thus inflation and high interest rates slow economic growth.

In recent years the Fed has been very successful in keeping down the rate of inflation, and as a result, keeping down overall interest rates as well. Low interest rates contributed to the nation's booming economy in the 1990s by encouraging businesses to borrow money for expansion and consumers to buy more on credit. The "soft" economy in 2001–2002 inspired the Fed to lower interest rates even further. As the economy strengthened, the Fed gradually raised interest rates. When the housing market suffered a setback in 2007 and recession threatened, the Fed again lowered interest rates.

Economic Globalization

The American economy is a major force in the global economy. **International trade**—the buying and selling of goods and services between individuals and firms located in different countries—has expanded rapidly in recent decades. Today almost one-quarter of the world's total output is sold in a country other than the one in which it was produced. The United States exports about 11 percent of the value of its gross domestic product (GDP) and imports about 12 percent. As late as 1970, exports and imports were only about 3 percent of GDP (see Figure 16.3).

Historic Protectionism   Historically, American business supported high tariffs—taxes on foreign imports. Prior to World War II, U.S. tariffs on imported goods averaged 30 to 50 percent in various decades. This eliminated most foreign

★ **international trade**
The buying and selling of goods and services between individuals or firms located in different countries.

Think
Again

Do you think the trend toward a global economy is a good thing or a bad thing for the United States?

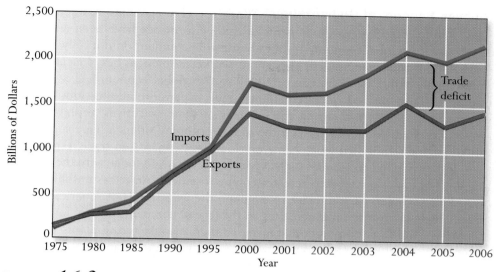

Figure *16.3*   The Trade Gap: U.S. World Trade

Each year the U.S. imports more goods than it exports, thereby creating annual trade deficits.

Source: U.S. Bureau of Economic Analysis, December, 2007.

competition from U.S. markets. American firms could raise prices to levels just below the price of imported goods with their high tariffs attached. Not only did this improve the profit margins of American manufacturers, it also allowed them to be less efficient than foreign producers and yet survive and prosper under the protection of tariffs. The pressure to cut wages and downsize workforces was less than it would be if U.S. firms had to face foreign competition directly. American consumers, of course, paid higher prices than they otherwise would if foreign goods could come into the country without tariffs. The policy of high tariffs and quotas—limits on the number of units of specific goods imported into the country—was referred to as **protectionism**.

Free Trade   But after World War II, the American economy became the most powerful in the world, and American businesses sought to expand their markets overseas. In order to lower trade barriers in other countries, the United States reduced or eliminated almost all of its own tariffs and import quotas. In effect, the United States became an open market. "Free trade" became a byword of American business, and "protectionism" became a derogatory term.

The argument for **free trade** is that it lowers the price of goods and improves the standard of living in nations that choose to trade with each other. Trade shifts resources (investment capital, jobs, technology, raw materials, and so on) in each nation toward what each does best. If one nation is much better at producing aircraft and another better at producing clothing, then each nation will benefit more from trading than from trying to produce both airplanes and clothing. The efficiencies achieved by trading are said to directly benefit consumers by making available cheaper imported goods. Export industries also benefit when world markets are opened to their products. It is also argued that the pressure from competition from foreign-made goods in the American marketplace forces our own industries to become more efficient—cutting their costs and improving the quality of their goods. Finally, trade expands the menu of goods and services available to trading countries. American consumers gain access to everything from exotic foods and foreign-language movies to Porsches, BMWs, and Toyotas.

★ **protectionism**
A policy of high tariffs and quotas on imports to protect domestic industries.

★ **free trade**
A policy of reducing or eliminating tariffs and quotas on imports to stimulate international trade.

Uneven Benefits of Globalization   While the U.S. economy has performed very well in recent years, the benefits of that performance have been unevenly distributed. A global economy inspires worldwide competition not only among corporations and businesses but also among workers. America's best educated and most highly skilled workers compete well in the global economy. U.S. export industries have thrived on international trade expansion, adding jobs to the American economy and raising the incomes of their executives, professionals, and skilled high-tech workers. But the global economy offers a huge supply of unskilled and semiskilled workers at very low wages. Increased trade, especially with less developed economies such as Mexico, China, and India, with their huge numbers of low-wage workers, creates competition with America's unskilled and semiskilled workers. It is difficult to maintain the wage levels of American jobs, especially in labor-intensive industries, in the face of competition from low-wage countries. And U.S. corporations can move their manufacturing plants to low-wage countries, for example to northern Mexico, where the transportation costs of moving these products back into the United States are minimal. Harvard economist Richard B. Freeman summarizes the problem:

> An economic disaster has befallen low-skilled Americans, especially young men. Researchers using several data sources—including household survey data from the Current Population Survey, other household surveys, and establishment surveys—have documented that wage inequality and skill differentials in earnings and employment increased sharply in the United States from the mid-1970s through the 1980s and into the 1990s. The drop in the relative position of the less skilled shows up in a number of ways: greater earnings differentials between those with more and less education; greater earnings differentials between older and younger workers; greater differentials between high-skilled and low-skilled occupations; in a wider earnings distribution overall and within demographic and skill groups; and in less time worked by low-skill and low-paid workers.[3]

Income inequality has worsened in America along with the growth of international trade (see "Inequality of Income and Wealth" in Chapter 2). Not all of the increases in inequality can be attributed to the growth of international trade. But, clearly, America's less educated and less skilled workers are at a disadvantage in global competition.[4]

The Politics of Free Trade   Over the years both Democratic and Republican presidential administrations have advanced free trade. And Congress has approved the major treaties and organizations designed to institutionalize the global economy (see Table 16.1). The task of the cabinet-level position, International Trade Representative, has been to open up foreign markets to American products. Occasionally, the United States has threatened to limit the importation of foreign products in order to force other nations to open up their own markets. And occasionally, Congress members from districts adversely affected by foreign competition have opposed specific trade arrangements or, alternatively, called upon the federal government to assist workers displaced by foreign competition. But the thrust of U.S. policy has been to expand free trade.

Democrats in Congress have expressed more reservations about free trade than Republicans. (Democrats often call for "fair trade" in lieu of "free trade.") Democratic Congress members often reflect the views of their party's core constituencies, including labor unions, that fear the adverse effect on wages created by globalization. Environmentalists also complain that foreign corporations are not governed by strong or well-enforced environmental laws in their own countries. An array of other groups frequently demonstrates against globalization at meetings of the World Trade Organization and other international bodies (see *What Do You Think?: "Does Globalization Help or Hurt America?"*).

Think
Again

Which is more important: holding down the size of government or providing needed services?

Table *16.1* Major International Trade Agreements

The World Trade Organization and GATT

The World Trade Organization (WTO) was created in 1993. Today the WTO includes 149 nations that agree to a governing set of global trade rules. (China joined in 2001.) The WTO is given power to adjudicate trade disputes among countries and monitor and enforce trade agreements, including GATT. GATT, the multinational General Agreement on Tariffs and Trade, was created following World War II for the purpose of encouraging international trade. Over the years GATT has been dominated by banking, business, and commercial interests in Western nations seeking multilateral tariff reductions and the relaxation of quotas. In 1993, the GATT "Uruguay Round" eliminated quotas on textile products; established more uniform standards for proof of dumping; set rules for the protection of intellectual property rights (patents and copyrights on books, movies, videos, and so on); reduced tariffs on wood, paper, and some other raw materials; and scheduled a gradual reduction of government subsidies for agricultural products.

The International Monetary Fund (IMF) and the World Bank

The IMF's purpose is to facilitate international trade, allowing nations to borrow to stabilize their balance of trade payments. When economically weak nations, however, incur chronic balance of trade deficits and perhaps face deferral or default on international debts, the IMF may condition its loans on changes in a nation's economic policies. It may require a reduction in a nation's government deficits by reduced public spending and/or higher taxes; or it may require a devaluation of its currency, making its exports cheaper and imports more expensive. It may also require the adoption of noninflationary monetary policies. Currently, the IMF as well as the World Bank are actively involved in assisting Russia and other states of the former Soviet Union to convert to free-market economies.

The World Bank makes long-term loans, mostly to developing nations, to assist in economic development. It works closely with the IMF in investigating the economic conditions of nations applying for loans and generally imposes IMF requirements on these nations as conditions for loans.

North American Free Trade Agreement (NAFTA)

In 1993, the United States, Canada, and Mexico signed the North American Free Trade Agreement (NAFTA). Objections by labor unions in the United States were drowned out in a torrent of support by the American corporate community, Democrats and Republicans in Congress, President Bill Clinton, and former President George H. W. Bush. NAFTA envisions the removal of tariffs on virtually all products by all three nations over a period of 10 to 15 years. It also allows banking, insurance, and other financial services to cross these borders.

FTAA and CAFTA

Currently the United States and the nations of North, Central, and South America are engaged in negotiations designed to create a free trade area throughout most of the Western Hemisphere. The Free Trade Area of the Americas (FTAA) is to resemble NAFTA. Barriers to trade and investment are to be progressively eliminated. The rules of the World Trade Organization will constitute a base for the FTAA agreements.

Recent U.S. presidents, both Democrats and Republicans, have pressed Congress for "fast-track authority" for trade agreements, essentially requesting that Congress pass presidentially negotiated trade agreements without amendments. In 2002, Congress granted President Bush's request for something quite similar—"trade promotion authority." While negotiations on FTAA continue, President Bush signed a trade agreement—the Central American Free Trade Agreement (CAFTA)—with five Central American nations (Guatemala, El Salvador, Honduras, Costa Rica, and Nicaragua). CAFTA is based on the NAFTA model and is looked upon in Washington as a stepping stone to the broader FTAA.

Government Spending, Budget Priorities, and Debt

The expenditures of all governments in the United States—federal, state, and local governments combined—today amount to about 30 percent of GDP. The federal government itself spends more than $3 trillion each year—about 20 percent of GDP.

"Mandatory" Spending Much of the growth of federal government spending over the years is attributed to **mandatory spending** items in the federal budget. These "uncontrollables" are budget items committed to by past policies of Congress that are not easily changed in annual budget making. Sources of mandatory spending include the following:

★ *Entitlement programs:* Federal programs that provide classes of people with a legally enforceable right to benefits are called **entitlement programs**. Entitlement programs account for more than half of all federal spending,

★ **mandatory spending**
Spending for program commitments made by past congresses.

★ **entitlement programs**
Social welfare programs that provide classes of people with legally enforceable rights to benefits.

What Do You *Think?*

Does Globalization Help or Hurt America?

While Democratic and Republican presidents and Congresses have supported free trade and given their approval to two major trade agreements, the American public appears to be divided over the benefits of economic globalization.

Q. "Globalization is the increase of trade, communication, travel, and other things among countries around the world. In general, has the United States gained more or lost more because of globalization?"

Gained	Lost	Both (vol.)	Unsure/No answer
36%	51%	1%	12%

Q. "Generally speaking, do you believe that free international trade has helped or hurt the economy or hasn't it made a difference to the economy one way or the other?"

Helped	Hurt	No Difference	Unsure
27%	44%	15%	13%

Q. "What do you think foreign trade means for America? Do you see foreign trade more as an opportunity for economic growth through increased U.S. exports or a threat to the economy from foreign imports?"

Opportunity	Threat	Both (vol.)	Neither (vol.)	Unsure
46%	45%	5%	2%	2%

Q. "Do you believe that the United States is benefiting from the global economy, is being harmed by the global economy, or do you think the global economy has had no impact on the United States one way or the other?"

Benefiting	Harmed	No Impact	Unsure
25%	48%	14%	13%

Source: Various polls as reported in *The Polling Report,* 2007, www.pollingreport.com

Farm Subsidies

★ **indexing**
Tieing of benefit levels in social welfare programs to the general price level.

★ **in-kind (noncash) benefits**
Benefits of a social welfare program that are not cash payments, including free medical care, subsidized housing, and food stamps.

★ **balanced budget**
Government budget in which expenditures and revenues are equal, so that no deficit or surplus exists.

including Social Security, Medicare and Medicaid, food stamps, federal employees' retirement pensions, and veterans' benefits (see *Politics Up Close:* "Transfers and Entitlements Drive Government Spending"). These entitlements are benefits that past Congresses have pledged the federal government to pay. Entitlements are not really uncontrollable. Congress can always amend the basic laws that established them, but doing so is politically difficult and might be regarded as abandonment of a public trust. As more people become "entitled" to government benefits—for example, as more people reach retirement ages and claim Social Security benefits, federal spending increases.

★ *Indexing of benefits:* Another reason that spending increases each year is that Congress has authorized automatic increases in benefits to match inflation. Benefits under such programs as Social Security are tied to the Consumer Price Index. This **indexing** pushes up the cost of entitlement programs each year, even when the number of recipients stays the same, thus running counter to federal efforts to restrain inflation. Moreover, because the Consumer Price Index includes interest payments for new housing and the cost of new cars and appliances, it generally overestimates the needs of older recipients for cost-of-living increases.

★ *Increasing costs of in-kind benefits:* Rises in the cost of major **in-kind (noncash) benefits**, particularly the medical costs of Medicaid and Medicare, also guarantee growth in federal spending. These in-kind benefit programs have risen faster in cost than cash benefit programs.

★ *Interest on the national debt:* The federal government has a long history of deficits. In 1998 the president sent the first **balanced budget** to the Congress in 30

Politics Up Close   Washington Bails Out Wall Street

For years Americans lived on easy credit. Families ran up credit card debt and borrowed heavily for cars, tuition, and especially home buying. Mortgage lenders approved loans for borrowers without fully examining their ability to pay. Federally chartered corporations, Fannie Mae and Freddie Mac, encouraged mortgage loans to low-income home buyers. Some mortgages were "predatory" with initial low payments followed by steep upwardly adjustable rates. To make matters worse, banks and financial institutions bundled mortgages together and sold these mortgage-backed securities as "derivatives." Banks, insurers, and lenders all assumed that housing prices would inevitably rise. Housing construction boomed.

Eventually the bubble burst. Housing prices fell dramatically. The number of houses for sale greatly exceeded the number of people willing to buy them. Homeowners found themselves holding "upside down" mortgages—mortgages that exceeded the value of their homes. Many were unable or unwilling to meet their mortgage payments. Foreclosures and delinquencies spiraled upward. Investors who held mortgage-backed securities began to incur heavy losses. Investment banks, such as Bear Stearns, and mortgage insurers, including Fannie Mae and Freddie Mac, found themselves in serious financial trouble. Bankruptcies and federal bailouts multiplied. The stock market plummeted.

President Bush sent Secretary of the Treasury Henry Paulson, Federal Reserve Chairman Ben Bernanke, and the Securities and Exchange Commission Chairman Chris Cox, to Congress to plead for a massive $700 billion bailout of banks, insurance companies, and investment firms that held mortgage-backed "illiquid assets." They argued that their proposal was absolutely essential to safeguard the financial security of the nation. Steep recession, if not a full-blown depression, would result if the federal government failed to purchase these troubled assets.

Congress responded with their own ideas: no Wall Street CEOs should benefit from government rescue (no "golden parachutes"); congressional oversight of the bailout; taxpayers must share in any recovery that might eventually occur; and the money must be made available in staggered amounts.

The nation's top leadership—President Bush, the Treasury Secretary, the Fed Chairman, House and Senate Democratic and Republican leaders, and even the presidential candidates—all supported the bill as amended. But polls show that most Americans oppose a "Wall Street bailout." Congress members were being asked by their leaders to ignore the folks back home. The initial House vote stunned Washington and Wall Street: "nay" votes prevailed. The stock market plunged alarmingly.

Predictions of economic catastrophe inspired a renewed effort to pass the bill. The Senate responded by passing it with a comfortable margin, while adding various sweeteners, mostly tax benefits to gain House support. Tensions were high when the House voted on the Senate version of the bill. In a sharp reversal of its earlier action, the House approved the Emergency Economic Stabilization Act of 2008. President Bush promptly signed it: "By coming together on this legislation, we have acted boldly to help prevent the crisis on Wall Street from becoming a crisis in communities across the country."

---

years. Deficit spending resumed in 2002. The accumulated deficits leave the government with a national debt of over $10 trillion. Interest payments on this debt now make up about 8 percent of total federal spending.

Federal Budget Priorities
Federal budget shares (the percentage of outlays devoted to various functions) reflect the spending priorities of the national government. Entitlements and other mandatory spending (principally interest on the national debt) heavily outweighs defense and **discretionary spending** combined (see Figure 16.4). Spending on programs designed to assist senior citizens (Social Security and Medicare) heavily outweighs defense spending, welfare spending, and all discretionary spending. Today Social Security payments are the largest single item in the federal budget. Over time, defense spending declined from more than 50 percent of the federal budget at the height of the Cold War in the early 1960s to 14 percent in the 1990s. The war on terror, including military operations in Iraq and Afghanistan, has increased defense spending to over 18 percent of the budget. Medical costs—Medicare for the elderly and Medicaid for the poor—are currently the fastest growing items in the federal budget.

★ **discretionary spending**
Spending for programs not previously mandated by law.

Figure *16.4*

Who Gets What?: Federal Budget Shares

Mandatory spending—spending commitments in existing laws, notably Social Security, Medicare, Medicaid, and other entitlements, plus interest on the national debt—accounts for over two-thirds of the federal budget. Discretionary spending, including defense, accounts for only about one-third of the budget.

Source: Budget of the United States Government, 2009.

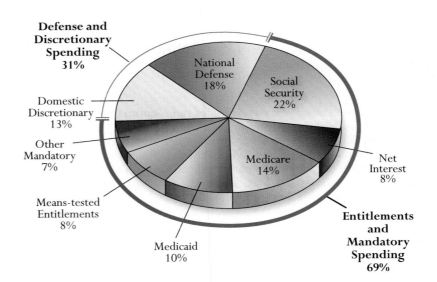

Defense and Discretionary Spending 31%

National Defense 18%

Social Security 22%

Domestic Discretionary 13%

Other Mandatory 7%

Medicare 14%

Net Interest 8%

Means-tested Entitlements 8%

Medicaid 10%

Entitlements and Mandatory Spending 69%

★ **deficits**
Imbalances in the annual federal budget in which spending exceeds revenues.

★ **national debt**
Total debt accumulated by the national government over the years.

The Debt Burden   The U.S. federal government regularly incurrs **deficits** every year—that is, its expenditures exceed its revenues (see Figure 16.5). The accumulated **national debt** is over $10 trillion, or $30,000 for every man, woman, and child in the nation. This government debt is owed mostly to U.S. banks and financial institutions and private citizens who buy Treasury bonds. Only about 15 percent of the debt is owed to foreign banks and individuals. As old debt comes due, the U.S. Treasury Department sells new bonds to pay off the old; that is, it continues to "roll over" or "float" the debt. Despite its size in dollars, the debt today is smaller as a percentage of GDP than at some periods in U.S. history. For example, to pay the costs of fighting World War II, the U.S. government ran up a debt equivalent to over 100 percent of GDP. The current $10 trillion debt, although the highest in history in dollar terms, is equal to about 70 percent of GDP.

The ability to float such a huge debt depends on public confidence in the U.S. government—confidence that it will continue to pay interest on its debt, that it will pay off the principal of bonds when they come due, and that the value of the bonds will not decline over time because of inflation.

Interest Burden for Future Generations   Interest payments on the national debt come from current taxes and so divert money away from *all* other government programs. Even if the federal government manages to balance future budgets, these payments will remain obligations of the children and grandchildren of the current generation of policy makers and taxpayers. Interest payments on the national debt, currently about 8 percent of the federal budget, do not purchase any government goods or services. This means that for every dollar paid in federal taxes, taxpayers currently receive only 92 cents in government goods and services.

The Long-Sought Balanced Budget   Economic growth began to shrink annual deficits after the 1991–92 recession. The nation's booming economy increased tax revenues. And in 1993, President Clinton succeeded in getting a Democratic-controlled Congress to pass a major increase in tax rates (see "Tax Politics," later in this chapter). After 1994, a Republican-controlled Congress slowed the growth of federal spending. Budget "caps" were enacted by Congress and worked surprisingly well during the 1990s in holding down overall spending. President Clinton did not introduce any major new spending programs after his comprehensive health care program failed to pass Congress in 1993 (see Chapter 17). So both Democrats and Republicans claimed credit for reducing annual deficits.

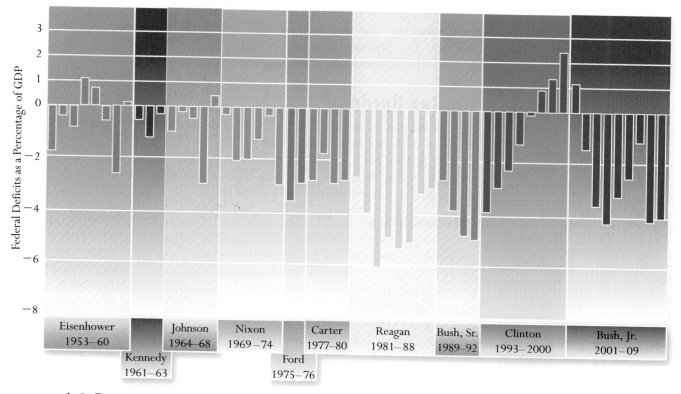

Figure *16.5*   Deeper in Debt Deficits Through the Years

This figure shows annual federal deficits as percentages of the GDP. Note that the federal government incurred deficits for 30 years, under both Republican and Democratic presidential administrations. A strong economy, and resulting increases in revenues flowing to the federal government, created budget surpluses from 1998 to 2001. An economic slowdown, the Iraq War, and added security costs after the "9/11" attack put the federal budget back in the red. Economic recession promises even larger deficits in the next few years.

Note: Figures for 2008 and 2009 are estimates.
Source: Budget of the United States Government, 2009.

Politics, Deficits, and Spending   Federal budget surpluses lasted for only 4 years, 1998–2001. During those years, Democrats and Republicans in Washington fought over what to do with the surplus revenues. Both parties pledged to use part of the surplus to strengthen Social Security and Medicare for the coming retirement of the "baby-boom" generation. But Republicans and conservatives argued that surpluses should also be used to reduce taxes or to pay off part of the national debt, or some combination of both. In contrast, Democrats argued that the surpluses should be used for investment in education, job skills, federal health insurance, and environmental protection. The result of the stalemate was a modest automatic reduction in the national debt.

But an economic slowdown, combined with the Iraq War and added security spending after the "9/11" attack on America, brought a return of red ink to federal budgets. Outlays for national defense increased dramatically, as did spending for homeland security—border and airport security, terrorism preparedness, aid to police, fire, and rescue teams, and the like. Democrats also blamed the return of deficits on Bush's tax cuts of 2001 and 2003 (see "Bush Tax Cuts" on page 600). But Republicans argued that these tax cuts helped avoid an even deeper economic recession.

Both parties now support increased spending for the military and for homeland security. Both seem willing to set aside the goal of a balanced budget in order to

Evaluating Federal Spending and Economic Policy

Growth of the Budget and Federal Spending

do so. But it is likely that conflict between Democrats, who seek to spend more on social programs, and Republicans, who seek further tax reductions, is likely to continue. The general public remains ambivalent over conflicting budget goals; they want both increased government services *and* reduced taxes.

The Tax Burden

The tax burden in the United States is modest compared to burdens in other advanced democracies (see *Compared to What?*: "Tax Burdens in Advanced Democracies"). Federal revenues are derived mainly from (1) individual income taxes, (2) corporate income taxes, (3) Social Security payroll taxes, (4) estate and gift taxes, and (5) excise taxes and custom duties.

Individual Income Taxes   The individual income tax is the federal government's largest source of revenue (see Figure 16.6). Following tax cuts enacted by Congress in 2001 and 2003, individual income is now taxed at six rates: 10, 15, 25, 28, 33, and 35 percent. These are *marginal rates*, a term that economists use to mean additional. That is, income up to the top of the lowest bracket is taxed at 10 percent; additional income in the next bracket is taxed at 15 percent, up to a top marginal rate of 35 percent on income over $349,700 (in 2007). A personal exemption for each taxpayer and dependent, together with a standard deduction for married couples and a refundable earned income tax credit, ensure that low income earners pay no income tax. (However, they still must pay Social Security taxes on wages.) Tax brackets, as well as the personal exemption and standard deduction, are indexed annually to protect against inflation.

The income tax is automatically deducted from the paychecks of employees. This "withholding" system is the backbone of the individual income tax. There is no withholding of nonwage income such as dividends on investments, but taxpayers with such income must file a "Declaration of Estimated Taxes" and pay this estimate in quarterly installments. Before April 15 of each year, all income-earning Americans must report their taxable income for the previous year to the Internal Revenue Service on its 1040 Form.

Americans are usually surprised to learn that half of all personal income is not taxed. To understand why, we must know how the tax laws distinguish between *adjusted gross income* (an individual's total money income minus expenses incurred in earning that income) and *taxable income* (that part of adjusted gross income subject to taxation). Federal tax rates apply only to *taxable* income.

Think Again

Do you believe all wage earners should pay the same percentage of income in taxes (a flat tax)?

★ **individual income tax**
Taxes on individuals' wages and other earned income, the primary source of revenue for the U.S. federal government.

You Are the President and Need to Get a Tax Cut Passed

Figure *16.6*
Where the Money Comes From: Sources of Federal Income
Individual income taxes make up the largest portion of the federal government's revenues (47 percent). The government also relies heavily on the second largest source of its revenues, Social Security taxes.

Source: Budget of the United States Government, 2009.

Compared to *What?*

Tax Burdens in Advanced Democracies

Americans complain a lot about taxes. But from a global perspective, overall tax burdens in the United States are relatively low (see figure). Tax revenues in the United States amount to about 25 percent of the gross domestic product (GDP). U.S. taxes are well below the burdens imposed in Sweden, Denmark, and other nations with highly developed welfare systems.

Top marginal tax rates in many nations were reduced during the 1980s and 1990s. For example, the top rate in Great Britain was lowered from 60 to 40 percent, in Japan from 70 to 30 percent, and in Sweden from 80 to 55 percent. Both in the United States and abroad, the notion that excessively high tax rates discourage work, savings, and investment, as well as slow economic growth, won acceptance (although how high is "excessive" is obviously open to different interpretations). Moreover, in a global economy, with increased mobility of individuals and firms, pressures push nations to keep their top tax rates within reasonable limits. Corporations can shift their assets to low-tax jurisdictions, and high personal income tax rates can even threaten a "brain drain" of talented individuals.

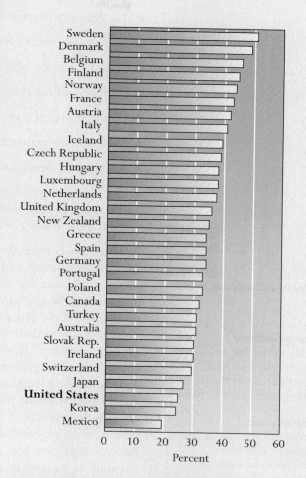

Tax Revenues as a Percentage of GDP

Source: OECD Factbook, 2007, www.oecd.org

Tax expenditures are tax revenues lost to the federal government because of exemptions, exclusions, deductions, and special treatments in tax laws. Federal government revenues from individual and business income taxes would be substantially higher were it not for special provisions in tax laws that enable taxpayers to avoid paying taxes on often substantial sums of income. Although each of these "loopholes" supposedly has a larger social goal behind it (for example, the deductibility of mortgage interest is supposed to stimulate the purchase and construction of homes, keeping up the value of those assets for current homeowners and keeping the construction industry employed), critics charge that many cost far more than they are worth to society. These are the major tax expenditures in federal tax law:

★ Personal exemptions for taxpayer, spouse, and children

★ Deductibility of mortgage interest on homes

★ Deductibility of property taxes on first and second homes

★ **tax expenditures**
Revenues lost to the federal government because of exemptions, exclusions, deductions, and special-treatment provisions in tax laws.

★ Deferral of capital gains on home sales

★ Deductibility of charitable contributions

★ Credit for child-care expenses

★ Tax-free deposits for educational savings accounts

★ Exclusion of employer contributions to pension plans and medical insurance

★ Partial exclusion of Social Security benefits

★ Exclusion of interest on public-purpose state and local bonds

★ Deductibility of state and local income taxes

★ Exclusion of income earned abroad

★ Accelerated depreciation of machinery, equipment, and structures

★ Deductible contributions to IRAs and 401(K) retirement plans, and accrued interest and profits in these plans. (But taxes must be paid when cash is taken from these plans.)

You Are an Environmental Activist

There is a continual struggle between proponents of special tax exemptions to achieve social goals and those who believe the tax laws should be simplified and social goals met by direct government expenditures. Much of the political infighting in Washington involves the efforts of interest groups to obtain exemptions, exclusions, deductions, and special treatments in tax laws.[5]

In addition to these multiple means of **tax avoidance** (legal means), an "underground economy" that facilitates **tax evasion** (illegal means of dodging taxes) costs the federal government many billions of dollars. The federal Internal Revenue Service itself estimates that it is losing about $200 billion per year in revenue due to the failure of people to report income and pay taxes on it. Independent estimates of the size of the underground economy are much higher, perhaps $450 billion, or 15 percent of all taxes due.[6] Many citizens receive cash for goods and services they provide, and it simply does not occur to them to report these amounts as income in addition to the wage statements they receive from their employer. Many others receive all or most of their income from cash transactions; they have a strong incentive to underreport their income. And, of course, illegal criminal transactions such as drug dealing are seldom reported on personal income tax forms. As tax rates rise, hiding income becomes more profitable.

★ tax avoidance
Taking advantage of exemptions, exclusions, deductions, and special treatments in tax laws (legal).

★ tax evasion
Hiding income and/or falsely claiming exemptions, deductions, and special treatments (illegal).

Corporate Income Taxes   The corporate income tax provides only about 13 percent of the federal government's total revenue. The Tax Reform Act of 1986 reduced the top corporate income tax from 46 to 34 percent (raised to 35 percent in 1993). However, corporations find many ways of reducing their taxable income—often to zero. The result is that many very large and profitable corporations pay little in taxes. Religious, charitable, and educational organizations, as well as labor unions, are exempt from corporate income taxes except for income they may derive from "unrelated business activity."

Who really bears the burden of the corporate income tax? Economists differ over whether the corporate income tax is "shifted" to consumers or whether corporations and their stockholders bear its burden. The evidence on the **incidence**—that is, who actually bears the burden—of this tax is inconclusive.[7]

★ incidence
Actual bearer of a tax burden.

Social Security Taxes   The second largest source of federal revenue is the Social Security tax. It is withheld from paychecks as the "FICA" deduction, an acronym that helps hide the true costs of Social Security and Medicare from wage earners. To keep up with the rising number of beneficiaries and the higher levels of benefits voted for by Congress, including generous automatic cost-of-living increases each year, the Social Security taxes rose to 15.3 percent. (The Social Security tax is 12.4 percent and the Medicare tax is 2.9 percent; all wage income is subject to the Medicare tax, but wage income above a certain level, $102,010 in 2008, is not subject to the Social Security tax.)

Taxes collected under FICA are earmarked (by Social Security number) for the account of each taxpayer. Workers thus feel they are receiving benefits as a right rather than as a gift of the government. However, less than 15 percent of the benefits being paid to current recipients of Social Security can be attributed to their prior contributions. Current taxpayers are paying more than 85 percent of the benefits received by current retirees.

Today a majority of taxpayers pay more in Social Security taxes than income taxes. Indeed, combined employer and employee Social Security taxes now amount to over $15,600 for each worker at the top of the wage base. If we assume that the employer's share of the tax actually comes out of wages that would otherwise be paid to the employee, then more than 75 percent of all taxpayers pay more in Social Security taxes than in income taxes.

Estate and Gift Taxes Taxation of property left to heirs is one of the oldest forms of taxation in the world. Federal estate taxes levy a tax rate that rises to 45 percent for estates worth more than $3 million. But these rates are scheduled to rise to 55 percent after 2010. Estates worth less than $1 million are exempt. Because taxes at death otherwise could be avoided by simply giving estates to heirs while the giver is still alive, a federal gift tax is also levied on anyone who gives gifts in excess of $12,000 annually. Gifts to spouses and charitable contributions are exempt.

Excise Taxes and Custom Duties Federal excise taxes on the consumption of liquor, tobacco, gasoline, telephones, air travel, and other so-called luxury items, together with customs taxes on imports, provide about 3 percent of total federal revenues.

Tax Politics

The politics of taxation centers around the question of who actually bears the heaviest burden of a tax—especially which income groups must devote the largest proportion of their income to taxes. **Progressive taxation** requires high-income groups to pay a larger percentage of their incomes in taxes than low-income groups. **Regressive taxation** takes a larger share of the income of low-income groups. **Proportional (flat) taxation** requires all income groups to pay the same percentage of their income in taxes. Note that the *percentage of income* paid in taxes is the determining factor. Most taxes take more money from the rich than the poor, but a progressive or regressive tax is distinguished by the percentages of income taken from various income groups.

The Argument for Progressivity Progressive taxation is generally defended on the principle of ability to pay; the assumption is that high-income groups can afford to pay a larger *percentage* of their incomes in taxes at no more of a sacrifice than that required of lower income groups to devote a smaller proportion of their income to taxation. This assumption is based on what economists call *marginal utility theory* as it applies to money; each additional dollar of income is slightly less valuable to an individual than preceding dollars. For example, a $5,000 increase in the income of an individual already earning $100,000 is much less valuable than a $5,000 increase to an individual earning only $10,000 or to an individual with no income at all. Hence, it is argued that added dollars of income can be taxed at higher rates without violating equitable principles.

★ **progressive taxation**
System of taxation in which higher income groups pay a larger percentage of their incomes in taxes than do lower income groups.

★ **regressive taxation**
System of taxation in which lower income groups pay a larger percentage of their incomes in taxes than do higher income groups.

★ **proportional (flat) taxation**
System of taxation in which all income groups pay the same percentage of their income in taxes.

The Argument for Proportionality   Opponents of progressive taxation generally assert that equity can only be achieved by taxing everyone at the same percentage of their income, regardless of the size of their income. Progressivity penalizes initiative, enterprise, and the risk taking necessary to create new products and businesses. It also reduces incentives to expand and develop the nation's economy. Highly progressive taxes curtail growth and make everyone poorer (see *A Conflicting View*: "We Should Enact a Flat Tax").

Reagan's Reductions in Progressivity   Certainly the most dramatic change in federal tax laws during the Reagan years was the reduction in the progressivity of individual income tax rates (see Figure 16.7). The top marginal tax rate fell from 70 percent when President Reagan took office to 28 percent following enactment of tax reform in 1986. The Tax Reform Act of 1986 reduced fourteen rate brackets to only two rate brackets, 15 and 28 percent.

"Read My Lips"   At the Republican national convention in 1988, presidential nominee George H. W. Bush made a firm pledge to American voters that he would veto any tax increases passed by the Democratic-controlled Congress: "Read my lips! No new taxes." Yet in a 1990 budget summit with Democratic congressional leaders, President Bush agreed to add a top marginal rate of 31 percent to the personal income tax. Breaking his solemn pledge on taxes contributed heavily to Bush's defeat in the 1992 presidential election.

"Soak the Rich"   Proposals to "soak the rich" are always politically very popular. President Clinton pushed Congress to raise the top marginal tax rates to 39.6 percent for families earning $250,000. But these new top rates do not raise much revenue, partly because very few people have annual incomes in these categories. Moreover, high rates encourage people to seek tax-sheltered investments—to use their capital less efficiently to create tax breaks for themselves rather than to promote new business and new jobs.

Bush Tax Cuts   George W. Bush came into office vowing *not* to make the same mistake as his father, raising tax rates in an effort to compromise with the Democrats. On the contrary, Bush was strongly committed to lowering taxes, arguing first in 2001 that the American people should receive some part of the government's surpluses. Congress initially responded with a small tax cut, bringing the top marginal rate from 39.6 percent to 38.6 percent.

Figure *16.7*

Top Personal Income Tax Rates, by President

The top marginal personal income tax rate fell dramatically during the Reagan administration, then began to creep upward again under Presidents Bush and Clinton. George W. Bush lowered the top rate in 2001 and again in 2003.

A Conflicting *View*

We Should Enact a Flat Tax

More than a hundred years ago, Supreme Court Justice Stephen J. Field, in striking down as unconstitutional a progressive income tax enacted by Congress, predicted that such a tax would lead to class wars: "Our political contests will become a war of the poor against the rich, a war constantly growing in intensity and bitterness."[a] But populist sentiment in the early twentieth century—the anger of Midwestern farmers toward Eastern rail tycoons and the beliefs of impoverished Southerners that they would never have incomes high enough to pay an income tax—helped secure the passage of the 16th Amendment to the U.S. Constitution. The federal income tax passed by Congress in 1914 had a top rate of 7 percent; less than 1 percent of the population had incomes high enough to be taxed. Today the top rate is 35 percent (actually over 42 percent when mandated phaseouts of deductions are calculated); about half of the population pays income taxes.

The current income tax progressively penalizes all the behaviors that produce higher incomes—work, savings, investment, and initiative. And whenever incomes are taxed at different rates, people will figure out ways to take advantage of the differential. They will hire lawyers, accountants, and lobbyists to find or create exemptions, exclusions, deductions, and preferential treatments for their own sources of income. The tax laws will become increasingly lengthy and complex. Today about half of all personal income is excluded from federal income taxation.

The Internal Revenue Service (IRS) is the most intrusive of all government agencies, overseeing the finances of every tax-paying citizen and corporation in America. It maintains personal records on more than 100 million Americans and requires them to submit more than a billion forms each year. It may levy fines and penalties and collect taxes on its own initiative; in disputes with the IRS, the burden of proof falls on the taxpayer, not the agency. Its 110,000 employees spend $8 billion per year reviewing tax returns, investigating taxpayers, and collecting revenue. Americans pay an additional $30 billion for the services of tax accountants and preparers, and they waste some $200 billion in hours of record keeping and computing their taxes.

We should replace the current federal income tax system with a simple flat tax that could be calculated on a postcard. The elimination of all exemptions, exclusions, deductions, and special treatments, and the replacement of current progressive tax rates with a flat 19 percent tax on all forms of income, even excluding family incomes under $25,000, would produce just as much revenue as the current complicated system. It would sweep away the nation's army of tax accountants and lawyers and lobbyists and increase national productivity by relieving taxpayers of millions of hours of record keeping and tax preparation. A flat tax could be filed on a postcard form (see below). Removing progressive rates would create incentives to work, save, and invest in America. It would lead to more rapid economic growth and improve efficiency by directing investments to their most productive uses rather than to tax avoidance. It would eliminate current incentives to underreport income, overstate exemptions, and avoid and evade taxation. Finally, by exempting a generous personal and family allowance, the flat tax would be made fair.

Form 1	Individual Wage Tax	2000
Your first name and initial (if joint return, also give spouse's name and initial)	Last name	Your social security number
Home address (number and street including apartment number or rural route)		Spouse's social security number
City, town, or post office, state, and ZIP code		Your occupation
		Spouse's occupation

1 Wages and salary	1	
2 Pension and retirement benefits	2	
3 Total compensation (*line 1 plus line 2*)	3	
4 Personal allowance		
(a) 0–$16,500 for married filing jointly	4a	
(b) 0–$9,500 for single	4b	
(c) 0–$14,000 for single head of household	4c	
5 Number of dependents, not including spouse	5	
6 Personal allowances for dependents (*line 5 multiplied by $4,500*)	6	
7 Total personal allowances (*line 4 plus line 6*)	7	
8 Taxable compensation (*line 3 less line 7, if positive; otherwise zero*)	8	
9 Tax (*19% of line 8*)	9	
10 Tax withheld by employer	10	
11 Tax due (*line 9 less line 10, if positive*)	11	
12 Refund due (*line 10 less line 9, if positive*)	12	

[a]*Pollock v. Farmer's Loan*, 158 U.S. 601 (1895).

Broken Promise
George Bush's pledge "Read my lips, no new taxes" helped him to victory in 1988. But breaking the pledge in 1990 contributed heavily to his defeat in 1992.

By 2003 the economy appeared to be in a slide. Bush argued that an "economic stimulus" package of additional tax cuts would revive the economy. He believed that federal deficits were the result of slow economic growth; tax reductions might temporarily add to deficits, but eventually the economic growth inspired by lower taxes would increase government revenues and eliminate deficits.[8]

Bush moved the Republican-controlled Congress to lower the top marginal rate to 35 percent, and restructure rates through six brackets—10, 15, 25, 28, 33, and 35 percent (see Table 16.2). And the Bush 2003 tax package also contained a variety of new credits and special treatments:

Dividends: Corporate stock dividends are to be taxed at a low 15 percent rather than at the same rate as earned income. Bush and the Republicans in Congress initially proposed eliminating all taxes on dividends. They argued that corporations already paid taxes on corporate profits, and inasmuch as dividends come out of profits, taxing them as personal income amounted to "double taxation." They also recognized that nearly one-half of all American families now own stock or mutual funds, and they hoped that this new tax break would be politically popular. The 15 percent tax rate on dividends is less than half of the top marginal rate of 35 percent on earned income.

Marriage penalty: For married couples the new law made the standard personal deduction twice that of a single person. This change corrected a flaw in the tax law that had long plagued married persons filing joint returns.

Child tax credit: The per child tax credit was raised to $1,000 (from $600). This was a politically popular change supported by many Democrats as well as Republicans.

Capital gains: Finally, the Bush tax package chipped away again at the tax on capital gains—profits from the sale of investments held at least 1 year. The capital gains tax was reduced from 20 to 15 percent, a rate less than half of the top marginal rate on earned income of 35 percent.

2010? The Bush tax cuts are scheduled to expire in 2010. Congress must act in order to continue them. But Democrats in Congress have expressed their opposition to these cuts, arguing that they primarily benefit the rich. Republicans counter that allowing these cuts to expire is actually a tax increase, and a tax increase will slow economic growth and threaten recession.

Who Pays the Federal Income Tax? The federal income tax continues to be highly progressive. Progressive rates, together with the personal and standard deductions for families and the earned income tax credit for low-income earners, combined to remove most of the income tax burden on middle- and low-income Americans. Indeed, the lower half of the nation's taxpayers pay less than 4 percent of total income taxes paid to the federal government (see Figure 16.8).

Table *16.2* **Progressive Taxation: Marginal Individual Income Tax Rates, by Income Bracket**

President George W. Bush succeeded in getting a Republican-controlled Congress to reduce the tax rate in 2001 and 2003, but these reductions are scheduled to expire in 2010.

	Before 2001	2001–2003	2003–2010
Lowest	15%	10%	10%
to	28	15	15
Highest	31	27	25
Income	36	30	28
Brackets	39.6	35	33
		38.6	35

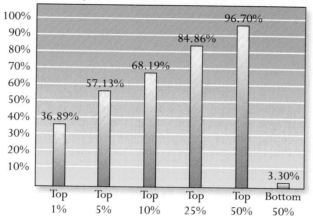

Percentage of Federal Personal Income Tax Paid by Different Income Percentiles—2004

	Top 1%	Top 5%	Top 10%	Top 25%	Top 50%	Bottom 50%
	36.89%	57.13%	68.19%	84.86%	96.70%	3.30%

Figure *16.8*

Who Pays the Federal Income Tax?

The federal income tax is steeply progressive in its effect. Almost all of it is paid by the upper half of income earners. Over two-thirds of it is paid by the top 10 percent of income earners.

Source: Joint Economic Committee, U.S. Congress, April 2007.

Even though marginal tax rates have been reduced substantially since 1980, upper-income Americans pay a much larger share of the federal income tax today than was previously the case. Although top marginal tax rates were reduced from 70 percent to 35 percent, the richest Americans are now paying more of the personal income tax even though their rates are lower than those in effect in 1980. How can one explain the fact that the rich are paying more now even though their tax rates are lower? The answer is that the incentive to earn additional income increases when tax rates decrease. Moreover, the incentive to find loopholes in the tax laws, to avoid receiving taxable income, and even to hide income (that is, to cheat), is reduced when top marginal rates are lowered.

Note that today the top 50 percent of income earners pay virtually all of the nation's personal income tax (See Figure 16.8). Indeed, the top 10 percent of income earners pay about 68 percent of all of the income taxes collected by the federal government, and the top 1 percent pay over a third of all income taxes. (This was not the case in 1980 when marginal tax rates were high. At that time the top 10 percent of income earners paid only 49 percent of all income taxes, and the top 1 percent paid only 19 percent of all income taxes.) This steep progressivity in the personal income tax means that tax reductions automatically benefit upper-income individuals.

Capital Gains Taxation   All income is *not* taxed equally under federal income tax laws. (Indeed, interest income from municipal bonds is totally tax free, encouraging many wealthy investors to put their money into these "munies.") The Tax Code distinguishes between earned income and **capital gains**—profits from the buying and selling of property, including stocks, bonds, and real estate. Currently, capital gains are taxed at a top marginal rate of 15 percent, compared to the top marginal rate of 35 percent for earned income.

Why should income earned from *working* be taxed at a higher rate than income earned from *investing*? The real estate industry, together with investment firms and stockbrokers, argue that high tax rates on capital gains discourage investment and economic growth. (But if it is true that high taxes discourage investment, high taxes must also discourage work, and both capital and labor are required for economic growth.) But the political power of investors, especially in the Republican Party, places heavy downward pressure on capital gains tax rates.

Capital gains are concentrated among the rich. More than half of all capital gains go to persons with incomes in excess of $1 million. That means that any reduction in capital gains taxes go disproportionately to the rich. The rich pay virtually all capital gains taxes.

★ **capital gains**
Profits from buying and selling property including stocks, bonds, and real estate.

A *Constitutional* Note

The Constitution and Private Property

The protection of private property was one of the principal motives in convening the Constitutional Convention of 1787. Among the powers set forth in Article I, Section 8, are the "power to lay and collect taxes, duties, imposts, and excises"; "to borrow money"; "to regulate commerce with foreign nations and among the several states and with the Indian Tribes"; "to establish . . . uniform rules of bankruptcy"; "to coin money, regulate the value thereof"; "to provide for the punishment of counterfeiting." And among the powers specifically denied to the states in Section 10 are the powers to "coin money; emit Bills of Credit; make any Thing but Gold and Silver Coin a Tender in Payment of Debts; pass any . . . Law impairing the Obligation of Contracts. . . ." In addition, the Constitution of 1787 created what we call today a *common market* or *free trade area* among the states: "No state shall . . . lay any Imports or Duties on Imports or Exports. . . ." This prevents states taxing goods or services moving across state lines or from taxing foreign commerce. In short, the Constitution places power over the economy in the hands of the national government and prevents the states from interfering with commerce. However, for well over a century the Supreme Court interpreted the Interstate Commerce Clause narrowly to include only the regulation of goods and services that actually moved across state lines. It was not until 1937 that the Court, in the important case of *National Labor Relations Board v. Jones and Loughlin Steel Co.*, extended the commerce power to include production and manufacturing which occurred *within* a state but nonetheless affected interstate commerce.

Summary
Who Gets What: The Economy

A central policy issue is deciding how much to rely on government versus the marketplace to produce and distribute goods and services. The United States is primarily a free-market economy, but federal fiscal and monetary policies exercise a strong influence over economic activity.

★ Fiscal policy—decisions about government taxing, spending, and deficits or surpluses—is decided in the president's budget recommendations and in the appropriations acts passed by Congress. Monetary policy is largely decided by the independent Federal Reserve Board.

★ The performance of the economy can be measured by GDP growth and the unemployment and inflation rates. Politically the unemployment rate may be the most important of these measures of economic performance.

★ Imports and exports grow each year as a percentage of the gross domestic product of the United States. This trend toward globalization has been fostered by U.S. participation in the World Trade Organization, the International Monetary Fund, the World Bank, the North American Free Trade Agreement, and other agreements and treaties in support of free trade. Free trade may benefit the economy as a whole, but it appears to disadvantage poorly educated, low-skilled American workers.

★ Annual federal budget deficits over 30 years led to a national debt of more than $5 trillion, an amount equal to almost half the nation's GDP. A strong economy produced budget surpluses from 1998 through 2001, but an economic slowdown combined with the effects of the "9/11" terrorist attack, and perhaps also the effects of tax cuts enacted by the Republican-controlled Congress and President George W. Bush, led to a return of annual budget deficits.

★ Tax politics centers on the question of who actually bears the burden of a tax. The individual income tax, the largest source of federal government revenue, is progressive, with higher rates levied at higher income levels. Progressive taxation is defended on the ability-to-pay principle. But half of all personal income, and a great deal of corporate income, is untaxed, owing to a wide variety of exemptions, exclusions, deductions, and special treatments on tax laws. These provisions are defended in Washington by a powerful array of interest groups.

★ The Reagan administration reduced top income tax rates from 70 to 28 percent, believing high rates discouraged work, savings, and investment, and thereby curtailed economic growth. But George Bush agreed to an increase in the top rate to 31 percent. Bill Clinton pushed Congress to raise the top rates to 39.6 percent, arguing that rich people had benefited from Reagan's "trickle down" policies and must now be forced to bear their "fair share." George W. Bush succeeded in getting two tax cut bills through Congress in 2001 and 2003. The bills lowered the top marginal income tax rate to 35 percent, eliminated the marriage penalty, increased child exemptions, and lowered the capital gain rate to 15 percent. These cuts require congressional renewal in 2010.

Key Terms

Suggested Readings

Balaam, David N., and Michael Veseth. *Introduction to International Political Economy*. 4th ed. Upper Saddle River, N.J.: Prentice Hall, 2008. Comprehensive intro to global politics and economics.

Issak, Robert A., *Globalization Gap*. Upper Saddle River, N.J.: Prentice Hall, 2005. Antiglobalization argument that rich nations get richer and poor nations get poorer as a result of international trade.

Jacobs, Laurence R., and Theda S. Skocpol, eds. *Inequality and American Democracy*. New York: Russell Sage Foundation, 2005. A series of essays describing increasing inequality in America and its political and social consequences.

Rothgeb, John M., Jr. *U.S. Trade Policy*. Washington, D.C.: CQ Press, 2001. Concise text on international trade, including history of GATT, WTO, and NAFTA.

Sowell, Thomas. *Basic Economics: A Citizen's Guide to the Economy*. New York: Basic Books, 2003. Introduction to economics with an emphasis on public policy. No jargon or equations.

Steger, Manfred B. *Globalism*. Boston: Rowman & Littlefield, 2002. The politics of pro- and antiglobalist groups, with a sharp critique of the ideology of globalism.

Wolff, Edward N. *Top Heavy* (updated edition). New York: Century Foundation, 2002. The study of the increasing inequality of wealth in United States and an argument for taxing financial wealth (bank accounts, stocks, bonds, property, houses, cars, and so on) as well as income.

Suggested Web Sites

Bureau of Economic Analysis   www.bea.gov
Source of official economic statistics, listed A–Z.

Bureau of Labor Statistics   www.bls.gov
The U.S. Department of Labor's Bureau of Labor Statistics site contains monthly information about the nation's employment rate plus a wealth of supporting data.

Center on Budget and Policy Priorities   www.cbpp.org
Data on budget items, projected costs of federal programs, and so on.

Concord Coalition   www.concordcoalition.org
Nonpartisan advocacy organization promoting fiscal responsibility and balanced federal budget.

Council of Economic Advisors (CEA)
www.whitehouse.gov/cea
Official CEA site, with latest Economic Report of the President and mostly economic indicators.

Federal Reserve System   www.federalreserve.gov
Official site of the Fed, with data on money supply, interest rates, and banking regulation.

Internal Revenue Service (IRS)   www.irs.gov
Official IRS site, with downloadable tax forms, information on tax laws, and tax statistics.

National Taxpayers Union   www.ntu.org
Advocacy organization for taxpayers "to keep what they have earned," with policy papers and data on tax burdens.

Tax Foundation Advocacy   www.taxfoundation.org
Organization devoted to making the public "tax conscious," with information, "fiscal facts," and "tax freedom day."

World Trade Organization (WTO)   www.wto.org
Official WTO site, with trade agreements, including General Agreement on Tariffs and Trade (GATT).

17 POLITICS AND SOCIAL WELFARE

> **"** Political analysis includes the class consequences of events. A class is a major social group of similar function, status, and outlook. **"**

Harold Lasswell

Chapter *Outline*

★ Power and Social Welfare
★ Poverty in the United States
★ Social Welfare Policy
★ Senior Power
★ Politics and Welfare Reform
★ Health Care in America
★ Politics and Health Care Reform

Power and Social Welfare

Social welfare policy largely determines who gets what from government—who benefits from government spending on its citizens and how much they get. This vast power has made the federal government a major *redistributor* of income from one group to another—from the working population to retirees, from the employed to the unemployed, from taxpayers to poor people. Direct payments to individuals—Social Security, welfare, pension, and other **transfer payments**—now account for about 60 percent of all federal government outlays.

When most Americans think of social welfare programs, they think of poor people. An estimated 35 million to 40 million people in the United States (11 to 15 percent of the population, or roughly one in eight Americans) have incomes below the official **poverty line**—that is, their annual cash income falls below what is required to maintain a decent standard of living (see Figure 17.1). If the approximately $1.8 trillion spent per year for social welfare were directly distributed to the nation's poor people, each poor person—man, woman, and child—would receive $45,000 per year.

Why does poverty persist in a nation where total social welfare spending is more than four times the amount needed to eliminate poverty? Because poor people are not the principal beneficiaries of social welfare spending. Most social welfare spending, including the largest programs—Social Security and Medicare—goes to the *non*-poor (see Figure 17.2). Less than one-third of federal social welfare spending is **means-tested spending**—that is, distributed on the basis of the recipient's income. The middle classes, not the poor, are the major beneficiaries of the nation's social welfare system.

Poverty in the United States

How much poverty really exists in the United States? It depends on how you define the term "poverty." The official definition used by the federal government focuses on the cash income needed to maintain a "decent standard of living." The official poverty line is only a little more than one-third of the median income of all American families. It takes into account the effects of inflation, rising each year with the rate of inflation. (For example, in 1990, the official poverty line for an urban family of four was $13,359 per year; by 2008 the poverty line had risen to about $21,200.)

Figure *17.1*

America's Poor: The Rate and Number

Roughly one in eight Americans lives below the official poverty level. The poverty rate has remained relatively stable since 1970, although the total number of people living in poverty has risen.

Source: www.census.gov/hhes/poverty00/pov00.html

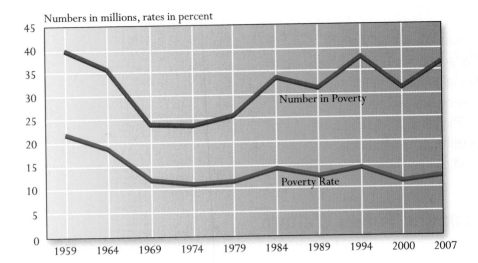

Numbers in millions, rates in percent

Number in Poverty

Poverty Rate

★ **transfer payments**
Direct payments (either in cash or in goods and/or services) by governments to individuals as part of a social welfare program, not as a result of any service or contribution rendered by the individual.

★ **poverty line**
Official standard regarding what level of annual cash income is sufficient to maintain a "decent standard of living"; those with incomes below this level are eligible for most public assistance programs.

★ **means-tested spending**
Spending for benefits that is distributed on the basis of the recipient's income.

★ **underclass**
People who have remained poor and dependent on welfare over a prolonged period of time.

Temporary Poverty   Poor people are often envisioned as a permanent "under-class" living most of their lives in poverty. But most poverty is not long term. Tracing poor families over time presents a different picture of the nature of poverty from the "snapshot" view taken in any 1 year. For example, over the last decade 11 to 15 percent of the nation's population has been officially classified as poor in any 1 year. However, only *some* poverty is persistent: about 6 to 8 percent of the population remains in poverty for more than 5 years. Thus about half of the people who are counted as poor are experiencing poverty for only a short period of time. For these temporary poor, welfare is a "safety net" that helps them through hard times.

Persistent Poverty   About half of the people on welfare rolls at any one time are *persistently poor,* that is, likely to remain on welfare for 5 or more years. For these people, welfare is a more permanent part of their lives.

Because they place a disproportionate burden on welfare resources, persistently poor people pose serious questions for social scientists and policy makers. Prolonged poverty and welfare dependency create an **underclass** that suffers from many social ills—teen pregnancy, family instability, drugs, crime, alienation, apathy, and irresponsibility.[1] Government educational, training, and jobs programs, as well as many other social service efforts, fail to benefit many of these people.

Family Structure   Poverty and welfare dependency are much more frequent among female-headed households with no husband present than among husband–wife households (see *Politics Up Close:* "Who Are the Poor?"). Traditionally, "illegitimacy" was held in check by powerful religious and social structures. But these structures weakened over time (see Figure 17.3 on page 604), and the availability of welfare cash benefits, food stamps, medical care, and government housing removed much of the economic hardship once associated with unwed motherhood. Indeed, it was sometimes argued that government welfare programs, however well meaning, ended up perpetuating poverty and social dependency. This argument inspired welfare reform in 1996 (see "Politics and Welfare Reform" later in this chapter).

The "Truly Disadvantaged"   The nation's largest cities have become the principal location of many of the social problems confronting our society—poverty,

Politics Up Close — **Who Are the Poor?**

Poverty occurs in many kinds of families and in all races and ethnic groups. However, some groups experience poverty (low income) in greater proportions than the national average (see figure).

Poverty is most common among families headed by women. The incidence of poverty among these families is four times greater than that for married couples. These women and their children constitute over two-thirds of all of the persons living in poverty in the United States. About one of every five children in the United States lives in poverty. These figures describe what has been labeled the "feminization of poverty" in the United States. Clearly, poverty is closely related to family structure. The disintegration of the traditional husband–wife family is the single most influential factor contributing to poverty today.

Blacks also experience poverty in much greater proportions than whites. Over the years, the poverty rate among blacks in the United States has been almost three times higher than the poverty rate among whites. Poverty among Hispanics is also significantly greater than among whites.

In contrast, elderly people in America experience less poverty than the non-aged. The aged are not poor, despite the popularity of the phrase "the poor and the aged." The percentage of persons over 65 years of age with low incomes is *below* the national

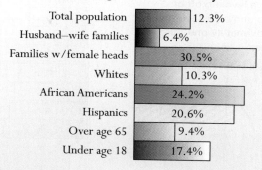

Percentage Living Below the Poverty Level

Total population	12.3%
Husband–wife families	6.4%
Families w/female heads	30.5%
Whites	10.3%
African Americans	24.2%
Hispanics	20.6%
Over age 65	9.4%
Under age 18	17.4%

average. Moreover, elderly people are much wealthier in terms of assets and have fewer expenses than the non-aged. They are more likely than younger people to own homes with paid-up mortgages. Medicare pays a large portion of their medical expenses. With fewer expenses, elderly people, even with relatively smaller cash incomes, experience poverty differently from the way a young mother with children experiences it. The declining poverty rate among elderly people is a relatively recent occurrence, however. Continuing increases in Social Security benefits over the years are largely responsible for this singular "victory" in the war against poverty

Source: U.S. Bureau of the Census, 2007.

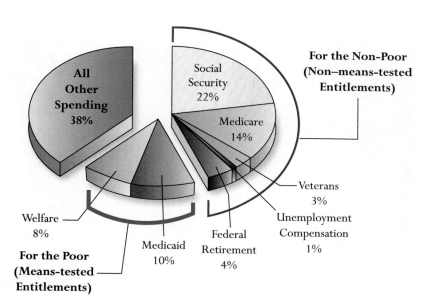

For the Non-Poor (Non–means-tested Entitlements)

All Other Spending 38%

Social Security 22%

Medicare 14%

Veterans 3%

Unemployment Compensation 1%

Federal Retirement 4%

Medicaid 10%

Welfare 8%

For the Poor (Means-tested Entitlements)

Figure *17.2*

Who's Entitled?

Welfare entitlement programs in the federal budget. Social welfare entitlement programs take up over 60 percent of the federal government's budget. But most of these payments go to the non-poor.

Source: Budget of the United States Government, 2009.

Figure *17.3*

Births to Unmarried Women

The rate of children born to unmarried women rose through 1995. Recent reports indicate a leveling off of births to unmarried women, at approximately one-third of all births.

Source: Centers for Disease Control, www.cdc.gov

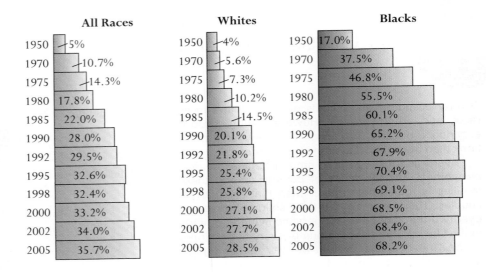

All Races		
1950	5%	
1970	10.7%	
1975	14.3%	
1980	17.8%	
1985	22.0%	
1990	28.0%	
1992	29.5%	
1995	32.6%	
1998	32.4%	
2000	33.2%	
2002	34.0%	
2005	35.7%	

Whites	
1950	4%
1970	5.6%
1975	7.3%
1980	10.2%
1985	14.5%
1990	20.1%
1992	21.8%
1995	25.4%
1998	25.8%
2000	27.1%
2002	27.7%
2005	28.5%

Blacks	
1950	17.0%
1970	37.5%
1975	46.8%
1980	55.5%
1985	60.1%
1990	65.2%
1992	67.9%
1995	70.4%
1998	69.1%
2000	68.5%
2002	68.4%
2005	68.2%

homelessness (see *Politics Up Close:* "Homelessness in America"), racial tension, drug abuse, delinquency, and crime. These problems are all made worse by their concentration in large cities. Yet the concentration of social ills in cities is a relatively recent occurrence; as late as 1970, there were higher rates of poverty in rural America than in the cities.

Why has the inner city become the locus of social problems? Some observers argue that changes in the labor market from industrial goods–producing jobs to professional, financial, and technical service–producing jobs have increasingly divided the labor market into low-wage and high-wage sectors.[2] The decline in manufacturing jobs, together with a shift in remaining manufacturing jobs and commercial (sales) jobs to the suburbs, has left inner-city residents with fewer and lower paying job opportunities. The rise in joblessness in the inner cities has in turn increased the concentration of poor people, added to the number of poor single-parent families, and increased welfare dependency.

Maria Luisa Juarez, 6, far right, kisses her niece, Glenda Beltran, 4, outside of the trailer home where they live in Earlimart, California, on Friday, June 6, 2003. Neighbor Lupe Chavez is sitting at left.

Politics Up Close   **Homelessness in America**

The most visible social welfare problem in the United States is the nation's homeless people, who wander about in the larger cities suffering from violence, exposure, alcoholism, drug abuse, and chronic mental illness.

The term "homeless" is used to describe many different situations. Many are *street people* who sleep in subways, bus stations, parks, or the streets. Some of them are temporarily traveling in search of work; some have left home for a few days or are youthful runaways; others have roamed the streets for months or years. In contrast, *sheltered homeless* people have obtained housing in shelters operated by local governments or private charities. As the number of shelters has grown over the years, the number of sheltered homeless people has also grown. But most of the sheltered homeless people come from other housing, not the streets. These are people who have recently been evicted from rental units or have previously lived with family or friends. They often include families with children; the street people are virtually all single persons.

About half of all street people are chronic alcohol and drug abusers; an additional one-fourth to one-third are mentally ill. Moreover, homeless people who are alcohol and drug abusers and/or mentally ill are by far the most likely to remain on the streets for long periods of time.

The current plight of homeless people is partly a result of various "reforms" in public policy, notably the "deinstitutionalization" of care for the mentally ill and the now recognized rights of individuals to refuse treatment; the "decriminalization" of vagrancy and public intoxication; and the push for urban renewal, which has eliminated many low-rent apartments and cheap hotels.

Deinstitutionalization, a policy advanced by mental health care professionals and social welfare activists in the 1960s and 1970s after the introduction of new psychotropic drug therapies, has resulted in the release of all but the most dangerous mental patients from state-run mental hospitals.

Decriminalization of public intoxication has also added to the numbers of street people. Involuntary confinement of substance abusers is now banned

A family eating a Christmas Eve lunch for the needy and homeless, prepared by a Washington, D.C., mission.

unless a person is arrested while possessing an illegal substance or is found in court to be "a danger to himself or others," which means a person must commit a serious act of violence before the courts will intervene.

Community-based care has failed for many substance abusers and chronically mentally ill street people. Many are "uncooperative"; they are isolated from society; they have no family members or doctors or counselors to turn to for help. The nation's vast social welfare system provides them little help. They cannot handle forms, appointments, or interviews; the welfare bureaucracy is intimidating. Lacking a permanent address, many receive no Social Security, welfare, or disability checks. Shelters provided by private charities, such as the Salvation Army, by churches, or by city governments are more helpful to the temporarily homeless than to chronic alcohol or drug abusers or mentally ill people. Few shelters offer treatment for alcohol or drug abusers, and many refuse disruptive people.

Comparing Social Welfare Systems

Where the Money Goes . . .

★ **social insurance programs**
Social welfare programs to which beneficiaries have made contributions so that they are entitled to benefits regardless of their personal wealth.

★ **public assistance programs**
Those social welfare programs for which no contributions are required and only those living in poverty (by official standards) are eligible; includes food stamps, Medicaid, and Family Assistance.

★ **entitlements**
Any social welfare program for which there are eligibility requirements, whether financial or contributory.

★ **Social Security**
Social insurance program composed of the Old Age and Survivors Insurance program, which pays benefits to retired workers who have paid into the program and their dependents and survivors, and the Disability Insurance program, which pays benefits to disabled workers and their families.

★ **unemployment compensation**
Social insurance program that temporarily replaces part of the wages of workers who have lost their jobs.

Social Welfare Policy

Public welfare has been a recognized responsibility of government in English-speaking countries for many centuries. As far back as the Poor Relief Act of 1601, the English Parliament provided workhouses for the "able-bodied poor" (the unemployed) and poorhouses for widows and orphans, elderly and handicapped people.[3] Today, nearly one-third of the U.S. population receives some form of government benefits: Social Security, Medicare or Medicaid, disability insurance, unemployment compensation, government employee retirement, veterans' benefits, food stamps, school lunches, job training, public housing, or cash public assistance payments (see Table 17.1). More than half of all families in the United States include at least one person who receives a government check. Thus the "welfare state" now encompasses a very large part of our society.

The major social welfare programs can be classified as either **social insurance** or **public assistance**. This distinction is an important one that has on occasion become a major political issue. If the beneficiaries of a government program are required to have made contributions to it before claiming any of its benefits, and if they are entitled to the benefits regardless of their personal wealth—as in Social Security and Medicare—then the program is said to be financed on the social insurance principle. If the program is financed out of general tax revenues and if recipients are required to show that they are poor before claiming its benefits—as in Temporary Assistance to Needy Families, Supplemental Security Income, and Medicaid—then the program is said to be financed on the public assistance principle. Public assistance programs are generally labeled as "welfare."

Entitlements   Entitlements are government benefits for which Congress has set eligibility criteria—age, income, retirement, disability, unemployment, and so on. Everyone who meets the criteria is "entitled" to the benefit.

Most of the nation's major entitlement programs were launched either in the New Deal years of the 1930s under President Franklin D. Roosevelt (Social Security, Unemployment Compensation, Aid to Families with Dependent Children, now called Temporary Assistance to Needy Families, and Aid to Aged, Blind, and Disabled, now called Supplemental Security Income) or in the Great Society years of the 1960s under President Lyndon B. Johnson (food stamps, Medicare, Medicaid).

Social Security   Begun during the Depression (1935), **Social Security** is now the largest of all entitlements; it comprises two distinct programs. The Old Age and Survivors Insurance program provides monthly cash benefits to retired workers and their dependents and to survivors of insured workers. The Disability Insurance program provides monthly cash benefits for disabled workers and their dependents. An automatic, annual cost-of-living adjustment (COLA) for both programs matches any increase in the annual inflation rate.

With more than 48 million beneficiaries, Social Security is the single largest spending program in the federal budget. The program is funded by a payroll tax on employers and employees. Retirees can begin receiving benefits at age 62 (full benefits at age 65), regardless of their personal wealth or income.

Unemployment Compensation   **Unemployment compensation** temporarily replaces part of the wages of workers who lose their jobs involuntarily and helps stabilize the economy during recessions. The U.S. Department of Labor oversees the system, but states administer their own programs, with latitude within federal guidelines to define weekly benefits and other program features. Benefits are funded by a combination of federal and state unemployment taxes on employers.

Table *17.1*   Who Gets Welfare?: Beneficiaries of Major Federal Social Welfare Programs

Social Insurance Programs	Beneficiaries (millions)	Public Assistance Programs	Beneficiaries (millions)
Social Security		**Cash Aid**	
Retirement	33.5	Assistance to Families	4.5
Survivors	6.7	Supplemental Security Income (SSI)	7.0
Disabled	8.3	**Medical Care**	
Total	47.3	Medicaid	37.5
Unemployment Compensation		SCHIP (State Children's Health Ins. Prog.)	9.0
Total	7.9	**Food Benefits**	
Government and Military Retirement		Food stamps	25.7
Military	3.5	School lunches	29.6
Federal employees	2.4	Women, Infants, Children (WIC)	8.0
State and local	14.1	Child and adult care food	3.1
Medicare		**Housing Benefit**	
Total	39.6	Total	3.3
		Education Aid	
		Pell Grants	5.2
		Opportunity Grants	1.3
		Loans	3.5
		Head Start	0.9
		Work Study	0.8
		Job Training	
		Total	0.8
		Energy Assistance	
		Total	4.6
		Earned Income Tax Credit	
		Total	19.1

Source: U.S. Bureau of the Census, *Statistical Abstract of the United States,* 2007, pp. 106, 352, 353, 357, 362.

Supplemental Security Income   Supplemental Security Income (SSI) is a means-tested, federally administered income assistance program that provides monthly cash payments to needy elderly (65 or older), blind, and disabled people. A loose definition of "disability"—including alcoholism, drug abuse, and attention deficiency among children—has led to a rapid growth in the number of SSI beneficiaries.

Family Assistance   Family Assistance, officially Temporary Assistance to Needy Families (formerly AFDC, or Aid to Families with Dependent Children), is a grant program to enable the states to assist needy families. States now operate the program and define "need"; they set their own benefit levels and establish (within federal guidelines) income and resource limits. Prior to welfare reform in 1996, AFDC was a *federal* entitlement program. The federal government now mandates a 2-year limit on benefits, a 5-year lifetime limit, and other requirements (see "Politics and Welfare Reform" later in this chapter).

Food Stamps   The **Food Stamp** program provides low-income household members with coupons that they can redeem for enough food to provide a minimal

★ **Supplemental Security Income (SSI)**
Public assistance program that provides monthly cash payments to the needy elderly (65 or older), blind, and disabled.

★ **Family Assistance**
Public assistance program that provides monies to the states for their use in helping needy families with children.

★ **Food Stamp program**
Public assistance program that provides low-income households with coupons redeemable for enough food to provide a minimal nutritious diet.

The Origins of Federal Welfare Programs

Most of America's social welfare programs began in either the Great Depression of the 1930s or the War on Poverty in the 1960s. At the outset of the Depression, millions of unemployed Americans, like the New Yorkers in a bread line in the photo at left, had only private charities to turn to for survival. The War on Poverty of the 1960s was a reaction to the persistence of extreme poverty, like that of the rural family in the photograph at right in the midst of the prosperity that followed World War II.

nutritious diet. The program is overseen by the federal government but administered by the states.

★ **Earned Income Tax Credit (EITC)**
Tax refunds in excess of tax payments for low-income workers.

Earned Income Tax Credit   The **Earned Income Tax Credit** (EITC) is designed to assist the working poor. It not only refunds their payroll taxes but also provides larger refunds than they actually paid during the previous tax year. Thus, the EITC is in effect a "negative" income tax. It was originally passed by a Democratic-controlled Congress and signed by Republican President Gerald Ford in 1975. Over the years EITC payments have increased substantially. However, the program applies only to those poor who actually work and who apply for the credit when filing their income tax.

★ **Medicaid**
Public assistance program that provides health care to the poor.

Medicaid   Medicaid is a joint federal-state program providing health services to low-income Americans. Most Medicaid spending goes to elderly and nonelderly disabled people. However, women and children receiving benefits under TANF automatically qualify for Medicaid, as does anyone who gets cash assistance under SSI. States can also offer Medicaid to the "medically needy"— those who face crushing medical costs but whose income or assets are too high to qualify for SSI or Family Assistance, including pregnant women and young children not receiving Family Assistance. Medicaid also pays for long-term nursing home care, but only after beneficiaries have used up virtually all of their savings and income.

✓ *Think* Again

Should all retirees receive Social Security benefits regardless of their personal wealth or income?

Senior Power

Senior citizens are the most politically powerful age group in the population. They constitute 28 percent of the voting-age population, but, more important, because of their high voter turnout rates, they constitute more than one-third of the voters on election day. Persons over age 65 average a 68 percent turnout rate in presidential elections and a 61 percent rate in congressional elections. By comparison, those aged 18–21 have a turnout rate of 36 percent in presidential elections and 19 percent in congressional elections, so the voting power of senior citizens is twice that of young people. Moreover, seniors are well represented in Washington; the American Association of Retired Persons (AARP) is the nation's largest organized interest group (see *Politics Up Close*: "AARP: The Nation's Most Powerful Interest Group" in Chapter 9). No elected officials can afford to offend seniors, and seniors strongly support generous Social Security benefits.

The Aged in the Future

The baby boom from 1945 to 1960 produced a large generation of people who crowded schools and colleges in the 1960s and 1970s and encountered stiff competition for jobs in the 1980s. During the baby boom, women averaged 3.5 births during their lifetime. Today, the birthrate is only 1.4 births per woman, less than the 2.1 figure required to keep the population from declining. (Current U.S. population growth is a product of immigration.) The baby-boom generation will be retiring beginning in 2010, and by 2030 they will constitute more than 80 million people, 20 percent of the population (see Figure 17.4). Changes in lifestyle—less smoking, more exercise, better weight control—may increase the aged population even more. Medical advances may also extend life expectancy.

The Generational Compact

The framers of the Social Security Act of 1935 created a "trust fund" with the expectation that a reserve would be built up from social insurance taxes paid by working persons. The reserve would earn interest, and the interest and principal would be used in later years to pay benefits. In theory, Social Security is an insurance program. (Payments are recorded by name and Social Security number.) Many people believe that they get back what they paid during their working years. Reality, however, has proven much different.

Social Security is actually financed on a pay-as-you-go system, rather than a reserve system. Today, the income from all social insurance premiums (taxes) pays for current Social Security benefits. This generation of workers is paying for the benefits of the last generation, and this generation must hope that its future benefits will be financed by the next generation of workers. Taxing current workers to pay benefits to current retirees may be viewed as a compact between generations. Each generation of workers in effect agrees to pay benefits to an earlier generation of retirees and expects the next generation will pay for its retirement.

The Rising Dependency Ratio

Because current workers must pay for the benefits of current retirees and other beneficiaries, the **dependency ratio** becomes an important component of evaluating the future of Social Security. The dependency ratio for Social Security is the number of recipients as a percentage of the number of contributing workers. Americans are living longer and increasing the dependency ratio. A child born in 1935, when the Social Security system was created, could expect to live only to age 61, 4 years *less* than the retirement age of 65. The life expectancy of a child born in 1990 is 74 years, 9 years beyond the retirement age. In the early years of Social Security, there were ten workers supporting each retiree—a dependency ratio of 10 to 1. But today, as the U.S. population has grown older—due to lower birthrates and longer life spans—the dependency ratio is closer to two workers for each retiree.

Social Security Taxes

Social Security taxes are levied on workers' earnings. Combined Social Security and Medicare taxes amount to 15.3 percent of wage earnings. (The Social Security tax is 12.4 percent and the Medicare tax is 2.9

Colin O'Leary, front, joins about 60 protesters chanting outside Charles Schwab Corp.'s annual stockholder meeting on Thursday, May 19, 2005, in San Francisco. O'Leary and the other demonstrators were calling on Schwab to stop its support for privatizing Social Security.

 Think Again

Do you believe the Social Security system will still be solvent when you retire?

 Think Again

Should the government pay for nursing home care without forcing beneficiaries to use up all their savings and income?

★ **dependency ratio**
In the Social Security system, the number of recipients as a percentage of the number of contributing workers.

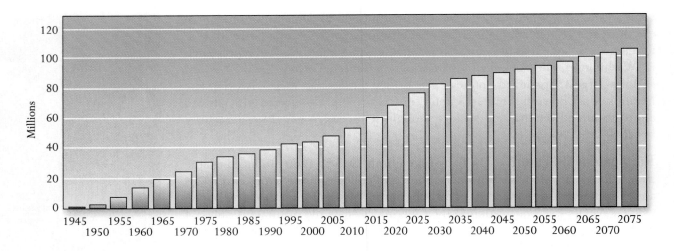

Figure *17.4*   The Aging of America: The Growing Number of Social Security Beneficiaries

Millions of Old-Age, Survivors, and Disability Insurance (OASDI) recipients, 1945–2075. As the "baby boom" generation (persons born from 1945 to 1960) ages, the burden on the Social Security system increases.

Note: Numbers for 2000 onwards are estimates based on intermediate assumptions.

Source: "2000 Annual Report." March 2000, Board of Trustees, Federal Old-Age and Survivors Insurance and Disability Insurance Trust Funds.

★ **COLAs**
Annual cost-of-living adjustments mandated by law in Social Security and other welfare benefits.

percent.) Half is paid directly by the employer, and half is deducted from the employees' check as the FICA deduction. All wage income is subject to the Medicare tax, but wage income above a certain level—$102,010 in 2008—is not subject to Social Security taxes. This wage limit increases every year.

Cost-of-Living Increases   Currently, the annual Social Security cost-of-living adjustments (**COLAs**) are based on the Consumer Price Index, which estimates the cost of all consumer items each year. These costs include home buying, mortgage interest, child rearing, and other costs that many retirees do not confront. Moreover, most workers do not have the same protection against inflation as retirees; average wage rates do not always match increases in the cost of living. Hence, over the years, COLAs have improved the economic well-being of Social Security recipients relative to all American workers.

Wealthy Retirees   Social Security benefits are paid to *all* eligible retirees, regardless of whatever other income they may receive. There is no means test for Social Security benefits. As a result, large numbers of affluent Americans receive government checks each month. They paid into Social Security during their working years, and they can claim these checks as an entitlement under the social insurance principle. But currently their benefits far exceed their previous payments.

Because elderly people experience less poverty than today's workers (see *Politics Up Close:* "Who Are the Poor?"on page 603) and possess considerably more wealth, Social Security benefits constitute a "negative" redistribution of income—that is, a transfer of income from poorer to richer people. The elderly are generally better off than the people supporting them.

"Saving" Social Security   The income from Social Security taxes *currently* exceeds payments to beneficiaries—that is, it produces a "surplus." But Social Security taxes are lumped together with general tax revenues in federal budgets; the Social Security surplus is used to hide a portion of overall federal deficits. Democrats and Republicans alike have promised to create a "lock box" and not "dip into Social Security" in order to fund current programs. But the Social Security "trust fund" is merely an accounting gimmick: current Social Security taxes are used to fund current government spending, and future retirement benefits will be paid from future revenues.

The Social Security system appears to be adequately financed for the next several decades. (In 1983 a National Commission on Social Security Reform, appointed by President Reagan, recommended an increase in Social Security taxes and a gradual increase in the retirement age from 65 to 67 beginning in 2000. Congress adopted these recommendations.) But with the aging of the population and the resulting increases in the dependency ratio expected in the twenty-first century, Social Security will become a heavy burden on working Americans.

"Saving" Social Security is a popular political slogan in Washington. But agreement on exactly how to reform the system continues to evade lawmakers. In theory, Congress could reform Social Security by limiting COLAs to the true increases in the cost of living for retirees, or it could introduce means tests to deny benefits to high-income retirees. But politically these reforms are very unlikely. Yet another approach to reform is to allow the Social Security trust fund to invest in the private stock market with the expectation that stock values will increase over time. But if stock market investment decisions were made by the government itself, presumably the Social Security Administration, controversies would be bound to arise over these decisions. And critics object to the idea of the government making private investment decisions for Americans. Another reform frequently recommended is to allow American workers to deposit all or part of their Social Security payroll tax into an individual retirement account to buy securities of their own choosing. But such a plan would expose those individuals to the risk of bad investment decisions. (See *Controversy:* "How Should We Reform Social Security?")

Politics and Welfare Reform

Americans confront a clash of values in welfare policy. Americans are a generous people; they believe government should aid those who are unable to take care of themselves, especially children, disabled people, and elderly people. But Americans are worried that welfare programs encourage dependency, undermine the work ethic, and contribute to illegitimate births and the breakup of families. Although social insurance programs (Social Security, Medicare, and Unemployment Compensation) are politically popular and enjoy the support of large numbers of active beneficiaries, public assistance programs (Family Assistance, SSI, Medicaid) are far less popular. A variety of controversies surround welfare policy in the United States.

Conflict Over What Causes Poverty   Americans have different ideas about what causes poverty (see Table 17.2). Some attribute poverty to characteristics of individuals—drug use, declining moral values, lack of motivation. Others blame the economy—too many part-time and low-wage jobs and a shortage of good jobs. Still others place blame on the welfare system itself. Indeed, prior to welfare reform in 1996, some scholars argued that government itself was a major cause of poverty—that social welfare programs destroyed incentives to work, encouraged

Think Again

Do you think government welfare programs perpetuate poverty?

Think Again

Should the states rather than the federal government decide about welfare policy?

Think Again

Should there be a time limit on how long a person can receive welfare payments?

The Evolution of Social Welfare Policy

Controversy

How Should We Reform Social Security?

Politicians want to make Social Security reform as pain-less as possible. The topic of Social Security reform in Washington is so sensitive that Congress has been unable to adopt any long-term reform proposals since 1983, when a presidential commission recommended a gradual increase in the retirement age. But most Ameri-cans do recognize the seriousness of the problem. Polls show that fewer than half of the American public believes the Social Security system will have money to provide benefits when they retire. Yet despite their skepticism about the future of Social Security, relatively few Americans save enough for retirement.

Specific proposals for reforming Social Security receive mostly negative support among the general public (see below). Americans do not want to cut Social Security benefits, or increase taxes, or raise the eligibility age. Support for allowing individuals to invest part of their Social Security taxes in pri-vate investments (stocks or bonds) has actually declined in recent years despite President George Bush's active support at the proposal. The reform proposals that get majority support are those that "tax the rich."

	Favor	Oppose
Changing Social Security from a system where the government collects the taxes to a system where individuals invest some of their payroll tax contributions themselves	40%	54%
Raise the retirement age	31	68
Reduce the rate of growth in benefits for future retirees	30	68
Increase the amount employers and workers pay in taxes	40	59
Increase the eligibility age to receive full benefits	35	63
Reduce benefits for people currently under age 65	29	67
Increase Social Security taxes for all workers	37	60
Limit benefits for wealthy retirees	68	29
Require higher income workers to pay taxes on all of their wages	67	30

Source: Various polls reported at Public Agenda, 2007, www.publicagenda.org

teenage pregnancies, and made people dependent on government handouts.[4] They argued that the combination of cash payments, food stamps, Medicaid, and housing assistance unintentionally discouraged people from forming families, taking low-paying jobs, and, perhaps, with hard work and perseverance, gradu-ally pulling themselves and their children into the mainstream of American life.

There is little doubt that poverty and welfare dependency are closely related to family structure. As noted earlier, poverty is much more frequent among female-headed households with no husband present than among husband–wife households. As births to unmarried women rose, poverty and social dependency increased. (In 1970 only 11 percent of births were to unmarried women; by 2005 this figure had risen to 37 percent of all births, 68 percent of African American births, and 46 percent of Hispanic births.) The troubling question was whether the welfare system ameliorated some of the hardships confronting unmarried mothers and their children, or whether it actually contributed to social depend-ency by mitigating the consequences of unmarried motherhood. For example, were teenage pregnancies more common because teenagers knew that govern-ment benefits were available to young mothers and their children?

Table *17.2*   Public Opinion: What Causes Poverty?

Americans have different ideas about what causes poverty.

Question: For each of the following, please tell me if this is a major cause of poverty, a minor cause of poverty, or not a cause at all.

	Major	Minor	Not a Cause	Don't Know
Drug abuse	70%	24%	5%	2%
Medical bills	58%	32%	7%	2%
Decline in moral values	57%	29%	12%	3%
Too many part-time or low-wage jobs	54%	32%	10%	4%
Too many single parents	54%	32%	12%	2%
Poor people lacking motivation	52%	35%	9%	4%
Poor public schools	47%	38%	13%	4%
The welfare system	46%	37%	11%	7%
A shortage of jobs	34%	41%	23%	2%

Source: Kaiser Family Foundation, poll reported in *Public Agenda,* 2007, www.publicagenda.org

The Politics of Welfare Reform

A political consensus grew over the years that long-term social dependency had to be addressed in welfare policy. The fact that most non-poor mothers work convinced many *liberals* that welfare mothers had no special claim to stay at home with their children. And many *conservatives* acknowledged that some transitional assistance—education, job training, continued health care, and day care for children—might be necessary to move welfare mothers into the workforce.

Although President Clinton had once promised "to end welfare as we know it," it was the Republican-controlled Congress elected in 1994 that proceeded to do so. The Republican-sponsored welfare reform bill ended the 60-year-old federal "entitlement" for low-income families with children—the venerable AFDC program. In its place the Republicans devised a "devolution" of responsibility to the states through federal block grants—**Temporary Assistance to Needy Families**—lump sum allocations to the states for cash welfare payments, with benefits and eligibility requirements decided by the states. Conservatives in Congress imposed tough-minded "strings" to state aid, including a 2-year limit on continuing cash benefits and a 5-year lifetime limit; a "family cap" that would deny additional cash benefits to women already on welfare who bear more children; the denial of cash welfare to unwed parents under 18 years of age unless they live with an adult and attend school. President Clinton vetoed the first welfare reform bill passed by Congress in early 1996, but as the presidential election neared, he reversed himself and signed the Welfare Reform Act, establishing the Temporary Assistance to Needy Families program. Food stamps, SSI, and Medicaid were continued as federal "entitlements" (see *Politics Up Close:* "Is Welfare Reform Working?").

More Reform?

Public sentiment is strongly behind the concept of working in exchange for receiving public assistance. It is unlikely that public policy will ever return to welfare as we used to know it.[5] But Democrats and liberals and Republicans and conservatives continue to argue over additional reforms. Democrats and liberals argue for expanded subsidized day care, increases in the minimum wage, spending more on medical care for the poor, and making food stamps more available. Republicans and conservatives propose toughening the work requirements

DEBATE

Welfare Reform

★ **Temporary Assistance to Needy Families**

Welfare reform program replacing federal cash entitlement with grants to the states for welfare recipients.

"As far as I'm concerned, they can do what they want with the minimum wage, just as long as they keep their hands off the maximum wage."

Source: © *The New Yorker Collection* *1989.* Robert Mankoff from cartoonbank.com. All rights reserved.

Up Close **Is Welfare Reform Working?**

Welfare reform, officially Temporary Assistance to Needy Families, was passed by Congress in 1996; its provisions took effect in 1997. By early 1998 the Clinton administration, as well as Republican congressional sponsors of welfare reform, was declaring it a success.

The number of cash welfare recipients in the nation has dropped below 5 million—the lowest number in more than 25 years. Only about 2 percent of Americans are now on cash welfare—the smallest proportion since 1970. No doubt some of this decline is attributable to growth of the economy: declines in welfare rolls began *before* Congress passed its welfare reform law, and some decline may have occurred without reform. Many states had initiated their own reforms under "waivers" from the federal government even before Congress acted.

All states have now developed work programs for welfare recipients. Applicants for welfare benefits are now generally required to enter job-search programs, to undertake job training, and to accept jobs or community service positions.

Yet, although nearly everyone agrees that getting people off welfare rolls and onto payrolls is the main goal of reform, there are major obstacles to the achievement of this goal. First of all, a substantial portion (perhaps 25 to 40 percent) of long-term welfare recipients have handicaps—physical disabilities, chronic illnesses, learning disabilities, alcohol or drug abuse problems—that prevent them from holding a full-time job. Many long-term recipients have no work

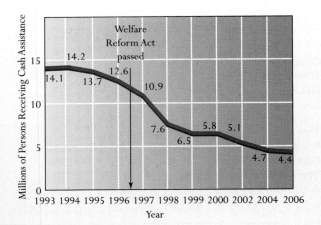

Source: Department of Health and Human Services, 2006.

experience (perhaps 40 percent), and two-thirds of them did not graduate from high school. Almost half have three or more children, making day-care arrangements a major obstacle. It is unlikely that any counseling, education, job training, or job placement programs could ever succeed in getting these people into productive employment.

Early studies of people who left the welfare rolls following welfare reform suggest that over half and perhaps as many as three-quarters have found work, although most at minimum or near-minimum wages.[a]

[a]*Governing* (April 1999), pp. 21–26.

Programs such as this Riverside "Jobs Club" in California try to help welfare recipients find jobs in the wake of reforms intended to reduce welfare dependency.

for cash welfare assistance and closing many of the loopholes that allow states to continue paying benefits to persons whose time limit has expired.

Health Care in America

The United States spends more of its resources on health care than any other nation (see *Compared to What?*: "Health and Health Care Costs in Advanced Democracies"). Nevertheless, the United States ranks well below other advanced democracies in key measures of the health of its people such as life expectancy and infant death rate. Moreover, unlike most other advanced democracies, which make provision for health care for all citizens, Americans have no guarantee of access to medical care. In short, the American health care system is the most expensive and least universal in its coverage in the world.

The Health of Americans   Historically, most reductions in death rates have resulted from public health and sanitation improvements, including immunizations, clean public water supplies, sanitary sewage disposal, improved diets, and increased standards of living. Many of the leading causes of death today (see Table 17.3), including heart disease, cancer, stroke, and AIDS, are closely linked to heredity, personal habits and lifestyles (smoking, eating, drinking, exercise, stress, sexual practices), and the physical environment—factors over which doctors and hospitals have no direct control. Thus some argue that the greatest contribution to better health is likely to be found in altered personal habits and lifestyles rather than in more medical care. Thanks to improved health care habits as well as breakthroughs in medical technology, Americans are living longer than ever before.

Access to Care   A major challenge in health care is to extend coverage to all Americans. Today, about 85 percent of the nation's population is covered by either government or private health insurance. Government pays about 43 percent of all health care costs—through Medicare for the aged, Medicaid for the poor, and other government programs, including military and veterans' care.

Comparing Health Systems

Should government provide health care insurance for all Americans?

Table *17.3*   Leading Causes of Death in America

Deaths from all causes are declining over time in relation to the population. Heart disease and cancer remain the most common cause of death.

	Deaths per 100,000 Population per Year				
	1960	**1970**	**1980**	**1990**	**2006**
All causes	954.7	945.3	883.4	863.8	816.7
Heart disease	369.0	362.0	336.0	368.3	293.8
Stroke (cerebrovascular)	108.0	101.9	75.5	57.9	51.8
Cancer	149.2	162.8	183.9	203.2	187.4
Accidents	52.3	56.4	46.7	37.0	37.0
Pneumonia/Influenza	37.3	30.9	24.1	32.0	35.9
Diabetes	16.7	18.9	15.5	19.2	24.8
Alzheimers	N.A.	N.A.	N.A.	N.A.	22.4
AIDS	N.A.	N.A.	N.A.	17.6	4.4
Suicide	10.6	11.6	11.9	12.4	10.8
Homicide	4.7	8.3	10.7	10.0	5.7

Source: Centers for Disease Control, www.cdc.gov/nchs/data

Compared to *What?*

Health and Health Care Costs in Advanced Democracies

Americans spend more than any other nation in the world for health care (see figure). Few people object to heavy spending for health care if they get their money's worth. But cross-national comparisons of health statistics indicate that Americans on the average are less healthy than citizens in other advanced democracies. The United States ranks *below* many other advanced nations in life expectancy and infant death rates—two commonly used measures of national health.

The United States offers some of the most advanced and sophisticated medical care in the world, attracting patients from the countries that rank well ahead of it in various health measures. The United States is the locus of some of the most advanced medical research, attracting medical researchers from throughout the world. But the high quality of medical care available in the United States, combined with the poor health statistics of the general public, suggests that the nation's health care problems center more on access to care and education and prevention of health problems than on the quality of care available.

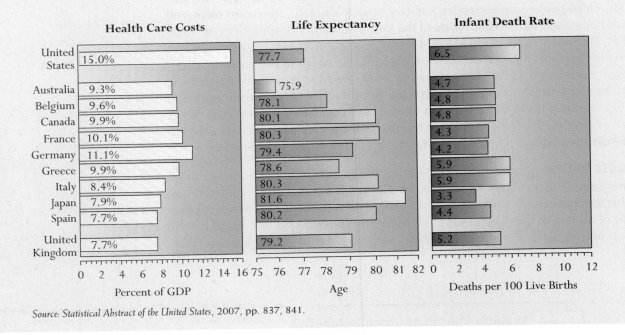

Source: *Statistical Abstract of the United States*, 2007, pp. 837, 841.

Private insurance pays for about 40 percent of the nation's health costs; the remaining 17 percent is paid directly by patients (see Figure 17.5).

But about 15 percent of the U.S. population—an estimated 45 million Americans—have *no* medical insurance. These include workers and their dependents whose employers do not offer a health insurance plan, as well as unemployed people who are not eligible for Medicare or Medicaid. People who lack health insurance may postpone or go without needed medical care or may be denied medical care by hospitals and physicians in all but emergency situations. Confronted with serious illness, they may be obliged to impoverish themselves in order to become eligible for Medicaid. Any unpaid medical bills must be absorbed by hospitals or shifted to paying patients and their insurance companies.

Coverage Gaps   Even people who *do* have health insurance often confront serious financial problems in obtaining medical care owing to inadequate coverage. Medicare, like most private insurance plans, requires patients to pay some

Who Pays the Bill?
Personal Health Care Spending by Source of Funds, 2005.

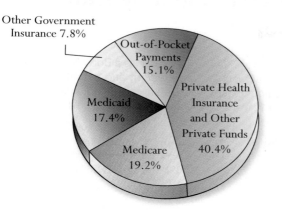

Figure *17.5*

Who Pays the Bill?: Personal Health Care Spending by Source of Funds, 2005.

Government insurance programs, primarily Medicare and Medicaid, pay the largest proportion of the nation's total health care bill; private health insurance payments follow closely.

Source: "National Health Expenditures Tables." Health Care Financing Administration.

initial charges called **deductibles**. The purpose of deductibles is to discourage unnecessary treatment. Patients must also make up any difference between doctors' actual charges and the rates allowed by their insurance plans. Indeed, only an estimated half of the doctors in the nation accept Medicare rates as payment in full. In addition, Medicare and many private insurance plans do not pay for eyeglasses, hearing aids, or routine physical examinations.

More important, perhaps, Medicare does *not* pay for long-term care or catastrophic illness. Medicare covers only the first 60 days of hospitalization; it covers nursing home care for 100 days only if the patient is sent there from a hospital. Yet as the number and proportion of the elderly population grows in the United States (80 years and over is the fastest growing age group in the nation), the need for long-term nursing home care grows. Medicaid assistance to needy people is paid for nursing home patients, but middle-class people cannot qualify for Medicaid without first "spending down" their savings. Long-term nursing home care threatens their assets and their children's inheritance. Private insurance policies covering long-term care are said to be too expensive. So senior citizen groups have lobbied heavily for long-term nursing home care to be paid for by taxpayers under Medicare.

★ **deductibles**
Initial charges in insurance plans, paid by beneficiaries.

Health Care Costs
No system of health care can provide as much as people will use. Anyone whose health and life may be at stake will want the most thorough diagnostic testing, the most constant care, the most advanced treatment. Sworn to preserve life, doctors, too, want the most advanced diagnostic and treatment facilities available for their patients. Under conditions of uncertainty in a medical situation—and there is always some uncertainty—physicians are trained to seek more consultations, run more tests, and try new therapeutic approaches. Any tendency for doctors to limit testing and treatment is countered by the threat of malpractice suits; it is always easier to order one more test or procedure than to risk even the tiniest chance that failing to do so will some day be cause for a court suit. So in the absence of restraints, both patients and doctors will push up the costs of health care. Currently, health care costs appear to have stabilized at about 15 percent of the nation's GDP.

Managed Care Controversies
Both private and government insurers have made efforts to counter rising costs through **managed care**. Private insurers have negotiated discounts with groups of physicians and with hospitals—**preferred provider organizations (PPOs)**—and have implemented rules to guide physicians

★ **managed care**
Programs designed to keep health care costs down by the establishment of strict guidelines regarding when and what diagnostic and therapeutic procedures should be administered to patients under various circumstances.

★ **preferred provider organizations (PPOs)**
Groups of hospitals and physicians who have joined together to offer their services to private insurers at a discount.

Controversy

Are Americans Too Fat?

Obesity is a contributing cause to many health problems, including heart disease, stroke, and diabetes. Over two-thirds of Americans are classified as "overweight," and one-third are classified as "obese." The U.S. Center for Disease Control uses a Body Mass Index (BMI) that adjusts for body weight and height in order to determine obesity. The BMI is calculated as weight in kilograms divided by height in meters squared.

	Underweight	Healthy weight	Overweight	Obese
Total	1.8%	32.9%	33.7%	31.6%
Sex				
Male	1.5	28.5	39.2	30.7
Female	2.0	36.6	28.7	32.8
Race				
White male	1.5	27.8	29.6	31.1
White female	2.2	39.2	28.4	30.2
Black male	NA	31.3	33.7	33.3
Black female	NA	18.3	22.3	53.0

Source: U.S. National Center for Health Statistics, *Statistical Abstract of the United States*, 2007, p. 131.

★ **health maintenance organizations (HMOs)**
Health care provider groups that provide a stipulated list of services to patients for a fixed fee that is usually substantially lower than such care would otherwise cost.

★ **Medicare**
Social insurance program that provides health care insurance to elderly and disabled people.

about when patients should and should not receive costly diagnostic and therapeutic procedures. Medicare no longer pays hospitals based on costs incurred; instead it pays fixed fees based on primary and secondary diagnoses at the time of admission. Both government and private insurers have encouraged the expansion of **health maintenance organizations (HMOs)**, groups that promise to provide a stipulated list of services to patients for a fixed fee and that are able to provide care at lower total costs than can other providers. Today over 30 percent of Americans are enrolled in HMOs.

But many of the efforts by both private insurers and governments to control costs have created new problems. These include cost-control regulations and restrictions that add to administrative costs and create a mountain of paperwork for physicians and hospitals, and frustration and anger among both health care workers and patients. Doctors and hospitals argue that the *administrative* costs imposed by these cost-control measures far exceed whatever savings are achieved. Patients and doctors complain that preapproval of treatment by insurance companies often removes medical decisions from the physician and patient and places them in the hands of insurance company employees.

Medicare   Medicare is a two-part program that helps elderly and disabled people pay acute-care (as opposed to long-term-care) health costs. Hospital insurance (Part A) helps pay the cost of hospital inpatient and skilled nursing care. Anyone 65 or older who is eligible for Social Security is automatically eligible for Part A benefits. Also eligible are people under 65 who receive Social Security disability or railroad retirement disability and people who have end-stage kidney disease. Part A is financed primarily by the 1.45 percent payroll tax collected with Social Security (FICA) withholding. Supplemental Medical Insurance (Part B) is an

Figure *17.6*

Projected Medicare Costs on the Rise

Medicare costs are rising dramatically with the aging of the baby boom generation and advances in Medical care.

Source: Congressional Budget Office.

* Includes prescription drug benefit costs.

optional add-on taken by virtually all those covered by Part A. It pays 80 percent of covered doctor and outpatient charges. Small monthly premiums are deducted from Social Security benefit checks to finance it.

Medicare has tried to control rising costs in a variety of ways. Currently, Medicare offers beneficiaries:

* *Original Medicare plan (fee-for-services).* Patients choose any physician or specialist, but pay a higher patient co-payment.

* *Managed care plans.* Patients join an HMO that receives the patient's monthly Medicare premiums from the government in exchange for an insurance plan that covers many items not covered by original Medicare, for example, eye exams, hearing aids, routine physicals, and (until newly enacted for 2006) prescription drugs. However, patients must see only HMO doctors and obtain their recommendation before seeing specialists.

* *Medicare plus Medigap plans.* Patients remain in original Medicare plan, choosing their own physicians and specialists but purchase a separate "medigap" plan from a private insurer to cover most of the gaps in Medicare.

But Medicare costs are expected to rise dramatically in future years as the baby boom generation expands the population age 65 and over and people live longer (see Figure 17.6). The addition of prescription drug coverage will add even more to Medicare costs.

Politics and Health Care Reform

Health care reform centers on two central problems: controlling costs and expanding access. These problems are related: expanding access to Americans who are currently uninsured and closing gaps in coverage requires increased costs, even while a central thrust of reform is to control overall health care costs.

National Health Insurance Plans Liberals have long sought the creation of a Canadian-style health care system in which the federal government would provide health insurance for all Americans in a single national plan paid for by

★ **national health insurance**
Government-provided insurance to all citizens paid from tax revenues.

general tax increases. Under **national health insurance** all Americans would be entitled to a stipulated list of services from physicians, hospitals, and nursing homes, regardless of their employment, age, medical status, or income level. The federal government would be the "single payer" of health care costs through increased taxes. Hospitals would operate on budgets periodically negotiated with the government. Government fee schedules would dictate payments to physicians. Patients also might have to pay some share of the costs at the time of illness. This approach to health care would shift most costs from the private to the public sector. Although these plans are generally popular in Canada and Western Europe, proposals for federal nationwide insurance systems have consistently failed to win political support in Washington (see *What Do You Think?:* "Should We Enact a National Health Care System Covering All Americans?").

Employer-Based Plans   Others have advanced the notion of universal coverage through mandated employer-based insurance for most workers combined with government subsidies to pay the insurance costs for people living below the poverty line and to assist others in purchasing insurance.

A majority of American employees are currently enrolled in employer-based plans, but these plans vary a great deal in coverage and cost to employees. And, of course, they do not cover the self-employed or unemployed. The federal government has never *mandated* employers to provide health insurance to their workers.

Modest Reforms   Some modest reforms were enacted in 1996 in the Kennedy–Kassebaum Act, named for its bipartisan sponsorship by liberal Democratic Senator Edward M. Kennedy and moderate Republican Senator Nancy Kassebaum. This act guarantees the "portability" of health insurance—allowing workers to maintain their insurance coverage if they lose or change jobs. Their new employer's health insurance company cannot deny them insurance for "pre-existing conditions."

The Plight of the Uninsured

Lack of health insurance forces many Americans to postpone regular visits to a doctor and to rely on crowded hospital emergency rooms when they become sick.

What Do You *Think?*

Should We Enact a National Health Care System Covering All Americans?

About 45 million Americans—almost one in six—are currently without health insurance. And this number climbs to about one in three uninsured persons who are between the ages of 19 and 24.

The millions of Americans who go uninsured often end up costing state and federal government a lot of money. Since those who are uninsured are much less likely to consult doctors when they experience serious medical symptoms, they end up catching their health problems later rather than sooner. And their (later) costs for emergency-room care, hospitalization at community-health centers, treatment at mental-health facilities, and Medicaid are all, of course, more expensive than the expense of prevention, early treatment, and routine health care.[a]

The average per capita cost of health insurance in the United States is the highest among advanced countries. Over the past 5 years health insurance premiums rose by 73 percent, even though American's wages rose just 15 percent over the same period. By 2015, health experts project that the cost of the health system will come to one-fifth—20 percent—of GDP. Despite the high costs of health in the United States, the overall health of Americans is not very good—ranking twenty-fourth among industrialized countries in terms of life expectancy. For good reason, then, many recommend that the state and national government exert much greater control on medical and hospital costs.

Yet there is considerable resistance to cost controls. Some economists fear that a system of cost controls on medical and hospital charges will make inventors less likely to come up with new medical devices, that U.S. companies will introduce fewer innovative and specialized drugs, and that many specialized services and elective surgeries will be in short supply—resulting in long waits and frustrated patients.

Americans are not fully agreed on what needs to be done about health care. But it appears that they do believe that health care should be readily available to the public, and believe that something has to be done.[b]

Q. "Now, here are six goals that could be considered to change our health care system. Which one of the following goals is most important for the country and should receive the greatest attention in reforming our health care system? Providing basic health insurance coverage to all Americans, making health care more affordable, maintaining the high quality of American health care, providing basic health insurance coverage to all American children, making sure people can select the doctor or hospital of their choice, making sure the system allows the development and adoption of new medical technologies."

Providing basic health insurance coverage to all Americans	41%
Making health care more affordable	32
Maintaining the high quality of American health care	8
Providing basic health insurance coverage to all American children	8
Making sure people can select the doctor or hospital of their choice	7
Making sure the system allows the development and adoption of new medical technologies	3
Don't know	2

But the public is not quite sure about who in particular should carry the burden for health care coverage. Some think the government should take the lead, others believe the burden should be on employers, and still others on individuals themselves. Interestingly, almost one in five persons responded—without being asked—that health insurance is a shared responsibility.[c]

Q. "Which of the following statements comes closest to your view? 'It is the government's responsibility to ensure that its citizens have health insurance.' 'It is the employer's responsibility to ensure that their employees have health insurance.' 'It is the responsibility of the individuals to secure their own health insurance without the help of the government or their employer.'"

Government's responsibility	29%
Individual's responsibility	24
Employer's responsibility	23
Shared responsibility (vol.)	19
Not sure	5

[a]See Marcia Clemmitt, "Rising Health Costs," CQ *Researcher*, April 2006.

[b]Survey by Robert Wood Johnson Foundation and Public Opinion Strategies, August 4–7, 2007. Retrieved February 7, 2008, from the iPOLL Databank, The Roper Center for Public Opinion Research, University of Connecticut. www.ropercenter.uconn.edu/ipoll.html

[c]Survey by Bloomberg and *Los Angeles Times*, October 19–October 22, 2007. Retrieved February 7, 2008, from the iPOLL Databank, The Roper Center for Public Opinion Research, University of Connecticut, www.ropercenter.uconn.edu/ipoll.html

A *Constitutional* Note

Rights Versus Entitlements

The Constitution *limits* government. It does not oblige the government to provide any benefits or services to people, such as education, welfare, Social Security, medical care, and so on. Constitutionally speaking, there is no *right* to these benefits. The states, for example, are not obliged by the Constitution to provide public education; the national government is not obliged by the Constitution to provide Social Security or Medicare. These governments do so as a matter of legislation, not as a mandate of the U.S. Constitution. (Of course, if the national or state governments decide to provide such services, they must provide them equally to all persons "similarly situated," that is, they cannot discriminate but must provide "equal protection of laws" under the 14th Amendment.) Political rhetoric often claims a *right* to an education, or to Social Security, or to medical care,

or to other important programs. But there are no such rights set forth in the Constitution. Although politically unthinkable, states could abolish public education altogether; Congress could abolish Social Security or Medicare.

However, governments over time have provided benefits and services that people have come to depend upon. The laws granting these benefits set eligibility requirements—age, income, disability, unemployment, and so forth. Everyone who meets these requirements is said to be *entitled* to these benefits by law. Indeed, we have come to refer to these benefits as *entitlements*. But it is important to distinguish between *rights*—limits on government power to protect individuals—and *entitlements*—benefits that governments have enacted for persons who meet specific requirements.

A Patients' Bill of Rights   The growth of managed care health plans, and their efforts to control costs, have fueled a drive for a "patients' bill of rights." Various proposals have been put forward for inclusion in a patients' bill of rights. The most common proposals are those allowing patients to see specialists without first obtaining permission from a representative of their health plan; providing emergency care without securing prior approval from a health plan representative; allowing immediate appeals when a patient is denied coverage for a particular treatment; and giving patients the right to sue their health plans for medical mistakes. The health insurance industry, including HMOs, argues that these proposals would significantly increase costs of health insurance. They oppose giving the federal government such a large role in overseeing health care plans. And they are particularly concerned about opening themselves to patients' lawsuits—"just a lawyers' bill of rights."

Prescription Drug Coverage Under Medicare   The long battle over adding prescription drug coverage to Medicare reached a turning point in 2004 when Congress finally passed by wide margins and President George W. Bush signed such a bill. Americans have long supported the addition of prescription drug benefits to Medicare. And in every election over the previous 20 years both Democrats and Republicans had pledged their support for such a benefit. But it was not until after a prolonged battle over the details of the legislation that Congress finally added the long-awaited prescription drug benefit to Medicare. (The Medicaid program for the poor has paid for prescription drugs since its inception.)

The bill was passed by a Republican-controlled Congress and signed by a Republican president; most Democrats in Congress opposed the bill, claiming that it failed to go far enough in protecting seniors. The AARP provided crucial support for the bill, arguing that later amendments could cure any defects.

Prescription Drug Costs   Prescription drugs are more costly in the United States than anywhere else in the developed world. The American pharmaceutical industry argues that the higher prices that Americans pay help to fund research on new drugs, and that forcing down drug prices would curtail the development of new and potentially life-saving drugs. In effect, Americans are asked to subsidize drug research that benefits the entire world.

Many Americans have resorted to importing drugs from Canada or other nations that have much lower prices than those being charged in the United States. The Food and Drug Administration contends that this practice is illegal, and both the FDA and drug companies claim that imported drugs may not be safe (a highly dubious claim, inasmuch as they are the same drugs shipped by American drug companies to Canada and other nations).

Interest-Group Battles   Interest-group battles over the details of health care policy have been intense. Virtually everyone has a financial stake in any proposal to reorganize the nation's health care system.

★ Employers, especially small businesses, are fearful of added costs.

★ Physicians strongly oppose price controls and treatment guidelines, as well as programs that take away patient choice of physician or force all physicians into health maintenance organizations (HMOs). Support is stronger among those physicians most likely to benefit from low-cost plans—general family practitioners—and weakest among those most likely to lose—medical specialists.

★ Psychiatrists, psychologists, mental health and drug abuse counselors, physical therapists, chiropractors, optometrists, and dentists all want their own services covered. Providing such "comprehensive" services greatly increases costs.

★ Drug companies want to see prescription drugs paid for, but they vigorously oppose price controls on drugs.

★ Hospitals want all patients to be insured but oppose government payment schedules.

★ Medical specialists fear that proposals for managed care will result in fewer consultations, and medical manufacturers fear it will limit use of high-priced equipment.

★ The powerful senior citizens' lobby wants added benefits—including coverage for drugs, eyeglasses, dental care, and nursing homes—but fears folding Medicare into a larger health care system.

★ Veterans' groups want to retain separate VA hospitals and medical services.

★ Opponents of abortion rights are prepared to do battle to keep national coverage from including such procedures, whereas many supporters of abortion rights will not back any plan that excludes abortion services.

Although polls show that a majority of Americans are willing to pay higher taxes for comprehensive health care, many are willing to see increases only in "sin taxes"—taxes on alcohol, tobacco, and guns.

Summary
Who Gets What: Social Welfare Policy

Social welfare policy largely determines who gets what from government; over half of the federal budget is devoted to "human resources." The government is a major redistributor of income from group to group.

★ The poor are *not* the principal beneficiaries of social welfare spending. Only about one-third of all federal social welfare spending is means tested. Most social welfare spending, including the largest programs—Social Security and Medicare—goes to the middle class.

★ About 11 to 15 percent of the U.S. population falls below the annual cash income level that the federal government sets as its official definition of poverty.

★ Poverty is temporary for many families, but some poverty is persistent—lasting 5 years to a lifetime. Prolonged poverty and welfare dependency create an "underclass" beset by many social and economic problems. Poverty is most frequent among families headed by single mothers.

★ Nearly one-third of the U.S. population receives some form of government payments or benefits. Entitlements are government benefits for which Congress has set eligibility criteria by law. Social Security and Medicare are the largest entitlement programs. The elderly are entitled to these benefits regardless of their income or wealth.

★ Senior citizens are politically powerful; they vote more often than younger people and they have powerful lobbying organizations in Washington. Social Security is the largest single item in the federal budget. Yet proposals to modify Social Security or Medicare benefits are politically dangerous.

★ Public assistance programs, including Family Assistance, Supplemental Security Income, and food stamps, require recipients to show that they are poor in order to claim benefits.

★ Social welfare policies seek to alleviate hardship; at the same time they seek to avoid creating disincentives to work. Cash welfare payments may, for example, encourage teenage pregnancies, undermine family foundations, and contribute to long-term social dependency. Welfare reform centers on moving former welfare recipients into the workforce. But doing so may require increased spending on education, job training, health care, and child care, and some recipients may never be able to work.

★ Welfare reform in 1996 replaced federal entitlements to cash payments with block grants to the states. It also set time limits on welfare enrollment.

★ Americans spend more on health care than citizens of any other nation, yet we fail to insure about 15 percent of the population. And the United States ranks below many other advanced nations in common health measures.

★ Health care reform centers on two related problems—extending health insurance coverage to all Americans and containing the costs of health care. Proposals for extending coverage have included national health insurance and mandatory employer-sponsored health insurance. But only more modest proposals, for example, extending government programs to children and making insurance "portable," have been enacted.

★ A modest prescription drug insurance plan was added to Medicare for seniors. It is administered through private insurance companies, but fails to cover all drug costs.

Key Terms

Suggested Readings

Altman, Nancy J. The *Battle for Social Security*. New York: Wiley, 2005. An overview of the history and partisan battles over Social Security, from its beginning under Franklin D. Roosevelt to George W. Bush's proposals to privatize part of the system.

DiNitto, Diana M., and Linda K. Cummins. *Social Welfare Politics and Policy*. 6th ed. New York: Allyn & Bacon, 2007. A comprehensive overview of social welfare programs—Social Security, Medicare, SSI, cash assistance, Medicaid, food stamps, and so on—and the political controversies surrounding them.

Gilens, Martin. *Why Americans Hate Welfare*. Chicago: University of Chicago Press, 2000. An argument that racial stereotypes, aided by the media, encourage opposition to welfare.

Hays, Sharon. *Flat Broke With Children: Women in the Age of Welfare Reform*. New York: Oxford Press, 2003. Stories of single mothers and welfare workers trying to cope with the harsher rules of welfare reform.

MacManus, Susan A. *Young v. Old*. Boulder, CO: Westview Press, 1996. An argument based on polling data that "generational combat" is likely in the twenty-first century over taxing and spending for Social Security, Medicare, education, health care, and so on.

Murray, Charles. *Losing Ground*. 10th American ed. New York: Basic Books, 1994. Controversial, classic thesis, first put forth in 1984, that government social welfare programs, by encouraging social dependence, had the unintended and perverse effect of slowing and even reversing earlier progress in reducing poverty, crime, ignorance, and discrimination. Often cited as the inspiration for welfare reform.

Schiller, Bradley R. *The Economics of Poverty and Discrimination*. 10th ed. Upper Saddle River, N.J.: Prentice Hall, 2008. Leading text on poverty and welfare in America.

Weissert, Carol S., and William G. Weissert. *Governing Health: The Politics of Health Policy*. 3rd ed. Baltimore, Md.: Johns Hopkins University Press, 2006. Health care policy making, including the roles of Congress, the president, interest groups, and the bureaucracy.

Wilson, William Julius. *The Truly Disadvantaged*. Chicago: University of Chicago Press, 1987. Classic thesis that the growth of the underclass is primarily a result of the decline of manufacturing jobs and their shift to the suburbs, and the resulting concentration of poor, jobless, isolated people in the inner city.

Suggested Web Sites

AARP Social Security www.aarp.org/socialsecurity
AARP's Social Security Center site provides information about the Social Security system including such items as the system's future solvency and a tutorial on how the system works.

Centers for Disease Control www.cdc.gov
Official site for health information and statistics.

Food Stamp Program www.fns.usda.gov/fsp
This U.S. Department of Agriculture's Food Stamp program site contains information about application procedures, recipient eligibility guidelines, and other relevant subjects.

Institute for Research on Poverty www.ssc.wsc.edv/irp
University of Wisconsin Institute leads in research on extent and causes of poverty.

Medicare www.medicare.gov
Official government site explaining eligibility, plan options, appeals, and so forth.

National Center for Children in Poverty www.nccp.org
Columbia University Center with studies and data on children in poverty.

Social Security Online www.ssa.gov
Find out all about your Social Security benefits.

Social Security Reform www.socialsecurity.org
CATO Institute think tank urges private investment of Social Security premiums.

18 POLITICS AND NATIONAL SECURITY

> " Specialists in violence obtain new lease on life when internal or external crises arise. It is notorious that every war and revolution leaves a legacy of military personages in its wake. "
>
> **Harold Lasswell**

Chapter *Outline*

- ★ Power Among Nations
- ★ The Legacy of the Cold War
- ★ Nuclear Threats
- ★ The War on Terrorism
- ★ The War in Iraq

✓Think About Politics

1. Has the United Nations been effective in maintaining world peace?
   YES ○ NO ○

2. Should the United States and NATO intervene in regional conflicts in Eastern Europe?
   YES ○ NO ○

3. Should the United States build a ballistic missile defense system even if it is very costly?
   YES ○ NO ○

4. Is the president justified in placing U.S. troops in danger where U.S. vital interests are not at stake?
   YES ○ NO ○

5. Do you approve of the military attacks led by the United States against terrorist targets in Afghanistan?
   YES ○ NO ○

6. Do you favor the immediate withdrawal of all U.S. troops from Iraq?
   YES ○ NO ○

7. Are U.S. military force levels today sufficient to deal with potential regional aggressors such as Iran and North Korea?
   YES ○ NO ○

8. Should the United States destroy all of its nuclear weapons now that the Cold War is over?
   YES ○ NO ○

America must decide how to use its national power in world affairs. Should we intervene with military forces in pursuit of humanitarian goals and to keep the peace in war-torn lands? Or should we only use military force when vital national interests are at stake?

Power Among Nations

International politics, like all politics, is a struggle for power. The struggle for power is global; it involves all the nations and peoples of the world, whatever their goals or ideals. As the distinguished political scientist Hans Morgenthau once observed,

> Whatever the ultimate aims of international politics, power is always the immediate aim. Statesmen and peoples may ultimately seek freedom, security, prosperity or power itself. They may define their goals in terms of a religious, philosophic, economic, or social ideal. . . . But whenever they strive to realize their goal by means of international politics, they are striving for power.[1]

The struggle for power among nations has led to many attempts to bring order to the international system.

Collective Security Originally, **collective security** meant that *all* nations would join together to guarantee each other's "territorial integrity and existing political independence" against "external aggression" by any nation. This was the idea behind the League of Nations, established in 1919. However, opposition to international involvement was so great in the United States after World War I that, after a lengthy debate, the Senate refused to enroll the United States in the League of Nations. More important, the League of Nations failed to deal with acts of aggression by the Axis Powers—Germany, Japan, and Italy—in the 1930s. During that decade, Japan invaded Manchuria, Italy invaded Ethiopia, and Germany dismembered Czechoslovakia. Finally, when Germany invaded Poland in 1939, World War II began. Japan bombed the U.S. Navy base at Pearl Harbor on December 7, 1941, and the United States joined in the war. World War II cost more than 40 million lives, both civilian and military.

Formation of the United Nations Even after World War II, the notion of collective security remained an ideal of the victorious Allied Powers. The Charter of the United Nations, signed in 1945, provided for the following organization:

★ The Security Council, with eleven member nations, five of them being permanent members—the United States, the **Soviet Union** (whose membership is now held by Russia), Britain, France, and China—and each having the power to veto any action by the Security Council.

★ The General Assembly, composed of all the member nations, each with a single vote.

★ **collective security**
Attempt to bring order to international relations by all nations joining together to guarantee each other's "territorial integrity" and "independence" against "external aggression."

★ **Soviet Union**
The Union of Soviet Socialist Republics (USSR) consisting of Russia and its bordering lands and ruled by the communist regime in Moscow, officially dissolved in 1991.

★ **superpowers**
Refers to the United States and the Soviet Union after World War II, when these two nations dominated international politics.

Standing Tall?
The UN building in New York City symbolizes the hope that nations can resolve problems through collective action. But the United Nations has achieved only limited success in the worldwide war on terror.

★ The Secretariat, headed by a Secretary General with a staff at United Nations headquarters in New York.

★ Separate organizations to handle specialized affairs—for example, the Economic and Social Council, the Trusteeship Council, and the International Court of Justice at The Hague in the Netherlands.

The Security Council has the "primary responsibility" for maintaining "international peace and security." The General Assembly has authority over "any matter affecting the peace of the world," although it is supposed to defer to the Security Council when the council has already taken up a particular security matter. No nation has a veto in the General Assembly; every nation has one vote regardless of its size or power. Most resolutions can be passed by a majority vote.

The United Nations in the Cold War The United Nations (UN) proved largely ineffective during the long Cold War confrontation between the communist nations, led by the Soviet Union, and the Western democracies, led by the United States. The UN grew from its original 51 member nations to 150 (192 in 2008), but many of those nations were headed by authoritarian regimes of one kind or another. The Western democracies were outnumbered in the General Assembly, and the Soviet Union frequently used its veto to prevent action by the Security Council. Anti-Western and antidemocratic speeches became common in the General Assembly.

During the Cold War, the UN was overshadowed by the confrontation of the world's two **superpowers**: the United States and the Soviet Union. Indeed, international conflicts throughout the world—in the Middle East, Africa, Latin America, Southeast Asia, and elsewhere—were usually influenced by some aspect of the superpower struggle.

The UN Today Following the disintegration of the Soviet Union in 1991, Russia inherited its UN Security Council seat. Many of the regional conflicts in the world were no longer "proxy" wars between superpowers. Over the years the UN has sent blue-helmeted "peacekeeping" forces to monitor cease-fires in many troubled areas of the world. Yet the United Nations and its Security Council must rely on "the last remaining superpower," the United States, to take the lead in enforcing its resolutions. However, a top-heavy bureaucracy at UN headquarters in New York, together with scandal and inefficiency in UN spending, has eroded support for the UN in the United States.

Regional Security—NATO The general disappointment with the United Nations as a form of collective security gave rise as early as 1949 to a different approach, **regional security**. In response to aggressive Soviet moves in Europe, the United States and the democracies of Western Europe created the **North Atlantic Treaty Organization (NATO)**. In the NATO treaty, fifteen Western nations agreed to collective regional security: they agreed that "an armed attack against one or more [NATO nations] . . . shall be considered an attack against them all." The United States made a specific commitment to defend Western Europe in the event of a Soviet attack. A joint NATO military command was established (with Dwight D. Eisenhower as its first commander) to coordinate the defense of Western Europe.

After the formation of NATO, the Soviets made no further advances into Western Europe. The Soviets themselves, in response to NATO, drew up the Warsaw Pact, a comparable treaty with their own Eastern European satellite nations. But for many years the real deterrent to Warsaw Pact expansion was not the weak NATO armies, but rather the pledge of the United States to use its strategic nuclear bomber force to inflict "massive retaliation" on the Soviet Union itself in the event of an attack on Western Europe.

The Warsaw Pact disintegrated following the dramatic collapse of the communist governments of Eastern Europe in 1989. Former Warsaw Pact nations—Poland, Hungary, Romania, Bulgaria, and East Germany—threw out their ruling communist regimes and demanded the withdrawal of Soviet troops from their territory. The Berlin Wall was dismantled in 1989, and Germany was formally reunified in 1990, bringing together the 61 million prosperous people of West Germany and the 17 million less affluent people of East Germany. (Unified Germany continues as a member of NATO.) The Communist Party was ousted from power in Moscow, and the Soviet Union collapsed in 1991.

NATO Expansion   The United States and its Western European allies agree that NATO continues to play an important role in the security of Europe. Indeed, the continued deployment of some level of U.S. troops to NATO is widely considered to be reassurance that the United States remains committed to this security.

In recent years NATO has made the key decision to expand its security protections to the newly democratic nations of Eastern Europe. Three nations—Poland, Hungary, and the Czech Republic—were admitted to NATO in 1998. At that time Russia strongly objected to NATO expansion, viewing it as an incursion of Western powers in the East and a threat to Russia's security. A NATO-Russia Council was created in 2002 to calm Russian fears about NATO's intentions. In 2004 seven additional countries—Bulgaria, Estonia, Latvia, Lithuania, Romania, Slovakia, and Slovenia—were admitted to membership. All of these nations were formerly under the domination of the Soviet Union. NATO now has 26 members (see Figure 18.1).

NATO and Ethnic Conflicts in the Balkans.   Traditionally, NATO forces were never deployed outside of Western Europe. Yet ethnic wars in the former communist nation of Yugoslavia, and the media coverage of the hardships endured by the people there, inspired NATO to intervene and deploy troops to Bosnia in 1995 to halt conflict raging among Serbs, Croats, and Muslims. The United States provided about one-third of the ground troops deployed in Bosnia as "peacekeepers." Yet some argued that U.S. national security interests were not at stake in southeastern European ethnic conflicts and therefore American troops should not be exposed to the dangers of intervention.

NATO again acted militarily to halt ethnic conflict in Kosovo in 1999. NATO's objective was to force Serbian troop withdrawal from the largely Muslim province. NATO relied exclusively on bombing from the air to force the Serbian withdrawal. Despite some controversy, even among NATO nations, as well as denunciations from Russia and China, NATO aircraft and missiles hit targets in both Kosovo and Serbia itself. (Even the Chinese embassy in the Serbian capital of Belgrade was bombed, apparently by mistake.) Eventually, Serbian troops were withdrawn from Kosovo; they were replaced by NATO troops (and a small contingent of Russian troops).

NATO in Afghanistan   The United States turned over command of its military forces in Afghanistan to NATO in 2003. NATO created an International Security

★ **regional security**
Attempt to bring order to international relations during the Cold War by creating regional alliances between a superpower and nations of a particular region.

★ **North Atlantic Treaty Organization (NATO)**
Mutual-security agreement and joint military command uniting the nations of Western Europe, initially formed to resist Soviet expansionism.

Figure *18.1*   NATO Nations of Europe*

NATO was originally created to protect the nations of Western Europe from Soviet expansion; the collapse of the Soviet Union in 1991 has led to the expansion of NATO into Eastern European nations formerly dominated by the old Soviet Union.

* NATO members, United States and Canada, not shown.

Comparing Foreign and Security Policy

Assistance Force, officially under UN auspices, "to assist the Islamic Republic of Afghanistan in creating a stable and secure environment for the people of Afghanistan." Some thirty-seven nations contribute troops to this Force, but the United States contributes the largest number. To date, NATO forces have failed to capture Osama bin Laden and failed to eliminate Taliban forces from Afghan mountainous regions along the Pakistani border.

The Legacy of the Cold War

★ **Cold War**
Political, military, and ideological struggle between the United States and the Soviet Union following the end of World War II and ending with the collapse of the Soviet Union's communist government in 1991.

For more than 40 years following the end of World War II, the United States and the Soviet Union confronted each other in the protracted political, military, and ideological struggle known as the **Cold War**.

Origins   During World War II, the United States and the Soviet Union joined forces to eliminate the Nazi threat to the world. The United States dismantled its military forces at the end of the war in 1945, but the Soviet Union, under the brutal dictatorship of Josef Stalin, used the powerful Red Army to install communist governments in the nations of Eastern Europe in violation of wartime agreements to allow free elections. Stalin also ignored pledges to cooperate in a unified allied occupation of Germany; Germany was divided, and in 1948 Stalin unsuccessfully tried to oust the United States, Britain, and France from Berlin in a year-long "Berlin Blockade." Former British Prime Minister Winston Churchill warned the United States as early as 1946 that the Soviets were dividing Europe with an "Iron Curtain." When Soviet-backed communist forces threatened Greece and Turkey in 1947, President Harry S Truman responded with a pledge to "support free people who are resisting attempted subjugation by armed minorities or by outside pressures," a policy that became known as the **Truman Doctrine**.

Containment   The United States had fought two world wars to maintain democracy in Western Europe. The new threat of Soviet expansionism and communist world revolution caused America to assume world leadership on behalf of the preservation of democracy. In an influential article in the Council on Foreign Relations' journal *Foreign Affairs*, the State Department's Russia expert George F. Kennan called for a policy of **containment**:

> It is clear that the main element of any United States policy toward the Soviet Union must be that of a long-term, vigilant containment of Russian expansive tendencies. . . .[2]

To implement the containment policy, the United States first initiated the **Marshall Plan**, named for Secretary of State George C. Marshall, to rebuild the economies of the Western European nations. Marshall reasoned that *economically* weak nations were more susceptible to communist subversion and Soviet intimidation. The subsequent formation of NATO provided the necessary *military* support to contain the Soviet Union.

The Korean War   The first military test of the containment policy came in June 1950, when communist North Korean armies invaded South Korea. President Truman assumed that the North Koreans were acting on behalf of their sponsor, the Soviet Union. The Soviets had already aided Chinese communists under the leadership of Mao Zedong in capturing control of mainland China in 1949. The United States quickly brought the Korean invasion issue to the Security Council. With the Soviets boycotting this meeting because the Council had refused to seat the new communist delegation from China, the Council passed a resolution calling on member nations to send troops to repel the invasion.

America's conventional (nonnuclear) military forces had been largely dismantled after World War II. Moreover, President Truman insisted on keeping most of the nation's forces in Europe, fearing that the Korean invasion was a diversion to be followed by a Soviet invasion of Western Europe. But General Douglas MacArthur, in a brilliant amphibious landing at Inchon behind North Korean lines, destroyed a much larger enemy army, captured the North Korean capital, and moved northward toward the Chinese border. Then in December 1950, disaster struck American forces as a million-strong Chinese army entered the conflict. Chinese troops surprised the Americans, inflicting heavy casualties, trapping entire units, and forcing U.S. troops to beat a hasty retreat. General MacArthur urged retaliation against China, but Truman sought to keep the war "limited." When MacArthur publicly protested political limits to military operations, Truman dismissed the popular general. The **Korean War** became a bloody stalemate.

Dwight Eisenhower was elected president in 1952 in large measure because he promised to "go to Korea" to end the increasingly unpopular war. He also

Think Again

Should the United States and NATO intervene in regional conflicts in Eastern Europe?

★ **Truman Doctrine**
U.S. foreign policy, first articulated by President Harry S Truman, that pledged the United States to "support free peoples who are resisting attempted subjugation by armed minorities or by outside pressures."

★ **containment**
Policy of preventing an enemy from expanding its boundaries and/or influence, specifically the U.S. foreign policy vis-à-vis the Soviet Union during the Cold War.

★ **Marshall Plan**
U.S. program to rebuild the nations of Western Europe in the aftermath of World War II in order to render them less susceptible to communist influence and takeover.

TIMELINE

The Evolution of Foreign Policy

★ **Korean War**
Communist North Korea invaded non-Communist South Korea in June 1950, causing President Harry S Truman to intervene militarily, with UN support. General Douglas MacArthur defeated the North Koreans, but with China's entry into the war, a stalemate resulted. An armistice was signed in 1953, with Korea divided along nearly original lines.

★ **Cuban Missile Crisis**
The 1962 confrontation between the Soviet Union and the U.S. over Soviet placement of nuclear missiles in Cuba.

Economic Sanctions and Cuba

You Are President John F. Kennedy

★ **Vietnam War**
War between non-communist South Vietnam and communist North Vietnam from 1956 to 1975, with increasing U.S. involvement, ending with U.S. withdrawal in 1973 and communist victory in 1975. The war became unpopular in the United States after 1968 and caused President Johnson not to run for a second term. More than 58,000 Americans died in the war.

threatened to use nuclear weapons in the conflict but eventually agreed to a truce along the original border between North and South Korea. Communist expansion in Korea was "contained," but at a high price: the United States lost more than 38,000 men in the war.

The Cuban Missile Crisis   The most serious threat of nuclear holocaust during the entire Cold War was the **Cuban Missile Crisis**. In 1962 Soviet Premier Nikita Khrushchev sought to secretly install medium-range nuclear missiles in Cuba in an effort to give the Soviet Union nuclear capability against U.S. cities. In October 1962 intelligence photos showing Soviet missiles at Cuban bases touched off a 13-day crisis. President Kennedy rejected advice to launch an air strike to destroy the missiles before they could be activated. Instead, he publicly announced a naval blockade of Cuba, threatening to halt Soviet missile-carrying vessels at sea by force if necessary. The prospect of war appeared imminent; U.S. nuclear forces went on alert. Secretly, Kennedy proposed to withdraw U.S. nuclear missiles from Turkey in exchange for Soviet withdrawal of nuclear missiles from Cuba. Khrushchev's agreement to the deal appeared to the world as a backing down; Kennedy would be hailed for his statesmanship in the crisis, while Khrushchev would soon lose his job.

The Vietnam War   When communist forces led by Ho Chi Minh defeated French forces at the battle of Dien Bien Phu in 1954, the resulting Geneva Accords divided that country into North Vietnam, with a communist government, and South Vietnam, with a U.S.-backed government. When South Vietnamese communist (Vietcong) guerrilla forces threatened the South Vietnamese government in the early 1960s, President Kennedy sent a force of more than 12,000 advisers and counterinsurgency forces to assist in every aspect of training and support for the Army of the Republic of Vietnam (ARVN) in South Vietnam and authorized a gradual increase in air strikes against North Vietnam. Washington committed more than 500,000 troops to a war of attrition, a war in which U.S. firepower was expected to inflict sufficient casualties on the enemy to force a peace settlement. But over time, the failure to achieve any decisive military victories eroded popular support for the **Vietnam War**.

On January 31, 1968, the Vietnamese holiday of Tet, Vietcong forces blasted their way into the U.S. embassy compound in Saigon and held the courtyard for 6 hours. The attack was part of a massive, coordinated Tet offensive against all major cities of South Vietnam. U.S. forces responded and inflicted very heavy casualties on the Vietcong. By any military measure, the Tet offensive was a "defeat" for the enemy and a "victory" for U.S. forces. Yet the Tet offensive was Hanoi's greatest *political* victory. Television pictures of bloody fighting in Saigon and Hue seemed to mock President Johnson's promises of an early end to the war.

On March 31, 1968, President Johnson went on national television to make a dramatic announcement: He halted the bombing of North Vietnam and asked Hanoi for peace talks, concluding, "I shall not seek, and I will not accept, the nomination of my party for another term as your president." Formal peace talks opened in Paris on May 13.

The new president, Richard Nixon, and his national security adviser, Henry Kissinger, knew the war must be ended, but they sought to end it "honorably." Even in the absence of a settlement with the communists in Vietnam, Nixon began the withdrawal of U.S. troops under the guise of "Vietnamization" of the war effort. Unable to persuade Hanoi to make even the slightest concession at Paris, President Nixon sought to demonstrate American strength and resolve. In

December 1972 the United States unleashed a devastating air attack directly on Hanoi for the first time. Critics at home labeled Nixon's action "the Christmas bombing," but when negotiations resumed in Paris in January, the North Vietnamese quickly agreed to peace on the terms that Kissinger and Le Duc Tho had worked out earlier.

The South Vietnamese government lasted 2 years after the agreement. In early 1975 Hanoi decided that the Americans would not "jump back in" and therefore "the opportune moment" was at hand for a new invasion. President Gerald Ford's requests to Congress for emergency military aid to the South Vietnamese fell on deaf ears. Saigon (now Ho Chi Minh City) fell to the North Vietnamese in April 1975, and the United States abandoned hundreds of thousands of loyal Vietnamese who had fought alongside the Americans for years.[3] The spectacle of U.S. Marines using their rifle butts to keep desperate Vietnamese from boarding helicopters on the roof of the U.S. embassy "provided a tragic epitaph for twenty-five years of American involvement in Vietnam."[4]

The Vietnam Syndrome America's humiliation in Vietnam had lasting national consequences. The United States suffered 47,393 battle deaths and missing-in-action among the 2.8 million U.S. personnel who served in Vietnam. A new isolationism permeated American foreign policy following defeat in Vietnam. The slogan "No More Vietnams" was used to oppose any U.S. military intervention, whether or not U.S. vital interests were at stake. Disillusionment replaced idealism. American leaders had exaggerated the importance of Vietnam; now Americans were unwilling to believe their leaders when they warned of other dangers.

Rebuilding America's Defenses The decision to rebuild Western military forces and reassert international leadership on behalf of democratic values gained widespread support in the Western world in the early 1980s. President Ronald Reagan, British Prime Minister Margaret Thatcher, French President François Mitterrand, and German Chancellor Helmut Kohl all pledged to increase their defense efforts and all held fast against a "nuclear freeze" movement that would have locked in Soviet superiority in European-based nuclear weapons.

The Reagan defense buildup extended through 1985—with increases in defense spending, improvements in strategic nuclear weapons, and, perhaps more important, the rebuilding and reequipping of U.S. conventional forces. The American and NATO defense buildup, together with the promise of a new, expensive, and technologically sophisticated race for ballistic missile defenses, forecast heavy additional strains on the weak economy of the Soviet Union. Thus, in 1985, when new Soviet President Mikhail Gorbachev came to power, the stage was set for an end to the Cold War.

Gorbachev announced reductions in the size of the Soviet military and reached agreements with the United States on the reduction of nuclear forces. More important, in 1988 he announced that the Soviet Union would no longer use its military forces to keep communist governments in power in Eastern European nations. This stunning announcement, for which he received the Nobel Peace Prize in 1990, encouraged opposition democratic forces in Poland (the Solidarity movement), Czechoslovakia, Hungary, Bulgaria, Romania, and East Germany. Gorbachev refused to intervene to halt the destruction of the Berlin Wall in 1989, despite pleas by the East German hard-line communist leader Erich Honecker.

A Costly Campaign
The Vietnam War inflicted more than 47,000 battle deaths on U.S. forces. Units of army infantry and marines slogged through the jungles of Southeast Asia for more than 8 years. The Paris Peace Accord, signed in 1973, was ignored by the communist regime in Hanoi; its renewed invasion in 1975 succeeded in capturing all of Vietnam.

VISUAL LITERACY

Evaluating Defense Spending

A Haunting Reminder

The Vietnam War Memorial in Washington, D.C., is inscribed with the names of the nearly 50,000 Americans who died in Vietnam. America's defeat fostered skepticism about the wisdom of foreign military intervention, leading to a new caution about intervention and to the idea that U.S. forces should be deployed only with overwhelming numbers—a lesson America followed in the 1991 Gulf War.

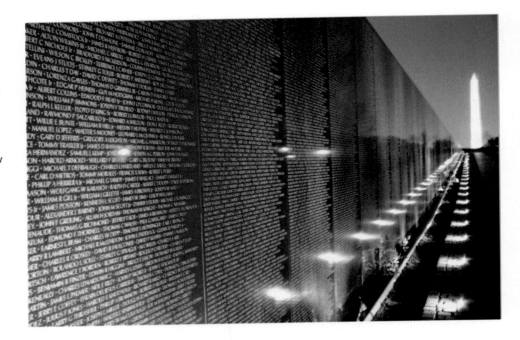

The Collapse of Communism

When hardliners in the Communist Party, the military, and the KGB attempted the forcible removal of Gorbachev in August 1991, democratic forces rallied to his support. Led by Boris Yeltsin, the first elected president of the Russian Republic, thousands of demonstrators took to the streets; Soviet military forces stood aside. Yeltsin emerged as the most influential leader in the nation. The failed coup hastened the demise of the Communist Party. The party lost legitimacy with the peoples of Russia and the other republics.

The Disintegration of the Soviet Union

Strong independence movements in the republics of the Soviet Union emerged as the authority of the centralized Communist Party in Moscow waned. Lithuania, Estonia, and Latvia—nations that had been forcibly incorporated into the Soviet Union in 1939—led the way to independence in 1991. Soon all of the fifteen republics of the Soviet Union declared their independence, and the Union of Soviet Socialist Republics offi-

Nuclear Drawdown

Presidents Vladimir Putin of Russia and George W. Bush of the United States reached agreement in 2002 to reduce their nations' nuclear stockpiles by over 80 percent from Cold War levels.

cially ceased to exist after December 31, 1991. The red flag with its hammer and sickle atop the Kremlin was replaced with the flag of the Russian Republic.

Russia After Communism   The transition from a centralized state-run economy to free markets turned out to be more painful for Russians than expected. Living standards for most people declined, alcoholism and death rates increased, and even average life spans shortened. Ethnic conflict and political separatism, especially in the largely Muslim province of Chechnya, added to Russia's problems. Yeltsin was able to overcome these political challenges and win reelection as president in 1996. But corruption, embezzlement, graft, and organized crime continue to undermine democratic reforms. Poor health eventually forced Yeltsin to turn over power to Vladimir Putin, who himself won election as president of Russia in 2000. Putin became a popular leader among Russians despite his recentralization of power and weakening of democratic institutions. Putin's protegee, Dmitry Medvedev, assumed the presidency of Russia in 2008; Putin occupies the post of Prime Minister.

Nuclear Threats

Nuclear weaponry has made the world infinitely more dangerous. During the Cold War, the nuclear arsenals of the United States and the Soviet Union threatened a human holocaust. Yet, paradoxically, the very destructiveness of nuclear weapons caused leaders on both sides to exercise extreme caution in their relations with each other. Scores of wars, large and small, were fought by different nations during the Cold War years, yet American and Soviet troops never engaged in direct combat against each other.

Deterrence   To maintain nuclear peace during the Cold War, the United States relied primarily on the policy of **deterrence**. Deterrence is based on the notion that a nation can dissuade a *rational* enemy from attacking by maintaining the capacity to destroy the enemy's homeland even *after* the nation has suffered a well-executed surprise attack by the enemy. Deterrence assumes that the worst may happen—a surprise first strike against a nation's nuclear forces. It emphasizes **second-strike capability**—the ability of a nation's forces to survive a surprise attack by the enemy and then to inflict an unacceptable level of destruction on the enemy's homeland. Deterrence is really a *psychological* defense against attack; no effective physical defense against a ballistic missile attack exists even today.

Limiting Nuclear Arms: SALT   The United States and the Soviet Union engaged in negotiations over nuclear arms control for many years. The development of reconnaissance satellites in the 1960s made it possible for each nation to monitor the strategic weapons possessed by the other. Space photography made cheating on agreements more difficult and thus opened the way for both nations to seek stability through arms control.

Following the election of Richard Nixon as president in 1968, the United States, largely guided by former Harvard professor Henry Kissinger (national security adviser to the president and later secretary of state), began negotiations with the Soviet Union over strategic nuclear arms. In 1972 the two nations concluded 2½ years of Strategic Arms Limitation Talks (SALT) about limiting the nuclear arms race. The agreement, **SALT I**, consisted of a treaty limiting antiballistic missiles (ABMs) and an agreement placing a numerical ceiling on offensive missiles. In the **ABM Treaty** both nations pledged *not* to build ballistic missile defenses. This meant that the populations of both nations in effect would be held hostage against a first strike by either nation.

Think Again

Should the United States destroy all of its nuclear weapons now that the Cold War is over?

★ **deterrence**
U.S. approach to deterring any nuclear attack from the Soviet Union by maintaining a second-strike capability.

★ **second-strike capability**
Ability of a nation's forces to survive a surprise nuclear attack by the enemy and then to retaliate effectively.

★ **SALT I**
First arms limitation treaty between the United States and the Soviet Union, signed in 1972, limiting the total number of offensive nuclear missiles; it included the ABM Treaty that reflected the theory that the population centers of both nations should be left undefended.

★ **ABM Treaty**
A formal treaty in 1972 between the United States and the Soviet Union in which each side agreed not to build or deploy antiballistic missiles.

Too Deadly a Weapon
Intercontinental Ballistic Missiles (ICBMs) with multiple nuclear warheads, like this MX Peacekeeper being test-fired, threatened a nuclear holocaust during the long Cold War. The START II Treaty in 1993 called for the dismantling of all multiple-warhead missiles, and the Treaty of Moscow in 2002 called for the reduction of total nuclear warheads by 80 percent from Cold War levels.

★ **SALT II**
Lengthy and complicated treaty between the United States and the Soviet Union, agreed to in 1979 but never ratified by the U.S. Senate, that set limits on all types of strategic nuclear launch vehicles.

★ **START I**
First treaty between the United States and the Soviet Union that actually reduced the strategic nuclear arms of the superpowers, signed in 1991.

★ **START II**
A treaty between the United States and Russia eliminating all multiwarhead land missiles and reducing nuclear weapons stockpiles, signed in 1993.

SALT I was the first step forward on the control of nuclear arms; both sides agreed to continue negotiations. After 7 years of difficult negotiations, the United States and the Soviet Union produced the lengthy and complicated **SALT II** treaty in 1979. It set an overall limit on "strategic nuclear launch vehicles"—ICBMs, SLBMs, bombers, and long-range cruise missiles—at 2,250 for each side. It also limited the number of missiles that could have multiple warheads (MIRVs). But when the Soviet Union invaded Afghanistan in 1979, President Carter withdrew the SALT II treaty from Senate consideration. However, President Carter, and later President Reagan, announced that the United States would abide by the provisions of the unratified SALT II treaty as long as the Soviet Union did so.

Reducing Nuclear Arms: START In negotiations with the Soviets, the Reagan administration established three central principles of arms control—reductions, equality, and verification. The new goal was to be *reductions* in missiles and warheads, not merely limitations on future numbers and types of weapons, as in previous SALT talks. To symbolize this new direction, President Reagan renamed the negotiations the Strategic Arms *Reduction* Talks, or START.

The **START I** Treaty signed in Moscow in 1991 by Presidents George H. W. Bush and Mikhail Gorbachev was the first agreement between the nuclear powers that actually resulted in the reduction of strategic nuclear weapons. The START I Treaty reduced the total number of deployed strategic nuclear delivery systems to no more than 1,600, a 30 percent reduction from the SALT II level.

A far-reaching **START II** agreement, signed in 1993 by U.S. President George H. W. Bush and Russian President Yeltsin, promised to eliminate the threat of a first-strike nuclear attack by either side. Its most important provision was the agreement to eliminate all multiwarhead (MIRVed) land-based missiles. START II also called for the reduction of overall strategic warheads to 3,500.

The Treaty of Moscow The capstone of strategic nuclear arms reductions is the Treaty of Moscow, signed by Russian President Vladimir Putin and U.S. President George W. Bush in 2002. This new treaty calls for an overall limit of nuclear warheads at 1,700–2,200 by 2012. Each side may determine for itself the composition and structure of its strategic forces consistent with this limit. The provisions of the START treaties remain unchanged. The effect of the Moscow Treaty, together with earlier reductions in nuclear weapons under the START treaties, will be to reduce the nuclear arsenals of the former adversaries by over 80 percent from Cold War levels (see Figure 18.2).

Nuclear Terrorism Even as the threat of a large-scale nuclear attack recedes, the threats arising from "nondeterrable" sources are increasing. Today, the principal nondeterrable threats are missiles launched by terrorist nations, possibly North Korea and Iran. Over time global nuclear and ballistic missile proliferation steadily increases the likelihood of these types of threats. Terrorist attacks are considered "nondeterrable" because the threat of nuclear retaliation is largely meaningless.

Defending against terrorist missile attacks requires the development and deployment of **ballistic missile defense (BMD)** systems, weapons capable of detecting, intercepting, and destroying ballistic missiles while they are in flight. At present there is no defense against a ballistic missile attack on American cities (see *A Conflicting View:* "We Should Defend Ourselves Against a Ballistic Missile Attack").

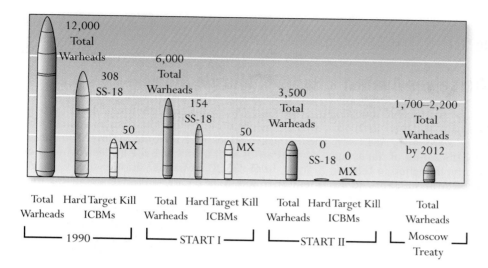

Figure *18.2*
Reducing Nuclear Arms
Implementation of the START II Treaty and the Treaty of Moscow will reduce the total number of warheads in both the United States and Russia by over 80 percent and will completely eliminate hard target kill ICBMs.

The War on Terrorism

Terrorism is a political act. The deliberate targeting of civilians, the infliction of widespread destruction, and the resulting media portrayals of the pain and suffering of victims are designed to call attention to political grievances and to instill fear in people. (The Latin root of the term, *terrere*, means "to frighten.") The horror of terrorist acts and their unpredictability add to public fear—people can neither anticipate nor prepare for tragedies inflicted upon them. Terrorists hope to undermine the confidence of people in their government to protect them, and so they will conclude that submission to the terrorists' demands is preferable to living in a continuing climate of anxiety and uncertainty.

Global Terrorism   Global terrorism has evolved over the years into highly sophisticated networks operating in many countries. Prior to the attacks on New York's World Trade Center and the Pentagon on September 11, 2001, most Americans thought of terrorism as foreign. Terrorist acts on American soil had been rare; the most destructive attack—the Oklahoma City bombing of a federal building in 1995—had been carried out by domestic terrorists. But the "9/11" attacks were on an unprecedented scale and they revealed a sophisticated global plot against America.

A loose-knit network of terrorist cells (Al Qaeda) organized by a wealthy Saudi Arabian, Osama bin Laden, was engaged in global terrorism. Their political grievances included America's support of Israel in Middle East conflicts and an American presence in Islamic holy lands, notably Saudi Arabia. Several nations share these grievances and, more important, provided support and haven to Al Qaeda and similar terrorist organizations. The principal base of support and sanctuary for Al Qaeda was the repressive and violent Taliban regime of Afghanistan.

Declaring War on Terrorism   On the evening of September 11, President George W. Bush spoke to the American people from the Oval Office in a nationally televised address:

> The pictures of airplanes flying into buildings, fires burning, huge structures collapsing, have filled us with disbelief, terrible sadness, and a quiet, unyielding anger. These mass murders were intended to frighten our nation into chaos and retreat. But they failed; our country is strong. . . . These deliberate and deadly attacks were more than acts of terror. They were acts of war.

The president outlined a broad "response to terrorism" to be fought both at home and abroad through diplomatic, military, financial, investigative, homeland

★ **ballistic missile defense (BMD)**
Weapons systems capable of detecting, intercepting, and destroying missiles in flight.

✔ *Think* Again

Is the president justified in placing U.S. troops in danger where U.S. vital interests are not at stake?

★ **terrorism**
Title 22 of the U.S. Code, Section 2656 (d): "The term 'terrorism' means premeditated, politically motivated violence perpetrated against noncombatant targets by subnational groups or clandestine agents, usually intended to influence an audience."

You Are the President of the United States

A Conflicting *View*

We Should Defend Ourselves Against a Ballistic Missile Attack

For over a half-century, since the terrible nuclear blasts at Hiroshima and Nagasaki in Japan in 1945, the world has avoided nuclear war. Peace has been maintained by deterrence—by the threat of devastating nuclear attacks that would be launched in retaliation to an enemy's first strike. But in 1983, President Ronald Reagan urged that instead of deterring war through fear of retaliation, the United States should seek a technological defense against nuclear missiles.

> Our nuclear retaliating forces have deterred war for forty years. The fact is, however, that we have no defense against ballistic missile attack. . . . In the event that deterrence failed, a president's only recourse would be to surrender or to retaliate. Nuclear retaliation, whether massive or limited, would result in the loss of millions of lives. . . .[a]

"Star Wars"

Reagan's Strategic Defense Initiative (SDI) was a research program designed to explore means of destroying enemy nuclear missiles in space before they could reach their targets. Following President Reagan's initial announcement of SDI in March 1983, the press quickly labeled the effort "Star Wars." In theory, a ballistic missile defense (BMD) system could be based in space, orbiting over enemy missile-launching sites. Should an enemy missile get through the space-based defense, a ground-based BMD system would attempt to intercept warheads as they reentered the atmosphere and approached their targets. SDI included research on laser beams, satellite surveillance, computerized battle-management systems, and "smart" and "brilliant" weapons systems. SDI under President Reagan was a very ambitious program with the goal of creating an "impenetrable shield" that would protect not only the population of the United States but the population of our allies as well.

Protection Against Nuclear Terrorism   The end of the Cold War refocused SDI away from defense against a massive Russian missile attack to more limited yet more likely threats. Today the principal nuclear threats are missiles launched by terrorists or a "rogue state." President George H. W. Bush redirected SDI toward defending against these more limited yet potentially devastating attacks.

The Gulf War experience demonstrated that deterrence may not protect the United States against a ballistic missile attack by a terrorist regime. The success of the Patriot antiballistic missile in destroying short-range Iraqi SCUD missiles during the Gulf War demonstrated that enemy missiles could be intercepted in flight. (The Patriot is a ground-based "tactical" weapon designed to protect specific military targets.) However, developing an effective antiballistic missile that can intercept and destroy another missile in space has proven to be more difficult, although not impossible.

The Future of BMDs

As a Reagan-era initiative, partisanship has tended to cloud the debate over BMDs. In 1993, President Clinton announced the termination of the separate SDI organization, but he reassured the nation that research would continue on the ground-based ballistic missile defenses. President George W. Bush notified the Russians in 2002 that the United States was withdrawing from provisions of the ABM Treaty of 1972 that prohibited the development, testing, or deployment of new ballistic missile defense systems.

Advanced testing has met with both successes and failures. Intercepting an incoming missile has been compared to "hitting a bullet with a bullet." Even this daunting challenge is further complicated by the likelihood of enemy decoys masking the real warhead; a reliable ballistic missile defense must be able to discriminate between decoys and actual warheads.

President George W. Bush announced a limited deployment of sea-based and ground-based missile interceptors and advanced Patriot missiles in 2004. The president envisioned an incremental growth of an anti-ballistic missile capability that would be directed at potential attacks from terrorist states. Currently, the United States has a limited BMD system based in Alaska, presumably to defend against missiles from North Korea. The United States has proposed to develop BMD sites in Poland and the Czech Republic, presumably to defend Europe against missiles from Iran. But Russian President Vladimir Putin has vigorously opposed such a development. In early 2008, the U.S. Navy successfully intercepted and destroyed a falling reconnaissance satellite with a sea-based anti-ballistic missile.

[a]President Ronald Reagan, *The President's Strategic Defense Initiative*, The White House, January 3, 1985.

What Do You *Think?*

When Should the United States Use Military Force?

All modern presidents have acknowledged that the most agonizing decisions they have made were to send U.S. military forces into combat. These decisions cost lives. The American people are willing to send their sons and daughters into danger—and even to see some of them wounded and killed—but *only* if a president convinces them that the outcome "is worth dying for." A president must be able to explain why they lost their lives and to justify their sacrifice.

Only to Protect Vital Interests?

The U.S. military learned many bitter lessons in its long bloody experience in Vietnam. Among those lessons are what became known as the Powell Doctrine, advanced by then Chair of the Joint Chiefs of Staff, General Colin Powell:

★ The United States should commit its military forces only in support of vital national interests.
★ If military forces are committed, they must have clearly defined military objectives—the destruction of enemy forces and/or the capture of enemy-held territory.
★ Any commitment of U.S. forces must be of sufficient strength to ensure overwhelming and decisive victory with the fewest possible casualties.
★ Before committing U.S. military forces, there must be some reasonable assurances that the effort has the support of the American people and their representatives in Congress.
★ The commitment of U.S. military forces should be a last resort, after political, economic, and diplomatic efforts have proven ineffective.

These guidelines for the use of military force are widely supported within the U.S. military itself.[5] Contrary to Hollywood stereotypes, military leaders are extremely reluctant to go to war when no vital interest of the United States is at stake, where there are no clear-cut military objectives, without the support of Congress or the American people, or without sufficient force to achieve speedy and decisive victory with minimal casualties. They are wary of seeing their troops placed in danger merely to advance diplomatic goals, or to engage in "peacekeeping," or to "stabilize governments," or to "show the flag." They are reluctant to undertake humanitarian missions while being shot at. They do not like to risk their soldiers' lives under "rules of engagement" that limit their ability to defend themselves.

In Support of Important Political Objectives?

In contrast to military leaders, political leaders and diplomats often reflect the view that "war is a continuation of politics by other means"—a view commonly attributed to nineteenth-century German theorist of war Karl von Clausewitz. Military force may be used to protect interests that are important but not necessarily vital. Otherwise, the United States would be rendered largely impotent in world affairs. A diplomat's ability to achieve a satisfactory result often depends on the expressed or implied threat of military force. The distinguished international political theorist Hans Morgenthau wrote, "Since military strength is the obvious measure of a nation's power, its demonstration serves to impress others with that nation's power."[6]

Currently American military forces must be prepared to carry out a variety of missions in addition to the conduct of conventional war:

★ Demonstrating U.S. resolve in crisis situations.
★ Demonstrating U.S. support for democratic governments.
★ Protecting U.S. citizens living abroad.
★ Peacemaking among warring factions or nations.
★ Peacekeeping where hostile factions or nations have accepted a peace agreement.
★ Providing humanitarian aid often under warlike conditions.
★ Assisting in an international war against drug trafficking.

In pursuit of such objectives, recent U.S. presidents have sent troops to Lebanon in 1982 to stabilize the government (Reagan), to Grenada in 1983 to rescue American medical students and restore democratic government (Reagan), to Panama in 1989 to oust drug-trafficking General Manuel Antonio Noriega from power and to protect U.S. citizens (Bush, Sr.); to Somalia in 1992–93 to provide emergency humanitarian aid (Bush, Sr., and Clinton); to Haiti in 1994 to restore constitutional government (Clinton) and again to Haiti in 2004 (Bush, Jr.); and to Bosnia and Kosovo for peacekeeping among warring ethnic factions (see the table on the next page).

Major Deployments of U.S. Military Forces Since World War II

Year	Area	President
1950–53	Korea	Truman
1958	Lebanon	Eisenhower
1961–64	Vietnam	Kennedy
1962	Cuban waters	Kennedy
1965–73	Vietnam	Johnson, Nixon
1965	Dominican Republic	Johnson
1970	Laos	Nixon
1970	Cambodia	Nixon
1975	Cambodia	Ford
1980	Iran	Carter
1982–83	Lebanon	Reagan
1983	Grenada	Reagan
1989	Panama	Bush, Sr.
1990–91	Persian Gulf	Bush, Sr.
1992–93	Somalia	Bush, Sr., Clinton
1994–95	Haiti	Clinton
1995–2000	Bosnia	Clinton
1999–2000	Kosovo	Clinton
2001–	Afghanistan	Bush, Jr.
2002–	Philippines	Bush, Jr.
2003–	Iraq	Bush, Jr.
2004	Haiti	Bush, Jr.

security, and humanitarian means. He warned that the new war on terrorism would require a long-term sustained effort. It would require Americans to accept new restrictions on their lives (see "Terrorism's Threat to Democracy" in Chapter 1). It would require new legislation—an Airport Security Act federalizing security at U.S. airports and instituting new strict security measures, and a Patriot (antiterrorism) Act expanding the authority of the attorney general and federal law-enforcement agencies to fight domestic terrorism (see *A Conflicting View*: "Terrorism Requires Restrictions on Civil Liberties" in Chapter 14). It would require the creation of a new Department of Homeland Security designed to coordinate many federal, state, and local law-enforcement agencies charged with responsibility for dealing with acts of terror.

Afghanistan—Operation "Enduring Freedom" The military phase of the war on terrorism began October 7, 2001, when U.S. Air Force and Navy aircraft began attacks on known Al Qaeda bases in Afghanistan and U.S. Special Forces organized and led anti-Taliban fighters, including several tribal groups, in a campaign against the Taliban regime. A coalition of nations participated in Operation "Enduring Freedom"; some, including Britain and Canada, contributed troops, while others, including Pakistan, Saudi Arabia, and Uzbekistan, informally allowed U.S. forces to base operations on their territory. Kabul, the capital of Afghanistan, was occupied by anti-Taliban forces on November 13, 2001.

President Bush made it clear that the United States was prepared to act militarily against governments that harbored or gave sanctuary to terrorists. The Taliban regime was ousted from power. By April 2002—6 months into Operation Enduring Freedom—Al Qaeda and Taliban forces had been scattered into small groups in the mountainous areas of Afghanistan and neighboring Pakistan. Osama bin Laden himself, however, escaped capture.

Politics Up Close — **The Use of Force: Operation Desert Storm**

Saddam Hussein's invasion of Kuwait on August 2, 1990, was apparently designed to restore his military prestige after an indecisive war against Iran, to secure additional oil revenues to finance the continued buildup of Iraqi military power, and to intimidate (and perhaps invade) Saudi Arabia and the Gulf states, thereby securing control over a major share of the world's oil reserves.

The Iraqi invasion met with a surprisingly swift response by the United Nations, with Security Council resolutions condemning the invasion, demanding an immediate withdrawal, and imposing a trade embargo and economic sanctions. President George H. W. Bush immediately set to work to stitch together a coalition military force that would eventually include thirty nations. Early on, the president described the U.S. military deployment as "defensive," but he soon became convinced that neither diplomacy nor an economic blockade would dislodge Saddam from Kuwait and so ordered the military to prepare an "offensive" option.

The top U.S. military commanders—including the chair of the Joint Chiefs of Staff, General Colin Powell, and the commander in the field, General Norman Schwarzkopf—had been field officers in Vietnam, and they were resolved not to repeat the mistakes of that war. They were reluctant to go into battle without the full support of the American people. If ordered to fight, they wanted to employ overwhelming and decisive military force; they wanted to avoid the gradual escalation, protracted conflict, target limitations, and political interference in the conduct of the war that had characterized the U.S. military's efforts in Vietnam. Accordingly, they presented the president with a plan that called for a very large military buildup involving nearly 500,000 troops. Coalition forces also included British and French heavy armored units, and Egyptian, Syrian, Saudi, and other Arab forces.

From Baghdad, CNN reporters Bernard Shaw and Peter Arnett were startled on the night of January 16 when Operation Desert Storm began with an air attack on key installations in the city. Iraqi forces were also surprised, despite the prompt timing of the attack; Saddam had assured them that the United States lacked the resolve to fight.

The success of the coalition air force was spectacular. American TV audiences saw videotapes of laser-guided bombs entering the doors and air shafts of enemy bunkers. Civilian damage was lower than in any previous air war. After 5 weeks of air war, intelligence estimated that nearly half the Iraqi tanks and artillery in the field had been destroyed, demoralized troops were hiding in deep shelters, and the battlefield had been isolated and "prepared" for ground operations.

The Gulf War, labeled "Operation Desert Storm" by the U.S. military, destroyed Iraqi troops in Kuwait and eastern Iraq. President George H. W. Bush ordered a ceasefire after only 100 hours of ground operations. It was hoped that the Iraqi defeat would lead to the ouster of Saddam Hussein, but he survived and strengthened his hold on the Iraqi people.

General Schwarzkopf's plan for the ground war emphasized deception and maneuver. While Iraqi forces prepared for attacks from the south and the east coast, he sent heavily armed columns in a "Hail Mary" play—a wide sweep to the west, outflanking and cutting off Iraqi forces in the battle area. On the night of February 24, the ground attack began. Marines breached ditches and minefields and raced directly to the Kuwait airport; army helicopter air assaults lunged deep into Iraq; armored columns raced northward across the desert to outflank Iraqi forces and then attack them from the west, while a surge in air attacks kept Iraqi forces holed up in their bunkers. Iraqi troops surrendered in droves, highways from Kuwait city became a massive junkyard of Iraqi vehicles, and Iraqi forces that tried to fight were quickly destroyed. After 100 hours of ground fighting, President George H. W. Bush ordered a cease-fire.

The United States had achieved a decisive military victory quickly and with remarkably few casualties. The president resisted calls to expand the original objectives of the war and go on to capture Baghdad, to destroy the Iraqi economy, to encourage Iraq's disintegration as a nation, or to kill Saddam, although it was expected that his defeat would lead to his ouster. Although the war left many political issues unresolved, it was the most decisive military outcome the United States had achieved since the end of World War II.[a] President Bush chose to declare victory and celebrate the return of American troops.

[a]See Harry G. Summers, Jr., *On Strategy II: A Critical Analysis of the Gulf War.* New York: Dell, 1992.

A meeting in Bonn, Germany, of various Afghan political and military groups produced general agreement on the installation of a new government in Kabul, headed by Hamid Karzai. But today the Karzai government has less than full control over Afghanistan; various tribal military chiefs, or "warlords," exercise independent power throughout the country.

Military Force in the War on Terrorism   The War on Terrorism creates new conditions for the use of military force.[7] Currently U.S. forces are prepared for:

★ Direct attacks against terrorist forces to capture or kill them. These operations are usually carried out by highly trained Special Forces.

★ Attacks on nations that harbor terrorists, allow terrorists to maintain bases, or supply and equip terrorist organizations. In 1986, the United States struck at Libya in a limited air attack in response to various Libyan-supported acts of terrorism around the world. In 1993, the United States struck Iraq's intelligence center in Baghdad in response to a foiled plot to assassinate former President George H. W. Bush. In 2001, the United States relied principally on Special Forces working in conjunction with tribal forces in Afghanistan to attack Al Qaeda terrorists and to topple the Taliban government that had harbored and supported Al Qaeda.

★ **preemptive attacks**
The initiation of military action by the United States to prevent terrorists or rogue nations from inflicting heavy damage on the United States.

★ **Preemptive attacks** on regimes that threaten to use weapons of mass destruction—chemical, biological, or nuclear weapons—against the United States or its allies, or to supply terrorist organizations with these weapons. Preemptive military action represents a reversal of traditional U.S. policy. Historically, the United States acted militarily only in response to a direct attack on its own forces or those of its allies. But it is argued that the Terrorist Attack of "9/11" initiated the current War on Terrorism and that American military actions in the Middle East, including those in Afghanistan and Iraq, are related to the "9/11" attack on America. The argument for preemptive military action was summarized by Secretary of State Condoleezza Rice: "We cannot wait until the smoking gun becomes a mushroom cloud."

Assymmetrical Warfare of the Future   Traditionally the United States structured its military tactics and forces to confront conventional threats—national armies with heavy armor, tanks and artillery, mechanized infantry, and combat aircraft. During the Cold War, U.S. forces were designed to confront heavy Soviet armor and artillery in Central Europe, in a manner similar, albeit more violent, to the armies that fought in World War II. The Gulf War in 1991 demonstrated the superiority of American forces in large-scale conventional operations.

The war on terror requires the United States to reshape its military planning to confront unconventional (or assymmetrical) wars—lightly armed, irregular enemy forces engaging in tactics such as ambushes, hidden explosives, suicide bombings, and hostage takings. America's enemies are fully aware of the overwhelming firepower of conventional U.S. military forces. Consequently they seek to minimize U.S. advantage in firepower in a variety of ways. They choose terrain that inhibits the use of conventional tank, artillery, and air power—jungles and mountains where these conventional forces cannot operate as effectively as in open country. They also choose built-up urban areas where civilian populations inhibit U.S. forces from employing their full firepower. They avoid direct confrontations with large American units, blending in with the population and seeming to disappear in the presence of U.S. combat forces.

Assymmetrical warfare is the approach of a weaker foe trying to overcome the advantages of a force that is superior in conventional forms of warfare. Traditionally the U.S. Army preferred that its opponents face it in massed formations on conventional battlefields where overwhelming American power could be brought to bear to destroy the opponent. But an inferior opponent would be foolhardy to cooperate in its own destruction by fighting the war that Americans prefer to fight. Guerrilla warfare, which United States encountered in Vietnam, is one form of a symmetrical warfare. Terrorism is another, which includes consciously targeting civilians.

In the future the United States is likely to confront a new and radically different form of warfare: ". . . in the future there will be no distinctions between civilians and military forces in terms of targeting: society is the battlefield in the new environment. There will be an absence of definable battlefields or fronts, and the places where fighting occurs will be disbursed and undefined: everywhere and nowhere is the front lines. . . . The goal will not be traditional military defeat but instead the internal political collapse of the opponent and its will to continue. The manipulation of the media will be a skill that is highly sought by practitioners [of this kind of warfare], and the targets of much of this activity will be popular support for the government or whatever force against which the campaign is waged."[8]

The War in Iraq

At the end of the Gulf War in 1991, the Iraqi regime of Saddam Hussein agreed to destroy all of its chemical and biological weapons and to end its efforts to acquire nuclear weapons. United Nations inspectors were to verify Iraqi compliance with these conditions. But Saddam's regime refused to cooperate; in 1998 he ordered the inspectors out of the country. Over a 12-year period Iraq violated at least a dozen UN resolutions. Following a U.S. military buildup in the region in late 2002, Saddam allowed UN inspectors to return but continued to obstruct their work. On March 19, 2003, after giving Saddam a 48-hour warning to leave Iraq, the United States and Great Britain launched air strikes designed to eliminate Saddam and his top command.

Operation Iraqi Freedom At different times President George W. Bush stated the purposes of "Operation Iraqi Freedom" as (1) the elimination of Iraq's weapons of mass destruction, (2) a "regime change" for Iraq to end the threat that Saddam posed for his neighbors and to free the Iraqi people from his oppressive rule, and (3) to ensure that Saddam would not harbor or assist terrorist organizations. But President Bush and Secretary of State Colin Powell failed to secure UN Security Council approval for military action. Among the permanent members of the Security Council, only the British, with the strong support of Prime Minister Tony Blair, were prepared to offer significant military support for the war against Saddam. Public opinion in America supported military action, but public opinion in Europe opposed it (see *Compared to What?* "World Opinion About America's War Against Terrorism"). France and Germany led the diplomatic opposition; Turkey refused to let U.S. troops use its territory to attack Iraq; and the United States was obliged to rely primarily on Kuwait, Qatar, and the other smaller Gulf states for regional support.

Turbulent Occupation

American and British soldiers and Marines swept into Baghdad in just 21 days in 2003 with relatively few casualties. But the subsequent occupation of that country was poorly prepared for, incompetently executed, and terribly costly in soldiers' lives lost.

The U.S. military wanted to wage war in the fashion of the successful Gulf War—a period of heavy air bombardment to "prepare the battlefield," followed by a massive ground attack using overwhelming military force. But Secretary of Defense Donald Rumsfeld wanted a "leaner" fighting force in Iraq. He deployed fewer than half of the air, ground, and naval forces that had been used in the Gulf War. And he began the air and ground attacks simultaneously.

American and British soldiers and Marines took just 21 days to sweep the 350 miles from the Kuwait border to downtown Baghdad. The British 3rd Armored Division, with Australian support, captured the port city of Basra; the U.S. 3rd Infantry Division moved up the west side of the Euphrates River; and the U.S. 1st Marine Division moved up the east side. Special Operations Forces, together with elements of the 101st Airborne Division, joined Kurdish forces in northern Iraq. Special Operations Forces also acted quickly to secure Iraq's oil fields and prevent their destruction. At first progress was hindered by the requirement that soldiers wear heavy chemical protection gear and carry decontamination equipment. But neither chemical nor biological weapons were used against U.S. forces. The advance on Baghdad was speeded up and the city was captured with precious few casualties.

The Occupation of Iraq The American occupation of Iraq started out poorly and proceeded over time to become worse. Planning for post-war Iraq appeared nonexistent. The U.S. administrator for Iraq, Paul Bremmer, began by dismissing the entire Iraqi Army, sending thousands of well-armed, unemployed young men into the streets. The United States promised to restore infrastructure—water, electricity, roads—yet Bremmer pursued a policy of dismissing virtually all Iraqi managers and technicians on the ground that they had been Baathists (Saddam's ruling party members). Later, the United States would be obliged to begin recruiting and training an Iraqi army and police force and bringing in U.S. contract workers, managers, and technicians. Bremmer was fired after 1 year.

Soon, Iraqi street mobs that had earlier torn down Saddam's statute began demonstrations against the American presence. An insurgent movement seemed to surprise Secretary of Defense Donald Rumsfeld. He steadfastly refused to send additional U.S. troops to Iraq to handle the insurgency and insisted that a new Iraqi government could eventually recruit and train enough troops to contain the insurgency. No weapons of mass destruction were found despite an intensive search. Saddam himself was captured and turned over to the Iraqis, who conducted a bizarre trial; 3 years after his capture he was convicted of mass murder and executed by hanging.

Bush's critics at home and abroad increasingly complained of the president's "unilateralism"—his willingness to go to war without the support of the United Nations, and they charged that he misled Congress, the UN and the American people about the existence of weapons of mass destruction.

Iraqi Governance The population of Iraq is composed of three major factions: the Kurds, who occupy most of northeastern Iraq; the Shiites, who occupy most of southern Iraq; and the Sunnis, who occupy central Iraq. Baghdad itself is divided between Sunni and Shiite neighborhoods (see Figure 18.3). The Sunnis have long dominated Iraq. Saddam's family was Sunni. Yet the Shiites are the largest faction with more than half of the total population of Iraq. Over the years, the Kurds have fought for a separate Kurdistan, an outcome strongly opposed by neighboring Turkey.

Iraq held its first nationwide election in 50 years in 2003, despite violence and threats of violence. Nearly 60 percent of the population participated, many proudly displaying their blue-inked thumbs to signal that they had voted. The result was a new constitution that was approved in a second vote that year. However, a substantial number of Sunnis boycotted the elections, fearing a loss of

Compared to *What?*

World Opinion About America's War Against Terrorism

Europeans were generally sympathetic with the United States following the terrorist attack of "9/11," and generally supported the U.S. military campaign against terrorists in Afghanistan. But opinion in Europe, as well as in the Muslim world, opposed U.S. military action in Iraq. Indeed, over time ratings of the United States have grown markedly less favorable among Europeans, and the United States is now strongly disliked in the Muslim world. An important factor in world opinion about America is the perception that the United States acts internationally without taking into account the interests of other nations.

Ratings of the United States

	2002		2006	
	Favorable	Unfavorable	Favorable	Unfavorable
Great Britain	75%	16%	56%	32%
France	63	34	39	60
Germany	61	35	37	58
Russia	61	33	43	45
Japan	72	22	63	30
Turkey	30	42	12	60
Pakistan	10	58	27	50
Jordan	25	57	15	65

Source: Pew Research Center for the People and the Press. www.people-press.org. Reprinted by permission of Pew Research Center for the People and the Press.

their power and the ascendancy of the Shiites. The United States officially turned over sovereignty to a new Iraqi government in 2004.

Civil War   Iraq gradually disintegrated into a bloody civil war, with Sunni and Shiite forces committing atrocities against each other. By 2006 most of the violence in Iraq was occurring among various factions; thousands of Iraqi were victims of sectarian killings. The Shiites, the majority of Iraq's population, gained power for the first time in more than 1,000 years. Above all, the Shiites are interested in preserving that power. The Sunnis fear displacement and the loss of their traditional position of power in Iraq. The Kurds seek at a minimum quasi-independence and control over the oil resources in their region. The Shiites also seek control over oil resources in southern Iraq. But the areas with the largest Sunni population lack oil resources, so the Sunnis fight to maintain control of all of Iraq. Corruption is rampant throughout; the judiciary is weak; oil production is down; and as of 2008 the U.S. backed government is unable to produce an acceptable plan of national reconciliation.

The Insurgency   Attacks on U.S. forces and Iraqi army and police grew in intensity and deadliness month after month. Most attacks against Americans came from disaffected Sunni Arabs including former elements of Saddam's regime. Al Qaeda was responsible for a portion of the violence including the more spectacular suicide attacks, truck bombs, and attacks on religious and political targets. The insurgency raised the flag of "Jihad" and brought in thousands of Islamic radical foreign fighters. The Shiites organized their own militia, the strongest being the Mahdi Army with as many as 60,000 fighters led by Moqtada al-Sadr. Large areas of Iraq came under the control of one or another of these insurgent groups.

Figure *18.3*

Distribution of Religious Groups in Iraq

Iraq encompasses multiple religious sects and minority groups. The principal divisions are between Sunnis, Shia, and Kurds.

Source: Iraq Study Group Report. 2006.

American military forces suffered a gruesome toll in lives and limbs. By 2008 over 4,000 American troops had been killed, many from "improvised explosive devices." U.S. Army and Marine forces approached the "breaking point." Nearly every Army and Marine combat unit, and several National Guard and Reserve units, were rotated into Iraq more than once. The strain on U.S. forces worldwide became clearly evident, with both personnel and equipment wearing down.

"Stay the Course"   U.S. policy in Iraq focused primarily on security. The key phrase was "clear, hold, and build." U.S. military forces were to clear neighborhoods and cities, towns, and regions of insurgents; then to hold the cleared areas with U.S. trained and equipped Iraqi army and police forces; and then to begin to rebuild infrastructure. U.S. forces were able to "clear" many areas, but there were too few troops to "hold" these areas. Iraqi forces were unable or unwilling to halt insurgents from reoccupying these areas after American troops left. Very little "building" took place. Many members of the Iraqi security forces remained loyal to their sectarian—Shiite or Sunni—goals, rather than the agenda of the national government. Many of these units simply refused to carry out assigned missions.

Nevertheless, President Bush continued to argue that the war in Iraq was central to the worldwide war against terrorism. He argued that an abrupt withdrawal ("cut and run") would encourage radical Islamic terrorists around the world.

> Failure is not an option. Iraq would become a safe haven from which terrorists could plan attacks against American interests abroad, and our allies. Middle East reformers would never again fully trust American assurances of support for democracy in human rights in the region. Iraq is the central front in the global war on terror.[9]

The "Surge" The sweeping Democratic victory in the congressional elections of 2006 was widely attributed to popular disaffection with the war in Iraq. Democrats gained control of both the House and the Senate. Many of their supporters expected them to end the war by cutting off funds for the prosecution of the war. At a minimum, opponents of the war wanted Congress to set a timetable for the reduction of U.S. troops in Iraq. But when staring directly at the prospect of cutting off funds for troops in the field, Congress blinked. Resolutions to end the war or to force U.S. troop reductions failed.

Instead, President Bush announced a "surge" in troop strength designed to improve security in Iraq and allow the Iraqi government to reach "benchmarks" in resolving civil strife. The "surge" involved increasing U.S. troop levels in Iraq from roughly 138,000 to 160,000. In January 2007, the president appointed a new commander for Iraq. General David Petraeus (see *People in Politics: "General David Petraeus"*). Petraeus was unanimously confirmed by the Senate, but Congress stipulated that in September 2007, the general was to report on progress in Iraq.

Petraeus reported to Congress that the "surge" was working, that progress was being made in stabilizing Iraq and in training Iraqi forces, that U.S. troop levels could be reduced to presurge levels, but that some U.S. forces may be needed in Iraq for 10 years or more. He argued that a timetable for troop reductions would be counterproductive.

"A Way Forward"? The Bush administration argued that a premature withdrawal would "embolden violent extremists" and leave our children a far more dangerous world." Al Qaeda would gain new recruits and sanctuaries. Iran would benefit from the chaos and be encouraged in its efforts to gain nuclear weapons and dominate the region. Iraq could face a humanitarian nightmare. Extremists

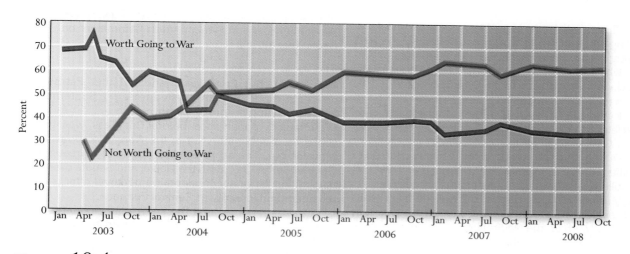

Figure *18.4* Public Opinion: Was the War in Iraq Worth It?

Q. *"All in all, do you think it was worth going to war in Iraq, or not?"*
Dates of Polls: 2003–March, May, August, October; December 2004–January, March, June, September; 2005–January, June, September, November; 2005–June.

Source: www.pollingreport.com

could control a key part of the global energy supply. Bush proposes "a way forward": "Over time, our troops will shift from leading operations to partnering with Iraqi forces and eventually to over-watching those forces. As this transition in our mission takes place, our troops will focus on a more limited set of tasks, including counterterrorism operations and training, equipping, and supporting Iraqi forces."[9]

Yet it is clear that the American public no longer supports the war and wants U.S. troops withdrawn as soon as possible (see Figure 18.4). There is frustration over the failure of the Iraqi government to make progress in resolving sectarian differences. The United States should not be involved in a civil war. U.S. military presence in Iraq is encouraging the growth of Al Qaeda. International opinion strongly opposes the continuation of U.S. military occupation of Iraq. Years after the start of the war, violence continues and there is no end in sight. The U.S. military has been weakened overall by the stresses placed upon it by the fighting in Iraq.

People in Politics   General David Petraeus

When General David Petraeus was given the assignment to carry out his Commander-in-Chief's "surge" policy in Iraq, the four-star general was thrust into the political cauldron in Washington. His success depended on his performance on two battlefields—Iraq and Capitol Hill.

David Petraeus was well suited for the politically difficult command he was given. As a West Point cadet Petraeus dated the Superintendent's daughter, proving his willingness to take risks. He married the General's daughter following graduation in 1974. Recognized as a rising star in the military, Petraeus was the top graduate of the U.S. Army Command and General Staff College in 1983. He subsequently earned a Master of Public Administration degree and a Ph.D. in International Relations from Princeton University. He rose through various commands in airborne infantry, and served in Haiti, Kuwait, and Bosnia.

His first combat was as a Major General and commanding officer of the 101st Airborne Division in the 2003 invasion of Iraq. He led his division in the battles of Karbala, Hilla, and Najaf. Following the fall of Baghdad the 101st cleared western Iraq to the Syrian border. When his division returned to the United States, Petraeus was given the task of training a new Iraqi army and security force. He would later come under criticism for distributing weapons to Iraqi forces, weapons that ended up in the hands of insurgents fighting U.S. troops. Later, Petraeus returned to the United States to oversee the Command and General Staff College and develop counterinsurgency doctrine.

In January 2007, as part of his revised Iraqi strategy, President Bush announced that Petraeus would take command of the Multi-National Force in Iraq. Congressional Democrats expressed strong misgivings against the "surge" but the Senate unanimously confirmed Petraeus as a four-star general and Commander of U.S. forces in Iraq. Congress failed to cut off funds for the war or to set a timetable for troop

Photographers swarm over General David Petraeus, Commanding General Multi-National Force, Iraq, and U.S. Ambassador to Iraq Ryan Crocker before they give their testimony, before a joint hearing of the House Armed Services and Foreign Affairs Committees on September 10, 2007.

withdrawal. But Congress mandated that Petraeus deliver a report directly to Congress by September 2007, assessing progress in Iraq.

Petraeus's appearance before Congress was preceded by a defamatory ad in the *New York Times* by MoveOn.org. The ad's headline: "General Petraeus or General Betray Us." Both the House and Senate passed resolutions "strongly condemning personal attacks on the honor and integrity of General Petraeus."

Petraeus reported that the surge was working and that U.S. troop levels could be reduced to presurge numbers. He argued against any timetables for withdrawal and acknowledged that U.S. involvement in Iraq could last another 10 years. Congressional Democrats were not pleased. The General remained loyal to his Commander-in-Chief.

Controversy

Opposition to the War in Iraq

Americans demand quick victory in war. With the exception of World War II, American public support for wars, notably Korea (1950–53) and Vietnam (1965–73), declined steadily as casualties rose and no end appeared in sight.[a] The initial "rally 'round the flag" support for military action begins to wane after the first year of combat. Quick victories with few casualties, as in the Gulf War (1991), inspire support for the president and his decision to go to war. Prolonged stalemates with mounting casualties gradually erode public support for war.

Shortly after the war in Iraq began, most Americans thought Iraq was worth going to war over. Indeed, this opinion climbed to a 76 percent approval rating immediately following the capture of Baghdad. But as American casualties mounted and no end to the fighting appeared in sight, mass opinion in support of the war declined rapidly.[b] By late 2004, a majority of Americans believed that Iraq was "not worth going to war over." By nearly two to one, the negative view has prevailed through 2008 (see Figure 18.4).

[a]John E. Mueller, *War Presidents and Public Opinion*. New York: Wiley, 1973.
[b]Scott Sigmund Gartner, "The Multiple Effects of Casualties on Public Support for War," *American Political Review* 102 (February 2008), 95–106.

A *Constitutional* Note

Congress Versus the Commander-in-Chief

The Constitution of 1787 divided war-making powers between the Congress and the president. Article I, Section 8, states that "Congress shall have Power . . . to provide for the common Defense . . . to declare War . . . to raise and support Armies . . . to provide and maintain a Navy . . . to make Rules for the Government and Regulation of the land and naval forces." However, Article II, Section 2, states that "the President shall be the Commander-in-Chief of the Army and Navy of the United States." But today wars are not "declared"; instead they begin with military action, and the president is responsible for the actions of the Armed Forces of the United States. Presidents have sent U.S. troops beyond the borders of the United States in military actions on more than 200 occasions. In contrast, Congress has formally declared war only five times: the War of 1812, the Mexican War in 1846, the Spanish-American War in 1898, World War I in 1917, and World War II in 1941. Congress did *not* declare war in the Korean War (1950–53), the Vietnam War (1965–73), the Persian Gulf War (1991), or the wars in Afghanistan (2002–) or Iraq (2003–). While presidents asked for the support of Congress in these wars, no formal declarations of war were ever made. The Supreme Court has consistently refused to hear cases involving the war powers of the president and Congress.

Summary
Who Gets What: National Security

The struggle for power is global. Leaders and peoples of the world protect and advance their goals and ideals through the exercise of power.

★ There is no world government capable of legislating and enforcing rules of international politics. But various efforts to stabilize relations among nations have been attempted, including the balance-of-power system of alliances in the eighteenth and nineteenth centuries, the collective security arrangements of the League of Nations and the United Nations in the twentieth century, and the regional security approach of the North Atlantic Treaty Organization.

★ The United Nations was largely ineffective during the Cold War, the confrontation between the Western democracies led by the United States and communist bloc nations led by the Soviet Union. During these years, the Western nations relied principally on the strength of the North Atlantic Treaty Organization (NATO) to deter war in Europe.

★ For nearly 50 years, the Cold War largely directed U.S. foreign and defense policy. The United States sought to contain Soviet military expansionism and world communist revolutionary forces in all parts of the globe. U.S. involvement in the Korean and Vietnam wars grew out of this containment policy.

★ During the Cold War years, U.S. and Soviet military forces never engaged in direct combat against each other, although many "proxy" conflicts took place throughout the world. The most serious threat of nuclear war occurred during the Cuban missile crisis in 1962.

★ To maintain nuclear peace, the United States relied primarily on the policy of deterrence—dissuading the Soviets from launching a nuclear attack by maintaining survivable second-strike forces capable of inflicting unacceptable levels of destruction in a retaliatory attack.

★ In 1970 President Richard Nixon and National Security Adviser Henry Kissinger began negotiations with the Soviet Union with a view to limiting the nuclear arms race. These Strategic Arms Limitation Talks produced the SALT I agreement in 1972, and later, under President Jimmy Carter, the SALT II agreement in 1979. Both agreements set limits on future strategic weapons development but failed to reduce existing weapons stockpiles.

★ President Ronald Reagan renamed the negotiations START, emphasizing the goal of reductions in weapons rather than limitations, and stressing equality and verification. The START I (1991) and START II (1993) treaties called for reducing nuclear arsenals by two-thirds from Cold War levels.

★ The end of the Cold War followed the ouster of communist governments in Eastern Europe in 1989, the unifica-

tion of Germany in 1990, the collapse of the Warsaw Pact communist military alliance in 1991, and the dissolution of the Soviet Union in 1991. Russia has inherited most of the nuclear weapons and military forces of the former Soviet Union as well as its seat on the UN Security Council.

★ Current threats to peace and security are likely to be posed by regional aggressors. U.S. involvement in the Gulf War in 1990–91 is representative of the type of military action required to confront regional powers such as Iran and North Korea.

★ The military phase of America's War on Terrorism began October 7, 2001, when U.S. aircraft began attacks on Al Qaeda bases in Afghanistan and U.S. special forces organized and led anti-Taliban Afghan fighters to oust the Taliban regime that had harbored the terrorists. These military actions largely destroyed the terrorist infrastructure in Afghanistan; yet scattered groups of terrorists remain in that country and neighboring Pakistan.

★ Military doctrine is increasingly focused on counterinsurgency—confronting irregular forces engaging in tactics such as ambushes, hidden explosives, and suicide bombings.

★ Following the Vietnam War, many military leaders argued that U.S. forces should be used only to protect vital American interests, only in support of clearly defined military objectives, only with sufficient strength to ensure decisive victory with the fewest possible casualties, only with the support of the American people and Congress, and only as a last resort.

★ Recent presidents, however, have used military forces to carry out a variety of missions in addition to conventional war, including peacekeeping, antiterrorist, and humanitarian activities. They have argued that the risks were worth taking in light of the importance of the goals.

Key Terms

collective security 628
Soviet Union 628
superpowers 628
regional security 629
North Atlantic Treaty
Organization
  (NATO) 629

Cold War 630
Truman Doctrine 631
containment 631
Marshall Plan 631
Korean War 632
Cuban Missile
  Crisis 632

Vietnam War 632
deterrence 635
second-strike
  capability 635
SALT I 635
ABM Treaty 635
SALT II 636

START I 636
START II 636
ballistic missile defense
  (BMD) 637
terrorism 637
preemptive attacks 642

Suggested Readings

Banks, William C., Renee deNevers, and Mitchel B. Wallerstein. *Combatting Terrorism Strategies and Approaches.* Washington, D.C.: CQ Press, 2007. Comprehensive description of a variety of counterterrorism strategies, including law enforcement, diplomacy, and military action.

Clausewitz, Karl von. *On War.* Edited and translated by Michael Howard and Peter Paret. Princeton, N.J.: Princeton University Press, 1984. The classic theory of war and military operations, emphasizing their political character; first published in 1832.

Hastedt, Glenn P. *American Foreign Policy: Past, Present, Future.* 7th ed. Upper Saddle River, N.J.: Prentice Hall, 2009. A foreign policy text that deals with national security issues within the broader context of foreign policy.

International Institute for Strategic Studies. *The Military Balance.* London: International Institute for Strategic Studies, published annually. Careful description of the military forces of more than 160 countries; this book is considered the most authoritative public information available.

Hook, Stephen W., and John Spanier. *American Foreign Policy Since World War II.* 17th ed. Washington, D.C.: CQ Press; 2006. Updated version of classic text on American Foreign Policy, concluding with "A World of Trouble".

Magstadt, Thomas M. *An Empire If You Can Keep It: Power and Principle in American Foreign Policy.* Washington, D.C.: CQ Press, 2004. Comprehensive text on American foreign policy, describing its history, the Cold War, the Gulf War, September 11, and the War on Terrorism.

Nacos, Brigitte L. *Terrorism and Counterterrorism.* 2nd ed. New York: Longman, 2008. Terrorism's causes, actors, and strategies as well as counterterrorism responses.

Snow, Donald M. *National Security for a New Era.* 3rd ed. New York: Longman, 2009. Comprehensive text examining United States national security issues following the end of the Cold War and following "9/11".

Summers, Harry G., Jr. *On Strategy II: A Critical Analysis of the Gulf War.* New York: Dell, 1992. Analysis of the Gulf War based on Clausewitz's classic principles of war. The strategic decisions leading to victory in the Gulf contrast markedly with the decisions in Vietnam that led to defeat, a topic covered in Summers's groundbreaking first book, *On Strategy: A Critical Analysis of the Vietnam War* (New York: Dell, 1984).

Suggested Web Sites

American Security Council www.ascusa.org
Organization providing summary information on national security threats.

CIA-Terrorism www.cia.gov/terrorism
Reports, news, and facts regarding terrorism.

CIA World Factbook www.cia.gov/publications/factbook
Nations listed A–Z with geography, people, economy, government, military, and so on.

Cuban Crisis www.cubacrisis.net
The October 1962 nuclear missile crisis described day to day, with photos.

Defenselink Terrorism www.defenselink.mil/terrorism
Official Defense Department site link to information on terrorism.

Korean War Project Organization www.koreanwar.org
Dedicated to the memory of sacrifices of Americans in Korea, with links to battles, units, and memorials.

NATO www.nato.int
The official "North Atlantic Treaty Organization" site contains basic facts about the alliance, current NATO news and issues, and important NATO policies.

Russia EIN News www.einnews.com/russia
Business, cultural, political, and scientific news from Russia.

State Department www.state.gov
This U.S. Department of State Web site contains background notes on the countries and regions of the world.

Terrorism Research Center www.terrorism.com
The "Terrorism Research Center" Web site is dedicated to "informing the public of the phenomena of terrorism and information warfare." It contains news, analytical essays on terrorist issues, and many links to other terrorism materials and research sources.

United Nations www.un.org
This United Nations site contains basic information about the world body's mission, member states, issues of concern, institutions, and accomplishments.

19 THE SOCIAL AND ECONOMIC MILIEU OF TEXAS POLITICS

> **"** Political life, in the narrowest sense of the word, is a life of conflict and presupposes who can bring themselves into active relationship to their surroundings. **"**

Harold Lasswell

Chapter *Outline*

✓Think About Politics

1. Are politics in Texas different from other states?
   YES ◯ NO ◯

2. Is the political culture of Texas changing as a consequence of demographic changes?
   YES ◯ NO ◯

3. Do race and ethnicity play a major role in Texas politics?
   YES ◯ NO ◯

4. Do some groups or interests in Texas have more influence or power than others in public policy decisions?
   YES ◯ NO ◯

5. Has Texas been successful in adapting to the global economy?
   YES ◯ NO ◯

6. Should a fence be constructed on the Texas border to reduce illegal immigration into Texas?
   YES ◯ NO ◯

Social and economic factors are directly related to the distribution of political power and help determine who gets what in Texas politics.

Decades of Change and Challenge

With a colorful history of cowboys and oilmen, Texas has a rugged, bigger-than-life mystique that annoys or amuses many non-Texans. In many obvious and not-so-obvious ways, Texans continue to manifest this legacy of the frontier in their speech, their can-do attitude, their celebration of their "Texan-ness," and their actions (see *Politics Up Close*: "Perpetuating an Image: The Cowboy President"). In what other state do you find the pervasive display of the state's flag or the pilgrimage of so many to the state's holy shrine—the Alamo? Behaviors and language with which others take umbrage and often misunderstand are viewed by most Texans to be simply part of the rich culture and legacy of the state.

The twenty-first century wasn't very old, however, before it became obvious that Texas also had oversized problems. Houston-based Enron Corp., a symbol of how to transform brash confidence into seemingly unlimited corporate wealth, came tumbling down, taking thousands of jobs and pensions with it and damaging public confidence in corporate America.

The terrorist attacks on the World Trade Center and the Pentagon on September 11, 2001, challenged Texans' and other Americans' long-held assumptions about the basic security of our country and our state. And throughout the decade, Texas was thrust into the center of renewed debate over illegal immigration, including concerns over how to improve the security of the border with Mexico and deal with thousands of undocumented workers seeking better lives for themselves and their families.

Back-to-back hurricanes in 2005 challenged Texas's ability to provide education, health care, and other social services for thousands of Katrina refugees from Louisiana (many of whom stayed in Texas rather than returning to their homes), and to help thousands of residents of southeast Texas rebuild their lives following Hurricane Rita.

Increasingly, the politics and economy of Texas are being challenged by global trends. The state's population continues to be transformed by immigration and other changing demographic patterns. The frontier, or rural society, characterized by the cowboy, is long gone. The "Oil Patch," where wildcatters and roughnecks once prevailed, has been replaced by what one author dubbed the "Silicon Prairie . . . where venture capitalists and software engineers roam."[1] Texas is now urban, with

Politics Up Close   Perpetuating an Image: The Cowboy President

Source: BBC News, June 6, 2003.

Throughout his administration, President George W. Bush has been described by some as the "cowboy president." At least two of his predecessors, Theodore Roosevelt and Ronald Reagan, also were portrayed as cowboys, either in cartoons or prose. The cowboy mythology resonates with most Americans, and it can be used by presidents to symbolize their style of leadership.

At the beginning of the invasion of Iraq, Bush branded former Iraqi leader Saddam Hussein an "outlaw" and declared that he wanted terrorist Osama bin Laden "dead or alive." At a conference in Aqaba on the Red Sea, Bush said that he was going to appoint a coordinator to "ride herd" on Middle East leaders along the peace trail. Many in his audience had no idea what he was talking about.

Bush owns a 1,600-acre ranch in Texas, which he purchased during his governorship, but he didn't grow up or work on a ranch. He also has been reported to be afraid of horses. While visiting the former president of Mexico, Vicente Fox, on his ranch, he was offered the opportunity to ride a horse but reportedly backed away from the animal. It was later reported that Fox referred to him as a "windshield cowboy."

Bush wears a stylish Stetson and a large belt buckle. He conveys an "aw shucks" demeanor, scrambles his words in a folksy manner, stages photo-ops on his ranch, and seems to enjoy driving his guests around in his Jeep. This cowboy imagery makes for good press, and some observers think that a great deal of this is orchestrated by his staff and consultants.

The president's characterization as a cowboy in articles, newscasts, and cartoons, meanwhile, continues to feed the perceptions others have of the frontier culture of Texas and its style of politics.

more than 83 percent of the population living in cities or suburban areas. The state includes three of the ten largest cities in the United States—Houston, San Antonio, and Dallas.

Texas is not immune from a host of nagging, down-to-earth problems confronting many other states, including the demands of population growth, economic uncertainties, and corporate mergers outsourcing thousands of jobs to the other side of the world. But a legacy of individualism and limited government makes it difficult to adjust to the new realities of a changing economy, a changing society, and a changing political landscape.

Like many other citizens across the country, Texans are woefully ignorant of their state and local governments. Many view government as something in Austin or at the county courthouse, where people do things to us, not for us. Government is often described in terms of red tape, inefficiency, and anonymous or rude bureaucrats. Political campaigns are perceived as a form of organized mud wrestling in which candidates characterize each other as despicable, immoral, incompetent, or whatever, and this perception results in large numbers of Texans tuning out politics. Many people distrust government—a traditionally strong sentiment in Texas—and hope it interferes with their lives as little as possible. Most Texans don't vote in elections, leaving the selection of public leaders to others.

Texans expect a wide variety of public services, but they are ill disposed to paying for them with increased taxes, an attitude perpetuated by many politicians who promise more services but are unwilling to address their costs.

Our past, marked by good times as well as bad, is a prelude to our future, and our decisions about politics, government, and public policies will determine how we adapt to inevitable changes.

Challenges of the Twenty-First Century

Sustained population growth; the continued transformation of the state's economy; environmental, transportation, and water problems; security; and increased demands for governmental services pose tremendous challenges to the resources, capabilities, and the very structure of Texas's governments. Federal mandates and reductions in federal funds have forced state and local governments to scramble to develop more effective and efficient means of assisting low-income people. Public officials are also challenged by a regressive and outdated tax system, high rates of unemployment and underemployment in various areas of the state, the influx of immigrants from Mexico and other countries, an aging population that requires long-term nursing care, large numbers of people who have no health insurance, and changes in welfare law. Inequities in public education persist and continue to pose a challenge for developing a workforce that can compete in the global economy. And the state's growth has aggravated environmental problems, including water use, that affect the health and well-being of everyone.

These problems and issues are the ingredients of contemporary Texas politics. They reflect the fundamental conflicts between competing interests and the way Texans decide who gets "what, when, and how."[2] Unfortunately, only a small part of the population is involved in developing solutions. The only time many people get excited or concerned about government is when it fails to meet their demands or expectations. Such indifference and ignorance are harmful to the public interest as Texas faces critical changes.

As we begin our analysis of Texas government and politics, we ask why Texans and their public officials make the political choices they do. Why, for example, do expenditures for public education rank so low in comparison to other states? How do we account for Texas's highly regressive tax system, which requires low-income citizens to pay a higher proportion of their income in state and local taxes than do the wealthy? Why are Texans so willing to fund the construction of highways and roads and yet their state ranks near the bottom nationally in expenditures for public welfare?[3]

These policy issues are directly linked to a variety of other questions about governmental institutions and the political system. Why are Texans content to live under a state constitution that most scholars regard as obsolete? Why, until recently, was Texas a one-party Democratic state? Why are state politics now dominated by Republicans? Does a small group of powerful individuals make the primary policy decisions for the state, or are there various competitive centers of power? Do Texans feel they are paying more but getting less for their tax dollars?

Most of these issues affect Texans personally. They pay the costs, even though they may not receive the benefits of every policy decision. The actions of governmental leaders can have an immediate and direct effect on people's lives, and, from time to time, those holding positions of power have made decisions that have cost Texans dearly. For example, the Enron debacle and the manipulation of energy markets were the result, in large part, of the failure of state and federal governments to regulate the energy industry adequately. And cuts in governmental services—or increases in tuition at state-supported universities—often result from the refusal of the Texas legislature to increase taxes. The fundamental changes in the social, economic, and political structure of the state have required new solutions. Funding public education in the days of the one-room schoolhouse was one thing. Funding today's educational system in a way that provides equity among the state's 1,000-plus school districts is much more complex.

The demographics, or population characteristics, of the state have changed dramatically since the 1940s, when Texas was still predominantly rural. With the state's population fast approaching 24 million residents, Texas now is second only to California in population. Its ethnic and racial composition has changed, and it is now home to a large number of individuals who were born and reared in other parts of the United States or outside the country—people who have a limited sense of Texas history and politics. Although oil and natural gas are still important to the state's economy, economic diversification is the dominant theme promoted by business leaders, government officials, and economists. Change places heavy demands on the state's basic governmental institutions, and Texans will need to give increased attention to modernizing and adapting government to new realities.

This chapter will introduce you to the people of Texas, the views they have of themselves, the state's political subcultures and economy, and the increased interdependence of Texas and Mexico. We refer to these factors generally as the political environment, a concept developed by political scientist David Easton to describe the milieu or context in which political institutions function.[4] While much of our discussion focuses on broad patterns or characteristics of the political environment, individual and collective behavior will determine how our governments respond to changing conditions.

Texas Myths

Although most Texans have only a cursory knowledge of the state's governmental institutions, political history, and contemporary public policy, they do have views—often ill-defined—of the state, its people, and its culture. Key elements of these views, shared by millions of Texans, are described by some scholars as political myths.

In recent years, serious scholarship has focused on myths as ways to assess the views people have of their common historical and cultural experiences. A myth can be regarded as a "mode of truth . . . that codifies and preserves moral and spiritual values" for a particular culture or society.[5] Myths are stories or narratives that are used to describe past events, explain their significance to successive generations, and provide an interpretive overview and understanding of a society. Myths provide a world picture or, in our case, a picture of the state of Texas. The relevance of a myth depends, in part, on the degree to which it approximates the event it is describing and its pervasiveness in the literature and popular culture of the state.

Texas has produced its own myth of origin, which continues to be a powerful statement about the political system and the social order on which it is based.[6] For many Texans, the battle of the Alamo clearly serves to identify the common experiences of independence and the creation of a separate, unique political order. No other state was a **republic** prior to joining the Union, and several scholars argue that independence and "going at it alone" from 1836 to 1845 resulted in a cultural experience that distinguishes the Texas political system from that of other states. The state's nickname—the Lone Star State—is a constant reminder of this unique history. A set of heroes came out of the formative period of Texas history, including many who fought and died at the Alamo or secured Texas independence on the San Jacinto battlefield. Texas

Pulp Fiction

The dime novel helped create the myth of Texas individualism by popularizing and exaggerating the image of the cowboy.

★ **republic**
Form of government in which representatives of the people, rather than the people themselves, govern.

school children are introduced to these heroes at an early age with field trips—"pilgrimages"—to the Alamo in San Antonio and visits to the San Jacinto monument in Houston.

The Texas mythology also includes the Texas Ranger and the cowboy. There is considerable lore of the invincible, enduring ranger defeating overwhelming odds. Newspapers and dime novels in the nineteenth century introduced readers throughout the United States to the cowboy, who often was portrayed as an honest, hardworking individual wrestling with the harsh Texas environment. The cowboy's rugged **individualism**, with strong connotations of self-help, symbolizes a political culture in Texas that does not like to look to government to solve its problems.[7] It is the kind of individualism that continues to be exploited by political candidates in campaign ads and public rhetoric and by the state legislature in limited appropriations for health care and other public assistance programs.

The frontier to which the Texas Ranger and the cowboy belong is part of a cultural myth of limited government and unlimited personal opportunity. The frontier in the Texas experience also perpetuates the myths of "land as wilderness and land as garden."[8] Space, distance, and size are pervasive in a great deal of literature on the state, reinforcing perceptions of the "wide open spaces" that shape Texans' views of their autonomy and independence (see *What Do You Think?*: "Do Size and Geography Shape Texas Politics?").

The Texas myths, however, have been primarily the myths of the white (Anglo) population and have limited relevance to the cultural and historical experiences of many African American, Hispanic, and Asian Texans. From

Hero or Villain?

The Texas Rangers played an important (but sometimes controversial) role in taming the Texas frontier.

★ **individualism**
Attitude, rooted in classical liberal theory and reinforced by the frontier tradition, that citizens are capable of taking care of themselves with minimal governmental assistance.

What Do You *Think?*

Do Size and Geography Shape Texas Politics?

Texas is a big state. Covering 267,339 square miles, it is second only to Alaska in land mass. Texans appear to have adjusted to long distances but many visitors from out of state are overwhelmed by Texas's size and diversity. The distance from Texarkana in Northeast Texas to El Paso in far West Texas is about 800 miles, and a person living in Texarkana is closer to Chicago than to El Paso. Brownsville in far South Texas is closer to Mexico City than it is to Texline in the Texas Panhandle.

Some argue that the state's size has helped shape political attitudes and perceptions of public needs and policy. Roads and highways, for example, historically received a significant—and, some argued, a disproportionate—share of the state's budget. Economic development in such a large, diverse state required a commitment to highway construction, and roads were regarded as essential to the development of an integrated economy.

One scholar argued that the great distances in Texas were politically important because they made it difficult for a politician to develop a personal following, such as could be cultivated in many Southern states. Size and distance deterred the development of a statewide political machine similar to those that developed in Virginia and Louisiana in the 1920s and 1930s. Although there have been regional or local political machines, such as the now-defunct Parr machine in South Texas, none extended statewide.

Size also contributes to the high cost of political campaigns. Candidates in the 2002 gubernatorial race spent more than $100 million to communicate with and mobilize Texas voters. There are twenty separate media markets in the state, and the cost of communicating with the voters is likely to increase.

Geography shaped historical migration and land use in Texas, and, although we are capable of partially compensating for climate and geography through modern technology, geography continues to shape the economies and population patterns of the state.

Source: Terry G. Jordan with John L. Bean, Jr., and William M. Holmes, *Texas: A Geography*. Boulder, Colo.: Westview Press, 1984, p. 7.

Marching to Remember

San Antonio hosts the largest Martin Luther King, Jr., march in the nation. The march is held in conjunction with many activities held throughout the city commemorating King's birthday, which is now a national and state holiday.

New Elements of the Political Culture?

Throughout Texas, Cinco de Mayo is celebrated by Hispanics in commemoration of Mexico's defeat of French troops at Puebla, Mexico, in 1862.

★ **political culture**
Widely shared set of views, attitudes, beliefs, and customs of a people as to how their government should be organized and run.

the 1840s to the mid-1960s, these latter groups were excluded from full participation in Texas politics and the state's economic and social life. To many Hispanics, for example, the Texas Ranger is not a hero but a symbol of ruthless suppression.

Over the past 30 years, African Americans, Hispanics, and Asian Americans have made significant political and economic gains. Their share of the population has been increasing as well, and these three groups combined constitute a majority of the state's population.

As this shift occurs, Hispanic and African American historical experiences are likely to be incorporated into the mythology of the state, and some components of the contemporary mythology will be challenged and redefined. These revisions may already be under way, as demonstrated by intermittent debates over what actually took place during the battle of the Alamo. According to recently published accounts, some of the Alamo's heroes surrendered to Mexican soldiers and were executed, rather than fighting to the death. African Americans in Texas have been successful, after several years of trying, in getting the legislature to make Martin Luther King, Jr.'s birthday a state holiday. And, for Hispanics, the *Cinco de Mayo* holiday speaks to common cultural and historical experiences with Mexico.

The Political Culture of Texas

Texas shares the common institutional and legal arrangements that have developed in all fifty states, including a commitment to personal liberties, equality, justice, the rule of law, and popular sovereignty with its limitations on government. But there are differences among the states and even among regions within individual states. Texas is a highly diverse state, with racial and ethnic differences from one region to another and divergences in political attitudes and behavior that are reflected in the state's politics and public policies.

The concept of political culture (see Chapter 2) helps us compare some of these differences. **Political culture** has been defined as "the set of attitudes, beliefs, and sentiments which give order and meaning to a political process and which provide the underlying assumptions and rules that govern behavior in the political system."[9] The political culture of the state includes fundamental beliefs about the proper role of government, the relationship of the government to its citizens, and who should govern.[10] These complex attitudes and behaviors are rooted in the historical experience of the nation, shaped by the groups that immigrated to the United States, and carried across the continent to Texas.

One authority on American political culture, Daniel Elazar, concluded that three political subcultures have emerged over time in the United States: the individualistic, the moralistic, and the traditionalistic. All three draw from the common historical legacy of the nation, but they have produced regional political differences. Sometimes they complement each other; at other times they produce conflict.[11]

The Individualistic Subculture

The political view of the **individualistic subculture** holds that politics and government function as a marketplace. Government does not have to be concerned with creating a good or moral society but exists for strictly "utilitarian reasons, to handle those functions demanded by the people it is created to serve."[12] Government should be limited, and its intervention in the private activities of its citizens kept to a minimum. The primary function of government is to ensure the stability of a society so that individuals can pursue their own interests.

In this view, politics is not a high calling or noble pursuit but is like any other business venture in which skill and talent prevail and the individual can anticipate economic and social benefits. Politics is often perceived by the general public to be a dirty business that should be left to those willing to soil their hands. This tradition may well contribute to political corruption, and members of the electorate who share this view may not be concerned when governmental corruption is revealed. New policies are more likely to be initiated by interest groups or private individuals than by public officials.

The Moralistic Subculture

The **moralistic subculture** regards politics as one of the "great activities of man in his search for the good society."[13] Politics, it maintains, is the pursuit of the common good. Unlike the attitude expressed in the individualistic subculture that governments are to be limited, the moralistic subculture considers government a positive instrument with a responsibility to promote the general welfare. Politics, therefore, is not to be left to the few but is a responsibility of every individual. Politics is a duty and possibly a high calling. This cultural tradition has a strong sense of service. It requires a high standard for those holding public office, which is not to be used for personal gain. Politics may be organized around political parties, but this tradition has produced nonpartisanship, in which party labels and organizations are eliminated or play a reduced role. This tradition produces a large number of "amateur" or "nonprofessional" political activists and officeholders and has little toleration for political corruption. From the moralistic perspective, governments should actively intervene to enhance the social and economic lives of their citizens. Public policy initiatives can come from officeholders as well as from those outside the formal governmental structure.

The Traditionalistic Subculture

The **traditionalistic subculture** holds the political view that there is a hierarchical arrangement to the political order. This hierarchy serves to limit the power and influence of the general public, while allocating authority to a few individuals who constitute a self-perpetuating **elite**. The elite may enact policies that benefit the general public, but that is secondary

★ **individualistic subculture**
View that government should interfere as little as possible in the private activities of its citizens while assuring that adequate public facilities and a favorable business climate are available to permit individuals to pursue their self-interests.

★ **moralistic subculture**
View that government's primary responsibility is to promote the public welfare and that it should actively use its authority and power to improve the social and economic well-being of its citizens.

★ **traditionalistic subculture**
View that political power should be concentrated in the hands of a few elite citizens who belong to established families or influential social groups. Public policy basically serves the interests of this small group.

★ **elite**
Small group of people who exercise disproportionate power and influence in the policy-making processes.

to its interests and objectives. Public policy reflects the interests of those who exercise influence and control, and the benefits of public policy go disproportionately to the elite.

Family, social, and economic relationships form the basis for maintaining this elite structure, rather than mass political participation. In fact, in many regions of the country where traditionalistic patterns existed, there were systematic efforts to reduce or eliminate the participation of the general public. Although political parties may exist in such a subculture, they have only minimal importance. The traditionalistic subculture characterized Southern states in which two-party politics was replaced by factionalism within the Democratic Party.[14]

Historical Origins of Political Subcultures   The historical origins of these three subcultures can be explained, in part, by the early settlement patterns of the United States and by the cultural differences among the groups of people who initially settled the eastern seaboard. In very general terms, the New England colonists, influenced by Puritan and congregational religious groups, spawned the moralistic subculture. Settlers with entrepreneurial concerns and individualistic attitudes tended to locate in the Middle-Atlantic states, whereas the initial settlement of the South was dominated by elites who aspired, in part, to re-create a semi-feudal society.

As expansion toward the frontiers progressed, there were identifiable migration patterns from the initial three settlement regions. Texas was settled primarily by people holding the individualistic and traditionalistic views of a political system. The blending of these two views, along with the historical experience of the republic and the frontier, contributed to the distinct characteristics of Texas's political culture.[15]

These two political subcultures have merged to shape Texans' general views of what governments should do, who should govern, and what constitutes good public policy. Given the characteristics of these two traditions, one might well conclude, as have many scholars, that the Texas political culture is conservative. Politics in Texas tends to minimize the role of governments in providing social and economic benefits for lower income groups, is hostile toward taxes—especially those allocated toward social services—and is often manipulated by the few for their narrow advantages at the expense of the general population.

Some scholars have reservations about the concept of political subcultures because the theory is difficult to test. Their reservations are legitimate, but we know of no other single theory that presents such a rich historical perspective on the relationship of settlement patterns in the state and the evolution of political attitudes and behavior.

The People of Texas

The Evolving Demographic Makeup of Texas

The politics and government of Texas can be understood, in part, from the perspective of the people living in the state. What follows is a descriptive analysis of a select number of demographic characteristics of Texans. In subsequent chapters, we examine the relationship of race, ethnicity, and other demographic characteristics to partisan behavior, public opinion, institutional power, and public policy.

Native Americans   There are only three small Native American groups (Alabama-Coushatta, Tigua, and Kickapoo) living on reservations in Texas, and the Native American population is less than one-half of 1 percent of the state's total population.[16] Unlike Native American populations in Oklahoma, New Mexico, and Arizona, those in Texas have little influence on governmental institutions, politics, or public policy.

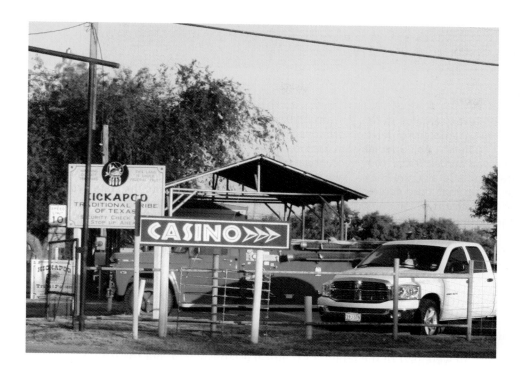

Betting on the Future
The Kickapoo tribe has staked its economic development on a limited gambling casino located on its reservation outside Eagle Pass.

In the early nineteenth century, there were at least twenty-three different Native American groups residing in Texas (see *What Do You Think?:* "What's in a Name?"). During the period of the republic (1836–45), President Sam Houston attempted to follow a policy of "peace and friendship" with the Native Americans, but he was followed by President Mirabeau B. Lamar, who set out to "expel, defeat or exterminate" them. As the European populations expanded to lands traditionally claimed by various Native American groups, conflict ensued, and most of the Native American population was eventually eliminated or displaced to other states.[17]

In recent years, Native American tribes have cooperated with officials in many states in establishing gambling casinos on tribal reservations. Such casinos are allowed under federal law, but some casino gambling comes into conflict with Texas law. The Kickapoos operate a limited casino outside of Eagle Pass, but the Tiguas and Alabama-Coushattas have been denied the right to run casinos on their reservations. Recent efforts to change the state law have been unsuccessful. Some Native American leaders consider casinos a major source of revenue, jobs, and economic development for their people.

Hispanics In the eighteenth and nineteenth centuries, neither Spain nor Mexico was very successful in convincing Hispanics to settle in the Tejas territory of Mexico. The Spanish regarded it as a border province with relatively little value except as a strategic buffer between Spanish colonies and those held by the British and the French. By the time Mexico declared its independence from Spain in 1821, the total Texas population under Spanish control was estimated to be approximately 5,000. With the rapid expansion of Anglo American immigration to Texas in the 1820s and 1830s, Hispanics became a small minority of the population.[18]

Some Hispanics were part of the Texas independence movement from Mexico, and after independence in 1836, men such as José Antonio Navarro and Juan

"Sworn to Be a Texan"
José Antonio Navarro (1795–1871) played a central role in the colonization and independence of Texas. Largely self-educated, he was a lawyer, merchant, and rancher and the only Hispanic or Tejano to serve as a delegate to the 1845 Texas Statehood Convention.

What Do You *Think?*

What's in a Name?

The Native American legacy of Texas remains in the state's name. The word "Texas" came from Tejas, which means "friends" or "allies." As Spanish explorers and missionaries moved across Texas, they confronted a Native American confederacy, the Hasinai. It was to this particular group that they applied the term, and eventually the Anglo form of the name became the permanent name of the region and then the state.

In 1989, the Texas Department of Transportation proposed changing the state's vehicle license plates to include the phrase "The Friendship State." The proposal was dropped, however, because of a generally hostile public reaction. Some Texans apparently found the phrase incompatible with the state's rugged frontier image. The irony is that the state's very name, which means friendship, is used almost every day by these same people.

Source: Rupert N. Richardson, Ernest Wallace, and Adrian N. Anderson, *Texas: The Lone Star State,* 6th ed. Upper Saddle River, N.J.: Prentice Hall, 1993, p. 1.

Seguin were part of the republic's political establishment. But the Anglo migration rapidly overwhelmed the Hispanic population and greatly reduced its political and economic power. There was even an effort at the Constitutional Convention of 1845 to strip Hispanics of the right to vote. The attempt failed, but it was an early indication of Anglo hostility toward the Hispanic population.[19]

By 1887, the Hispanic population had declined to approximately 4 percent of the state's total. In 1930, it was 12 percent and was concentrated in the border counties from Brownsville to El Paso (see Figure 19.1). There were modest increases in the Hispanic population until it reached 18 percent of the state's population in 1970, after which it grew at a more rapid rate. By 2000, it had reached 32 percent, spurred by immigration from Mexico and other Latin American countries as well as by higher birth rates among Hispanic women. These growth patterns continued in the first decade of the twenty-first century, and by 2006, Hispanics were estimated to make up approximately 35.7 percent of the state's population.[20] In addition to their traditional concentrations in the Rio Grande Valley and South-Central Texas, large Hispanic populations are found in most metropolitan areas. Except for the Asian population, which is still considerably smaller, the Hispanic population is growing at a significantly higher rate than other populations in Texas.

Hispanics will continue to increase at a higher rate than most other populations, and by 2030, the Hispanic population is likely to exceed 50 percent of the state's total.[21] This growth already has produced significant political power and influence. Six Hispanics have been elected to statewide office. And, after successful redistricting and legal challenges to city, county, school board, and state legislative districts, Hispanics in 2006 held some 2,169 elected positions in Texas, the highest number of any state.[22]

The regions of the state where Hispanics were concentrated (South Texas and along the Mexican border) before their more widespread migration to cities were areas heavily influenced by the traditionalistic subculture. Extreme poverty, low levels of education, and local economies based on agriculture contributed to the development of political systems dominated by a few Anglos, who often considered Hispanics second-class citizens. Hispanics' increasing political clout, however, has produced major political and governmental changes in those regions.

Figure **19.1** Ethnic and Racial Composition of Texas, 1860–2006

*White, not of Hispanic origin (2000 Census)

Note: Data for Asian and other populations not tabulated by the Bureau of the Census prior to 1980. Spanish total for 1970 based on "Persons of Spanish language or surname."

Sources: Terry G. Jordan with John L. Bean, Jr., and William M. Holmes, *Texas: A Geography*. Boulder: Westview Press, 1984, pp. 81–83; U.S. Census Bureau, U.S Censuses, 1860–2000; U.S Census Bureau, 2006 *American Community Survey*.

African Americans

Relatively few African Americans lived in Texas during the colonization period, and the modern story of African American settlement did not begin until after independence in 1836. When Texas was part of Mexico, Mexican law restricted slavery within the territory. During the period of the republic and early statehood prior to the U.S. Civil War, there was a significant increase in the African American population as Americans settling in Texas brought cotton cultivation and the slavery system with them. At the time of the Civil War, 30 percent of the state's residents were African American, but that percentage declined after the war. By 1960, it had leveled off to 12 percent, about the same level counted in the 2000 Census (see Figure 19.1). African Americans are expected to comprise between 11 percent and 12 percent of the state's population through the 2020 Census.

There is a large concentration of African Americans in East Texas, where white Southerners and their slaves originally settled. African Americans are

Successful Despite the Hostile Environment
Norris Wright Cuney (1846–1898), born to a slave mother and white planter father, became an influential African American political leader during Reconstruction and the years following. Active in the Texas Republican party, he was selected national committeeman in 1886 and derived much of his power from his ties to the national Republican party, appointed offices, and as a dispenser of political patronage.

also concentrated in the urban areas of Dallas, Fort Worth, Austin, and Houston. Relatively few African Americans live in the western counties or in the counties along the border with Mexico. The increased number of African American state legislators, city council members, county commissioners, and school board trustees representing urban communities is an indication of the political power of the African American population in selected areas. In 2002, the most recent year for which data were available, there were 466 African American elected officials in Texas. Four African Americans have been elected to statewide office.[23]

The slaveholding whites who migrated to Texas from the lower Southern states brought with them the dominant values of the traditionalistic political subculture. Although slaves were freed after the Civil War, continued political and economic discrimination against African Americans was commonplace in the eastern part of Texas into the 1960s. As in South Texas, the politics of East Texas served the interests of the white elites, by reducing or eliminating African American participation in the political process through election laws and outright physical intimidation.

Anglos   In the vernacular of Texas politics, the white population is referred to as "Anglos," although there is no census designation by that name. The term includes Jews, Irish, Poles, and just about any other individual who is designated by the U.S. Census Bureau as "non-Hispanic white."

Scholars have identified two distinct early patterns of Anglo migration into Texas from other states. These patterns, as well as population movements through much of the late nineteenth and early twentieth centuries, largely explain the regional locations of the state's two dominant political subcultures.

In the early nineteenth century, the first Anglos moving to Texas were from the upper South—Tennessee, Kentucky, Arkansas, and North Carolina—a region significantly influenced by the individualistic subculture of limited government. The earliest settlements were primarily in what is now Northeast Texas in the Red River Valley. After Mexican independence from Spain, there was a second wave of immigration from the upper South. Few of the early colonists were slaveholders from the lower South.

After Texas became independent, slavery was legalized, and settlers from the lower South began arriving. By the outbreak of the Civil War, Anglos who had moved to Texas from the lower South were roughly equal in number to those from the upper South. Arrivals from the slaveholding lower South initially settled in southeastern Texas near Louisiana, but soon they began to move northward and westward.

A line between Texarkana and San Antonio in effect divides Texas subcultures. Most of those Anglos who settled north and west of this line were from the upper South and heavily influenced by the individualistic subculture, which favors limited government. Anglos who settled south and east of the line were by and large from the lower South and shaped by its traditionalistic subculture.

This pattern of immigration and settlement continued after the Civil War. It was primarily those populations from the upper South who pushed westward to the Panhandle and West Texas. This expansion introduced into the western part of the state the cultural experience of those who resisted the notion that government existed to solve society's ills. To this day, West Texas is still one of the most politically conservative areas of the state.[24]

In 1860, Anglos constituted approximately 63 percent of Texas' population (see Figure 19.1). The Anglo population increased until it reached 74 percent in 1950.

But by 1990 the stabilization of the African American population and the increase in the Hispanic population had reduced the Anglo proportion to 60 percent. Anglos accounted for only 53.1 percent of Texas's population in 2000 and slightly less than 50 percent in 2006. Although the number of Anglos will continue to increase with Texas's continued population growth, their share of the total population will continue to decrease.

The Anglo population is diverse, as exhibits in the Institute of Texan Cultures in San Antonio remind us. Towns throughout Texas are identified with immigrants of national origin other than Anglo-Saxon, and these national groups brought with them a rich heritage. Castroville, for example, is identified with the Alsatians; New Braunfels and Fredericksburg, the Germans; Panna Maria, the Poles; West and Hallettsville, the Czechs.

The Asian American Population

In 1980, Asian Americans accounted for 0.8 percent of Texas's population. By 2006, this group had grown to 3.2 percent of the population and was projected to increase to 4.2 percent by 2020. This rapid increase parallels national trends. Changes in immigration policy and the dislocation of Asians because of war and political persecution have resulted in larger numbers of Asian immigrants entering the United States and Texas since the 1970s. Moreover, the Asian population is increasingly diverse and includes individuals from Vietnam, China, Iran, Iraq, India, Pakistan, South Korea, and a number of other countries.

The largest concentration of Asian Americans in Texas is in Houston, where several Asian Americans have been elected to major public offices. Among them, community activist Martha Wong was elected to the Houston City Council in 1993 and then to the Texas House of Representatives in 2002. Wong apparently was the second Asian American to serve in the Texas House. Tom Lee of San Antonio, who served in the 1960s, was believed to be the first. Another Houstonian, Hubert Vo, a Vietnamese American, was elected to the Texas House in 2004. Asian Americans hold or have held public offices in several other Texas cities as well.

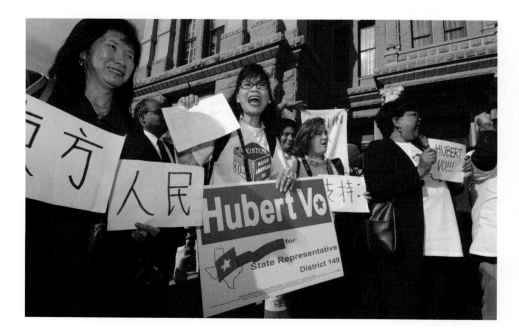

An Emerging Political Force

The rapid increase in the Asian American populations has produced circumstances in which members of these populations can now win public office. Houston Vietnamese Americans rally at the Texas Capitol in 2004 as Houston businessman Hubert Vo took his seat in the Texas House of Representatives as the first Vietnamese American ever to be elected to the Texas House. Vo was reelected in 2006 and 2008.

Politics, Race, and Ethnicity

Today, few Texans go running around the state wearing Ku Klux Klan robes, burning crosses or marching in support of white supremacy. But there still are occasions of extreme racial violence and cruelty, such as the murder of James Byrd, Jr., an African American who was dragged to death by three white men in a pickup truck in early 1999 near Jasper in East Texas. Despite such incidents, the state has made progress in creating a more equitable society. A state law barring African Americans from voting in party primaries was declared unconstitutional in the 1940s, and many other laws intended to reduce the political participation of African Americans and Hispanics have been eliminated. The federal Voting Rights Act, which was enacted in 1965 and extended to Texas in 1975, has also helped open up state and local electoral systems to minorities. There is still evidence of employment and housing discrimination, and opposition to the desegregation of a public housing project in Vidor received national publicity in 1993. But restrictive codes prohibiting specific groups of people from buying residential property have been declared unconstitutional, and federal and state laws have given minorities greater access to jobs.

Nonetheless, race and ethnicity are implicit in many contemporary political and policy issues. Throughout the long struggle to restructure the school finance system, the protagonists are identified as the "rich" and "poor" school districts of the state. But, in large part, these are alternative terms for "non-minority" and "minority" school systems. There have been bitter debates about redrawing political districts to increase Hispanic and African American representation on city councils, school boards, and special districts, and in the state legislature and the U.S. Congress. And although many poor Anglos live in Texas, the disproportionately high poverty rates among minority groups often influence discussions about social services.

The budget crisis of 2003 produced a particularly contentious legislative session, when funding was reduced for many of the state's health and social services programs. Many state and local elections show evidence of polarized voting along ethnic lines. Race and ethnicity also emerge in racial profiling by police, employment patterns, and contracts with state and local governments. Admissions policies of Texas colleges and universities resulted in a succession of legal challenges centering on affirmative action and reverse discrimination.

More than 50 years ago, V. O. Key, a Texan scholar of American politics, concluded that Texas politics was moving from issues of race to issues of class and economics. He argued that voters in Texas "divide along class lines in accord with their class interests as related to liberal and conservative candidates."[25] In part, he was correct, in that unabashed racial bigotry and public demagoguery are no longer acceptable. In part, though, he was incorrect and much too optimistic. If the state divides on economic issues, this division puts the majority of Anglos on one side and the majority of Hispanics and African Americans on the other.[26]

The Political Implications of Demographics

Population Increase Over the past 50 years, the population of Texas has increased much faster than the national average. According to the 2000 census, the state's population was 20,851,820, an increase of approximately four million people in 10 years. This growth rate of 22.8 percent was significantly higher than the national growth rate of 13.2 percent.[27] In the first 6 years of this century, the population increased by some 2.7 million people or 12.7 percent, a rate also higher than the national average. With a population approaching 24 million, Texas is now the second most populous state.[28]

High birth rates explain part of the population increase, but migration from other states has also been a significant factor. In recent decades, demographers (those who study populations) have described a nationwide shift in population from the Northeast and Midwest to the South and West. For each of the censuses from 1940 to 1970, in-migration accounted for less than 10 percent of Texas's growth. But in-migration jumped to 58.5 percent of the total growth between 1970 and 1980. Between 1980 and 1990, it contributed 34.4 percent.[29] In-migration slowed down somewhat between 1990 and 2000, but at the beginning of this decade, approximately 23 percent of Texas residents reported other states as their place of birth, and this increased to 26 percent in 2006.[30]

Although it is expected to become less significant in the future, in-migration from other states has already contributed to the transformation of Texas's traditional one-party, Democratic political system into a Republican-dominated system. Many new residents came from states with strong Republican Party traditions and brought their party affiliation with them. In the long run, in-migration may affect additional elements of the state's political culture.

Texas also attracts individuals from other countries. Approximately 2.9 million, or 14 percent of Texas residents, were identified as foreign-born in the 2000 census, and this number increased to 16 percent in 2006. Between 1990 and 2000, approximately 1.4 million, or 6.4 percent, of the state's population arrived from other countries. More than 75 percent of Texans born in other countries come from Latin America. Approximately 11 percent of all Texas residents are not U.S. citizens, a fact that has several implications.[31]

Citizenship is directly related to political participation, and noncitizens, while counted in the census for reapportionment of congressional seats, cannot vote. The overwhelming majority of noncitizens in Texas are Hispanic, thus reducing the number of eligible Hispanic voters in relation to their population.

Under current federal policy, noncitizens have been denied access to some public social services that are funded in whole or in part by the national government. Needy immigrants are especially affected by such policies, and in some instances, the state has found it necessary to use its own funds to provide services.

Are There Any More Seats?

While some school districts are experiencing declines in enrollment, many larger urban districts are seeing a rapid rise in school enrollment, making it difficult for these districts to provide permanent classrooms. Opened in 1998, Sandra Day O'Connor High School, located in the northern part of Bexar County, had inadequate space the day it opened and now houses students in some 30 temporary or portable buildings.

Some 7.3 million Texans older than five speak languages other than English at home, and 43 percent of them report that they don't speak English well.[32] Some states have adopted English as their official language, but there has not been a significant English language movement in Texas. Nonetheless, language is a policy issue for Texas in terms of bilingual education, official documents and publications, translators for court proceedings, and a host of related language issues in the workplace.

The increase in population places demands on all levels of government, and many local governments throughout Texas are hard-pressed to provide adequate services. Many Texas cities, for example, are running out of landfill space. Environmental laws make it difficult to obtain new licenses for garbage and waste disposal, and without these additional facilities, new population growth cannot be serviced. The increased population has also raised questions about the adequacy of water supplies throughout the state with different cities, regions, and industries competing intensely for the resources now available. Even though the state has been engaged in a massive road construction program, streets and highways in urban and suburban areas are clogged with traffic (see *Controversy*: "Toll Roads and the Trans Texas Corridor"). A driving survey, released in the fall of 2003, indicated significant increases in daily commute time in metropolitan areas. This means additional gasoline consumption, pollution, and costs of time.[33] Other possible transportation solutions include managing road systems more efficiently, restructuring demand, and increasing use of public transportation.[34]

The Aging Population   Texans, along with other Americans, are aging. In 2006, the median age of the state's population was 33.1 years, compared to 36.4 for the entire country. Approximately 10 percent of the state's population was older than 65 in 2006, and that group was expected to increase to 17 percent by 2030.[35] This aging population will place unprecedented demands on the public and private sectors for goods and services, including expanded health care and long-term care. In recent years, increasing state expenditures under the Medicaid program for long-term nursing care have strained the state's budget and forced the state to shift priorities in public programs.

Urbanization   Although Texas was a rural state during the first 100 years of its history, 83 percent of the state's population in 2000 resided in areas classified by the Bureau of the Census as urban (Table 19.1). **Urbanization** and suburban sprawl now characterize Texas's settlement patterns, and many urban corridors and suburban areas cross county boundaries (see *Politics Up Close*: "The Texas Urban Triangle"). Residents of these areas often encounter problems that cut across political jurisdictions, and local governments sometimes find it difficult to resolve them.

The dramatic growth of Texas's largest cities is shown in Table 19.2. From 1960 to 2006, the populations of Houston, San Antonio, and El Paso more than doubled. Dallas increased by approximately 82 percent. Arlington had a population of only 44,775 in 1960, but in 2006 its population was 372,566, an increase of more than 730 percent. During this period, Austin's population increased by 284 percent.

Three of the ten largest cities in the United States are in Texas, and, like urban areas throughout the country, Texas's largest cities increasingly are home to minority and low-income populations. This trend results from higher birth rates among minority populations, urban migration patterns, and what is often referred to as "white flight" from the cities to suburban areas. Minority groups now account for the majority of the population in five of Texas's ten largest cities (Houston, San Antonio, Dallas, El Paso, and Corpus Christi). These minority residents include Hispanics, African Americans, and Asian Americans—groups

★ **urbanization**
Process by which a predominantly rural society or area becomes urban.

Controversy

Toll Roads and the Trans Texas Corridor

Study after study, coupled with the experiences of millions of Texas drivers, point to increased congestion on Texas roads and highways. The interstate highway system has served the state well, but Texas's increased population, projected to reach 50 million in the next 50 years, will make many existing highways impossible to negotiate.

Governor Rick Perry proposed the idea of dedicated transportation corridors during his 2002 election campaign. In 2003, the legislature enacted the general outline of the proposal, which was expected to take 50 years and, according to some estimates, $184 billion to complete. The Texas Department of Transportation (TxDot) presented its plan in 2004 and signed a contract with a consortium led by a Spanish company to build the first stage of a corridor project that will run parallel to Interstate Highway 35. The corridors will be up to one-quarter of a mile wide in some places, include "six high-speed toll lanes for cars and trucks, six rail lines, and easements for petroleum, natural gas, and water pipelines as well as electric, broadband, and other telecommunications lines."

These facilities are to be constructed and maintained by private companies. Rather than raising the state tax on gasoline (one of the lowest in the nation) to finance the new roads, the state will allow private corporations to collect tolls and generate revenue from their control over concessions along the routes. The corridors will be constructed in phases, based on current needs.

TxDot argues that these new roads will permit motorists to drive faster, circumvent congestion, and save time. The agency says the roads will be built more quickly with borrowed money—to be repaid in tolls by the people who use the roads—than they would by relying on tax revenues. If you don't want to use the roads, you won't have to, TxDot says.

But many Texans, including some of Perry's fellow Republicans, oppose the plan. They say there was too

For Whom the Bell Tolls, or Just Tolling Along
Toll roads, such as Texas Toll Road 45 in Round Rock, are seen by many political leaders as the solution to the ever-increasing congestion on state highways.

much ambiguity and secretiveness about the proposals and the initial contract. They question why a foreign company was included in the consortium that got the first contract. Critics also have accused TxDot's leadership of being arrogant and indifferent to community needs.

Environmentalists are concerned about the project's potential impact, and farmers fear their land will be taken for highway right of way. Some communities also fear that the new roads will bypass them and hurt their local economies. Some studies have suggested there is a relationship between income and toll road usage, raising concerns about the discriminatory effects of a massive road system on lower income groups. One state audit warned that costs could be much higher than official estimates.

Questions also have been raised about TxDot's use of public funds to pitch its proposals to the public. Two groups—the Texas Toll Party and Corridor Watch—formed to oppose the proposal, and other established groups, such as the Texas Farm Bureau, also announced their opposition.

The public hostility forced TxDot to modify its tactics, but it is clear that decisions for future transportation will have winners and losers.

Sources: Texas Department of Transportation, *Benefits of a Toll Road;* Sylvia Moreno, "Texans are Divided over Plan for Miles of Wide Toll Roads," *Washington Post,* February 8, 2005, A03.

Table *19.1* Urban-Rural Population of Texas, 1850–2000

Year	Urban		Rural		Total
	Percentage	*Population*	*Percentage*	*Population*	
1850	4%	7,665	96%	204,927	212,592
1860	4	26,615	96	577,600	604,215
1870	7	54,521	93	764,058	818,579
1880	9	146,795	91	1,444,954	1,591,749
1890	16	359,511	84	1,886,016	2,245,527
1900	17	520,759	83	2,527,951	3,048,710
1910	24	938,104	76	2,958,438	3,896,542
1920	32	1,512,689	68	3,150,539	4,663,228
1930	41	2,389,148	59	3,435,367	5,824,715
1940	45	2,911,389	55	3,503,435	6,414,824
1950	63	4,838,050	37	2,873,134	7,711,194
1960	75	7,187,470	25	2,392,207	9,579,677
1970	80	8,922,211	20	2,274,519	11,196,730
1980	80	11,333,017	20	2,836,174	14,229,191
1990	80	13,634,517	20	3,351,993	16,986,510
2000	83	17,204,073	17	3,647,747	20,851,820

Source: U.S. Census Bureau, *U.S. Censuses 1850–2000.*

that do not always constitute a cohesive bloc of interests. As minority growth continues, areas of potential conflict will emerge among these groups.

Population Density   Population density refers to the number of people per square mile in a specific political jurisdiction, and it provides another measure of urbanization. As people crowd into smaller areas living in close proximity to each other, problems are inevitable. Noise, land use, property maintenance, traffic patterns, and numerous other issues must be addressed There are marked differences in the population and density of Texas's 254 counties. Loving County in West Texas has a population of about 60 persons living in an area of 677 square miles. The most populous county is Harris County (Houston), with more than 3.8 million people living in 1,777 square miles.[36] Clearly, the problems and issues that Loving County faces are significantly different from those encountered in Harris County, yet both counties function with the same form of government created by the Texas Constitution of 1876.

★ **population density**
Number of residents living within the boundaries of a city, county, or state in relationship to the land area. Population density is a significant factor in determining the level of local public services.

Table *19.2* Ten Largest Texas Cities, 1920–2006

City	1920	1940	1960	1980	1990	2000	2006
Houston	138,276	384,514	838,219	1,595,138	1,630,553	1,953,631	2,112,671
San Antonio	161,379	253,854	587,718	785,880	935,933	1,144,646	1,296,265
Dallas	158,976	294,734	679,684	904,078	1,006,877	1,188,580	1,233,970
Austin	34,876	87,960	186,545	345,496	465,622	656,562	716,344
Fort Worth	106,482	177,662	356,268	385,164	447,619	534,694	650,344
El Paso	77,560	96,810	276,687	425,259	515,342	563,662	608,395
Arlington	3,031	4,240	44,775	160,113	261,721	332,969	372,566
Corpus Christi	10,522	57,301	167,690	231,999	257,453	277,454	283,700
Plano	1,715	1,582	3,695	72,331	128,713	222,030	262,722
Garland	1,421	2,233	38,501	132,857	180,650	215,768	219,141

Sources: U.S. Census Bureau, *U.S. Censuses, 1920–2000; Texas State Data Center, Population Estimates and Projections, 2007.*

Politics Up Close The Texas Urban Triangle

About 80 percent of the state's population lives within or near a triangular area (often referred to as the central Texas triangle or the Texas Urban triangle) formed by linking the metropolitan areas of Dallas–Fort Worth, Houston, and San Antonio. Population from the core cities is expected to continue expanding into neighboring counties. This area dominates the state's economy and is projected to play a greater role in the future. The area has major research and educational institutions, investment capital, an ample supply of low-cost labor, available energy, a pro-business tax structure, affordable housing, medical facilities, cultural venues, and other amenities. Each of the metropolitan areas has its own distinct characteristics, but there will be increased integration and interdependence in their economies.

Continued growth, however, also will be affected by the availability of water and other utilities at reasonable costs as well as state and local governmental policies, including regulatory restrictions and transportation improvements. Many people oppose unregulated or unplanned growth, and they can be influential in electing public officials and setting governmental policies. Texas's ability to provide the public infrastructure also will be affected by its tax structure. Public outrage continues to grow over local property taxes, the major revenue source for most local governments. Texas doesn't have a personal income tax. So state government relies on a regressive tax system heavily dependent on sales taxes. This tax structure leaves little room for new programs, which is one reason Governor Rick Perry has been advocating more toll roads as a solution to the state's growing transportation problems. Changes in federal immigration laws also could affect Texas's population growth.

Sources: Federal Reserve Bank of Texas, "Houston Business—A Perspective on the Houston Economy," April 2004; James P. Gaines, "Looming Boom: Texas Through 2030," Texas A&M University, Real Estate Center.

Texas politics has often divided along urban-rural lines, creating conflict, a trend compounded by suburban areas of the state taking on more importance. Redistricting battles and a host of other public policy issues are evidence of that. Until recently, the Texas legislature was dominated by rural lawmakers, many of whom were often insensitive to urban needs. To make matters more difficult, suburban legislators with a different constituency base and interests often pursue policies in conflict with both the central city and rural legislators. Moreover, many of urban Texas's problems are aggravated by constitutional restrictions written when Texas was still a rural state.

Wealth and Income Distribution There is a wide disparity in the distribution of income and wealth across the state. In 2006, the median household income in Texas was $44,922, and the median family income was $52,355, both below national income levels (see Table 19.3). Approximately 28 percent of Texas households reported incomes of less than $25,000 per year. By contrast, 16.5 percent of Texas households reported incomes in excess of $100,000. Income disparities are evident among the different regions of the state. The median household income for Collin County, north of Dallas, was $71,419 in 2005. The median household income for Starr County on the border with Mexico was $17,843. Of the ten counties reporting household incomes of less than $25,000 in 2005, nine were in South and Southwest Texas. Eight of the border counties fell below the $25,000 figure.[37]

Although many Texans are suffering economically, others make large salaries and have significant assets, including those on *Forbes's* annual list of the 400

Table *19.3* U.S and Texas Income Figures, 2006 Estimates

	U.S.	TEXAS				
	All Persons	**All Persons**	**Anglos**	**Hispanics**	**African Americans**	**Asian Americans**
Median Income						
Household	$48,451	$44,922	$55,506	$33,354	$32,159	$60,159
Families	58,526	52,355	69,863	34,758	37,941	66,500
Per Capita Income	25,267	22,501	31,063	12,815	16,333	25,423
Percent of Persons Below Poverty Level	13.3%	16.9%	8.9%	25.7%	25.4%	11.8%

Source: U.S. Census Bureau, 2006 *American Community Survey.*

richest Americans. Thirty-seven Texans made the list in 2007, with a reported net worth ranging from $1.3 billion to $17.2 billion.[38] The vast majority of Texans, however, have incomes or assets that are nowhere near those of the super wealthy (see *Compared to What?*: "Texas and Other States").

On all measures of income, Hispanics and African Americans fall significantly below the Anglo population. According to the 2006 *American Community Survey*, 36.5 percent of Hispanic households and 40 percent of African American households in Texas reported incomes less than $25,000, but only 21 percent of Anglo households and a similar portion of the Asian American population reported incomes below that level. By contrast, 36 percent of Anglo households but only 14.5 percent of Hispanic and 16.6 percent of African American households reported incomes of more than $75,000.[39]

Many Texans live in severe poverty. Some of the nation's poorest counties are in Texas. These are border counties (Dimmit, Hidalgo, Maverick, Starr, Willacy,

For Sale—Two Bedrooms, Two Baths and Air Conditioning

There are some 1,200 colonias or settlements along the Texas-Mexico border with substandard housing and little or no access to running water, sewer lines, or paved roads.

Compared to *What?*

Texas and Other States

If you compare Texas to other states, it ranks:

#1 in exports to Mexico ($56 billion in 2007); in the percentage of people five and older who speak Spanish at home (29.1 percent in 2006); in percentage of the population without health insurance (24.5 percent in 2006)

#2 in total resident population (23.5 million in 2006); in total Hispanic population (8,385,139 in 2006); in members of the U.S. House of Representatives (32 in 2008)

#3 in the size of its economy ($1.3 trillion in 2006 in current dollars); in the number of immigrants (3.74 million in 2006); in the percentage of the foreign-born population born in Mexico (62.5 percent in 2006); in the percentage of people 5 and over who speak a language other than English at home (33.8 percent in 2006)

#4 in total number of African American residents (2,687,401 in 2006); in average household size (2.83 in 2006)

#5 in the percentage of total population classified as minorities (52 percent in 2007)

#6 in registered boats per 1,000 population in 2002 (29)

#7 in the percentage of children below the poverty level in 2006 (23.9 percent); in the percentage of people who are foreign born (15.9 percent in 2006)

#8 in the percentage of the population below the poverty level (16.9 percent in 2006); in the number of superfund sites (45 in 2008)

#9 in the percentage of people 65+ below the poverty level (12.3 percent in 2006); births financed by Medicaid as a percent of total births (49.2 percent in 2002)

#10 in the unemployment rate in 2004 (6 percent of the workforce)

BUT . . .

#41 in physicians per 100,000 people in 2003 (220)

#42 in elementary and secondary per pupil spending in 2005–06 ($7,561 per pupil); in the percentage of occupied housing units that are owner occupied (65.2 percent in 2006)

#43 in federal money for public elementary and secondary school systems in 2005–06 ($4.7 billion)

#44 in health care expenditures per capita ($4,601 in 2004)

#45 in percentage of children aged 19–35 months who are immunized (76 percent in 2006)

#46 in average math SAT scores in school year 2005 (502); in Medicaid payments per enrollee ($3,598 in 2007)

#47 in the percentage of the population over 65 (9.9 percent in 2006); in mental health expenditures per capita ($36.70 in 2004)

#48 in employer-provided health insurance in 2006

#49 in average verbal SAT scores in the school year 2005 (493); in the percentage of people 25+ who have completed high school (78.6 percent in 2006)

#50 in the median age of the population (33.1 years in 2006); in government per capita expenditures ($3,441 in 2004)

Sources: Texas Comptroller of Public Accounts, *Texas–Where We Stand*, February 2006; U.S. Census Bureau, *Statistical Abstract*, 2006; U.S. Census Bureau, 2006 *American Community Survey*; U.S. Census Bureau, *Income, Poverty, and Health Insurance Coverage in the United States 2006*; U.S. Census Bureau, *Federal Aid to States for Fiscal Year 2006*; The Kaiser Family Foundation, statehealthfacts.org; Green Media Toolshed, *Scorecard*; Kendra A. Hovey and Harold A. Hovey, *CQ's State Fact Finder 2004*. Washington, D.C.: CQ Press, 2004; Indiana Business Research Center, Indiana University Kelley School of Business, *Stats Indiana*.

Zapata, and Zavala) with large Hispanic populations and unemployment rates that are twice the state average. The per capita income (total state income divided by the population) for Texas was $22,501 in 2006. For the Anglo population, it was significantly higher, $31,063, but for African Americans, the figure was $16,333, and for Hispanics, $12,815.

In 2006, the poverty-level guidelines used in Texas to establish eligibility for many federal and state programs were $20,614 for a family of four and $10,294 for one person. According to the U.S. Census Bureau, 16.9 percent of the state's population, or some 3.8 million people, fell below the poverty level. Nationally, 13.3 percent or 38.8 million persons fell below the poverty level in 2006.[40] The impact of poverty disproportionately affected children, particularly those living in one-parent households, and those who were Hispanic and African American. In the seven counties mentioned above, 25 percent or more of the population fell below the poverty level in 2005 with 39 percent or more of all children living in families below the poverty line.[41] In Hidalgo County, approximately 52 percent of the children fell below the poverty line, and in Starr County, 55.5 percent. Many of these families don't have adequate housing or health care and depend on food stamps or charities for food. Some 25 percent of Texans don't have health insurance, including some individuals who can afford it but choose not to purchase coverage.

Although the state's economic growth over the past several decades has reduced poverty somewhat, scholars who study demographic trends fear that poverty is likely to worsen in Texas if several policy issues are not addressed. Without significant changes in educational levels and expanded economic opportunities, it is possible that approximately 20 percent of the state's households will fall below the poverty line by 2030, and income disparity will be especially problematic for minorities.[42]

Financial resources can be translated into political power and influence through campaign contributions, funding one's own campaign for public office, access to the mass media, and active support for policy think tanks, interest groups, and lobbying activities. Wealth is not the only dimension of political power, but some Texans obviously have the potential for much greater clout than others.

Education and Literacy   Public education has been a dominant issue in state politics for many years now. Litigation has forced the legislature to struggle with changes in the funding of public schools, and education will be a primary factor in determining whether Texas can successfully compete in a new global economy.

Over the next decade, many of the new jobs created in Texas will be in service industries. Most of these jobs will require increased reading, writing, and math skills, and high school dropouts will find fewer and fewer opportunities for decent-paying jobs. Across the nation, millions of low-skilled jobs have been outsourced to other countries, and most of the higher paying jobs now require a college education. Texas faces a crisis in public education, and the state's ability to resolve it will directly affect the financial well-being of many Texans (see *Politics Up Close*: "How Is Immigration Impacting Public Education in Texas?").

According to the 2006 American Community Survey, 78.6 percent of Texans ages 25 and older had completed high school, and 24.7 percent had completed college (Table 19.4). Educational attainment improved between 2000 and 2006, and positive changes were reported for all racial or ethnic groups in the state.[43]

Table *19.4*   United States and Texas: Educational Attainment by Race and Ethnicity for Population 25 and Older, 2006

	United States		Texas	
	High School Diploma	**College Degree**	**High School Diploma**	**College Degree**
Anglo*	88.9%	29.9%	90.2%	32.5%
Hispanic	60.2	12.3	56.0	10.3
African American	79.3	16.9	82.1	17.8
Asian	85.6	49.2	85.4	51.9
All Persons	84.1	27.0	78.6	24.7

*White, not of Hispanic origin
Source: U.S. Census Bureau, 2006 American Community Survey.

Politics Up Close

How Is Immigration Impacting Public Education in Texas?

States have long complained that the failure of the national government to develop an effective immigration policy is having a significant impact on their ability to improve their educational systems and provide the resources necessary to train young people for the twenty-first century job market. President George W. Bush called for immigration reforms in his 2004 State of the Union Address, renewing debate within Congress and the public. The Texas legislature, meanwhile, was faced with a court-mandated requirement to restructure the state's funding of the public schools. Proposals for significant increases in education funding during a special session in 2006 were shoved aside as Governor Rick Perry and the Republican legislative majority instead focused more attention on reducing local school property taxes.

Immigration, both legal and illegal, is having a profound impact on public education in Texas, and it will require much more than the funding changes approved in 2006.

An estimated 3.7 million of the nation's 37.5 million immigrants lived in Texas in 2006. About half of these immigrants were believed to be in Texas illegally, but public school districts were still obligated to admit those of school age.

On a significant number of educational rankings, Texas has fallen into the bottom half of the states, partly because of the economic disadvantages of many students, including immigrants, and their limited knowledge of English. Texas was next to last in

2006 in the percentage of Texans 25 and older who had graduated from high school. The state ranked forty-sixth in average math SAT scores in 2005 and forty-ninth in verbal SAT scores. It ranked thirty-fifth in the percentage of eighth graders scoring at or above proficient in reading in 2005. And the story goes on and on.

Many students across Texas are getting an excellent education, but if public officials do not address the impact of immigration on educational achievement, there will be serious problems in the near future. Approximately 47 percent of immigrants 25 and above did not have a high school education. Some seven million Texans report that languages other than English are spoken in their homes, and some 60 percent indicate they do not speak English well.

It is commonly understood that educational attainment is linked to earning potential. Moreover, changes in the nation's economy require increased levels of education. Low educational levels relegate people to low-paying jobs. Persons with limited income are more likely to use public assistance programs, have more limited access to health care and affordable housing, and fall below the poverty level.

The Texas legislature in 2006 failed to address many of the problems facing the state's public schools. If this neglect continues, it will bode ill for Texas in the future.

Sources: Steven Camarota, *Backgrounder: Immigrants at Mid-Decade,* December 2005, Center for Immigration Studies; Jeffrey S. Passel, *Estimates of the Size and Characteristics of the Undocumented Worker,* March 21, 2005, Pew Hispanic Center; Gordon H. Hanson, *Why Does Immigration Divide America? Public Finance and Political Opposition to Open Borders,* December 2005, The Center for Comparative Immigration Studies; U.S. Census Bureau, 2006 *American Community Survey.*

Although there have been incremental gains since 2000, there are still wide disparities in the educational levels of the three major ethnic-racial groups. In 2006, 90 percent of the Anglo population reported that they had completed high school, and 32.5 percent had college degrees. By contrast, 56 percent of the Hispanic population had high school diplomas and only 10.3 percent reported having college degrees. Some 82 percent of African Americans graduated from high school, with approximately 18 percent indicating they had college degrees. Particularly compelling is the Asian population, which reported that 52 percent of those 25 and older had college degrees.

Education not only helps determine a person's employment and income potential but also affects his or her participation in politics. Individuals with high educational levels are much more likely to believe they can influence the actions of policy makers, be informed about politics, and participate in the political process.

The Economy of Texas

Politics, government, and economics are inextricably linked. An economy that is robust and expanding provides far more options to government policy makers than an economy in recession. A healthy tax base is dependent on an expanding economy, and when the economy goes through periods of recession, state and local governments are confronted with the harsh realities of having to increase taxes or cut back on public services, usually at a time when more people are in need of governmental assistance.

Historically, the health of the Texas economy had been linked to oil and natural gas, but by the last decade of the twentieth century, the state's economy had undergone significant diversification. In 1981, for example, 27 percent of the economy was tied to energy-related industries. The decade started with rapid increases in the world price of oil, and there was an economic boom throughout the financial, construction, and manufacturing sectors of the state's economy.[44]

Changes in international fuel markets, particularly a big drop in oil prices in the 1980s, staggered the Texas petroleum industry. Natural gas prices also fell. Thousands of energy-related jobs were lost, and many exploration and drilling companies went out of business. Cheaper foreign oil weakened the demand for Texas oil, and a decline in recoverable reserves further reduced the importance of fossil fuels to the state's commerce. Within two decades, oil and gas-related industries were contributing only 10 percent of the Texas economy.[45]

Other factors also hurt the situation. The Mexican peso experienced a precipitous decline, which had a negative impact on the economies of border cities and counties. In 1983, a harsh freeze in South Texas and a severe drought in West Texas had serious adverse effects on the agricultural sector. Some regions of the state were insulated from these conditions, but other areas experienced a significant economic downturn.[46]

There also was a worldwide slump in the electronics industry. These events hurt the construction and real estate sectors of the economy and, in turn, manufacturing and retail trade. For 16 straight months in 1986 and 1987, the state's employment rate dropped, with a loss of an estimated 233,000 jobs.[47]

Boom, Decline, and Diversification

Oil played a dominant role in the Texas economy for much of the twentieth century. When wildcatter Columbus M. "Dad" Joiner struck oil near the city of Kilgore, it started a boom that saw the city grow from 500 to 12,000 and the completion of more than 1,100 producing wells within the city. By the end of the twentieth century, oil and gas reserves declined, the Texas economy diversified, and this industry played a reduced role in the overall economy.

These reversals had a disastrous effect on Texas's banks and savings and loan institutions. "In 1987 and 1988, more Texas financial institutions failed than at any other time since the Great Depression," the state comptroller's office reported. And the pattern of bank failures continued through 1990. The federal government eventually developed a plan to bail out institutions that were covered by federal deposit insurance, and the state's banking system ultimately was restructured. But as the magnitude of the problem became clearer, there was a bitter debate over its causes, including the deregulation of the savings and loan and banking industries, inadequate government scrutiny of banking practices, a frenzy of speculation with questionable or unsecured loans, and outright fraud and malfeasance.[48]

State and local governments consequently suffered declines in revenues. With falling property values, local governments that depended on the property tax were particularly vulnerable. The legislature convened in a special session in 1986 to pass an $875 million tax bill and cut the state budget by about $580 million in an attempt to "patch up" the widening holes in projected state revenues. In 1987, the legislature, mandated by the state constitution to a "pay as you go" system of government and denied the option of deficit financing, enacted a $5.6 billion tax bill, including an increase in the sales tax, a regressive tax that most adversely affects low-income people.[49]

With the exception of three years, the Texas economy has outpaced the overall national economy since 1990. There have been ups and downs, including the impact of the recession of 2001 and financial problems spawned by subprime lending practices in 2007, but the state's economy is now in much better shape than it was in the late 1980s. In 2007, Texas had a gross state product of $896 billion in 2000 dollars (dollars are "chained" to an earlier period to permit meaningful comparisons and control for the effect of inflation). In current dollars, the gross state product in 2007 was $1.3 trillion. By comparison, the gross domestic product of the United States in 2007 was $11.5 trillion in 2000 dollars. The Texas economy was the third largest among the states, following California and New York. If Texas were a nation, its economy would rank eleventh in the world.[50]

Several lessons can be drawn from the state's economic history. Because of economic diversification, a number of experts believe that the state is now less vulnerable to the volatility of the energy industry. So, even in recessionary periods, not all regions of the state or sectors of its economy are affected the same way. It remained to be seen, though, what kind of lasting, economic impact the rapid increase in oil prices in 2007 and 2008 would have on Texas.

Another dimension of the state's economic success has been an ever-increasing shift to high-tech industries. Many economic and political leaders believe that the state's future must be tied directly to these developing industries, and the state and many cities have developed aggressive recruitment programs that include economic development bonds and tax abatements for high-tech companies.

The term *high-tech* is generally used to describe business activities that produce new technology based on highly sophisticated scientific research and computer applications. Companies that make semiconductors, microprocessors, and computer hardware and software clearly fall into this category, as do companies that produce telecommunications devices, fiber optics, aerospace guidance systems, and some medical instruments. These industries have been joined by new biotechnology industries involved in producing new medicines, vaccines, and genetic engineering of plants and animals. Houston and Dallas have emerged as centers for biotechnology, with some development also occurring in San Antonio, Austin, and Fort Worth.[51] With the cooperation and support of state universities and two major research consortia in the area, Austin also has attracted a significant number of computer-related industries.

★ **globalization of the economy**
Increased interdependence in trade, manufacturing, and commerce as well as most other business activities between the United States and other countries.

Texas and the United States also are contributing to what is often referred to as the **globalization of the economy**. Throughout the 1980s, as world oil prices directly affected the state's economy, Texans were made keenly aware of their increased dependence on the world economy. Foreign investment in Texas business has become increasingly common. In 1999, Texas exported some $83 billion in merchandise to other countries. By 2007, total exports were $168 billion with approximately 33 percent going to Mexico.[52] The North American Free Trade Agreement (NAFTA) among the United States, Mexico, and Canada, which will be discussed later in this chapter, has already produced changes in the economic relationships among these countries, and more economic interdependence for North America is anticipated.

Economic Regions of Texas

One approach to understanding the complexities of the Texas economy is to think in terms of thirteen distinct economic regions, as defined by the Office of the Comptroller (see Figure 19.2). There are marked differences among these areas.[53] One may be undergoing rapid growth, while another may be experiencing a recession. Regions vary in population, economic infrastructures, economic performance, and rates of population growth. One region's economy may be heavily dependent on only two or three industries. If one or two of those industries suffers an economic downturn, that region may have a more severe recession than the state overall. There also are marked differences in personal income, poverty levels, and geography among the regions. All regions, meanwhile, share in one economic sector—fairly significant levels of government employment.

The *High Plains Region*, for example, is comprised of forty-one counties in the Panhandle. It includes Amarillo and Lubbock, but many of the counties in this

Figure *19.2*
Economic Regions of Texas

Source: Texas Comptroller of Public Accounts.

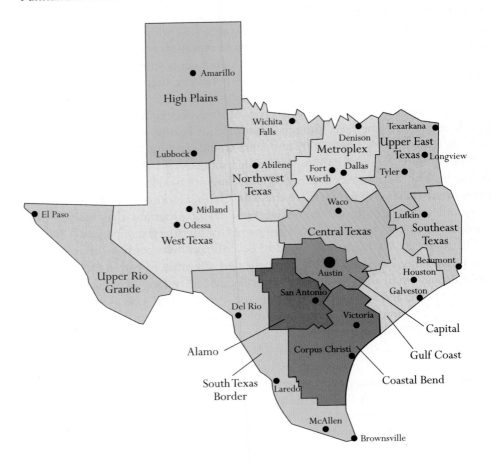

region are sparsely populated. Agricultural production, whose major source of water is the Ogallala Aquifer, is a dominant industry. Related businesses include agricultural services, food processing, and the manufacturing of feed, fertilizers, and farm machinery and equipment. Oil and gas production remains an important component of the region's economy.

By contrast, the nineteen counties defined as the *Metroplex* have the greatest concentration of large and middle-size cities in the state, including Dallas, Fort Worth, Plano, Garland, and Arlington. This area is a major financial center, with regional offices of the Federal Reserve Bank and the Federal Home Loan Bank. Its manufacturing base is the most diversified in the state, including a number of high-tech industries. It is home to the Dallas Market Center (one of the world's largest trade complexes) and the Dallas–Fort Worth International Airport, a major hub for transportation and shipping. The metroplex experienced the largest population growth in 2007 of all metropolitan statistical areas in the nation.

The *South Texas Border Region* includes the Lower Rio Grande Valley and other border counties upriver to Val Verde County. This area includes some of the poorest counties in the state and has high unemployment, although it has received a boost from the construction of manufacturing plants in Mexico and trading benefits from the North American Free Trade Agreement (NAFTA). Laredo is now the state's primary point of imports from Mexico. Agriculture, livestock, and food processing are major industries in the region. The economy of the six-county *Upper Rio Grande Region* is directly tied to the economy of Mexico. El Paso (the oldest city in Texas) is across the border from Juarez, Mexico, a major manufacturing center. NAFTA is believed to have played a major role in the rapid industrialization of this area over the past two decades. This region is located in the Chihuahuan Desert, and its potential for future growth also is directly related to water issues.

The geographic characteristics of these regions, including the presence of natural resources, contribute to their economic diversity. These factors help shape the policies of local governments and the policy priorities of state legislators elected from the various regions.

Transnational Regionalism

Texas shares a 1,248-mile border with Mexico, and common problems and interests that bond the two neighbors, called **transnational regionalism**, have taken on increased importance since the mid-1980s.

Historically, relations between the United States and Mexico were often strained. The United States fought a war against Mexico in 1846–48, and on subsequent occasions, American troops entered Mexican territory, ostensibly to protect U.S. economic and national security interests. Apprehension about U.S. objectives resulted in Mexican policies on trade, commerce, and foreign ownership of property that were designed to insulate the country from excessive foreign influence and domination. Nevertheless, the interests of the two countries have long been bound by geopolitical factors, economics, and demographics. One Mexican author has compared the interdependence of the two countries to Siamese twins, warning that "if one becomes gangrenous, the other twin will also be afflicted."[54]

Maquiladoras Changes in the economic relationships between Mexico and the United States began with the **maquiladora program**, an initiative under Mexico's Border Industrialization Program in 1965 to boost employment, foreign exchange, and industrial development. It was also designed to transfer technology to Mexico, help train workers, and develop managerial skills among Mexican nationals.[55]

★ **transnational regionalism**
Expanding economic and social interdependence of South Texas and Mexico.

★ **maquiladora program**
Policies initiated by Mexico in 1964 to stimulate economic growth along the U.S.–Mexico border.

Economic Changes South of the Border
Hundreds of thousands of workers are now employed in the maquiladora assembly and manufacturing plants that have been constructed in Mexico over the past 40 years. Some economic experts argue that further stimulation of the Mexican economy will help stem the flow of illegal immigrants to the United States.

★ **North American Free Trade Agreement (NAFTA)**
Treaty among the United States, Canada, and Mexico that created the world's largest trading bloc. Approved by the U.S. Congress in 1993, the treaty is designed to reduce tariffs and increase trade among the three countries.

The concept was to develop twin plants, one in the United States and one in Mexico, under a single management. The plant in the United States would manufacture parts, and its Mexican counterpart would assemble them into a product, which, in turn, would be sent back to the United States for further processing or for shipping to customers.[56] Parts shipped into Mexico would not be subject to the normal tariffs, and the tax imposed on the assembled product would be minimal. In 1984, Mexico changed its laws to permit the United States and other foreign countries to establish these relationships throughout Mexico, rather than just on the border, and to permit 100 percent foreign ownership of the assembly plants in Mexico. The latter step was a radical departure from previous Mexican law, which prohibited such foreign ownership.[57]

The maquiladora program has not resulted in the construction of a significant number of manufacturing plants on the Texas side of the border because American companies have used existing plants throughout the United States to produce parts to be assembled in Mexico. Nevertheless, Texas's border counties have benefited through the creation of thousands of support jobs in transportation, warehousing, and services.[58] Some 4,700 maquiladora plants were in operation in 2004, providing hundreds of thousands of jobs but also contributing to increased population density along the Mexican side of the border, where most of the Mexican assembly plants are located.[59]

The maquiladora program continues to play a major role in transnational economic development. American organized labor opposes the program, arguing that the maquiladoras drain jobs from the United States. But the program provides a source of inexpensive labor for American businesses, which have complained for years that they cannot compete against cheap foreign labor costs.

The North American Free Trade Agreement (NAFTA) Negotiations on a free trade agreement in 1991 marked another significant change in the relationship between Mexico and the United States. The negotiations were precipitated, in part, by world economics and the emergence of regional trading zones. But the administration of Mexican President Carlos Salinas de Gortari also was reacting to the failure of Mexico's economic policies of the 1980s and a fear of economic isolation. The end of the Cold War, a reduction in Central American conflicts, and internal population pressures also were factors.[60]

The convergence of interests of the United States, Mexico, and Canada produced the **North American Free Trade Agreement (NAFTA)** to reduce tariffs and increase trade among the three countries. It created one of the world's largest trading blocs, which now has a combined population of approximately 447 million and a combined gross national product of $16.1 trillion.[61] Other regions of the world have recognized the value of creating large trading blocs, and the European Union, which now includes 27 nations, is estimated to have a combined population of 491 million and a combined GDP of $16.4 trillion.[62]

Approved by the U.S. Congress in late 1993, NAFTA has increased trade among the United States and its two neighbors, strengthened previous economic ties, and created new ones. Texas has experienced significant economic changes from these new relationships, but the benefits have not been uniformly distributed throughout the state.

NAFTA's Infrastructure The Free Trade Commission, based in Mexico City, is the central agency responsible for implementing NAFTA. Assisted by some twenty committees, subcommittees, and advisory groups, it is charged with resolving disputes and developing and administering procedures, measures, and standards authorized by the agreement.[63]

Three agencies were created under side agreements to NAFTA to help address common problems arising under the treaty. The Border Environmental Cooperation Commission (BECC) is responsible for tackling international environmental issues that face the three nations. Working with states and local communities along the U.S.–Mexican border, the agency is charged with developing plans to improve such things as water supplies, wastewater treatment, and waste disposal. It is responsible for certifying infrastructure projects for funding by the North American Development Bank (NADBank), or other financial institutions. By the spring of 2006, it had certified 105 environmental projects with a total cost of $2.4 billion.[64]

NADBank, which is located in San Antonio, was created by the United States and Mexico to fund infrastructure and environmental projects along the U.S.–Mexico border. In response to complaints about NADBank's early performance, a change was made in 2006 to have the bank and the BECC share the same board of directors. By early 2006, NADBank had participated in 88 infrastructure projects with loans and grants of $675 million. The total cost for these projects is estimated to be $2.25 billion.[65]

The Commission for Labor Cooperation is charged with improving working conditions and living standards and strengthening the enforcement of domestic labor laws with trade sanctions and other penalties. It takes complaints from interested parties and conducts quasijudicial proceedings with recommendations based on the labor laws of the three treaty participants.[66]

Continued Concerns About NAFTA   Some people on both sides of the U.S.–Mexico border believe that NAFTA is harming their respective countries. Labor unions in the United States are particularly concerned that lower labor costs in Mexico have moved jobs from the United States. Some manufacturers argue that labor and capital costs in Mexico threaten their American markets. Some Texas officials and many Texas residents fear that opening up the state's highways to Mexican trucks will create safety problems, and American trucking interests, including owners and drivers, oppose the additional competition.

In Mexico, there is concern that American corporations will dominate and reduce Mexico's control over its own economy, since approximately 82 percent of Mexico's exports are going to the United States. Human rights advocates have expressed concerns about working conditions, workers' benefits, and the broader social impact of the maquiladora plants on the lives of hundreds of thousands of Mexican citizens. Environmentalists have argued that increased commerce is worsening air and water pollution in both countries.[67]

Trade Patterns Between Texas and Mexico   The United States, including Texas, does a lot of business with Mexico. U.S. exports to Mexico were $12.4 billion in 1986 and $137 billion in 2007 (see Table 19.5). Imports from Mexico, now the United States' third largest trading partner, were $170 billion in 2007. Mexico accounted for 8.7 percent of all goods imported into the United States in 2007 and 11.7 percent of U.S. exports.[68]

Texas exported more than $56 billion worth of goods, 6.2 percent of the state's gross economy, to Mexico in 2007, a dramatic increase over the $8.8 billion exported in 1987.

The sheer volume of goods, services, and people is obvious on the highways leading into Mexico and in the long lines of autos and trucks at border crossings in Brownsville, Laredo, and El Paso. There were approximately 98 million legal crossings between Mexico and the United States in 2007. This included 32.5 million pedestrians, 59 million cars, and approximately six million trucks. More than eight thousand trucks cross the border each day at Laredo, the nation's

Table *19.5* Texas and U.S. Exports to Mexico, 1993–2007

Year	Texas Exports to Mexico (in billions of dollars)	U.S. Exports to Mexico (in billions of dollars)	Texas Exports as a percentage of U.S. Exports
1993	20.4	41.6	49%
1994	23.8	50.8	47
1995	21.9	46.3	47
1996	27.0	56.8	48
1997	31.2	71.4	44
1998	36.3	79.0	46
1999*	37.9	87.0	44
2000	47.8	111.7	43
2001	41.6	101.5	41
2002	41.6	97.5	43
2003	41.6	97.5	43
2004	45.7	110.8	41
2005	50.1	120.0	42
2006	54.9	134.2	41
2007	56.0	136.5	41

*Note: The Massachusetts Institute for Social and Economic Research applied a more advanced algorithim to data beginning in 1999. Thus, the post-1998 export figures more accurately account for unreported exports by states and therefore more accurately reflect actual export revenue that do pre-1999 figures.

Sources: Massachusetts Institute of Social and Economic Research and the U.S. Census Bureau (based on "origin of movement to port" state-level data series); Texas Department of Economic Development, April 2000; International Trade Administration, *Trade Stats* program.

largest inland port, and this number will continue to increase.[69] Billions of dollars are required to upgrade and expand the roads, highways, bridges, water and sanitation systems, and other facilities on both sides of the border. Some initiatives have been taken by both countries, but many facilities will not be completed for years, contributing to delays and gridlock in both countries. As noted above, NADBank was established, in part, to address these needs.

Illegal Immigration   Population growth in Texas has always been affected by migration from other states and foreign countries. But the proximity of Texas to Mexico has put the state in the center of a long-running dispute over the illegal immigration of large numbers of Mexicans and other Latin Americans. The dispute erupted anew in 2005 and 2006 as President George W. Bush and the U.S. Congress debated changes in immigration law. With Democrats in control of both houses of Congress after the 2006 elections, no resolution was forthcoming, and the issue spilled over into the 2008 election cycle.

In late 2005, the U.S. House approved a bill to improve border security and make criminals of undocumented immigrants, ignoring a proposal by President Bush to provide illegal immigrants already in the country a way to become citizens. The U.S. Senate rejected the House bill and approved legislation providing a so-called pathway to citizenship for illegal immigrants who paid fines, learned to speak English and met certain other requirements. Meanwhile, the controversy also played out in peaceful, but noisy, demonstrations in many American cities, including Dallas, Houston, and San Antonio, and in numerous political campaigns. Thousands of immigrants, their descendants and supporters took to the streets to wave American and Mexican flags for their cause, while many Texans and other Americans, including some political leaders, advocated building a high wall along the U.S.–Mexico border. President Bush also ordered several thousand National

Holding the Line?
In its efforts to increase border security and reduce illegal immigration, Congress increased the number of Border Patrol officers. But there continues to be a steady stream of illegal immigrants, such as this group, crossing the Mexico–U.S. border near Brownsville, Texas.

Guard troops to the border to help the Border Patrol. It was widely believed the president took that additional step to "secure" the border to boost support for his proposal to allow immigrants already in the country illegally to earn citizenship.

Congress authorized and funded the construction of a fence on the border between the United States and Mexico in 2005, and when the details of the fence became public in 2007, there was another round of intense political controversy. More fuel was added to the political fire in 2008, when the Department of Homeland Security announced it would pursue construction despite potential conflicts with some 34 existing laws.

In 2006, there were an estimated 11.3 million people, mostly from Mexico and other Latin American countries, living in the United States illegally.[70] Many enter through Texas and continue on to other areas of the country, but others remain in the state. According to the most recent estimates, Texas has some 3.7 million immigrants. Some 1.7 million, or 50 percent, are believed to be in the state illegally.[71]

The failure of the Mexican economy and the attraction of employment opportunities north of the border have been major reasons for this migration, although political instability and persecutions in Central America have also been significant factors. Large portions of the Texas and U.S. economies were built on the availability of cheap, low-skilled Mexican labor.[72] If arrested, illegal workers were returned to Mexico, but, until 1986, it was not illegal for U.S. employers to hire them.

In 1986, the U.S. Congress enacted the Immigration Reform and Control Act, which imposed fines on employers who hired undocumented workers and provided jail sentences for flagrant violators. Potential employees had to provide documentation, and employers had to verify their employees' citizenship or residency status. The new law also provided a means for giving legal status, or amnesty, to hundreds of thousands of illegal immigrants who had moved to the United States prior to January 1, 1982. It also granted temporary legal status for agricultural workers who could satisfy specific residency requirements.[73]

Additional legislation was passed in 1996 to increase funds for border guards and inspectors, to increase penalties for smuggling people into the United States and using fraudulent documents, to construct fences along the border, and to make it easier to detain and deport illegal immigrants.[74] But it soon became obvious that these laws had not stemmed the tide of illegal immigration. There were many reasons for the failure of these policies, including lax enforcement of the penalties on American companies, a need for cheap labor to fill many jobs in the United States, and insufficient funding and staffing of the Border Patrol.

According to recent surveys by the Census Bureau, educational attainment for the immigrant population is much lower than for people born in the United States. Income levels also are lower. A larger percentage of the immigrant workforce is comprised of unskilled labor. Poverty levels for families of immigrants are higher than for native-born Americans. Fewer immigrants are covered by health insurance, and more of the immigrant population has been served by the welfare system than the native population.[75]

Children of illegal immigrants can represent a heavy financial burden for many school districts and taxpayers along the border. Undocumented workers also increase demands on public health care programs. Some citizens, particularly unskilled workers, view the illegal arrivals as a threat to their jobs and standard of living.[76]

One of the unspoken realities of illegal immigration is that many native Texans have no desire to curtail the flow of people from the south. Within blocks of where one of the authors works, there are household domestics, nannies, and yardmen who are in the country illegally, and neighbors know their status. Numerous businesses throughout the state hire illegal immigrants for low-wage labor, despite the legal and financial risks. Good, "law-abiding" citizens have hired undocumented workers for temporary, contract jobs and never asked their status, as required by law. There are so many undocumented workers in Texas that the responsible federal agencies cannot always enforce the law. As a source of cheap labor, the illegal immigrant is, in effect, subsidizing business interests and others throughout Texas. State funds that are spent for social services for the immigrants also are a subsidy.

Other Border Controversies   Many Americans also are concerned about other issues affecting the United States' relationship with its neighbor to the south, including Mexican political corruption, the long-time domination of Mexican politics by the Institutional Revolutionary Party (PRI), the stability of the country, increased drug smuggling into the United States, and human rights violations.

Drug-related violence and alleged collusion between high-ranking Mexican officials and drug smugglers have raised questions about Mexico's ability to fight the drug problem. Americans also fear that violence among the competing drug cartels in Mexico's border cities could spill over into the United States. Nuevo Laredo, the neighboring city of Laredo, has seen numerous shootings. Several Mexican government officials responsible for enforcing drug laws have been murdered, as have members of the Mexican press who have reported on the drug cartels.

The potential for political instability in Mexico surfaced dramatically with the uprising on January 1, 1994, of the Zapatistas, a peasant-based guerrilla movement centered in Chiapas. Although some efforts were made to address the Zapatistas's grievances, the massacre of forty-five people in late December of 1997 by gunmen with alleged links to the ruling party cast more shadows on Mexico's political system.

Presidential candidate Luis Donaldo Colosio was assassinated in March 1994, and José Francisco Ruiz Massieu, secretary general of the ruling party, was murdered in September of that year. There are still widespread suspicions in the United States and Mexico that officials of PRI, the then-ruling party, were involved in these murders.

When Vicente Fox Quesada, a candidate of the largest opposition party, the National Action Party (PAN), captured the Mexican presidency in 2000, ending the 70-year domination by the Institutional Revolutionary Party (PRI), there was hope that he would initiate widespread reforms in the economy, the bureaucracy, the military, and law enforcement. Some changes have occurred, but the task he faced was daunting, with formidable entrenched opposition. PAN's presidential nominee, Felipe Calderon, won the presidency in 2006 in a highly contentious election that produced an election challenge by his opponent, Andres Manuel Lopez Obrador. For two months, Lobez Obrador's supporters took to the streets of Mexico City in an effort to influence the decision of the Federal Electoral Tribunal, but on September 6, 2006, Calderon was declared the winner.

President Fox and President George W. Bush had developed a cooperative relationship when they served as governors of their respective states, and initially their cooperation extended into their presidencies. But their relationship soured in 2003 when Mexico, along with most other members of the United Nations, refused to endorse U.S. military action against Iraq. Relations between the two countries further eroded because of a renewed debate over immigration, a dispute over water allocations from the Rio Grande, and the perception that the Bush administration was giving little attention to the interests of Mexico and other Latin American countries. The construction of the fence along the border has further exacerbated tension between the two countries.

Common Borders, Common Problems To anyone living on the border, the economic interdependence of the United States and Mexico is evident every day. Tens of thousands of pedestrians, cars, and trucks move across the international bridges, to and from the commercial centers on both sides of the Rio Grande. When the Mexican economy suffered a precipitous decline in 1982, the peso devaluation severely disrupted the Texas border economy, causing unemployment to skyrocket and a considerable number of U.S. businesses to fail.

Much of the effort toward improving relations between the United States and Mexico has focused on potential economic benefits, but other complex problems confronting both countries also merit attention. One is health care. On both sides of the border, many children have not been immunized against basic childhood diseases. On the Texas side are more than 1,200 *colonias*—rural, unincorporated slums that have substandard housing, roads, and drainage and, in many cases, lack water and sewage systems. These conditions have contributed to severe health problems, including hepatitis, dysentery, and tuberculosis. Higher than normal numbers of both Texan and Mexican children along the border also have been born with serious birth defects. Public health facilities in Texas report that Mexican women come across the border to give birth to their children in U.S. facilities. This practice, which has the effect of creating "binational families," increases the burden on public hospitals—and taxpayers—in Texas. Children born in the United States are U.S. citizens and are eligible for various public services.[77]

Industrial development and population growth along the border also increase environmental problems. U.S. anti-pollution laws have been more stringent than those of Mexico, but air and water pollution generated in Mexico does not stop at the border. The side agreements to NAFTA provide a basic framework for addressing these problems, but some have argued that a country such as Mexico, under enormous pressure to industrialize rapidly, is less likely to be concerned with environmental issues. In addition, U.S. efforts to impose its environmental standards on Mexico could be interpreted as another American effort to dominate the country.[78] In June 1994, several maquiladora plants in Matamoras, across the border from Brownsville, settled lawsuits alleging that pollution caused rare birth defects in children born in Texas. There have been numerous initiatives by both governments and private groups to deal with these common health and environmental problems, but it will take years to see widespread improvements.

Regional interdependence, although perhaps not recognized by most people on both sides of the border, has taken on greater importance in the press and in academic, business, and labor communities in the United States. Transnational public policies are emerging, creating legal issues in product liability, insurance, copyrights, and patents that must still be resolved. The governors of Mexican and U.S. border states have their own association, the Border Governors Conference, which meets regularly to discuss such issues as free trade, the environment, education, and tourism.

Summary
Who Gets What: The Social and Economic Milieu of Texas Politics

Politics, public policies, and the actions of decision makers are shaped by the complex environments in which governments function. People individually and collectively, "bring themselves into active relations to their surroundings" and often engage in conflict as well as compromise in pursuit of their self-interests.

★ Texas has distinct historic, geographic, and social features that shape its "brand" or style of politics. New generations of Texans, including those native to the state and those born outside the state, are confronted by the core features of the political culture, but they add to this complex mix, producing incremental changes that take years to identify. Change often generates intense conflict between competing groups with different interests or values. It also produces new or expanded demands of government.

★ The conservative politics of the state are rooted in its individualistic and traditionalistic political subcultures. The beliefs Texans hold about what government should do, who should govern, and what constitutes good public policy are rooted in these cultural patterns. These attitudes or beliefs are often articulated in the cultural myths that provide Texans with generalized views of the state, its common historical experience, and its people.

★ Demographically, Texans are diverse. Despite views shaped by the wide open spaces, more than 80 percent of Texans live in urban areas. The population continues to grow at a rapid pace, with the most significant increases among Hispanics and Asian Americans. Based on the 2006 American Community Survey, the state now has a "majority minority" population.

★ Race and economics have historically shaped Texas's politics. Disparities in wealth and income levels among Texans point to the political influence of class as well as of race and ethnicity. Largely excluded from participation in the past, racial and ethnic minority groups are quickly acquiring political influence and power that will continue to increase in the future.

★ Educational disparities among Texans follow race, ethnicity, and economics. With the exception of Asian Americans, minorities in Texas report lower levels of educational attainment than the Anglo population. Improved literacy and the development of a technologically competent workforce are essential to the state's ability to compete in the global economy.

★ Over the past 30 years, Texas has experienced the normal business cycles of "booms and busts." But the state's economy has diversified, giving the state greater flexibility in dealing with economic downturns.

★ The economy of Texas is the third largest in the nation, and it is helpful to view it in terms of thirteen distinct economic regions, with significant variations in population, basic industries, growth rates, and overall productivity. Periods of economic downturn and recovery are not felt uniformly across the state. With the pattern of urbanization that has occurred over the past three decades, the emerging "Texas urban triangle" points to new configurations and relationships in the Texas economy.

★ The Texas economy is bound to the economy of Mexico and the world. This development has occurred rapidly over the past 20 years, stimulated, in part, by Mexico's maquiladora program, the North American Free Trade Agreement, and the globalization of the state's economy.

★ Texas shares a 1,200-mile border with Mexico. The two countries also share many common problems, including illegal immigration, drug smuggling, and environmental concerns. Transnational regionalism speaks to the increased interdependence of the two countries and the necessity for governments on both sides of the Rio Grande to collaborate on solutions.

Key Terms

republic 656
individualism 657
political culture 658
individualistic subculture 659

moralistic subculture 659
traditionalistic subculture 659
elite 659
urbanization 668

population density 670
globalization of the economy 678
transnational regionalism 679

maquiladora program 679
North American Free Trade Agreement (NAFTA) 680

Suggested Readings

Barr, Alwyn. *Black Texans: A History of African Americans in Texas, 1528–1995*. Norman: University of Oklahoma Press, 1996.

Buenger, Walter L., and Robert A. Calvert, eds. *Texas through Time: Evolving Interpretations*. College Station, Tex.: Texas A&M University Press, 1991. An analysis of Texas myths, emphasizing potential distortions of the state's history and the need to utilize critical historical analysis to provide a more accurate understanding of Texans and their historical experiences.

Elazar, Daniel. *American Federalism: A View from the States*. New York: Thomas Y. Crowell, 1966. A groundbreaking analysis of American federalism focusing on the collaborative aspects of state-federal relationships with emphasis on the political culture of states.

Erikson, Robert S., Gerald Wright, and John P. McIver. *Statehouse Democracy: Public Opinion and Policy in the American States*. New York: Cambridge University Press, 1993. Using ideology "to assess the correspondence between public opinion and politics across the states," the authors demonstrate the utility of political subcultures to explain the conservative politics of Texas.

Fehrenbach, T. R. *Lone Star: A History of Texas and the Texans*. New York: Macmillan, 1968. One of the most comprehensive histories of Texas. A must for the serious student of Texas history and politics.

Frymier, Jack, and Arliss Roaden. *Cultures of the States: A Handbook on the Effectiveness of State Governments*. Lanham, Md.: The Scarecrow Press, 2003. Provides rankings across the fifty states with an emphasis on core problems facing state governments.

Hill, Kim Quaile. *Democracy in the Fifty States*. Lincoln: University of Nebraska Press, 1994. A provocative "comprehensive, empirical, theory-based analysis of the extent to which the governments of the fifty states can be judged to be democratic and of the policy consequences of the degree to which they are democratic."

Jordan, Terry G., with John L. Bean, Jr., and William M. Holmes. *Texas: A Geography*. Boulder, Colo.: Westview Press, 1984. An excellent introduction to the physical, demographic, economic, and cultural geography of Texas.

Langley, Lester D. *MexAmerica: Two Countries, One Future*. New York: Crown, 1988. A highly readable perspective on the impact of Mexican immigration on the politics, economy, policies, and culture of the United States.

McComb, David G. *Texas: A Modern History*. Austin, Tex.: University of Texas Press, 1989. A brief narrative history that provides a quick introduction to Texans, their culture, and their experiences.

Metz, Leon C. *Border: The U.S.-Mexico Line*. El Paso, Tex.: Mangan Books, 1989. A chronicle of the nearly 2,000-mile U.S.–Mexican border through "the eyes and experiences of government agents, politicians, soldiers, revolutionaries, outlaws, Indians, developers, illegal aliens, business people, and people looking for work."

Murdock, Steve H., Md. Nazrul Hoque, Martha Michael, Steve White, and Beverly Pecotte. *The New Texas Challenge: Population Change and the Future of Texas*. College Station, Tex.: Texas A&M University Press, 2003. Using extensive demographic data, the authors point to future problems for the state if significant educational and economic disparities among racial, ethnic, and economic groups are not addressed.

O'Connor, Robert F., ed. *Texas Myths*. College Station, Tex.: Texas A&M University Press, 1986. Utilizing the general concept of myth, these fourteen essays address various aspects of the state's history and political culture.

Richardson, Rupert N., Ernest Wallace, and Adrian N. Anderson. *Texas: The Lone Star State*. 9th ed. Upper Saddle River, N.J.: Prentice Hall, 2005. A comprehensive text on the history of Texas.

Wright, Bill. *The Tigua: Pueblo Indians of Texas*. El Paso, Tex.: Texas Western Press, 1993. A pictorial history of the Tiguas.

Zamora, Emilio. *The World of the Mexican Worker in Texas*. College Station, Tex.: Texas A&M University Press, 1993. A history of Mexican labor in the early part of the twentieth century.

Suggested Web Sites

State of Texas—Texas Online www.state.tx.us
Provides links to state agencies, local and county governments, and councils of states, with a wide array of governmental, demographic, and economic data.

U.S. Bureau of the Census www.census.gov
Population and economic data for the state are provided by the Bureau of the Census, which conducts the decennial census and a wide range of demographic studies between censuses. For state and county data, use "State and County Quick Facts" or "American Factfinder."

State Data Center and Demographer http://txsdc.utsa.edu
The Texas State Data Center "functions as a focal point for the distribution of Census information for Texas."

Office of the Comptroller www.cpa.state.tx.us
The comptroller's office produces reports on state finances and studies of select facets of the state's economy.

Economic Development and Tourism, Office of the Governor www.governor.state.tx.us/ecodevo/
This agency provides extensive economic and market data to businesses and promotes tourism in the state.

International Trade Administration
http://ita.doc.gov/td/industry/otea/state/indexhtml
This is a federal agency in the Department of Commerce that provides detailed trade data through its *TradeStats Express* program.

20 THE TEXAS CONSTITUTION

> 66 The constitution, written or unwritten, embodies the practices which are deemed most fundamental to the governmental and the social order. 99

Harold Lasswell

Chapter *Outline*

★ The Constitutional Legacy
★ General Principles of the Texas Constitution
★ Weaknesses and Criticisms of the Constitution of 1876
★ Constitutional Change and Adaptation
★ Constitutional Restraints and the Ability to Govern

The Constitutional Legacy

The year was 1874, and unusual events marked the end of the darkest chapter in Texas history—the Reconstruction era and the military occupation that followed the Civil War. Texans, still smarting from some of the most oppressive laws ever imposed on American citizens, had overwhelmingly voted their governor out of office, but he refused to leave the Capitol and hand over his duties to his elected successor. For several tense days, the city of Austin was divided into two armed camps of people—those supporting the deposed governor, Edmund J. Davis, and those supporting the man who defeated him at the polls, Richard Coke. Davis finally gave up only after the Texas militia turned against him and marched on the Capitol.

That long-ago period bears little resemblance to modern Texas, but the experience still casts a long shadow over state government. The state constitution written by Texans at the close of Reconstruction was designed to put strong restraints on government to guard against future abuses, and most of those restraints remain in place today. The Texas Constitution, adopted in 1876 and amended many times since, is so restrictive that many scholars and politicians believe it is counterproductive to effective modern governance. They believe the document, which is bogged down with statutory detail, is a textbook example of what a constitution should not be. State government functions despite its constitutional shackles: a weak chief executive, an outdated and part-time legislature, a poorly organized judiciary, and dedicated funds that limit the state's budgetary options. But a total rewriting of the constitution has been elusive, thanks to numerous special interests that find security in the present document—from holders of obsolete offices to beneficiaries of dedicated funds and bureaucrats who fear change. Public ignorance and indifference to the problems created by the restrictive constitutional provisions also thwart an overhaul of the document.

It is our opinion, shared by others who study state governments, that one cannot develop a clear understanding of Texas government or its politics without some familiarity and understanding of the Texas Constitution.[1] Constitutions are more than the formal frameworks that define the structure, authority, and responsibilities of governmental institutions. They also reflect fundamental political, economic, and power relationships as determined by the culture, values, and interests of the people who create them and the events of the period in which they were written.[2]

The constitution of Texas is not an easy read, and one can quickly get bogged down in details that make little sense to the casual reader. But a careful study of the document will provide insights into the distribution of power among competing groups and regions within the state. The

✓ Think About Politics

1. Should constitutional amendments be required to address strictly local issues, such as whether a particular county should have a hospital district?
   YES ◯   NO ◯

2. Should Texas prepare its budgets each year rather than for 2-year periods?
   YES ◯   NO ◯

3. Should Texas make it more difficult to amend its constitution?
   YES ◯   NO ◯

4. Should voters in Texas be able to sign petitions to put specific policy issues on the ballot?
   YES ◯   NO ◯

5. Should judges be appointed rather than elected?
   YES ◯   NO ◯

6. Does Texas need a new constitution?
   YES ◯   NO ◯

The Texas Constitution does more than define the institutions of government. It structures the power and influence that groups and individuals can wield in deciding who gets what, when, and how.

constitution outlines the powers of the state and local governments, and it defines the limitations imposed on these governments. The constitution also speaks to "the relation of the state to economic activity, including both the extent of direct governmental support for enterprise and the appropriate balance between promotion and regulation of economic development."[3]

Texas has had seven constitutions, and understanding that legacy is critical to understanding contemporary Texas politics and public policy (see Table 20.1). The first constitution was adopted in 1827, when the state was still part of Mexico. The second was drafted when Texas declared its independence from Mexico in 1836 and became a republic, and the third was adopted in 1845, when the state joined the Union. The fourth constitution was written when Texas joined the Confederacy in 1861, and the fifth was adopted when the state rejoined the Union in 1866. The sixth constitution was adopted in 1869 to satisfy the Radical Reconstructionists' opposition to the 1866 constitution, and the seventh constitution was adopted in 1876 after the termination of Reconstruction policies. Each of Texas's seven constitutions was written in a distinct historical setting. And although there are significant differences among these documents, each contributed to the state and local governments that exist in Texas today.

The Texas Constitution in a Comparative Perspective

The formal legal language of a **constitution** often obscures the general objectives of the document and its relevance to contemporary issues of political power and public policy. Scholars believe, first, that constitutions should be brief and should include general principles rather than specific legislative provisions. In other words, constitutions should provide a basic framework for government and leave the details to be developed in **statutory law.** Second, these experts say, constitutions should make direct grants of authority to specific institutions, so as to increase the responsiveness and the accountability of individuals elected or appointed to public office. Scholars also believe that constitutions should provide for orderly change but should not be written in such a restrictive fashion that they require continual modifications to meet contemporary needs.[4]

Amended only twenty-seven times since its ratification in 1788, the U.S. Constitution is a concise 7,000-word document that outlines broad basic principles of authority and governance. No one would argue that the government of the 2000s is comparable to that of the 1790s, yet the flexibility of the U.S. Constitution makes it as relevant now as it was in the eighteenth century. It is often spoken of as "a living charter or document" that does not have to be continually amended to meet society's ever-changing needs and conditions. As discussed in Chapter 3, its reinterpretations by the courts, the Congress, and the president have produced an expansion of powers and responsibilities within the framework of the original language of the document.

By contrast, the Texas Constitution—like those of many other states—is an unwieldy, restrictive document. With more than 90,000 words, it has been on a life-support system—the piecemeal amendment process—for most of its existence (see *Across the USA:* "States Frequently Amend Their Constitutions"). It is less a set of basic governmental principles than a compilation of detailed statutory language reflecting the distrust of government that was widespread in Texas when it was written. In effect, it attempts to diffuse political power among many different institutions. As drafted in 1875, it also included restrictions on elections and civil rights that were later invalidated by the U.S. Supreme Court. Those early provisions were efforts to limit the power of minority groups to fully participate in state government (see Table 20.2).[5]

★ **constitution**
Legal structure of a political system, establishing government bodies and defining their powers.

★ **statutory law**
Law enacted by a legislative body.

Table *20.1*   The Seven Texas Constitutions

1827: Constitution of Coahuila y Tejas

The first Texas constitution, adopted in 1827. It recognized Texas as a Mexican state with Coahuila.

1836: Constitution of the Republic

The constitution, adopted March 16, 1836, by Texas colonists declaring independence from Mexico. Under this constitution, Texas functioned as an independent republic for 9 years.

1845: Constitution of 1845

The constitution under which Texas was admitted to the United States.

1861: Civil War Constitution

The constitution adopted by Texans after the state seceded from the Union and joined the Confederacy in 1861.

1866: Constitution of 1866

The short-lived constitution under which Texas sought to be readmitted to the Union after the Civil War and before the Radical Reconstructionists took control of the U.S. Congress.

1869: Reconstruction Constitution

The constitution centralizing power in state government and weakening local governments. It reflected the sentiments of Radical Reconstructionists, not of most Texans.

1876: Texas Constitution

The constitution adopted at the end of Reconstruction, amended many times since, and still in effect. Highly restrictive and antigovernment, this constitution places strict limitations on the powers of the governor, the legislature, and other state officials.

The historical constitutional experiences of Texas parallel those of many southern states that have had multiple constitutions in the post–Civil War era. The southern states, Texas included, are the only states whose constitutions formally acknowledge the supremacy of the U.S. Constitution, a provision required by the Radical Reconstructionists for readmission of the former Confederate states to the Union.

The Constitution of Coahuila y Tejas, 1827

Sparsely populated Texas was part of Mexico when that country secured its independence from Spain in 1821, about the same time that Stephen F. Austin and others initiated Anglo colonization of Texas. Initially, Anglo Texans appeared to be willing to be incorporated into the Mexican political system as long as there was limited intrusion by the Mexican government into their daily affairs. In 1824 the new Republic of Mexico adopted a constitution for a federal system of government that recognized as a single state Texas and Coahuila, its neighbor south of the Rio Grande. Saltillo, Mexico, was the state capital.

The Constitution of Coahuila y Tejas, completed in 1827, provided for a **unicameral** legislature of twelve deputies, including two from Texas, elected by the people. Most of the legislators were from the more populous, Spanish-speaking Coahuila, and the laws were published in Spanish, which few Texas colonists understood. The executive department included a governor and a vice-governor. The governor enforced the law, led the state militia, and granted pardons. The constitution

★ **unicameral**
A legislature consisting of a single chamber.

Across the USA   States Frequently Amend Their Constitutions

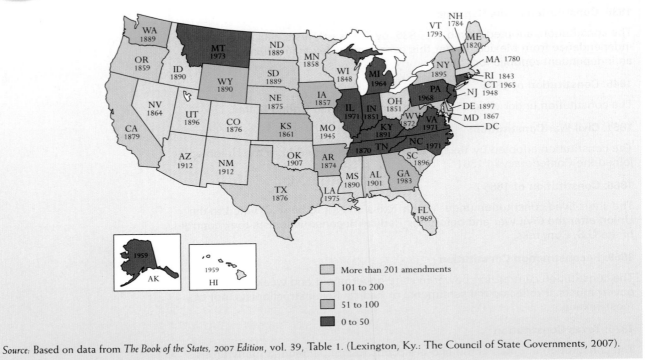

More than 201 amendments

101 to 200

51 to 100

0 to 50

Source: Based on data from *The Book of the States, 2007 Edition,* vol. 39, Table 1. (Lexington, Ky.: The Council of State Governments, 2007).

made Catholicism the state religion, although that requirement was not enforced among Texas's Anglo settlers. Additionally, Anglo Texans were not subject to military service, taxes, or custom duties. In effect, Texas served as a buffer between Mexico and various Native American peoples and the United States.

But with increased Anglo immigration and the perceived threat of U.S. imperial or expansionary policies, Mexico soon attempted to extend its control over Texas. This effort reinforced cultural differences between the Anglo and Spanish populations and would eventually lead to revolution by Anglo Texans.[6]

This formative period produced some enduring contributions to the Texas constitutional tradition. Elements of the Mexican legal system are still found in property and land laws, water laws and water rights, and community property laws. One justification for the Revolution of 1836 was the failure of the Mexican government to provide sufficient funding for public education. But while there were expectations of funding by the central government, a "concept of local control over school development was firmly established."[7] This paradox has raised a continuing constitutional question and is central to the current issue of funding public education.

The Constitution of the Republic of Texas, 1836

During the late 1820s and the early 1830s, increased immigration from the United States into the territory of Texas heightened tensions between the Anglo settlers and the Mexican government. Mexico's efforts to enforce its laws within Texas produced conflicts

Table *20.2* Comparison of the Texas Constitution
and the U.S. Constitution

	U.S. Constitution	Texas Constitution
General principles	Popular sovereignty	Popular sovereignty
	Limited government	Limited government
	Representative government	Representative government
	Social contract theory	Social contract theory
	Separation of powers	Separation of powers
Context of adoption	Reaction to weakness of Articles of Confederation—strengthened national powers significantly	Post-Reconstruction—designed to limit powers of government
Style	General principles stated in broad terms	Detailed provisions
Length	7,000 words	90,000 words
Date of implementation	1789	1876
Amendments	27	456
Amendment process	Difficult	Relatively easy
Adaptation to change	Moderately easy through interpretation	Difficult; often requires constitutional amendments
Bill of Rights	Amendments to the Constitution—adopted in 1791	Article 1 of the Constitution of 1876
Structure of government	Separation of powers, with a unified executive based on provisions of Articles I, II, III	Separation of powers with plural executive defined by Article 2
Legislature	Bicameral	Bicameral
Judiciary	Creation of one Supreme Court and other courts to be created by the Congress	Detailed provisions creating two courts of last resort and other state courts
Distribution of powers	Federal	Unitary
Public policy	Little reference to policy	Detailed policy provisions

between cultures, legal traditions, and economic interests that resulted in open rebellion by the colonists.

At the same time, Mexico was embroiled in its own internal dissension. It struggled to stabilize its political system but did not have the legacy or social and political institutions to ensure a successful democratic system. In many respects, the events in Texas were a footnote to the power politics in Mexico. Had the autonomy of Texas that was provided for under the Mexican Constitution of 1824 been maintained, the history of this region might well have been different.

Increased internal conflict among competing Mexican interests resulted in the seizure of power by the popular general, Antonio López de Santa Anna Perez de Lebron. Santa Anna began to systematically suspend the powers of the Mexican Congress and local governments, and in October 1835, the national Constitution of 1824 was voided. Mexico adopted a new constitution providing for a **unitary system** with power centralized in the national Congress and the presidency. The principle of **federalism**, which divided power and authority between the national government and the states, was repudiated. This major change intensified conflict

★ **unitary system**
Constitutional arrangement whereby authority rests with the national government; subnational governments have only those powers given them by the national government.

★ **federalism**
Constitutional arrangement in which power is formally divided between national and subnational governments.

Birth of the Republic

Faced with the advancing Mexican armies, Texans hastily met in the small settlement of Washington-on-the-Brazos, declared their independence on March 2, 1836, and wrote the constitution of the Republic, which was adopted on March 16, 1836.

between the national government and the Mexican states. Texas was not the only area of Mexico where the principles of federalism were highly regarded, and although Texas was eventually successful in establishing its autonomy, several other rebellious Mexican states were subjected to harsh military retaliation.

As the Mexican government under Santa Anna attempted to regain control over Texas, colonists who initially supported the national government and those who expressed ambivalence were slowly converted to the cause of independence. Stephen F. Austin had consistently supported the position that Texas was a Mexican state, and he represented the views of a large part of the Anglo population living in Texas. But when Mexican troops moved across the Rio Grande into Texas in the autumn of 1835, Austin sent out a call for resistance.

The numerous special interests that later were to obstruct the course of constitutional development in Texas were missing at the small settlement of Washington-on-the-Brazos in 1836. The fifty-nine male colonists who convened to declare Texas's independence from Mexico on March 2 and to adopt a constitution for the new republic two weeks later had two overriding interests: the preservation of their fledgling nation and the preservation of their own lives. By the time they had completed their work, the Alamo—only 150 miles away—had fallen to a large Mexican army under Santa Anna, and a second Mexican force had arrived north of the Rio Grande. Accordingly, the constitution writers wasted little time on speech making.

Consequently, the Constitution of the Republic, adopted on March 16, 1836, was not cluttered with the details that weaken the present Texas Constitution. It drew heavily on the U.S. Constitution and, since forty-four of the fifty-nine delegates were from the South, from the constitutions of several southern states. The document created an elected **bicameral** Congress and provided for an elected president. Members of the clergy were prohibited from serving as president or in Congress, and there was no official, state-preferred religion. Slavery was legal, but importation of slaves from any country other than the United States was illegal. Free African Americans had to have Congress's permission to leave Texas.

Approximately 6 weeks after the disastrous defeat at the Alamo, the Texas army, under Sam Houston, defeated Santa Anna's army at the battle of San Jacinto on April 21, 1836. The war of independence had been relatively short and involved limited casualties, but the problems of creating a stable political system under the new constitution were formidable. There was no viable government in place, no money for paying the costs of government, and no party system. And,

★ **bicameral**
A legislature consisting of two chambers.

although defeated, Mexico did not relinquish its claim to Texas and was to demonstrate in subsequent actions that it wanted to regain this lost territory. Nevertheless, the "transition from colony to constitutional republic was accomplished quickly and with a minimum of disorganization."[8]

Independence and national autonomy from 1836 to 1845 contributed significantly to the development of a sense of historical uniqueness among Texans. Although the effects on the state's political psyche may be difficult to measure, the "Lone Star" experience has been kept alive through school history texts, the celebration of key events, and the development of a mythology of the independence period.

The Constitution of 1845

During the independence movement and immediately thereafter, some Texans made overtures to the United States to annex Texas, but they were initially blocked by the issue of slavery and its relationship to economic and regional influence in U.S. politics. Increased immigration to Texas in the late 1830s and early 1840s, more interest among Texans in joining the Union, and expansionist policies of the U.S. government stepped up pressures for annexation. It was a major issue in the U.S. presidential campaign of 1844, and the election of James K. Polk accelerated the move toward Texas's admission to the United States in 1845.

The annexation bill approved by the U.S. Congress included a compromise that allowed slavery to continue in Texas.[9] Racial issues that emerged from this period continue to shape contemporary politics and public policy in the state. Texas still struggles with voting rights issues, inequities in funding of education, and the maldistribution of economic resources that directly affect the quality of life of many minorities.

The terms of Texas's admission into the Union also provided that Texas could divide itself into as many as five states, a provision largely forgotten until state representative David Swinford, a Republican from Dumas, made such a proposal in 1991. The idea attracted some newspaper headlines and some interest in the Panhandle, which is geographically isolated from most of Texas, but was not given serious consideration by Swinford's colleagues.

The state constitution drafted to allow Texas's annexation was about twice as long as the Constitution of 1836. It borrowed not only from its predecessor but also from the constitutions of other southern states, particularly Louisiana.

The Constitution of 1845 created an elected legislature that met biennially and included a House of Representatives and a Senate. It provided for an elected governor and an elected lieutenant governor, and it empowered the governor to appoint a secretary of state, attorney general, and state judges, subject to Senate confirmation. The legislature chose a comptroller, treasurer, and land commissioner. But in 1850, Texas voters amended the constitution to make most state offices elective. In this respect, Texas was following a national pattern of fragmenting the powers of the executive branch of state government. Today Texas still has a plural executive system under which practically all statewide officeholders are elected independently of the governor, a system that contrasts sharply with the appointive cabinet system of executive government enjoyed by the president of the United States (see Chapter 11).

The Constitution of 1845 protected private homesteads from foreclosure, guaranteed separate property rights for married women, and established a permanent fund for the support of public schools—provisions also found in the present constitution. The 1845 charter also recognized slavery, prohibited anyone who had ever participated in a duel from holding public office, and prohibited state-chartered banks. This constitution "worked so well that after several intervening constitutions, the people of Texas recopied it almost in toto as the Constitution of 1876."[10]

Transition President

Anson Jones was the last president of the Republic of Texas, serving from December 1844 to February 1846.

A Proponent of Annexation

President James K. Polk, a proponent of westward expansion and the annexation of Texas, signed a joint resolution to admit Texas as a state on December 29, 1845.

His Opposition to Secession Cost Him His Job

Governor Sam Houston, who played a pivotal role throughout the formative period of Texas history, opposed the state's secession from the Union and was replaced on March 16, 1861, by Ed Clark.

★ **confederacy**
National government created by states that relies on the states for its authority.

★ **Radical Reconstructionists**
The group of Republicans who took control of the U.S. Congress in 1866 and imposed military governments on the former Confederate states after the Civil War.

The Civil War Constitution, 1861

When Texas seceded from the Union in 1861, just before the outbreak of the Civil War, the state constitution was again revised. Although most of the provisions of the 1845 document were retained, significant changes were made in line with Texas's new membership in the Confederacy. Public officials were required to pledge their support of the Confederate Constitution, greater protection was given to slavery, and the freeing of slaves was prohibited.

Any semblance of a two-party system had been destroyed by the issues of slavery and secession during the 1850s, and state politics was dominated by personalities and factions. Factionalism within the Democratic Party persisted for more than 100 years, until the emergence of a two-party system in the 1980s.

The Civil War era also contributed to a legacy of states' rights, which was to persist well into the next century and spark an extended struggle for desegregation. Theoretically, the constitutional issue of the Civil War was whether a state, once having joined the Union, could leave it. The southern states subscribed to a view of the national government as a **confederacy**, and it was their position that a state could withdraw, or secede. Although the northern victory dispelled this interpretation, Texas, along with other southern states, found ways to thwart national policy through the 1960s. Their efforts were based, in part, on their continued arguments for states' rights.

The Constitution of 1866

After the Civil War, Texas was subject to national control through, first, a military government, then a provisional government headed by A. J. Hamilton, a former U.S. congressman who had remained loyal to the Union. These were dark days for Texans. Although the state had experienced relatively few battles and had not suffered from the scorched-earth tactics used by Union generals elsewhere, the economy was in disarray. Many Texas families had also lost loved ones, and many surviving Confederate veterans had been wounded physically or psychologically. Although the national government developed policies to assist the newly freed slaves, these policies were never fully funded and were halfheartedly—and often dishonestly—carried out. And the presence of an occupation army heightened tension and shaped subsequent political attitudes.

The reconstruction plan initiated by President Abraham Lincoln but never fully implemented envisioned a rapid return to civilian government for the southern states and their quick reintegration as equals into the national political system. Requirements were modest: the abolition of slavery, the repudiation of the Secession Ordinance of 1861, and the repudiation of all debts and obligations incurred under the Confederacy.[11]

Texas voters revived the Constitution of 1845 and amended it to include the stipulations required by the national government. Although slavery was eliminated and the freed slaves were given the right to hold property and were accorded legal rights before a jury, black people could not testify in any court case involving whites. And African Americans were denied the right to vote. The new constitution was adopted in June 1866, a new government was elected, and on August 20, 1866, President Andrew Johnson "declared the rebellion in Texas at an end."[12]

In short order, however, the mild reconstruction policies of Johnson were replaced by the severe policies of the **Radical Reconstructionists** who captured control of Congress in 1866. The new Texas Constitution was invalidated by Congress, which passed, over the president's veto, the Reconstruction Acts that established military governments throughout the South. The civilian government initiated by the state Constitution of 1866 was short-lived, and Texas functioned for 2 years under a reinstituted military government.

This period had an enduring impact on Texas constitutional law and politics. In a broad sense, it prolonged the full reintegration of Texas into the national political system, and, in specific terms, it transformed the constitutional tradition of Texas into one of hostility and suspicion toward government.

The Reconstruction Constitution, 1869

The Reconstruction Acts required a Texas constitution that would grant African Americans the right to vote and include other provisions acceptable to the U.S. Congress. A Republican slate of delegates to a new state constitutional convention produced a new charter that was published in 1869. It did not reflect the majority Texas sentiment of the time, but it conformed to Republican wishes. Centralizing more powers in state government while weakening local government, it gave the governor a 4-year term and the power to appoint other top state officials, including members of the judiciary. It provided for annual legislative sessions, gave African Americans the right to vote, and, for the first time, provided for a centralized, statewide system of public schools. Texans were unhappy enough with their new constitution, but the widespread abuses of the document that followed under the oppressive and corrupt administration of Radical Republican Governor Edmund J. Davis paved the way for the shackles on state government that are still in place today.

Detested by Many Texans

A Union general and later governor of Texas (1870–74), Edmund J. Davis conducted one of the most oppressive administrations in U.S. history. Texans reacted to such practices by building restrictions into the Constitution of 1876.

In the 1869 election, the first under the new constitution, the military governor certified that Davis, a former Union Army officer, beat conservative Republican A. J. Hamilton by 39,901 to 39,092 votes. This outcome was allowed despite widespread, flagrant incidents of voter fraud, which were also ignored by President Ulysses S. Grant and the U.S. Congress. A radical majority in the new Texas legislature then approved a series of authoritarian—and, in some respects, unconstitutional—laws proposed by Davis. They gave the governor the power to declare martial law and suspend the laws in any county and created a state police force under the governor's control that could deprive citizens of constitutional protections. The governor also was empowered to appoint mayors, district attorneys, and hundreds of other local officials. Another law that designated newspapers as official printers of state documents in effect put much of the press under government control.

Davis exercised some of the most repressive actions ever imposed on U. S. citizens. And Texans responded. First, in 1872, they elected a Democratic majority to the legislature, which abolished the state police and repealed other oppressive laws. Then, in 1873, they elected a Confederate veteran, Democrat Richard Coke, governor by more than a 2 to 1 margin over Davis. Like the Radical Republicans in the previous gubernatorial election, the Democrats were not above abusing the democratic process, and, once again, voting fraud was rampant.

As was described earlier in the chapter, Davis initially refused to leave office and appealed to President Grant for federal troops to help him retain power. Grant refused, and Davis finally gave up after the Texas militia turned against him and marched on the Capitol in January 1874. Bloodshed was avoided, Reconstruction was ending, and the Constitution of 1869 was doomed.

The Constitution of 1876: Retrenchment and Reform

The restored Democratic majority promptly took steps to write a new constitution. A new constitutional convention convened in Austin on September 6, 1875. The delegates were all men. Most were products of a rural and frontier South, and, still smarting from Reconstruction abuses, they considered government a necessary evil that had to be heavily restricted. Many, however, had previous governmental experience. Initially, seventy-five Democrats and fifteen Republicans were elected delegates, but one Republican resigned after only limited service and was replaced by a Democrat.[13]

The vast majority of the delegates were white, and some disagreement remains over how many African Americans served in the convention. Some historians say there were six. According to one account, however, six African Americans were elected but one resigned after only one day of service and was replaced in a special election by a white delegate. All of the African American delegates were Republicans.[14]

Only four of the delegates were native Texans. Most had immigrated to Texas from other southern states, including nineteen—the largest single group—from Tennessee, which one author called the "breeding ground" of Texas delegates. Their average age was 45. The oldest was 68; the youngest was 23.[15] Eleven of the delegates had been members of previous constitutional conventions in Texas, but there is disagreement over whether any had participated in drafting the Reconstruction Constitution of 1869. In any event, the influences of the 1869 Constitution were negative, not positive.

At least thirty of the delegates had served in the Texas legislature. Two others had served in the Tennessee and Mississippi legislatures, two had represented Texas in the U.S. Congress, and two had represented Texas in the Confederate Congress. Delegates also included a former attorney general, a former lieutenant governor, and a former secretary of state of Texas; at least eight delegates had judicial experience. Many delegates had been high-ranking Confederate military officers. One, John H. Reagan, had been postmaster general of the Confederacy.[16] Reagan later would become a U.S. senator from Texas and would serve as the first chair of the Texas Railroad Commission.

Another delegate who epitomized the independent, frontier spirit of the time was John S. "Rip" Ford, a native of South Carolina who had come to Texas in 1836 as a physician. He later became a lawyer, journalist, state senator, mayor of Austin, and Texas Ranger captain. In 1874, he was a leader of the militia that marched on the Capitol and forced Edmund J. Davis to relinquish the governor's office to his elected successor. Ford had been a secessionist delegate to the 1861 convention, which voted for secession and drafted a constitution. During the Civil War he had commanded a makeshift cavalry regiment that fought Union soldiers along the Texas–Mexico border.[17]

According to one account, delegates to the 1875 convention included thirty-three lawyers, twenty-eight farmers, three physicians, three merchants, two teachers, two editors, and one minister. At least eleven other delegates were part-time farmers who also pursued other occupations.[18] Other historians have come up with slightly different breakdowns, but all agree that the influence of agricultural interests was substantial in the writing of the new Texas charter.

About half the delegates were members of the Society of the Patrons of Husbandry, or the **Grange**. An organization formed to improve the lot of farmers, the Grange became politically active in the wake of national scandals involving abuses by big business and government. The Grange started organizing in Texas in 1873, and its influence was felt directly in constitutional provisions limiting taxes and governmental expenditures and restricting banks, railroads, and other corporations.

The delegates did not try to produce a document that would be lauded as a model of constitutional perfection or mistaken for a literary classic. They faced the reality of addressing serious, pressing problems—an immediate crisis that did not encourage debate over the finer points of academic or political theory or produce any prophetic visions of the future.

The Civil War and Reconstruction had plunged the state into economic ruin and state government into deep debt, despite the heavy taxation of Texas citizens,

★ **Grange**
Organization formed in the late nineteenth century to improve the lot of farmers. The Grange influenced provisions in the Texas Constitution of 1876 limiting taxes and government spending and restricting big business, including banks and railroads.

Toward a New Texas

Ninety delegates, including six recently emancipated African Americans, were elected to the 1875 Constitutional Convention.

particularly property owners. The bottom had fallen out of land prices, a disaster for what was still an agricultural state. Governmental corruption had been pervasive under the Davis administration, and the dictatorial powers that Davis had exercised, particularly the abuses of his hated state police, had left deep scars. Moreover, the national political scene under President Grant's two administrations (1869–77) had also been plagued by corruption and scandal.

The framers of the Texas Constitution of 1876 reacted accordingly. In seeking to restore control of their state government to the people and reestablish economic stability, they fashioned what was essentially an anti-government charter. Centralization was replaced with more local control, strict limits were placed on taxation, and short leashes were put on the legislature, the courts, and, especially, the governor.[19]

Texas's traditional agricultural interests, which had been called on to finance industrial development and new social services during the Reconstruction era, were once again protected from onerous governmental intrusion and taxation. The retrenchment and reform embodied in the new charter would soon hamper the state's commercial and economic development. But post-Reconstruction Texans applauded the multitude of restrictive details that the new constitution carried. They ratified the document in February 1876 by a vote of 136,606 to 56,052.

General Principles of the Texas Constitution

The Texas Constitution of 1876 draws from the national constitutional tradition discussed earlier and embodies four dominant principles: popular sovereignty, contract theory, limited government, and separation of powers (see Table 20.2).

A relatively short Preamble and the first two sections of the Bill of Rights express the document's underlying principle. It is a social compact, formed by free men (no women participated in its drafting), in which "all political power is inherent in the people and all free governments are founded on their authority, and instituted for their benefit." These brief sections are based on the principles of **popular sovereignty** and **social contract theory**, both of which were part of a legacy of constitutional law in the United States. Although the language articulates the noble aspirations of a free and just society, it was limited in scope and application. Women and minorities were initially denied full citizenship rights. And although women gained the right to vote by amendment to the U.S. Constitution in 1920, it has taken years for African Americans and Hispanics to receive the full protections implicit in these statements.

A third major principle is **limited government**. The Texas Bill of Rights and other provisions throughout the constitution place limits on governmental authority and power. The constitution spells out the traditional rights of religious freedom, procedural due process of law, and other rights of the citizen in relation to the government.

A fourth major principle is **separation of powers**. Unlike the U.S. Constitution, in which this principle emerges through powers defined in the three articles related to the Congress, the president, and the judiciary, Article II of the Texas Constitution specifically provides for it.

The Constitution of 1876 created three branches of government—legislative, executive and judicial—and provided for a system of checks and balances that assured that no single branch would dominate the others. This principle originated with the U.S. Constitution, whose drafters were concerned about the so-called "mischief of factions." They feared that groups or special interests would be able to capture governmental institutions and pursue policies that were not in

★ **popular sovereignty**
Constitutional principle of self-government; belief that the people control their government and governments are subject to limitations and constraints.

★ **social contract theory**
Political theory that holds that the legitimacy of the state is based on the obligations and responsibilities that individuals and the state have toward each other.

★ **limited government**
Constitutional principle restricting governmental authority and spelling out personal rights.

★ **separation of powers**
Division of powers among three distinct branches of government—the legislative, the executive, and the judicial—which serve as checks and balances on each other's actions.

the national interest. So institutional power was fragmented to guard against that potential problem. In some respects, this was an issue of even greater concern to the framers of the Texas Constitution. Reacting to the highly centralized authority and abuses of the Davis administration, they took the separation of powers principle to its extreme.

Law-making authority is vested in an elected legislature that includes a 150-member House of Representatives and a 31-member Senate. The Texas legislature meets in regular sessions in odd-numbered years and in special sessions of limited scope and duration when called by the governor. The sixty-five sections of Article III spell out in detail the powers granted to and the restrictions imposed on the legislature.

An elected governor shares authority over the executive branch with several other independently elected, statewide officeholders. The governor, who has limited constitutional powers, can veto bills approved by the legislature and can call and set the agendas for special legislative sessions. A gubernatorial veto can be overridden only by a two-thirds vote of the House and the Senate.

Also elected are members of the judiciary—from justices of the peace, with limited jurisdiction at the county level, to judges on the highest statewide appellate courts. This provision reflects the strong sentiment of post-Reconstruction Texans for an independent judiciary and is a major difference from the federal government, in which judges are appointed by the president. Also unlike the federal system, in which the U.S. Supreme Court is the court of last resort in both civil and criminal appeals, Texas has two courts of last resort. The Texas Supreme Court has final jurisdiction over civil matters, and the Texas Court of Criminal Appeals has final review of criminal cases.

Weaknesses and Criticisms of the Constitution of 1876

Executive Branch Many experts believe that the Texas Constitution excessively fragments governmental authority and responsibility, particularly in the executive branch. Although there is a natural disposition for the public to look to the governor to establish policy priorities, the governor does not have control over other elected state executives but rather shares both authority and responsibility for policy with them. This situation can be problematic, as when former Republican Governor Bill Clements, for example, shared executive responsibilities with Democrats who sharply disagreed with his priorities. Even when the governor and other elected officials are of the same party, differences in personality, political philosophy, and policy objectives can produce tension and sometimes deadlock. Political divisiveness and feuding at the highest levels of state government became particularly strident in 2006, when Comptroller Carole Keeton Strayhorn, a Republican, became an independent candidate to unsuccessfully challenge Republican Governor Rick Perry's reelection.

The governor's power has been further diffused by the creation over the years of numerous boards and commissions that set policy for executive agencies not headed by elected officials. Although the governor appoints most of those board members, they serve staggered 6-year terms, which are longer than a governor's term. A newly elected governor—who cannot fire a predecessor's appointees—usually has to wait through most of his or her first term to gain a majority of appointees to most boards.

Fragmented authority and responsibility are also found in county governments, which are administrative agents of the state (see Chapter 25). Various elected county officials often clash over public policy, producing inefficiencies or failing to meet public needs. And just as voters are faced with a long ballot for statewide offices, they must also choose among a long, often confusing list of county officers. Because a long ballot discourages many people from voting, this obstacle reduces public accountability, an end result that the framers of the Constitution of 1876 certainly never intended.

Legislative Branch   The constitution created a low-paid, part-time legislature to ensure the election of citizen-lawmakers who would be sensitive to the needs of their constituents, not of professional politicians who would live off the taxpayers. Unwittingly, however, the constitution writers also produced a law-making body easily influenced by special interest groups. And the strict limitations placed on the legislature's operations and powers slow its ability to meet the increasingly complex needs of a growing, modern Texas.

In 1972, voters approved a constitutional change to lengthen the terms of the governor and other executive officeholders from 2 to 4 years. This change gives the governor more time to develop public policies with the prospect of seeing those policies implemented. But voters have repeatedly rejected proposals to provide for regular, annual legislative sessions, and legislative pay remains among the lowest in the country.

Judicial Branch   The Texas Constitution also created numerous locally elected judicial offices, including justice of the peace and county and district courts. Although there are appeal procedures, these judges have a great deal of autonomy, power, and influence through their local constituencies.

Education   Another example of decentralization is the public school system. The centralized school system authorized under the Reconstruction Constitution of 1869 was abolished, and local authorities were given primary responsibility for supervising public education. The concept of local control over their schools is

Diversity on the Rise
Minority participation at all levels of Texas government has increased significantly since the 1980s as a result of the Voting Rights Act and the reversal of federal court decisions that kept minorities from registering and voting. Democratic senatorial nominee Rick Noriega, a former member of the Texas House, is shown campaigning in 2008.

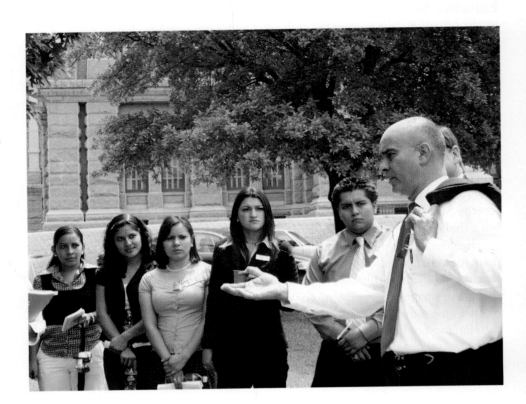

important to many Texans, but decentralization and wide disparities in local tax bases have produced an inequitable public education system.

Budgeting and Finances   The Texas Constitution, including key amendments adopted after 1876, requires a balanced state budget but also heavily restricts the legislature's choices over state spending. The dedication of large amounts of revenue to specific purposes has made it increasingly difficult for lawmakers to address changing state needs (see *Politics Up Close*: "Budget Restrictions").

Individual Rights   Although articulating a general commitment to democracy and individual rights, the constitution initially retarded democratic development in Texas. Like many other southern states, Texas had restrictive laws on voter participation. It levied a poll tax, which reduced the voting of minorities and poor whites until 1966, when an amendment to the U.S. Constitution and a decision by the U.S. Supreme Court outlawed it. Federal courts also struck down a Texas election system that excluded African Americans from voting in the Democratic primary, which was where elections were decided when Texas was a one-party, Democratic state. The elimination of significant numbers of people from participating in elections helped perpetuate the one-party political system for approximately 100 years.[20]

Consequence of Details   The Texas Constitution is burdened with excessive detail. Although few individuals are disposed to read the 90,000-plus-word document, a person casually perusing it can find language, for example, governing the

Politics Up Close   Budget Restrictions

Like most other states and unlike the federal government, Texas—thanks to a constitutional requirement—operates on a pay-as-you-go basis that prohibits deficit financing. The comptroller must certify that each budget can be paid for with anticipated revenue from taxes, fees, and other sources. Although that provision is designed to protect taxpayers and keep state government solvent, other sections of the constitution make it more difficult for the legislature to meet the state's budgetary needs adequately and fairly.

One handicap is the 2-year budget period, necessitated by the fact that the legislature meets in regular session only every other year. Critics, including many legislators and state agency directors, say 2-year budgets require too much guesswork and cause inadequate funding of some programs and wasteful spending in other areas. Voters in 1985 approved a constitutional amendment to allow the governor and legislative leaders to transfer funds between programs or agencies to meet emergencies when the legislature is not in session. But that provision only partially addressed the problem.

The legislature's control over the budget-setting process is further restricted by constitutional requirements that dedicate significant portions of state revenue to specific purposes. Three-fourths of the revenue from the motor fuels tax is automatically set aside for highways and the remaining one-fourth for public education. The Permanent School Fund and the Permanent University Fund are land- and mineral-rich endowments that help support the public schools and boost funding for the University of Texas and Texas A&M University systems.

The legislature can bend the pay-as-you-go requirement by issuing general obligation bonds, serviced by future tax revenues, to build prisons and other public facilities. Such bonds require voter approval in the form of constitutional amendments, several of which, totaling billions of dollars, have been approved in recent years for numerous needs, from prisons to cancer research. That debt will have to be paid off with tax dollars over the next generation.

operation of hospital districts in Ochiltree, Castro, Hansford, and Hopkins counties. There also is a provision dealing with expenditures for relocating or replacing sanitary sewer laterals on private property. Whereas the 7,000-word U.S. Constitution leaves the details of implementation to congressional legislation, the Texas Constitution often spells out the authority and power of a governmental agency in specific detail. Most experts agree that many constitutional articles are of a legislative nature and have no business in a constitution.[21] The excessive detail limits the adaptability of the constitution to changing circumstances and places undue restrictions on state and local governments.

Consequently, there are obsolete and contradictory provisions in the constitution. Some have been superseded by subsequent state and federal constitutional amendments. And, periodically, state constitutional amendments have been approved to clean up such deadwood, but the problem persists.[22]

Another important criticism of the Texas Constitution focuses on the amendments and the amendment process. Alabama has had more constitutional amendments than any other state, but Texas ranked third, with 456 amendments from 1876 through 2007 (see Table 20.3). In contrast, the U.S. Constitution has been amended only twenty-seven times since 1789, and ten of those amendments were adopted as the Bill of Rights immediately after the government organized. The numerous restrictions and prohibitions in the Texas Constitution require excessive amendments to enable state government to adapt to social, economic, and political changes.

Table **20.3**   Ten Shortest and Ten Longest State Constitutions (As of January 1, 2007)

State	Number of Constitutions	Effective Date of Current Constitution	Estimated Number of Words	Amendments Submitted to Voters	Amendments Adopted
Ten Shortest State Constitutions					
New Hampshire	2	1784	9,200	287	145
Vermont	3	1793	10,286	211	53
Indiana	2	1851	10,379	78	46
Rhode Island	2	1986	10,908	11	10
Utah	1	1896	11,000	158	107
Minnesota	1	1858	11,547	214	119
Kansas	1	1861	12,296	123	93
Iowa	2	1857	12,616	57	52
Montana	2	1973	13,145	54	30
Tennessee	3	1870	13,300	61	38
Ten Longest State Constitutions					
Florida	6	1969	51,456	141	110
New York	4	1895	51,700	291	216
Oregon	1	1859	54,083	477	238
Louisiana	11	1975	54,112	210	150
California	2	1879	54,645	870	514
Arkansas	5	1874	59,500	190	92
Oklahoma	1	1907	74,075	340	175
Colorado	1	1876	74,522	315	150
Texas	7	1876	90,000	631	456
Alabama	6	1901	340,136	1,088	794

Source: The Book of the States, 2007 Edition, Vol. 39. Lexington, Ky.: The Council of State Governments, 2007.

Constitutional Change and Adaptation

Amendment   The drafters provided a relatively easy method of amending the constitution, which has enabled state government to meet some changing needs. But it also has added thousands of words to the document.

Proposed constitutional amendments can be submitted only by the legislature. Approval by two-thirds of the House and the Senate puts them on the ballot, where adoption requires a majority vote. Although voters had approved 456 amendments through 2007, they had rejected 175 others. Since the present charter was ratified in 1876, there have been only a few years in which voters have not been asked to change it. The first amendment was adopted on September 2, 1879. A record twenty-five amendments were on the November 3, 1987, ballot. Seventeen were adopted, and eight were defeated.

Some amendments are of major statewide importance, but many have affected only a single county or a handful of counties or have been offered simply to rid the constitution of obsolete language (see *Politics Up Close*: "A Lot of Trouble for a Minor Office"). One amendment approved by voters in 1993 affected only about 140 families, two church congregations, and one school district in Fort Bend and Austin counties. It cleared up a title defect to their land.

Unlike voters in many other states, Texas citizens cannot force the placement of constitutional amendments on the ballot because Texas does not have the **initiative** or **referendum** on a statewide level. On taking office in January 1979 as Texas's first Republican governor since Reconstruction, Bill Clements made adoption of the initiative and referendum a priority. But these innovations could not take effect without a constitutional amendment, and the legislature—which did not want to give up such a significant policy prerogative to the electorate—ignored Clements.

At times, however, the legislature has demonstrated a tendency to seek political cover by selectively letting the voters decide some particularly controversial issues, such as a binding referendum in 1987 on the legalization of pari-mutuel betting on horse and dog racing. In 1993 the legislature proposed a constitutional amendment, which voters overwhelmingly endorsed, to prohibit a personal income tax in Texas without voter approval.

Constitutional Convention   The constitution also provides for revision by constitutional convention, which the legislature can call with the approval of the voters. Convention delegates have to be elected, and their terms also are subject to voter approval. In 1919, voters overwhelmingly rejected a proposal for a constitutional convention. Subsequent efforts, including an attempt by Governor John Connally in 1967, to initiate reforms using a constitutional convention were also defeated.[23] Connally's efforts did, however, result in adoption of a "cleanup" amendment in 1969 that removed many obsolete provisions from the constitution, and they laid the groundwork for a constitutional convention in 1974.

Constitutional Reform Efforts of 1971–1975   The 1974 convention, the only one ever held under the present 1876 charter, ended in failure. Its delegates were the 181 members of the legislature. The constitutional convention of 1974 had its beginning in 1971, when state representative Nelson Wolff of San Antonio and several other first-term legislators won the leadership's backing for a full-scale revision effort. In 1972 voters approved the necessary constitutional amendment that specified that the convention would comprise House members and senators elected the same year.

SIMULATION

You Are Attempting to Revise the Texas Constitution

TIMELINE

Initiatives and Referendums

★ **initiative**
Procedure by which voters propose constitutional amendments or other laws through petitions subject to adoption by a popular vote.

★ **referendum**
Vote by the general electorate on a public policy issue, such as a constitutional amendment or statute.

Politics Up Close   A Lot of Trouble for a Minor Office

Roberts County Judge Vernon H. Cook was convinced that his rural county near the top of the Texas Panhandle did not need a constable. He believed the sheriff provided enough law enforcement for the county's 1,500 residents. For years, the county had not had a constable, but the office, which was created in the Texas Constitution, remained on the books. Unexpectedly, in 1992 a write-in candidate ran for constable and was elected. The office then became an extra expense for county taxpayers, as county commissioners felt obliged to pay the new officeholder a $600-a-month salary plus a $200-a-month car allowance and health insurance benefits.

Convinced they were not getting their money's worth—"As near as we can tell, he served two official papers in his first year in office," Cook complained—commissioners later reduced his salary, and the

constable left town. To avoid a recurrence of the problem, commissioners had to ask the state legislature to put a constitutional amendment abolishing the Roberts County constable's office on a statewide ballot. Thus voters in Houston—600 miles away—would have a greater say on abolishing the office than Roberts County's own taxpayers, because Houston's 1.6 million residents cast many more votes. Although that may not seem fair—Houston taxpayers, after all, did not pay the Roberts County constable's salary—it is just one of many obstacles and inconveniences imposed on modern government by a nineteenth-century constitution. Most amendments abolishing obsolete county offices are approved by Texas voters, including amendments abolishing the constables' offices in Roberts County and two other rural counties in 1995.

Source: Houston Chronicle, November 6, 1995.

In 1973 the legislature created a thirty-seven-member Constitutional Revision Commission to hold public hearings around the state and make recommendations to the convention. The constitutional convention, or "con-con," as it came to be called by legislators and members of the media, began on January 8, 1974. House Speaker Price Daniel, Jr., was elected president, and Lieutenant Governor Bill Hobby, in an address to delegates, offered a prophetic warning: "The special interests of today will be replaced by new and different special interests tomorrow, and any attempt to draft a constitution to serve such interests would be futile and also dishonorable."[24]

Hobby's plea was ignored. Special interests dominated the convention, which finally adjourned in bitter failure on July 30, failing by three votes to get the two-thirds vote necessary to send a new constitution to Texas voters for ratification. The crucial fight was over a business-backed attempt to lock the state's right-to-work law into the constitution. The **right-to-work law** prohibits union membership as a condition of employment, so the effort was fought by organized labor. Then as now, business was politically stronger than labor in Texas, but the two-thirds vote necessary to put a new constitution on the ballot was too great an obstacle.

★ **right-to-work law**
Law prohibiting the requirement of union membership in order to hold or get a job.

Other factors also worked against the revision effort (see *What Do You Think?:* "Do Most Voters Really Care?"). One was Governor Dolph Briscoe's refusal to exercise any significant leadership on behalf of a new state charter. Except for opposing proposals that he thought would further weaken the authority of the governor, he provided little input to the convention and did not attempt to twist delegates' arms to get enough votes to send the document to the electorate. Louisiana voters approved a new state constitution in 1974, and Governor Edwin Edwards's strong support was considered instrumental. Gubernatorial leadership in other states also appears to have been critical to successful constitutional conventions.

Another major obstacle was the convention's makeup. Texas, unlike most other states, chose to use the 181 members of the legislature as its constitutional

After three years of preparation and deliberations, the proposed constitution of 1974 failed by three votes in the final hectic session of the constitutional convention, when the gallery was filled with interested onlookers, including many representatives of labor.

convention. Soon after the convention began its work, many of them were facing reelection campaigns in the party primaries, which diverted their attention from the business of the convention.

Additionally, a minority of legislators—dubbed "cockroaches" by President Daniel—did not want a new constitution and attempted to delay or obstruct the convention's work at every opportunity. Most legislators, even those who wanted a new constitution, reacted on the basis of their own political fears and ambitions. They were very susceptible to the influence of special interests, far more susceptible than most private-citizen delegates would likely have been. And special interests were legion at the convention. In addition to various business and professional groups and organized labor, many county officeholders whose jobs—protected by the Constitution of 1876—were suddenly in jeopardy put pressure on the delegates.

During its next regular session, in 1975, the legislature, with the strong support of House Speaker Bill Clayton and Lieutenant Governor Bill Hobby, resurrected the constitutional revision effort. Lawmakers voted to present to Texans the basic document that the convention had barely rejected the previous summer in the form of eight separate constitutional amendments. The first three articles dealing with the separation of powers and the legislative and executive branches were combined into one ballot proposition. Each of the remaining seven propositions was a separate article, each to be independently approved or rejected by the voters. The most controversial issues that the 1974 convention had debated, such as right-to-work, were excluded. The streamlined amendments would have considerably shortened the constitution and provided some major changes, including annual legislative sessions, a unified judicial system, and more flexibility in county government. It would have been a much more flexible, modern constitution than the 1876 document and had cost several million tax dollars and countless hours to produce. But voters rejected all eight propositions on November 4, 1975, some by margins of more than 2 to 1.

A stock fraud scandal in the legislature in 1971 (see Chapter 22) and the Watergate scandal that had forced the resignation of President Richard Nixon in

What Do You *Think?*

Do Most Voters Really Care?

State Senator Bill Ratliff, R-Mount Pleasant, believed that many Texans were so tired of being asked to vote on constitutional amendments that they would support an effort to shorten the document. So Ratliff and State Representative Rob Junell, D-San Angelo, proposed a shorter, more modern constitution for the Texas Legislature to consider during its 1999 session. As chairmen that year of the legislature's key budget-writing committees, Ratliff and Junell usually had enough clout to get their legislative priorities passed. They didn't have enough influence, however, to remove the public apathy that greeted their constitutional revision effort. Legislative committees held public hearings on the proposal, but lawmakers did not feel an urgency to write a new constitution because the idea aroused no interest among their constituents. Halfway through the session, for example, Lieutenant Governor Rick Perry, the state Senate's presiding officer, had received only two letters on the proposed new constitution, compared to thousands of letters and electronic messages on other issues. The Ratliff-Junell proposal also included some controversial features, including more powers for the governor and term limits for legislators, which most lawmakers were in no hurry to address. Governor George W. Bush, who was anticipating a race for president, was also cool toward the new document. "Can this Legislature tackle a matter of the gravity of the constitution in the absence of a crisis?"[a] Ratliff asked.

During the 1999 legislative session, former Senator Bill Ratliff, R-Mount Pleasant, (left) and former Representative Rob Junell, D-San Angelo, chairmen of their respective budget committees, proposed rewriting the Constitution of 1876.

Apparently, it couldn't. But the Legislature approved seventeen more constitutional amendments—including an amendment to remove obsolete language—to put on the November 1999 ballot. Voters approved thirteen of the amendments, including the "cleanup" measure, and rejected four. Turnout was extremely low. Less than 10 percent of registered voters cast ballots on the amendments.[b]

[a]*Houston Chronicle*, March 14, 1999.
[b]*Houston Chronicle*, November 4, 1999.

1974 had raised Texans' distrust of government, and the proposed new constitution had been drafted by state officials, not by private citizens.

Efforts to enact these proposals were further thwarted by Governor Briscoe. Although he had never taken an active role in the revision effort, three weeks before the 1975 election, he openly opposed the eight propositions and suggested that the existing constitution had served the state well and would continue to be adequate for the future.[25]

Further Piecemeal Reforms So it was back to piecemeal constitutional changes. Between 1975 and 2007, 235 amendments were approved by Texas voters and 39 were rejected. Propositions winning approval included the creation of the state lottery in 1991, the 1993 amendment to ban a personal income tax without voter approval and a series of propositions authorizing $3 billion in tax-backed bonds for a huge prison expansion program. In 1985, voters approved an amendment to give the governor and legislative leaders the authority to deal with budgetary emergencies between legislative sessions. Martha Whitehead, the state's last treasurer, ran on a promise in 1994 to seek the elimination of the office on the grounds that it was obsolete. In 1995, voters approved an amendment to abolish the state treasurer's office and transfer its duties to the comptroller. During its 1999 session, the legislature rejected a proposal—the first of its kind in more than 20 years—to rewrite the constitution. But legislators approved an amendment, which voters approved, to remove more obsolete language from the document. One of the more controversial amendments in recent years, Proposition 12, ratified new limits on some monetary damages in medical malpractice lawsuits. It was narrowly approved by voters in 2003 (see *Politics Up Close*: "High Stakes over Lawsuits"). And tackling another controversial issue, voters overwhelmingly approved a constitutional amendment in 2005 to ban same-sex marriages in Texas (see *Controversy*: "The Constitution Is Still a Battleground").

Constitutional Provisions, Interest Groups, and Elites   Only a small percentage of registered voters—often less than 10 percent—participate in elections when

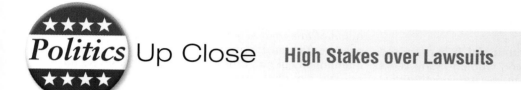

Politics Up Close   High Stakes over Lawsuits

Supporters said Proposition 12 was a cure for high medical malpractice insurance premiums that were forcing some doctors, particularly in rural areas, to close their practices. Opponents argued that medical malpractice coverage was high because state regulators weren't effectively clamping down on bad doctors. They warned that Proposition 12 was instead an effort by business and insurance interests to further restrict access to the courts for injured or aggrieved consumers. In any event, Texas voters narrowly approved the constitutional amendment in 2003 after a multimillion-dollar advertising war. Doctors, hospitals, nursing homes and other business interests primarily financed the campaign promoting the amendment. Plaintiffs' lawyers, who make their living suing doctors, hospitals, and businesses on behalf of injured consumers, picked up most of the tab for the media campaign against it, although numerous consumer advocacy groups also opposed the proposal.

The amendment did two things. First, it ratified a 2003 law enacted by the legislature to put new limits on non-economic damages—money awarded for things such as pain, suffering, and disfigurement—in medical malpractice suits. Such damages, which are in addition to medical costs and other actual economic losses that could be awarded a patient who suffered from a botched medical procedure or misdiagnosis, were capped at $750,000 for each case. Of that amount, only $250,000 can be recovered from physicians or other medical personnel. The remainder would come from hospitals, nursing homes, or other health care facilities that may be involved. Additionally—and potentially more far-reaching—Proposition

12 included language clearing the way for future sessions of the legislature to enact new limits on damages in other civil lawsuits.

Legislative sponsors of Proposition 12 also were accused of trying to sneak the proposal past the voters by scheduling the constitutional amendments election for September 13, rather than November 4, the general election date on which constitutional amendments were traditionally set for voter review. Supporters of the amendment said it was important to win voter approval earlier than normal to remove any legal uncertainty over the new malpractice limits. But opponents argued that the early election, with no other issues to attract voters, was designed to avoid the higher voter turnout that would be generated by a hotly contested mayoral race in Houston on November 4. Voters in Houston, the state's largest city, usually are a major factor in determining state elections, and a high voter turnout there could prove to be pivotal in determining the fate of Proposition 12. According to this argument, the higher the voter turnout in Houston, the greater the likelihood that the amendment would be defeated, because Democrats and plaintiffs lawyers still had some clout over elections in that city. Opponents of Proposition 12, as it turned out, had reason to fear the early election date. The proposal narrowly passed statewide, but 58 percent of Houston voters—turning out in far fewer numbers than would vote two months later in the mayor's race—cast ballots against it. "It (the statewide result) would have been a real horse race if it had been held in conjunction with the Houston mayor's race," said University of Houston political scientist Richard Murray.

Source: Houston Chronicle, September 16, 2003, p. 13A.

Controversy

The Constitution Is Still a Battleground

Texas has functioned under the same constitution for more than 125 years, and during this time the document has been amended some 450 times. Many non-controversial amendments have removed outdated provisions from the constitution. Others have affected only one county or a handful of people with no significant statewide importance. But other amendments have generated a great deal of conflict, pitting significant parts of the electorate against others. Some of the more contentious amendments have centered on the rights and liberties of individuals who were denied full access to the electoral system or protections under the law.

Although the Texas Constitution of 1876 espoused equality, it took minorities and women many years and numerous court battles to see the constitutional provisions become a reality for them. And today, the struggle over political rights and civil rights continues in debates over immigration, voter identification, abortion, and even the time-honored, personal institution of marriage.

There also has been a similar historical disconnect between the theories and actual practices of civil and individual rights in the United States as a whole. A colleague, an expert on English and American constitutional law, once asserted that "rights are not something that are given to you but something you take." In effect, majorities are not disposed to extend rights on the basis of democratic principles to those it deems outsiders. The extension of rights comes with intense conflict that often persists over long periods of time.

Women did not receive the right to vote in all elections until 1920 when the 19th Amendment to the U.S. Constitution was adopted by the required number of states. The arduous and torturous path to full suffrage for the state's minority populations continued through the 1970s, and it took an additional three decades for the discriminatory effects of election systems to be eliminated by the Voting Rights Act and many court decisions.

There are groups that see themselves as second-class citizens and continue to be embroiled in contentious battles over constitutional amendments. For example, Texas became the eighteenth state to add a ban on same-sex marriage to its constitution when voters approved Proposition 2 in 2005. The amendment had the strong support of Governor Rick Perry and many church leaders, who argued that it was necessary to guard against any legal challenges to an already existing state law that defined marriage as a union of one man and one woman. Opponents, however, contended the measure was unnecessary and, intentionally or not, promoted hostility toward homosexuals, a minority group.

"I'm not sure the right to desegregate schools, the freedom to marry another race or even access to contraception in many states would exist if those issues were put up for a vote," said Matt Foreman, executive director of the National Gay and Lesbian Task Force.

But Garrett Booth, pastor of Grace Community Church in Clear Lake and a supporter of the amendment, had a different viewpoint.

"It's important we do not sit idly by and let an extreme minority set aside what God has set in place. We are living in a day when the things that you and I hold precious are being redefined," Booth said. The proposition, one of nine amendments on the ballot, was approved by a 3–1 margin.

The Texas Constitution does more than define the institutions of government and their responsibilities. It structures the power, influence, and control that groups and individuals can wield in deciding who gets what, when, and how. Whenever there are contentious proposals to change the document, there is political conflict.

Sources: Houston Chronicle, November 7, 2005, p. 1B; *Houston Chronicle,* November 9, 2005, p. 1A.

constitutional amendments are the only issues on the ballot (see Figure 20.1). When amendments are submitted to the voters during gubernatorial or presidential elections, the turnout is much higher. But in many instances, a relative handful of Texans ultimately decides on fundamental changes in government, which enhances their influence over the constitutional revision process.

Interest groups, which historically have been strong in Texas, work diligently to protect their concerns and objectives. They develop strategies to get provisions into the constitution that would benefit them and to keep provisions out of the constitution that they fear would hurt them. Because most amendments represent nonpartisan issues, a well-financed public relations campaign is likely to produce public support for an amendment.[26]

Type of Election	Number of Elections	Percent of Registered Voters	Percent of Voting-Age Population
Special[a]	17	12.8%	8.7%
General (Gubernatorial)	9	42.7%	28.2%
General (Presidential)	9	63.2%	45.3%

[a]Only constitutional amendments on the ballot.

Figure *20.1* Turnout for Constitutional Amendment Elections, 1970–2007

Source: Texas Secretary of State, Elections Division.

Interest groups are able to kill many proposed constitutional changes in the legislature, where the two-thirds vote requirement works to their advantage. Only a small fraction of constitutional amendments proposed by legislators get put on the ballot. Those that do usually have the support of one or more special interest groups, which often finance publicity campaigns to promote the propositions to the voters. Few amendments attract organized opposition after being put on the ballot, but there have been exceptions. In 2003, doctors, insurance companies, and business interests heavily promoted Proposition 12, the ratification of new medical malpractice limits. They were successful, despite a media campaign against the amendment financed primarily by plaintiffs' lawyers.

Many recent constitutional changes have reflected a pro-industry and economic development push that contrasts sharply with the anti-business sentiment of the original constitutional framers. Recent amendments also have helped build up a public bonded indebtedness that the nineteenth-century constitution writers would have been unable to comprehend. Texas was rural then. It is now largely urban and is working to diversify and expand its economy as well as provide the infrastructure required to support the large increases in its population.

Nine of the record twenty-five amendments on the November 1987 ballot were actively promoted as an economic development package by the Build Texas Committee, a bipartisan group of business and civic leaders. Voters approved most of the amendments, including bonds for new water projects and prisons. In 2007, voters—encouraged by Gov. Rick Perry and cycling champion Lance Armstrong, a cancer survivor—approved $3 billion in bonds to boost state funding for cancer research.

Industry, with the unusual support of organized labor and environmentalists, won a major tax break through a constitutional amendment approved by Texas voters in 1993. It requires local governments to grant property tax exemptions for expensive pollution control equipment that businesses are required by state or federal law to install in their plants and other facilities. The business community supported the amendment because it represented untold millions of dollars in potential tax savings. Labor supported it because money not spent on taxes could mean more money spent on jobs. And environmentalists viewed it as an anti-pollution measure. Some local officials were fearful of the potential loss of large amounts of revenue to counties, school districts, and other local governments, but they were clearly overpowered. Sometimes, however, relief can turn into heartburn, as it did in 2001, when lawmakers and Texas voters accidentally put a new tax into the constitution when they thought they were repealing one (see *Politics Up Close: "Oops! How Did That Happen?"*).

It has been argued that the Texas Constitution serves the interests of a small number of elites—those individuals who control businesses and other dominant institutions in the state. This argument suggests that the severe constraints built

Politics Up Close   Oops! How Did That Happen?

People who have any doubts that an election ballot loaded with constitutional amendments is an accident waiting to happen need only consider Proposition 14, one of nineteen amendments on the November 2001 ballot, all of which were approved by voters. The proposal was promoted as a means of allowing local governments, except for school districts, to exempt registered, non–income-producing travel trailers from local property taxes. Supporters said the tax break was needed to encourage the so-called winter Texans to continue making their seasonal homes in the Rio Grande Valley. These people, who travel south to escape the cold winters up north, have become an important part of the South Texas economy and represent an important financial boost to some of Texas's poorest counties. Many of the winter visitors are senior citizens who live in recreational vehicles.

Everybody was sure the amendment did what it was intended to do. No one—legislative sponsors,

legislative analysts, local officials, the media—noticed a problem, until after the amendment was approved and then became part of the constitution. Only then did someone discover that the amendment had inadvertently imposed a new tax on travel trailers, rather than removed one. The new provision labeled trailers as taxable, whereas the constitution previously had said nothing about them. And because the exemption didn't apply to school districts, legal experts believed that travel trailers had been made subject to school taxes.

The goof prompted Governor Rick Perry and legislative sponsors to start scrambling. Perry asked school districts to refrain from taxing travel trailers until the legislature had a chance to correct the mistake, which it did in 2003.

"I guess it moved through the process and went and went and went," the amendment's sponsor, state representative Kino Flores of Mission, said of the blunder.

Source: Associated Press, March 8, 2002.

into the constitution limit the policy options of state government and historically have thwarted the efforts of larger public-interest groups to restructure or improve the tax system, education policy, social services, health care, and other policies and programs that would benefit low- and middle-income Texans. Power is so fragmented that these groups have had to turn to the courts to force change. This same argument, incidentally, has often been made about the U.S. Constitution.

If this interpretation is accurate, it is ironic that those who framed the Texas Constitution of 1876 directed much of their wrath against railroads, banks, and other institutions that today are considered elitist. The tumultuous last quarter of the nineteenth century witnessed high levels of class and economic conflict, with the emergence of the Greenback and Populist political parties, which articulated the interests of lower-income groups. But monied business interests eventually were able to use the state constitution and subsequent legislation to reestablish their dominance over Texas government. Although the elite structure of the state has changed since 1876, some scholars argue that there has been a gradual transfer of power and control to new elites, who continue to exercise enormous influence over public policy.

Change Through Court Interpretation   Some evidence indicates that Texas courts are now prepared to play a more expansive role in the interpretation of the constitution and, in turn, effect major changes in state policy. The best-known example is the Edgewood school finance case, in which the courts invalidated the system of funding public education and ordered the legislature to provide more equity in tax resources among the state's more than 1,000 school districts. Wide disparities in spending on students between rich and poor districts—the result of wide disparities in local property values—violated the state constitution's requirement for an "efficient" system of public schools, the Texas Supreme Court ruled.

Constitutional Restraints and the Ability to Govern

The nonpartisan League of Women Voters of Texas has been a steadfast advocate of a total rewrite of the state constitution. Nevertheless, before each constitutional amendments election, it normally announces which propositions it endorses for the sake of good government and which it opposes. But league leaders lost their patience in 1987 with the placement of a record twenty-five amendments on the same ballot. They announced they would neither support nor oppose any amendment that year. Instead, they urged voters to examine the propositions carefully and complain to their legislators about the length of the ballot. "Enough is enough. Let us work together to halt this ridiculous system of running the government by means of the constitution," the league said. But without a new constitution, the only way state government can prepare for the challenges of the twenty-first century under a highly restrictive constitution written in the nineteenth is to continue this pattern of "amendomania."[27]

Prospects for Future Change   Experts can point out the many flaws of the Texas Constitution, but attempts at wholesale revision have not been successful. Numerous piecemeal changes have been made, but they have not addressed the fundamental criticisms of the charter. What is to be made of all this?

First, Texas has a long history of suspicion of government, and this tradition continues. Most people fear government abuses and excesses more than they worry about government's inability to respond quickly and efficiently to the needs of its citizens. In the vernacular of the layperson, "If it ain't broke, don't fix it." And it is not clear that the layperson regards the constitution as "broke." Second, many groups and interests benefit from the existing constitution, and they have demonstrated a collective resolve to minimize change. Finally, most Texans give little thought to changing the constitution because they are ill-prepared to deal with the complexities of the document. Enormous problems must be overcome if citizens are to be educated and motivated to press for constitutional revision.

Summary
Who Gets What: The Texas Constitution

Institutional arrangements and processes are core elements of the Texas Constitution, but its often arcane and confusing language must be interpreted and implemented. Through its application, the constitution becomes a political document, often mobilizing people in defense or opposition to the interpretation of specific provisions. The formal arrangements, while expressed in neutral terms, structure power and influence.

★ Few Texans have read the Texas Constitution with its 90,000-plus words, and they are not likely to do so in the future. It's extremely long. With all of its amendments, it often is difficult to understand its provisions. Some of the provisions of the document outline the formal powers of governing agencies, and others outline specific procedures to be followed by those holding public office. Still other provisions define the limits on governmental authority and power, providing for relief or remedies when those in public office exceed or abuse their powers. The adroit use of these provisions helps influential groups and individuals—the state's elites—to shape and influence actions of governmental institutions at all levels. A group that can convince the legislature to write a constitutional provision promoting its interests will have a strong advantage in the policy-making process.

★ Texas has functioned under seven constitutions, each reflecting the political, social and economic conditions of the period in which it was adopted. Texas's current constitution, its seventh, was adopted following the Civil War and the Radical Reconstruction era. The enduring legacy of these events has been a deep suspicion of government, limited government, and fragmented governmental institutions. Those who drafted this constitution thought that governmental excesses or abuses could be minimized by carefully defining in detailed provisions what governments could and could not do.

★ The framers of the 1876 Constitution failed to anticipate that the limitations they imposed on governmental institutions would ultimately allow major economic interests within the state to dominate the policy-making process, often to the detriment of the lower socioeconomic groups. They also failed to recognize that fragmented authority, detailed limitations on the power of governmental institutions, and decentralization—all of which they regarded as the strengths of the constitution—have served to limit the ability of state and local governments to adapt effectively to economic and demographic changes of the twenty-first century. Their decisions contributed to unintended consequences with which the state and its local governments contend today.

★ Efforts to overhaul the Texas Constitution have failed. Consequently, the state has been forced to amend the document continually on a piecemeal basis. This process has produced some success in modernizing the charter, but many structural problems of state government require major institutional changes that cannot be resolved through this amendment process.

★ In many ways, the Texas Constitution reflects the values of the state's conservative political culture, which continues to be suspicious of far-reaching constitutional changes. Moreover, constitutions and the debates that surround them are complex, and most people give little attention to these issues.

★ Over the years, numerous groups have attempted to protect their interests through constitutional amendments. But the same groups usually oppose any proposed changes that threaten their influence, power, or benefits. Consequently, the interests of small segments of the state's population often prevail over the interests of the majority. It is much easier to mobilize public opinion against rather than for wholesale change.

Key Terms

constitution 690
statutory law 690
unicameral 691
unitary system 693
federalism 693

bicameral 694
confederacy 696
Radical Reconstructionists 696
Grange 698

popular sovereignty 700
social contract theory 700
limited government 700
separation of powers 700
initiative 705

referendum 705
right-to-work law 706

Suggested Readings

Braden, George D., et al. *The Constitution of the State of Texas: An Annotated and Comparative Analysis.* 2 vols. Austin, Tex.: Texas Advisory Commission on Intergovernmental Relations, 1977. Originally designed as a research tool for delegates to the 1974 Constitutional Convention, this work provides an explanation of the historical development of the Texas Constitution and a comparative perspective on other state constitutions.

Bruff, Harold H. "Separation of Powers under the Texas Constitution." *Texas Law Review* 68 (June 1990): 1337–67. Summarizes leading state court cases pertaining to the separation of powers clause of the Texas Constitution and addresses issue of judicial review.

Cnudde, Charles F., and Robert E. Crew, Jr. *Constitutional Democracy in Texas.* St. Paul, Minn.: West, 1989. A constitutional perspective on Texas government and politics.

Lutz, Donald S. "The Texas Constitution." In *Perspectives on American and Texas Politics: A Collection of Essays,* eds. Donald S. Lutz and Kent L. Tedin, pp. 193–211. Dubuque, Iowa: Kendall/Hunt, 1987. An analysis of the 1876 Texas Constitution that argues the document reflects the dominant subcultures of the state with a tilt toward individualism.

Mauer, John Walker. "State Constitutions in a Time of Crisis: The Case of the Texas Constitution of 1876." *Texas Law Review* 68 (June 1990): 1615–47. Focuses on the enactment of post-Reconstruction constitutions in Texas and the South, arguing that the constitutional framers of 1875 were reacting not only to Republican Reconstruction but also to the recently elected Democratic administration.

May, Janice C. *The Texas Constitution Revision Experience in the 70s*. Austin, Tex.: Sterling Swift, 1975. Written by an expert on state constitutions, this work provides a historical perspective on the efforts to rewrite the Texas Constitution in the 1970s.

McKay, Seth Shepard. *Seven Decades of the Texas Constitution of 1876*. Lubbock, Tex.: Texas Technical College, 1943. A historical perspective on the impact of the 1876 constitution.

Tarr, Alan. *Understanding State Constitutions*. Princeton, N.J.: Princeton University Press, 1998. An introduction to state constitutional theory that addresses a series of issues, including the differences among state constitutions and between federal and state constitutions and state constitutions within the federal context.

Wolff, Nelson. *Challenge of Change*. San Antonio, Tex.: Naylor, 1975. Written by a delegate to the 1974 Constitutional Convention, this book discusses divisive issues and provides an abbreviated history of the convention proceedings.

Suggested Web Sites

Texas Legislative Council www.tlc.state.tx.us

The entire text of the Texas Constitution can be downloaded from this site (see Publications). It also provides an index to the constitution and allows the text of the constitution to be searched using key words.

Cornell University Law School
www.law.cornell.edu/statutes.html

If you are interested in the constitutions of other states, this is one of several sites that provide you access to these documents as well as a wealth of historical information on state constitutions.

Texas Legislature Online www.capitol.state.tx.us

Access to legislative resolutions providing for constitutional amendments can be found here. Legislative intent and legislative histories of proposed constitutional amendments are also available by searching Bill Action and Vote History on the homepage.

Secretary of State www.sos.state.tx.us

This office is responsible for compiling state election returns, including constitutional amendments. County-level returns for constitutional amendments since 1993 can be accessed from this site.

21 INTEREST GROUPS, POLITICAL PARTIES, AND ELECTIONS IN TEXAS

" Political analysis is partly concerned with the discovery of which people act which way under which conditions. **"**

Harold Lasswell

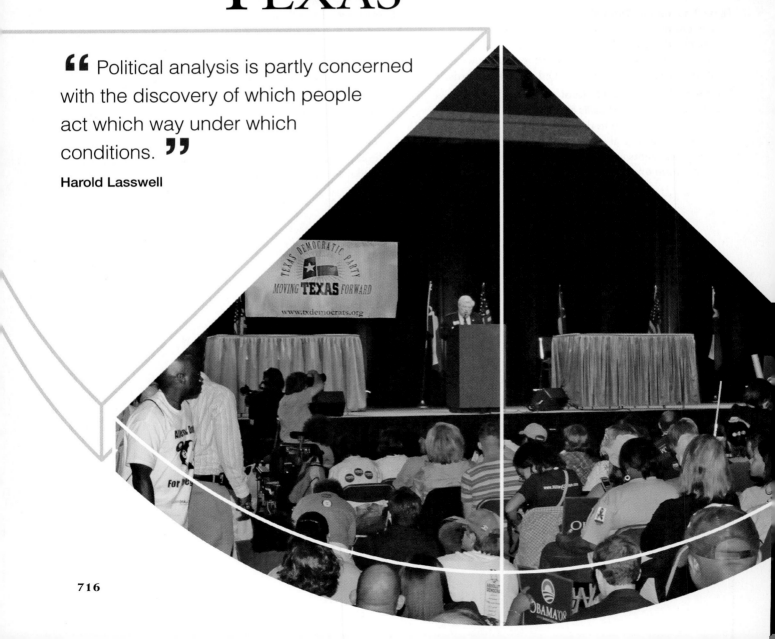

Chapter *Outline*

★ The Power of Interest Groups
★ Pluralism or Elitism?
★ Dominant Interest Groups in Texas
★ The Development of a Two-Party System in Texas
★ Changing Patterns of Party Support and Identification
★ The Party Organization
★ Parties and Government
★ Minorities and Political Participation
★ Political Gains by Minorities and Women
★ Elections in Texas
★ Campaign Finances

Think About Politics

1. Do your elected officials care what you think about public policy and their decisions?
   YES ◯ NO ◯

2. Do working people have the same access to their state legislators as bank presidents do?
   YES ◯ NO ◯

3. Should a political party have the right to determine who can vote in its primary elections?
   YES ◯ NO ◯

4. Is there really any difference between the two major political parties in Texas?
   YES ◯ NO ◯

5. Should a candidate for public office be allowed to accept unlimited amounts of money from special interest groups?
   YES ◯ NO ◯

6. Should people be permitted to register to vote the day an election is held?
   YES ◯ NO ◯

7. Should minority groups be represented in the Texas legislature in proportion to their share of the state's population?
   YES ◯ NO ◯

Democracy is as much a struggle among competing interests at the state and local level as it is in Washington. How are the power and influence that affect the quality of life for millions of people distributed in Texas?

The Power of Interest Groups

The business community, through endorsements and political contributions, was influential in Republicans capturing a majority of Texas House of Representatives seats in 2002, giving the GOP control of that body for the first time since Reconstruction and leading to the election of the first Republican House speaker of modern times. The Texas Association of Business, or TAB, an umbrella group representing many businesses, was one of the most visible backers of Republican candidates who supported business priorities, including more restrictions on civil lawsuits, fewer governmental regulations, and holding the line on state taxes. In pursuit of its policy agenda, TAB took the unusual—and controversial—step of spending $2 million in corporate contributions on political advertising in twenty-four legislative races. Most candidates supported by TAB won, but the tactic prompted a criminal investigation of the business group and precipitated a debate over free speech versus undue corporate influence over elections.

State law allows officers and employees of corporations to make personal contributions to political candidates or to contribute through political action committees established for that purpose. It is illegal, however, for corporate funds to be given directly to a candidate, and soon after the election, Travis County District Attorney Ronnie Earle began investigating TAB's contributions. TAB argued that the corporate donations were legal because they weren't given directly to candidates but instead were used to purchase advertising that educated voters on issues important to the group. The ads didn't directly advocate the election or defeat of any candidates, although they obviously influenced election results. TAB fought the investigation with a series of legal maneuvers, arguing that the ads amounted to constitutionally protected free speech. National business groups also rallied to TAB's defense, claiming that Earle, a Democrat, was letting politics influence his investigation. But Earle argued that he was merely investigating "allegations of crime."[1] The organization was later indicted by a Travis County grand jury on charges of violating state campaign finance laws. The investigation resulted in related charges against then-U.S. House Majority Leader Tom DeLay of Sugar Land and two associates, who also had been active in securing the Republican takeover of the Texas House. TAB eventually pleaded to a misdemeanor charge of unlawful campaign expenditures and paid a $10,000 fine. None of the other defendants had come to trial by late 2008, but the controversy prompted DeLay's resignation from Congress.

TAB's ad campaign was one of the more visible examples of an interest group's influence in Austin in recent years. But under both Democratic and Republican statehouse control, interest groups have long dominated Texas's policy-making process and most likely will continue to do so.

★ **interest groups**
Organizations seeking to influence government policy.

Interest groups have priorities that usually cross partisan lines. Their organizational strengths and initiatives are reflected in public policy, and those segments of Texas society that are unorganized are likely to have little, if any, impact on governmental decisions. The discussion of national interest groups in Chapter 9 is applicable to Texas, and many interest groups that function on the state and local level are linked to some extent to the national system.

Just as they do at the national level, interest groups in Texas spend millions of dollars a year trying to elect favored candidates or to influence the outcome of governmental decisions through a number of direct and indirect lobbying activities. Campaign contributions have always raised ethical questions of undue influence on policy makers and are a continuing source of controversy, as TAB's involvement demonstrates. Moreover, aggressive and often heavy-handed lobbying efforts contribute to the view that state and local governments are dominated by a few big interests looking out for themselves.

Two studies, conducted more than 40 years apart, placed Texas among states with strong interest-group systems.[2] Powerful pressure groups usually evolve in states with weak political parties, a condition that characterized Texas during most of the twentieth century.[3] During the many years that Texas was a one-party, Democratic state, the Republican Party posed no serious challenge to the Democratic monopoly, and the Democratic Party was marked by intense factionalism. Although the conservative Democratic wing dominated state politics through the 1970s, interest groups often played a greater role in the policy-making process. Subsequent Republican growth has changed Texas's party system, but interest groups remain strong and, more often than not, still have a greater impact on the policy-making process than the political parties.

Pluralism or Elitism?

There are thousands of interest groups at the state and local level in Texas. Some have long histories and a durable presence in the policy process, whereas others are formed to address a specific need and then disappear after a relatively short period. Although most groups have the potential to participate in policy making, many will not.

★ **pluralism**
Political system in which power is distributed among multiple groups.

One can find evidence in Texas to support the pluralist view of power discussed in Chapter 1. **Pluralism** holds that significant numbers of diverse and competing interest groups serve to limit the power of any single group. Although most people do not actively participate in the policy-making process, they have access to the process through their group leaders. Pluralists believe that there are numerous leadership opportunities within groups for people who want active roles.

★ **lobbyists**
Individuals who attempt, directly or indirectly, to shape and influence the decisions of policy makers.

The number of **lobbyists** has grown significantly over the past three decades, and the hundreds now registered in Austin represent a wide assortment of economic, social, civic, and cultural organizations. Supporters of the pluralist view say this growth proves that the political system is open and accessible to new organizations. They argue that public officeholders are responsive to the needs and interests of a greater diversity of Texans than ever before.

Others insist that pluralist theories simply do not describe the realities of power and policy making in Texas. Convinced of the persuasiveness of **elitism**, they contend that the ability to influence the most important policy decisions is monopolized by a few individuals who derive power from their leadership positions in organizations or institutions with great financial resources. In one view, from 1938 to 1957 Texas was "governed by conservatives, collectively dubbed **the Establishment**." This was a "loosely knit plutocracy comprised mostly of Anglo businessmen, oilmen, bankers and lawyers" that emerged in the late 1930s, in part, as a response to the liberal policies of the New Deal. They were extremely conservative, producing a "virulent" strain of conservatism marked by "Texanism" and "super-Americanism."[4]

That's Why It Is Called Lobbying

Lobbyists and visitors, who are denied access to the floor of the Senate chamber while the body is in session, are seen mingling outside the chamber during a tax debate. Upon careful observation, one can often see lobbyists and legislators talking with each other in this area of the Capitol.

The traditionalistic-individualistic political culture described in Chapter 19 was especially conducive to the dominance of the conservative establishment, which had little interest in the needs of the lower socioeconomic groups and minorities within the state. The exclusion of minorities from participation in elections and the low rates of voter turnout, particularly among the lower socioeconomic groups, resulted in the election of public officials who were sympathetic to the views of the conservative elites. In addition, public opinion was manipulated by "unprincipled public relations men" and "the rise of reactionary newspapers."[5]

A more recent study of Texas politics argues that there is a group of Texans—extraordinarily wealthy or linked to large corporations—who constitute "an upper class in the precise meaning of the term: a social group whose common background and effective control of wealth bring them together politically."[6] While warning against the hasty conclusion that this upper class is a ruling class, the study describes their shared values, group cohesiveness, and interlocking relationships.[7] The upper class has enormous political power. When united on specific policy objectives, its members have usually prevailed against "their liberal enemies concentrated in the working class."[8] Moreover, the institutional arrangements of the state's economic and political structure work to produce upper-class unity that contributes to their successes in public policy.[9]

These sharply contrasting views of political power in Texas have produced an ongoing debate. To a large extent, the issue of who really controls Texas politics has not been resolved because of insufficient data to support one position over the other. There also is evidence that power relationships have changed over time. Historically, Texas government and public policy were dominated by an "upper class" or a "conservative establishment." But with the enormous social and economic changes that have taken place over the past 20 years, Texans may well be moving from an elitist system to some variation of pluralism.

★ **elitism**
Political system in which power is concentrated in the hands of a relatively small group of individuals or institutions.

★ **"The Establishment"**
In the days of one-party Democratic politics in Texas, the Establishment was a loosely knit coalition of Anglo business and oil company executives, bankers, and lawyers who controlled state policy making through the dominant conservative wing of the Democratic Party.

Dominant Interest Groups in Texas

You Are a Restaurant Owner

Throughout much of the twentieth century, state government was dominated by large corporations, banks, oil companies, and agricultural interests that backed the conservative Democratic officeholders who had a stranglehold on the legislature, the courts, and the executive branch. Big business still carries a lot of weight in Austin and can purchase a lot of influence through major political contributions. State officials who want to build public support for new policy proposals usually solicit the support of the business community first.

But beginning in the 1970s, influence began to be more diffused. **Single-member districts** increased the numbers of minorities, Republicans, and liberal Democrats elected to the legislature (see Chapter 22). Consumer, environmental, and other public advocacy groups emerged. Organized labor, which had been shut out by the corporate establishment, found some common interests with the trial lawyers, who earn fees suing businesses on behalf of consumers and other plaintiffs claiming damages or injuries caused by various companies or products. The decline of oil and gas production and the emergence of high-tech manufacturing and service industries also helped diffuse the business lobby into competing factions.

★ single-member district
Election system in which one person is elected to represent the people living within one geographic district.

Business Groups   The diverse business interests in Texas organize themselves in several ways to influence the policy-making process. First, broad-based associations, including the Texas Association of Business and the Texas Taxpayers and Research Association, represent business and industry in general. Their overall goal is to maintain, and improve on, a favorable business climate.

The business community also organizes through trade associations, such as the Texas Bankers Association, the Texas Automobile Dealers Association, the Texas Independent Producers and Royalty Owners Association, the Wholesale Beer Distributors of Texas, and the Texas Chemical Council. These groups represent and seek to advance the interests of specific industries.

Finally, many individual companies retain their own lobbyists to represent them before the legislature and administrative agencies. Some wealthy individuals even hire their own lobbyists.

Although most business groups band together against organized labor, consumer advocates, and trial lawyers on major political and philosophical issues, the business lobby is far from monolithic (see *What Do You Think?*: "Do Texas Lobbyists Look Out for Your Interests?"). There are numerous issues, including tax policy and utility regulation, on which companies or trade associations differ.

★ political action committee (PAC)
Committee organized by a corporation, labor union, trade association, ideological or issue-oriented group, cooperative, or nonprofit corporation for the purpose of collecting campaign contributions and distributing the money to political candidates.

Professional Groups   A number of professional groups have played dominant roles in Texas politics and the policy-making process. One of the best known is the Texas Medical Association (TMA), which in recent years has joined forces with business interests against trial lawyers in support of laws that would limit malpractice suits and other damage claims against physicians and the business community. The TMA's political action committee is a major contributor of campaign dollars to candidates for the legislature and other state offices, and it won a major victory in 2003, with legislative and voter approval of a constitutional amendment imposing new limits on monetary damages in medical malpractice cases.

Litigation over medical malpractice, product liability, and workers' compensation has also expanded the influence of trial lawyers, who make their living representing injured persons. Individually and through their **political action committee (PAC)**, trial lawyers have contributed millions of dollars to judicial, legislative, and other selected candidates since the 1970s. In the early 1980s, they succeeded in electing several Texas Supreme Court justices who shared

★ tort
A wrongful act or injury for which a damage lawsuit can be brought.

What Do You *Think?*

Do Texas Lobbyists Look Out for Your Interests?

During each regular session of the Texas legislature, hundreds of individuals representing businesses, trade associations, and other interests register as lobbyists. They run the gamut from well-dressed corporate lobbyists with generous expense accounts to volunteer consumer and environmental advocates. Most are male, although the number of women lobbyists has increased in recent years, and many women now hold major lobbying positions. Most lobbyists came to their career by way of other occupations and jobs, but they have, on the whole, an acute understanding of the policy-making process and the points of access and influence in that process. The most successful lobbyists have developed the ability to pursue a wide range of tactics based on a comprehensive strategy.

Many lobbyists are former legislators. They bring to the process their legislative skills, personal relationships with former legislative colleagues, and expertise in substantive policy areas. A number of other lobbyists are former legislative staffers. Many trade and professional associations, labor unions, and public interest groups have full-time staffers in Austin who function as their lobbyists. Many corporations also use their own employees to lobby in Austin. Some

companies have governmental affairs departments or offices staffed by employees with experience in government or public affairs. In large corporations that do business across the country, the governmental affairs staffs may be rather large because such companies will attempt to follow the actions of numerous state legislatures, city councils, and the U.S. Congress.

A number of lawyers have developed successful lobby practices. Some of these professional freelancers, or "hired guns," specialize in specific policy areas, whereas others represent a wide array of clients. Many work for the state's largest law firms, which have established permanent offices in Austin. Some of the top-notch freelancers are not attorneys, but they have a strong knowledge of the governmental process. There are also some public relations firms that offer their services to interest groups.

These companies specialize in "image creation" or "image modification." While they may not handle the groups' direct lobbying efforts, they are often retained to assist in indirect lobbying. They are particularly adroit in developing relationships with the press, planning media campaigns, and assisting in political campaigns.

their viewpoint, and the court issued major, precedent-setting opinions making it easier for plaintiffs to win large damage awards from businesses, doctors, and insurance companies. The business and medical communities retaliated by boosting their own political contributions and lobbying efforts and, by 1990, had succeeded in tipping the Supreme Court's philosophical scale back to its traditional business-oriented viewpoint. Although the war over **tort** law, as these types of damage suits are called, continued to rage, trial lawyers usually were on the defensive in the new era of Republican statehouse control.

Education Groups

In the past several years, educational interests have been very visible in the policy-making process in Austin, and higher education lobbying has been particularly effective. The changing global economy has enhanced the role of higher education in developing the state's future, and there is widespread public support for expanded access to higher education.

Most university regents, chancellors, and presidents are well connected politically. Universities also are capable, through the use of donations and other non-tax funds, of hiring a well-paid cadre of lobbyists. Another effective lobbying source for universities, particularly the larger ones, are the armies of alumni—many of them politically influential—who are ready to make phone calls, send e-mails, or

Concentration of Interests

Austin does not have its K Street, but the offices of hundreds of associations and lobbyists can be found within a short distance of the Capitol. More than thirty interest groups or lobbyists maintain offices in the three buildings shown a short distance from the Capitol.

write letters on behalf of their alma mater when the need arises. The business community is also a strong supporter of higher education. The influence of the University of Texas system, in particular, was instrumental in the legislature's enactment of a law in 2003 giving university governing boards the authority, for the first time in Texas, to raise student tuition independently of legislative control.

The struggle for equity and quality in public elementary and secondary education in Texas, a major issue since the 1940s, has been complicated by more than two dozen groups representing various—and often conflicting—interests within the educational community. There are at least four different teachers' groups, one for school boards, one for school administrators, and still others for elementary and secondary school principals. Separate groups have also been formed for urban school districts, suburban districts, rural districts, and districts with large numbers of special needs students. Virtually all these groups employ paid lobbyists, and although all claim to support educational quality, their primary goals are to protect the specific interests of their members.

Public Interest Groups   Most public interest groups represented in Austin are concerned with protecting consumers and the environment from big business, promoting stronger ethical standards for public officials, and increasing funding for health and human services programs for the poor, the elderly, the young, and the disabled. Many have full-time lobbyists, but these groups are seldom able to match the financial resources of business and professional organizations. Grassroots volunteer efforts and the adroit use of the mass media are crucial to their success. Among the most active are Common Cause, the Sierra Club, Consumers Union, Texas Citizen Action, Texas Watch, the Gray Panthers, Americans Disabled for Attendant Programs Today (ADAPT), and Public Citizen, a Texas affiliate of the national public interest group founded by consumer advocate Ralph Nader.

Minority Interest Groups   The advent of single-member, urban legislative districts in the 1970s significantly increased the number of African American and Hispanic lawmakers and strengthened the influence of minority interest groups. These groups have often found that the courthouse is a shorter route to success than the statehouse, but the legislature has become increasingly attentive to their voices.

The League of United Latin American Citizens (LULAC) and the Mexican American Legal Defense and Educational Fund (MALDEF) are two of the better-known Hispanic organizations. LULAC, founded in 1929, is the oldest and largest Hispanic organization in the United States and continues to be particularly influential in causes such as education and election reform in Texas. MALDEF, formed in San Antonio in 1968, fights in the courtroom for the civil rights of Hispanics. It has been successful in numerous battles over the drawing of political boundaries for governmental bodies in Texas and in lengthy litigation over public school finance. MALDEF represented the property-poor school districts that won a unanimous landmark Texas Supreme Court order in 1989 (*Edgewood v. Kirby*) for a more equitable distribution of education aid between rich and poor school districts. The victory led to major legislative changes in the school finance system.

The National Association for the Advancement of Colored People (NAACP) is a leader in promoting and protecting the interests of African Americans. The NAACP initiated many of the early court attacks on educational inequality and the disfranchisement of minorities. More recently, this group has worked hard to increase employment opportunities for African Americans in state agencies, particularly in higher-paying administrative jobs.

In recent years, the Industrial Areas Foundation, a collection of well-organized, church-supported community groups, has become a strong and effective voice for low-income minorities. Member groups include Valley Interfaith in South Texas, Communities Organized for Public Service (COPS) in San Antonio, The Metropolitan Organization (TMO) in Houston, and the El Paso Interreligious Sponsoring Organization (EPISO).

Organized Labor Groups Organized labor has traditionally taken a back seat to business in Texas, a strong right-to-work state in which union membership cannot be required as a condition of employment. Anti-labor sentiment ran particularly high in the 1940s and 1950s, at the height of the conservative Democratic establishment's control of Texas politics. Labor-baiting campaigns in which unions were portrayed as evil communist sympathizers were not uncommon then.[10]

Today, about 500,000 Texans are members of labor unions. Among the largest unions in the state are the Communications Workers of America; the Texas Federation of Teachers; the American Federation of State, County and Municipal Employees; and the United Auto Workers.

Unions can provide strong grassroots support for political candidates through endorsements, the distribution of campaign literature, the use of union phone banks, and other get-out-the-vote efforts. Such union support historically has gone to Democratic candidates. Labor generally sides with the trial lawyers on such issues as workers' compensation, worker safety, and business liability for faulty products.

Government Lobbyists Local governments are significantly affected by state laws and budgetary decisions. The stakes are particularly high now because most governments are finding revenue harder to raise—especially with the federal government passing the cost of numerous programs on to the state, and the state issuing similar mandates to local governments. As a result, counties, cities, prosecutors, metropolitan transit authorities, and various special districts are represented by lobbyists in Austin as well as Washington, D.C. State and local governments have increasingly used their lobbyists to influence the earmarking of federal funds, and there is increased evidence that local governments are using their lobbyists to influence similar budget decisions in Austin.[11]

Many local governments belong to umbrella organizations, such as the Texas Municipal League, the Texas Association of Counties, and the Texas District and County Attorneys Association, which have full-time lobbyists. Several of the larger cities and counties also retain their own lobbyists. Mayors, city council members, and county judges also frequently travel to Austin to visit with legislators and testify for or against bills.

Agriculture Groups Although Texas is now predominantly urban, agriculture is still an important part of the state's economy, and a number of agriculture groups are represented in Austin. Their influence is obviously strongest among rural legislators. But the Texas Farm Bureau—the largest such group and probably the most conservative—was instrumental in the 1990 defeat of liberal Democratic Agriculture Commissioner Jim Hightower, who had angered many agricultural producers and the chemical industry with tough stands on farm worker rights and pesticide regulation. Other producer groups include the Texas and Southwestern Cattle Raisers Association, the Texas Poultry Federation, and the Texas Corn Producers Board.

★ **Religious Right**
Political movement, based
primarily in evangelical
Protestant churches, that has
played an increasingly
prominent role in Texas and
national politics.

Religious Groups   Many people, influenced in part by their views on separation of church and state, think religious groups have little or no legitimate role in the political process. Nevertheless, religious groups have helped influence policy in Texas, and the abortion issue and other social and economic issues have increased the presence of religious groups in Austin.

A number of religious groups emerged in the 1940s with an identifiable right-wing orientation. These groups, predecessors to what is now known as the **Religious Right**, combined Christian rhetoric and symbols with anti-communist, anti-labor, anti–civil rights, anti-liberal, or anti–New Deal themes. Although these groups were often very small, they were linked to the extreme right wing of the Texas establishment, and they were the precursors of many of the conservative ideological groups that have emerged in American politics in the past twenty years.[12] Many of these organizations have gravitated toward the Republican Party[13] (see *Politics Up Close*: "The Religious Right and Republican Growth"). With a strong organizational effort, religious conservatives were influential in a right-wing takeover of leadership positions in the Texas Republican Party in 1994.

Many religious denominations have boards or commissions responsible for monitoring governmental action. Although staff members or volunteers serving in this capacity may not register as lobbyists, they function much like lobbyists.

Churches across the state have formed community-based organizations to address the social and economic needs of the poor. In many regards, this is a redefinition of the Social Gospel, a church-based social movement of the late nineteenth and early twentieth centuries.

The Development of a Two-Party System in Texas

The Texas party system has been restructured by the social and economic changes that the state has experienced over the past 30 years. Texas now has a strong Republican Party and a competitive **two-party system**, but for more than a century, Texas was a **one-party** Democratic state. There was no organized opposition party to mobilize those who felt excluded from the Democratic Party. Electoral politics were based on factions and personalities; the interests of the lower socioeconomic classes—especially minorities—were blatantly neglected.

★ **two-party system**
Political system that has two
dominant parties, such as that
of the United States.

★ **one-party system**
Domination of elections and
governmental processes by a
single party, which may be
split into different ideological,
economic, or regional
factions. In Texas, the phrase
is used to describe the period
from the late 1870s to the late
1970s, when the Democratic
Party claimed virtually all
elected, partisan offices.

One-Party Democratic Politics   Texas's long domination by the Democratic Party can be traced to the period immediately after the Civil War, when the Republican Party was able to capture control of Texas's government for a short period. Strong anti-Republican feelings were generated by the Reconstruction administration of Radical Republican Governor Edmund J. Davis, and the Republican Party was perceived by most Texans of that era to be the party of conquest and occupation. By the time the Constitution of 1876 was implemented, the Republican Party's influence in state politics was negligible. From 1874 to 1961, no Republican won a statewide office in Texas, and Republicans were elected to local offices in only a few scattered districts.

The anti-Republicanism that evolved from the Civil War and Reconstruction, however, is only a partial explanation for the Democratic Party's long-time control of Texas politics. One classic study presents the provocative thesis that Texas politics might be better understood in terms of "modified class politics."[14]

As Texas's conservative agricultural leaders attempted to regain control over the state's political system after Reconstruction, the postwar economic devastation was dividing Texans along class lines. Small farmers, African Americans, and an emerging urban labor class suffered disproportionately from the economic

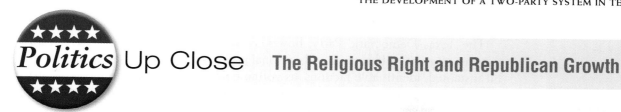

Politics Up Close   The Religious Right and Republican Growth

As the Republican Party expanded its support in Texas, it experienced sharp, often bitter, philosophical and ideological differences among its members. Overwhelmingly conservative, Republicans were split along the lines of economic conservatism and the "lifestyle" conservatism advocated by the Religious Right.

The Religious Right has long been part of the Texas political landscape.[a] Although its influence was occasionally manifested in conservative Democratic politics, it found far greater potential in the Republican Party for shaping electoral politics. It has strong religious overtones and draws considerable support from evangelical groups across the state. Some scholars attribute much of its success to its ability to mobilize voters who were traditionally inactive and bring them into the Republican Party. The Republicans' difficulty in attracting minority groups also gave the social conservative wing greater influence in the party.

Low voter turnout in the 1994 Republican primary enabled well-organized social conservatives to gain control of the party's precinct conventions and therefore a majority of delegates to the June state convention. Sensing defeat, Fred Meyer, a traditional Republican who had guided the state party for 6 years during a period of growth and electoral success, stepped down and was replaced by Tom Pauken, a Dallas lawyer and former Reagan administration official who courted Christian activists. Delegates also elected a new party vice chair, Christian activist Susan Weddington of San Antonio, and put other members of the Religious Right on the State Republican Executive Committee.

The Religious Right also was instrumental in the election of Republican George W. Bush over Democrat Ann Richards in the 1994 gubernatorial race. According to a survey of voters as they left the polls, 20 percent of the 4.4 million Texans who voted in that election identified themselves as white Christian fundamentalists. Of those, 84 percent said they voted for Bush. They also voted heavily for other Republican candidates.[b]

The State Republican Executive Committee elected Susan Weddington state party chair after Pauken resigned in 1997 to seek the Republican nomination for state attorney general. Weddington served in that post and was an outspoken advocate for social conservative causes until 2003, when she resigned to take a job directing a new state charitable foundation. She was succeeded by another conservative party activist, Houston attorney Tina Benkiser.

Governor Rick Perry actively courted the Religious Right as an important part of his electoral base. In 2005, on the eve of his 2006 reelection campaign, he successfully promoted a state constitutional amendment banning same-sex marriages in Texas, a proposition that attracted large numbers of social conservatives to the polls. And he visited a church school to sign a law requiring minors to have their parents' permission before obtaining abortions.

[a]George Norris Green, *The Establishment in Texas Politics, 1938–1957.* Westport, Conn.: Greenwood Press, 1979, ch. 5.

[b]*Dallas Morning News*, November 11, 1994.

depression of this period. They turned their discontent into support for agrarian third parties, particularly the Populist Party, which began to threaten the monopoly of the traditional Texas power structure.

To protect their political power, the established agricultural leaders moved to divide the lower social groups by directing the discontent of lower-income whites against blacks. The rural elites, who manifested traditionalistic political values and wanted to consolidate power in the hands of the privileged few, also created alliances with the mercantile, banking, and emerging industrial leaders, who reflected the individualistic view of a limited government that served to protect their interests. Over the years, these two dominant forces consolidated political power and merged the politics of race with the politics of economics.

The elites were able to institutionalize their control through the adoption of constitutional restrictions and segregation legislation, called **Jim Crow laws**, designed to reduce the size of the electorate and the potential of a popular challenge to the establishment's political monopoly.[15]

★ **Jim Crow laws**
Legislation enacted by many states after the Civil War to limit the rights and power of African Americans.

The Texas Democratic Party, however, was not homogeneous. There were factions, regional differences, and personal political rivalries. Initially, there were no sustained, identifiable factions, as voting coalitions changed from election to election through much of the first third of the twentieth century. But the onset of the Great Depression in 1929, the election of President Franklin D. Roosevelt in 1932, and the policies of the New Deal reshaped Texas politics in the 1930s.

Factionalism in the Democratic Party

Franklin Roosevelt's administrations (1933–1945) articulated and developed a policy agenda radically different from that of the Republican Party, which had dominated national politics from 1860 to 1932. Government was to become a buffer against economic downturns as well as a positive force for change. Under Roosevelt, the regulatory function of the federal government was expanded to exercise control and authority over much of the nation's economy. The federal government also enacted programs such as Social Security, public housing, and labor legislation to benefit lower socioeconomic groups.

These national policies produced an active philosophical split within the Texas Democratic Party that was to characterize Texas politics for the next two generations. A majority of Texas voters supported Roosevelt in his four elections, and the Democratic Party maintained its monopoly over Texas politics. But competing economic interests clearly—and often bitterly—divided Texas Democrats along liberal and conservative lines.

A strong Republican Party did not emerge at this time in Texas or any other southern state because "southern conservative Democratic politicians, who would have been expected to lead such a realignment, or any politicians for that matter, did not relish jumping from a majority-status party to one in the minority."[16]

Despite some liberal successes under Governor James Allred, who was elected in 1934 and again in 1936, the conservative wing of the Democratic Party prevailed in state elections from the 1940s to the late 1970s. Democratic presidential candidates carried Texas in 1944, 1948, 1960, 1964, 1968, and 1976, even though some of them were too liberal to suit the tastes of the state's conservative Democratic establishment.

At first glance, it might appear that the **bifactionalism** in the Democratic Party partially compensated for the lack of a competitive two-party system, but one scholar argued against that perception, concluding that factionalism resulted in "no-party politics." Factionalism results in discontinuity in leadership and group support, and the voter has no permanent reference point from which to judge the performance of the party or selected candidates. Because there are no clear distinctions between who holds power and who does not, the influence of pressure groups increases.[17] In one-party Democratic Texas, as noted, state government and public policy were susceptible to control by wealthy and corporate interests.

★ **bifactionalism**
Presence of two dominant factions organized around regional, economic, or ideological differences within a single political party. For much of the twentieth century, Texas functioned as a one-party system with two dominant factions.

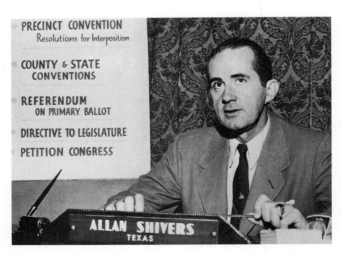

A Governor Who Broke with His Party

Governor Allan Shivers led conservative Democrats in support of Republican Dwight D. Eisenhower in the 1952 presidential elections.

This bifactional pattern of state Democratic politics was tested by a number of factors, including the national party's increased commitment after 1948 to civil rights legislation. That development alienated segments of the white population and prompted many voters eventually to leave the Democratic Party and align with the Republicans. Efforts by Texas oil interests to reestablish state control over the oil-rich tidelands also played a key role in the demise of one-party politics and the development of a two-party system. President Harry Truman, concerned about national security and federal access to these offshore oil resources, refused to accede to state demands and vetoed legislation favorable to Texas oil interests in 1952. That veto prompted a series of maneuvers orchestrated by Democratic Governor Allan Shivers to take the support of conservative Democrats to the Republican Party.

The "Shivercrats," as they were called, were successful in carrying Texas for the 1952 Republican presidential nominee, Dwight D. Eisenhower. This election helped establish a pattern of Texas's retaining its Democratic leanings in state and local elections but voting Republican in many presidential elections. Moreover, this election marked a shift in the state leadership of the Republican Party and led to efforts to create a party capable of winning local and statewide elections.[18]

In 1960, Democrat Lyndon B. Johnson ran both for election as vice president and for reelection as U.S. senator from Texas—a dual candidacy permitted under state law—and won both offices. His Republican opponent in the Senate race was John Tower, a relatively unknown college professor from Wichita Falls, who received 41 percent of the vote. After Johnson won the vice presidency and resigned from the Senate, a special election to fill the Senate seat was called in 1961. It attracted seventy-one candidates, including Tower, who defeated conservative Democrat William Blakely with 50.6 percent of the vote in a runoff.[19] Some evidence indicates that liberal Democrats, in retaliation for having been locked out of the power centers of their party and in anticipation of an ideological realignment of the party system, supported Tower in this election. The *Texas Observer*, an influential liberal publication, endorsed Tower with an argument for a two-party system. "How many liberals voted for Tower will never be known, nor will it be known how many 'went fishing,'" wrote a Republican campaign consultant.[20] Tower was reelected in 1966, 1972, and 1978, but no other Texas Republican won a statewide office until 1978, when Bill Clements was elected governor. Nevertheless, many students of Texas politics regard Tower's election in 1961 as a key factor in the development of the state's two-party system.[21]

Although Republicans made some gains in suburban congressional districts and local elections in the 1960s—including the election to Congress of a Houston Republican named George Herbert Walker Bush—the numbers were inconsequential. Most significant election battles continued to take place for a while longer within the Democratic Party, in which the conservative wing generally prevailed until 1978.

Two-Party Politics in Texas

On the national level, **realignment** of political parties (see Chapter 7) is often associated with a critical election in which economic or social issues cut across existing party allegiances and produce a permanent shift in party support and identification.[22] What apparently has happened in Texas is that the state party system has been integrated into the national party system and now more closely approximates the political divisions that exist in states outside the South. Rather than occurring in a single election, this process has occurred over many years.

A major contributor to this change was the civil rights movement. African Americans and Hispanics went to federal court to attack state laws that enforced segregation and restricted minority voting rights. Successful lawsuits were brought against the white primary, the preprimary endorsement, the poll tax (all discussed later in this chapter), and racial **gerrymandering** of political districts.

★ **realignment**
Major shift in political party support or identification that usually occurs around a critical election. In Texas, realignment took place as a gradual transformation from a one-party system dominated by Democrats to a two-party system in which Republicans became competitive in elections.

★ **gerrymandering**
Drawing the boundaries of legislative districts in such a way as to increase the power of one group over another.

His Election Was a Precursor to Realignment

John Tower's surprise election to the U.S. Senate in 1961 was the first statewide victory by a Republican since Reconstruction.

★ **Voting Rights Act**
Federal law designed to protect the voting rights of minorities by requiring the Justice Department's approval of changes in political districts and certain other electoral procedures. The 1965 act, as amended, has eliminated most of the restrictive practices that limited minority political participation.

Minorities then turned to the U.S. Congress for civil rights legislation, a process that produced the 1965 **Voting Rights Act**, which Congress extended to cover Texas after 1975.

Economic factors have also shaped minority political support and, in turn, have contributed to two-party development. African Americans and Hispanics are disproportionately low-income populations and generally support such governmental services as public housing, public health care, day care, and income support. These policies are associated with the liberal wing of the Democratic Party.

Minority organizations have made concerted efforts to register, educate, and mobilize the people in their communities. As the numerical strength of minorities increased, conservative Anglo Democrats found their position within the party threatened and began to look to the Republican Party as an alternative.

The large number of people who migrated to Texas from other states, particularly when the Sun Belt economy of the 1970s and early 1980s was booming and many northern industrial states were struggling, also contributed to two-party development in Texas. Many of these new arrivals were Republicans from states with strong Republican parties, and many of them settled in high-income, suburban, Anglo areas in Texas. Other significant factors were Presidents Ronald Reagan's and George Bush's popularity in the 1980s and the 1978 election of Republican Governor Bill Clements, who encouraged many conservative Democratic officeholders to switch parties.

Other events of the 1970s and the 1980s demonstrated that the transformation of the Texas party system was well on its way. After a major stock fraud scandal, the Texas House elected a liberal Democrat, Price Daniel, Jr., as speaker in 1973. Three other moderate-to-liberal Democrats were also elected to statewide office in the early 1970s: Bob Armstrong as land commissioner in 1970, John Hill as attorney general in 1972, and Bob Bullock as comptroller in 1974.

In 1978, John Hill defeated Governor Dolph Briscoe, a conservative, in the Democratic primary and was subsequently defeated by Republican Bill Clements, then a political unknown, in the general election by a narrow margin of 17,000 votes. Four years later, Clements lost to Democratic Attorney General Mark White, but in 1986 he returned to defeat White in an expensive, bitter campaign. In the 1982 election, Democratic candidates who were considered liberal won additional statewide offices: Ann Richards was elected state treasurer; Jim Mattox, attorney general; Jim Hightower, agriculture commissioner; and Garry Mauro, land commissioner.

The 1990 election further demonstrated how far the realignment process had gone. Democratic gubernatorial nominee Ann Richards defeated conservative business executive Clayton Williams, who had spent $6 million of his own money to win the Republican primary. But Republican Kay Bailey Hutchison was elected state treasurer, and Republican Rick Perry unseated Democrat Jim Hightower to become agriculture commissioner. Republicans also retained one of the U.S. Senate seats from Texas when Phil Gramm easily won reelection to the seat once held by John Tower, and the GOP claimed eight of the twenty-seven congressional seats that Texas then had in Congress.

In a special election in 1993 to fill the U.S. Senate seat vacated by Democrat Lloyd Bentsen when he was appointed secretary of the treasury by President Bill Clinton, Kay Bailey Hutchison defeated Democrat Bob Krueger, thus giving the Republicans both U.S. Senate seats from Texas. Hutchison easily won reelection in 1994, despite a political and legal controversy over her administration of the state treasurer's office.

Also in 1994, Democratic Governor Ann Richards was unseated by Republican nominee George W. Bush, the son of former President George H. W. Bush and a future president himself. Republicans that year also captured four other statewide offices that had been held by Democrats, marking the most statewide gains by Republicans in any single election since Reconstruction. Meanwhile, Republicans also were increasing their share of seats in the Texas legislature.

Toward Republican Dominance   The political transformation of Texas accelerated even more in 1996, when Republicans swept all statewide offices on the general election ballot and captured a majority of the state Senate for the first time since Reconstruction. Republican presidential nominee Bob Dole also carried the Lone Star State, despite a poor national showing against President Clinton. Republicans also increased their numbers in the Texas House and in the Texas congressional delegation. When the electoral dust had cleared, Republicans held twenty of Texas's twenty-nine statewide elected offices, including the top three. That number increased to twenty-one in 1997, when presiding judge Michael McCormick of the Texas Court of Criminal Appeals switched from the Democratic to the Republican Party.

Lieutenant Governor Bob Bullock and Attorney General Dan Morales, both Democrats, chose not to seek reelection or any other office in 1998, and Republicans cashed in on the opportunity. With Governor Bush winning reelection in a landslide, Republicans again swept all statewide offices on the ballot. And a few weeks after the 1998 election, the GOP secured all statewide offices in Texas for the first time since Reconstruction when Texas Supreme Court Justice Raul A. Gonzalez, a Democrat, retired in midterm and was replaced by a Republican appointee of Bush. Republicans did not capture control of the Texas House but picked up four seats to narrow the Democratic margin to six seats. In the governor's race, Bush carried 69 percent of the vote against Democratic challenger Garry Mauro, the longtime land commissioner.

Democrats fielded candidates for only three of the nine statewide offices up for election in 2000. They lost all three but held their ground in legislative races.

Republicans also swept all statewide races in 2002, including Governor Rick Perry's victory over Democratic nominee Tony Sanchez and former Texas attorney general John Cornyn's victory over former Dallas mayor Ron Kirk in a race to succeed retiring U.S. Senator Phil Gramm. Republicans also finally gained control of the Texas House of Representatives in 2002, capturing 88 of the 150 seats after the Legislative Redistricting Board in 2001 had drawn new districts that favored Republicans (see Chapter 22). Additionally, the GOP increased its margin in the state Senate by winning 19 of the 31 seats. All statewide elected officials remained Republican.

The statewide losses in 2002 were particularly disappointing for Democratic leaders, who had carefully assembled a racially diverse ticket with an eye toward increasing minority turnout. Kirk, the U.S. Senate candidate, was African American, and Sanchez, a wealthy businessman from Laredo, was Hispanic. The Democratic nominee for lieutenant governor, John Sharp, a former state comptroller, was Anglo. Sanchez was unexpectedly challenged in the Democratic primary by former Texas attorney general Dan Morales. The race was historic because it was the first gubernatorial contest in Texas between two Hispanics, and it was extremely contentious. Sanchez was supported by most party leaders because the party was banking on his wealth to help finance the Democrats' general election campaign.

Republicans achieved still another long-sought goal in 2004—a majority of Texas's congressional delegation—after the legislature, in a bitter partisan fight in

The Senior Senator from Texas

U.S. Senator Kay Bailey Hutchison (R), first elected in a special election in 1993, is now in her third term. She is part of the Republican leadership in the Senate, and the only woman from Texas elected to the U.S. Senate.

The Junior Senator from Texas

U.S. Senator John Cornyn (R), a former Texas attorney general and state Supreme Court justice, was first elected in 2002 and reelected in 2008.

2003, redrew congressional district boundaries to favor GOP candidates (see Chapter 22).

The GOP also has made significant gains across Texas at the county level. In 1974, Republicans held 53 county offices but had claimed 1,814 by 2006, paralleling the dramatic statewide realignment that was occurring (see Table 21.1). Democrats still held most county offices, and regained a handful of local offices in Dallas County in 2004.

Republicans again swept all statewide offices in 2006. Governor Rick Perry won reelection—but with only 39 percent of the vote—over three major opponents, including Democratic nominee Chris Bell, a former congressman and former city councilman from Houston. Republican Comptroller Carole Keeton Strayhorn and musician-author Kinky Friedman challenged Perry as independents. Bell headed a Democratic ticket that was much less experienced and more poorly financed than the party's slate of candidates in 2002. Barbara Ann Radnofsky, the Democratic nominee against Republican U.S. Senator Kay Bailey Hutchison, was a Houston lawyer making her first race for elected office.

But in local and district races in 2006, Democrats narrowed the Republicans' majority in the Texas House and swept all local offices in Dallas County, including several judgeships and the district attorney's race.

Republicans retained their control of all statewide elected offices in the 2008 general election. U.S. Senator John Cornyn turned back a challenge by Democrat Rick Noriega, a state representative from Houston and a veteran of the war in Afghanistan. Republicans gained one congressional seat, but Democrats picked up at least one seat in the state Senate and three seats in the Texas House.

Table *21.1* Growth of Republican Officeholders in Texas, 1974–2006

Year	U.S. Senate	Other Statewide	U.S. Congress	Texas Senate	Texas House	County Offices	Total
1974	1	0	2	3	16	53	75
1976	1	0	2	3	19	67	92
1978	1	1	4	4	22	87	119
1980	1	1	5	7	35	166	215
1982	1	0	5	5	36	191	238
1984	1	0	10	6	52	287	356
1986	1	1	10	6	56	410	484
1988	1	5	8	8	57	485	564
1990	1	6	8	8	57	547	627
1992	1	8	9	13	58	634	723
1994	2	13	11	14	61	734	835
1996	2	18	13	17	68	938	1056
1998	2	27	13	16	72	1,108	1,238
2000	2	27	13	16	72	1,299	1,429
2002	2	27	15	19	88	1,443	1,594
2004	2	27	21	19	87	1,608	1,764
2006	2	27	21	20	81	1,814	1,965

Source: Republican Party of Texas.

Politics Up Close   La Raza Unida

La Raza Unida, led by José Angel Gutierrez and Mario Compean, began in 1969 to organize in Crystal City in Zavala County and then extended its influence to Dimmit, La Salle, and Hildago counties. Overwhelmingly Hispanic and poor, these counties were characteristic of many South Texas counties where the Anglo minority controlled both the political and economic institutions, and there was little sensitivity to the needs of low-income residents. In 1972, Ramsey Muniz ran as the party's gubernatorial candidate. During the general election campaign, there was considerable speculation in the press and apprehension among conservative Democrats that La Raza would drain a sufficient number of votes away from Dolph Briscoe, the Democratic nominee, to give Henry "Hank" Grover, a right-wing Republican, the governorship. Briscoe won the election, but without a majority of the votes. The subsequent growth of liberal and minority influence within the Democratic Party, internal dissension within La Raza Unida, and legal problems encountered by Muniz contributed to the demise of this third party after 1978.

Source: Juan Gomez Quinones, *Chicano Politics.* Albuquerque, N.M.: University of New Mexico Press, 1990, pp.128–31.

Third Parties   There has been a tradition of third parties in Texas, including Grangers, Populists, Progressives, Socialists, Dixiecrats, the American Independent Party, Libertarians, and La Raza Unida (see *Politics Up Close:* "La Raza Unida"). None has had statewide electoral success, a situation that can be explained in part by the cultural consensus supporting the two-party and winner-take-all election systems (see "Why the Two-Party System Persists" in Chapter 7). Most Americans do not have highly cohesive political views, which are part of the appeal of many third parties.

The most successful third party in Texas in recent years has been the Libertarian Party. Libertarians have qualified for a place on the ballot in every Texas general election since 1986 because the party has succeeded in winning at least 5 percent of the vote in at least one statewide race during each election year. But the party has never won an elected office in Texas. Another minor party, the Green Party, which puts a high priority on environmental protection, also qualified for the Texas ballot in 2002.

In addition to statewide third parties, local political organizations connected to neither the Democratic nor the Republican Party have been influential in some cities. Elections for city offices are nonpartisan, and most are held during odd-numbered years, when there are no state offices on the ballot. Cities such as San Antonio and Dallas developed citizens' associations, which controlled city governments for decades and maintained a virtual monopoly over city elections. But these local political parties have disappeared in recent years.

Changing Patterns of Party Support and Identification

The changes in party affiliations over the past 40 years illustrate Texas's political realignment. In 1952, 66 percent of Texans called themselves Democrats, and only 6 percent claimed to be Republicans,[23] a pattern that changed little from 1952 to 1964. During the next decade, however, Republican Party identification increased to 16 percent, and Democratic Party identification declined to 59 percent (see Figure 21.1).

Figure *21.1*

Changing Party
Affiliation in Texas,
1964–2008

Sources: The Texas Poll, Summer
1993, Fall 1993, Winter 1996,
Spring 1996, Fall 1996, Spring
1999, Summer 1999, Fall 1999,
Winter 2000, Summer 2003, Fall
2003, Winter 2004, Spring 2004:
Pew Research Center, "Fewer
Voters Identify as Republicans,"
March 20, 2008; 1,476 interviews
were conducted in 2007 and 2008.

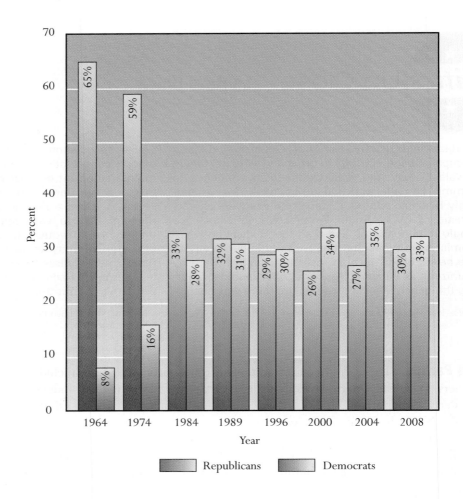

| | Republicans | | Democrats |

Between 1975 and 1984, there was a dramatic decline in voter identification with the Democratic Party and a significant increase in Republican Party identification. By 2008, approximately 33 percent of Texas voters called themselves Republicans, and 30 percent identified as Democrats. The remainder called themselves independents, third-party affiliates, or undecided. This shift in party identification is further proof that Texas is now Republican-dominant on a statewide level. But party identification does not always translate into winning elected offices in some counties.

As noted above, a large number of voters identify themselves as independents. Independents don't have their own party, and their choices in most elections are limited to candidates from the two major parties. Further survey research, moreover, suggests that most self-proclaimed Independents vote consistently for Republican candidates.

Ticket splitting, a practice associated with the realignment process, has been common in recent Texas elections. It explains, in part, why Democrats have still been able to keep most local offices despite Republican sweeps statewide. Many Texans cast their votes selectively as they go down the general election ballot.

The *Texas Poll* and other studies indicate marked differences in the social and economic characteristics of party identifiers. From these data, analysts have made the following generalizations:

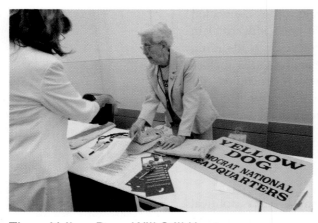

These Yellow Dogs Will Still Hunt

Although growing scarcer in Texas, yellow dog
Democrats—voters who swore by the phrase, "I'd vote
for a yellow dog if he ran on the Democratic ticket"—
remain fiercely loyal to their party.

1. The Republican Party is composed disproportionately of voters who fall into one or more of the following categories:

   ★ College educated

   ★ Persons who have come to Texas from other states

   ★ Anglos

   ★ Large metropolitan area residents, particularly the suburbs

   ★ Higher income earners

   ★ Middle aged

   ★ Protestant

2. Democrats are strongly represented among:

   ★ Hispanics

   ★ African Americans

   ★ Central city residents

   ★ Older people

   ★ Native Texans

   ★ Lower-income earners

   ★ Less-educated people

   ★ Catholic.[24]

Seeking to expand the Republican Party's base, Governor George W. Bush made a strong appeal to Hispanics during his 1998 reelection campaign and was rewarded with about 40 percent of the Hispanic vote. Some Republican strategists have been arguing for years that the GOP must strengthen its appeal to the growing Hispanic population—and chip away at Hispanics' traditional support for the Democratic Party—if the GOP is to maintain its control over state politics.[25] Anglo Protestants, who form the core of the Republican Party, are declining in proportion to the increased number of Hispanics in Texas. To maintain dominance, it has been argued, Republicans must embrace issues, such as improved health care and educational opportunities, which are central to Hispanic voting interests. And they may need to develop a more tolerant attitude toward immigration than what was expressed in the 2006 Texas Republican Party platform, which advocated, among other things, a wall between Texas and Mexico. It is premature to conclude that there will be an erosion of Hispanic support from the Democratic Party, but both parties will be battling for the Hispanic vote over the next two decades. Republicans also have spoken about the need to appeal to African American Texans who share their core values, but the GOP has had little success attracting African Americans from the Democratic Party.

The Party Organization

To carry out their functions, the two major parties in Texas have developed permanent and temporary organizations (see "Where's the Party?" in Chapter 7), structured by state law, state and national party rules, and a series of court decisions protecting voters' rights. Party organizations are built around geographic election districts, starting with the precinct. There is, however, no hierarchical arrangement to party organization. The party structure has been described as a "system of layers of organization," with each level—county, state, and federal—concentrating on the elections within its jurisdiction.[26]

There are no membership requirements for either the Democratic or the Republican Party. Party members do not have to pay dues, attend meetings, campaign for candidates, or make contributions. When people register to vote in Texas, they are not required to state their party preference. The right to participate in a party's

★ **precincts**
Specific local voting areas created by county commissioners courts. The state election code provides detailed requirements for drawing up these election units.

★ **precinct chair**
Local officer in a political party who presides over the precinct convention and serves on the party's county executive committee. Voters in each precinct elect a chair in the party's primary election.

★ **county executive committee**
Panel responsible on the local level for the organization and management of a political party's primary election. It includes the party's county chair and each precinct chair.

electoral and nominating activities is based simply on voting in that party's primary election. When a person votes in one of the major party primaries, his or her voter registration card is stamped "Democrat" or "Republican."

The Permanent Organization Election **precincts** (there were an estimated 8,400 in Texas in 2008) are created by the county commissioners of each of the 254 counties.[27] Voters in each precinct elect a **precinct chair** in the party primary (see Figure 21.2). Any eligible voter within the precinct can file for this position, or the names of write-in candidates can be added to the ballot. The chair calls to order the precinct convention (discussed later) and serves as a member of the county executive committee. Many people do nothing with the position, but others contribute a great deal of time and energy to deliver the precinct's votes for their party's candidates in the general election.

The second level of the party organization is the **county executive committee**, which includes each precinct chair and the **county chair**, who is elected to a 2-year term by primary voters countywide. A major responsibility of the county chair and the executive committee is the organization and management of the primary election in their county. The county executive committee accepts filings by candidates and is also responsible for planning the county or district conventions. Funds for the management of primary elections are provided to the county party by the state through the secretary of state's office.

TEMPORARY ORGANIZATION

PERMANENT ORGANIZATION

State Convention
Delegates are selected from the district or senatorial conventions to attend the state convention, held in June.

State Chair and Vice Chair
State Executive Committee
The State Executive Committee and the chair and the vice chair are selected by the state convention, held in June of the even-numbered years.

County or District Convention
Delegates from the precinct conventions are selected to attend the county convention or the senatorial district convention, held the second Saturday after the second Tuesday in March.

County Chair
The county chair is elected by the voters countywide in the primary and, if required, the runoff primary.

County Executive Committee
The precinct chairs and the county chair comprise the party's County Executive Committee.

Precinct Convention
Any person who has participated in a party primary may attend the precinct convention, held the same day as the primary.

Precinct Chair
A precinct chair is selected by voters participating in the primary and, if required, the runoff primary.

Voters in the Party Primary
Any registered voter may participate in the primaries, held in even-numbered years on the second Tuesday in March.

Figure *21.2* Organization of Texas Political Parties

County committees may be well organized and may actively work to carry out a wide range of organizational and electoral activities, or they may meet irregularly and have difficulty getting a quorum of members to attend. The county chair is an unpaid position. But party organizations in some counties have successful ongoing fund-raising operations, and they support a party headquarters, retain professional staff, and are engaged in various party activities between elections.

At the state level, a party's permanent organization is the **state executive committee**, which is composed of sixty-four members, including the party's state chair and vice chair. When the parties meet in their biennial state conventions, two committee members—a man and a woman—are selected by delegation caucuses from each of the thirty-one state senatorial districts. The **state chair and the vice chair**, one of whom must be a woman, also are selected by the convention. The two top state party leaders and other executive committee members serve 2-year terms and are unpaid.

Statewide candidates file for office with the executive committee, which is also responsible for planning and organizing the party's state convention and helps raise funds for the ongoing operations of the party. The committee serves to establish party policy, but day-to-day party operations are entrusted to the party's executive director and professional staff. The Texas Democratic Party and the Texas Republican Party have permanent staffs and headquarters in Austin.

Temporary Organizations

The temporary organizations of the political parties are the series of conventions that are held every 2 years, beginning on the day of the party primaries. They are particularly significant in presidential election years because they help select the state's delegates to the national party conventions. The convention system also helps organize the permanent party structure and brings party activists together to share common political concerns and shape party policies. Most Texans, however, have little knowledge of the convention system, and few participate in it.

Precinct Conventions

Anyone who votes in a party primary, held on the second Tuesday in March of even-numbered years, is eligible to participate in that party's **precinct convention**, normally held in the same place as the primary after voting stops at 7 P.M. The main business of the convention is the selection of delegates and alternate delegates to the county or senatorial district convention. Since 1972, the Democrats have used complex procedures designed to assure broad-based delegate representation by ethnicity, gender, and age. A precinct convention can also adopt resolutions to be submitted at the county or district conventions for possible inclusion in the party's platform.

In presidential election years, the presidential preference primary and the precinct conventions are the first steps in the selection of delegates to the national nominating conventions. They attracted thousands of participants and sparked more controversy than normal in 2008 because of the hotly contested Democratic presidential primary race between Hillary Clinton and Barack Obama (see *Controversy*: "The Texas Two-Step"). Precinct conventions held in non-presidential election years, however, are often poorly attended, and in many precincts no one shows up. Such low participation rates are cited by those who conclude that the political parties are in decline.

County or Senatorial District Conventions

County or state senatorial district conventions are held 2 weeks after the precinct conventions. District conventions are held in the larger urban counties that include more than one state senatorial district. Delegates elected at the precinct conventions constitute the

★ **county chair**
Presiding officer of a political party's county executive committee. He or she is elected countywide by voters in the party primary.

★ **state executive committee**
Statewide governing board of a political party. It includes a man and a woman from each of the thirty-one state senatorial districts and the state chair and vice chair, who are selected by delegates to the party's biennial state convention.

★ **state chair and vice chair**
Two top state leaders of a political party, one of whom must be a woman. They are selected every two years by delegates to the party's state convention.

★ **precinct convention**
Meeting held by a political party in each precinct on the same day as the party primary. In presidential election years, the precinct conventions and the primaries are the first steps in the selection of delegates to the major parties' national nominating conventions.

membership of this second level of the convention process, which, in turn, elects delegates to the state convention.

★ **state convention**
Meeting held in June of even-numbered years by each of the two major political parties. Delegates to this convention elect the party's state leadership and adopt a party platform. In presidential election years, the state convention selects the delegates to the party's national nominating convention.

State Conventions   The two major parties hold their **state conventions** in June of even-numbered years. Convention delegates certify to the secretary of state the names of those individuals who were nominated to statewide offices in the March primaries, adopt a party platform, and elect the state party chair, the vice chair, and the state executive committee.

In presidential election years, the state conventions also select delegates to their respective parties' national nominating conventions, elect members to their parties' national committees, and choose presidential electors. Electors from the party that carries Texas in the presidential race will formally cast the state's electoral votes for that party's presidential candidate in December after the general election.

The allocation of Texas delegates to the Republican national convention is determined by the presidential primary, but the actual delegates are selected at the state convention.

Texas delegates to the Democratic national convention are determined through a more complicated process based both on the primary vote and on candidate support from attendees at the series of party conventions, beginning at the precinct level.

Parties and Government

Political parties in Texas do not produce cohesive, policy-oriented coalitions in government, and they have been unable to hold their elected officials accountable or make them responsive to those supporting the party. Under ideal circumstances, some students of government believe, the two major parties would articulate clearly defined political philosophies and policies they would pursue if their candidates were elected. Once elected, persons supported by the party would be committed to these programs, giving the voters a clear standard by which to evaluate their performances in office. This perspective is often referred to as the responsible party model (see Chapter 7).

There are several reasons why Texas parties are incapable of functioning in this manner, none of which lessens the disenchantment and disgust that many voters feel toward political parties and politicians. First, the political parties in Texas are highly decentralized and unable to discipline members who pursue goals that conflict with the party's stated objectives. The large number of elected officials at both the state and the local level serves to diffuse party leadership. Furthermore, most of these elected officials rely primarily on their own fund-raising skills and receive very limited direct financial support through the parties.

Moreover, the coalitions that parties form with groups harboring different objectives, interests, and agendas make it next to impossible to develop clearly stated positions that would always differentiate one party from another. Philosophical, ideological, and programmatic differences among members and supporters of the same party result, for example, in ideological voting patterns in the legislature that cross party lines.

Another explanation for the lack of partisan accountability is the long-standing anti-party tradition of American politics. Many voters are ambivalent—even outright hostile—toward political parties, and the parties make only limited efforts to include a large number of individuals in their organizational activities.

Controversy

The Texas Two-Step

One political consultant called it a "tsunami." Democratic officials were delighted but also overwhelmed by the response to the March 2008 Texas Democratic primary and related precinct conventions, the so-called "Texas Two-Step" that helped decide the tight race between Hillary Clinton and Barack Obama for the 2008 Democratic presidential nomination.

Thousands of Texas voters were so confused or frustrated that party officials soon began examining ways to overhaul or replace the delegate selection process. Texas wasn't even supposed to be in play in the presidential nominating campaign that year. Both Democratic and Republican nominations were expected to be all but decided by the time the March 4, 2008, Texas primary was held, following, as it did, the better-known caucuses in Iowa, the New Hampshire and South Carolina primaries and a host of "Super Tuesday" contests stretching from New York to California.

But the Democratic battle between Clinton and Obama was still wide open, focusing national attention on the Texas Democratic Party's bifurcated system of picking delegates that had been put to the test only once before—in 1988, when Michael Dukakis had won the nomination over the Rev. Jesse Jackson.

More than 2.8 million Texans (a record) voted in the 2008 Democratic primary, and about 1 million of them (also a record) returned after the polls closed for their precinct conventions. Clinton won the primary by about 101,000 votes over Obama and was awarded 65 delegates to Obama's 61.

Another 67 delegates were awarded on the basis of support demonstrated in party caucuses, beginning with more than 8,000 precinct conventions held that evening after the primary vote had ended. A preliminary count of precinct convention results indicated that Obama would get most of those delegates, 37, and Clinton would get 30. The count, however, wasn't made official until the State Democratic Convention in June 2008.

Both the primary and the caucuses drew criticism.

Delegates based on the primary vote were allocated according to the 31 state senatorial districts, and some districts were worth proportionately more delegates than others because they had had a higher Democratic turnout in the 2006 and 2004 elections. Senatorial districts, for example, in heavily Hispanic South Texas, where Clinton had a strong lead in the primary vote, didn't have as many delegates as some districts in Houston and Dallas, where Obama got more votes.

Most of the criticism, however, was leveled at the caucus system. Some participants complained of long lines and confusion. Others said they had been locked out of their meeting places by delegates for the opposing candidate. Other people argued that it was "undemocratic" to allow caucus attendees to, in effect, vote twice for their candidates, once in the primary and again in the caucus.

The whole system was widely misunderstood, and the huge turnout slowed the delegate count. "The turnout was a tsunami. There's no other way to describe it," said Democratic consultant Ed Martin.

Adding to the confusion was the fact that Clinton and Obama supporters still had to compete a few weeks later at county and state senatorial conventions before the delegate allocation was finally ratified at the state convention.

Minorities and Political Participation

At a time when millions of people around the world have eliminated authoritarian political systems and made great sacrifices to win free and open elections, Texans congratulate themselves if one-third of the eligible population votes. Such a poor turnout cannot be blamed on a lack of opportunity. After decades of denying voting rights to large parts of the population, Texas now has one of the most progressive voter registration laws in the United States. Contemporary political campaigns, especially those for national and statewide offices, have high media visibility. People are bombarded by sophisticated television advertising campaigns, direct mail, e-mail messages, phone bank solicitations for candidates, and daily news coverage. Yet something fundamental is disturbing Texas voters as well as voters across the nation. Statewide turnout rates in Texas are consistently low, and turnout rates in many local elections are downright appalling.

★ **poll tax**
A tax that Texas and some other states required before people were allowed to vote. The purpose was to discourage minorities and poor whites from participating in the political process. The tax was declared unconstitutional in the 1960s.

★ **white primary**
Series of state laws and party rules that denied African Americans the right to vote in the Democratic primary in Texas in the first half of the twentieth century.

Texas has had a dark history of voter disfranchisement. The systematic exclusion of African Americans, Hispanics, and low-income whites was clearly undemocratic and created a political system in which the interests of a few could prevail over the interests of the majority.

Texas enacted a **poll tax** in 1902. Although not a large sum of money by today's standards, the $1.50 to $1.75 people had to pay in order to vote eliminated large numbers of potential voters, especially those who were likely to support liberal social and economic policies and undermine the political establishment.[28] The poll tax was in effect for more than 60 years in Texas. It was outlawed for federal elections by the 24th Amendment to the U.S. Constitution, adopted in 1964, but Texas retained it for state and local elections until November 1966.

In 1923, the Texas legislature enacted a law that denied African Americans the right to vote in the Democratic primary. After a series of challenges in the U.S. Supreme Court, the so-called **white primary** was finally eliminated in 1944 as a result of the court's decision in *Smith v. Allwright*.[29] But those who were intent on keeping African Americans from voting began to utilize a restrictive pre-primary selection process to pick candidates, who then would be formally nominated in the Democratic primary and subsequently elected in the general election. Finally, in 1953, the Supreme Court also declared this arrangement unconstitutional.[30]

Until 1971, Texas had one of the nation's most restrictive voter registration systems. Voters had to register annually between October 1 and January 31. Voters who did not register in person at the county courthouse could be registered by deputy registrars. But deputy registrars could not mail a large number of registrations together; they were required to deliver or mail in only one registration form at a time. This requirement thwarted coordinated voter registration drives that targeted minorities and low-income populations.[31]

Court action eliminated this system, and the legislature—pressured by Common Cause, the League of Women Voters, and minority groups—enacted one of the most progressive voter registration systems in the country.[32] Permanent registration was implemented, and citizens could register by mail or in person up to 30 days prior to an election. The law also made it easier to organize large voter registration drives. In 1993, the U.S. Congress enacted "motor-voter registration," which requires states to provide facilities for voter registration where a person obtains a driver's license.

Women were not given the right to vote until the adoption of the 19th Amendment to the U.S. Constitution in 1920, and the adoption of the 26th Amendment lowered the voting age from 21 to 18 in 1971. Until the 1970s, property qualifications were used to exclude many voters from voting in local bond elections.

Even after the most obvious discriminatory practices against minorities were eliminated, there were more subtle, but just as pervasive, techniques for reducing the political power and influence of these same groups.

One technique is racial gerrymandering of political boundaries. State legislators and many city council members are elected from single-member districts, each of which represents a specific number of people in a designated area. To minimize the possibilities of minority candidates being elected, policy makers could divide minority communities and attach them to predominantly non-minority communities. This tactic is called cracking. Or, the minority communities could be consolidated into one district, a tactic called packing, with an 80 to 90 percent minority population, which would reduce the number of other districts in which minorities might have a chance of winning office.

At-large elections also have been used to reduce minority representation. At one time, members of the Texas House from urban counties were elected in multi-member districts, which required candidates to win election in countywide races, a very difficult prospect for most minority candidates. The practice was eliminated in legislative races in the 1970s as a result of federal lawsuits. But until recently, many cities, school districts, and special districts across Texas with significant minority populations continued to use at-large elections requiring candidates to run for office citywide or districtwide. The system dilutes minority representation in most communities in which it is used because of the higher costs of campaigning and the prevalence of polarized voting, in which minorities vote for minority candidates and Anglo voters, the majority, vote for white candidates.

Political Gains by Minorities and Women

Over the past 30 years, nevertheless, minorities have made substantial gains in the electoral process. Elimination of restrictive voting laws and adoption of a liberal voter registration system have contributed to an increase in minority voters across the state, as have voter registration and mobilization drives coordinated by groups such as the National Association for the Advancement of Colored People and the Southwest Voter Registration Education Project. The federal Voting Rights Act, which was passed by the U.S. Congress in 1965 and extended to Texas 10 years later, also has played a key role. Minority groups have used the Voting Rights Act to challenge discriminatory state and local election systems in the federal courts. An election system that dilutes minority voting strength is illegal, and the Voting Rights Act requires changes in the election systems of state or local governments, including redistricting plans, to be reviewed and pre-cleared by the U.S. Justice Department or approved by the U.S. District Court in Washington, D.C. This law has been used with considerable success to eliminate at-large elections and attack racial gerrymandering of political districts. These changes enhanced election opportunities for African Americans and Hispanics, but the fight continued.

By the mid-1990s, the Voting Rights Act was under attack by conservatives. And the U.S. Supreme Court, in "reverse-discrimination" cases from Texas and Georgia, ruled that some congressional districts had been illegally gerrymandered to elect minority candidates.[33] In the Texas case, three federal judges held that the Texas legislature had violated the U.S. Constitution by designing two districts in Houston and one in the Dallas area to favor the election of African American or Hispanic candidates. The court redrew 13 congressional districts in Texas—the three minority districts and ten districts adjoining them—and ordered special elections to fill the seats. Despite the redrawn boundaries, two incumbent African American congresswomen in the affected districts were reelected.

Hispanics   According to 2006 population estimates, Hispanics made up 35.7 percent of Texas's population. But the Hispanic population is younger than the Anglo and African American populations, and Hispanics accounted for only 32.1 percent of Texans of voting age (Figure 21.3).

Hispanics also include many immigrant noncitizens, thus reducing to 27 percent the Hispanic portion of adults eligible to register and vote. In the 2004 presidential election, the U.S. Census Bureau estimated that 22 percent of registered voters in Texas were Hispanic and 20 percent of those voting were Hispanic. By comparison, Anglos comprised 65 percent of those voting and African Americans, 12 percent.[34] According to analyses of elections in the early 1990s, Hispanics accounted for only 12 to 15 percent of Texans casting ballots.[35] Voter turnout rates among Hispanics are lower, in part, because of lower education and income levels.

It Took a Constitutional Amendment to Effect Change

President Lyndon Johnson, in a White House ceremony in 1964, signs the 24th Amendment to the Constitution barring the levying of a poll tax in federal elections. Texas soon followed with the elimination of the poll tax in state elections.

	Total Population	Percent of Total	Population of Voting Age	Percent of Total
Anglo	11,309,011	48.1%	8,852,437	52.1%
Hispanic	8,385,118	35.7%	5,462,072	32.1%
Black	2,676,626	11.4%	1,864,237	11.0%
Other	1,137,028	4.8%	826,183	4.9%
Total	22,507,783	100%	17,004,929	100%

Figure *21.3* Population and Voting Age Population of Texas, 2006

Source: U.S. Census Bureau, 2006 *American Community Survey*.

Approximately 44 percent of Hispanic adults interviewed in the 2003–2004 *Texas Polls* said they identified with the Democratic Party, but this percentage tells only part of the story.[36] Until Governor George W. Bush made substantial inroads into the Hispanic vote in 1998, Democratic candidates for president and governor consistently received more than 70 percent of the Hispanic vote in Texas.[37]

Hispanic voters dominated the 2002 Democratic primary, which for the first time featured two Hispanic gubernatorial candidates, Laredo businessperson Tony Sanchez and former Attorney General Dan Morales. One of three major candidates for the party's U.S. Senate nomination also was Hispanic—Victor Morales, a schoolteacher who had shocked party leaders by winning the 1996 nomination. The William C. Velasquez Institute, which specializes in Hispanic-related voting activity, reported that preliminary figures indicated that Hispanics cast a record 33 percent of the 2002 Democratic primary votes.[38] Spending heavily from his wealth on television advertising, Sanchez easily defeated Dan Morales for the gubernatorial nomination. Tapping into the Hispanic vote, Victor Morales got into a runoff for the Senate nomination with former Dallas mayor Ron Kirk, an African American. Each received about one-third of the vote. But Kirk, who was supported by most party leaders and swamped Victor Morales in fund-raising, won the Senate runoff, when Hispanic voter turnout had fallen off. Both Sanchez and Kirk later lost their general election races to Republicans.

The increased electoral strength of the Hispanic population is borne out in Table 21.2, which compares the number of Hispanic elected officials in Texas

Table *21.2* Latino Elected Officials in Texas, 1974–2006

	1974	1996	2001	2006
Federal	2	5	6	6
State	13	35	36	38
County	102	203	213	276
Municipal	251	536	555	575
Judicial/Law Enforcement	172	323	280	413
School Board	—	536	701	807
Special District	—	51	37	54
Total	540	1,689	1,828	2,169

Sources: Juan A. Sepulveda, Jr., *The Question of Representative Responsiveness for Hispanics*, Cambridge, Mass.: Harvard College, Honors Thesis, March 1985; National Association of Latino Elected and Appointed Officials, *National Roster of Hispanic Elected Officials*, 1996, 2001, 2006.

in 1974 to those holding office in 2006. Some 540 Hispanics held elected office in 1974. By 2006, there were 2,169 Hispanic elected officials, the highest in any state. The marked increase can be attributed to a more equitable apportionment of city, county, and school district political boundaries (see Chapter 22); the growth of the Hispanic population; and increased organizational efforts among Hispanics.

By 2006, only six Hispanics—Texas Supreme Court Justices Raul A. Gonzalez, Alberto R. Gonzales, and David M. Medina; Attorney General Dan Morales; and Texas Railroad Commissioners Tony Garza and Victor Carrillo—had been elected to statewide office in Texas. Victor Morales, a Hispanic schoolteacher from Crandall, a small town in North Texas, generated some excitement and received national publicity when he ran for the U.S. Senate in 1996. Operating on a shoestring budget in the primary, Morales campaigned across Texas in a white pickup truck that became a symbol of his long-shot effort. To the surprise of most political observers, he defeated two incumbent congressmen and a politically experienced lawyer to win the Democratic nomination. But this David-versus-Goliath challenge of Republican Senator Phil Gramm fell short in the general election campaign. Gramm outspent his Democratic challenger 6 to 1 and easily won reelection. As noted above, Victor Morales also ran for the Democratic Senate nomination in 2002 but lost a runoff that year.

African Americans African Americans constitute approximately 11 percent of the state's population, 11 percent of the voting-age population, and 10 to 12 percent of those who vote. Approximately 61 percent of Texas African Americans call themselves Democrats, but 80 to 90 percent of the African American vote is normally cast for Democratic candidates. Voting cohesively as a group, African Americans, like Hispanics, have considerable potential to influence the outcome of both primaries and general elections.

The increased political clout of the African American population is also manifested in the number of African American elected officials (Table 21.3). In 1970, there were only 29 African Americans elected to public office in Texas. The number increased to 196 in 1980 and to 466 in 2002, the latest year for which data were available. Only four African Americans have been elected to statewide office in Texas. They are Railroad Commissioner Michael Williams, Texas Supreme Court Chief Justice Wallace Jefferson, and Texas Supreme Court Justice Dale Wainwright, all Republicans; and former Texas Court of Criminal Appeals

Table *21.3* African American Elected Officials in Texas, 1970–2002

	1970	1980	2002
Federal	—	1	2
State	3	14	17
County	—	5	21
Municipal	16	75	285
Judicial/Law Enforcement	—	21	47
School Board	10	78	94
Special District	—	2	—
Total	29	196	466

Sources: Metropolitan Applied Research Center, Inc. and Voter Regional Council, Inc., *National Roster of Black Elected Officials;* Joint Center for Political and Economic Studies, *National Roster of Black Elected Officials,* 1980, 1998, and 2002.

Judge Morris Overstreet, a Democrat. As noted earlier, former Dallas mayor Ron Kirk, an African American, won the Democratic nomination for the U.S. Senate in 2002 but lost to Republican John Cornyn in the general election.

Women   Historically, the world of Texas politics has been dominated by men. Prior to Ann Richards's election as state treasurer in 1982, only two other women had been elected to statewide office. Richards was elected governor in 1990, and Kay Bailey Hutchison, who had succeeded Richards as state treasurer, was elected to the U.S. Senate in 1993. As governor, Richards also appointed more women to key positions on state boards and commissions than her predecessors.

By 2006, nine women were holding statewide offices in Texas, including Hutchison, who was still in the U.S. Senate; state Comptroller Carole Keeton Strayhorn; state Agriculture Commissioner Susan Combs; Railroad Commissioner Elizabeth Ames Jones; one member of the Texas Supreme Court; and four members of the Texas Court of Criminal Appeals. That same year, there were four women in the state Senate and thirty-three in the Texas House, a significant increase over 1981, when the legislature included only one woman in the Senate and eleven in the House.

Women are playing an increased role in local government as well, and this pattern can be expected to continue. Over the past three decades, the state's three largest cities—Houston, Dallas, and San Antonio—had women mayors. A 2006 survey by the Texas Municipal League counted 198 women mayors (or 16 percent) in the state's 1,211 cities. The 6,021 council members in the cities included 1,588 women, or 26 percent of the total. Of the 254 county judges in 2002, 26 (or 10 percent) were women, and women held 67 (or 6.6 percent) of 1,016 county commissioner posts.[39] Of the 7,207 elected school board trustees in 2008, some 1,835 (or 25 percent) were women. Of the 1,036 school superintendents, 166 (or 16 percent) were women in 2008.[40]

There has been little increase in the number of African American elected officials over the past few years, but there has been an increase in the number of African American women elected to public office. Of the 460 black elected officials in 2001, 30 percent were women.[41]

Elections in Texas

Texans have numerous opportunities to vote, often as many as three or four times a year. Despite various rationales for this election scheduling by the legislature, there is evidence that it contributes to "voter fatigue," reduced voter turnout, and the disproportionate influence of a few individuals in many local and special elections in which voter turnout is usually the lowest. Turnout and interest are highest in the general election in presidential election years but can be abysmally low in elections for school boards and the governing bodies of other single-purpose districts, such as hospital and water districts.

★ **direct primary election**
Selection of candidates for government office through direct election by the voters of a political party.

★ **open primary**
Primary election in which a voter may cast a ballot in either party's primary election.

Primary Elections   Texas uses the **direct primary election**, adopted in 1903, to nominate major party candidates for public office. Administered by the political parties, primaries are held on the second Tuesday in March in even-numbered years. If no candidate receives a majority, the two top vote-getters must face each other in a runoff election. For practical purposes, Texas utilizes an **open primary** in which voters do not register by party. People who vote in one party's primary, however, cannot vote in the other party's runoff election.

Voter turnout in the primary is traditionally lower than in the general election, but the emergence of a two-party system in Texas is producing appreciable changes in participation patterns in the Democratic and Republican primaries (Table 21.4).

Table *21.4* Democratic and Republican Primary Turnout, 1970–2008

Year	Race	Republican Primary Vote	Percent of Voting Age Population	Percent of Registered Voters	Democratic Primary Vote	Percent of Voting Age Population	Percent of Registered Voters
1970	Governor	109,021	1.5%	2.6%	1,011,300	14.1%	24.4%
1972	President/Governor	114,007	1.5	2.9	2,192,903	28.4	56.6
1974	Governor	69,101	0.8	1.3	1,521,306	18.4	28.4
1976	President	356,307	4.0	6.6	1,529,168	17.3	28.5
1978	Governor	158,403	1.7	3.1	1,812,896	19.4	35.8
1980	President	526,769	5.3	9.8	1,377,767	13.8	25.7
1982	Governor	265,794	2.5	4.4	1,318,663	12.3	21.6
1984	President	336,814	3.0	4.9	1,463,449	12.9	21.3
1986	Governor	544,719	4.6	6.9	1,096,552	9.3	13.8
1988	President	1,014,956	8.3	13.1	1,767,045	14.4	22.8
1990	Governor	855,231	6.8	10.3	1,487,260	11.9	18.0
1992	President	797,146	6.2	10.0	1,482,075	11.5	18.6
1994	Governor	557,340	4.3	6.2	1,036,944	7.9	11.5
1996	President	1,019,803	7.4	10.5	921,256	6.7	9.5
1998	Governor	596,839	4.2	5.4	664,532	4.7	6.0
2000	President	1,126,757	7.8	9.7	786,890	5.4	6.9
2002	Governor	622,423	4.0	5.1	1,003,388	6.5	8.2
2004	President	687,615	4.3	5.6	839,231	5.2	6.8
2006	Governor	655,919	3.9	5.2	508,602	3.1	4.0
2008	President	1,362,322	7.7	10.7	2,874,986	16.2	22.5

Source: Secretary of State, Elections Division.

During the period of one-party, Democratic politics, the candidate who won the Democratic primary usually won the general election. From the 1920s through 1970, the rate of turnout for the Democratic primary never exceeded 35 percent of the voting-age population. Over the past 30 years, it has eroded, reflecting the realignment of the state's party system. About 28 percent of the voting-age population (persons 18 or older) voted in the hotly contested Democratic gubernatorial primary in 1972. After that year, turnout in Democratic primaries fell below 20 percent.[42] From 1994 through 2006, it dropped below 10 percent.

But the battle between Hillary Clinton and Barack Obama for the 2008 Democratic presidential nomination sparked a record numerical turnout of more than 2.8 million voters in the Democratic primary that year. Almost 1.4 million voters cast ballots in the Republican primary for a record, total primary turnout of more than 4.2 million.

Prior to 1980, participation in the Republican primaries in Texas never exceeded 5 percent of the voting-age population or 7 percent of the registered voters.[43] That rate has increased somewhat since then, but the percentage of Texans voting in a Republican primary has never reached the level of participation that the Democratic Party experienced when it dominated state politics. Since 1980, the Republicans' share of the voting-age population participating in their primaries has never exceeded 10 percent. One million voters, or 8.3 percent of voting-age Texans, cast ballots in the 1988 Republican presidential primary, when Texan George Bush was on the ballot. That is the highest turnout percentage among registered voters and voting-age population in a Republican primary in Texas so far. More voters participated in the 2008 Republican primary, but the participation rate was lower.

Only a small percentage of the population normally participates in the selection of the political parties' nominees. And those who participate in party primaries tend to be more ideological than the general population. This often prompts candidates to take more extreme positions on issues during their primary campaigns, only to try to move to the center in the general election campaign to appeal to more moderate voters.

General Elections General elections for state and federal offices are held on the first Tuesday after the first Monday in November in even-numbered years. The names of the candidates nominated in the primaries by the two major parties are placed on a ballot, along with the names of Libertarians, other third-party candidates and independents who have submitted petitions bearing the names of eligible registered voters equal to 1 percent of the vote in the last gubernatorial election.

In the 1896 presidential election, the turnout rate was more than 80 percent of the eligible voting-age population, but in 1908, 4 years after the effective date of the poll tax, turnout had fallen to approximately 35 percent. During much of the period from 1910 to 1958, turnout rates in non-presidential elections were less than 20 percent. Presidential elections generated a somewhat higher turnout, but in very few instances did the turnout rate exceed 40 percent of eligible voters.

Turnout rates in presidential elections are considerably higher than in years when the governor and other statewide officials are elected. Since 1970, the average turnout in gubernatorial elections in Texas has been 28.2 percent of the voting age population and 42.7 percent of registered voters. Average turnout in presidential elections has been 45.3 percent of the voting age population and 63.2 percent of registered voters. These turnout rates are higher than turnout in the party primaries, but a significant number of Texans do not participate in either state or national elections (see Table 21.5).

Table 21.5 Turnout in Texas General Elections

Year	Type of Election	Total Registered Voters	Total Votes Cast	Percent Turnout of Voting Age Population	Percent Turnout of Registered Voters
1970	Governor	4,149,250	2,235,847	31.1%	53.9%
1972	President	3,872,462	3,471,281	44.9	66.6
1974	Governor	5,348,393	1,654,984	20.0	30.9
1976	President	6,281,149	4,071,884	46.1	64.8
1978	Governor	5,681,875	2,369,764	25.3	41.7
1980	President	6,639,661	4,541,637	45.6	68.4
1982	Governor	6,414,988	3,191,091	29.8	49.7
1984	President	7,900,167	5,397,571	47.6	68.3
1986	Governor	7,287,173	3,441,460	29.1	47.2
1988	President	8,201,856	5,427,410	44.3	66.2
1990	Governor	7,701,449	3,892,746	31.1	50.6
1992	President	8,439,874	6,154,018	47.6	72.9
1994	Governor	8,641,848	4,396,242	33.6	50.9
1996	President	10,540,678	5,611,644	41.0	53.3
1998	Governor	11,538,235	3,738,078	26.5	32.4
2000	President	12,365,235	6,407,637	44.3	51.8
2002	Governor	12,563,459	4,553,979	29.4	36.2
2004	President	13,098,329	7,410,749	46.1	56.6
2006	Governor	13,074,279	4,399,068	26.4	33.6
2008	President	13,575,062	8,053,036	45.4	59.3

Source: Texas Secretary of State, Elections Division.

City, School Board, and Single-Purpose District Elections   Most local elections, which are nonpartisan, are held in May in odd-numbered years to minimize the convergence of issues in state and local races. Across the state, there are wide variations in the competitiveness of these elections, campaign costs, and turnout. But turnout rates rarely match those in the general election and are often very low.

Special Elections   The legislature can submit constitutional amendments to the voters in a general election or schedule them in a special statewide election. Local governments also conduct special elections for bond issues, local initiatives and referenda, and the recall of public officials. Although these elections occasionally arouse high interest, turnout rates tend to be extremely low. The governor also can call special elections to fill vacancies in certain offices, including legislative and congressional seats.

Extended Absentee Balloting   In 1988 Texas made a major change in the requirements for **absentee (or early) voting** to permit any voter to cast a ballot from the twentieth day to the fourth day prior to an election. Special early voting areas are established, including many at shopping malls and other convenient locations, and voters do not have to provide a reason for casting their ballots early. Consequently, there has been a notable increase in the number of early votes—20 to 30 percent of all votes in some areas. Extended early voting has forced candidates to identify two different sets of voters and develop strategies that require campaigns to "peak" twice. Several other states have followed Texas's lead in eliminating another barrier to political participation.

★ **absentee (or early) voting** Period before the regularly scheduled election date, during which voters are allowed to cast ballots. With recent changes in election law, a person does not have to offer a reason for voting absentee.

Campaign Finances

Campaign Costs   No one knows precisely how much is spent on political campaigns in Texas because there is no single place where all this information is collected. Candidates for state office file campaign finance reports with the state Ethics Commission, but candidates for city councils, county offices, and school boards file reports with the jurisdictions in which they are running. Costs vary across the more than 2,000 governmental units, but modern campaign technology and paid media are extremely expensive, even on the local level. A few recent examples of campaign costs in selected races are illuminating.

In the 2006 election cycle, candidates for state offices reported political contributions totaling $157.6 million. Some $59.6 million was raised by candidates who ran for the Texas House of Representatives. Winners of House races raised, on average, $280,000—for a job that pays $7,200 a year. Some received $1 million or more in campaign donations.[44]

Some $27 million was contributed to state Senate candidates, including some who were not up for election. Senate winners received, on average, $917,000; losers, $287,000.[45] Campaign contributions raised by the winners ranged from $530,000 to $1.9 million. Among the losers, there were many who raised inconsequential funds, but there were at least three candidates who raised over $800,000 and still lost.

Candidates for governor in 2006 reported total campaign contributions of more than $42 million. The winner, incumbent Republican Rick Perry, received almost half of that—$21 million. His three major rivals spent more than $6 million each in the general election.[46] The most expensive gubernatorial race in the state's history was in 2002, when Perry and unsuccessful Democratic challenger

Tony Sanchez spent more than $82 million. Sanchez's expenditures included more than $50 million from his own pocket.[47]

The high costs of campaigns also have spilled over into local elections. It is increasingly common for mayoral candidates in major cities to spend a million dollars or more in their bids for office.[48] Expenditures in city council races in the large cities can easily exceed $100,000. Races for county judge or district clerk in the large counties can cost hundreds of thousands of dollars. Although some candidates can win office with modest campaign budgets, they have become the exception rather than the rule.

There are a number of explanations for the increased costs. The population has increased, requiring more money to be spent to reach more voters. Candidates increasingly rely on the electronic media, which is very costly. So is the increased use of consultants to organize and run political campaigns. Meanwhile, the growing number of interest groups and political action committees (PACs) has made more money available to candidates.

Fund-Raising   Soaring campaign costs have raised considerable concern about campaign fund-raising and contributions in Texas, as they have also nationally (see "Raising Campaign Cash," in Chapter 8). There is concern that elections are being bought and that major campaign contributors are purchasing influence in the policy-making process. Some critics of contemporary campaigns have argued that current practices are a form of legalized bribery, implying that public officials are available to the highest bidder. Other critics have asserted that some officeholders engage in "shaking down" organizations for campaign contributions with implied threats.

Unlike the federal government, Texas places no limits on the amount of money a single individual or political action committee can contribute to most political candidates (see *People in Politics*: "James Leininger: He Doesn't Like to Lose"). The only exceptions in Texas are campaign contribution limits in judicial races, which were imposed by the legislature in 1995. There are no limits on how much a candidate in any race can contribute to his or her own campaign. Large contributions have long played a role in Texas politics, and, over the years, most large contributions have gone to the conservative candidates, both Democratic and Republican.

People in Politics   000 James Leininger: He Doesn't Like to Lose

Wealthy businessperson James Leininger of San Antonio has contributed millions of dollars to conservative candidates and causes, but one of his major unfulfilled goals in 2005 was a state law allowing tax dollars to be spent on vouchers for private school tuition. A voucher proposal was defeated in the Texas House that year, prompting Leininger to target five Republicans who had joined Democratic legislators in voting against the bill. He gave more than $2 million to their opponents in the 2006 Republican primaries, and two of the incumbents were unseated.

Voucher opponents were grateful that three Republicans survived Leininger's cash assault. "I think we've learned that legislators can stand up for neighborhood public schools and against vouchers, despite James Leininger's millions of dollars pumped into elections," said Kathy Miller, president of the Texas Freedom Network, which opposes vouchers and frequently criticizes political activities of the Religious Right. Despite Leininger's spending, a pro-voucher bill never came to a vote during the 2007 legislative session.

Source: Houston Chronicle, March 8, 2006, page 12A.

Table *21.6* Campaign Contributions in 2006 Election Cycle

Economic Interests of Individual, PAC and Business Contributors

Economic Interests	Individuals	PACS/Business	Totals	Rank
Agriculture	$2,165,505	$1,425,626	$3,591,131	12
Communications	1,948,690	2,256,163	4,204,853	10
Computers and Electronics	1,437,552	471,454	1,909,006	15
Construction	9,183,781	2,845,752	12,029,533	6
Energy and Natural Resources	8,446,689	4,467,587	12,914,276	5
Finance	8,905,771	5,504,820	14,410,591	3
Health	5,600,420	5,921,329	11,521,749	7
Ideological and Single Issue	262,267	13,320,758	13,583,025	4
Insurance	1,623,007	1,395,894	3,018,901	13
Labor	105,481	2,311,526	2,417,007	14
Lawyers & Lobbyists	11,662,642	11,709,686	23,372,328	1
Miscellaneous Business	11,883,533	4,095,647	15,979,180	2
Other	1,557,589	2,123,959	3,681,548	11
Real Estate	5,613,614	2,509,340	8,122,954	8
Transportation	3,571,079	1,780,483	5,351,562	9
Unknown	17,770,602	1,395,157	19,165,759	
Totals	$91,738,222	$63,535,181	$155,273,403	

Campaign Contributions by Individuals and Couples

	Total	Industry
Bob & Doylene Perry	$7,167,064	Construction
James & Cecilia Leininger	5,551,966	Health
Fred & Lisa Baron	2,100,821	Law
George & Amanda Ryan	1,390,354	Finance
Charles C. Butt	1,205,921	Food
John Herschell McCall	1,201,545	Miscellaneous
T. Boone Pickens, Jr.	1,200,348	Energy
Harold Simmons	1,129,400	Finance
John M. O'Quinn	1,116,556	Law
David & Martha Alameel	766,300	Health
Total	$22,830,275	

Sources: Texans for Public Justice, "54 More Rich Donors Join the '$100,000 Club,'" *Lobby Watch,* April 19, 2007; Texans for Public Justice, *Money in Politics: A Guide to Money in the 2006 Texas Elections,* September 2007.

Political Action Committees and Fat Cats Just as they have nationally, political action committees (PACs) have increased their importance at the state and local level by bringing sophisticated fund-raising skills to political campaigns. Representing special interest groups or individual companies, PACs collect money from their members and are a ready source of campaign dollars. They are in the business of influencing elections.

More than 100,000 campaign contributions were recorded by candidates in their campaign reports in 2006. Many gave only modest amounts, but the lion's share of the money came from PACs, party committees, and individuals associated with key sectors of the state's economy (see Table 21.6). Ten individuals or couples gave approximately $22.8 million—6.9 percent of all campaign contributions—in the 2006 election cycle (see *People in Politics:* "Bob Perry: Homebuilder and Big Contributor").

Texans for Lawsuit Reform, a PAC that has lobbied successfully for limits on damage lawsuits and judgments against businesses, contributed $3.9 million to candidates. Two-thirds of all contributions in 2006 (some $103 million) came from individuals, corporations or associations linked to twelve sectors of the state's economy.[49]

These figures are cited by those who argue that political power in Texas is concentrated in the hands of a small number of elites.

Attempts at Reform   On the heels of the Sharpstown scandal, in which high-ranking state officials were given preferential treatment in the purchase of stock in an insurance company (see Chapter 22), the legislature enacted a major campaign finance disclosure law in 1973 that, with some changes, is now administered by the state Ethics Commission. Although it did not limit the size of political contributions, for the first time it required candidates to list the addresses as well as the names of donors and the amounts and dates of contributions. It also required PACs contributing to candidates or officeholders to report the sources of their donations, which in the past had usually been hidden. Also for the first time, officeholders were required to file annual reports of their political contributions and expenditures—even during years when they were not seeking reelection—and candidates were required to report contributions and other financial activity that occurred after an election. A candidate also had to formally designate a campaign treasurer before he or she could legally accept political contributions. Campaign finance reform, however, remains a difficult and seemingly endless struggle.

People in Politics   Bob Perry: Homebuilder and Big Contributor

Houston homebuilder Bob Perry tries to maintain a low public profile, but in recent years he has received significant publicity for emerging as one of Texas's most generous political contributors. In 2002, he was the biggest donor to state political candidates and causes, contributing at least $3.8 million during that election cycle, mostly to Republicans. He also was the largest contributor in 2006 with some $4.6 million in donations, which again went primarily to Republicans. Texas Land Commissioner Jerry Patterson, a former state senator and one of many candidates backed by Perry, said the homebuilder had never asked for favors. "He's a reserved, serious and principled guy who has never tried to influence my vote. He truly is a philosophical contributor, who wants to improve the Republican Party," Patterson said.[a]

But Perry's voice obviously is heard. He was believed to be influential in the legislature's creation in 2003 of a new state agency, the Residential Construction Commission, to develop performance standards for builders and discourage lawsuits against builders by unhappy homebuyers. Governor Rick Perry (who isn't related to the homebuilder) appointed an executive of Bob Perry's company to the new agency's board, less than one month after the governor had received a $100,000 contribution from Bob Perry. The homebuilder had contributed more than half a million dollars to Rick Perry since 1997. The governor's office said the appointment wasn't influenced by the contributions, but by the appointee's experience in the homebuilding industry.[b]

[a]*Houston Chronicle*, December 22, 2002, p. 1A.
[b]*Houston Chronicle*, September 30, 2003, p. 1A.

Summary
Who Gets What and How: Interest Groups, Political Parties, and Elections in Texas

Texans engage in a wide range of political behavior and activity. Many individuals are not engaged in the political processes, but there are others who attempt to maximize their political influence and calculate what venue or arena will best serve their interests and goals.

★ People get involved in politics for a variety of reasons, and there is a rich body of research that deals with most facets of political behavior. For many lobbyists, its their business or livelihood. Others are motivated by a cause, a conviction or ideology. Some people derive benefits from their participation in a political campaign, a political protest, or the activities of an interest group. Others pursue power or influence through their social networks, campaign contributions, recruiting candidates, or running for office. And the list of reasons goes on.

★ Pluralist theorists argue that political power in Texas is distributed among a wide range of groups and interests, none of which has a monopoly on the institutions of government. Despite marked differences in the resources of groups, there is sufficient competition and interaction among groups to achieve the goals of a democratic society. Public policy, in this view, reflects the compromise of competing interests.

★ Advocates of elitist theory argue that political power in Texas is concentrated in the hands of a relatively small number of individuals who derive their resources from powerful institutional bases. These institutions are tied together with complex interlocking relationships, and access to their leadership positions is limited. Called the "Texas Establishment," those who monopolized power in the past were predominantly white males from the higher socioeconomic groups. Although there is some competition among these elites, there also is a great deal of consensus. Historically, the Establishment has expressed indifference, if not hostility, toward the interests of labor, minorities, and the lower socioeconomic groups.

★ The interest-group system in Texas was historically dominated by oil and gas, agriculture, and financial institutions. Dramatic changes in the state's economy, the political mobilization of minorities, and the development of public interest groups have produced considerable change in the configuration of this system. More groups now participate in the political process and policy arena, and some of the traditionally dominant groups apparently have experienced a dilution of their power. Policies directed to the interests of the lower socioeconomic groups are modest indications of these changes.

★ Texas was a one-party, Democratic state for most of its political history. But there were major political conflicts between factions within the Democratic Party. This weak party system, based in part on the systematic exclusion of many citizens through discriminatory election laws, contributed to a powerful interest-group system. In Austin, as well as at the local level, the raw power of interest groups is seen in most aspects of the decision-making process, often to the detriment of the general public.

★ There have been significant changes in the state's party structure since the 1960s. One-party Democratic control has been transformed by complex economic, social, and political changes, and Texas is now a two-party state dominated by the Republican Party. Texas voters are divided among Democrats, Republicans, and Independents, but the GOP has an edge. This change, or realignment, is similar to partisan changes in most of the states that were part of the Confederacy.

★ Historically, politics in Texas was configured around class and race, and these two factors are still primary dimensions of partisan alliances.

★ Parties have rarely functioned as highly cohesive, disciplined organizations, either in the electorate or in government. With candidate-centered campaigns, many elected officials act as free agents, aligning with other groups and having little fear of recrimination from the political party.

★ One of the most disturbing aspects of the contemporary Texas political system is the low voter turnout in most elections, despite the elimination of discriminatory election laws, the creation of an extended voting period, and easy voter registration.

★ Although most discriminatory election barriers have been eliminated, racial gerrymandering and at-large election systems continue to generate controversy over the fairness and equity of state and local elections.

★ Over the past 30 years, Hispanics and African Americans have realized substantial gains in the electoral process and increased success in winning election to public office. There has also been a dramatic increase in the number of women elected to public office.

★ With varied election cycles for multiple levels of government, Texans are subjected to a continuous election process, contributing to "voter fatigue" and indifference.

★ The costs of statewide campaigns, as well as many regional and local campaigns, have escalated over the past three decades. While money may not buy public officials, it certainly buys access to them, and it creates the impression that well-organized interests, corporations, and wealthy individuals have a disproportionate influence on policy makers.

★ Despite changes in the partisan lineup, Texans have not expressed a significant shift in their philosophical orientations over the past 20 years. Most Texans still classify themselves as moderate to conservative.

Key Terms

interest groups 718	Religious Right 724	precinct chair 734	state convention 736
pluralism 718	two-party system 724	county executive committee 734	poll tax 738
lobbyists 718	one-party system 724		white primary 738
elitism 719	Jim Crow laws 725	county chair 735	direct primary election 742
"The Establishment" 719	bifactionalism 726	state executive committee 735	open primary 742
single-member district 720	realignment 727	state chair and vice chair 735	absentee (or early) voting 745
political action committee (PAC) 720	gerrymandering 727	precinct convention 735	
tort 720	Voting Rights Act 728		
	precincts 734		

Suggested Readings

Anders, Evan. *Boss Rule in South Texas: The Progressive Era.* Austin, Tex.: University of Texas Press, 1982. Utilizing recent perspectives on political machines, the author provides a comprehensive analysis of political bosses in South Texas counties during the Progressive Era.

Barnes, Ben. *Barn Burning, Barn Building.* Albany, Tex.: Bright Sky Press, 2006. An insider's assessment of party realignment in Texas.

Black, Earl, and Merle Black, *The Rise of Southern Republicanism.* Cambridge, Mass.: Belknap Press, 2002. A comprehensive assessment of Republican realignment in the southern states.

Davidson, Chandler. *Race and Class in Texas Politics.* Princeton, N.J.: Princeton University Press, 1990. An adaptation of V.O. Key's earlier analysis to contemporary Texas politics, this work assesses the dimensions of race and class and addresses the issue of a governing elite.

Dyer, James A., Jan E. Leighley, and Arnold Vedlitz. "Party Identification and Public Opinion in Texas, 1984–1994: Establishing a Competitive Two-Party System," in *Texas Politics,* ed. Anthony Champagne and Edward J. Harpham. New York: W.W. Norton, 1997. A pre-2000 analysis of party realignment in Texas, offering various scenarios for the configuration of party politics in the state.

Elliott, Charles P. "The Texas Trial Lawyers Association: Interest Group Under Siege," in *Texas Politics,* ed. Anthony Champagne and Edward J. Harpham. New York: W.W.

Norton, 1997. Examines the activities of the Texas Trial Lawyers Association, the organization's relationships with like-minded interest groups, and the problems faced battling the dominant business interests in the state.

Garcia, Ignacio. *United We Win: The Rise and Fall of La Raza Unida Party.* Tucson: Mexican American Studies and Research Center at the University of Arizona, 1989. Written from the perspective of an activist, this book is an "interpretive essay" tracing the development of La Raza Unida with the formation of MAYO (Mexican American Youth Organization) to its demise in the early 1980s.

Green, George Norris. *The Establishment in Texas Politics: 1938–1957.* Westport, Conn.: Greenwood Press, 1979. A historical perspective that concludes Texas politics was controlled by corporate elites who, in their reaction to the New Deal, developed and fostered a form of reactionary conservatism permitting predatory interest groups to dominate the electoral and policy processes.

Hrebenar, Robert J., and Clive S. Thomas, eds. *Interest Group Politics in Southern States.* Tuscaloosa, Ala.: University of Alabama Press, 1992. A twelve-state study of interest groups in which the authors conclude that interest groups in Texas have moved from personalized lobbying to information-based communications.

Key, V. O. *Southern Politics*. New York: Vintage Books, 1949. This classic study of southern politics details the politics in each of the states of the Confederacy and provides a historical framework for understanding contemporary political changes in the region.

Knaggs, John R. *Two-Party Texas: The John Tower Era, 1961–1984*. Austin, Tex.: Eakin Press, 1986. An assessment of the early development of the modern Republican Party in Texas.

Lenchner, Paul. "The Party System in Texas," in *Texas Politics*, eds. Anthony Champagne and Edward J. Harpham. New York: W.W. Norton, 1997. In addition to a brief overview of Republican successes since the 1960s, this article raises the issue of the potential of Texas becoming a one-party Republican state.

Navarro, Armando. *La Raza Unida Party: A Chicano Challenge to the U.S. Two-Party Dictatorship*. Philadelphia: Temple University Press, 2000. An assessment of the La Raza Unida Party grounded in third party literature.

San Miguel, Guadalupe, Jr. *Let Them Take Heed: Mexican Americans and the Campaign for Educational Equality in Texas, 1910–1981*. Austin, Tex.: University of Texas Press, 1987. Describes Mexican American organizational efforts to promote educational equality over a 70-year period.

Suggested Web Sites

Texas Ethics Commission   www.ethics.state.tx.us

Under Texas law, individuals and organizations that lobby the legislature are required to file with the Ethics Commission. This source provides names of registered lobbyists and their clients, as well as lobbyists organized by legislative subject matter. Candidates and political action committees are also required to file their financial statements with this agency.

Texas Democratic Party   www.txdemocrats.org

This site provides a range of information on state party organization, county chairs, affiliate organizations, candidates, and policy issues.

Republican Party of Texas   www.texasgop.org

In addition to information about the Republican Party and links to other state party organizations, this site provides information about Republican candidates, the party platform, and a calendar of party events.

Green Party of Texas   www.txgreens.org

A third party committed to social justice, nonviolence, ecology, and grass-roots democracy.

Libertarian Party of Texas   www.tx.lp.org

Libertarians tend to advocate a very limited role of governments, and they are particularly vocal in supporting "the right of individuals to live in whatever manner they choose, so long as they do not interfere with the right of others."

The Pew Research Center for the People and the Press
www.people-press.org

This research center produces numerous studies of public opinion and media habits of Americans.

National Institute on Money in State Politics
www.followthemoney.org

This is a nonpartisan organization that provides information on campaign finances at a state level. For the state of Texas, data is taken from the records of the Ethics Commission.

Center for Responsive Politics   www.opensecrets.org

This nonpartisan research center, located in Washington, D.C., tracks money in politics with an emphasis on its effect on elections and public policy. Most of the data generated by this organization focuses on candidates running for national offices.

Project Vote Smart   www.vote-smart.org

Project Vote Smart is a national nonpartisan organization that tracks the performance of approximately 40,000 national and state elected officials and candidates. Information on policy positions, campaign finances and expenditures, and job performance is provided about the governor and state legislators.

Secretary of State   www.sos.state.tx.us

In addition to compiling county election data for state offices, this office provides information on election laws, election procedures, county officials, and a program for voter education (Project V.O.T.E.).

Texans for Public Justice   www.tpj.org

"A nonpartisan, nonprofit research organization which tracks the influence of money and corporate power in Texas politics."

22 THE TEXAS LEGISLATURE

❝ We look first for the organs authorized to lay down general rules in the name of the body politic. In democratic countries the most conspicuous organ relatively specialized to the prescribing function is a Congress or Parliament (or State Legislature). ❞

Harold Lasswell

Chapter *Outline*

✓ Think About Politics

1. Does it make sense to limit the Texas legislature to 140 days every 2 years?
   YES ◯ NO ◯

2. Would our state representatives and senators do a better job if we paid them more than their current salary of $7,200 per year?
   YES ◯ NO ◯

3. Should candidates for the Texas state legislature be limited in the amount of money they can spend to get elected?
   YES ◯ NO ◯

4. Should Texas state legislators be limited in the number of terms they can hold office?
   YES ◯ NO ◯

5. Should the legislature be allowed to borrow money to pay for current budget expenditures?
   YES ◯ NO ◯

6. Do the men and women making laws in Texas really care about you?
   YES ◯ NO ◯

7. Should members of the Texas legislature be required to publicly identify all groups or individuals who lobby them on legislation?
   YES ◯ NO ◯

Even a part-time legislature still has considerable power over the laws that affect your life. And your interests often compete with those of other people and groups.

The Texas Legislature: A Time of Change

The Republican takeover of the Texas House of Representatives in 2003 was a watershed event in state politics. It marked the first GOP majority of that body since the 1870s and assured Tom Craddick's election as the first Republican House speaker since Reconstruction. Moreover, it gave Republicans control of all major power points in the statehouse because they also maintained their majority in the state Senate and their hold on the governor's office. The conservative GOP agenda dominated legislative deliberations, including the crucial balancing of a new state budget. Despite a $10 billion revenue shortfall, Republican leaders held the line against higher state taxes, drawing applause from many middle-income and wealthy Texans. But lawmakers imposed spending cuts that reduced the availability of health care and other services for low-income and disadvantaged Texans and further widened the divide between the privileged and the underprivileged.

Legislative partisanship also increased in 2003, thanks primarily to a bitter fight over congressional redistricting that took the regular session and three special sessions to resolve. The battle over redrawing district lines to elect more Republicans from Texas to the U.S. Congress focused national attention on the legislature when Democratic lawmakers, on two separate occasions, fled to neighboring states to shut down the legislative process and block action on redistricting bills. Eventually, the Republicans prevailed.

But despite the GOP victories, Craddick's leadership was soon under attack, not only from Democrats, but also from Republican House members unhappy with his autocratic style. Within a few years, Craddick was fighting to hang on to power.

These recent legislative experiences reflect some of the enormous social, political, and economic changes that have occurred in Texas during the past generation. Forty years ago, a rural-dominated legislature showed little concern for the problems of urban areas and minority groups. Operating within the context of one-party Democratic control and an interest group system dominated by oil, finance, and agriculture, legislative leaders tied to conservative factions in the Democratic Party pursued selected policies that benefited those sectors of the Texas economy.

Today, Texas is the country's second most populous state and is more than 80 percent urban. The ethnic and racial characteristics of its population have changed, and still more changes are projected in its social composition. Texas is now dominated by the Republican Party, its economy is diversifying, and there are more demands today on the legislature than in the past. The issues and policy questions that confront lawmakers are more complex, and the special interests demanding attention are more numerous and diverse.

Despite these major demographic and political changes, however, lawmakers still have to operate under outdated constitutional restrictions—including strict limits on when they can meet—that were written for a rural state in a bygone era.

Legislative Functions

The legislature, whose members are elected from districts throughout Texas, is the chief policy-making branch of state government. Its basic role is similar to that of Congress at the federal level, although there are major differences between the two institutions. The Texas legislature performs a variety of functions, but its primary task is to decide how conflicts between competing groups and interests are to be resolved, that is, who gets what, when, and how. Although often taken for granted, this orderly, institutionalized process of conflict management and resolution is critical to a stable political system.[1]

Explaining Differences in State Laws

Enacting Laws Every 2 years, the legislature enacts several hundred laws governing our behavior; allocating resources, benefits, and costs; and defining the duties of those institutions and bureaucrats responsible for putting these laws into effect. From local legislation that affects only a city or county to general statewide policies and proposals for constitutional amendments, there are literally thousands of ideas advanced for new laws every legislative session. The legislative arena includes a wide range of players in addition to legislators, and law-making requires compromise and accommodation of competing ideas and interests.

Budgets and Taxes The legislature establishes programs providing a variety of public services and sets priorities through the budgetary process. It sets the budgets for the governor, the bureaucracy, and the state courts. It decides whether state taxes should be increased, how high they should be increased, and how the tax burden should be distributed. Indirectly, its actions affect local tax rates as well.

Overseeing State Agencies Hundreds of laws are passed each legislative session, and the legislature assigns to specific state agencies and local governments the responsibility of carrying out the laws on a day-to-day basis. It is ultimately the legislature's responsibility to make sure agencies and bureaucrats are doing what they are charged with by law, and this review, or "oversight," process is achieved through legislative budget hearings, other committee investigations, and program audits. The Senate further influences policy by confirming or rejecting the governor's appointees to hundreds of state boards and commissions that administer public programs.

Educating the Public   The 181 members of the Texas Legislature certainly do not speak with one voice, and on major policy issues it is inevitable that there will be a variety of opinions and proposed solutions. Individual lawmakers try to inform the public about their own actions and the collective actions of the legislature. They use speeches, letters to constituents, news releases, telephone calls, newsletters, Web sites, e-mails, and other techniques to explain the legislative process, substantive policy issues, and their views on issues.

Representing the Public   The legislature is a representative body whose members are chosen in free elections. This process provides legitimacy to legislative actions and decisions. People may disagree over how "representative" the legislature is in terms of race, ethnicity, gender, or class. And many Texans may be indifferent toward or ignorant about public policy. But successful lawmakers must demonstrate concern for the attitudes and demands of their constituents. Legislators use many methods to learn how their constituents feel, including public opinion polls, questionnaires, phone calls, town hall meetings, and personal visits with people.

Institutionalization of the Texas Legislature

As noted at the beginning of this chapter, the Texas Legislature has undergone significant institutional changes over the past 130 years. Some changes have been due to external factors, such as the development of a two-party system within the electorate, changes in the state's interest-group system, and complex social and economic problems. Other changes were internal. They included the increased tenure of the membership, changing career and leadership patterns, expanded workload, the development and enforcement of complex rules and procedures, and the emergence of partisan divisions. Political scientists describe these developments as **institutionalization**.[2]

Institutionalization varies throughout the fifty states. Some state legislatures are highly professional; others are not (see Figure 22.1). In some states, salaries are

★ **institutionalization**
In the context of political science, the development of a legislative body into a formally structured system with stable membership, complex rules, expanded internal operations, and the delineation of staff functions.

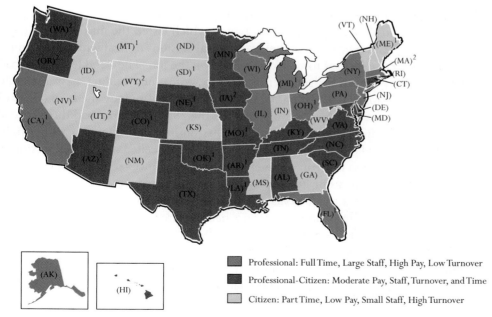

Figure *22.1*

How Professional Is the Texas Legislature?

Several criteria determine how professional or amateur a legislature is considered. Texas falls somewhere in between.

Sources: National Conference of State Legislatures, "The Term Limited States," February 2006, www.ncsl.org/programs/legismgt/aboutstates/htm; "Three Kinds of State Legislatures," *State Legislatures,* 30 (July/August 2004): p. 7; James D. King, "Changes in Professionalism in U.S. State Legislatures," *Legislative Studies Quarterly* 25 (May 2000): pp. 327–43.

■ Professional: Full Time, Large Staff, High Pay, Low Turnover
■ Professional-Citizen: Moderate Pay, Staff, Turnover, and Time
■ Citizen: Part Time, Low Pay, Small Staff, High Turnover

[1] States currently with term limits (15 total).
[2] States in which term limits have been repealed by legislative or court action (6 total).

high, turnover is limited, and legislative service becomes a career. Similarly, some legislatures have developed sophisticated staff and support services. By contrast, in other legislatures, members are poorly paid, turnover is high, legislative service is regarded as a part-time activity, and support services are limited. The Texas Legislature falls somewhere between those legislatures that can be classified as highly professional and those that can be classified as amateur or citizen law-making bodies.[3] The institutionalization process has produced a more professional legislature in Texas, and this development is likely to continue in the future.

The Organization and Composition of the Texas Legislature

Following the oppressive efforts of Governor Edmund J. Davis and the Reconstruction Republicans to centralize power (see Chapter 20), the delegates to the constitutional convention in 1875 were distrustful, even fearful, of the excesses and abuses of big government. They created a part-time, **bicameral legislature** that included a 31-member Senate and a 150-member House of Representatives, and they placed strong restrictions on it. All other states also have bicameral legislatures except Nebraska, which has only one law-making body with 49 members. The sizes of other state senates range from 20 in Alaska to 67 in Minnesota; houses of representatives vary in size from 40 in Alaska to 400 in New Hampshire.[4]

★ bicameral legislature
Law-making body, such as the Texas Legislature, that includes two chambers.

★ regular session
One-hundred-forty-day period in the odd-numbered years in which the legislature meets and can consider and pass laws on any issue or subject.

★ special session
Legislative session that can be called at any time by the governor. This session is limited to 30 days and to issues or subjects designated by the governor.

Legislative Sessions   To curb lawmakers' power, the Texas constitutional framers limited **regular sessions** of the legislature to a maximum of 140 days every 2 years but gave the governor the authority to call **special sessions** when necessary. Lawmakers convene in regular session on the second Tuesday of January in odd-numbered years. Special sessions are limited to 30 days each and to subjects submitted by the governor, but there is no limit on the number of special sessions a governor can call.

There have been periods of frequent special sessions. From midsummer of 1986 through midsummer of 1987, for example, during a lingering budgetary crisis spawned by a depressed oil industry, the legislature convened for its regular 140-day session plus four special sessions, two of which lasted the maximum 30 days. The 71st legislature in 1989–90 held six special sessions to deal with school funding and medical expenses for workers injured on the job. The 72nd legislature had two special sessions in the summer of 1991 to write a new budget, pass a tax bill, make major changes in the criminal justice system, and redraw the boundaries of congressional districts. And, as noted earlier, the 78th legislature had three special sessions in the summer and early fall of 2003 during a protracted, partisan fight over congressional redistricting. Governor Rick Perry called one special session in spring 2004 and two more in summer 2005 to try to lower school property taxes and change the education funding system, but all three were unsuccessful. The legislature finally met those goals in still another special session in spring 2006, but only after the Texas Supreme Court had declared the school finance system unconstitutional and given lawmakers a deadline.

Some state officials and government experts believe that the Texas Legislature should have annual regular sessions, at least for budgetary purposes. Only six other state legislatures do not. The change, however, would require a constitutional amendment.

Terms of Office and Qualifications   Article III of the Texas Constitution contains the provisions pertaining to the structure, membership, and selection of the

Texas Legislature. Representatives serve 2-year terms, and senators are elected to 4-year, staggered terms. A senator has to be a qualified voter, at least 26 years old, a resident of Texas for 5 years preceding his or her election, and a resident of the district from which he or she is elected for at least one year. A representative must be a qualified voter, at least 21 years old, a Texas resident for 2 years, and a resident of the district represented for 1 year. There is no limit on the number of terms an individual can serve in the legislature.

Pay and Compensation   Members of both the House and the Senate and their presiding officers have a base pay of $7,200 per year. This figure is set by the state constitution and can be raised only with voter approval. This is one of the lowest legislative pay levels in the country and was last increased in 1975 by a constitutional amendment that also set lawmakers' per diem, or personal expense allowance, at $30 a day while they were in session. The House and the Senate authorize additional expense allowances for members to cover staff salaries and other costs of operating legislative offices.

In 1991, Texas voters approved a constitutional amendment creating a state Ethics Commission that could recommend legislative pay raises to the voters and change legislative per diem on its own. The commission has never recommended a pay raise, but it has increased per diem several times. The allowance has been $125 per day for recent sessions.

By 2008, only Texas, Alabama, New Hampshire, and Rhode Island had limits on legislative pay that could be changed only by constitutional amendment. Compensation commissions now recommend legislative pay levels in some states, and legislatures in other states set their own salaries, often with the approval of voters.[5] In 2008, legislative pay ranged from a high of $113,098 a year in California, where lawmakers set their own salaries and are considered a full-time legislature, to a low of $200 a year in New Hampshire, which has annual sessions but a constitutional limit on salaries[6] (see *What Do You Think?:* "How Much Is a Legislator Worth?").

Physical Facilities   The House chamber and representatives' offices have traditionally been located in the west wing of the state Capitol, and the Senate

What Do You *Think?*

How Much Is a Legislator Worth?

Supporters of higher legislative pay in Texas say a raise is only fair because legislative service has become much more than a part-time job for many lawmakers, particularly during periods of frequent special sessions. They argue that the present low compensation level effectively restricts legislative service to wealthy individuals or those who have law practices or who own businesses in which their partners or employees can help take up the slack while they are in Austin. They believe higher pay would broaden the potential pool from which legislators are drawn—and perhaps improve the prospects for quality—by encouraging more salaried working people to run for legislative office.

The outside personal income of many legislators obviously does suffer while they are in office, but legislative service can enhance business and professional connections. Critics of higher legislative pay also note that candidates, many of whom spend thousands of dollars to get elected to the legislature, know the pay level before they run for the office. And Texas lawmakers have provided themselves with one of the best legislative retirement plans in the country. Retirement is computed on the basis of state district judges' salaries, which legislators periodically raise, thereby increasing their own retirement benefits as well. Many former legislators receive pensions that are much larger than their paychecks were while they were in office.

Figure 22.2

Corridors of Power

The legislative chambers and the governor's office are located on the second floor of the state Capitol, while committee meeting rooms and the offices of legislators and legislative support services are dispersed throughout the Capitol complex and in state office buildings nearby.

chamber and senators' offices in the east wing (see Figure 22.2). The pink granite building was completed in 1888, but the growth of state government and periodic renovations created a hodgepodge of cramped legislative offices. After one visitor died in a fire behind the Senate chamber in 1983, it also became obvious that the building had become a firetrap. So in 1990 the state launched a $187 million Capitol restoration and expansion project that included a four-story underground addition to the building. Legislative committee hearing rooms and many lawmakers' offices were relocated from the main building to the underground extension, which is connected to the original Capitol and nearby office buildings by tunnels.

When the legislature is in session, access to the floor of each chamber on the second floor of the Capitol is restricted to lawmakers, certain state officials, some staff members, and accredited media representatives. The galleries, to which

It Cost 3 Million Acres

Completed in 1888 and paid for by 3 million acres of land in the Texas Panhandle, Texas's Capitol has a Renaissance Revival architectural style. Recently renovated, it houses the governor's office and meeting chambers for the House of Representatives and the Senate.

the public is admitted, overlook the chambers from the third floor of the Capitol. In both the House and Senate chambers, members have desks facing the presiding officer's podium, which, in turn, is flanked by desks of the clerical staff. Unlike the U.S. Congress, where seating is arranged by party affiliation, seats are assigned to state legislators by seniority.

Membership and Careers   In 1971, the Texas Legislature was overwhelmingly white, male, and Democratic. There were two African Americans in the 150-member House and one in the 31-member Senate. The one African American senator was also the only woman in the Senate. She was Barbara Jordan of Houston, who 2 years later would begin a distinguished career in the U.S. Congress. Frances Farenthold of Corpus Christi was the only woman in the House. She was a reform-minded lawmaker who was often referred to as "the Den Mother of the Dirty Thirty," a coalition of liberal Democrats and conservative Republicans who challenged the power of Speaker Gus Mutscher while a major political scandal in which he was involved was unfolding. In 1972, Farenthold ran a strong race for governor in the Democratic primary but lost a runoff election to Uvalde rancher Dolph Briscoe. There were eleven Hispanic members of the House and only one Hispanic senator in 1971. Only twelve legislators were Republicans—ten in the House and two in the Senate.

By 2007, changing political patterns and attitudes, redrawn political boundaries, and court-ordered single-member districts for urban House members had significantly altered the composition of the legislature (see Table 22.1). That year, Republicans had a 20–11 majority in the Senate. The Senate also had two African American members, six Hispanics, and four women. The House in 2007 had an 81–69 Republican majority, a smaller Republican majority than the 88–62 margin the GOP had in 2003, when it had gained its first House majority of modern times. The House in 2007 included fourteen African Americans, thirty-one Hispanics, one Asian American, and thirty-three women. Representation from the urban and suburban areas of the state had grown, reflecting the population shifts accommodated by redistricting.

Business has been the dominant occupation of legislators serving in recent years, followed by law. The House in 2007 included one pharmacist, one automobile dealer, a drive-in restaurant owner, and a hearing aid specialist. One senator was a family physician, one was an anesthesiologist, and one was a retired firefighter. Like the House, the Senate also had a pharmacist among its membership.

Table *22.1*   Legislative Face Has Changed Comparative Profile of Texas Legislators, 1971–2007

	House				Senate			
	1971	**1981**	**2001**	**2007**	**1971**	**1981**	**2001**	**2007**
Democrats	140	112	78	69	29	24	15	11
Republicans	10	38	72	81	2	7	16	20
Males	149	139	120	117	30	30	27	27
Females	1	11	30	33	1	1	4	4
Hispanics	11	17	28	31	1	4	7	6
African Americans	2	13	14	14	1	0	2	2
Asian Americans				1				
Anglos	137	120	108	104	29	27	22	23

Source: Texas House and Senate rosters, 1971, 1981, 2001, 2007.

Senators' ages ranged from 41 to 69, with an average age of 54. The age range for members of the House was 26 to 80, with an average age of 51.

Various career patterns lead to election to the legislature.[7] Lawmakers include former members of city councils and school boards, former prosecutors, former legislative aides, and long-time Democratic and Republican party activists. Eighteen of the thirty-one senators in 2007 had previously served in the House. Many first-term legislators, however, arrive in Austin with relatively little political experience (See *People in Politics*: "Melissa Noriega, Valerie Corte, and Cheri Isett: Wartime Legislators").

Legislative Turnover   Compared to other states, turnover in the Texas legislature is moderate. Relatively few individuals who serve can be considered career legislators. Only six senators and nine House members entered the 2005 regular session with 20 or more years of legislative service. The average legislative experience in the Senate was 13 years; House members had served an average of 8 years. In addition to the effects of redistricting of legislative seats every 10 years, turnover is due to the low pay and the personal costs involved in running for public office. While in session, many legislators lose income from their regular sources of employment. Political ambition is also a factor. Many lawmakers who want to move up the political ladder serve only a few terms in the Texas House before running for the Texas Senate, the U.S. Congress, or other state or local offices. Other legislators quit after a few sessions to become lobbyists.

Five senators, including three of the chamber's more senior members, ended their legislative careers in 2006, taking with them a cumulative 112 years of experience in the House and the Senate. Democrats Ken Armbrister of Victoria and Gonzalo Barrientos of Austin and Republican Jon Lindsay of Houston voluntarily retired. Democrat Frank Madla of San Antonio was unseated in his party's primary, and Republican Todd Staples of Palestine was elected state agriculture commissioner. In the House, former speaker Pete Laney, a Democrat, also retired after 34 years in the legislature. In addition, twenty-six other House members did not return for the 2007 legislative session.[8] Madla died in a fire at his home in San Antonio a few months after leaving office, and Armbrister joined Governor Rick Perry's staff as legislative liaison for the 2007 session.

People in Politics   Melissa Noriega, Valerie Corte, and Cheri Isett: Wartime Legislators

The wars in Afghanistan and Iraq interrupted the political careers of three Texas legislators in 2005 and 2006, but they appointed their wives to temporarily step in while they were overseas.

Melissa Noriega of Houston served in the Texas House during the 2005 regular session after her husband, Representative Rick Noriega, an officer in the Texas Army National Guard, was called up for 14 months of active duty in Afghanistan.

Representative Frank Corte of San Antonio, a Marine reservist, was on duty in Iraq, and Representa-

tive Carl Isett of Lubbock, a Navy reservist, was on assignment in Kuwait, during a 2006 special session on school finance. Corte appointed his wife, Valerie, and Isett designated his wife, Cheri, to serve in their absence.

"It's nothing more than another military wife stepping up to the plate and doing what has to be done to get the job done," said Valerie Corte, an assistant bank vice president.

Source: San Antonio Express–News, February 3, 2006, p. 2B.

Representation and Redistricting

Many European legislatures use a system called proportional representation, in which legislative seats are allocated on the basis of each party's percentage of the total vote in an election. By contrast, the Texas legislature and most other American legislatures allocate seats geographically on the basis of **single-member districts**. The long legal and political battles over apportionment and redistricting address some fundamental questions of who should be represented and how they should be represented (see Chapter 10).

The Texas Constitution of 1876 provided that the legislature redraw state representative and senatorial districts every 10 years, "at its first session after the publication of each United States decennial census," to reflect changing population patterns. But members of earlier rural-dominated legislatures were reluctant to apportion the legislative seats equitably to reflect the increased urbanization of the state, and inequities grew. In 1948, Texas voters approved a constitutional amendment creating the **Legislative Redistricting Board** to carry out redistricting responsibilities if the legislature failed to do so during the required session. The board includes the lieutenant governor, the speaker of the house, the attorney general, the comptroller, and the land commissioner.

But for many more years, the urban areas of the state were still denied equality in representation. In 1960, House districts ranged in size from 23,062 to 155,393 persons, and Senate districts, 131,970 to 1,243,158 persons.[9] With these disparities in population, it was possible for approximately 33 percent of the state's population to elect a majority of both the Texas House and the Senate.[10] And rural legislators tended to neglect urban problems.

Equality in redistricting finally came to Texas as a result of federal court intervention. In 1962, the U.S. Supreme Court, in the case of *Baker v. Carr*, applied the principle of equality to congressional districts. Then, in the case of *Reynolds v. Sims* (1964), the court held that state legislative districts had to be apportioned on the "one person, one vote" principle. Litigation in 1965 (*Kilgarlin v. Martin*) extended this ruling to Texas, and the "reapportionment revolution" was to produce dramatic changes in the composition and structure of the Texas Legislature.[11] To a large degree, the increased representation of minorities and Republicans in Texas's lawmaking body is a result of the legal and political redistricting battles.

The Texas Senate has always been elected by single-member districts, and after the 1970 Census, the application of the "equality principle" to the Senate resulted in districts that were comparable in size. The issues of racial and partisan gerrymandering—the practice of drawing lines to favor a particular individual or group (see Chapters 10 and 21)—were still to be resolved through subsequent litigation and federal legislation.

Rural members of the Texas House were also elected from single-member districts, but in the urban counties that had been allocated more than one representative, the elections were held in multimember districts. Each candidate for a House seat in an urban area had to run for election countywide, a practice that put ethnic and political minorities at a disadvantage because their votes were diluted by the dominant Anglo and Democratic populations.

In 1972, a three-judge federal court ruled that multimember districts in Dallas and Bexar counties were unconstitutional because they diluted the voting strength of African Americans in Dallas and Hispanics in Bexar. Coincidentally, the **at-large districts** diluted the voting strength of Republicans in both counties.

Despite the fact that 50 percent of Bexar County's population was Hispanic, under the at-large election system only one Hispanic from Bexar had

★ **single-member district**
System in which a legislator, city council member, or other public official is elected from a specific geographic area.

★ **Legislative Redistricting Board**
A board created by constitutional amendment charged to redistrict the Texas Legislature if it is not accomplished in the regular session following the release of the census.

★ **at-large district**
Legislative or other political district, sometimes called a multimember district because two or more officials are elected from it, that includes an entire county, city, or other political subdivision.

served in the Texas House in 1971. Dallas County, which had a large African American population, had only one African American House member. Single-member districts in Harris County had been drawn by the Legislative Redistricting Board in 1971, and after the U.S. Supreme Court upheld the lower court's decision regarding Dallas and Bexar counties, multimember legislative districts were soon eliminated in all other urban counties. After 1975, the U.S. Congress put Texas under the provisions of the federal Voting Rights Act, which prohibits the dilution of minority voting strength, requires clearance in advance of redistricting plans by the Department of Justice, and gives African Americans and Hispanics an effective weapon to use in challenging a redistricting plan in court.

At the beginning of the twenty-first century, however, minorities believed their fight for equal representation was still far from over. The Voting Rights Act was under attack by conservatives. The U.S. Supreme Court, in "reverse discrimination" cases from Texas and Georgia, ruled that some congressional districts had been illegally gerrymandered to elect minority candidates. And in another case from Georgia, the high court held in 2003 that states have the right to determine how best to draw legislative and congressional districts to protect minority voters.[12]

Texas Republicans scored huge redistricting victories in 2001, after the legislature failed to redraw its own districts during that year's regular session. Under the state constitution, the task then fell to the five statewide elected officials, four of whom were Republicans, on the Legislative Redistricting Board. The panel drew new legislative maps that helped increase Republican strength in the 31-member Senate to 19 GOP senators. It also enabled Republicans to capture their first majority of modern times in the 150-member House. With legislative candidates running under the new plan in the 2002 elections, the GOP increased its strength in the House from 72 seats to 88 seats, a margin that cleared the way for state representative Tom Craddick of Midland, a Republican, to be elected speaker after the regular session convened in 2003. The GOP takeover of the Texas House also gave Republicans the opportunity to redraw the boundaries for Texas's congressional districts later that year. Republicans prevailed after a bitter partisan fight that included two walkouts by Democratic legislators. The new congressional map gave Republicans a 21–11 majority among members of the U.S. Congress elected from Texas in 2004, ending the congressional careers of several Democratic incumbents. Most of the plan was later upheld by the U.S. Supreme Court. The court, however, ordered the redrawing of some district lines in South Texas to protect minority voting rights. Those changes led to the unseating of a Republican incumbent in 2006, reducing the GOP majority to 20–12 (see *Politics Up Close*: "Redistricting: Partisans at War").

Legislative Leadership

The highly institutionalized leadership structure found in the U.S. Congress (see Chapter 10) is only now beginning to emerge in the Texas Legislature—and to only a limited extent. Until recent years, the Texas Legislature was dominated by a small group of Democratic lawmakers. With no significant party opposition or minority representation for much of the state's history, legislative leadership was highly personal and dependent on the political relationships between the presiding officers and key legislators. Recent Republican growth in the statehouse, however, is beginning to force changes.

Politics Up Close   **Redistricting: Partisans at War**

The contentious, nationally publicized fight over congressional redistricting in 2003 was not the Texas Legislature's finest hour. But the drama of Democratic lawmakers fleeing across state lines to shut down legislative business in Austin, the bitter partisan rhetoric, and the persistence of the eventual Republican victors vividly illustrated the huge political stakes that were involved.

The Republican takeover of the Texas House in 2003 gave the GOP control of state government, but Democrats still held a 17–15 edge among members of the U.S. Congress elected from Texas. The lines for congressional districts had been redrawn to reflect new census data in 2001 by a federal court, not by the legislature, because the Texas House, which still had a Democratic majority in 2001, couldn't agree on a new map with the Republican-dominated Senate. Once Republicans had control of both legislative chambers, the then-Republican leader of the U.S. House, Congressman Tom DeLay, began urging Texas Republican leaders to redraw the congressional lines to favor more Republican candidates. But a redistricting bill died late in the regular legislative session that spring when more than fifty Democratic members of the Texas House fled to Ardmore, Oklahoma, to break a House quorum and prevent the body from conducting business for 4 days—long enough to miss a deadline for action on the redistricting measure. The Democrats, outnumbered 88–62, didn't have enough votes in the House to defeat the bill outright, but they had enough members to shut down work, because a quorum required two-thirds of the members to be present. The Democrats left the state in order to avoid being arrested by state troopers and forced to return to the Capitol. In their absence, Speaker Tom Craddick and the remaining members had placed a "call" on the House, authorizing the sergeant-at-arms to enlist the aid of law enforcement officers to round up the missing members.

Republican leaders, most notably DeLay and Governor Rick Perry, didn't give up. Perry called the legislature back into a 30-day special session in June to tackle redistricting again. This time, Democrats didn't bolt, and the House easily approved the bill. But the measure died in the Senate, where Democratic senators used the two-thirds rule to block action on it. That traditional procedure required two-thirds of the senators to approve debate on any legislation, and Republicans, although they were in the majority, didn't constitute two-thirds of the body. At the end of the first special session, Lieutenant Governor David Dewhurst, a Republican who earlier had been reluctant to force a vote on redistricting, announced that he would bypass the two-thirds requirement during a second special session. That prompted eleven Democratic senators to fly to Albuquerque, New Mexico, breaking a Senate quorum, only

minutes before Perry issued a proclamation calling the second special session. The Democrats remained holed up in New Mexico for more than a month, outlasting the entire second session. The only Democratic senator who didn't flee was Ken Armbrister of Victoria, who represented a strongly Republican district.

While the national media listened and watched, the Democrats in Albuquerque and the Republicans in Austin exchanged a barrage of partisan charges and countercharges. The dissident Democrats—who included nine minorities and two Anglos who represented predominantly minority districts—accused the Republicans of trying to redraw congressional districts to dilute the voting strength of Hispanics and African Americans. "This is a shameful return to the days of the Jim Crow laws designed to prevent electoral participation of minorities in the South," said state senator Leticia Van de Putte of San Antonio, chair of the Senate Democratic Caucus. Dewhurst and the Republican senators denied the charges. They said redistricting would enhance minority voting strength. And they argued that Republicans, who had a majority in Texas, were entitled to a majority of congressional seats from the state.

The stalemate finally ended when one of the Democrats, state senator John Whitmire of Houston, returned to Texas, announcing that he would continue the fight on the Senate floor. Because Whitmire's return restored the Senate's two-thirds quorum, the remaining dissidents returned as well. Perry called a third special session in September, and Republican majorities in the House and the Senate approved different versions of a redistricting map. Final approval was delayed for several days because House and Senate Republicans, ironically, continued to fight among themselves over a handful of districts. The main hangup was over West Texas, where Speaker Craddick insisted that his hometown, Midland, get a congressional district it could dominate. In the end, Craddick got his wish, but not before DeLay visited Austin to personally help negotiate between House and Senate members of the conference committee that drew the final map.

The third special session ended on October 12, and Perry quickly signed the new redistricting plan. Democrats filed suit in federal court to block the law, but a three-judge federal panel approved it in time for the 2004 elections, which gave Republicans 21 of Texas's 32 congressional seats. Ruling in 2006, the United States Supreme Court upheld most of the plan. The high court, however, held that one South Texas district was unconstitutional because it didn't protect the voting rights of Hispanics. Subsequent revisions in the plan led to the election defeat of one Republican congressman in 2006, trimming the Republican edge in the Texas congressional delegation to 20–12.

Source: Houston Chronicle, August 14, 2003, p. 25A.

★ **speaker**
Presiding officer of the
House of Representatives.

House Leadership

The presiding officer of the House of Representatives is the **speaker**, who is elected by the House from among its membership. With the long tenures of Gib Lewis and his immediate predecessor in the speaker's office, Bill Clayton, there was not a contested speaker's race between 1975 and 1991. Lewis's decision not to seek reelection in 1992 prompted several House members to announce their candidacy for the post. But veteran Democratic Representative James E. "Pete" Laney, a farmer/businessman from Hale Center, secured the support of the necessary majority of House members several weeks before the 1993 legislature convened, and his election on the opening day of the session was unopposed.

Laney served five terms as speaker and, although he was a Democrat, enjoyed the support of many Republican House members. Continuing a bipartisan tradition, he appointed several Republicans to chair House committees. But Republicans, after winning a strong majority of House seats in the 2002 elections, elected state representative Tom Craddick, a Republican from Midland, to succeed Laney as presiding officer in 2003. Laney, who had won reelection to his West Texas district in 2002, remained in the House, becoming the first former speaker in years to return to a seat on the House floor after having been presiding officer. Laney also was reelected from his district in 2004 but didn't seek reelection in 2006, ending a 34-year legislative career.

It is illegal for a speaker candidate to make outright promises in return for members' support. But, continuing a tradition, Craddick gave his key supporters choice leadership positions when the new speaker exercised one of his most significant, formal powers and made his committee assignments. Legislators know that the earlier they hop onto a winning bandwagon in a speaker's race, the better chance they will have of getting their preferred committee assignments or the opportunity to advance their legislative programs. Sometimes, however, choosing the winning candidate is difficult because the campaigning is conducted largely behind the scenes, with candidates making personal pleas to individual House members.

Until the 1950s, it was unusual for a speaker to serve more than one 2-year term (see Table 22.2). The position was circulated among a small group of legislators who dominated the House. Clayton, a lawmaker from Springlake in West Texas, set a record by serving four consecutive terms before retiring in 1983. Lewis of Fort Worth and Laney each surpassed Clayton's record by serving five terms.

Unlike most of their predecessors, Clayton, Lewis, Laney, and Craddick devoted long hours to the job and kept large full-time staffs. With the complexities of a growing state putting more demands on the legislative leadership, recent Senate leaders (lieutenant governors) have also made their jobs virtually full-time and, like the speaker, have hired large staffs of specialists to research issues and help develop legislation. The presiding officers also depend on key committee chairs to take the lead in pushing their legislative priorities.

During Laney's speakership, the state completed a multibillion-dollar expansion of its prison system, overhauled criminal justice laws, and enacted a school finance law that addressed a Texas Supreme Court order for more equity in education spending. In a bipartisan endeavor, Laney actively supported then-Governor George W. Bush's unsuccessful effort to replace a large chunk of local school property taxes with higher state taxes in 1997. He also encouraged opposing sides to find common ground on other major issues, but one of his own priorities was to improve the way the House conducted its business. Laney won significant changes in House rules that produced, in the view of many House members, a more democratic law-making process than under previous speakers.

Limits of Power
Speaker Tom Craddick
(R-Midland) was elected
speaker in 2003 when
Republicans gained control
of the House. A forceful
leader, he was confronted
with several challenges in
2007 from members who felt
he had overstepped his
leadership role.

Table *22.2* They Stay Busy

Most recent presiding officers of the House and Senate have served in these positions for several legislative sessions.

Lieutenant Governors	When Served	Home
Ben Ramsey	1951–1961*	San Augustine
Preston Smith	1963–1969	Lubbock
Ben Barnes	1969–1973	DeLeon
Bill Hobby, Jr.	1973–1991	Houston
Bob Bullock	1991–1999	Hillsboro
Rick Perry	1999–2000	Haskell
Bill Ratliff	2000–2003	Mt. Pleasant
David Dewhurst	2003–	Houston

Speakers	When Served	Home
Reuben Senterfitt	1951–1955	San Saba
Jim T. Lindsey	1955–1957	Texarkana
Waggoner Carr	1957–1961	Lubbock
James A. Turman	1961–1963	Gober
Byron M. Tunnell	1963–1965	Tyler
Ben Barnes	1965–1969	DeLeon
Gus Mutscher	1969–1972	Brenham
Rayford Price	1972–1973	Palestine
Price Daniel, Jr.	1973–1975	Liberty
Bill Clayton	1975–1983	Springlake
Gib Lewis	1983–1993	Fort Worth
James E. "Pete" Laney	1993–2003	Hale Center
Tom Craddick	2003–	Midland

* Ben Ramsey resigned as lieutenant governor on September 18, 1961, upon his appointment to the Railroad Commission. The office was vacant until Preston Smith took office in 1963.

Sources: Texas Legislative Council, *Presiding Officers of the Texas Legislature, 1846–1982.* Austin, Tex.: Texas Legislative Council, 1982; Texas Legislature Online.

Backed by a Republican majority, Craddick was a key figure in the legislature's tight-fisted approach to drafting the new state budget in 2003, which cut spending in many areas to bridge a $10 billion revenue shortfall. He was a strong opponent of raising state taxes, although he insisted the legislature enact a separate law allowing university governing boards to raise college tuition. Craddick also was a key figure in the legislature's enactment of the redistricting bill to increase the number of Republicans elected to Congress from Texas. He was a consistently tough negotiator. "He's the toughest, hardest trader I've ever met. When you start trading with the speaker, it's tough trading," said state senator Steve Ogden, a Republican from Bryan and a long-time friend of Craddick's.[13]

Craddick continued to deal a difficult hand with the Senate and Lieutenant Governor David Dewhurst in prolonged attempts during 2005 to draft a new school funding system. During the regular session and two special sessions that year, the House and the Senate repeatedly failed to agree on how to trade higher state taxes for reductions in local school property taxes. Finally, faced with a Texas Supreme Court order for school funding changes during a 2006 special session, Craddick endorsed a plan promoted by Governor Rick Perry and helped win enactment of an expanded business tax and a higher cigarette tax to help pay for school tax reductions. He also led the House in reaching agreement with Dewhurst and the Senate for a teacher pay raise and other educational changes.

But by 2007, Craddick's speakership was under attack from some Republicans as well as Democrats. His iron-fisted style was partly blamed for the defeat of several incumbent Republican House members in 2006. Critics said the speaker had forced the lawmakers to vote against the best interests of their districts on such important issues as education, thus making them vulnerable to challengers. Craddick survived a challenge at the beginning of the 2007 session, when he was reelected to a third term as presiding officer. In the closing days of the session, however, he faced an open rebellion on the House floor, hanging on to the speaker's post by refusing to recognize motions to depose him. By the time the session adjourned in late spring, several Republican and Democratic House members had announced they would challenge Craddick for speaker when the next regular session convened in January 2009. Consequently, the developing speaker's race overshadowed many legislative races in 2008 (see *Controversy:* "Speaker Craddick Under Fire").

The speaker appoints a speaker pro tempore, or assistant presiding officer, who is usually a close ally. In 1981, Speaker Clayton named the first African American, Representative Craig Washington of Houston, to the post. Although Clayton was

Controversy

Speaker Craddick Under Fire

Just as a law-making body is a major "organ" in a democracy, the speaker of the House is a major "organ" in the Texas legislature. The holder of that office is a pivotal player in determining what does and doesn't become law and which programs are funded and which aren't. The stakes—as well as the controversy—have been particularly high during the tenure of Republican Speaker Tom Craddick.

Dissent over Craddick's leadership, which had been building among some Republican and Democratic House members alike during the 2007 session, finally erupted into an open rebellion on the House floor late one night in May.

Tempers flared when Craddick said he would refuse to recognize a motion to remove him as speaker. Some legislators charged toward the podium, shouting, "No! No! No!" while Craddick's supporters angrily rallied to his defense. The conflict was verbal, not physical, but one lawmaker said the turmoil reminded him of a "scene out of *Lord of the Flies.*"

Craddick ordered the House to stand "at ease" and walked off the floor to the shelter of his private office. When he returned 2 1/2 hours later, order had been restored, but his opponents' unhappiness hadn't been quelled.

The House's two parliamentarians had resigned and been replaced with two former House members close to Craddick—Republican Terry Keel of Austin and Democrat Ron Wilson of Houston. Supported by

their rulings and physical presence on the dais, Craddick held on to the speakership for the remaining 10 days of the session, refusing to recognize any legislator who wanted to make a motion challenging his leadership. No one knew for sure if Craddick could have survived a vote.

But the stage had been set for another challenge to Craddick's tenure at the beginning of the 2009 session. Craddick announced he would seek a fourth term as presiding officer, but several other House members, Republicans and Democrats, said they also would be candidates for his job.

Some lawmakers predicted Craddick's reaction to the late-session revolt would cost him the speakership in 2009. "There's no way he can lead this House after tonight because people don't trust him," said Representative Joaquin Castro, D-San Antonio. Representative Todd Smith, R-Euless, said Craddick's refusal to recognize his challengers was "clearly an abuse of power in an office."

Because House members elect the speaker, Craddick's future would be determined by the 2008 races for House seats. His leadership became an issue in several of those races with opponents complaining that Craddick's rule over the House was too autocratic and his priorities were detrimental to the needs of many Texans. But Craddick remained popular among conservative Republicans, including major contributors to legislative races.

Source: Houston Chronicle, May 26, 2007, p. 1A.

a rural conservative and Washington was an urban liberal, Washington proved to be a critical member of the speaker's team. He also exercised considerable influence in the House on a wide range of issues of importance to minorities. Ten years later, Gib Lewis named another African American legislator, Representative Wilhelmina Delco of Austin, as the first woman speaker pro tempore.

The membership of most House committees is determined partly by seniority. The speaker has total discretion, however, in naming committee chairs and vice chairs and in appointing all the members of procedural committees, including the influential Calendars Committee, which will be described in more detail later in this chapter. Under a rules change in 2003, Craddick also had total discretion—without regard for seniority—in appointing the budget-writing House Appropriations Committee. The new speaker bumped some senior Democratic members from the panel.

Senate Leadership The **lieutenant governor** is chosen by the voters in a statewide election to serve a 4-year term as presiding officer of the Senate. Unlike the vice president of the United States—his or her counterpart in the federal government, who has only limited legislative functions—the lieutenant governor has traditionally been the Senate's legislative leader. This office, which is elected independently of the governor, has often been called the most powerful office in state government because of the lieutenant governor's opportunity to merge a statewide electoral base into a dominant legislative role.[14] Lieutenant governors, however, get most of their power from rules set by the senators, not from the constitution.

The lieutenant governor's power is based in part on the same coalitional strategies that are used by the speaker through committee assignments and relationships with interest groups. But the lieutenant governor has traditionally had more direct control over the Senate's agenda than the speaker has over the House's agenda. Under long-standing Senate rules, the lieutenant governor determines when—and if—a committee-approved bill will be brought up for a vote by the full Senate. In the House, the order of floor debate is determined by the Calendars Committee. Although that key panel is appointed by the speaker and is sensitive to the speaker's wishes, it represents an intermediate step that the lieutenant governor does not have to encounter.

The lieutenant governor also has had more formal control over the membership of Senate committees than the speaker has over House panels. Under its rules, the Senate traditionally has allowed the lieutenant governor to appoint members of all standing committees without regard to seniority or any other restrictions.

The Senate has a president pro tempore, who is chosen by senators from among their membership. This position is rotated among the senators on a seniority basis. It is held for a limited period, and the holder of the position is third in line of succession to the governorship. There is a tradition that the governor and the lieutenant governor both allegedly "leave" the state on the same day so that the president pro tempore can serve as "governor for a day" at one point during his or her term.

Bill Hobby, a quiet-spoken media executive who served a record 18 years as lieutenant governor before voluntarily leaving office in January 1991, patiently sought consensus among senators on most major issues and rarely took the lead in promoting specific legislative proposals. One notable exception occurred in 1979, when Hobby, a Democrat, tried to force Senate approval of a presidential primary bill opposed by most Democratic senators. After Hobby served notice that he would alter the Senate's traditional operating procedure to give the bill

★ **lieutenant governor**
Presiding officer of the Senate. This officeholder would become governor if the governor were to die, be incapacitated, or removed from office.

special consideration, twelve Democratic senators, dubbed the "Killer Bees," hid out for several days to break a quorum and keep the Senate from conducting business. They succeeded in killing the primary bill and reminding Hobby that the senators set the rules.

Hobby's successor, Bob Bullock, had demonstrated strong leadership and a mercurial temperament during 16 years as state comptroller. On taking office as lieutenant governor, he had major policy and structural changes in mind for state government and was impatient to see them carried out by the legislature. Unlike Hobby, Bullock took the lead in making proposals and then actively lobbying for them. During his first session in 1991, he reportedly had shouting matches with some lawmakers behind closed doors and one day abruptly and angrily adjourned the Senate when not enough members were present for a **quorum** at the scheduled starting time. But his experience and knowledge of state government and his tireless work habits won the respect of most senators and their support for most of his proposals.

Bullock, a Democrat, strengthened his leadership role during the 1993 and 1995 sessions and was actively involved in every major issue that the Senate addressed. Recognizing that increases in Republican strength after the 1992 and 1994 elections made the Senate more conservative than it had been in several years, and eager to strengthen his support in the business community, Bullock saw to it that compromises on major issues—including some long sought by business—were reached behind closed doors before they were made public. This approach kept controversy to a minimum and defused partisanship, but it distressed consumer advocates and environmentalists, who felt excluded from the process. It also prompted remarks that the Senate had abandoned democracy. There were so many unanimous or near-unanimous votes in the Senate in 1993 that some House members joked that senators who wanted to show dissent voted aye with their eyes closed.[15]

Bullock played a less active role during the 1997 session, after Republicans, for the first time this century, had won a majority of Senate seats. He was strongly supportive of some key legislation, including a statewide water conservation and management plan, but he did little to promote a property-tax relief effort that Governor Bush had made his highest priority for the session. One key element of Bush's proposal, an increase in state taxes as a partial tradeoff for lower school district taxes, died primarily because of strong Senate opposition, which Bullock did not try to defuse.

A few days after the 1997 session ended, Bullock surprised the Texas political community by announcing that he would not seek reelection in 1998. The former state leader, who had a history of health problems, was later diagnosed with lung cancer, and he died in June 1999.

After defeating Democrat John Sharp in a hard-fought race in 1998, former Agriculture Commissioner Rick Perry became Texas's first Republican lieutenant governor of modern times in 1999. Perry not only had to follow in Bullock's legendary footsteps, he also had to preside over the Senate during a session overshadowed by Governor George W. Bush's anticipated presidential race. The new lieutenant governor had the advantage, though, of entering the 1999 session with a $6 billion state surplus and a rare absence of emergencies. Perry lost one of his biggest priorities, a pilot project to allow students in low-performing public schools to use state-paid vouchers to transfer to private schools. But generally he received high marks for his performance during the session from both Democrats and Republicans. As one senator observed, "He might not have used the Bullock style of cracking heads or the woodshed" to

★ **quorum**
Required number of the members of a governing body who must be present so that official business, such as voting, can be conducted. In Texas, a quorum of the House and the Senate is two-thirds of the membership. For committees, it is a majority of the members.

A Legislator's Legislator
Former Lieutenant Governor Bob Bullock, who retired in 1999 and died later that year, was often perceived to be more powerful than the governors with whom he served as he adroitly led the Senate to support policies that he deemed important for the state.

force legislative solutions. "He did effectively bring people together and kept us from having any meltdowns."[16] Perry was more low-key than Bullock, perhaps choosing to learn more about the Senate and its members before plunging into potential controversies. Nevertheless, he was credited with helping Republican and Democratic lawmakers negotiate a compromise on one key legislative package of the session—a series of tax cuts, teacher pay raises, and other increased education spending.

Perry was elected to a lieutenant governor's term that wasn't to expire until January 2003. But in anticipation of Governor Bush's presidential race, the legislature in 1999 approved a constitutional amendment—which Texas voters later endorsed—to make it clear that Perry would have to give up the lieutenant governor's job in midterm if he were promoted to fill a vacancy in the governor's office. After Bush resigned the governorship in December 2000 to become president, Perry was promoted to governor. And, acting under the new constitutional amendment, senators elected state Senator Bill Ratliff, R-Mount Pleasant, to serve as lieutenant governor during the 2001 session.

Ratliff, a former chair of the Senate Education and Finance committees, was business-like in his role as presiding officer, and he generally received favorable reviews. He appointed the first African American, state Senator Rodney Ellis, D-Houston, to chair the budget-writing Finance Committee. He also parted ways with most Republican senators and supported Ellis's bill to strengthen the state law against hate crimes, which passed that session. And Ratliff blocked a bill that would have removed state legal restrictions against Native Americans operating casinos on their reservations in Texas. At the end of the 2001 session, Ratliff announced that he would seek election to the lieutenant governor's post in 2002. But several days later, admitting he didn't have the stomach for the compromises often involved in a statewide race, he announced that he had changed his mind and would seek reelection to his Senate seat instead. "I do love policy-making, but I do not love politics," he said.[17] After winning reelection to the Senate in 2002 and serving during the regular and special sessions in 2003, Ratliff resigned in early 2004, expressing weariness after 15 years in the legislative arena.

Republican David Dewhurst won the 2002 lieutenant governor's race over Democrat John Sharp, who had narrowly lost the same office to Rick Perry in 1998. A wealthy businessman, Dewhurst had no legislative experience when he became the Senate's presiding officer in January 2003. His only experience in elected office had been his 4 previous years as state land commissioner, but he moved quickly to establish credibility as a leader. He appointed respected legislative insiders to key staff positions and spent many hours studying issues and meeting with individual senators. Although Republicans held a 19–12 Senate majority, he continued the tradition of appointing both Republicans and Democrats to leadership positions. Dewhurst agreed with Governor Rick Perry and Speaker Tom Craddick that the legislature would close a $10 billion revenue shortfall and write a new state budget without increasing state taxes. But he and the Senate helped to minimize some of the spending cuts by insisting that lawmakers tap into non-tax revenue, such as the state's Rainy Day savings account. On such budgetary details and other matters, including how quickly the legislature should move to improve the school finance system, Dewhurst sometimes differed with Perry and Craddick. Their differences stemmed partly from Dewhurst's independent nature, which was bolstered by the fact that he, not special interest groups, had largely funded his election to the state's number two office. The Senate's rules and traditions also required the lieutenant governor to seek more consensus among senators than the speaker normally has to do in the

It's More Than Presiding
Lieutenant Governor David Dewhurst, elected in 2002 and reelected in 2006, presides over the Senate. Strongly independent and skillful in his use of the resources of his office, he has led the Senate on issues that have come into conflict with the speaker and the governor.

House. Legislation traditionally wasn't approved without the consent of two-thirds of the senators, which meant that the twelve Democratic senators had enough clout to force some budgetary concessions.

Dewhurst orchestrated the Senate's biggest show of independence during the 2003 regular session by hammering out in a series of private meetings a new public education funding plan that would have raised the state sales tax in exchange for sharp reductions in local property taxes, which were increasingly under fire, particularly in many suburban and heavily Republican school districts. Dewhurst won unanimous Senate approval of the proposal, but the House never acted on it. Craddick and Perry insisted instead that lawmakers conduct another study of school finance, which had already been studied several times in recent years, and attempt to tackle the issue later.

Senate unanimity disappeared—and Dewhurst's leadership was severely challenged—during the bitter partisan fight over congressional redistricting that took three special sessions in summer and fall 2003 to resolve. Democratic senators blocked a House-passed redistricting bill during the first special session by using a Senate tradition that required two-thirds of the senators to approve debate on any legislation. After Dewhurst announced that he would bypass that procedure, known as the "two-thirds rule," to allow a redistricting bill to be passed on a simple majority vote during the second special session, eleven of the Senate's twelve Democrats fled to Albuquerque, New Mexico, where they remained for more than a month. Their flight, which received national media coverage, deprived the Senate of a quorum and the ability to conduct any business during the entire, 30-day second special session. It also severely damaged the Senate's tradition of personal and partisan cooperation as Democratic and Republican senators exchanged verbal attacks across state lines. The boycotting senators eventually returned to Austin, and the legislature approved a congressional redistricting bill favoring Republicans during a third special session. Dewhurst immediately began working behind the scenes to restore the Senate's ability to conduct business in a civil, bipartisan fashion, and he was largely successful.

As noted earlier, Dewhurst was unable in 2005 to negotiate a compromise with Speaker Craddick over changes in the school funding system. But faced with the Texas Supreme Court order, he joined Craddick in backing the governor's tax trade-off proposal during the 2006 special session. And Dewhurst was instrumental in getting a teacher pay raise and other educational changes included in the legislation.

Dewhurst was successful in getting several legislative goals passed in 2007, but he lost one of his and his fellow Republicans' top priorities, a bill that would have required Texas voters to have photo identification cards before voting. That bill, which sparked a major partisan fight, was approved by the House but died in the Senate, where Democratic senators used the two-thirds rule to block it (see *Politics Up Close:* "A Voter ID Bill Contracts a Fatal Senate Disease").

Influence and Control over the Legislative Process

The power of each presiding officer to appoint committees and determine which committee will have jurisdiction over a specific bill gives the speaker and the lieutenant governor tremendous influence over the law-making process.

The speaker and the lieutenant governor control the legislative process through the application of the rules, including those set in the state constitution and those adopted by the House and the Senate. Each presiding officer is advised on procedures by a parliamentarian. The speaker and the lieutenant governor do not participate in House or Senate debate on bills and usually attempt

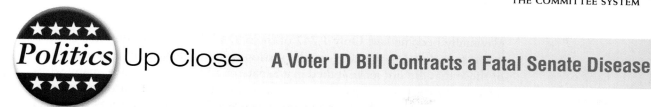

Politics Up Close   A Voter ID Bill Contracts a Fatal Senate Disease

Republicans had a strong majority in the Texas legislature during the 2007 session, but one of their top priorities—a bill that would have required Texas voters to produce a form of photo identification before casting ballots—died, thanks to the Senate's two-thirds "rule" and two ailing Democratic senators.

Republicans said the voter ID bill was an essential protection against voter fraud, but Democratic opponents argued that it was an effort to discourage minority and elderly voters, who primarily vote for Democratic candidates, from going to the polls. The bill won easy approval in the Republican-dominated House but ran aground in the Senate, where the 11 Democratic senators, the minimum needed to block legislation, remained steadfast against it.

The Senate's rules, in effect, require two-thirds of the senators present to approve debate on any bill.

One of the Democrats, Senator Mario Gallegos of Houston, missed much of the session while recuperating from a liver transplant, and Republican Lieutenant Governor David Dewhurst could have won approval of the bill in Gallegos's absence. But Dewhurst agreed to give Gallegos advance notice and time to get to Austin before taking a vote on the controversial measure.

After Gallegos had returned to Austin, Dewhurst tried to win Senate approval of the bill one day when another Democratic senator, Carlos Uresti of San Antonio, was out of action (or so Dewhurst thought) with a stomach virus. Notified by other Democrats of the pending vote, Uresti rushed to the Senate chamber in time to cast a vote against the bill and then hurried to the senators' private lounge to vomit.

Uresti soon recovered, but the voter ID bill didn't.

Source: Houston Chronicle, May 17, 2007, p. 10B.

---

to present an image of neutral presiding officers. Their formal powers, however, are further strengthened by their informal relationships with their committee leaders and interest groups. And, with the notable exceptions of the separate walkouts by House and Senate Democrats during the 2003 redistricting battle and the recent turmoil over the House leadership, the speaker and the lieutenant governor rarely lose control of the process.

In the Senate, the lieutenant governor can vote only to break a tie. The speaker can vote on any issue in the House but normally abstains from voting except to break a tie or to send a signal to encourage reluctant or wavering House members to vote a particular way on an issue.

Leadership Teams   Traditionally, there has been no formal division along party lines or a formal system of floor leaders in either the Texas House or the Senate. The long-time, Democrat-dominated legislative system with the speaker's and lieutenant governor's control of committee appointments did not produce a leadership structure comparable to that of the U.S. Congress. The committee chairs constitute the speaker's and lieutenant governor's teams and usually act as their unofficial floor leaders in developing and building support for the leadership's legislative priorities. Most chairs are philosophically, if not always politically, aligned with the presiding officers.

The Committee System

The committee system is the backbone of the legislative process, and it is molded by the lieutenant governor and the speaker.[18] It is a screening process that decides the fate of most legislation.

The **committee** is where technical drafting errors and oversights in bills can be corrected and where compromise can begin to work for those bills that do

★ **committee**
In the legislature, a group of lawmakers who review and hold public hearings on issues or bills they are assigned by the presiding officer. Committees that specialize in bills by subject matter are designated as standing committees. A bill has to win committee approval before it can be considered by the full House or Senate. Most bills die in committees, which perform as a legislative screening process.

eventually become law. Only 1,742 of the 6,374 bills and constitutional amendments introduced in the 2007 regular session won final legislative approval. Most of those that did not make it died in a Senate or a House committee, many without ever being heard. Rarely does a committee kill a bill on an outright vote, because there are much easier, less obvious ways to scuttle legislation. A bill can be gutted, or so drastically amended or weakened, that even its sponsor can hardly recognize it. Or, it can be simply ignored.

Committee chairs have considerable power over legislation that comes to their committees. They may kill bills by refusing to schedule them for a hearing. Or, after a hearing, a chair may send a bill to a **subcommittee** that he or she stacks with members opposed to the legislation, thus allowing the bill to die slowly and quietly in the legislative deep freeze. Even if a majority of committee members want to approve a bill, the chair can refuse to recognize such a motion. Most chairs, however, are sensitive to the wishes of the presiding officers. If the speaker or the lieutenant governor wants a bill to win committee approval or wants another measure to die in committee, the chair will usually comply.

Referral to a subcommittee does not always mean the death of a bill. Subcommittees also help committees distribute the workload. They work out compromises, correct technical problems in bills, or draft substitute legislation to accommodate competing interest groups.

Standing Committees   The number and names of committees are periodically revised under House and Senate rules, but there have been relatively few major changes in the basic committee structure in recent years. During the 2007 session, the Senate had fifteen **standing committees**, varying in membership from five to fifteen.

There were forty standing committees in the House, with memberships ranging from five to twenty-nine (Table 22.3). Additionally, there was the Committee of the Whole Senate. Most committees are substantive. That is, they hold public hearings and evaluate bills related to their areas, such as higher education, natural resources, or public health. A few committees are procedural, such as the Rules and Resolutions Committee, which handles many routine congratulatory resolutions, and the **Calendars Committee**, which schedules bills for debate by the full House.

Some committees play more dominant roles in the law-making process than others, particularly in the House. The House State Affairs Committee, for example, handles many more major statewide bills than the Committee on Culture, Recreation, and Tourism or the Committee on Agriculture and Livestock. The House Urban Affairs and County Affairs committees handle several hundred bills of importance to local governments each session. The importance of a committee is determined by the area of public policy over which it has jurisdiction or by its role in the House's operating procedure.

The House Calendars Committee historically has had more life-and-death power over legislation than any other committee because it sets the order of debate on the House floor. During each regular session, it kills hundreds of bills that have been approved by various substantive committees by refusing to schedule them for debate by the full House or scheduling them so late in the session they don't have time to win Senate approval. This committee traditionally works closely with the speaker and is one means by which the speaker and the speaker's team control the House. Although many legislators complain about the committee killing their priority bills, some lawmakers defend the panel as a means of keeping controversial legislation—on which many members would rather not have to cast votes—from reaching the House floor.

★ **subcommittee**
A few members of a larger committee appointed to review a particular bill and make recommendations on its disposition to the full committee.

★ **standing committee**
Committee that is created by House or Senate rules to consider legislation or perform a procedural role in the law-making process.

★ **Calendars Committee**
Special procedural committee that schedules bills that already have been approved by other committees for floor debate in the House.

Table **22.3** Senate and House Standing Committees, 80th Legislature, 2007 Regular Session

Committees, whose membership is appointed by the presiding officers, are where most legislative work is completed. Size, importance, and workload of the committees vary, and legislators cultivate their relationships with the leadership to gain plum committee assignments.

Senate Committee	Number of Members	Bills Referred to Committee in 80th Legislature	Bills Out of Committee
Administration	7	*	*
Business & Commerce	9	297	171
Criminal Justice	7	352	217
Education	9	356	198
Finance	15	259	88
Government Organization	7	101	74
Health & Human Services	9	285	190
Intergovernmental Relations	5	409	303
International Relations and Trade	7	27	22
Jurisprudence	7	280	203
Natural Resources	11	348	254
Nominations	7	*	*
State Affairs	9	381	208
Transportation and Homeland Security	9	296	192
Veteran Affairs & Military Installations	5	39	38

House Committee	Number of Members	Bills Referred to Committee in 80th Legislature	Bills Out of Committee
Agriculture & Livestock	7	45	30
Appropriations	29	89	19
Border and International Affairs	7	45	32
Business & Industry	9	158	87
Calendars	11	*	*
Civil Practices	9	73	34
Corrections	7	116	73
County Affairs	9	150	101
Criminal Jurisprudence	9	294	142
Culture, Recreation, and Tourism	7	95	72
Defense Affairs and State-Federal Relations	9	83	54
Economic Development	7	76	51
Elections	7	168	76
Energy Resources	7	43	26
Environmental Regulation	7	108	43
Financial Institutions	7	79	38
General Investigating and Ethics	5	*	*
Government Reform	7	111	60
Higher Education	9	190	100
House Administration	11	*	*
Human Services	9	179	75
Insurance	9	172	77
Judiciary	9	204	143
Juvenile Justice & Family Issues	9	133	89
Land & Resource Management	9	100	54
Law Enforcement	7	146	82
Licensing & Administrative Procedures	9	174	88
Local & Consent Calendars	11	*	*
Local Government Ways and Means	7	143	90
Natural Resources	9	326	245
Pensions & Investments	7	90	38
Public Education	9	378	148

(Continued)

Table 22.3 (Continued)

House Committee	Number of Members	Bills Referred to Committee in 80th Legislature	Bills Out of Committee
Public Health	9	285	127
Redistricting	15	8	0
Regulated Industries	9	92	24
Rules & Resolutions	11	*	*
State Affairs	9	182	81
Transportation	9	334	175
Urban Affairs	7	133	90
Ways & Means	9	235	85

*Procedural or administrative committees.

Source: Texas Legislature Online, *Legislative Reports for the 80th Legislature, Regular Session* (2007).

The state budget is the single most important bill enacted by the legislature because, through it, lawmakers determine how much money is spent on the state's public programs and services. In the House, the Appropriations Committee takes the lead in drafting state budgets, whereas the Ways and Means Committee normally is responsible for producing any tax or revenue measures necessary to balance the budget. The two most important committees in the Senate are the Finance Committee, which handles the budget and, usually, tax bills, and the State Affairs Committee, which, like its House counterpart, handles a variety of legislation of major, statewide importance.

Although committees have general subject areas of responsibility, legislative rules allow the lieutenant governor and the speaker some latitude in assigning bills. The presiding officer can ensure the death of a bill by sending it to a committee known to oppose it or can guarantee quick action on a measure by referring it to a receptive, or friendly, panel.

Standing Subcommittees

The formal, standing subcommittee structure of the U.S. Congress has only begun to develop in the Texas Legislature, in which committee chairs traditionally have appointed subcommittees as needed to handle specific bills.

Conference Committees

Legislation must be passed in exactly the same form by the House and the Senate. If one chamber refuses to accept the other's version

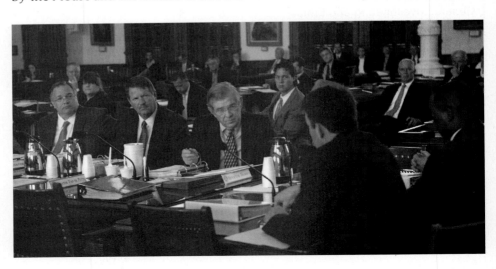

Where the Work Is Done

Sometimes committees meet in the Senate chamber. Shown here is a meeting of the Senate Committee on State Affairs.

of a bill, a **conference committee** can try to resolve the differences. Conference committees of five senators and five representatives are appointed by the presiding officers. A compromise bill has to be approved by at least three senators and three House members who serve on the conference committee before it is sent back to the full House and the full Senate for subsequent approval or rejection. Over the years, conference committees have drafted legislation in forms dramatically different from earlier versions approved by the House or the Senate. But because a conference committee is supposed to do no more than adjust the differences between the House and the Senate versions of a bill, both chambers have to pass a concurrent resolution to allow a conference committee to add significant new language.

Special Committees Special, or select, committees are occasionally appointed by the governor, the lieutenant governor, and the speaker to study major policy issues, such as tax equity or school finance. These panels usually include private citizens as well as legislators, and they usually recommend legislation. Standing legislative committees also study issues in their assigned areas during the **interims** between sessions, and the presiding officers can ask committees to conduct special investigations or inquiries pertaining to governmental matters.

Rules and Procedures

Laws are made in Texas according to the same basic process followed by the U.S. Congress and other state legislatures.[19] But as the discussion of the committee system already has indicated, legislative rules are complex and are loaded with traps in which legislation can be killed. One often hears the remark around the Capitol that "there are a lot more ways to kill a bill than to pass one." Legislators and lobbyists who master the rules can wield a tremendous amount of influence over the law-making process. Both the House and the Senate have detailed rules governing the disposition of legislation, and each has a parliamentarian to help interpret them.

How a Bill Becomes a Law The simplified outline of the process by which a bill becomes a law (Figure 22.3) starts with the introduction of a bill in the House or the Senate and its referral to a committee by the presiding officer, which constitutes **first reading**. That is the only reading most bills ever get.

A bill that wins committee approval can be considered on **second reading** by the full House or Senate, where it is debated and often amended. Some amendments are designed to improve a bill, but others are designed to kill it by loading it down with controversial or objectionable provisions. Amendments that may be punitive toward particular individuals or groups are also sometimes offered. Such an amendment, which may be temporarily added to a bill only to be removed before the measure becomes law, is designed to give a group or perhaps a local official a message that the sponsoring legislator expects his or her wishes to be heeded on a particular issue. Lawmakers also may offer amendments that they know have little chance of being approved merely to make favorable political points with constituents or special interest groups.

If a bill is approved on second reading, it has to win one more vote on **third reading** before it goes to the other chamber for the same process. If the second chamber approves the bill without any changes, or amendments, it then goes to the governor for signature into law or for **veto**. The governor also can allow a bill

★ **conference committee**
Panel of House members and senators appointed to work out a compromise on a bill if different versions of the legislation were passed by the House and the Senate.

★ **special, or select, committees**
Special panels appointed to study major policy issues.

★ **interims**
Periods between legislative sessions.

★ **first reading**
Introduction of a bill in the House or the Senate and its referral to a committee by the presiding officer.

★ **second reading**
Initial debate by the full House or Senate on a bill that has been approved by a committee.

★ **third reading**
Final presentation of a bill before the full House or Senate.

★ **veto**
The power of the governor to reject, or kill, a bill passed by the legislature.

HOUSE　　　　　　　　　　　　　　　**SENATE**

Bill Introduction

First Reading
Bill is introduced, numbered, and referred to committee by speaker.

First Reading
Bill is referred to committee by lieutenant governor.

Committee Action

Committee
After public hearing, committee approves bill, possibly with amendments, and sends to the Calendars Committee to schedule for debate by full house.

Committee
After public hearing, committee approves bill, possibly with amendments.

Floor Action

Second Reading
Bill is debated by full House, amended by majority vote, and given preliminary approval.
Third Reading
Bill can be amended by 2/3 vote and given final approval.

Second Reading
Bill is debated by full Senate, amended by majority vote, and given preliminary approval.
Third Reading
Bill can be amended by 2/3 vote and given final approval.

Conference Action

Conference Action
In many cases in which House and Senate bills differ, one chamber will accept the other chamber's version. If not, a conference committee is appointed to work out the differences. The House and Senate must then approve the conference committee report.

Gubernatorial Action

Governor
The governor signs the bill, lets it become law without signing it, or vetoes it.

LAW

Figure *22.3*　　Basic Steps in the Texas Legislative Process

The basic steps for enacting legislation are similar to those found in other states and the U.S. Congress. But legislative rules, tactics, and strategies make the process very complex. It requires strong political and parliamentary skills.

to become law without his or her signature. This procedure is just the opposite of the pocket veto power afforded the president of the United States. If the president does not sign a bill approved by Congress by a certain deadline, it is automatically vetoed. If the governor of Texas does not sign or veto a bill by a certain deadline, it becomes law. A veto can be overridden and the bill allowed to become law by a two-thirds vote of both houses, although this process is rarely attempted.

The governor must accept or reject a bill in its entirety except for the general **appropriations bill**, or state budget, from which the governor can delete specific spending proposals while approving others. This power is called a **line-item veto**. The budget or any other bill approved by the legislature that appropriates money has to be certified by the comptroller before it is sent to the governor. Texas has a **pay-as-you-go** government, and the comptroller has to certify that there will be enough revenue available to fund the bill.

If the second chamber amends the bill, the originating chamber must approve the change or request a conference committee. Any compromise worked out by a conference committee has to be approved by both houses, without further changes, before it is sent to the governor.

All bills except revenue-raising measures can originate in either the House or the Senate. Tax bills must originate in the House, although the legislative leadership severely bent that rule to win approval, in a special session in 1991, of a tax bill necessary to balance a new state budget. After the House had dismantled a $3.3 billion revenue bill recommended by its Ways and Means Committee and sent the Senate nothing but a $30 million shell, Lieutenant Governor Bob Bullock and the Senate, in consultation with lobbyists, took over the writing of a new tax bill, which the House later approved.

Procedural Obstacles to Legislation

Pieces of legislation also encounter other significant procedural obstacles. In the House, there is the Calendars Committee, discussed earlier in this chapter. In the Senate, there is the so-called **two-thirds rule**.

The two-thirds requirement for debating bills on the Senate floor is a strong obstacle to controversial bills because it means that only eleven senators, if they are determined enough and one is not absent at the wrong time, can keep any measure from becoming law. This tradition also has been a source of the lieutenant governor's power. After a bill is approved by a committee, its sponsor can have it placed on the daily **intent calendar**. If the sponsor is recognized by the lieutenant governor, he or she will seek Senate permission to consider the bill. A sponsor can have majority Senate support for a measure but will watch it die if he or she cannot convince two-thirds of the senators to let the body formally debate it.

The two-thirds tradition also gives a senator the opportunity to vote on both sides of an issue. Sometimes a senator will vote to bring up a bill and then vote against the measure when it is actually passed, as only a majority vote is required for approval. This procedure enables the senator to please the bill's supporters, give the sponsor a favor that can be repaid later, and, at the same time, tell the bill's opponents that he or she voted against the measure.

As noted earlier in this chapter, Lieutenant Governor David Dewhurst suspended the two-thirds tradition to break a partisan impasse and win Senate approval of a Republican-backed congressional redistricting bill during a special session in 2003. But the procedure still enjoyed strong support among senators, and a proposal to change it at the beginning of the 2007 session was defeated, 30–1.

The Senate rules also provide for tags and filibusters, both of which can be effective in killing bills near the end of a legislative session. A **tag** allows an individual senator to postpone a committee hearing on any bill for at least 48 hours, a delay that is often fatal in the crush of unfinished business during a session's closing days. The **filibuster**, a procedure that allows a senator to speak against a

★ **appropriations bill**
Bill that authorizes the expenditure of money for a public program or purpose. In Texas, the general appropriations bill approved by the legislature every 2 years is the state budget.

★ **line-item veto**
The power of the Texas governor to reject certain parts of the general appropriations, or spending, bill without killing the entire measure.

★ **pay-as-you-go**
Constitutional requirement that prohibits the legislature from borrowing money for the state's operating expenses.

★ **two-thirds rule**
Procedure under which the Texas Senate has traditionally operated that requires approval of at least two-thirds of senators before a bill can be debated on the Senate floor. It allows a minority of senators to block controversial legislation.

★ **intent calendar**
Daily list of bills eligible for debate on the floor of the Texas Senate, if the sponsor is recognized by the lieutenant governor.

★ **tag**
Rule that allows an individual senator to postpone a committee hearing on any bill for at least 48 hours, a delay that can be fatal to a bill during the closing days of a legislative session.

★ **filibuster**
Procedure that allows a senator to speak against a bill for as long as he or she can stand and talk. A filibuster can become a formidable obstacle or threat against controversial bills near the end of a legislative session.

Talking a Bill to Death
Former Senator Gonzalo Barrientos of Austin puts on comfortable shoes in anticipation of a lengthy filibuster.

★ **calendar**
Agenda or the list of bills to be considered by the House or the Senate on a given day.

★ **record vote**
Vote taken in the House or the Senate of which a permanent record is kept, listing how individual legislators voted.

★ **division votes**
Votes taken on the computerized voting boards in the Texas House but erased without being permanently recorded.

bill for as long as he or she can stand and talk, is usually little more than a nuisance to a bill's supporters early in a session, but it, too, can become a potent and ever-present threat against controversial legislation near the end of a session. Sometimes the mere likelihood of a filibuster against a bill is sufficient to kill the measure. Late in a session, the lieutenant governor may refuse to recognize the sponsor of a controversial bill for fear a filibuster will fatally delay other major legislative proposals. State senator Bill Meier of Euless spoke for 43 hours in 1977 against a bill dealing with the public reporting of on-the-job accidents. In so doing, he captured the world's record for the longest filibuster, which he held for years.

Shortcuts, Obfuscation, and Confusion

Sponsors of legislation languishing in an unfriendly committee or subcommittee often try to resurrect their proposals by attaching them as amendments to related bills being debated on the House or Senate floor. Such maneuvers often are successful, particularly if opponents are absent or if the sponsor succeeds in "mumbling" the amendment through without challenge. But the speaker or the lieutenant governor must find that such amendments are germane to the pending bill if an alert opponent raises a point of order against them.

To facilitate the passage of noncontroversial and local pieces of legislation, the House and the Senate have periodic local and consent, or local and uncontested **calendars**, which are conducted under special rules that enable scores of bills to be routinely and quickly approved by the full House or Senate without debate. Bills of major statewide significance, even controversial measures, sometimes get placed on these calendars, but it takes only one senator or three representatives to have any bill struck. Legislators will sometimes knowingly let a controversial bill slip by on a local calendar without moving to strike it so as not to offend the sponsor or the presiding officer. But to protect themselves politically, should the bill become an issue later, they will quietly register a vote against the measure in the House or Senate journal.

As noted earlier in this chapter, compromises on controversial legislation are often worked out behind closed doors long before a bill is debated on the House or Senate floor or even afforded a public hearing. It can be argued that this approach to consensus building is an efficient, business-like way to enact legislation, but it also serves to discourage the free and open debate that is so important to the democratic process.

Recent speakers also have discouraged the taking of **record votes** during House floor debate on most bills. A constitutional amendment approved by Texas voters in 2007 requires record votes on final House or Senate passage of all legislation, except some local bills. But many important amendments offered to bills in the House are decided with **division votes**, which are taken on the computerized voting boards but leave no formal record once the boards are cleared. This approach saves the taxpayers some printing costs and can give lawmakers some respite from lobby pressure. But it also serves to keep the public in the dark about significant decisions made by their elected representatives. The fewer record votes legislators have to make, the more easily they can dodge accountability to their constituents.

Often, legislators have made up their minds on an issue before the matter is debated on the floor. But when they are not familiar with a bill and have no political interest in it, they may simply vote the way the sponsor votes or the way the House or Senate leadership wants them to vote. Despite what tourists in the gallery may think, legislators who raise their fingers above their heads when a vote is taken are not asking the presiding officer for a rest break. They are signaling the way they are voting and encouraging other lawmakers to vote the same way. One finger means yes; two fingers mean no.

When record votes are taken, House rules prohibit members from punching the voting buttons on other members' desks, but the practice occurs regularly. Sometimes members instruct a desk mate or another legislator to cast a specific vote for them if they expect to be off the floor when the vote is called for. Other legislators make a habit of punching the voting buttons at all the empty desks within reach. This practice is normally challenged only in cases of close votes, when members of the losing side request a roll-call verification of the computerized vote and the votes of members who do not answer the roll call are struck. The House was embarrassed in 1991 when a dead lawmaker was recorded as answering the daily roll call and voting on several record votes. The legislator had died in his Austin apartment, but his body was not discovered for several hours. Meanwhile, colleagues had been pushing his voting button. This practice is not a problem in the Senate, where the secretary of the Senate orally calls the roll on record votes.

Partly because of the rules under which the legislature operates, partly because of the heavy volume of legislation, and partly because of political maneuvering, the closing weeks of a regular session are hectic. Legislators in both houses are asked to vote on dozens of conference committee reports they do not have time to read. With hundreds of bills being rushed through the legislature to the governor's desk, mistakes occur. And deliberate attempts are made—often successfully—to slip major changes in law through the confusion. For every surprise bill or special interest amendment that is caught, dozens slip through and become law.

The Emerging Party System

Unlike the U.S. Congress, the Texas Legislature is not organized along party lines, with rules automatically giving leadership positions to members of the majority party. The arrangement in Texas is due primarily to the absence of Republican legislators for many years and the more recent practice—before Republicans gained a House majority in 2003—of rural Democrats aligning themselves with Republicans to produce a conservative coalition. As recently as 1971, the year before a federal court declared urban, countywide House districts unconstitutional, there were only ten Republicans in the House and two in the Senate. As Republicans increased their numbers, they aligned themselves with conservative Democrats to attempt to control the policy-setting process, particularly in the House. This ideological coalition became increasingly important as single-member districts boosted not only the number of Republican lawmakers but also the number of moderate and liberal Democratic legislators elected from urban areas. The coalition became a means of maintaining some legislative control for conservative Democrats as the base of power shifted in their own party.

Republicans and conservative Democrats formally organized the Texas Conservative Coalition in the House in the 1980s. The coalition remained a strong force in the 1990s, chaired for several years by Representative Warren Chisum of Pampa, who switched from the Democratic to the Republican Party in 1995. Chisum's mastery of the rules blocked many pieces of legislation on technicalities.

On occasion, liberal Democrats and conservative Republicans have formed "unholy alliances," but these coalitions were usually short-lived. During the controversy over the Sharpstown stock fraud scandal in 1971, liberal Democrats and Republicans formed a loose coalition called the "Dirty Thirty" that continually harassed Speaker Gus Mutscher, who not only was a key figure in the scandal but also epitomized the rural conservative Democratic tradition of the statehouse.

The Growth of Partisanship With the growth of the Republican Party in Texas in the 1980s, Speaker Gib Lewis, a conservative urban Democrat, appointed Republicans to major committee chairs in the House. But partisan divisions increased in 1987 when Lewis, Democratic Lieutenant Governor Bill Hobby, and Republican Governor Bill Clements fought over a new state budget in the face of a huge revenue shortfall. On one side of the debate were moderate and liberal Democratic legislators, including inner-city and South Texas minorities whose constituents had the most to gain from a tax increase and the most to lose from deep cuts in spending on human services and educational programs. On the other side were a handful of conservative, primarily rural Democrats and Republicans with middle- and upper-middle-class suburban constituents who insisted on fiscal restraint. Clements eventually gave in and supported a tax increase, but most of the House Republicans continued to fight the measure until it was approved in a summer special session.

In 1989, Republicans formed their first caucus in the House, and soon both parties had active caucuses in both the House and the Senate, which began to play key roles in marshaling legislative support on selected issues. They also became active in legislative races as Republicans began to mount aggressive, well-financed challenges of Democratic incumbents.

During the 1995 legislative session, when Democrats still held a majority of House and Senate seats, Lieutenant Governor Bob Bullock and Speaker Pete Laney, both Democrats, continued the practice of naming Republicans, as well as Democrats, to committee chairs. Bullock and Laney also were strongly supportive of Republican Governor George W. Bush's legislative priorities. All three leaders cooperated in making major changes in public education and juvenile justice and setting limits on civil liability lawsuits.

After many bitterly contested legislative races, Republicans won their first Senate majority in modern times during the 1996 elections and gained four seats in the House to narrow the Democratic majority in that body to 82–68. Bipartisanship still prevailed for the most part in the 1997 session. Bullock, the Democratic lieutenant governor, gave Republicans some new leadership positions in the Senate but named Democrats to chair most committees. But legislative fights with strong partisan overtones increased in 1997 and subsequent sessions over such issues as abortion, gay rights, and whether tax dollars should be spent on private school tuition for some students (see *Politics Up Close:* "The 'Memorial Day Massacre'").

Another partisan-charged issue in 1999 and 2001 was an attempt by some Democrats to strengthen the state law against hate crimes, after three white men in East Texas were accused and later convicted of dragging an African American man, James Byrd, Jr., to death behind a pickup truck. Most Republicans opposed the bill because it increased penalties for crimes motivated by prejudice against homosexuals as well as prejudice over race or religion. That provision was opposed by social conservatives, and in 1999 Governor Bush—who did not want to anger conservatives on the eve of his race for the Republican presidential nomination—called the bill unnecessary. The measure, which sponsors named for Byrd, died in the Senate in 1999 but was passed in 2001.

Republicans Take Control Aided by the redrawn legislative districts discussed earlier in this chapter, Republicans made major gains in the 2002

Politics Up Close   The "Memorial Day Massacre"

Partisan differences, which were building in the years leading up to the Republican takeover of the Texas House in 2003, erupted on Memorial Day in 1997, one week before the regular legislative session ended. They were ignited by fights over a bill to require parents to be notified before their minor daughters could receive abortions and a measure that would have prohibited the recognition of gay marriages in Texas. Both measures were to be approved in later years, but they died in 1997, despite the strong support of social conservatives, who formed a significant bloc among Republicans in the House.

After abortion rights supporters and other Democratic House members used parliamentary maneuvers to block debate on both bills, Representative Arlene Wohlgemuth, a Republican from Burleson, used a technical procedural point to block consideration of fifty-two other bills remaining on the House's Memorial Day calendar. Wohlgemuth's move effectively killed most of the bills because that day was the deadline for the House to consider them on second reading. Sponsors managed to save only a few of the measures, including an education bill strongly supported by then-Governor George W. Bush, by tagging them on as amendments to related bills that had already won House approval.

Wohlgemuth said she was simply retaliating against House members who killed the bills on abortion restrictions and same-sex marriages, which social conservatives believed would have passed had they been able to vote on them. "I think that a statement needs to be made about why measures that are important to families, important to the people of this state, have not been heard, have not been voted on," she said.

Wohlgemuth's action wasn't entirely partisan because some of the bills that she killed or jeopardized, including Bush's education priority, were sponsored by other Republican legislators. But the action had strong partisan overtones and was a preview of future legislative sessions.

Representative Kent Grusendorf of Arlington, an outspoken Republican critic of then-Democratic Speaker Pete Laney, supported Wohlgemuth. He said committees controlled by Democrats had stalled bills that were important to Republicans and that had majority support in the House.

But longtime Democratic Representative Dan Kubiak of Rockdale, in a speech on the House floor, strongly criticized Wohlgemuth's tactic. Kubiak said the incident—which he dubbed the "Memorial Day Massacre"—"was only the latest outbreak of the cancer that threatens not only this body, but the democratic process itself."

Kubiak died the next year, and the voters in his central Texas district replaced him with a Republican. Partisanship remained a threat in the statehouse.

Source: Dallas Morning News, May 28, 1997.

elections. They increased their majority in the state Senate to 19–12, captured an 88–62 majority in the Texas House, their first since Reconstruction, and elected Republican Tom Craddick of Midland as speaker. Those victories, plus the elections of Governor Rick Perry and Lieutenant Governor David Dewhurst, gave Republicans control of all the points of power in the statehouse. They controlled the budget-setting process in 2003, making significant cuts in services to close a $10 billion revenue shortfall, enacted significant new restrictions on civil lawsuits, and won the fight over congressional redistricting. Throughout the year, partisanship was stronger than it had been since the GOP became a competitive party in Texas.

Craddick and Dewhurst appointed Democrats, as well as Republicans, to chair committees and serve in other leadership positions. Democrats chaired six of the Senate's fifteen standing committees and thirteen of the forty-three committees in the House. Craddick also appointed a Democrat, state representative Sylvester Turner of Houston, as speaker pro tempore. But Craddick stacked the key chairmanships and the membership of the budget-writing House Appropriations Committee with Republicans who clearly reflected his conservative viewpoint. After winning a change in House rules that removed seniority as a factor in appropriations appointments, the new speaker bumped from the panel three outspoken Democrats who opposed budget cuts.

Democrats regained some of their lost House seats in subsequent elections and, sooner or later, likely will recapture majorities in both the House and the Senate. So, partisanship will remain part of the legislative process for the foreseeable future. Before too many more years, the legislature may even organize itself along the same partisan lines as the U.S. Congress, with distinct party positions, such as floor leaders, caucus leaders, and whips. If this were to happen, the legislative rules and powers of the presiding officers discussed earlier in this chapter would be significantly changed. But this development will depend on how long Republicans continue to dominate the statehouse, on how Democrats continue to react, and on the future leadership personalities that emerge in both parties. Another factor will be how well the two factions in the Republican Party—the traditional, fiscal conservatives and the social conservatives—are able to accommodate each other's interests.

Other Legislative Caucuses

★ **bloc**
Group of legislators who act together for a common goal regardless of party affiliation.

Hispanic and African American House members formed their own caucuses as their numbers began to increase in the 1970s in the wake of redistricting and the creation of urban single-member districts. Their cohesive **blocs** of votes have proved influential in speaker elections and the resolution of major statewide issues, such as health care for the poor, public school finance, and taxation. Their ability to broker votes has won committee chairs and other concessions they may not otherwise have received (see *People in Politics*: "Gregory Luna and Irma Rangel: Champions of Education").

Some urban delegations, such as the group of legislators representing Harris County, the state's most populous county, have formed their own caucuses to discuss and seek consensus on issues of local importance. In Harris County's case, consensus is often difficult to achieve on local controversies because of the political, ethnic, and urban–suburban diversity within the delegation. Twenty-five House members—one-sixth of the body's membership—represent various parts of Houston and Harris County, and seven senators have districts that are wholly within or include part of the county.

Legislators and Their Constituents

Although representative government is an essential component of American society, there are continued debates as to how people elected to public office should identify the interests and preferences of the people they represent.[20] Political theorists as well as legislators struggle with the problem of translating the will of the people into public policy. Most legislators represent diverse groups and interests in their districts. During a normal legislative session, there are thousands of proposed laws to consider, and legislators must constantly make decisions that will benefit or harm specific constituents.

Except for an occasional emotional issue—such as whether motorcycle riders should have to wear safety helmets or whether private citizens should be allowed to carry pistols—most Texans pay little attention to what the legislature is doing. That is why they are often surprised to discover they have to pay a few extra dollars to register their cars or learn that the fee for camping in a state park has suddenly been increased. Very few Texans can identify their state representatives or

People in Politics Gregory Luna and Irma Rangel: Champions of Education

Gregory Luna and Irma Rangel made important contributions to young people, particularly minorities, in the legislature and other public forums.

Luna, whose father died when he was an infant, knew firsthand the difficulties that many Texas children faced in securing an education and a chance at a better life. He was only 11 when he got his first job as a busboy in a restaurant. After working as a police officer to help put himself through college and law school, Luna then devoted much of his adult life to improving civil rights and educational opportunities for Hispanics and all Texans.

As an attorney in San Antonio in 1968, Luna helped found the Mexican American Legal Defense and Educational Fund (MALDEF), which has waged successful courtroom fights for civil rights. MALDEF has forced school boards and other governments to redraw political boundaries to assure minority representation on governing bodies. And in the 1980s, MALDEF filed a landmark lawsuit against the state that forced the Texas Legislature to distribute state education dollars more equitably among wealthy and poor school districts.

Luna served in the Texas House from 1985 to 1992 and in the state Senate from 1993 until illness forced his resignation in September 1999. He died a few weeks later of complications related to diabetes. He was 66.

Luna was chair of the Senate Hispanic Caucus and vice chair of the Senate Education Committee, and throughout his legislative career he fought for improvements in school funding and for better educational opportunities. His legislative style was usually low-key, but he was effective. He knew what he had to do to accomplish a goal and quietly went about doing it.

"He was a monument of many, many people who were able to benefit from his efforts for a better education system for everyone," said the Reverend Virgil Elizondo. "He was in the ministry of public service."[a]

Rangel, a Democrat from Kingsville, was a schoolteacher and a prosecutor before becoming, in 1976, the first Hispanic woman elected to the Texas House. She chaired the House Higher Education Committee for several years and sponsored a state law to boost affirmative action by requiring Texas colleges and universities to automatically admit students who graduated in the top 10 percent of their high school classes. She also was instrumental in boosting state funding for higher education institutions along the border with Mexico.

Rangel was still a member of the House—its fifth most senior member—when she died of cancer in March 2003 at age 71. State representative Pete Gallego (D-Alpine), chairman of the Mexican American Legislative Caucus, called Rangel's life a "testament to everything that is good about public service."[b]

[a]The *Associated Press*, as published in the *Houston Chronicle*, November 10, 1999.

[b]*Houston Chronicle*, March 19, 2003, p. 25A.

Caucuses and Informal Alignments

In addition to the political parties, other common interests bring legislators together in caucuses. This is a meeting of the Hispanic Caucus of the Texas House.

senators by name, and far fewer can tell you what their legislators have voted for or against. This public inattention gives a legislator great latitude when voting on public policies. It also is a major reason that most incumbent lawmakers who seek reelection are successful. Most legislative turnover is the result of voluntary retirements, not voter retribution.

Several Democratic incumbents, however, fell victim to redistricting that favored Republican challengers in 2002. Some were unseated at the polls, and others didn't seek reelection because of the redrawn district lines. And several incumbents of both parties have been unseated in their own party primaries in recent elections because of the controversy over Tom Craddick's speakership.

Media coverage of the legislature is uneven. The large daily newspapers with reporters in Austin make commendable efforts to cover the major legislative issues and players and provide both spot news accounts and in-depth interpretation of the legislature's actions. All too frequently, however, they are limited by insufficient space and rarely publish individual voting records or attempt to evaluate the performance of individual legislators. Most television and radio news shows provide only cursory legislative coverage.

Although legislators are aware of latent public opinion, they tend to be more responsive to the interest groups, or attentive publics, that operate in their individual districts or statewide.[21] People who are well informed and attentive to public policy issues are a relatively small portion of the total population, but they can be mobilized for or against an individual legislator. In some instances, they are community opinion leaders who, directly or indirectly, are able to communicate information to other individuals about a legislator's performance. Or they may belong to public interest and special interest groups that compile legislative voting records on selected issues of importance to their memberships. Although these records are only sporadically disseminated by the news media to the general public, they are mailed or e-mailed to the sponsoring groups' members.

Many special interest groups contribute thousands of dollars to a legislator's reelection campaign or to the campaign of an opponent. But politically astute legislators duly take note of all the letters, phone calls, e-mail messages, petitions, and visits by their constituents—plus media coverage—lest they lose touch with a significant number of voters with different views on the issues and become politically vulnerable.

A favorite voter-contact tool of many legislators is an occasional newsletter, which they can mail to households in their districts at state expense. These mailings usually include photos of the lawmaker plus articles summarizing, in the best possible light, his or her accomplishments in Austin. Sometimes legislators also include a public opinion survey seeking constituent responses on a number of issues.

Legislative Decision Making

In addition to the formal rules of each legislative body, there are unwritten rules, or norms, that shape the behavior of legislators and other actors in the law-making process. The legislature is like most other social institutions in that its members have perceptions of the institution and the process as well as the way they are expected to behave or carry out their responsibilities. Other participants also impose their views and expectations on lawmakers.[22]

The legislative process is designed to institutionalize conflict, and the rules and norms of the legislature are designed to give this conflict an element of civility. Debate is often intense and vigorous, and it may be difficult for some lawmakers to separate attacks on their positions from attacks on their personalities. But most legislators have learned the necessity of decorum and courtesy. Even if lawmakers believe some of their opponents in the House and Senate are deceitful, personal attacks on other legislators are considered unacceptable. Personal attacks, even to the point of fistfights, occasionally occur, but they are rare.

With about 6,300 pieces of legislation introduced during a regular session—the level reached in 2007—no legislator could possibly read and understand each bill, much less the hundreds of amendments offered during floor debate. And despite moments of high drama when issues of major statewide importance are being debated, most legislative work is tedious and dull and produces little direct political benefit for most senators and representatives. But many of those bills contain hidden traps and potential controversies that can haunt a legislator later, often during a reelection campaign. So legislators use numerous information sources and rely on the norms of the process to assist them in decision making.

To make the process work, legislators must accommodate the competing interests they represent and achieve considerable reciprocity among themselves. An individual legislator usually will have no direct political or personal interest in most bills because much legislation is local in nature and affects only a limited number of lawmakers and constituents. A legislator accumulates obligations as he or she supports another lawmaker's bill, with the full expectation that his or her consideration will be returned in kind.

A number of factors, however, help shape lawmakers' decisions on major legislation.[23] The wishes of constituents will be considered, particularly if there is a groundswell of dominant opinion coming from a legislator's district. Legislators also exchange information with other lawmakers, particularly with members of the same caucus, members who share the same political philosophy, and colleagues from the same counties or regions of the state. Lawmakers often take their cues from bill sponsors or the speaker's and lieutenant governor's leadership teams. Identifiable patterns of giving and taking cues also are emerging along party lines, particularly on budgetary, taxation, and redistricting issues.

A legislator's staff also assists in the decision-making process, not only by evaluating the substantive merits of legislation but also by assessing the political implications of a lawmaker's decisions. The Legislative Budget Board and the Legislative Council provide technical information and expertise that can also be weighed by legislators.

Interest groups are major sources of information and influence. Although an individual legislator will occasionally rail against a specific group, most lawmakers consider interest groups absolutely essential to the legislative process. Through their lobbyists, interest groups provide a vast amount of technical information and can signal the level of constituency interest, support, or opposition to proposed laws. A senator or representative can use interest groups to establish coalitions of support for a bill, and some legislators become closely identified with powerful interest groups because they almost always support a particular lobby's position.

The governor can also influence the legislature in several ways. He or she can raise the public's consciousness of an issue or need and can promote solutions through speeches and through the media. The governor can communicate indirectly to individual lawmakers through the governor's staff, party leaders, and influential persons in a lawmaker's district. The governor can also personally appeal to lawmakers in direct one-on-one meetings or in meetings with groups of legislators. At the beginning of each regular session, the governor outlines his or her legislative priorities in a State of the State address to a joint session of the House and the Senate, and the governor usually has frequent meetings with the lieutenant governor and the speaker throughout a session.

The Governor's Personal Touch

Governor Rick Perry "works the floor" of the Texas House of Representatives during a recent legislative session.

The governor may also visit the House or Senate chamber in a personal show of support when legislation that he or she strongly advocates is being debated. Unlike most recent governors, former Governor Ann Richards personally testified before legislative committees on several of her priorities, including ethics reform and government reorganization, during her first year in office. The severity of a governor's arm-twisting is often in the eye of the beholder, but it can include appeals to a lawmaker's reason or conscience, threats of retaliation, appeals for party support, and promises of a quid pro quo. The greatest threat that a governor can hang over a legislator is the possible veto of legislation or a budget item of importance to him or her. In special sessions, the governor also can negotiate with a lawmaker over whether to add a bill that is important to the legislator to the special session's agenda, which is controlled by the governor.

Legislators also get information and support from other elected statewide office-holders, such as the attorney general, the comptroller, or the land commissioner. These officials and lawmakers can assist each other in achieving political agendas.

The news media provide information and perspective on issues in broader political terms. In part, the policy agenda is established by those issues the media perceive to be important.

The relative importance of any groups or actors on decision making is difficult to measure and varies from lawmaker to lawmaker and from issue to issue. Outside influences can also be tempered by a legislator's own attitude and opinion. On many issues, legislators get competing advice and pressure. As much as a lawmaker may like to be all things to all people, that cannot be. She cannot please a chemical lobbyist, who is seeking a tax break for a new plant

Politics Up Close   Legislative Reputations: Not All the Same

Some legislators become known for their commitment to producing good legislation. They spend endless hours developing programs and are repeatedly turned to by presiding officers to handle tough policy issues. Other lawmakers tend to look to their leadership for direction and cues, giving them considerable influence and power. And they are also essential to a productive legislative session.

Other legislators earn reputations as grandstanders. Almost every legislator has shown off for the media or the spectators in the gallery at one time or another, but a number have developed a distinct reputation for this style of behavior. They appear to be more interested in scoring political points with their constituents or interest groups—with the objective of being reelected or seeking higher office—than with mastering the substance of legislation. Many of these lawmakers are lightweights who contribute little to the legislature's product. And although they may introduce many bills during a session, they are not interested in the details of the law-making

process and are unable to persuade other legislators to support their legislation.

The legislature also has a number of opportunists, including members who pursue issues to produce personal or political benefits for themselves. They may sponsor legislation or take a position on an issue to curry favor with a special interest group or benefit their personal businesses or professions. Legislative rules prohibit legislators from voting on issues in which they have a personal monetary interest, but individual lawmakers can interpret that prohibition as they see fit. Many lawmakers will try to cash in on their legislative experience by becoming lobbyists after they leave office at considerably higher pay than they received as legislators.

Still other legislators appear to be little more than spectators. They enjoy the receptions and the other perks of the office much more than the drudgery of the committee hearings, research, and floor debates. Some quickly become weary of the legislative process and, after a few sessions, decide against seeking reelection.[a]

[a]These legislative styles are similar to those developed by James David Barber, *The Lawmakers*. New Haven, Conn.: Yale University Press, 1965, Chs. 2–5.

on the Gulf Coast and also happens to be a large campaign contributor, and environmentalists, who fear the facility would spoil a nearby wildlife habitat. He cannot please the governor, who is promoting a lottery as a new state revenue source, and most of the voters in his district, who have consistently voted against gambling. The ultimate decision and its eventual political consequences are the legislator's.

Should lawmakers cast particular votes on the basis of the specific concerns of their districts, their personal convictions, the position of their political party, or the wishes of the special interest groups that helped fund their campaigns? These issues reflect complex relationships between the legislator and the people represented. And since the overriding consideration for most lawmakers is to get reelected, the legislator must balance them carefully (see *Politics Up Close:* "Legislative Reputations: Not All the Same").

The Development of Legislative Staff

The quality of a legislator's staff can help determine his or her success, and both the quality and quantity of legislative staffs have been significantly enhanced since the early 1970s.[24] This growth reflects an emerging professional approach to lawmaking and meeting the needs of an increasingly complex urban state. During recent regular sessions, the House has had about 900 employees, including part-time workers, and the Senate about 800. These figures included Capitol and district office staff for individual senators and representatives, committee staffs, assistants to the lieutenant governor and the speaker, and other support staff hired directly by the House and the Senate.

Additionally, there are permanent staff members assigned to the Legislative Budget Board, the legislature's financial research arm; the Legislative Council, which researches issues and drafts bills and resolutions for introduction by legislators; and the Legislative Reference Library, which provides resource materials for lawmakers, their staffs, and the general public. Other support staff is assigned to the Sunset Advisory Commission, which assists the legislature in periodic reviews of state agencies, and the state auditor, who is chosen by and reports to the legislative leadership.

Legislative staffers range from part-time secretaries and clerks to lawyers and other professionals who draft bills and direct research resulting in major state laws. There are limits on the number of staff members and funds allocated for legislators' personal staffs. As a general rule, senators have larger staffs than House members. Staffing levels are usually reduced between sessions, and some members shut down their Capitol offices entirely. Most lawmakers, however, maintain offices both in Austin and in their districts, even if staffs function only to answer the phone.

A key support group in the House is the House Research Organization, which was organized as the House Study Group in the 1970s by a handful of primarily liberal lawmakers. The group's name was later changed, and its structure was reorganized to represent the entire House, but it still fills a strong research role. It is supported by funds from the House budget and is governed by a steering committee that represents a cross section of Democratic and Republican House members. During legislative sessions, its staff provides detailed analyses, including pro and con arguments, of many bills on the daily House calendar. During interims between sessions, it provides periodic analyses of proposed constitutional amendments and other issues. The Senate formed a similar organization, the Senate Research Center, in 1991.

Assisting in the Heavy Workload

As the legislative workload has become increasingly complex, legislators have expanded their Capitol and district staff. Senator Jeff Wentworth (R-San Antonio) meets with a legislative aide in the Senate chamber.

The quality of other resources available to lawmakers has also improved in recent years. Legislators and their staffs can routinely check the status or texts of bills online, and so can the public. The Legislative Council maintains a Web site on the Internet that includes committee schedules, bill texts and analyses, and other legislative information. Private citizens also can use the Web site to identify their state representatives and senators.

Legislative Ethics and Reforms

The majority of legislators are honest, hardworking individuals. But the weaknesses of a few and the millions of dollars spent by special interests to influence the law-making process undermine Texans' confidence in their legislature and their entire state government. Although legislators cannot pass laws guaranteeing ethical behavior, they can set strong standards for themselves, other public officials, and lobbyists; and they can institute stiff penalties for those who fail to comply. Such reform efforts are periodically attempted, but, unfortunately, they usually are the result of scandals and fall short of creating an ideal ethical climate.

Fallout from the Sharpstown stock scandal helped an outsider, Uvalde rancher Dolph Briscoe, win the 1972 gubernatorial race and helped produce a large turnover in legislative elections. In 1973, the legislature responded with a series of ethics reform laws, including requirements that lobbyists register with the secretary of state and report their expenditures. State officials were required to file public reports identifying their sources of income, although not specific amounts.

Weaknesses in those laws, however, were vividly demonstrated in 1989, when wealthy East Texas poultry producer Lonnie "Bo" Pilgrim distributed $10,000 checks to several senators in the Capitol while lobbying them on workers' compensation reform, and the Travis County district attorney could find no law under which to prosecute him. There also were published reports that lobbyists had spent nearly $2 million entertaining lawmakers during the 1989 regular session without having to specify which legislators received the "freebies," thanks to a large loophole in the lobby registration law. News stories about lobbyists treating lawmakers to golf tournaments, ski trips, a junket to Las Vegas for a boxing match, and limousine service to a concert created an uproar.

Some senators had angrily rejected Pilgrim's checks on the spot; others returned them after the media pounced on the story. But the very next year, Pilgrim—a longtime political contributor—again contributed thousands of dollars to several statewide officeholders and candidates. This time, the checks were sent more traditionally through the mail, and they were gratefully accepted.

Despite all the headlines over ethical problems, legislative turnover was minimal in 1990. But in early December, about a month after the general election, a Travis County grand jury began investigating Speaker Gib Lewis's ties to a San Antonio law firm, Heard Goggan Blair and Williams. The firm had made large profits collecting delinquent taxes for local governments throughout Texas under a law that allowed it to collect an extra 15 percent from the taxpayers as its fee. For several years, it had successfully defeated legislation that would have hurt its business. The *Fort Worth Star–Telegram* reported that Heard Goggan had paid about half of a $10,000 tax bill owed to Tarrant County by a business that Lewis partly owned.[25] And the *Houston Chronicle* reported that the grand jury was also looking into a trip that Lewis had taken to a Mexican resort during the 1987 legislative session with four Heard Goggan partners and a lobbyist (all males) and six women (including a waitress from a topless nightclub in Houston).[26] The trip had been taken while a bill opposed by Heard Goggan was dying in a House committee.

On December 28, only 12 days before the 1991 regular legislative session was to convene and Lewis was to be reelected to a fifth term as the House's presiding officer, grand jurors indicted him on two misdemeanor ethics charges. He was accused of soliciting, accepting, and failing to report an illegal gift from Heard Goggan—the partial payment of the tax bill. Lewis insisted he was innocent and vowed to fight the charges. He said the tax payment was the settlement of a legal dispute, and he angrily accused Travis County District Attorney Ronnie Earle, who headed the prosecution and had been publicly advocating stronger ethics laws, of using the grand jury to "influence the speaker's election." Lewis said that Earle was guilty of "unethical and reprehensible behavior."[27] Lewis won a postponement of his trial under a law that automatically grants delays to legislators when they are in session. The grand jury investigation continued for several more weeks, but no more indictments were issued.

Meanwhile, Governor Ann Richards urged the legislature to pass a law imposing tougher ethical requirements on state officials and lobbyists. The Senate approved an ethics bill fairly early in the session, but the House did not act on its version until late in the session. The final bill was produced by a conference committee on the last night of the regular session in a private meeting and was approved by the House and the Senate only a few minutes before the legislature adjourned at midnight. There was no time to print and distribute copies, and few legislators knew for sure what was in the bill. Despite the secrecy and complaints that the measure was not strong enough, Richards signed the bill. She called the new law a "very strong step in the direction of openness and ethics reform in this state."[28]

The measure required additional reporting of lobby expenditures and conflicts of interest between lobbyists and state officials, prohibited special interests from treating legislators to pleasure trips, prohibited lawmakers from accepting fees for speaking before special interest groups, and created a new state Ethics Commission to review complaints about public officials.

But the new law did not put any limits on financial contributions to political campaigns, nor did it prohibit legislator-attorneys from representing clients before state agencies for pay. Moreover, it authorized the Ethics Commission to slap a bigger fine ($10,000) on someone who filed a frivolous complaint against a public official than the maximum fine ($5,000) that could be levied on an officeholder for violating the ethics law. That latter provision was viewed by many critics as an unreasonable effort to discourage citizen complaints. The new law also provided that complaints filed with the Ethics Commission would remain confidential unless the commission took action, a provision that would allow the commission to dismiss or sit on legitimate complaints without any public accounting.

In January 1992, Lewis announced that he would not seek reelection to another term in the House. In a plea bargain later the same month, prosecutors dropped the two ethics indictments against him in return for the speaker's "no contest" plea to two minor, unrelated charges. Lewis paid a $2,000 fine for failing to publicly disclose a business holding in 1988 and 1989, for which he had already paid a minor civil penalty to the secretary of state.

The legislature enacted other significant changes in ethics laws in 2003. The new provisions required officeholders and candidates to identify the occupations and employers of people who contribute more than $500, required financial reports to be filed with the Ethics Commission electronically, increased penalties for people who filed their reports late, and required—for the first time—officeholders and candidates for municipal offices in the large cities to file personal financial disclosure statements, similar to those already filed by state officeholders.

Also in 2003, Travis County District Attorney Ronnie Earle began a lengthy investigation of how corporate contributions were used to affect several legislative elections in the Republican takeover of the House (see Chapter 21). Republicans accused Earle, a Democrat, of playing politics, but Earle said that he was investigating the possibility that corporate funds had been illegally spent on political activity.

The investigation produced several criminal indictments, including charges against Tom DeLay of Sugar Land, the then-powerful Republican leader of the U.S. House of Representatives, and the Texas Association of Business, one of the state's largest business groups. The business group was charged with illegally using corporate money to help Republicans win several House races in 2002. And DeLay and two associates were charged with money laundering and conspiracy relating to alleged improper campaign fundraising for Republican candidates for the Texas House. DeLay and the other defendants said they were innocent of the charges, but the politically charged controversy raged for months. The 2002 legislative elections had been crucial because they not only enabled Republicans to gain a majority of the Texas House, they also gave Republicans enough clout to redraw congressional district lines in Texas, at DeLay's urging, to favor GOP candidates.

A state district judge dismissed charges against the business group and dismissed the conspiracy indictment against DeLay and his two associates, political consultants John Colyandro and Jim Ellis. But the judge let the money laundering charge against the three men stand. By mid-2008, no one had yet come to trial, but the Texas charges and ethical questions in Washington had taken a political toll on DeLay. He stepped down from his leadership position in January 2006 and resigned from Congress later that year.

Summary
Who Gets What: Texas Legislature

Texas, the nation's second most populous state and third largest economy, has a part-time legislature that operates under detailed anti-government restrictions drafted by nineteenth-century Texans in the wake of the repressive Reconstruction era. It is a law-making body that is not structured to respond readily to twenty-first century needs and crises.

★ As recently as 1971, there was only a handful of African Americans, Hispanics, Republicans, and women in the 150-member House of Representatives and the 31-member Senate. But political realignment and federal court intervention in redistricting—particularly the ordering of single-member House districts for urban counties in 1972—have significantly increased the number of women, ethnic minorities, and Republicans in the legislature.

Republicans now have a majority of both legislative bodies.

★ Unlike the U.S. Congress, the Texas Legislature is not organized along party lines and has only the tentative beginnings of an institutionalized leadership structure. The presiding officer of the House is the speaker, who is elected by the other House members. The presiding officer of the Senate is the lieutenant governor, who is elected by the voters statewide.

★ The most significant powers of the speaker and the lieutenant governor are the appointment of House and Senate committees, which screen and draft legislation, and the assignment of bills to committees. The fate of most legislation is decided at the committee level. Most House committees are partially appointed on the basis of seniority, but the lieutenant governor has absolute control over the composition of Senate committees. The presiding officers also play key roles in the development of major legislative proposals and, to a great extent, depend on their handpicked committee chairs to sell their legislative programs to House and Senate colleagues.

★ Traditionally, the powers of the presiding officers have been enhanced by the Calendars Committee in the House and the two-thirds rule in the Senate. The Calendars Committee, composed entirely of speaker appointees, sets the schedule for floor debate in the House. The two-thirds rule provides that two-thirds of the Senate must approve before any bill can be debated on the floor of that body. That means that eleven senators can block, or kill, any piece of legislation that has majority support. The lieutenant governor decides which Senate sponsors are recognized for consideration of specific bills.

★ To be sent to the governor for signature into law, a bill must be approved after three readings in both the House and the Senate. Referral to committee is the first reading, which is as far as most bills progress. Many are never scheduled for a public hearing by the chairs of the committees to which they are assigned. Many others die in subcommittees to which they are sent after being heard by the full committee. And others do not survive the Calendars Committee in the House or the two-thirds requirement in the Senate. Those that do win committee approval are often amended, or changed.

★ For those bills that survive the committee process, second reading is a crucial step. That is where most floor debate on legislation occurs and where many bills are further amended. If a bill is approved on second reading, it advances to a third reading and then to the other legislative chamber, where it is referred to a committee and has to repeat the process.

★ A bill must be approved in exactly the same form by both chambers. If the Senate, for example, approves a House bill after making some changes in it, the House will have to concur in—or accept—the Senate version, or a conference committee of House and Senate members will have to be appointed to try to work out a compromise.

★ The governor can sign a bill, veto it, or let it become law without his or her signature. The governor can use the line-item veto to delete specific spending provisions from the general appropriations bill, or state budget. All other bills have to be accepted or rejected in their entirety.

★ Tax bills have to originate in the House. All other bills can originate in either chamber.

★ The legislative rules and heavy volume of bills considered sometimes enable lawmakers to sneak major, controversial proposals into law by adding little-noticed amendments to other bills.

★ The growth of Republican strength has increased partisan activity in the legislature and fueled speculation that, sooner or later, attempts may be made to organize the legislature along the partisan lines of the U.S. Congress. Both major parties already have active legislative caucuses.

★ Legislators' decisions are influenced by a number of factors, including constituents, interest groups, colleagues, staff, the governor, and the media.

★ Legislators have increasingly come to rely on their staffs to develop legislation, perform constituent services, and act as liaisons to interest groups.

★ Although most legislators are honest, hardworking individuals, the weaknesses of a few and the millions of dollars spent by special interests to influence the law-making process have undermined Texans' confidence in state government. Lawmakers make periodic efforts to strengthen their ethical standards, but usually only after well-publicized scandals.

Key Terms

institutionalization   755
bicameral legislature   756
regular session   756
special session   756

single-member
   district   761
Legislative Redistricting
   Board   761

at-large district   761
speaker   764
lieutenant governor   767
quorum   768

committee   771
subcommittee   772
standing committee   772
Calendars Committee   772

Suggested Readings

Ansolabehere, Stephen, and James M. Snyder, Jr. *The End of Inequality: One Person, One Vote and the Transformation of American Politics.* New York, N.Y.: W.W. Norton, 2008. An engaging analysis of the "reapportionment revolution" and its impact on the American political system.

Bickerstaff, Steve. "State Legislative and Congressional Reapportionment in Texas: A Historical Perspective." *Public Affairs Comment* 37 (Winter 1991): 1–13. An excellent overview of three decades of reapportionment litigation in Texas.

Boulard, Garry. "Lobbyists as Outlaws." *State Legislatures* 22 (January 1996): 20–25. A short essay focusing on issues facing state legislatures in the regulation of lobbyists.

Burka, Paul. "Bob Bullock: The Man Who Runs Texas Politics." *Texas Monthly* (September 1994): 100, 162–63. An informative essay on the leadership style of the late Bob Bullock.

Deaton, Charles. *The Year They Threw the Rascals Out.* Austin, Tex.: Shoal Creek Press, 1973. A detailed account of the 1971 Sharpstown Bank scandal.

Hamm, Robert, and Robert Harmel. "Legislative Party Development and the Speaker System: The Case of the Texas House." *Journal of Politics* 55 (November 1993): 1140–51. Traces the development of the Republican Party in the Texas House, emphasizing the potential for the reduction of the power of the speaker.

Jewell, Malcolm E., and Marcia Lynn Whicker. *Legislative Leadership in the American States.* Ann Arbor: University of Michigan Press, 1994. A comparative study of state legislative leadership focusing on leaders' goals, leadership styles, and efforts to be more effective.

Jones, Nancy Baker, and Ruthie Winegarten. *Capitol Women: Texas Female Legislators, 1923–1999.* Austin, Tex.: University of Texas Press, 2000. A compilation of biographies and biographic sketches of the eighty-six females who served in the Texas Legislature from 1923 to 1999, with a focus on their impact on the legislative process and public policy.

Moncrief, Gary F., Joel A. Thompson, and Karl T. Kurtz. "The Old Statehouse, It Ain't What It Used to Be." *Legislative Studies Quarterly* 21 (February 1996): 57–72. A comparative study based on a survey of 330 veteran state legislators summarizing their perceptions of changes in state legislatures.

Mooney, Christopher Z. "Citizens, Structures and Sister States: Influences on State Legislative Professionalism." *Legislative Studies Quarterly* 20 (February 1995): 47–67. Discusses from a comparative perspective the development of "legislative professionalism in terms of a state's population, its governance structures, and the level of professionalism in its peer group states."

Texas Legislative Council. *Presiding Officers of the Texas Legislature, 1846–1995.* Austin, Tex.: Texas Legislative Council, 1995. Brief biographic sketches of presiding officers.

Thorburn, Wayne. "The Growth of Republican Representation in the Texas Legislature: Coattails, Incumbency, Special Elections, and Urbanization." *Texas Journal of Political Studies* 11 (Spring/Summer 1989): 16–28. An early study of the gains made by Republicans in the Texas Legislature.

Suggested Web Sites

Texas Legislature Online   www.capitol.state.tx.us

In addition to providing links to other legislative Web sites, such as the House, Senate, Legislative Budget Board, state auditor, and the Sunset Commission, TLOL provides legislative histories, access to bills, amendments, and statutes affected by proposed legislation.

National Conference of State Legislatures   www.ncsl.org

This national organization provides a wide range of reports and data on state legislatures.

Texas House of Representatives   www.house.state.tx.us

This site provides direct access to live broadcasts of legislative proceedings, information pertaining to the legislative process in the House, information from the speaker's office, and general information about the Capitol complex. Biographical information, committee assignments, district data, and addresses are provided for each member of the House.

Texas Senate   www.senate.state.tx.us

In addition to information from the lieutenant governor's office, biographic information, committee assignments, district data, and addresses are provided for each member of the Senate.

Texas Legislative Council   www.tlc.state.tx.us

The Texas Legislative Council (TLC) is a state agency within the legislative branch. The TLC drafts bills and other legislative documents, conducts legal and public policy research, and produces informational publications for the Senate and the House.

23 THE TEXAS EXECUTIVE AND BUREAUCRACY

❝ We note, too, that the intelligence function is provided for. The Chief Executive is usually charged with responsibility for factual reports and estimates of the future. **❞**

Harold Lasswell

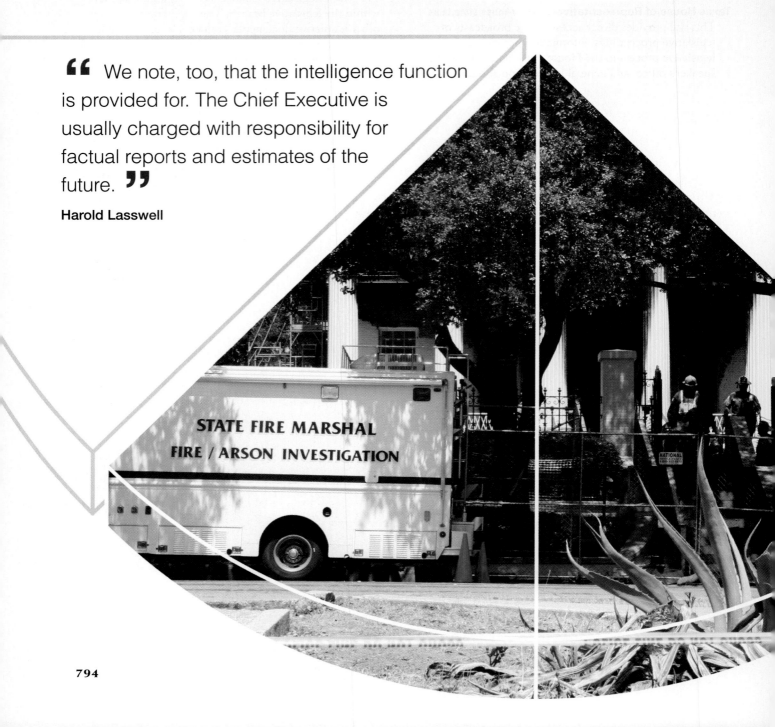

STATE FIRE MARSHAL
FIRE / ARSON INVESTIGATION

Chapter *Outline*

★ A Fragmented Government
★ The Structure of the Plural Executive
★ The Formal Powers of the Governor
★ Informal Resources Available to the Governor
★ Other Offices of the Executive Branch
★ Elected Boards and Commissions
★ The Texas Bureaucracy
★ The Growth of Government in Texas
★ Bureaucrats and Public Policy
★ Strategies for Controlling the Bureaucracy

A Fragmented Government

"One thing Texans have today is a state government that doesn't work very well," the state comptroller concluded after an exhaustive study of state agencies and programs. "It is time to rethink Texas government and how it provides basic services to the state's citizens."[1]

When that study was conducted in 1991, Texas had already been operating under an inefficient, fragmented government for more than a century. Yet no changes in what could be considered the root of the problem—the basic governmental structure—have been made since.

For starters, in Texas no single, elected official is ultimately responsible for the executive branch of state government, that is, for the quality of public services performed by thousands of state workers. Despite public perception to the contrary, Texas has one of the weaker governors in the country. Unlike the president of the United States, the governor of Texas has no formal appointive cabinet through which to impose policy on the governmental bureaucracy. Several major state agencies are headed by independently elected officeholders who don't answer to the governor and sometimes don't even belong to the same political party. Approximately 250 other state agencies and universities are headed by boards and commissions appointed by the governor, but the governor has only indirect—and often spotty—influence over them.

The office of governor is not without prestige and leadership opportunities. Candidates spend millions of dollars and countless hours campaigning for the job. Clearly, it is the most visible state office. But it is institutionally weak, thanks to constitutional restrictions ensuring that no governor repeat the oppressive abuses of Governor Edmund J. Davis and his Reconstruction administration.[2]

Over the years, the governor's lot has improved somewhat. By constitutional amendment, voters empowered the legislature to raise the governor's salary, and the terms of office for the governor and most other statewide executive officeholders were lengthened from 2 to 4 years. In 1980, the governor was given the power, with the approval of the Texas Senate, to remove board members he or she had personally appointed.[3] Nevertheless, these changes have not significantly enhanced the governor's authority. When Governor Ann Richards in 1991 tried to revive

✓ Think About Politics

1. Should the governor and lieutenant governor be elected as a ticket?
   YES ⬭ NO ⬭

2. Should the governor be able to appoint an attorney general and other executive officeholders of his or her choosing?
   YES ⬭ NO ⬭

3. Should a governor be limited to a certain number of terms in office?
   YES ⬭ NO ⬭

4. Should a new governor be able to fire policy makers appointed by a predecessor and replace them with his or her own appointees?
   YES ⬭ NO ⬭

5. Should a nursing home owner be allowed to serve on a state board that regulates the quality of patients' care in nursing homes?
   YES ⬭ NO ⬭

6. Do you believe mismanagement and waste are common in state agencies?
   YES ⬭ NO ⬭

7. Should an elected official be able to hire anyone he or she wants, regardless of the individual's qualifications for a particular job?
   YES ⬭ NO ⬭

Voters perceive the Texas governor to have a great deal of power and influence over public policy and the administration of state programs. But a constitutional legacy of the plural executive limits the governor's formal powers, forcing the chief executive to rely on informal resources to strengthen a weak office.

interest in giving the governor cabinet-style appointment powers over major state agencies, she had only limited success.

The governor can veto legislation and has the exclusive authority to schedule special sessions of the legislature and set their agendas. And, despite its limitations, the appointment power offers the governor an opportunity to make a strong mark on state government. The high visibility of the office also offers a ready-made public forum. Although the Texas Constitution limits the formal powers of the office, a governor's influence is shaped by his or her personality, political adroitness, staff appointments, and ability to define and sell an agenda that addresses broad needs and interests.

The Structure of the Plural Executive

★ **plural executive**
A fragmented system of authority under which most statewide executive officeholders are elected independently of the governor.

You Are a Governor

Article IV, Section 1, of the 1876 Constitution created a **plural executive** branch, which "shall consist of a Governor, who shall be the Chief Executive Officer of the State, a Lieutenant Governor, Secretary of State, Comptroller of Public Accounts, Treasurer, Commissioner of the General Land Office, and Attorney General." Elected officials added later to the executive branch were the agriculture commissioner, the three-member Railroad Commission, and the fifteen-member State Board of Education. The office of treasurer was eliminated by constitutional amendment in 1993. Only the secretary of state is appointed by the governor. Members of the education board are elected from districts; other officeholders are elected statewide (see Figure 23.1). Article IV, Section 4, of the Texas Constitution requires most of these officials to be at least 30 years old and a resident of Texas for at least 5 years.

Agencies headed by these elected officials are autonomous and, except for limited budgetary review, independent of the governor. In a confrontation with the governor over policy, agency heads can claim their own electoral mandates. For many years, there were only "scattered incidents of hostility within the executive branch," and elected officials generally "cooperated remarkably well with their chief executives"—at least while Texas was a one-party Democratic state.[4] During that period, party politics was dominated by conservatives, whose interests were generally served by state officials who believed it was in their own best political interests to cooperate with one another.

But the potential for conflict between the governor and other executive officials increased as Texas became a two-party state, and conflict is likely to become more common in the future, even among officials from the same party. During Republican Governor Bill Clements's first term (1979–83), the other elected officers in the executive branch were Democrats, including Attorney General Mark White, who frequently feuded with the governor. White jockeyed for the political advantage that allowed him to unseat Clements in 1982.

In 2003, budgetary differences erupted between Republican Comptroller Carole Keeton Strayhorn and other Republican officeholders, including Governor Rick Perry. They resulted in the legislature's approval of a bill, signed by Perry, transferring two key programs from the comptroller's office to the Legislative Budget Board. The political animosity between Strayhorn and Perry intensified, and in 2006 the comptroller unsuccessfully challenged the governor's reelection as an independent candidate. Throughout the year, official actions and pronouncements by both officeholders often had sharp political edges. Strayhorn, in particular, jumped on every opportunity to criticize her opponent. Despite the distraction, Perry called a special legislative session and won lawmakers' enactment of school finance changes necessary to meet a Texas Supreme Court deadline in a major education lawsuit. Performing her official duties, the comptroller

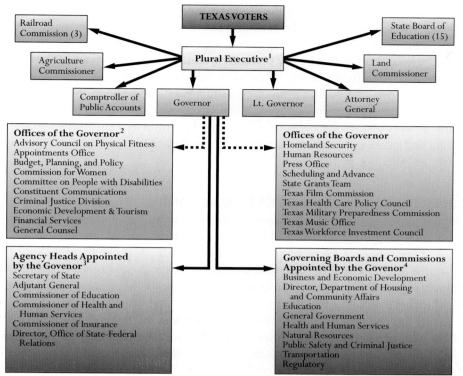

Figure *23.1*

Shared Powers and Responsibilities: The Plural Executive in Texas

The governor shares power with five other statewide elected officials and two elected boards. With a combination of elected and appointed officials who administer more than 200 state agencies, it is often confusing as to who is in charge.

[1] Defined by the constitution or statutory law, the heads of these agencies are elected independently of the governor.

[2] The Offices of the Governor are created under statutory authority and serve to assist the governor in policy development, budgeting and planning, and coordination of policy among agencies and governments. Some 200 persons serve in these offices and are appointed by the governor.

[3] With the exception of the Secretary of State which is authorized under the Texas Constitution, these administrative positions were created under statutory law giving the appointment authority to the governor.

[4] Some two hundred state agencies, including universities, are assigned by statutory law the responsibilities for the administration of public policy in these areas. The members of the governing bodies are appointed by the governor with the approval of the legislature. In turn, the agency executives are appointed by the governing boards.

certified the legislature's action, but she also repeatedly attacked the governor and second-guessed his priorities. She said the school property tax cuts approved by lawmakers and touted by the governor were inadequate, and she criticized Perry for endorsing higher state taxes to help pay for the local tax relief. (This dispute will be discussed further in the section on the comptroller of public accounts later in this chapter.)

When those holding office in a plural executive system have sharply different or competing agendas, it is difficult to develop coordinated policies, even when officials aren't involved in election campaigns against each other. The governor, in an effort to avoid conflict, may pursue policies that are not likely to be disruptive, innovative, or responsive to pressing issues. But proponents of the plural executive contend that it does what it was intended to do: control and constrain the governor. Although collegial or collective decision making is often inefficient and can lead to deadlock, the advocates of the plural executive contend that democracy, in most instances, is to be preferred over efficiency.

The Governor

Gubernatorial leadership styles have been as varied as the personalities that the chief executives have brought to their jobs. Some governors come to the office with well-defined policy agendas and attempt to exploit every resource available to achieve them. Other governors take a more limited view of the office. They adopt an administrative or managerial posture while leaving policy initiatives to other institutions or elected officials. Such governors tend to pursue new programs, especially those with far-reaching tax or social implications, with considerable caution.

Some governors thrive on the constant attention and political and social interactions that go with the office. They work long hours and continually engage in public relations and coalition building. Strange as it may seem, however, there also have been governors who were introverted, even shy, and apparently found many aspects of the office distasteful. They often insulated themselves from the public and other political officials and seemed detached from the activities necessary to influence public policy.[5]

Backgrounds and Requirements for Governorship

The Texas Constitution has few requirements for a person who desires to run for governor. A governor must be at least 30 years old, a U.S. citizen, and a resident of Texas for at least 5 years. There also is a vague requirement that no individual can be excluded from office for religious beliefs, "provided he acknowledges the existence of a Supreme Being" (Article I, Section 4). The constitution, however, does not spell out all the roadblocks to winning the office.

Until the election of Republican Bill Clements in 1978, every governor since 1874 had been a Democrat (see Table 23.1). Clements served two terms (1979–83 and 1987–91). Republican George W. Bush was elected to the office in 1994 and again in 1998, and Republican Rick Perry was elected in 2002 and reelected in 2006, after Republican strength had increased in Texas.

Most governors have been well-educated, middle-aged, and affluent white Protestant males. In many cases, their families also were active in public life and helped shape their careers. No minorities have been elected to the office, but two women, Miriam A. "Ma" Ferguson, whose husband, James E. "Pa" Ferguson, had earlier been governor, served two terms (1925–27 and 1933–35), and Ann Richards served one term (1991–95). By the time Richards became governor, only three women had ever been elected to any other statewide executive office in Texas. Richards, a Democrat, served two terms as state treasurer before being elected governor. She was succeeded as treasurer by Republican Kay Bailey Hutchison. From 1919 to 1923, Annie Webb Blanton was state superintendent of schools, an elective office that no longer exists.

With the rising costs of statewide political campaigns, a candidate's personal wealth or ability to raise large sums of money has taken on increased importance. Otherwise-qualified individuals are dissuaded from running for governor and other offices because of the difficult burden of fund-raising. Former Governor Bill Clements and fellow Republican Clayton Williams, a Midland businessman who lost the 1990 gubernatorial race to Richards, spent millions of dollars out of their own pockets on gubernatorial races that were their first bids for elective office (see *People in Politics*: "Governor Bill Clements: On-the-Job Training"). Similarly, Democrat Tony Sanchez, a wealthy Laredo businessman, spent more than $56 million of his personal fortune in an unsuccessful race for governor in 2002. Their experience raises the possibility that personal wealth and the willingness to spend it on one's own election campaign will take on more importance in future races.

Previous public service has provided gubernatorial aspirants with public recognition and ties to party leaders, interest groups, and public officials around the state. Texas governors have previously served in local and statewide offices, the legislature, and Congress. Preston Smith (1969–73) was a legislator and lieutenant governor before being elected governor. Dolph Briscoe (1973–79) also served in the legislature. Mark White (1983–87) served as secretary of state and

Breaking New Ground
Miriam A. "Ma" Ferguson was the first woman to serve as governor of Texas (1925–27 and 1933–35).

Table *23.1* Governors of Texas Since 1870: The End of
Democratic Dominance

For over 100 years following Reconstruction, governors of Texas came from the
Democratic party. With party realignment, this pattern was broken in 1978 with
the election of Governor William P. Clements, Jr.

	Party	Years Served
Edmund J. Davis	R	1870–1874
Richard Coke	D	1874–1876
Richard B. Hubbard	D	1876–1879
Oran M. Roberts	D	1879–1883
John Ireland	D	1883–1887
Lawrence Sullivan Ross	D	1887–1891
James Stephen Hogg	D	1891–1895
Charles A. Culberson	D	1895–1899
Joseph D. Sayers	D	1899–1903
Samuel W. T. Lanham	D	1903–1907
Thomas Mitchell Campbell	D	1907–1911
Oscar Branch Colquitt	D	1911–1915
James E. Ferguson*	D	1915–1917
William Pettus Hobby	D	1917–1921
Pat Morris Neff	D	1921–1925
Miriam A. Ferguson	D	1925–1927
Dan Moody	D	1927–1931
Ross S. Sterling	D	1931–1933
Miriam A. Ferguson	D	1933–1935
James V. Allred	D	1935–1939
W. Lee O'Daniel	D	1939–1941
Coke R. Stevenson	D	1941–1947
Beauford H. Jester	D	1947–1949
Allan Shivers	D	1949–1957
Price Daniel	D	1957–1963
John Connally	D	1963–1969
Preston Smith	D	1969–1973
Dolph Briscoe, Jr.**	D	1973–1979
Williams P. Clements, Jr.	R	1979–1983
Mark White	D	1983–1987
William P. Clements, Jr.	R	1987–1991
Ann Richards	D	1991–1995
George W. Bush	R	1995–2000
Rick Perry	R	2000–

R = Republican, D = Democrat

* Only governor of Texas to be impeached and convicted.

** Prior to 1974, governors were elected for 2-year terms of office.

Sources: Texas Almanac, 1996–1997 (Dallas, Tex.: The Dallas Morning News, Inc., 1995); Secretary of
State, Elections Division.

then as attorney general. Ann Richards was a county commissioner and then
state treasurer. Although he had never previously held elective office, Clements
was a deputy U.S. secretary of defense prior to winning his first gubernatorial
race. George W. Bush was elected governor in 1994 without any previous formal
government experience. He had been an unofficial adviser to his father, former

People in Politics   Governor Bill Clements: On-the-Job Training

Bill Clements, a self-made multimillionaire who had founded an international oil drilling firm, personally funded much of his first campaign for governor in 1978. The man who shocked the Democratic establishment by defeating John Hill by 17,000 votes had held no previous elected office. His only governmental experience had been as deputy secretary of defense under Presidents Richard Nixon and Gerald Ford. Clements was an outsider, a Republican, a highly opinionated and blunt person, but he had a reputation for solid management skills. All the other elected statewide officials were Democrats, as were most legislators, although many lawmakers shared Clements's conservative views.

On arriving in Austin, Clements did not understand the limitations on the powers of the governor. In his election campaign, he had tapped a rather widely held view that state government was wasteful by proposing that 25,000 state jobs be eliminated. He also appealed to the popular notion of limited government and proposed that the Texas Constitution be amended to allow private citizens to propose laws through a statewide initiative and referendum process. But he gradually learned that he could not run the statehouse and the bureaucracy single-handedly the way he had run the corporate boardroom, and he did not accomplish either of these goals.

In an interview years later, Clements admitted that he did not fully understand how state government worked when he first took office:

> Until I came to Austin and until I actually was in office and everything, I really didn't understand the detailed nuances of how the state government really functioned. I'd say it took me at least through that first legislative session. And by the time that was over, well, I began to understand exactly how the state government works[a].

Clements eagerly exercised his veto power. During his first legislative session in 1979, he vetoed fifty-one bills. He also struck $252 million from the $20.7 billion state budget for 1980–81.

Clements generally received high marks for the quality of his staff and board appointments during his first term. He naturally appointed many fellow Republicans, who for years had been shut out of appointments to boards and commissions, and he also appointed many conservative Democrats. In part, his appointment strategies were designed to convert conservative Democrats to the Republican Party, thus extending and consolidating Republican gains across the state.

But Clements never developed effective ways of communicating with the legislature, the news media, and the general public, and he often found himself at odds with other elected officials and interest groups, primarily because of his outspokenness. He was often portrayed as insensitive, as someone inclined to "shoot from the lip" and worry about the consequences later.

By the end of his first term in 1982, Clements's job performance rating had dropped, his image had suffered, and the Texas economy had begun to show signs of weakness. A revitalized Democratic statewide political effort helped Mark White unseat Clements in a bitterly fought campaign.

In 1986 Clements became only the second person in Texas history to regain the governor's office after losing it. He spent his first 6 months back in Austin battling Lieutenant Governor Bill Hobby and Democratic legislators over the state budget. The problem was critical because revenue from existing taxes had fallen in the midst of a recession. Clements insisted on deep service cuts that would have enabled him to keep a 1986 campaign promise not to raise taxes, but he finally gave in during a summer special session in 1987 and signed a record $5.6 billion tax increase. The public's opinion of Clements, meanwhile, was plummeting. Two-thirds of the respondents to the Texas Poll that summer said they disapproved of the governor's job performance. And Clements's negative ratings remained high throughout the remainder of his term. By the time he left the governor's office the second time, in 1991, he was widely viewed more as an obstructionist who would rather fight the Democratic majority in the legislature than as a leader who was ready to seek solutions to significant state problems.

Clements's two terms coincided with the emergence of a two-party system in Texas, and his candidacy and elections contributed significantly to this historic development. By proving that a Republican could win the governorship, Clements made the Republican Party attractive to many conservative Democrats, and many switched to the GOP.

In an interview shortly before leaving office for the last time, Clements assessed his contribution to the development of a two-party system:

> The electorate out there breaks down into about one-third Democrats, one-third Republicans, and one-third independents. Well, that is a significant change in the political profile of Texas. That's a historic change, and I guess I'd like to say that I put a brick in place to bring that about[b].

[a]Quoted in *Houston Chronicle*, December 2, 1990.
[b]Quoted in *Houston Chronicle*, December 2, 1990.

President George H.W. Bush. Rick Perry was a state representative, agriculture commissioner, and lieutenant governor before becoming governor.

Impeachment and Incapacitation   A governor can be removed from office through **impeachment** proceedings initiated in the House of Representatives and conviction by the Senate in a trial on the impeachment charges. Texas is one of only a few states that have removed a governor with this procedure. In 1917, a controversy erupted over Governor James E. "Pa" Ferguson's efforts to remove five University of Texas (UT) faculty members. The governor vetoed the UT appropriations, and when he called a special legislative session to consider other funding, he was immediately faced with articles of impeachment based primarily on the misuse of public funds. He was ultimately convicted and removed from office, a landmark in the two decades of controversy that surrounded the husband-and-wife team of Pa and Ma Ferguson.[6]

If the governor dies, is incapacitated, is impeached and convicted, or leaves office for another reason in midterm, the lieutenant governor replaces the governor until the next general election. When the governor leaves the state, the lieutenant governor serves as acting governor.

Some other states, such as California, can remove a governor through recall, as well as impeachment. Through a process that begins with petitions signed by a defined number of voters, a special election can be held on the question of removing the governor from office. If the governor is removed by popular vote, a new governor is then elected. This occurred in California in late 2003, when Democrat Gray Davis was recalled as governor, and voters in the same election chose movie star Arnold Schwarzenegger, a Republican, to replace him. Texas doesn't have the recall process for the governor or other statewide officeholders.

Salary and Perks of the Office   In 2008, the governor of Texas was paid $115,345. The state also provides the governor with a mansion and a staff to maintain it, a security detail, travel expenses, and access to state-owned planes and cars.

The Formal Powers of the Governor

Texans appear to have high expectations of their governor. Governors are evaluated in terms of their policy agendas and the leadership they exercise in achieving these goals. But how does a governor meet such expectations when the formal powers of the office are limited? The following discussions analyze the formal or legal powers of the governor's office and the informal resources that the governor can use to complement them.

Legislative Powers of the Governor   Governors have the opportunity to outline their legislative priorities at the beginning of each regular biennial session through the traditional State of the State Address to the legislature. The governor can also communicate with lawmakers, collectively or individually, throughout the session. In this fashion, the governor can establish a policy agenda, recommend specific legislation, and set the stage for negotiations with legislative leaders, other state officials, and interest groups. The governor's addresses and other formal messages to the legislature are well covered by the media. They give governors the opportunity to mobilize the public support that may be essential to the success of their initiatives.

★ **impeachment**
A procedure by which the legislature can remove a governor or certain other public officials from office for misconduct.

Impeachment Politics

Governor James E. "Pa" Ferguson was the only governor to be removed from office through the impeachment process. Ferguson was impeached and convicted in 1917 during a controversy over his efforts to remove five University of Texas faculty members.

★ **special session**
A legislative session that can be called at any time by the governor. This session is limited to 30 days and to issues or subjects designated by the governor.

The governor's effectiveness can be enhanced by the office's two major constitutional powers over the legislature: the veto and the authority to call and set the agenda for special legislative sessions.

The governor can call any number of **special sessions**, which can last as long as 30 days each, and designate the issues to be considered during each one. Sometimes the mere threat of a special session can be enough to convince reluctant lawmakers to approve a priority program of the governor or reach an acceptable compromise during a regular session. Most legislators, who are paid only part-time salaries by the state, dread special sessions because they interfere with their regular occupations and disrupt their personal lives. Governor Bill Clements, who called two special sessions on workers' compensation reform in 1989, used the threat of a third to convince a handful of senators to break a year-long impasse and approve legislation backed by the governor, a majority of the House, and the business community. Governor Rick Perry called three special sessions in 2003 to win approval of a congressional redistricting bill that favored Republican candidates. The bill wouldn't have passed without Perry's persistence (see Chapter 22).

There also are risks in calling special sessions. The governor's influence and reputation are on the line, and further inaction by the legislature can become a political liability or embarrassment. In some instances, the legislative leadership has liberally interpreted the subject matter of a governor's special session proclamation and considered bills not sought by the governor. Because the speaker and the lieutenant governor make the parliamentary rulings that determine whether a specific piece of legislation falls within the governor's call, the governor has to draft proclamations setting special session agendas very carefully. Once a special session is called, the governor can increase his or her bargaining power by adding legislators' pet bills to the agenda in exchange for the lawmakers' support of the governor's program.

★ **veto**
The power of the governor to reject, or kill, a bill passed by the legislature.

The governor of Texas has one of the strongest **veto** powers of any governor. While the legislature is in session, the governor has 10 days to veto a bill or let it become law without his or her signature. A veto can be overridden by a two-thirds vote of both the House and the Senate. During the past 50 years, Governor Clements was the only governor to have a veto overridden. It was a local bill related to game management that the Democrat-dominated legislature voted to override during the Republican governor's first term. The governor has 20 days after the legislature adjourns to veto bills passed in the closing days of a session. Such vetoes are absolute because the only way the legislature can respond is to have the bill reintroduced in the next session.

★ **line-item veto**
The power of the governor to reject certain parts of an appropriations, or spending, bill without killing the entire measure.

The governor also has **line-item veto** authority over the state budget; that is, the governor can strike specific spending items without vetoing the entire bill. All other bills have to be accepted or rejected in their entirety.

A governor may veto a bill for a number of reasons, including doubts about its constitutionality, objections to its wording, concerns that it duplicates existing law, or substantive differences with its policy. A governor's threat of a veto is often as effective as an actual veto because such threats can prompt legislators to make changes in their bills to meet the governor's objections.

Historic records on gubernatorial vetoes are not complete, but Governor Rick Perry is believed to have set a single-year record by vetoing eighty-two bills at the end of the 2001 legislative session. Those vetoes sparked a lot of anger from doctors, criminal justice reformers, state employees, advocates for the poor, and others. One veto, the striking down of a bill that would have banned the execution of mentally retarded convicts in Texas, received international attention. And although that veto was sharply criticized by death penalty opponents, it drew praise from crime victims' advocates. Perry attempted to milk the most favorable publicity that he could from the event by inviting more than a dozen relatives of people murdered by mentally retarded convicts to join him at a state Capitol news conference to announce the veto. Despite his veto, however, the U.S. Supreme Court later had the final say on the issue when it ruled the execution of mentally retarded convicts was unconstitutional. Perry vetoed forty-eight bills after the 2003 regular session, nineteen bills in 2005 and about fifty bills in 2007.

Governor Dan Moody also was a frequent veto user. He vetoed 117 bills and resolutions between 1927 and 1931. Governor Ann Richards vetoed 36 bills and resolutions in one regular and two special sessions in 1991 and allowed 228 bills to become law without her signature.

Budgetary Powers of the Governor

The governor of Texas has weaker budgetary authority than the governors of most states and the president of the United States. These budgetary constraints limit the governor's ability to develop a comprehensive legislative program. The legislature has the lead in budget setting, with a major role played by the **Legislative Budget Board (LBB)**, a ten-member panel that includes the lieutenant governor, the speaker, and eight key lawmakers.

To meet emergencies between legislative sessions, the governor can propose the transfer of funds between programs or agencies, with the approval of the LBB. Or the LBB can recommend a funds transfer, subject to the governor's approval.

★ **Legislative Budget Board (LBB)**
The panel that makes budgetary recommendations to the full legislature. It is chaired by the lieutenant governor and includes the speaker of the House and eight other key lawmakers.

Appointive and Removal Powers of the Governor

Much of the state bureaucracy falls under more than 200 boards and commissions that oversee various agencies created by state law. Most are part-time, unpaid positions whose occupants are heavily dependent on agency staffs and constituents for guidance. Although members of these boards are appointed by the governor and confirmed by the Senate, the structure creates the potential for boards and commissions to become captives of the narrow constituencies they are serving or regulating and reduces their accountability to both the governor and the legislature.

Most board members serve 6-year **staggered terms**, an arrangement under which the terms of one-third of a board's membership expire every 2 years. That means it takes new governors at least 2 years to get majorities favoring their policies on most boards. Resignations or deaths of board members may speed up the process, but a governor cannot remove a predecessor's appointees. Governors, with the approval of two-thirds of the Senate, can fire only their own appointees.

★ **staggered terms**
Terms that begin on different dates, a requirement for members of state boards and commissions appointed by the governor.

During her first year in office in 1991, Governor Ann Richards asked the legislature to give her the power to appoint the executive directors of state agencies directly. These officials historically had been hired by the various boards and commissions. In reorganizing a handful of agencies, the legislature gave the governor a small taste of the cabinet-style authority she had sought, but it hardly changed the system. The governor was given the authority to appoint a new commissioner to oversee several health and human services agencies, the executive director of the Department of Commerce, and the executive director of a new Department of Housing and Community Affairs. The governor retained her previous authority to appoint the secretary of state, the adjutant general, and the director of the Office of State-Federal Relations (see *People in Politics:* "Governor Ann Richards: Saleswoman").

The governor appoints individuals to boards and commissions with the approval of two-thirds of the Senate. **Senatorial courtesy**, an unwritten norm of the Senate, permits a senator to block the governor's nomination of a person who lives in that senator's district. The governor and staff members involved in

★ **senatorial courtesy**
An unwritten practice that permits a senator to block the confirmation of a gubernatorial appointee who lives in the senator's district.

People in Politics   Governor Ann Richards: Saleswoman

Taking her oath in January 1991, Ann Richards attempted to convince the public that her election marked the emergence of a "New Texas." She invited supporters to join her in a march up Congress Avenue to symbolically retake the Capitol for "the people." And, hitting on the progressive Democratic themes of her campaign, she promised in her inaugural address a user-friendly, compassionate state government that would expand opportunities for everyone, particularly minorities and women. But the euphoria of the day was tempered by the reality of a $4 billion-plus potential deficit, a court order for school finance reform that could make the shortfall even greater, and a grand jury investigation into legislative behavior that had eroded public confidence in state government.

Richards moved quickly to establish herself as an activist governor. The day after her inauguration, she continued a campaign assault on high insurance rates by marching over to a meeting of the State Board of Insurance to speak publicly against a proposed increase in auto insurance premiums. Unlike her recent predecessors, she also testified for her priorities before House and Senate committees and used the media to attack the state bureaucracy.

Richards also quickly fulfilled a campaign promise to appoint more women and minorities to key positions in state government. She appointed the first African American to the University of Texas System Board of Regents, the first African American woman to the Texas A&M University governing board, and the first Hispanic to the Texas Court of Criminal appeals. Some 25 percent of her appointees during her first three months in office were Hispanic, 21 percent were African American, and 49 percent were women. Richards also named a disabled person to the Board of Human Services and a crime victim to the Board of Criminal Justice.[a]

With the state facing a revenue crunch, Richards took the lead in lobbying legislators for a constitutional amendment to create a state lottery. The lottery was a relatively safe issue on which to stake a leadership claim because polls indicated it had the strong support of most Texans as a new source of revenue for state government.

Most other major issues before the legislature during Richards's first year in office, however, were not so simple, and the new governor was less willing to strike specific policy positions on them. She preferred to support the initiatives of Democratic legislative leaders—or take the best bill they were willing to give her—rather than demand that legislators enact a specific plan. Detractors would say Richards's leadership

wilted in the heat of legislative battle. Supporters would say she was a pragmatist who knew the limits of her office and recognized the necessity of political compromise.

The progressive goals that Richards had outlined in her campaign were also tempered by the reality that Texas was a predominantly conservative state. Despite promoting a vision of a "New Texas" that offered more compassion for the poor, improved health care for the sick, and greater educational opportunity for all, Richards took pains to establish credentials for fiscal restraint. She opposed a proposal for a personal income tax, even though it could have provided funds for a big boost in spending on health and human services programs and education. And she eagerly embraced a thorough review of state spending practices that helped reduce the size of the revenue and tax bill she eventually signed during her first year in office.

Although Richards entered the 1993 legislative session with one of the highest public approval ratings of any governor in Texas history, she remained cautious during the entire session, apparently to save political capital for a 1994 reelection race. She joined Lieutenant Governor Bob Bullock and Pete Laney, the new House speaker, in insisting that a new state budget be written without an increase in state taxes. There was no tax bill, but the new budget did not enable the legislature to give teachers a pay raise, which had been another Richards priority, and it did not keep up with growing caseloads in health and human services programs.

In one of the most emotional issues of the session, Richards sided with police chiefs, mayors, physicians, and members of the clergy—and against a majority of the legislature—in killing a proposal to allow private citizens to carry handguns. (It was revived and approved under Governor George W. Bush 2 years later.) She successfully advocated an immunization program for children and actively promoted the legislature's efforts to comply with a Texas Supreme Court order for a constitutional school finance system but did not propose a plan of her own.

Richards staked out a strong anti-crime position early in her term. In 1991 she ordered her appointees to the Board of Pardons and Paroles to sharply curtail a high rate of releases from state prisons, and she supported a huge prison expansion program. Richards also made economic development a major goal. She actively recruited companies to locate or expand in Texas and was instrumental in lobbying the U.S. Congress for approval of the North American Free Trade Agreement (NAFTA), even though NAFTA was bitterly opposed by organized labor, one of her key longtime supporters.

Richards was a national figure who was readily welcomed on Wall Street, at Hollywood parties, and in corporate boardrooms throughout the country. Many analysts believed her role as Texas's chief salesperson, or ambassador, was her greatest contribution to the state, along with the appointments that opened up the state policy-making process to a record number of women, Hispanics, and African Americans.

Richards, who had no legislative experience, did not seem to relish the often bloody give-and-take of the legislative process, but she obviously enjoyed her celebrity role as governor. During the 1993 session, Richards told reporters that she was not the kind of leader who could force results. Instead, she said, she tried to contribute to "an atmosphere in which good things can happen."[b]

Although Richards was unseated by Republican George W. Bush in 1994, polls indicated she remained personally popular with her constituents. But most conservative, independent voters had never been comfortable with Richards politically. Her defeat coincided with voter discontent with the Democratic Party that swept the country that year. A number of other Democratic governors were also defeated, and Republicans captured control of both houses of the U.S. Congress. Richards's opposition to the handgun bill during the 1993 legislative session was another factor, particularly in key conservative areas of the state. Richards died of cancer in 2006.

[a]*Texas Government Newsletter*, February 25, 1991.
[b]Quoted in *Houston Chronicle*, June 2, 1993.

appointments spend considerable time clearing potential nominees with senators because political considerations are as important in the confirmation process as a nominee's qualifications.

Individuals seek gubernatorial appointments for a variety of reasons, and the appointments process can be hectic, particularly at the beginning of a new governor's administration. Potential nominees are screened by the governor's staff to determine their availability, competence, political acceptability, and support by key interest groups. And although most governors would deny it, campaign contributions are a significant factor. A number of Governor Clements's appointees had made substantial contributions to his campaign.[7] Governors Richards, Bush, and Perry also appointed major contributors to important posts. Governor Perry made the most controversial appointment of his first year in office, former Enron Corporation executive Max Yzaguirre as chairman of the Public Utility Commission, one day before receiving a $25,000 political donation from then-Enron chairman Ken Lay in 2001. Perry insisted the timing was coincidental, but it generated much controversy after Enron filed for bankruptcy a few months later, prompting Yzaguirre's resignation from the post. Then, in 2003, less than one month after receiving a $100,000 contribution from homebuilder Bob Perry of Houston, Governor Perry appointed a top executive of the homebuilder's company to a new state commission charged with developing building performance standards. The commission had been created by the legislature to reduce consumer lawsuits against builders. Since June 1997, Bob Perry, who wasn't related to the governor, had contributed $580,000 to Rick Perry[8] (see *People in Politics:* "Governor Rick Perry: Claiming His Inheritance").

The governor appoints individuals to fill vacancies on all courts at the district level or higher. If a U.S. senator dies or resigns, the governor appoints a replacement. When a vacancy occurs in another statewide office, except for the lieutenant governor, the governor also appoints a replacement. All appointees must later win election to keep their seats.

Governor Richards was particularly sensitive to constituencies that had historically been excluded from full participation in the governmental process and appointed a record number of women and minorities to state posts. About 45 percent of Richards's appointees during her 4-year term were women, and about 35 percent were minorities.

People in Politics   Governor Rick Perry: Claiming His Inheritance

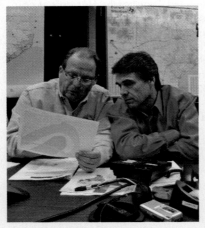

Republican Rick Perry came to the governor's office in December 2000 with much more governmental experience than his immediate and more famous predecessor, George W. Bush. He had served 6 years as a state representative, 8 years as state agriculture commissioner, and almost 2 years as lieutenant governor before succeeding Bush as governor after Bush resigned to become president. But Perry wasn't blessed with Bush's politically powerful name or his popularity, and he hadn't been elected governor. He had inherited the job.

Perry, however, survived his first session mostly unscarred. Lawmakers wrote a new state budget without having to raise taxes and, at Perry's urging, even found enough money to triple funding for a grant program to help thousands of young Texans from low-income families attend college.

The legislature also enacted one of Perry's criminal justice priorities, a law to give inmates the ability to obtain court-ordered DNA testing if they could demonstrate that there was a substantial possibility that the results would prove them innocent. But the governor didn't get his way on another criminal justice issue with significant political overtones. In one of the most emotional and partisan issues of the session, the legislature approved a bill, backed by most Democrats and opposed by most Republicans, to strengthen penalties for crimes motivated by hate or prejudice. It was a fight that had begun in earnest 2 years earlier, after three white assailants had dragged an African American, James Byrd, Jr., to death behind a pickup in East Texas. At one point, Perry convinced a Republican senator to help delay action on the bill because he opposed a provision that listed protected classes of people, including homosexuals, which was strongly opposed by social conservatives in the Republican Party. But after the measure won final legislative approval, Perry signed it within a few hours after it reached his desk. He said he still had doubts about it. "But I also believe that as governor, and as a Texan, I have an obligation to see issues from another person's perspective, to walk in another person's shoes," he said.[a]

Some legislators criticized Perry's mostly low-key style during the 2001 session and complained that he didn't let them know early enough and clearly enough what he wanted. Shortly after the legislative session had ended, however, Perry flexed his muscles and vetoed a record eighty-two bills, including a measure that would have banned the execution of mentally retarded convicts in Texas. Aware that international attention was focused on his decision, Perry invited relatives of murder victims to join him at a state Capitol news conference announcing the veto. Crime victims' advocates praised the veto, but death penalty opponents criticized it. A year later, the U.S. Supreme Court, acting in a case from another state, would prohibit the execution of mentally retarded inmates throughout the country.

Other vetoes drew sharp criticism from a range of people. During his first year as governor, Perry also had to dodge political fallout from the spectacular collapse of Enron Corp., the Houston-based energy-trading giant, which had been a major source of political donations during his public career.

Despite his rural roots—Perry grew up in Paint Creek, a tiny town in West Texas—the governor was acutely aware of the clogged freeways that plagued the daily lives of urban and suburban Texans and, early on, sought to make improved transportation a signature issue of his administration. In early 2002, he proposed a massive, $175 billion transportation network for Texas, which would include toll roads, railroads, and underground utility tunnels grouped in corridors stretching across the state. The plan, which Perry called the Trans Texas Corridor, would take an estimated 50 years to complete.

Perry defeated Democratic nominee Tony Sanchez, a multimillionaire Laredo businessman, in a bruising campaign to win a full term in the governor's office in 2002. Perry's victory and the first Republican takeover of the Texas House in modern times put the GOP in undisputed control of state government, and Perry acted accordingly. The governor joined Republican legislative leaders in demanding that a $10 billion revenue shortfall be closed by cutting spending, not raising taxes, and Republicans prevailed. Advocates of health care programs and other services protested the spending reductions, and many of the state's daily newspapers editorialized for limited tax increases to help minimize the cuts in services. The legislature raised some state fees and enacted legislation to allow university governing boards to increase tuition, but Perry refused to budge on taxes, apparently convinced that most middle-class Texans agreed with him. He also argued that the state's relatively low tax burden had to be protected to keep the state attractive to businesses looking for places to expand. Perry also won from the legislature a special economic development fund that could be used to provide economic incentives for business recruitment.

The governor also advocated and won significant new restrictions on medical malpractice claims and other civil lawsuits. He said the so-called tort reform changes were essential to easing a crisis in health care, particularly in rural areas, and improving the state's business climate, although opponents argued that they put unnecessary new restrictions on consumers' access to the courts.

As was more fully discussed in Chapter 22, Perry also played a dominant role in a bitter, partisan fight over congressional redistricting in 2003. Perry fully supported an effort, initiated by U.S. House Majority Leader Tom DeLay of Sugar Land, to increase the number of Republicans elected to the U.S. House from Texas. Under a 2001 redistricting plan drawn by a federal court, Democrats still held a 17–15 majority in the Texas congressional delegation, despite recent Republican sweeps of all statewide offices and Republican majorities in both the Texas House and the state Senate. DeLay, Perry, and other GOP leaders argued that the congressional delegation should more accurately reflect the state's Republican strength. A bill that would have redrawn congressional districts to favor more Republican candidates died during the 2003 regular session after more than fifty Democratic members of the Texas House fled to Ardmore, Oklahoma, to break a quorum and keep the House from acting on the measure. Using one of his strongest constitutional powers, Perry then called the legislature back into special session that summer to try again. Eventually it took three special sessions to complete the task, but Perry was persistent. He even waited out a second Democratic boycott, when eleven Democratic senators flew to Albuquerque, New Mexico, to hold out for more than a month and shut down the Senate during the entire second special session. A redistricting bill that the legislature finally passed during the third special session gave Republicans a majority in the Texas congressional delegation after the 2004 elections. Several incumbent Democrats lost their seats in the turnover.

Perry's job approval ratings were sub-par during most of that term, partly because of the controversy over redistricting and partly because he and legislative leaders failed repeatedly during 2004 and 2005 to agree on a plan for cutting local property taxes, which the governor had vowed to do during his 2002 election campaign. Finally, in the fall of 2005, Perry enlisted the help of former Comptroller John Sharp, an old friend from his college days at Texas A&M but more recently a political rival, whom Perry had defeated in a hard-fought race for lieutenant governor in 1998. He appointed Sharp, a Democrat, to chair a study commission to make recommendations for restructuring the state tax structure and reducing local property taxes. Within a few weeks of the appointment, the Texas Supreme Court, in a widely anticipated ruling, held that the school finance system was unconstitutional because of a heavy reliance on local property taxes.

The court gave the state until June 1, 2006, to fix the problem or face the prospect of cutting off state funds to the public schools in an election year.

In early 2006, Sharp's commission recommended an expanded business tax and an increase in the cigarette tax to help pay for reductions in local school taxes. Perry endorsed the plan, solicited widespread support from the business community for it, and called the legislature into special session in April. This time, faced with a court deadline, Perry and Republican legislative leaders worked closely together and were successful in getting the plan passed. Democrats and educator groups criticized the tax trade-off because it didn't significantly increase overall funding for education, and Perry also was accused of overstating the significance of the property tax cuts for most Texans. But the plan satisfied the court order.

Perry, meanwhile, had worked to strengthen his support among conservative Republican voters in preparation for his 2006 reelection race. In 2005, he advocated a state constitutional amendment banning same-sex marriage, which Texans overwhelmingly approved, with strong support from fundamentalist churches. He also backed a new state law to require minors to have their parents' permission before obtaining an abortion. Perry also courted nationally prominent conservatives, prompting speculation that he was trying to open the door to a vice-presidential invitation on the 2008 Republican ticket.

Perry attracted three high-profile reelection opponents, an unusually high number, in 2006. They included Democratic nominee Chris Bell, a former congressman and city councilman from Houston, and independents Carole Keeton Strayhorn, the state comptroller, and Kinky Friedman, an author-musician whose campaign was punctuated by satirical one-liners. Strayhorn, who had openly feuded with Perry on budgetary matters, ran as an Independent because she knew she couldn't unseat the governor in the Republican primary. Perry was reelected, but with only 39 percent of the vote.

That low margin may have contributed to the rocky relationship the governor had with many Republican lawmakers during the 2007 legislative session. He infuriated many conservatives by issuing an executive order to require schoolgirls to be vaccinated against a virus linked to cervical cancer. Perry said his order was an important health care initiative. But opponents said it interfered with parental rights and questioned the governor's authority to issue it. With Republicans taking the lead, legislators overwhelmingly approved a bill to rescind it. Many Republican lawmakers, particularly from rural areas, also fought the governor over the expanded use of toll roads, an important, but controversial, part of Perry's transportation plan. Several toll road projects were allowed to continue, but lawmakers placed new limits on privately financed toll projects.

[a]*Houston Chronicle*, May, 12, 2001, p. 1A.

Her successor, Governor George W. Bush, appointed women to 37 percent and minorities to 22 percent of the posts he filled during his first 5 years in office. Bush appointed the first African American, Michael Williams, to the Texas Railroad Commission, and, at different times during his administration, appointed two Hispanics—Tony Garza and Alberto R. Gonzales—secretary of state. Bush later appointed Gonzales to fill a vacancy on the Texas Supreme Court and, after Bush became president, he first appointed Gonzales to the important post of White House counsel, then to United States attorney general. Tony Garza became U.S. ambassador to Mexico.

Governor Perry appointed the first African American, Wallace Jefferson of San Antonio, to the Texas Supreme Court.

Judicial Powers of the Governor Texas has a seven-member Board of Pardons and Paroles appointed by the governor. This panel, which was reduced from eighteen members by a 2003 law, decides when prisoners can be released early, and its decisions do not require action by the governor. The governor, however, can influence the board's overall approach to paroles. The governor has the authority to grant executive clemency—acts of leniency or mercy—toward convicted criminals. One is a 30-day stay of execution for a condemned murderer, which a governor can grant without a recommendation of the parole board. The governor, on recommendation of the board, can grant a full pardon to a criminal, a conditional pardon, or the commutation of a death sentence to life imprisonment.

If a person flees a state to avoid prosecution or a prison term, the U.S. Constitution, under the **extradition** clause, requires that person, on arrest in another state, to be returned to the state from which he or she fled. The governor is legally responsible for ordering state officials to carry out such extradition requests.[9]

★ **extradition**
A process by which a person in one state is returned to another state to face criminal charges.

Military Powers of the Governor The Texas Constitution authorizes the governor to function as the "commander-in-chief of the military force of the state, except when they are called into actual service of the United States" (Article IV, Section 7). The governor appoints the adjutant general to carry out this duty. Texas cannot declare war on another country, and the president of the United States has the primary responsibility for national defense. But when riots or natural disasters occur within the state, the governor can mobilize the Texas National Guard to protect lives and property and keep the peace. Should the United States go to war, the National Guard can be mobilized by the president as part of the national military forces. After the September 11, 2001, terrorist attacks on the World Trade Center and the Pentagon, some National Guard members from Texas were activated to temporarily bolster security at airports. Others went overseas to participate in the military operations in Afghanistan and Iraq. And some were assigned to support the U.S. Border Patrol along the U.S.–Mexico border after President George W. Bush ordered the National Guard's assistance in securing the border during political debate over illegal immigration.

Informal Resources Available to the Governor

Governors can compensate for the constitutional limitations on their office with their articulation of problems and issues, leadership capabilities, personalities, work habits, and administrative styles. Some governors relish being involved in the minutiae of building policy coalitions and devote much of their personal time to bringing about compromises and agreements. Other governors find such hands-on involvement distasteful, inefficient, and time consuming and leave such detail work to subordinates. As the most visible state official, the governor some-times gets credit that belongs to others but can just as readily be blamed for problems beyond his or her control. For example, falling oil prices that had dev-astated the state's economy were a major factor in Mark White's loss in his 1986 reelection bid. White had no choice but to call a special legislative session only a few months before the November election and, under the circumstances, proba-bly exercised the best leadership that he could in convincing lawmakers to cut the budget and raise taxes. But it was not the type of leadership appreciated by most voters.

The Governor's Staff   Nineteenth-century governors had only three or four individuals to assist them, but staffs have grown with the increased complexity of state government and greater demands on the governor's time. By 1963, under John Connally, the governor's staff had grown to 68 full-time and 12 part-time employees.[10] Under the administration of Dolph Briscoe in the 1970s, the staff had further expanded to more than 300, but staff sizes were smaller in most sub-sequent administrations. At one point in her term, Ann Richards had almost 300 people on her staff. The number decreased to about 200 under George W. Bush, but Bush approved higher salaries for some of his key staffers. Governor Perry also has had approximately 200 employees.

The critical question involving staff is whether the governor has access to suf-ficient information on which to make decisions that produce good public policy and minimize the potential for controversy, conflict, and embarrassment. Under ideal circumstances, the staff enhances the governor's political, administrative, and policy-making capabilities. There have been instances, however, when gov-ernors have permitted staff to insulate them by denying access to persons with significant information or recommendations.

Governors generally choose staffers who are loyal and share their basic politi-cal attitudes. Because communication with the governor's various constituencies is fundamental to success, some staffers are chosen for their skills in mass com-munications and public relations. Others are hired for their expertise in specific policy areas. In many respects, staff members function as the governor's surro-gates. Thus, if one makes a mistake—particularly a serious mistake—the public perceives it as the governor's error.

The staff collects, organizes, and screens information, helps decide who sees the governor, and otherwise schedules the governor's time. Staffers also work on strategies to garner support for the governor's proposals from legislators, agen-cies, and interest groups. Because the governor often lacks the time to conduct discussions and negotiations, key staff members represent the governor in such meetings and in personal lobbying of lawmakers. Sometimes governors get involved personally, particularly if their participation is needed to break an impasse and bring about a solution.[11]

The Governor and the Mass Media   The mass media help shape the political and policy options of the governor. Governors who have failed to understand the impact of the media often have courted disaster. A governor who is readily acces-sible to reporters and understands the constraints under which the media operate is likely to develop a good working relationship with the press. But success with the media involves more than being accessible and friendly.

Governors call press conferences to announce new policies or to explain their positions on pending issues. They stage pseudo "news events," such as visits to classrooms to emphasize concern for educational quality or appearances at high-tech facilities to demonstrate a commitment to economic development. They or their staffers sometimes leak information to selected reporters to embarrass the opposition, put an action of the administration in the best possible light, or float a trial balloon to gauge legislative or public reaction to a proposal. Some governors have spent political funds to purchase radio or television time in an attempt to mobilize public opinion in support of pet proposals before the legislature. Overall, the timely use of the media can contribute significantly to the power and influence of a governor.

The Governor and the Political Party

Historically, the political factions within one-party Democratic Texas were somewhat ill defined. Factionalism was often described in terms of liberal or conservative, but there also were complex urban-rural, regional, and economic differences. Democratic governors built policy coalitions around these factions, but there was little stability or continuity, and most governors derived only limited power from their position as party leader. Under the two-party system, however, the political party is taking on more importance and may provide greater resources to the governor (see *Across the USA:* "Party Control of the Governor's Office, 2008"). During his second term in the late 1980s, Bill Clements often had enough Republican votes in the House to thwart the will of the Democratic majority. After Republicans had gained legislative control, Rick Perry had strong support from Republican lawmakers and party officials during the budgetary and redistricting battles of 2003 (see Chapter 22).

On taking office in 1995, Republican Governor George W. Bush enjoyed the support of party leaders for his own priorities—efforts to improve education, restrict civil lawsuits, reform juvenile justice, and change the welfare system. Initially, he kept his distance from much of the agenda advocated by the social conservatives who had taken control of leadership positions in the Texas Republican Party in 1994. But in 1999, when he was preparing for a presidential race, Bush strengthened his anti-abortion credentials with social conservatives by convincing the legislature to enact one of their major priorities—a law requiring parents to be notified before their minor daughters could have abortions. Governor Perry courted social conservatives from the beginning of his administration. He solidified their support for his 2006 reelection race with enactment of a state constitutional amendment banning same-sex marriages and a law that required parental approval, not just notification, for minors to get abortions. Perry, however, encountered much opposition from Republican legislators and other conservatives in 2007 to his effort to expand the use of toll roads and his unsuccessful attempt to order schoolgirls to be vaccinated against a virus linked to cervical cancer (see *Controversy:* "A Political Fight over Women's Health"). Part of Perry's troubles that year may have stemmed from his low reelection margin in 2006. He was reelected with only 39 percent of the vote over three major opponents, including two Independents.

The Governor and Interest Groups

Successful governors must be consummate political animals who continually nurture relationships throughout the political system. A gubernatorial candidate aggressively solicits the endorsements and contributions of various groups. These groups, in turn, develop stakes in gubernatorial elections and usually assume that the candidates they support will be responsive to their interests. A governor's policy initiatives often include legislation of benefit to key support groups, which maintain active roles throughout the policy process. Business groups, for example, were major contributors to Governor Perry's successful election race in 2002, and the governor strongly supported their priorities, including additional limits on civil lawsuits, during the 2003 regular legislative session.

Across the USA — Party Control of the Governor's Office, 2008

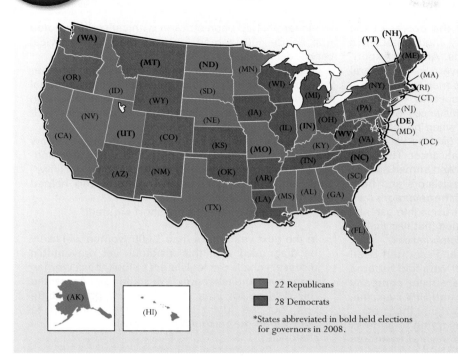

Governors in many states are faced with one or both Legislative houses controlled by the opposition party. Both houses of the Texas Legislature are controlled by the Republican Party, providing the recently elected Republican governors a significant base of support in the policy-making process.

Sources: Democratic Governors Association, "Post Election Governors"; Republican Governors Association, "2008 Gubernatorial Seats Up."

- 22 Republicans
- 28 Democrats

*States abbreviated in bold held elections for governors in 2008.

Other Offices of the Executive Branch

Lieutenant Governor   The **lieutenant governor** is the second highest-ranking official in the state, but the executive powers of this office are limited. Were the governor to die, be incapacitated, be removed from office, or voluntarily leave office in midterm, the lieutenant governor would become governor. That eventuality has occurred only four times. In 1917, William P. Hobby replaced James E. Ferguson, who was impeached. Governor W. Lee O'Daniel resigned in 1941 to enter the U.S. Senate and was succeeded by Coke Stevenson. Governor Beauford Jester died in office in 1949 and was replaced by Allan Shivers. And George W. Bush resigned in December 2000 after being elected president and was succeeded by Rick Perry.

In Texas, the office of lieutenant governor is primarily a legislative office. Many experts consider this position, because of its key legislative role and statewide constituency, the most powerful office in state government. The lieutenant governor, who need not belong to the same party as the governor and is elected independently of the governor, presides over the Senate and has traditionally been given enormous power over the legislative process by the Senate rules. The legislative powers and prerogatives far exceed those of the vice president on the federal level. The lieutenant governor also chairs the Legislative Budget Board, which plays a key role in the state budgetary process.

Democrat Bill Hobby, son of the former governor, served a record 18 years as lieutenant governor before retiring in 1991. He was succeeded by Democrat Bob Bullock, a former state comptroller and one of the most influential state officials

★ **lieutenant governor**
The presiding officer of the Senate. This officeholder would become governor if the governor were to die, be incapacitated, be removed from office, or leave office voluntarily in midterm.

Controversy

A Political Fight over Women's Health

The strict constitutional limits on the power of the governor of Texas are periodically highlighted in a modern era with modern problems. And the experience can be frustrating for the governor. On several occasions, Governor Rick Perry has tried to loosen his restraints but has had only limited success.

One of the most controversial instances of Perry's "muscle flexing" occurred in 2007, when he issued an executive order that all sixth-grade girls be vaccinated against HPV, a virus linked to cervical cancer. The order was legally questionable, and it provoked immediate and loud opposition from Republican legislators and from many other conservative members of the governor's own political base, who viewed it as an intrusion into parental rights. Some conservatives also argued that vaccinating girls against HPV might encourage premarital sex.

Some critics questioned whether Perry had been influenced by a former chief of staff who had become a lobbyist for Merck, the pharmaceutical company that manufactured Gardasil, an anti-HPV vaccine. Merck had been lobbying states to require the shots.

But the governor insisted he was trying to address a critical health care issue. He said several members

of his family had been stricken with cancer and noted that nearly 400 women in Texas died from cervical cancer each year.

The courts never got a chance to determine whether the order exceeded the governor's constitutional authority because the legislature, which was in session that year, made that determination unnecessary. It overwhelmingly approved a law to rescind the order.

"This drug has not been properly studied to know the impact on eleven-year-olds and what the long-term impact might be on those young girls' fertility," said Rep. Dennis Bonnen, R-Angleton, who helped lead the fight against the order.[a]

Perry said lawmakers were short-sighted:

In the next year, more than 1,000 women will likely be diagnosed with this insidious yet preventable disease. I challenge legislators to look these women in the eyes and tell them, "We could have prevented this disease for your daughters and granddaughters, but we just didn't have the gumption to address all the misguided and misleading political rhetoric."[b]

[a]Quoted in *Houston Chronicle*, May 9, 2007, p. 1A.
[b]Quoted in *Houston Chronicle*, May 9, 2007, p. 1A.

in recent history (see Chapter 22). Bullock, who chose not to seek reelection in 1998 and died the next year, was succeeded by Republican Rick Perry, a former state agriculture commissioner.

Perry generally received high marks from senators for his work as presiding officer, but he presided over the Senate for only one session before succeeding Bush as governor after the 2000 presidential election. State senators then elected Senator Bill Ratliff (R-Mt. Pleasant) to complete Perry's term as lieutenant governor and preside over the Senate during the 2001 session. Republican David Dewhurst was elected lieutenant governor in 2002. The former land commissioner had no legislative experience but made a quick, yet thorough, study of major issues and legislative procedures (see Chapter 22). Dewhurst was reelected to a second term as lieutenant governor in 2006.

★ **attorney general**
The state's chief legal officer, who represents Texas in lawsuits and is responsible for enforcing the state's antitrust, consumer protection, and other civil laws.

Attorney General As the state's chief legal officer, the **attorney general** is called on to defend state laws enacted by the legislature and orders adopted by regulatory agencies. The office also enforces the state's anti-trust and consumer protection laws and helps collect child support payments from delinquent non-custodial parents. Recent attorneys general have been kept busy defending the state or negotiating settlements in lawsuits challenging the constitutionality of state prisons, the public school finance system, the method of selecting state judges, and other major policies. The attorney general also gives opinions on the legality of actions of other state and local officials and is at the center of the policy-making process.[12]

Unlike counterparts in the federal government and some other states, the Texas attorney general is primarily a civil lawyer. Except for representing the state in the appeals of death penalty cases and assisting local prosecutors, the attorney general has relatively little responsibility for criminal law enforcement. Many candidates for the office campaign on tough law and order platforms, but responsibilities for criminal prosecution are vested in locally elected county and district attorneys. Reacting to the times, however, Attorney General Greg Abbott created a "cyber crimes unit," which went online to crack down on sexual predators prowling Internet chat rooms, posing as teenagers to lure young victims into personal meetings. His unit, with the assistance of local law enforcement officers, has made numerous arrests.

Dan Morales, a former Democratic state representative from San Antonio, was elected attorney general in 1990, becoming the second Hispanic elected to statewide office in Texas. He won reelection in 1994 but chose not to run for a third term in 1998. He was succeeded by former Texas Supreme Court Justice John Cornyn, Texas's first Republican attorney general in modern times. Cornyn was elected to the U.S. Senate in 2002 and was succeeded by Abbott, another former Texas Supreme Court justice. Abbott was reelected in 2006.

In a major policy decision made independently of the governor, the legislature, and other state officials, Morales in 1996 filed a multibillion-dollar damage suit against tobacco companies, seeking reimbursement for public health care costs associated with smoking. Some state officials supported Morales's decision, although others had reservations about the state jumping into the tobacco controversy. But Morales acted within his authority as the state's chief legal officer. The decision was his alone to make, and it resulted in a $17.3 billion settlement for the state. The tobacco suit also sparked a controversy over legal fees that, several years after Morales had left office, resulted in his being sentenced to federal prison for 4 years for mail fraud and filing a false income tax return (see *People in Politics:* "Dan Morales: A Spectacular Rise and Fall").

Comptroller of Public Accounts

The **comptroller** is the state's primary tax administrator, accounting officer, and revenue estimator. Texas functions under a **pay-as-you-go principle**, which means that the state cannot adopt an operating budget that exceeds anticipated revenue. The comptroller is responsible for providing the revenue estimates on which biennial state budgets are drafted by the legislature. A budget cannot become law without the comptroller's certification that it falls within the official revenue projection. The comptroller's office produces a revenue estimate of all projected state income for the 2-year budget period by using sophisticated models of the state's economy.[13]

The comptroller's powerful role in budgetary affairs was enhanced by the legislature in 1990 with the additional authority to conduct management audits of local school districts, and again in 1991 with similar oversight authority over other state agencies. Through this process, Comptroller John Sharp, a Democrat, and his successor, Republican Carole Keeton Strayhorn, identified billions of dollars' worth of potential savings for legislative budget writers and local school boards.

Strayhorn, who changed her name from Rylander after marrying in early 2003, was a strong supporter of—and reaped favorable publicity from—the management audits. But the legislature, in a 2003 special session, transferred those programs to the Legislative Budget Board after the comptroller had become involved in a series of budgetary disputes with legislators and other Republican leaders. Always outspoken and widely viewed as politically ambitious, Strayhorn had surprised the governor and the legislature with a larger-than-anticipated revenue shortfall of $10 billion at the beginning of the 2003

The State's Chief Legal Officer

Former Texas Supreme Court Justice Greg Abbott, a Republican, was elected attorney general in 2002 and reelected in 2006.

★ **comptroller**
The state's primary tax administrator, accounting officer, and revenue estimator.

★ **pay-as-you-go principle**
A principle written into the Texas Constitution prohibiting state government from borrowing money to meet its operating budget.

People in Politics   Dan Morales: A Spectacular Rise and Fall

Dan Morales was one of state government's biggest vote-getters during two terms as attorney general and, as only the second Hispanic ever elected to statewide office in Texas, was considered a rising star of the Democratic Party. He chose not to seek reelection in 1998. But before leaving office, he sued the tobacco industry over smoking-related health care costs and won a $17.3 billion settlement for the state from cigarette manufacturers. The settlement, to be paid out over many years, would generate huge amounts of revenue for health care or any other programs the legislature chose.

The settlement was clearly the highlight of Morales's political career, but, ironically, it also contributed to his eventual downfall. The settlement sparked much controversy over $3.3 billion in legal fees awarded to five private lawyers whom Morales had hired under a contingency contract to represent the state in the litigation. Although tobacco companies agreed to pay the lawyers' fees, Attorney General John Cornyn, Morales's Republican successor, called the payments excessive. He also questioned the legality of the outside lawyers' agreement with Morales and spent much of his first year in office investigating the lawyers' work. The legal fees also were attacked by business groups seeking limits on civil court judgments and lawyers' payments. These same groups—so-called tort reformers—had contributed heavily to Cornyn's election campaign.

Neither Cornyn nor federal prosecutors found any illegalities in Morales's dealings with the five lawyers or in the outside lawyers' work for the state. But Morales's attempt to steer as much as $520 million in

legal fees to a sixth lawyer, Marc Murr of Houston, resulted in a lengthy federal investigation. Morales said Murr, a personal friend, was an important part of his anti-tobacco legal team, but other lawyers said Murr did little, if any, work on the case.

While the investigation, which stretched over 4 years, was still pending, Morales attempted a political comeback by running for governor in the 2002 Democratic primary. He lost to Laredo businessman Tony Sanchez and later crossed party lines to endorse Republican Governor Rick Perry, who defeated Sanchez in the general election.

Finally, in March 2003, a federal grand jury indicted Morales, accusing him of trying to improperly steer millions of dollars in legal fees from the tobacco settlement to Murr. The indictment also charged the former attorney general with misappropriating campaign money to make a down payment on a $775,000 house while he was still in office, lying on a loan application for a $600,000 mortgage and filing a false income tax return for 1998, his last year in office. Seven months later, Morales was sentenced to 4 years in federal prison after pleading guilty to mail fraud and filing a false income tax return. He admitted backdating a government contract and forging government records related to the tobacco suit. In a separate deal with prosecutors, Murr pleaded guilty to one count of mail fraud.

Morales expressed "sincere regret and remorse" at his sentencing before U.S. District Judge Sam Sparks of Austin. But he said that the "vast majority of misdeeds" he had been accused of were untrue. Most political observers were left scratching their heads.

Source: Houston Chronicle, November 1, 2003, p. 29A.

---

regular session. And, to make matters worse, she announced that the no-new-taxes budget about which the governor and Republican lawmakers had bragged actually included $2.7 billion in higher fees to be paid by millions of Texans. Strayhorn blamed Governor Rick Perry for the decision to strip the management audit programs from her agency. The governor's office denied the allegation, but Perry had signed the bill. As noted earlier in this chapter, Strayhorn was so angry—or ambitious—that she unsuccessfully challenged Perry's reelection in 2006 as an independent candidate.

Republican Susan Combs, a former agriculture commissioner, was elected comptroller in 2006.

Commissioner of the General Land Office
Texas retains ownership, including the mineral rights, to approximately 22 million acres of public lands, which are managed by the state **land commissioner**. Revenues generated by mineral leases and other land uses are earmarked for education through the Permanent

★ **land commissioner**
The elected official who manages the state's public lands and administers the Veterans Land Program, which provides low-interest loans to veterans for the purchase of land and houses.

University Fund and the Permanent School Fund. This agency is also responsible for the Veterans Land Program, which provides low-interest loans to veterans for the purchase of land and houses.

During 16 years in office, Land Commissioner Garry Mauro, a Democrat, developed several environmental initiatives, including beach cleanup efforts and a program for cleaning up oil spills off the Texas coast. After Mauro unsuccessfully ran for governor in 1998, the next land commissioner, Republican David Dewhurst, a businessman from Houston, continued the beach cleanup efforts. Dewhurst also won legislative approval of a program to replenish beaches and protect them from erosion. Dewhurst was elected lieutenant governor in 2002 and was succeeded as land commissioner by Republican Jerry Patterson, a former state senator from Harris County. Patterson's priorities included development of new nursing homes for veterans and new veterans' cemeteries. Patterson was reelected to a second term in 2006.

Commissioner of Agriculture

The **agriculture commissioner** is responsible for carrying out laws regulating and benefiting the agricultural sector of the state's economy. In addition to providing support for agricultural research and education, the agency is responsible for the administration of consumer protection laws in the areas of weights and measures, packaging and labeling, and marketing. Republican Rick Perry aggressively promoted Texas agricultural products during two terms as commissioner. Republican Susan Combs, a former state representative from Austin, was elected to the office in 1998. She also urged Texans to buy more produce grown in the Lone Star State and, concerned about obesity among Texas children, she led a campaign to reduce the sales of soft drinks and junk foods in the public schools. After Combs ran for comptroller in 2006, she was succeeded by Republican Todd Staples, a former state senator from Palestine.

Secretary of State

The **secretary of state**, the only constitutional official appointed by the governor, has a variety of duties, including granting charters to corporations and processing the extradition of prisoners to other states. The primary function of this office, however, is to administer state election laws. That responsibility includes reviewing county and local election procedures, developing statewide policy for voter registration, and receiving and tabulating election returns.

State Treasurer

The Constitution of 1876 created a **state treasurer** to be the custodian of state funds. Shortly after taking office in 1993, however, Treasurer Martha Whitehead came to believe the office was no longer needed. She convinced the legislature and the voters to abolish it with a constitutional amendment, which was adopted in 1995. The agency's duties were transferred to the comptroller's office.

Elected Boards and Commissions

Only two of the more than 200 boards and commissions that head most state agencies are elected. They are the Texas Railroad Commission and the State Board of Education.

Texas Railroad Commission

The **Railroad Commission** was originally designed to regulate intrastate (within Texas) operations of railroads. It also regulated intrastate trucking for many years. But it lost its trucking responsibilities and most of its railroad regulation to the federal government. It still regulates oil and natural gas production and lignite mining in Texas.

Keeping the Numbers Straight

Comptroller Susan Combs, a former state legislator and agriculture commissioner, was elected in 2006. In addition to providing revenue estimates required to balance the biennial budget, the comptroller is the state's primary tax administrator and accounting officer.

★ **agriculture commissioner**
The elected official responsible for administering laws and programs that benefit agriculture.

★ **secretary of state**
The official who administers state election laws, grants charters to corporations, and processes the extradition of prisoners to other states. This officeholder is appointed by the governor.

★ **state treasurer**
This elective office was created by the Constitution of 1876 to manage state funds. It was abolished by the voters in 1995, and its duties were transferred to the comptroller's office.

★ **Railroad Commission**
A three-member, elected body that regulates oil and natural gas production and lignite mining in Texas.

Land, Lots of Land
Republican Jerry Patterson, a former state senator, was first elected land commissioner in 2002 and reelected in 2006. Texas owns some 22 million acres of land, including mineral rights, which are administered by this office.

★ **State Board of Education**
An elected panel that oversees the administration of public education in Texas.

The commission includes three elected members who serve 6-year staggered terms and rotate the position of chair among themselves. The oil and gas industry has historically focused much attention on this agency and made large campaign contributions to commission members. Many critics claim the commission is a prime example of a regulatory body that has been co-opted by those interests it was created to regulate. And, in recent years, it has become a staging area for opportunistic politicians who seek election to the commission primarily as a stepping-stone to higher office. A commissioner doesn't have to resign in the middle of his or her 6-year term to seek another office and, as an incumbent regulator, has little trouble collecting large contributions from the oil and gas industry that can be used to further political ambitions. Both Democrat John Sharp and Republican Carole Keeton Strayhorn used seats on the commission to strengthen their political bases for successful races for state comptroller in 1990 and 1998, respectively. Other recent commission members haven't been as successful, but not because they didn't try. Between 1980 and 2002, fifteen people served on the commission, and only four actually completed a full 6-year term. One recent commissioner, Tony Garza, resigned in midterm to accept President George W. Bush's appointment as ambassador to Mexico.

The game of musical chairs has prompted calls in recent years for the commission to be abolished and its duties transferred to other agencies appointed by the governor, including the Public Utility Commission, which already has oversight over electric utilities, and the Texas Commission on Environmental Quality, the state's main environmental protection agency. Democrat Hector Uribe, a former state senator, ran for the commission in 1996, promising to work to abolish it. But Strayhorn, his Republican opponent, argued that the agency was important and needed to be retained. Strayhorn defeated Uribe for a 6-year term on the commission, but 2 years later she ran for and won election to the comptroller's office.

State Board of Education   Prior to educational reforms enacted in 1984, the **State Board of Education** was made up of 27 members elected from congressional districts across the state. At the urging of reformers dissatisfied with student performance, the legislature provided for a new education board of 15 members to be appointed by the governor and confirmed by the Senate. The idea was to reduce the board's independence while new education reforms ordered by the legislature were being carried out. But the law also mandated that the board once again become an elected body within a few years. Some state leaders later proposed that the board remain appointive and put the question to the voters, who opted for an elected board in 1986. The present board has 15 members elected from districts established by the legislature.

Philosophical and partisan bickering on the board in recent years prompted the legislature to reduce its powers. The panel's main remaining duties include investment of education dollars in the Permanent School Fund and some oversight of textbook selection and curriculum standards. The day-to-day administration of the Texas Education Agency, the agency responsible for public education, is under the direction of the commissioner of education, who is appointed by the governor.

The Texas Bureaucracy

A loosely connected, highly fragmented, and often confusing network of approximately 250 state agencies and universities with more than 300,000 full- and part-time employees is responsible for carrying out programs and policies approved and funded by the legislature and the governor. In addition, more than

950,000 other full- and part-time workers are employed by school districts, cities, counties, and special districts in Texas.

This **bureaucracy** is often on the receiving end when someone complains about government. But without it, government would come to a grinding halt. The bureaucracy issues drivers' licenses, builds highways, administers health care benefits for the poor, and performs myriad other public services. On an individual basis, the bureaucracy is the clerk, the inspector, the highway patrol officer, the computer programmer, the engineer, or one of hundreds of other occupational specialists delivering state services on a daily basis. On a larger scale, it is an assortment of agencies, some employing thousands of individuals, with designated responsibilities for specific public programs and services. Although it is overstating the case to say that the bureaucracy runs state government, its role is enhanced in Texas because the legislature meets in regular session only 5 months every other year and the governor has only limited powers over the executive branch. The part-time boards and commissions that oversee most state agencies can exercise considerable independence in interpreting policies and determining the character and the quality of public services. Many boards depend heavily on the guidance of veteran administrators and career bureaucrats within their agencies.

★ **bureaucracy**
The agencies of government and their employees responsible for carrying out policies and providing public services approved by elected officials.

The Growth of Government in Texas

In 1972, there were 504,000 full-time state and local government employees in Texas.[14] Thirty-five years later, there were 2½ times that many (Table 23.2). By 2002, the latest year for which we have comprehensive data, Texas had 574 full-time state and local government employees per 10,000 residents, making it the eighteenth highest in that category among the 50 states. Texas had only 124 state employees per 10,000 population, forty-fourth among the states. But its 450 local government workers per 10,000 population ranked sixth highest.[15] The number of employees has increased along with the state's population since the 2002 *Census of Governments*, but the rankings have remained much the same. Many services

Table *23.2* Measure of Government Growth: Employment by Type of Government, 1972–2002

With the expanding population and increased demands for public services, governments at all levels have increased the number of employees since the 1970s. Privatization and contracting for services may slow the increase in public employees; it will not reduce significantly government expenditures.

Unit of Government	Full-Time Equivalent Employees			
	1972	**1982**	**1992**	**2002**
State	124,560	175,660	238,974	269,674
Total Local	*380,038*	*557,082*	*744,325*	*979,164*
Counties	37,302	67,228	94,145	120,885
Municipalities	93,107	127,794	147,812	172,846
School Districts	223,646	335,855	460,212	634,589
Special Districts	25,983	26,205	42,156	50,844
Total Texas	**504,598**	**732,742**	**983,299**	**1,248,838**

Sources: U.S. Department of Commerce, Bureau of the Census, *Census of Governments, 1972*, vol. 3, no. 2, table 14; *Census of Governments, 1982*, vol. 3, no. 2, table 13; *Census of Governments, 1992*, vol. 3, no. 2, table 14; *Census of Governments, 2002*, vol. 3, table 9.

Politics Up Close   Privatization Hits a "Black Hole"

The legislature in 2003 ordered a controversial restructuring of Texas's health and human services agencies with an eye toward privatizing some functions, such as screening applicants for public assistance, which had previously been done by state employees. Republican state leaders predicted the changes would promote efficiency and save money for taxpayers, but the reorganization and privatization got off to a rough start. Within a few years, thousands of children had been dropped from Medicaid and the Children's Health Insurance Program (CHIP), to the dismay of health care advocates who blamed the problem on changes in eligibility rules and problems with the transition to private contractors.

Accenture LLP, a company given an $899 million state contract to screen applicants for children's health coverage and other welfare programs, came under fire from legislators and advocates angry that Texans in need were losing benefits because of inadequate staffing and training at private call centers operated by the company.

Then, in 2006, the *Houston Chronicle* reported that, for 3 months, dozens of documents from applicants seeking food stamps and other public assistance in Texas were mistakenly routed to a fax machine in a warehouse in Seattle, Washington, because a wrong phone number had been listed on an information memo. The applicants thought they were sending their faxes, which included personal financial information, to the Texas Health and Human Services Commission or its private contractor in Midland.

"There was a black hole in Seattle, Washington," a clerk at the warehouse told the newspaper. "People send us check stubs. They send us bills. We've gotten letters from people asking why they haven't been approved for food stamps yet. They were faxing in their personal information."[a] The state ended the contract with Accenture the next year.

[a] Quoted in *Houston Chronicle*, June 2, 2006, p. 1A.

performed by local governments—including education, fire and police protection, and sanitation services—require large numbers of professionals and other workers.

Over the past two decades, there also has been more privatization of government. Governments continue to raise taxes, but they contract with private companies to carry out some services. Contractors' employees aren't public employees and aren't counted in the public employment census data. Supporters of privatization say it can reduce governmental costs by promoting efficiency. But critics argue that contracting out government functions can be more costly. It also results in less public scrutiny and control (see *Politics Up Close*: "Privatization Hits a 'Black Hole'").

There has been a substantial expansion of programs at all levels of government in recent years. State spending during the 1982–83 biennium was $25.6 billion, and 26 years later, the legislature appropriated $152.5 billion for the 2008–2009 biennium. Nevertheless, Texas still ranks low in per capita expenditures. Texas was forty-ninth among the states in per capita spending by state government alone—$3,441 per person—in 2004. When combined state and local spending was compared, Texas's ranking rose slightly, thanks partly to the large share of public school costs borne by local taxpayers. In such key areas as per capita state spending on public health, education, and welfare, Texas ranked below many other states.[16]

Efforts to curtail government growth and spending have met with only marginal success. Texas citizens have come to expect a wide range of public services, and these expectations increase as the population grows. The federal government also has imposed mandates on state and local governments that require additional expenditures and personnel. Moreover, the success of interest groups in winning approval of new programs adds to the growth of public employment. The legislature reduced spending on many programs to help bridge a $10 billion revenue shortfall in 2003.

Table *23.3* They Don't Do the Same Thing: State and Local Employment by General Functions, 2002

Governments in Texas have some overlapping functions, but there are some significant differences assigned to them by the constitution or statutory law. The state, for example, has the primary responsibility for higher education while the school districts have the responsibility for primary and secondary education.

	State Employees		County Employees		City Employees		School Employees		Special District Employees	
Education	99,088	36.7%	1,138	0.9%	5,123	3.0%	634,589	100%	0	0
Social Services	69,192	25.7%	35,583	29.4%	9,522	5.5%	0	0	26,778	52.7%
Public Safety and Corrections	49,240	18.3%	40,005	33.1%	63,288	36.6%	0	0	261	0.5%
Transportation	15,562	5.8%	9,566	7.9%	14,979	8.7%	0	0	866	1.7%
Government Administration	16,754	6.2%	27,924	23.1%	18,121	10.5%	0	0	0	0
Environment/ Housing	12,749	4.7%	3,192	2.6%	31,030	18.0%	0	0	7,828	15.4%
Utilities	0	0	65	0.1%	20,079	11.6%	0	0	14,643	28.8%
All Other	7,089	2.6%	3,412	2.8%	10,704	6.2%	0	0	468	0.9%
Total Number of Employees	**269,674**	100.0%	**120,885**	100.0%	**172,846**	100.0%	**634,589**	100%	**50,844**	100.0%

Source: Bureau of the Census, *Census of Governments* 2002, *Public Employment*, vol. 3, table 15.

And that same year, it ordered a major reorganization of health and human services agencies, with the goal of privatizing some services. But the long-term effect of those changes on overall state government employment remained to be seen.

Some 80 percent of state government employees work in three areas: higher education; public safety and corrections; and social services (including public welfare and health care). Most employees of county governments work in social services, public safety and corrections, and general governmental administration (Table 23.3). More than one-third of city employees are engaged in fire and police protection, and another 30 percent work for city utilities and in housing, sewerage, sanitation, parks and recreation, and natural resources departments. Elementary and secondary school teachers are employees of local school districts. One-third of the special district employees work for hospital districts, and close to 30 percent work for utility districts.

Bureaucrats and Public Policy

The bureaucracy does more than carry out the policies set by the legislature. It is involved in virtually every stage of the policy-making process. The legislature usually broadly defines a program and gives the affected agency the responsibility for filling in the details.[17] Administrative agencies can sometimes interpret a vaguely worded law differently from its original legislative purpose. Although the legislature can use oversight committees and the budgetary process to control the bureaucracy (see Chapter 12), agencies often have resources and political influence that protect their prerogatives. Many appointed agency heads have political ties to interest groups affected by the work of their agencies, and these officials help develop policy alternatives and laws because legislators depend on their technical expertise.

Policy Implementation   Although one state agency may be primarily responsible for translating legislative intent into a specific program, other governmental bodies are also involved. The courts, for example, shape the actions of bureaucrats through their interpretation of statutes and administrative rules. And there may be jurisdictional and political battles between different agencies over program objectives.

In some cases, a new agency may have to be organized and staffed to carry out the goals of a new law. More often, however, the new responsibilities are assigned by the legislature to an existing agency, which develops the necessary rules, procedures, and guidelines for operating the new program. Additional employees are hired if the legislature provides the necessary funding. If not, responsibilities are reassigned among existing personnel. Sometimes tasks are coordinated with other agencies. Ultimately, all this activity translates into hundreds of thousands of daily transactions between governmental employees—or an agency's private contractors—and the public.

Almost everyone has heard horror stories about persons who have suffered abuse or neglect at the hands of public employees and agencies. Whether they involve an indigent family that fell through the cracks of the welfare system or a county jail prisoner who was lost in the administrative process of the judicial system, these stories tend to reinforce the suspicion and hostility that many people have toward bureaucracies and public employees. Unquestionably such abuses deserve attention and demand correction, yet thousands of governmental programs are successfully carried out with little or no fanfare and are fully consistent with the purpose of the authorizing legislation.

Most public employees take pride in what they do and attempt to be conscientious in translating policy objectives into workable public services. They are citizens and taxpayers who also receive services from other state and local agencies. A complex, interdependent state that is home to some 24 million people depends on the effectiveness and efficiency of governmental agencies. That activity appears, on the whole, to be mutually satisfactory or beneficial to most parties.

Obstacles to Policy Implementation   When things go wrong in state government and problems go unresolved, there is a tendency to blame the bureaucrats for excessive red tape, inefficiency, mismanagement, or incompetence. "Bureaucrat bashing" plays well politically, and many candidates for public office run on such campaigns. But in many cases they are unfairly blaming government employees for complex problems that policy makers have been unable, or unwilling, to resolve. One high-profile issue is the perennial struggle to improve the quality of the public education system. Some of the criticism directed at educational bureaucrats has been justified, but the legislature and the governor are ultimately responsible for the enactment of sound educational policies—and the development of a sufficient and equitable system of paying for them.

Some legislative policies may be misdirected, with little potential for producing the intended results. Or economic and social conditions may change, making programs inappropriate. In hindsight, administrators may also find that approaches different from those outlined by the legislature would have worked better. The legislature also frequently fails to fund programs adequately. In some cases, those charged with carrying out a new policy may not have the know-how or the resources to make it work. And, finally, programs often produce unanticipated results.

The accountability and responsiveness of state and local agencies are also affected by other factors, including the influence of special interests. Thanks to the clout of special interest lobbyists with the legislature, regulatory agencies are often headed by boards with a majority of members from the professions or industries they are supposed to regulate. Many taxpayers may feel this system is merely a legalized way of letting the foxes guard the henhouse. It is an extension of the **iron triangle** concept, whereby special interests seek to influence not only the legislators responsible for enacting laws but also the agencies responsible for enforcing them.

★ **iron triangle**
Mutually supportive interrelationships among the interest groups, administrative agencies, and legislative committees involved in drafting the laws and regulations affecting a particular area of the economy or a specific segment of the population.

Business and professional groups argue that their professions can be regulated effectively only by individuals knowledgeable in their fields. Although that argument has some validity, it also increases the potential for incestuous relationships that mock the regulatory process. There is always the possibility—and often the likelihood—that industry representatives serving on boards, commissions, or in agencies will be inclined to protect their industries against the best interests of consumers. This pattern of influence and control is often referred to as co-optation, underscoring the possibility that agencies may be captured by the industries they are supposed to regulate. Licensing agencies may also seek to adopt unfair regulations designed to restrict new competitors from entering an industry.

Historically, many nine-member state regulatory boards included only industry representatives. But under the sunset review process, discussed in more detail later in this chapter, laws have gradually been changed to turn over some positions on most of those boards to members of the public. The Sunset Advisory Commission has concluded:

> Boards consisting only of members from a regulated profession or group affected by the activities of an agency may not respond adequately to broad public interests. This potential problem can be addressed by giving the general public a direct voice in the activities of the agency through representation on the board.[18]

The "fox and the henhouse" approach to state regulation was highlighted when Governor Ann Richards demanded that the Texas Department of Health crack down on deplorable conditions in some nursing homes. It was revealed that state inspectors had repeatedly found unsanitary conditions in three nursing homes partly owned by a member of the Texas Board of Health. The board member, an appointee of former governor Bill Clements, denied any allegations of improper care but resigned after moving to another state.[19] Texas law in effect then required that one member of the eighteen-member health board be involved in the nursing home industry and the other members represent other health care professions. The board has since been restructured.

Strategies for Controlling the Bureaucracy

Elected policy makers can use several strategies to control bureaucracies and help ensure that policies are implemented as intended:

★ Change the law or make legislation detailed enough to reduce or eliminate the discretionary authority of an agency.

★ Overrule the bureaucracy and reverse or rescind an action or decision of an agency. With the independence of many agencies, boards, and commissions at the state level, the governor can reverse few agency decisions. Consequently, this step often requires legislative action.

★ Transfer the responsibility for a program to another agency through administrative reorganization.

★ Replace an agency head who refuses to or is incapable of carrying out program objectives. (There are, however, only a few agencies over which the governor can directly exercise such authority in Texas.)

★ Cut or threaten to reduce the budget of an agency to force compliance with policy objectives.

★ Abolish an agency or program through sunset legislation.

★ Pressure the bureaucracy to change with legislative hearings and public disclosures of agency neglect or inadequacies.

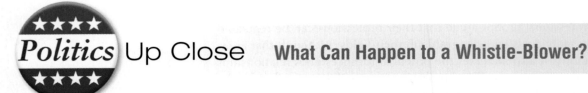

Politics Up Close   What Can Happen to a Whistle-Blower?

Governmental agencies make mistakes that can be very costly to the public in terms of financial waste or neglect. Texas has a whistle-blower protection law, which is designed to protect public employees who report wrongdoing within their agencies to their supervisors. If an employee is subjected to retaliation after having come forward, the law permits the worker to file a lawsuit against the offending agency.

A major test of the law's effectiveness was the case of George Green, an architect for the Texas Department of Human Services (DHS). Green complained of shoddy construction on agency facilities, kickbacks, and non-compliance with contracts. He said his supervisors refused to take action against the offending contractors. After he went public with his charges, Green was fired by the agency for allegedly abusing sick-leave time and making one unauthorized call on his state telephone—a 13-cent call to his father. Criminal charges were brought against him, and, although they were eventually dropped, he had spent $130,000 in legal fees, could not find a new job, and had depleted many of his personal assets.

Green sued the state and won a $13.6 million judgment from a Travis County jury in 1991. The amount included $3.6 million in actual damages that Green had suffered and $10 million in punitive damages to punish the state for the way he had been treated. The state appealed, dragging out a resolution of the case, until the judgment was upheld by the Texas Supreme Court in 1994. But the legislature was not in session that year, and state leaders said there was no money in the state budget to pay Green. So the whistle-blower had to wait for the legislature to convene in 1995. Green, meanwhile, was still unemployed and living off the generosity of friends and family and a personal loan he had taken out against a portion of his judgment.

By the time the legislature convened in January 1995, Green's judgment, with interest, had grown to almost $20 million, and interest continued to grow at the rate of more than $4,500 a day. The whistle-blower's case also was receiving considerable media attention, nationally as well as in Texas. But many legislators, particularly in the House, did not want to pay him the full amount, which they considered

excessive. They particularly objected to the $10 million the jury had awarded as punitive damages and pointed out that taxpayers would ultimately have to pick up the tab.

Green refused to accept an amount smaller than the judgment and interest, and the 1995 session ended in late May without Green receiving any payment. Legislators, however, took steps to ensure that such a large whistle-blower judgment would never be awarded again. They changed the law to limit whistle-blower suit damages against the state to $250,000. Critics of the change warned it would seriously curtail whistle-blower suits—and damage an important taxpayer protection—because the best lawyers, whose fees are based on the size of a judgment, would no longer accept these cases.

Finally, in November 1995, Green reached a compromise with legislative leaders. The Legislative Budget Board (LBB), which can transfer funds when the full legislature is not in session, approved a $13.8 million settlement, which Green accepted. Part of the money went to lawyers and a lobbyist who had helped Green collect payment, and $1 million went to an investor who had loaned Green money during his battle. Lieutenant Governor Bob Bullock, who chaired the LBB, apologized to Green and called his ordeal a "black mark on the history of Texas."[a]

Even then, Green's story continued. A former consultant sued Green for allegedly failing to pay him for helping Green collect the judgment from the state. In December 1996, another Travis County jury awarded the former consultant more than $600,000 in actual and punitive damages against Green. The whistle-blower also became embroiled in a lengthy dispute with the Internal Revenue Service over federal income taxes.

Green's experience speaks to a major problem. Few public employees can afford to be subjected to this type of retaliation, and few have the resources to fight state government. Although the original intent of the law was to protect whistle-blowers and to encourage their coming forward with inside information, most state and local employees may have received a different message from the Green case and the legislature's decision to weaken the law.

[a]Quoted in *Houston Chronicle*, November 16, 1995.

★ **whistle-blower**
A public employee who reports illegal activities or "blows the whistle" on agency wrongdoing.

★ Protect public employees who reveal incompetence, mismanagement, and corruption through **whistle-blower** legislation (see *Politics Up Close:* "What Can Happen to a Whistle-Blower?").

★ Enact **revolving door** restrictions to reduce or eliminate the movement of former state employees to industries over which they had regulatory authority.[20]

The Revolving Door   Over the years—at least until 1991—many regulatory agencies had become training grounds for young attorneys and other professionals taking their first jobs out of college or law school. They would work for state agencies for a few years for relatively low pay while gaining valuable experience in a particular regulatory area and making influential contacts in the state bureaucracy. They then would leave state employment for higher-paying jobs in the industries they used to regulate and would represent their new employers before the state boards and commissions for which they had once worked—or they would become consultants or join law firms representing regulatory clients. Former gubernatorial appointees to boards and commissions, not just hired staffers, also participated in this revolving-door phenomenon, which raised ethical questions about possible insider advantages (see Chapter 12, and earlier discussion of iron triangles in this chapter, p. 820).

An early step in restricting the revolving door was part of the Public Utility Regulatory Act (PURA) of 1975 that created the Public Utility Commission (PUC); this law prohibited PUC members and key staffers from going to work for regulated utilities immediately after leaving the agency. The ethics reform law of 1991 expanded the restrictions to other agencies.

Legislative Budgetary Control   Every 2 years, the legislature sets the budgets for state agencies but subsequently provides little oversight as to how effectively the money is spent, unless there is a financial crisis requiring a special legislative session or an emergency transfer of funds by the governor and the Legislative Budget Board. Perhaps the most control that lawmakers exercise over agency spending, besides setting the bottom line, is their approval of a number of line items in agency budgets that restrict portions of the funds to specific programs.

Sunset Legislation   Texas was one of the first states to require formal, exhaustive reviews of how effectively agencies are doing their jobs. The sunset law enacted in 1977 was so named because most agencies have to be periodically re-created by the legislature or automatically go out of business. Relatively few agencies—except for a number of inactive ones such as the Pink Bollworm Commission and the Stonewall Jackson Memorial Board—have been abolished. But the obligatory review has produced some significant structural and policy changes in the state bureaucracy that the legislature may not have otherwise ordered. It also has expanded employment opportunities for lobbyists, because special interest groups have much to win or lose in the sunset process. In many cases, special interests have succeeded in protecting the status quo.

Each agency is usually up for review every 12 years, under a rotating order set out in the sunset law. The review begins with the Sunset Advisory Commission, which includes four state representatives appointed by the speaker of the House; four senators appointed by the lieutenant governor; and two public members, one named by the speaker and the other by the lieutenant governor. The commission employs a staff that studies each agency up for review during the next regular, biennial legislative session and reports its findings to the panel, which makes recommendations to the legislature.

In a few cases, the commission proposes that an agency (usually a minor one) be terminated or consolidated with another agency. In most cases, however, the commission recommends the continuation of an agency but outlines suggested changes in its organizational structure and/or operations. The future of the agency is then debated by the full legislature. If lawmakers fail to approve a sunset bill for any agency by September 1 of the year the agency is scheduled for

★ **revolving door**
A term describing the practice of former members of state boards and commissions or key employees of agencies leaving state government for more lucrative jobs with the industries they used to regulate.

★ **sunset**
The process under which most state agencies have to be periodically reviewed and recreated by the legislature or go out of business.

review, the agency will be phased out of existence over the next year, or it will be terminated abruptly on September 1 if the legislature also refuses to approve a new budget for the agency. In recent years, however, the legislature has postponed controversial sunset decisions by passing special laws to allow some agencies to stay open past their review dates.

The Texas Higher Education Coordinating Board is subject to sunset review, but individual universities are not. Also exempted from sunset review are the courts and state agencies created by the constitution, such as the governor's office, the attorney general, the comptroller, and the General Land Office.

The sunset process has not reduced the size of the bureaucracy. By 2006, there were more than 300,000 state employees, compared to about 164,000 in 1977, the year the sunset law was approved. Although more than sixty agencies have been terminated or merged, others have been created (see Table 23.4). But Bill Wells, the Sunset Advisory Commission's former executive director, once remarked that statistics did not tell the full story. He believed the sunset process had served to slow down the creation of new agencies. "You can't say how many [new agencies] would have been created if sunset hadn't heightened the awareness of the fact that we've got maybe too many agencies now," he said. "There is a heightened awareness of the fact that you need to go a little slower and you need to really have a problem before you create an agency."[21]

The sunset review process has helped rid state government of some deadwood, modernized some state laws and bureaucratic procedures, and made some agencies more responsive and accountable to the public. Under a sunset policy discussed earlier in this chapter, public members have been added to the boards of regulatory agencies that previously had included only representatives of the professions or industries that they regulated.

The largest agencies and those with influential constituencies are usually the most difficult to change because special interests are working overtime and making large political contributions to protect their turf. In 1993, for example, the insurance lobby succeeded in weakening some regulatory reforms in the Department of Insurance sunset bill. In another case, there was such a high-stakes battle involving

---

Table *23.4* Agency Reviews: Sunset Action from 1979 to 2007, 66th to 80th Legislative Sessions

As part of the ongoing efforts to assess the effectiveness of state agencies and their programs, Texas created a formal review process assigned to the Texas Sunset Advisory Commission. Since 1979, close to 400 agencies have been reviewed. Some agencies have been abolished outright. Other agencies have been merged or seen their functions transferred elsewhere. As might be expected, 80 percent of the agencies have been continued.

Actions Taken	Total	Percent
Agencies Reviewed	398*	
Agencies Continued	316	80%
Agencies Abolished Outright	33	8
Agencies Abolished and Functions Transferred	21	5
Agencies Combined	12	3
Agencies Separated	2	1

*Some agencies reviewed were not subject to continuation or abolishment. Also includes other special reviews and projects. Totals and percentages based on the 384 agencies where action was taken.

Source: Texas Sunset Advisory Commission, "Guide to the Texas Sunset Process," July 2008.

telephone companies, newspaper publishers, electric utilities, and consumers over the Public Utility Commission sunset bill that the legislature postponed action for 2 years. The lobby's influence over the 1993 sunset bills prompted Governor Ann Richards and some legislative leaders to suggest that the sunset process should be changed or repealed because it was being abused by special interests. But consumer advocates, who value the sunset process, blamed the problem on legislators who had difficulty saying "no" to special interest lobbyists.

Performance Reviews Facing a large revenue shortfall in 1991, the legislature directed Comptroller John Sharp to conduct unprecedented performance reviews of all state agencies to determine ways to eliminate mismanagement and inefficiency and to save tax dollars. Sharp recommended $4 billion in spending cuts, agency and funds consolidations, accounting changes, some minor tax increases, and increases in various state fees to reflect more accurately the costs of providing services. Pressure from special interests killed many of the recommendations, but the legislature adopted about $2.4 billion of them. Sharp produced follow-up reports in 1993, 1995, and 1997, and his successor, Carole Keeton Strayhorn, continued the performance reviews after she took office. At the beginning of the 2003 regular legislative session, Strayhorn made sixty-four recommendations for further restructuring of state agencies and their operations, some of which were adopted by lawmakers. The comptroller also similarly reviewed the operations of a number of local school districts.

The performance reviews generally have been considered instrumental in improving administrative practices. But as discussed earlier in this chapter, the legislature, with Governor Rick Perry's approval, transferred the work from the comptroller's office to the Legislative Budget Board after a series of budgetary disputes with Strayhorn in 2003. The move was criticized by those who believed the reviews should have remained under the oversight of an independently elected officeholder, but it remained to be seen what the ultimate effect of the transfer would be.

Merit Systems and Professional Management One hundred years ago, public employees in Texas were hired on the basis of **political patronage**, or the personal relationships they had with elected or appointed officials. Little consideration was given to their skills, competence, or expertise. Few rules dictated terms of employment, advancement, or the rights or conduct of public employees, and wages and salaries varied widely from agency to agency. There also were high rates of employee turnover.

To serve the public and state workers more effectively, some reform advocates pushed for a **merit system** based, in part, on the Civil Service Commission created by the federal government for its workers in 1883 (see Chapter 12). Although some other states have developed comprehensive statewide employment or personnel systems administered by a single agency, the reform movement in Texas has not been as successful. Improvements have been made, but state government here continues to function under a decentralized personnel system, in part because the various elected executive officeholders have jealously guarded their prerogatives to hire and fire the people who work for them.

Texas's personnel "system" is not a merit system but a highly fragmented arrangement with different agencies assigned various personnel responsibilities. Ultimately, the legislature has the legal authority to define personnel practices, and the biennial budget is the major tool used by legislators to establish some 1,300 job classifications and corresponding salary schedules. The legislature also establishes policies on vacations, holidays, and retirement. But the primary responsibility for carrying out personnel policies is still delegated to the various

★ **political patronage**
The hiring of government employees on the basis of personal friendships or favors rather than ability or merit.

★ **merit system**
A personnel system in which public employees are selected for government jobs through competitive examinations and are systematically evaluated after being hired.

state agencies. An administrator can develop specific policies for an agency as long as the agency works within the general framework defined by the legislature.

All state job openings are required to be listed with the Texas Workforce Commission. Agencies also advertise for workers through the mass media and college placement centers. But many jobs still are filled as a result of friendships, other personal contacts, and the influence of key political players. Higher and public education employees are subject to different employment policies, which are determined by individual university governing boards and local school districts. Unlike state government, many cities across Texas have adopted centrally administered merit systems organized around the accepted principles of modern personnel management.

Summary
Who Gets What: Texas Executive and Bureaucracy

The public believes the governor of Texas has considerable power and can act quickly and effectively when necessary. But, in fact, the office of governor is weak in terms of formal powers and limited by the structure of the "plural executive," which includes several other statewide officeholders elected independently of the governor.

★ Although the lieutenant governor is part of the executive branch, the duties of that office are primarily legislative. The top appointed official in the executive branch is the secretary of state.

★ Administrative responsibilities are further fragmented through approximately 250 boards and commissions authorized by statutory law. Although the governor appoints individuals to these boards, the governor's control is diluted by board members' staggered terms, the need for senatorial approval of the governor's appointments, and legal requirements relating to the composition of these boards.

★ Besides appointments, the governor's main formal powers are the veto of legislation, line-item veto authority over the budget, and the authority to call and set the agenda for special sessions of the legislature.

★ As part of the judicial powers, a governor can stay executions and, with the recommendation of the Board of Pardons and Paroles, grant full or conditional pardons or commute a death sentence to life imprisonment. The governor is the commander-in-chief of the state's military force and is responsible for maintaining order within the state and responding to various disasters by mobilizing the National Guard.

★ Potentially, the governor also has a number of informal resources that can be used to shape public policy and the administrative process. Governors have used their staffs, their access to the mass media, their party roles, and their relationships to key interest groups to bring pressure to bear on legislators and other elected officials.

★ More than one million Texans are employed by state and local governments. Collectively, we refer to them and the agencies for which they work as the bureaucracy. The bureaucracy has the primary responsibility of carrying out

public policies adopted by the legislature and local governing bodies. But administrative agencies also are involved in virtually every stage of the policy-making process. Legislators depend on administrative agencies for counsel and advice when they draft public policies, and they rely on them to help assess the success or failure of policies.

★ When things go wrong and problems go unresolved, there is a tendency to blame bureaucrats. But often, government employees are unfairly blamed for complex problems that elected policy makers have been unwilling or unable to resolve. The fragmented structure of the executive branch of state government is, in itself, a major obstacle to the efficient, responsive delivery of public services. There also is the potential for agencies headed by appointed, part-time boards to become unaccountable to the electorate and susceptible to the influence of special interest groups.

★ Through sunset legislation, Texas became one of the first states to require formal reviews of how effectively state agencies are doing their jobs. Most state agencies are subject to periodic review and reauthorization by the legislature. The process has not reduced the size of the bureaucracy, but it has helped rid state government of obsolete agencies and produced greater accountability. Texas also has adopted revolving-door restrictions. Former board members and key employees of regulatory agencies are prohibited from going to work for regulated companies within a certain period after leaving their state posts.

★ Although many local governments have adopted merit employment systems, state government functions under a decentralized personnel system. It is highly fragmented, with each agency largely free to set its own personnel policies.

Key Terms

plural executive   796

impeachment   801

special session   802

veto   802

line-item veto   802

Legislative Budget
   Board   803

staggered terms   803

senatorial courtesy   803

extradition   808

lieutenant governor   811

attorney general   812

comptroller   813

pay-as-you-go
   principle   813

land commissioner   814

agriculture
   commissioner   815

secretary of state   815

state treasurer   815

Railroad Commission   815

State Board of
   Education   816

bureaucracy   817

iron triangle   820

whistle-blower   822

revolving door   823

sunset   823

political patronage   825

merit system   825

Suggested Readings

Barta, Carolyn. *Bill Clements: Texian to His Toenails.* Austin, Tex.: Eakin Press, 1996. A detailed account of Bill Clements's three campaigns for governor and his two terms in office.

Beyle, Thad. "Governors: The Middlemen and Women in Our Political System." In *Politics in the American States: A Comparative Analysis,* 6th ed., eds. Virginia Gray and Herbert Jacob. Washington, D.C.: CQ Press, 1996. A comparative analysis of the formal and informal powers of U.S. governors.

Frederick, Douglas W. "Reexamining the Texas Railroad Commission." In *Texas Politics: A Reader,* eds. Anthony Champagne and Edward J. Harpham. New York, N.Y.: W.W. Norton, 1997. Using theories of capture, authors address the issue of the Railroad Commission's domination by the oil and gas industries that it regulates.

Gantt, Fred, Jr. *The Chief Executive in Texas: A Study in Gubernatorial Leadership.* Austin, Tex.: University of Texas Press, 1964. An extensive analysis of the governorship of Texas, including the development of the office and roles played by governors in the administrative and policy processes.

Hendrickson, Kenneth E. *Chief Executives of Texas: From Stephen F. Austin to John B. Connally, Jr.* College Station, Tex.: Texas A&M University Press, 1995. Brief biographic sketches of the political careers of forty-three individuals who have held the office of governor or president of the republic.

Morris, Celia. *Storming the Statehouse: Running for Governor with Ann Richards and Dianne Feinstein.* New York, N.Y.: Scribner's Sons, 1992. An analysis of the hotly contested 1990 governor's race.

Prindle, David. *Petroleum Politics and the Texas Railroad Commission.* Austin, Tex.: University of Texas Press, 1981. An assessment of energy policy in Texas and the role of the Railroad Commission in policy development and industry regulation.

Texas General Land Office. *The Land Commissioners of Texas.* Austin, Tex.: Texas General Land Office, 1986. Brief biographic sketches of past land commissioners.

Tolleson-Rinehart, Sue. *Claytie and the Lady: Ann Richards, Gender and Politics in Texas.* Austin, Tex.: University of Texas Press, 1994.

Suggested Web Sites

Governor of Texas   www.governor.state.tx.us

The governor's Web site offers up-to-date and archived news releases and speeches, ongoing initiatives, and a detailed description of the structure and functions of the governor's office. Links are provided to the important divisions or sections of the governor's office as well as to other state agencies.

National Governors Association (NGA)   www.nga.org

This bipartisan organization provides information on key state issues and monitors and analyzes the progress of important state policy issues. Information on the governors of all fifty states is also available.

State of Texas   www.state.tx.us

The state's Web page provides links to over 200 state agencies. Most state agencies have their own sites, with detailed information about their organizational structures, programs, budgets, reports, and recent activities.

Office of the Comptroller   www.window.state.tx.us

In addition to providing links to other state agencies, the comptroller's office provides a wide array of information pertaining to state taxes, management and accounting systems, and performance reviews of state operations and agencies.

24 THE TEXAS JUDICIARY

> **"** Objectivity, or at least the appearance of objectivity, is especially useful in courts and quasi-judicial tribunals. **"**
>
> **Harold Lasswell**

Chapter *Outline*

★ The Power of the Courts in Texas
★ The State Courts in the Federal System
★ The Legal Framework of the Judicial System
★ The Structure of the Texas Court System
★ The Jury System
★ Judicial Procedures and Decision Making
★ Judicial Concerns and Controversies
★ Crime and Punishment
★ The Politics of Criminal Justice
★ Increased Policy Role of the State Courts

The Power of the Courts in Texas

Although most people would like to think that justice in Texas is blind, it is not. Most judges try to be fair, but, even so, their decisions are molded by their political and ideological views, life experiences, ethnicity, and gender. In recent years, moreover, Texas courts have been beset by a series of controversies that have severely strained the popular notion that the scales of justice are weighed in an atmosphere that is above reproach. Large campaign contributions to elected state judges from lawyers who practice before them and from other special interests fueled a high-stakes war for philosophical and political control of the judiciary, raising questions in the media about whether Texas courtrooms are "for sale."

Women and minorities, meanwhile, remain grossly underrepresented among the ranks of Texas judges. And the basic structure of the judicial system—an assortment of about 2,600 courts of various, often overlapping jurisdictions—is so outdated that many experts believe it should be overhauled. But change doesn't come easily.

State courts resolve civil disputes over property rights and personal injuries. They also determine guilt or innocence and set punishment in criminal cases involving offenses against people, their property, and public institutions. And, to a more limited extent than the federal judiciary, they help set public policy by reviewing the actions of the executive and legislative branches of government. A civil dispute may stem from something as simple as a tenant's breaking an apartment lease to something as complex and potentially expensive as a manufacturer's liability for defective tires that contribute to the deaths or injuries of dozens of motorists. Criminal cases range from traffic offenses, punishable by fines, to capital murder, for which the death penalty can be imposed.

Some streamlining of Texas's judicial processes, especially at the appellate level, was accomplished in 1981. But the Texas judiciary, particularly in urban areas, has become overloaded by criminal cases and an increasingly litigious approach to civil disputes. It can take months to get a civil or a criminal case—one that is not settled out of court or in a plea bargain with prosecutors—to trial.

✓ Think About Politics

1. Should an accused serial murderer be considered innocent until proven guilty?
   YES ◯ NO ◯

2. Do you believe that the death penalty is "cruel and unusual punishment" in all circumstances?
   YES ◯ NO ◯

3. Should a judge be required to try a lawsuit within one month after the suit is filed?
   YES ◯ NO ◯

4. Do you think that a nonlawyer could be a good judge?
   YES ◯ NO ◯

5. Is it wrong to use one's influence to "fix" a traffic ticket?
   YES ◯ NO ◯

6. Should the close relatives of a murder victim be allowed to witness the execution of their loved one's murderer?
   YES ◯ NO ◯

7. Does the Ku Klux Klan have the same constitutional rights as the National Association for the Advancement of Colored People?
   YES ◯ NO ◯

The courts often have the final say in how power is distributed. Understanding how they work can be crucial in gaining a share of that power.

The State Courts in the Federal System

Like people in every state, Texans are subject to the jurisdiction of both state and federal courts. The federal judiciary has jurisdiction over violations of federal laws, including criminal offenses that occur across state lines, and over banking, securities, and other activities regulated by the federal government (see Chapter 13). Federal courts have also had major effects on state government policies and Texas's criminal justice system through interpretations and applications of the U.S. Constitution and federal laws, including the Bill of Rights.

Although Texas has a bill of rights in its constitution, the federal courts have taken the lead in protecting many civil and political rights, as when the U.S. Supreme Court declared the white primary election unconstitutional in *Smith v. Allwright* in 1944 (see Chapter 21).[1] Federal court intervention continues in the redistricting of legislative and congressional district lines. The federal judiciary also has ordered far-reaching improvements in the state prison system. And when police officers read criminal suspects their rights, the officers are complying with constitutional requirements determined by the U.S. Supreme Court in the *Miranda* case.[2]

Nevertheless, it is estimated that more than 97 percent of all litigation is based on state laws or local ordinances. Thus anyone involved in litigation is likely to be found in a state rather than a federal court.

The Legal Framework of the Judicial System

The U.S. and Texas constitutions form the basic legal framework of the Texas court system. Building on that framework, the Texas Legislature has enacted codes of criminal and civil procedure to govern conduct in the courtroom and statutory laws for the courts to apply. Most criminal activities are defined and their punishments established in the Texas **penal code**. In criminal cases, the state—often based on charges made by another individual—initiates action against a person accused of a crime. The most serious criminal offenses, for which prison sentences can be imposed, are called **felonies**. More minor offenses, punishable by fines or short sentences in county jails, are called **misdemeanors**. Many property crimes and drug offenses are classified as state jail felonies and are punishable by community service work or time in a state jail, a prison-like facility operated by the state.

Civil lawsuits, which can be brought under numerous **statutes**, involve conflicts between two or more parties—individuals, corporations, governments, or other entities. Civil law governs contracts and property rights between private citizens, affords individuals an avenue for relief against corporate abuses, and determines liability for personal injuries. Administrative law includes enforcement powers over many aspects of the state's economy.

An individual with a grievance to be addressed has to take the initiative of going to court. A person can experience problems with a landlord who refuses to return a deposit, a dry cleaner that lost a suit, or a friend who borrowed and wrecked a car. But in a civil dispute, there is no legal issue to be resolved unless a lawsuit is filed. An injured person filing a lawsuit is a **plaintiff**. Because even the most minor disputes in the lowest courts can require professional assistance from a lawyer, a person will soon discover that the pursuit of justice can be very costly and time consuming.

Statutes and constitutional laws are subject to change through legislative action and popular consent of the electorate, and over the years there have been significant changes in what is legal and illegal, permissible and impermissible. At one time, for

★ **penal code**
Body of law that defines most criminal offenses and sets a range of punishments that can be assessed.

★ **felonies**
Serious criminal offenses that can be punished by imprisonment and/or a fine.

★ **misdemeanors**
Minor criminal offenses punishable by a fine and/or a short sentence in the county jail.

★ **civil lawsuits**
Noncriminal legal disputes between two or more individuals, businesses, governments, or other entities.

★ **statutes**
Laws enacted by a legislative body.

★ **plaintiff**
Individual or party who initiates a lawsuit.

example, state law provided for a potential life prison sentence for the possession of a few ounces of marijuana. Small amounts are now considered a misdemeanor punishable by a fine. The legal drinking age was lowered to 18 for a few years but was reestablished at 21 after parents and school officials convinced the legislature that the younger age limit had helped increase alcohol abuse among teenagers.

The Structure of the Texas Court System

There are five levels of Texas courts, but some courts at different levels have overlapping authority and jurisdiction (see Figure 24.1). Some courts have only **original jurisdiction**; that is, they try or resolve only those cases being heard for the first time. They weigh the facts presented as evidence and apply the law in reaching a decision or verdict. Other courts have only **appellate jurisdiction**. They review the decisions of lower courts to determine whether constitutional and statutory principles and procedures were correctly interpreted and followed. Appellate courts are empowered to reverse the judgments of the lower courts and to order cases to be retried if constitutional or procedural mistakes were made. Still other courts have both original and appellate jurisdiction.

At the highest appellate level, Texas has a **bifurcated court system**, with the nine-member Texas Supreme Court serving as the court of last resort in civil cases and the nine-member Texas Court of Criminal Appeals functioning as the court of last resort in criminal cases. Only one other state, Oklahoma, has a similar structure.[3]

Unlike federal judges, who are appointed by the president to lifetime terms, state judges, except for those on municipal courts, are elected to limited terms in partisan elections. Midterm vacancies, however, are filled by appointment. Vacancies on the justice of the peace and county courts are filled by county commissioners courts; vacancies on the district and appellate benches are filled by the governor.

Courts of Limited Jurisdiction
The lowest-ranking courts in Texas are **municipal courts** and **justice of the peace courts**. You or someone you know has probably appeared before a judge in one of these courts because both handle a large volume of traffic tickets. Some of these courts are big revenue raisers for local governments, and they are often accused of subordinating justice and fairness to financial considerations.

★ **original jurisdiction**
Authority of a court to try or resolve a civil lawsuit or a criminal prosecution being heard for the first time.

★ **appellate jurisdiction**
Authority of a court to review the decisions of lower courts to determine whether the law was correctly interpreted and legal procedures were correctly followed.

★ **bifurcated court system**
Existence of two courts at the highest level of the state judiciary. The Texas Supreme Court is the court of last resort in civil cases, and the Texas Court of Criminal Appeals has the final authority to review criminal cases.

★ **municipal courts**
Courts of limited jurisdiction that hear cases involving city ordinances and primarily handle traffic tickets.

★ **justice of the peace courts**
Low-ranking courts with jurisdiction over minor civil disputes and criminal cases.

Limited, but Important Jurisdiction
Justice of the Peace Courts have limited jurisdiction in civil and criminal matters, such as small claims, evictions, or Class C misdemeanors. Judge Monica Caballero presides over JP Court 1, Place 1 in Bexar County.

Figure *24.1* The Texas Court System (2008)

The state's highly fragmented and decentralized court system has five levels of courts. The structure and jurisdiction of the courts are defined by the 1876 Constitution and statutory law. There are now approximately 2,700 courts and over 3,200 judges.

Some 916 municipal courts are established under state law, including some with multiple judges.[4] The qualifications, terms of office, and methods of selecting municipal judges are determined by the individual cities, but they are generally appointed by the city council. Municipal courts have original and exclusive jurisdiction over city **ordinances**, but most of these courts are not courts of record, in which a word-for-word transcript is made of trial proceedings. Only very rudimentary information is officially recorded in most of these courts, and any appeal from them is heard *de novo* by the higher court. That is, the second court has to conduct a new trial and hear the same witnesses and evidence all over again because no official record of the original proceedings was kept. The informality of these proceedings and the absence of a record add to the confusion and cost of using the system.[5] In response to these problems, the legislature in recent years has created municipal courts of record for some cities.

Each county in Texas is required to provide for one justice of the peace court, and each county government in the larger metropolitan areas may create sixteen (see Chapter 25). There are 821 of these courts in Texas. Justices of the peace are elected to 4-year terms from precincts, or subdivisions of the county drawn by the commissioners court, which also sets their salaries. Justices of the peace are not required to be licensed attorneys, a situation that has generated much criticism of these courts.

Although their duties vary from county to county, justice of the peace courts, with certain restrictions, have original jurisdiction in civil cases when the amount in dispute is $10,000 or less and have original jurisdiction over criminal offenses that are punishable by fines only. In some areas of criminal law, they have overlapping jurisdiction with municipal courts. Justices of the peace also sit as judges of small-claims courts, and in many rural counties they serve as coroners. They also function as state magistrates with the authority to hold preliminary hearings to determine whether there is probable cause to hold a criminal defendant.

These are not courts of record, and cases appealed from these courts are tried *de novo* in county courts, county courts-at-law, or district courts. Each justice court has an elected constable to serve warrants and perform other duties for the court.

County Courts

If there is confusion about the authority and jurisdiction of municipal and justice of the peace courts, it is compounded by the county courts. They were created by the Texas Constitution to serve the needs of the sparsely populated, rural society that existed when the charter was written in 1875. But population growth and urbanization have placed enormous demands on the judicial system, and rather than modernize the system, the state has added courts while making only minor changes in the structure and jurisdiction of the older courts.

Each county has a **constitutional county court**. The holder of this office, the county judge, is elected countywide to a 4-year term. This individual is the chief executive officer of the county and presides over the county commissioners court, the policy-making body of county government (see Chapter 25). Most urban county judges do not perform judicial duties, but county judges in many rural counties perform both executive and judicial functions, a dual responsibility that some experts believe is inconsistent with the Texas Constitution's separation-of-powers doctrine. Although a large number of county judges are lawyers, they are not required to be. They are required only to be "well informed in the law" and to take appropriate courses in evidence and legal procedures.

The constitutional county court shares some original civil jurisdiction with both the justice of the peace and the district court. It has original criminal jurisdiction over misdemeanors punishable by fines of more than $500 and jail sentences of 1 year or less. These courts also probate wills and have appellate jurisdiction over cases tried originally in justice of the peace and municipal courts.

★ **ordinances**
Local laws enacted by a city council.

★ **de novo**
In a civil lawsuit or criminal trial, evidence is presented again before an appellate court because no record was kept of the evidence presented to the trial court.

★ **constitutional county court**
County court created by the Texas Constitution, presided over by the county judge.

★ **statutory county court**
Court that exercises limited jurisdiction over criminal and/or civil cases. The jurisdiction of these courts varies from county to county.

Over the years, the legislature also has created 240 **statutory county courts**, or county courts-at-law, in more than 90 counties. Some specialize in probate cases and are called probate courts. These courts were designed to deal with specific local problems and, consequently, have inconsistent jurisdictions. Judges on these courts are elected countywide and have to be lawyers, but the authority of a particular court is defined by the legislation creating it. Some cannot hear civil disputes involving more than $2,500, whereas others can hear disputes involving as much as $100,000. Drunken driving cases are the primary criminal cases tried before these courts, but some also hear appeals *de novo* from lower courts.

County courts across the state disposed of more than 850,000 civil and criminal cases during the 2007 fiscal year but saw more than 884,000 cases added to their dockets. At the end of the year, more than 969,000 cases were pending before the county courts.[6]

★ **district court**
Primary trial court in Texas. It has jurisdiction over criminal felony cases and civil disputes.

Courts of General Jurisdiction   The primary trial court in Texas is the **district court**. Although there is some overlapping jurisdiction with county courts, the district courts have original jurisdiction over civil cases involving $200 or more in damages, divorce cases, contested elections, suits over land titles and liens, suits for slander or defamation, all criminal felony cases, and misdemeanors involving official misconduct. In recent years, the legislature has created district courts with specialized jurisdictions over criminal or civil law or over such specialties as family law (i.e., divorces and child custody cases). In some large metropolitan counties that have numerous district courts, the jurisdictions of the respective courts are determined by informal agreements among the judges. District court judges are elected to 4-year terms, must be at least 25 years old, and must have practiced law or served as a judge of another court for 4 years prior to taking office.

The Texas Constitution gives the legislature the responsibility to define judicial districts, and as the expanding population produced greater caseloads, new districts were created. In 1981, there were 328 district courts. In 2008, there were 443. A single county may be allocated more than one district court with overlapping geographic jurisdiction. Harris County, the state's most populous county, has fifty-nine district courts, each covering the entire county. By contrast, one rural district court may include several counties. As these courts evolved, there was little systematic consideration of the respective workloads of individual courts, and there are now great disparities in the number of people that district courts serve.

The Court Is Now in Session
Judge Phillip A. Kazen presides over a murder case in the 227th District Court in Bexar County, Texas. While there is some overlapping jurisdiction with county courts, the 443 state district courts have general jurisdiction in both civil and criminal matters.

Many urban counties suffer from a heavy backlog of cases that can delay a trial date in civil lawsuits and even some criminal cases for months or years. The district courts disposed of 862,605 civil and criminal cases during the 2007 fiscal year, but new cases were added, and the courts began 2008 with 902,222 pending cases.[7]

Delays in criminal cases have prompted a widespread use of **plea bargains**. In plea bargaining, a criminal defendant, through a lawyer, negotiates with prosecutors a guilty plea that will get a lesser sentence than he or she could expect to receive if convicted in a trial. The process saves the state the time and expense of a full-blown trial and has become an essential tool in clearing urban court dockets.

Former District Attorney John B. Holmes, Jr., estimated that 90 percent of the thousands of felony cases filed in Harris County (Houston) each year were disposed of through plea bargains. Without plea bargains, the caseload would simply overwhelm the twenty-two Harris County district courts that handle criminal cases.

Harris County's civil district courts disposed of more than 97,000 lawsuits—divorces, personal injuries, tax disputes, and others—in fiscal year 2007 but left more than 89,000 other cases pending.[8] Many civil lawsuits are resolved through negotiations between the opposing parties, but those that are tried and appealed can take several years to be resolved.

The wide disparities in populations and caseloads served by the various district courts prompted the adoption of a constitutional amendment in 1985 that created the Judicial Districts Board. That panel was responsible for redrawing judicial districts with an eye toward a more equitable distribution of the workload. But in 1994, yielding to pressure from incumbent judges who did not want to lose their offices, it issued recommendations that primarily preserved the status quo. Extensive changes by the legislature were considered unlikely.

Although the district court is the state's primary trial court and the state pays the district judges' base salaries, the counties pick up virtually all other district court expenses. The counties provide courtrooms, pay the courts' operating expenses, and supplement the judges' state pay.

Intermediate Courts of Appeals

Fourteen intermediate **courts of appeals** cover thirteen multicounty regions that hear appeals of both civil and criminal cases from the district courts. Two courts, the First Court of Appeals and the Fourteenth Court of Appeals, are based in Houston and cover the same area. The Texas Constitution provides that each court shall have a chief justice and at least two other justices, but the legislature can add to that number and has done so for most courts. Each Houston court has nine judges, and the Fifth Court of Appeals in Dallas has thirteen judges. Five of these intermediate courts, however, have only three members. Appellate judges are elected to 6-year terms. They must be at least 35 years old and have at least 10 years of experience as an attorney or a judge on a court of record.

Although the appellate courts disposed of more than 11,000 civil and criminal cases during fiscal 2007, they left more than 7,000 other cases pending on their dockets at the end of the year, with criminal cases accounting for more than half of the unfinished business.[9] But there are wide disparities in the caseloads between individual courts, with those in Houston and Dallas handling the lion's share, although the Texas Supreme Court partially balances the load by transferring cases among courts. The courts of appeals normally decide cases in panels of three judges, but an entire court can hear some appeals *en banc*.

The Highest Appellate Courts

The creation of separate courts of last resort for civil and criminal cases was part of the effort by the constitutional framers of 1875 to fragment political power and decentralize the structure of state and local government.

★ **plea bargains**
Procedures that allow persons charged with crimes to negotiate guilty pleas with prosecutors in exchange for lighter sentences than they would expect to receive if convicted in trials.

★ **court of appeals**
Intermediate-level court that reviews civil and criminal cases from the district courts.

Cases on Appeal

Civil cases reach the Texas Supreme Court on appeal from the lower courts and are argued on points of law. The justices read briefs and listen to oral arguments from opposing attorneys. Justices can interrupt and query an attorney at any time.

★ **Texas Supreme Court**
Nine-member court with final appellate jurisdiction over civil lawsuits.

★ **Texas Court of Criminal Appeals**
Nine-member court with final appellate jurisdiction over criminal cases.

It was also based on the rationale that criminal cases should be tried more expeditiously, and the way to accomplish this was through a separate appellate court.

Although it decides only civil appeals, the **Texas Supreme Court** is probably viewed by most Texans as the titular head of the state judiciary, and it has been given some authority to coordinate the state judicial system.[10] The Supreme Court is charged with developing administrative procedures for the state courts and rules of civil procedure. It appoints the Board of Law Examiners, which is responsible for licensing attorneys, and has oversight of the State Bar, the professional organization to which all lawyers in Texas must belong. The Supreme Court also has disciplinary authority over state judges through recommendations of the State Commission on Judicial Conduct.

The Texas Supreme Court includes a chief justice and eight justices who serve staggered 6-year terms. Three members are up for election every 2 years on a statewide ballot. Members must be at least 35 years old and must have been a practicing attorney, a judge of a court of record, or a combination of both for at least 10 years.

The **Texas Court of Criminal Appeals**, which hears only criminal cases on appeal, includes a presiding judge and eight other judges elected statewide to staggered 6-year terms. The qualifications for members of this court are the same as those for the Texas Supreme Court.

Under the federal system, some decisions of the Texas Supreme Court and the Texas Court of Criminal Appeals can be appealed to the U.S. Supreme Court. Those cases have to involve a federal question or a right assured under the U.S. Constitution.

Texas Judges Many judges on the intermediate and highest appellate courts previously served on lower courts. Most district judges came to their offices from private law practice or from a prosecutor's office.

With the partisan realignment of Texas, Republicans have seen election gains and more appointments to judicial vacancies. A number of judges also have switched from the Democratic Party. By 2003, almost two-thirds of the judges at the district court level and higher were Republicans, including all nine members of the Texas Supreme Court and all nine members of the Texas Court of Criminal Appeals.

Most Texas judges are white males. More women, Hispanics, and African Americans are entering the legal profession and running for judicial offices, but they are still proportionately underrepresented in the judiciary. As will be discussed later in this chapter, minorities have pressed for changes in the judicial selection process to enhance their chances to serve on the bench.

Judicial elections have been diluted by a large number of appointments to judicial vacancies. The governor appoints judges to fill midterm vacancies on the district and appellate courts. County commissioners courts fill midterm vacancies on county court-at-law and justice of the peace courts. Appointees are required to run for office in the next general election to keep their seats, but their incumbency can enhance their election chances.

Other Participants in the State Judiciary   County and district clerks, both elected offices, are custodians of court records. Bailiffs are peace officers assigned to the courts to help maintain order and protect judges and other parties from physical attacks. Other law enforcement officers play critical roles in the arrest, detention, and investigation of persons accused of crimes.

County attorneys and district attorneys are responsible for prosecuting criminal cases. Both positions are elected. Some counties do not have a county attorney. In those that do, the county attorney is the chief legal adviser to the commissioners court, represents the county in civil lawsuits, and may prosecute misdemeanors. The district attorney prosecutes felonies and, in some counties, also handles misdemeanors. The district attorney represents one county in metropolitan areas and several counties in less populated areas of the state (see Chapter 25).

Other important players in the judicial process are the private citizens who serve on juries. Although there is some debate about the competency of a jury of ordinary citizens to make reasonable decisions on complex and technical civil and criminal matters, no acceptable alternatives have been found.

Efforts to Reform the Judicial System   Judicial reform has been a recurring issue in Texas politics. Small, incremental changes have been made since the 1970s, but many jurists and scholars continue to push for an overhaul of the state courts. In September 1989, Texas Supreme Court Chief Justice Thomas R. Phillips requested an in-depth study of the Texas judiciary by the Texas Research League, a privately financed, nonprofit group specializing in studies of state government.

The league concluded that the court system was fundamentally flawed and sorely in need of an overhaul. It made twenty-seven recommendations, including one that the legislature rewrite the judiciary article of the Texas Constitution to provide a fundamental framework for a unified court system.[11]

Despite a series of similar studies and reports, however, reform of Texas courts has been difficult. The public may have a lot to gain from judicial restructuring, but the primary stakeholders—the judges, the attorneys, the court administrative personnel, and the litigants who benefit from delays, confusion, and inefficiency—have resisted change. Unless there is a popular demand for improvement, there will be few structural changes in the judiciary until some or all of these participants perceive some advantages from reform.

The Jury System

The Grand Jury   Citizens serve on two kinds of juries, grand juries and trial, or petit, juries. The **grand jury** functions, in theory, to ensure that the government has sufficient reason to proceed with a criminal **prosecution** against an individual. It includes twelve persons selected by a district judge from a list

★ **grand jury**
Panel that reviews evidence submitted by prosecutors to determine whether to indict, or charge, an individual with a criminal offense.

★ **prosecution**
Conduct of legal proceedings against an individual charged with a crime.

proposed by a jury commission appointed by the local district judge or judges. Although the grand jury evolved to protect the individual against arbitrary and capricious behavior by governmental officials, a district attorney can exercise great control over a grand jury through deciding what evidence and which witnesses jurors will hear. There also have been allegations over the years that grand juries over-represent the interests of upper social and economic groups and under-represent minorities. Grand jury meetings and deliberations are conducted in private, and the accused is not allowed to have an attorney present during grand jury questioning.

A grand jury usually meets on specified days of the week and serves for the duration of the district court's term, usually from 3 to 6 months. If at least nine grand jurors believe there is enough evidence to warrant a trial in a case under investigation, they will issue an **indictment**, or a "true bill"—a written statement charging a person or persons with a crime. A grand jury investigation also may result in no indictment, or a "no bill." (See *What Do You Think?*: "A Grand Jury Challenges the DA.")

In some cases—especially when an investigation fails to produce a strong enough case for a felony indictment—grand juries issue indictments alleging misdemeanors. Most misdemeanors, however, are not handled by grand juries. They are handled by the district or county attorney, who prepares an **information**—a document formally charging an individual with a misdemeanor, on the basis of a complaint filed by a private citizen.

★ **indictment**
Written statement issued by a grand jury charging a person with a punishable offense.

★ **information**
Document formally charging a person with a misdemeanor.

What Do You *Think?*

A Grand Jury Challenges the DA

No one was injured, but the damage was extensive after a fire broke out in June 2007 at the suburban Houston home of Texas Supreme Court Justice David Medina. The justice's house and a neighbor's home were destroyed, and a third house was damaged. Medina wasn't home when the fire started, but his wife, Francisca, and one of their children were. Investigators, who spent several months on the case, determined the fire was intentionally set. Medina was called to testify before a grand jury, but he said neither he nor any member of his family had done anything wrong. And then-Harris County District Attorney Chuck Rosenthal said the justice wasn't a suspect in the arson.

Although district attorneys normally have a lot of influence over grand juries, Rosenthal and this grand jury soon parted company, sparking a politically charged controversy and allegations of a "runaway grand jury." In January 2008, the grand jury indicted Francisca Medina on an arson charge and David Medina on a charge of tampering with evidence. Within

hours, Rosenthal said he would move to have the charges dismissed due to "insufficient evidence."

A judge dismissed the charges the next day, angering grand jurors and raising allegations of political favoritism. Rosenthal and Medina were both Republicans.

For several more weeks, controversy continued to dog Rosenthal, a strong, law-and-order advocate whose office had sent more convicts to death row than any other prosecutor's office in the country. No sooner had the Medina dispute started to subside than Rosenthal became embroiled in a controversy over the public disclosure of office e-mails that included some sexually explicit and racist content.

Under increasing pressure, Rosenthal resigned in February 2008, saying a combination of prescription drugs had impaired his judgment. The publicity over the e-mails also had taken a toll on his family, he said.

"I am hopeful that, in my retirement, the media will accord my family the privacy we need to heal," Rosenthal said.

Source: Houston Chronicle, February 16, 2008, p. 1A.

The Petit Jury   The jury on which most people are likely to be called to serve is the trial jury, or **petit jury**. Citizens who are at least 18 years old and meet other minimal requirements are eligible for jury duty, and anyone refusing to comply with a jury summons can be fined for contempt of court (see *What Do You Think?*: "Is This Any Way to Round Up a Jury?"). Persons older than 70, individuals with legal custody of young children, and full-time students are exempted from jury duty. The legislature in 1991 increased the likelihood of an individual's being called to jury duty by providing that county and district clerks prepare jury summonses from lists of those Texans who have drivers' licenses or hold Department of Public Safety identification cards. Previously, prospective jurors were chosen from voter registration lists, and it was believed that some Texans had not been registering to vote in order to avoid jury duty.

Six persons make up a jury in a justice of the peace or county court, and twelve in a district court. Attorneys for both sides in a criminal or civil case screen the prospective jurors, known as veniremen, before a jury is seated. In major felony cases, such as capital murder, prosecutors and defense attorneys may take several days to select a jury from among hundreds of prospects.

Attorneys for each side in a criminal case are permitted a certain number of peremptory challenges, which allow them to dismiss a prospective juror without having to explain the reason, and an unlimited number of challenges for cause. In the latter case, the lawyer has to state why he or she believes a particular **venireman** would not be able to evaluate the evidence in the case impartially. The judge decides whether to grant each challenge for cause but can rule against a peremptory challenge only if he or she believes a prosecutor is trying to exclude prospective jurors because of their race, such as keeping African Americans off a jury that is to try an African American defendant. If that happens, the defendant is entitled to a new group, or panel, of prospective jurors.

In civil cases, attorneys for both sides determine whether any persons on the jury panel should be disqualified because they are related to one of the parties,

★ **petit jury**
Panel of citizens that hears evidence in a civil lawsuit or a criminal prosecution and decides the outcome by issuing a verdict.

★ **venireman**
Member of a panel from which a petit, or trial, jury is chosen.

What Do You *Think?*

Is This Any Way to Round Up a Jury?

Some people called it "street justice." Others said it was bad public relations. It was probably both, and it was certainly unusual.

Justice of the Peace Mark Fury had scheduled a night jury trial for a minor traffic case in his southwest Houston courtroom but, at the last minute, discovered he didn't have enough jurors. So he issued a writ, ordering deputy constables to go across the street and round up some shoppers in a grocery store parking lot.

Nineteen people soon found themselves unexpectedly pressed into jury duty. Not all were chosen for the jury, but all had to report to the courtroom and had their evening plans disrupted. Several weren't too happy about it.

"It just seemed everybody was a little crusty toward everybody. They were just all mad," one draftee said.

Lisa Sedgwick, who had planned to go to a soccer game that night, ended up being the jury foreman instead.

The jury roundup, although rare, was legal. But people caught in the judge's net couldn't understand why he didn't just simply postpone the trial of such a minor case.

Fury said he believed the jurors had "a positive experience. . . . I thought it went very smoothly. I expected there to be a larger number of acrimonious people."

The jury convicted the defendant, a teenager, of speeding.

Source: Houston Chronicle, August 22, 1997.

Cornerstone of the Judicial Process

It is a citizen's duty to show up for jury duty when summoned. Despite many criticisms of the petit jury, no alternative has gained widespread support. An attorney is shown addressing a jury in a state court in Dallas.

have some other personal or business connection, or could otherwise be prejudiced. For example, a lawyer defending a doctor in a malpractice suit probably would not want to seat a prospective juror who had been dissatisfied with his own medical treatment. Such potential conflicts are discovered by attorneys' careful screening and questioning of veniremen.

Unanimous jury verdicts are required to convict a defendant in a criminal case. And jurors have to be convinced "beyond a reasonable doubt" that a defendant is guilty before returning a guilty verdict. In contrast, agreement of only ten of the twelve members of a district court jury and five of the six on a county court jury are sufficient to reach a verdict in a civil suit.

Judicial Procedures and Decision Making

Civil litigants and criminal defendants (except those charged with capital murder) can waive their right to a jury trial if they believe it would be to their advantage to have their cases decided by a judge. Following established procedures, which differ between civil and criminal cases and are enforced by the judge, the trial moves through the presentation of opening arguments by the opposing attorneys, examination and cross-examination of witnesses, presentation of evidence, rebuttal, and summation. Some trials can be completed in a few hours, but the trial of a complex civil lawsuit or a sensational criminal case can take weeks or months. Convicted criminal defendants or parties dissatisfied with a judge or jury's verdict in a civil lawsuit can then appeal their case to higher courts.

The procedure in appellate courts is markedly different from that in trial courts. There is no jury at the appellate level to rehear evidence. Instead, judges review the decisions and the procedures of the lower court for conformance to constitutional and statutory requirements. The record of the trial court proceedings and legal briefs filed by the attorneys are available for appellate judges to review.

Most civil and criminal appeals are initially made to one of the fourteen intermediate courts of appeals. Parties dissatisfied with decisions of the courts of appeals can appeal to the Texas Supreme Court or the Texas Court of Criminal Appeals.

Cases reach the Texas Supreme Court primarily on **petitions for review**, usually filed by the losing parties, claiming that legal or procedural mistakes were

★ **petition for review**
Petition to the Texas Supreme Court claiming that legal or procedural mistakes were made in the lower court.

made in the lower courts. These petitions are distributed among the nine Supreme Court justices. The justices and their briefing attorneys then prepare memoranda on their assigned cases for circulation among the other court members. Meeting in private conference, the court decides which applications to reject outright—thus upholding the lower court decisions—and which to schedule for attorneys' oral arguments. A case will not be heard without the approval of at least four of the nine justices.

Oral arguments, in which the lawyers present their perspectives on the legal points that are at issue in their case and answer questions from the justices, are presented in open court. Most hearings are held in the Supreme Court chambers in Austin, but since 1998 the court, in an effort to try to educate more people about its work, has been holding occasional hearings in other Texas cities. The responsibility for writing the majority opinions that state the court's decisions is determined by lot among the justices. It often takes several months after oral arguments before a decision is issued. Legal points and judicial philosophies are debated among the justices behind the closed doors of their conference room. But differences sometimes spill out for public view through split decisions and strongly worded dissenting opinions.

Most cases taken to the Texas Supreme Court on appeal are from one of the courts of appeals, but occasionally the Supreme Court receives a direct appeal from a district court. In recent years, the court has been hearing about 10 percent of the petitions for review it receives.

The Texas Supreme Court also acts on petitions for **writs of mandamus,** or orders directing a lower court or another public official to take a certain action. Many involve disputes over procedure or evidence in cases still pending in trial courts.

> ★ **writ of mandamus**
> Court order directing a lower court or another public official to take a certain action.

The Texas Court of Criminal Appeals has appellate jurisdiction in criminal cases that originate in the district and county courts. Death penalty cases are appealed directly to the Court of Criminal Appeals. Other criminal cases are appealed first to the intermediate courts of appeals. Either the defendant or the prosecution can appeal the courts of appeals' decisions to the Court of Criminal Appeals by filing petitions for discretionary review, which the high court may grant if at least four judges agree. The court sets one day a week aside for lawyers' oral arguments in the cases it agrees to review. The task of writing majority opinions is rotated among the nine judges.

Judicial Concerns and Controversies

For more than 20 years, Texas courts often have been beset with conflict and controversy. Large campaign contributions from lawyers and other special interests to judges and judicial candidates periodically raise allegations that Texas has the best justice that money can buy. With millions of dollars at stake in crucial legal decisions, the Texas Supreme Court has been a philosophical and political battleground. Meanwhile, minorities, who hold a disproportionately small number of judicial offices, continue to press for greater influence in electing judges. Lengthy ballots, particularly in urban areas, make it increasingly difficult for most voters to choose intelligently among judicial candidates (see *People in Politics:* "Steve Mansfield: An Election Day Surprise"). Although these issues and concerns may seem unrelated, they all share one important characteristic: they cast a cloud over the Texas judiciary. Each, in its own way, undermines public confidence in the state courts and makes many Texans question how just their system of justice is.

Judicial Activism   In earlier chapters, we noted the historical domination of Texas politics and policies by the conservative, business-oriented establishment.

People in Politics Steve Mansfield: An Election Day Surprise

Like most other candidates for the Texas Court of Criminal Appeals, Houston attorney Steve Mansfield received little publicity when he began a campaign in 1994 to unseat Democratic judge Charles Campbell, a 12-year incumbent. Running as a crime victims' advocate, he defeated an equally unknown attorney for the Republican nomination and then got more publicity than he wanted—all of it negative. In the middle of his campaign, it was revealed that Mansfield had lied about his personal and political background and had exaggerated his legal experience. He was primarily an insurance lawyer with little experience in criminal law. But he unseated Campbell, thanks to heavy straight-ticket Republican voting in a GOP landslide.

Bad publicity continued to dog Mansfield even after he took office. Texas Republican Party officials shunned him at a party fund-raiser, and the Board of Law Examiners investigated the circumstances under which he had obtained a Texas law license, which he had to have to serve on the court. But at his swearing-in ceremony in January 1995, Mansfield promised to be a hardworking judge, and he spent his first year in office living up to his promise by authoring thirty-three opinions, slightly more than the court average. It was unknown how much of the actual research and writing could be credited to Mansfield and how much to the experienced staff he inherited from Campbell and was wise enough to retain. But, as he had promised during his campaign, Mansfield usually sided with the prosecution.

Several months after Mansfield took office, the State Bar publicly reprimanded him for his campaign lies. But the Board of Law Examiners did not challenge his law license, which cleared the way for him to remain on the court. Many judges, prosecutors, and other state officials considered Mansfield's election an embarrassment and a good argument for appointing, rather than electing, judges. But despite the controversy, Mansfield said he enjoyed his new job. "It's certainly been the greatest challenge I've ever faced. I've worked very hard to live up to the trust the people of Texas put in me," he said.[a]

Mansfield didn't seek reelection in 2000 and left the court after 6 years. Attempting a comeback, he ran for another Court of Criminal Appeals seat in the 2002 Republican primary, but lost.

[a]Quoted in *Houston Chronicle*, June 28, 1995.

For decades, that domination also applied to the judiciary, as insurance companies, banks, utilities, and other large corporate entities became accustomed to favorable rulings from a Democratic, but conservative, Texas Supreme Court.

Establishment-oriented justices, usually elected with the support of the state's largest law firms, tended to view their role as strict constructionists. The legislature had the authority to enact public policy; the responsibility of the courts, they believed, was to narrowly interpret and apply the law. Judges were not to engage in setting policy but were to honor legal precedent and prior case law, which in general had favored the interests of corporations over those of consumers, laborers, and the lower social classes.

The establishment began to feel the first tremors of a philosophical earthquake in the 1970s. The Texas Trial Lawyers Association, whose members represent consumers in lawsuits against businesses, doctors, and insurance companies, increased its political activity. And in 1973, the legislature, with increased minority and female membership from single-member House districts ordered by the federal courts (see Chapter 22), enacted the Deceptive Trade Practices–Consumer Protection Act, which encouraged plaintiffs, or injured parties, to take their grievances to court. Among other things, the new law allowed plaintiffs to sue for attorneys' fees as well as compensatory and punitive damages.

Trial, or plaintiffs', attorneys, who usually receive a healthy percentage of monetary damages awarded their clients, began contributing millions of dollars to successful Texas Supreme Court candidates, and judicial precedents started falling. A revamped court issued significant decisions that made it easier for consumers to win large judgments for medical malpractice, faulty products, and other complaints against businesses and their insurers. The new activist, liberal interpretation of the law contrasted sharply with the traditional record of the court. "All of a sudden, we have a magnificent Supreme Court, which is not controlled by a sinister, rich, opulent elite," trial attorney Pat Maloney of San Antonio, a major contributor to Supreme Court candidates, said in a 1983 interview with the *Fort Worth Star–Telegram*.[12]

The business community and defense lawyers accused the new court majority of exceeding its constitutional authority by trying to write its own laws. Some business leaders contended that the court's activism endangered the state's economy by discouraging new businesses from moving to Texas, a fear that was soon to be put to partisan advantage by Republican leaders.

Judicial Impropriety Controversy over the Texas Supreme Court escalated into a full-blown storm in 1986 when the Judicial Affairs Committee of the Texas House investigated two justices, Democrats C. L. Ray and William Kilgarlin, for alleged improper contact with attorneys practicing before the court. The two justices denied the allegations, made largely by former briefing attorneys, but never testified before the legislative panel. Both justices had consistently sided with plaintiffs' lawyers and had received considerable campaign support from them, and they contended the investigation was politically motivated and orchestrated by defense lawyers and corporate interests opposed to their judicial activism.

The committee eventually concluded its investigation without recommending any action against the justices. But in June 1987, the State Commission on Judicial Conduct issued public sanctions against both. Ray was reprimanded for seven violations of the Code of Judicial Conduct, including the acceptance of free airplane rides from attorneys practicing before the court and improper communication with lawyers about pending cases. Kilgarlin received a milder admonishment because two of his law clerks had accepted a weekend trip to Las Vegas from a law firm with cases pending before the court. Both justices were cited for soliciting funds from attorneys to help pay for litigation the justices had brought against the House Judicial Affairs Committee and a former briefing attorney who testified against them.

Later in 1987, the Texas judiciary, particularly the Texas Supreme Court, received negative publicity on a national scale when the high court upheld a record $11 billion judgment awarded Pennzoil Company in a dispute with Texaco, Inc. Several members of the Supreme Court were even featured on a network television program that questioned whether justice was "for sale" in Texas. The record judgment was awarded to Pennzoil after a state district court jury in Houston had determined that Texaco had wrongfully interfered in Pennzoil's attempt to acquire Getty Oil Company in 1984. Texaco, which sought protection under federal bankruptcy laws, later reached a settlement with Pennzoil, but it also waged a massive public relations campaign against the Texas judiciary.

In a segment on CBS-TV's *60 Minutes*, correspondent Mike Wallace pointed out that plaintiffs' attorney Joe Jamail of Houston, who represented Pennzoil, had contributed $10,000 to the original trial judge in the case and thousands of dollars more to Texas Supreme Court justices. The program also generally criticized the elective system that allowed Texas judges legally to accept large campaign contributions from lawyers who practiced before them. The program presented what had already been reported in the Texas media, but after the national exposure, Governor Bill Clements and other Republicans renewed

Advocate of Change
Texas Supreme Court Chief Justice John L. Hill, a Democrat, was highly critical of the costs of judicial campaigns and actively lobbied for the merit selection of judges with retention elections after he left the court in 1988.

★ **merit selection**
Proposal under which the governor would appoint state judges from lists of potential nominees recommended by committees of experts. Appointed judges would have to run later in retention elections to keep their seats but would not have opponents on the ballot. Voters would simply decide whether a judge should remain in office or be replaced by another gubernatorial appointee.

attacks on the activist, Democratic justices. And some Texas newspapers published editorials calling for changes in the judicial selection process.

Campaign Contributions and Republican Gains

Texas Supreme Court Chief Justice John L. Hill, a former attorney general who had narrowly lost a gubernatorial race to Clements in 1978, had been a strong supporter of electing state judges and had spent more than $1 million winning the chief justice's seat in 1984. As did his colleagues on the court, he accepted many campaign contributions from lawyers. But in 1986, Hill announced that the "recent trend toward excessive political contributions in judicial races" had prompted him to change his mind.[13] He now advocated a so-called **merit selection** plan of gubernatorial appointments and periodic retention elections. But the other eight Supreme Court justices—like Hill, all Democrats—still favored the elective system, and the legislature ignored pleas for change.

Hill resigned from the court on January 1, 1988, to return to private law practice and lobby as a private citizen for changing the judicial selection method. His resignation and the midterm resignations of two other Democratic justices before the 1988 elections gave Republicans a golden opportunity to make historic inroads on the high court, and also helped the business community regain control of the court from plaintiffs' attorneys.

Party realignment, including midterm judicial appointments by Clements, had already increased the number of Republican judges across the state, particularly on district court benches in urban areas. But only one Republican had ever served on the Supreme Court in modern times. Will Garwood was appointed by Clements in 1979 to fill a vacancy on the court but was defeated by Democrat C. L. Ray in the 1980 election. GOP leaders already had been planning to recruit a Republican slate of candidates for the three Supreme Court seats that normally would have been on the ballot in 1988. Now, six seats were contested, including those held by three new Republican justices appointed by Clements to fill the unexpected vacancies. Even though a full Texas Supreme Court term is 6 years, the governor's judicial appointees have to run in the next election to keep their seats. Clements appointed Thomas R. Phillips, a state district judge from Houston, to succeed Hill and become the first Republican chief justice since Reconstruction.

The competing legal and financial interests in Texas also understood that the six Texas Supreme Court races on the 1988 ballot would help set the philosophy of the court for years to come. Consequently, these were the most expensive court races Texas had ever experienced, with the twelve Republican and Democratic nominees raising $10 million in direct campaign contributions. Contributions to the winners averaged $836,347. Phillips, one of three Republican winners, spent $2 million, the most by a winning candidate. Some individual donations to other candidates were as large as $65,000.[14] Reformers argued that such large contributions created an appearance of impropriety and eroded public confidence in the judiciary's independence.

But the successes of Republicans and conservative Democrats in the 1988 races probably hindered, more than helped, the cause of reforming the judicial selection process. The business and medical communities, which had considerable success fighting the plaintiffs' lawyers under the existing rules—with large campaign contributions of their own—were pleased with the election results. "I'm a happy camper today," said one lobbyist for the Texas Medical Association, whose political action committee had supported two conservative Democratic winners and the three Republican victors.[15]

In several key liability cases over the next few years, the Supreme Court began to demonstrate a rediscovered philosophy favoring business defendants over plaintiffs.[16]

Republicans won a fourth seat on the court in 1990 and a fifth in 1994, to give the GOP a majority for the first time since Reconstruction. Republican challengers in 1994 also unseated nineteen incumbent Democratic district judges in Harris County in strong straight-party voting. Republicans completed their sweep of the Supreme Court in 1998 when Justice Rose Spector, one of two remaining Democratic justices, was unseated by Republican Harriet O'Neill and Democrat Raul A. Gonzalez retired in midterm and was replaced by Alberto R. Gonzales, an appointee of Governor George W. Bush who later would follow Bush to the White House.

Phillips, the chief justice since 1988, resigned in mid-term in 2004 to become a visiting professor at the South Texas College of Law in Houston. Phillips believed the court's reputation had been enhanced during his tenure, but, as his predecessor had done on stepping down sixteen years earlier, he criticized the money-driven, partisan election system for judges. He said it "creates great instability in the judiciary and erodes public confidence in the fairness of our decisions."[17]

Legislative Reaction to Judicial Activism

The business community had also moved its war against the trial lawyers to the legislature, which in 1987 enacted a so-called **tort reform** package that attempted to put some limits on personal-injury lawsuits and damage judgments entered by the courts. (A tort is a wrongful act over which a lawsuit can be brought.) Insurance companies, which had been lobbying nationwide for states to set limits on jury awards in personal-injury cases, were major proponents of the legislation. They were joined by the Texas Civil Justice League, an organization of trade and professional associations, cities, and businesses formed in 1986 to seek similar changes in Texas tort law. The high-stakes campaign for change was enthusiastically supported by Governor Bill Clements but was opposed by consumer groups and plaintiffs' lawyers, who had been making millions of dollars from the judiciary's new liberalism.

Cities, businesses, doctors, and even charitable organizations had been hit with tremendous increases in insurance premiums, which they blamed on greedy trial lawyers and large court awards in malpractice and personal-injury lawsuits. Trial lawyers blamed the insurance industry, which, they said, had started raising premiums to recoup losses in investment income after interest rates had fallen.

Among other things, the 1987 tort-reform laws limited governmental liability, attempted to discourage frivolous lawsuits, and limited the ability of claimants to collect damages for injuries that were largely their own fault. They also set limits on punitive damages, which are designed to punish whoever caused an accident or an injury and are often awarded in addition to an injured party's compensation for actual losses.

Other limits on lawsuits were enacted in later legislative sessions, including 1995 and 2003. The 1995 changes, major priorities of Governor George W. Bush, imposed even stricter limits on punitive damages and limited the liability of a party who is only partially responsible for an injury. The 2003 legislation, actively sought by Governor Rick Perry and a new Republican majority in the Texas House, set new restrictions on class action lawsuits, which are brought on behalf of large groups of people, and imposed new limits on money that could be awarded for non-economic damages (e.g., pain, suffering, or disfigurement) in medical malpractice cases. Lawsuits, or the threat of lawsuits, had been blamed for rising medical malpractice insurance premiums, which some doctors and other advocates of civil justice changes had characterized as a "crisis" in health care in Texas.

A leading proponent for the civil justice restrictions in 2003 was Texans for Lawsuit Reform (TLR), a Houston-based business group whose political action committee gave more than $1 million to successful legislative candidates during

Advocate of Retention Elections

Texas Supreme Court Chief Justice Thomas R. Phillips, the first Republican to serve as chief justice since Reconstruction, resigned in 2004. Like his predecessor, he also was critical of the impact of campaign contributions in the state's partisan election system.

★ **tort reform**
Changes in state law to put limits on personal injury lawsuits and damage judgments entered by the courts.

the 2002 campaigns.[18] The group, which has given the lion's share of its contributions to Republicans, experienced some noteworthy reversals in the 2006 elections. TLR contributed $3.8 million, primarily in highly contested legislative races, including $2.7 million to candidates who lost.[19]

Winners and Losers In a study released in 1999, Texas Watch, a consumer advocacy group, said that doctors, hospitals, and other business-related litigants had been big winners before the Texas Supreme Court during the previous 4 years and that consumers had fared poorly. The group studied more than 625 cases in which the court had written opinions between January 1, 1995, and April 14, 1999, a period during which most court members had received substantial campaign funding from doctors, insurers, and other business interests. The opinions also were issued after the Texas Legislature had begun enacting tort reform laws setting limits on civil lawsuits. The study determined that physicians and hospitals had won 86 percent of their appeals, most of which involved medical malpractice claims brought by injured patients or their families. Other consistent winners were insurance companies (73 percent), manufacturers (72 percent), banks (67 percent), utilities (65 percent), and other businesses (68 percent). Insurance policyholders, injured workers, injured patients, and other individual litigants won only 36 percent of the time.[20] The report covered only cases in which the Supreme Court had written opinions. Hundreds of other cases in which the high court upheld lower courts without issuing its own opinions weren't studied. "Individuals are the lowest link in the legal food chain that ends in the Texas Supreme Court," said Walt Borges, who directed the study. "The study raises a question about the fairness of the Texas Supreme Court and state law," he added.[21]

CBS-TV's *60 Minutes*, which had turned the national spotlight on plaintiffs' lawyers and their political contributions to Texas judges in 1987, revisited the Texas judiciary in a follow-up program in 1998. Noting that the partisan system of electing judges had remained unchanged, the new *60 Minutes* segment suggested that justice may still be for sale in Texas, but with different people— the business community—now wielding the influence. The Texas legislature in 1995 had imposed modest limits on campaign contributions to judges and judicial candidates and restricted the periods during which judges and their challengers could raise funds. But a judge could still receive as much as $30,000 from members of the same law firm and as much as $300,000 in total contributions from special interests through political action committees. The 1996 races for the Texas Supreme Court—the first conducted under the new law— demonstrated how weak the new reforms were. Four Republican incumbents still raised a combined $4 million, easily swamping fund-raising efforts by their unsuccessful challengers.

Texas Watch, the consumer advocacy group, issued a follow-up report on the Supreme Court's 2000–2001 term, which found that consumers were beginning to fare better in some court decisions. But the group determined that businesses, insurance companies, and other defendants still won 52 percent of cases pitting consumers against businesses. Consumers won 41 percent of the cases, and the remaining decisions were split, according to the new study.[22] Some observers attributed the moderating influence to appointees whom Governor George W. Bush had made to midterm vacancies on the court in the late 1990s. As some of those justices began to leave the court, however, consumer advocates complained of another philosophical shift against plaintiffs. Texas Watch issued still another report in October 2006, noting that the Supreme Court had ruled for business defendants and against workers and other consumers in about 80 percent of the cases it had decided during the previous 12 months.[23]

Minorities and the Judicial System   As the high-stakes battles were being waged over the Texas Supreme Court's philosophical and political makeup, minorities were actively seeking more representation in the Texas judiciary. But instead of pouring millions of dollars into judicial races, Hispanics and African Americans filed lawsuits to try to force change through the federal courts.

Throughout Texas history, Hispanics and African Americans have had difficulty winning election to state courts. The high cost of judicial campaigns, polarized voting along ethnic lines in the statewide or countywide races that are required of most judges, and low rates of minority participation in elections have minimized their electoral successes. The first Hispanic was seated on the Texas Supreme Court in 1984 and on the Court of Criminal Appeals in 1991. The first African American was seated on the Texas Court of Criminal Appeals in 1990 and on the Texas Supreme Court in 2001.

Another factor limiting the number of minority judges is a proportional shortage of minority attorneys, from whose ranks judges are drawn. State leaders' efforts to increase the number of minority lawyers were thwarted for several years by an anti-affirmative action federal court ruling in 1996 and a related state attorney general's opinion, which prohibited Texas law schools and universities from giving preferential treatment to minorities in admissions, student aid, and other programs. Those restrictions were eased in 2003, when the U.S. Supreme Court ruled that college admissions policies could include race as a factor, provided racial quotas weren't established (see *Politics Up Close:* "An Attack on Affirmative Action").

As of February 1989, a few months before a major lawsuit went to trial over the issue, only 35 of 375 state district judges were Hispanic, and only seven were African American. Only three Hispanics and no African Americans were among the eighty judges on the fourteen intermediate courts of appeals. Although they constituted at least one-third of the Texas population at the time, African Americans and Hispanics held only 11.2 percent of the district judgeships and less than 4 percent of the intermediate appellate seats.[24]

Three African American judges in Dallas, who had been appointed by Governor Mark White to fill judicial vacancies, had been unseated in countywide elections. One was Jesse Oliver, a former legislator who had won election to the Texas House from a sub-district within Dallas County but could not win a 1988 judicial race countywide. Oliver, a Democrat, had overwhelming African American support but lost about 90 percent of Dallas's white precincts.[25]

In a lawsuit tried in September 1989 in federal district court in Midland, attorneys for the League of United Latin American Citizens (LULAC) and other minority plaintiffs argued that the countywide system of electing state district judges violated the Voting Rights Act by diluting the voting strength of minorities. That federal law allows a federal court to strike down an electoral system that denies a protected class of voters an equal opportunity to elect officeholders of their choice. This case, *League of United Latin American Citizens et al. v. Mattox et al.*, took almost 5 years and two appeals to the U.S. Supreme Court to resolve. It did not change Texas's judicial selection system, but a summary of the case and its bumpy journey through the judicial process highlights the political stakes involved in the issue.

In November 1989, U.S. District Judge Lucius Bunton ruled that the countywide system was illegal in nine of the state's largest counties: Harris, Dallas, Tarrant, Bexar, Travis, Jefferson, Lubbock, Ector, and Midland. Those counties elected 172 district judges, almost half of the state's total, but had only a handful of minorities serving on the district courts. Bunton did not order an immediate remedy but strongly urged the legislature to address the issue. After the legislature failed to act, Bunton the next year ordered judges in the nine counties to run

Politics Up Close An Attack on Affirmative Action

The power of the federal courts over state policy was clearly demonstrated by a reverse discrimination lawsuit filed by four white students who had been denied admission to the University of Texas School of Law. For a few years, it thwarted efforts to promote racial and ethnic diversity in some of Texas's colleges and universities. Ruling in the so-called *Hopwood* case, the Fifth U.S. Circuit Court of Appeals in 1996 said a law school admissions policy that had given preferences to minority applicants was unconstitutional. The decision later was upheld by the U.S. Supreme Court.[a] The nation's high court, however, did not reverse its earlier landmark opinion in the *Bakke* case from California, which had held that race could be a factor in university admissions policies,[b] thus allowing other states to continue using affirmative action programs.

In a related legal opinion in 1997, Texas Attorney General Dan Morales held that the *Hopwood* restrictions applied to admissions, student aid, and all other student policies at all colleges and universities in Texas. Morales's opinion was attacked as overly broad by many civil rights leaders and minority legislators, but it had the force of law. The Texas legislature, which met in 1997, attempted to soften the blow to affirmative action by enacting a new law that guaranteed automatic admissions to state universities for high school graduates who finished in the top 10 percent of their classes, regardless of their scores on college entrance examinations. The law was designed to give the best students from poor and predominantly minority school districts an equal footing in university admissions with better-prepared graduates of wealthier school districts. The new law also allowed university officials to consider other admissions criteria, including a student's family income and parents' education level.

There was little change in minority enrollments at many Texas universities after the *Hopwood* decision because many universities hadn't used race as a factor

in admissions anyway. But the two largest—the University of Texas at Austin (UT) and Texas A&M University—did. The drop-off in minority enrollment was particularly troubling at the UT law school the first year after the *Hopwood* restrictions went into effect. The first-year law class of almost 500 students in the fall of 1997 included only four African Americans and twenty-five Hispanics. There had been thirty-one African Americans and forty-two Hispanics in the previous year's entering class. And the more flexible admissions standards set by the legislature applied only to entering undergraduate students, not to those seeking admission to law school and other professional schools.

Many higher education administrators and civil rights leaders said it was wrong to dismantle affirmative action programs that had been designed to improve the educational and professional opportunities of minorities, who had historically suffered from segregation and were still overrepresented among the nation's poor. They said it was particularly short-sighted to deemphasize minority recruitment efforts at a time when Hispanics and African Americans were only a few years away from making up a majority of the Texas population.

But Morales urged university officials to redouble their efforts to recruit disadvantaged students of all races. "We must express to young Texans the reality that in this country one is capable of rising as high as his or her individual talents, ability and hard work will allow," he said.[c]

The U.S. Supreme Court refused to hear two appeals by Texas of the *Hopwood* decision. But ruling in a separate case from Michigan in 2003, the high court held that college admissions policies could include race as a factor, provided the policies didn't set racial quotas. University officials in Texas then began revising admissions policies to once again include affirmative action.

[a]*Hopwood v. Texas*, 135 L.Ed. 1095 (1996).
[b]*University of California Regents v. Bakke*, 438 U.S. 265 (1978).
[c]Quoted in *Houston Chronicle*, February 7, 1997.

for election from districts in nonpartisan elections. But the state won a stay of Bunton's order from the Fifth U.S. Circuit Court of Appeals, and partisan, countywide judicial elections were held as scheduled in 1990.

Ironically, one minority judge was outspoken in his opposition to district elections. State District Judge Felix Salazar of Houston, a Democrat who didn't seek reelection in 1990, lived in a predominantly non-Hispanic white neighborhood and in previous elections had been endorsed by a diversity of groups. He claimed that small districts could work against the interests of minorities because a judge from a conservative Anglo district could feel political pressure to sentence minority criminal defendants more harshly than whites. "The judge will have to espouse the feeling of the community. His district may think that's all right, and it will be hell unseating him," he told the *Houston Chronicle*.[26]

Other opponents of district elections argued that districts could also put undue pressure from minority communities on judges. But Jesse Oliver, the former African American legislator and judge who had been unseated in a countywide race in Dallas, did not agree that judicial districts would distort the administration of justice any more than countywide elections. "For one thing, if the community does exert pressure, then the white community is exerting all the pressure now because they are electing the judges in Dallas County," he said.[27]

Ruling in the Texas case and one from Louisiana in June 1991, the U.S. Supreme Court held that the Voting Rights Act applied to elections for the judiciary. But the high court did not strike down the at-large election system. "We believe that the state's interest in maintaining an electoral system—in this case, Texas's interest in maintaining the link between a district judge's (countywide) jurisdiction and the area of residency of his or her voters—is a legitimate factor to be considered" in determining whether the Voting Rights Act has been violated, the court wrote. But it also emphasized that the state's interest was only one factor to be considered and did not automatically outweigh proof of diluting minority votes.[28]

The U.S. Supreme Court returned the Texas lawsuit to the Fifth U.S. Circuit Court of Appeals for more deliberations, and, in January 1993, a three-judge panel of the Fifth Circuit ruled 2–1 that countywide elections illegally diluted the voting strength of minorities in eight counties: Harris, Dallas, Bexar, Tarrant, Jefferson, Lubbock, Ector, and Midland. Under pressure from minority legislators, Attorney General Dan Morales agreed to a settlement with the plaintiffs that would have required district elections for most of the judges in those counties and a ninth, Travis County. The settlement was endorsed by Governor Ann Richards, Democratic legislative leaders, and Democratic majorities in the Texas House and Senate. But it was opposed by Texas Supreme Court Chief Justice Thomas R. Phillips and state District Judges Sharolyn Wood of Houston and Harold Entz of Dallas, Republican defendants in the lawsuit.

The full Fifth Circuit rejected the settlement in a 9–4 vote in August 1993, holding that the "evidence of any dilution of minority voting power [in countywide judicial elections] is marginal at best."[29] The Fifth Circuit said partisan affiliation was a more significant factor than ethnicity in judicial elections. Then in January 1994, the U.S. Supreme Court brought the lawsuit to an end by upholding the Fifth Circuit's opinion. That left the issue of judicial selection in the hands of the Texas legislature, which for years had refused to change the elective system. State Senator Rodney Ellis, a Houston Democrat and a leading proponent of district elections, called the decision "devastating" and said it amounted to a "wholesale assault on civil rights." State District Judge Sharolyn Wood, a Houston Republican who had fought district elections, had a different reaction. "Hooray for Texas!" she said.[30]

By late 2007, about 13 percent of the state judges at the county court level and higher were Hispanic and about 3 percent were African American.[31]

Minority Judicial Appointments   Democratic Governor Mark White appointed the first Hispanic, Raul A. Gonzalez, the son of migrant workers, to the Texas Supreme Court in 1984 to fill a vacancy created by a resignation. Gonzalez made history a second time in 1986 by winning election to the seat and becoming the first Hispanic to win a statewide election in Texas. A native of Weslaco in the Rio Grande Valley, Gonzalez had been a state district judge in

Brownsville and had been appointed to the Thirteenth Court of Appeals in Corpus Christi by Republican Governor Bill Clements in 1981.

Despite his background, Gonzalez, a Democrat, was one of the most conservative members of the Supreme Court during his tenure. Consequently, he came under frequent attack from plaintiffs' lawyers and, ironically, from many of the constituent groups within his own party who advocated increasing the number of minority judges. Gonzalez's bitterly contested reelection race in 1994 proved that ethnicity can quickly take a backseat to judicial philosophy and partisanship.

Gonzalez defeated a strong challenge in the Democratic primary from Corpus Christi attorney Rene Haas, who was supported by trial lawyers, women's groups, consumer advocates, several key Democratic legislators, and a number of African American and Hispanic leaders in the Democratic Party. Gonzalez drew heavy financial support from business interests, insurance companies, and defense attorneys. He had angered many Democrats by siding with the Republican justices in a 5–4 decision upholding a state Senate redistricting plan that favored Republicans in the 1992 legislative elections. And he angered many women, as well as trial lawyers, by voting with the court majority in two cases overturning damages awarded women who had complained of being emotionally and physically abused by men.

Raul Gonzalez resigned from the Supreme Court in midterm in late 1998 and was replaced by Alberto R. Gonzales, an appointee of Governor George W. Bush and only the second Hispanic to serve on the high court. As had Raul Gonzalez, Alberto Gonzales came from a modest background. His parents were migrant workers when he was born in San Antonio, but they soon moved to Houston, where his father became a construction worker. The young Gonzales, one of eight children, joined the Air Force after graduating from high school, attended the Air Force Academy, and earned degrees from Rice University and Harvard Law School. He had never been a judge before Governor Bush named him to the Supreme Court. But he had been a partner in one of Houston's largest law firms, had been Bush's top staff lawyer, and had served under Bush as Texas secretary of state.

Alberto Gonzales's appointment came at a time when Governor Bush was actively trying to increase the Republican Party's appeal to Hispanics, and Bush acknowledged that it was important to him that Gonzales was Hispanic. "Of course, it mattered what his ethnicity is, but first and foremost what mattered is, I've got great confidence in Al. I know him well. He's a good friend. He'll do a fine job," Bush said.[32] Bush's confidence in Gonzales continued after Bush became president in 2001. He appointed Gonzales White House counsel and later U.S. attorney general.

On succeeding Bush, Republican Governor Rick Perry named minorities to the first two vacancies he had the opportunity to fill on the Texas Supreme Court in 2001. One was Wallace Jefferson, an appellate lawyer from San Antonio who became the first African American to serve on the high court. Perry named Jefferson to succeed Alberto Gonzales, who had resigned to become the White House counsel. Jefferson, a Republican, was the great-great-great-grandson of a slave. Later the same year, Perry appointed Xavier Rodriguez, a San Antonio labor lawyer, to the Supreme Court to succeed former Justice Greg Abbott, who had resigned to run for Texas attorney general. Rodriguez became the third Hispanic to serve on the court, but he was unseated in the 2002 Republican primary by Austin lawyer Steven Wayne Smith, an Anglo. Jefferson was elected in 2002 to keep his seat on the high court, and a second African American, Republican Dale Wainwright, a state district judge from Houston, was elected to an open Supreme Court seat the same year. Perry appointed another Hispanic, David M. Medina, to the Supreme Court in 2004.

Governor Ann Richards appointed the first Hispanic, Fortunato P. Benavides, to the Texas Court of Criminal Appeals in 1991 to fill a vacancy. Benavides had been a justice on the Thirteenth Court of Appeals and a district judge and a county court-at-law judge in Hidalgo County. But his tenure on the statewide court was short-lived. He was narrowly unseated in 1992 by Republican Lawrence Meyers of Fort Worth, an Anglo, who became the first Republican elected to the criminal court. Benavides later was appointed by President Bill Clinton to the Fifth U.S. Circuit Court of Appeals.

Governor Bill Clements appointed the first African American, Louis Sturns, a Republican state district judge from Fort Worth, to the Texas Court of Criminal Appeals on March 16, 1990. Because the vacancy that Sturns filled had occurred after the 1990 party primaries, the State Republican Executive Committee put Sturns on the general election ballot as the GOP nominee for the seat. The State Democratic Executive Committee nominated another African American, Morris Overstreet, a county court-at-law judge from Amarillo. Overstreet narrowly defeated Sturns in the November general election to become the first African American elected to a statewide office in Texas. Overstreet served on the court until 1998, when he lost a race for the Democratic nomination for Texas attorney general.

Women in the Judiciary The first woman to serve as a state district judge in Texas was Sarah T. Hughes of Dallas, who was appointed to the bench in 1935 by Governor James V. Allred and served until 1961, when she resigned to accept an appointment by President John F. Kennedy to the federal district bench. Ironically, Hughes is best known for swearing a grim-faced Lyndon B. Johnson into office aboard Air Force One on November 22, 1963, following Kennedy's assassination in Dallas.

Ruby Sondock of Houston was the first woman to serve on the Texas Supreme Court. She had been a state district judge before Governor Bill Clements named her to the high court on June 25, 1982, to fill a vacancy temporarily. Sondock chose not to seek election to the seat and served only a few months. She later returned to the district bench. Democrat Rose Spector, a state district judge from San Antonio, became the first woman elected to the Supreme Court when she defeated Republican Justice Eugene Cook in 1992. She was unseated in 1998 by Republican Harriet O'Neill.

In 1994, Republican Sharon Keller, a former Dallas County prosecutor, became the first woman elected to the Texas Court of Criminal Appeals. She was elected presiding judge in 2000. Four women, including Keller, were serving on the nine-member court in 2007. And more than 260 women were judges at the county court level or higher in Texas.[33]

The Search for Solutions The debates and lawsuits over judicial elections and representation in Texas emphasize the significant role of the courts in policy making as well as day-to-day litigation. The composition of the courts makes a difference. Although some may argue that the role of a judge is simply to apply the law to the facts and issues of a specific case, judges bring to the courts their own values, philosophical views, and life experiences, and these factors serve to filter their interpretations of the law and determine the shape of justice for millions of people.

There is no one simple solution to all the problems and inequities outlined above. Strict limits on the amount of campaign funds that judges and judicial candidates could raise from lawyers and other special interests, for example, could reduce the appearance of influence peddling in the judiciary and temper the high-stakes war between the trial lawyers and the business community for philosophical control of the courts. Campaign finance reform could also help build or restore public confidence in the impartiality of the judiciary. Such reform, however, may not improve opportunities for minorities to win election to the bench. Nor would it shorten the long election ballots that discourage Texans from casting informed votes in judicial races.

The same shortcomings could be anticipated with nonpartisan judicial elections or a merit selection system—two frequently mentioned alternatives to Texas's system of partisan judicial elections. In nonpartisan elections, judges and judicial candidates would not run under Democratic, Republican, or other party labels. This arrangement would guard against partisan bickering on the multimember appellate courts and eliminate the possibility that a poorly qualified candidate could be swept into office by one-party, straight ticket voting.

★ **retention elections**
Elections in which judges run on their own records rather than against other candidates. Voters cast their ballots on the question of whether the incumbent judge should stay in office.

Under the merit selection plan (sometimes referred to as the Missouri Plan), the governor would appoint judges from lists of nominees recommended by nominating commissions. The appointed judges would have to run later in **retention elections** to keep their seats, but they would not have opponents on the ballot. Voters would simply decide whether a judge should remain in office or be removed, to be replaced by another gubernatorial appointee.

Texas was one of only eight states in 2008 with a partisan election system for judges (see *Across the USA:* "Judicial Selection in the States"). Thirteen states had nonpartisan judicial elections, and half used some form of judicial nominating commission, usually in conjunction with a gubernatorial appointment. Only sixteen states, however, combined the use of nominating commissions with retention elections, as provided for in the Missouri Plan. Each alternative has its advantages, but none would necessarily eliminate undue political influence on the judiciary.[34]

Under a merit selection system, interest groups could still apply pressure on the governor and the members of the committees making recommendations for appointments. Although a merit selection plan could be written to require the nominating panels to make ethnically diverse recommendations to the governor, that would not answer the question of how to structure the retention elections. Minority appointees could still be at a disadvantage in retention elections if they have to run countywide, rather than in smaller geographic districts. Despite their popularity among minority leaders, district elections for judges are still viewed by many decision makers as a form of **ward politics** that may be appropriate or desirable for legislative seats but not for judges. Judges, they argue, do not represent a particular constituency.

★ **ward politics**
Term, often with negative connotations, that refers to partisan politics linked to political favoritism.

Attempts were made to overhaul the judicial selection process during recent legislative sessions, but they failed. In 1995, as discussed earlier in this chapter, lawmakers set modest limits on campaign contributions to judges and judicial candidates and restricted the periods during which judges and judicial candidates could accept political donations.

Crime and Punishment

Under both the U.S. Constitution and the Texas Constitution, a person charged with a crime is presumed innocent until the state can prove guilt beyond a reasonable doubt to a judge or a jury. The state also has the burden to prosecute fairly, that is, to follow principles of procedural due process outlined in constitutional and statutory law and interpreted by the courts. Even persons charged with the most heinous crimes retain these fundamental rights, and although there is often a public outcry about "coddling criminals," the process is designed to protect an individual from governmental abuses, to lessen the chance that an innocent person will be wrongly convicted of a crime.

Across the USA   Selection of State Appellate Judges

There is no uniformity in the manner states select judges. In an effort to reduce the impact of politics and campaign contributions, many states have moved toward nonpartisan elections or gubernatorial appointments with retention elections. With the exception of municipal judges, Texas selects judges by partisan election. This map shows how states select their appelate judges.

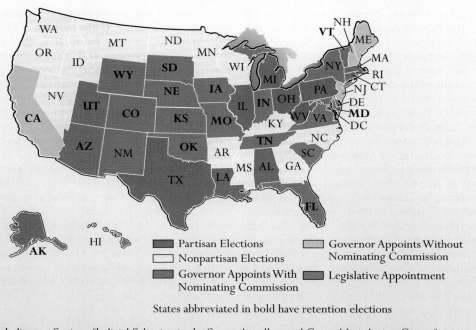

Partisan Elections
Nonpartisan Elections
Governor Appoints With Nominating Commission
Governor Appoints Without Nominating Commission
Legislative Appointment

States abbreviated in bold have retention elections

Source: American Judicature Society, "Judicial Selection in the States: Appellate and General Jurisdiction Courts."

In Texas, as well as in other states, these rights have sometimes been violated (see *Politics Up Close*: "A Huge Injustice in Tulia"). But over the years, the federal courts, in particular, have strengthened their enforcement. Through a case-by-case process, the U.S. Supreme Court has applied the Bill of Rights to the states by way of the Due Process and the Equal Protection clauses of the 14th Amendment to the U.S. Constitution. The failure of police or prosecutors to comply with specific procedures for handling a person accused of a crime may result in charges against an individual being dropped or a conviction reversed on appeal.

Arrested suspects must be taken before a magistrate—usually a justice of the peace or a municipal court judge—to be formally informed of the offense or offenses with which they are charged and to be told their legal rights. Depending on the charges, a bond may be set to allow them to get out of jail and remain free pending their trials. They have the right to remain silent, to consult with an attorney and have an attorney present during questioning by law enforcement officers or prosecutors, and to be warned that any statement they make can be used against them in a trial. Defendants who cannot afford to hire a lawyer must be provided with court-appointed attorneys at taxpayer expense. Many of these protections were extended to the states by the U.S. Supreme Court in the landmark *Miranda* ruling in 1966.[35]

★ *Miranda* ruling
Far-reaching decision of the U.S. Supreme Court that requires law enforcement officers to warn a criminal suspect of his or her right to remain silent and to have an attorney present before questioning.

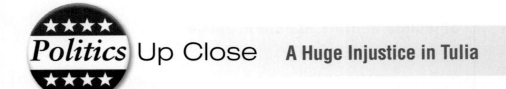

Politics Up Close   A Huge Injustice in Tulia

What began as a drug sting in Tulia, a small town in the Texas Panhandle, quickly escalated into one of the biggest miscarriages of justice in recent Texas history. After belated, but intense, media coverage, help finally arrived for thirty-five victims, but not before they had paid a high price.

In July 1999, forty-six Tulia residents, including thirty-nine African Americans, were arrested on drug charges. Thirty-eight of the defendants were later convicted, all on the testimony of Tom Coleman, an undercover officer and the only prosecution witness against them. After the *Texas Observer* newspaper, followed by other media, focused attention on the arrests and raised questions about whether they were racially motivated, special evidentiary hearings into the drug sting were convened in March 2003. Retired state District Judge Ron Chapman of Dallas presided over the hearings, during which Coleman's testimony was discredited. Chapman recommended that the Texas Court of Criminal Appeals overturn all thirty-eight convictions. In a separate proceeding, Coleman was later indicted on three counts of perjury stemming from his testimony before Chapman.

The Texas legislature then stepped in, passing a law that allowed fourteen Tulia defendants who were still in prison to be released on bond while the Court of Criminal Appeals considered their cases. And, finally, Governor Rick Perry pardoned thirty-five of the defendants in August 2003, more than 4 years after their arrests. "Questions surrounding testimony from the key witnesses in these cases, coupled with recommendations from the Board of Pardons and Paroles, weighed heavily in my final decision," the governor said. "Texans demand a system that is tough but fair. I believe my decision to grant pardons in these cases is both appropriate and just," he added. Perry's office said three of the Tulia defendants weren't eligible for pardons.

Jeff Blackburn of Amarillo, an attorney for the Tulia defendants, also filed a civil lawsuit in federal court, seeking damages against a regional drug task force and several local government officials in Swisher County, where Tulia is located. Will Harrell, who then was executive director for Texas of the American Civil Liberties Union, said systemic flaws in the criminal justice system, such as police misconduct, abuse of authority and inadequate legal representation of the poor, still needed to be addressed.

Source: Houston Chronicle, August 23, 2003, p. 1A.

★ **nolo contendere**
Plea of "no contest" to a criminal charge.

All criminal defendants have the right to a trial by jury but, except in capital murder cases, may waive a jury trial and have their cases decided by a judge. Defendants may plead guilty, not guilty, or **nolo contendere** (no contest). Prosecutors and defense attorneys settle many cases through plea bargaining, a process described earlier in this chapter. The trial judge does not have to accept a plea bargain but usually does. When defendants choose to have their guilt or innocence determined by the judge, the judge also determines the punishment if they are convicted. A jury can return a guilty verdict only if all jurors agree that the defendant is guilty beyond a reasonable doubt. If a jury cannot reach a unanimous verdict, even after lengthy negotiations and prodding from the judge, the judge must declare a mistrial. In that case, the prosecution has to seek a new trial with another jury or drop the charges. In a jury trial, a defendant may choose to have the punishment also set by the jury. If not, it is determined by the judge.

In 1991, the Texas Court of Criminal Appeals took the major step of ordering, for the first time, an official definition of "reasonable doubt" that was to be submitted to every jury deciding a criminal case. According to the definition, evidence against a criminal defendant had to be so convincing that jurors would be willing to rely on it "without hesitation" in the most important events in their own lives.[36] But, reflecting a change in philosophy, a more conservative Court of Criminal

Appeals eliminated that definition in 2000, to the dismay of some criminal defense lawyers. "We find the better practice is to give no definition of reasonable doubt at all to the jury," said the new opinion written by Judge Mike Keasler.[37]

Jury trials are required in **capital murder** cases, which are punishable by death or life in prison without parole. Executions in Texas used to be carried out by electrocution at the state prison unit in downtown Huntsville. Some 361 individuals were executed in Texas from 1924 to 1964, when executions were suspended because of legal challenges.

In 1972, the U.S. Supreme Court halted executions in all the states by striking down all the death penalty laws then on the books as unconstitutional. The high court held that capital punishment, as then practiced, violated the constitutional prohibition against "cruel and unusual punishment" because it could be applied in a discriminatory fashion.[38] Not only could virtually any act of murder be punished by death under the old Texas law, but so could rape and certain other crimes.

In 1973, the Texas Legislature rewrote the death penalty statute to try to meet the Supreme Court's standards by defining capital crimes as murder committed under specific circumstances. The list was expanded later and now includes the murder of a law enforcement officer or firefighter who is on duty, murder committed during the course of committing certain other major crimes, murder for hire, murdering more than one person, murder of a prison guard or employee, murder committed while escaping or attempting to escape from a penal institution, or murder of a child younger than 6.

A jury that has found a person guilty of capital murder must answer certain questions about the defendant before choosing between death or life imprisonment, the only punishments available. Jurors are required to consider whether a convicted murderer will be a continuing danger to society as well as mitigating circumstances, including evidence of mental retardation, before deciding punishment.[39]

The first execution under the 1973 Texas law was carried out in 1982. By then the legislature, acting in 1977, had changed the method of execution from the electric chair to the intravenous injection of a lethal substance. By 2008, more than 300 men and two women had been executed in Texas by

★ **capital murder**
Murder committed under certain circumstances for which the death penalty or life in prison must be imposed.

Emerging Patterns Among Women Jurists
In 2008, four women, including Sharon Keller, the presiding judge, served on the state's highest court for criminal appeals.

Opposition to Executions

Death penalty opponents outside the state Capitol protesting a 2008 U.S. Supreme Court ruling that death by lethal injection does not violate the federal Constitution's prohibition against cruel and unusual punishment.

lethal injection. Karla Faye Tucker, the first woman executed in Texas since the Civil War, was put to death in 1998 for killing two people with a pickax almost 15 years earlier. The second woman was executed in early 2000 for the murder of her husband.

After considerable controversy in Texas and other states, the U.S. Supreme Court in June 2002 banned the execution of mentally retarded convicts. Death penalty opponents had argued that, before the high court ruling, Texas had executed at least six inmates who were demonstrably retarded. The Texas Legislature, in its first session after the Supreme Court ban, failed to revise its death penalty statute to comply with the court's order, requiring defense attorneys to continue the battle, case by case. Some feared that, without new state guidelines for evaluating and trying convicts, additional mentally retarded persons would be executed in Texas, despite the Supreme Court's ban.[40]

In 2008, the nation's high court, deciding two appeals from Kentucky, ruled that the chemicals used in lethal injections did not amount to cruel and unusual punishment and did not violate the U.S. Constitution. Death penalty opponents had argued that the chemicals may cause the condemned to feel intense pain. Texas uses the same chemicals as Kentucky (see *Controversy*: "Shutting the Court Door on a Condemned Inmate's Last-Gasp Appeal").

After capital murder, the most serious criminal offense is a first-degree felony (e.g., aggravated sexual assault and non-capital murder), punishable by a prison sentence of 5 to 99 years or life. Second-degree felonies, such as burglary of someone's home and bribery, are punishable by 2 to 20 years in prison. Third-degree felonies, including intentional bodily injury to a child and theft of trade secrets, are punishable by 2 to 10 years in prison. State jail felonies—which include many property crimes, such as burglary of an office building, and minor drug offenses—are punishable by up to 2 years in a state-run jail or time in a community corrections program, each of which is supposed to emphasize rehabilitation as well as punishment.

Controversy

Shutting the Court Door on a Condemned Inmate's Last-Gasp Appeal

Despite the controversy it provokes, the death penalty still has strong political support in Texas, which has executed more than 300 convicts by lethal injection—more than all other states combined—since 1982. And few, if any, public officials in Texas are stronger supporters of the death penalty than is Sharon Keller, presiding judge of the Texas Court of Criminal Appeals, which upholds the vast majority of the death sentences it reviews. But, in the view of many lawyers and other Texans as well, Keller went too far when she cut off

Over in a Few Minutes

Hanging and electrocution were used by the state to execute convicted prisoners prior to lethal injection, which is now used by Texas. Condemned prisoners are strapped to this gurney, two needles are inserted, the inmate is injected with three solutions, which produce an anesthetic overdose and respiratory and cardiac arrest.

a condemned inmate's attempt to file a last-gasp appeal only a few hours before he was executed.

Lawyers for Michael Richard, a convicted murderer and rapist, attempted to halt his execution by lethal injection on September 25, 2007, following the United States Supreme Court's decision earlier that day to accept two Kentucky cases challenging the constitutionality of chemicals used for lethal injection. Death penalty opponents have argued that the execution method may amount to cruel and unusual punishment, prohibited by the U.S. Constitution, because the condemned may feel intense pain as the mixture of drugs is administered. Texas used the same chemicals as Kentucky.

Richard's attorneys tried to get a stay of execution for their client until the nation's high court decided the Kentucky cases, but computer problems at one lawyer's office slowed the preparation of their appeal. When they asked the Court of Criminal Appeals for more time, Keller ordered the court clerk's office to close at the normal time, 5 P.M. Richard's lawyers didn't have time to file his appeal, and he was executed later that evening.

After the controversy over Keller's decision erupted during subsequent days, three other judges on the nine-member court said they had been available for work on the evening of Richard's execution and could have handled his appeal had they known about it. Twenty lawyers from across Texas, including many prominent names, later filed a formal complaint against Keller with the State Commission on Judicial Conduct. The complaint accused the judge of violating the constitutional due process of a condemned man.

"Judge Keller's actions denied Michael Richard two constitutional rights, access to the courts and due process, which led to his execution," the complaint said.

Keller blamed Richard's lawyers.

"I think the question ought to be why didn't they file something on time. They had all day," she said.[a]

A few weeks later, the Court of Criminal Appeals announced it would accept emergency e-mail filings of appeals in death penalty cases in an effort to avoid something like the Richard's case from occurring again.[b]

[a]Quoted in *Houston Chronicle*, October 11, 2007, p. 1A

[b]*Houston Chronicle*, November 7, 2007, p. 1A

The most minor crimes are classified as Class A, B, or C misdemeanors. Crimes such as public lewdness and harboring a runaway child are examples of Class A misdemeanors and are punishable by a maximum $4,000 fine and/or one year in a county jail. The unauthorized use of television cable decoding equipment or falsely claiming to be a police officer are examples of Class B misdemeanors and carry a maximum sentence of 180 days in a county jail and a $2,000 fine. Class C misdemeanors include illegal gambling and the issuance of a bad check. They are punishable by a maximum $500 fine.

★ **probation**
Procedure under which a convicted criminal is not sent to prison if he or she meets certain conditions, such as restrictions on travel and associates.

★ **parole**
Early release of an inmate from prison, subject to certain conditions.

People convicted of crimes can be sentenced to **probation** (also called community supervision); they are not sent to prison but must meet certain conditions, such as restrictions on where they travel and with whom they associate. Except for those under the death penalty and some capital murderers serving life sentences, convicted felons sentenced to prison can become eligible for **parole**—or early release under supervisory restrictions—after serving a portion of their sentence. Capital murderers sentenced to life in prison before a significant change in state law in 2005 can be considered for parole after serving 40 years. Those sentenced after the 2005 law, which imposed life without parole for capital murderers who aren't sentenced to death, cannot be paroled. Parole decisions are made by the Board of Pardons and Paroles, which is appointed by the governor.

A landmark federal court order in 1980 forced the state to spend billions of dollars expanding and improving its prison system and forced the legislature to reevaluate the punishment of some criminals (see *Politics Up Close:* "Criminal Justice: An Expensive Headache") In 2007, Texas's juvenile justice system erupted into controversy with reports that staff members at some state schools for delinquent offenders had been sexually abusing inmates. The legislature responded by placing the Texas Youth Commission under a conservator. New administrators were hired and reforms ordered.

Politics Up Close   Criminal Justice: An Expensive Headache

An overcrowded and inadequately staffed prison system prompted U.S. District Judge William Wayne Justice of Tyler to declare Texas's prisons unconstitutional in 1980 in a landmark lawsuit brought by inmates (*Ruiz v. Estelle*). Among other things, the court ordered the population of prison units limited to 95 percent of capacity. That limit and an increase in the violent crime rate in the 1980s helped produce a criminal justice crisis that saw hundreds of dangerous convicts released from prison early and thousands of other criminals backlogged in overcrowded county jails.

The *Ruiz* lawsuit was settled in 1992, with the state promising to maintain constitutional prisons. In 1993 the legislature enacted a major package of criminal justice reforms. The minimum time that violent criminals would have to serve in prison before being eligible for parole was doubled, from one-fourth to

one-half of their sentences. To make sure there was enough room to keep the most dangerous felons in prison longer, thousands of property and drug offenders were to be diverted into community corrections programs or a new system of state jails, where education, drug abuse treatment, and other rehabilitation programs were to be emphasized.

Financed by bond issues totaling $3 billion, a huge prison expansion program was completed in the mid-1990s. With more than 140,000 spaces, Texas finally had enough room for all its prisoners in its corrections system. Some counties had sufficient jail space to permit them to lease space to house convicts from other states. But criminal justice experts warned that the relief was only temporary, and before long, lower parole rates and long prison sentences were once again taking their toll on the state's resources.

The Politics of Criminal Justice

The Texas Court of Criminal Appeals must try to balance the constitutional rights of convicts against the public welfare, a role that puts the court at the center of major philosophical and political battles.

The combatants on one side of the debate include the prosecutors—the elected district and county attorneys—who do not like to see the convictions they have won reversed, partly because too many reversals could cost them reelection. Judges of the trial courts, who also periodically face the voters, are sensitive to reversals, too. So are the police and sheriffs' departments that arrest the defendants and provide the evidence on which criminal convictions are based (see *Politics Up Close:* "A Crime Lab Scandal").

On the other side of the debate are defense attorneys, who have an obligation to protect the rights and interests of their clients and who in their appeals often attack procedures used by police, prosecutors, and trial judges. Also on this side are civil libertarians, who insist that a criminal defendant's every right—even the most technical—be protected, and minority groups, who have challenged the conduct of trials when minorities have been excluded from juries weighing the fate of minority defendants (see *Politics Up Close:* "More Is Involved than Technicalities").

Throughout much of its early history, the Texas Court of Criminal Appeals was accused of excessive concern with legal technicalities that benefited convicted criminals.[41] The court reversed 42 percent of the cases appealed to it during the first quarter of the twentieth century, when Texas and many other states had a harsh system of criminal justice that often reflected class and racial bias at the trial level. By 1966, the reversal rate had dropped to 3 percent. But changes in the court's makeup and changes in political attitudes produced fluctuations in that record in subsequent years.

Politics Up Close   A Crime Lab Scandal

Recent scientific advances can improve the administration of justice, as demonstrated by a growing number of criminal cases in which DNA samples have been used to help convict or clear suspects. Texas Governor Rick Perry has issued pardons for several men after DNA evidence proved they had been wrongfully convicted of crimes. One man was pardoned after serving 18 years in prison after being wrongfully convicted of aggravated sexual assault.[a]

Convictions in a number of other cases were thrown into question with the exposure of errors in the work of some crime labs, particularly the crime lab operated by the Houston Police Department. The Houston lab's DNA division was shut down in 2002 because of serious problems, which were reported in numerous articles by the *Houston Chronicle*. Independent investigators later discovered errors in the handling of DNA, body fluids, controlled substances, and other evidence in hundreds of cases. Poor training and inadequate standards contributed to the problems. By 2006, two men had been released from prison, with one receiving a pardon from the governor, after it was determined the lab had mishandled evidence in their cases. The investigation continued.[b]

The controversy also prompted the legislature to create the Texas Forensic Science Commission to oversee crime labs. The new commission had the power to investigate allegations of misconduct or negligence.[c]

[a]*Houston Chronicle*, March 18, 2006, p. 1A.

[b]*Houston Chronicle*, May 12, 2006, p. 1A.

[c]*Houston Chronicle*, January 24, 2006, p. 4B.

Politics Up Close   More Is Involved than Technicalities

Randall Dale Adams and Clarence Lee Brandley owe their lives to the appellate process. Both men came perilously close to being executed for murders they apparently did not commit. Adams spent more than a decade behind bars before he was released in 1989, after a documentary film argued he had been wrongfully convicted of the murder of a Dallas police officer. The Texas Court of Criminal Appeals ordered a new trial, but the Dallas County district attorney chose not to retry him.

Brandley, an African American janitor at Conroe High School, was convicted by an all-white jury of the rape and murder of a 16-year-old girl, but the Court of Criminal Appeals reversed the conviction after being presented with evidence that Brandley had not received a fair trial and had been a victim of racial prejudice. Neither man would have lived long enough to win freedom had not the appellate process, which many prosecutors attack as too time-consuming and too "technical," worked to delay their scheduled executions.

The court signaled a shift toward a conservative philosophy after the 1994 elections of Judges Sharon Keller and Steve Mansfield increased the number of Republicans on the court to three. During the first 13 months the new judges were in office, for example, the court ordered the reinstatement of two death sentences it had reversed before Keller's and Mansfield's arrival. The court's conservatism was solidified with a Republican sweep of all three court seats on the 1996 ballot. A 6–3 Democratic majority had become a 6–3 Republican majority, the first GOP majority on the court since Reconstruction. Republicans increased their majority to 7–2 in 1997, when long-time Presiding Judge Mike McCormick, one of the court's most conservative members, switched from the Democratic to the Republican Party. The Republican takeover of the court was completed in 1998, when Democrats lost their last two seats on the panel. McCormick did not seek reelection in 2000 and was replaced as presiding judge by Sharon Keller, a former prosecutor.

After the GOP takeover, the Court of Criminal Appeals quickly began compiling a strong pro-prosecutorial record, particularly in death penalty cases. The court upheld a number of death sentences that later were overturned by federal courts. In one case, later reversed by a federal court, it affirmed a capital conviction even though the defendant's attorney had slept through part of his trial (see *What Do You Think?*: "Can Justice Afford a Nap?"). In another case, it upheld a death sentence despite the fact that a prosecution witness had argued improperly

What Do You *Think?*

Can Justice Afford a Nap?

Justice is supposed to be blind, but it isn't supposed to be asleep. At least that was the conclusion of one of the more controversial death penalty convictions to emerge from Texas in recent years. Calvin Burdine was convicted and sentenced to death for the 1983 murder of his roommate, W. T. "Dub" Wise. His conviction was

upheld by the Texas Court of Criminal Appeals, and he spent 18 years on death row before the Fifth U.S. Circuit Court of Appeals overturned the sentence because Burdine's defense attorney had slept through portions of his trial. In a plea bargain with prosecutors, Burdine then was sentenced to life in prison.

Source: Houston Chronicle, June 20, 2003, p. 29A.

that the defendant was a future danger to society partly because he was Hispanic. That ruling prompted then-Texas attorney general John Cornyn, a Republican and strong law-and-order advocate, to admit to the U.S. Supreme Court that the prosecution had committed reversible error in the case. Such rulings prompted defense lawyers and civil libertarians to heap much criticism on the court. "They're so far gone they're barely even a court anymore," lawyer Jeff Blackburn of Amarillo said in an interview with the *Houston Chronicle*.[42]

Increased Policy Role of the State Courts

The federal judiciary has traditionally had more influence than the state courts in molding public policy. Over the years, it has been at the center of political debate over the proper role of the judiciary in the policy-making process (see Chapter 13).

Much of the Texas Supreme Court's time is spent refereeing disputes between trial lawyers and insurance companies. But in recent years this court has sometimes played an active role in shaping broader public policies and addressing significant constitutional issues.

The Courts and Education   In one of its most significant and best-known rulings, the Texas Supreme Court in the Edgewood school finance case in 1989 unanimously ordered major, basic changes in the financing of public education to provide more equity between rich and poor school districts.[43] The lawsuit was brought against the state by poor districts after years of legislative inaction against a property tax–based finance system that had produced huge disparities in local education resources and in the quality of local schools.

The unanimity of the opinion, written by Justice Oscar Mauzy, a Democrat, surprised many legislators and school officials because two of the three Republican justices on the court at that time had initially been appointed by Governor Bill Clements, who had insisted that the courts had no business trying to tell the legislature what to do about school finance. The decision, which held that the school finance law violated a constitutional requirement for an efficient education system, was obviously the product of considerable compromise among the nine justices. Their deliberations were secret, but Justice Franklin Spears, a Democrat, told the *Fort Worth Star–Telegram*: "We wanted to speak with one voice. The opinion is a composite of many ideas, much brainstorming, much compromising." Mark Yudof, then dean of the University of Texas School of Law, said the court may have been determined to offer a united front because it attached as much importance to the school finance case as a united U.S. Supreme Court had to the landmark *Brown v. Board of Education of Topeka* desegregation case in the 1950s.[44]

Compliance with the school finance order did not come easily, however. A 1990 school finance law failed to meet the court's standards, so the court issued another order in 1991 and a third order in 1992 after the legislature again came up short. The court lost its unanimity on the third order, which struck down a 1991 law that had established special county education districts with a minimum property tax. In a challenge brought this time by wealthy school districts, a 7–2 court majority ruled that the tax was a statewide property tax prohibited by the Texas Constitution. Mauzy and fellow Democratic Justice Lloyd Doggett sharply dissented.

The legislature responded with still another school finance law in 1993. This law gave wealthy school districts several options for sharing revenue with poor districts, and it was challenged by both rich and poor districts. The rich districts objected to sharing their property wealth, whereas the poor districts argued that the new law was inadequately funded and did not sufficiently reduce the funding gap between rich and poor districts. The Texas Supreme Court upheld the law in a 5–4 decision in January 1995. By that time, a majority of the court's members were Republicans. In the majority opinion, Justice John Cornyn, a Republican, wrote:

> Children who live in property-poor districts and children who live in property-rich districts now have substantially equal access to the funds necessary for a general diffusion of knowledge. It is apparent from the court's opinions that we have recognized that an efficient system does not require equality of access to revenue at all levels.[45]

But Republican Justice Craig Enoch, who dissented, wrote that the state had failed to adequately provide for the public schools. He said the new law contributed to further "constitutional tensions" by promoting continued use of local property taxes.[46]

By 2003, the school finance law was under attack again, this time from school districts contending that the "Robin Hood" share-the-wealth requirement and inadequate state aid were forcing many districts to raise local school maintenance tax rates to the maximum $1.50 per $100 valuation. They argued that it amounted to an unconstitutional statewide property tax, and in fall 2005 the Texas Supreme Court, in a subsequent decision, agreed. This time, the court gave the state until June 1, 2006, to correct the problem, which the Legislature did in a special session that spring. Lawmakers enacted Governor Rick Perry's proposal to cut school maintenance tax rates by as much as one-third over the next 2 years, replacing the lost revenue with money from a budgetary surplus, an expanded business tax, a $1 per pack increase in the cigarette tax and tightened collections of sales taxes on used cars.

In 1992, a state district judge in Brownsville ruled that the state's system of funding higher education also was unconstitutional because it shortchanged Hispanics in South Texas. But the Texas Supreme Court reversed that decision and upheld the higher education system.[47]

In another education case with major implications, the Texas Supreme Court in 1994 upheld the right of Texas parents to educate their own children. Ending a 10-year legal battle, the court overturned a Texas Education Agency ruling that home schools were illegal. The court held that a home school was legitimate if parents used books, workbooks, or other written materials and met "basic education goals" by teaching basic subjects.[48]

The Courts and Abortion Rights   In 1998, the Texas Supreme Court upheld $1.2 million in damages against anti-abortion protesters who had staged massive demonstrations at Houston abortion clinics during the 1992 Republican National Convention. Some clinics had been vandalized and patients harassed. The high court also upheld most of the restrictions a lower court had set on protests near the clinics and the homes of several doctors who performed abortions. The court said it was trying to balance free speech rights with the rights of the clinics to conduct business, the rights of women to have access to pregnancy counseling and abortion services, and privacy rights of physicians. The court prohibited demonstrators from blocking access to clinics, intimidating patients, and engaging in other forms of aggressive behavior.[49] In a case from Florida, the U.S. Supreme Court had ruled in 1994 that judges could limit protests near abortion clinics but that restrictions had to be strictly limited.[50]

The Texas Supreme Court became embroiled in the abortion issue again in 2000 after a state law went into effect requiring parents to be notified by doctors before their minor daughters could have abortions. The law included a "judicial bypass" provision, giving a young woman who didn't want her parents to be told an opportunity to convince a judge that she was mature and well-informed enough to make an abortion decision by herself or that notifying her parents would be harmful. Acting on several early cases, the Texas Supreme Court set guidelines for district judges to follow in making bypass decisions.

In another abortion case, decided in 2002, the Texas Supreme Court held that the state's refusal to pay for medically necessary abortions for poor women didn't violate the Texas Constitution. The court ruled that the restriction on funding abortions for women on Medicaid didn't discriminate by gender and advanced a legitimate government interest of favoring childbirth over abortion.

The Courts and Gay Rights   Deciding still another controversial issue, the Texas Supreme Court in 1996 ruled against the Log Cabin Republicans, a gay GOP group that had been denied a booth at the Republican State Convention in San Antonio. The court said the group had no grounds to sue the Republican Party for deprivation of rights under the Texas Constitution because the party was not a governmental agency.[51]

Summary
Who Gets What: Texas Judiciary

The Texas court system has a confusing array of courts, many with overlapping jurisdictions. State judges, elected in partisan elections, often must raise significant sums of money to run their campaigns. The people or groups who contribute to judicial campaigns often have a direct stake in the outcome of cases, giving rise to a view that "Texas has the best justice money can buy."

★ Criticism of judicial elections, both statewide and nationally, has produced some intermittent efforts to change the selection process of state judges. Possible alternatives are nonpartisan elections, elections from geographic districts, or a merit selection plan under which the governor would appoint judges from lists of nominees recommended by experts. The latter plan would require the appointed judges to run later in retention elections to keep their seats, but they would not have opponents on the ballot.

★ Civil and criminal procedures are defined by statutory law, the rules of the courts, and constitutional rights. Decisions of the federal courts also have an impact on the state's judicial process. The lower courts have original jurisdiction in both civil and criminal matters. Civil and criminal trials include opening statements, examination and cross-examination of witnesses, presentation of evidence, rebuttal, summation, and verdict. In a criminal case, a defendant has the right to trial by jury, but this right can be waived except for capital murder cases. There are instances of jury trials in civil matters, but this

is the exception rather than the rule. When cases are appealed, there are no juries; and appellate courts review the decisions and procedures of lower courts for conformity to constitutional and statutory requirements.

★ The controversies surrounding the highest appellate courts include judicial activism (a view held by some jurists that their role is to take a more expansive view of the law by putting broad policy implications into their decisions), large campaign contributions to those running for judicial office, and the intense conflict among competing interests to influence the partisan and philosophical composition of the courts.

★ Only a handful of women and minorities have ever served on the state's highest appellate courts, and historically they have been under-represented on the lower-court benches as well. Hispanics and African Americans have argued through litigation that the current system of countywide elections is inherently discriminatory, but the U.S. Supreme Court rejected this argument in 1994.

Key Terms

penal code 830
felonies 830
misdemeanors 830
civil lawsuits 830
statutes 830
plaintiff 830
original jurisdiction 831
appellate jurisdiction 831
bifurcated court
  system 831
municipal courts 831

justice of the peace
  courts 831
ordinances 833
de novo 833
constitutional county
  court 833
statutory county
  court 834
district court 834
plea bargains 835
court of appeals 835

Texas Supreme Court 836
Texas Court of
  Criminal Appeals 836
grand jury 837
prosecution 837
indictment 838
information 838
petit jury 839
venireman 839
petition for review 840
writ of mandamus 841

merit selection 844
tort reform 845
retention elections 852
ward politics 852
Miranda ruling 853
nolo contendere 854
capital murder 855
probation 858
parole 858

Suggested Readings

Baum, Lawrence. "Supreme Courts in the Policy Process." In *The State of the States*, ed. Carl E. Van Horn, pp. 143–60. Washington, D.C.: Congressional Quarterly Press, 1996. Recent state court decisions indicate increased judicial activism producing a counterreaction by those adversely affected by the actions of the courts.

Champagne, Anthony. "Judicial Selection in Texas: Democracy's Deadlock." In *Texas Politics: A Reader*, eds. Anthony Champagne and Edward J. Harpham, pp. 97–110. New York, N.Y.: W. W. Norton, 1997. Addresses issues and problems related to the partisan selection of Texas state judges.

Hill, John. "Taking Texas Judges Out of Politics: An Argument for Merit Election." *Baylor Law Review* 40 (Summer 1988): 340–66. A former chief justice of the Texas Supreme Court argues for nonpartisan elections of state judges.

Jacob, Herbert, "Courts: The Invisible Branch." In *Politics in the American States: A Comparative Analysis*, 6th ed., eds. Virginia Gray and Herbert Jacob, pp. 253–85. Washington, D.C.: CQ Press, 1996. A comparative analysis of state court systems.

Texas Judicial Council, Office of Court Administration. *Texas Judicial System, 79th Annual Report*. Austin, Tex.: Texas Judicial Council, 2007. Annual compilation of data on the activities of state courts.

Texas Research League. *The Texas Judiciary: A Structural-Functional Overview*. Report 1. Austin, Tex.: Texas Research League, 1990. Describes the court structure of Texas with a focus on its primary weaknesses.

Texas Research League. *Texas Courts: A Proposal for Structural-Functional Reform*. Report 2. Austin, Tex.: Texas Research League, 1991. Recommendations for a major overhaul of the state's court system.

Suggested Web Sites

Office of Court Administration www.courts.state.tx.us
This agency provides administrative support and technical assistance to all courts in Texas. Links to state and local courts are found here along with information about the state court system, court records, and court rules.

Texas Bar Association www.texasbar.com
This site provides access to a wide range of information relevant to the legal profession.

Texas Department of Criminal Justice
www.tdcj.state.tx.us
This agency is responsible for the administration of the state's prison/jail system. Organizational data can be found at this site along with statistics and reports on the prison population, prison sites, paroles, and programs designed to prevent recidivism.

Bureau of Justice Statistics www.ojp.usdoj.gov/bjs

The Bureau of Justice Statistics, a division of the U.S. Department of Justice, is a primary source for criminal justice statistics in the United States.

Texas Juvenile Probation Commission

www.tjpc.state.tx.us

This agency works with local juvenile probation departments to rehabilitate juvenile offenders. This site provides information about state funding, standards, training, certification, and monitoring of caseworkers, and statistics on juvenile offenders.

Texas Youth Commission www.tyc.state.tx.us

The Texas Youth Commission is responsible for "secure care, custody and control of juveniles who are committed to state custody" for criminal behavior. This site includes information on facilities, programs, correctional treatment, and juvenile crime in Texas.

25 LOCAL GOVERNMENT IN TEXAS

Cities, Towns, Counties, and Special Districts

" Has the (local) government been alert enough to arrest the disintegration of residential neighborhoods by using its planning authority to give protection against non-residential encroachments? And to make sites available for community facilities needed for a constructive common life? **"**

Harold Lasswell

Chapter *Outline*

★ The Legacy of Local Government
★ Local Governments in the Texas Political System
★ Municipal Government in Texas
★ Forms of City Government in Texas
★ Municipal Election Systems
★ City Revenues and Expenditures
★ Urban Problems in Texas
★ County Government in Texas
★ Criticisms of County Government
★ Special Districts in Texas
★ Independent School Districts
★ Councils of Government
★ Solutions to the Problems of Local Government

The Legacy of Local Government

Texans have an affinity for local government, and the mosaic of local governments with overlapping jurisdictions is confusing to many citizens. There are more than 4,800 local governments, of all sizes, across the state. Some operate with a handful of employees and budgets of one or two hundred thousand dollars a year, whereas others have tens of thousands of employees with billion dollar-plus budgets. Their governmental structures range from the simple to the complex. Some special districts perform one basic function; large cities perform any number of services that are limited only by budgetary and legal restraints. Some counties have fewer than 1,000 people, but Harris County has more than 3.8 million residents. One school district in West Texas has only twenty students; the Houston Independent School District has more than 202,000. Three of the ten largest cities in the United States are in Texas, but many cities across the state have fewer than 1,000 residents.

The key to understanding local governments in Texas is to understand what responsibilities have been assigned to them by the Texas Constitution and statutory law. Once the institutional structures and functions of local governments have been studied, attention will be directed to a number of core problems confronting them and their political capacities to address these issues. Two themes underlie this analysis: what changes can make local governments more effective, and is it possible or desirable to reduce the fragmentation in local governments?

A tradition of localism is rooted in the fabric of our political history. Since the founding of the nation, Americans have expressed a strong belief in the right to local self-government.[1] In many areas of the young country, local governments existed long before there was a viable state or federal government. Early communities had to fend for themselves and had limited expectations of services or protections to be provided by state or federal governments.

This history of local self-help has led to the popular notion that local governments have fundamental rights based on the concept of local

✓ Think About Politics

1. Are local governments more responsive to their citizens than the national government?
   YES ◯ NO ◯

2. Should cities be able to choose any form of government they want?
   YES ◯ NO ◯

3. Would we get more qualified county elected officials if candidates ran without party labels?
   YES ◯ NO ◯

4. Should Texas cities have the power to enact a local income tax to replace the sales and property tax?
   YES ◯ NO ◯

5. Should the Texas Legislature extend home rule powers to counties?
   YES ◯ NO ◯

6. Should Texas enact laws giving school districts greater authority over local education?
   YES ◯ NO ◯

7. With so many special districts in Texas, should the state attempt to consolidate local governments into larger, more comprehensive governmental units?
   YES ◯ NO ◯

Local governments are often described as the governments closest to the people, but constitutional and legislative restrictions often hamper them in their efforts to carry out their basic responsibilities. How can local government be improved, and is there the political interest or will to make such improvements?

★ **unitary system**
Constitutional arrangement whereby authority rests with the central government; regional governments have only those powers given them by the central government.

★ **Dillon rule**
Principle holding that local governments are creations of state government and that their powers and responsibilities are defined by the state.

Comparing State and Local Governments

You Are the Mayor and Need to Get a Town Budget Passed

sovereignty, or ultimate power. Thomas Jefferson, for example, developed a theory of local government, designed in part to strengthen the powers of the states, in which local sovereignty was rooted in the sovereignty of the individual.[2] Some scholars suggest that this cultural legacy persists in grassroots politics, the flight to suburbia, and the creation of neighborhood organizations. Today it is common to hear the argument that local government is closest to the people and best represents their interests and desires.[3]

Although this view is widely held, the prevailing constitutional theory on the relationship of local governments to the state is the **unitary system**. Simply stated, this theory holds that local governments are the creations of the state. The powers, functions, and responsibilities that they exercise have been delegated or granted them by the state government, and no local government has sovereign powers. There have been numerous court cases enunciating this principle, which is referred to as the **Dillon rule**, but the best summary is derived from an Iowa case in which a court held the following:

> The true view is this: Municipal corporations owe their origin to, and derive their powers and rights wholly from, the legislature. It breathes into them the breath of life, without which they cannot exist. As it creates, so it may destroy. If it may destroy, it may abridge and control. Unless there is some constitutional limitation on the right, the legislature might by a single act sweep from its existence all of the municipal corporations in the State, and the corporations could not prevent it. We know of no limitation on this right so far as the corporations are concerned.[4]

The Dillon rule is now the prevailing theory defining the relationships of states and local governments, and it is applicable to local governments in Texas.

Local Governments in the Texas Political System

Local governments—counties, cities, school districts, and special districts—are created by the state and operate under limits set by the Texas Constitution and the legislature. They have found their capabilities and resources increasingly burdened by the pressing needs of a growing, urban state. Some of this pressure has come from the state and federal governments ordering or mandating significant improvements in environmental, educational, health, and other programs but letting cities, counties, and school districts pick up much of the tab. Prior to the state's commitment to an extensive prison construction program in the 1990s, for example, the Texas government forced counties to spend millions of local taxpayer dollars to house state prisoners in county jails because it had failed to adequately address a criminal justice crisis. Local school districts and their property-tax payers also are at the mercy of the legislature, which has ordered expensive educational programs and has raised classroom standards without fully paying for them. Cities, too, find their budgetary problems exacerbated by state mandates. Local governments are the governments closest to the people, but they have to shoulder much of the responsibility—and often take much of the public outrage—for policy decisions made in Austin and Washington.

Although the legal position expressed by the Dillon rule subordinates local governments to the state, there are practical and political limitations on what the state can do with local governments. More importantly, the state relies on local governments to carry out many of its responsibilities.[5]

Texas granted cities home rule authority in 1912. Home rule cities, discussed in more detail later, have considerable authority and discretion over their own local policies, but within limits set by state law. Texas voters approved a constitutional amendment in 1933 that also gave counties home rule authority, but no county established home rule government before the amendment was repealed in 1969.[6] County home rule provisions were again introduced in the 1997 and 1999 legislative sessions by several urban legislators but were defeated because of opposition from a variety of state and local interests. As a general observation, Texas has given its cities considerable discretionary powers permitting them to provide services not specifically defined by state statutes. By contrast, the discretionary powers of counties are limited.[7]

The states vary considerably in the major responsibilities assigned to different levels of government. Texas, like most other states, assigns the primary responsibility for public education to local school districts while retaining the primary responsibility for highways, public welfare, and public health at the state level. Police and fire protection, water and sanitation services, parks, recreation, and libraries are the primary responsibility of city governments. Public hospitals are a shared function of the state, county, and special districts.[8] Texas counties share with the state a primary responsibility for the court and criminal justice system. Altogether, there are some 4,800 local governments in Texas (see Table 25.1).

Municipal Government in Texas

Despite popular images of wide-open spaces dotted with cattle and oil wells, Texas is an urban state. Some areas, particularly in West Texas, still offer a good deal of room to roam, but most Texans live in cities. First-time visitors to the state often express surprise at the size and diversity of Houston and Dallas and the more relaxed charm of San Antonio, whose Riverwalk reminds many tourists of some European cities. Austin, the seat of state government and location of a world-class university, is highly attractive to young professionals and high-tech businesses.

When the Texas Constitution was adopted in 1876, the state was rural and agrarian; less than 10 percent of the population lived in cities. According to the 1880 Census, Galveston was the largest city, with a population of 22,248, followed by San Antonio with 20,550. Dallas, a relatively new settlement, had 10,358 residents, and Houston had 16,513. For most of the period from 1880 to 1920, San Antonio was Texas's largest city, but since the 1930 Census, Houston has held that distinction.[9] In 1940, only 45 percent of Texans lived in urban

---

Table *25.1* Governments in the United States and Texas, 2007

With each Census of Governments, the number of government units in Texas and the United States increases. In the past 20 years, Texas has seen an increase of over 400 governments, most of which are special districts.

	U.S.	**Texas**
U.S. Government	1	—
State Government	50	1
Counties	3,033	254
Municipalities	19,492	1,209
Townships and Towns	16,519	—
School Districts	13,051	1,081
Special Districts	37,381	2,291
Total	89,527	4,836

Source: U.S. Census Bureau, 2007 *Census of Governments,* "Local Governments and Public School Systems by Type and State: 2007."

areas, but by 1950, 60 percent of the population resided in cities. Since the 1970 Census, eight of every ten Texans have been living in cities, and the more recent population growth continues to be overwhelmingly urban.

Houston, San Antonio, and Dallas are among the ten largest cities in the United States. According to 2006 population estimates, Houston had a population of 2,074,828; San Antonio, 1,273,374; and Dallas 1,192,538.[10] Six additional Texas cities—Austin, Fort Worth, El Paso, Arlington, Corpus Christi, and Plano—each had more than 250,000. Seven of Texas's ten largest cities—Houston, San Antonio, Dallas, Fort Worth, El Paso, Corpus Christi, and Garland—have minority populations exceeding 50 percent (see Table 25.2).

The more than 1,200 incorporated municipalities in Texas are diverse, and urban life, politics, and local governments have developed different styles across the state. The basic forms of city government are defined by statutory and constitutional law, but cities vary in their demographic makeup, their economies, the historical experiences that shaped their development, and their quality of life. There are local differences in economic stability, public safety, public education, health and environmental quality, housing, transportation, culture, recreation, and politics.[11]

★ **general law cities**
Cities allowed to exercise only those powers specifically granted to them by the legislature. General law cities have fewer than 5,000 residents.

★ **home rule cities**
Cities with a population of more than 5,000, which can adopt any form of government residents choose, provided they do not conflict with the state constitution or statutes.

General Law and Home Rule Cities   The Texas Constitution provides for two general categories of cities: general law and home rule. **General law cities** have fewer than 5,000 residents and have more restrictions in organizing their governments, setting taxes, and annexing territory than do **home rule cities**. They are allowed only those powers specifically granted to them by the legislature. Most Texas cities—approximately 875—are general law cities.[12]

Table *25.2* The Differences Tell a Story: Select Characteristics for the Ten Largest Cities in Texas, 2006

Cities across Texas differ in terms of their demographic makeup, economies, and politics. The mix of these factors provides the unique characteristics, images, and lifestyles associated with the urban areas of the state.

City	Total Population in 2006	% Over 65	% Under 18	Median Age	% African American	% Hispanic	% Asian	Median Household Income, 2006	% of Persons Below Poverty Level, 2006	% of Children Below Poverty Level, 2006
Houston	2,074,828	8.5%	27.1%	32.2	24.7%	41.9%	5.0%	$39,682	21.3%	32.1%
San Antonio	1,273,374	10.2	27.8	32.6	6.7	61.3	2.1	$40,650	18.1	26.7
Dallas	1,192,538	8.3	27.1	31.9	24.2	43.1	2.3	$38,276	22.1	34.1
Austin	717,100	6.8	23.5	31.2	8.5	35.9	5.5	$47,212	17.7	25.2
Fort Worth	637,178	8.3	27.5	32.3	17.7	32.4	3.2	$45,276	16.6	22.5
El Paso	596,189	11.2	31.0	31.7	2.8	81.0	1.2	$33,103	26.4	37.5
Arlington	357,370	7.4	27.9	31.6	17.4	26.3	6.0	$50,582	12.8	19.7
Corpus Christi	285,174	11.8	27.3	34.2	4.3	58.3	1.6	$36,245	21.9	30.4
Plano	266,021	6.9	26.6	35.1	6.1	14.4	14.7	$77,038	5.1	5.7
Garland	240,876	8.1	29.1	33.9	13.3	35.1	9.8	$50,682	13.6	20.1
State Totals	23,507,783	9.9%	27.7%	33.1	11.6%	35.7%	3.3%	$44,922	16.6%	23.9%

Source: U.S. Census Bureau, 2006 *American Community Survey*.

What Do You *Think?*

Is This Any Way to Change a City Charter?

Boerne, Texas, which is just northwest of San Antonio, held a special election in May 2002 to amend its charter to bring it in line with a law recently enacted by the Texas Legislature. The new law permits local governments to purchase items valued at $25,000 or less without seeking bids. Prior to its enactment, the limit was $15,000, and the charter of Boerne included this figure. To permit the city to follow the state law and to anticipate future increases in the cap, a charter amendment would have permitted the city council to change spending caps each year as allowed by state law.

In a cliff-hanging election in which only 57 of 4,836 registered voters participated, the charter amendment was defeated, 29–28. The election occurred when there were no city or school board elections to draw voters to the polls. Few voters apparently were even aware the issue was on the ballot, and some just didn't care or believe the issue was important to them.

What happened in Boerne occurs throughout the state in charter elections. Just as is true for changes to the state constitution, all too often a small minority of a city's voters decide on changes in its fundamental law. We have no empirical evidence, but it might be argued that most changes are well-intentioned and necessary. But it is evident that a few individuals can use charter elections for their own self-interest.

Source: "Boerne Rejects Charter Change," *San Antonio Express-News*, May 7, 2002.

A city with more than 5,000 inhabitants can adopt any form of government its residents choose, provided it does not conflict with the state constitution (Article XI, Sections 4, 5) or statutes. This option is called home rule and is formalized through the voters' adoption of a **charter**, which is the fundamental document (something like a constitution) under which a city operates. A charter establishes a city's governing body, the organization of its administrative agencies and municipal courts, its taxing authority, and procedures for conducting elections, annexing additional territory, and revising the charter (see *What Do You Think?*: "Is This Any Way to Change a City Charter?"). As of 2006, there were 334 home rule cities in Texas.[13]

> ★ **charter**
> Document, based on state authorization, which defines the structure, powers, and responsibilities of a city government.

Forms of City Government in Texas

Texas cities have experimented with three forms of government: the mayor-council, the commission, and the council-manager (see *What Do You Think?*: "Why Different Forms of City Government?"). According to the Texas Municipal League, there were 1,211 municipal governments in Texas in 2006. More than 900 cities operated with some variation of the mayor-council form; approximately 280 used some form of council-manager or commission-manager government; and only a handful used the commission form of government.[14]

Mayor-Council The **mayor-council**, the most common form of municipal government in Texas, was derived from the English model of city government. The legislative function of the city is vested in the city council, and the executive function is assigned to the mayor. This type of government is based on the separation-of-powers principle, which also characterizes the state and federal governments. In theory, the mayor, who is elected citywide, is the chief executive officer. In terms of power, however, there are two distinguishable forms of mayor—the **weak mayor** and the **strong mayor**—and in most Texas cities, the mayor is weak.

The city charter determines a mayor's strength. The weak mayor has little control over policy initiation or implementation. The mayor's powers may be constrained by one or more of the following: limited or no appointment or

> ★ **mayor-council**
> Form of city government in which the legislative function is vested in the city council and the executive function in the mayor.
>
> ★ **weak mayor**
> Form of city government in which the mayor shares authority with the city council and other elected officials but has little independent control over city policy or administration.
>
> ★ **strong mayor**
> Form of city government that gives the mayor considerable power, including budgetary control and appointment and removal authority over city department heads.

What Do You *Think?*

Why Different Forms of City Government?

Most major Texas cities have functioned under more than one form of government. Both Houston and San Antonio have functioned under all three primary forms described in this chapter. Changes in city charters often follow periods of intense political conflict, inertia, or an inability to respond to long-term problems. Proposed changes in governmental structures and election systems often threaten groups and interests that have a stake in the way business is currently being conducted, and charter revisions have a tendency to polarize a community.

Does the form of government under which a city operates make any significant difference? Political scientists have spent a lot of time trying to answer that question, and although there is some consensus on the general weaknesses of the city commission, opinions are divided on the other forms of local government. The general public appears to pay little attention to city charters or government structures, but elected officials and other city leaders, public employees, special interest groups, minority leaders, and some reform-minded citizens consider the structure of city government a crucial issue.

A city charter spells out how a city will run its affairs and helps determine which citizens will have access to policy making. In part, a charter is an expression of a city's social, economic, and political structure. Some scholars have concluded that the urban reform movements advocating nonpartisan, at-large elections, which often were tied to council-manager government, were advancing middle- and upper-middle-class views and interests. The original intent of these changes may have been to encourage managerial efficiencies, but many urban governments became less responsive to the needs and interests of lower-income groups and minority populations.

Sources: William Lyons, "Reform and Response in American Cities: Structure and Policy Reconsidered," *Social Science Quarterly* 59 (June 1978): 130; Robert Lineberry and Edmund Fowler, "Reformism and Public Policies in American Cities," *American Political Science Review* 61 (September 1967): 701–17; Willis D. Hawley, *Nonpartisan Elections and the Case for Party Politics.* New York: John Wiley and Sons, 1973.

removal power over city offices, limited budgetary authority, and the election of other city administrators independently of the mayor (Figure 25.1). Under these circumstances, the mayor shares power with the city council over city administration and policy implementation and "is the chief executive in name only."[15] These restrictions limit both the political and the administrative leadership of

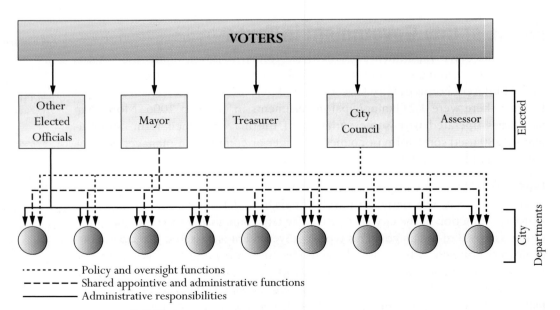

Figure *25.1* Limited Powers: The Weak Mayor Form of Government

Mayors have limited budget and administrative power under the weak mayor form of government.

the mayor. Although it is possible for a mayor to use informal or non-institutional resources to influence the city council and other administrators and to provide energetic leadership, there are formidable obstacles to overcome.[16]

A strong mayor has real power and authority, including appointive and removal powers over city agency heads (see Figure 25.2). Such appointments often require city council approval, but the appointees are responsible to the mayor and serve at mayoral discretion. The mayor has control over budget preparation and exercises some veto authority over city council actions. This form of city government clearly distinguishes between executive and legislative functions.

The strong mayor form of government is found in many of the larger American cities, but it is now used by only one major city in Texas—Houston. El Paso functioned under this form of government until 2004, when the city changed to council-manager government. This form may be unpopular in the state because the strong mayor often was associated with urban political machines, ward politics,

Organization Chart

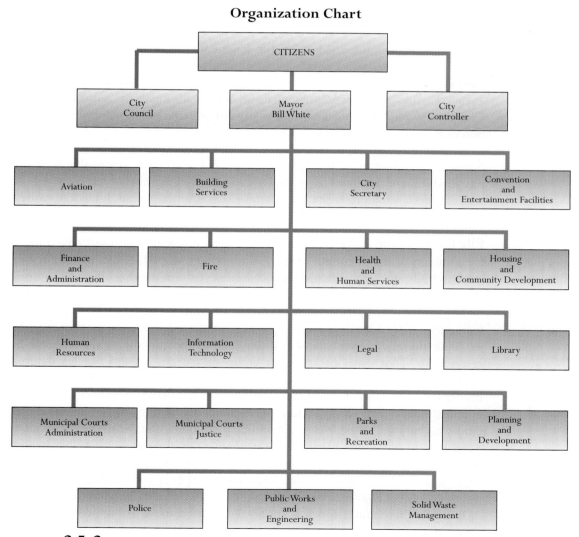

Figure *25.2* The Office Really Has Power: The Strong Mayor Form of Government

Houston is the only large Texas city that utilizes the strong mayor form of government in which the mayor has major day-to-day administrative responsibilities.

Source: Office of the mayor, city of Houston.

Swearing In
Bill White, a lawyer, businessman, and former Deputy Secretary of Energy of the United States, was elected to his third term in 2007 as mayor of Houston.

and political corruption. Moreover, the fragmentation of authority and responsibility in local government parallels that found in state government and is another reminder of the deep distrust of government that Reconstruction produced in Texas. Finally, the state's individualistic and traditionalistic subcultures (see Chapter 19) reinforce hostile attitudes toward governmental institutions that are potentially more responsive to lower socioeconomic groups.

As might be expected, the salaries of the mayors and council members of a city with the strong mayor system are generally higher than under other forms of city government. In many cities, mayors and council members receive no pay or only modest reimbursement for services. But the mayor of Houston earned $176,762 in 2007, and council members, $51,337.[17]

City Commission   The commission and council-manager forms of government are products of the twentieth century. Both reflect, in part, efforts to reform city governments through administrative efficiency, the reduction of partisan conflict, and the adaptation of a business-like approach to running city government.

★ **city commission**
Form of city government in which elected commissioners collectively serve as a city's policy-making body and individually serve as administrative heads of different city departments.

The origin of the **city commission** is usually traced to the Texas island city of Galveston. After a hurricane and subsequent flooding devastated most of the city in 1900, the government then in office proved incompetent and incapable of responding. That crisis prompted a group of citizens to win the legislature's approval of a new form of government designed to be more responsive by combining the city's legislative and administrative functions in the offices of five city commissioners. City commissions were soon adopted by other major Texas cities, including Dallas, Houston, and San Antonio. But with the subsequent development of council-manager government as an alternative, there has been a marked decline in the city commission's popularity. It has been replaced in Houston, Dallas, and San Antonio, and only a few cities in Texas still have this form of government (see Figure 25.3).

Initially, the commission was supported as a business-like approach to running city government. By eliminating partisan elections and combining the executive, administrative, and legislative functions, it was argued, cities could provide services more efficiently. But critics have identified several problems. The commission minimizes the potential for effective political leadership because no single individual can be identified as the person in charge.

```
                              VOTERS

                          CITY COMMISSION
  Commissioner   Commissioner   Commissioner   Commissioner   Commissioner

   Public          Water &        Streets &       Parks         Finance
   Safety         Sanitation      Drainage
```

Figure **25.3**

Falling into Disuse: The Commission Form of Government

Commissioners combine policy and administrative functions under the commission form of government developed in Galveston after the 1900 hurricane. Few Texas cities use this form of government, and many that do have added a manager.

Moreover, there is minimal oversight and review of policies and budgets. Commissioners are elected primarily as policy makers, not administrators, and there are downsides to electing amateurs to administer increasingly technical and complex city programs.

The few cities in Texas that use the pure form of commission government generally have three members, a mayor and two commissioners, who are assigned responsibilities for specific city functions, such as water, sanitation, and public safety. Several of the commission cities now use a city administrator or manager, hired by the commission, to run the daily affairs of the city.

Council-Manager   After enthusiasm for the city commission waned, urban reformers, both in Texas and nationally, looked to the **council-manager** form of government. Its specific origins are disputed, but it was influenced by the same reform principles on which the city commission was based. The first cities in Texas to use council-manager government were Amarillo and Terrell in 1913, and it soon became popular among home rule cities. Dallas and San Antonio have been the largest cities in the state to adopt it (see Figure 25.4). Its principal characteristics are professional city management, nonpartisan city elections, and a clear distinction between policy making and administration. But in recent years, it has become evident that this policy-administration distinction has been modified by the increased roles of mayors and council members in the day-to-day operations of city government.

In some council-manager cities, the mayor is chosen by the city council from among its membership to preside over council meetings and fulfill a primarily symbolic role. But in other cities, the mayor is elected citywide, an arrangement that enhances the political position of the office without necessarily vesting it with formal legal authority. The mayor is usually a voting member of the city council but has few other institutional powers in a council-manager government. The mayor does, however, have the opportunity to become a visible spokesperson for the city and has a forum from which to promote ideas and programs.

The city council is primarily responsible for developing public policy (see *Politics Up Close:* "The Job of the City Council Member"). It creates, organizes, and restructures city departments, approves the city budget, establishes the tax rate, authorizes the issuance of bonds (subject to voter approval), enacts local laws (ordinances), and conducts inquiries and investigations into the operations and functions of city agencies.[18]

The council hires a full-time city manager, who is responsible for administering city government on a day-to-day basis. The manager hires and fires assistants and department heads, supervises their activities, and translates the policy directives

★ **council-manager**
Form of city government in which policy is set by an elected city council, which hires a professional city manager to head the daily administration of city government.

Just a Tree-Hugging Mayor

Mayor Phil Hardberger (2005–2009) of San Antonio, an ardent advocate of parks and other public spaces, is seen hugging a tree at the announcement of the city's purchase of new park land. Prior to his election as mayor, Hardberger, who is a lawyer, served in the Kennedy and Johnson administrations and served as an associate justice and chief justice on the Texas Fourth Court of Appeals.

CITY OF AUSTIN

Figure 25.4 Preference of City Reformers: The Council-Manager Government

Austin, as do all major Texas cities with the exception of Houston, functions with a council-manager form of government. In theory, there is a sharp distinction between policy formulation by the city council and policy implementation by the city manager who is hired by the council.

Politics Up Close   The Job of the City Council Member

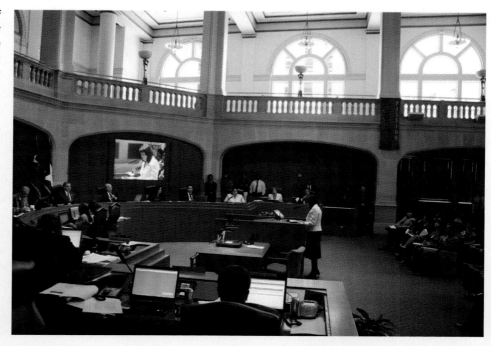

Regardless of the form of government, most city councils in Texas are small, with five to fifteen members elected for 2-year terms. Most council seats are elected at-large, or citywide, and council elections are nonpartisan. Council members in most cities can serve for an unlimited number of terms. Recent referenda on term limitations, however, have been held in several Texas cities. San Antonio limits its council members and mayor to four terms, and Houston, three terms.

In most cities, a council office is part time with little or no compensation, and although some large cities (e.g., Houston, Austin, and Dallas) have recently increased salaries significantly, many council members do not consider their pay to be commensurate with the time spent on the job. Council members in San Antonio are still paid $20 per meeting. Low salaries were part of the early urban reform tradition. The idea was that people would run for office out of a sense of civic duty rather than to advance themselves financially.

The frequency of council meetings varies. In many small towns, councils may meet for only a few hours each month, but councils in large cities meet much more frequently, usually weekly, with meetings lasting several hours. Cities are dealing with a wider range of complex issues than ever before, and demands on a council member's time are great. In addition to their policy-making roles, council members in large cities are faced with increased demands for constituent services. Many council members are finding that public service is extremely costly in terms of time lost from their families and the jobs or professions that provide their livelihoods.

Council members often complain that they had no idea how much time the public would demand of them and no idea of the personal costs of public service. Yet, public service has its rewards, and they often come from a sense that one has made a significant contribution to the future well-being of his or her city. And there are some prescriptions for effectiveness:

1. Learn all you can about your city—its history, its operations, its finances, and those responsible for carrying out the policies of the council. But recognize that change occurs in political institutions and the political climate of a community.

2. Don't let honest differences of opinion with other council members or staff degenerate into personality conflicts. Remember that "there are no permanent friends or permanent enemies in politics."

3. Take the budget and budgetary process seriously. The budget is at the heart of all policy decisions.

4. Don't be misled by the strong demands of special interest groups that want action now, their way. Remember, you represent the whole city.

5. Listen to what your constituents, your fellow council members, and staff have to say. Don't give quick answers until you are confident that you understand the issue. Keep your constituents informed and encourage citizen participation. Balancing interests among your constituents can produce breakthroughs in city policies.

6. Don't spring surprises on your fellow council members or staff. Spend time before a public discussion soliciting information, ascertaining interests in your issue or concerns, and soliciting others' perspectives.

7. Don't bypass the system and don't let others bypass the system. Procedures, when used appropriately, assure openness and consistency in decision-making and policy implementation.

8. Recognize that in some situations there will be winners and losers.

(*continued*)

9. Develop a vision for the future of your city, along with short-term and long-term goals.
10. Celebrate when good things—of which you have been a part—happen. Let the public share in

these successes. Your constituents often hear only about the problems of the city, which, in turn, contributes to negative attitudes toward government.

Sources: Ernie Mosher, "Suggestions for Public Service," *Texas Town and City* 92 (June 2005): 14–16; Nelson Wolff, "How I See It: Lessons for Leadership," in L. Tucker Gibson and Clay Robison, *Government and Politics in the Lone Star State: Theory and Practice.* 6th ed. Upper Saddle River, N.J.: Prentice Hall, 2008, pp. 397–98.

of the city council into concrete action by city employees (see *People in Politics:* "Is This Any Job for a Woman?"). The city manager is also responsible for developing a city budget for council approval and then supervising its implementation. Professionalism is one of the key attributes of the council-manager form of government. Initially, many city managers were engineers, but in recent years there has been a tendency for managers to be generalists with solid skills in public finance. City managers are fairly well paid. In 2006, the salary of the city manager of Dallas was $263,000. San Antonio's city manager, who was hired in late 2005, was paid $250,000 with a $10,000 raise at the end of her first year and a $35,000 bonus the second year, and the city manager of Austin earned $232,502 along with other benefits.[19] The city manager of even a small city such as Seguin received $127,779.[20]

At one time in the not-too-distant past, the salaries of mayors and council members serving in council-manager cities were very low, but there has been a trend in recent years to increase salaries in response to the expanded workload. Salaries of the mayor and city council members in Austin are $67,981 and $57,736, respectively.[21] Until recently, the mayor and council members in Dallas received $50 per meeting, but voters approved a charter amendment in 2001 to raise the mayor's pay to $60,000 a year and council members to $37,500. By contrast, San Antonio's council members and mayor earn $20 per meeting (up to $1,040 a year) and the mayor, an additional $3,000 per year.[22]

There is a delicate line between policy making and administration, and a city manager is, in principle, supposed to be politically neutral. The overall effectiveness of city managers depends on three main factors: their relationships with their city councils; their ability to develop support for their recommendations within the council and the community at large without appearing to have gone beyond the scope of their authority; and the overall perception of their financial and managerial skills. In the real world of municipal government, city managers play a central role in setting policy as well as carrying it out. Managers' adroit use of their resources and sensitivity to political factions and the personal agendas of elected officials are key to determining their success.

Municipal Election Systems

Nonpartisan City Elections Virtually every city in Texas elects its council members in **nonpartisan elections**. Claiming that there was no Democratic or Republican way to pave a street, city reformers who were part of the nonpartisan movement (1920s to 1950s) expressed a strong aversion to political parties and particularly to the urban political machines. To enforce separation of city

★ **nonpartisan elections**
Elections in which candidates do not represent a political party.

People in Politics   Is This Any Job for a Woman?

When the council-manager form of government was first adopted, there was a general perception that the job of the city manager required an engineer or someone from a related field of training to address the basic infrastructure problems of a city. At that time, city officials concentrated most of their work on basic services: streets, water systems, wastewater treatment plants, utilities, public safety, and other public facilities. Budgets were relatively modest, and few cities provided what we now call "social services." So, city councils tended to hire engineers who understood the development and maintenance of infrastructures, and in those days, engineering was almost exclusively a male career.

Over the years, as city populations increased and demands for public services became more complex, budgetary and management skills came to be perceived as more critical for a city manager than engineering, and the next generation of city managers was trained in finance and budgeting. Yet, until recently, it was still a male-dominated career.

But urban management in Texas has undergone a sea change over the past two decades. Women,

Sources: City Web sites.

especially those with training in finance and budgeting, began to work their way up the ranks of city agencies. As the older generation of city managers retired or moved on, these women established their own reputations for management and leadership.

In 2006, the city managers of four of Texas's largest cities—San Antonio, Dallas, Austin, and El Paso—were women. Two—Sheryl Sculley (San Antonio) and Joyce Wilson (El Paso)—were recruited from other cities. Mary K. Suhm (Dallas) and Toby Hammett Futrell (Austin) worked their way up through the ranks of their own cities. Their undergraduate degrees were in somewhat diverse disciplines, but they had master's degrees in public or business administration. As have many of their recent male counterparts, they had considerable experience in public finance and budgeting.

All four were appointed to their current positions in 2004 or later, and while the verdict was still out on their performances, early signs indicated they could hold their own in the rough-and-tumble world of city management and politics. After a long career with the city of Austin, Futrell retired in 2008.

Sheryl Sculley, San Antonio City Manager

Mary K. Suhm, Dallas City Manager

Joyce Wilson, El Paso City Manager

elections from party politics, most municipal elections are held at times other than the party primaries or the general election.

The nonpartisan ballot—combined with at-large, citywide elections—has historically benefited higher social and economic groups. Parties and party labels normally serve as cues for voters. When they are eliminated in city elections, voters are forced to find different sources of information about candidates. Many local newspapers, which endorse candidates and decide how much coverage to give them, have ties to the dominant urban elites. Candidates from lower socioeconomic groups historically have had few contacts with the influential organizations that recruit, support, and endorse candidates. Although no longer in existence, San Antonio's Good Government League and Dallas's Citizens Charter Association controlled the recruitment and election of candidates in those two cities for several decades. Both organizations drew members from the Democratic and the Republican parties, but they reflected and pursued the interests of higher socioeconomic groups, often to the detriment of lower-income and minority populations.

★ **at-large elections**
Election systems under which officeholders are elected by voters in the entire city, school district, or single-purpose district.

At-Large Elections Another notable feature of city politics in Texas is the general use of citywide or **at-large elections**. In 1992, there were 6,409 individuals elected to the governing bodies of 1,171 cities and towns in Texas. Some 5,649, or 88 percent, were elected at large. Only 12 percent were elected from single-member districts, discussed in the following section.[23] Of the 1,204 Texas cities in 2002, some 207, or 14 percent, had single-member districts.[24]

In an at-large election, all of a city's voters participate in the selection of all members of the city council. In a pure at-large system, every candidate runs against every other candidate. If there are eight candidates running for five positions on the city council, the candidates with the five highest vote totals are the winners. Many of these election systems have been struck down by the federal courts or by the U.S. Justice Department under the Voting Rights Act as discriminatory against minorities.

★ **place system**
Form of at-large election in which candidates run for specific positions, or places, on a city council or other governing body.

A variation of the at-large system is the **place system**. Candidates file for a specific council seat and run citywide for places, or positions. Cities using the place system may require that the winning candidate receive a simple plurality of votes (more votes than any other candidate running for the same position) or an absolute majority of votes (more than half the votes cast). If a city requires the latter and there are more than two persons in a race, **runoff elections** between the two highest vote-getters are often required.

★ **runoff elections**
Elections that are required if no candidate receives an absolute majority of the votes cast in a city council, school district, or party primary race. The runoff is between the two top vote-getters.

★ **single-member district**
System in which city council members, legislators, or other public officials are elected from specific geographic areas.

Single-Member Districts An alternative to at-large elections is the **single-member district**, or ward. Under this system, a city is divided into separate geographic districts, each represented by a different council member. A candidate must live in and run for election from a specific district, and voters can cast a ballot only in the race for the council seat that represents their district. A person elected from a single-member district can, depending on the city's charter, be elected by a plurality or an absolute majority of votes.[25] Electoral systems using single-member districts are usually found in cities or towns that have significant minority populations approaching or exceeding 20 percent.

Legal Attacks on At-Large Elections Hispanics and African Americans, through various advocacy groups such as the NAACP, Mexican American Legal Defense and Educational Fund, Texas Rural Legal Aid, and the Southwest Voter Registration and Education Project, have challenged in federal courts the election systems used by numerous Texas cities. From the small East Texas town of Jefferson to El Paso, Houston, and Dallas, minority groups have, with considerable success, challenged the inequities of at-large elections and forced city governments to adopt electoral plans that give minorities a better chance of electing candidates to city councils. The ethnic and racial composition of city councils has changed dramatically over the past 20 years, with a marked increase in the number of Hispanics and African Americans elected to these governing bodies (see Chapter 21).

City Revenues and Expenditures

Despite a growing number of expensive needs that they are expected to address, Texas cities have limited financial options. Unlike counties and school districts, they receive no state appropriations. City governments are disproportionately dependent on **regressive taxes**, such as property taxes and a one-cent sales tax (see Figure 25.5). Other revenue sources include franchise fees, court fines, hotel occupancy taxes, taxes on amusements, fees on various permits, and transfers from funds generated by locally owned utilities.[26]

Texas cities have been given considerable discretion to determine what taxes they will impose, and to a large extent the state has not depended on the cities to fund state programs. But cities are continually threatened by legislative proposals to place caps or other restrictions on their taxing authority.[27] Through their associations and lobbyists, cities work hard to thwart such restrictions.

State law limits the property tax rate that a city can impose and permits citizens to petition their city council for a **rollback election** to nullify any tax increase of more than 8 percent a year. Although there have been few rollback elections in recent years, the potential for such citizen initiatives serves to restrain local officials. A proposal to lower the cap on annual increases in property appraisals, a key element in determining property tax bills, was defeated in the legislature in 2005.[28]

City revenues tend to track the state's economy. When the economy is robust and expanding, city revenues usually grow. Although all areas of the state do not share equally in good economic times, a strong economy eases the pressure for cities to raise property taxes, increase fees, lay off city workers, freeze the hiring of new employees, or reduce services. Conversely, when the state's economy sours, as it did in the late 1980s and in 2001, the opposite occurs.[29]

Although cities are required by law to balance their operating budgets, many municipal construction projects are financed by loans through the issuance of

★ **regressive taxes**
Taxes that impose a disproportionately heavier burden on low-income people than on the more affluent.

★ **rollback election**
Election in which local voters can nullify a property tax increase that exceeds 8 percent in a given year.

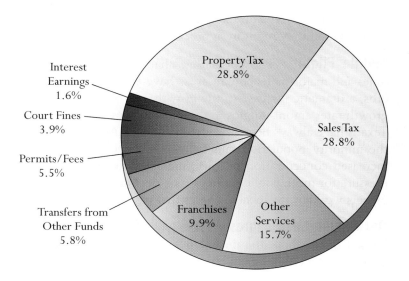

Figure *25.5*

Where Do Texas Cities Get Their Money?

The sales and property taxes—both regressive taxes—provide approximately 60 percent of the revenues collected by Texas cities.

Interest Earnings 1.6%

Court Fines 3.9%

Permits/Fees 5.5%

Transfers from Other Funds 5.8%

Franchises 9.9%

Other Services 15.7%

Property Tax 28.8%

Sales Tax 28.8%

★ **general obligation bonds**
Method of borrowing money to pay for new construction projects, such as prisons, mental hospitals, or school facilities. The bonds, which require voter approval, are repaid with tax revenue.

★ **revenue bonds**
Bonds that are used to finance construction of a public facility and are repaid with income produced by the facility.

★ **infrastructure**
Streets, waste disposal systems, libraries, and other public facilities built and operated by governments.

★ **homestead exemption**
Reduction in property taxes that some local governments grant on a taxpayer's residence.

general obligation bonds, which are subject to voter approval. These bonds are secured by the city's taxing power. The city pledges its full faith and credit to the lender and, over a number of years, repays the bonds with tax revenue. Cities also fund various projects through **revenue bonds** that are payable solely from the revenues derived from an income-producing facility.[30] The poor economy of the late 1980s made it more difficult for cities to borrow money. And with a pent-up demand for improving **infrastructure** (streets, waste disposal systems, libraries, and other facilities), cities have entered an era of bond financing that has been radically altered by the performance of Wall Street and changes in state and federal tax laws.[31] Although city finances had improved by 2008, cities continued to postpone capital spending for streets, water systems, and a variety of other infrastructure improvements. Additionally, there were concerns about the crisis in the mortgage markets that increased home foreclosures across the state. A significant decline in home values would have a direct impact on revenues generated from the property tax.

Urban Problems in Texas

During the 1970s and through the early 1980s, Texas cities were key participants in the dramatic economic growth of the state. Many older cities across the country, particularly in the East and the Midwest, "looked at their Texas counterparts and envied their capacity to attract population and business."[32] Texas cities had low taxes, a pro-business tradition, few labor unions with significant economic clout, an abundant workforce, proximity to natural resources, and governing bodies that favored economic growth and development. At the beginning of the twenty-first century, however, many Texas cities were confronted with many of the problems associated with older urban areas outside of Texas.

The Graying of Texas Cities The Texas population is aging, or graying. Texans are living longer, and as the population ages, additional pressures are placed on city governments for public services. The local property tax, a major source of revenue for city governments as well as other local governments, is stretched almost to its limits in many communities. Moreover, many Texas cities have granted, in addition to the standard **homestead exemption**, additional property tax exemptions for individuals older than 65. As more and more people become old enough to claim these exemptions, younger taxpayers will be called on to shoulder the burden through higher tax rates. There is also the looming possibility that older citizens on fixed incomes will be much more reluctant to support bond issues if they result in significant property tax increases.

"White Flight" The population characteristics of Texas cities change over time, and major metropolitan areas have experienced "white flight" to the suburbs, a dramatic increase in the growth rate of minority populations, and small growth rates among Anglos in the central cities. Income levels for most minority Texans have always been lower than those of Anglos, and a larger proportion of the minority population falls below the poverty level (see Chapter 19). The increased concentration of lower-income people in the central cities increases pressure for more public services, as a declining proportion of affluent property owners weakens the local tax bases that pay for the services.

Declining Infrastructures There has been much concern across Texas and the United States about the declining infrastructures of local governments. Streets, bridges, water and sewer systems, libraries, and other facilities must be continually maintained or expanded to support a growing population. Moreover, many Texas cities are out of compliance with federal standards for treating water and sewage and disposing of solid waste and must spend millions of dollars on physical improvements to avoid or reduce fines. Some capital improvements are paid for out of current operating budgets, but a more common practice is for cities to borrow money to improve roads, streets, water systems, and the like. These bonds are repaid from property taxes. When property values decline, as they did in the late 1980s, the cities' ability to finance the improvements is curtailed. By the end of the 1990s, property values were increasing across most of the state, and cities had more opportunities to borrow money. A construction boom that began in the 1990s and continued through much of the first decade of the twenty-first century added a significant new tax base, but a growing population increased the demand for roads, utilities, water and wastewater systems, and an array of other capital needs. Cities were having trouble keeping up with these new demands.

Crime and Urban Violence

Crime is a major problem facing Texas cities and counties, just as it is in many other parts of the country. Although crime rates in most offense categories declined in the 1990s and through the early part of the twenty-first century, many Texans continue to believe that crime is on the rise. Much of the problem is related to drug abuse, gang violence, and juvenile crime. Political candidates and officeholders often propose the hiring of more police, but many cities can't afford the additional cost—or can't afford to pay their police enough to attract the most qualified officers.

Federal and State-Mandated Programs

Both federal and state governments have increasingly used mandates to implement public policy in recent years. A **mandate** is a law or regulation enacted by a higher level of government that compels a lower level of government to carry out a specific action. In simpler terms, it is a form of "passing the buck." Federal mandates, along with preemptions, cover a wide range of governmental functions, including transportation, education for the disabled, water and air quality, and voter registration (see Chapter 4). States, meanwhile, have shifted much of the cost of public education to local governments.

Despite a decrease in federal funding for many urban problems during the 1980s, there has been an increase in federal mandates on the states, counties, and cities and an increase in state mandates on local governments, often with no

★ **mandate**
Law or regulation enacted by a higher level of government that compels a lower level of government to carry out a specific function.

financial support. In some cases, the state simply passes on the responsibility for—and the costs of—carrying out federal mandates to local governments. Congress enacted a law in 1995 to restrict unfunded mandates, but the law applied only to future, not existing, mandates. And such restrictions can still be circumvented if Congress chooses.

Although this practice may seem unfair and illogical, it is politically attractive to policy makers because they can "appease a large and vocal interest group that demands an extensive program without incurring the wrath of their constituents." They get the credit for such programs, but they do not get the blame for their costs.[33] Cities and other local governments across Texas claim that these unfunded requirements are excessively expensive, force them to rearrange their priorities, and limit local initiatives dealing with their most pressing issues. If local governments do not comply with mandates, they will be subject to litigation and face the prospect of losing federal or state funds. If they comply with mandates, they are then likely to reduce other services or to seek alternative sources of funding now denied them.

Environmental Issues

Texas is one of the most polluted states in the nation. Petrochemical industries generate a large amount of pollutants as by-products in processing fossil fuels or in manufacturing chemicals. The indiscriminate disposal of much of this waste in years past has produced toxic waste dumps in many cities, often in low-income, minority neighborhoods. Heavy automobile traffic and coal-burning power plants spew tons of pollutants into the air; fertilizers and herbicides threaten local water supplies. Cities are frequently on "ozone alert" days, which could trigger additional federal and state requirements to contain the problems. Some cities are addressing these issues through broad "smart growth" initiatives, but there are many political and jurisdictional hurdles to overcome.

Public Employment

As the baby boom generation begins to retire, government agencies are beginning to face serious personnel and financial issues. They will need to find new, qualified public employees at a time of growing hostility toward government, brought about in large part by bureaucrat-bashing political candidates and also by media reports of governmental corruption and inefficiency. Retiring public employees also have accumulated expensive pensions, including health care benefits, that many cities may have trouble paying.

Can You See Me Now?
The haze of pollution over an industrial zone is one of the many environmental problems facing Texas cities today.

County Government in Texas

Texas has 254 counties, more than any other state. Counties are administrative subunits of the state that were developed initially to serve a predominantly rural population. Created primarily to administer state law, they possess powers delegated to them by the state, but they have relatively few implied powers. Unlike home rule cities, counties lack the basic legislative power of enacting ordinances. They can carry out only those administrative functions granted them by the state. Counties administer and collect some state taxes and enforce a variety of state laws and regulations. They also build roads and bridges, administer local welfare programs, aid in fire protection, and perform other functions primarily local in nature.[34] All counties function under the same constitutional restrictions and basic organizational structure despite wide variations in population, local characteristics, and public needs.

According to the 2006 population estimates, Loving County, the state's least populous, had only 60 residents, compared to 3.8 million in Harris County, the most populous (see Table 25.3). Rockwall County includes only 147 square miles, whereas Brewster County covers 6,204 square miles. Some 58 percent of the state's population lives in the ten most populous counties.[35]

Motley County, with a population of about 1,400, had a 2007 budget of $727,673 and paid its county judge $15,226 and its commissioners $11,786 a year. Dallas County had a $750 million budget and paid its county judge $147,935 and its commissioners $121,925. Harris County's 2007 budget was $1.98 billion. Its county judge was paid $141,544, and each of its commissioners received $134,472.[36] Although there is an obvious relationship between the population of a county and salaries paid to its officials, the county's tax base is also a significant factor.

Structure of County Government The organizational structure of county government is highly fragmented, reflecting the principles of Jacksonian democracy (see Chapter 7) and the reaction of late nineteenth century Texans to Radical Reconstruction. The governing body of a county is the **commissioners court**, but it shares administrative functions with other independently elected officials (see Figure 25.6). Moreover, the name "commissioners court" is somewhat misleading because that body has no judicial functions.

★ **commissioners court**
Principal policy-making body for county government. It sets the county tax rate and supervises expenditures.

Table *25.3* Some Are Big and Others, Very, Very Small: Populations of the Ten Largest and Ten Smallest Texas Counties, 1980–2006

Some 80 percent of the state's population is concentrated in the central Texas triangle, which includes most of the urban counties with large populations. Counties in the Panhandle and western part of the state comprise a large land mass but are sparsely populated.

	1980 Population	1990 Population	2000 Population	2006 Population
Harris County	2,409,547	2,818,199	3,400,578	3,830,130
Dallas County	1,556,390	1,852,810	2,218,899	2,340,063
Tarrant County	860,880	1,170,103	1,446,219	1,667,306
Bexar County	988,800	1,185,394	1,392,391	1,550,160
Travis County	419,573	576,407	812,280	928,037
El Paso County	479,899	591,610	679,622	743,319
Hidalgo County	283,229	383,545	569,463	708,235
Collin County	144,576	264,036	491,675	696,306
Denton County	143,126	273,525	432,976	590,120
Fort Bend County	130,846	225,421	354,452	487,047
Glasscock County	1,304	1,447	1,406	1,241
Sterling County	1,206	1,438	1,393	1,223
Terrell County	1,595	1,410	1,081	1,006
McMullen County	789	817	851	863
Roberts County	1,187	1,025	887	860
Kent County	1,145	1,010	859	815
Borden County	859	799	729	710
Kenedy County	543	460	414	392
King County	425	354	356	359
Loving County	91	107	67	60

Sources: U.S. Census Bureau, *U.S. Censuses, 1980, 1990, 2000;* Texas State Data Center, *Total Population Estimates for Counties, 2006.*

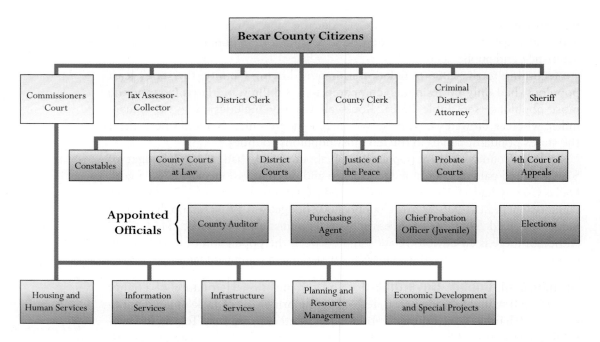

Figure *25.6* It's Confusing—The Structure of County Government

While urban counties such as Bexar County function with many employees and provide a wide array of services, all counties in Texas function under a similar structure, which provides for the election of many officials and fragments authority among these elected officials.

The Commissioners Court and County Judge

The commissioners court comprises a county judge, who is elected countywide, and four county commissioners, who are elected from a county's four commissioners precincts. Like other elected county officials, the judge and the commissioners serve 4-year terms and are elected in partisan elections.

Until recent years, there were gross inequities in the population distributions among commissioners precincts in most counties. This issue of malapportionment came to a head in the 1968 case of *Avery v. Midland County*, in which the U.S. Supreme Court applied the "one person, one vote" principle to the counties and required districts to be equally apportioned.[37] Subsequently, Congress forced Texas to comply with the Voting Rights Act in 1975, and counties were required to consider the interests of minority populations in drawing up the boundaries for commissioners precincts. African Americans and Hispanics across the state have challenged county electoral systems and have increased minority representation on county commissioners courts. After the 2000 Census, most Texas counties quickly redistricted their commissioner precincts in compliance with state and federal law.

The **county judge** presides over commissioners court, participates in the court's deliberations, and votes on issues before it. If there is a vacancy among the commissioners, the county judge appoints a replacement. If the county judge vacates the office, the commissioners choose a replacement.

The Texas Constitution also gives the county judge some judicial responsibilities but does not require the officeholder to be a lawyer. Most urban counties have county courts-at-law that relieve the county judge of judicial duties. However, county judges in some rural counties perform a judicial as well as an executive role, combining two sets of duties in one office.

★ **county judge**
Presiding officer of a county commissioners court. This office also has some judicial authority, which is assumed by separate county courts-at-law in most urban counties.

It's Becoming a Full-Time Job

The problems and complexities of governments in urban counties have transformed the responsibilities of the county judge and commissioners into full-time jobs. County Judge Nelson Wolff, a former mayor of the city of San Antonio, a city council member, a state legislator and a delegate to the 1974 constitutional convention, presides over the Bexar County Commissioners Court, which generally meets at least once a week.

The commissioners court fills midterm vacancies in other county offices. It also has authority over the county budget, which permits the court to exercise some influence, if not control, over other officeholders.[38] The court sets the annual tax rate, which is limited by the Texas Constitution, approves the tax roll, and supervises all expenditures of county money. Other county officials must obtain the court's authorization for personnel positions, salaries, and office expenses. Consequently, the budgetary process often sparks political disputes and other conflicts.

Historically, county road construction and maintenance were primary functions of commissioners courts. The Optional Road Law of 1947 gave counties the authority to create a consolidated road system under the supervision of a county engineer, who relieved commissioners of road maintenance and construction headaches. But the importance of roads to the commissioners and their constituents still generates political disputes.

County Clerk The Texas Constitution provides for an elected **county clerk** to serve as the clerk of the commissioners court, the clerk of the county courts, and (in the smaller counties) the clerk of the district court. Over the years, the legislature has enacted hundreds of statutory provisions defining specific responsibilities of the office, prompting one writer to describe the office as the "dumping ground for miscellaneous functions of the county."[39] The office is the depository of a county's vital statistics, such as birth and death records, and documents related to real estate transactions. It issues marriage licenses and various other licenses required by state law.[40] The county clerk also serves as a county's chief elections administrator if the commissioners court has not created a separate elections administrator's office.[41]

District Clerk The **district clerk**, also elected countywide, assists the district court by maintaining custody of court documents and records.[42] In small counties, the county clerk is authorized to double as the district clerk, and sixty-three counties combined these two offices in 2007.[43]

County and District Attorneys The state's legal interests in both civil and criminal matters are represented at the local level by one of three officers: the **county attorney**, the **district attorney**, or the criminal district attorney. The legislature has enacted numerous provisions for legal departments that vary from county to county. Some counties have no county attorney but have a criminal

★ **county clerk**
Chief record-keeping officer of a county.

★ **district clerk**
Elected county official who maintains custody of state district court records.

★ **county attorney**
Elected official who is the chief legal officer of some counties. He or she also prosecutes lesser criminal offenses, primarily misdemeanors, in county courts.

★ **district attorney**
Elected official who prosecutes more serious criminal offenses, usually felonies, before state district courts.

district attorney. Under state law, other counties are authorized both a county attorney and a district attorney. District attorneys prosecute more serious cases, usually felonies, in the district courts, whereas the county attorneys usually prosecute lesser offenses, primarily misdemeanors, in the county courts.[44]

These officers can also provide legal advice and opinions to other county officials and give legal counsel to public officials or employees who have been sued for acts committed in carrying out their official duties. At the request of the commissioners court, the district attorney or county attorney may initiate lawsuits on behalf of the county. Various other laws charge these attorneys with protecting the public health, assisting the state attorney general in cases involving deceptive trade practices, enforcing the state's election laws, collecting delinquent taxes, and even enforcing the Texas Communist Control Act of 1951.[45]

Tax Assessor-Collector

★ **tax assessor-collector**
Elected official who determines how much property tax is owed on the different pieces of property within a county and then collects the tax.

The property tax is the primary source of revenue for counties. Although the commissioners court sets property tax rates, the **tax assessor-collector**, another elected county officer, has the task of ascertaining who owns what property, determining how much tax is owed on that property, and then collecting the tax. In counties with fewer than 10,000 people, these responsibilities are assigned to the sheriff, unless voters decide to create a separate tax assessor-collector's office. Thirteen counties, mainly those below 5,000 in population, continue to let the sheriff handle the job.

Prior to reforms enacted in the 1970s, the tax assessor-collector also was responsible for appraising property or determining its value. This process was often steeped in politics because the higher the value of a piece of property, the more taxes its owner has to pay. Lowering property values for select friends or supporters gave people holding this office considerable power, which often was abused. In an effort to move toward greater consistency across the state and to enhance the professionalism of tax appraisals, the legislature now requires each county to create an **appraisal district** separate from the tax office.[46] Property tax appraisals are now conducted countywide by an appraisal district whose members represent other governmental units in the county. The district also certifies the tax rolls, and other governmental units are required by law to use its appraisals.[47]

★ **appraisal district**
Local agency that determines the value of pieces of property in a county. All local governments are required to use its evaluations, or appraisals, for tax purposes.

County Law Enforcement

★ **sheriff**
Elected official who is the chief law enforcement officer of a county.

★ **constable**
Elected law enforcement officer who is primarily responsible for executing court judgments, serving subpoenas, and delivering other legal documents.

Sheriffs and **constables**, a county's law enforcement officers, are part of an old tradition under the Anglo-Saxon legal system. Each county has one sheriff with countywide jurisdiction, but the number of constables can vary. In counties with fewer than 18,000 residents, the commissioners court can designate the entire county as a single justice of the peace precinct or can create as many as four precincts, with each precinct assigned one constable. In the large counties, as many as eight justice of the peace precincts can be created, with a constable assigned to each. Most counties have four constables.[48]

In a small rural county, the sheriff is the primary law enforcement officer for the entire county. But in urban counties, city police departments generally assume exclusive jurisdiction in the incorporated municipal areas, leaving the sheriff jurisdiction over the unincorporated areas. Most sheriffs have considerable discretion in the hiring, promotion, and firing of deputies and other employees, although some counties have adopted a merit employment system for the sheriff's office. The sheriff also serves as the administrative officer for the district and county courts.

★ **subpoenas**
Court orders requiring people to testify in court or before grand juries or to produce certain documents.

Constables are authorized to patrol their precincts, make arrests, and conduct criminal investigations, but their primary function is to serve as administrative officers of the justice of the peace courts. They are responsible for serving **subpoenas**, executing judgments of the court, and delivering other legal documents.[49]

County governments are responsible for constructing and staffing county jails, which are managed in most counties by the sheriff and in some counties by a jail administrator. During the late 1980s and early 1990s, counties across the state pursued an aggressive policy of jail construction in response to court decisions, increased crime rates, and a shortage of state prison space. Jail construction was a growth industry during this period, but by the mid-1990s, some counties found that they had overextended their finances to construct these jails. They also were left with excess jail capacity after an increase in state-built prison facilities. To compensate for these problems, several counties contracted with other states to house their prisoners in Texas jails.

All counties are authorized to create an office of **medical examiner**. This individual is appointed by the commissioners court and determines the cause of death of murder victims or others who die under suspicious or unusual circumstances. In counties that do not have a medical examiner, the justice of the peace is charged with conducting an **inquest** to determine whether there are conditions to merit an autopsy.

Counties, either individually or as part of multicounty judicial districts, are required to provide facilities for a criminal probation office. Funded by the state, the chief adult probation officer of a county is chosen by the district judges, who supervise the office.

County Auditor

All counties with 10,000 or more people are required to have a **county auditor**, and smaller counties may have one if the commissioners court chooses. Two counties with fewer than 25,000 residents may jointly agree to hire an auditor to serve both counties. The county auditor is appointed by the district judges of the county for a 2-year term. He or she is primarily responsible for reviewing every bill and expenditure of a county to ensure its correctness and legality. Such oversight can, in effect, impose budgetary restrictions on the commissioners court and produce political conflict with other county officers.

The role of the auditor varies from county to county. In counties with more than 225,000 people, the auditor is the budget officer and prepares the county budget for submission to the commissioners court, unless an alternative has been authorized by the legislature.[50] In smaller counties, the commissioners court prepares the budget, based on estimates provided by the auditor.

County Treasurer

The **county treasurer** is responsible for receiving and disbursing county funds. Although this office has existed since 1846, its primary functions are now carried out by the county auditor, and constitutional amendments have eliminated the office in a number of counties.

Criticisms of County Government

The structure of county government in Texas, designed for a rural state, has inhibited efforts of urban counties to respond to growing needs for public services. The state experimented with county home rule years ago, but the provisions were so poorly written, confusing, and contradictory that local self-rule at the county level was never given a real chance. Efforts were made in the 1997 and 1999 sessions of the legislature to amend the constitution to once again allow counties to adopt home rule, but there was limited statewide support for this change.

Even though the county functions primarily as an extension, or administrative subdivision, of state government, there is limited supervision of the counties by the state and a wide disparity in the way counties interpret and administer their functions. Some counties do a very good job; others have a dismal record. The fragmentation

Do You Want to Spend a Night Here?
Prior to federal court intervention, many local governments maintained jails that were small, crowded, and often unsanitary. Maverick County's old jail, now boarded up, is located between the old and new county courthouses.

★ **medical examiner**
Appointed official who is responsible for determining the cause of death of murder victims or others who die under suspicious or unusual circumstances.

★ **inquest**
Examination by a justice of the peace or a medical examiner of unusual circumstances under which someone has died.

★ **county auditor**
Appointed officer who is primarily responsible for reviewing every bill and expenditure of a county to assure it is correct and legal.

★ **county treasurer**
Elected officer who is responsible for receiving and disbursing county funds.

represented by several independently elected officers always poses a danger of jurisdictional conflict, administrative inefficiency, and even government deadlock. Like other local governments in Texas, counties rely heavily on the property tax for revenue but cannot exceed tax rate limits set by the state constitution. Those limits reflected a general apprehension about government when they were initially set in 1875. They now further restrict the counties' ability to provide services.

Historically, county courthouses have been associated with political patronage and the **spoils system**. Victorious candidates have claimed the right to appoint personal and political friends to work for them, and state courts have held that elected county officials have wide discretion in the selection of their employees. Reformers have advocated a **civil service system** for county employees based on merit and competitive examinations and offering job security from one election to the next. A 1971 law allows counties with more than 200,000 residents to create a civil service system, but it excludes several county offices, including the district attorney. An elected public official retains considerable control over the initial hiring of employees through a probationary period of six months.[51]

Special Districts in Texas

Every day, Texans use the services of municipal utility districts (MUDs), water conservation and improvement districts (WCIDs), hospital districts, and a host of other local governments, which have been deemed by some as the "invisible governments" of the state.[52] There are approximately 3,400 such governmental units across Texas classified as **special purpose districts**, and almost every year additional ones are created. These include drainage districts, navigation districts, freshwater supply districts, river authorities, underground water districts, sanitation districts, housing authorities, soil conservation districts, MUDs, and WCIDs. School districts are also considered a form of special purpose district.

Functions and Structures Special districts are units of local government created by the state to perform specific functions. Wide variations in their functions, taxing and borrowing authority, governance, and performance limit generalizations about them. Most special districts are authorized to perform a single function and are designated single-purpose districts. But some are multipurpose districts because the laws creating them permit them to provide more than one service to constituents. For example, in addition to providing water to people in their service areas, MUDs may assume responsibility for drainage, solid waste collection, firefighting, and parks and other recreational facilities.[53] Some districts, such as hospital districts, normally cover an entire county. Others, such as MUDs, cover part of one county; still others, such as river authorities, cover a number of counties.

A special district is governed by a board either appointed by other governmental units or elected in nonpartisan elections. The board members of hospital districts are appointed by county commissioners courts; city housing authority boards are appointed by mayors or city councils. Many of these districts have taxing and borrowing authority, but others have no taxing powers and are supported by user fees or funds dedicated to them by other government agencies. Many special districts are eligible for federal grants-in-aid.

Special districts exist for a variety of reasons. Independent school districts were created, in part, to depoliticize education and remove the responsibility for it from county and city governments. In some cases, existing governments are unwilling or unable—because of state restrictions on their tax, debt, or jurisdictional authority—to provide essential services to developing communities. So special districts were created to fill the gap.

★ **spoils system**
System of filling public jobs by hiring friends and other politically connected applicants, regardless of their abilities.

★ **civil service system**
System under which public employees are hired and promoted on their abilities. It features competitive examinations and offers job security from one election to another.

★ **special purpose districts**
Units of local government created by the state to perform specific functions not met by cities or counties, including the provision of public services to unincorporated areas.

The cost of providing a particular governmental service is another reason for the growth of special districts. By creating a special district that includes a number of governmental units and a larger population and tax base, the costs can be spread over a wider area. Special districts often are promoted by individuals, groups, or corporations for selfish gains (see *Controversy:* "The Ambitious Little Water District"). Builders, for example, sometimes develop plans for large tracts of land in the unincorporated areas of a county and then get local governments or the legislature to create municipal utility or water districts to provide water and sewer services.

Controversy

The Ambitious Little Water District

Most Texans have never heard of sparsely populated Roberts County, which sits over the Ogallala Aquifer in the Texas Panhandle. And it is highly unlikely that they have heard of Roberts County Water District #1, a "fresh water supply district" approved in 2007 by voters owning land in the eight square miles comprising the district. Yet, high stakes politics over water supplies and private property rights are being played out in the district's organization.

Communities throughout the Southwest are facing severe water shortages that, if not cured, will limit their abilities to continue to grow and prosper. There also has been a quiet effort by some wealthy individuals, including oilman T. Boone Pickens of Dallas, to fill their needs and reap profits by purchasing water rights in sparsely populated areas that have access to underground water.

Roberts County Water District #1 sits over land to which Pickens has water rights and is the vehicle he has designed to pump water from the Ogallala through a pipeline to Dallas, some 300 miles away. He also may build transmission lines to transmit power from wind farms to metropolitan areas in the central part of the state.

Pickens initially tried to organize this water district in 2002 but was rebuffed by a group of Roberts County residents, who initiated a plan for a county-wide water district over which he would have little control. So Pickens pursued another strategy.

During the 2006 election cycle, he gave $1.2 million to political candidates and political committees, including 16 state senators and one-third of the members of the Texas House. Pickens also spent some $1 million on lobbyists working the Texas Legislature in 2007.

During that session, the legislature enacted changes in state law to give Pickens virtual carte blanche to organize a special district with wide-ranging powers. The law pertaining to special districts was modified to permit people who owned property within the district but lived elsewhere to vote in the organization election. At the same time, lawmakers resisted efforts to make substantive changes in eminent domain laws, which give governments the power to take private property for public use. Consequently, the water district contemplated by Pickens would have eminent domain powers extending hundreds of miles beyond the small district's boundaries.

There was no doubt what the outcome of the election on the district's creation in November 2007 would be. Only five voters owned land in the district, and all had business relationships with Pickens. He had sold them small parcels of his huge holdings shortly after the end of the 2007 legislative session and before the November election. Two were residents of Roberts County, and three lived hundreds of miles away from the district.

In the future, Pickens's water supply district will provide him with a wide range of legal powers to expedite the delivery of water to customers hundreds of miles away. Using the so-called right of recapture (access to water under one's own property), Pickens anticipates pumping 200,000 acre feet of water out of the aquifer each year, which could place additional stress on the primary water source of West Texas. Using the power of eminent domain, he can force landowners to sell him access to their land for a pipeline. And as Pickens's plans for pumping water from the Ogallala unfold, it may become evident how a special district can be used by individuals or corporations to advance their own economic interests. Indeed, if his plans for a wind farm materialize, he also could use those easements to build power lines.

Moreover, the actions of the legislature weakened the public's control over the organization and governance of special districts, opening the way for individuals or corporations to pursue actions that could be potentially harmful to a large number of Texans.

Sources: Jim Landers, "T. Boone Pickens to Import Water, Wind Power to North Texas," *Dallas Morning News,* April 18, 2008; Texans for Public Justice, "Watch Your Assets: T. Boone Pickens Land Grab," October 4, 2007.

Some special districts have been designed to serve specific geographic areas. River basins that extend for thousands of square miles and cover ten or twenty counties have presented a particular problem. Because no existing governments had jurisdiction over the use of water resources in these basins, river authorities with multicounty jurisdictions were created.[54]

Consequences of Single-Purpose Districts   From one perspective, special districts compensate for the fragmentation of local government that exists throughout Texas. But, ironically, these districts contribute to further fragmentation and delay the more difficult development of comprehensive, multipurpose governmental units that could more efficiently provide public services. A special district has been called a "halfway house between cityhood and non-cityhood, between incorporation and non-incorporation."[55] Residents of a developing community or subdivision may not want to create a new city or become part of a nearby existing city, but they need certain fundamental services, such as water, electricity, and fire protection, some of which can be provided through the creation of special districts.

Many special districts are small operations with limited financial resources and few employees. Salaries often are low, and some districts have difficulty retaining the licensed technical people required to perform daily operations. In some cases, record-keeping and management operations are shoddy and amateurish, and the costs of providing services by many of these operations may actually be higher than what similar services cost in larger governmental systems. Special districts may also use outside legal and professional assistance, which can be very costly, and many districts lack the expertise to maximize their investments or borrowing potential.[56]

Some special districts expand their functions beyond the purpose for which they were created. The Metropolitan Transit Authority in San Antonio, for example, authorized under state law to impose a 1 percent sales tax for public transportation, became involved in building the Alamodome, a multipurpose convention and sports facility. As governments expand their functions, there is a greater potential for intergovernmental rivalry, conflict, deadlock, and duplication of costs.

Except for the 1,000-plus independent school districts and a small number of other highly visible districts, such as river authorities, most special districts operate in anonymity. The public has only limited knowledge of their jurisdiction, management, operations, or performance. Many taxpayers may not even be aware they are paying taxes to some of these entities. There is little media coverage of their work, few individuals attend their board meetings, and turnout for their elections is extremely low. In the case of the governing boards that are appointed by other governmental agencies, the appointment process is often dominated by a small number of individuals or groups who also dominate the activities of the special district. This domination is probably the most damning indictment of special districts.

Independent School Districts

★ **independent school district**
Specific form of special district that administers the public schools in a designated area.

The **independent school district**, currently the basic organizational structure for public education in Texas, had its origins in the Constitution of 1876. Cities and towns were allowed to create independent school districts and to impose a tax to support them. Initially, the city government served as the school board, but in 1879, school districts were permitted to organize independently of the city or town, elect their own boards of trustees, and impose their own school tax. But residents of rural areas, where most nineteenth-century Texans lived, were denied these powers and only had the option of forming community schools. So, in effect, Texas operated under a dual school system, with the majority of students subject to the discretionary and often arbitrary powers of county governments.

Inequities in the Public Education System From the very beginning, the inequities in the school system were clear to many parents, elected officials, and educators, and there were early efforts to reform and modernize public schools. Most were linked to national education reform movements. For example, the Peabody Education Board, a national organization, provided financial aid and technical support to the leaders of the state reform movement during the early part of the twentieth century. More recently, national attention was directed to the problems of public education through widely publicized studies such as *A Nation at Risk: The Imperative for Educational Reform* (1983), which was conducted by the National Commission on Excellence in Education. Many national, state, and local organizations have attempted to identify the most serious problems in public education, develop alternatives for resolving these problems, and initiate related litigation or legislative and administrative initiatives. Although education is primarily a local responsibility, three recent presidents have made educational policy one of their top priorities.

Reformers have focused much of their attention on compulsory education laws, adequacy and equity in school funding, quality curricula, and teacher preparation. Some reform efforts also have been directed at the structure and governance of local school districts. The diverse and fragmented structure of Texas schools has been modified over the years through consolidation, greater uniformity in the organization of school districts, and the extension of the independent school district to virtually every community in the state.

Differences Among School Districts Although regulation and coordination are provided on a statewide level through the State Board of Education and the Texas Education Agency (TEA), public education is now administered through more than 1,000 local school districts. In the 2006–2007 school year, one of the smallest districts, the San Vicente ISD in far West Texas, had twenty-one students. The largest, the Houston Independent School District, had 202,000 students. The fifteen largest districts—with more than 50,000 students each—enrolled approximately 1.2 million or 27 percent of the 4.6 million students attending prekindergarten through grade 12 in Texas public schools during the 2006–2007 school year. By contrast, 471 districts had fewer than 500 students each, serving a total of only 113,076 students. Students from minority ethnic or racial groups constituted 46 percent of the public school population in Texas in 2006–2007, and their numbers are projected to increase.[57]

School District Governance A school district is governed by a **school board**, ranging in size from three to nine members; most have seven. Trustees are elected in nonpartisan elections for terms that vary from 2 to 6 years, with most serving 3-year terms. In 2008, 161 of the 1,000-plus school districts elected their boards from single-member districts.[58] School districts with significant minority populations have shifted from at-large elections to single-member districting, primarily as a consequence of lawsuits or the threats of lawsuits by minority plaintiffs under the Voting Rights Act.

Most school board elections are held on the first Saturday in May, the same day most cities hold their elections. School board election turnouts are low, usually less than 10 percent of registered voters. But turnout increases when there are highly visible issues, such as the firing of a superintendent or a dramatic increase in taxes.

Recruiting qualified candidates for school boards is often difficult, and many times elections are uncontested. Individuals are encouraged to run by the superintendent, other members of the board, or key community leaders, many of whom point out that it is difficult to find people who are willing to give the required time and energy. Individuals often have little knowledge of what school board members do, and because many trustees serve for only one term, some boards have high turnover rates. Moreover, there is no way for a potential trustee

★ **school board**
Governing body of a school district. Its responsibilities include the development or approval of educational policies, approval of the budget, hiring of the superintendent, and other personnel matters.

School Days, School Days

School boards, such as the North East Independent School District Board shown here, are responsible for policy and budgeting, leaving the day-to-day management of a school district to the superintendent.

★ **school superintendent**
Top administrator of a school district. He or she is hired by the elected school board to direct the district's daily operations.

to anticipate the amount of time it will take for briefings by the superintendent and staff, preparing for and participating in board meetings, and taking phone calls from parents and taxpayers. A board member must also deal with the political aspects of the job, including attendance at community functions and major school programs and meeting with teachers and taxpayer groups. Board members receive no salaries but are reimbursed for travel related to board business.

The most important decision that a school board makes is the hiring of a **school superintendent**. In organization and management structure, the school district is similar to the council-manager form of government. The board hires a superintendent, who is in charge of the district's day-to-day operations. Although the board has the primary policy-making responsibility for a district, part-time board members are often dominated by the superintendent and the superintendent's staff. School trustees and superintendents tend to talk about "keeping politics out of education," and superintendents often attempt to convey the impression that they serve simply to carry out the will of their boards. In most instances, however, a school board's agenda is established by the superintendent, and the board members depend on the superintendent and other professional staff members for information and policy recommendations. Very few board members have much time to give to the district, and most have only limited knowledge of the laws affecting education. State law, in fact, restricts the intrusion of board members into the daily management and administration of a district. An excessively politicized school board that becomes involved in day-to-day administration can be called to task by the Texas Education Agency. In an extreme case, the TEA can even take over the management of a school district.

Councils of Government

Local issues or problems do not start or stop at the boundaries of local governments. Water issues, for example, are usually of a regional nature and transcend the boundaries of cities and counties. Land use, crime, and transportation issues similarly affect multiple governments, and, in fact, there are relatively few policy issues that do not impact more than one government. Under the complex system of local government that has evolved in Texas and throughout the United States, it has long been argued by policy makers and students of government that greater coordination and collaboration is imperative if sound public policy is to be developed in response to these mutual issues.

Councils of government (**COGs**), or regional planning commissions, were created under the Texas Regional Planning Act of 1965 (see Figure 25.7). That law was enacted, in part, to comply with federal regulations requiring local planning and review procedures.[59] These organizations evolved over the years to take

★ **council of government (COG)**
Council comprised of representatives of other governments in a defined region of the state.

on additional duties, including comprehensive planning and service responsibilities for employment and job training, criminal justice, economic development, health, aging, early childhood development, alcoholism, drug abuse, transportation, land resource management, environmental quality, and rural development.[60]

Although councils of government are "defined by law as political subdivisions of the state, they have no regulatory power or other authority possessed by cities, counties, or other local governments."[61] Stated another way, they do not have jurisdictional authority with police and taxing powers. They cannot enact local legislation, nor do they have the power to force compliance. Decisions of the COGs are not binding on their members.[62]

The councils, instead, are support agencies designed to promote voluntary collaboration and coordination of public services among local governments. Their

01 Panhandle Regional Planning Commission
02 South Plains Association of Governments
03 Nortex Regional Planning Commission
04 North Central Texas Council of Governments
05 Ark-Tex Council of Governments
06 East Texas Council of Governments
07 West Central Texas Council of Governments
08 Rio Grande Council of Governments
09 Permian Basin Regional Planning Commission
10 Concho Valley Council of Governments
11 Heart of Texas Council of Governments
12 Capital Area Council of Governments

13 Brazos Valley Council of Governments
14 Deep East Texas Council of Governments
15 South East Texas Regional Planning Commission
16 Houston-Galveston Area Council
17 Golden Crescent Regional Planning Commission
18 Alamo Area Council of Governments
19 South Texas Development Council
20 Coastal Bend Council of Governments
21 Lower Rio Grande Valley Development Council
22 Texoma Council of Governments
23 Central Texas Council of Governments
24 Middle Rio Grande Valley Development Council

Figure *25.7* Can't We All Agree? State Planning Regions

Councils of governments, which have no enforcement powers, were created to bring some level of coordination and collaboration among local governments in the development of plans and policies that were regional in scope.

Source: Office of the Governor.

effectiveness varies across the state and appears to be related, in part, to their members' willingness to engage in serious intergovernmental policy planning and implementation, their staffs' technical expertise, and their leaders' political effectiveness.

Twenty-four regional councils of government in Texas each serve a specific geographic area. Membership is voluntary; in 2008, more than 2,000 counties, cities, school districts, and other special districts were members of COGs.[63] Each COG decides the composition and structure of its governing body, so long as two-thirds of its members are elected officials from counties or cities.

Member governments pay dues, but the primary sources of funding for COGs have been the state and federal governments. The state pays a regional council a flat fee for each county that is a member and provides a per capita payment for each person residing in the COG. At one time, the regional councils relied extensively on federal grants-in-aid, but there was a 70 percent decrease in direct federal funding of COGs during the 1980s. Indirect federal pass-through funds administered by state agencies also provide funds for the COGs.[64] Several COGs have expanded their technical support and some management services to offset these lost revenues.[65] In recent years, state COGs have turned their attention to emergency planning in the aftermath of the 2001 terrorist attacks and the hurricanes of 2005 and are working with the governor's Division of Emergency Management to develop and implement a regional strategy for emergency responses. Environmental issues are also receiving increased attention, and COGs are now engaged in statewide planning for a potential bird flu epidemic.[66]

Solutions to the Problems of Local Government

Privatization of Functions   As local governments have juggled their financial problems with increased demands for public services, they have tended to contract out some services to private companies. Many governments believe **privatization** can reduce costs through business-like efficiency, and they consider it an attractive alternative in the face of voter hostility toward higher taxes. Cities, for example, are contracting for garbage pickup, waste disposal, towing, food services, security, and a variety of other services. Privatization also provides a way for cities that have reached their limit on bonded indebtedness to make new capital improvements by leasing a facility from a private contractor. A civic center or school facility can be constructed by a private contractor and leased back to the government for an extended period.

Annexation and Extraterritorial Jurisdiction   Population growth in the areas surrounding most large Texas cities has forced municipalities and counties to wrestle with urban sprawl. El Paso covered 26 square miles in 1950 but had expanded to 250 square miles by 2000. Houston grew from 160 square miles in 1950 to 594 square miles in 2008, with its **extraterritorial jurisdiction** encompassing 1,312 square miles, excluding the cities that lie within this area.[67]

The cities' ability to expand their boundaries beyond suburban development derives from their annexation powers and extraterritorial jurisdiction over neighboring areas. With the Municipal Annexation Act of 1963, the legislature granted cities considerable discretionary authority over nearby unincorporated areas. Specific annexation powers and extraterritorial jurisdiction vary with the size and charter of a city. Generally, cities have extraterritorial jurisdiction over unincorporated areas within one-half mile to five miles of the city limits, making development in those areas subject to the city's building codes, zoning and land use restrictions, utility easement requirements, and road and street specifications. This authority restricts the use of unincorporated land and requires those building outside the city to build according to at least minimal standards. Later, when those areas are annexed by the city, they are less likely to degenerate quickly into suburban slums that will require a high infusion of city dollars for basic services.

★ **privatization**
Contracting by government with private companies to provide some public services.

★ **annexation powers**
Authority of cities to add territory, subject to restrictions set by state law.

★ **extraterritorial jurisdiction**
Power of an incorporated city to control development within nearby unincorporated areas.

Cities can annex areas equivalent to 10 percent of their existing territory in a given year, and if this authority is not exercised in 1 year, it can be carried over to subsequent years. Annexation usually does not require a vote of those people who are to be incorporated into the city. However, within 2½ years, a city is required to provide annexed areas with services comparable to those provided in its older neighborhoods. Otherwise, individuals living in these newly annexed areas can exercise an option to be de-annexed, a situation that rarely occurs.

Aggressive use of annexation has permitted several large cities to expand geographically with population growth, thus often limiting the development of small suburban towns that would potentially limit future expansion. Cities have even annexed thin strips of land, miles from urban development, along major roads and highways leading into them. Given that a city's extraterritorial jurisdiction extended as far as five miles on either side of the strip that was annexed, this practice has enabled a city to control future development in a large area. In San Antonio, these annexation policies have often been referred to as "spoke annexation," and it has taken more than 30 years for much of the territory brought under the city's jurisdiction to be developed and annexed by the city.[68]

In recent legislative sessions, many lawmakers have demonstrated an anti-city sentiment with proposals that would have eroded municipal authority, reduced municipal revenues, and imposed costly new mandates. Of particular concern to cities were attacks on annexation powers. The legislature in 1999 enacted a major overhaul of annexation authority, including a provision that requires cities to outline their annexation plans 3 years in advance. But cities felt, through their lobbying efforts, that they were able to obtain a relatively "well-balanced" law.[69] The legislature in 2001 continued to reflect growing suburban-rural hostility toward the cities. It enacted a law that modified the extraterritorial jurisdiction of cities by requiring city-county agreements on the regulation of subdivisions.[70]

Modernization of County Government   City governments provide most basic public services in urban areas, and as cities expand to county boundaries and beyond, there is increased overlapping jurisdiction of county and city governments and a reduction of county services in the annexed areas. Counties, nevertheless, still play an important role in Texas. Rural Texans, in particular, continue to rely on counties to provide a number of services, and demands on many counties will increase. Recommendations to modernize county government include further attempts at county home rule, granting counties some legislative or ordinance-making authority, and creating an office of county administrator, appointed by the commissioners court to run the departments now assigned to commissioners. Another recommendation is to extend the civil service system to smaller counties and to all county employees.[71] Many rural counties are making significant strides in computer applications for managing court records, budgeting, purchasing, auditing, mapping, and inventory control.

Economic Development   Historically, cities have collaborated with the private sector to stimulate local economies. Private sector initiatives have come from chambers of commerce or economic development foundations, and local governments have participated. Cities also are using a variety of new financing techniques to assist in economic development, including development impact taxes and fees, user charges, creation of special district assessments, tax increment financing, and privatization of governmental functions.[72] A state law was enacted in 1989 to permit cities, with the approval of local voters, to impose a 0.5 percent sales tax for local economic development. By 2005, voters in more than 500 Texas cities had approved this tax option.

Texas cities, as well as some counties, aggressively court American and foreign companies to relocate or develop new plants or operations in their communities.

★ **tax abatements**
Exemptions from property taxes granted to certain businesses, usually to encourage them to move to or expand their operations in a city or county. The exemptions are granted for specific periods.

Cities and local chambers of commerce sponsor public relations campaigns touting local benefits and attractions. Local governments offer **tax abatements**—exemptions from property taxes on a business for a specified period—to encourage a company to locate or expand in a community (see *Politics Up Close:* "Expensive Tax Breaks"). Other financial incentives to companies being courted include lowered utility bills and assistance in obtaining housing for employees.

The legislature has permitted counties to form industrial development corporations or enterprise zones and to relax state regulatory policies to encourage the redevelopment of depressed areas. Portions of a county may be designated as reinvestment zones, in which tax abatements can be offered to attract new businesses. Counties also can create county boards of development, civic centers, foreign trade zones, and research and development authorities.[73]

Interlocal Contracting Because many small governments have limited tax bases and staffs, they enter into contracts with larger governments for various public services. In 1971, the legislature, following a constitutional amendment, enacted the Interlocal Cooperation Act, which gave cities, counties, and other political subdivisions rather broad authority for such contracts.[74] The law has been amended several times to expand the scope of these agreements, and local governments are now contracting with each other for services in twenty-five functional areas, ranging from aviation to water and wastewater management.[75] Contracting is not an alternative to consolidation of local governments, but it does hold out some promise for improving the quality of local services and reducing their costs.

Metro Government and Consolidation In the metropolitan areas of Houston, Dallas, and San Antonio, there are literally hundreds of cities and special districts providing public services. In Harris County (Houston) alone, there are 487 separate governmental units (see Table 25.4). Legislators, scholars, and reform groups have extensively studied the duplication and other problems produced by such proliferation and fragmentation and have made numerous recommendations over the years.

Politics Up Close **Expensive Tax Breaks**

As the Texas economy was diversifying in the 1990s, economic development was very important to many communities. Texas towns and cities competed with each other and with cities in other states for industries that would provide jobs and help their communities grow. They offered incentives for companies to build new plants or expand existing facilities. One popular incentive was a form of tax break called a tax abatement: companies receiving tax abatements from local governments did not have to pay property taxes on their new facilities for a designated number of years. Proponents defended such breaks as an important economic development tool and argued that abatements eventually paid for themselves in the form of an expanded tax base. But some legislators and other critics believed school districts and other local governments were

giving away too much potential tax revenue. There also was fear that a company could go out of business or move its operations out of a community before it had paid any taxes or hired the projected number of people it claimed it would employ.

According to a staff report prepared for the Senate Economic Development Committee in 1996, 186 of the state's 1,050 school districts had given tax abatements since 1985. The state comptroller's office said those abatements had cost $480 million in lost property tax revenue. "Our children's future should not be traded for new jobs now," said state senator David Sibley of Waco, the committee chairman.[a] The lost money, he said, could have been spent on supplies, teacher salaries, and other educational needs. The legislature, however, let tax abatements continue.

[a]Quoted in *Austin American-Statesman*, October 31, 1996.

Table 25.4 Why All These Governments? Local Governments in the Ten Largest and the Ten Smallest Texas Counties, 2002

The number of governments within a county is shaped by the size of the population, early and subsequent settlement patterns, school district consolidations, initiatives by developers to provide services in non-urban areas, and specific policy issues for which no government had responsibility.

	Population (2006)	Total	County	Municipal	School Districts	Special Districts
State	23,507,783	4,784	254	1,196	1,089	2,245
Harris	3,830,130	487	1	28	24	434
Dallas	2,340,063	63	1	25	16	21
Tarrant	1,667,306	67	1	34	18	14
Bexar	1,550,160	51	1	22	16	12
Travis	928,037	79	1	15	8	55
El Paso	743,319	36	1	6	10	19
Hidalgo	708,235	77	1	22	16	38
Collin	696,306	51	1	24	15	11
Denton	590,120	69	1	33	11	24
Fort Bend	487,047	138	1	16	5	116
Glasscock	1,241	4	1		1	2
Sterling	1,223	5	1	1	1	2
Terrell	1,006	4	1		1	2
McMullen	863	5	1		1	3
Roberts	860	4	1	1	1	1
Kent	815	5	1	1	1	2
Borden	710	2	1		1	
Kenedy	392	2	1		1	
King	359	3	1		1	1
Loving	60	2	1			1

Sources: U.S. Census Bureau, Census of Governments, 2002, Government Organization, Table 16; U.S. Census Bureau, 2006 American Community Survey; Texas State Data Center, Estimates of the Total Populations of Texas Counties for July 1, 2006, and January 1, 2007, September 2007.

One proposed solution is a consolidation of city and county governments known as **metro government**, which has been tried in a dozen or so areas outside Texas. Efforts initiated by San Antonio and Bexar County to obtain constitutional authority to propose city-county consolidation to voters in the county failed in the 1997 legislative session. Other metropolitan areas joined Bexar County and San Antonio in an expanded effort to obtain this authority from the legislature in 1999, but again it failed. Without such authority, county-city collaboration is more likely to take the form of increased intergovernmental contracting and the informal cooperation that local governments develop out of necessity and mutual self-interest.[76]

★ **metro government**
Local government in which city and county governments consolidate to avoid duplication of public services.

Public Improvement Districts Under one state law, property owners in a specific area of a city or its extraterritorial jurisdiction can petition the city to create a special **public improvement district**. These districts can undertake a wide range of improvements—landscaping, lighting, signs, sidewalks, streets, pedestrian malls, libraries, parking, and water, wastewater, and drainage facilities. Public improvement districts do not have the same autonomy as other special districts. They are created solely through the discretionary powers of a city and are funded by assessments on property within their boundaries.[77] Although their budgets and assessments must be approved by the city, they can be operated and managed by private management companies or by the citizens themselves. Fort Worth created a public improvement district for its downtown area in 1986, and other cities have considered the option.

★ **public improvement district**
Specific area of a city in which property owners pay special taxes in return for improvements to streets and other public facilities in their neighborhood.

Summary
Who Gets What: Local Government in Texas

Local governments across the state struggle to keep up with the demands of ever-increasing populations. But they function under a number of restraints, including state laws that limit their authority, sources of revenue that are primarily regressive, and an array of state and federal mandates for which there are no funds.

★ Texas cities with fewer than 5,000 people are designated general law cities and are limited as to the form of government they can use. Cities with more than 5,000 residents can function as home rule cities, choosing a form of government that satisfies community needs as long as it does not conflict with the state constitution or statutes. Within this legal framework, Texas cities have experimented with three forms of government—mayor-council, city commission, and council-manager.

★ A notable feature of city politics in Texas is the widespread use of nonpartisan, at-large elections. Prompted by legal attacks on at-large elections under the Voting Rights Act, many cities, as well as special purpose districts, have adopted single-member districts, thus increasing minority representation on local governing bodies.

★ County governments, initially created to serve a rural population, function primarily as administrative subdivisions of the state, but many are now urban and face the same problems as cities. Much like state government, county government is highly fragmented, with administrative powers shared by a variety of elected officials.

★ Hundreds of special purpose districts provide numerous public services and add to the fragmentation of local government. Most people know little about their jurisdiction, structure, functions, and leadership, making them the "invisible governments" of Texas. Texas has approximately 1,050 independent school districts, which are working to improve the quality of education against a backdrop of social, cultural, and financial problems.

★ Texas cities are now experiencing many of the same problems as the older cities of the East and Midwest. Populations are aging, and there is evidence of white flight from the core urban centers. A disproportionately larger share of the population in the central cities is low income and least able to pay taxes to support municipal services. Crime rates are high, and cities are faced with significant problems of deteriorating infrastructures. Federal and state governments have imposed additional requirements, or mandates, on the cities that are increasingly difficult to meet.

★ Local governments are experimenting with a variety of techniques to deal with their problems. Cities have used their annexation powers and extraterritorial jurisdiction to expand their tax bases and exercise limited controls over development in adjacent areas. Cities are also using public improvement districts to permit targeted areas to impose additional taxes for needed services. Both counties and cities are privatizing governmental functions to decrease costs and increase efficiency. Interlocal contracting permits governments to provide services to each other on a contractual basis, and many counties and cities are engaged in aggressive economic development programs. Some people advocate governmental consolidation, but there is limited support for this alternative in Texas.

Key Terms

unitary system 868
Dillon rule 868
general law cities 870
home rule cities 870
charter 871
mayor-council 871
weak mayor 871
strong mayor 871
city commission 874
council-manager 875
nonpartisan elections 878
at-large elections 880
place system 880
runoff elections 880

single-member district 880
regressive taxes 881
rollback election 881
general obligation
 bonds 882
revenue bonds 882
infrastructure 882
homestead exemption 882
mandate 883
commissioners court 885
county judge 886
county clerk 887
district clerk 887
county attorney 887

district attorney 887
tax assessor-collector 888
appraisal district 888
sheriff 888
constable 888
subpoenas 888
medical examiner 889
inquest 889
county auditor 889
county treasurer 889
spoils system 890
civil service system 890
special purpose
 districts 890

independent school
 district 892
school board 893
school superintendent 894
council of government
 (COG) 894
privatization 896
annexation powers 896
extraterritorial
 jurisdiction 896
tax abatements 898
metro government 899
public improvement
 district 899

Suggested Readings

Bridges, Amy. *Morning Glories: Municipal Reform in the Southwest.* Princeton, N.J.: Princeton University Press, 1997. Traces the development and successes of urban reformers in the Southwest.

Brooks, David B. *Texas Practice: County and Special District Law.* Vols. 35 and 36. St. Paul, Minn.: West, 1989. The definitive legal analysis of county and local governments in Texas.

Burns, Nancy. *The Formation of American Local Governments: Private Values in Public Institutions.* New York: Oxford University Press, 1994. A study of the political and economic reasons citizens create local governments.

Feagin, Joe R. *Free Enterprise City: Houston in Political-Economic Perspective.* New Brunswick, N.J.: Rutgers University Press, 1988. History of the economic development of Houston and its politics.

Johnson, David R., John A. Booth, and Richard J. Harris, eds. *The Politics of San Antonio: Community, Progress, and Power.* Lincoln: University of Nebraska Press, 1983. Essays written to assess changes in San Antonio based on concepts of political community, power, and progress.

Miller, Char, and Heywood T. Sanders, eds. *Urban Texas.* College Station, Tex.: Texas A&M University Press, 1990. Essays provide multiple perspectives on the development of urban Texas.

Norwood, Robert E., and Sabrina Strawn. *Texas County Government: Let the People Choose.* 2nd ed. Austin, Tex.: Texas Research League, 1984. A summary of the structure, powers, and duties of Texas county governments.

Orum, Anthony M. *Power, Money and the People: The Making of Modern Austin.* Austin, Tex.: Texas Monthly Press, 1987. A study of the dramatic growth of Austin, providing reasons for expansion and development, an analysis of political events linked to this period of growth, and an assessment of the "episodic struggles" between the business community and proponents of controlled growth and more inclusive politics.

Perrenod, Virginia Marion. *Special Districts, Special Purposes: Fringe Governments and Urban Problems in the Houston Area.* College Station, Tex.: Texas A&M University Press, 1984. Focuses on Harris County but provides generalizations about the development of special districts, their benefits, and their weaknesses.

Suggested Web Sites

State of Texas www.state.tx.us

This site provides access to Web sites for all counties in Texas as well as the Councils of Government. Select cities have developed Web pages that can also be accessed through this site. Information varies, with some sites providing more comprehensive information than others.

Texas Municipal League www.tml.org

The purpose of this organization is to provide services to Texas cities. In addition to providing links to twenty-two affiliate organizations, this site provides information on the association's publications, programs, and services, including its legislative policy program.

Nelson A. Rockefeller Institute of Government

www.rockinst.org

This institute is located at the State University of New York and is actively involved nationally in research and special projects on the role of state governments in American federalism. In addition to providing a link to other public policy Web sites, this site references numerous studies related to federalism.

Texas Association of Counties www.county.org

This association serves county governments throughout the state. Links to related organizations can be found here, as well as information on recent legislation and laws pertaining to counties, support services, news releases, and educational programs for county officials.

Texas Association of School Boards www.tasb.org

The Texas Association of School Boards serves the 1,000-plus school districts through policy advocacy and support services. This site includes links to many school districts as well as information pertaining to services, programs, and publications.

Texas Association of Regional Councils

www.txregionalcouncil.org

This site provides links to regional councils of governments and provides general information on statewide initiatives in which the councils of government are involved.

Urban Institute www.urban.org

The Urban Institute focuses on a range of social policies. It has developed a multiyear research project entitled, "Assessing the New Federalism."

Federal Web Sites www.fedworld.gov

This site, FEDWORLD.GOV, provides links to major federal agencies whose activities directly impact states and local governments.

GENERAL TIMELINE OF TEXAS

1500s

1520s
Spanish conquests of Texas begin

1600s

1700s

1800s

1821
Mexico wins independence from Spain

1827
Constitution of the state of Coahuila y Tejas

1830
Mexican government bans further American immigration

1834
Santa Ana dismantles federal system, threatening autonomy of Texans

1836
Texans win war of independence and establish the Republic of Texas

1846
Texas annexed by the United States

Start of war with Mexico which ends in 1848 with Treaty of Hildago

1900s

1900s
Progressive reforms of election laws, child labor laws, and business regulations

1920
Women given right to vote

1930s
Great Depression dominates state's politics, producing sharp political divisions

1952
Democratic Governor Allan Shivers leads many conservative Democrats to vote for Republican presidential nominee Dwight D. Eisenhower

1961
Senator John Tower is the first Republican elected to a statewide office in Texas since Reconstruction

1970s
Period of rapid economic expansion

2000s

2002
Republicans win control of all statewide elected offices and both houses of the Texas Legislature

2006
Republicans again win all statewide elected offices

2008
John McCain carries Texas in the presidential election

1685
French attempt to
establish claim to
Texas

1861
Texas secedes from
the Union and joins
the southern
Confederacy

1865
End of Civil War
and the beginning
of Reconstruction

1869
New post-Civil War
constitution adopted
to meet demands of
U.S. government

1875
New constitution
written in reaction
to Radical
Reconstruction

1880s
Populist and Reform
Politics

1890s
Enactment of
Jim Crow Laws

1974
Constitutional
Convention fails to
adopt a new
Constitution

1975
Texas included under
the provisions of the
Voting Rights Act

1978
Bill Clements elected
first Republican
governor since
Reconstruction,
leading the way for the
transformation of the
state's party system

1980s
Early evidence of the
transformation of the
Texas economy from
its heavy dependence
on oil and gas to a
highly diversified
economy

1990s
Accelerated party
realignment to the
Republican Party

Robust economic
growth based on an
increasingly diverse
economy

1993
North American Free
Trade Agreement that
established closer
economic ties to
Mexico

The *Declaration* of Independence

Drafted mainly by Thomas Jefferson, this document, adopted by the Second Continental Congress and signed by John Hancock and fifty-five others, outlined the rights of man and the rights to rebellion and self-government. It declared the independence of the colonies from Great Britain, justified rebellion, and listed the grievances against George III and his government. What is memorable about this famous document is not only that it declared the birth of a new nation, but that it set forth with eloquence our basic philosophy of liberty and representative democracy.

IN CONGRESS, JULY 4, 1776 (The unanimous Declaration of the Thirteen United States of America)

PREAMBLE

When, in the course of human events, it becomes necessary for one people to dissolve the political bands which have connected them with another, and to assume, among the powers of the earth, the separate and equal station to which the laws of nature and of nature's God entitle them, a decent respect to the opinions of mankind requires that they should declare the causes which impel them to the separation.

New Principles of Government

We hold these truths to be self-evident; that all men are created equal, that they are endowed by their Creator with certain unalienable rights, that among these are life, liberty, and the pursuit of happiness.

That, to secure these rights, governments are instituted among men, deriving their just powers from the consent of the governed.

That whenever any form of government becomes destructive of these ends, it is the right of the people to alter or to abolish it, and to institute new government, laying its foundation on such principles, and organizing its powers in such form, as to them shall seem most likely to effect their safety and happiness. Prudence, indeed will dictate that governments long established should not be changed for light and transient causes; and accordingly all experience hath shown that mankind are more disposed to suffer while evils are sufferable, than to right themselves by abolishing the forms to which they are accustomed. But when a long train of abuses and usurpations, pursuing invariably the same object, evinces a design to reduce them under absolute despotism, it is their right, it is their duty, to throw off such government, and to provide new guards for their future security.

Reasons for Separation

Such has been the patient sufferance of these colonies; and such is now the necessity which constrains them to alter their former systems of government. The history of the present king of Great Britain is a history of repeated injuries and usurpations, all having in direct object the establishment of an absolute tyranny over these states. To prove this, let facts be submitted to a candid world.

He has refused his assent to laws, the most wholesome and necessary for the public good.

He has forbidden his governors to pass laws of immediate and pressing importance unless suspended in their operation till his assent should be obtained; and when so suspended, he has utterly neglected to attend to them.

He has refused to pass other laws for the accommodation of large districts of people, unless those people would relinquish the right of representation in the legislature, a right inestimable to them, and formidable to tyrants only.

He has called together legislative bodies at places unusual, uncomfortable, and distant for the depository of their public records, for the sole purpose of fatiguing them into compliance with his measures.

He has dissolved representative houses repeatedly, for opposing, with manly firmness, his invasions on the rights of people.

He has refused, for a long time after such dissolutions, to cause others to be elected; whereby the legislative powers incapable of annihilation, have returned to the people at large for their exercise; the state remaining, in the mean-time, exposed to all the dangers of invasion from without and convulsions within.

He has endeavored to prevent the population of these states; for that purpose obstructing the laws of naturalization of foreigners, refusing to pass others to encourage their migration hither, and raising the conditions of new appropriations of lands.

He has obstructed the administration of justice, by refusing his assent to laws for establishing judiciary powers.

He has made judges dependent on his will alone for the tenure of their offices, and the amount and payment of their salaries.

He has erected a multitude of new offices, and sent hither swarms of officers to harass our people and eat out their substance.

He has kept among us, in times of peace, standing armies, without the consent of our legislature.

He has affected to render the military independent of, and superior to, the civil power.

He has combined with others to subject us to jurisdiction foreign to our constitution and unacknowledged by our laws, giving his assent to their acts of pretended legislation:

For quartering large bodies of armed troops among us;

For protecting them, by a mock trial, from punishment for any murders which they should commit on the inhabitants of these states;

For cutting off our trade with all parts of the world;

For imposing taxes on us without our consent;

For depriving us, in many cases, of the benefits of trial by jury;

For transporting us beyond seas, to be tried for pretended offenses;

For abolishing the free system of English laws in a neighboring province, establishing therein an arbitrary government, and enlarging its boundaries, so as to render it at once an example and fit instrument for introducing the same absolute rule into these colonies;

For taking away our charters, abolishing our most valuable laws, and altering, fundamentally, the forms of our governments;

For suspending our own legislatures, and declaring themselves invented with power to legislate for us in all cases whatsoever.

He has abdicated government here, by declaring us out of his protection and waging war against us.

He has plundered our seas, ravaged our coasts, burned our towns, and destroyed the lives of our people.

He is at this time transporting large armies of foreign mercenaries to complete the works of death, desolation, and tyranny already begun with circumstances of cruelty and perfidy scarcely paralleled in the most barbarous ages and totally unworthy of the head of a civilized nation.

He has constrained our fellow-citizens, taken captive on the high seas, to bear arms against their country, to become the executioners of their friends and brethren, or to fall themselves by their hands.

He has excited domestic insurrections among us, and has endeavored to bring on the inhabitants of our frontiers the merciless Indian savages, whose known rule of warfare is an undistinguished destruction of all ages, sexes, and conditions.

In every stage of these oppressions we have petitioned for redress in the most humble terms; our repeated petitions have been answered only by repeated injury. A prince whose character is thus marked by every act which may define a tyrant is unfit to be the ruler of a free people.

Nor have we been wanting in attention to our British brethren. We have warned them, from time to time, of attempts by their legislature to extend an unwarrantable jurisdiction over us. We have reminded them of the circumstances of our emigration and settlement here. We have appealed to their native justice and magnanimity; and we have conjured them, by the ties of our common kindred, to disavow these usurpations, which would inevitably interrupt our connections and correspondence. They, too, have been deaf to the voice of justice and of consanguinity. We must, therefore, acquiesce in the necessity which denounces our separation, and hold them, as we hold the rest of mankind, enemies in war, in peace, friends.

We, therefore, the representatives of the United States of America, in General Congress assembled, appealing to the Supreme Judge of the world for the rectitude of our intentions, do, in the name and by authority of the good people of these colonies, solemnly publish and declare, that these united colonies are, and of right ought to be, free and independent states; that they are absolved from all allegiance to the British crown, and that all political connection between them and the state of Great Britain is, and ought to be, totally dissolved; and that, as free and independent states, they have full power to levy war, conclude peace, contract alliances, establish commerce, and do all other acts and things which independent states may of a right do. And, for the support of this declaration, with a firm reliance on the protection of Divine Providence, we mutually pledge to each other our lives, our fortunes, and our sacred honor.

The *Federalist, No. 10,*
James Madison

To the People of the State of New York: Among the numerous advantages promised by a well-constructed union, none deserves to be more accurately developed than its tendency to break and control the violence of faction. The friend of popular governments, never finds himself so much alarmed for their character and fate, as when he contemplates their propensity to this dangerous vice. He will not fail, therefore, to set a due value on any plan which, without violating the principles to which he is attached, provides a proper cure for it. The instability, in justice, and confusion introduced into the public councils, have, in truth, been the mortal diseases under which popular governments have everywhere perished; as they continue to be the favourite and fruitful topics from which the adversaries to liberty derive their most specious declamations. The valuable improvements made by the American constitutions on the popular models, both ancient and modern, cannot certainly be too much admired; but it would be an unwarrantable partiality, to contend that they have as effectually obviated the danger on this side, as was wished and expected. Complaints are everywhere heard from our most considerate and virtuous citizens, equally the friends of public and private faith, and of public and personal liberty, that our governments are too unstable; that the public good is disregarded in the conflicts of rival parties; and that measures are too often decided, not according to the rules of justice, and the rights of the minor party, but by the superior force of an interested and over-bearing majority. However anxiously we may wish that these complaints had no foundation, the evidence of known facts will not permit us to deny that they are in some degree true. It will be found, indeed, on a candid review of our situation, that some of the distresses under which we labour have been erroneously charged on the operation of our governments; but it will be found, at the same time, that other causes will not alone account for many of our heaviest misfortunes; and, particularly, for that prevailing and increasing distrust of public engagements, and alarm for private rights, which are echoed from one end of the continent to the other. These must be chiefly, if not wholly, effects of the unsteadiness and injustice, with which a factious spirit has tainted our public administrations.

By a faction, I understand a number of citizens, whether amounting to a majority or minority of the whole, who are united and actuated by some common impulse of passion, or of interest, adverse to the rights of other citizens, or to the permanent and aggregate interests of the community.

There are two methods of curing the mischiefs of faction: the one, by removing its causes; the other, by controlling its effects.

There are again two methods of removing the causes of faction: the one, by destroying the liberty which is essential to its existence; the other, by giving to every citizen the same opinions, the same passions, and the same interests.

It could never be more truly said, than of the first remedy, that it was worse than the disease. Liberty is to faction what air is to fire, an aliment without which it instantly expires. But it could not be a less folly to abolish liberty, which is essential to political life, because it nourishes faction, than it would be to wish the annihilation of air, which is essential to animal life, because it imparts to fire its destructive agency.

The second expedient is as impracticable, as the first would be unwise. As long as the reason of man continues fallible, and he is at liberty to exercise it, different opinions will be formed. As long as the connection subsists between his reason and his self-love, his opinions and his passions will have a reciprocal influence on each other; and the former will be objects to which the latter will attach themselves. The diversity in the faculties of men, from which the rights of property originate, is not less an insuperable obstacle to an uniformity of interests. The protection of these faculties is the first object of government. From the protection of different and unequal faculties of acquiring property, the possession of different degrees and kinds of property immediately results; and from the influence of these on the sentiments and views of the respective proprietors, ensues a division of the society into different interests and parties.

The latent causes of faction are thus sown in the nature of man; and we see them everywhere brought into different degrees of activity, according to the different circumstances of civil society. A zeal for different opinions concerning religion, concerning government, and many other points, as well of speculation as of practice; an attachment to different leaders ambitiously contending for preeminence and power; or to persons of other descriptions whose fortunes have been interesting to the human passions, have, in turn, divided mankind into parties, inflamed them with mutual animosity, and rendered them much more disposed to vex and oppress each other, than to cooperate for their common good. So strong is this propensity of mankind, to fall into mutual animosities, that where no substantial occasion presents itself, the most frivolous and fanciful distinctions have been sufficient to kindle their unfriendly passions and excite their most violent conflicts. But the most common and durable source of factions, has been the various and unequal distribution of property. Those who hold, and those who are without property, have ever formed distinct interests in society. Those who are creditors, and those who are debtors, fall under a like discrimination. A landed interest, a manufacturing interest, a mercantile interest, a moneyed interest, with many lesser interests, grow up of necessity in civilized nations, and divide them into different classes, actuated by different sentiments and views. The regulation of these various and interfering interests forms the principal task of modern legislation, and involves the spirit of the party and faction in the necessary and ordinary operations of the government.

No man is allowed to be a judge in his own cause; because his interest will certainly bias his judgment, and, not improbably, corrupt his integrity. With equal, nay, with greater reason, a body of men are unfit to be both judges and parties at the same time; yet what are many of the most important acts of legislation, but so many judicial determinations, not indeed concerning the right of single persons, but concerning the rights of large bodies of citizens? And what are the different classes of legislators, but advocates and parties to the causes which they determine? Is a law proposed concerning private debts? It is a question to which the creditors are parties on one side, and the debtors on the other. Justice ought to hold the balance between them. Yet the parties are, and must be, themselves the judges; and the most numerous party, or, in other words, the most powerful faction, must be expected to prevail. Shall domestic manufacturers be encouraged, and in what degree, by restrictions on foreign manufacturers are questions which would be differently decided by the landed and the manufacturing classes; and probably by neither with a sole regard to justice and the public good. The apportionment of taxes, on the various descriptions of property, is an act which seems to require the most exact impartiality; yet there is, perhaps, no legislative act, in which greater opportunity and temptation are given to a predominant party to trample on the rules of justice. Every shilling, with which they overburden the inferior number, is a shilling saved to their own pockets.

It is in vain to say, that enlightened statesmen will be able to adjust these clashing interests, and render them all subservient to the public good. Enlightened statesmen will not always be at the helm; nor, in many cases, can such an adjustment be made at all, without taking into view indirect and remote considerations, which will rarely prevail over the immediate interest which one party may find in disregarding the rights of another, or the good of the whole.

The inference to which we are brought is, that the *causes* of faction cannot be removed; and that relief is only to be sought in the means of controlling its *effects*.

If a faction consists of less than a majority, relief is supplied by the republican principle, which enables the majority to defeat its sinister views, by regular vote. It may clog the administration, it may convulse the society; but it will be unable to execute and mask its violence under the forms of the Constitution. When a majority is included in a faction, the form of popular government, on the other hand, enables it to sacrifice to its ruling passion or interest, both the public good and the rights of other citizens. To secure the public good, and private rights, against the danger of such a fac-

tion, and at the same time to preserve the spirit and the form of popular government, is then the great object to which our inquiries are directed. Let me add, that it is the great desideratum, by which alone this form of government can be rescued from the opprobrium under which it has so long laboured, and be recommended to the esteem and adoption of mankind.

By what means is this object attainable? Evidently by one of two only. Either the existence of the same passion or interest in a majority, at the same time, must be prevented; or the majority, having such coexistent passion or interest, must be rendered, by their number and local situation, unable to concert and carry into effect schemes of oppression. If the impulse and the opportunity be suffered to coincide, we well know that neither moral nor religious motives can be relied on as an adequate control. They are not found to be such on the injustice and violence of individuals, and lose their efficacy in proportion to the number combined together; that is, in proportion as their efficacy becomes needful.

From this view of the subject, it may be concluded, that a pure democracy, by which I mean a society consisting of a small number of citizens, who assemble and administer the government in person, can admit of no cure for the mischiefs of faction. A common passion or interest will, in almost every case, be felt by a majority of the whole; a communication and concert, results from the form of government itself; and there is nothing to check the inducements to sacrifice the weaker party, or an obnoxious individual. Hence, it is, that such democracies have ever been spectacles of turbulence and contention; have ever been found incompatible with personal security, or the rights of property; and have in general been as short in their lives, as they have been violent in their deaths. Theoretic politicians, who have patronized this species of government, have erroneously supposed, that by reducing mankind to a perfect equality in their political rights, they would, at the same time, be perfectly equalized and assimilated in their pos-

sessions, their opinions, and their passions.

A republic, by which I mean a government in which the scheme of representation takes place, opens a different prospect, and promises the cure for which we are seeking. Let us examine the points in which it varies from pure democracy, and we shall comprehend both the nature of the cure and the efficacy which it must derive from the union.

The two great points of difference, between a democracy and a republic, are, first, the delegation of the government, in the latter, to a small number of citizens, elected by the rest; secondly, the greater number of citizens, and greater sphere of country, over which the latter may be extended.

The effect of the first difference is, on the one hand, to refine and enlarge the public views, by passing them through the medium of a chosen body of citizens, whose wisdom may best discern the true interest of their country, and whose patriotism and love of justice, will be least likely to sacrifice it to temporary or partial considerations. Under such a regulation, it may well happen, that the public voice, pronounced by the representatives of the people, will be more consonant to the public good, than if pronounced by the people themselves, convened for the purpose. On the other hand the effect may be inverted. Men of factious tempers, of local prejudices, or of sinister designs, may by intrigue, by corruption, or by other means, first obtain the suffrages, and then betray the interest of the people. The question resulting is, whether small or extensive republics are most favourable to the election of proper guardians of the public weal; and it is clearly decided in favour of the latter by two obvious considerations.

In the first place, it is to be remarked that, however small the republic may be, the representatives must be raised to a certain number, in order to guard against the cabals of a few; and that however large it may be, they must be limited to a certain number, in order to guard against the confusion of a multitude. Hence, the number of representatives in the two cases not being in proportion to that of the constituents, and being proportionally greatest in the small republic, it follows, that if the proportion of fit characters be not less in the large than in the small republic, the former will present a greater option, and consequently a greater probability of a fit choice.

In the next place, as each representative will be chosen by a greater number of citizens in the large than in the small republic, it will be more difficult for unworthy candidates to practice with success the vicious arts, by which elections are too often carried; and the suffrages of the people being more free, will be more likely to centre in men who possess the most attractive merit, and the most diffusive and established characters.

It must be confessed, that in this, as in most other cases, there is a mean, on both sides of which inconveniences will be found to lie. By enlarging too much the number of electors, you render the representatives too little acquainted with all their local circumstances and lesser interests; as by reducing it too much, you render him unduly attached to these, and too little fit to comprehend and pursue great and national objects. The federal constitution forms a happy combination in this respect; the great and aggregate interests being referred to the national, the local and particular to the state legislatures.

The other point of difference is, the greater number of citizens, and extent of territory, which may be brought within the compass of republican, than of democratic government; and it is this circumstance principally which renders factious combinations less to be dreaded in the former, than in the latter. The smaller the society, the fewer probably will be the distinct parties and interests composing it; the fewer the distinct parties and interests, the more frequently will a majority be found of the same party; and the smaller the number of individuals composing a majority, and the smaller the compass within which they are placed, the more easily will they concert and execute their plans of oppression. Extend the sphere, and you take in a greater variety of parties and interests; you make it less probable that a majority of the whole will have a common motive to invade the rights of other citizens; or if such a common motive exists, it will be more difficult for all who feel it to discover their own strength, and to act in unison with each other. Besides other impediments, it may be remarked, that where there is a consciousness of unjust or dishonourable purposes, communication is always checked by distrust, in proportion to the number whose concurrence is necessary.

Hence, it clearly appears, that the same advantage, which a republic has over a democracy, in controlling the effects of faction, is enjoyed by a large over a small republic—is enjoyed by the union over the states composing it. Does this advantage consist in the substitution of representatives, whose enlightened views and virtuous sentiments render them superior to local prejudices, and to schemes of injustice? It will not be denied that the representation of the union will be most likely to possess these requisite endowments. Does it consist in the greater security afforded by a greater variety of parties, against the event of any one party being able to outnumber and oppress the rest? In an equal degree does the increased variety of parties, comprised within the union, increase the security? Does it, in fine, consist in the greater obstacles opposed to the concert and accomplishment of the secret wishes of an unjust and interested majority? Here, again, the extent of the union gives it the most palpable advantage.

The influence of factious leaders may kindle a flame within their particular states, but will be unable to spread a general conflagration through the other states; a religious sect may degenerate into a political faction in a part of the confederacy; but the variety of sects dispersed over the entire face of it, must secure the national councils against any danger from that source; a rage for paper money, for an abolition of debts, for an equal division of property, or for any other improper or wicked project, will be less apt to pervade the whole body of the union than a particular member of it; in the same proportion as such a malady is more likely to taint a particular county or district, than an entire state.

In the extent and proper structure of the union, therefore, we behold a republican remedy for the diseases most incident to republican government. And according to the degree of pleasure and pride we feel in being republicans, ought to be our zeal in cherishing the spirit, and supporting the character of federalists.

The *Federalist, No. 51,* James Madison

To what expedient, then, shall we finally resort, for maintaining in practice the necessary partition of power among the several departments as laid down in the Constitution? The only answer that can be given is that as all these exterior provisions are found to be inadequate the defect must be supplied, by so contriving the interior structure of the government as that its several constituent parts may, by their mutual relations, be the means of keeping each other in their proper places. Without presuming to undertake a full development of this important idea I will hazard a few general observations which may perhaps place it in a clearer light, and enable us to form a more correct judgment of the principles and structure of the government planned by the convention.

In order to lay a due foundation for that separate and distinct exercise of the different powers of government, which to a certain extent is admitted on all hands to be essential to the preservation of liberty, it is evident that each department should have a will of its own; and consequently should be so constituted that the members of each should have as little agency as possible in the appointment of the members of the others. Were this principle rigorously adhered to, it would require that all the appointments for the supreme executive, legislative, and judiciary magistracies should be drawn from the same fountain of authority, the people, through channels having no communication whatever with one another. Perhaps such a plan of constructing the several departments would be less difficult in practice than it may in contemplation appear. Some difficulties, however, and some additional expense would attend the execution of it. Some deviations, therefore, from the principle must be admitted. In the constitution of the judiciary department in particular, it might be inexpedient to insist rigorously on the principle: first, because peculiar qualifications being essential in the members, the primary consideration ought to be to select that mode of choice which best secures these qualifications; second, because the permanent tenure by which the appointments are held in that department must soon destroy all sense of dependence on the authority conferring them.

It is equally evident that the members of each department should be as little dependent as possible on those of the others for the emoluments annexed to their offices. Were the executive magistrate, or the judges, not independent of the legislature in this particular, their independence in every other would be merely nominal.

But the great security against a gradual concentration of the several powers in the same department consists in giving to those who administer each department the necessary constitutional means and personal motives to resist encroachments of the others. The provision for defense must in this, as in all other cases, be made commensurate to the danger of attack. Ambition must be made to counteract ambition. The interest of the man must be connected with the constitutional rights of the place. It may be a reflection on human nature that such devices should be necessary to control the abuses of government. But what is government itself but the greatest of all reflections on human nature? If men were angels, no government would be necessary. If angels were to govern men, neither external nor internal controls on government would be necessary. In framing a government which is to be administered by men over men, the great difficulty lies in this: you must first enable the government to control the governed; and in the next place oblige it to control itself. A dependence on the people is, no doubt, the primary control on the government; but experience has taught mankind the necessity of auxiliary precautions.

This policy of supplying, by opposite and rival interests, the defect of better motives, might be traced through the whole system of human affairs, private as well as public. We see it particularly displayed in all the subordinate distributions of power, where the constant aim is to divide and arrange the several offices in such a manner as that each may be a check on the other—that the private interest of every individual may be a sentinel over the public rights. These inventions of prudence cannot be less requisite in the distribution of the supreme powers of the State.

But it is not possible to give to each department an equal power of self-defense. In republican government, the legislative authority necessarily predominates. The remedy for this inconveniency is to divide the legislature into different branches; and to render them, by modes of election and different principles of action, as little connected with each other as the nature of their common functions and their common dependence on the society will admit. It may even be necessary to guard against dangerous encroachments by still further precautions. As the weight of the legislative authority requires that it should be thus divided, the weakness of the executive may require, on the other hand, that it should be fortified. An absolute negative on the legislature appears, at first view, to be the natural defense with which the executive magistrate should be armed. But perhaps it would be neither altogether safe nor alone sufficient. On ordinary occasions it might not be exerted with the requisite firmness, and on extraordinary occasions it might be perfidiously abused. May not this defect of an absolute negative be supplied by some qualified connection between this weaker de partment and the weaker branch of the stronger department, by which the latter may be led to support the constitutional rights of the former, without being too much detached from the rights of its own department?

If the principles on which these observations are founded be just, as I persuade myself they are, and they be applied as a criterion to the several State constitutions, and to the federal Constitution, it will be found that if the latter does not perfectly correspond with them, the former are infinitely less able to bear such a test.

There are, moreover, two considerations particularly applicable to the federal system of America, which place that system in a very interesting point of view.

First. In a single republic, all the power surrendered by the people is submitted to the administration of a single government; and the usurpations are guarded against by a division of the government into distinct and separate departments. In the compound republic of America, the power surrendered by the people is first divided between two distinct governments, and then the portion allotted to each subdivided among distinct and separate departments. Hence a double security arises to the rights of the people. The different governments will control each other, at the same time that each will be controlled by itself.

Second. It is of great importance in a republic not only to guard the society against the oppression of its rulers, but to guard one part of the society against the injustice of the other part. Different interests necessarily exist in different classes of citizens. If a majority be united by a common interest, the rights of the minority will be insecure. There are but two methods of providing against this evil: the one by creating a will in the community independent of the majority—that is, of the society itself; the other, by comprehending in the society so many separate descriptions of citizens as will render an unjust combination of a majority of the whole very improbable, if not impracticable. The first method prevails in all governments possessing an hereditary or self-appointed authority. This, at best, is but a precarious security; because a power independent of the society may as well espouse the unjust views of the major as the rightful interests of the minor party, and may possibly be turned against both parties. The second method will be exemplified in the federal republic of the United States. Whilst all authority in it will be derived from and dependent on the society, the society itself will be broken into so many parts, interests and classes of citizens, that the rights of individuals, or of the minority, will be in little danger from interested combinations of the majority. In a free government the security for civil rights must be the same as that for religious rights. It consists in the one case in the multiplicity of interests, and in the other in the multiplicity of sects. The degree of security in both cases will depend on the number of interests and sects; and this may be presumed to depend on the extent of country and number of people comprehended under the same government. This view of the subject must particularly recommend a proper federal system to all the sincere and considerate friends of republican government, since it shows that in exact proportion as the territory of the Union may be formed into more circumscribed Confederacies, or States, oppressive combinations of a majority will be facilitated; the best security, under the republican forms, for the rights of every class of citizen, will be diminished; and consequently the stability and independence of some member of the government, the only other security, must be proportionally increased. Justice is the end of government. It is the end of civil society. It ever has been and ever will be pursued until it be obtained, or until liberty be lost in the pursuit. In a society under the forms of which the stronger faction can readily unite and oppress the weaker, anarchy may as truly be said to reign as in a state of nature, where the weaker individual is not secured against the violence of the stronger; and as, in the latter state, even the stronger individuals are prompted, by the uncertainty of their condition, to submit to a government which may protect the weak as well as themselves; so, in the former state, will the more powerful factions or parties be gradually induced, by a like motive, to wish for a government which will protect all parties, the weaker as well as the more powerful. It can be little doubted that if the State of Rhode Island was separated from the Confederacy and left to itself, the insecurity of rights under the popular form of government within such narrow limits would be displayed by such reiterated oppressions of factious majorities that some power altogether independent of the people would soon be called for by the voice of the very factions whose misrule had proved the necessity of it. In the extended republic of the United States, and among the great variety of interests, parties, and sects which it embraces, a coalition of a majority of the whole society could seldom take place on any other principles than those of justice and the general good; whilst there being thus less danger to a minor from the will of a major party, there must be less pretext, also, to provide for the security of the former, by introducing into the government a will not dependent on the latter, or, in other words, a will independent of the society itself. It is no less certain that it is important, notwithstanding the contrary opinions which have been entertained that the larger the society, provided it lie within a practicable sphere, the more duly capable it will be of self-government. And happily for the *republican cause*, the practicable sphere may be carried to a very great extent by a judicious modification and mixture of the *federal principle*.

PRESIDENTS AND VICE PRESIDENTS

1. George Washington (1789)
   John Adams (1789)

2. John Adams (1797)
   Thomas Jefferson (1797)

3. Thomas Jefferson (1801)
   Aaron Burr (1801)
   George Clinton (1805)

4. James Madison (1809)
   George Clinton (1809)
   Elbridge Gerry (1813)

5. James Monroe (1817)
   Daniel D. Tompkins (1817)

6. John Quincy Adams (1825)
   John C. Calhoun (1825)

7. Andrew Jackson (1829)
   John C. Calhoun (1829)
   Martin Van Buren (1833)

8. Martin Van Buren (1837)
   Richard M. Johnson (1837)

9. William H. Harrison (1841)
   John Tyler (1841)

10. John Tyler (1841)

11. James K. Polk (1845)
    George M. Dallas (1845)

12. Zachary Taylor (1849)
    Millard Fillmore (1849)

13. Millard Fillmore (1850)

14. Franklin Pierce (1853)
    William R. King (1853)

15. James Buchanan (1857)
    John C. Breckinridge (1857)

16. Abraham Lincoln (1861)
    Hannibal Hamlin (1861)
    Andrew Johnson (1865)

17. Andrew Johnson (1865)

18. Ulysses S. Grant (1869)
    Schuyler Colfax (1869)
    Henry Wilson (1873)

19. Rutherford B. Hayes (1877)
    William A. Wheeler (1877)

20. James A. Garfield (1881)
    Chester A. Arthur (1881)

21. Chester A. Arthur (1881)

22. Grover Cleveland (1885)
    T.A. Hendricks (1885)

23. Benjamin Harrison (1889)
    Levi P. Morton (1889)

24. Grover Cleveland (1893)
    Adlai E. Stevenson (1893)

25. William McKinley (1897)
    Garret A. Hobart (1897)
    Theodore Roosevelt (1901)

26. Theodore Roosevelt (1901)
    Charles Fairbanks (1905)

27. William H. Taft (1909)
    James S. Sherman (1909)

28. Woodrow Wilson (1913)
    Thomas R. Marshall (1913)

29. Warren G. Harding (1921)
    Calvin Coolidge (1921)

30. Calvin Coolidge (1923)
    Charles G. Dawes (1925)

31. Herbert C. Hoover (1929)
    Charles Curtis (1929)

32. Franklin D. Roosevelt (1933)
    John Nance Garner (1933)
    Henry A. Wallace (1941)
    Harry S Truman (1945)

33. Harry S Truman (1945)
    Alben W. Barkley (1949)

34. Dwight D. Eisenhower (1953)
    Richard M. Nixon (1953)

35. John F. Kennedy (1961)
    Lyndon B. Johnson (1961)

36. Lyndon B. Johnson (1963)
    Hubert H. Humphrey (1965)

37. Richard M. Nixon (1969)
    Spiro T. Agnew (1969)
    Gerald R. Ford (1973)

38. Gerald R. Ford (1974)
    Nelson A. Rockefeller (1974)

39. James E. Carter Jr. (1977)
    Walter F. Mondale (1977)

40. Ronald W. Reagan (1981)
    George H.W. Bush (1981)

41. George H.W. Bush (1989)
    James D. Quayle III (1989)

42. William J.B. Clinton (1993)
    Albert Gore (1993)

43. George W. Bush (2001)
    Richard Cheney (2001)

44. Barack H. Obama (2009)
    Joseph R. Biden (2009)

Glossary

ABM Treaty Treaty in 1972 between the U.S. and the Soviet Union in which each side agreed not to build or deploy antiballistic missiles.

abolition movement Social movement before the Civil War whose goal was to abolish slavery throughout the United States.

absentee (or early) voting Period before the regularly scheduled election date, during which voters are allowed to cast ballots. With recent changes in election law, a person does not have to offer a reason for voting absentee.

access Meeting and talking with decision makers, a prerequisite to direct persuasion.

adjudication Decision making by the federal bureaucracy as to whether or not an individual or organization has complied with or violated government laws and/or regulation.

adversarial system Method of decision making in which an impartial judge or jury or decision maker hears arguments and reviews evidence presented by opposite sides.

advice and consent The constitutional power of the U.S. Senate to reject or ratify (by a two-thirds vote) treaties made by the president.

affirmative action Any program, whether enacted by a government or by a private organization, whose goal is to overcome the results of past unequal treatment of minorities and/or women by giving members of these groups preferential treatment in admissions, hiring, promotions, or other aspects of life.

affirmative racial gerrymandering Drawing district boundary lines to maximize minority representation.

agenda setting Deciding what will be decided, defining the problems and issues to be addressed by decision makers.

amendment Formal change in a bill, law, or constitution.

amicus curiae Literally, "friend of the court"; a person, private group or institution, or government agency that is not a party to a case but participates in the case (usually through submission of a brief) at the invitation of the court or on its own initiative.

amnesty Government forgiveness of a crime, usually granted to a group of people.

Annapolis Convention A 1786 meeting at Annapolis, Maryland, to discuss interstate commerce, that recommended a larger convention—the Constitutional Convention of 1787.

annexation powers Authority of cities to add territory, subject to restrictions set by state law.

Anti-Federalists Those who opposed the ratification of the U.S. Constitution and the creation of a strong national government.

appeal In general, requests that a higher court review cases decided at a lower level. In the Supreme Court, certain cases are designated as appeals under federal law; formally, these must be heard by the Court.

appellate jurisdiction Particular court's power to review a decision or action of a lower court.

apportionment The allocation of legislative seats to jurisdictions based on population. Seats in the U.S. House of Representatives are apportioned to the states on the basis of their population after every ten-year census.

appraisal district Local agency that determines the value of pieces of property in a county. All local governments are required to use its evaluations, or appraisals, for tax purposes.

appropriations act Congressional bill that provides money for programs authorized by Congress.

appropriations bill Bill that authorizes the expenditure of money for a public program or purpose. In Texas, the general appropriations bill approved by the legislature every two years is the state budget.

at-large district Legislative or other political district, sometimes called a multimember district because two or more officials are elected from it, that includes an entire county, city, or other political subdivision.

at-large elections Election systems under which officeholders are elected by voters in the entire city, school district, or single-purpose district.

authoritarianism Monopoly of political power by an individual or small group that otherwise allows people to go about their private lives as they wish.

authorization Act of Congress that establishes a government program and defines the amount of money it may spend.

backdoor spending Spending by agencies of the federal government whose operations are not included in the federal budget.

bail Release of an accused person from custody in exchange for promise to appear at trial, guaranteed by money or property that is forfeited to court if defendant does not appear.

***Bakke* case** U.S. Supreme Court case challenging affirmative action.

balanced budget Government budget in which expenditures and revenues are equal, so that no deficit or surplus exists.

ballistic missile defense (BMD) Weapons systems capable of detecting, intercepting, and destroying missiles in flight.

beliefs Shared ideas about what is true.

bicameral Any legislative body that consists of two separate chambers or houses; in the United States, the Senate represents 50 statewide voter constituencies, and the House of Representatives represents voters in 435 separate districts.

bicameral legislature Lawmaking body, such as the Texas legislature, that includes two chambers.

bifactionalism Presence of two dominant factions organized around regional, economic, or ideological differences within a single political party. For much of the twentieth century, Texas functioned as a one-party system with two dominant factions.

bifurcated court system Existence of two courts at the highest level of the state judiciary. The Texas Supreme Court is the court of last resort in civil cases, and the Texas Court of Criminal Appeals has the final authority to review criminal cases.

big-state strategy Presidential political campaign strategy in which a candidate focuses on winning primaries in large states because of their high delegate counts.

bill of attainder Legislative act inflicting punishment without judicial trial; forbidden under Article I of the Constitution.

Bill of Rights Written guarantees of basic individual liberties; the first ten amendments to the U.S. Constitution.

bipartisanship Agreement by members of both the Democratic and the Republican parties.

bloc Group of legislators who act together for a common goal regardless of party affiliation.

block grant A federal grant to state or local governments for a general governmental function, allowing greater flexibility in the use of the money.

bribery Giving or offering anything of value in an effort to influence government officials in the performance of their duties.

briefs Documents submitted by an attorney to a court, setting out the facts of the case and the legal arguments in support of the party represented by the attorney.

budget maximization Bureaucrats' tendencies to expand their agencies' budgets, staff, and authority.

budget resolution Congressional bill setting forth target budget figures for appropriations to various government departments and agencies.

bureaucracy Departments, agencies, bureaus, and offices that perform the functions of government.

cabinet The heads (secretaries) of the executive departments together with other top officials accorded cabinet rank by the president; only occasionally does it meet as a body to advise and support the president.

calendar Agenda or the list of bills to be considered by the House or the Senate on a given day.

Calendars Committee Special procedural committee that schedules bills that already have been approved by other committees for floor debate in the House.

campaign strategy Plan for a political campaign, usually including a theme, an attempt to define the opponent or the issues, and an effort to coordinate images and messages in news broadcasts and paid advertising.

capital gains Profits from buying and selling property including stocks, bonds, and real estate.

capital murder Murder committed under certain circumstances for which the death penalty or life in prison must be imposed.

capitalism Economic system asserting the individual's right to own private property and to buy, sell, rent, and trade that property in a free market.

capture theory of regulation Theory describing how some regulated industries come to benefit from government regulation and how some regulatory commissions come to represent the industries they are supposed to regulate rather than representing "the people."

careerism In politics, a reference to people who started young working in politics, running for and holding public office, and made politics their career.

casework Services performed by legislators or their staff on behalf of individual constituents.

categorical grant A federal grant to a state or local government for a specific purpose or project; it may be allocated by a formula or by project.

caucus Nominating process in which party leaders select the party's nominee.

censure Public reprimand for wrongdoing, given to a member standing in the chamber before Congress.

centralized federalism Model of federalism in which the national government assumes primary responsibility for determining national goals in all major policy areas and directs state and local government activity through conditions attached to money grants.

chain of command Hierarchical structure of authority in which command flows downward; typical of a bureaucracy.

challengers In politics, a reference to people running against incumbent officeholders.

charter Document, based on state authorization, which defines the structure, powers, and responsibilities of a city government.

checks and balances Constitutional provisions giving each branch of the national government certain checks over the actions of other branches.

circuit courts The twelve appellate courts that make up the middle level of the federal court system.

city commission Form of city government in which elected commissioners collectively serve as a city's policy-making body and individually serve as administrative heads of different city departments.

civil cases Noncriminal court proceedings in which a plaintiff sues a defendant for damages in payment for harm inflicted.

civil disobedience Form of public protest involving the breaking of laws believed to be unjust.

civil lawsuit Noncriminal legal dispute between two or more individuals, businesses, governments, or other entities.

civil service system System under which public employees are hired and promoted on their abilities. It features competitive examinations and offers job security from one election to another.

class action suits Cases initiated by parties acting on behalf of themselves and all others similarly situated.

class conflict Conflict between upper and lower social classes over wealth and power.

class consciousness Awareness of one's class position and a feeling of political solidarity with others within the same class in opposition to other classes.

classical liberalism Political philosophy asserting the worth and dignity of the individual and emphasizing the rational ability of human beings to determine their own destinies.

clear and present danger doctrine Standard used by the courts to determine whether speech may be restricted; only speech that creates a serious and immediate danger to society may be restricted.

closed primaries Primary elections in which voters must declare (or have previously declared) their party affiliation and can cast a ballot only in their own party's primary election.

closed rule Rule that forbids adding any amendments to a bill under consideration by the House.

cloture Vote to end debate—that is, to end a filibuster—which requires a three-fifths vote of the entire membership of the Senate.

coalition A joining together of interest groups (or individuals) to achieve a common goal.

COLAs Annual cost-of-living adjustments mandated by law in Social Security and other welfare benefits.

Cold War Political, military, and ideological struggle between the United States and the Soviet Union following the end of World War II and ending with the collapse of the Soviet Union's communist government in 1991.

collective security Attempt to bring order to international relations by all nations joining together to guarantee each other's "territorial integrity" and "independence" against "external aggression."

commercial speech Advertising communications given only partial protection under the First Amendment to the Constitution.

commissioners court Principal policy-making body for county government. It sets the county tax rate and supervises expenditures.

committee In the legislature, a group of lawmakers who review and hold public hearings on issues or bills they are assigned by the presiding officer. Committees that specialize in bills by subject matter are designated as standing committees. A bill has to win committee approval before it can be considered by the full House or Senate. Most bills die in committees, which perform as a legislative screening process.

common market Unified trade area in which all goods and services can be sold or exchanged free from customs or tariffs.

communism System of government in which a single totalitarian party controls all means of production and distribution of goods and services.

comparable worth Argument that pay levels for traditionally male and traditionally female jobs should be equalized by paying equally all jobs that are "worth about the same" to an employer.

concurrent powers Powers exercised by both the national government and state governments in the American federal system.

concurring opinion Opinion by a member of a court that agrees with the result reached by the court in the case but disagrees with or departs from the court's rationale for the decision.

confederacy National government created by states that relies on the states for its authority.

confederation Constitutional arrangement whereby the national government is created by and relies on subnational governments for its authority.

conference committee Meeting between representatives of the House and Senate to reconcile differences over provisions of a bill passed by both houses.

confirmation The constitutionally required consent of the Senate to appointments of high-level executive officials by the president and appointments of federal judges.

congressional hearings Congressional committee sessions in which members listen to witnesses who provide information and opinions on matters of interest to the committee, including pending legislation.

congressional investigation Congressional committee hearings on alleged misdeeds or scandals.

congressional session Each Congress elected in November of even-numbered years meets the following January 3 and remains in session for two years. Since the first Congress to meet under the Constitution in 1789, Congresses have been numbered by session (for example, 107th Congress 2001–2003, 108th Congress 2003–2005, 109th Congress 2005–2007).

Connecticut Compromise A constitutional plan that merged elements of a Virginia plan and a New Jersey plan into the present arrangement of the U.S. Congress: one house in which each state has an equal number of votes (the Senate) and one house in which states' votes are based on population (the House of Representatives).

conservatism Belief in the value of free markets, limited government, and individual self-reliance in economic affairs, combined with a belief in the value of tradition, law, and morality in social affairs.

constable Elected law enforcement officer who is primarily responsible for executing court judgments, serving subpoenas, and delivering other legal documents.

constituency The votes in a legislator's home district.

constitution The legal structure of a political system, establishing governmental bodies, granting their powers, determining how their members are selected, and prescribing the rules by which they make their decisions. Considered basic or fundamental, a constitution cannot be changed by ordinary acts of governmental bodies.

constitutional government Government limited by rule of law in its power over the liberties of individuals.

constitutionalism A government of laws, not people, operating on the principle that governmental power must be limited and government officials should be restrained in their exercise of power over individuals.

containment Policy of preventing an enemy from expanding its boundaries and/or influence, specifically the U.S. foreign policy vis-à-vis the Soviet Union during the Cold War.

contempt In law, willful disobedience to, or open disrespect of, a court or congressional body.

contingency fees Fees paid to attorneys to represent the plaintiff in a civil suit and receive in compensation an agreed-upon percentage of damages awarded (if any).

continuing resolution Congressional bill that authorizes government agencies to keep spending money for a specified period at the same level as in the previous fiscal year; passed when Congress is unable to enact final appropriations measures by October 1.

convention Nominating process in which delegates from local party organizations select the party's nominees.

cooperative federalism Model of federalism in which national, state, and local governments work together exercising common policy responsibilities.

council of government (COG) Council comprised of representatives of other governments in a defined region of the state.

council-manager Form of city government in which policy is set by an elected city council, which hires a professional city manager to head the daily administration of city government.

county attorney Elected official who is the chief legal officer of some counties. He or she also prosecutes lesser criminal offenses, primarily misdemeanors, in county courts.

county auditor Appointed officer who is primarily responsible for reviewing every bill and expenditure of a county to assure it is correct and legal.

county chair Presiding officer of a political party's county executive committee. He or she is elected countywide by voters in the party primary.

county clerk Chief record-keeping officer of a county.

county executive committee Panel responsible on the local level for the organization and management of a political party's primary election. It includes the party's county chair and each precinct chair.

county judge Presiding officer of a county commissioners court. This office also has some judicial authority, which is assumed by separate county courts-at-law in most urban counties.

county treasurer Elected officer who is responsible for receiving and disbursing county funds.

court of appeals Intermediate-level court that reviews civil and criminal cases from the district courts.

covert action Secret intelligence activity outside U.S. borders undertaken with specific authorization by the president; acknowledgment of U.S. sponsorship would defeat or compromise its purpose.

Cuban Missile Crisis The 1962 confrontation between the Soviet Union and the U.S. over Soviet placement of nuclear missiles in Cuba.

de facto segregation Racial imbalances not directly caused by official actions but rather by residential patterns.

de novo In a civil lawsuit or criminal trial, evidence is presented again before an appellate court because no record was kept of the evidence presented to the trial court.

dealignment Declining attractiveness of the parties to the voters, a reluctance to identify strongly with a party, and a decrease in reliance on party affiliation in voter choice.

deductibles Initial charges in insurance plans, paid by beneficiaries.

defendants Parties against whom a criminal or civil suit is brought.

deferrals Items on which a president wishes to postpone spending.

deficit Imbalance in the annual federal budget in which spending exceeds revenues.

delegated, or enumerated, powers Powers specifically mentioned in the Constitution as belonging to the national government.

delegates Accredited voting members of a party's national presidential nominating convention.

democracy Governing system in which the people govern themselves, from the Greek term meaning "rule by the many."

democratic ideals Individual dignity, equality before the law, widespread participation in public decisions, and public decisions by majority rule, with one person having one vote.

Democratic Leadership Council Organization of party leaders who sought to create a "new" Democratic Party to appeal to middle-class, moderate voters.

Democratic Party One of the main parties in American politics; it traces its origins to Thomas Jefferson's Democratic-Republican Party, acquiring its current name under Andrew Jackson in 1828.

dependency ratio In the Social Security system, the number of recipients as a percentage of the number of contributing workers.

deregulation Lifting of government rules and bureaucratic supervision from business and professional activity.

deterrence U.S. approach to deterring any nuclear attack from the Soviet Union by maintaining a second-strike capability.

devolution Passing down of responsibilities from the national government to the states.

diplomatic recognition Power of the president to grant "legitimacy" to or withhold it from a government of another nation (to declare or refuse to declare it "rightful").

direct democracy Decisions are made directly by the people usually by popular initiative and referendum voting, as opposed to decisions made by elected representatives.

direct discrimination Now-illegal practice of differential pay for men versus women even when those individuals have equal qualifications and perform the same job.

discharge petition Petition signed by at least 218 House members to force a vote on a bill within a committee that opposes it.

discretionary funds Budgeted funds not earmarked for specific purposes but available to be spent in accordance with the best judgment of a bureaucrat.

discretionary spending Spending for programs not previously mandated by law.

dissenting opinion Opinion by a member of a court that disagrees with the result reached by the court in the case.

district attorney Elected official who prosecutes more serious criminal offenses, usually felonies, before state district courts.

district clerk Elected county official who maintains custody of state district court records.

district court Primary trial court in Texas. It has jurisdiction over criminal felony cases and civil disputes.

diversity Term in higher education that refers to racial and ethnic representation among students and faculty.

divided party government One party controls the presidency while the other party controls one or both houses of Congress.

division of labor Division of work among many specialized workers in a bureaucracy.

division votes Votes taken on the computerized voting boards in the Texas House but erased without being permanently recorded.

drafting a bill Actual writing of a bill in legal language.

dual federalism Early concept of federalism in which national and state powers were clearly distinguished and functionally separate.

Earned Income Tax Credit (EITC) Tax refunds in excess of tax payments for low-income workers.

economic cycles Fluctuations in real GDP growth followed by contraction.

economic diversification Development of new and varied business activities. New businesses were encouraged to relocate or expand in Texas after the oil and gas industry, which had been the base of the state's economy, suffered a major recession in the 1980s.

Electoral College The 538 presidential electors apportioned among the states according to their congressional representation (plus 3 for the District of Columbia) whose votes officially elect the president and vice president of the United States.

elite Small group of people who exercise disproportionate power and influence in the policy-making processes.

elitism Political system in which power is concentrated in the hands of a relatively small group of individuals or institutions.

Emancipation Proclamation Lincoln's 1862 Civil War declaration that all slaves residing in rebel states were free. It did not abolish all slavery; that would be done by the Thirteenth Amendment.

end of history The collapse of communism and the worldwide movement toward free markets and political democracy.

Enlightenment, The Also known as the "Age of Reason," was a philosophical movement in 18th century Western thought based upon a belief in reason and the capacities of individuals, a faith in a scientific approach to knowledge, and a confidence in human progress.

entitlement programs Social welfare programs that provide classes of people with legally enforceable rights to benefits.

entitlements Any social welfare program for which there are eligibility requirements, whether financial or contributory.

enumerated powers Powers specifically mentioned in the Constitution as belonging to the national government.

Equal Rights Amendment (ERA) Proposed amendment to the Constitution guaranteeing that equal rights under the law shall not be denied or abridged on account of sex. Passed by Congress in 1972, the amendment failed to win ratification by three of the necessary three-fourths of the states.

equality of opportunity Elimination of artificial barriers to success in life and the opportunity for everyone to strive for success.

equality of results Equal sharing of income and material goods regardless of one's efforts in life.

equal-time rule Federal Communications Commission (FCC) requirement that broadcasters who sell time to any political candidate must make equal time available to opposing candidates at the same price.

ex post facto law Retroactive criminal law that works against the accused; forbidden under Article I of the Constitution.

exclusionary rule Rule of law that evidence found in an illegal search or resulting from an illegally obtained confession may not be admitted at trial.

executive agreement Agreement with another nation signed by the president of the United States but less formal (and hence potentially less binding) than a treaty because it does not require Senate confirmation.

executive order Formal regulation governing executive branch operations issued by the president.

executive privilege Right of a president to withhold from other branches of government confidential communications within the executive branch; although posited by presidents, it has been upheld by the Supreme Court only in limited situations.

externalities Costs imposed on people who are not direct participants in an activity.

extraterritorial jurisdiction Power of an incorporated city to control development within nearby unincorporated areas.

extremism Rejection of democratic politics and the assertion of the supremacy of the "people" over laws, institutions, and individual rights.

Fair Deal Policies of President Harry Truman extending Roosevelt's New Deal and maintaining the Democratic Party's voter coalition.

Family Assistance Public assistance program that provides monies to the states for their use in helping needy families with children.

fascism Political ideology in which the state and/or race is assumed to be supreme over individuals.

Federal Election Commission (FEC) Agency charged with enforcing federal election laws and disbursing public presidential campaign funds.

Federal Reserve Board (the Fed) Independent agency of the executive branch of the federal government charged with overseeing the nation's monetary policy.

federalism A constitutional arrangement whereby power is divided between national and subnational governments, each of which enforces its own laws directly on its citizens and neither of which can alter the arrangement without the consent of the other.

Federalists Those who supported the U.S. Constitution during the ratification process and who later formed a political party in support of John Adams's presidential candidacy.

"feeding frenzy" Intense media coverage of a scandal or event that blocks out most other news.

filibuster Delaying tactic by a senator or group of senators, using the Senate's unlimited debate rule to prevent a vote on a bill.

first reading Introduction of a bill in the House or the Senate and its referral to a committee by the presiding officer.

fiscal policy Economic policies involving taxing, spending, and deficit levels of the national government.

fiscal year Yearly government accounting period, not necessarily the same as the calendar year. The federal government's fiscal year begins October 1 and ends September 30.

focus group In a political context, a small number of people brought together in a comfortable setting to discuss and respond to themes and issues, allowing campaign managers to develop and analyze strategies.

Food Stamp Program Public assistance program that provides low-income households with coupons redeemable for enough food to provide a minimal nutritious diet.

franking privilege Free use of the U.S. mails granted to members of Congress to promote communication with constituents.

Free Exercise Clause Clause in the First Amendment to the Constitution that prohibits government from restricting religious beliefs and practices.

free market Free competition for voluntary exchange among individuals, firms, and corporations.

free-riders People who do not belong to an organization or pay dues, yet nevertheless benefit from its activities.

free trade A policy of reducing or eliminating tariffs and quotas on imports to stimulate international trade.

freedom of expression Collectively, the First Amendment rights to free speech, press, and assembly.

front-end strategy Presidential political campaign strategy in which a candidate focuses on winning early primaries to build momentum.

front loading The scheduling of presidential primary elections early in the year.

gender gap Aggregate differences in political opinions of men and women.

general election Election to choose among candidates nominated by parties and/or independent candidates who gained access to the ballot by petition.

general law city City allowed to exercise only those powers specifically granted to it by the legislature. General law cities have fewer than 5,000 residents.

general obligation bonds Method of borrowing money to pay for new construction projects, such as prisons, mental hospitals, or school facilities. The bonds, which require voter approval, are repaid with tax revenue.

generation gap Differences in politics and public opinion among age groups.

generational effects Historical events that affect the views of those who lived through them.

gerrymandering Drawing district boundary lines for political advantage.

glass ceiling "Invisible" barriers to women rising to the highest positions in corporations and the professions.

globalization of the economy Increased interdependence in trade, manufacturing, and commerce as well as most other business activities between the United States and other countries.

GOP "Grand Old Party"—popular label for the Republican Party.

government Organization extending to the whole society that can legitimately use force to carry out its decisions.

government bonds Certificates of indebtedness that pay interest and promise repayment on a future date.

grand jury Jury charged only with determining whether sufficient evidence exists to support indictment of an individual on a felony charge; the grand jury's decision to indict does not represent a conviction.

grant of immunity from prosecution Grant by the government to an individual of freedom from prosecution on a particular charge in return for testimony by that individual that might otherwise be self-incriminating.

grants-in-aid Payments of funds from the national government to state or local governments or from a state government to local governments for specific purposes.

grass-roots lobbying Attempts to influence government decision making by inspiring constituents to contact their representatives.

Great Society Policies of President Lyndon Johnson that promised to solve the nation's social and economic problems through government intervention.

gridlock Political stalemate between the executive and legislative branches arising when one branch is controlled by one major political party and the other branch by the other party.

gross domestic product (GDP) Measure of economic performance in terms of the nation's total production of goods and services for a single year, valued in terms of market prices.

halo effect Tendency of survey respondents to provide socially acceptable answers to questions.

health maintenance organizations (HMOs) Health care provider groups that provide a stipulated list of services to patients for a fixed fee that is usually substantially lower than such care would otherwise cost.

home rule city City with a population of more than 5,000, which can adopt any form of government residents choose, provided it does not conflict with the state constitution or statutes.

home rule Power of local government to pass laws affecting local affairs, so long as those laws do not conflict with state or federal laws.

home style Activities of Congress members specifically directed at their home constituencies.

homestead exemption Reduction in property taxes that some local governments grant on a taxpayer's residence.

honeymoon period Early months of a president's term in which his popularity with the public and influence with the Congress are generally high.

horse-race coverage Media coverage of electoral campaigns that concentrates on who is ahead and who is behind, and neglects the issues at stake.

ideological organizations Interest groups that pursue ideologically based (liberal or conservative) agendas.

ideological party Third party that exists to promote an ideology rather than to win elections.

ideology Consistent and integrated system of ideas, values, and beliefs.

immigration policy Regulating the entry of noncitizens into the country.

impeachment Formal charges of wrongdoing brought against a government official, resulting in a trial and, upon conviction, removal from office.

impersonality Treatment of all persons within a bureaucracy on the basis of "merit" and of all "clients" served by the bureaucracy equally according to rules.

implementation Development by the federal bureaucracy of procedures and activities to carry out policies legislated by Congress; it includes regulation as well as adjudication.

implied powers Powers not mentioned specifically in the Constitution as belonging to Congress but inferred as necessary and proper for carrying out the enumerated powers.

impoundment Refusal by a president to spend monies appropriated by Congress; outlawed except with congressional consent by the Budget and Impoundment Control Act of 1974.

inalienable rights The rights of all people derived from natural law and not bestowed by governments, including the rights to life, liberty, and property.

incidence Actual bearer of a tax burden.

income transfers Government transfers of income from taxpayers to persons regarded as deserving.

incorporation In constitutional law, the application of almost all of the Bill of Rights to the states and all of their subdivision through the Fourteenth Amendment.

incremental budgeting Method of budgeting that focuses on requested increases in funding for existing programs, accepting as legitimate their previous year's expenditures.

incumbent Candidate currently in office seeking reelection.

incumbent gerrymandering Drawing legislative district boundaries to advantage incumbent legislators.

independent counsel ("special prosecutor") A prosecutor appointed by a federal court to pursue charges against a president or other high official. This position was allowed to lapse by Congress in 1999 after many controversial investigations by these prosecutors.

independent school district Specific form of special district that administers the public schools in a designated area.

indexing Tying of benefit levels in social welfare programs to the general price level.

indictment Determination by a grand jury that sufficient evidence exists to warrant trial of an individual on a felony charge; necessary before an individual can be brought to trial.

individual income tax Taxes on individuals' wages and other earned income, the primary source of revenue for the U.S. federal government.

individualism Attitude, rooted in classical liberal theory and reinforced by the frontier tradition, that citizens are capable of taking care of themselves with minimal governmental assistance.

individualistic subculture View that government should interfere as little as possible in the private activities of its citizens while assuring that adequate public facilities and a favorable business climate are available to permit individuals to pursue their self-interests.

inflation Rise in the general level of prices; not just the prices of some products.

information Document formally charging a person with a misdemeanor.

information overload Situation in which individuals are subjected to so many communications that they cannot make sense of them.

infrastructure Streets, waste disposal systems, libraries, and other public facilities built and operated by governments.

initiative Allows a specified number or percentage of voters by use of a petition to place a state constitutional amendment or a state law on the ballot for adoption or rejection by the state electorate.

in-kind (noncash) benefits Benefits of a social welfare program that are not cash payments, including free medical care, subsidized housing, and food stamps.

inquest Examination by a justice of the peace or a medical examiner of unusual circumstances under which someone has died.

institutionalization In the context of political science, the development of a legislative body into a formally structured system with stable membership, complex rules, expanded internal operations, and the delineation of staff functions.

intent calendar Daily list of bills eligible for debate on the floor of the Texas senate, if the sponsor is recognized by the lieutenant governor.

interest group Organization seeking to influence government policy.

interest-group entrepreneurs Leaders who create organizations and market memberships.

intergovernmental relations Network of political, financial, and administrative relationships between units of the federal government and those of state and local governments.

interims Periods between legislative sessions.

international trade The buying and selling of goods and services between individuals or firms located in different countries.

iron triangles Mutually supportive relationships among interest groups, government agencies, and legislative committees with jurisdiction over a specific policy area.

issue ads Ads that advocate policy positions rather than explicitly supporting or opposing particular candidates.

Jim Crow Second-class-citizen status conferred on blacks by Southern segregation laws; derived from a nineteenth-century song-and-dance act (usually performed by a white man in blackface) that stereotyped blacks.

Jim Crow laws Legislation enacted by many states after the Civil War to limit the rights and power of African Americans.

judicial activism Making of new law through judicial interpretations of the Constitution.

judicial review Power of the courts, especially the Supreme Court, to declare laws of Congress, laws of the states, and actions of the president unconstitutional and invalid.

judicial self-restraint Self-imposed limitation on judicial power by judges deferring to the policy judgments of elected branches of government.

jurisdiction Power of a court to hear a case in question.

justice of the peace court Low-ranking court with jurisdiction over minor civil disputes and criminal cases.

Korean War Communist North Korea invaded non-Communist South Korea in June, 1950, causing President Harry S Truman to intervene militarily, with U.N. support. General Douglas MacArthur defeated the North Koreans, but with China's entry into the war, a stalemate resulted. An armistice was signed in 1953, with Korea divided along nearly original lines.

laboratories of democracy A reference to the ability of states to experiment and innovate in public policy.

left A reference to the liberal, progressive, and/or socialist side of the political spectrum.

legal equality Belief that the law should apply equally to all persons.

Legislative Redistricting Board A board created by constitutional amendment charged to redistrict the Texas legislature if it is not accomplished in the regular session following the release of the census.

legitimacy Widespread acceptance of something as necessary, rightful, and legally binding.

Lemon test To be constitutional, a law must have a secular purpose; its primary effect must neither advance nor inhibit religion; and it must not foster excessive government entanglement with religion.

Leninism The theories of Vladimir Lenin, among them that advanced capitalist coun-

tries turned toward war and colonialism to make their own workers relatively prosperous.

libel Writings that are false and malicious and are intended to damage an individual.

liberalism Belief in the value of strong government to provide economic security and protection for civil rights, combined with a belief in personal freedom from government intervention in social conduct.

libertarian Opposing government intervention in both economic and social affairs, and favoring minimal government in all sectors of society.

lieutenant governor Presiding officer of the senate. This officeholder would become governor if the governor were to die, be incapacitated, or removed from office.

life-cycle effects Changes in life circumstances associated with age that affect one's views.

limited government Principle that government power over the individual is limited, that there are some personal liberties that even a majority cannot regulate, and that government itself is restrained by law.

line-item veto Power of the chief executive to reject some portions of a bill without rejecting all of it.

literacy test Examination of a person's ability to read and write as a prerequisite to voter registration, outlawed by Voting Rights Act (1965) as discriminatory.

litigation Legal dispute brought before a court.

litmus test In political terms, a person's stand on a key issue that determines whether he or she will be appointed to public office or supported in electoral campaigns.

lobbying Activities directed at government officials with the hope of influencing their decisions.

lobbyist Person working to influence government policies and actions.

logrolling Bargaining for agreement among legislators to support each other's favorite bills, especially projects that primarily benefit individual members and their constituents.

machine Tightly disciplined party organization, headed by a boss, that relies on material rewards—including patronage jobs—to control politics.

majoritarianism Tendency of democratic governments to allow the faint preferences of the majority to prevail over the intense feelings of minorities.

majority Election by more than 50 percent of all votes cast in the contest.

majority leader In the House, the majority-party leader and second in command to the Speaker; in the Senate, the leader of the majority party.

majority opinion Opinion in a case that is subscribed to by a majority of the judges who participated in the decision.

malapportionment Unequal numbers of people in legislative districts resulting in inequality of voter representation.

managed care Programs designed to keep health care costs down by the establishment of strict guidelines regarding when and what diagnostic and therapeutic procedures should be administered to patients under various circumstances.

mandate Perception of popular support for a program or policy based on the margin of electoral victory won by a candidate who proposed it during a campaign; direct federal orders to state and local governments requiring them to perform a service or to obey federal laws in the performance of their functions.

mandatory spending Spending for program committments made by past congresses.

maquiladora program Policies initiated by Mexico in 1964 to stimulate economic growth along the U.S.-Mexico border.

markup Line-by-line revision of a bill in committee by editing each phrase and word.

Marshall Plan U.S. program to rebuild the nations of Western Europe in the aftermath of World War II in order to render them less susceptible to communist influence and takeover.

Marxism The theories of Karl Marx, among them that capitalists oppress workers and that worldwide revolution and the emergence of a classless society are inevitable.

mass media All means of communication with the general public, including television, newspapers, magazines, radio, books, recordings, motion pictures, and the Internet.

mayor-council Form of city government in which the legislative function is vested in the city council and the executive function in the mayor.

means-tested spending Spending for benefits that is distributed on the basis of the recipient's income.

Medicaid Public assistance program that provides health care to the poor.

medical examiner Appointed official who is responsible for determining the cause of death of murder victims or others who die under suspicious or unusual circumstances.

Medicare Social insurance program that provides health care insurance to elderly and disabled people.

merit selection Proposal under which the governor would appoint state judges from lists of potential nominees recommended by committees of experts. Appointed judges would have to run later in retention elections to keep their seats but would not have opponents on the ballot. Voters would simply decide whether a judge should remain in office or be replaced by another gubernatorial appointee.

merit system Selection of employees for government agencies on the basis of competence, with no consideration of an individual's political stance and/or power.

metro government Local government in which city and county governments consolidate to avoid duplication of public services.

minority leader In both the House and Senate, the leader of the opposition party.

Miranda ruling Far-reaching decision of the U.S. Supreme Court that requires law enforcement officers to warn a criminal suspect of his or her right to remain silent and have an attorney present before questioning.

Miranda warning Requirement that persons arrested be informed of their rights immediately after arrest.

misdemeanor Minor criminal offense punishable by a fine and/or a short sentence in the county jail.

mobilize In politics, to activate supporters to work for candidates and turn out on Election Day.

monetary policy Economic policies involving the money supply, interest rates, and banking activity.

moralistic subculture View that government's primary responsibility is to promote the public welfare and that it should actively use its authority and power to improve the social and economic well-being of its citizens.

"Motor Voter Act" Federal mandate that states offer voter registration at driver's licensing and welfare offices.

muckraking Journalistic exposés of corruption, wrongdoing, or mismanagement in government, business, and other institutions of society.

municipal court Court of limited jurisdiction that hears cases involving city ordinances and primarily handles traffic tickets.

name recognition Public awareness of a candidate—whether they even know his or her name.

national debt Total debt accumulated by the national government over the years.

national health insurance Government-provided insurance to all citizens paid from tax revenues.

National Security Council (NSC) "Inner cabinet" that advises the president and coordinates foreign, defense, and intelligence activities.

National Supremacy Clause Clause in Article VI of the U.S. Constitution declaring the constitution and laws of the national government "the supreme law of the land" superior to the constitutions and laws of the states.

nationalism Belief that shared cultural, historical, linguistic, and social characteristics of a people justify the creation of a government encompassing all of them, the resulting nation-state should be independent and legally equal to all other nation-states.

natural law The law that would govern humans in a state of nature before governments existed.

Necessary and Proper Clause Clause in Article I, Section 8, of the U.S. Constitution granting Congress the power to enact all laws that are "necessary and proper" for carrying out those responsibilities specifically delegated to it. Also referred to as the Implied Powers Clause.

negative campaigning Speeches, commercials, or advertising attacking a political opponent during a campaign.

New Deal Policies of President Franklin D. Roosevelt during the Depression of the 1930s that helped form a Democratic Party coalition of urban working-class, ethnic, Catholic, Jewish, poor, and Southern voters.

new federalism Attempts to return power and responsibility to the states and reduce the role of the national government in domestic affairs.

newsmaking Deciding what events, topics, presentations, and issues will be given coverage in the news.

No Establishment Clause Clause in the First Amendment to the Constitution that is interpreted to require the separation of church and state.

nolo contendere Plea of "no contest" to a criminal charge.

nomination Political party's selection of its candidate for a public office.

nominee Political party's entry in a general election race.

nonpartisan elections Elections in which candidates do not officially indicate their party affiliation; often used for city, country, school board, and judicial elections.

nonviolent direct action Strategy used by civil rights leaders such as Martin Luther King Jr., in which protesters break "unjust" laws openly but in a "loving" fashion in order to bring the injustices of such laws to public attention.

North American Free Trade Agreement (NAFTA) Treaty among the United States, Canada, and Mexico that created the world's largest trading bloc. Approved by the U.S. Congress in 1993, the treaty is designed to reduce tariffs and increase trade among the three countries.

North Atlantic Treaty Organization (NATO) Mutual-security agreement and joint military command uniting the nations of Western Europe, initially formed to resist Soviet expansionism.

obligational authority Feature of some appropriations acts by which an agency is empowered to enter into contracts that will require the government to make payments beyond the fiscal year in question.

one-party system Domination of elections and governmental processes by a single party, which may be split into different ideological, economic, or regional factions. In Texas, the phrase is used to describe the period from the late 1870s to the late 1970s, when the Democratic Party claimed virtually all elected, partisan offices.

open primaries Primary elections in which a voter may cast a ballot in either party's primary election.

open rule Rule that permits unlimited amendments to a bill under consideration by the House.

open seat Seat in a legislature for which no incumbent is running for reelection.

organizational sclerosis Society encrusted with so many special benefits to interest groups that everyone's standard of living is lowered.

original intent Judicial philosophy under which judges attempt to apply the values of the Founders to current issues.

original jurisdiction Refers to a particular court's power to serve as the place where a given case is initially argued and decided.

outlays Actual dollar amounts to be spent by the federal government in a fiscal year.

outsourcing Government contracting with private firms to perform public services.

override Voting in Congress to enact legislation vetoed by the president; requires a two-thirds vote in both the House and Senate.

oversight Congressional monitoring of the activities of executive branch agencies to determine if the laws are being faithfully executed.

packing Redistricting in which partisan voters are concentrated in a single district, "wasting" their majority vote and allowing the opposition to win by modest majorities in other districts.

paradox of democracy Potential for conflict between individual freedom and majority rule.

parole Early release of an inmate from prison, subject to certain conditions.

partial preemption Federal government's assumption of some regulatory powers in a particular field, with the stipulation that a state law on the same subject as a federal law is valid if it does not conflict with the federal law in the same area.

party identification Self-described identification with a political party, usually in response to the question, "Generally speaking, how would you identify yourself: as a Republican, Democrat, independent, or something else?"

party organization National and state party officials and workers, committee members, convention delegates, and others active in the party.

party-in-the-electorate Voters who identify themselves with a party.

party-in-the-government Public officials who were nominated by their party and who identify themselves in office with their party.

party polarization The tendency of the Democratic Party to take more liberal positions and the Republican Party to take more conservative positions on key issues.

party unity Percentage of Democrats and Republicans who stick with their party on party votes.

party vote Majority of Democrats voting in opposition to a majority of Republicans.

passport Evidence of U.S. citizenship, allowing people to travel abroad and reenter the United States.

patronage Appointment to public office based on party loyalty.

pay-as-you-go Constitutional requirement that prohibits the legislature from borrowing money for the state's operating expenses.

penal code Body of law that defines most criminal offenses and sets a range of punishments that can be assessed.

perjury Lying while under oath and sworn to tell the truth.

petit (regular) jury Panel of citizens that hears evidence in a civil lawsuit or a criminal prosecution and decides the outcome by issuing a verdict.

petition for review Petition to the Texas Supreme Court claiming that legal or procedural mistakes were made in the lower court.

photo ops Staged opportunities for the media to photograph the candidate in a favorable setting.

place system Form of at-large election in which candidates run for specific positions, or places, on a city council or other governing body.

plaintiffs Parties initiating suits and claiming damages. In criminal cases, the state acts as plaintiff on behalf of an injured society and requests fines and/or imprisonment as damages. In civil suits, the plaintiff is the injured party and seeks monetary damages.

platform Statement of principles adopted by a political party at its national convention (specific portions of the platform are known as planks); a platform is not binding on the party's candidates.

plea bargaining Practice of allowing defendants to plead guilty to lesser crimes than those with which they were originally charged in return for reduced sentences.

pluralism Theory that democracy can be achieved through competition among multiple organized groups and that individuals can participate in politics through group memberships and elections.

plurality Election by at least one vote more than any other candidate in the race.

pocket veto Effective veto of a bill when Congress adjourns within ten days of passing it and the president fails to sign it.

policy networks Interaction in a common policy area among lobbyists, elected officials, staff personnel, bureaucrats, journalists, and private-sector experts.

political action committees (PACs) Organizations that solicit and receive campaign contributions from corporations, unions, trade associations, and ideological and issue-oriented groups, and their members, then distribute these funds to political candidates.

political alienation Belief that politics is irrelevant to one's life and that one cannot personally affect public affairs.

political culture Widely shared views about who should govern, for what ends, and by what means.

political equality Belief that the law should apply equally to all and that every person's vote counts equally.

political organizations Parties and interest groups that function as intermediaries between individuals and government.

political parties Organizations that seek to achieve power by winning public office.

political science The study of politics: who governs, for what ends, and by what means.

politically correct (PC) Repression of attitudes, speech, and writings that are deemed racist, sexist, homophobic (anti-homosexual), or otherwise "insensitive."

politics Deciding who gets what, when, and how.

poll taxes Taxes imposed as a prerequisite to voting; prohibited by the Twenty-fourth Amendment.

popular sovereignty Constitutional principle of self-government; belief that the people control their government and governments are subject to limitations and constraints.

population density Number of residents living within the boundaries of a city, county, or state in relationship to the land area. Population density is a significant factor in determining the level of local public services.

pork barreling Legislation designed to make government benefits, including jobs and projects used as political patronage, flow to a particular district or state.

poverty line Official standard regarding what level of annual cash income is sufficient to maintain a "decent standard of living"; those with incomes below this level are eligible for most public assistance programs.

power of the purse Congress's exclusive, constitutional power to authorize expenditures by all agencies of the federal government.

precedent Legal principle that previous decisions should determine the outcome of current cases; the basis for stability in law.

precinct Subdivision of a city, county, or ward for election purposes.

precinct chair Local officer in a political party who presides over the precinct convention and serves on the party's county executive committee. Voters in each precinct elect a chair in the party's primary election.

preemption Total or partial federal assumption of power in a particular field, restricting the authority of the states.

preferred position Refers to the tendency of the courts to give preference to the First Amendment rights to speech, press, and assembly when faced with conflicts.

preferred provider organizations (PPOs) Groups of hospitals and physicians who have joined together to offer their services to private insurers at a discount.

presidential primaries Primary elections in the states in which voters in each party can choose a presidential candidate for its party's nomination. Outcomes help determine the distribution of pledged delegates to each party's national nominating convention.

primary elections Elections to choose party nominees for public office; may be open or closed.

prior restraint Government actions to restrict publication of a magazine, newspaper, or books on grounds of libel, obscenity, or other legal violations prior to actual publication of the work.

privatization Contracting by government with private companies to provide some public services.

professionalism In politics, a reference to the increasing number of officeholders for whom politics is a full-time occupation.

program budgeting Identifying items in a budget according to the functions and programs they are to be spent on.

progressive taxation System of taxation in which higher income groups pay a larger percentage of their incomes in taxes than do lower income groups.

proportional (flat) taxation System of taxation in which all income groups pay the same percentage of their income in taxes.

proportional representation Electoral system that allocates seats in a legislature based on the proportion of votes each party receives in a national election.

prosecution Conduct of legal proceedings against an individual charged with a crime.

protectionism A policy of high tariffs and quotas on imports to protect domestic industries.

protest party Third party that arises in response to issues of popular concern which have not been addressed by the major parties.

protests Public marches or demonstrations designed to call attention to an issue and motivate others to apply pressure on public officials.

public assistance programs Those social welfare programs for which no contributions are required and only those living in poverty (by official standards) are eligible; includes food stamps, Medicaid, and Family Assistance.

public goods Goods and services that cannot readily be provided by markets, either because they are too expensive for a single individual to buy or because if one person bought them, everyone else would use them without paying.

public improvement district Specific area of a city in which property owners pay special taxes in return for improvements to streets and other public facilities in their neighborhood.

public-interest groups Interest groups that claim to represent broad classes of people or the public as a whole.

public opinion Aggregate of preferences and opinions of individuals on significant issues.

public relations Building and maintaining goodwill with the general public.

quorum Required number of the members of a governing body who must be present so that official business, such as voting, can be conducted. In Texas, a quorum of the House and the Senate is two-thirds of the membership. For committees, it is a majority of the members.

quota Provision of some affirmative action programs in which specific numbers or percentages of positions are open only to minorities and/or women.

Radical Reconstructionists The group of Republicans who took control of the U.S. Congress in 1866 and imposed hated military governments on the former Confederate states after the Civil War.

radicalism Advocacy of immediate and drastic changes in society, including the complete restructuring of institutions, values, and beliefs. Radicals may exist on either the extreme left or extreme right.

raiding Organized efforts by one party to get its members to cross over in a primary and defeat an attractive candidate in the opposition party's primary.

ranking minority member The minority-party committee member with the most seniority.

ratification Power of a legislature to approve or reject decisions made by other bodies. State legislators or state conventions must ratify constitutional amendments submitted by Congress. The U.S. Senate must ratify treaties made by the president.

Reagan Coalition Combination of economic and social conservatives, religious fundamentalists, and defense-minded anti-communists who rallied behind Republican President Ronald Reagan.

realignment Major shift in political party support or identification that usually occurs around a critical election. In Texas, realignment took place as a gradual transformation from a one-party system dominated by Democrats to a two-party system in which Republicans became competitive in elections.

record vote Vote taken in the House or the Senate of which a permanent record is kept, listing how individual legislators voted.

recession Decline in the general level of economic activity.

Reconstruction The Post–Civil war period when the Southern states were occupied by federal troops and newly freed African Americans occupied many political offices and exercised civil rights.

redistricting Drawing of legislative district boundary lines following each ten-year census.

referenda Proposed laws or constitutional amendments submitted to the voters for their direct approval or rejection, found in state constitutions but not in the U.S. Constitution.

regional security Attempt to bring order to international relations during the Cold War by creating regional alliances between a superpower and nations of a particular region.

registration Requirement that prospective voters establish their identity and place of residence prior to an election in order to be eligible to vote.

regressive taxation System of taxation in which lower income groups pay a larger percentage of their incomes in taxes than do higher income groups.

regular session 140-day period in the odd-numbered years in which the legislature meets and can consider and pass laws on any issue or subject.

regulation Development by the federal bureaucracy of formal rules for implementing legislation.

Religious Right Political movement, based primarily in evangelical Protestant churches, that has played an increasingly prominent role in Texas and national politics.

remedies and reliefs Orders of a court to correct a wrong, including a violation of the Constitution.

representational federalism Assertion that no constitutional division of powers exists between the nation and the states but the states retain their constitutional role merely by selecting the president and members of Congress.

representative democracy Governing system in which public decision making is delegated to representatives of the people chosen by popular vote in free, open, and periodic elections.

republic Form of government in which representatives of the people, rather than the people themselves, govern.

Republican Party One of the two main parties in American politics, it traces its origins to the antislavery and nationalist forces that united in the 1850s and nominated Abraham Lincoln for president in 1860.

republicanism Government by representatives of the people rather than directly by the people themselves.

rescissions Items on which a president wishes to cancel spending.

reserved powers Powers not granted to the national government or specifically denied to the states in the Constitution that are recognized by the Tenth Amendment as belonging to the state governments. This guarantee, known as the Reserved Powers Clause, embodies the principle of American federalism.

responsible party model System in which competitive parties adopt a platform of principles, recruiting candidates and directing campaigns based on the platform, and holding their elected officials responsible for enacting it.

restricted rule Rule that allows specified amendments to be added to a bill under consideration by the House.

retail politics Direct candidate contact with individual voters.

retention elections Elections in which judges run on their own records rather than against other candidates. Voters cast their ballots on the question of whether the incumbent judge should stay in office.

retrospective voting Voting for or against a candidate or party on the basis of past performance in office.

revenue bonds Bonds that are used to finance construction of a public facility and are repaid with income produced by the facility.

revolving doors The movement of individuals from government positions to jobs in the private sector, using the experience, knowledge, and contacts they acquired in government employment.

rider Amendment to a bill that is not germane to the bill's purposes.

right A reference to the conservative, traditional, anticommunist side of the political spectrum.

right-to-work law Law prohibiting the requirement of union membership in order to hold or get a job.

rollback election Election in which local voters can nullify a property tax increase that exceeds 8 percent in a given year.

roll-call vote Vote of the full House or Senate on which all members' individual votes are recorded and made public.

rule Stipulation attached to a bill in the House of Representatives that governs its consideration on the floor, including when and for how long it can be debated and how many (if any) amendments may be appended to it.

rule of four At least four justices must agree to hear an appeal (writ of certiorari) from a lower court in order to get a case before the Supreme Court.

runoff elections Elections that are required if no candidate receives an absolute majority of the votes cast in a city council, school district, or party primary race. The runoff is between the two top vote-getters.

runoff primary Additional primary held between the top two vote-getters in a primary where no candidate has received a majority of the vote.

safe seat Legislative district in which the incumbent regularly wins by a large margin of the vote.

salient issues Issues about which most people have an opinion.

SALT I First arms limitation treaty between the United States and the Soviet Union, signed in 1972, limiting the total number of offensive nuclear missiles; it included the ABM Treaty that reflected the theory that the population centers of both nations should be left undefended.

SALT II Lengthy and complicated treaty between the United States and the Soviet Union, agreed to in 1979 but never ratified by the U.S. Senate, that set limits on all types of strategic nuclear launch vehicles.

school board Governing body of a school district. Its responsibilities include the development or approval of educational policies, approval of the budget, hiring of the superintendent, and other personnel matters.

search warrant Court order permitting law-enforcement officials to search a location in order to seize evidence of a crime; issued only for a specified location, in connection with a specific investigation, and on submission of proof that "probable cause" exists to warrant such a search.

second reading Initial debate by the full House or Senate on a bill that has been approved by a committee.

second-strike capability Ability of a nation's forces to survive a surprise nuclear attack by the enemy and then to retaliate effectively.

secular In politics, a reference to opposition to religious practices and symbols in public life.

selective perception Mentally screening out information or opinions with which one disagrees.

senatorial courtesy Custom of the U.S. Senate with regard to presidential nominations to the judiciary to defer to the judgment of senators from the president's party from the same state as the nominee.

seniority system Custom whereby the member of Congress who has served the longest on the majority side of a committee becomes its chair and the member who has served the longest on the minority side becomes its ranking member.

separate but equal Ruling of the Supreme Court in the case of *Plessy v. Ferguson* (1896) to the effect that segregated facilities were legal as long as the facilities were equal.

separation of powers Constitutional division of powers among the three branches of the national government—legislative, executive, and judicial.

set-aside program Program in which a specified number or percentage of contracts must go to designated minorities.

Shays's Rebellion An armed revolt in 1786, led by a Revolutionary War Officer Daniel Shays, protesting the discontent of small farmers over debts and taxes, and raising concerns about the ability of the U.S. government under the Articles of Confederation to maintain internal order.

sheriff Elected official who is the chief law enforcement officer of a county.

shield laws Laws in some states that give reporters the right to refuse to name their sources or to release their notes in court cases; may be overturned by the courts when such refusals jeopardize a fair trial for a defendant.

single-issue groups Organizations formed to support or oppose government action on a specific issue.

single-issue party Third party formed around one particular cause.

single-member district Election system in which one person is elected to represent the people living within one geographic district.

slander Oral statements that are false and malicious and are intended to damage an individual.

social contract The idea the government originates from an implied contract among people who agree to obey laws in exchange for the protection of their natural rights.

social insurance programs Social welfare programs to which beneficiaries have made contributions so that they are entitled to benefits regardless of their personal wealth.

social mobility Extent to which people move upward or downward in income and status over a lifetime or generations.

Social Security Social insurance program composed of the Old Age and Survivors Insurance program, which pays benefits to retired workers who have paid into the program and their dependents and survivors, and the Disability Insurance program, which pays benefits to disabled workers and their families.

socialism System of government involving collective or government ownership of economic enterprise, with the goal being equality of results, not merely equality of opportunity.

socialization The learning of a culture and its values.

soft money Campaign contributions, not subject to regulated limits, given to a party for activities such as party building or voter registration, but not directly for campaigns. Soft-money contributions to national parties were banned in 2002.

soft news News featured in talk shows, late-night comedy and TV news magazines—reaches more people than regular news broadcasts.

solicitor general Attorney in the Department of Justice who represents the U.S. government before the Supreme Court and any other courts.

sound bites Concise and catchy phrases that attract media coverage.

sovereign immunity Legal doctrine that individuals can sue the government only with the government's consent.

Soviet Union The Union of Soviet Socialist Republics (USSR) consisting of Russia and its bordering lands and ruled by the communist regime in Moscow, officially dissolved in 1991.

Speaker of the House Presiding officer of the House of Representatives.

special purpose districts Units of local government created by the state to perform specific functions not met by cities or counties, including the provision of public services to unincorporated areas.

spin doctor Practitioner of the art of spin control, or manipulation of media reporting to favor one's own candidate.

splinter party Third party formed by a dissatisfied faction of a major party.

splintering Redistricting in which a strong minority is divided up and diluted to prevent it from electing a representative.

spoils system Selection of employees for government agencies on the basis of party loyalty, electoral support, and political influence.

standard partial preemption Form of partial preemption in which the states are permitted to regulate activities already regulated by the federal government if the state regulatory standards are at least as stringent as the federal government's.

standing Requirement that the party who files a lawsuit have a legal stake in the outcome.

standing committee Permanent committee of the House or Senate that deals with matters within a specified subject area.

stare decisis Judicial precept that the issue has already been decided in earlier cases and the earlier decision need only be applied in the specific case before the bench; the rule in most cases, it comes from the Latin for "the decision stands."

START I First treaty between the United States and the Soviet Union that actually reduced the strategic nuclear arms of the superpowers, signed in 1991.

START II A treaty between the United States and Russia eliminating all multiwarhead land missiles and reducing nuclear weapons stockpiles; signed in 2003.

state chair and vice chair Two top state leaders of a political party, one of whom must be a woman. They are selected every two years by delegates to the party's state convention.

state convention Meeting held in June of even-numbered years by each of the two major political parties. Delegates to this convention elect the party's state leadership and adopt a party platform. In presidential election years, the state convention selects the delegates to the party's national nominating convention.

state executive committee Statewide governing board of a political party. It includes a man and a woman from each of the thirty-one state senatorial districts and the state chair and vice chair, who are selected by delegates to the party's biennial state convention.

statutes Laws enacted by a legislative body.

statutory county court Court that exercises limited jurisdiction over criminal and/or civil cases. The jurisdiction of these courts varies from county to county.

statutory laws Laws made by act of Congress or the state legislatures, as opposed to constitutional law.

strict scrutiny Supreme Court holding that race-based actions by government can be done only to remedy past discrimination or to further a "compelling" interest and must be "narrowly tailored" to minimize effects on the rights of others.

strong mayor Form of city government that gives the mayor considerable power, including budgetary control and appointment and removal authority over city department heads.

subcommittees Specialized committees within standing committees; subcommittee

recommendations must be approved by the full standing committee before submission to the floor.

subcultures Variations on the prevailing values and beliefs in a society.

subpoenas Court orders requiring people to testify in court or before grand juries or to produce certain documents.

suffrage Legal right to vote.

Sullivan rule Court guideline that false and malicious statements regarding public officials are protected by the First Amendment unless it can be proven they were known to be false at the time they were made or were made with "reckless disregard" for their truth or falsehood.

superdelegates Delegates to the Democratic Party national convention selected because of their position in the government or the party and not pledged to any candidate.

superpowers Refers to the United States and the Soviet Union after World War II, when these two nations dominated international politics.

Supplemental Security Income (SSI) Public assistance program that provides monthly cash payments to the needy elderly (sixty-five or older), blind, and disabled.

survey research Gathering of information about public opinion by questioning a representative sample of the population.

swing states States that are not considered to be firmly in the Democratic or Republican column.

symbolic speech Actions other than speech itself but protected by the First Amendment because they constitute political expression.

tag Rule that allows an individual senator to postpone a committee hearing on any bill for at least forty-eight hours, a delay that can be fatal to a bill during the closing days of a legislative session.

takings clause The Fifth Amendment's prohibition against government taking of private property without just compensation.

tariff Tax imposed on imported products (also called a customs duty).

tax abatements Exemptions from property taxes granted to certain businesses, usually to encourage them to move to or expand their operations in a city or county. The exemptions are granted for specific periods.

tax assessor-collector Elected official who determines how much property tax is owed on the different pieces of property within a county and then collects the tax.

tax avoidance Taking advantage of exemptions, exclusions, deductions, and special treatments in tax laws (legal).

tax evasion Hiding income and/or falsely claiming exemptions, deductions, and special treatments (illegal).

tax expenditures Revenues lost to the federal government because of exemptions, exclusions, deductions, and special-treatment provisions in tax laws.

taxes Compulsory payments to the government.

television malaise Generalized feelings of distrust, cynicism, and powerlessness stemming from television's emphasis on the negative aspects of American life.

Temporary Assistance to Needy Families Welfare reform program replacing federal cash entitlement with grants to the states for welfare recipients.

terrorism Title 22 of the U.S. Code, Section 2656 (d): "The term 'terrorism' means premeditated, politically motivated violence perpetrated against noncombatant targets by subnational groups or clandestine agents, usually intended to influence an audience."

Texas Court of Criminal Appeals Nine-member court with final appellate jurisdiction over criminal cases.

Texas Supreme Court Nine-member court with final appellate jurisdiction over civil lawsuits.

"The Establishment" In the days of one-party Democratic politics in Texas, the Establishment was a loosely knit coalition of Anglo business and oil company executives, bankers, and lawyers who controlled state policy making through the dominant conservative wing of the Democratic Party.

third party Political party that challenges the two major parties in an election.

third reading Final presentation of a bill before the full house or senate.

Three-Fifths Compromise A compromise in the Constitutional Convention of 1787 between free and slave states in which slaves would be counted as three-fifths of a person for both taxation and representation.

ticket splitter Person who votes for candidates of different parties for different offices in a general election.

Title IX A provision in the Federal Education Act forbidding discrimination against women in college athletic programs.

tort A wrongful act or injury for which a damage lawsuit can be brought.

tort reform Changes in state law to put limits on personal injury lawsuits and damage judgments entered by the courts.

total preemption Federal government's assumption of all regulatory powers in a particular field.

totalitarianism Rule by an elite that exercises unlimited power over individuals in all aspects of life.

trade associations Interest groups composed of businesses in specific industries.

traditionalistic subculture View that political power should be concentrated in the hands of a few elite citizens who belong to established families or influential social groups. Public policy basically serves the interests of this small group.

transfer payments Direct payments (either in cash or in goods and/or services) by governments to individuals as part of a social welfare program, not as a result of any service or contribution rendered by the individual.

transnational regionalism Expanding economic and social interdependence of South Texas and Mexico.

Truman Doctrine U.S. foreign policy, first articulated by President Harry S Truman, that pledged the United States to "support free

peoples who are resisting attempted subjugation by armed minorities or by outside pressures."

trustees Legislators who feel obligated to use their own best judgment in decision making.

turnout Number of voters who actually cast ballots in an election, as a percentage of people eligible to register and vote.

turnover Replacement of members of Congress by retirement or resignation, by reapportionment, or (more rarely) by electoral defeat, usually expressed as a percentage of members newly elected.

two-party system Political system that has two dominant parties, such as that of the United States.

unanimous consent agreement Negotiated by the majority and minority leaders of the Senate, it specifies when a bill will be taken up on the floor, what amendments will be considered, and when a vote will be taken.

underclass People who have remained poor and dependent on welfare over a prolonged period of time.

unemployment compensation Social insurance program that temporarily replaces part of the wages of workers who have lost their jobs.

unemployment rate Percentage of the civilian labor force who are not working but who are looking for work or waiting to return to or to begin a job.

unfunded mandates Mandates that impose costs on state and local governments (and private industry) without reimbursement from the federal government.

unicameral A legislature consisting of a single chamber.

unitary system Constitutional arrangement whereby authority rests with the national government; subnational governments have only those powers given to them by the national government.

U.S. Solicitor General The U.S. government's chief legal council, presenting the government's arguments in cases in which it is a party or in which it has an interest.

urbanization Process by which a predominantly rural society or area becomes urban.

values Shared ideas about what is good and desirable.

veniremen Members of a panel from which a petit, or trial, jury is chosen.

veto Rejection of a legislative act by the executive branch; in the U.S. federal government, overriding of a veto requires a two-thirds majority in both houses of Congress.

Vietnam War War between non-Communist South Vietnam and Communist North Vietnam from 1956 to 1975, with increasing U.S. involvement, ending with U.S. withdrawal in 1973 and Communist victory in 1975. The war became unpopular in the U.S. after 1968 and caused President Johnson not to run for a second term. More than 58,000 Americans died in the war.

visa A document or stamp on a passport allowing a person to visit a foreign country.

Voting Rights Act Federal law designed to protect the voting rights of minorities by

requiring the Justice Department's approval of changes in political districts and certain other electoral procedures. The 1965 act, as amended, has eliminated most of the restrictive practices that limited minority political participation.

wall-of-separation doctrine The Supreme Court's interpretation of the No Establishment Clause that laws may not have as their purpose aid to one religion or aid to all religions.

War Powers Resolution Bill passed in 1973 to limit presidential war-making powers; it restricts when, why, and for how long a president can commit U.S. forces and requires notification of and, in many cases, approval by Congress.

ward Division of a city for electoral or administrative purposes or as a unit for organizing political parties.

Watergate The scandal that led to the forced resignation of President Richard M. Nixon. Adding "gate" as a suffix to any alleged corruption in government suggests an analogy to the Watergate scandal.

weak mayor Form of city government in which the mayor shares authority with the city council and other elected officials but has little independent control over city policy or administration.

Whig Party Formed in 1836 to oppose Andrew Jackson's policies; elected President Harrison in 1840 and Taylor in 1848 but disintegrated over the issue of slavery.

whips In both the House and Senate, the principal assistants to the party leaders and next in command to those leaders.

whistle-blower Employee of the federal government or of a firm supplying the government who reports waste, mismanagement, and/or fraud by a government agency or contractor.

White House press corps Reporters from both print and broadcast media assigned to regularly cover the president.

white primary Democratic Party primary elections in many Southern counties in the early part of the twentieth century that excluded black people from voting.

writ of certiorari Writ issued by the Supreme Court, at its discretion, to order a lower court to prepare the record of a case and send it to the Supreme Court for review. Most cases come to the Court as petitions for writs of certiorari.

writ of habeas corpus Court order directing public officials who are holding a person in custody to bring the prisoner into court and explain the reasons for confinement; the right to habeas corpus is protected by Article I of the Constitution.

writ of mandamus Court order directing a lower court or another public official to take a certain action.

zero-based budgeting Method of budgeting that demands justification for the entire budget request of an agency, not just its requested increase in funding.

NOTES

All chapter opening quotes are from Harold Lasswell, *Politics: Who Gets What, When, How* (New York: McGraw-Hill, 1936).

Chapter 1

1. Harold Lasswell, *Politics: Who Gets What, When, How* (New York: McGraw-Hill, 1936).
2. For an update on the continuing discussion of whether political science is a "science", see Jon R. Bond, "The Scientification of the Study of Politics," *Journal of Politics* 69 (November 2007): 897–907.
3. For a discussion of various aspects of legitimacy and its measurement in public opinion polls, see M. Stephen Weatherford, "Measuring Political Legitimacy," *American Political Science Review* 86 (March 1992): 140–55.
4. Thomas Hobbes, *Leviathan* (1651).
5. John Locke, *Treatise on Government* (1688).
6. See Barbara S. Gamble, "Putting Civil Rights to a Popular Vote," *American Journal of Political Science* 41 (January 1997): 245–69. For an essay on the "paradox" of democracy, see Bonnie Honig, "Between Decision and Deliberation: Political Paradox in Democratic Theory," *American Political Science Review* 101 (February 2007): 1–25.
7. James Madison, Alexander Hamilton, and John Jay, *The Federalist Papers* (New York: Mentor Books, 1961), No. 10, p. 81. Madison's *Federalist Papers*, No. 10 and No. 51, are reprinted in the Appendix.
8. E. E. Schattschneider, *Two Hundred Million Americans in Search of a Government* (New York: Holt, Rinehart & Winston, 1969), p. 63.
9. Harold Lasswell and Daniel Lerner, *The Comparative Study of Elites* (Stanford, Calif.: Stanford University Press, 1952), p. 7.
10. C. Wright Mills's classic study, *The Power Elite* (New York: Oxford University Press, 1956), is widely cited by Marxist critics of American democracy, but it can be read profitably by anyone concerned with the effects of large bureaucracies—corporate, governmental, or military—on democratic government.
11. In *Who Rules America?* (New York: Prentice Hall, 1967) and its sequel, *Who Rules America Now?* (New York: Prentice Hall, 1983), sociologist G. William Domhoff argues that America is ruled by an "upper class" who attend the same prestigious private schools, intermarry among themselves, and join the same exclusive clubs. In *Who's Running America?* (New York: Prentice Hall, 1976) and *Who's Running America? The Bush Restoration* (New York: Prentice Hall, 2002), political scientist Thomas R. Dye documents the concentration of power and the control of assets in the hands of officers and directors of the nation's largest corporations, banks, law firms, networks, foundations, and so forth. Dye argues, however, that most of these "institutional elites" were not born into the upper class but instead climbed the ladder to success.
12. Yale political scientist Robert A. Dahl is an important contributor to the development of pluralist theory, beginning with his *Preface to Democratic Theory* (Chicago: University of Chicago Press, 1956). He often refers to a pluralist system as a *polyarchy*—literally, a system with many centers of power. See his *Polyarchy* (New Haven, Conn.: Yale University Press, 1971), and for a revised defense of pluralism, see his *Democracy and Its Critics* (New Haven, Conn.: Yale University Press, 1989).

Chapter 2

1. Gunnar Myrdal, *An American Dilemma* (New York: Harper, 1944).
2. See Martin Luther King, Jr., "Letter from Birmingham City Jail," April 16, 1963.
3. For a discussion of the sources and consequences of intolerance in the general public, see James L. Gibson, "The Political Consequences of Intolerance: Cultural Conformity and Political Freedom," *American Political Science Review* 86 (June 1992): 338–52.
4. Alexis deTocqueville, *Democracy in America*, orig. 1835 (New York: Penguin Classic Books, 2003). See also Aurelian Craiutu and Jeremy Jennings, "The Third Democracy: Tocqueville's Views of America After 1840," *American Journal of Political Science* 98 (August 2004): 391–404.
5. Quoted in *The Ideas of Equality*, ed. George Abernathy (Richmond, Va.: John Knox Press, 1959), p. 185; also in Herbert McClosky and John Zaller, *The American Ethos: Public Attitudes toward Capitalism and Democracy* (Cambridge, Mass.: Harvard University Press, 1984), p. 72. For a more recent discussion of the American identity see Deborah J. Schildkraut, "Defining American Identity in Twenty-First Century," *Journal of Politics* 69 (August 2007): 597–615.
6. Quoted in Richard Hofstadter, *The American Political Tradition* (New York: Knopf, 1948), p. 45. Historian Hofstadter describes the thinking of American political leaders from Jefferson and the Founders to Franklin D. Roosevelt.
7. For a discussion of how people balance the values of individualism and opposition to big government with humanitarianism and the desire to help others, see Stanley Feldman and John Zaller, "The Political Culture of Ambivalence: Ideological Responses to the Welfare State," *American Journal of Political Science* 36 (February 1992): 268–307.
8. Lawrence R. Jacobs and Theda Skocpol, eds., *Inequality and American Democracy* (New York: Russell Sage Foundation, 2005).
9. Greg J. Duncan, *Years of Poverty, Years of Plenty* (Ann Arbor: University of Michigan Press, 1984); Isabel Sawhill, *Income Mobility in the United States* (Washington, D.C.: Urban Institute, 1996).
10. American Security Council, *The Illegal Immigration Crisis* (Washington, D.C.: ASC, 1994).
11. *Sale v. Haitian Centers Council*, 125 L. Ed. 2d 128 (1993).
12. Poll figures in this section are derived from the Pew Research Center for the People and the Press, "Religion and American Life," August 24, 2004. *www.people-press.org*
13. *Congressional Quarterly*, March 7, 2005.
14. See Stephen Earl Bennett, "Americans' Knowledge of Ideology, 1980–92," *American Politics Quarterly* 23 (July 1995): 259–78.
15. For evidence that ideological consistency increases with educational level, see William G. Jacoby, "Ideological Identification and Issue Attitude," *American Journal of Political Science* 35 (February 1991): 178–205.
16. Francis Fukuyama, *The End of History and the Last Man* (New York: Free Press, 1992).
17. See Robert Kimball, *Tenured Radicals* (New York: Harper & Row, 1990).
18. Herbert Marcuse, *One-Dimensional Man* (Boston: Beacon Press, 1964).
19. Allan Bloom, *The Closing of the American Mind* (New York: Simon & Schuster, 1987), p. 15.

Chapter 3

1. In *Federalist Papers*, No. 53, James Madison distinguishes a "constitution" from a law: a constitution is "established by the people and unalterable by the government, and a law established by the government and alterable by the government."
2. Another important decision on opening day of the Constitutional Convention was to keep the proceedings secret. James Madison made his own notes on the convention proceedings, and they were published many years later. See Max Ferrand, ed., *The Records of the Federal Convention of 1787* (New Haven, Conn.: Yale University Press, 1911).
3. See Edward Millican, *One United People: The Federalist Papers and the National Idea* (Lexington: University Press of Kentucky, 1990).
4. See David Brian Robertson, "Madison's Opponents and Constitutional Design," *American Political Science Review* 99 (May 2005): 225–43.
5. Charles A. Beard, *An Economic Interpretation of the Constitution* (New York: Macmillan, 1913).
6. Robert E. Brown, *Charles Beard and the Constitution* (Princeton, N.J.: Princeton University Press, 1956).
7. James Madison, *Federalist Papers*, No. 10, reprinted in the Appendix.
8. Alexander Hamilton, *Federalist Papers*, No. 78.

Chapter 4

1. The states are listed in the order in which their legislatures voted to secede. While occupied by Confederate troops, secessionist legislators in Missouri and Kentucky also voted to secede, but Unionist representatives from these states remained in Congress.
2. *Texas v. White*, 7 Wallace 700 (1869).
3. James Madison, *Federalist Papers*, No. 51, reprinted in the Appendix.
4. Ibid.
5. The arguments for "competitive federalism" are developed at length in Thomas R. Dye, *American Federalism: Competition among Governments* (Lexington, Mass.: Lexington Books, 1990).
6. David Osborne, *Laboratories of Democracy* (Cambridge, Mass.: Harvard Business School, 1988).
7. Morton Grodzins, *The American System* (Chicago: Rand McNally, 1966), pp. 8–9.
8. Ibid., p. 265.
9. Charles Press, *State and Community Governments in the Federal System* (New York: Wiley, 1979), p. 78.
10. *Garcia v. San Antonio Metropolitan Transit Authority*, 469 U.S. 528 (1985).
11. See Michael S. Greve, *Real Federalism: Why It Matters, How It Could Happen* (Washington, D.C.: AEI Press, 1999).
12. *U.S. v. Lopez*, 514 U.S. 549 (1995).
13. *Seminole Tribe of Florida v. Florida*, 517 U.S. 44 (1996).
14. *Alden v. Maine*, 67 U.S.L.W. 1401 (1999).
15. *Printz v. U.S.* 521 U.S. 890 (1997).
16. *Brzonkala v. Morrison* (2000).
17. *Federal-State-Local Relations: Federal Grants in Aid*, House Committee on Government Operations, 85th Cong., 2d sess., p. 7.
18. Craig Volden, "Intergovernmental Political Competition in American Federalism," *American Journal of Political Science* 49 (April 2005): 327–42.

Chapter 5

1. See James A. Stimson, Michael B. MacKuen, and Robert S. Erikson, "Dynamic Representation," *American Political Science Review* 89 (September 1995): 543–61.
2. Robert S. Erikson and Kent L. Tedin, *American Public Opinion*, 7th ed. (New York: Longman, 2007).
3. Ibid., p. 35.
4. For a summary of literature on public opinion, see James Stimson, "Opinion and Representation," *American Political Science Review* 89 (March 1995): 179–83.
5. Sandra K. Schwartz, "Preschoolers and Politics," in *New Directions in Political Socialization*, eds. David C. Schwartz and Sandra K. Schwartz (New York: Free Press, 1975), p. 242.
6. David O. Sears and Carolyn Funk, "Evidence of the Long-Term Persistence of Adults' Political Predispositions," *Journal of Politics* 61 (February 1999): 1–28.
7. Robert D. Hess and Judith V. Torney, *The Development of Political Attitudes in Children* (Chicago: Aldine, 1977), p. 42.
8. See also Ted G. Jelen, "The Political Consequences of Religious Group Attitudes," *Journal of Politics* 55 (February 1993): 178–90.
9. Geoffrey C. Longman, "Religion and Political Behavior in the United States," *Public Opinion Quarterly* 61 (Summer 1997): 288–316.
10. See John C. Green, "The Christian Right in the 1994 Elections," *P.S.: Political Science and Politics* 28 (March 1995): 5–23.
11. See also James A. Stimson, *Public Opinion in America: Moods, Cycles, and Swings* (Boulder, Colo.: Westview Press, 1991).
12. Janet M. Box-Steffensmeier, Suzanna De Boef, and Tse-Min Lin, "The Dynamics of the Partisan Gender Gap," *American Political Science Review* 98 (August 2004): 515–28.
13. Jon Horwitz and Mark Peffley, "Explaining the Great Racial Divide: Perceptions of Fairness in the U.S. Criminal Justice System," *Journal of Politics* 67 (August 2005): 768–83.
14. See Marissa A. Abrajano, R. Michael Alvarez, and Jonathan Nagler, "The Hispanic Vote in the 2004 Presidential Election" *Journal of Politics* 70 (April, 2008): 368–382; Marco Battaglini, Rebecca Morton, and Thomas Palfrey, "*Si Se Puede!* Latino Candidates and the Mobilization of Latino Voters," *American Political Science Review* 101 (August 2007): 409–24.
15. V.O. Key Jr., *Public Opinion and American Democracy* (New York: Knopf, 1967), p. 536.
16. *Smith V. Allwright*, 321 U.S. 649 (1944).
17. *Harper v. Virginia State Board of Elections*, 383 U.S. 663 (1966).
18. Staci L. Rhine, "Registration Reform and Turnout," *American Politics Quarterly* 23 (October 1995): 409–26; Stephen Knack, "Does 'Motor Voter' Work?" *Journal of Politics* 57 (August 1995): 796–811; Michael D. Martinez and David B. Hill, "Did Motor Voter Work?" *American Politics Quarterly* 27 (February 1997): 296–315.
19. Richard G. Niemi and Paul S. Herrnson, "Beyond the Butterfly: The Complexity of U.S. Ballots," *Perspectives on Politics* 1 (June, 2003): 317–26.
20. *Crawford v. Marion County Election Board* April 28, 2008.
21. See Dennis F. Thompson, "Election Time: Normative Implications of Temporal Properties of the Election Process in the United States," *American Political Science Review* 98 (February 2004); 51–64.
22. *General Social Survey, 1998* (Chicago: National Opinion Research Center, 1999).
23. John E. Filer, Lawrence W. Kenny, and Rebecca B. Morton, "Redistribution, Income, and Voting," *American Journal of Political Science* 37 (February 1993): 63–87.
24. Sidney Verba, Kay Scholzman, Henry Brady, and Norman Nie, "Citizen Activity: Who Participates? What Do They Say?" *American Political Science Review* 87 (June 1993): 303–18.
25. John Stuart Mill, *Considerations on Representative Government* (Chicago: Regnery, Gateway, 1962; original publication 1859), p. 144.
26. Ibid., p. 130.
27. Quotation from Austin Ranney in "Non-Voting Is Not a Social Disease," *Public Opinion* 6 (November/December 1983): 18.
28. Martin Luther King Jr., "Letter from Birmingham City Jail," April 16, 1963.

Chapter 6

1. For an overview of the mass media in American politics, see Doris A. Graber, *Mass Media and American Politics*, 7th ed. (Washington, D.C.: CQ Press, 2005).
2. Pew Research Center for People and the Press. http://people-press.org June, 2000.
3. See Lance Bennett, *News: The Politics of Illusion*, 5th ed. (New York: Longman, 2007).
4. E. E. Schattschneider, *The Semisovereign People* (New York: Holt, Rinehart & Winston, 1961), p. 68.
5. William A. Henry, "News as Entertainment," in *What's News*, ed. Elie Abel (San Francisco: Institute for Contemporary Studies, 1981), p. 133.
6. Shanto Iyengar, *Is Anyone Responsible? How Television Frames Political Issues* (Chicago: University of Chicago Press, 1991).
7. Graber, *Mass Media*, p. 35.
8. Matthew A. Baum, "Sex, Lies, and War: How Soft News Brings Foreign Policy to the Inattentive Public," *American Political Science Review* 96 (March 2002): 91–109.
9. Larry Sabato, Mark Stencel, and S. Robert Lichter, *Peep Show? Media Politics in an Age of Scandal* (Lanham, Md.: Rowman & Little-field, 2001).
10. Ben J. Wattenberg, *The Good News Is the Bad News Is Wrong* (New York: Simon & Schuster, 1984).
11. Ted Smith, "The Watchdog's Bite," *American Enterprise* 2 (January/February 1990): 66.
12. Larry Sabato, *Feeding Frenzy: How Attack Journalism Has Transformed American Politics* (New York: Free Press, 1991).
13. Graber, *Mass Media*, p. 946.
14. S. Robert Lichter, Stanley Rothman, and Linda S. Lichter, *The Media Elite* (Bethesda, Md.: Adler and Adler, 1986).
15. David Prindle, "Hollywood Liberalism" *Social Science Quarterly* 71 (March 1993): 121.
16. David C. Barker, "Rushed Decisions: Political Talk Radio and Vote Choice," *Journal of Politics* 61 (May 1999): 527–39.
17. Diana C. Mutz and Byron Reeves, "The New Videomalaise: Effects of Televised Incivility on Political Trust," *American Political Science Review* 99 (February 2005): 1–15.
18. Marcus Prior, "News Versus Entertainment; How Increasing Media Choice Widens Gaps in Political Knowledge and Turnout," *American Journal of Political Science* 49 (July 2005): 577–592.
19. Shanto Iyengar, et al., "Selective Exposure to Campaign Communication" *Journal of Politics* 70 (January 2008): 186–200.
20. Julianne F. Flowers, Audrey A. Haynes, and Michael H. Crespin, "The Media, the Campaign, and the Message," *American Journal of Political Science* 47 (April 2003): 259–73.
21. See also Martin Gilens, Lynn Vavreck, and Martin Cohen, "The Mass Media and the Public's Assessment of Presidential Candidates, 1952–2000." *Journal of Politics* 69 (November 2007): 1160–75.
22. See David S. Castle, "Media Coverage of Presidential Primaries," *American Politics Quarterly* 19 (January 1991): 13–42; Christine F. Ridout, "The Role of Media Coverage of Iowa and New Hampshire," *American Politics Quarterly* 19 (January 1991): 43–58.
23. *Media Monitor*, Vol. 14 (November/December 2000).
24. *New York Times v. U.S.*, 376 U.S. 713 (1971).
25. *New York Times v. Sullivan*, 376 U.S. 254 (1964).
26. See Arthur Lupia and Tasha S. Philpot "Views from Inside the Net," *Journal of Politics* 67 (November 2005): 1122–42.
27. *Reno v. American Civil Liberties Union* 117 S.Ct. 2329 (1997).
28. Bernard Cohen, *The Press and Foreign Policy* (Princeton, N.J.: Princeton University Press, 1963), p. 16.
29. Austin Ranney, *Channels of Power* (New York: Basic Books, 1983), p. 81.
30. Benjamin J. Page, Robert Y. Shapiro, and Glen R. Dempsey, "What Moves Public Opinion," *American Political Science Review* 81 (March 1987): 23–43.
31. National Institute of Mental Health, *Television and Behavior* (Washington, D.C.: Government Printing Office, 1982).
32. Brandon Centerwall, "Exposure to Television as a Risk Factor for Violence," *American Journal of Epidemiology* 129 (April 1989): 643–52.

Chapter 7

1. Gaetano Mosca, *The Ruling Class* (New York: McGraw-Hill, 1939), p. 51.
2. James Madison, *Federalist Papers*, No. 10, reprinted in the Appendix.
3. George Washington, Farewell Address, September 17, 1796, in *Documents on American History*, 10th ed., eds. Henry Steele Commager and Milton Cantor (Upper Saddle River, N.J.: Prentice Hall, 1988), 1: 172.
4. Colleen A. Sheehan and *Madison v. Hamilton*, "The Battle over Republicanism and the Role of Public Opinion," *American Political Science Review* 98 (August 2004), 405–24.
5. Samuel Merrill III, Bernard Grofman, and Thomas L. Brunell, "Cycles in American Electoral Politics, 1854–2006" *American Political Science Review* 102 (February 2008): 1–18.
6. E. E. Schattschneider, *Party Government* (New York: Holt, Rinehart & Winston, 1942), p. 1.
7. Geofrey C. Layman and Thomas M. Carsey, "Party Polarization and Conflict Extension in the American Electorate," *American Journal of Political Science* 46 (October 2002): 786–802.
8. See Thomas R. Dye and Susan MacManus, *Politics in States and Communities*, 13th ed. (Upper Saddle River, N.J.: Prentice Hall, 2008).
9. *National Election Study*, 2000.
10. Conventions continue to play a modest role in nominations in some states:
    - Colorado: Parties may hold a preprimary convention to designate a candidate to be listed first on the primary ballot. All candidates receiving at least 30 percent of the delegate vote will be listed on the primary ballot.
    - Connecticut: Party conventions are held to endorse candidates. If no one challenges the endorsed candidate, no primary election is held. If a challenger receives 20 percent of the delegate vote, a primary election will be held to determine the party's nominee in the general election.
    - New York: Party conventions choose the party's "designated" candidate in primary elections. Anyone receiving 25 percent of the delegates also appears on the ballot.
    - Utah: Party conventions select party's nominees.
    - Illinois, Indiana, Michigan, and South Carolina: Party conventions nominate candidates for some minor state offices.
11. For an argument that primary elections force parties to be more responsive to voters, see John G. Geer and Mark E. Shere, "Party Competition and the Prisoner's Dilemma: An Argument for the Direct Primary," *Journal of Politics* 54 (August 1992): 365–74.
12. For an up-to-date listing of state primaries and relevant information about them, see *The Book of the States*, published biannually by the Council of State Governments, Lexington, Kentucky.
13. The U.S. Supreme Court declared that the "blanket primary" violated the First Amendment freedom of association right of political parties to choose their own candidates. California had adopted a primary system that gave all voters, regardless of party affiliation, ballots that included the names of *all* candidates in

both parties. Candidates of each party who received the most votes were to become the nominees of those parties and move on to face each other in the general election. But the Supreme Court held that the blanket primary violated the First Amendment right of association *California Democratic Party v. Jones*, 530 U.S. 567 (2000).

14. Congressional Quarterly, *National Party Conventions 1811–1996* (Washington, D.C.: CQ Press, 1997).

15. For evidence that the national party conventions raise the poll standings of their presidential nominees, see James E. Campbell, Lynna L. Cherry, and Kenneth A. Wink, "The Convention Bump," *American Politics Quarterly* 20 (July 1992): 287–307.

16. See John A. Clark, John M. Bruce, John H. Kessel, and William G. Jacoby, "I'd Rather Switch Than Fight: Lifelong Democrats and Converts to Republicanism among Campaign Activists," *American Journal of Political Science* 35 (August 1991): 577–97.

17. For a scholarly debate over realignment, see Byron E. Schafer, ed., *The End of Realignment: Interpreting American Election Eras* (Madison: University of Wisconsin Press, 1991).

18. Gary Miller and Norman Schofield, "Activists and Partisan Realignment in the United States," *American Political Science Review* 97 (May 2003): 245–60.

Chapter 8

1. Gerald Pomper, *Elections in America* (New York: Dodd, Mead, 1968).

2. Morris P. Fiorina, *Retrospective Voting in American National Elections* (New Haven, Conn.: Yale University Press, 1988).

3. Quoted in *Congressional Quarterly Almanac, 1965* (Washington, D.C.: Congressional Quarterly, Inc., 1966), p. 267.

4. Alan Ehrenhalt, *The United States of Ambition: Politicians, Power and the Pursuit of Office* (New York: Random House, 1991), p. 22.

5. See Jamie L. Carson, "Strategy, Selection and Candidate Competition in U.S. House and Senate Elections", *Journal of Politics* 67 (February 2005): 1–26.

6. Alan I. Abramowitz, "Incumbency, Campaign Spending, and the Decline of Competition in U.S. House Elections," *Journal of Politics* 53 (February 1991): 55–70.

7. Herbert Alexander, as quoted in Richard R. Lau et al., "The Effects of Negative Political Advertisements," *American Political Science Review* 93 (December 1999): 851–75.

8. Lee Sigelman and Emmett H. Buell Jr., "You Take the High Road and I'll Take the Low Road? The Interplay of Attack Strategies and Tactics in Presidential Campaigns," *The Journal of Politics* 46 (May 2003): 518–31; Richard R. Lau and Gerald M. Pomper, "Effectiveness of Negative Campaigning in U.S. Senate Elections," *American Journal of Political Science* 46 (January 2002): 47–66; Daniel Stevens, et al., "What's Good for the Goose is Bad for the Gander: Negative Political Advertising, Partisanship and Turnout," *Journal of Politics* 70 (April 2008): 527–41.

9. Ted Brader, "Striking a Responsive Chord: How Political Ads Motivate and Persuade Voters by Appealing to Emotions," *American Journal of Political Science* 49 (April 2005): 388–405.

10. Paul Friedman, Michael Franz, and Kenneth Goldstein, "Campaign Advertising and Democratic Citizenship," *American Journal of Political Science* 48 (October 2004): 723–41. But see also Jonathan S. Krasno and Donald P. Green, "Do Televised Presidential Ads Increase Voter Turnout?", *Journal of Politics* 70 (January, 2008): 245–61.

11. Thomas M. Holbrook and Scott D. McClung, "The Mobilization of Core Supporters," *American Journal of Political Science*, 49 (October 2005): 689–703.

12. Center for Responsive Politics, *The Big Picture: The Money Behind the 2000 Elections* (Washington, D.C., 2001).

13. In the important U.S. Supreme Court decision in *Buckley v. Valeo* in 1976, James L. Buckley, former U.S. senator from New York, and his brother, William F. Buckley, the well-known conservative commentator, argued successfully that the laws limiting an individual's right to participate in political campaigns—financially or otherwise—violated First Amendment freedoms. Specifically, the U.S. Supreme Court held that no government could limit individuals' rights to spend money or publish or broadcast their own views on issues or elections. Candidates can spend as much of their own money as they wish on their own campaigns. Private individuals can spend as much as they wish to circulate their own views on an election, although their contributions to candidates and parties can still be limited. The Court, however, permitted governmental limitations on parties and campaign organizations and allowed the use of federal funds for financing campaigns. *Buckley v. Valeo*, 424 U.S. 1 (1976).

14. Sanford C. Gordon and Catherine Hafer, "Flexing Muscles: Corporate Political Expenditures As Signals to the Bureaucracy," *American Political Science Review* 99 (May 2005): 245–61.

15. *Buckley v. Valeo*, 424 US. 1 (1976).

16. *McConnell v. F.E.C.*, 540 US. 93 (2003).

17. *F.E.C. v. Wisconsin Right to Life*, June 25, 2007.

18. *Randall v. Sorrell*, June 26, 2006.

19. See Paul-Henri Guvian and Audrey A. Haynes, "Presidential Nominating Campaigns," *P.S. Political Science and Politics* 36 (April 2003): 175–80.

20. Lynn Vavreck, Constantine J. Spiliotes and Linda L. Fowler, "The Effects of Retail Politics in the New Hampshire Primary," *American Journal of Political Science* 46 (July 2002): 595–610.

21. Matthew A. Baum, "Talking the Vote: Why Presidential Candidates Hit the Talk Show Circuit," *American Journal of Political Science* 49 (April 2005): 213–34.

22. University-based political scientists rely heavily on a series of National Election Studies, originated at the Survey Research Center at the University of Michigan, which have surveyed the voting-age population in every presidential election and most congressional elections since 1952.

23. See Martin P. Wattenberg, *The Rise of Candidate-Centered Politics* (Cambridge, Mass.: Harvard University Press, 1991).

24. Responsibility for the economy, however, is also affected by the voters' partisanship, ideology and views about whether the president or Congress is chiefly responsible. See Joseph J. Rudolph, "Who's Responsible for the Economy?," *American Journal of Political Science* 47 (October 2003): 698–713.

25. For an argument that voters look ahead to the economic future and reward or punish the president based on rational expectations, see Michael B. MacKuen, Robert S. Erickson, and James A. Stimson, "Peasants or Bankers? The American Electorate and the U.S. Economy," *American Political Science Review* 86 (September 1992): 680–95.

26. See Herbert F. Weisberg, "The Structure and Effects of Moral Predispositions in Contemporary American Politics," *Journal of Politics* 67 (August 2005): 646–68.

Chapter 9

1. Political scientist David Truman's classic definition of an interest group: "any group that is based on one or more shared attitudes and makes certain demands upon other groups or organizations in society." See *The Governmental Process* (New York: Knopf, 1971), p. 33.
2. James Madison, *Federalist Papers*, No. 10, reprinted in the Appendix.
3. Gale Research Company, *Encyclopedia of Associations* (Detroit: Gale Research, 2004).
4. Frank R. Baumgartner and Beth L. Leech, "Interest Niches and Policy Bandwagons: Patterns of Interest Group Involvement in National Politics," *The Journal of Politics* 63 (November 2001): 1191–1213.
5. Jeffrey M. Berry, *The New Liberalism: The Rising Power of Citizen Groups* (Washington, D.C.: Brookings Institution Press, 1999).
6. For both theory and survey data on the sources of interest-group mobilization, see Jack L. Walker, *Mobilizing Interest Groups in America: Patrons, Professions, and Social Movements* (Ann Arbor: University of Michigan Press, 1991).

7. Kay Lehmann Scholzman, "What Accent the Heavenly Chorus? Political Equality and the American Pressure System," *Journal of Politics* 46 (November 1984): 1006–32; see also Jeffrey M. Berry, Kent E. Portney, and Ken Thomson, *The Case for Participatory Democracy* (Washington, D.C.: Brookings Institution Press, 1994).
8. Center for Responsive Politics, *Influence, Inc. 2000* (Washington, D.C., 2001).
9. Jeffrey M. Berry, *The New Liberalism* (Washington D.C.: Brookings Institution Press, 1999).
10. Quotation from Roger Kersh, "Corporate Lobbyists as Political Actors," in *Interest Group Politics*, 6th ed., ed. Allan J. Cigler and Burdett A. Loomis (Washington, D.C.: CQ Press, 2002).
11. For evidence that vote buying on congressional roll calls is rare, see Janet M. Grenzke, "Shopping in the Congressional Supermarket: The Currency Is Complex," *American Journal of Political Science* 33 (February 1989): 1–24. But for evidence that committee

participation by members of Congress is influenced by political action committee money, see Richard L. Hall and Frank W. Wayman, "Buying Time: Moneyed Interests and the Mobilization of Bias in Congressional Committees," *American Political Science Review* 84 (September 1990): 797–819.
12. See, for example, Mark E. Patterson, "The Presidency and Organized Interests: White House Patterns of Interest Group Liaison," *American Political Science Review* 86 (September 1992): 612–22.
13. Robert H. Salisbury, "Who You Know versus What You Know: The Use of Government Experience by Washington Lobbyists," *American Journal of Political Science* 33 (February 1989): 175–95.
14. *Brown v. Board of Education of Topeka*, 349 U.S. 294 (1955).
15. Samuel Huntington, *Political Order in Changing Societies* (New Haven, Conn.: Yale University Press, 1965), p. 28.
16. Mancur Olson, *The Rise and Decline of Nations*. (New Haven, Conn.: Yale University Press, 1982).

Chapter 10

1. James Madison, *Federalist Papers*, No. 10, reprinted in the Appendix.
2. Quoted in Jay M. Schafritz, *The Harper Collins Dictionary of American Government and Politics* (New York: HarperCollins, 1992), p. 56.
3. See David Auerswald and Forrest Maltzman, "Policymaking through Advice and Consent: Treaty Consideration by the United States Senate," *Journal of Politics* 65 (November 2003): 1097–1110.
4. *McGrain v. Doughtery*, 273 U.S. 13J (1927).
5. *Baker v. Carr*, 369 U.S. 186 (1962), *Wesberry v. Sanders*, 370 U.S. 1 (1964).
6. *Gray v. Sanders*, 322 U.S. 368 (1963).
7. *Department of Commerce v. U.S. House of Representatives*, 525 U.S. 316 (1999).
8. *Gaffney v. Cummings*, 412 U.S. 763 (1973).
9. *Davis v. Bandemer* 478 U.S. 109 (1986).
10. *Vieth v. Jubelirer* 241 F. Supp. 2d 478 (2004).
11. *League of United Latin American Citizens v. Perry*, June 28, 2006.
12. Scott W. Desposato and John R. Petrocik, "The Variable Incumbency Advantage: New Voters, Redistricting, and Personal Vote," *American Journal of Political Science* 47 (January 2003): 18–32
13. *Thornburg v. Gingles*, 478 U.S. 30 (1986).
14. *Shaw v. Reno*, 125 I. Ed. 2d 511 (1993).
15. *Miller v. Johnson*, 115 S. Ct. 2475 (1995).
16. See Roger H. Davidson and Walter J. Oleszek, *Congress and Its Members*, 9th ed. (Washington, D.C.: CQ Press, 2004).

17. David Lublin, *The Paradox of Representation: Racial Gerrymandering and Minority Interests in Congress* (Princeton, N.J.: Princeton University Press, 1997). See also David Lublin and D. Stephen Voss, "The Missing Middle," *Journal of Politics* 65 (February 2003). 227–37.
18. *Georgia v. Ashcroft*, 539 U.S. 461 (2003).
19. For an in-depth analysis of who decides to run for Congress and who does not, see Linda L. Fowler and Robert D. McClure, *Political Ambition: Who Decides to Run for Congress* (New Haven, Conn.: Yale University Press, 1990).
20. See Michael K. Moore and John R. Hibbing, "Situational Dissatisfaction in Congress: Explaining Voluntary Departures," *Journal of Politics* 60 (November 1998): 1088–1107.
21. *U.S. Term Limits v. Thornton*, 115 S.C. 1842, (1995).
22. See Gary Jacobson, *The Politics of Congressional Elections*, 5th ed. (New York: HarperCollins, 2000).
23. See David Epstein and Peter Zemsky, "Money Talks: Deterring Quality Challengers in Congressional Elections," *American Political Science Review* 89 (June 1995): 295–322.
24. See Thomas E. Mann and Raymond Wolfinger, "Candidates and Parties in Congressional Elections," *American Political Science Review* 84 (September 1990): 545–64.
25. See Mary T. Hanna, "Political Science Caught Flat-Footed by Midterm

Elections," *Chronicle of Higher Education*, November 30, 1994, pp. B1–2.
26. See Richard Fenno, *Going Home: Black Representatives and Their Constituents* (Chicago: University of Chicago Press, 2003).
27. Paul S. Herrnson, J. Celeste Lay, and Atiya Kai Stokes, "Women Running 'As Women'," *Journal of Politics* 65 (February 2003): 244–55; see also Jennifer Lawless and Kathryn Pearson, "The Primary Reason for Women's Underrepresentation? Re-evaluating the Conventional Wisdom," *Journal of Politics* 70 (January 2008): 67–82.
28. See Glen S. Krutz, "Issues and Institutions: 'Winnowing' in the U.S. Congress," *American Journal of Political Science* 49 (April 2005) 313–26.
29. U.S. House of Representatives, Commission on Administrative Review, *Administrative Reorganization and Legislative Management*, 95th Cong., 1st sess, H. Doc. 95–232, pp. 17–19.
30. Richard F. Fenno, *Home Style* (Boston: Little, Brown, 1978).
31. Roger H. Davidson and Walter J. Oleszek, *Congress and Its Members* 814 (Washington, D.C.: CQ Press, 2000).
32. Glenn R. Parker, *Characteristics of Congress* (Upper Saddle River, N.J.: Prentice Hall, 1989), p. 30.
33. Richard F. Fenno, *The Making of a Senator: Dan Quayle* (Washington, D.C.: CQ Press, 1989), p. 119. Also cited in

34. Davidson and Oleszek, *Congress and Its Members*, 9th ed., p. 120.

34. Davidson and Oleszek, *Congress and Its Members*, 9th ed., p. 129.

35. Barbara Sinclair, "The Emergence of Strong Leadership in the House of Representatives," *Journal of Politics* 54 (August 1992): 657–84.

36. Gary W. Cox and Eric Magar, "How Much Is Majority Status in the U.S. Congress Worth?" *American Political Science Review* 93 (June 1999): 299–310.

37. Davidson and Oleszek, *Congress and Its Members*, 9th ed. p. 161.

38. John R. Hibbing, *Congressional Careers* (Chapel Hill: University of North Carolina Press, 1991).

39. See Charles Stewart and Tim Groseclose, "The Value of Committee Seats in the United States Senate," *American Journal of Political Science* 43 (July 1999): 963–73; see also Kevin M. Esterling, "Buying Expertise: Campaign Contributions and Attention to Policy Analysis in Congressional Committees," *American Political Science Review* 101 (February 2007): 93–110.

40. See John W. Patty, "The House Discharge Procedure and Majoritarian Politics," *Journal of Politics* 69 (August 2007): 678–88.

41. Nathan W. Monroe and Gregory Robinson, "Do Restrictive Rules Produce Nonmedian Outcomes?," *Journal of Politics* 70 (January 2008): 217–31.

42. Larry Markinson, *The Cash Constituents of Congress* (Washington, D.C.: CQ Press, 1992).

43. Donald Matthews, *U.S. Senators and Their World* (New York: Vintage Books, 1960).

44. David Rohde, Norman J. Ornstein, and Robert L. Peabody, "Political Change and Legislative Norms," in *Studies of Congress*, ed. Glenn R. Parker (Washington, D.C.: CQ Press, 1985), p. 175.

45. See John R. Hibbing, "Contours of the Modern Congressional Career," *American Political Science Review* 85 (June 1991): 405–28.

46. Richard Fenno, *Power of the Purse* (Boston: Little, Brown, 1965), p. 620.

47. See David R. Mayhew, *Divided We Govern* (New Haven, Conn.: Yale University Press, 1991); Sarah A. Binder, "The Dynamics of Legislative Gridlock," *American Political Science Review* 93 (September 1999): 519–33.

48. *Congressional Quarterly Weekly Report*, November 23, 1991, p. 3437.

Chapter 11

1. For an argument that presidents encourage people to think of them as "the single head of government and moral leader of the nation who speaks for all of the people," see Barbara Hinckley, *The Symbolic Presidency: How Presidents Portray Themselves* (New York: Routledge, 1991).

2. See Theodore Lowi, *The Personal President* (Ithaca, N.Y.: Cornell University Press, 1987).

3. Presidential address to Congress, September 20, 2001.

4. See Michael Less Benedict, *The Impeachment and Trial of Andrew Johnson* (New York: Norton, 1973).

5. William Howard Taft, *Our Chief Magistrate and His Powers* (New York: Columbia University Press, 1938), p. 138, reprinted in *The Presidency*, ed. John P. Roche (New York: Harcourt Brace Jovanovich, 1964), p. 23.

6. Quoted in Arthur B. Tourtellot, *Presidents on the Presidency* (New York: Doubleday, 1964), pp. 55–56.

7. *Youngstown Sheet & Tube Co. v. Sawyer*, 343 U.S. 579 (1952).

8. *United States v. Nixon*, 418 U.S. 683 (1974).

9. *Nixon v. Fitzgerald*, 457 U.S. 731 (1982).

10. *Clinton v. Jones*, 520 U.S. 681 (1997).

11. Quoted in Richard Neustadt, *Presidential Power* (New York: Wiley, 1960), p. 9.

12. See Paul Brace and Barbara Hinckley, "The Structure of Presidential Approval," *Journal of Politics* 53 (November 1991): 993–1017.

13. See Suzanne L. Pancer, "Toward an Understanding of 'Rally' Effect," *Public Opinion Quarterly* 59 (September 1995): 526–46; Wave J. Aetherington and Michael Nelson: "Anatomy of a Rally Effect," *P.S. Political Science and Politics* 36 (January 2003): 37–42.

14. John Mueller, *War, Presidents, and Public Opinion* (New York: Wiley, 1973).

15. See George C. Edwards and B. Dan Wood, "Who Influences Whom," *American Political Science Review* 93 (June 1999): 327–44.

16. Garry Young and William B. Perkins, "Presidential Rhetoric, the Public Agenda, and the End of Presidential Television's 'Golden Age,'" *Journal of Politics* 67 (November 2005): 1190–1205.

17. Michael Bailey, Lee Sigelman, and Clyde Wilcox, "Presidential Persuasion on Social Issues," *Political Research Quarterly* 56 (March 2003): 49–58.

18. George C. Edwards and Stephen J. Wayne, *Presidential Leadership*, 6th ed. (Belmont, Calif.: Wadsworth, 2003), p. 118.

19. Lawrence R. Jacobs and Robert Y. Schapiro, *Politicians Don't Pander* (Chicago: University of Chicago Press, 2000).

20. Brandice Canes-Wrone and Kenneth W. Shotts, "The Conditional Nature of Presidential Responsiveness to Public Opinion," *American Journal of Political Science* 48 (October 2004): 690–706.

21. *Youngstown Sheet & Tube Co. v. Sawyer*, 343 U.S. 579 (1952).

22. Kenneth R. Mayer, "Executive Orders and Presidential Power," *Journal of Politics* 61 (May 1999): 445–66; Christopher J. Deering and Forrest Maltzman, "The Politics of Executive Orders," *Political Research Quarterly* 52 (December 1999): 767–83.

23. See also Jeffrey E. Cohen, *The Politics of the U.S. Cabinet* (Pittsburgh: University of Pittsburgh Press, 1988).

24. John Kingdon, *Agenda, Alternatives, and Public Policies* (Boston: Little, Brown, 1984), p. 25.

25. Mathew N. Beckmann, "The President's Playbook: White House Strategies for Lobbying Congress," *Journal of Politics* 70 (April 2008): 407–19.

26. See Daniel E. Ingberman and Dennis A. Yao, "Presidential Commitment and the Veto," *American Journal of Political Science* 35 (May 1991): 357–89; and Samuel B. Hoff, "Saying No," *American Politics Quarterly* 19 (July 1991): 310–23.

27. *Clinton v. City of New York*, 524 U.S. 417 (1998).

28. Brandice Canes-Wrone, William G. Howell, David E. Lewis, "Toward a Broader Understanding of Presidential Power," *Journal of Politics* 70 (January 2008): 1–16.

29. G.J.A. O'Toole, *Honorable Treachery: A History of U.S. Intelligence from the American Revolution to the CIA* (New York: Atlantic Monthly Press, 1991).

30. National Commission on Terrorist Attacks upon the United States, *The 9/11 Commission Report*, New York: W.W. Norton, 2004.

31. *Mora v. McNamara*, 389 U.S. 934 (1964); *Massachusetts v. Laird*, 400 U.S. 886 (1970). The Court specifically refused to intervene in the conduct of the Vietnam War by presidents Johnson and Nixon.

32. Jules Witcover, *Crap Shoot: Rolling the Dice on the Vice Presidency* (New York: Crow Publishing, 1992).

Chapter 12

1. "Red tape" derives its meaning from the use of reddish tape by seventeenth-century English courts to bind legal documents. Unwrapping court orders entangled one in "red tape." See Herbert Kaufman, *Red Tape: Its Uses and Abuses* (Washington, D.C.: Brookings Institution, 1977).

2. H. H. Gerth and C. Wright Mills, *From Max Weber* (New York: Oxford Press, 1958).

3. Max Neiman, *Defending Government: Why Big Government Works* (Upper Saddle River, N.J.: Prentice Hall, 2000).

4. James Q. Wilson, *Bureaucracy: What Government Agencies Do and Why They Do It* (New York: Basic Books, 1989).

5. William Niskanen, *Bureaucracy and Representative Government* (Chicago: Aldine, 1971).

6. The constitutional question of whether Congress can establish an executive branch commission and protect its members from dismissal by the president was settled in *Humphrey's Executor v. United States* (1935). Franklin Roosevelt fired Humphrey from the Federal Trade Commission despite a fixed term set by Congress. Humphrey died shortly afterward, and when the executors of his estate sued for his back pay, the Supreme Court ruled that his firing was illegal.

7. See Nicholas Henry, *Public Administration and Public Affairs*, 7th ed. (Upper Saddle River, N.J.: Prentice Hall, 1999), Chapter 11.

8. Quoted in U.S. Civil Service Commission, *Biography of an Ideal: A History of the Civil Service System* (Washington, D.C.: Government Printing Office, 1973), p. 16.

9. See John D. Huber and Nalan McCarty, "Bureaucratic Capacity, Delegation, and Political Reform," *American Political Science Review* 98 (August 2004) 481–494.

10. Paul C. Light, *Thickening Government: Federal Hierarchy and the Diffusion of Accountability* (Washington, D.C.: Brookings Institution, 1995).

11. David Osborne and Ted Gaebler, *Reinventing Government* (New York: Addison-Wesley, 1992).

12. Al Gore, *Creating a Government That Works Better and Costs Less* (Washington, D.C.: Government Printing Office, 1993).

13. William G. Howell and David E. Lewis, "Agencies by Presidential Design," *Journal of Politics* 64 (November 2002): 1098–1114.

14. OMB also forecasts economic activity, government spending and debt; see George A. Krause and J. Kevin Corder, "Explaining Bureaucratic Optimism," *American Political Science Review* 101 (February 2007): 129–42.

15. Daniel P. Carpenter, "Protection Without Capture," *American Political Science Review* 98 (November 2004): 613–31.

16. Robert Crandell and Jerry Ellig, *Economic Deregulation and Consumer Choice* (Fairfax, Va.: Center for Market Processes, 1997).

17. General Accounting Office, *Regulatory Enforcement Fairness Act Report*, 1999.

18. Thomas D. Hopkins, *Regulatory Costs in Profile* (Washington, D.C.: Center for the Study of American Business, 1996).

19. Richard K. Vedder, "Federal Regulation's Impact on the Productivity Slowdown: A Trillion Dollar Drag," *Policy Study*, Center for the Study of American Business, July 1996.

20. For research suggesting that the appointive power is a more important instrument of political control of the bureaucracy than budgets or legislation, see B. Dan Wood and Richard W. Waterman, "The Dynamics of Political Control of the Bureaucracy," *American Political Science Review* 83 (September 1991): 801–28.

21. Evidence of the effectiveness of interventions by members of Congress in local offices of federal agencies is provided by John T. Scholz, Jim Twombly, and Barbara Headrick, "Street-Level Political Controls over Federal Bureaucracy," *American Political Science Review* 85 (September 1991): 829–50.

22. Bradley Cannon and Michael Giles, "Recurring Litigants: Federal Agencies before the Supreme Court," *Western Political Quarterly* 15 (September 1972): 183–91; Reginald S. Sheehan, "Federal Agencies and the Supreme Court," *American Politics Quarterly* 20 (October 1992): 478–500.

Chapter 13

1. Alexis de Tocqueville, *Democracy in America* (1835; New York: Mentor Books, 1956), p. 75.

2. Felix Frankfurter, "The Supreme Court and the Public," *Forum* 83 (June 1930): 332.

3. Alexander Hamilton, *Federalist Papers*, No. 78 (New York: Modern Library, 1937), p. 505.

4. *Marbury v. Madison*, 1 Cranch 137 (1803).

5. *Brown v. Board of Education of Topeka*, 347 U.S. 483 (1954).

6. *Roe v. Wade*, 410 U.S. 113 (1973).

7. *Lawrence v. Texas* (June 26, 2003).

8. *Buckley v. Valeo*, 424 U.S. 1 (1976).

9. *U.S. v. Morrison* 529 U.S. 598 (2000).

10. *Ex parte Milligan*, 4 Wallace 2 (1866).

11. *Youngstown Sheet & Tube Co. v. Sawyer*, 343 U.S. 579 (1952).

12. *United States v. Nixon*, 418 U.S. 683 (1974).

13. *Clinton v. Jones*, 520 U.S. 681 (1997).

14. *West Virginia Board of Education v. Barnette*, 319 U.S. 624 (1943).

15. Quoted in Henry J. Abraham, *Justices and Presidents*, 3rd ed. (New York: Oxford University Press, 1992), p. 7.

16. Quoted in Charles P. Curtis, *Lions under the Throne* (Boston: Houghton Mifflin, 1947), p. 281.

17. Lee Epstein and Thomas G. Walker, *Constitutional Law for a Changing America*, 3rd ed. (Washington, D.C.: CQ Press, 1998), pp. 33–34.

18. William O. Douglas, "Stare Decisis," *Record*, April 1947, cited in Henry J. Abraham, *The Judicial Process* (New York: Oxford University Press, 1968), p. 58.

19. *Flast v. Cohen*, 392 U.S. 83 (1968).

20. *Gideon v. Wainwright*, 372 U.S. 335 (1963).

21. *Missouri v. Jenkins*, 110 S.C. 1651 (1990).

22. *Morrison v. Olson*, 487 U.S. 654 (1988).

23. Robert Scigliano, *The Supreme Court and the Presidency* (New York: Free Press, 1971), pp. 147–48.

24. See Bryon J. Moraski and Charles R. Shipan, "The Politics of Supreme Court Nominations," *American Journal of Political Science* 43 (October 1999): 1069–95.

25. See Charles R. Shipan and Megan L. Shannon, "Delaying Justices, *American Journal of Political Science* 47 (October 2003): 654–68; Sarah A. Binder and Forrest Maltzman, "Senatorial Delay in Confirming Federal Judges," *American Journal of Political Science* 46 (January 2002): 190–99; David W. Rohde and Kenneth A. Shepsle, "Advising and Consenting in the 60-Vote Senate: Strategic Appointments to the Supreme Court," *Journal of Politics* 69 (August 2007): 664–77.

26. At one time the U.S. Supreme Court was legally required to accept certain "writs of appeal," but today very few cases come to the Court in this fashion.

27. *University of California Regents v. Bakke*, 438 U.S. 265 (1978).

28. See Lee Epstein et al., *The Supreme Court Compendium*, 3rd ed. (Washington, D.C.: CQ Press, 2002).

29. Thomas Marshall, *Public Opinion and the Supreme Court* (New York: Unwin Hyman, 1989), p. 97; see also Michael W. Giles, Bethany Blackstone, and Richard L. Vining, Jr., "The Supreme Court in

American Democracy: Unraveling the Linkages Between Public Opinion and Judicial Decision Making," *Journal of Politics* 70 (April 2008): 293–06.

30. Lee Epstein and C. K. Rowland, "Debunking the Myth of Interest Group Invincibility," *American Political Science Review* 85 (1991): 205–17.

31. James L. Gibson et al., "Measuring Attitudes toward the United States Supreme Court," *American Journal of Political*

Science 47 (April 2003): 354–67; Stephen P. Nicholson and Robert H. Howard, "Framing Support for the Supreme Court in the Aftermath of *Bush v. Gore,*" *Journal of Politics* 65 (August 2003): 676–95.

32. President Andrew Jackson's comments came in response to the Court's ruling in the case of *Cherokee Nation v. Georgia* (1831) and *Worcester v. Georgia* (1832), which forbade the federal or state governments from seizing Native American lands and

forcing the people to move. Refusal by Jackson, an old "Indian fighter," to enforce the Court's decisions resulted in the infamous "Trail of Tears," the forced march of the Georgia Cherokees that left one-quarter of them dead along the path west.

33. *Grove City College v. Bell,* 465 U.S. 555 (1984).

34. *Pollock v. Farmer's Loan,* 158 U.S. 601 (1895).

Chapter 14

1. James Madison, *Federalist Papers,* No. 10, reprinted in the Appendix.

2. *West Virginia Board of Education v. Barnette,* 319 U.S. 624 (1943).

3. *Slaughter-House Cases,* 16 Wallace 36 (1873).

4. *Hurtado v. California,* 110 U.S. 516 (1884).

5. *Gitlow v. New York,* 268 U.S. 652 (1925).

6. For an argument that Madison and some other framers not only were concerned with lessening religious conflict but also were hostile to religion generally, see Thomas Lindsay, "James Madison on Religion and Politics," *American Political Science Review* 85 (December 1991): 1051–65.

7. *Reynolds v. United States,* 98 U.S. 145 (1879).

8. *Pierce v. Society of Sisters,* 268 U.S. 510 (1925).

9. *Cantwell v. Connecticut,* 310 U.S. 296 (1940).

10. *Employment Division v. Smith,* 494 U.S. 872 (1990).

11. *Wisconsin v. Yoder,* 406 U.S. 295 (1972).

12. *Church of Lukumi Babalu Aye v. City of Hialeah* 508 U.S. 520 (1993).

13. *City of Borne v. Flores* 521 U.S. 507 (1997).

14. *Bob Jones University v. United States,* 461 U.S. 574 (1983).

15. *Employment Division of Oregon v. Smith,* 494 U.S. 872 (1990).

16. *Goldman v. Weinberger,* 475 U.S. 503 (1986).

17. *Everson v. Board of Education,* 330 U.S. 1, 15, 16 (1947).

18. *Zorach v. Clausen,* 343 U.S. 306 (1952).

19. Opening public meetings with prayer was ruled constitutional as "a tolerable acknowledgment of beliefs widely held among the people of this country." *Marsh v. Chambers,* 463 U.S. 783 (1983).

20. *Lemon v. Kurtzman,* 403 U.S. 602 (1971).

21. *Muebler v. Adams,* 463 U.S. 388 (1983).

22. *Tilton v. Richardson,* 403 U.S. 672 (1971).

23. *Lambs Chapel v. Center Moriches Union Free School District,* 508 U.S. 384 (1993).

24. *Rosenberger v. University of Virginia,* 515 U.S. 819 (1995).

25. *Walz v. Tax Commission,* 397 U.S. 664 (1970).

26. *Board of Education v. Mergens,* 497 U.S. 111 (1990).

27. *McGowan v. Maryland,* 366 U.S. 429 (1961), and *Braunfeld v. Brown,* 366 U.S. 599 (1961).

28. *County of Allegheny v. ACLU,* 492 U.S. 573 (1989).

29. *Edwards v. Aguillard,* 482 U.S. 578 (1987).

30. *VanOrden v. Perry* 545 U.S. 677 (2005).

31. *Engel v. Vitale,* 370 U.S. 421 (1962).

32. *Abington School District v. Schempp,* 374 U.S. 203 (1963).

33. *Wallace v. Jaffree,* 472 U.S. 38 (1985).

34. *Lee v. Weisman,* 505 U.S. 577 (1992).

35. *Santa Fe Independent School District v. Doe,* 120 S.Ct. 2266 (2000).

36. *Zelman v. Simmons-Harris,* June 27, 2002.

37. *Schenck v. United States,* 249 U.S. 47 (1919).

38. *Gitlow v. New York,* 268 U.S. 652 (1925).

39. *Schenck v. United States,* 249 U.S. 47, 52 (1919).

40. *Whitney v. California,* 274 U.S. 357, 377 (1927), concurring opinion.

41. *Thomas v. Collins,* 323 U.S. 516 (1945).

42. *Dennis v. United States,* 341 U.S. 494 (1951).

43. *Yates v. United States,* 354 U.S. 298 (1957).

44. *Albertson v. Subversive Activities Control Board,* 382 U.S. 70 (1965).

45. *Whitehill v. Elkins,* 389 U.S. 54 (1967).

46. *United States v. Robel,* 389 U.S. 258 (1967).

47. *Aptheker v. Secretary of State,* 378 U.S. 500 (1964).

48. *Tinker v. Des Moines Independent Community School District,* 393 U.S. 503 (1969).

49. *Texas v. Johnson,* 491 U.S. 397 (1989).

50. *Texas v. Johnson* 491 U.S. 397 (1989).

51. *Virginia v. Black* 538 U.S. 343 (2003).

52. *Chaplinsky v. New Hampshire,* 315 U.S. 568 (1942).

53. *Terminiello v. Chicago,* 337 U.S. 1 (1949).

54. *Cohen v. California,* 403 U.S. 15 (1971).

55. *Hill v. Colorado* 530 U.S. 703 (2000).

56. Justice Louis D. Brandeis opinion in *Whitney v. California,* 274 U.S. 357 (1927).

57. *R. A. V. v. City of St. Paul, Minnesota,* 505 U.S. 377 (1992).

58. *Wisconsin v. Mitchell,* 508 U.S. 476 (1993).

59. *Virginia State Board of Pharmacy v. Virginia Consumer Council, Inc.,* 425 U.S. 748 (1976).

60. *Bates v. Arizona State Bar,* 433 U.S. 350 (1977).

61. *Linmark Associates, Inc. v. Township of Willingboro,* 431 U.S. 85 (1977).

62. *New York Times v. Sullivan,* 376 U.S. 254 (1964).

63. *Griswold v. Connecticut,* 381 U.S. 479 (1965).

64. *Roe v. Wade,* 410 U.S. 113 (1973).

65. *Harris v. McRae,* 448 U.S. 297 (1980).

66. *Planned Parenthood v. Casey,* 510 U.S. 110 (1992).

67. *Gonzales v. Carhart,* April 18, 2007.

68. *Bowers v. Hardwick,* 478 U.S. 186 (1986).

69. *Lawrence v. Texas* (June 26, 2003).

70. *Stanley v. Georgia* 394 U.S. 557 (1969).

71. *Washington v. Glucksberg,* 117 S.Ct. 2258 (1997).

72. *Cruzan v. Missouri Department of Health,* 497 U.S. 261 (1990).

73. *Gertz v. Robert Welch, Inc.,* 418 U.S. 323 (1974).

74. *Roth v. United States,* 354 U.S. 476 (1957).

75. *Jacobellis v. Ohio,* 378 U.S. 184 (1964).

76. *Jacobellis v. Ohio,* 378 U.S. 184 (1964).

77. Bob Woodward and Scott Armstrong, *The Brethren* (New York: Avon, 1979), p. 233.

78. *Miller v. California,* 5413 U.S. 15 (1973).

79. *Barnes v. Glenn Theatre,* 501 U.S. 560 (1991).

80. *Reno v. American Civil Liberties Union,* 117 S.Ct. 2329 (1997).

81. *Near v. Minnesota,* 283 U.S. 697 (1931).

82. *New York Times v. United States,* 403 U.S. 713 (1971).

83. *Mutual Film Corp. v. Industrial Commission,* 236 U.S. 230 (1915).

84. *Times Film Corporation v. Chicago,* 365 U.S. 43 (1961).

85. *Freedman v. Maryland,* 380 U.S. 51 (1965).

86. *Young v. American Mini Theaters, Inc.,* 427 U.S. 50 (1976).

87. *Red Lion Broadcasting Co. v. Federal Communications Commission,* 395 U.S. 367 (1969).

88. *Miami Herald Publishing Co. v. Tornillo,* 418 U.S. 241 (1974).

89. *Branzburg v. Hayes,* 408 U.S. 665 (1972).

90. *NAACP v. Alabama ex rel. Patterson,* 357 U.S. 449 (1958).

91. *Aptheker v. Secretary of State,* 378 U.S. 500 (1964).

92. *Roberts v. United States Jaycees,* 468 U.S. 609 (1984).

93. *Hurley v. Irish-American Gay Lesbian and Bisexual Group of Boston*, 515 U.S. 557 (1995).
94. *Bay Scouts of America v. Dale*, 530 U.S. 640 (2000).
95. *California Democratic Party v. Jones*, 530 U.S. 567 (2000).
96. *Healy v. James*, 408 U.S. 169 (1972).
97. *National Socialist Party of America v. Skokie*, 432 U.S. 43 (1977).
98. *Frisby v. Schultz*, 487 U.S. 474 (1988).
99. *Schenck v. Pro Choice Network of Western New York*, 519 U.S. 357 (1997).
100. *Kelo v. New London*, June 23, 2005.
101. *Village of Euclid v. Amber Realty*, 272 U.S. 365 (1954).
102. *Lucas v. South Carolina Coastal Council*, 112 Sup. Ct. 2886 (1992).
103. James Madison, *Federalist Papers*, No. 46.
104. *Ex parte Milligan*, 4 Wallace 2 (1866).
105. *Duncan v. Kahanamosby*, 327 U.S. 304 (1946).
106. *Illinois v. Gates*, 462 U.S. 213 (1983).

107. *Arizona v. Hicks*, 480 U.S. 321 (1987).
108. *Knowles v. Iowa*, 525 U.S. 113 (1998).
109. *Katz v. U.S.*, 309 U.S. 347 (1967).
110. *Youngstown Sheet & Tube Co. v. Sawyer*, 343 U.S. 579 (1952).
111. *Veronia School District v. Acton*, 515 U.S. 646 (1995).
112. *Chandler v. Miller*, 520 U.S. 305 (1997).
113. *United States v. Watson*, 423 U.S. 411 (1976).
114. *Payton v. New York*, 445 U.S. 573 (1980).
115. *Spano v. New York*, 360 U.S. 315 (1959).
116. *Gideon v. Wainwright*, 372 U.S. 335 (1963).
117. *Escobedo v. Illinois*, 378 U.S. 478 (1964).
118. *Miranda v. Arizona*, 384 U.S. 436 (1966).
119. *Mapp v. Ohio*, 367 U.S. 643 (1961).
120. *United States v. Leon*, 468 U.S. 897 (1984).
121. *Illinois v. Perkins*, 497 U.S. 177 (1990).
122. *United States v. Salerno*, 481 U.S. 739 (1987).
123. *U.S. v. Marion*, 404 U.S. 307 (1971).

124. *Barker v. Wingo*, 407 U.S. 514 (1972).
125. *Illinois v. Allen*, 397 U.S. 337 (1970).
126. *Maryland v. Craig*, 497 U.S. 1 (1990).
127. *Brady v. Maryland*, 373 U.S. 83 (1963).
128. *Batson v. Kentucky*, 476 U.S. 79 (1986).
129. *Sheppard v. Maxwell*, 384 U.S. 333 (1966).
130. *Williams v. Florida*, 399 U.S. 78 (1970).
131. *Johnson v. Louisiana*, 406 U.S. 356 (1970); *Apodaca v. Oregon*, 406 U.S. 404 (1972).
132. U.S. Department of Justice, *The Prevalence of Guilty Pleas* (Washington, D.C.: Government Printing Office, 1984).
133. *U.S. v. Perez*, 9 Wheat 579 (1824).
134. *Heath v. Alabama*, 474 U.S. 82 (1985).
135. *Furman v. Georgia*, 408 U.S. 238 (1972).
136. *Gregg v. Georgia*, 428 U.S. 153 (1976); *Proffitt v. Florida*, 428 U.S. 242 (1976); *Jurek v. Texas*, 428 U.S. 262 (1976).
137. *Ring v. Arizona*, June 24, 2002.
138. *Atkins v. Virginia*, June 20, 2002.
139. *Roper v. Simmons*, March 1, 2005.

Chapter 15

1. *Dred Scott v. Sandford*, 60 U.S. 393 (1857).
2. See C. Vann Woodward, *Reunion and Reaction* (Boston: Little, Brown, 1951), and Woodward, *The Strange Career of Jim Crow* (New York: Oxford University Press, 1957).
3. *Civil Rights Cases*, 100 U.S. 3 (1883).
4. *Plessy v. Ferguson*, 163 U.S. 537 (1896).
5. *Sweatt v. Painter*, 339 U.S. 629 (1950).
6. *Brown v. Board of Education of Topeka*, 347 U.S. 483 (1954).
7. Kenneth Clark, *Dark Ghetto* (New York: Harper & Row, 1965), p. 75.
8. The Supreme Court ruled that Congress was bound to respect the Equal Protection Clause of the Fourteenth Amendment even though the amendment is directed at states, because equal protection is a liberty guaranteed by the Fifth Amendment. *Bolling v. Sharpe*, 347 U.S. 497 (1954).
9. *Brown v. Board of Education of Topeka* (II), 349 U.S. 294 (1955).
10. *Alexander v. Holmes Board of Education*, 396 U.S. 19 (1969).
11. *Swann v. Charlotte-Mecklenburg County Board of Education*, 402 U.S. (1971).
12. *Milliken v. Bradley*, 418 U.S. 717 (1974).
13. *Board of Education v. Dowell*, 498 U.S. 550 (1991).
14. Martin Luther King Jr., "Letter from Birmingham City Jail," April 16, 1963.
15. *University of California Regents v. Bakke*, 438 U.S. 265 (1978).
16. Bakke's overall grade point average was 3.46, and the average for special admissions students was 2.62. Bakke's MCAT scores were verbal, 96; quantitative, 94; science, 97; general information, 72. The average MCAT scores for special admissions students were verbal, 34; quantitative, 30; science, 37; general information, 18.
17. *United Steelworkers of America v. Weber*, 443 U.S. 193 (1979).
18. *United States v. Paradise*, 480 U.S. 149 (1987).
19. *Firefighters Local Union 1784 v. Stotts*, 467 U.S. 561 (1984).
20. *City of Richmond v. Crosen Co.*, 488 U.S. 469 (1989).
21. *Adarand Construction v. Pena*, 132 L. Ed., 2d 158 (1995).
22. *Parents Involved in Community Schools v. Seattle School District*, June 28, 2007.
23. *Hopwood v. Texas*, 116 S.Ct. 2581 (1996).
24. *Grutter v. Bollinger* (June 23, 2003).
25. *Gratz v. Bollinger* (June 23, 2003).
26. U.S. Department of Education, Office of Civil Rights, "Race-neutral Alternatives in Postsecondary Education," March 2003.
27. State of California, Proposition 209 "Prohibition Against Discrimination or Preferential Treatment by State and Other Public Entities," http://vote96.ss.ca.gov.
28. *Coalition for Economic Equity v. Pete Wilson*, Ninth Circuit Court of Appeals, April 1997.
29. Rodolfo O. de la Garza et al., *Latino Voices: Mexican, Puerto Rican, and Cuban Perspectives on American Politics* (Boulder, Colo.: Westview Press, 1992).
30. See F. Luis Garcia, *Latinos in the Political System* (Notre Dame, Ind.: Notre Dame University Press, 1988). John D. Griffin and Brian Newman, "The Unequal Representation of Latinos and Whites," *Journal of Politics* 69 (November, 2007), 1032–1046; Matt A. Barreto, "Si Se Puede! Latino Candidates and the Mobilization of Latino Voters," *American Political Science Review*, 101 (August, 2007): 425–38.
31. Linda Chavez, "Tequila Sunrise: The Slow but Steady Progress of Hispanic Immigrants," *Policy Review* (Spring 1989): 64–67.
32. Peter Mathiessen, *Sal Si Puedes: Cesar Chavez and the New American Revolution* (New York: Random House, 1969).
33. *Plyer v. Doe*, 457 U.S. 202 (1982).
34. See Marisa A. Abrajano, R. Michael Alvarez, Jonathan Nagler, "The Hispanic Vote in the 2004 Presidential Election," *Journal of Politics* 70 (April 2008): 368–82.
35. *Morton v. Mancari*, 417 U.S. 535 (1974).
36. See Joseph P. Shapiro, *No Pity: People with Disabilities Forging a New Civil Rights Movement* (New York: Times Books/Random House, 1993).
37. *U.S. News & World Report*, February 9, 1998.
38. *The Chronicle of Higher Education*, December 8, 2000.
39. *Bradwell v. Illinois*, 16 Wall 130 (1873).
40. *Reed v. Reed*, 404 U.S. 71 (1971).
41. *Michael M. v. Superior Court of Sonoma County*, 450 U.S. 464 (1981).
42. *Rostker v. Goldberg*, 453 U.S. 57 (1981).
43. *Statistical Abstract of the United States*, 2007, p. 379.
44. Susan Fraker, "Why Women Aren't Getting to the Top," *Fortune*, April 16, 1984, pp. 40–45.

Chapter 16

1. Paul Samuelson, *Economics*, 12th ed. (New York: McGraw-Hill, 1985), p. 5.
2. GDP differs very little from gross national product, GNP, which is often used to compare the performance of national economies.
3. Richard B. Freeman, "Are Your Wages Set in Beijing?" *Journal of Economic Perspectives* 9 (Summer 1995): 15.

4. Laurence R. Jacobs and Theda Skocpol, eds., *Inequality and American Democracy* (New York: Russell Sage Foundation, 2005).
5. For a revealing case study of interest-group efforts to maintain tax breaks during the struggle over the Tax Reform Act of 1986, see Jeffrey H. Birnbaum and Alan S. Murray, *Showdown at Gucci Gulch* (New York: Random House, 1986).

6. "The Underground Economy," National Center for Policy Analysis, 1998.
7. Joseph A. Pechman, *Federal Tax Policy*, 5th ed. (Washington, D.C.: Brookings Institution, 1987).
8. See Peter R. Orszag, *Taxing the Future* (Washington D.C.: Brookings Institute, 2006).

Chapter 17

1. Christopher Jenks and Paul E. Peterson, eds., *The Urban Underclass* (Washington, D.C.: Brookings Institution, 1991). See also William A. Kelso, *Poverty and the Underclass* (New York: New York University Press, 1994).

2. See William Julius Wilson, *The Truly Disadvantaged* (Chicago: University of Chicago Press, 1987).
3. See Michael B. Katz, *In the Shadow of the Poorhouse* (New York: Basic Books, 1996).

4. See Charles Murray, *Losing Ground* (New York: Basic Books, 1984).
5. See Joe Soss and Stanford F. Schram. "A Public Transformed? Welfare Reform as Policy Feedback," *American Political Science Review* 101 (February 2002): 111–22.

Chapter 18

1. Hans Morgenthau, *Politics among Nations*, 5th ed. (New York: Knopf, 1973), p. 27.
2. George F. Kennan, writing under the pseudonym "X," "Sources of Soviet Conduct," *Foreign Affairs* 25 (July 1947): 25.
3. Frank Snepp, *Decent Interval* (New York: Random House, 1977).
4. George C. Herring, *America's Longest War* (New York: Random House, 1979), p. 262.

5. See Caspar W. Weinberger, "The Uses of Military Force," *Defense* (Arlington, Va.: American Forces Information Services Survey, 1985), pp. 2–11.
6. Morgenthau, *Politics among Nations*, p. 80.
7. President George W. Bush, *National Security Strategy 2006*, March 16, 2006, www.whitehouse.gov.

8. Donald M. Snow, *National Security in a New Era* (New York: Pearson, 2008) p. 309.
9. President George W. Bush, *National Strategy for Victory in Iraq*, November 1, 2005, www.whitehouse.gov.
10. www.whitehouse.gov/infocus/Iraq.

Chapter 19

1. *New York Times*, November 11, 1997.
2. Harold Lasswell, *Politics: Who Gets What, When, How* (New York: McGraw-Hill, 1936).
3. Texas Comptroller of Public Accounts, *Fiscal Notes*, June 1998, p. 6; Texas Comptroller of Public Accounts, *Texas—Where We Stand*, February 2006.
4. David Easton, *A Framework for Political Analysis* (Englewood Cliffs, N.J.: Prentice Hall, 1965), Chap. 5.
5. Louise Cowan, "Myth in the Modern World," in *Texas Myths*, ed. Robert F. O'Connor (College Station: Texas A&M University Press, 1986), p. 4.
6. Ibid., p. 14. For an excellent analysis of the concept of the "myth of origin" as integrated into the American mythology, see Robert N. Bellah, *The Broken Covenant: American Civil Religion in Time of Trial* (New York: The Seabury Press, 1975).
7. T. R. Fehrenbach, "Texas Mythology: Now and Forever," in *Texas Myths*, pp. 210–17.
8. Robin Doughty, "From Wilderness to Garden: Conquering the Texas Landscape," in *Texas Myths*, p. 105.
9. Lucian W. Pye, "Political Culture," *International Encyclopedia of the Social Sciences*,

Vol. 12 (New York: Crowell, Collier and Macmillan, 1968), p. 218.
10. Ellen M. Dran, Robert B. Albritton, and Mikel Wyckoff, "Surrogate versus Direct Measures of Political Culture: Explaining Participation and Policy Attitudes in Illinois," *Publius* 21 (Spring 1991): 17.
11. Daniel Elazar, *American Federalism: A View from the States* (New York: Thomas Y. Crowell, 1966), p. 86.
12. Ibid., pp. 86–89.
13. Ibid., pp. 90–92.
14. Ibid., pp. 92–94.
15. Ibid., pp. 97, 102, 108.
16. U.S. Census Bureau, *Census 2000 and 2006 American Community Survey*.
17. Ellen N. Murray, "Sorrow Whispers in the Winds," *Texas Journal*, 14 (Spring/Summer 1992): 16.
18. Terry G. Jordan with John L. Bean, Jr., and William M. Holmes, *Texas: A Geography* (Boulder, Colo.: Westview Press, 1984), pp. 79–86.
19. David Montejano, *Anglos and Mexicans in the Making of Texas, 1836–1986* (Austin: University of Texas Press, 1987), p. 38.
20. Hispanics can be of any race.

21. Texas State Data Center, *Population Estimates and Projections Program*, 2004.
22. National Association of Latino Elected and Appointed Officials, *2006 National Roster of Hispanic Elected Officials*.
23. Joint Center for Political Studies, *National Roster of Black Elected Officials*, 2002.
24. Jordan et al., *Texas*, pp. 71–7.
25. V. O. Key, *Southern Politics in State and Nation* (New York: Vintage Books, 1949), p. 261.
26. For an excellent analysis of Key's projections for political change in Texas, see Chandler Davidson, *Race and Class in Texas Politics* (Princeton, N.J.: Princeton University Press, 1990).
27. U.S. Census Bureau, *Census 2000*.
28. U.S. Census Bureau, *2006 American Community Survey*.
29. Office of the Governor, Texas 2000 Commission, *Texas Trends*, pp. 5–6; Office of the Governor, Texas 2000 Commission, *Texas Past and Future: A Survey*, p. 6.
30. U.S. Census Bureau, *2006 American Community Survey*.
31. U.S. Census Bureau, *Census 2000*; U.S. Census Bureau, *2006 American Community Survey*.

32. U.S. Census Bureau, *2006 American Community Survey*.

33. *San Antonio Express—News*, October 1, 2003, p. 1A.; Texas Transportation Institute, Texas A&M University, *2003 Mobility Study*, September 2003.

34. David Schrank and Tim Lomax, *2005 Mobility Report*, Texas Transportation Institute, Texas A&M University, College Station.

35. Steve H. Murdock, Nazrul Hoque, Martha Michael, Steve White, and Beverly Pecotte, *The Texas Challenge: Population Change and the Future of Texas* (College Station: Texas A&M University Press, 1997), p. 29; U.S. Census Bureau, *2006 American Community Survey*.

36. U.S. Census Bureau, *Census 2000*; Texas State Data Center, *Population Estimates and Projections Program*, 2007.

37. U.S. Census Bureau, *Small Area Income and Poverty Estimates*, 2005.

38. *Forbes*, "The Four Hundred Richest Americans," Special Edition, September 20, 2007.

39. U.S. Census Bureau, *2006 American Community Survey*.

40. U.S. Census Bureau, "Poverty Thresholds 2006," U.S. Census Bureau, *2006 American Community Survey*.

41. U.S. Census Bureau, *Small Area Income and Poverty Estimates*, 2005.

42. Murdock et al., *The Texas Challenge*, pp. 64–5.

43. U.S. Census Bureau, *2006 American Community Survey*.

44. For an expanded analysis of the Texas economy and the dominant role played by larger corporations, see James W. Lamare, *Texas Politics: Economics, Power and Policy*, 7th ed. (Belmont, Calif.: Wadsworth, 2001), Chap. 2.

45. "Texas Economic Outlook," *Texas Economic Quarterly* (December 1996): 2.

46. "Boom, Bust and Back Again: Bullock Tenure Covers Tumultuous Era," *Fiscal Notes* (December 1990): 6–7.

47. Ibid.

48. "Road to Recovery Long and Bumpy, but Positive Signs Begin to Appear," *Fiscal Notes* (March 1989): 4.

49. "Boom, Bust and Back Again," p. 7.

50. Texas Comptroller of Public Accounts, *The Texas Economy, Fall 2007 Forecasts*, www.cpa.state.tx.us/.

51. "Biotechnology: New Science Brings Jobs to Texas as Biotech-related Efforts Blossom," *Fiscal Notes* (April 1990): 1–8.

52. U.S. Department of Commerce, International Trade Administration, *TradeStats Express: National Trade Data*. http://ita.doc.gov/td/industry/otea/state/index.html.

53. The following discussion is based on a series of reports published by the Texas Comptroller of Public Accounts titled *Texas Regional Outlook*, 2002.

54. M. Delal Baer, "North American Free Trade," *Foreign Affairs* 70 (Fall 1991): 138.

55. Joan B. Anderson, "Maquiladoras and Border Industrialization: Impact on Economic Development in Mexico," *Journal of Borderland Studies* V (Spring 1990): 5.

56. Michael Patrick, "Maquiladoras and South Texas Border Economic Development," *Journal of Borderland Studies* IV (Spring 1989): 90.

57. Martin E. Rosenfeldt, "Mexico's In Bond Export Industries and U.S. Legislation: Conflictive Issues," *Journal of Borderland Studies* V (Spring 1990): 57.

58. Patrick, "Maquiladoras and South Texas Border Economic Development," p. 90.

59. United States, International Trade Data System, *Importing/Exporting Resources*, http://itds.teas.gov/maquiladora.html.

60. Baer, "North American Free Trade," pp. 132–49.

61. Central Intelligence Agency, *The World Factbook—2008*, www.cia.gov/library/publications/the-world-factbook/index.html.

62. Ibid.

63. Augustin Redwine, "A Bureaucracy is Born: International Departments Being Organized to Oversee NAFTA," *Fiscal Notes* (April 1994): 12.

64. Border Environment Cooperation Commission and the North American Development Bank, *Joint Status Report*, March 2006.

65. Ibid.; *San Antonio Express–News*, June 22, 2006.

66. Commission for Labor Cooperation, April 2003, www.NAALC.org.

67. U.S. Department of State, Bureau of Western Hemisphere Affairs, "Background Note: Mexico," April 2008. www.state.gov/r/pa/ei/bgn/35749.htm.

68. International Trade Administration, *Industry, Trade and the Economy*, http://ita.doc.gov/td/industry/otea/usfth/aggregate/H04T07.html.

69. Texas Center for Border Economic and Enterprise Development, Texas A&M International University, *Border Crossings*, http://texascenter.tamiu.edu/texcen_services/datavehicle.asp.

70. Stephen A. Camarota, "Immigrants in the United States, 2007: A Profile of America's Foreign-Born Population," Center for Immigration Studies, November, 2008, p. 3.

71. Ibid., Tables 1 and 21.

72. James F. Pearce and Jeffery W. Gunther, "Illegal Immigration from Mexico: Effects on the Texas Economy," *Federal Reserve Bank of Dallas Economic Review* (September 1985): 4.

73. "Congress Clears Overhaul of Immigration Law," *Congressional Quarterly Almanac*, 1986 (Washington, D.C.: Congressional Quarterly, 1987), pp. 61–7.

74. Dan Carney, "Law Restricts Illegal Immigration," *Congressional Quarterly Weekly Report* 54 (November 16, 1996): 3287.

75. Camarota, "Immigrants in the United States, 2007."

76. Pearce and Gunther, "Illegal Immigration from Mexico: Effects on the Texas Economy," p. 2.

77. Joan Anderson and Martin de la Rosa, "Economic Survival Strategies of Poor Families on the Mexican Border," *Journal of Borderland Studies* VI (Spring 1991): 51.

78. Howard G. Applegate, C. Richard Bath and Jeffery T. Trannon, "Binational Emissions Trading in an International Air Shed: The Case of El Paso, Texas and Ciudad and Juarez," *Journal of Borderland Studies* IV (Fall 1989): 1–25.

Chapter 20

1. G. Alan Tarr, *Understanding State Constitutions* (Princeton, N.J. Princeton University Press, 1998), pp. 3–4.

2. Daniel Elazar, "The Principles and Traditions Underlying American State Constitutions," *Publius* 12 (Winter 1982): 23.

3. Tarr, pp. 4–5.

4. David Saffell, *State Politics* (Reading, Mass.:Addison-Wesley, 1984), pp. 23–4.

5. Elazar, pp. 20–1.

6. T. R. Fehrenbach, *Lone Star: A History of Texas and the Texans* (New York: Macmillan, 1968), pp. 152–73.

7. Richard Gambitta, Robert A. Milne, and Carol R. Davis, "The Politics of Unequal Educational Opportunity," in *The Politics of San Antonio*, eds. David R. Johnson, John A. Booth, and Richard J. Harris (Lincoln: University of Nebraska Press, 1983), p. 135.

8. Joe B. Frantz, *Texas: A Bicentennial History* (New York: W.W. Norton, 1976), pp. 73, 76.

9. Fehrenbach, *Lone Star*, p. 265.

10. Frantz, *Texas*, p. 92.

11. Fehrenbach, *Lone Star*, p. 396.

12. Ibid, pp. 398–99, 401.

13. J. E. Ericson, "The Delegates to the Convention of 1875: A Reappraisal," *Southwestern Historical Quarterly* 67 (July 1963), p. 22.

14. Ibid., p. 23

15. Ibid.

16. Ibid, pp. 25–6.

17. Fehrenbach, *Lone Star*, pp. 374, 431, 434.

18. Ericson, "The Delegates to the Convention of 1875," pp. 24–5.
19. Fehrenbach, *Lone Star*, p. 435.
20. Janice May, "Constitutional Revision in Texas," in *The Texas Constitution: Problems and Prospects for Revision* (Arlington, Texas: Urban Development Commission, 1971), p. 82.
21. David Berman, *State and Local Politics*, 6th ed. (Dubuque, Iowa: Wm. C. Brown, 1991), p. 61.

22. May, "Constitutional Revision in Texas," p. 76.
23. John E. Bebout, "The Problem of the Texas Constitution," in *The Texas Constitution: Problems and Prospects for Revision* (Arlington, Texas: Urban Development Commission, 1971), pp. 9, 11.
24. Bill Hobby, quoted in the *Houston Chronicle*, January 8, 1974.

25. Dolph Briscoe, reported in the *Houston Chronicle*, October 15, 1975.
26. Lewis A. Froman, Jr., "Some Effects of Interest Group Strength in State Politics," *American Political Science Review* 60 (December 1966); 952–63.
27. "California's Constitutional Amendomania," *Stanford Law Review* 1 (1949); 279–88.

Chapter 21

1. *Houston Chronicle*, October 2, 2003, p. 19A.
2. Belle Zeller, *American State Legislatures* (New York: Thomas Y. Crowell, 1954), p. 603; and Clive S. Thomas and Ronald J. Hrebenar, "Interest Groups in the States," in *Politics in the American States*, 6th ed., eds. Virginia Gray and Herbert Jacob (Washington, D.C.: Congressional Quarterly Press, 1996), p. 152.
3. Harmon L. Zeigler and Hendrik van Dalen, "Interest Groups in State Politics," in *Politics in the American States*, 3rd ed., eds. Herbert Jacob and Kenneth N. Vines (Boston: Little, Brown, 1976), pp. 93–136.
4. George Norris Green, *The Establishment in Texas Politics: 1938–1957* (Westport, Conn.: Greenwood Press, 1979), pp. 1, 17.
5. Ibid., p. 30.
6. Chandler Davidson, *Race and Class in Texas Politics* (Princeton, N.J.: Princeton University Press, 1990), p. 54.
7. Ibid., Chs. 4 and 5
8. Ibid., p. 83.
9. Ibid., p. 108.
10. See Green, *The Establishment in Texas Politics*, for an excellent analysis of the labor-bashing techniques used by Texas business in the 1940s and 1950s.
11. Jodi Rudoren and Aron Pilhofer, "Hiring Lobbyists for Federal Aid, Towns Learn That Money Talks," *The New York Times*, July 2, 2006, p. 1.
12. Ibid., Ch. 5.
13. See Davidson, Ch. 10.
14. V. O. Key, *Southern Politics* (New York: Vintage Books, 1949), p. 255.
15. Davidson, *Race and Class in Texas Politics*, p. 21.
16. Alexander P. Lamis, *The Two-Party South*, expanded ed. (New York: Oxford University Press, 1988), p. 23.
17. Key, pp. 302–10.
18. Green, pp. 142–48.
19. Lamis, p. 195.

20. John R. Knaggs, *Two-Party Texas: The John Tower Era, 1961–1984* (Austin, Tex.: Eakin Press, 1986), p. 15.
21. Davidson, p. 199.
22. For an excellent summary of realignment theory and conditions under which realignment is likely to take place, see James L. Sundquist, *Dynamics of the Party System* (Washington, D.C.: The Brookings Institution, 1973).
23. James A. Dyer, Arnold Vedlitz, and David Hill, "New Voters, Switchers, and Political Party Realignment in Texas," *Western Political Quarterly* 41 (March 1988): 156.
24. Ibid., pp. 165–66; *Texas Poll*, Summer 2003, Fall 2003, Winter 2003, Spring 2004.
25. See the homepage of the Texas Republican Party for policy statements designed to appeal to Hispanic and African American voters.
26. V. O. Key, Jr., *Parties, Politics, and Pressure Groups*, 4th ed. (New York: Thomas Y. Crowell, 1958), p. 347.
27. Texas Office of Secretary of State, "March 2008 Voter Registration Figures," www.sos.state.tx.us/elections/historical.
28. Wilbourn E. Benton, *Texas Politics: Constraints and Opportunities*, 5th ed. (Chicago: Nelson-Hall, 1984), pp. 72–3.
29. *Smith v. Allwright*, 321 U.S. 649 (1944).
30. John Terry et al., *Petitioners v. A. J. Adams et al.*, 345 U. S. 461.
31. Beryl E. Pettus and Randall W. Bland, *Texas Government Today: Structures, Functions, Political Processes*, 3rd ed. (Homewood, Ill.: Dorsey, 1984), pp. 85–6.
32. *Beare et al. v. Preston Smith, Governor of Texas*, 321 F. Supp. 1100 (1971).
33. *Miller v. Johnson*, 115 S.Ct 2475 (1995); *Bush v. Vera*, 116 S.Ct. 1941 (1996).
34. U.S Census Bureau, "Voting and Registration in the Election of November 2004," *Current Population Reports*, P20-556, March, 2006.

35. Robert R. Brischetto, Southwest Voter Research Institute, Inc., San Antonio, telephone conversations, November 1, 1991.
36. *The Texas Poll*, Summer 2003, Fall 2003, Winter 2004, Spring 2004.
37. Brischetto, telephone conversation; and Robert Brischetto, *The Political Empowerment of Texas Mexicans, 1974–1988* (San Antonio, Tex.: Southwest Voter Research Institute, Latino Electorate Series, 1988), pp. 1–19.
38. William C. Valasquez Institute news release, March 13, 2002.
39. Texas Municipal League, *Directory of City Officials*, 2006 (Austin: Texas Municipal League, 2006); survey conducted by the V. G. Young Institute of County Government, Texas A&M University, 2002.
40. Texas Association of School Boards, data provided by the courtesy of the association.
41. David A. Bositis, *Black Elected Officials, 2001* (Washington, D.C.: Joint Center for Political and Economic Studies, 2003), p. 18.
42. Chandler Davidson, *Race and Class in Texas Politics* (Princeton, N.J.: Princeton University Press, 1990), p. 24.
43. Davidson, p. 24.
44. Texans for Public Justice, *Money in Politex: A Guide to Money in the 2006 Texas Elections*, September 2007.
45. Ibid.
46. Ibid.
47. Texans for Public Justice, *Money in Politex: A Guide to Money in the 2002 Texas Elections*, November 2003.
48. *Houston Chronicle*, December 2, 1997; *Associated Press*, December 7, 2003.
49. Texans for Public Justice, "Voters Rebuked Texas' Biggest PAC," *Lobby Watch*, January 11, 2007; Texans for Public Justice, *Money in Politex: A Guide to Money in the 2006 Texas Elections*, September 2007.

Chapter 22

1. For an extended discussion of legislative functions, see William J. Keffe and Morris S. Ogul, *The American Legislative Process*, 8th ed. (Englewood Cliffs, N.J.: Prentice Hall, 1993), pp. 16–37.

2. On the general concept of institutionalization, see Nelson W. Plosby, "The Institutionalization of the U.S. House of Representatives," *American Political Science Review* 62 (March 1968): 144–68. For a more recent assessment of state legislative developments, see Alan Rosenthal, "State Legislative Development: Observations from Three Perspectives," *Legislative Studies Quarterly* XXI (May 1996): 169–98.

3. Thomas R. Dye and Susan MacManus, *Politics in States and Communities*, 12th ed. (Englewood Cliffs, N.J.: Prentice Hall, 2007), pp. 209–12. In a recent study of state legislatures, Texas ranked 13th in terms of professionalization. Other studies place it somewhat lower. See Peverell Squire, "Uncontested Seats in State Legislative Elections," *Legislative Studies Quarterly* XXV (February 2000): 143; and James D. King, "Changes in Professionalism in U.S. State Legislatures," *Legislative Studies Quarterly* XXV (May 2000): 327–43.

4. Council of State Governments, *The Book of the States* 2007, 39 (Lexington, Ky.: The Council of State Governments, 2008), Table 3.4.

5. Ibid., Table 3.8.

6. Ibid., Table 3.9.

7. For a comprehensive analysis of the literature on legislative recruitment and careers, see Donald R. Matthews, "Legislative Recruitment and Legislative Careers," *Legislative Studies Quarterly* IX (November 1984): 547–85.

8. Council of State Governments, *The Book of the States* 2007, Table 3.4.

9. Paul T. David and Ralph Eisenberg, *Devaluation of the Urban and Suburban Vote* (Charlottesville, Va.: Bureau of Public Administration, University of Virginia, 1961).

10. Stephen Ansolabehere and James M. Snyder, Jr., *The End of Inequality: One Person, One Vote and the Transformation of American Politics* (New York, N.Y.: W.W. Norton, 2008), pp. 50–1.

11. *Baker v. Carr*, 369 U.S. 186 (1992); *Reynolds v. Sims*, 377 U.S. 533 (1964); *Kilgarlin v. Martin*, 252 F. Supp 404 (S.D. Tex 1966).

12. *Georgia v. Ashcroft*, 539 U.S. 539 (2003).

13. *Houston Chronicle*, October 12, 2003, p. 33A.

14. Fred Gantt, Jr., *The Chief Executive in Texas: A Study of Gubernatorial Leadership* (Austin, Tex.: University of Texas Press, 1964), p. 238.

15. *Houston Chronicle*, January 6, 1993.

16. State Senator Bill Ratliff, quoted in the *Houston Chronicle*, June 6, 1999, p. 1E.

17. *Houston Chronicle*, June 6, 2001, p. 1A.

18. For an earlier summary of the scholarly work on legislative committees, see Heinz Eulau and Vera McCluggage, "Standing Committees in Legislatures: Three Decades of Research," *Legislative Studies Quarterly* IX (May 1984): 195–270. For a more recent summary of research on state legislatures, see Malcom Jewell, "Trends in Research on U.S. State Legislatures: A Review Article," *Legislative Studies Quarterly* XXII (May 1997): 265–74.

19. See Malcolm E. Jewell and Samuel C. Patterson, *The Legislative Process in the United States* (New York: Random House, 1966), Ch. 11, for a summary of the function of legislative rules and procedures.

20. For a brief overview of the representative problem, see Neil Reimer, ed., *The Representative: Trustee? Delegate? Partisan? Politico?* (Boston: D.C. Heath, 1967). For a more comprehensive treatment of the subject, see Hanna F. Pitkin, *The Concept of Representation* (Berkeley: University of California Press, 1967).

21. For an excellent treatment of the relationship of U.S. legislators to their districts and constituencies, see Richard F. Fenno, Jr., *Home Style: House Members in Their Districts* (Boston: Little, Brown, 1978).

22. There have been a considerable number of studies of these informal norms within the legislative process. Donald R. Matthews, *U.S. Senators and Their World* (New York: Vintage Books, 1960) was the seminal work in this area. For the adaptation of this concept to state legislature see Alan Rosenthal, *Legislative Life: People, Process, and Performance of the States* (New York: Harper & Row, 1981), pp. 123–27.

23. The general concepts for this discussion are based on John W. Kingdon, *Congressmen's Voting Decisions*, 2nd ed. (New York: Harper & Row 1981).

24. For a general discussion of staff in state legislatures, see Rosenthal, *Legislative Life: People, Process, and Performance in the States* Ch. 10.

25. *For Worth Star–Telegram*, December 4, 1990.

26. *Houston Chronicle*, December 12, 1990

27. *Houston Chronicle*, January 1, 1991

28. Statement issued by Governor Ann Richards, May 1991.

Chapter 23

1. State Comptroller's Office, *Breaking the Mold: A Report of the Texas Performance Review*, vol. 1 (Austin, Tex.: Texas Comptroller's Office, 1991), p.1.

2. Joseph A. Schlesinger, "The Politics of the Executive," in Herbert Jacob and Kenneth N. Vines eds., *Politics in the American States*, 2nd ed. (Boston: Little, Brown, 1971), Ch. 6; Thad L. Beyle "The Governors, 1988–89," in *The Book of the States, 1990–1991* (Lexington, Ky.: The Council of State Governments, 1990), p. 54.

3. Charles F. Cnudde and Robert E. Crew, *Constitutional Democracy in Texas* (St. Paul, Minn.: West, 1989), p. 90.

4. Fred Gantt, Jr., *The Chief Executive in Texas* (Austin, Tex.: University of Texas Press, 1964), p. 116.

5. See James E. Anderson, Richard W. Murray, and Edward L. Farley, *Texas Politics*, 6th ed. (New York: HarperCollins, 1992), pp. 166–91, for an excellent analysis of the leadership styles of Governors Allan Shivers, Price Daniel, John Connally, Preston Smith, and Dolph Briscoe.

6. Gantt, Chief Executive in Texas, pp. 229–30.

7. *Dallas Morning News*, April, 1987, p. H-2.

8. *Houston Chronicle*, September 30, 2003, p. 15A.

9. Wilbourn E. Benton, *Texas Politics: Constraints and Opportunities*, 5th ed. (Chicago: Nelson-Hall, 1984), pp. 164–67.

10. Gantt, Chief Executive in Texas, pp. 90–107.

11. Robert S. Lorch, *State and Local Politics*, 3rd ed. (Englewood Cliffs, N.J.: Prentice Hall, 1989), pp. 115–19.

12. Daniel Elazar, "The Principles and Traditions Underlying State Constitutions," *Publius* 12 (Winter 1982): 17.

13. Texas Comptroller of Public Accounts, *Fiscal Notes*, December 1990, pp. 8–9.

14. The Bureau of the Census conducts a census of all U.S. governments every 5 years. In compiling employment data, part-time and full-time employees are counted. There were a total of 1,386,524 persons working for the state and local governments in 2002. Using payroll data, this total is recalculated as "full-time equivalent" employees.

15. U.S. Department of Commerce, Bureau of the Census, *Census of Governments* 2002,

vol. 3, *Public Employment* (Washington, D.C.: Government Printing Office, 2004), Table 9.

16. U.S. Bureau of the Census, *Statistical Abstract of the U.S.: 2006*, 125th ed. (Washington, D.C., 2005), Tables 440 and 441.

17. Theodore J. Lowi, *The End of Liberalism*, 2nd ed. (New York, N.Y.: W.W. Norton, 1979), p. 274.

18. Texas Sunset Advisory Commission, *Sunset Review in Texas: Summary of Process and Procedures* (Austin, Tex.: Texas Sunset Advisory Commission, 1991).

19. *Dallas Morning News*, October 24, 1991.

20. Robert Lineberry, *American Public Policy* (New York: Harper and Row, 1977), pp. 84–5.

21. Bill Wells, quoted in Associated Press Story, *Dallas Times Herald*, August 14, 1983.

Chapter 24

1. *Smith v. Allwright*, 321 U.S. 649 (1944).

2. *Miranda v. Arizona*, 384 U.S. 436 (1966).

3. Texas Research League, *The Texas Judiciary: A Structural-Functional Overview*, Report 1 (Austin, Tex.: Texas Research League, August 1990).

4. Office of Court Administration, Texas Judicial System, 79th Annual Report, 2007.

5. Allen E. Smith, *The Impact of the Texas Constitution on the Judiciary* (Houston, Tex.: University of Houston, Institute for Urban Studies, 1973), p. 45.

6. Office of Court Administration, Texas Judicial System, 79th Annual Report.

7. Ibid.

8. Ibid.

9. Ibid.

10. Smith, *The Impact of the Texas Constitution on the Judiciary*, pp. 28–31.

11. Texas Research League, *Texas Courts: A Proposal for Structural-Functional Reform*, Report 2 (Austin, Tex.: Texas Research League, May 1991), pp. 1–15.

12. *Fort Worth Star–Telegram*, September 4, 1983.

13. *Houston Post*, May 18, 1986.

14. Anthony Champagne, "Campaign Contributions in Texas Supreme Court Races," *Crime, Law and Social Change* 17 (1992): 91–106.

15. Kim Ross, quoted in the *Houston Post*, November 10, 1988.

16. *Austin American-Statesman*, December 9, 1993.

17. *Houston Chronicle*, April 30, 2004, p. 1A.

18. *Houston Chronicle*, August 21, 2003, p. 24A.

19. Texans for Public Justice, "Voters Rebuked Texas' Biggest Pac," *Lobby Watch*, January 11, 2007.

20. Texas Watch, *The Food Chain: Winners and Losers in the Texas Supreme Court, 1995–1999* (Austin, Tex.: Texas Watch, 1999).

21. Texas Watch press release, May 3, 1999.

22. Texas Watch, *Access Denied, the Texas Supreme Court in 2000–2001* (Austin, Tex.: Texas Watch 2001).

23. Texas Watch, "Texas Supreme Court Fails Consumers," October 5, 2006.

24. Samuel Issacharoff, *The Texas Judiciary and the Voting Rights Act: Background and Options* (Austin, Tex.: Texas Policy Research Forum, 1989), pp. 2, 13.

25. *Texas Lawyer*, September 18, 1989.

26. *Houston Chronicle*, December 24, 1989.

27. *Texas Lawyer*, September 18, 1989.

28. *League of United Latin American citizens, et al. v. Mattox, et al.*, 501 U.S. 419 (1991); *Chisom v. Roemer*, 501 U.S. 380 (1991).

29. *League of United Latin American Citizens v. Clements*, 999 F2d 831 (1993).

30. *Houston Chronicle*, January 19, 1994.

31. Office of Judicial Administration, "Profile of Appellate and Trial Judges," September 1, 2007.

32. *Houston Chronicle*, November 13, 1998, p. 1A.

33. Office of Judicial Administration, "Profile of Appellate and Trial Judges," September 1, 2007.

34. American Judicature Society, "Judicial Selection Methods in the States, 2008.

35. *Miranda v. Arizona*, 384 U.S. 436 (1966).

36. *Texas Lawyer*, November 11, 1991.

37. *Paulson v. State*, Texas Court of Criminal Appeals, October 4, 2000.

38. *Furman v. Georgia*, 408 U.S. 238 (1972).

39. *Texas Lawyer*, June 3, 1991.

40. *Houston Chronicle*, May 11, 2003, p. 1A.

41. Paul Burka. "Trial by Technicality," *Texas Monthly* (April 1982): 126–31, 210–18, 241.

42. *Houston Chronicle*, August 27, 2003, p. 23A.

43. *Edgewood v. Kirby*, 777 S.W.2d 391 (1989).

44. *Fort Worth Star–Telegram*, October 4, 1982; *Brown v. Board of Education of Topeka*, 347 U.S. 483 (1954).

45. *Edgewood v. Meno*, 893 S.W.2d 450 (1995).

46. Ibid.

47. *Richards v. LULAC*, 868 S.W. 2d 306 (1993); *Houston Chronicle*, June 16, 1994.

48. *Texas Education Agency v. Leeper*, 893 S.W. 2d 432 (1994).

49. *Operation Rescue—National v. Planned Parenthood of Houston and Southeast Texas, Inc.*, 975 S.W. 2d 546 (1998). See also *Houston Chronicle*, July 4, 1998.

50. *Madsen v. Women's Health Clinic, Inc.*, 512 U.S. (1994).

51. *Republican Party of Texas v. Dietz*, 924 S.W. 2d 932 (1996).

Chapter 25

1. Anwar Hussain Syed, *The Political Theory of American Local Government* (New York: Random House, 1966), p. 27.

2. Ibid., pp. 38–52. Syed presents a summary of Jefferson's theory of local government.

3. Roscoe C. Martin, *Grass Roots* (Tuscaloosa: University of Alabama Press, 1957), p. 5.; Robert C. Wood, *Suburbia* (Boston: Houghton Mifflin, 1958), p. 18.

4. *City of Clinton v. The Cedar Rapids and Missouri River Railroad Co.*, 24 Iowa 455 (1868).

5. Roscoe C. Martin, *The Cities in the Federal System* (New York: Atherton Press, 1965), pp. 28–35.

6. David B. Brooks, *Texas Practice: County and Special District Law*, Vol. 35 (St. Paul, Minn.: West, 1989), pp. 41–46. A good part of the materials presented on county government rely on this comprehensive work.

7. Advisory Commission on Intergovernmental Relations, *Measuring Local Government Discretionary Authority*, Report M–131 (Washington, D.C.: ACIR, 1981). This earlier report ranked Texas first as to the discretionary powers granted to cities but forty-third in those powers granted to counties. No similar current ranking has been developed.

8. Advisory Commission on Intergovernmental Relations, *State and Local Roles in the Federal System*, (Washington, D.C.: ACIR, 1982), pp. 32–3.

9. For an excellent overview of urban development in Texas, see Char Miller and David R. Johnson, "The Rise of Urban Texas," in Char Miller and Heywood T. Sanders, *Urban Texas: Politics and Development* (College Station: Texas A&M University Press, 1990), pp. 3–29.

10. U.S. Census Bureau, *2006 American Community Survey*.

11. See Richard L. Cole, Ann Crowley Smith, and Delbert A. Taebel, with a foreword by Marlan Blissett, *Urban Life in Texas: A Statistical Profile and Assessment of the Largest Cities* (Austin, Tex.: University of Texas Press, 1986), for an earlier example of rankings of larger Texas cities on various dimensions measuring aspects of urban quality of life. Rankings of all types are generated each year by academics, magazines, corporations, and individuals on a wide range of topics.

12. Texas Municipal League, July 2006, Austin, Texas.

13. Ibid.

14. Ibid.; Texas Municipal League, May 2002, Austin, Texas.

15. Murray S. Stedman, *Urban Politics*, 2nd ed. (Cambridge, Mass.: Winthrop, 1975), p. 51.

16. Beryl E. Pettus and Randall W. Bland, *Texas Government Today*, 3rd ed. (Homewood, Ill.: The Dorsey Press, 1984), p. 347.

17. City of Austin, Charter Revision Committee, "Mayor Council Survey," October 2007. www.ci.austin.tx.us/charter/downloads/2007_mayor_council_salary_info.pdf.

18. Wilbourn E. Benton, *Texas Politics*, 5th ed. (Chicago: Nelson-Hall, 1984), p. 260.

19. Greg Jackson, "Sculley's Reputation Built on Tough Jobs," *San Antonio Express–News*, September 4, 2005, B1; Kate Alexander, "With Praise, City Tells Futrell She's Valued," *Austin American– Statesman*, February 17, 2006, p. A1.

20. Telephone calls to budget staff in Dallas, San Antonio, and Seguin, Texas, July 2006.

21. City of Austin, Charter Revision Committee, "Mayor Council Survey," October 2007.

22. See the city charters of Dallas, Chapter 3, Section 4, and San Antonio Article II, Sections 6 and 9.

23. U.S. Census Bureau, *1992 Census of Government, Popularly Elected Officials*, vol. 2, no. 1, Table 11.

24. Texas Municipal League, Austin, Texas; telephone conversation with research staff, May 2002.

25. Texas Municipal League, Austin, Texas; telephone conversation with research staff, July 2006.

26. "Where Do Texas Cities Get Their Money?" *Texas Town and City* 92 (January 2005): 20–1.

27. Ibid.; Frank Sturzl, "The Courses of Municipal Revenue," *Texas Town and City* 93 (June 2006): 14–6.

28. Karen Brooks, "For Uphill Battle, Legislator Was Up to Challenge," *Texas Town and City* 92 (July 2005): 14–5.

29. "Municipal Fiscal Conditions are Improving," *Texas Town and City* 92 (March 2005): 10–3.

30. "Texas Cities Continue to Face Fiscal Squeeze," *Texas Town and City* 79 (March 1991): 26, 32–4.

31. Lawrence E. Jordan, "Municipal Bond Issuance in Texas: The New Realities," *Texas Town and City* 79 (December 1991): 12, 25.

32. Miller and Sanders, *Urban Texas: Politics and Development*, p. xiv.

33. Frank Sturzl, "The Tyranny of Environmental Mandates," *Texas Town and City* 79 (September 1991): 14–5.

34. Robert E. Norwood and Sabrina Strawn, *Texas County Government: Let the People Choose*, 2nd ed. (Austin, Tex.: The Texas Research League, 1984), p. 9. For a sample of Texas court decisions that affirm the general principle of the Dillon rule that the county can perform only those functions allocated to it by law, see pp. 11–2.

35. Texas State Data Center, "Estimates of the Total Populations of Counties and Places for July 1, 2006 and January 1, 2007," September 2007.

36. Texas Association of Counties, *2007 Salary Survey* (Austin, Tex.: Texas Association of Counties, 2008).

37. *Avery v. Midland*, 88 S. Ct. 1114 (1968).

38. Norwood and Strawn, *Texas County Government*, p. 22.

39. Brooks, *Texas Practice* 35: 331.

40. Texas Commission on Intergovernmental Relations, *An Introduction to Texas County Government* (Austin: TCIR, 1980), p. 10.

41. Brooks, *Texas Practice* 35: 392–93.

42. David B. Brooks, *Texas Practice: County and Special District Law*, Vol. 36 (St. Paul, Minn.: West, 1989), pp. 104–5.

43. Texas Association of Counties, *2007 Salary Survey*.

44. Brooks, *Texas Practice* 36: 49–50.

45. Ibid., 18–49.

46. Norwood and Strawn, *Texas County Government*, p. 24.

47. Brooks, *Texas Practice* 35: 273–74.

48. Brooks, *Texas Practice* 36: 122–23.

49. TCIR, *An Introduction to County Government*, p. 22.

50. Norwood and Strawn, *Texas County Government*, p. 27.

51. Brooks, *Texas Practice* 35: 273–74.

52. Virginia Marion Perrenod, *Special Districts, Special Purposes: Fringe Governments and Urban Problems in the Houston Area* (College Station, Tex.: Texas A&M University Press, 1984), p. 4.

53. Ibid., 34.

54. Woodworth G. Thrombley, *Special Districts and Authorities in Texas* (Austin, Tex.: Institute of Public Affairs, The University of Texas, 1959), p. 13.

55. Robert S. Lorch, *State and Local Politics*, 3rd ed. (Englewood Cliffs, N.J.: Prentice Hall, 1989), p. 246.

56. Ibid., p. 247.

57. Texas Education Agency, *Snapshot: School District Profiles*, 2007. www.tea.state.tx.us/perfreport/snapshot/.

58. Texas Association of School Boards, Membership Services, Telephone Conversation on 4–22–2008; Summary

documents of membership provided by the TASB.

59. Governor's Planning and Budget Office, *Regional Councils in Texas: A Status Report and Directory, 1980–1981*, p. 9.

60. Governor's Budget and Planning Office, *Regional Councils in Texas: Annual Report and Directory, 1990–1991*, p. 8.

61. Texas Association of Regional Councils, "What is a COG?" www.txregionalcouncil.org.

62. Governor's Budget and Planning Office, *Regional Councils in Texas: Annual Report and Directory, 1992–1993*.

63. Texas Association of Regional Councils, "What is a COG?" www.txregionalcouncil.org.

64. Telephone interview by author on March 21, 2000, with staff in the governor's office.

65. Brooks, *Texas Practice* 36: 380–84.

66. See the Web site of the Texas Association of Regional Councils, www.txregional-council.org

67. www.texasbest.com/houston/houston.html.

68. For a more detailed discussion of annexation authority, see Wilbourn E. Benton, *Texas Politics*, pp. 264–66.

69. "Texas Legislature Adjourns," *Texas Town and City* 86 (July 1999): 10.

70. "Texas Legislature Adjourns," *Texas Town and City* 89 (July 2001): 11.

71. Norwood and Strawn, *Texas County Government*, pp. 75–81.

72. Joel B. Goldsteen and Russell Fricano, *Municipal Finance Practices and Preferences for New Development: Survey of Texas Cities* (Arlington, Tex.: Institute of Urban Studies, The University of Texas at Arlington, 1988), pp. 3–11.

73. Brooks, *Texas Practice*, 36: 229–42.

74. Tom Adams, "Introduction and Recent Experience with the Interlocal Contract," in *Interlocal Contract in Texas*, eds. Richard W. Tees, Richard L. Cole, and Jay G. Stanford. (Arlington, Tex.: Institute of Urban Studies, University of Arlington, 1990), p. 1.

75. Tees, et al., *Interlocal Contract in Texas*, pp. B1–B7.

76. Vincent Ostrom, *The Meaning of American Federalism* (San Francisco: Institute for Contemporary Studies, 1991), p. 161. Ostrom suggests that advocates of metropolitan government often overlook the "rich and intricate framework for negotiating, adjudicating, and deciding questions" that are now in place in many urbanized areas with multiple governmental units.

77. Ann Long Lively and Dwight A. Shupe, "Public Improvement Districts: An Alternative for Financing Public Improvements and Services," *Texas Town and City* 79 (September 1991): 6–10, 30, 66.

PHOTO CREDITS

INDEX

Page numbers in **bold** refer to definitions of terms.